About the Authors

Kym Anderson is George Gollin Professor of Economics and foundation Executive Director of the Wine Economics Research Centre at the University of Adelaide. He has published numerous articles on the economics of wine for industry and academic journals as well as a 2004 book on *The World's Wine Markets: Globalization at Work*. He is also the senior author of several editions of a 500-page statistical compendium on *Global Wine Markets*, the most recent one being published by University of Adelaide Press in 2011. He has served on the Board of Directors of Australia's Grape and Wine Research and Development Corporation (2000-05), and is a co-founder and Vice-President of the American Association of Wine Economists and a Co-Editor of Cambridge University Press's *Journal of Wine Economics*.

Nanda R. Aryal is a Research Assistant in the Wine Economics Research Centre at the University of Adelaide. He has MSc degrees in mathematics and statistics from both the University of York in England and Tribhuvan University in Nepal.

This book is available as a free fully-searchable PDF from
www.adelaide.edu.au/press

Which Winegrape Varieties are Grown where?

A Global Empirical Picture

Kym Anderson

with the assistance of Nanda R. Aryal

This volume, which is freely available as an ebook at **www.adelaide.edu.au/press/titles/winegrapes**, provides winegrape area data for the major winegrape regions of the world. It complements a volume on global wine markets which was published in 2011 by University of Adelaide Press as:

K. Anderson and S. Nelgen, ***Global Wine Markets, 1961 to 2009: A Statistical Compendium***, Adelaide: University of Adelaide Press, 2011 (also freely available as an ebook at **www.adelaide.edu.au/press/titles/global-wine**).

The data are also freely available in Excel spreadsheets at **www.adelaide.edu.au/wine-econ/databases**

The author welcomes comments on how to improve the quality and coverage of data and the way they have been summarized. Please send feedback to:

Professor Kym Anderson, Executive Director
Wine Economics Research Centre
School of Economics
University of Adelaide
Adelaide SA 5005 Australia
Phone (+61 8) 8313 4712
Fax   (+61 8) 8223 1460
kym.anderson@adelaide.edu.au

www.adelaide.edu.au/wine-econ

Which Winegrape Varieties are Grown where?

A Global Empirical Picture

Kym Anderson

with the assistance of Nanda R. Aryal

Wine Economics Research Centre
School of Economics
University of Adelaide
Adelaide, South Australia

THE UNIVERSITY *of* ADELAIDE

UNIVERSITY OF
ADELAIDE PRESS

Published in Adelaide by

University of Adelaide Press
The University of Adelaide
Level 1, 254 North Terrace
South Australia 5005
press@adelaide.edu.au
www.adelaide.edu.au/press

The University of Adelaide Press publishes externally refereed scholarly books by staff of the University of Adelaide. It aims to maximise access to the University's best research by publishing works through the internet as free downloads and for sale as high quality printed volumes.

© 2013 Kym Anderson

This work is licenced under the Creative Commons Attribution 3.0 Unported License. To view a copy of this licence, visit http://creativecommons.org/licenses/by/3.0/ or send a letter to Creative Commons, 444 Castro Street, Suite 900, Mountain View, California, 94041, USA. This licence allows for copying any part of the work for personal and commercial use, providing author attribution is clearly stated. Address all inquiries to the Director at the above address.

For the full Cataloguing-in-Publication data please contact the National Library of Australia:

cip@nla.gov.au

ISBN (paperback) 978-1-922064-67-7
ISBN (ebook) 978-1-922064-68-4

Cover image: iStockphoto
Cover design: Emma Spoehr
Paperback printed by Griffin Press, South Australia

Table of contents

	Page
List of charts	x
List of tables	xi
Authors' preface and acknowledgements	xvii
Statistical sources	xix
Technical notes	xxiii

A guide to where in the world various winegrape varieties are grown	1
Charts: World's winegrape varieties and wine regions at a glance	13

Table sections:

I.	**Country coverage**	31
II.	**Regional coverage of each country**	91
III.	**Winegrape varietal coverage globally**	109
IV.	**Winegrape areas for world's top varieties, by country**	303
V.	**Winegrape areas and Varietal Intensity Indexes for national top 45 varieties**	357
VI.	**Regional Varietal Intensity Indexes for world's top varieties**	439
VII.	**Index of Varietal Similarity, by region and country**	529
VIII.	**Summary charts for each of the world's top 50 varieties**	573
IX.	**Summary charts for each of the 44 countries**	625

About Adelaide's Wine Economics Research Centre (inside back cover)

List of charts

	Page
1. National shares of global winegrape area, 2000 and 2010	14
2. National shares of global winegrape area, wine production volume and wine production value, 2010	14
3. Cumulative national shares of global winegrape area and of wine production volume, 2010	15
4. Cumulative national shares of global wine production volume, 1909-13, 1961-64 and 2009-11	15
5. Largest increases and decreases in national winegrape bearing area, 2000 to 2010	16
6. Share of total agricultural crop area under winegrapes, 2009-11	16
7. Cumulative varietal shares of global winegrape area, 1990, 2000 and 2010	17
8. Cumulative shares of Old World and New World winegrape areas by variety, 2000 and 2010	17
9. World's fastest-expanding winegrape varieties, 2000 to 2010	18
10. World's fastest-contracting winegrape varieties, 2000 to 2010	18
11. World's top 35 varieties in 1990 (c.f. 2000 and 2010)	19
12. World's top 35 varieties in 2010 (c.f. 1990 and 2000)	19
13. Top 30 red varieties' shares of global wine area, 2000 and 2010	20
14. Top 30 white varieties' shares of global wine area, 2000 and 2010	20
15. Red and white shares of global winegrape area, 2000 and 2010	21
16. Share of red varieties in national winegrape area, 2000 and 2010	21
17. Percentage point changes in shares of red and white varieties in national winegrape area, 2000 to 2010	22
18. Change in national hectares of red varieties, 2000 to 2010	22
19. Cumulative varietal shares of world red and white winegrape area, 2000 and 2010	23
20. Shares of French varieties in national winegrape areas, 2000 and 2010	23
21. Shares of Spanish varieties in national winegrape areas, 2000 and 2010	24
22. Shares of Italian varieties in national winegrape areas, 2000 and 2010	24
23. Shares of Syrah in national winegrape area, 2000 and 2010	25
24. National shares of global winegrape area of Syrah, 2000 and 2010	25
25. Cumulative national shares of world Syrah area, 2000 and 2010	26
26. Varietal Intensity Index for Syrah, 2000 and 2010	26
27. Varietal Intensity Index for Australia's 15 largest varieties, 2000 and 2010	27
28. Index of Varietal Similarity of each country with the world, 2000 and 2010	27
29. Index of Varietal Similarity between 2000 and 2010 for each country	28
30. Index of Varietal Similarity of each country with the country with closest varietal mix, 2010	28

List of tables

Page

I.	**Country coverage**	31

1. Number of regions and prime varieties, by country, 2000 and 2010 — 32
2. National shares of global winegrape area and global wine production volume, 2000 and 2010 — 33
3. Key indicators of national grape area and production, 1990, 2000 and 2010 — 34
4. National winegrape areas and change between 2000 and 2010 — 37
5. Global winegrape area, share of global area, and global ranks of each prime variety (alphabetic), 1990, 2000 and 2010 — 38
6. Ranking of prime varieties by global winegrape area and decadal changes, 1990, 2000 and 2010 — 67
7. Red winegrape area and share of all varieties, by country, 2000 and 2010 — 88
8. White winegrape area and share of all varieties, by country, 2000 and 2010 — 89

II.	**Regional coverage of each country**	91

9. Winegrape area by region for each country, 2000 — 92
10. Winegrape area by region for each country, 2010 — 98
11. Winegrape area by region for the United States, 1990, 2000 and 2010 — 106
12. Large regions or regions within each state in Australia and Italy, 2010 — 108

III.	**Winegrape varietal coverage globally**	109

13. Prime varieties' colour, country of origin, synonyms, and 2010 global area, share and rank — 110
14. Prime varieties' global area and share of each synonym, and synonym's share of each prime variety, 2000 — 142
15. Prime varieties' global area and share of each synonym, and synonym's share of each prime variety, 2010 — 154
16. Synonyms' global area and share of each prime variety, 2000 — 174
17. Synonyms' global area and share of each prime variety, 2010 — 187
18. Shares of number of prime varieties, and of global winegrape area, by country of origin, 2000 and 2010 — 206
19. Prime varieties' global area and share of all varieties globally, by prime's country of origin, 2000 — 207
20. Prime varieties' global area and share of all varieties globally, by prime's country of origin, 2010 — 221
21. Shares of national winegrape area by varietal country of origin, 2000 — 238
22. Shares of national winegrape area by varietal country of origin, 2010 — 242
23. National shares of top, top 3, top 5, top 10 and top 20 varieties, by winegrape area, 2000 — 247
24. National shares of top, top 3, top 5, top 10 and top 20 varieties, by winegrape area, 2010 — 248
25. Source of prime varietal name and its main synonym, and their shares of prime — 249

variety's global area, 2000

26. Source of prime varietal name and its main synonym, and their shares of prime variety's global area, 2010 — 273

IV. Winegrape areas for world's top varieties, by country — 303

27. National winegrape area (hectares) for world's top 30 red varieties, 2000 — 304
28. National shares (%) of global winegrape area for world's top 30 red varieties, 2000 — 308
29. Shares (%) of world's top 30 red varieties in national winegrape area, by country, 2000 — 312
30. National winegrape area (hectares) for world's top 30 red varieties, 2010 — 316
31. National shares (%) of global winegrape area for world's top 30 red varieties, 2010 — 320
32. Shares (%) of world's top 30 red varieties in national winegrape area, by country, 2010 — 324
33. National winegrape area (hectares) for world's top 30 white varieties, 2000 — 328
34. National shares (%) of global winegrape area for world's top 30 white varieties, 2000 — 332
35. Shares (%) of world's top 30 white varieties in national winegrape area, by country, 2000 — 336
36. National winegrape area (hectares) for world's top 30 white varieties, 2010 — 340
37. National shares (%) of global winegrape area for world's top 30 white varieties, 2010 — 344
38. Shares (%) of world's top 30 white varieties in national winegrape area, by country, 2010 — 348
39. National winegrape area (hectares) for world's top 6 non-red/white varieties, 2000 — 352
40. National shares (%) of global winegrape area for world's top 6 non-red/white varieties, 2000 — 353
41. National winegrape area (hectares) for world's top 6 non-red/white varieties, 2010 — 354
42. National shares (%) of global winegrape area for world's top 6 non-red/white varieties, 2010 — 355

V. Winegrape areas and Varietal Intensity Indexes for national top 45 varieties — 357

43. Winegrape areas and national and global shares (and Varietal Intensity Indexes) for national top 45 varieties, 2000 — 358
44. Winegrape areas and national and global shares (and Varietal Intensity Indexes) for national top 45 varieties, 2010 — 376
45. Varietal Intensity Indexes (and winegrape areas and national and global shares) for national top 45 varieties, 2000 — 398
46. Varietal Intensity Indexes (and winegrape areas and national and global shares) for national top 45 varieties, 2010 — 416

VI.	**Regional Varietal Intensity Indexes for world's top varieties**	439
47.	Varietal Intensity Indexes for the top 25 regions for the world's top 30 red varieties, 2000	440
48.	Varietal Intensity Indexes for the top 25 regions for the world's top 30 red varieties, 2010	448
49.	Varietal Intensity Indexes for the top 25 regions for the world's top 30 white varieties, 2000	456
50.	Varietal Intensity Indexes for the top 25 regions for the world's top 30 white varieties, 2010	464
51.	Varietal Intensity Indexes for the top 25 regions for the world's top 6 non-red/white varieties, 2000	472
52.	Varietal Intensity Indexes for the top 25 regions for the world's top 6 non-red/white varieties, 2010	473
53.	Winegrape areas and Varietal Intensity Indexes for each region's top 6 varieties, by region and country, 2010	474
VII.	**Indexes of Varietal Similarity, by country and region**	529
54.	Index of Varietal Similarity of each country and region relative to the world, 2000	530
55.	Index of Varietal Similarity of each country and region relative to the world, 2010	535
56.	Index of Varietal Similarity of each region in 2010 relative to that region in 2000	543
57.	Each country's 10 most-similar winegrape countries in the world according to the Varietal Similarity Index, 2000	548
58.	Each country's 10 most-similar winegrape countries in the world according to the Varietal Similarity Index, 2010	550
59.	Each region's 3 most-similar winegrape regions in the world according to the Varietal Similarity Index, 2000	552
60.	Each region's 3 most-similar winegrape regions in the world according to the Varietal Similarity Index, 201	561
VIII.	**Summary charts for each of the world's top 50 varieties**	573
61.	Airen	574
62.	Alicante Henri Bouschet	575
63.	Aligote	576
64.	Barbera	577
65.	Blaufrankisch	578
66.	Bobal	579
67.	Cabernet Franc	580
68.	Cabernet Sauvignon	581
69.	Catarratto Bianco	582
70.	Cayetana Blanca	583
71.	Cereza	584

72.	Chardonnay	585
73.	Chenin Blanc	586
74.	Cinsaut	587
75.	Colombard	588
76.	Cot	589
77.	Criolla Grande	590
78.	Douce Noire	591
79.	Doukkali	592
80.	Feteasca Alba	593
81.	Gamay Noir	594
82.	Garganega	595
83.	Garnacha Tinta	596
84.	Grasevina	597
85.	Gruner Veltliner	598
86.	Isabella	599
87.	Macabeo	600
88.	Mazuelo	601
89.	Merlot	602
90.	Monastrell	603
91.	Montepulciano	604
92.	Muller Thurgau	605
93.	Muscat Blanc A Petits Grains	606
94.	Muscat of Alexandria	607
95.	Nero D'Avola	608
96.	Palomino Fino	609
97.	Pinot Gris	610
98.	Pinot Noir	611
99.	Prosecco	612
100.	Riesling	613
101.	Rkatsiteli	614
102.	Sangiovese	615
103.	Sauvignon Blanc	616
104.	Semillon	617
105.	Syrah	618
106.	Tempranillo	619
107.	Trebbiano Romagnolo	620
108.	Trebbiano Toscano	621
109.	Tribidrag	622
110.	Verdejo	623

IX. Summary charts for each of the 44 countries   625

111. Algeria	626
112. Argentina	627
113. Armenia	628
114. Australia	629
115. Austria	630
116. Brazil	631
117. Bulgaria	632
118. Canada	633
119. Chile	634
120. China	635
121. Croatia	636
122. Cyprus	637
123. Czech Rep.	638
124. France	639
125. Georgia	640
126. Germany	641
127. Greece	642
128. Hungary	643
129. Italy	644
130. Japan	645
131. Kazakhstan	646
132. Luxembourg	647
133. Mexico	648
134. Moldova	649
135. Morocco	650
136. Myanmar	651
137. New Zealand	652
138. Peru	653
139. Portugal	654
140. Romania	655
141. Russia	656
142. Serbia	657
143. Slovakia	658
144. Slovenia	659
145. South Africa	660
146. Spain	661
147. Switzerland	662
148. Thailand	663
149. Tunisia	664
150. Turkey	665
151. Ukraine	666
152. United Kingdom	667
153. United States	668
154. Uruguay	669

Authors' preface and acknowledgements

Over the past 15 years the University of Adelaide has provided numerous editions of a global statistical compendium of annual time series data and various key indicators of national markets for grape wines. The eighth version was published by the University of Adelaide Press in 2011 as a paperback and ebook (www.adelaide.edu.au/press/titles/global-wine) and the data are freely available at the University's Wine Economics Research Centre (www.adelaide.edu.au/wine-econ/databases). However, very little of the data in that compendium relate to the grapes that are the key ingredient in winemaking. Nor are data included by wine region within each of the countries covered. One reason is space: that compendium is already 500 pages long, so subdividing each country's area and production data into regions would have turned the volume into a brick. Also, the readily available annual data for grapes do not distinguish winegrapes from grapes for fresh consumption or drying. The more-detailed data sets that focus specifically on winegrape area data by region and variety are far less frequently published in most countries.

Another reason for that compendium including little information on winegrapes is that the relatively scant data on bearing area (and the even scanter data on winegrape production, yield and price) refer to varieties that have different names in different countries – and sometimes in different regions within countries – even though they may have the same DNA. This challenge has recently been reduced greatly, however, thanks to new DNA research. In particular, the new and already well-known Robinson/Harding/Vouillamoz 2012 book called *Wine Grapes* provides a detailed guide to nearly 1400 commercially grown 'prime' varieties – and it also identifies their various synonyms. The 'prime' name is chosen by those authors according to the name used in its country or region of origin. In addition, the Julius Kühn-Institute for Grapevine Breeding at the Federal Research Centre for Cultivated Plants, Geilweilerhof, Germany, is maintaining a *Vitis International Variety Catalogue* (www.vivc.de) that provides additional DNA-based varietal information.

With that now-far-greater capacity to avoid spuriously indicating diversity of winegrape varieties across regions and countries, and with the European Union recently publishing census data on bearing area by variety and region circa 2010 for most of its winegrape-producing member countries, the time is right to bring together for the first time a global compendium of data on bearing area by variety and region (and hence also by country). This can be treated as a supplement to *Wine Grapes* and *The World Atlas of Wine* (or similar atlases) for readers seeking an idea of the relative importance of the world's wine regions and varieties at least as reflected in winegrape bearing area data circa 2010 and 2000 (and, in more limited form, 1990).

Assembling those data has been a time-consuming task, but it would have taken much longer (and in some cases been impossible) without the generous assistance of a large number of people in numerous countries. First and foremost, grateful thanks go to Jancis Robinson MW, Julia Harding MW and José Vouillamoz for promptly responding to endless emailed questions and for sharing their vast knowledge by reacting to drafts of numerous tables and charts, as well as for providing data for such countries as China, Japan, Russia and Ukraine.

We are also grateful to Patrick Fegan of the Chicago Wine School, whose 2003 book *The Vineyard Handbook: Appellations, Maps and Statistics* helped with its 1990 varietal data (see Table 3) and also circa 2000 data for several small wine-producing countries, for which we otherwise would have had only circa 2010 information.

At the risk of accidentally omitting some names (for which we humbly apologize in advance), our sincere thanks for providing or leading us to the following national data go to, in author alphabetical order, Julian Alston, Kate Fuller and Sandro Steinbach (California and Washington States, USA), Georgi Apkhazava (Georgia), Peter Bailey, Sheralee Davies, Alan Nankivell and Mark Rowley (Australia), Stefan Bojnec (Croatia, Serbia and Slovenia), Bruce Bordelon (Indianan, USA), Jasna Čačić (Croatia), Mark Chien (Pennsylvania, USA), Donald Cyr (Canada), Dominique Desbois (for carefully assembling French survey data for 2009, pending the publication of the official census data which have yet to be released), Christy Eckstein (Ohio, USA), Denis Gastin (Thailand), Anatassios Haniotis and Kargarita Koumanioti (for advance access to the 2009 Greek census data), Giulia Meloni (EUROSTAT data plus Brazil, Italy, Peru), Javier Merino and Jimena Estrella (Argentina), Taner Öğütoğlu (Turkey), Sergey Oleichenko, Dauren Oshakbaev and Alfinura Sharafeyeva (Kazakhstan), Bruce Reisch (New York State, USA), Jorge Tenotio (Mexico), Gabriel Tinguely (Switzerland), Áron Török (for advance access to the 2010 Hungarian census data), Angeliki Tsiolo of the OIV (for contacts in various countries), and last but definitely not least, the trio of Annalisa Zezza, Roberta Sardone and Eugenio Pomarici (for advance access to and heroic efforts to polish the 2010 Italian census data).

We acknowledge and thank Australia's Grape and Wine Research and Development Corporation for assisting with funding the research project that produced this data collection. We are grateful also to Lachlan Deer and Claire Hollweg for earlier research assistance with circa 2000 winegrape varietal data compilation for a dozen key countries that provided a prototype for the present much more comprehensive study (see Anderson, K., "Varietal Intensities and Similarities of the World's Wine Regions", *Journal of Wine Economics* 5(2): 270-309, Winter 2010).

While we have made every effort to ensure the accuracy and currency of information within this compendium, we cannot accept responsibility for information which may later prove to be misrepresented or inaccurate, or for any reliance placed on the information by readers. We warmly welcome comments on the raw data and the indicators derived from them, and we would gratefully receive any new databases for omitted countries or updated, expanded or revised databases for those countries already included.

Kym Anderson
Adelaide, South Australia
December 2013

Statistical sources

The most important source of winegrape bearing area data for this compendium is EUROSTAT, because it provides data by region for the European Union's member countries for the two most-recent decadal censuses, which were circa 2000 and 2010. They can be found at http://epp.eurostat.ec.europa.eu/portal/page/portal/statistics/search_database [In the Data Navigation Tree, click on "Agriculture, forestry and fisheries" then "Agriculture" then "Structure of orchards and vineyards" then "Vineyard " and then "Basic vineyard survey".] Since that source provides data for a large share of the world's winegrape production, those years are the ones targeted for all other countries. For the majority of the EU countries the census dates were a year earlier, so 1999 and 2009 were the vintages targeted for other Northern Hemisphere countries while 2000 and 2010 were targeted for Southern Hemisphere countries (bearing in mind that harvesting is late in the calendar year in the north and early in the calendar year in the south).

Not all EU-27 countries have their latest census data uploaded on that EUROSTAT website yet, so we approached government officials in the missing member countries (France, Greece, Hungary, Italy) to secure advance copies of the circa 2010 data that have yet to be uploaded even in those countries. In the case of France, its less-detailed 2009 annual survey rather than the decadal census data had to be used for the latest numbers, but at least France's detailed census data are available at EUROSTAT for 1999.

The national and regional data sources, and the exact years to which they relate, are listed in Table A of this section.

The choice of countries to include was determined by national shares of global wine production. The 44 countries for which data are available for circa 2010 account for 99% of global grapewine output in 2010. The only other country producing more than 0.1% of the world's wine is Macedonia (0.3%), for which we were unable to locate data. Of those 44 countries, we were unable to secure reliable data for 2000 for 9 of them (China, Japan, Kazakhstan, Mexico, Myanmar, Peru, Thailand, Turkey, and Ukraine). The combined share of global wine production of those 9 countries in 2000 was only 1.6% (compared with 5.1% in 2010), but to retain their unusual varietal contributions we included them as a group (called "Missing 9 in 2000") by assuming each of them had (i) the same varietal distribution then as in 2010 and (ii) a national acreage that was the same fraction of its 2010 acreage as was its national wine production volume.

In addition to national data, bearing area data by variety are available for regions within 29 of our 44 countries in 2010, and for 14 of those countries in 2000. In aggregate there are 521 unique regions represented in 2010 and 414 in 2000.

As for winegrape varieties, our key source for identifying DNA-identical varieties is the Robinson/Harding/Vouillamoz 2012 book called *Wine Grapes* (hereafter RHV). It provides a detailed guide to 1368 commercially grown 'prime' varieties, and it also identifies their various synonyms used in various countries. Those authors chose the 'prime' name according to the name used in its country or region of origin. In addition, the *Vitis International Variety Catalogue* (www.vivc.de) provides additional DNA-based varietal information. The RHV book's prime varieties account for 93% of the global winegrape area in 2010 and 86% in 2000, VIVC accounts for 2%, and the rest were listed in neither of those sources. We also adopt RHV's berry colours, although we simplify their five categories to just three: the darkest two we call red, the lightest two we call white, and the middle grey colour we call 'non-red/white' (which accounts for just 2.1% of the global area in 2010, of which almost half is Pinot Gris/Grigio, and 1.3% in 2000).[1]

There are two exceptions to our use of RHV prime names. One concerns Pinot, which is thought to have existed for two millennia and which therefore has many clones. Until recently the most popular clones – which include all three of our colour categories – were thought to be distinct varieties, and have been marketed separately to different niches in the market. For that reason we retain separately the following five, each of which has several synonyms identified by RHV: Pinot Blanc, Pinot Gris, Pinot Meunier, Pinot Noir, and Pinot Noir Précoce. The other exception is Garnacha, which also has both red and white mutations. In that case we retain separately the following four, each of which has several synonyms identified by RHV: Garnacha Blanca, Garnacha Peluda, Garnacha Roja, and Garnacha Tinta.

Apart from the bearing area data, various other variables are included in some of the tables. Their sources are as follows:

Tables 2 and 3: FAOSTAT data for total grapevine area, total grape production, grape yield per hectare, and agricultural land (arable land and land used for permanent crops) (http://faostat.fao.org).

Table 4: Varietal bearing area data for 1990 are from Fegan, P.W. (2003), *The Vineyard Handbook: Appellations, Maps and Statistics,* revised edition, Springfield IL: Phillips Brothers. We estimate the global winegrape bearing area in 1990 based on total and winegrape production data and taking into account that the global winegrape yield per hectare averages 15% less than the total grape yield, based on data in Anderson, K. and D. Norman, *Global Wine Production, Consumption and Trade, 1961 to 2001: A Statistical Compendium,* Adelaide: Centre for International Economic Studies, 2003.

In some tables we also provide aggregate data for the Old World and the New World sets of countries. For that purpose we define the Old World as all of continental Europe (not including the United Kingdom but including Cyprus, Lebanon, Turkey and all the countries that were part of the former Yugoslavia or Soviet Union). All other countries are considered here as the New World (including therefore, if somewhat unusually, the Asian winegrape-growing countries for which we have data, which are China, Japan, Myanmar and Thailand).

---

[1] Numerous countries have an 'other varieties' category for each region, only some of which sub-divide that category according to berry colour. When no sub-division is provided, we assume the proportions of 'other varieties' that are red and white are the same as the proportions in the named varieties for that region.

Table A: Sources of national winegrape bearing area data[a]

Country	Actual years	Data sources (latest, then earlier date)
Algeria	2001	Fegan (2003); and assumed unchanged for 2010
Argentina	2000, 2011	www.areadelvino.com; provides more-detailed data in 2011 than 2010
Armenia	2001	Fegan (2003); and assumed unchanged for 2010
Australia	2001, 2010	http://www.wineaustralia.com; more-detailed series begins in 2001
Austria	1999, 2009	EUROSTAT
Brazil	2000, 2010	http://vitibrasil.cnpuv.embrapa.br/index.php?opcao=opt_03, and Fegan (2003)
Bulgaria	2001, 2009	EUROSTAT, and Fegan (2003)
Canada	2001, 2009	www.grapegrowersofontario.com/sites/default/files/2012%20annual%20report.pdf, and Fegan (2003); British Columbia data are 2011 not 2009, from www.winebc.com
Chile	2000, 2009	www.odepa.gob.cl/odepaweb/servicios-informacion/publica/catastro-vides-2009.pdf
China	2009	*China Agricultural Yearbook 2010*, via Julia Harding, personal communication
Croatia	2001, 2011	Croatian Ministry of Agriculture, and Fegan (2003)
Cyprus	2000, 2009	EUROSTAT, and Fegan (2003)
Czech Rep	2001, 2009	EUROSTAT, and Fegan (2003)
France	1999, 2009	Personal communication with Dominique Desbois, and EUROSTAT
Georgia	2004	Georgian Wine Association; assumed unchanged for 2000 and small growth by 2009
Germany	1999, 2009	EUROSTAT
Greece	1999, 2009	Hellenic Statistical Authority, and EUROSTAT
Hungary	2000, 2010	Hungarian Ministry of Agriculture, and Fegan (2003)
Italy	2000, 2010	Italian Ministry of Agriculture, and EUROSTAT
Japan	2009	Julia Harding, personal communication
Kazakhstan	2007	Dauren Oshakbaev, personal communication; assumed unchanged for 2010
Luxembourg	1999, 2009	EUROSTAT
Mexico	2011	Mexican Ministry of Agriculture, www.siap.gob.mx
Moldova	2009	Moldovan Ministry of Agriculture, via Julia Harding, personal communication
Morocco	1999	http://agriculture.ovh.org; and assumed almost unchanged for 2010
Myanmar	2012	http://redmountain-estate.com/varieties.html
New Zealand	2000, 2009	http://wineinf.nzwine.com/statistics_outputs.asp?id=89&cid=6&type=n; survey not conducted in 2010
Peru	2008	www.minag.gob.pe/portal/download/pdf/herramientas/boletines/DocumentoFinalVid.pdf
Portugal	1999, 2009	EUROSTAT
Romania	2001, 2009	EUROSTAT, and Fegan (2003)
Russia	2000, 2009	Julia Harding, personal communication, and Fegan (2003)
Serbia	2001	Fegan (2003)); and assumed unchanged for 2010
Slovakia	2000, 2009	EUROSTAT, and Fegan (2003)
Slovenia	2000, 2009	EUROSTAT, and Fegan (2003)
South Africa	2002, 2011	http://www.wosa.co.za/sa/stats_sawis_annual.php
Spain	1999, 2009	EUROSTAT
Switzerland	1999, 2009	http://www.blw.admin.ch/themen/00013/00084/00344/index.html?lang=de
Thailand	2010	Thailand Grape Vine Survey, from Denis Gastin, personal communication
Tunisia	2000	Fegan (2003); and assumed unchanged for 2010
Turkey	2010	Taner Öğütoğlu of Wines of Turkey, personal communication
Ukraine	2009	Ukranian Ministry of Agriculture via Julia Harding, personal communication
UK	1999, 2009	EUROSTAT
United States[b]	1999, 2009	www.nass.usda.gov
Uruguay	2000, 2012	http://www.inavi.com.uy/categoria/38-estada-sticas-de-via-edos.html, and Robinson, J. *The Oxford Companion to Wine*, 3rd edition, 2006, p. 723

Table A (continued): Sources of national winegrape bearing area data[a]

[a] EUROSTAT data are available at http://epp.eurostat.ec.europa.eu/portal/page/portal/statistics/search_database. In addition, some data for 1990 are provided from Fegan, P.W. (2003), *The Vineyard Handbook: Appellations, Maps and Statistics,* revised edition, Springfield IL: Phillips Brothers, for the Chicago Wine School.

[b] Dates for the various US states vary according to availability, shown below, with additional sources as follows:
www.oda.state.or.us/oass/oass.html
http://gwi.missouri.edu/publications/mo-winery-impact.pdf
www.virginiawine.org/system/datas/320/original/2010_Commercial_Grape_Report.pdf?1312838511
www.nass.usda.gov/Statistics_by_State/Illinois/Publications/Special_Surveys/12Grape_Wine_Final_Publication.pdf
Arizona-2008, Arkansas-2009, California-1991, 1999 and 2009, Colorado-2009, Georgia-2009, Illinois-2011, Indiana-2011, Iowa-2006, Kentucky-2010, Michigan-2002 and 2011, Minnesota-2007, Missouri-2010, New York-1990, 2001 and 2011, North-Carolina-2009, Ohio-2008, Oregon-1990, 2000 and 2010, Pennsylvania-2008, Texas-2010, Virginia-2008, Washington-1990, 1999 and 2011

Technical notes

This section provides definitions of the units used in, and the various indicators generated from, the raw data in this compendium.

Definitions of unit measures

Variable	Unit (per year)
Grape vine bearing area	'000ha
Volume of grape production	kt
Grape yield	t/ha
Volume of wine production	ML
Volume of wine consumption	ML
Volume of wine exports and imports	ML
Value of wine exports and imports	current $USm
Unit value of wine exports and imports	current $US/L

Explanations of unit measures

Abbreviation	Definition	Conversion
ha	hectare	10,000 square metres or 2.471 acres
t	tonne	1,000 kilograms or 2,205 pounds
kt	kilotonne	1,000 tonnes
L	litre	1,000 millilitres or 0.2642 US gallons
ML	megalitre	1 million litres

Definition of Varietal Intensity Index

A Varietal Intensity Index is defined as a variety's share of a region's winegrape area divided by that variety's share of the global winegrape bearing area. The Varietal Intensity Index is thus a complement to share information in that it indicates the importance of a variety in a region not relative to other varieties in that region but rather relative to that variety in the world.

Specifically, define f_{im} as the proportion of bearing area of grape variety m in the total winegrape bearing area in region or country i such that the proportions fall between zero and one and sum to one (i.e., there is a total of M different grape varieties across the world, and $0 \leq f_{im} \leq 1$ and $\Sigma_m f_{im} = 1$). For the world as a whole, f_m is the bearing area of grape variety m as a proportion of the total global winegrape area, and $0 \leq f_m \leq 1$ and $\Sigma_m f_m = 1$. Then the Varietal Intensity Index, V_{im} for variety m in region i, is:

$$(1) \quad V_{im} = f_{im} / f_m$$

Definition of Index of Varietal Similarity

An Index of Varietal Similarity has been defined by Anderson (2010) to measure the extent to which the varietal mix of one region or country matches that of another region or country or the world. It can also be used to compare the varietal mix of a region or country over time. In defining the index, Anderson (2010) borrows and adapts an approach introduced by Jaffe (1986) and Griliches (1979). That approach has been used subsequently by Jaffe (1989), and by others including Alston, Norton and Pardey (1998) and Alston et al. (2010, Ch. 4), to measure inter-firm or inter-industry or inter-regional technology spillover potential.[2]

The mix of grape varieties is a form of revealed preference or judgement by vignerons about what is best to grow in their region. That judgement is affected by not only terroir but also past and present economic considerations, including current expectations about future price trends plus the sunk cost that would be involved in grafting new varieties onto existing rootstocks or grubbing out and replacing existing varieties.

The vector of grape varietal shares defined above, $f_i = (f_{i1}, \ldots, f_{iM})$, locates region i in M-dimensional space. Noting that proximity is defined by the direction in which the f-vectors are pointing, but not necessarily their length, Jaffe (1989) proposes a measure called the angular separation of the vectors which is equal to the cosine of the angle between them. If there were just two varieties, m and n, and region i had 80 percent of its total vine area planted to variety m whereas only 40 percent of region j was planted to variety m, then their index of regional similarity is the cosine of the arrowed angle between the two vectors. When there are M varieties, this measure is defined as:

$$(2) \quad \omega_{ij} = \frac{\sum_{m=1}^{M} f_{im} f_{jm}}{\left(\sum_{m=1}^{M} f_{im}^2\right)^{1/2} \left(\sum_{m=1}^{M} f_{jm}^2\right)^{1/2}},$$

where again f_{im} is the area of plantings of grape variety m as a proportion of the total grape plantings in region i such that these proportions fall between zero and one and sum to one (i.e., there is a total of M different grape varieties across the world, and $0 \leq f_{im} \leq 1$ and $\Sigma_m f_{im} = 1$). This makes it possible to indicate the degree of varietal mix "similarity" of any pair of regions. The index also can be generated for each region relative to the average of the world's N regions, call it ω. In short, ω_{ij} measures the degree of overlap of f_i and f_j. The numerator of equation (2) will be large when i's and j's varietal mixes are very similar. The denominator normalizes the measure to be unity when f_i and f_j are identical. Hence, ω_{ij} will be zero for pairs of regions with no overlap in their grape varietal mix, and one for pairs of regions with

---

[2] Alston, J.M., Andersen, M.A., James, J.S. and Pardey, P.G. (2010), *Persistence Pays: U.S. Agricultural Productivity Growth and the Benefits from Public R&D Spending,* New York: Springer.
Alston, J.M., Norton, G.W. and Pardey, P. (1998), *Science under Scarcity: Principles and Practice for Agricultural Research Evaluation and Priority Setting,* London: CAB International.
Anderson, K. (2010), 'Varietal intensities and similarities of the world's wine regions', *Journal of Wine Economics* 5(2): 270-309, Winter.
Griliches, Z. (1979), 'Issues in assessing the contribution of R&D to productivity growth', *Bell Journal of Economics* 10: 92-116.
Jaffe, A.B. (1986), 'Technological opportunity and spillovers of R&D: evidence from firms' patents profits and market value', *American Economic Review* 76(5): 984-1001,
Jaffe, A.B. (1989), 'Real effects of academic research', *American Economic Review* 79(5): 957-70.

an identical varietal mix. For cases in between those two extremes, $0 < \omega_{ij} < 1$. It is conceptually similar to a correlation coefficient. Like a correlation coefficient, it is completely symmetric in that $\omega_{ij} = \omega_{ji}$ and $\omega_{ii} = 1$. Thus the results can be summarized in a symmetric matrix with values of 1 on the diagonal, plus a vector that reports the index for each region relative to the global varietal mix. n

A guide to where in the world various winegrape varieties are grown

The dramatic globalization of the world's wine markets over the past two or three decades (see Anderson 2004) has generated countless new wine consumers. This has added to both the opportunities and competitive challenges for producers seeking to differentiate their product to attract the attention of consumers. Consumers in turn are always looking for new types of wines, and more so as wines within at least the lower-priced product ranges become more homogeneous with multinationalization of both wineries and wine retailers.

One strategy for producers has been to display grape varietal names on wine bottle labels. Its success, especially for lower-priced New World wines, has led to demands in the European Union for freeing up labelling laws so as to allow such labelling there also. Meanwhile, producers in the New World are increasingly realizing the marketing value of going beyond country of origin to regional (and even single-vineyard) labelling as another form of product differentiation – something that has long been practiced by Europe's traditional producers.

In addition to striving to differentiate their product, producers are also well aware of the impact climate changes (higher temperatures, more extreme weather events) are having on their winegrapes. Adaptation strategies include switching to warmer-climate or more-resilient grape varieties, and re-locating to a higher latitude or altitude to retain the current mix of grape varieties. Especially in the New World, where regions are still trying to identify their varietal comparative advantages and where regulations do not restrict varietal choice, winegrowers are continually on the lookout for attractive alternative varieties that do well in climates similar to what they expect theirs to become in the decades ahead. Moreover, the biotechnology revolution is providing breeders with new opportunities, which is increasing the interest in exploring traits of little-known varieties.

These marketing and climate adaptation needs are generating a rapidly growing demand for information on which winegrape varieties are grown in the world's various wine regions. Since 1971 *The World Atlas of Wine* has provided a great deal of information about where winegrapes are grown (the 7th Edition is by Johnson and Robinson 2013). That has been complemented by the new book called *Wine Grapes*, by Robinson, Harding and Vouillamoz (2012), which provides a detailed guide to 1368 commercially grown 'prime' varieties – and to their various synonyms, based on the latest DNA research. (The authors chose each 'prime' name according to the name used in its country or region of origin.) Neither of those seminal books, nor any other wine atlas or wine encyclopaedia, provides comprehensive global data on the bearing areas of winegrapes by region and variety. This is not surprising because, to our knowledge, no such global compendium of data has been readily available before now.[3]

---

[3] The handbook by Fegan (2003) provides information circa 2000 on key regions in the main wine-producing countries, and on the key varieties in those countries, but it does not provide a matrix of variety by region data. A preliminary matrix is provided for circa 2000 by Anderson (2010), but it covers just 166 regions and 258 varieties in a dozen countries – and many of those 258 varieties are not unique, because that study did not re-name the synonyms of primes.

Another reason for compiling a comprehensive global matrix of winegrape bearing areas by variety and region is because concern has been expressed that the diversity of winegrapes is narrowing to a few 'international' varieties. Johnson and Robinson (2013, page 8) note that vignerons are at last beginning to respond by reverting to neglected local varieties in the Old World and by exploring alternatives to the main 'international' varieties in the New World. But how severe is the current concentration compared with earlier times; and how different is the concentration in the Old World compared with the New World? Answering that question requires first re-naming synonyms by their prime, to avoid understating the degree of concentration.[4] That task is now possible, thanks to the book by Robinson, Harding and Vouillamoz (2012),[5] which in turn has been made possible by the DNA profiling of recent years that has added hugely to traditional ampelography (identification based on physical characteristics of the vine's appearance).[6]

With the above concerns in mind, this volume draws on a newly compiled global database (Anderson and Aryal 2013) to estimate numerous indicators that capture changes over the first decade of this century in the varietal mix of the world's wine regions. It builds directly on an earlier study that examined data for circa 2000 for just 12 countries (Anderson 2010). That paper defined two helpful indicators: a varietal intensity index, which captures the degree of each region's specialization in certain varieties; and a varietal-based regional similarity index, which captures the degree of similarity of each region's varietal mix with that of any other region (or of the nation or world). Those and several other indicators are used in the present study too.

Apart from adding an extra year's data, the present volume significantly advances the Anderson (2010) study in several ways: it has 32 additional countries so that the sample now covers all but 1% of global wine production; it is far more detailed in terms of having 521 regions and 2019 varieties (of which 1271 are 'primes' and 748 are their synonyms) compared with only 166 regions and 258 varieties previously; and it has removed spurious differences in varietal mixes resulting from different varietal names being used for what have been shown since to be DNA-identical varieties.

The years chosen correspond to the agricultural census periods of the European Union, which were 1999 or 2000 and 2009 or 2010. For the non-EU countries data have been sought for the earlier year in the Northern Hemisphere and the latter year in the Southern Hemisphere, so they refer to vintages that were less than 6 months apart. Inevitably not all

---

[4] Some varieties are not as rare as previously believed. For example, Zinfandel is genetically identical not only to Pimitivo (in Puglia) but also to Tribidrag (in Croatia). Also identical are the two 'varieties' in Italy's Liguria region, near Genoa, of Pigato and Vermentino – which are also genetically identical to Favorita (in Italy's Piedmont) and Rolle (in southern France). Their prime name, according to Robinson et al. is Vermentino.

[5] The Vitis listing compiled by JKI (2013) for European countries provided a few more primes. There is also a list of varieties maintained by the OIV (2012), but because OIV is an inter-governmental organization it uses only the names adopted by each member country.

[6] Scientific publications from that vine profiling began in South Australia in 1993 and in California at UC Davis in 1997, and have surged ahead since then. When one parent is missing, it is still possible for DNA profiling to identify parent-offspring relationships. And even when both parents are unknown, a probabilistic approach can be used to detect siblings, grandparents or grandchildren. The latter has been done for Syrah, for example: its parents were discovered barely a decade ago to be Mondeuse Blanche and Dureza, its great grandparent is very likely Pinot (according to Vouillamoz and Grando 2006), and it is either a grandchild or a half-sibling of both Mondeuse Noire and Viognier. Undoubtedly further DNA profiling will reduce this uncertainty and add to our stock of knowledge of these and the other 10,000 or so grape varieties currently available globally.

countries or regions had data for exactly those vintages, but those exceptions account for a very small fraction of the data.

The database on which this volume draws thus involves two years (2000 and 2010, plus some 1990 data) by up to 521 regions (in 44 countries), by up to 1271 varieties. Such a large three-dimensional database of 1.3 billion cells (many of which are zeros) is difficult to digest as large spreadsheets, hence the present volume which summarizes the data in numerous ways including though calculating various shares and indexes.

This Introduction provides a guide to the summary charts and tables, and is structured as follow. The next section describes the coverage of the database in more detail. The following two sections discuss the two key empirical indicators that are derived from the share data: a varietal intensity index to highlight the varietal specialization of each region or country; and a varietal similarity index to distinguish between regions and countries according to their overall mix of varieties. Select findings from the report's many tables are then provided, with the help of charts that provide visual images of key features of various tables. The final section draws out some implications and discusses other prospective uses of the database.

Coverage of countries and varieties

Data on bearing area of winegrapes are available by variety and region for most key wine-producing countries. In the case of the European Union countries, plantings are available from one source (Eurostat 2013), while for other countries they are typically available online from a national wine industry body or the national statistical agency. The United States and Canada are key exceptions, where data are collected at the state/provincial level and only for those with significant wine production. The raw data have been compiled, and varietal synonyms have been changed to prime varietal names, by Anderson and Aryal (2013).

Table 1 lists the 44 countries included in the dataset and shows the number of regions and prime varieties in each country in 2000 and 2010. The relative importance of those countries in global winegrape area and global wine production is reported in Table 2 (which also shows the other countries reported to be producing wine, although collectively they account for just 1% of global wine output). A more-extensive set of key indicators of grape production over the past two decades is provided in Table 3.

The data in Tables 2 and 3 are three-year averages based around the year shown, that is, they refer to 1989-91, 1999-2001 and 2009-11, so as to reduce seasonal variation. Of the 44 countries included, reliable area data for 2000 were unavailable for nine of them (China, Japan, Kazakhstan, Mexico, Myanmar, Peru, Thailand, Turkey, and Ukraine). The combined share of global wine production of those nine countries in 2000 was only 1.6% (compared with 5.1% in 2010), but their varietal contributions are included as a group (called "Missing 9 in 2000") by assuming each of them had (i) the same varietal distribution in 2000 as in 2010 and (ii) a national area that was the same fraction of its 2010 area then as was its national wine production volume. As for 1990, the data refer only to countries (no regional detail) and only to the world's most important 50 or so varieties.

The **vast differences between countries in their winegrape bearing areas** are depicted in Chart 1. The biggest three, Spain, France and Italy, account for 54% of the world's winegrape vineyard area in both 2000 and 2010. The next biggest is the United States, but its share is less than 5%.

The same four countries dominate global wine production volume and value[7] (accounting for 60% in aggregate). However, the 2010 rankings among them in wine production differ considerably from that in winegrape area: France and Italy are ahead of Spain in wine production volume, and France and the United States are well ahead of Italy and Spain in terms of pre-tax value of wine production, followed by Germany and Australia (Chart 2). One reason for these differing rankings is that the huge La Mancha region of Spain has bush vines sparsely planted to the drought-resistant but low-quality Airén variety, much of whose grapes are used to produce brandy rather than wine.

When expressed as cumulative shares by the 30 largest producing countries, it is evident from Chart 3 that the **differences between countries are greater in global wine production volume than they are in winegrape area**.

The globalization of the world's wine markets has meant that the curve linking the cumulative shares of global wine production by the 30 largest producing countries has been falling substantially (Chart 4). That is, **with the industry's globalization, the national concentration of the world's vineyards has been gradually diminishing over the past century**.

The global area of winegrapes has declined by almost 6% over the first decade of this millennium (Table 4). This is despite increases of around 30% in the United States and Georgia, 40% in the Czech Republic, and 220% in New Zealand. The biggest falls were in Spain (13%), Portugal (20%) and several countries in southeastern Europe (Chart 5). That overall decline continues an earlier trend: **the global area fell 8% in the final decade of the 20th century** (last row of Table 6).

These changes in bearing area are also reflected in changes in the winegrape intensity of cropland usage. Chart 6 reveals a **huge variance across countries in the shares of national cropland under winegrapes**. It ranges from 6-13% in the six countries where this indicator is highest (Portugal, Chile, Italy, Georgia, Moldova and Spain) to less than 0.2% in Australia, China and the United States.

Drilling down from total winegrape area to the area under different varieties, Table 5 lists alphabetically all the prime varieties in the dataset in 1990, 2000 and 2010, while Table 5 ranks all but the smallest of them according to their 2010 shares of global area. The data for 1990 are limited to little more than 50 varieties, but they cover three-quarters of that year's global winegrape area (last page of Table 6). The varieties with less than 100 ha globally are included in Table 6 only if there are data for both 2000 and 2010, as the right-hand half of Table 6 is devoted to reporting the decadal changes (in both hectares and as a percentage) in individual varieties' global bearing area.

The extent of varietal concentration in the world's vineyard has increased non-trivially over the decade to 2010. This is a reversal of the trend of the previous decade (Chart 7). Half the world's plantings in 2000 were accounted for by 21 varieties but, by 2010, that total had dropped to 15 varieties. This **varietal concentration is more apparent in New**

---

[7] The value data are estimated for 2009 by Anderson and Nelgen (2011, Table 175).

World countries, where the top seven varieties accounted for over half of all plantings in 2010, whereas 16 varieties were needed in the Old World to get to the half-way point (Chart 8).

Those changes in varietal concentration in the world's vineyard are reflected in the **marked changes in the global rankings of varieties over the period since 1990** (Tables 5 and 6). Cabernet Sauvignon and Merlot have more than doubled their shares to take them from 8th and 7th to 1st and 2nd places, and Tempranillo and Chardonnay have more than trebled their shares to take 4th and 5th places, while Syrah has jumped from 35th to 6th. Sauvignon Blanc and Pinot Noir are the other two to move into the top ten. These have all been at the expense of Airén which has fallen from 1st to 3rd, Garnacha from 2nd to 7th, and Trebbiano from 5th to 9th. The fastest-growing and fastest-contracting varieties are depicted in Charts 9 and 10.

These changes ensure that the chart of the world's top 35 varieties as ranked in 1990 shows a quite different mix and rank ordering to the comparable chart for 2010 (Charts 11 and 12). The decline in varietal concentration in the world's vineyard in the 1990s was due to the large fall in the importance of the six most-common winegrape varieties in 1990 (especially low-quality Airén and Sultaniye) and the beginning of the rise in importance of Merlot, Cabernet Sauvignon, Chardonnay and Syrah as regions sought to improve the quality of their winegrapes. Even in just the decade to 2010 there have been considerable changes in the relative importance globally of the top 30 red and top 30 white varieties (Charts 13 and 14).

These changes have meant that the overall **share of red varieties in the global winegrape area has risen considerably: from 49% to 55% in the decade to 2010** (Chart 15). That share varies hugely across countries though, from 96% in China and even higher in North Africa to just 12% in Georgia and 8% in Luxembourg (Chart 16 and Tables 7 and 8). And it has changed far more in some countries than in others, whether looked at in terms of red's share of the national total or in national hectares. Of the countries that have increased the share of red varieties in their national mix, the majority are in the Old World (Chart 17). In actual area, the largest rises in red's share are in Spain, the United States and Italy while the largest falls are in Romania, Bulgaria and France (Chart 18).

Within the red and white winegrape categories, the cumulative share curves in Chart 19 indicate that the **varietal concentration has increased almost equally for red and white winegrapes over the 2000 to 2010 period**.

The availability of area data by region within each country varies considerably across countries, and is not identical in the two periods (Tables 9 and 10). The available data for France has more regions in 2010 than in 2000 while the opposite is true of Italy, for example. For the United States the greatest regional detail is of course for California, where 80-90% of the winegrapes are grown, but there was also regional detail within New York State and Oregon by 2000 and also for what is now the state with the second-largest winegrape area, Washington, by 2010 (Table 11). Australia has an unusually large number of regions because data began to be collected by Geographical Indication following the introduction of that GI legal institutional arrangement in the 1990s (Table 12). In 2010, there are just 12 of our 44 countries for which no regional breakdown is available, and most of them are small wine producers.

The colour, synonyms and country of origin of each of the alphabetically listed 1271 prime winegrape varieties are shown in Table 13, along with their 2010 global area, share, and rank. The relative importance of each of the synonyms of each prime variety is indicated in Tables 14 and 15 for 2000 and 2010, respectively. One of the more-extreme cases is Cot, better known by the synonym Malbec which accounted for 74% of Cot's global area in 2000 and 84% in 2010. To make for easy reference, Tables 16 and 17 show those same data but with the synonyms listed alphabetically. Included in those tables are the names of those primes that have synonyms. As the last page of those tables show, **a little over one-quarter of the global winegrape area is devoted to varieties that are known locally by their synonyms rather than their prime**; and just under one-quarter is planted to primes that have no synonym.

Mention has been made earlier of the concern that the diversity of winegrapes has been narrowing to a few 'international' varieties. Certainly there are very few winegrape varieties that are not from the *Vitis vinifera* species.[8] They account for just under 1.5% of the total global area in our database in 2010 (and 1.3% in 2000), of which more than half are in Brazil and one-sixth are in each of Moldova and the United States.

One way to explore the diversity issue is to examine what share of the global area is devoted to varieties by their country of origin. **Between 2000 and 2010 the global winegrape share devoted to French varieties rose from 26% to 36%** (Table 18), which contrasts with France's own shares of the global bearing area and wine production which were just 18% in 2000 and 21% in 2010 (Table 2). **The next most important country of origin is Spain, accounting for 26% of the world's area in 2010, down from 28% in 2000**, which is just a little above Spain's own share of the global bearing area of 22-24%. **Third is Italy**, whose country of origin share is almost the same as Italy's share of global area of 13% -- **but in terms of number of varieties, Italy's global winegrape share is more than three times that of Spain**. No other country can lay claim to being the origin of more than 3% of the world's winegrape varieties in terms of bearing area. However, in terms of number of varieties Portugal appears to have a large share, but that is because it has introduced a particularly detailed reporting system that by 2010 captured many of its varieties that are planted to a small fraction of 1% of its total plantings. That is revealed in Tables 19 and 20, which list alphabetically the prime varieties from each country of origin and their global area and share.[9] Where those various varieties are planted is shown in the columns of Tables 21 and 22 for each of our 44 countries, as well as for the Old World and the New World aggregates. **Particularly striking is the high and increasing dominance of winegrapes of French origin in the New World's vineyards: that share averaged 67% in 2010, up from 53% in 2000. It compares with an increase from 20% to 27% for the Old World's vineyards.** The shares of French, Spanish and Italian winegrape varieties in various countries' vineyards are shown in Charts 20 to 22, respectively.

---

[8] A total of just 22 varieties have been identified as not *Vitis vinifera*: Baco Blanc, Bailey, Bordo, Campbell Early, Catawba, Concord, Couderc, Couderc Noir, Delaware, Fredonia, Herbemont, Isabella, Jacquez, Juliana, Landot Noir, Niagara, Noah, Norton, Oberlin, Patricia, Seibel, and Venus.

[9] Of the 1271 prime varieties identified for 2010, the most popular country of origin is Italy with 328, followed by Portugal (196), France (120), and Spain (88). Then three other countries contribute between 55 and 70 varieties each (Hungary, the United States and Croatia). Most of the remaining varieties are from Southeastern Europe and the countries surrounding the Black and Caspian seas (Table 19).

Another way to consider varietal concentration is to review the share of the top variety or the cumulative shares of the top few varieties globally and in a country's total area of winegrapes. Globally, the top 35 varieties accounted for 59% of the world's winegrape bearing area in 2000 but by 2010 that share was 66%. At the national level, in 2010 as many as 12 of our 44 countries have more than one-third of their total area under just their top variety; but perhaps even more striking is that **only 6 of the 44 countries have less than one-third of their total winegrape area under their top three varieties**. Those numbers of countries had changed from 7 and 7 in 2000, respectively, again indicating a rapid increase in varietal concentration (Tables 23 and 24), as already noted globally in Charts 7 and 8.

Tables 25 and 26 record the source of the prime name and main synonym if any for each variety (and thus also its country of origin). The Robinson, Harding and Vouillamoz (2012) volume is the source of close to 90% of named prime varieties in our database, with just 2% from www.vivc.de. As for the rest (just 6% in 2010), they have not been identified in either of those sources and so are assumed to have the name and origin of the country in which they are recorded.

Given the heavy concentration in just a few varieties in each country, Tables 27 to 42 provide details for the world's top 30 reds, top 30 whites, and top 6 other (greyish) coloured winegrapes. They reveal which varieties are dominating the vineyards of each country. For example, Table 29 shows that almost one-third of France's area was devoted to what were the three top reds globally in 2000, namely Cabernet Sauvignon, Garnacha Tinta and Merlot.

Varietal Intensity Indexes and global varietal shares

The Varietal Intensity Index is defined by Anderson (2010) as a variety's share of a region's total winegrape area divided by that variety's share of the global winegrape area. This index is thus a complement to national share information in that it indicates the importance of a variety in a region not relative to other varieties in that region but rather relative to that variety in the world. It also complements information on a country's share of the global area for a variety: like that share, the VII can change for a region – even if its area remains unchanged – when that variety's area in the rest of the world changes.

That complementarity is exposed in Tables 43 to 46. In Tables 43 and 44, for example, the top 45 varieties for each country are shown in order of their national share in 2000 or 2010, and alongside that is shown the country's global share of that variety and its Varietal Intensity Index. For example, France's total area and varietal mix altered relatively little over the decade to 2010, yet its VIIs altered considerably. On the one hand, the VIIs for its four biggest varieties of French origin (Merlot, Syrah, Cabernet Sauvignon and Chardonnay) each fell by 10% or more, in each case because bearing areas of those varieties expanded considerably in the rest of the world. On the other hand, France's VIIs for two of its three biggest varieties of non-French origin (Garnacha Tinta and Trebbiano Toscana) rose by about 10%, in those cases because their bearing areas fell much more in the rest of the world than in France. Mazuelo was the big exception: its area in France fell 45% over that decade, compared with a fall of 37% globally, so France's VII for that variety VII fell (from 4.3 to 3.6).

By contrast, the global area of each of Spain's seven biggest varieties apart from Tempranillo contracted, and so even though the Spanish areas of each of those seven also contracted, the contractions were smaller in Spain than globally and hence Spain's VII rose for almost all of them (the exception being Garnacha Tinta, whose VII fell slightly).

Another example of global interest relates to Argentina, where Cot (main synonym: Malbec) was the country's 3rd biggest variety in 2000 but its biggest in 2010 (15.4% of the national winegrape area), when it accounted for 76% of the world's Cot plantings. Since that variety represented only 0.88% of the global area of all varieties in that year, Argentina's Varietal Intensity Index for that variety was (0.154/0.088 =) 17.5 in 2010. But that was only slightly larger than its VII of 16.2 in 2000, because over that decade the global area of Cot rose by two-thirds. Note also that for Argentina, Cot is not even ranked in the top 25 varieties in terms of VIIs in 2010 (Table 46), because there are numerous varieties that are unique to Argentina and that therefore have the even higher VII of 23. (When a variety is grown only in one country, its VII is necessarily the inverse of the proportion of the global winegrape area accounted for by that country – and so is identical for each unique variety in that country and year.)

To illustrate the difference between the national share of a variety and its VII, consider as a further example the national shares and the VII's for Syrah (main synonym: Shiraz). This is the most important variety in Australia, and its share of Australia's total winegrape area has risen from 22% to 28% in the decade to 2010. However, Charts 23 and 24 reveal that Syrah has become more important in numerous other countries as well since 2000. Its share of the global vineyard area thus rose from 2.1% in 2000 to 4.0% in 2010. As a result, Australia's share of Syrah's global area has fallen from 29% to 23% (Chart 25) and so Syrah's VII for Australia has fallen from 11 to 7 over that decade (Chart 26).

Even so, Australian regions continues to dominate the list of the top 25 regions in the world in terms of regional VIIs for Syrah – just as regions within the United States dominate the list for Tribidrag (main synonym: Zinfandel), Spanish regions dominate the Airen list, and Argentinean regions dominate the Cereza list (Tables 47 to 53).

The fall in the VII for Australia is not unique to Syrah. Indeed of all 15 varieties for which there were more than 1000 hectares in Australia in 2010, there are only four whose VII has risen since 2000 (Chart 27). Only a small fraction of that can be explained by Australia's share of the global area becoming larger, since its share has risen only marginally over that decade (from 2.7% to 3.3%). The much more important reason for the VII falling for most of the key varieties in Australia is that the country's mix of varieties is becoming more similar to the global average. The next section provides a way of quantifying the extent of varietal mix similarity of regions and countries with the world (and also with each other).

Varietal Similarity Indexes

While the Varietal Intensity Index is helpful in indicating the extent of specialization of a region or country in any particular variety vis-à-vis the rest of the world, it is also helpful to have a measure of how similar or different a region's overall mix of varieties is to that of other regions or the world. For that purpose an index of similarity of varietal mix between regions or countries or over time has been developed. As defined and explained in the Technical Notes at the front of this volume, this Varietal Similarity Index provides an indication of how closely the shares of different varieties in the winegrape area in one location match the shares in another location or in the world (or in that same location in another time period). The closer (further away) that match, the closer the index is to one (zero). That is, the index will be zero for pairs of regions with no overlap in their winegrape varietal mix, and one for pairs of regions with an identical varietal mix. For the in-between cases, the index is conceptually similar to a correlation coefficient. Like a correlation coefficient, it is completely symmetric so the results can be summarized in a symmetric matrix with values of 1 on the diagonal, plus a vector that reports the index for each region relative to the global varietal mix.

Various questions can be addressed with the help of this Varietal Similarity Index (VSI), given the heterogeneity across regions and even countries in their winegrape varietal mixes. The most obvious is: how similar is each country to the global average mix of varieties? The range of national-world VSI's is quite wide (Tables 54 and 55), with a handful of countries above 0.55 and another handful below 0.15. Not surprisingly, the mix in France is closest to the global mix, but there have been major changes since 2000: France's is now closer to the world average, reflecting the fact that many other countries have adopted more French varieties over that decade. That global move toward French varieties has also contributed to the sharp rise in the VSI for the United States and the small drop for Spain. Australia's VSI has risen in part because so many other countries have expanded their plantings of Australia's most-popular variety, namely Syrah.

The fact that the VSI with the world rose between 2000 and 2010 for each of the five biggest New World countries and for two of the three biggest Old World countries (Chart 28) is a further reflection of the recent increase in varietal concentration in the world's vineyard over that decade. Meanwhile, the VSIs for many of the former communist countries of the Old World have fallen substantially since 2000 as those countries continue to restructure their vineyards and move toward more-profitable (including local) varieties. Hungary, for example had just under a quarter of its winegrape area under varieties of Hungarian origin in 2000, but by 2010 that share was 37%. The countries with the lowest VSIs vis-à-vis the world include those that are highly specialized in just white wines (e.g., Austria, Georgia, Luxembourg).

The VSI is also useful for indicating, for any one region or country, how close its varietal mix in 2010 is to that in 2000. Chart 29 lays that out for each country for which there are comparable data for the two periods. While some countries have an across-time VSI close to one (Switzerland 0.99, France and Austria 0.97), others are much lower (United Kingdom 0.32, Russia 0.25) which reflects considerable changes in their varietal mix of bearing areas over that decade.

The main use of the VSI is in examining the extent to which a region or country has a varietal mix similar to that of other regions or countries. In both 2000 and 2010, the New World countries have varietal mixes closest to other New World countries, whereas the varietal mixes of Old World countries are closest to one of their neighbours (Table 57 and 58, including last rows). The latter is especially the case among the countries of Eastern Europe and the former Soviet Union. This shows up in Chart 30, which ranks countries according to their VSI with the country that has the closest varietal mix to theirs: eleven of the first 14 countries are former communist countries of the Old World, and their closest-matched country is also from that region – as are several of their other nine closest-matched countries shown in Table 58. So even though those countries tend to have varietal mixes very different from the world average (they are biased toward the right-hand side of Chart 28), those mixes are very similar to each other. By contrast, several West European countries have no other country with a similar varietal mix, notably Italy, Portugal, Spain and Greece. Such varietal distinctiveness may or may not be a good thing economically, depending on how unique their terroir is and how valued their varieties are by consumers.

There are of course considerable differences in varietal mixes between regions within each country as well. For example, the VSIs across the regions within Australia, even vis-à-vis the world, range from 0.30 to 0.70 in 2010. That information may be helpful for producers in that region thinking of altering their varietal mix or re-locating to a region with a higher latitude or altitude so as to maintain their firm's current varietal mix in the wake of global warming. Tables 59 and 60 show that for some countries such as Italy, the regions with the closest mix to theirs are neighbouring Italian regions, whereas the closest matches for many French regions are in other countries.

Summary data for each key variety and country

To assist readers wishing to focus on a particular variety or country, Section VIII of the tables provides, in alphabetical order, a one-page graphical summary of information about each of the world's top 50 varieties, while Section XI provides, again in alphabetical order, a one-page summary of information about each of the 44 countries in the database.

Final word

While this volume provides a great deal of information about which winegrapes have been grown in various regions during the first decade of the 21st century, it leaves open the question of *why* those varieties have been produced where they are. Is it driven mainly by what grows best in each location (the terroir explanation)? Gergaud and Ginsgurgh (2008) argue that even in Bordeaux that has not been the main explanation. Is the increasing concentration on major French varieties because non-French producers – particularly in newly expanding wine-producing countries – find it easier to market them because of France's strong reputation with those varieties? Might part of the explanation be that those varieties do well in a wide range of growing environments, or have been found to be desirable for blending with the traditional varieties of a region? These and other centripetal forces during the first decade of this century apparently have dominated the possible centrifugal forces mentioned at the start of this Introduction. It remains to be seen whether the latter will be strong enough to dominate the former over the next decade or so. If China is the country with the greatest expansion of winegrape area in the next few years, and if its new plantings continue to concentrate on key French red varieties, the concentration of the world's varietal mix may continue to increase for some time yet.

References

Anderson, K. (ed.) (2004), *The World's Wine Markets: Globalization at Work*, London: Edward Elgar.

Anderson, K. (2010), 'Varietal Intensities and Similarities of the World's Wine Regions', *Journal of Wine Economics* 5(2): 270-309, Winter.

Anderson, K. and N.R. Aryal (2013), *Database of Regional, National and Global Winegrape Bearing Areas by Variety, 2000 and 2010*, freely available in Excel files at the University of Adelaide's Wine Economics Research Centre, at www.adelaide.edu.au/wine-econ/databases.

Anderson, K. and S. Nelgen (2011), *Global Wine Markets, 1961 to 2009: A Statistical Compendium,* Adelaide: University of Adelaide Press, freely available as an e-book at www.adelaide.edu.au/press/titles/global-wine.

Eurostat (2013), *Basic Vineyard Survey,* accessible by navigating ["Agriculture, forestry and fisheries "à"Agriculture"à"Vineyard survey"à"Basic vineyard survey"] at http://epp.eurostat.ec.europa.eu/portal/page/portal/statistics/search_database

Fegan, P.W. (2003), *The Vineyard Handbook: Appellations, Maps and Statistics,* revised edition, Springfield IL: Phillips Brothers, for the Chicago Wine School.

Gergaud, O. and V. Ginsgurgh (2008), 'Endowments, Production Technologies and the Quality of Wines in Bordeaux: Does Terroir Matter?, *The Economic Journal* 118: F142-57. Reprinted in *Journal of Wine Economics* 5: 3-21, 2010.

JKI (Julius Kühn-Institut) (2013). *Vitis International Variety Catalogue.* Institute for Grapevine Breeding, Federal Research Centre for Cultivated Plants, Geilweilerhof. www.vivc.de

Johnson, H. and J. Robinson (2013), *World Atlas of Wine,* 7th edition, London: Mitchell Beasley.

OIV (2012), *International List of Vine Varieties and Their Synonyms,* Paris: Organisation Internationale de la Vigne et du Vin (International Organisation of Vine and Wine). www.oiv.org

Robinson, J., J. Harding and J. Vouillamoz (2012), *Wine Grapes: A Complete Guide to 1,368 Vine Varieties, Including their Origins and Flavours,* London: Allen Lane.

Vouillamoz, J.F. and M.S. Grando (2006), 'Genealogy of Wine Grape Cultivars: Pinot is Related to Syrah', *Heredity* 97(2): 102-10.

World's winegrape varieties and wine regions at a glance

1. National shares of global winegrape area, 2000 and 2010 (%)

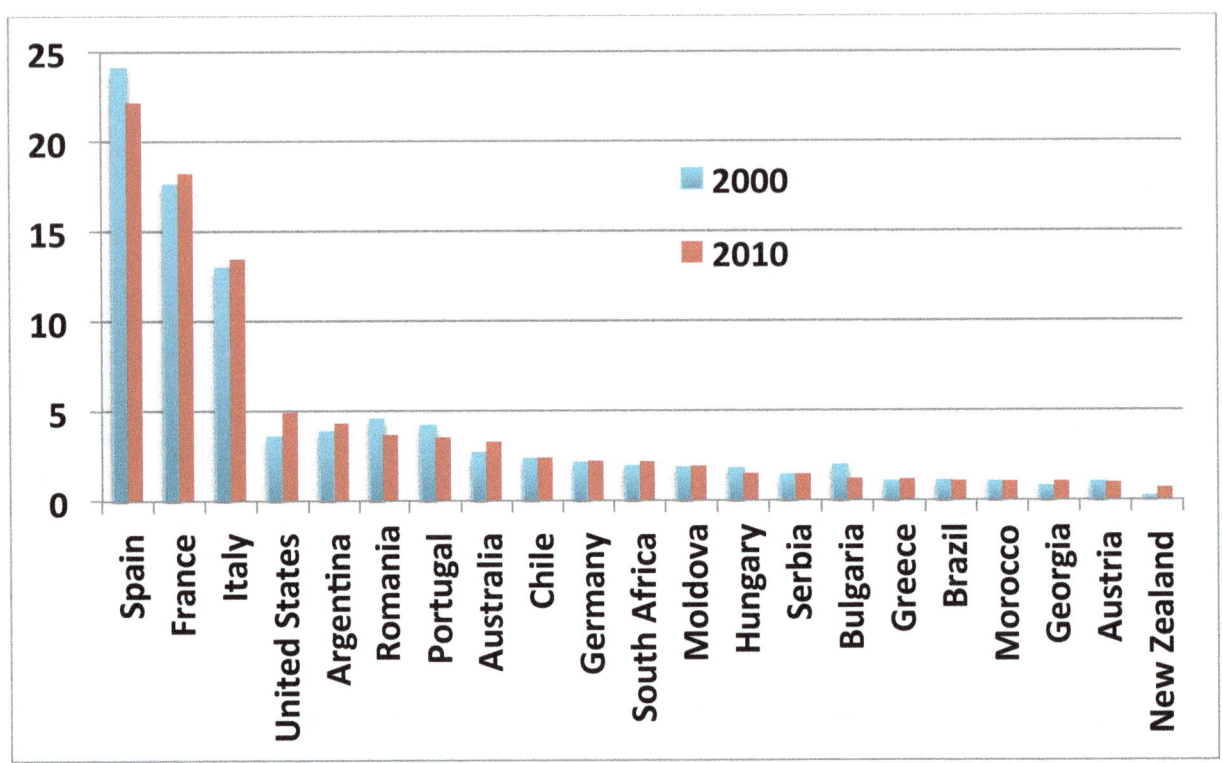

2. National shares of global winegrape area, wine production volume and wine production value, 2010 (%)

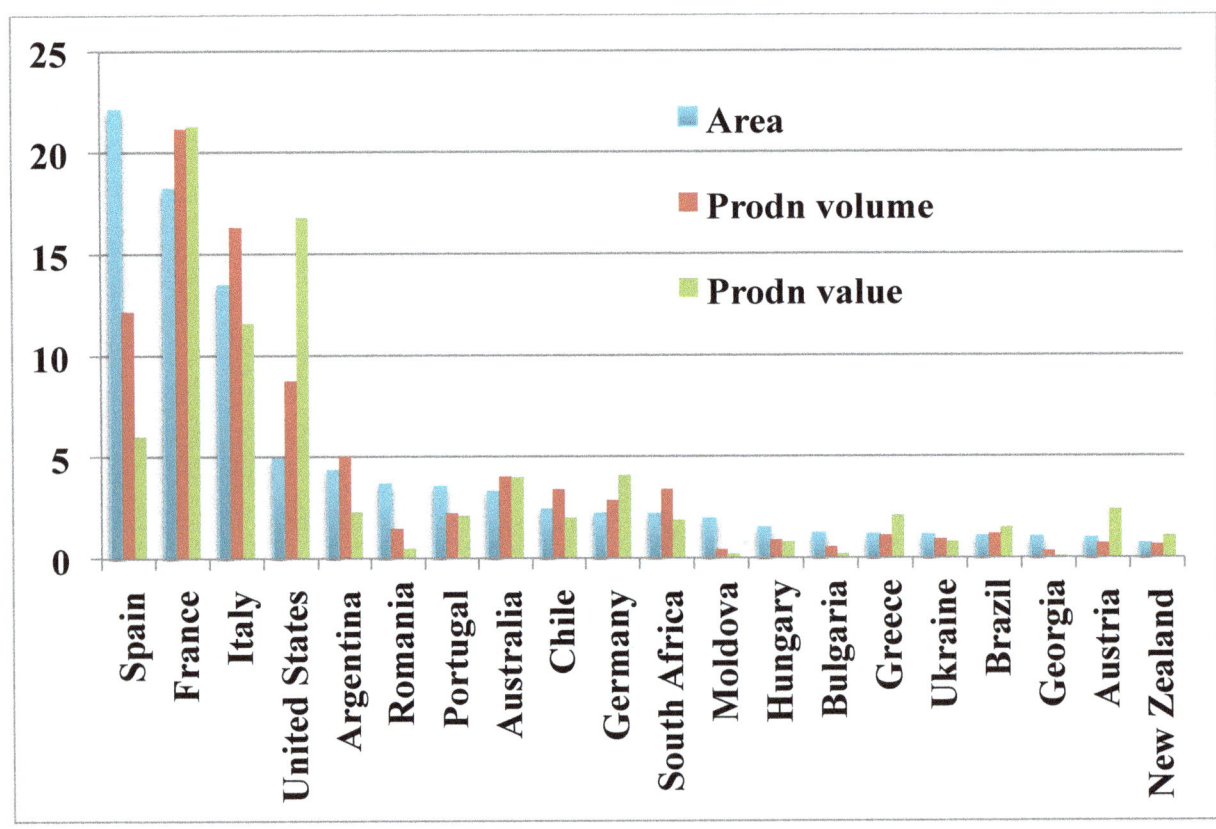

3. Cumulative national shares of global winegrape area and of wine production volume, 2010 (%)

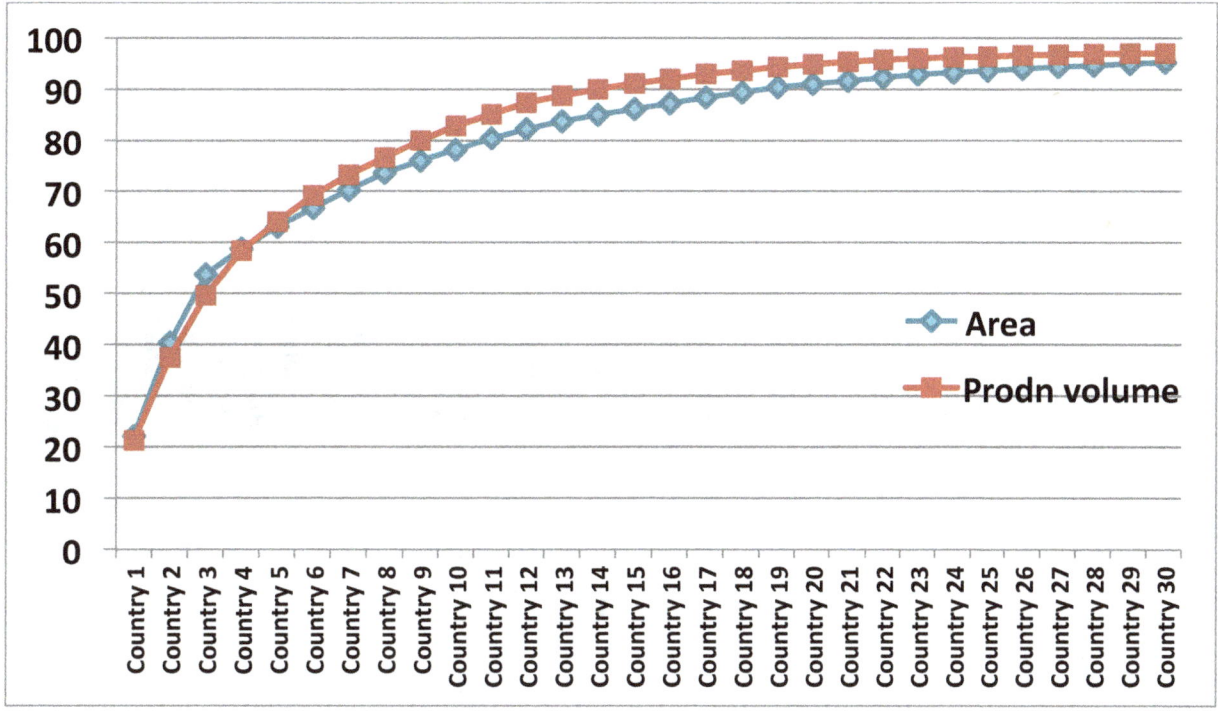

4. Cumulative national shares of global wine production, 1909-13, 1961-64 and 2009-11 (%)

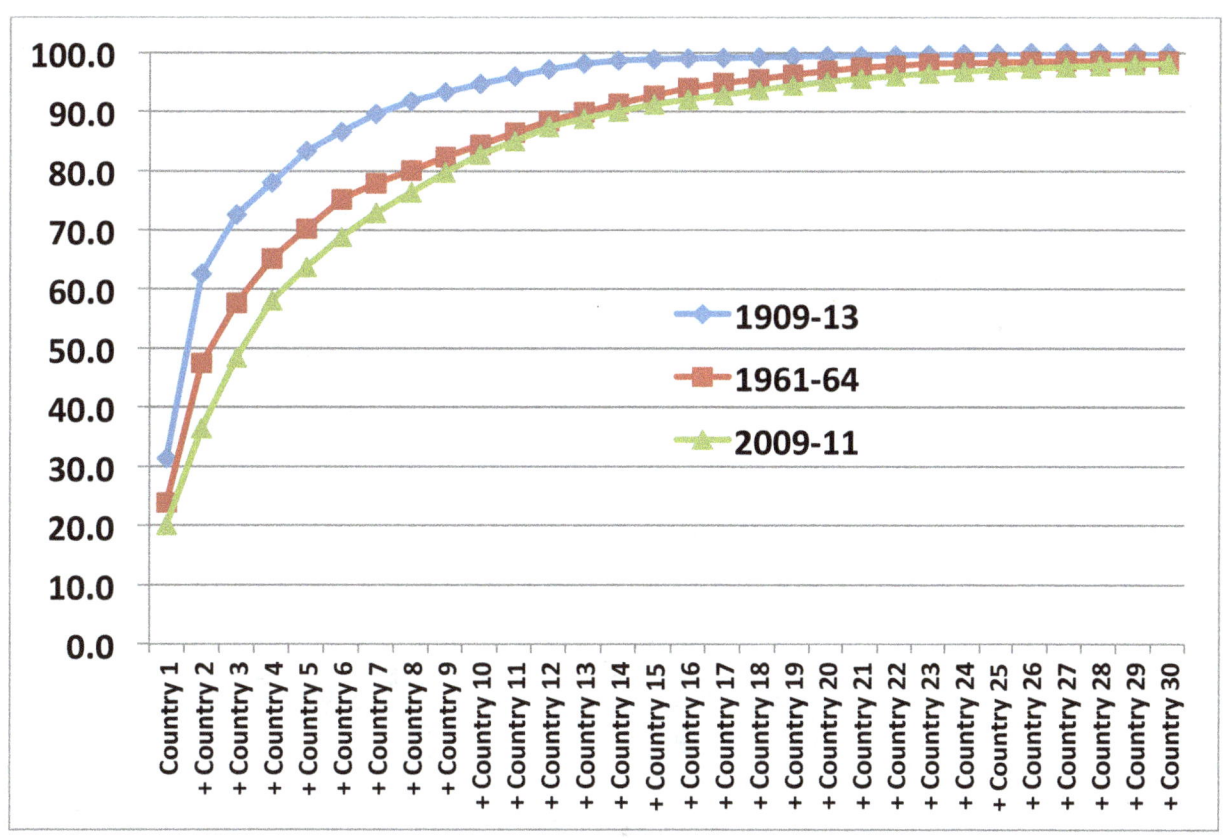

5. Largest increases and decreases in national winegrape bearing area, 2000 to 2010(ha)

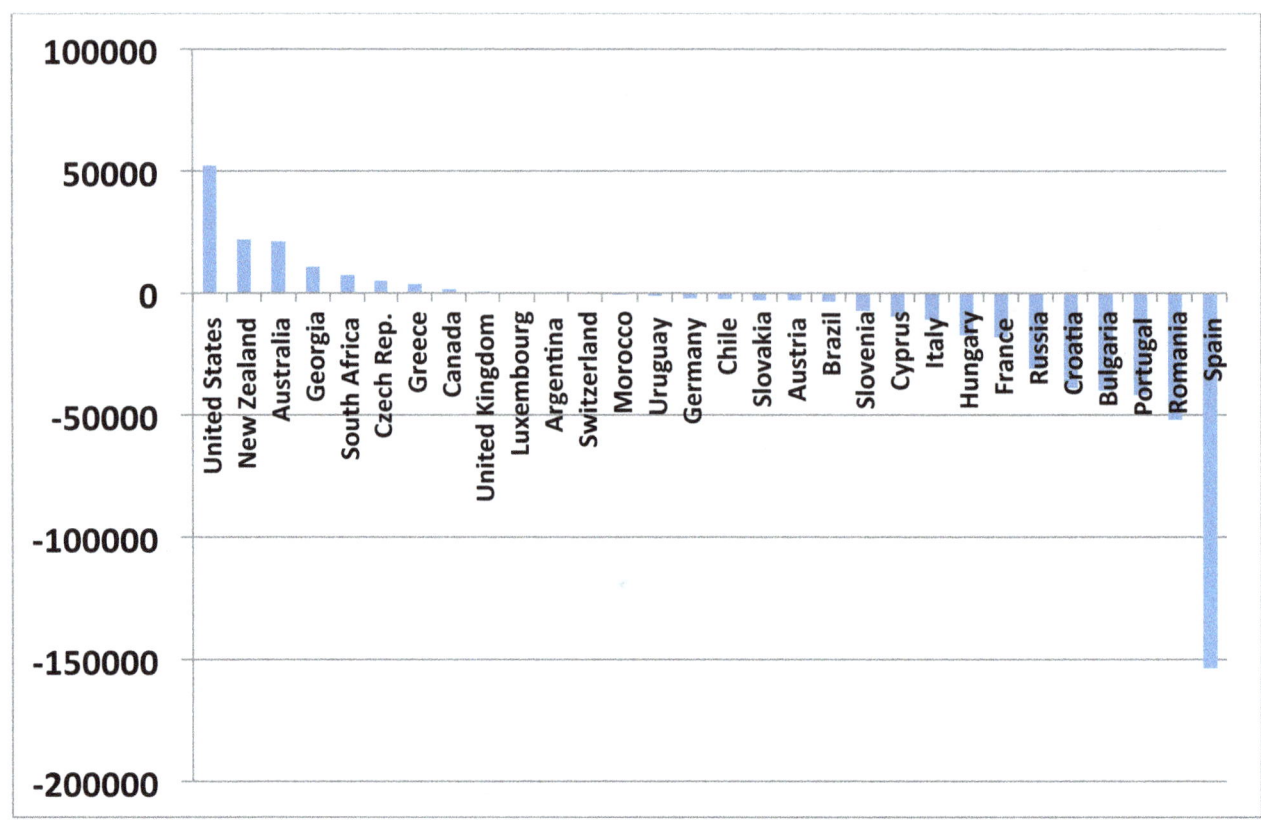

6. Share of total agricultural crop area under winegrapes, 2009-11 (%)

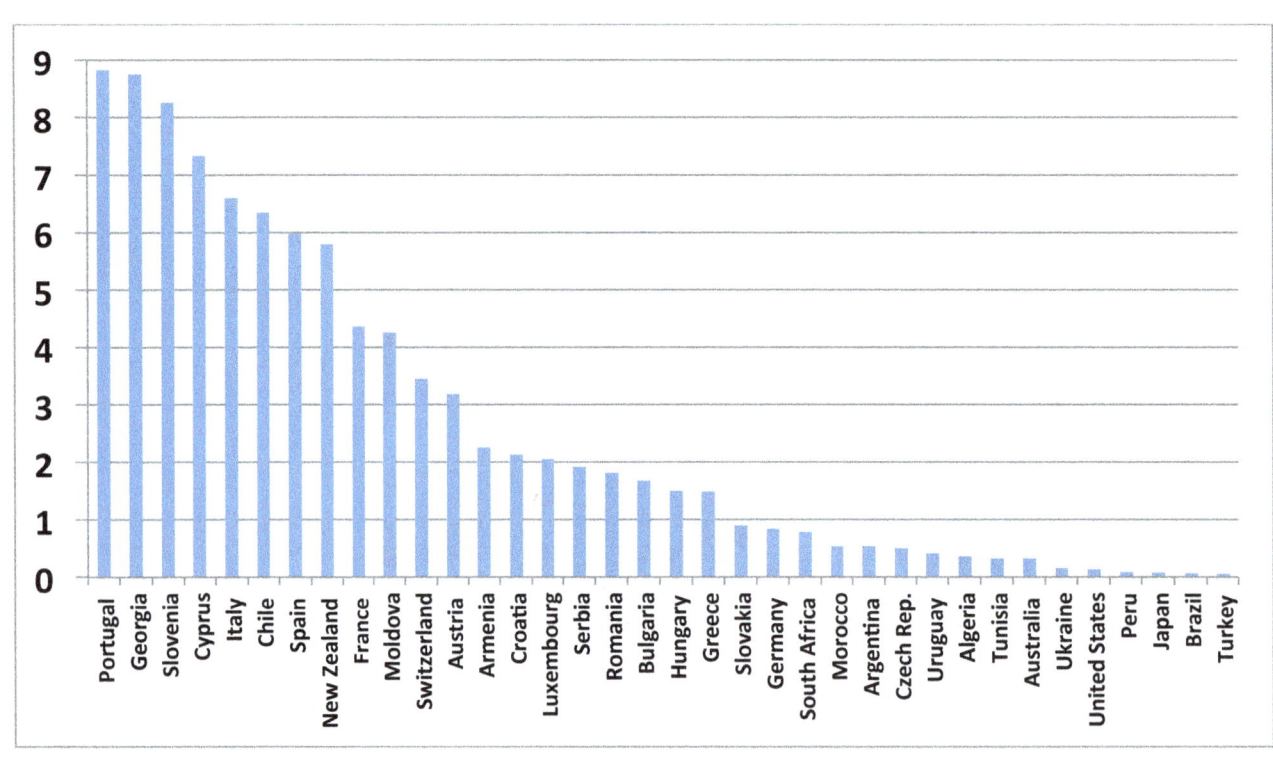

7. Cumulative varietal shares of global winegrape area, 1990, 2000 and 2010 (%)

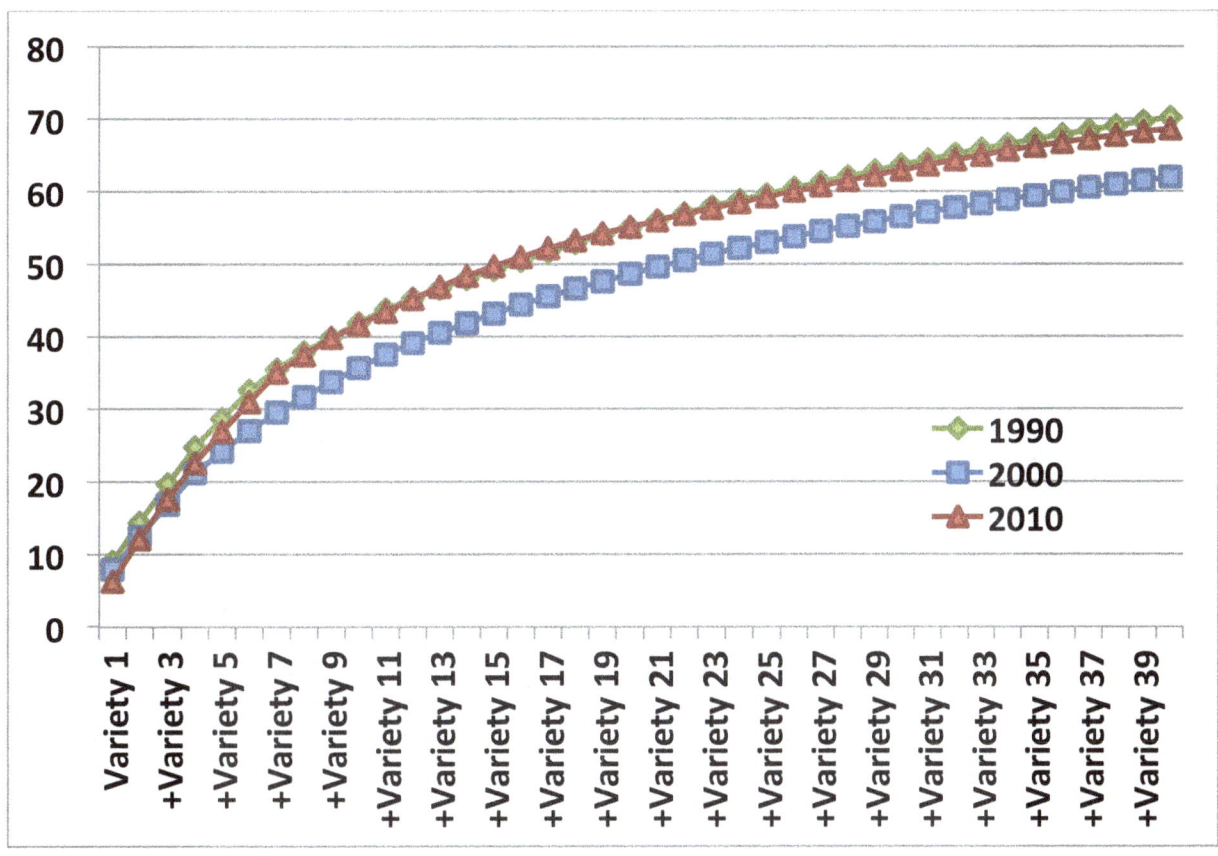

8. Cumulative shares of Old World and New World winegrape areas by variety, 2000 and 2010 (%)

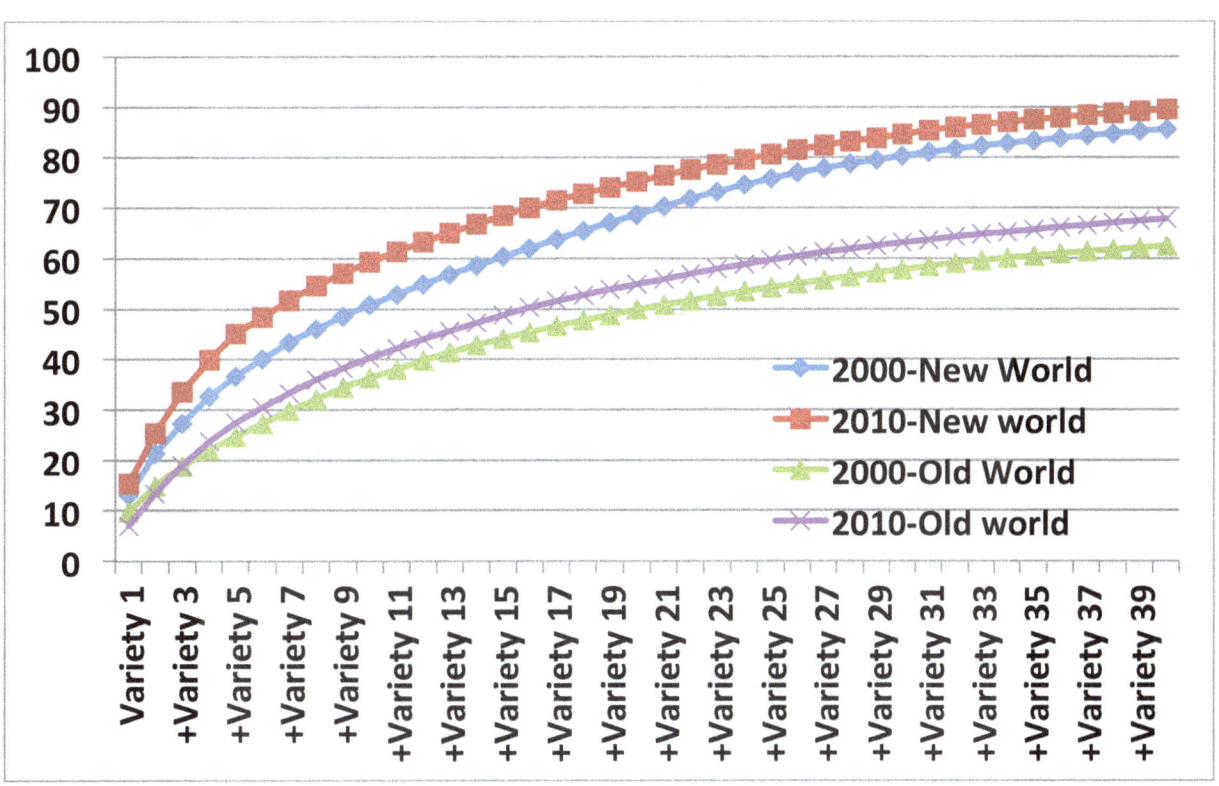

9. World's fastest-expanding winegrape varieties, 2000 to 2010 (ha)

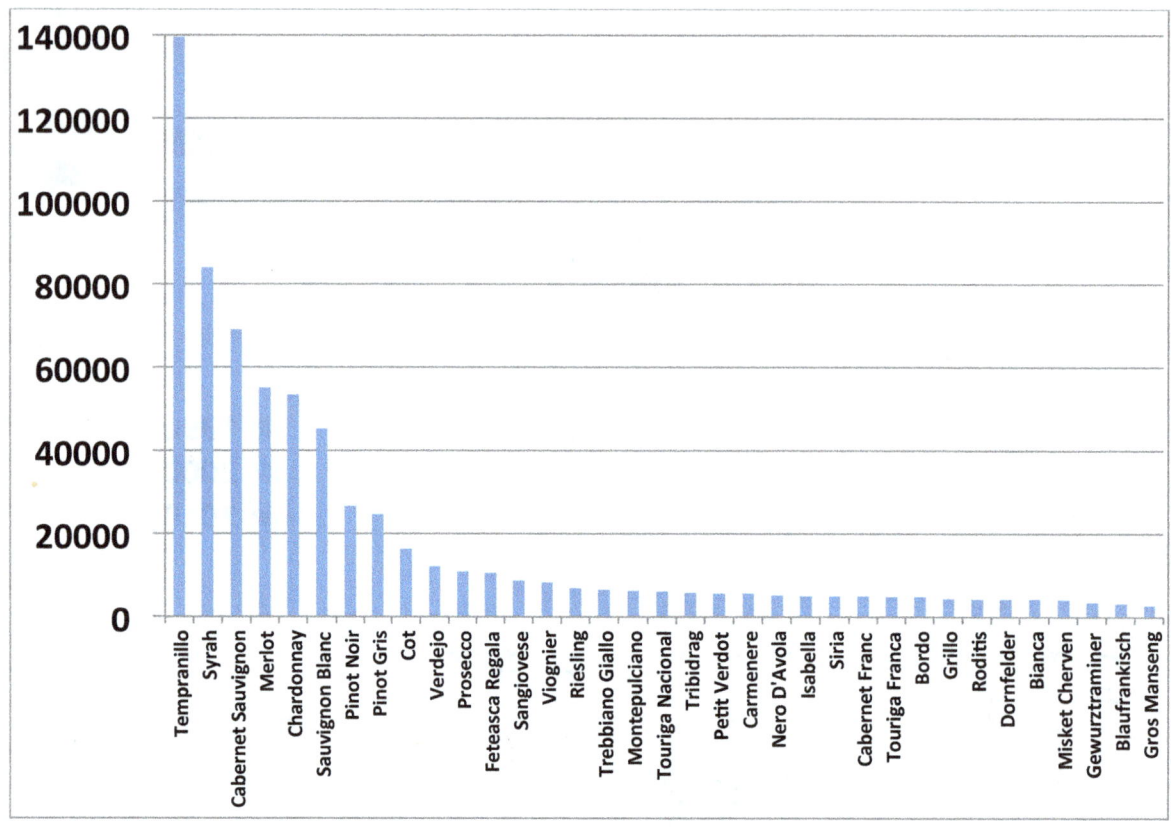

10. World's fastest-contracting winegrape varieties, 2000 to 2010 (ha)

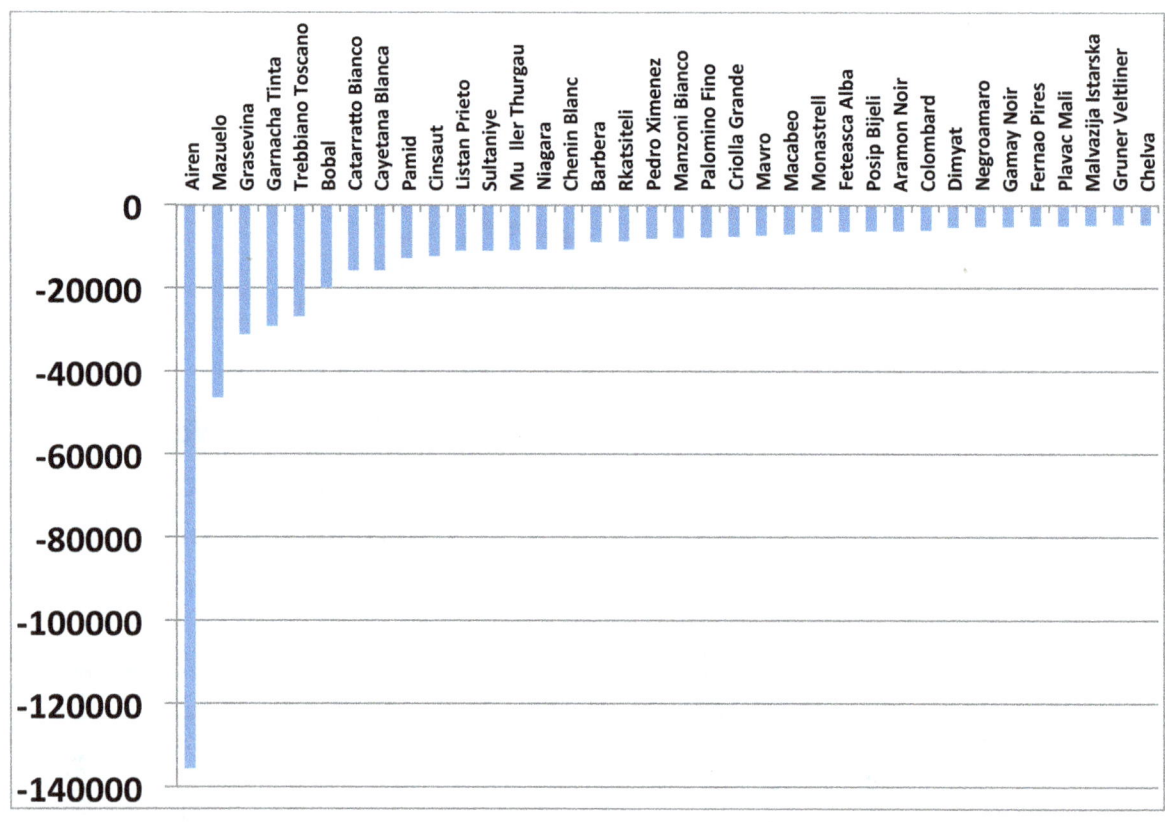

11. World's top 35 varieties in 1990, compared with 2000 and 2010 (ha)

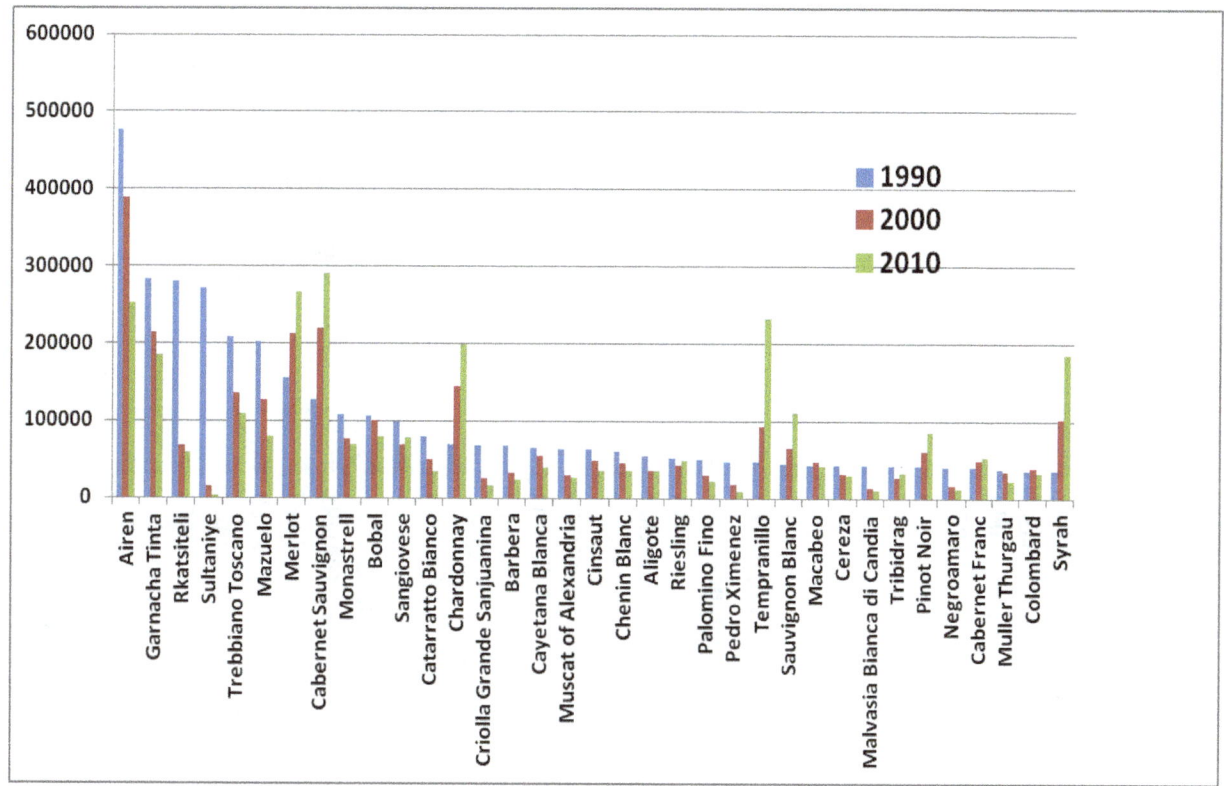

12. World's top 35 varieties in 2010, compared with 1990 and 2000 (ha)

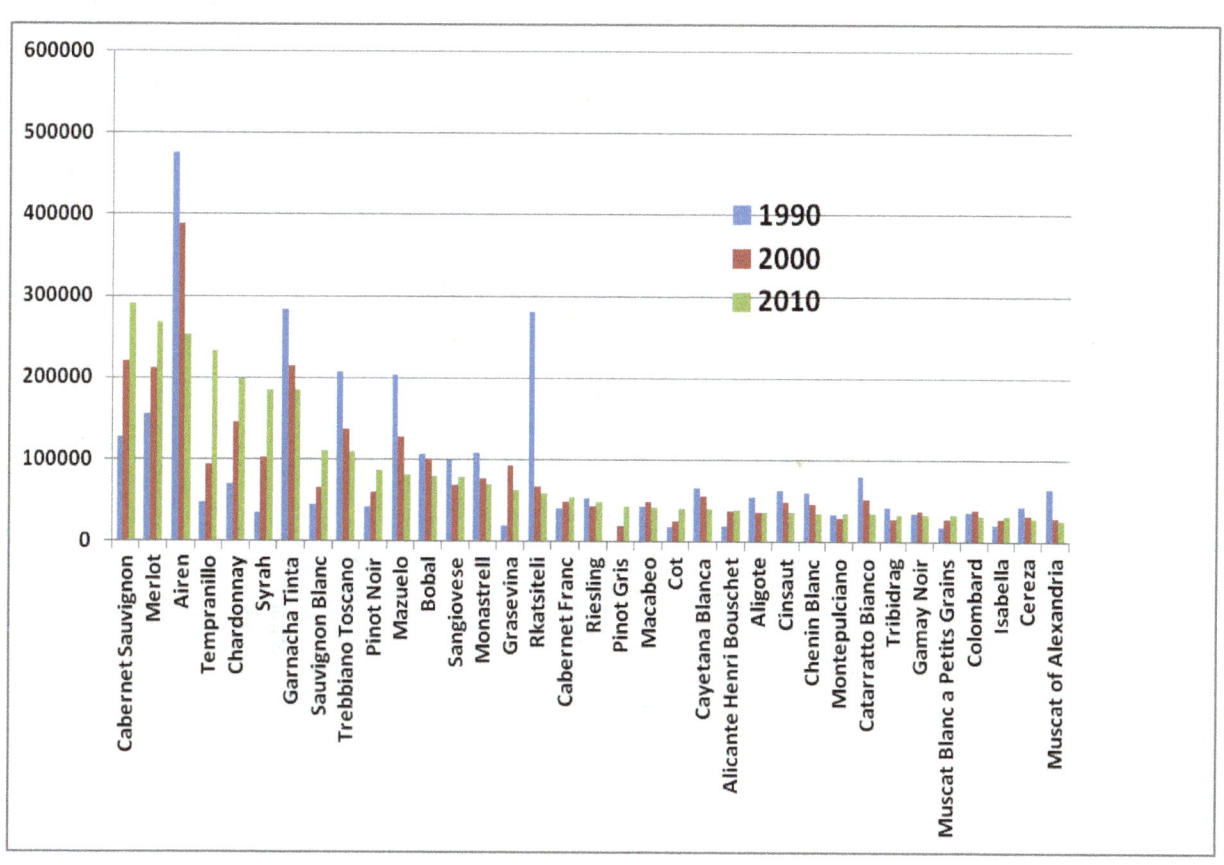

13. Top 30 red varieties' shares of global wine area, 2000 and 2010 (%)

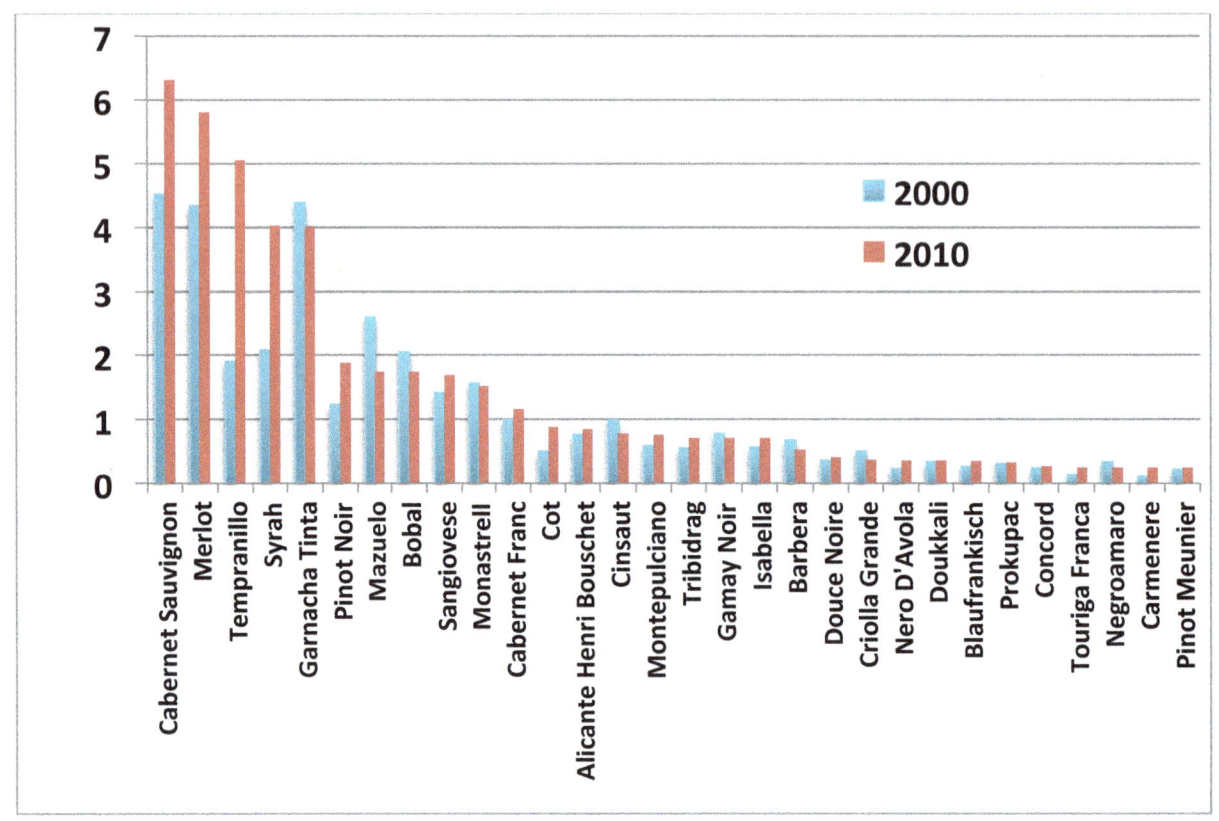

14. Top 30 white varieties' shares of global wine area, 2000 and 2010 (%)

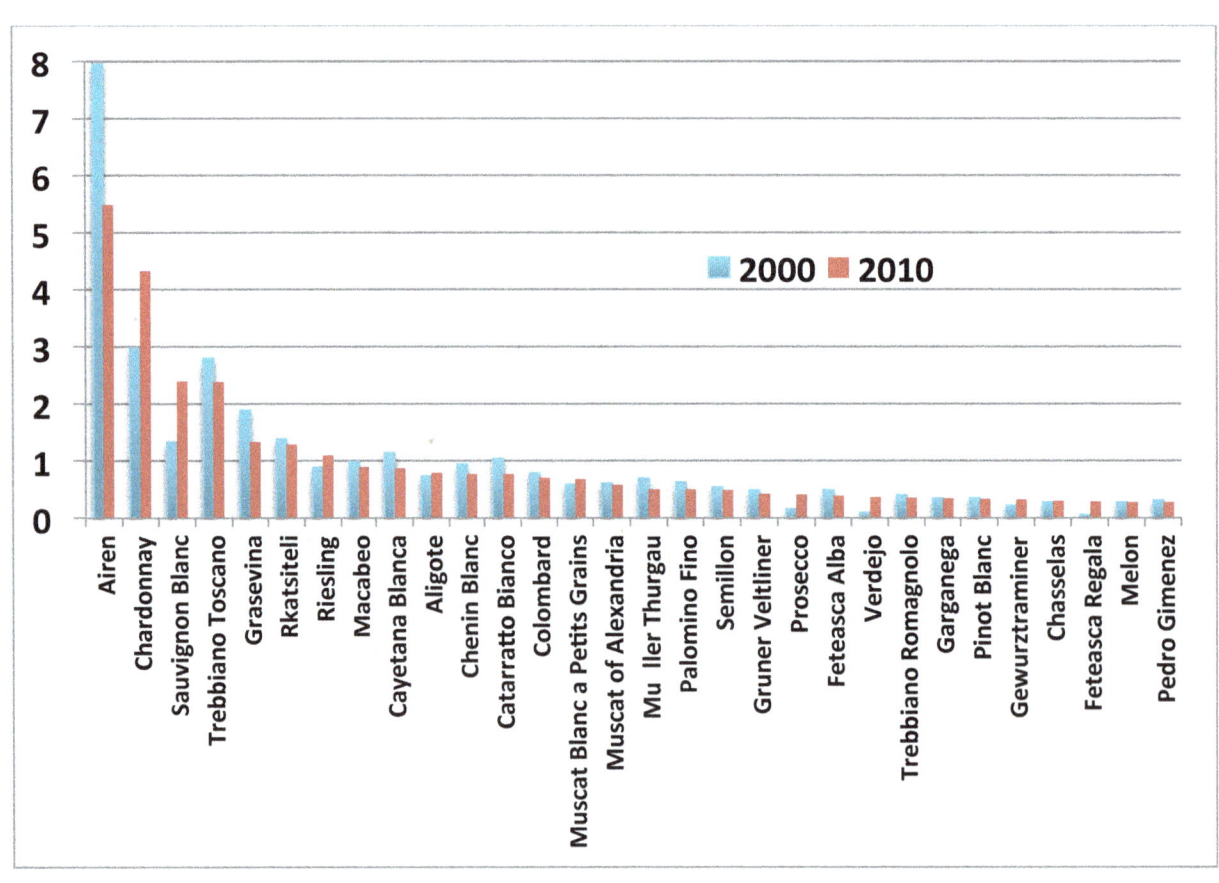

15. Red and white shares of global winegrape area, 2000 and 2010 (%)

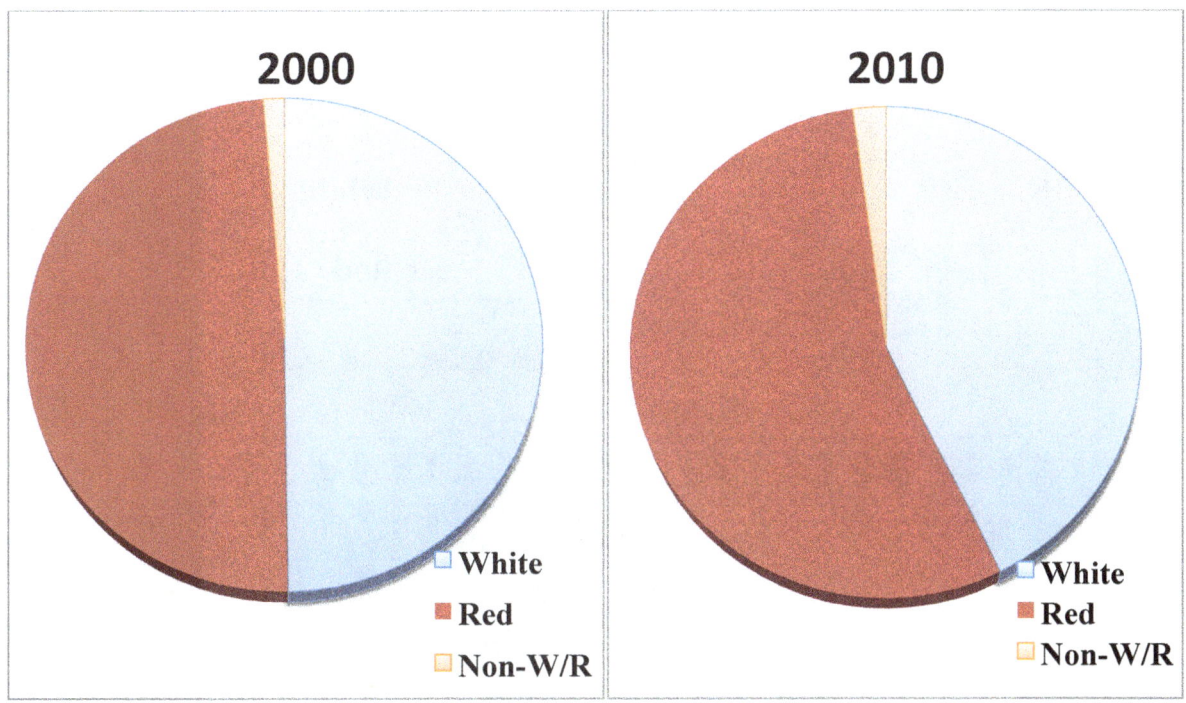

16. Share of red varieties in national winegrape area, 2000 and 2010 (%)

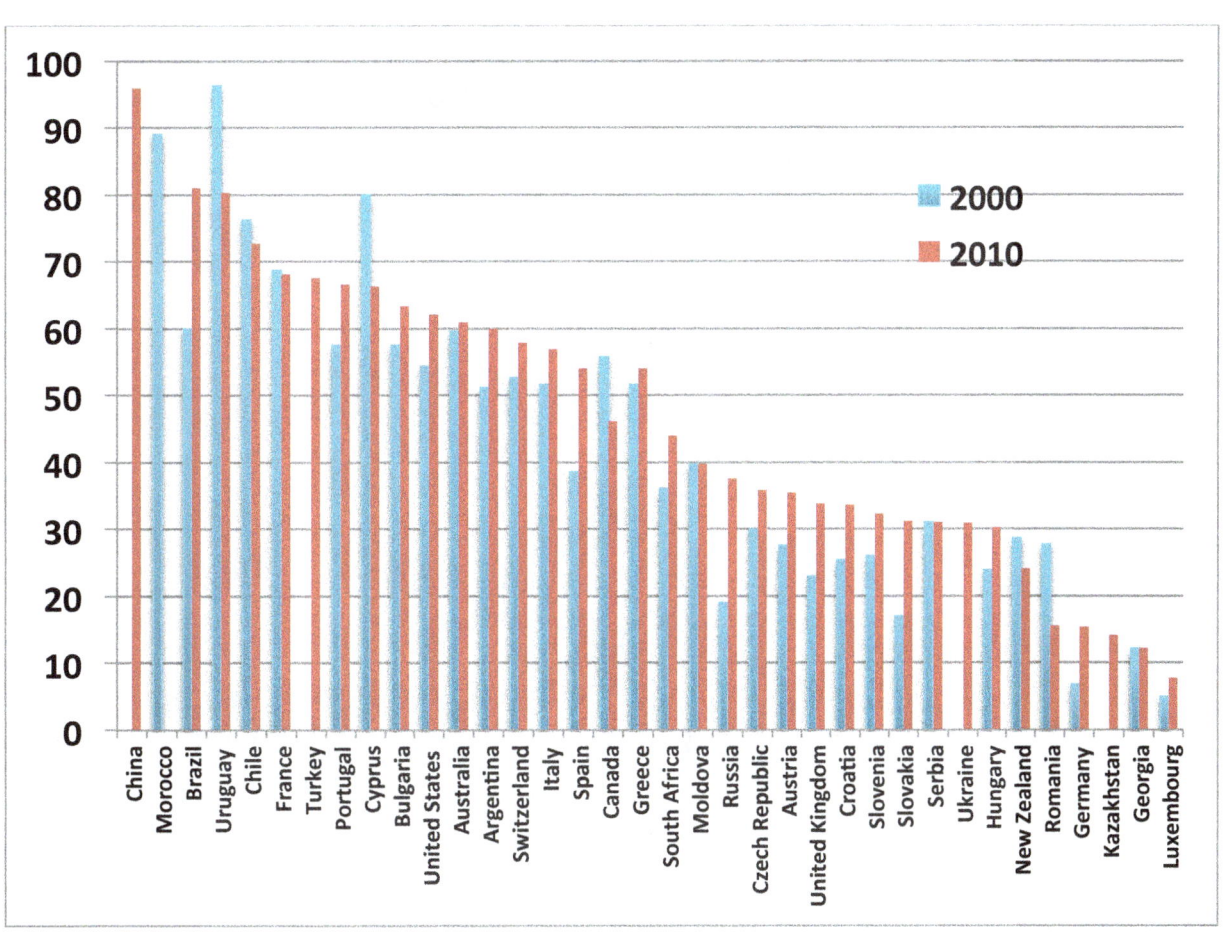

17. Percentage point changes in shares of red and white varieties in national winegrape area, 2000 to 2010 (%)

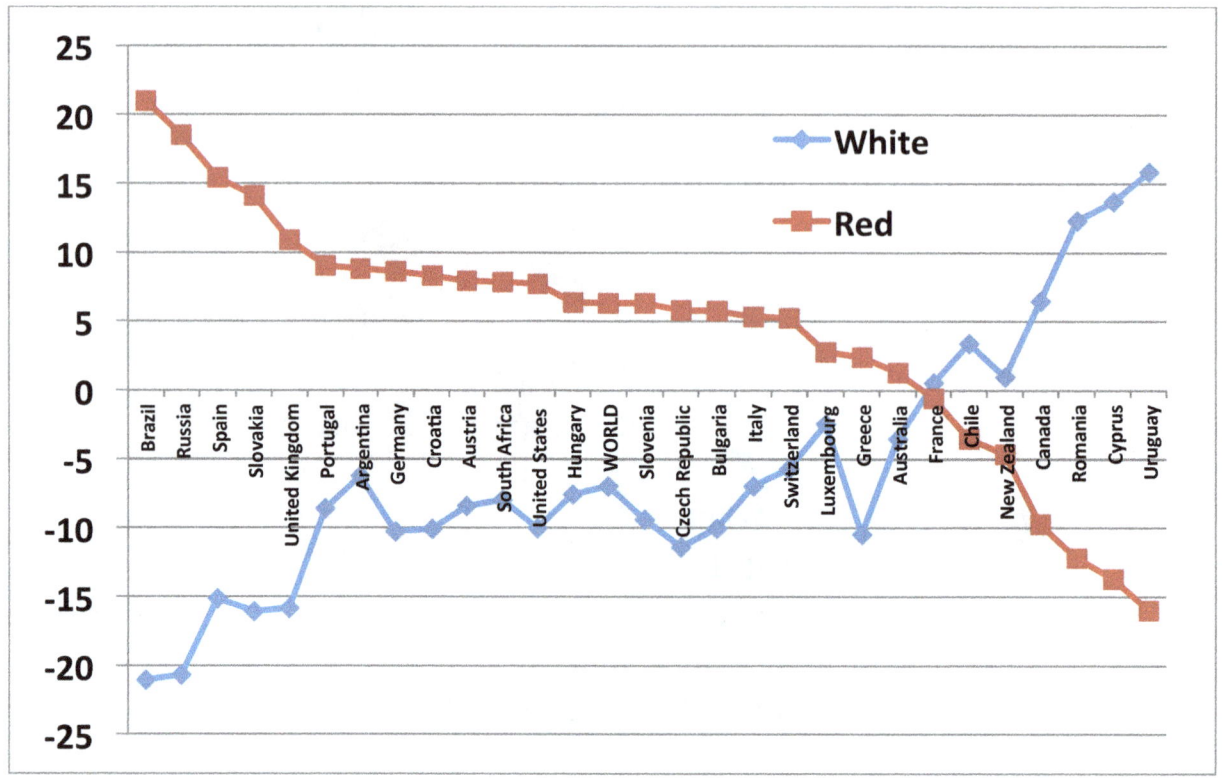

18. Change in national hectares of red varieties, 2000 to 2010 (ha)

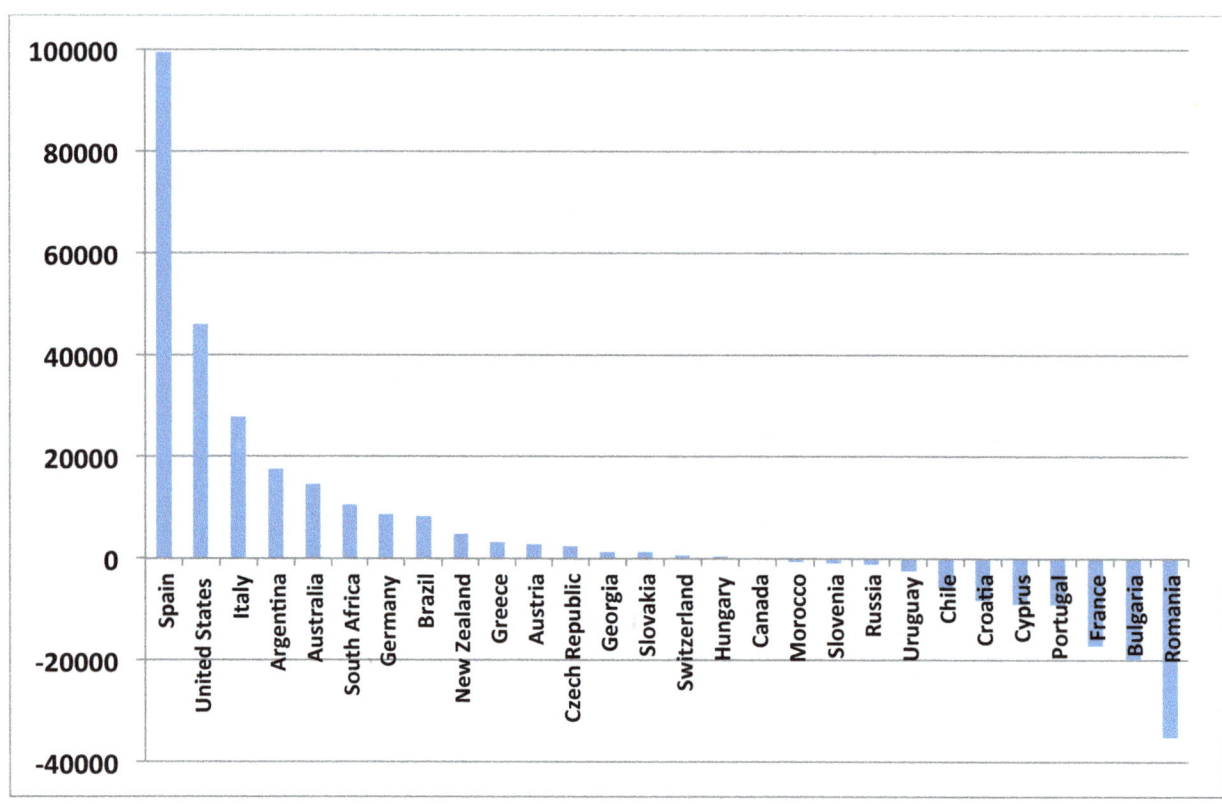

19. Cumulative varietal shares of world red and white winegrape area, 2000 and 2010 (%)

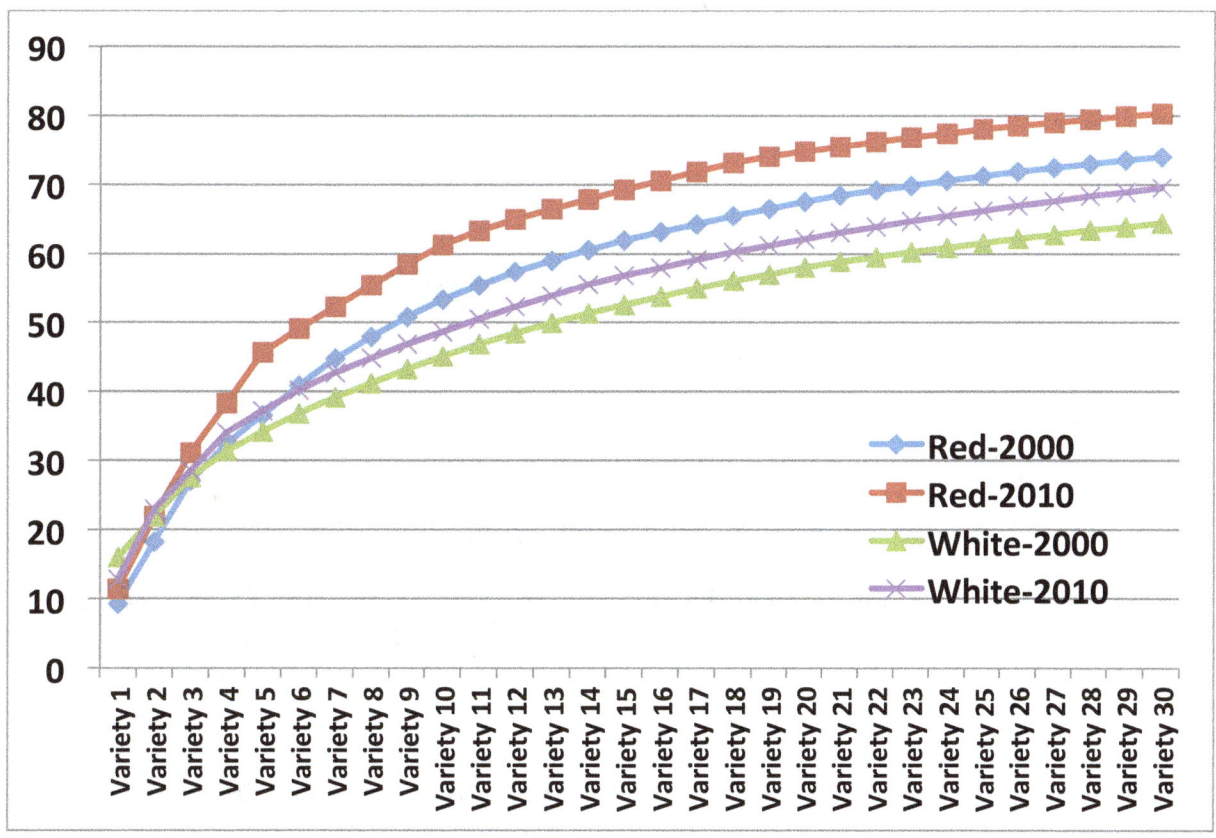

20. Shares of French varieties in national winegrape areas, 2000 and 2010 (%)

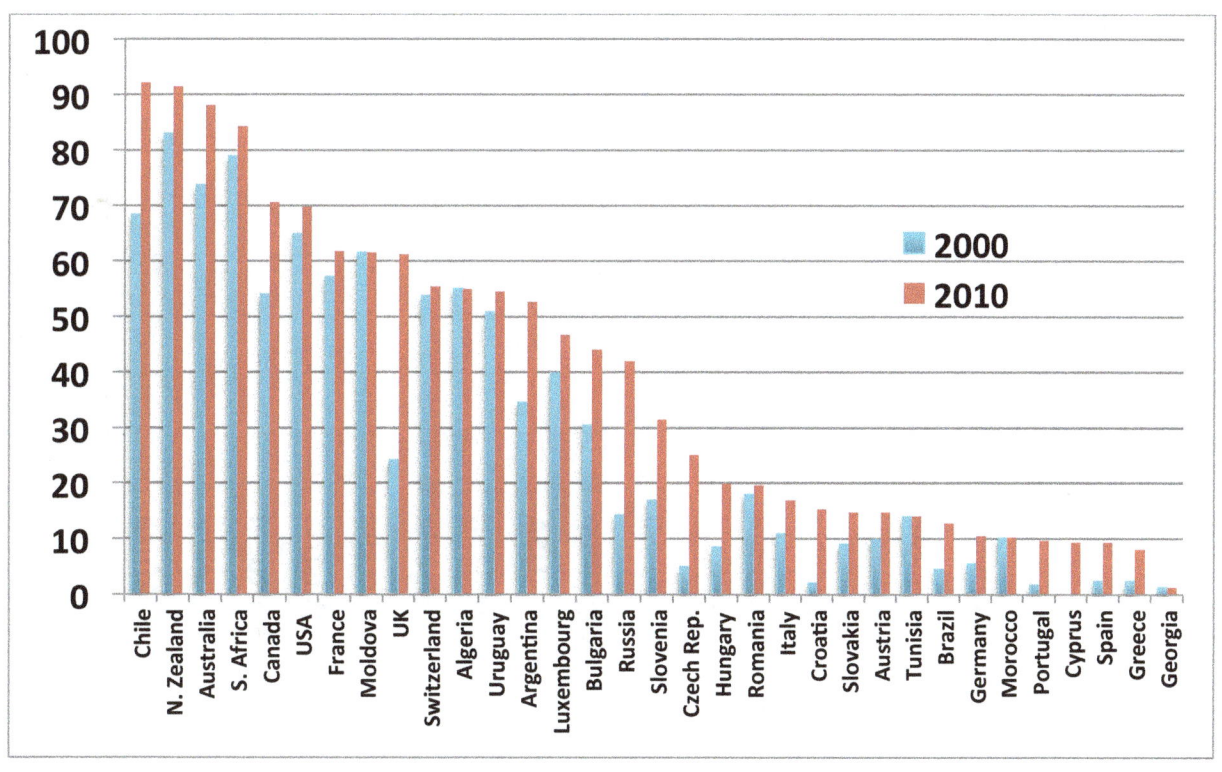

21. Shares of Spanish varieties in national winegrape areas, 2000 and 2010 (%)

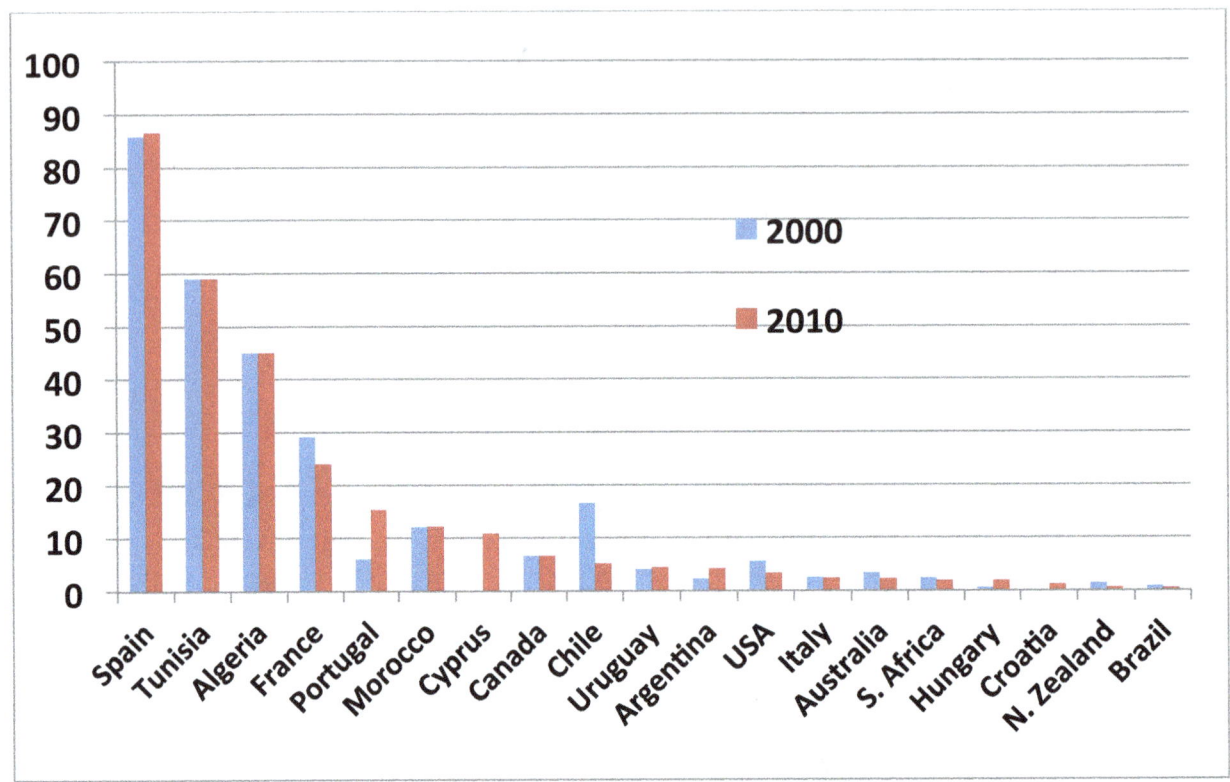

22. Shares of Italian varieties in national winegrape areas, 2000 and 2010 (%)

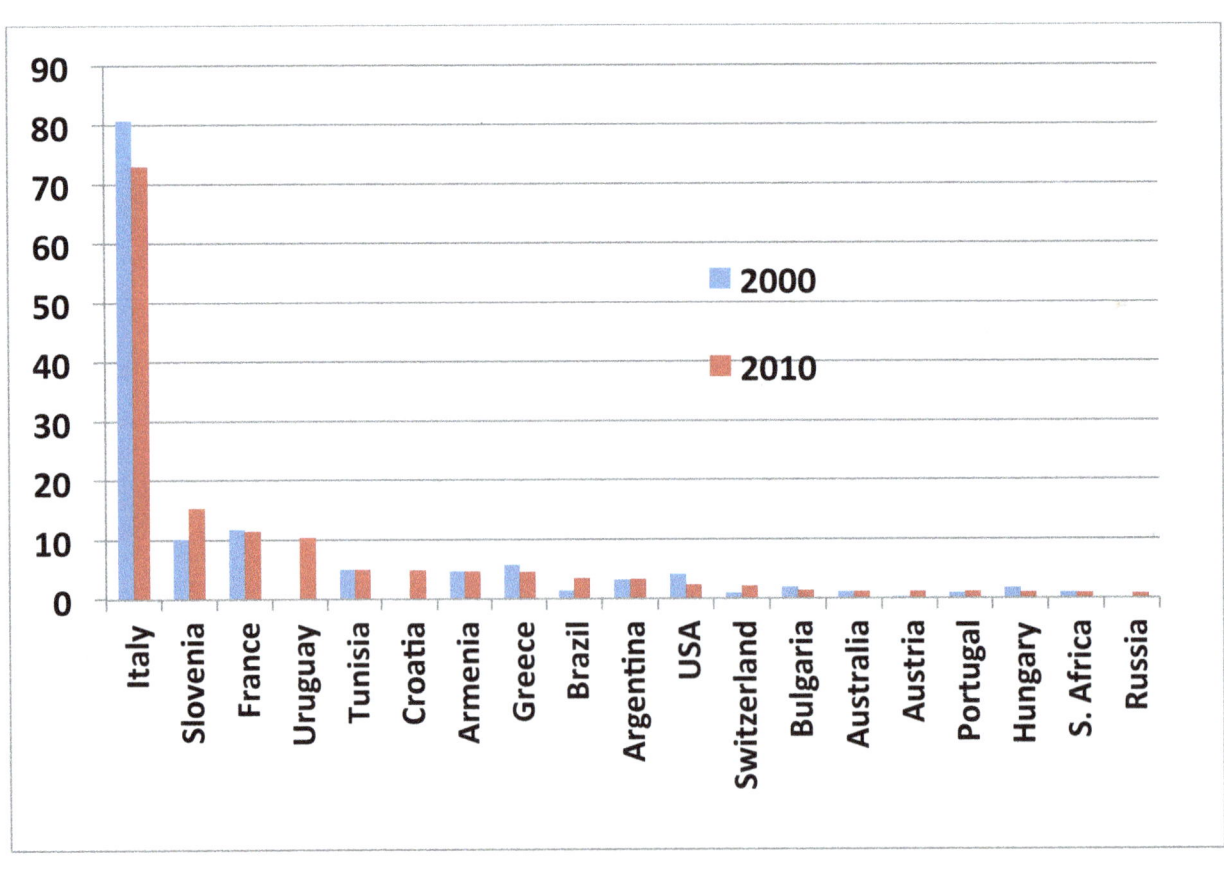

23. Shares of Syrah in national winegrape area, 2000 and 2010 (%)

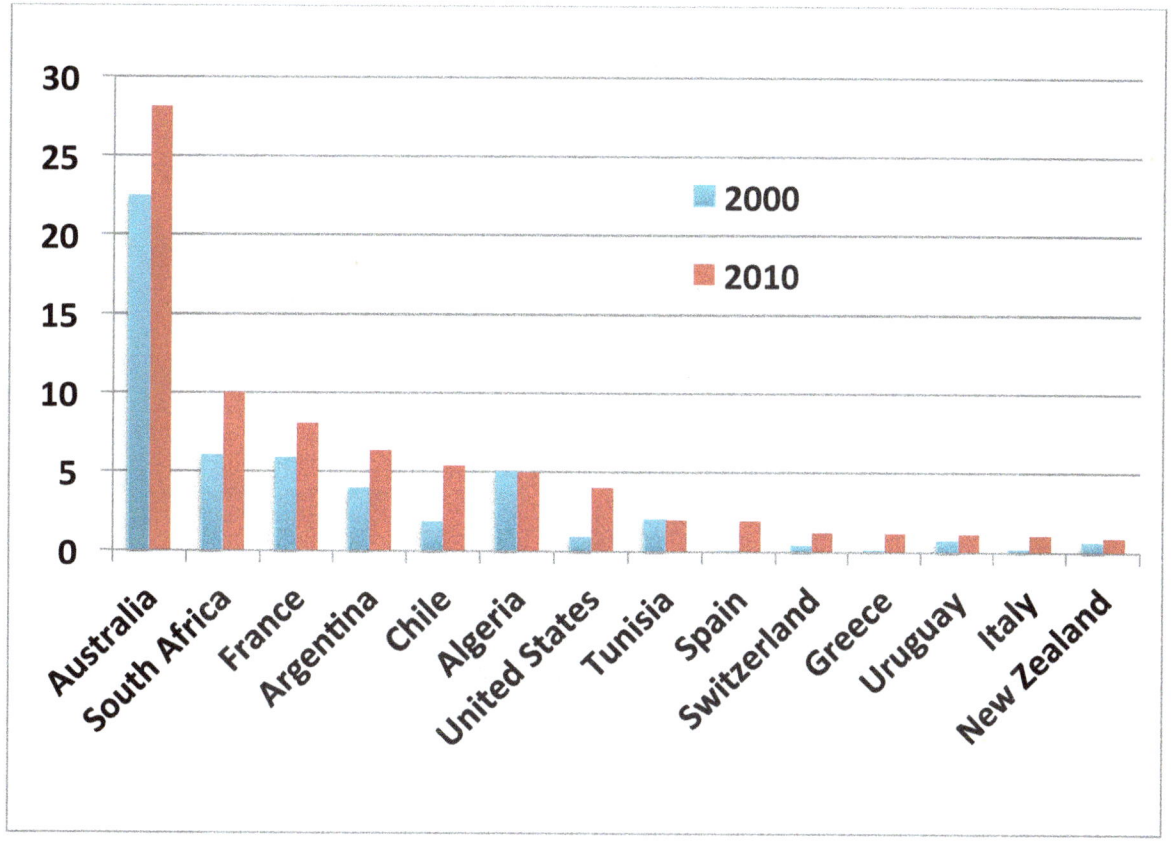

24. National shares of global winegrape area of Syrah, 2000 and 2010 (%)

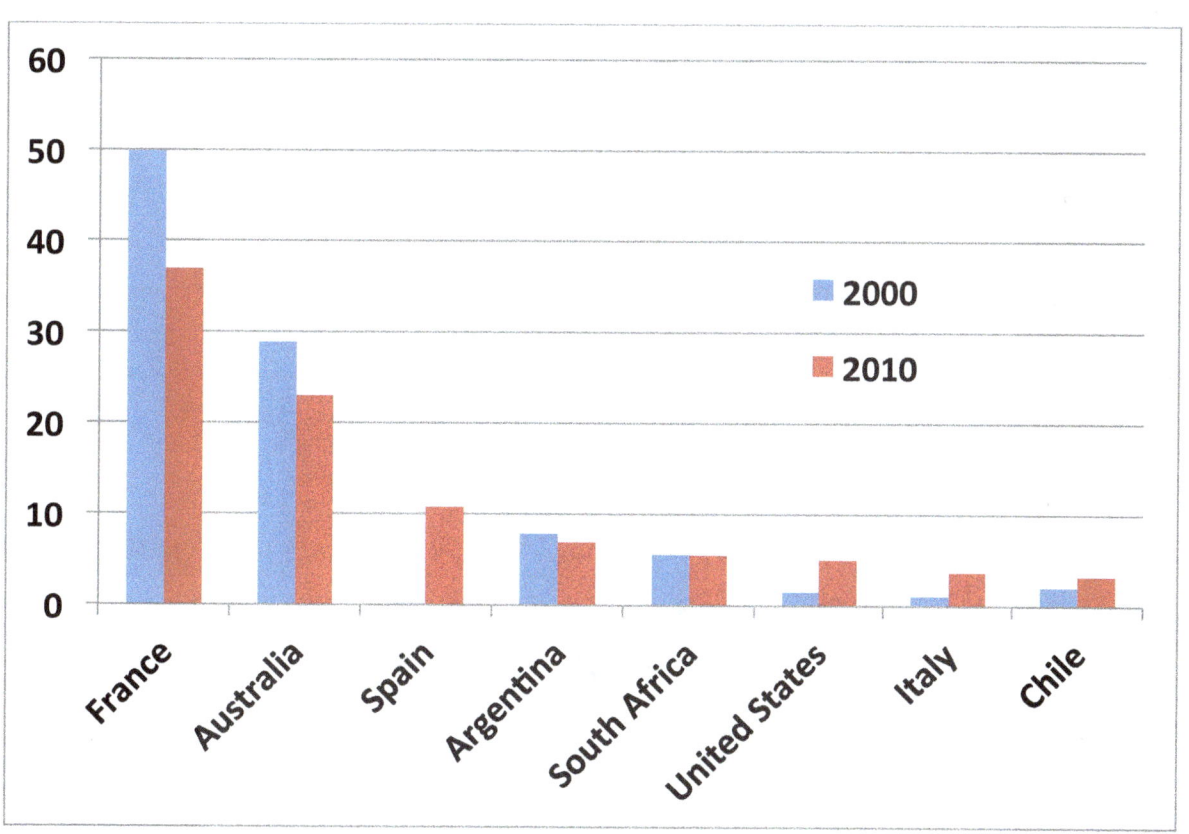

25. Cumulative national shares of world Syrah area, 2000 and 2010 (%)

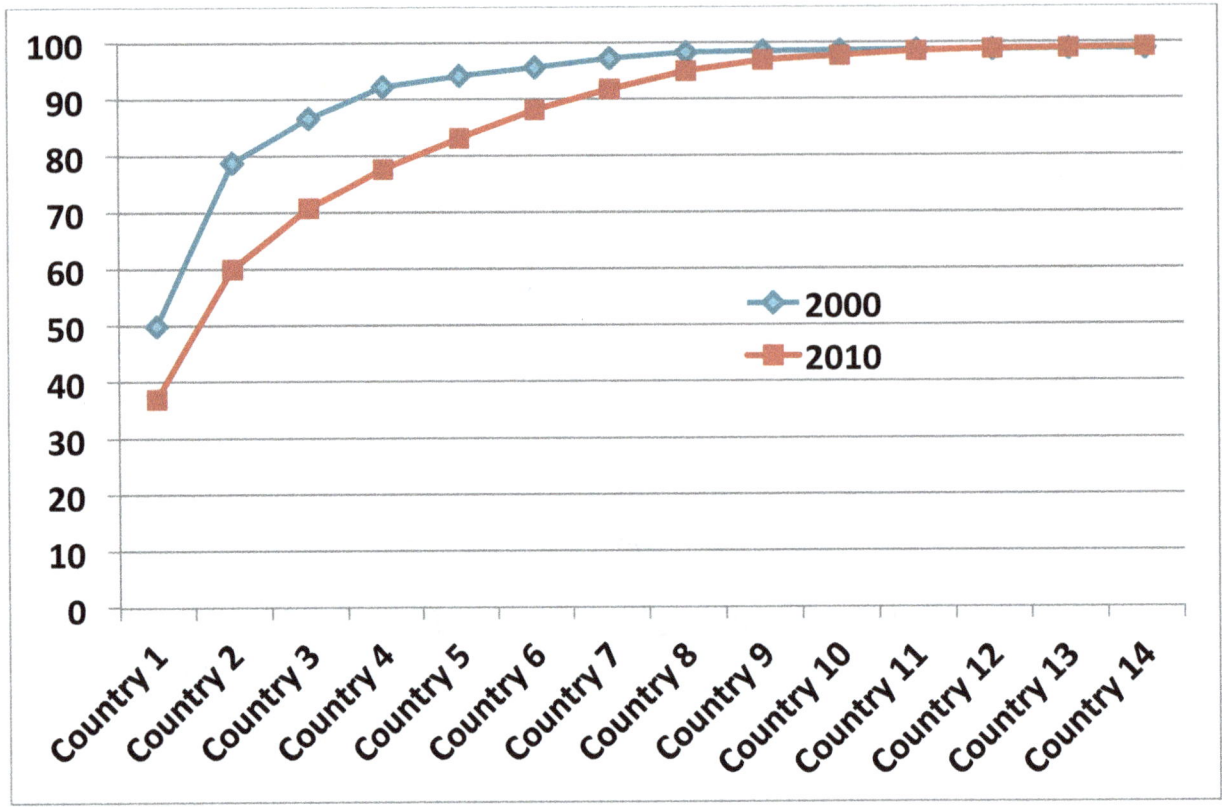

26. Varietal Intensity Index for Syrah, 2000 and 2010

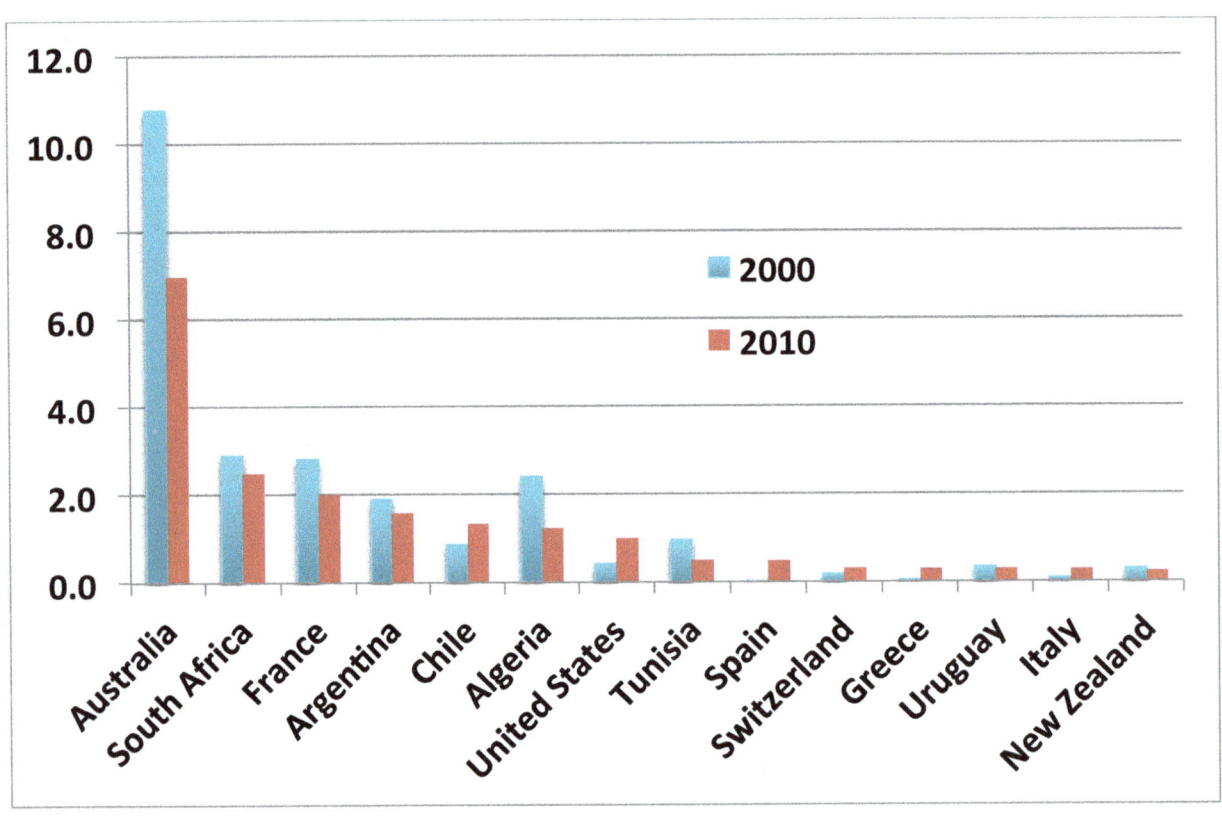

27. Varietal Intensity Index for Australia's 15 largest varieties, 2000 and 2010

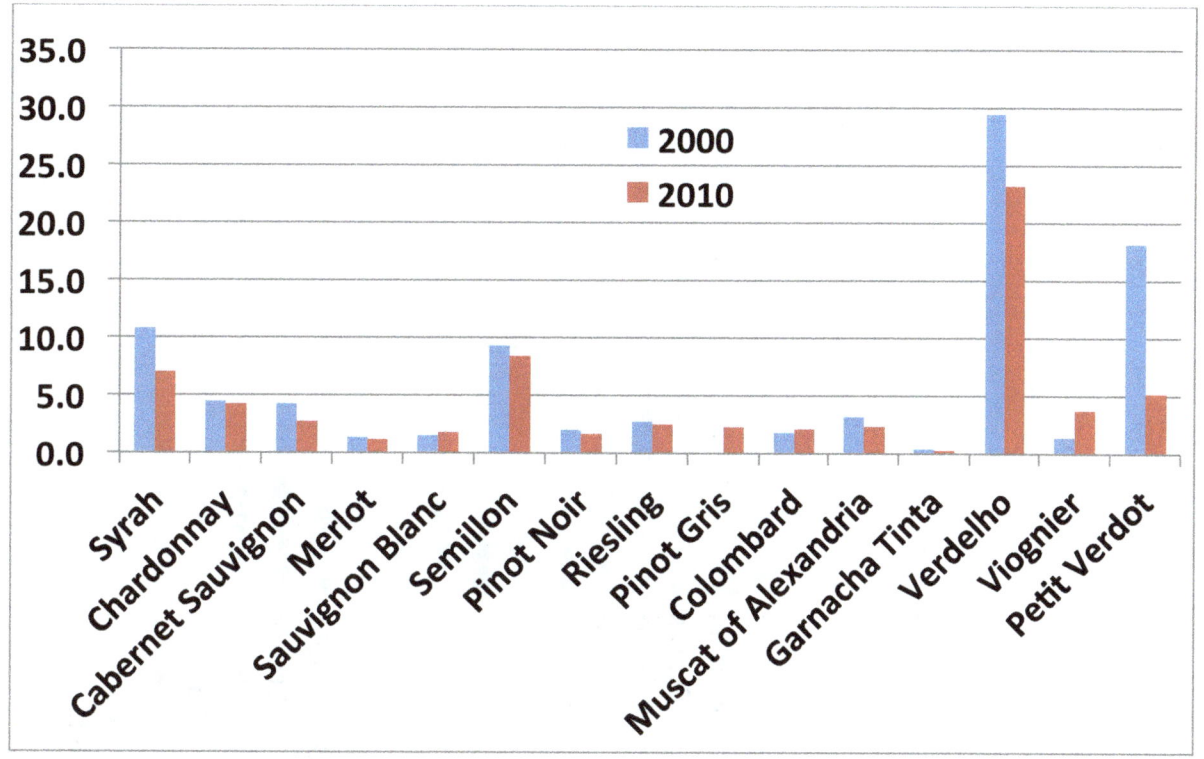

28. Index of Varietal Similarity of each country with the world, 2000 and 2010

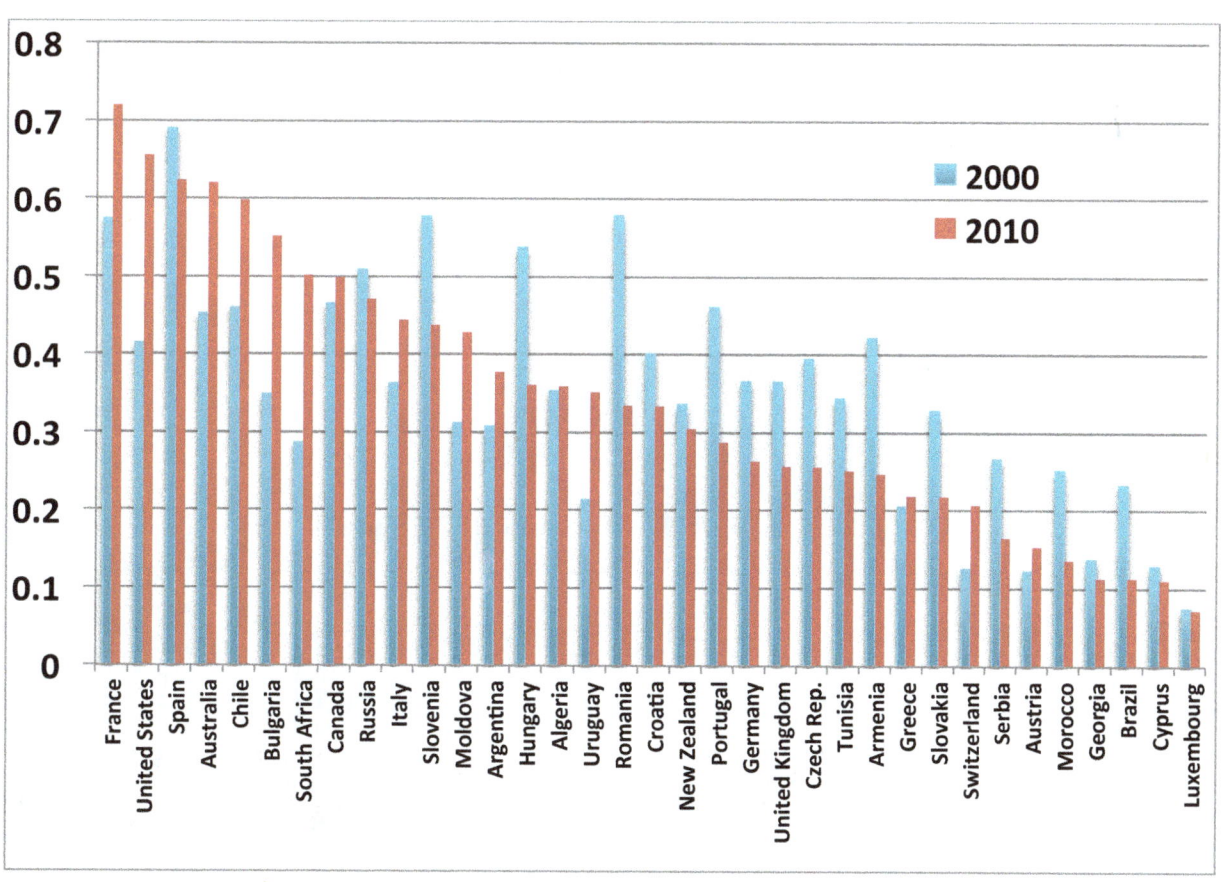

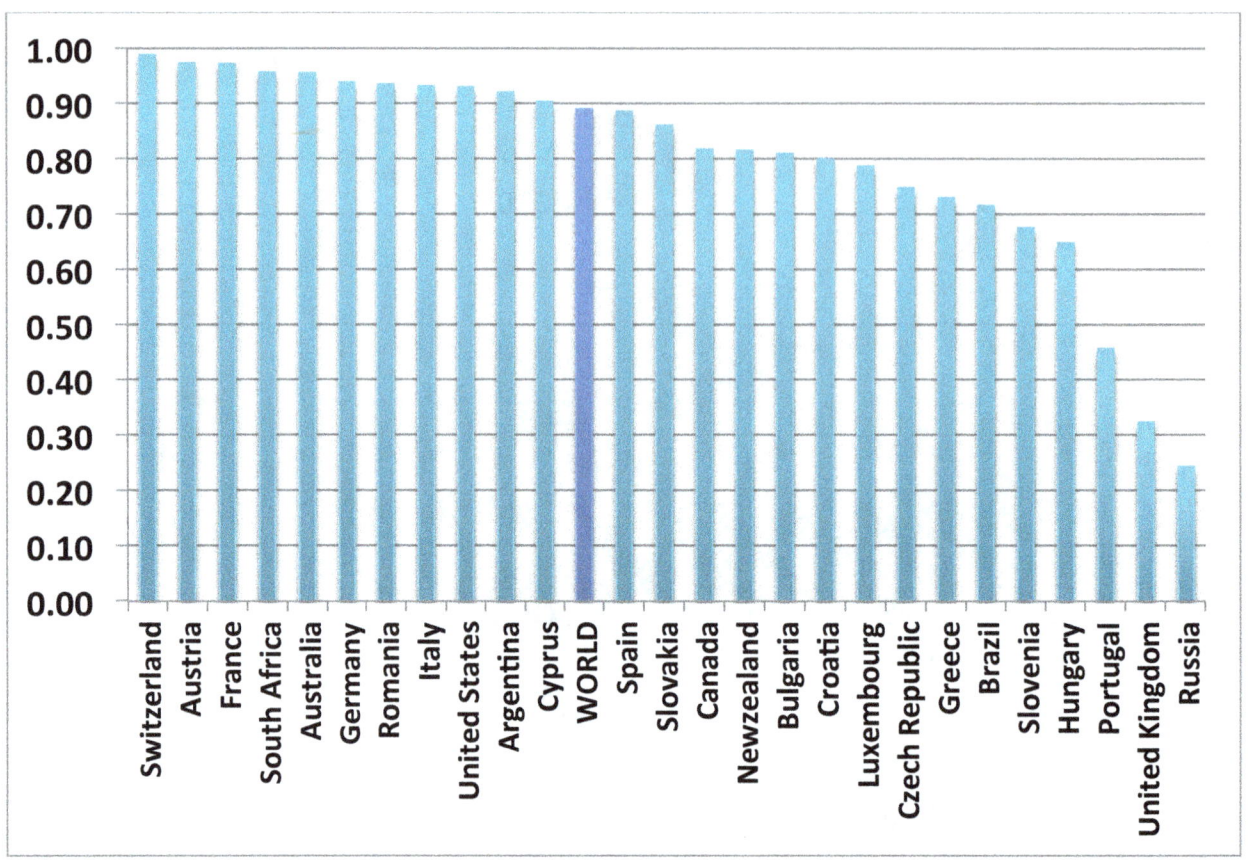

29. Index of Varietal Similarity between 2000 and 2010 for each country

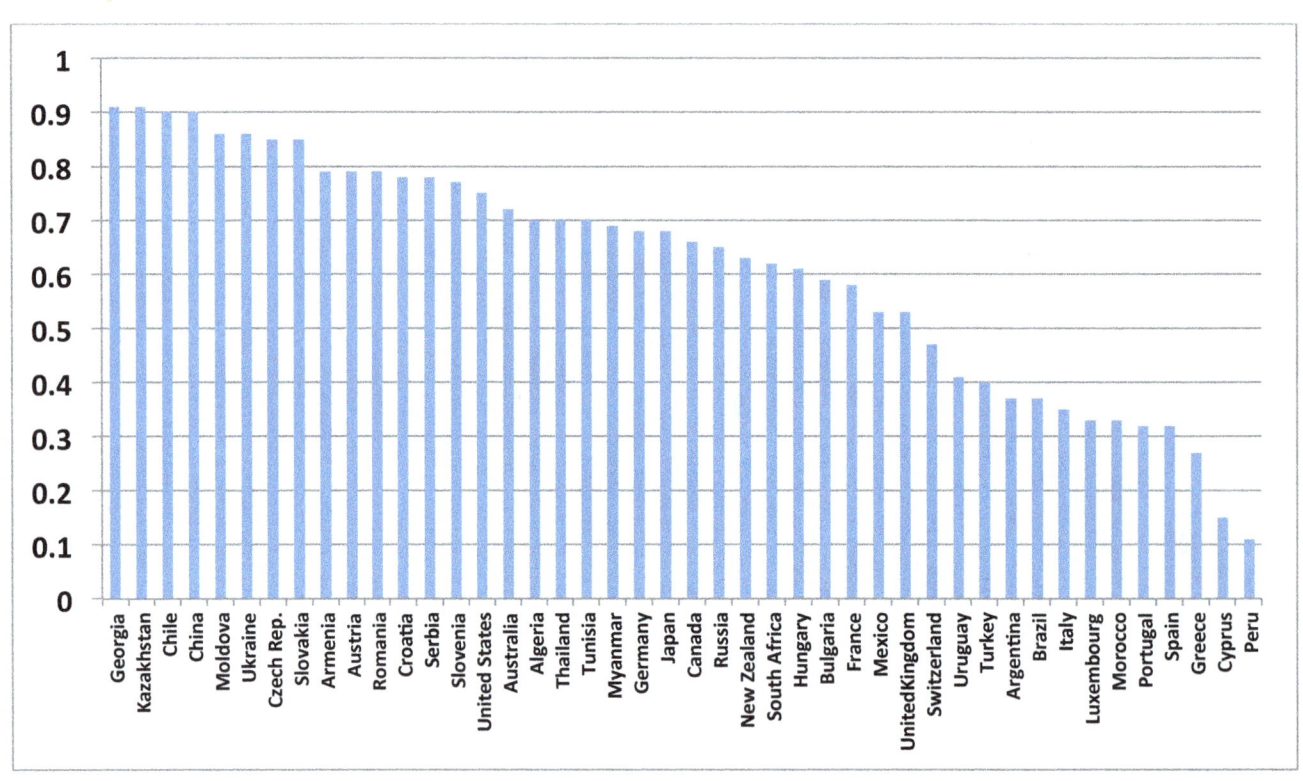

30. Index of Varietal Similarity of each country with the country with closest varietal mix, 2010

Table sections:

I. Country coverage

II. Regional coverage of each country

III. Winegrape varietal coverage globally

IV. Winegrape areas for world's top varieties, by country

V. Winegrape areas and Varietal Intensity Indexes for national top 45 varieties

VI. Regional Varietal Intensity Indexes for world's top varieties

VII. Index of Varietal Similarity, by region and country

VIII. Summary charts for each of the world's top 50 varieties

IX. Summary charts for each of the 44 countries

Table Section I: Country coverage

Table 1: Number of regions and prime varieties, by country, 2000 and 2010

Country	Code	2000 No. of regions	2000 No. of prime varieties	2010 No. of regions	2010 No. of prime varieties
Algeria	DZ	1	8	1	8
Argentina	AR	3	31	28	111
Armenia	AM	1	6	1	6
Australia	AU	76	43	94	40
Austria	AT	4	33	4	35
Brazil	BR	1	19	1	101
Bulgaria	BG	1	21	6	16
Canada	CA	1	20	2	76
Chile	CL	8	38	9	54
China	CN			10	17
Croatia	HR	1	7	13	72
Cyprus	CY	1	2	1	15
Czech Rep.	CZ	1	10	2	32
France	FR	29	285	45	96
Georgia	GE	1	21	1	21
Germany	DE	13	57	13	48
Greece	EL	13	60	13	56
Hungary	HU	1	32	22	137
Italy	IT	103	323	20	396
Japan	JP			5	15
Kazakhstan	KZ			6	15
Luxembourg	LU	1	11	1	10
Mexico	MX			5	17
Moldova	MD	1	39	1	39
Morocco	MA	1	8	1	8
Myanmar	MM			1	11
New Zealand	NZ	10	22	11	45
Peru	PE			4	30
Portugal	PT	9	80	9	266
Romania	RO	1	18	8	25
Russia	RU	1	11	2	55
Serbia	RS	1	4	1	4
Slovakia	SK	1	11	6	35
Slovenia	SI	1	6	10	21
South Africa	ZA	9	68	9	68
Spain	ES	36	159	36	150
Switzerland	CH	18	51	18	58
Thailand	TH			1	13
Tunisia	TN	1	9	1	9
Turkey	TR			7	35
Ukraine	UA			1	22
United Kingdom	UK	1	9	1	44
United States	US	61	84	89	129
Uruguay	UY	1	8	1	41
"Missing 9 in 2000"	M9	1	101	na	na
Sample total		**414**	**1012**	**521**	**1271**

Table 2: National shares of global winegrape area and wine production volume, 2000 and 2010

Sampled wine-producing countries	Share (%) of global winegrape area		Share (%) of global wine production		Non-sampled wine-producing countries	Share (%) of global wine prodn, 2010
	2000	2010	2000	2010		
Spain	23.97	22.13	13.11	12.16	Macedonia	0.31
France	17.54	18.23	21.19	21.19	Belarus	0.08
Italy	12.91	13.47	19.72	16.31	Uzbekistan	0.08
United States	3.56	4.91	8.02	8.76	Albania	0.06
Argentina	4.08	4.33	5.00	5.03	Montenegro	0.06
Romania	4.51	3.67	1.95	1.46	Turkmenistan	0.06
Portugal	4.16	3.52	2.72	2.24	Lebanon	0.05
Australia	2.65	3.27	2.91	4.03	Cuba	0.04
Chile	2.31	2.40	2.02	3.40	Madagascar	0.03
Germany	2.11	2.20	3.93	2.86	Egypt	0.03
South Africa	1.90	2.17	2.62	3.40	Azerbaijan	0.03
Moldova	1.82	1.93	0.33	0.45	Bolivia	0.03
Hungary	1.76	1.50	1.34	0.90	Lithuania	0.02
Serbia	1.40	1.49	0.59	0.78	Israel	0.02
Bulgaria	1.95	1.21	0.62	0.56	Bosnia and Herz.	0.01
Greece	1.03	1.17	1.41	1.13	Belgium	0.01
Ukraine		1.13		0.93	Zimbabwe	0.01
Brazil	1.07	1.06	1.09	1.20	Malta	0.01
Morocco	1.01	1.05	0.14	0.11	Paraguay	0.01
Georgia	0.76	1.03	0.25	0.33	Latvia	0.01
Austria	0.98	0.98	0.90	0.72	Kyrgyzstan	0.01
New Zealand	0.20	0.69	0.21	0.65	Ethiopia	0.01
Algeria	0.61	0.65	0.15	0.19		
China		0.64		5.68		
Russia	1.14	0.55	0.99	2.24		
Croatia	1.21	0.45	0.70	0.18		
Tunisia	0.34	0.36	0.15	0.08		
Slovenia	0.48	0.35	0.14	0.09		
Czech Rep.	0.23	0.35	0.19	0.17		
Switzerland	0.31	0.32	0.45	0.38		
Turkey		0.28		0.09		
Slovakia	0.32	0.27	0.16	0.10		
Armenia	0.23	0.24	0.02	0.02		
Canada	0.17	0.22	0.17	0.19		
Cyprus	0.37	0.19	0.20	0.04		
Uruguay	0.18	0.16	0.34	0.22		
Kazakhstan		0.15		0.06		
Mexico		0.12		0.15		
Japan		0.08		0.26		
Peru		0.08		0.22		
Luxembourg	0.03	0.03	0.05	0.04		
United Kingdom	0.02	0.03	0.00	0.00		
Thailand		0.00		0.00		
Myanmar		0.00		0.00		
"Missing 9 in 2000"	1.63	n.a.	5.14	n.a.		
Rest of the world	1.06	0.96	1.06	0.96		
Sample total	**98.94**	**99.04**	**98.94**	**99.04**	**Non-sample total**	**0.96**

Table 3: Key indicators of national grape area and production, 1990, 2000 and 2010

1990	Total grapevine area harvested ('000ha)	Share of world grapevine area harvested (%)	Total wine-grape area ('000ha)	Share of world wine-grape area (%)	Share of wine-grapes in total grapevine area (%)	Share (%) of national agr. crop area under grapevine	Grape yield (tonnes per ha.)	Total grape prod'n (kt)	Share of world grape prod'n (%)
Algeria	91	1.1				1.2	2.9	262	0.4
Argentina	223	2.8	151	2.8	68	0.8	11.0	2465	4.2
Armenia	24*	0.3					6.1	142*	0.2
Australia	59	0.7	46	0.9	78	0.1	15.6	845	1.5
Austria	54	0.7	54	1.0	99	3.6	7.1	387	0.7
Brazil	58	0.7				0.1	12.2	715	1.2
Bulgaria	139	1.7	125	2.4	90	3.4	5.3	741	1.3
Canada	6	0.1	6	0.1	100	0.0	8.5	55	0.1
Chile	120	1.5	65	1.2	55	3.9	9.5	1131	1.9
China	125	1.6				0.1	7.1	883	1.5
Croatia	56*	0.7					5.5	380*	0.7
Cyprus	25	0.3				16.1	6.0	153	0.3
Czech Rep.	10	0.1					6.3	74	0.1
France	911	11.4	887	16.8	97	4.8	7.8	7114	12.2
Georgia	87	1.1					5.8	380	0.7
Germany	96	1.2	96	1.8	100	0.8	16.0	1535	2.6
Greece	147	1.8	78	1.5	53	3.7	9.0	1334	2.3
Hungary	121	1.5	102	1.9	84	2.3	6.3	734	1.3
Italy	1018	12.7	914	17.3	90	8.5	8.9	9095	15.6
Japan	24	0.3	2	0.0	10	0.5	11.5	274	0.5
Kazakhstan	17	0.2					4.9	63	0.1
Luxembourg									
Mexico	48	0.6	30	0.6	63	0.2	10.2	487	0.8
Moldova	167*	2.1					5.3	824*	1.4
Morocco	49	0.6				0.5	5.1	249	0.4
Myanmar									
New Zealand	5.0	0.1	5.0	0.1	100	0.2	13.3	65	0.1
Peru	9	0.1				0.2	6.8	59	0.1
Portugal	276	3.4	276	5.2	100	8.8	4.9	1338	2.3
Romania	221	2.8	200	3.8	91	2.2	4.1	899	1.5
Russia	107*	1.3					5.2	529*	0.9
Serbia	89*^	1.1					5.0	394*^	0.7
Slovakia	24*	0.3					5.4	126*	0.2
Slovenia	20*	0.3					5.2	115*	0.2
South Africa	98	1.2	98	1.9	100	0.7	13.2	1300	2.2
Spain	1405	17.6	1364	25.8	97	7.0	4.0	5568	9.6
Switzerland	15	0.2	14	0.3	94	3.5	13.0	192	0.3
Thailand	2	0.0				0.0	9.9	21	0.0
Tunisia	30	0.4				0.6	2.9	85	0.1
Turkey	588	7.3	15	0.3	3	2.1	6.0	3510	6.0
Ukraine	140*	1.7					5.4	657*	1.1
United Kingdom	1	0.0				0.0	3.3	2	0.0
United States	300	3.7	118	2.2	40	0.2	17.3	5185	8.9
Uruguay	17	0.2	12	0.2	70	1.3	7.1	116	0.2
Rest of the world	978	12.2	632	12.0	65	0.5	8.1	7709	13.2
World	**8000**	**100.0**	**5290**	**100.0**	**66**	**0.5**	**7.3**	**58194**	**100.0**

* 1992 data because it is the nearest year for which data are available.

^including Montenegro

Table 3 (cont.) Key indicators of national grape area and production, 1990, 2000 and 2010

2000	Total grapevine area harvested ('000ha)	Share of world grapevine area harvested (%)	Total wine-grape area ('000ha)	Share of world wine-grape area (%)	Share of wine-grapes in total grapevine area (%)	Share (%) of national agr. crop area under grapevine	Grape yield (tonnes per ha.)	Total grape prod'n (kt)	Share of world grape prod'n (%)
Algeria	51	0.7	30	0.6	59	0.4	3.8	193	0.3
Argentina	201	2.7	201	4.1	100	0.7	12.6	2461	3.9
Armenia	15	0.2	11	0.2	76	2.3	7.9	116	0.2
Australia	137	1.9	131	2.6	95	0.3	12.3	1374	2.2
Austria	48	0.7	48	1.0	100	3.3	7.0	332	0.5
Brazil	61	0.8	53	1.1	87	0.1	16.5	1005	1.6
Bulgaria	117	1.6	96	1.9	82	2.5	3.6	419	0.7
Canada	8	0.1	8	0.2	100	0.0	9.2	69	0.1
Chile	160	2.2	114	2.3	71	5.4	11.0	1758	2.8
China	280	3.8					11.6	3223	5.2
Croatia	59	0.8	59	1.2	100	5.9	6.5	369	0.6
Cyprus	18	0.2	18	0.4	100	13.0	5.7	103	0.2
Czech Rep.	12	0.2	11	0.2	97	0.3	5.8	67	0.1
France	865	11.8	865	17.5	100	4.4	8.9	7676	12.3
Georgia	62	0.9	37	0.8	60	3.5	3.1	193	0.3
Germany	104	1.4	104	2.1	100	0.9	14.0	1415	2.3
Greece	126	1.7	51	1.0	40	1.3	9.8	1242	2.0
Hungary	90	1.2	87	1.8	97	1.8	7.8	688	1.1
Italy	870	11.9	637	12.9	73	5.6	10.4	9073	14.5
Japan	20	0.3	2	0.0	10	0.0	11.6	235	0.4
Kazakhstan	10	0.1					4.2	44	0.1
Luxembourg	1	0.0	1	0.0	100	3.2	9.5	12	0.0
Mexico	39	0.5					11.1	430	0.7
Moldova	146	2.0	90	1.8	61	4.1	3.8	558	0.9
Morocco	50	0.7	50	1.0	100	0.5	5.8	277	0.4
Myanmar									
New Zealand	10	0.1	10	0.2	97	0.6	7.6	77	0.1
Peru	11	0.1					10.3	111	0.2
Portugal	235	3.2	205	4.2	87	8.6	4.3	1014	1.6
Romania	248	3.4	222	4.5	90	2.3	4.8	1178	1.9
Russia	61	0.8	56	1.1	93	0.0	4.2	254	0.4
Serbia	69	0.9	69	1.4	100	1.8	5.2	34	0.1
Slovakia	18	0.2	16	0.3	88	1.0	3.7	65	0.1
Slovenia	23	0.3	23	0.5	100	11.6	7.3	111	0.2
South Africa	108	1.5	94	1.9	87	0.7	13.4	1446	2.3
Spain	1182	16.1	1182	24.0	100	6.5	5.1	5806	9.3
Switzerland	15	0.2	15	0.3	100	3.4	10.8	163	0.3
Thailand	3	0.0					16.8	44	0.1
Tunisia	28	0.4	17	0.3	60	0.3	5.0	139	0.2
Turkey	532	7.3	14	0.3	3	0.1	6.4	3417	5.5
Ukraine	100	1.4	71	1.4	71	0.2	3.9	385	0.6
United Kingdom	1	0.0	1	0.0	100	0.0	1.7	1	0.0
United States	376	5.1	176	3.6	47	0.1	16.5	6197	9.9
Uruguay	9	0.1	9	0.2	97	0.6	13.3	122	0.2
Rest of the world	744	10.2	45	0.9	6	0.0	8.3	8509	13.6
World	**7323**	**100.0**	**4930**	**100.0**	**67**	**0.3**	**8.5**	**62408**	**100.0**

Table 3 (cont.) Key indicators of national grape area and production, 1990, 2000 and 2010

2010	Total grapevine area harvested[a] ('000ha)	Share of world grapevine area harvested (%)	Total wine-grape area ('000ha)	Share of world wine-grape area (%)	Share of wine grapes in total grapevine area (%)	Share (%) of national agr. crop area under grapevine	Grape yield (tonnes per ha.)	Total grape prod'n (kt)	Share of world grape prod'n (%)
Algeria	70	1.0	30	0.6	43	0.4	6.9	485	0.7
Argentina	223	3.1	201	4.3	90	0.5	11.3	2516	3.7
Armenia	14	0.2	11	0.2	77	2.3	15.2	220	0.3
Australia	158	2.2	152	3.3	96	0.3	10.4	1732	2.5
Austria	46	0.6	46	1.0	100	3.2	6.9	307	0.5
Brazil	82	1.2	49	1.1	60	0.1	17.2	1421	2.1
Bulgaria	88	1.2	56	1.2	64	1.7	2.9	252	0.4
Canada	11	0.2	10	0.2	94	0.0	6.7	72	0.1
Chile	200	2.8	112	2.4	56	6.3	14.4	2884	4.2
China	547	7.7	30	0.6	5	0.0	15.6	8519	12.5
Croatia	33	0.5	21	0.4	63	2.1	6.2	206	0.3
Cyprus	9	0.1	9	0.2	100	7.3	3.3	28	0.0
Czech Rep.	16	0.2	16	0.3	100	0.5	4.3	69	0.1
France	847	11.9	847	18.2	100	4.4	7.9	6162	9.1
Georgia	49	0.7	48	1.0	99	8.8	2.9	143	0.2
Germany	102	1.4	102	2.2	100	0.8	11.5	1146	1.7
Greece	100	1.4	54	1.2	54	1.5	9.4	938	1.4
Hungary	75	1.1	70	1.5	93	1.5	5.7	432	0.6
Italy	768	10.8	626	13.5	81	6.6	10.0	7715	11.4
Japan	18	0.3	4	0.1	21	0.1	10.3	187	0.3
Kazakhstan	10	0.1	7	0.1	72	0.0	5.8	56	0.1
Luxembourg	1	0.0	1	0.0	100	2.1	13.7	17	0.0
Mexico	27	0.4	5	0.1	20	0.0	10.8	288	0.4
Moldova	132	1.9	90	1.9	68	4.3	4.4	587	0.9
Morocco	49	0.7	49	1.1	100	0.5	7.9	355	0.5
Myanmar			0	0.0		0.0			
New Zealand	33	0.5	32	0.7	97	5.8	7.3	238	0.4
Peru	15	0.2	4	0.1	25	0.1	18.5	281	0.4
Portugal	180	2.5	164	3.5	91	8.8	4.6	826	1.2
Romania	179	2.5	170	3.7	95	1.8	4.9	870	1.3
Russia	43	0.6	26	0.6	59	0.0	7.9	345	0.5
Serbia	69	1.0	69	1.5	100	1.9	6.9	362	0.5
Slovakia	13	0.2	13	0.3	100	0.9	4.0	37	0.1
Slovenia	16	0.2	16	0.4	100	8.3	7.0	114	0.2
South Africa	113	1.6	101	2.2	89	0.8	11.5	1305	1.9
Spain	1028	14.5	1028	22.1	100	6.0	5.8	5817	8.6
Switzerland	15	0.2	15	0.3	100	3.5	9.0	134	0.2
Thailand	4	0.1	0	0.0	3	0.0	17.5	77	0.1
Tunisia	29	0.4	17	0.4	58	0.3	3.5	103	0.2
Turkey	476	6.7	13	0.3	3	0.1	9.0	4272	6.3
Ukraine	69	1.0	52	1.1	76	0.2	6.7	466	0.7
United Kingdom	1	0.0	1	0.0	100	0.0	1.5	1	0.0
United States	385	5.4	228	4.9	59	0.1	17.4	6721	9.9
Uruguay	8	0.1	8	0.2	96	0.4	13.5	108	0.2
Rest of the world	748	10.5	49	1.1	7	0.0	8.8	9142	13.5
World[a]	**7103**	**100.0**	**4651**	**100.0**	**65**	**0.3**	**9.6**	**67955**	**100.0**

[a]Non-sample countries, which have a high (mostly non-wine) grape area harvested in 2009-11, are (in '000ha): Iran-230, Uzbekistan-108, India-991, Egypt-64, Afghanistan-61, Syria-51, Tajikistan-35, Macedonia-20, Turkmenistan-18, Korea-18, Pakistan-15, Yemen-14, Azerbaijan-11, Saudi Arabia-11, Lebanon-11

Table 4: National winegrape areas and change between 2000 and 2010

Country	Area in 2000 (hectares)	Area in 2010 (hectares)	Changes in area (hectares)	Changes in %
Algeria	30200	30200	0	0.0
Argentina	201113	201060	-54	0.0
Armenia	11206	11206	0	0.0
Australia	130602	151788	21,186	16.2
Austria	48496	45533	-2,963	-6.1
Brazil	52840	49412	-3,428	-6.5
Bulgaria	95997	56133	-39,864	-41.5
Canada	8498	10096	1,598	18.8
Chile	113966	111525	-2,441	-2.1
China		29545		
Croatia	59448	20754	-38,694	-65.1
Cyprus	18282	8608	-9,674	-52.9
Czech Rep.	11331	16242	4,911	43.3
France	864846	846880	-17,966	-2.1
Georgia	37419	48001	10,582	28.3
Germany	104207	102060	-2,147	-2.1
Greece	50878	54389	3,511	6.9
Hungary	86886	69715	-17,171	-19.8
Italy	636662	625700	-10,962	-1.7
Japan		3715		
Kazakhstan		6938		
Luxembourg	1348	1304	-44	-3.3
Mexico		5465		
Moldova	89844	89844	0	0.0
Morocco	49600	49000	-600	-1.2
Myanmar		75		
New Zealand	9942	31964	22,022	221.5
Peru		3831		
Portugal	205003	163522	-41,481	-20.2
Romania	222173	170292	-51,881	-23.4
Russia	56332	25628	-30,704	-54.5
Serbia	68999	68999	0	0.0
Slovakia	15580	12637	-2,944	-18.9
Slovenia	23472	16354	-7,118	-30.3
South Africa	93656	101016	7,361	7.9
Spain	1181805	1028258	-153,547	-13.0
Switzerland	15042	14820	-222	-1.5
Thailand		149		
Tunisia	16836	16836	0	0.0
Turkey		12856		
Ukraine		52293		
United Kingdom	873	1198	325	37.2
United States	175693	227948	52,255	29.7
Uruguay	8880	7657	-1,223	-13.8
"Missing 9 in 2000"	80221	(114867)	(34646)	(43.2)
Old World subtotal	**3955600**	**3568965**	**-386,635**	**-9.8**
New World subtotal	**922575**	**1032480**	**109,905**	**11.9**
World total	**4878175**	**4601445**	**-276,730**	**-5.7**

Table 5: Global winegrape area, share of global area, and global ranks of each prime variety, 1990, 2000 & 2010

Prime vairiety	Col	1990 Global area (ha)	1990 Global share %	1990 Global rank	2000 Global area (ha)	2000 Global share %	2000 Global rank	2010 Global area (ha)	2010 Global share %	2010 Global rank
Abbo	R				2375	0.05	183	2375	0.05	167
Abbuoto	R				696	0.01	328	37	0.00	767
Abondant	W				0	0.00	980			
Abouriou	R				419	0.01	396	364	0.01	414
Abrusco	R				399	0.01	402	423	0.01	393
Acolon	R							449	0.01	388
Adakarasi	R				48	0.00	647	69	0.00	674
Afus Ali	W				328	0.01	426	8	0.00	980
Agadai	W				1265	0.03	262			
Agiorgitiko	R				2320	0.05	189	2905	0.06	149
Aglianico	R				9264	0.19	75	9963	0.22	69
Aglianicone	R				148	0.00	513	62	0.00	687
Agni	R							6	0.00	1012
Agronomica	R				19	0.00	746	327	0.01	436
Agua Santa	R							78	0.00	657
Airen	W	476396	9.01	1	387978	7.95	1	252364	5.48	3
Aladasturi	R				46	0.00	649	59	0.00	699
Alarije	W				1686	0.03	219	1726	0.04	195
Alb de Ialoveni	W				2	0.00	910	2	0.00	1104
Albalonga	W				57	0.00	631			
Albana	W				2487	0.05	180	1523	0.03	206
Albanello	W				117	0.00	539	18	0.00	885
Albaranzeuli Bianco	W				72	0.00	600	7	0.00	999
Albaranzeuli Nero	R				40	0.00	666	49	0.00	735
Albarin Blanco	W							23	0.00	851
Albarola	W				4090	0.08	127	1453	0.03	213
Albarossa	R				5	0.00	853	80	0.00	649
Albillo Mayor	W				5	0.00	849	1319	0.03	229
Albillo Real	W				3368	0.07	145	861	0.02	290
Alcanon	W				54	0.00	637	60	0.00	695
Aleatico	R				458	0.01	386	333	0.01	432
Aledo	W							7	0.00	995
Aleksandrouli	R				219	0.00	474	281	0.01	460
Aletta	W							723	0.02	313
Alfrocheiro	R				523	0.01	375	1188	0.03	244
Alicante Henri Bouschet	R	19587	0.37	47	37043	0.76	26	38985	0.85	23
Aligote	W	54430	1.03	20	35668	0.73	27	36119	0.78	24
Alionza	W				41	0.00	663	11	0.00	947
Almafre	W							0	0.00	1242
Alminhaca	W							1	0.00	1184
Alphonse Lavallee	R				15	0.00	770	883	0.02	287
Altesse	W				294	0.01	442	356	0.01	419
Alvar Branco	W							0	0.00	1239
Alvar Roxo	O							2	0.00	1123
Alvarelhao	R				159	0.00	506	180	0.00	530
Alvarelhao Ceitao	R							0	0.00	1266
Alvarinho	W				5113	0.10	111	5523	0.12	103
Amaral	R				582	0.01	359	92	0.00	623
Amigne	W				21	0.00	737	43	0.00	
Amur	R							146	0.00	554
Ancellotta	R				4391	0.09	119	4774	0.10	111

Table 5 (cont.) Global winegrape area, share of global area, and global ranks of each variety, 1990, 2000 & 2010

Prime vairiety	Col	1990 Global area (ha)	1990 Global share %	1990 Global rank	2000 Global area (ha)	2000 Global share %	2000 Global rank	2010 Global area (ha)	2010 Global share %	2010 Global rank
Andre	R							472	0.01	378
Antao Vaz	W				376	0.01	408	1252	0.03	234
Ar110	O				1	0.00	954	1	0.00	1160
Ar99	O				3	0.00	866	5	0.00	1028
Aramon Bouschet	R				10	0.00	808			
Aramon Gris	W				72	0.00	601			
Aramon Noir	R				9084	0.19	77	2892	0.06	151
Aramont	W				1	0.00	944			
Aranel	W				22	0.00	732			
Arany Sarfeher	W				2914	0.06	160	1133	0.02	250
Arbane	W				1	0.00	933			
Argelina	R				3	0.00	872	1	0.00	1161
Ariana	R							3	0.00	1071
Arinarnoa	R				149	0.00	512	32	0.00	793
Arinto de Bucelas	W				3966	0.08	131	4446	0.10	118
Arinto Roxo	R							36	0.00	771
Arjuncao	R							1	0.00	1177
Arneis	W				738	0.02	323	1122	0.02	252
Arnsburger	W				3	0.00	883	30	0.00	804
Aromon Blanc	W				43	0.00	655			
Arriloba	W				59	0.00	626	7	0.00	997
Arrufiac	W				126	0.00	528			
Arvesiniadu	W				147	0.00	515	30	0.00	809
Arvine	W				61	0.00	622	172	0.00	535
Asirtiko Red	R				22	0.00	734	5	0.00	1036
Aspiran Bouschet	R				308	0.01	432	3042	0.07	144
Asprouda	W				433	0.01	391	113	0.00	591
Assaraky	W							1	0.00	1159
Assyrtiko	W				1106	0.02	278	902	0.02	282
Athiri	W				1273	0.03	258	748	0.02	308
Athiri (Red)	R				40	0.00	667			
Aubin Blanc	W				2	0.00	918			
Aubun	R				1411	0.03	242	648	0.01	330
Aurelius	W							70	0.00	672
Aurore	W				299	0.01	437	268	0.01	468
Auxerrois	W				2302	0.05	192	2741	0.06	154
Avana	R				53	0.00	641	28	0.00	819
Avarengo	R				1453	0.03	236	987	0.02	268
Avesso	W				636	0.01	340	685	0.01	326
Azal	W				3302	0.07	146	1072	0.02	262
Babeasca Gris	W							328	0.01	435
Babeasca Neagra	R				3722	0.08	136	3122	0.07	141
Babic	R				1189	0.02	270	359	0.01	418
Babica	R							18	0.00	884
Babosa de Madere	W							2	0.00	1103
Bacchus	W				3392	0.07	143	2047	0.04	180
Baco Blanc	W				2137	0.04	202	773	0.02	303
Baco Noir	R				397	0.01	403	467	0.01	382
Baga	R				6730	0.14	95	4108	0.09	122
Bailey	R							34	0.00	783
Bakator Roz	R							2	0.00	1118
Baleille	W				1	0.00	926			

Table 5 (cont.) Global winegrape area, share of global area, and global ranks of each variety, 1990, 2000 & 2010

Prime vairiety	Col	1990 Global area (ha)	Global share %	Global rank	2000 Global area (ha)	Global share %	Global rank	2010 Global area (ha)	Global share %	Global rank
Baratuciat	W							2	0.00	1124
Barbarossa	O				16	0.00	763			
Barbaroux	O				79	0.00	585			
Barbera	R	67987	1.29	15	33048	0.68	29	24178	0.53	36
Barbera Bianca	W				251	0.01	461	181	0.00	529
Barbera Sarda	R				326	0.01	427	84	0.00	639
Barcelo	W				34	0.00	685	23	0.00	853
Bariadorgia	W				0	0.00	978			
Barkhatnyi	W							30	0.00	807
Baroque	W				169	0.00	496	90	0.00	627
Barreto de Semente	R							3	0.00	1090
Barsaglina	R				20	0.00	739	17	0.00	890
Bastardillo	R				3	0.00	874			
Bastardo Branco	W							15	0.00	908
Bastardo Magarachsky	R				1969	0.04	209	2370	0.05	168
Batili	W				27	0.00	706			
Batily	R				38	0.00	673	54	0.00	713
Batoca	W				80	0.00	583	11	0.00	937
Bayanshira	W				451	0.01	389	645	0.01	331
Beba	W				4762	0.10	115	3036	0.07	146
Beclan	R				0	0.00	991			
Bellandais	R				2	0.00	921			
Bellone	W				1315	0.03	253	511	0.01	364
Bequignol Noir	R				1	0.00	938	698	0.02	321
Bianca	W				2180	0.04	200	6450	0.14	92
Biancame	W				1330	0.03	250	2599	0.06	161
Bianchetta Trevigiana	W				53	0.00	639	13	0.00	916
Bianco d'Alessano	W				941	0.02	298	419	0.01	396
Biancolella	W				385	0.01	405	164	0.00	542
Biancone di Portoferraio	W				67	0.00	616	78	0.00	656
Biancu Gentile	W				1	0.00	943			
Biborkadarka	R				202	0.00	478	136	0.00	567
Bical	W				912	0.02	302	924	0.02	275
Black Queen	R				340	0.01	421	486	0.01	374
Blanc Dame	W				0	0.00	987			
Blanc du Bois	W							28	0.00	816
Blanca Ovoide	W				107	0.00	551	40	0.00	756
Blanqueiro	W				1	0.00	963			
Blattner Reds	R							39	0.00	761
Blattner Whites	W							25	0.00	831
Blauburger	R				1002	0.02	290	1337	0.03	226
Blauer Portugieser	R				4278	0.09	121	3798	0.08	128
Blauer Wildbacher	R				472	0.01	383	368	0.01	412
Blaufrankisch	R				12879	0.26	62	16141	0.35	48
Blush Seedless	R				10	0.00	806			
Boal Barreiro	W							1	0.00	1198
Boal Vencedor	W							2	0.00	1095
Bobal	R	106149	2.01	10	100128	2.05	9	80120	1.74	12
Bogazkere	R				773	0.02	317	1106	0.02	253
Bogdanusa	W							48	0.00	
Boiziau	R				1	0.00	932			
Bombino Bianco	W				2893	0.06	161	1239	0.03	235

Table 5 (cont.) Global winegrape area, share of global area, and global ranks of each variety, 1990, 2000 & 2010

Prime vairiety	Col	1990 Global area (ha)	1990 Global share %	1990 Global rank	2000 Global area (ha)	2000 Global share %	2000 Global rank	2010 Global area (ha)	2010 Global share %	2010 Global rank
Bombino Nero	R				1156	0.02	275	1201	0.03	243
Bonamico	R				83	0.00	580	193	0.00	521
Bonarda Grande	R				538	0.01	370			
Bonda	R				3	0.00	877	7	0.00	1000
Bondola	R				17	0.00	757	13	0.00	923
Bordo	R				3379	0.07	144	8287	0.18	80
Borracal	R				2654	0.05	175	683	0.01	327
Bosco	W				88	0.00	574	82	0.00	644
Bouchales	R				108	0.00	548			
Bouillet	R				2	0.00	904			
Bourboulenc	W				772	0.02	318	597	0.01	344
Bousquet Precoce	W				16	0.00	765			
Bouvier	W				365	0.01	412	250	0.01	481
Bracciola Nera	R				89	0.00	572	26	0.00	827
Brachetto del Piemonte	R				1534	0.03	230	1460	0.03	211
Branco Especial	W							3	0.00	1069
Branco Sr. Joao	W							0	0.00	1213
Branco Valente	W							0	0.00	1240
Brandam	W							312	0.01	444
Braquet Noir	R				8	0.00	824			
Breidecker	W				28	0.00	698	7	0.00	996
Brianna	W							12	0.00	928
Bric	R				21	0.00	738	2	0.00	1099
Brocada	W				2	0.00	896			
Bronner	W							6	0.00	1014
Brun Argente	R				14	0.00	777			
Budai Zold	W							6	0.00	1007
Bukettraube	W				280	0.01	445	71	0.00	670
Burdin	W				0	0.00	993			
Bussanello	W				8	0.00	828	12	0.00	936
Busuioaca de Bohotin	O							268	0.01	467
Caberinta	R							47	0.00	742
Cabernet Cortis	R							20	0.00	867
Cabernet Cubin	R							40	0.00	757
Cabernet Diane	R							0	0.00	1215
Cabernet Dore	W							1	0.00	1141
Cabernet Dorio	R							20	0.00	868
Cabernet Dorsa	R				43	0.00	656	223	0.00	501
Cabernet Franc	R	39619	0.75	32	48551	1.00	19	53599	1.16	17
Cabernet Jura	R							19	0.00	876
Cabernet Malbec	R				34	0.00	684			
Cabernet Mitos	R							282	0.01	459
Cabernet Moravia	R							212	0.00	505
Cabernet Sauvignon	R	127678	2.41	8	220890	4.53	2	290091	6.30	1
Cabinda	R							362	0.01	416
Cabral	R							2	0.00	1119
Caddiu	R				978	0.02	293	309	0.01	448
Cainho de Moreira	W							7	0.00	988
Caino Blanco	W				69	0.00	611	121	0.00	581
Caladoc	R				1427	0.03	240	3675	0.08	129
Calagrano	W				8229	0.17	80	4794	0.10	110
California	O							252	0.01	480
Calitor Blanc	W				8	0.00	830			

Table 5 (cont.) Global winegrape area, share of global area, and global ranks of each variety, 1990, 2000 & 2010

Prime vairiety	Col	1990 Global area (ha)	1990 Global share %	1990 Global rank	2000 Global area (ha)	2000 Global share %	2000 Global rank	2010 Global area (ha)	2010 Global share %	2010 Global rank
Calitor Gris	W				2	0.00	901			
Calitor Noir	R				75	0.00	594			
Calkarasi	R				436	0.01	390	625	0.01	339
Callet	R				151	0.00	510	154	0.00	547
Caloria	R				129	0.00	524	108	0.00	599
Calrao	R							1	0.00	1156
Camaralet de Lasseube	W				691	0.01	329	515	0.01	361
Campanario	R							2	0.00	1117
Campbell Early	R				43	0.00	657	61	0.00	692
Canada Muscat	W				49	0.00	645			
Canadice	R							0	0.00	1235
Canaiolo Nero	R				2304	0.05	191	1068	0.02	263
Canaiolo Rosa	W				114	0.00	543	1	0.00	1187
Canari Noir	R							152	0.00	549
Canela	R							2	0.00	1122
Canelon	O							8	0.00	981
Canorroyo	W				157	0.00	508			
Capolongo	W							5	0.00	1027
Caracol	W				14	0.00	778	33	0.00	792
Caramela	W							0	0.00	1207
Cardinal	R				3190	0.07	151	545	0.01	354
Carica l'Asino	W				299	0.01	436	17	0.00	887
Carignan Blanc	W				1035	0.02	287	3061	0.07	143
Carignan Bouschet	R				16	0.00	768			
Carignan Gris	W				25	0.00	716			
Carmenere	R				5711	0.12	108	11360	0.25	62
Carmine	R				10	0.00	811			
Carminoir	R							10	0.00	951
Carnelian	R				625	0.01	344	316	0.01	442
Carrega Branco	W							507	0.01	367
Carrega Tinto	R							17	0.00	889
Carricante	W				252	0.01	460	205	0.00	514
Cartouche	W				31	0.00	691			
Casavecchia	R							136	0.00	566
Casculho	R							267	0.01	469
Casetta	R							12	0.00	926
Castalia	W							0	0.00	1243
Castel	R				0	0.00	998	2	0.00	1102
Castela	R							8	0.00	983
Castelao	R				14424	0.30	56	11088	0.24	64
Castelao Branco	W							37	0.00	765
Castelino	R							147	0.00	553
Castelo Branco	W							5	0.00	1042
Castets	R				0	0.00	1005			
Castiglione	R				83	0.00	579	18	0.00	881
Castonotal	W				0	0.00	981			
Catalanesca	W							54	0.00	714
Catanese Nero	R				76	0.00	591	15	0.00	907
Catarratto Bianco	W	80128	1.51	12	50711	1.04	18	34863	0.76	28
Catawba	R				635	0.01	342	633	0.01	337
Cavrara	R							23	0.00	850
Cavus	W				2	0.00	916	3	0.00	1091

Table 5 (cont.) Global winegrape area, share of global area, and global ranks of each variety, 1990, 2000 & 2010

Prime vairiety	Col	1990			2000			2010		
		Global area (ha)	Global share %	Global rank	Global area (ha)	Global share %	Global rank	Global area (ha)	Global share %	Global rank
Cayetana Blanca	W	65276	1.23	16	55502	1.14	17	39741	0.86	22
Cayuga White	W				108	0.00	549	212	0.00	506
Cellerina	R							2	0.00	1127
Centenial Seedless	W				2	0.00	894			
Centesimino	R							24	0.00	841
Centurian	R				134	0.00	517	34	0.00	784
Cep Rouge	R				0	0.00	1000			
Cerceal Branco	W				597	0.01	354	379	0.01	404
Cereza	O	42937	0.81	27	31666	0.65	30	29189	0.63	34
Cesanese	R				1024	0.02	289	679	0.01	329
Cesar	R				8	0.00	822			
Cetinka	W							35	0.00	782
Chambourcin	R				257	0.01	457	1130	0.02	251
Chancellor	R				27	0.00	705	49	0.00	734
Chardonel	W							144	0.00	556
Chardonnay	W	69282	1.31	13	145344	2.98	5	198793	4.32	5
Charmont	W				7	0.00	834	10	0.00	966
Chasan	W				914	0.02	301	801	0.02	301
Chasselas	W				13318	0.27	58	13186	0.29	54
Chasselas Rouge	R				11	0.00	797	7	0.00	1001
Chasselas Sabor	W							0	0.00	1262
Chatus	R				15	0.00	771	13	0.00	917
Chelois	R							1	0.00	1179
Chelva	W				10877	0.22	69	6168	0.13	97
Chenanson	R				636	0.01	341	506	0.01	368
Chenel	W				339	0.01	422	79	0.00	653
Chenin Blanc	W	59974	1.13	19	45806	0.94	22	35164	0.76	26
Chenivesse	R				1	0.00	925			
Chinuri	W				955	0.02	296	1225	0.03	239
Chkhaveri	O				20	0.00	740	26	0.00	829
Cianorie	R							2	0.00	1093
Cidreiro	R							0	0.00	1250
Ciliegiolo	R				2527	0.05	179	1830	0.04	189
Cinsaut	R	63171	1.19	18	48419	0.99	20	36040	0.78	25
Cinsaut Blanc	W				41	0.00	661	7	0.00	994
Cinsaut Seedless	R				9	0.00	816	13	0.00	920
Citronny Magarach	W							307	0.01	449
Cividin	W							4	0.00	1048
Clairette	W				4003	0.08	129	2900	0.06	150
Clairette Rose	W				356	0.01	414	260	0.01	473
Clarin	W				11	0.00	798			
Claverie	W				3	0.00	867			
Cococciola	W				887	0.02	305	983	0.02	269
Coda di Volpe Bianca	W				980	0.02	292	586	0.01	347
Codega de Larinho	W				4058	0.08	128	629	0.01	338
Codivarta	W				3	0.00	891			
Codrinski	R				5	0.00	844	5	0.00	1029
Colgadero	R				6	0.00	840	5	0.00	1030
Colobel	R				3	0.00	878	0	0.00	1236
Colombana Nera	R				126	0.00	526	38	0.00	764
Colombard	W	36138	0.68	34	38146	0.78	24	32076	0.70	32
Colomino	W				16	0.00	764	5	0.00	1040

Table 5 (cont.) Global winegrape area, share of global area, and global ranks of each variety, 1990, 2000 & 2010

Prime vairiety	Col	1990 Global area (ha)	1990 Global share %	1990 Global rank	2000 Global area (ha)	2000 Global share %	2000 Global rank	2010 Global area (ha)	2010 Global share %	2010 Global rank
Coloraillo	R				614	0.01	346	374	0.01	407
Completer	W				2	0.00	907	3	0.00	1074
Complexa	R				6	0.00	838	103	0.00	610
Concieira	R							52	0.00	722
Concord	R	30513	0.58	39	11816	0.24	65	12238	0.27	58
Coracao de Galo	R							1	0.00	1182
Corbina Vicentina	R							12	0.00	929
Cordenossa	R							5	0.00	1025
Cornalin	R				93	0.00	568	256	0.01	475
Cornarea	R				22	0.00	735	13	0.00	918
Cornifesto	R				259	0.01	455	499	0.01	372
Corot Noir	R							27	0.00	826
Corropio	R							1	0.00	1143
Cortese	W				3113	0.06	158	2953	0.06	148
Corvina Veronese	R				4781	0.10	114	7496	0.16	87
Corvinone	R				88	0.00	573	930	0.02	274
Corvo	R							0	0.00	1208
Cot	R	16997	0.32	52	24402	0.50	39	40688	0.88	21
Couderc	W				4	0.00	855	834	0.02	297
Couderc Noir	R				610	0.01	349	2691	0.06	157
Counoise	R				638	0.01	339	443	0.01	391
Courbu Blanc	W				47	0.00	648			
Courbu Noir	R				2	0.00	920			
Cove	W				56	0.00	633	6	0.00	1003
Cramposie Selectionata	W							409	0.01	397
Crimson Cabernet	R							1	0.00	1142
Crimson Seedless	R				1	0.00	929	2	0.00	1105
Criolla Grande	R	68513	1.30	14	24641	0.51	38	17080	0.37	44
Criolla Mediana	R							9	0.00	975
Croatina	R				3116	0.06	157	5700	0.12	102
Crouchen	W				2259	0.05	194	724	0.02	312
Crovassa	R				2	0.00	922	0	0.00	1234
Crystal	W				1	0.00	930	175	0.00	534
Cs.2	R							0	0.00	1260
Csaba Gyongye	W							89	0.00	630
Cserszegi Fuszeres	W				2185	0.04	199	3609	0.08	131
Csillam	W							20	0.00	872
Csokaszolo	R							2	0.00	1100
Csomorika	W							0	0.00	1210
Dakapo	R							53	0.00	720
Dalkauer	W				100	0.00	561			
Damaschino	W				2360	0.05	186	2083	0.05	178
Danlas	W							254	0.01	478
Dawn Seedless	W				5	0.00	851			
De Chaunac	R				186	0.00	484	91	0.00	625
De Cilindro	W				15	0.00	769			
Debina	W				455	0.01	388	239	0.01	489
Debit	W							403	0.01	398
Deckrot	R				30	0.00	693	10	0.00	953
Decuerno	R				4	0.00	859			
Dekabrskii	R							78	0.00	655
Delaware	O				134	0.00	518	127	0.00	579

Table 5 (cont.) Global winegrape area, share of global area, and global ranks of each variety, 1990, 2000 & 2010

Prime vairiety	Col	1990 Global area (ha)	1990 Global share %	1990 Global rank	2000 Global area (ha)	2000 Global share %	2000 Global rank	2010 Global area (ha)	2010 Global share %	2010 Global rank
Deliciosa	R							0	0.00	1257
Devin	W							133	0.00	573
Diagalves	W				1088	0.02	282	1156	0.03	248
Dimrit	R				602	0.01	350	863	0.02	288
Dimyat	W				7718	0.16	82	2401	0.05	166
Dindarella	R				9	0.00	820	7	0.00	998
Diolinoir	R				31	0.00	690	114	0.00	590
Diseca Ranina	W							2	0.00	1120
Docal	R							0	0.00	1246
Doina	R							227	0.00	498
Dolcetto	R				7191	0.15	90	6333	0.14	94
Dolciame	W				6	0.00	839	11	0.00	948
Domina	R				187	0.00	483	361	0.01	417
Dominga	W				0	0.00	988	1	0.00	1162
Dona Branca	W				296	0.01	439	276	0.01	462
Dona Joaquina	W							24	0.00	844
Donzelinho Branco	W				59	0.00	628	65	0.00	682
Donzelinho Roxo	R							0	0.00	1255
Donzelinho Tinto	R							33	0.00	789
Doradilla	W				24	0.00	717	40	0.00	758
Doradillo	W				249	0.01	464			
Doral	W				3	0.00	880	27	0.00	824
Dorinto	W							115	0.00	588
Dornfelder	R				3766	0.08	134	8101	0.18	84
Dostoinyi	R							65	0.00	683
Douce Noire	R				17653	0.36	45	18976	0.41	40
Doukkali	R				16557	0.34	49	16557	0.36	47
Doux d'Henry	R				26	0.00	707	9	0.00	967
Drenak Crven	R	20275	0.38	45						
Droujba	W				3	0.00	875	3	0.00	1072
Drupeggio	W				617	0.01	345	286	0.01	456
Duna Gyongye	R							63	0.00	685
Dunaj	R							46	0.00	744
Dunavski Lazur	W							483	0.01	375
Dunkelfelder	R				280	0.01	447	329	0.01	434
Dunze	R				1	0.00	959			
Duras	R				972	0.02	295	923	0.02	276
Durasa	R				23	0.00	721	6	0.00	1015
Durella	W				599	0.01	353	470	0.01	379
Durif	R				1197	0.02	269	3557	0.08	133
Edelweiss	W							32	0.00	798
Ederena	R				0	0.00	969			
Egiodola	R				315	0.01	430	372	0.01	408
Ehrenbreitsteiner	W				13	0.00	783			
Ehrenfelser	W				289	0.01	444	79	0.00	654
Ekigaina	R				5	0.00	843	1	0.00	1151
Ekim Kara	R				19	0.00	750	27	0.00	825
Elbling	W				1864	0.04	212	1418	0.03	217
Elbling Rot	R				4	0.00	863			
Elvira	W				344	0.01	420	263	0.01	471
Emerald Riesling	W				593	0.01	356	164	0.00	541
Emerald Seedless	W				16	0.00	767			

Table 5 (cont.) Global winegrape area, share of global area, and global ranks of each variety, 1990, 2000 & 2010

Prime vairiety	Col	1990 Global area (ha)	1990 Global share %	1990 Global rank	2000 Global area (ha)	2000 Global share %	2000 Global rank	2010 Global area (ha)	2010 Global share %	2010 Global rank
Emir	W				480	0.01	382	688	0.01	324
Enantio	R				1062	0.02	284	724	0.02	311
Encruzado	W				291	0.01	443	282	0.01	458
Ensanyo Tintas	R							27	0.00	822
Ensayo Blancas	W							1	0.00	1163
Erbaluce	W				329	0.01	425	319	0.01	441
Erbamat	W							24	0.00	843
Erbanno	R							0	0.00	1259
Ervi	R				5	0.00	842	4	0.00	1045
Esganacao Preto	R							0	0.00	1267
Esganinho	W							0	0.00	1252
Espadeiro	R				1682	0.03	220	469	0.01	380
Espadeiro Mole	R							0	0.00	1221
Estreito Macio	W							3	0.00	1083
Etraire de l'Adui	R				8	0.00	831			
Ezerfurtu	W				405	0.01	400	377	0.01	405
Ezerjo	W				3157	0.06	156	1074	0.02	261
Faberrebe	W				1586	0.03	228	524	0.01	356
Falanghina	W				1658	0.03	221	3037	0.07	145
Famoso	W							6	0.00	1009
Farinheira	R							3	0.00	1075
Fenile	W							5	0.00	1022
Fepiro	R							0	0.00	1268
Fer	R				1278	0.03	257	1817	0.04	190
Fernao Pires	W				14545	0.30	55	9511	0.21	74
Fernao Pires Rosado	R							98	0.00	615
Fertilia	R				13	0.00	784	3	0.00	1064
Feteasca Alba	W	18373	0.35	49	23828	0.49	40	17469	0.38	43
Feteasca Neagra	R				1214	0.02	266	1719	0.04	196
Feteasca Regala	W				2578	0.05	178	13136	0.29	55
Feunate	R				0	0.00	1006			
Fiano	W				758	0.02	319	1377	0.03	222
Fiesta	W				161	0.00	505	230	0.00	493
Fileri	W				249	0.01	462	97	0.00	618
Fino de Ribera del Fresno	W				332	0.01	424	45	0.00	746
Fintendo	R							183	0.00	526
Fioletovy Ranny	R							50	0.00	730
Flame Seedless	R	20194	0.38	46	541	0.01	369	42	0.00	754
Flavis	W				12	0.00	791	3	0.00	1067
Flora	O				6	0.00	841	8	0.00	985
Florental	R				1	0.00	961			
Fogarina	R							5	0.00	1026
Foglia Tonda	R				40	0.00	664	101	0.00	611
Fogoneu	R				36	0.00	680	35	0.00	778
Fokiano	R				162	0.00	504	262	0.01	472
Fokiano (White)	W				57	0.00	630			
Folgasao	W				409	0.01	399	182	0.00	528
Folgasao Roxo	R							18	0.00	879
Folha de Figueira	W							3	0.00	1062
Folle Blanche	W				2648	0.05	176	1845	0.04	188
Fontan	R				0	0.00	990			
Fontanara	W				2	0.00	897			

Table 5 (cont.) Global winegrape area, share of global area, and global ranks of each variety, 1990, 2000 & 2010

Prime vairiety	Col	1990 Global area (ha)	1990 Global share %	1990 Global rank	2000 Global area (ha)	2000 Global share %	2000 Global rank	2010 Global area (ha)	2010 Global share %	2010 Global rank
Fonte Cal	W				355	0.01	416	111	0.00	595
Forastera	W				543	0.01	368	208	0.00	512
Forcallat Tinta	R				2690	0.06	174	1163	0.03	247
Forgiarin	R				2	0.00	917	4	0.00	1051
Forsellina	R				9	0.00	814	7	0.00	992
Fortana	R				1252	0.03	264	642	0.01	334
Francavidda	W				86	0.00	576	13	0.00	924
Francusa	W							621	0.01	340
Frappato	R				784	0.02	315	752	0.02	307
Fredonia	R				86	0.00	575	37	0.00	769
Freisa	R				1436	0.03	238	1049	0.02	264
Freisamer	W				17	0.00	759	4	0.00	1044
Frontenac	R							135	0.00	568
Frontenac Gris	W							59	0.00	701
FruHroter Veltliner	R				632	0.01	343	846	0.02	294
Fubiano	W				2	0.00	898	9	0.00	970
Fuella Nera	R				4	0.00	858			
Fumin	R				73	0.00	597	31	0.00	800
Furmint	W				3481	0.07	141	5259	0.11	104
Gaglioppo	R				3592	0.07	138	4214	0.09	120
Gaillard	R				0	0.00	1001			
Galbena de Odobesti	W				546	0.01	367	385	0.01	402
Galego Dourado	W				51	0.00	643	16	0.00	897
Galotta	R							13	0.00	919
Gamaret	R				71	0.00	606	399	0.01	399
Gamay de Teinturier Bouze	R				318	0.01	429	225	0.00	500
Gamay Noir	R	35005	0.66	36	37796	0.77	25	32671	0.71	30
Gamay Teinturier de Chaudenay	R				267	0.01	451	24	0.00	846
Gamay Teinturier Freaux	R				132	0.00	519	55	0.00	706
Gamba Rossa	R							0	0.00	1232
Ganson	R				28	0.00	697			
Garandmak	W				931	0.02	299	931	0.02	273
Garanoir	R				76	0.00	593	216	0.00	503
Garganega	W				16549	0.34	50	15402	0.33	50
Gargiulo	R							47	0.00	741
Garnacha Blanca	W	28409	0.54	40	10821	0.22	71	7370	0.16	88
Garnacha Peluda	R				2024	0.04	207	1232	0.03	236
Garnacha Roja	W				2761	0.06	170	1784	0.04	192
Garnacha Tinta	R	282997	5.35	2	213987	4.39	3	184735	4.01	7
Garonnet	R				7	0.00	835			
Garrido Fino	W				174	0.00	492	59	0.00	700
Gascon	R				0	0.00	1011			
Gateta	R				7	0.00	833	2	0.00	1106
Gegic	W							11	0.00	941
Geisenheim	R							106	0.00	605
Generosa	W				9	0.00	815	107	0.00	603
Gesztus	W							0	0.00	1230
Gewurztraminer	W	16511	0.31	53	10670	0.22	72	14269	0.31	53
Gibi	W							917	0.02	278
Ginestra	W							4	0.00	1054
Giro	R				537	0.01	371	200	0.00	516
Gm 322	R							17	0.00	891

Table 5 (cont.) Global winegrape area, share of global area, and global ranks of each variety, 1990, 2000 & 2010

Prime vairiety	Col	1990 Global area (ha)	1990 Global share %	1990 Global rank	2000 Global area (ha)	2000 Global share %	2000 Global rank	2010 Global area (ha)	2010 Global share %	2010 Global rank
Godello	W				1489	0.03	234	1094	0.02	255
Goecseji Zamatos	W							55	0.00	705
Goher	W							1	0.00	1194
Goldburger	W				309	0.01	431	140	0.00	560
Golden Muscat	W							1	0.00	1183
Goldriesling	W				10	0.00	810	20	0.00	869
Goldtraminer	W							9	0.00	973
Golubok	R				50	0.00	644	87	0.00	632
Goncalo Pires	R							1	0.00	1189
Goruli Mtsvane	W				224	0.00	473	287	0.01	454
Gosen	R							1	0.00	1138
Gouais Blanc	W				1	0.00	936			
Gouget Noir	R				1	0.00	952			
Goustolidi	W				112	0.00	544	68	0.00	675
Gouveio Preto	R							0	0.00	1226
Gouveio Real	W							582	0.01	348
Gouveio Roxo	R							238	0.01	491
Gr 7	R							32	0.00	796
Grachen	W				3	0.00	879	2	0.00	1098
Graciano	R				1910	0.04	211	3102	0.07	142
Graisse	W				22	0.00	728			
Gramon	R				14	0.00	782			
Grand Manchen	W							8	0.00	982
Grand Noir	R				945	0.02	297	955	0.02	271
Grangeal	R							1	0.00	1150
Granho	W							0	0.00	1233
Grapariol	W							2	0.00	1101
Grasa de Cotnari	W				850	0.02	309	685	0.01	325
Grasevina	W	19384	0.37	48	92306	1.89	11	61200	1.33	15
Grassen	R				1	0.00	945			
Grechetto di Orvieto	W				1177	0.02	272	1501	0.03	208
Grechetto Rosso	R				111	0.00	545	49	0.00	737
Greco	W				1325	0.03	251	158	0.00	546
Greco Bianco	W				660	0.01	333	1604	0.03	202
Greco Nero	R				2715	0.06	172	1223	0.03	240
Grenache Rose	R				22	0.00	729	645	0.01	332
Grignolino	R				1353	0.03	249	915	0.02	279
Grillo	W				1803	0.04	214	6295	0.14	95
Gringet	W				74	0.00	596			
Grolleau Gris	W				806	0.02	314	454	0.01	386
Grolleau Noir	R				2201	0.05	198	2350	0.05	170
Groppello di Mocasina	R				120	0.00	534	81	0.00	648
Groppello di Revo	R							12	0.00	931
Groppello Gentile	R				219	0.00	475	326	0.01	437
Gros Bec	R				1	0.00	949			
Gros Manseng	W				2160	0.04	201	4995	0.11	108
Grossa	R							73	0.00	662
Gruner Veltliner	W	20760	0.39	43	23604	0.48	41	18842	0.41	41
Guardavalle	W				168	0.00	498	33	0.00	788
Guillemot	W				0	0.00	1002			
Gutenborner	W							2	0.00	1107
Gyongyrizling	W							23	0.00	848

Table 5 (cont.) Global winegrape area, share of global area, and global ranks of each variety, 1990, 2000 & 2010

Prime vairiety	Col	1990 Global area (ha)	1990 Global share %	1990 Global rank	2000 Global area (ha)	2000 Global share %	2000 Global rank	2010 Global area (ha)	2010 Global share %	2010 Global rank
Hajnalka	W							0	0.00	1264
Harslevelu	W				1296	0.03	254	1856	0.04	187
Hegel	R				10	0.00	802			
Helfensteiner	R				26	0.00	709	10	0.00	954
Herbemont	R				1453	0.03	237	764	0.02	306
Heroldrebe	R				199	0.00	479	140	0.00	561
Himbertscha	W				0	0.00	992			
Himrod	W							0	0.00	1209
Holder	W				13	0.00	789			
Hondarrabi Beltza	R				11	0.00	799	53	0.00	716
Hrvatica	R				245	0.01	465	116	0.00	586
Huerta del Rey	W				35	0.00	682	2	0.00	1108
Humagne	W				9	0.00	817	30	0.00	805
Huxelrebe	W				1289	0.03	256	607	0.01	343
Ilichevskii Rannii	R				5	0.00	845	5	0.00	1031
Imperial Napoleon	R							12	0.00	935
Imperial Seedless	O				1	0.00	955	1	0.00	1164
Impigno	W				60	0.00	624	7	0.00	993
Incrocio Bianco Fedit 51	W				11	0.00	796	5	0.00	1037
Incrocio Bruni 54	W				12	0.00	790	12	0.00	932
Incrocio Manzoni 2.15	R				166	0.00	503	86	0.00	636
Incrocio Terzi 1	R				65	0.00	618	44	0.00	749
Invernenga	W				32	0.00	689	7	0.00	1002
Inzolia	W				9259	0.19	76	6133	0.13	98
Irsai Oliver	W							1414	0.03	218
Isabella	R	21003	0.40	42	27376	0.56	35	32494	0.71	31
Italia	W				706	0.01	327	1145	0.02	249
Italica	W				178	0.00	489	367	0.01	413
Ives	R				23	0.00	726	16	0.00	896
J Ibanez	R							35	0.00	779
Jacquere	W				1086	0.02	283	1028	0.02	265
Jacquez	R				226	0.00	472	2368	0.05	169
Jampal	W				127	0.00	525	71	0.00	668
Joannes Seyve	R				3	0.00	892			
Johanniter	W							51	0.00	725
Joubertin	R				0	0.00	1003			
Juan Garcia	R				2077	0.04	204	1707	0.04	198
Jubilaumsrebe	W				30	0.00	692	14	0.00	914
Jubileum 75	R							194	0.00	520
Juhfark	W							186	0.00	525
Juliana	W							0	0.00	1237
Jurancon Blanc	W				24	0.00	720			
Jurancon Noir	R				1294	0.03	255	706	0.02	319
Jurie	W				0	0.00	1010			
Juwel	W				42	0.00	658	10	0.00	955
K.35	W							0	0.00	1245
Kabar	W							18	0.00	883
Kadarka	R				2630	0.05	177	1087	0.02	258
Kakotrygis	W							103	0.00	608
Kalecik Karasi	R				601	0.01	351	861	0.02	291
Kanaan	W				172	0.00	494	25	0.00	835
Kangun	W				850	0.02	310	850	0.02	293

Table 5 (cont.) Global winegrape area, share of global area, and global ranks of each variety, 1990, 2000 & 2010

Prime vairiety	Col	1990			2000			2010		
		Global area (ha)	Global share %	Global rank	Global area (ha)	Global share %	Global rank	Global area (ha)	Global share %	Global rank
Kanzler	W				53	0.00	640	10	0.00	956
Karalahna	R				3	0.00	887	4	0.00	1055
Karasakiz	R				3	0.00	888	4	0.00	1056
Karat	W							50	0.00	729
Karinian	W				14	0.00	780			
Karmin	R							36	0.00	774
Kay Gray	W							1	0.00	1140
Kek Bakator	W							3	0.00	1088
Keknyelu	W							43	0.00	751
Kerner	W				7111	0.15	91	3994	0.09	125
Kernling	W				18	0.00	753	15	0.00	901
Khikhvi	W				5	0.00	846	6	0.00	1004
Kiralyleanyka	W							855	0.02	292
Kisi	W				20	0.00	741	26	0.00	830
Knipperle	W				2	0.00	909			
Koenigin der Weingaerten	W				750	0.02	321	61	0.00	691
Koksis Irma	W							11	0.00	945
Kokur Bely	W				641	0.01	338	918	0.02	277
Kolor	R							2	0.00	1109
Korinthiaki	R	28126	0.53	41	834	0.02	312	54	0.00	711
Korona	W							1	0.00	1200
Koshu	O				118	0.00	537	168	0.00	538
Kotsifali	R				1148	0.02	276	2330	0.05	171
Kovidinka	O				1214	0.02	267	1075	0.02	260
Krakhuna	W				36	0.00	678	46	0.00	743
Kraljevina	W							447	0.01	389
Krasnostop Zolotovsky	R							562	0.01	352
Krassato	R				38	0.00	672	52	0.00	723
Kreaca	W							3	0.00	1081
Kujundzusa	W							206	0.00	513
Kuldzhinskii	O				269	0.01	450	385	0.01	401
Kunbarat	W							9	0.00	979
Kunleany	W				1376	0.03	247	1211	0.03	242
Kurucver	R							0	0.00	1249
La Crescent	W							77	0.00	658
La Crosse	W							25	0.00	832
Labrusco	R							81	0.00	647
Lacoste	R				1	0.00	940			
Lacrima Christi	R							85	0.00	637
Lacrima di Morro d'Alba	R				652	0.01	335	421	0.01	395
Lado	W				1	0.00	958	1	0.00	1165
Lafnetscha	W				1	0.00	931			
Lagarino Bianco	W							23	0.00	855
Lagrein	R				471	0.01	384	717	0.02	315
Lairen	W				298	0.01	438	214	0.00	504
Lakhegyi Mezes	W				567	0.01	364	306	0.01	451
Lambrusca di Alessandria	R				888	0.02	304	137	0.00	565
Lambrusco	R				42	0.00	660	45	0.00	745
Lambrusco Barghi	R							18	0.00	880
Lambrusco di Sorbara	R				1409	0.03	243	1606	0.03	201
Lambrusco Grasparossa	R				1720	0.04	217	2738	0.06	156
Lambrusco Maestri					1362	0.03	248	2272	0.05	172

Table 5 (cont.) Global winegrape area, share of global area, and global ranks of each variety, 1990, 2000 & 2010

Prime vairiety	Col	1990			2000			2010		
		Global area (ha)	Global share %	Global rank	Global area (ha)	Global share %	Global rank	Global area (ha)	Global share %	Global rank
Lambrusco Marani	R				2280	0.05	193	1394	0.03	221
Lambrusco Montericco	R				262	0.01	453	70	0.00	671
Lambrusco Oliva	R							112	0.00	593
Lambrusco Salamino	R				4147	0.09	126	5003	0.11	107
Lambrusco Viadanese	R				277	0.01	449	240	0.01	486
Lameiro	W							0	0.00	1218
Landal	R				16	0.00	766			
Landot	W				0	0.00	983			
Landot Noir	R				0	0.00	1008	2	0.00	1094
Lariao	W							4	0.00	1059
Lasina	R							14	0.00	910
Laska	R				1	0.00	939			
Laurot	R							6	0.00	1013
Lauzet	W				1	0.00	942			
Leanyka	W							838	0.02	296
Lecinaro	R							1	0.00	1192
Leira	W							1	0.00	1197
Len de l'El	W				734	0.02	324	640	0.01	335
Leon Millot	R				17	0.00	756	23	0.00	849
Leopoldo III	R				2	0.00	915			
Levokumski Sustainable	O							170	0.00	536
Levokumsky	R							720	0.02	314
Liatiko	R				2476	0.05	181	1211	0.03	241
Liatiko(White)	W				70	0.00	610			
Liliorila	W				3	0.00	890			
Limnio	R				95	0.00	565	372	0.01	409
Limnio(White)	W				27	0.00	701			
Listain de Huelva	W				596	0.01	355	350	0.01	422
Listan Negro	R				3291	0.07	147	2666	0.06	160
Listan Prieto	R				15532	0.32	51	4564	0.10	115
Listrao Roxo	R				10	0.00	807			
Lorena	W							519	0.01	359
Louise Swenson	W							3	0.00	1076
Loureiro	W				4392	0.09	118	4054	0.09	124
Lourela	R							0	0.00	1238
Lumassina	W				111	0.00	547	98	0.00	617
Lusitano	R							0	0.00	1256
Luzidio	W							0	0.00	1231
Macabeo	W	43504	0.82	26	48125	0.99	21	41046	0.89	20
Maceratino	W				122	0.00	530	177	0.00	532
Madeleine Angevine	W							52	0.00	724
Madeleine Sylvaner	W							7	0.00	991
Magliocco Canino	R				579	0.01	361	539	0.01	355
Magliocco Dolce	R				243	0.00	466	87	0.00	633
Magyarfrankos	R							0	0.00	1216
Maiolica	R				70	0.00	607	26	0.00	828
Maiolina	R							1	0.00	1131
Maiskii Chernyi	R				77	0.00	590	110	0.00	598
Malaga Blanc	W				11	0.00	795	16	0.00	894
Malagousia	W				23	0.00	724	182	0.00	527
Malbo Gentile	R				106	0.00	552	211	0.00	508
Malegue	R				1	0.00	941			

Table 5 (cont.) Global winegrape area, share of global area, and global ranks of each variety, 1990, 2000 & 2010

Prime vairiety	Col	1990 Global area (ha)	1990 Global share %	1990 Global rank	Global area (ha)	Global share %	Global rank	2010 Global area (ha)	2010 Global share %	2010 Global rank
Maliverne	W				0	0.00	974			
Malvarisco	R							3	0.00	1066
Malvasia Amarela	W							14	0.00	911
Malvasia Bianca di Basilicata	W				875	0.02	306	210	0.00	509
Malvasia Bianca di Candia	W	42654	0.81	28	12889	0.26	61	9891	0.21	71
Malvasia Bianca Lunga	W				3937	0.08	132	2544	0.06	163
Malvasia Branca de Sao Jorge	W				55	0.00	634	110	0.00	596
Malvasia Candida Roxa	R							3	0.00	1079
Malvasia del Lazio	W				2366	0.05	185	590	0.01	346
Malvasia di Candia Aromatica	W				1643	0.03	223	895	0.02	284
Malvasia di Casorzo	R				98	0.00	563	107	0.00	601
Malvasia di Lipari	W				516	0.01	376	310	0.01	447
Malvasia di Schierano	R				181	0.00	487	89	0.00	629
Malvasia Fina	W				7102	0.15	92	3416	0.07	137
Malvasia Fina Roxa	R							25	0.00	833
Malvasia Nera di Basilicata	R				754	0.02	320	114	0.00	589
Malvasia Nera di Brindisi	R				3174	0.07	153	1314	0.03	230
Malvasia Nera Lunga	R							38	0.00	763
Malvasia Parda	W							1	0.00	1132
Malvasia Preta	R				1157	0.02	274	1003	0.02	266
Malvasia Romana	W							0	0.00	1247
Malvasia Rosa	R				111	0.00	546	32	0.00	799
Malvasia Trigueira	R							12	0.00	930
Malvazija Istarska	W				7559	0.15	83	2740	0.06	155
Malvia	W							0	0.00	1241
Mammolo	R				777	0.02	316	825	0.02	298
Mandilaria	R				845	0.02	311	885	0.02	286
Mandon	R				261	0.01	454			
Manseng Noir	R				10	0.00	804	56	0.00	704
Manteudo Preto	R							16	0.00	893
Manto Negro	R				470	0.01	385	273	0.01	464
Manzoni Bianco	W				8290	0.17	79	382	0.01	403
Manzoni Moscato	R							20	0.00	871
Manzoni Rosa	O							29	0.00	811
Maratheftiko	R							152	0.00	550
Marechal Foch	R				173	0.00	493	344	0.01	428
Mariensteiner	W				9	0.00	812			
Mario Feld	R							0	0.00	1263
Marmajuelo	W				37	0.00	674	24	0.00	838
Marquette	R							88	0.00	631
Marquinhas	W							11	0.00	944
Mars	R							2	0.00	1114
Marsanne	W				1512	0.03	231	1742	0.04	194
Marselan	R				176	0.00	491	2497	0.05	164
Marufo	R				6339	0.13	101	6579	0.14	91
Marzemina Bianca	W				78	0.00	588	54	0.00	712
Marzemino	R				994	0.02	291	1091	0.02	257
Maticha	W							275	0.01	463
Matrai Muskotaly	W							67	0.00	678
Matrasa	R				20	0.00	744	28	0.00	818
Maturana Blanca	W							18	0.00	886
Mauzac Blanc	W				3251	0.07	150	1991	0.04	182

Table 5 (cont.) Global winegrape area, share of global area, and global ranks of each variety, 1990, 2000 & 2010

Prime vairiety	Col	1990			2000			2010		
		Global area (ha)	Global share %	Global rank	Global area (ha)	Global share %	Global rank	Global area (ha)	Global share %	Global rank
Mauzac Noir	R				10	0.00	809			
Mauzac Rose	W				59	0.00	627			
Mavro	R				10969	0.22	68	3575	0.08	132
Mavro Messenikola	R				3	0.00	873			
Mavrodafni	R				537	0.01	372	345	0.01	427
Mavrouda	R				349	0.01	418	520	0.01	358
Mavrud	R				647	0.01	337	1296	0.03	232
Mayolet	R				4	0.00	860	7	0.00	990
Mazuelo	R	202869	3.83	6	126650	2.60	7	80178	1.74	11
Mazzese	R				80	0.00	584	76	0.00	659
Mecle de Bourgoin	R				2	0.00	905			
Medina	R							159	0.00	545
Melara	W				13	0.00	788	3	0.00	1084
Melhorio	R							0	0.00	1261
Melon	W				13253	0.27	59	12365	0.27	56
Mencia	R	17321	0.33	51	13138	0.27	60	10658	0.23	65
Menoir	R							65	0.00	680
Menu Pineau	W				380	0.01	407	212	0.00	507
Merille	R				131	0.00	521			
Merlese	R							14	0.00	909
Merlo	W				3	0.00	871			
Merlot	R	154752	2.93	7	211967	4.35	4	267169	5.81	2
Merlot Blanc	W				176	0.00	490	31	0.00	801
Merseguera	W				7460	0.15	85	3946	0.09	126
Merzling	W				5	0.00	854			
Meslier Saint-Francois	W				55	0.00	635			
Mezes Feher	W							2	0.00	1097
Michele Parlieri	W				3	0.00	893	1	0.00	1166
Michurinetz	R							0	0.00	1214
Miguel del Arco	R				1267	0.03	261	468	0.01	381
Milgranet	R				2	0.00	902			
Milia	R							1	0.00	1135
Mindelo	R							1	0.00	1202
Minella Bianca	W				73	0.00	598	65	0.00	681
Misket	W				3764	0.08	135			
Misket Cherven	O							4159	0.09	121
Misket Varnenski	W							336	0.01	430
Molette	W				30	0.00	694			
Molinara	R				1634	0.03	225	717	0.02	316
Mollard	R				23	0.00	722			
Monastrell	R	108213	2.05	9	76304	1.56	12	69850	1.52	14
Monbadon	W				0	0.00	986			
Mondet	R							0	0.00	1227
Mondeuse Blanche	W				22	0.00	731			
Mondeuse Grise	W				0	0.00	970			
Mondeuse Noire	R				1404	0.03	245	306	0.01	450
Monemvassia	W				418	0.01	397	481	0.01	377
Monerac	R				2	0.00	923			
Monica Nera	R				2835	0.06	166	1404	0.03	219
Monstruosa	W				2	0.00	899	1	0.00	1167
Montepulciano	R	32982	0.62	37	28679	0.59	33	34947	0.76	27
Montils	W				131	0.00	520			

Table 5 (cont.) Global winegrape area, share of global area, and global ranks of each variety, 1990, 2000 & 2010

Prime vairiety	Col	1990 Global area (ha)	1990 Global share %	1990 Global rank	2000 Global area (ha)	2000 Global share %	2000 Global rank	2010 Global area (ha)	2010 Global share %	2010 Global rank
Montonico Bianco	W				656	0.01	334	734	0.02	310
Montu	W				1091	0.02	281			
Monvedro	R				14	0.00	779	6	0.00	1020
Moore's Diamond	W				19	0.00	748	42	0.00	753
Moradella	R							6	0.00	1019
Moravia Agria	R				1092	0.02	280	550	0.01	353
Morenillo	R				39	0.00	670			
Moreto	R				1053	0.02	286	900	0.02	283
Morio-Muskat	W				1188	0.02	271	509	0.01	365
Moristel	R							112	0.00	592
Mornen Noir	R				1	0.00	947			
Morone	R				22	0.00	730	13	0.00	922
Morrastel Bouschet	R				1	0.00	951			
Moscadet	W							4	0.00	1058
Moscargo	R							0	0.00	1253
Moscatel Branco	W				1419	0.03	241	30	0.00	808
Moscatel Lilaz	W							0	0.00	1269
Moscatel Rosada	O				10656	0.22	73	7329	0.16	89
Moscatello Selvatico	W				105	0.00	553	35	0.00	780
Moscato di Scanzo	R				73	0.00	599	53	0.00	717
Moscato di Terracina	W				229	0.00	471	138	0.00	563
Moscato Embrapa	W							862	0.02	289
Moscato Giallo	W				410	0.01	398	1470	0.03	210
Moscato Nazareno	W							68	0.00	677
Moscato Rosa del Trentino	R				93	0.00	569	81	0.00	646
Moscatuel	R							61	0.00	689
Moschofilero	R				423	0.01	395	934	0.02	272
Moschofilero	O				46	0.00	651	80	0.00	651
Moschomavro	R				2305	0.05	190	1428	0.03	215
Mostosa	W				95	0.00	566	24	0.00	842
Mourisco de Semente	R							60	0.00	694
Mourisco de Trevoes	R							2	0.00	1115
Mourvaison	R				9	0.00	818			
Mouyssagues	R				0	0.00	1007			
Mskhali	W				1093	0.02	279	1093	0.02	256
Mtsvane Kakhuri	W				249	0.01	463	319	0.01	440
Müller Thurgau	W	36381	0.69	33	33572	0.69	28	22753	0.49	37
Muscadel (Red)	R				360	0.01	413	371	0.01	410
Muscadelle	W				2207	0.05	197	1656	0.04	199
Muscardin	R				19	0.00	749			
Muscat a Petits Grains Noirs	R							108	0.00	600
Muscat a Petits Grains Roses	R				116	0.00	540			
Muscat a Petits Grains Rouge	R				500	0.01	379	613	0.01	341
Muscat Amber	O							21	0.00	862
Muscat Bailey A	R				72	0.00	602	122	0.00	580
Muscat Blanc a Petits Grains	W	17806	0.34	50	28401	0.58	34	31112	0.68	33
Muscat de Ialoveni	W				20	0.00	742	20	0.00	870
Muscat Fleur d'Oranger	W				36	0.00	676	91	0.00	626
Muscat of Alexandria	W	64224	1.21	17	29411	0.60	32	26336	0.57	35
Muscat of Alexandria Red	R				11	0.00	800	6	0.00	1017
Muscat of Hamburg	R				7066	0.14	93	8137	0.18	81
Muscat Ottonel	W				12259	0.25	64	10234	0.22	68

Table 5 (cont.) Global winegrape area, share of global area, and global ranks of each variety, 1990, 2000 & 2010

Prime vairiety	Col	1990 Global area (ha)	1990 Global share %	1990 Global rank	2000 Global area (ha)	2000 Global share %	2000 Global rank	2010 Global area (ha)	2010 Global share %	2010 Global rank
Muscat Rose	O				159	0.00	507	227	0.00	497
Muscat Swenson	W							24	0.00	836
Muscat Violet	R				19	0.00	747	27	0.00	821
Muskat Moravsky	W							514	0.01	362
Mustoasa de Maderat	W							255	0.01	476
Naia	W							0	0.00	1211
Naparo	R				0	0.00	982	1	0.00	1168
Narince	W				537	0.01	373	769	0.02	305
Nascetta	W							21	0.00	860
Nasco	W				166	0.00	502	141	0.00	558
Nebbiera	R				20	0.00	743	12	0.00	934
Nebbiolo	R				5047	0.10	112	5992	0.13	99
Negoska	R				96	0.00	564	143	0.00	557
Negramoll	R				3557	0.07	139	3193	0.07	139
Negrette	R				1319	0.03	252	1228	0.03	237
Negretto	R				280	0.01	446	75	0.00	660
Negroamaro	R	40064	0.76	31	16619	0.34	48	11460	0.25	60
Negroamaro Precoce	R							32	0.00	797
Negru de Ialoveni	R				15	0.00	772	15	0.00	902
Nektar	W							21	0.00	859
Ner d'Ala	R				8	0.00	827	30	0.00	806
Nerello Cappuccio	R				1501	0.03	233	508	0.01	366
Nerello Mascalese	R				4167	0.09	124	2883	0.06	152
Neretta Cuneese	R				374	0.01	409	132	0.00	574
Neretto di Bairo	R				53	0.00	642	34	0.00	785
Nero	R							50	0.00	728
Nero Buono di Cori	R				114	0.00	541	135	0.00	569
Nero d'Avola	R				11318	0.23	66	16596	0.36	45
Nero di Troia	R				1765	0.04	215	2572	0.06	162
Neronet	R							72	0.00	664
Neuburger	W				1434	0.03	239	964	0.02	270
Nevoeira	R							0	0.00	1220
New York Muscat	R							5	0.00	1035
Neyret	R				76	0.00	592	41	0.00	755
Niagara	W				15343	0.31	52	4670	0.10	112
Nieddera	R				58	0.00	629	107	0.00	602
Nigra	R				7	0.00	832	3	0.00	1092
Nincusa	R							17	0.00	892
Noah	W				71	0.00	605	71	0.00	666
Nobling	W				102	0.00	559	50	0.00	731
Nocera	R				27	0.00	703	15	0.00	904
Noir Fleurien	R				0	0.00	996			
Noiret	R							33	0.00	791
Noria	W							1	0.00	1136
Norton	R				0	0.00	985	329	0.01	433
Nosiola	W				191	0.00	481	79	0.00	652
Nosztori Rizling	W							1	0.00	1193
Notardomenico	R				13	0.00	787	10	0.00	963
Noual	W				1	0.00	966			
Nouvelle	W				2	0.00	914	422	0.01	394
Nuragus	W				3186	0.07	152	1345	0.03	225
Oberlin	R				0	0.00	997			

Table 5 (cont.) Global winegrape area, share of global area, and global ranks of each variety, 1990, 2000 & 2010

Prime vairiety	Col	1990			2000			2010		
		Global area (ha)	Global share %	Global rank	Global area (ha)	Global share %	Global rank	Global area (ha)	Global share %	Global rank
Oberlin White	W				1	0.00	946			
Odessky Cherny	R				1694	0.03	218	2686	0.06	158
Odola	R				1	0.00	928			
Odysseus	W							4	0.00	1043
Oeillade Bousche	R				10	0.00	805			
Ofthalmo	R							141	0.00	559
Ohanes	W				0	0.00	971	1	0.00	1169
Ojaleshi	R				25	0.00	713	32	0.00	794
Okuzgozu	R				1033	0.02	288	1479	0.03	209
Olivette Noire	R				0	0.00	975			
Ondarrabi Zuri	W				189	0.00	482	492	0.01	373
Ondenc	W				12	0.00	792			
Onitskanskii Belyi	W				5	0.00	847	71	0.00	667
Optima	W				239	0.00	468	37	0.00	770
Ora	W							0	0.00	1225
Oraniensteiner	W							3	0.00	1086
Orion	W				8	0.00	821	10	0.00	957
Orpheus	W							0	0.00	1228
Orpicchio	W							1	0.00	1205
Ortega	W				1054	0.02	285	637	0.01	336
Ortrugo	W				485	0.01	381	611	0.01	342
Oseleta	R							15	0.00	906
Osteiner	W				3	0.00	868	1	0.00	1170
Otskhanuri Sapere	R				5	0.00	848	6	0.00	1005
Padeiro	R							86	0.00	635
Palatina	W							6	0.00	1016
Palava	O							230	0.00	494
Pallagrello Bianco	W							55	0.00	709
Pallagrello Nero	R							169	0.00	537
Palomino Fino	W	50545	0.96	22	30297	0.62	31	22510	0.49	38
Palot	W				4	0.00	865			
Pamid	R				22718	0.47	42	9827	0.21	73
Pampanaro	W							5	0.00	1041
Pampanuto	W				277	0.01	448	356	0.01	420
Pannon Frankos	R							16	0.00	895
Panse Valenciano	W				649	0.01	336	1	0.00	1171
Paolina	W							1	0.00	1134
Papazkarasi	R				122	0.00	529	175	0.00	533
Pardillo	W				7272	0.15	87	4364	0.09	119
Parellada	W				11188	0.23	67	8847	0.19	77
Parraleta	R				167	0.00	500	346	0.01	424
Parreira Matias	R							1	0.00	1188
Pascal Blanc	W				0	0.00	994			
Pascale	R				1573	0.03	229	375	0.01	406
Passau	R				12	0.00	793	5	0.00	1024
Passerina	W				715	0.01	325	894	0.02	285
Patagonia	W							24	0.00	847
Patorra	R							10	0.00	960
Patria	W							3	0.00	1077
Patricia	R							1	0.00	1180
Pavana	R				69	0.00	612	32	0.00	795
Pe Comprido	W							1	0.00	1153

Table 5 (cont.) Global winegrape area, share of global area, and global ranks of each variety, 1990, 2000 & 2010

Prime vairiety	Col	1990 Global area (ha)	1990 Global share %	1990 Global rank	2000 Global area (ha)	2000 Global share %	2000 Global rank	2010 Global area (ha)	2010 Global share %	2010 Global rank
Pecorello	R				16	0.00	762	34	0.00	786
Pecorino	W				166	0.00	501	1228	0.03	238
Pecsi Szagos	W							1	0.00	1154
Pedral	R				179	0.00	488	151	0.00	551
Pedro Gimenez	W				15101	0.31	54	12250	0.27	57
Pedro Ximenez	W	47915	0.91	23	17272	0.35	46	9243	0.20	76
Pelaverga	R				28	0.00	699	55	0.00	708
Pelaverga Piccolo	R				24	0.00	719	6	0.00	1018
Peloursin	R				0	0.00	968			
Pelso	W							1	0.00	1191
Pepella	W							3	0.00	1078
Perdea	W				13	0.00	785			
Perera	W				25	0.00	715	4	0.00	1052
Perigo	W							4	0.00	1050
Perla dei Vivi	R							1	0.00	1186
Perle	O				121	0.00	531	21	0.00	863
Perlette	W				1	0.00	956	1	0.00	1172
Perlita	W				1	0.00	934	1	0.00	1173
Perola	W				68	0.00	615			
Perricone	R				580	0.01	360	228	0.00	495
Perruno	W				2831	0.06	167	1509	0.03	207
Persan	R				3	0.00	876	3	0.00	1073
Pervenets Magaracha	W				2837	0.06	165	2881	0.06	153
Pervomaisky	R				64	0.00	619	64	0.00	684
Petit Bouschet	R				1	0.00	964	15	0.00	899
Petit Courbu	W				75	0.00	595	36	0.00	776
Petit Manseng	W				613	0.01	347	1327	0.03	228
Petit Meslier	W				3	0.00	869			
Petit Rouge	R				100	0.00	560	84	0.00	640
Petit Verdot	R				1481	0.03	235	7202	0.16	90
Pexem	R							3	0.00	1089
Phoenix	W				24	0.00	718	51	0.00	726
Picapoll Blanco	W				34	0.00	683	37	0.00	768
Piccola Nera	O				17	0.00	755	17	0.00	888
Picolit	W				93	0.00	570	128	0.00	577
Piculit Neri	W				126	0.00	527	22	0.00	857
Piedirosso	R				896	0.02	303	699	0.02	320
Pignola Valtellinese	R				70	0.00	609	49	0.00	738
Pignoletto	W				6009	0.12	104	1707	0.04	197
Pignolo	R				18	0.00	752	93	0.00	622
Pineau d'Aunis	R				430	0.01	392	435	0.01	392
Pinella	W				66	0.00	617	72	0.00	665
Pinot Blanc	W				16990	0.35	47	14724	0.32	52
Pinot Gris	O				18879	0.39	44	43563	0.95	19
Pinot Meunier	R				10832	0.22	70	11267	0.24	63
Pinot Noir	R	41539	0.79	30	60099	1.23	16	86662	1.88	10
Pinot Noir Precoce	R				86	0.00	577	209	0.00	511
Pinotage	R				6574	0.13	98	6404	0.14	93
Pintes	W							3	0.00	1085
Pintosa	W							2	0.00	1121
Piquepoul Blanc	W				975	0.02	294	1455	0.03	212
Piquepoul Bousch	R				0	0.00	972			

Table 5 (cont.) Global winegrape area, share of global area, and global ranks of each variety, 1990, 2000 & 2010

Prime vairiety	Col	1990			2000			2010		
		Global area (ha)	Global share %	Global rank	Global area (ha)	Global share %	Global rank	Global area (ha)	Global share %	Global rank
Piquepoul Gris	W				9	0.00	813			
Piquepoul Noir	R				103	0.00	556	10	0.00	964
Plant Droit	R				40	0.00	668			
Planta Mula	R				1	0.00	935	24	0.00	839
Planta Nova	W				2029	0.04	206	1395	0.03	220
Plantet	R				209	0.00	477	1105	0.02	254
Plassa	R				41	0.00	662	91	0.00	624
Plavac Mali	R				6539	0.13	99	1569	0.03	205
Plavay	W							60	0.00	693
Plavec Zuti	W							13	0.00	921
Plavina	R							643	0.01	333
Podarok Magaracha	W				148	0.00	514	504	0.01	369
Poeloeske Muskotaly	W							103	0.00	609
Pollera Nera	R				19	0.00	745	54	0.00	710
Portan	R				368	0.01	411	311	0.01	445
Portland	W				9	0.00	819	12	0.00	927
Posip Bijeli	W				6539	0.13	100	253	0.01	479
Pougnet	R				0	0.00	979			
Poulsard	R				295	0.01	440	311	0.01	446
Poulsard Blanc	W				14	0.00	781			
Pozsonyi	W							10	0.00	949
Praca	W							166	0.00	539
Prairie Star	W							21	0.00	861
Precoce de Malingre	W				3	0.00	885			
Prensal	W				114	0.00	542	105	0.00	607
Preto Cardana	R							5	0.00	1038
Preto Martinho	R				428	0.01	394	163	0.00	543
Prie	W				36	0.00	679	33	0.00	790
Prieto Picudo	R				3256	0.07	149	4587	0.10	114
Primavera	R							40	0.00	760
Primetta	R				17	0.00	754	24	0.00	845
Prodest	R				2	0.00	895			
Prokupac	R				15180	0.31	53	15180	0.33	51
Promissao	W							6	0.00	1008
Prosecco	W				7498	0.15	84	18437	0.40	42
Prosecco Lungo	W							1367	0.03	223
Provareau	R				2	0.00	913			
Prunelard	R				2	0.00	903			
Prunesta	R				92	0.00	571	36	0.00	775
Pugnitello	R							28	0.00	814
Putzscheere	W				0	0.00	1009			
Quagliano	R				8	0.00	823	9	0.00	971
Quebranta	R				230	0.00	470	345	0.01	425
Rabigato	W				1133	0.02	277	1273	0.03	233
Rabigato Moreno	W							1	0.00	1181
Rabo de Anho	R							99	0.00	613
Rabo de Lobo	R							3	0.00	1065
Rabo de Ovelha	W				2330	0.05	188	908	0.02	281
Raboso Piave	R				1270	0.03	259	771	0.02	304
Raboso Veronese	R				307	0.01	433	277	0.01	461
Raffiat de Moncade	W				16	0.00	761			
Raisaine	W				1	0.00	937			

Table 5 (cont.) Global winegrape area, share of global area, and global ranks of each variety, 1990, 2000 & 2010

Prime vairiety	Col	1990 Global area (ha)	1990 Global share %	1990 Global rank	2000 Global area (ha)	2000 Global share %	2000 Global rank	2010 Global area (ha)	2010 Global share %	2010 Global rank
Ramisco	R				72	0.00	603	34	0.00	787
Ranfol	W							134	0.00	572
Ranna Melnishka Loza	R							249	0.01	482
Rathay	R							9	0.00	977
Ratinho	W							84	0.00	638
Rauschling	W				23	0.00	723	23	0.00	854
Ravat	R				1	0.00	948			
Ravat Blanc	W				2	0.00	906			
Rayon d'Or	W				1	0.00	950			
Rebo	R				37	0.00	675	120	0.00	582
Recantina	R							9	0.00	968
Red Globe	R				2068	0.04	205	240	0.01	487
Red Semillon	R				4	0.00	861	10	0.00	958
Refosco	R				1267	0.03	260	1420	0.03	216
Refosco dal Peduncolo Rosso	R				711	0.01	326	1076	0.02	259
Refosco di Faedis	R				256	0.01	458	217	0.00	502
Refren	W							0	0.00	1217
Regent	R				16	0.00	760	69	0.00	673
Regina	W				1509	0.03	232	321	0.01	439
Regner	W				150	0.00	511	44	0.00	748
Reichensteiner	W				319	0.01	428	228	0.00	496
Reliance	R							4	0.00	1061
Retagliado Bianco	W				26	0.00	710	28	0.00	815
Reze	W				1	0.00	953			
Ribolla Gialla	W				1406	0.03	244	1178	0.03	246
Rieslaner	W				70	0.00	608	60	0.00	696
Rieslina	W							127	0.00	578
Riesling	W	52164	0.99	21	43166	0.88	23	50060	1.09	18
Riesus	W							115	0.00	587
Rio Grande	W				4	0.00	862	1	0.00	1203
Ripolo	W							1	0.00	1149
Riton	W				2	0.00	911	257	0.01	474
Rkatsiteli	W	280569	5.30	3	67354	1.38	14	58641	1.27	16
Robola	W				356	0.01	415	465	0.01	383
Roditis	O				299	0.01	435	4661	0.10	113
Roditis(Red)	R				6945	0.14	94	3834	0.08	127
Roesler	R							160	0.00	544
Rojal Tinta	R				2845	0.06	162	1801	0.04	191
Rollo	W				117	0.00	538	51	0.00	727
Rombola Red	R				3	0.00	870	6	0.00	1021
Rome	R				2	0.00	919	297	0.01	452
Romeiko	R				382	0.01	406	1597	0.03	203
Romorantin	W				81	0.00	582			
Rondinella	R				2797	0.06	168	2481	0.05	165
Rondo	R							40	0.00	759
Roobernet	R				78	0.00	589	139	0.00	562
Rosa Arica	R				1	0.00	957	1	0.00	1174
Rosciola Rose	O							2	0.00	1096
Rose du Var	O				129	0.00	523			
Rossara Trentina	R				29	0.00	696	8	0.00	984
Rossese	R				232	0.00	469	312	0.01	443
Rossese Bianco	W							7	0.00	987

Table 5 (cont.) Global winegrape area, share of global area, and global ranks of each variety, 1990, 2000 & 2010

Prime vairiety	Col	1990 Global area (ha)	1990 Global share %	1990 Global rank	2000 Global area (ha)	2000 Global share %	2000 Global rank	2010 Global area (ha)	2010 Global share %	2010 Global rank
Rossignola	R				295	0.01	441	188	0.00	524
Rossola Nera	R				102	0.00	558	86	0.00	634
Rotberger	R							1	0.00	1145
Roter Veltliner	O				258	0.01	456	199	0.00	517
Rotgipfler	W				118	0.00	535	105	0.00	606
Roublot	W				0	0.00	973			
Rougeon	R				36	0.00	677	42	0.00	752
Roussanne	W				874	0.02	307	1746	0.04	193
Roussette d'Ayze	W				3	0.00	884			
Roussin	R				3	0.00	882	3	0.00	1068
Roviello Bianco	W							2	0.00	1130
Roxo de Vila Flor	R							0	0.00	1244
Roxo Rei	R							0	0.00	1223
Royal de Alloza	R							29	0.00	812
Royalty	R				338	0.01	423	97	0.00	619
Rozala Bianca	W							2	0.00	1129
Rozsakoe	W							19	0.00	878
Rual	R							1	0.00	1146
Rubea	R							81	0.00	645
Rubilande	R				3	0.00	886			
Rubin Golodrigi	R							82	0.00	643
Rubin Tairovsky	R				2	0.00	912	2	0.00	1110
Rubinovy Magaracha	R				0	0.00	999	0	0.00	1251
Rubintos	R							18	0.00	882
Rubired	R				4153	0.09	125	4556	0.10	116
Ruby	R				6	0.00	837	9	0.00	969
Ruby Cabernet	R				7419	0.15	86	5730	0.12	101
Ruby Seedless	R				0	0.00	1012			
Ruche	R				46	0.00	650	100	0.00	612
Rufete	R				3397	0.07	142	4833	0.11	109
Ruggine	W							1	0.00	1133
S. Mamede	W							1	0.00	1195
S.V. 23-512	R							29	0.00	813
Sabrevois	R							10	0.00	959
Sacy	W				63	0.00	620			
Sagrantino	R				351	0.01	417	995	0.02	267
Saint Jeannet	R							44	0.00	747
Saint Macaire	R				1	0.00	965			
Saint-Pierre Dore	W				1	0.00	967			
Salvador	R				572	0.01	362	394	0.01	400
Samarrinho	W							1	0.00	1139
San Giuseppe Nero	R				348	0.01	419	192	0.00	522
San Lunardo	W				22	0.00	733	10	0.00	965
San Martino	R				44	0.00	653	21	0.00	865
San Michele	R				120	0.00	532	57	0.00	703
Sanforte	R							1	0.00	1204
Sangiovese	R	98946	1.87	11	68877	1.41	13	77709	1.69	13
Sankt Laurent	R				2370	0.05	184	3007	0.07	147
Santa Maria	W				15	0.00	774	3	0.00	1080
Santarena	R							739	0.02	309
Santoal	W							9	0.00	972
Sao Saul	R							1	0.00	1178

Table 5 (cont.) Global winegrape area, share of global area, and global ranks of each variety, 1990, 2000 & 2010

Prime vairiety	Col	1990 Global area (ha)	1990 Global share %	1990 Global rank	2000 Global area (ha)	2000 Global share %	2000 Global rank	2010 Global area (ha)	2010 Global share %	2010 Global rank
Saperavi	R				6707	0.14	96	8126	0.18	82
Saperavi Severny	R				25	0.00	714	350	0.01	421
Sauvignon Blanc	W	44677	0.84	25	64889	1.33	15	110138	2.39	8
Sauvignon Gris	W				44	0.00	654	483	0.01	376
Sauvignon Rose	O				26	0.00	708			
Sauvignonasse	W				5494	0.11	110	4449	0.10	117
Savagnin Blanc	W				430	0.01	393	1898	0.04	186
Savagnin Rose	W				35	0.00	681			
Savatiano	W	20396	0.39	44	12747	0.26	63	9920	0.22	70
Scheurebe	W				3655	0.07	137	1984	0.04	183
Schiava	R				1231	0.03	265	517	0.01	360
Schiava Gentile	R				1158	0.02	273	694	0.02	322
Schiava Grigia	R				79	0.00	587	66	0.00	679
Schiava Grossa	R				1259	0.03	263	580	0.01	350
Schioppettino	R				93	0.00	567	154	0.00	548
Schonburger	O				39	0.00	669	59	0.00	698
Sciaglin	W				4	0.00	864	6	0.00	1006
Sciascinoso	R				253	0.01	459	94	0.00	621
Scimiscia	W							5	0.00	1034
Seara Nova	W				1213	0.02	268	681	0.01	328
Segalin	R				54	0.00	638			
Seibel	R				1991	0.04	208	591	0.01	345
Seibel White	W				15	0.00	773			
Seinoir	R				15	0.00	775			
Select	W				8	0.00	829			
Semebat	R				2	0.00	900			
Semidano	W				48	0.00	646	36	0.00	772
Semillon	W	31687	0.60	38	26230	0.54	37	22156	0.48	39
Sennen	R							10	0.00	952
Serbina	R							6	0.00	1011
Sercial	W				306	0.01	434	106	0.00	604
Sercialinho	W							9	0.00	978
Serna	O							10	0.00	961
Servanin	R				0	0.00	984			
Servant	W				530	0.01	374	54	0.00	715
Sevilhao	R							14	0.00	912
Seyval Blanc	W				389	0.01	404	464	0.01	384
Sgavetta	R				61	0.00	623	47	0.00	740
Shiroka Melnishka	R				3804	0.08	133	1580	0.03	204
Siegerrebe	O				167	0.00	499	120	0.00	583
Silcher	W				7	0.00	836			
Silvaner	W				4185	0.09	123	2255	0.05	173
Siria	W				2791	0.06	169	7898	0.17	86
Sirio	W				23	0.00	725	14	0.00	913
Skrlet	W							61	0.00	690
Slankamenka	W							31	0.00	803
Solaris	W							20	0.00	873
Soperga	R				32	0.00	688	22	0.00	856
Sovereign Opal	W							3	0.00	1082
Spergola	W							110	0.00	597
St Croix	R							25	0.00	834
St Pepin	W							19	0.00	875

Table 5 (cont.) Global winegrape area, share of global area, and global ranks of each variety, 1990, 2000 & 2010

Prime vairiety	Col	1990 Global area (ha)	1990 Global share %	1990 Global rank	2000 Global area (ha)	2000 Global share %	2000 Global rank	2010 Global area (ha)	2010 Global share %	2010 Global rank
St Vincent	R							23	0.00	852
Stavroto	R				104	0.00	555	11	0.00	942
Stepnyak	W							144	0.00	555
Steuben	R							39	0.00	762
Storgozia	R							295	0.01	453
Sugra Five	W				118	0.00	536	2	0.00	1111
Sukholimanskiy Bely	W				1631	0.03	226	2156	0.05	175
Sultaniye	W	271828	5.14	4	14351	0.29	57	3407	0.07	138
Sumoll	R				1401	0.03	246	83	0.00	642
Superior Seedless	W				2842	0.06	163	9	0.00	976
Suscan	R							5	0.00	1023
Susumaniello	R				62	0.00	621	50	0.00	733
Swenson Red	R							11	0.00	940
Symphony	W				184	0.00	486	324	0.01	438
Syrah	R	35086	0.66	35	101516	2.08	8	185568	4.03	6
Szeremi Zold	W							0	0.00	1219
Taltos	W							1	0.00	1158
Tamarez	W				585	0.01	357	343	0.01	429
Taminga	W				46	0.00	652			
Tannat	R				5557	0.11	109	5940	0.13	100
Tarrango	R				120	0.00	533	72	0.00	663
Tavkveri	R				29	0.00	695	37	0.00	766
Taylor	R				0	0.00	995			
Tazzelenghe	R				68	0.00	614	55	0.00	707
Teinturier	R				1	0.00	924	7	0.00	986
Telti Kyryk	W				172	0.00	495	246	0.01	484
Tempranillo	R	47429	0.90	24	92985	1.91	10	232561	5.05	4
Tempranillo Blanco	W							5	0.00	1032
Teneron	R				3488	0.07	140	3488	0.08	135
Teoulier Noir	R				1	0.00	960			
Termarina Rossa	O							20	0.00	866
Teroldego	R				682	0.01	331	839	0.02	295
Terrano	R				194	0.00	480	500	0.01	371
Terrantez	W				27	0.00	704	12	0.00	933
Terrantez do Pico	W							0	0.00	1224
Terras 20	R				13	0.00	786			
Terret Blanc	W				2703	0.06	173	1451	0.03	214
Terret Gris	W				262	0.01	452			
Terret Noir	R				370	0.01	410			
Therona	W				185	0.00	485	99	0.00	614
Thrapsathiri	W							31	0.00	802
Tibouren	R				457	0.01	387	445	0.01	390
Timorasso	W				19	0.00	751	129	0.00	575
Tinta Aguiar	R							75	0.00	661
Tinta Barroca	R				6052	0.12	103	6172	0.13	96
Tinta Bragao	R							63	0.00	686
Tinta Carvalha	R				1920	0.04	210	1311	0.03	231
Tinta da Barca	R							345	0.01	426
Tinta da Melra	R							1	0.00	1199
Tinta de Alcoa	R							24	0.00	840
Tinta de Cidadelhe	R							1	0.00	1190
Tinta de Pegoes								195	0.00	519

Table 5 (cont.) Global winegrape area, share of global area, and global ranks of each variety, 1990, 2000 & 2010

Prime vairiety	Col	1990 Global area (ha)	1990 Global share %	1990 Global rank	2000 Global area (ha)	2000 Global share %	2000 Global rank	2010 Global area (ha)	2010 Global share %	2010 Global rank
Tinta de Porto Santo	R							2	0.00	1125
Tinta do Rodo	R							3	0.00	1063
Tinta Engomada	R							4	0.00	1053
Tinta Francisca	R							53	0.00	718
Tinta Malandra	R							0	0.00	1270
Tinta Martins	R							11	0.00	946
Tinta Mesquita	R							1	0.00	1147
Tinta Penajoia	R							53	0.00	719
Tinta Pereira	R							1	0.00	1155
Tinta Pomar	R							30	0.00	810
Tinta Roseira	R							4	0.00	1060
Tinta Valdosa	R							1	0.00	1201
Tinta Varejoa	R							1	0.00	1157
Tintem	R							9	0.00	974
Tintilia del Molise	R							111	0.00	594
Tinto Basto	R				2331	0.05	187	62	0.00	688
Tinto Cao	R				556	0.01	366	369	0.01	411
Tinto de la Pampana Blanca	R				4726	0.10	116	5145	0.11	105
Tinto de Zafra	R				4	0.00	856	2	0.00	1112
Tinto do Aurelio	R							0	0.00	1271
Tinto Jeroma	R				1	0.00	927			
Tinto Velasco	R				3272	0.07	148	2684	0.06	159
Torbato	W				168	0.00	497	19	0.00	874
Torrontes Mendocino	W							713	0.02	317
Torrontes Riojano	W				8187	0.17	81	8115	0.18	83
Torrontes Sanjuanino	W				3166	0.06	154	2052	0.04	179
Tortosina	W				930	0.02	300	503	0.01	370
Touriga Branca	W							36	0.00	773
Touriga Femea	R							15	0.00	905
Touriga Franca	R				6674	0.14	97	11586	0.25	59
Touriga Nacional	R				4263	0.09	122	10435	0.23	67
Trajadura	W				2416	0.05	182	2169	0.05	174
Traminette	W				5	0.00	850	240	0.01	488
Trbljan	W							231	0.01	492
Trebbianina	W							128	0.00	576
Trebbiano	W				685	0.01	330	248	0.01	483
Trebbiano d'Abruzzo	W				8435	0.17	78	5091	0.11	106
Trebbiano Giallo	W				3984	0.08	130	10609	0.23	66
Trebbiano Modenese	W				583	0.01	358	363	0.01	415
Trebbiano Romagnolo	W				19492	0.40	43	15893	0.35	49
Trebbiano Spoletino	W				242	0.00	467	200	0.00	515
Trebbiano Toscano	W	207442	3.92	5	136572	2.80	6	109772	2.39	9
Trepat	R				1763	0.04	216	1358	0.03	224
Tressot	R				0	0.00	989			
Trevisana Nera	R				33	0.00	687	15	0.00	898
Tribidrag	R	41683	0.79	29	26915	0.55	36	32745	0.71	29
Trilla	W							1	0.00	1152
Trincadeira	R				7265	0.15	88	9270	0.20	75
Trincadeira das Pratas	W				216	0.00	476	239	0.01	490
Trincadeiro Branco	W							59	0.00	697
Triomphe	R							15	0.00	903
Triplett Blanc	W							244	0.01	485

Table 5 (cont.) Global winegrape area, share of global area, and global ranks of each variety, 1990, 2000 & 2010

Prime vairiety	Col	1990			2000			2010		
		Global area (ha)	Global share %	Global rank	Global area (ha)	Global share %	Global rank	Global area (ha)	Global share %	Global rank
Triunfo	R							2	0.00	1116
Trnjak	R							15	0.00	900
Trobat	R				83	0.00	581	1	0.00	1175
Tronto	R							2	0.00	1126
Trousseau	R				2120	0.04	203	3431	0.07	136
Trousseau Gris	O				28	0.00	700			
Tsimlyansky Cherny	R							451	0.01	387
Tsitska	W				2839	0.06	164	3642	0.08	130
Tsolikouri	W				6161	0.13	102	7903	0.17	85
Tsulukidzis Tetra	W				152	0.00	509	195	0.00	518
Tsvetochny (Floral)	W							89	0.00	628
Tsvetochny (Flowery)	W							80	0.00	650
Turan	R							177	0.00	531
Turchetta	R							3	0.00	1070
Ucelut	W				10	0.00	803	10	0.00	962
Uni Blan	R				26	0.00	711	1	0.00	1144
Urreti	W							0	0.00	1258
Usakhelouri	R				8	0.00	826	10	0.00	950
Uva Cao	W				33	0.00	686	1	0.00	1185
Uva del Fantini	R							0	0.00	1254
Uva del Tunde	R							2	0.00	1128
Uva Longanesi	R							512	0.01	363
Uva Rara	R				570	0.01	363	460	0.01	385
Uva Tosca	R				84	0.00	578	71	0.00	669
Uvalino	R							1	0.00	1137
Valais Noir	R				4	0.00	857			
Valbom	R							166	0.00	540
Valdiguie	R				79	0.00	586	138	0.00	564
Valenci Tinto	R				5	0.00	852	27	0.00	823
Valentino Nero	R				56	0.00	632	21	0.00	864
Valerien	W				2	0.00	908			
Valiant	R							11	0.00	943
Valveirinha	W							0	0.00	1229
Valvin Muscat	W							6	0.00	1010
Varousset	R				12	0.00	794			
Vasilaki	W				3	0.00	889	4	0.00	1057
Vega	W				27	0.00	702	35	0.00	781
Ventura	W				39	0.00	671	24	0.00	837
Venus	R							1	0.00	1148
Verdea	W				107	0.00	550	83	0.00	641
Verdealbara	W							0	0.00	1212
Verdeca	W				2208	0.05	196	796	0.02	302
Verdejo	W				4453	0.09	117	16578	0.36	46
Verdelet	W							1	0.00	1196
Verdelho	W				1639	0.03	224	2005	0.04	181
Verdelho Roxo	R							4	0.00	1047
Verdelho Tinto	R				1	0.00	962	28	0.00	817
Verdello	W				662	0.01	332	287	0.01	455
Verdesse	W				8	0.00	825	7	0.00	989
Verdial	W							1	0.00	1206
Verdial Tinto	R							3	0.00	1087
Verdicchio Bianco	W				5043	0.10	113	3532	0.08	134

Table 5 (cont.) Global winegrape area, share of global area, and global ranks of each variety, 1990, 2000 & 2010

Prime vairiety	Col	1990 Global area (ha)	1990 Global share %	1990 Global rank	2000 Global area (ha)	2000 Global share %	2000 Global rank	2010 Global area (ha)	2010 Global share %	2010 Global rank
Verdil	W				131	0.00	522	57	0.00	702
Verdiso	W				71	0.00	604	68	0.00	676
Verdoncho	W				3092	0.06	159	2124	0.05	176
Verduschia	W				15	0.00	776	11	0.00	938
Verduzzo Friulano	W				1592	0.03	227	812	0.02	299
Verduzzo Trevigiano	W				1657	0.03	222	708	0.02	318
Vermentino	W				5835	0.12	107	8617	0.19	78
Vermentino Nero	R				143	0.00	516	210	0.00	510
Vernaccia di Oristano	W				565	0.01	365	272	0.01	465
Vernaccia di San Gimignano	W				854	0.02	308	522	0.01	357
Vertes Csillaga	W							21	0.00	858
Vertzami	R				491	0.01	380	335	0.01	431
Veruccese	R							0	0.00	1222
Vespaiola	W				105	0.00	554	94	0.00	620
Vespolina	R				103	0.00	557	134	0.00	571
Victoria	W							52	0.00	721
Vidal	W				611	0.01	348	1644	0.04	200
Vidal Red	R				0	0.00	976			
Vidvizhenets	O							271	0.01	466
Vien de Nus	R				25	0.00	712	13	0.00	925
Vignoles	W				68	0.00	613	254	0.01	477
Vijariego	W				510	0.01	377	285	0.01	457
Viktor	W							0	0.00	1248
Viktoria Gyongye	W							190	0.00	523
Vilana	W				506	0.01	378	579	0.01	351
Vilana(Red)	R				60	0.00	625			
Villard Blanc	W				746	0.02	322	689	0.01	323
Villard Noir	R				601	0.01	352	1328	0.03	227
Vincent	R							11	0.00	939
Vineti	W				0	0.00	977			
Vinhao	R				5937	0.12	106	3160	0.07	140
Viognier	W				3160	0.06	155	11400	0.25	61
Violeta	R							98	0.00	616
Viorica	W				40	0.00	665	347	0.01	423
Viosinho	W				17	0.00	758	225	0.00	499
Vital	W				2246	0.05	195	1182	0.03	245
Vitovska	W				42	0.00	659	50	0.00	732
Voskeat	W				809	0.02	313	809	0.02	300
Vranac	R							149	0.00	552
Vugava	W							36	0.00	777
Vuillermin	R				0	0.00	1004	4	0.00	1046
Vulcanus	W							5	0.00	1039
Weldra	W				54	0.00	636	14	0.00	915
Wurzer	W							5	0.00	1033
Xara	R							0	0.00	1265
Xarello	W				10288	0.21	74	8393	0.18	79
Xarello Rosado	W				10	0.00	801	1	0.00	1176
Xinomavro	R				1816	0.04	213	1971	0.04	184
Xinomavro (White)	W				3	0.00	881			
Xynisteri	W				2742	0.06	171	2092	0.05	177
Yaqui	R				22	0.00	727	2	0.00	1113
Zalagyongye	W				4330	0.09	120	1948	0.04	185

Table 5 (cont.) Global winegrape area, share of global area, and global ranks of each variety, 1990, 2000 & 2010

Prime vairiety	Col	1990 Global area (ha)	1990 Global share %	1990 Global rank	2000 Global area (ha)	2000 Global share %	2000 Global rank	2010 Global area (ha)	2010 Global share %	2010 Global rank
Zalema	W				5969	0.12	105	4097	0.09	123
Zametovka	R							914	0.02	280
Zefir	W							49	0.00	736
Zengo	W							264	0.01	470
Zenit	W				405	0.01	401	580	0.01	349
Zeta	W							118	0.00	584
Zeusz	W							28	0.00	820
Zierfandler	O				98	0.00	562	117	0.00	585
Zlahtina	W							135	0.00	570
Zlatarica Vrgorska	W							19	0.00	877
Zoumiatiko Red	R				22	0.00	736			
Zupljanka	W							4	0.00	1049
Zweigelt	R				7230	0.15	89	9847	0.21	72
Other		1321510	24.98					1639	0.04	
Other Red					205292	4.21		77687	1.69	
Other White					364216	7.47		179844	3.91	
Total		**5290000**	**100**		**4878176**	**100**		**4601445**	**100**	

Table 6: Ranking of prime varieties by global grape area, and decadal changes, 1990, 2000 and 2010

Prime variety	Col	1990 Global area (ha)	1990 Global share %	1990 Global rank	2000 Global area (ha)	2000 Global share %	2000 Global rank	2010 Global area (ha)	2010 Global share %	2010 Global rank	2000-1990 Change (ha)	2010-2000 Change (ha)	2010-1990 Change (ha)	2000-1990 Changes %	2010-2000 Changes %	2010-1990 Changes %
Cabernet Sauvignon	R	127678	2.41	8	220890	4.53	2	290091	6.30	1	93212	69201	162412	73	31	127
Merlot	R	154752	2.93	7	211967	4.35	4	267169	5.81	2	57215	55202	112418	37	26	73
Airen	W	476396	9.01	1	387978	7.95	1	252364	5.48	3	-88419	-135614	-224032	-19	-35	-47
Tempranillo	R	47429	0.90	24	92985	1.91	10	232561	5.05	4	45556	139576	185131	96	150	390
Chardonnay	W	69282	1.31	13	145344	2.98	5	198793	4.32	5	76062	53449	129510	110	37	187
Syrah	R	35086	0.66	35	101516	2.08	8	185568	4.03	6	66430	84051	150482	189	83	429
Garnacha Tinta	R	282997	5.35	2	213987	4.39	3	184735	4.01	7	-69010	-29252	-98262	-24	-14	-35
Sauvignon Blanc	W	44677	0.84	25	64889	1.33	15	110138	2.39	8	20212	45248	65460	45	70	147
Trebbiano Toscano	W	207442	3.92	5	136572	2.80	6	109772	2.39	9	-70870	-26799	-97670	-34	-20	-47
Pinot Noir	R	41539	0.79	30	60099	1.23	16	86662	1.88	10	18561	26563	45124	45	44	109
Mazuelo	R	202869	3.83	6	126650	2.60	7	80178	1.74	11	-76219	-46472	-122691	-38	-37	-60
Bobal	R	106149	2.01	10	100128	2.05	9	80120	1.74	12	-6021	-20008	-26029	-6	-20	-25
Sangiovese	R	98946	1.87	11	68877	1.41	13	77709	1.69	13	-30068	8832	-21236	-30	13	-21
Monastrell	R	108213	2.05	9	76304	1.56	12	69850	1.52	14	-31909	-6454	-38363	-29	-8	-35
Grasevina	W	19384	0.37	48	92306	1.89	11	61200	1.33	15	72921	-31106	41815	376	-34	216
Rkatsiteli	W	280569	5.30	3	67354	1.38	14	58641	1.27	16	-213215	-8713	-221928	-76	-13	-79
Cabernet Franc	R	39619	0.75	32	48551	1.00	19	53599	1.16	17	8932	5049	13980	23	10	35
Riesling	W	52164	0.99	21	43166	0.88	23	50060	1.09	18	-8998	6894	-2104	-17	16	-4
Pinot Gris	O				18879	0.39	44	43563	0.95	19		24684			131	
Macabeo	W	43504	0.82	26	48125	0.99	21	41046	0.89	20	4621	-7078	-2457	11	-15	-6
Cot	R	16997	0.32	52	24402	0.50	39	40688	0.88	21	7406	16285	23691	44	67	139
Cayetana Blanca	W	65276	1.23	16	55502	1.14	17	39741	0.86	22	-9774	-15761	-25535	-15	-28	-39
Alicante Henri Bouschet	R	19587	0.37	47	37043	0.76	26	38985	0.85	23	17457	1942	19398	89	5	99
Aligote	W	54430	1.03	20	35668	0.73	27	36119	0.78	24	-18763	451	-18312	-34	1	-34
Cinsaut	R	63171	1.19	18	48419	0.99	20	36040	0.78	25	-14752	-12379	-27132	-23	-26	-43
Chenin Blanc	W	59974	1.13	19	45806	0.94	22	35164	0.76	26	-14169	-10642	-24811	-24	-23	-41
Montepulciano	R	32982	0.62	37	28679	0.59	33	34947	0.76	27	-4303	6268	1965	-13	22	6
Catarratto Bianco	W	80128	1.51	12	50711	1.04	18	34863	0.76	28	-29417	-15848	-45265	-37	-31	-56
Tribidrag	R	41683	0.79	29	26915	0.55	36	32745	0.71	29	-14767	5829	-8938	-35	22	-21
Gamay Noir	R	35005	0.66	36	37796	0.77	25	32671	0.71	30	2791	-5125	-2334	8	-14	-7
Isabella	R	21003	0.40	42	27376	0.56	35	32494	0.71	31	6372	5118	11491	30	19	55
Colombard	W	36138	0.68	34	38146	0.78	24	32076	0.70	32	2008	-6070	-4063	6	-16	-11
Muscat Blanc a Petits Grains	W	17806	0.34	50	28401	0.58	34	31112	0.68	33	10595	2711	13306	60	10	75

Table 6 (cont.) Ranking of prime varieties by global grape area, and decadal changes, 1990, 2000 and 2010

Prime variety	Col	1990 Global area (ha)	1990 Global share %	1990 Global rank	2000 Global area (ha)	2000 Global share %	2000 Global rank	2010 Global area (ha)	2010 Global share %	2010 Global rank	2000-1990 Change (ha)	2000-1990 Changes %	2010-2000 Change (ha)	2010-2000 Changes %	2010-1990 Change (ha)	2010-1990 Changes %
Cereza	O	42937	0.81	27	31666	0.65	30	29189	0.63	34	-11272	-26	-2476	-8	-13748	-32
Muscat of Alexandria	W	64224	1.21	17	29411	0.60	32	26336	0.57	35	-34813	-54	-3075	-10	-37888	-59
Barbera	R	67987	1.29	15	33048	0.68	29	24178	0.53	36	-34940	-51	-8870	-27	-43810	-64
Muller Thurgau	W	36381	0.69	33	33572	0.69	28	22753	0.49	37	-2809	-8	-10819	-32	-13628	-37
Palomino Fino	W	50545	0.96	22	30297	0.62	31	22510	0.49	38	-20248	-40	-7787	-26	-28035	-55
Semillon	W	31687	0.60	38	26230	0.54	37	22156	0.48	39	-5457	-17	-4074	-16	-9531	-30
Douce Noire	R				17653	0.36	45	18976	0.41	40			1323	7		
Gruner Veltliner	W	20760	0.39	43	23604	0.48	41	18842	0.41	41	2844	14	-4762	-20	-1918	-9
Prosecco	W				7498	0.15	84	18437	0.40	42			10939	146		
Feteasca Alba	W	18373	0.35	49	23828	0.49	40	17469	0.38	43	5455	30	-6359	-27	-904	-5
Criolla Grande	R	68513	1.30	14	24641	0.51	38	17080	0.37	44	-43872	-64	-7561	-31	-51434	-75
Nero d'Avola	R				11318	0.23	66	16596	0.36	45			5277			
Verdejo	W				4453	0.09	117	16578	0.36	46			12126	272		
Doukkali	R				16557	0.34	49	16557	0.36	47			0	0		
Blaufrankisch	R				12879	0.26	62	16141	0.35	48			3262	25		
Trebbiano Romagnolo	W				19492	0.40	43	15893	0.35	49			-3598	-18		
Garganega	W				16549	0.34	50	15402	0.33	50			-1147	-7		
Prokupac	R				15180	0.31	53	15180	0.33	51			0	0		
Pinot Blanc	W				16990	0.35	47	14724	0.32	52			-2266	-13		
Gewurztraminer	W	16511	0.31	53	10670	0.22	72	14269	0.31	53	-5841	-35	3599	34	-2242	-14
Chasselas	W				13318	0.27	58	13186	0.29	54			-131	-1		
Feteasca Regala	W				2578	0.05	178	13136	0.29	55			10558	410		
Melon	W				13253	0.27	59	12365	0.27	56			-888	-7		
Pedro Gimenez	W				15101	0.31	54	12250	0.27	57			-2851	-19		
Concord	R	30513	0.58	39	11816	0.24	65	12238	0.27	58	-18697	-61	422	4	-18275	-60
Touriga Franca	R				6674	0.14	97	11586	0.25	59			4912	74		
Negroamaro	R	40064	0.76	31	16619	0.34	48	11460	0.25	60	-23445	-59	-5159	-31	-28604	-71
Viognier	W				3160	0.06	155	11400	0.25	61			8241	261		
Carmenere	R				5711	0.12	108	11360	0.25	62			5649	99		
Pinot Meunier	R				10832	0.22	70	11267	0.24				435	4		
Castelao	R				14424	0.30	56	11088	0.24	64			-3336	-23		

Table 6 (cont.) Ranking of prime varieties by global grape area, and decadal changes, 1990, 2000 and 2010

		1990			2000			2010			2000-1990		2010-2000		2010-1990	
Prime vairiety	Col	Global area (ha)	Global share %	Global rank	Global area (ha)	Global share %	Global rank	Global area (ha)	Global share %	Global rank	Change (ha)	Change (ha)	Changes %	Changes %	Change (ha)	Changes %	
Mencia	R	17321	0.33	51	13138	0.27	60	10658	0.23	65	-4183	-2479	-24	-19	-6662	-38
Trebbiano Giallo	W				3984	0.08	130	10609	0.23	66		6625		166		
Touriga Nacional	R				4263	0.09	122	10435	0.23	67		6172		145		
Muscat Ottonel	W				12259	0.25	64	10234	0.22	68		-2025		-17		
Aglianico	R				9264	0.19	75	9963	0.22	69		699		8		
Savatiano	W	20396	0.39	44	12747	0.26	63	9920	0.22	70	-7649	-2827	-38	-22	-10477	-51
Malvasia Bianca di Candia	W	42654	0.81	28	12889	0.26	61	9891	0.21	71	-29765	-2998	-70	-23	-32763	-77
Zweigelt	R				7230	0.15	89	9847	0.21	72		2616		36		
Pamid	R				22718	0.47	42	9827	0.21	73		-12891		-57		
Fernao Pires	W				14545	0.30	55	9511	0.21	74		-5034		-35		
Trincadeira	R				7265	0.15	88	9270	0.20	75		2005		28		
Pedro Ximenez	W	47915	0.91	23	17272	0.35	46	9243	0.20	76	-30643	-8028	-64	-46	-38672	-81
Parellada	W				11188	0.23	67	8847	0.19	77		-2341		-21		
Vermentino	W				5835	0.12	107	8617	0.19	78		2782		48		
Xarello	W				10288	0.21	74	8393	0.18	79		-1895		-18		
Bordo	R				3379	0.07	144	8287	0.18	80		4908		145		
Muscat of Hamburg	R				7066	0.14	93	8137	0.18	81		1072		15		
Saperavi	R				6707	0.14	96	8126	0.18	82		1418		21		
Torrontes Riojano	W				8187	0.17	81	8115	0.18	83		-71		-1		
Dornfelder	R				3766	0.08	134	8101	0.18	84		4335		115		
Tsolikouri	W				6161	0.13	102	7903	0.17	85		1742		28		
Siria	W				2791	0.06	169	7898	0.17	86		5107		183		
Corvina Veronese	R				4781	0.10	114	7496	0.16	87		2715		57		
Garnacha Blanca	W	28409	0.54	40	10821	0.22	71	7370	0.16	88	-17588	-3451	-62	-32	-21039	-74
Moscatel Rosada	O				10656	0.22	73	7329	0.16	89		-3327		-31		
Petit Verdot	R				1481	0.03	235	7202	0.16	90		5722		386		
Marufo	R				6339	0.13	101	6579	0.14	91		240		4		
Bianca	W				2180	0.04	200	6450	0.14	92		4270		196		
Pinotage	R				6574	0.13	98	6404	0.14	93		-170		-3		
Dolcetto	R				7191	0.15	90	6333	0.14	94		-858		-12		
Grillo	W				1803	0.04	214	6295	0.14	95		4491		249		
Tinta Barroca	R				6052	0.12	103	6172	0.13	96		120		2		
Chelva	W				10877	0.22	69	6168	0.13	97		-4709		-43		
Inzolia	W				9259	0.19	76	6133	0.13	98		-3127		-34		

Table 6 (cont.) Ranking of prime varieties by global grape area, and decadal changes, 1990, 2000 and 2010

Prime variety	Col	1990 Global area (ha)	1990 Global share %	1990 Global rank	2000 Global area (ha)	2000 Global share %	2000 Global rank	2010 Global area (ha)	2010 Global share %	2010 Global rank	2000-1990 Change (ha)	2010-2000 Change (ha)	2010-1990 Change (ha)	2000-1990 Changes %	2010-2000 Changes %	2010-1990 Changes %
Nebbiolo	R				5047	0.10	112	5992	0.13	99		946			19	
Tannat	R				5557	0.11	109	5940	0.13	100		383			7	
Ruby Cabernet	R				7419	0.15	86	5730	0.12	101		-1688			-23	
Croatina	R				3116	0.06	157	5700	0.12	102		2585			83	
Alvarinho	W				5113	0.10	111	5523	0.12	103		410			8	
Furmint	W				3481	0.07	141	5259	0.11	104		1777			51	
Tinto de la Pampana Blanca	R				4726	0.10	116	5145	0.11	105		419			9	
Trebbiano d'Abruzzo	W				8435	0.17	78	5091	0.11	106		-3345			-40	
Lambrusco Salamino	R				4147	0.09	126	5003	0.11	107		856			21	
Gros Manseng	W				2160	0.04	201	4995	0.11	108		2836			131	
Rufete	R				3397	0.07	142	4833	0.11	109		1436			42	
Calagrano	W				8229	0.17	80	4794	0.10	110		-3435			-42	
Ancellotta	R				4391	0.09	119	4774	0.10	111		383			9	
Niagara	W				15343	0.31	52	4670	0.10	112		-10673			-70	
Roditis	O				299	0.01	435	4661	0.10	113		4362			1459	
Prieto Picudo	R				3256	0.07	149	4587	0.10	114		1331			41	
Listan Prieto	R				15532	0.32	51	4564	0.10	115		-10968			-71	
Rubired	R				4153	0.09	125	4556	0.10	116		403			10	
Sauvignonasse	W				5494	0.11	110	4449	0.10	117		-1045			-19	
Arinto de Bucelas	W				3966	0.08	131	4446	0.10	118		480			12	
Pardillo	W				7272	0.15	87	4364	0.09	119		-2908			-40	
Gaglioppo	R				3592	0.07	138	4214	0.09	120		622			17	
Misket Cherven	O							4159	0.09	121		4159				
Baga	R				6730	0.14	95	4108	0.09	122		-2621			-39	
Zalema	W				5969	0.12	105	4097	0.09	123		-1872			-31	
Loureiro	W				4392	0.09	118	4054	0.09	124		-339			-8	
Kerner	W				7111	0.15	91	3994	0.09	125		-3117			-44	
Merseguera	W				7460	0.15	85	3946	0.09	126		-3514			-47	
Roditis(Red)	R				6945	0.14	94	3834	0.08	127		-3111			-45	
Blauer Portugieser	R				4278	0.09	121	3798	0.08	128		-481			-11	
Caladoc	R				1427	0.03	240	3675	0.08	129		2248			158	
Tsitska	W				2839	0.06	164	3642	0.08	130		803			28	
Cserszegi Fuszeres	W				2185	0.04	199	3609	0.08	131		1423			65	
Mavro	R				10969	0.22	68	3575	0.08	132		-7394			-67	

Table 6 (cont.) Ranking of prime varieties by global grape area, and decadal changes, 1990, 2000 and 2010

Prime variety	Col	1990 Global area (ha)	1990 Global share %	1990 Global rank	2000 Global area (ha)	2000 Global share %	2000 Global rank	2010 Global area (ha)	2010 Global share %	2010 Global rank	Change (ha) 2000-1990	Change (ha) 2010-2000	Change (ha) 2010-1990	Changes % 2000-1990	Changes % 2010-2000	Changes % 2010-1990
Durif	R				1197	0.02	269	3557	0.08	133		2359			197	
Verdicchio Bianco	W				5043	0.10	113	3532	0.08	134		-1511			-30	
Teneron	R				3488	0.07	140	3488	0.08	135		0			0	
Trousseau	R				2120	0.04	203	3431	0.07	136		1311			62	
Malvasia Fina	W				7102	0.15	92	3416	0.07	137		-3686			-52	
Sultaniye	W	271828	5.14	4	14351	0.29	57	3407	0.07	138	-257477	-10944	-268420	-95	-76	-99
Negramoll	R				3557	0.07	139	3193	0.07	139		-364			-10	
Vinhao	R				5937	0.12	106	3160	0.07	140		-2777			-47	
Babeasca Neagra	R				3722	0.08	136	3122	0.07	141		-600			-16	
Graciano	R				1910	0.04	211	3102	0.07	142		1192			62	
Carignan Blanc	W				1035	0.02	287	3061	0.07	143		2027			196	
Aspiran Bouschet	R				308	0.01	432	3042	0.07	144		2734			887	
Falanghina	W				1658	0.03	221	3037	0.07	145		1379			83	
Beba	W				4762	0.10	115	3036	0.07	146		-1726			-36	
Sankt Laurent	R				2370	0.05	184	3007	0.07	147		638			27	
Cortese	W				3113	0.06	158	2953	0.06	148		-161			-5	
Agiorgitiko	R				2320	0.05	189	2905	0.06	149		586			25	
Clairette	W				4003	0.08	129	2900	0.06	150		-1103			-28	
Aramon Noir	R				9084	0.19	77	2892	0.06	151		-6193			-68	
Nerello Mascalese	R				4167	0.09	124	2883	0.06	152		-1284			-31	
Pervenets Magaracha	W				2837	0.06	165	2881	0.06	153		44			2	
Auxerrois	W				2302	0.05	192	2741	0.06	154		439			19	
Malvazija Istarska	W				7559	0.15	83	2740	0.06	155		-4818			-64	
Lambrusco Grasparossa	R				1720	0.04	217	2738	0.06	156		1019			59	
Couderc Noir	R				610	0.01	349	2691	0.06	157		2082			341	
Odessky Cherny	R				1694	0.03	218	2686	0.06	158		991			59	
Tinto Velasco	R				3272	0.07	148	2684	0.06	159		-588			-18	
Listan Negro	R				3291	0.07	147	2666	0.06	160		-625			-19	
Biancame	W				1330	0.03	250	2599	0.06	161		1269			95	
Nero di Troia	R				1765	0.04	215	2572	0.06	162		807			46	
Malvasia Bianca Lunga	W				3937	0.08	132	2544	0.06	163		-1393			-35	
Marselan	R				176	0.00	491	2497	0.05	164		2321			1321	
Rondinella	R				2797	0.06	168	2481	0.05	165		-316			-11	
Dimyat	W				7718	0.16	82	2401	0.05	166		-5318			-69	

Table 6 (cont.) Ranking of prime varieties by global grape area, and decadal changes, 1990, 2000 and 2010

Prime vairiety	Col	1990 Global area (ha)	1990 Global share %	1990 Global rank	2000 Global area (ha)	2000 Global share %	2000 Global rank	2010 Global area (ha)	2010 Global share %	2010 Global rank	Change (ha) 2000-1990	Change (ha) 2010-2000	Change (ha) 2010-1990	Changes % 2000-1990	Changes % 2010-2000	Changes % 2010-1990
Abbo	R				2375	0.05	183	2375	0.05	167		0			0	
Bastardo Magarachsky	R				1969	0.04	209	2370	0.05	168		401			20	
Jacquez	R				226	0.00	472	2368	0.05	169		2142			949	
Grolleau Noir	R				2201	0.05	198	2350	0.05	170		150			7	
Kotsifali	R				1148	0.02	276	2330	0.05	171		1183			103	
Lambrusco Maestri	R				1362	0.03	248	2272	0.05	172		910			67	
Silvaner	W				4185	0.09	123	2255	0.05	173		-1930			-46	
Trajadura	W				2416	0.05	182	2169	0.05	174		-246			-10	
Sukholimanskiy Bely	W				1631	0.03	226	2156	0.05	175		526			32	
Verdoncho	W				3092	0.06	159	2124	0.05	176		-968			-31	
Xynisteri	W				2742	0.06	171	2092	0.05	177		-650			-24	
Damaschino	W				2360	0.05	186	2083	0.05	178		-277			-12	
Torrontes Sanjuanino	W				3166	0.06	154	2052	0.04	179		-1114			-35	
Bacchus	W				3392	0.07	143	2047	0.04	180		-1344			-40	
Verdelho	W				1639	0.03	224	2005	0.04	181		366			22	
Mauzac Blanc	W				3251	0.07	150	1991	0.04	182		-1261			-39	
Scheurebe	W				3655	0.07	137	1984	0.04	183		-1671			-46	
Xinomavro	R				1816	0.04	213	1971	0.04	184		155			9	
Zalagyongye	W				4330	0.09	120	1948	0.04	185		-2382			-55	
Savagnin Blanc	W				430	0.01	393	1898	0.04	186		1468			342	
Harslevelu	W				1296	0.03	254	1856	0.04	187		560			43	
Folle Blanche	W				2648	0.05	176	1845	0.04	188		-803			-30	
Ciliegiolo	R				2527	0.05	179	1830	0.04	189		-697			-28	
Fer	R				1278	0.03	257	1817	0.04	190		539			42	
Rojal Tinta	R				2845	0.06	162	1801	0.04	191		-1044			-37	
Garnacha Roja	W				2761	0.06	170	1784	0.04	192		-978			-35	
Roussanne	W				874	0.02	307	1746	0.04	193		873			100	
Marsanne	W				1512	0.03	231	1742	0.04	194		229			15	
Alarije	W				1686	0.03	219	1726	0.04	195		40			2	
Feteasca Neagra	R				1214	0.02	266	1719	0.04	196		505			42	
Pignoletto	W				6009	0.12	104	1707	0.04	197		-4302			-72	
Juan Garcia	R				2077	0.04	204	1707	0.04	198		-370			-18	
Muscadelle	W				2207	0.05	197	1656	0.04	199		-551			-25	
Vidal	W				611	0.01	348	1644	0.04			1033			169	

Table 6 (cont.) Ranking of prime varieties by global grape area, and decadal changes, 1990, 2000 and 2010

Prime variety	Col	1990 Global area (ha)	1990 Global share %	1990 Global rank	2000 Global area (ha)	2000 Global share %	2000 Global rank	2010 Global area (ha)	2010 Global share %	2010 Global rank	2000-1990 Change (ha)	2010-2000 Change (ha)	2010-1990 Change (ha)	2000-1990 Changes %	2010-2000 Changes %	2010-1990 Changes %
Lambrusco di Sorbara	R				1409	0.03	243	1606	0.03	201		196			14	
Greco Bianco	W				660	0.01	333	1604	0.03	202		944			143	
Romeiko	R				382	0.01	406	1597	0.03	203		1215			318	
Shiroka Melnishka	R				3804	0.08	133	1580	0.03	204		-2224			-58	
Plavac Mali	R				6539	0.13	99	1569	0.03	205		-4970			-76	
Albana	W				2487	0.05	180	1523	0.03	206		-964			-39	
Perruno	W				2831	0.06	167	1509	0.03	207		-1322			-47	
Grechetto di Orvieto	W				1177	0.02	272	1501	0.03	208		324			28	
Okuzgozu	R				1033	0.02	288	1479	0.03	209		446			43	
Moscato Giallo	W				410	0.01	398	1470	0.03	210		1060			259	
Brachetto del Piemonte	R				1534	0.03	230	1460	0.03	211		-74			-5	
Piquepoul Blanc	W				975	0.02	294	1455	0.03	212		480			49	
Albarola	W				4090	0.08	127	1453	0.03	213		-2636			-64	
Terret Blanc	W				2703	0.06	173	1451	0.03	214		-1252			-46	
Moschomavro	R				2305	0.05	190	1428	0.03	215		-877			-38	
Refosco	R				1267	0.03	260	1420	0.03	216		153			12	
Elbling	W				1864	0.04	212	1418	0.03	217		-446			-24	
Irsai Oliver	W							1414	0.03	218		1414				
Monica Nera	R				2835	0.06	166	1404	0.03	219		-1431			-50	
Planta Nova	W				2029	0.04	206	1395	0.03	220		-634			-31	
Lambrusco Marani	R				2280	0.05	193	1394	0.03	221		-886			-39	
Fiano	W				758	0.02	319	1377	0.03	222		619			82	
Prosecco Lungo	W							1367	0.03	223		1367				
Trepat	R				1763	0.04	216	1358	0.03	224		-405			-23	
Nuragus	W				3186	0.07	152	1345	0.03	225		-1841			-58	
Blauburger	R				1002	0.02	290	1337	0.03	226		335			33	
Villard Noir	R				601	0.01	352	1328	0.03	227		728			121	
Petit Manseng	W				613	0.01	347	1327	0.03	228		714			117	
Albillo Mayor	W				5	0.00	849	1319	0.03	229		1314			26886	
Malvasia Nera di Brindisi	R				3174	0.07	153	1314	0.03	230		-1859			-59	
Tinta Carvalha	R				1920	0.04	210	1311	0.03	231		-609			-32	
Mavrud	R				647	0.01	337	1296	0.03	232		649			100	
Rabigato	W				1133	0.02	277	1273	0.03	233		139			12	
Antao Vaz	W				376	0.01	408	1252	0.03	234		876			233	

Table 6 (cont.) Ranking of prime varieties by global grape area, and decadal changes, 1990, 2000 and 2010

		1990			2000			2010			2000-1990	2010-2000	2010-1990	2000-1990	2010-2000	2010-1990
Prime variety	Col	Global area (ha)	Global share %	Global rank	Global area (ha)	Global share %	Global rank	Global area (ha)	Global share %	Global rank	Change (ha)	Change (ha)	Change (ha)	Changes %	Changes %	Changes %
Bombino Bianco	W				2893	0.06	161	1239	0.03	235		-1654			-57	
Garnacha Peluda	R				2024	0.04	207	1232	0.03	236		-792			-39	
Negrette	R				1319	0.03	252	1228	0.03	237		-91			-7	
Pecorino	W				166	0.00	501	1228	0.03	238		1062			639	
Chinuri	W				955	0.02	296	1225	0.03	239		270			28	
Greco Nero	R				2715	0.06	172	1223	0.03	240		-1493			-55	
Liatiko	R				2476	0.05	181	1211	0.03	241		-1265			-51	
Kunleany	W				1376	0.03	247	1211	0.03	242		-165			-12	
Bombino Nero	R				1156	0.02	275	1201	0.03	243		45			4	
Alfrocheiro	R				523	0.01	375	1188	0.03	244		665			127	
Vital	W				2246	0.05	195	1182	0.03	245		-1065			-47	
Ribolla Gialla	W				1406	0.03	244	1178	0.03	246		-229			-16	
Forcallat Tinta	R				2690	0.06	174	1163	0.03	247		-1527			-57	
Diagalves	W				1088	0.02	282	1156	0.03	248		68			6	
Italia	W				706	0.01	327	1145	0.02	249		439			62	
Arany Sarfeher	W				2914	0.06	160	1133	0.02	250		-1781			-61	
Chambourcin	R				257	0.01	457	1130	0.02	251		872			339	
Arneis	W				738	0.02	323	1122	0.02	252		385			52	
Bogazkere	R				773	0.02	317	1106	0.02	253		334			43	
Plantet	R				209	0.00	477	1105	0.02	254		896			429	
Godello	W				1489	0.03	234	1094	0.02	255		-395			-27	
Mskhali	W				1093	0.02	279	1093	0.02	256		0			0	
Marzemino	R				994	0.02	291	1091	0.02	257		97			10	
Kadarka	R				2630	0.05	177	1087	0.02	258		-1544			-59	
Refosco dal Peduncolo Rosso	R				711	0.01	326	1076	0.02	259		365			51	
Kovidinka	O				1214	0.02	267	1075	0.02	260		-139			-11	
Ezerjo	W				3157	0.06	156	1074	0.02	261		-2083			-66	
Azal	W				3302	0.07	146	1072	0.02	262		-2230			-68	
Canaiolo Nero	R				2304	0.05	191	1068	0.02	263		-1237			-54	
Freisa	R				1436	0.03	238	1049	0.02	264		-387			-27	
Jacquere	W				1086	0.02	283	1028	0.02	265		-59			-5	
Malvasia Preta	R				1157	0.02	274	1003	0.02	266		-154			-13	
Sagrantino	R				351	0.01	417		0.02	267		644			183	
Avarengo	R				1453	0.03	236	987	0.02	268		-466			-32	

Table 6 (cont.) Ranking of prime varieties by global grape area, and decadal changes, 1990, 2000 and 2010

		1990			2000			2010			2000-1990	2010-2000	2010-1990	2000-1990	2010-2000	2010-1990
Prime variety	Col	Global area (ha)	Global share %	Global rank	Global area (ha)	Global share %	Global rank	Global area (ha)	Global share %	Global rank	Change (ha)	Change (ha)	Change (ha)	Changes %	Changes %	Changes %
Cocacciola	W				887	0.02	305	983	0.02	269		96			11	
Neuburger	W				1434	0.03	239	964	0.02	270		-470			-33	
Grand Noir	R				945	0.02	297	955	0.02	271		10			1	
Moschofilero	R				423	0.01	395	934	0.02	272		511			121	
Garandmak	W				931	0.02	299	931	0.02	273		0			0	
Corvinone	R				88	0.00	573	930	0.02	274		842			953	
Bical	W				912	0.02	302	924	0.02	275		12			1	
Duras	R				972	0.02	295	923	0.02	276		-49			-5	
Kokur Bely	W				641	0.01	338	918	0.02	277		277			43	
Gibi	W							917	0.02	278		917				
Grignolino	R				1353	0.03	249	915	0.02	279		-438			-32	
Zametovka	R							914	0.02	280		914				
Rabo de Ovelha	W				2330	0.05	188	908	0.02	281		-1422			-61	
Assyrtiko	W				1106	0.02	278	902	0.02	282		-204			-18	
Moreto	R				1053	0.02	286	900	0.02	283		-153			-15	
Malvasia di Candia Aromatica	W				1643	0.03	223	895	0.02	284		-748			-46	
Passerina	W				715	0.01	325	894	0.02	285		179			25	
Mandilaria	R				845	0.02	311	885	0.02	286		39			5	
Alphonse Lavallee	R				15	0.00	770	883	0.02	287		868			5737	
Dimrit	R				602	0.01	350	863	0.02	288		260			43	
Moscato Embrapa	W							862	0.02	289		862				
Albillo Real	W				3368	0.07	145	861	0.02	290		-2507			-74	
Kalecik Karasi	R				601	0.01	351	861	0.02	291		260			43	
Kiralyleanyka	W							855	0.02	292		855				
Kangun	W				850	0.02	310	850	0.02	293		0			0	
FruHroter Veltliner	R				632	0.01	343	846	0.02	294		214			34	
Teroldego	R				682	0.01	331	839	0.02	295		157			23	
Leanyka	W							838	0.02	296		838				
Couderc	W				4	0.00	855	834	0.02	297		829			20229	
Mammolo	R				777	0.02	316	825	0.02	298		48			6	
Verduzzo Friulano	W				1592	0.03	227	812	0.02	299		-780			-49	
Voskeat	W				809	0.02	313	809	0.02	300		0			0	
Chasan	W				914	0.02	301	801	0.02	301		-112			-12	
Verdeca	W				2208	0.05	196	796	0.02	302		-1413			-64	

Table 6 (cont.) Ranking of prime varieties by global grape area, and decadal changes, 1990, 2000 and 2010

Prime variety	Col	1990 Global area (ha)	1990 Global share %	1990 Global rank	2000 Global area (ha)	2000 Global share %	2000 Global rank	2010 Global area (ha)	2010 Global share %	2010 Global rank	2000-1990 Change (ha)	2010-2000 Change (ha)	2010-1990 Change (ha)	2000-1990 Changes %	2010-2000 Changes %	2010-1990 Changes %
Baco Blanc	W				2137	0.04	202	773	0.02	303		-1364			-64	
Raboso Piave	R				1270	0.03	259	771	0.02	304		-499			-39	
Narince	W				537	0.01	373	769	0.02	305		232			43	
Herbemont	R				1453	0.03	237	764	0.02	306		-688			-47	
Frappato	R				784	0.02	315	752	0.02	307		-31			-4	
Athiri	W				1273	0.03	258	748	0.02	308		-525			-41	
Santarena	R							739	0.02	309		739				
Montonico Bianco	W				656	0.01	334	734	0.02	310		78			12	
Enantio	R				1062	0.02	284	724	0.02	311		-338			-32	
Crouchen	W				2259	0.05	194	724	0.02	312		-1535			-68	
Aletta	W							723	0.02	313		723				
Levokumsky	R							720	0.02	314		720				
Lagrein	R				471	0.01	384	717	0.02	315		246			52	
Molinara	R				1634	0.03	225	717	0.02	316		-918			-56	
Torrontes Mendocino	W							713	0.02	317		713				
Verduzzo Trevigiano	W				1657	0.03	222	708	0.02	318		-949			-57	
Jurancon Noir	R				1294	0.03	255	706	0.02	319		-588			-45	
Piedirosso	R				896	0.02	303	699	0.02	320		-198			-22	
Bequignol Noir	R				1	0.00	938	698	0.02	321		697			63946	
Schiava Gentile	R				1158	0.02	273	694	0.02	322		-465			-40	
Villard Blanc	W				746	0.02	322	689	0.01	323		-57			-8	
Emir	W				480	0.01	382	688	0.01	324		207			43	
Grasa de Cotnari	W				850	0.02	309	685	0.01	325		-164			-19	
Avesso	W				636	0.01	340	685	0.01	326		50			8	
Borracal	R				2654	0.05	175	683	0.01	327		-1972			-74	
Seara Nova	W				1213	0.02	268	681	0.01	328		-532			-44	
Cesanese	R				1024	0.02	289	679	0.01	329		-345			-34	
Aubun	R				1411	0.03	242	648	0.01	330		-764			-54	
Bayanshira	W				451	0.01	389	645	0.01	331		195			43	
Grenache Rose	R				22	0.00	729	645	0.01	332		623			2838	
Plavina	R							643	0.01	333		643				
Fortana	R				1252	0.03	264	642	0.01	334		-610			-49	
Len de l'El	W				734	0.02	324	640	0.01			-94			-13	

Table 6 (cont.) Ranking of prime varieties by global grape area, and decadal changes, 1990, 2000 and 2010

Prime variety	Col	1990 Global area (ha)	1990 Global share %	1990 Global rank	2000 Global area (ha)	2000 Global share %	2000 Global rank	2010 Global area (ha)	2010 Global share %	2010 Global rank	Change 2000-1990 (ha)	Change 2010-2000 (ha)	Change 2010-1990 (ha)	Changes 2000-1990 %	Changes 2010-2000 %	Changes 2010-1990 %
Ortega	W				1054	0.02	285	637	0.01	336		-417			-40	
Catawba	R				635	0.01	342	633	0.01	337		-2			0	
Codega de Larinho	W				4058	0.08	128	629	0.01	338		-3429			-85	
Calkarasi	R				436	0.01	390	625	0.01	339		189			43	
Francusa	W							621	0.01	340						
Muscat a Petits Grains Rouge	R				500	0.01	379	613	0.01	341		112			22	
Ortrugo	W				485	0.01	381	611	0.01	342		126			26	
Huxelrebe	W				1289	0.03	256	607	0.01	343		-682			-53	
Bourboulenc	W				772	0.02	318	597	0.01	344		-175			-23	
Seibel	R				1991	0.04	208	591	0.01	345		-1400			-70	
Malvasia del Lazio	W				2366	0.05	185	590	0.01	346		-1775			-75	
Coda di Volpe Bianca	W				980	0.02	292	586	0.01	347		-393			-40	
Gouveio Real	W							582	0.01	348		582				
Zenit	W				405	0.01	401	580	0.01	349		175			43	
Schiava Grossa	R				1259	0.03	263	580	0.01	350		-679			-54	
Vilana	W				506	0.01	378	579	0.01	351		73			14	
Krasnostop Zolotovsky	R							562	0.01	352		562				
Moravia Agria	R				1092	0.02	280	550	0.01	353		-542			-50	
Cardinal	R				3190	0.07	151	545	0.01	354		-2645			-83	
Magliocco Canino	R				579	0.01	361	539	0.01	355		-40			-7	
Faberrebe	W				1586	0.03	228	524	0.01	356		-1062			-67	
Vernaccia di San Gimignano	W				854	0.02	308	522	0.01	357		-332			-39	
Mavrouda	R				349	0.01	418	520	0.01	358		171			49	
Lorena	W							519	0.01	359		519				
Schiava	R				1231	0.03	265	517	0.01	360		-714			-58	
Camaralet de Lasseube	W				691	0.01	329	515	0.01	361		-175			-25	
Muskat Moravsky	W							514	0.01	362		514				
Uva Longanesi	R							512	0.01	363		512				
Bellone	W				1315	0.03	253	511	0.01	364		-804			-61	
Morio-Muskat	W				1188	0.02	271	509	0.01	365		-678			-57	
Nerello Cappuccio	R				1501	0.03	233	508	0.01	366		-993			-66	
Carrega Branco	W							507	0.01	367		507				
Chenanson	R				636	0.01	341	506	0.01	368		-130			-20	

Table 6 (cont.) Ranking of prime varieties by global grape area, and decadal changes, 1990, 2000 and 2010

Prime variety	Col	1990 Global area (ha)	1990 Global share %	1990 Global rank	2000 Global area (ha)	2000 Global share %	2000 Global rank	2010 Global area (ha)	2010 Global share %	2010 Global rank	2000-1990 Change (ha)	2010-2000 Change (ha)	2010-1990 Change (ha)	1990-2000 Changes %	2000-2010 Changes %	2010-1990 Changes %
Podarok Magaracha	W				148	0.00	514	504	0.01	369		356			240	
Tortosina	W				930	0.02	300	503	0.01	370		-427			-46	
Terrano	R				194	0.00	480	500	0.01	371		307			158	
Cornifesto	R				259	0.01	455	499	0.01	372		239			92	
Ondarrabi Zuri	W				189	0.00	482	492	0.01	373		303			161	
Black Queen	R				340	0.01	421	486	0.01	374		147			43	
Dunavski Lazur	W							483	0.01	375		483				
Sauvignon Gris	W				44	0.00	654	483	0.01	376		439			998	
Monemvassia	W				418	0.01	397	481	0.01	377		62			15	
Andre	R							472	0.01	378		472				
Durella	W				599	0.01	353	470	0.01	379		-130			-22	
Espadeiro	R				1682	0.03	220	469	0.01	380		-1213			-72	
Miguel del Arco	R				1267	0.03	261	468	0.01	381		-799			-63	
Baco Noir	R				397	0.01	403	467	0.01	382		70			18	
Robola	W				356	0.01	415	465	0.01	383		109			31	
Seyval Blanc	W				389	0.01	404	464	0.01	384		75			19	
Uva Rara	R				570	0.01	363	460	0.01	385		-111			-19	
Grolleau Gris	W				806	0.02	314	454	0.01	386		-352			-44	
Tsimlyansky Cherny	R							451	0.01	387		451				
Acolon	R							449	0.01	388		449				
Kraljevina	W							447	0.01	389		447				
Tibouren	R				457	0.01	387	445	0.01	390		-12			-3	
Counoise	R				638	0.01	339	443	0.01	391		-195			-31	
Pineau d'Aunis	R				430	0.01	392	435	0.01	392		5			1	
Abrusco	R				399	0.01	402	423	0.01	393		24			6	
Nouvelle	W				2	0.00	914	422	0.01	394		420			22241	
Lacrima di Morro d'Alba	R				652	0.01	335	421	0.01	395		-231			-35	
Bianco d'Alessano	W				941	0.02	298	419	0.01	396		-522			-55	
Cramposie Selectionata	W							409	0.01	397		409				
Debit	W							403	0.01	398		403				
Gamaret	R				71	0.00	606	399	0.01	399		329			463	
Salvador	R				572	0.01	362	394	0.01	400		-178			-31	
Kuldzhinskii	O				269	0.01	450	385	0.01	401		116			43	
Galbena de Odobesti	W				546	0.01	367	385	0.01	402		-161			-30	

Table 6 (cont.) Ranking of prime varieties by global grape area, and decadal changes, 1990, 2000 and 2010

Prime variety	Col	1990 Global area (ha)	1990 Global share %	1990 Global rank	2000 Global area (ha)	2000 Global share %	2000 Global rank	2010 Global area (ha)	2010 Global share %	2010 Global rank	2000-1990 Change (ha)	2010-2000 Change (ha)	2010-1990 Change (ha)	2000-1990 Changes %	2010-2000 Changes %	2010-1990 Changes %
Manzoni Bianco	W				8290	0.17	79	382	0.01	403		-7907			-95	
Cerceal Branco	W				597	0.01	354	379	0.01	404		-218			-37	
Ezerfurtu	W				405	0.01	400	377	0.01	405		-27			-7	
Pascale	R				1573	0.03	229	375	0.01	406		-1198			-76	
Coloraillo	R				614	0.01	346	374	0.01	407		-240			-39	
Egiodola	R				315	0.01	430	372	0.01	408		57			18	
Limnio	R				95	0.00	565	372	0.01	409		277			292	
Muscadel (Red)	R				360	0.01	413	371	0.01	410		11			3	
Tinto Cao	R				556	0.01	366	369	0.01	411		-188			-34	
Blauer Wildbacher	R				472	0.01	383	368	0.01	412		-104			-22	
Italica	W				178	0.00	489	367	0.01	413		189			106	
Abouriou	R				419	0.01	396	364	0.01	414		-55			-13	
Trebbiano Modenese	W				583	0.01	358	363	0.01	415		-221			-38	
Cabinda	R							362	0.01	416		362				
Domina	R				187	0.00	483	361	0.01	417		174			93	
Babic	R				1189	0.02	270	359	0.01	418		-830			-70	
Altesse	W				294	0.01	442	356	0.01	419		62			21	
Pampanuto	W				277	0.01	448	356	0.01	420		78			28	
Saperavi Severny	R				25	0.00	714	350	0.01	421		325			1300	
Listain de Huelva	W				596	0.01	355	350	0.01	422		-246			-41	
Viorica	W				40	0.00	665	347	0.01	423		307			768	
Parraleta	R				167	0.00	500	346	0.01	424		179			107	
Quebranta	R				230	0.00	470	345	0.01	425		115			50	
Tinta da Barca	R							345	0.01	426		345				
Mavrodafni	R				537	0.01	372	345	0.01	427		-192			-36	
Marechal Foch	R				173	0.00	493	344	0.01	428		170			98	
Tamarez	W				585	0.01	357	343	0.01	429		-243			-41	
Misket Varnenski	W							336	0.01	430		336				
Vertzami	R				491	0.01	380	335	0.01	431		-156			-32	
Aleatico	R				458	0.01	386	333	0.01	432		-125			-27	
Norton	R				0	0.00	985	329	0.01	433		329			131697	
Dunkelfelder	R				280	0.01	447	329	0.01	434		49			18	
Babeasca Gris	W							328	0.01	435		328				

Table 6 (cont.) Ranking of prime varieties by global grape area, and decadal changes, 1990, 2000 and 2010

Prime variety	Col	1990 Global area (ha)	1990 Global share %	1990 Global rank	2000 Global area (ha)	2000 Global share %	2000 Global rank	2010 Global area (ha)	2010 Global share %	2010 Global rank	1990-2000 Change (ha)	2000-2010 Change (ha)	2010-1990 Change (ha)	1990-2000 Changes %	2000-2010 Changes %	2010-1990 Changes %
Agronomica	R				19	0.00	746	327	0.01	436		308			1612	
Groppello Gentile	R				219	0.00	475	326	0.01	437		108			49	
Symphony	W				184	0.00	486	324	0.01	438		140			76	
Regina	W				1509	0.03	232	321	0.01	439		-1189			-79	
Mtsvane Kakhuri	W				249	0.01	463	319	0.01	440		70			28	
Erbaluce	W				329	0.01	425	319	0.01	441		-9			-3	
Carnelian	R				625	0.01	344	316	0.01	442		-308			-49	
Rossese	R				232	0.00	469	312	0.01	443		80			34	
Brandam	W							312	0.01	444		312				
Portan	R				368	0.01	411	311	0.01	445		-56			-15	
Poulsard	R				295	0.01	440	311	0.01	446		15			5	
Malvasia di Lipari	W				516	0.01	376	310	0.01	447		-206			-40	
Caddiu	R				978	0.02	293	309	0.01	448		-669			-68	
Citronny Magarach	W							307	0.01	449		307				
Mondeuse Noire	R				1404	0.03	245	306	0.01	450		-1098			-78	
Lakhegyi Mezes	W				567	0.01	364	306	0.01	451		-261			-46	
Rome	R				2	0.00	919	297	0.01	452		295			18697	
Storgozia	R							295	0.01	453		295				
Goruli Mtsvane	W				224	0.00	473	287	0.01	454		63			28	
Verdello	W				662	0.01	332	287	0.01	455		-374			-57	
Drupeggio	W				617	0.01	345	286	0.01	456		-331			-54	
Vijariego	W				510	0.01	377	285	0.01	457		-225			-44	
Encruzado	W				291	0.01	443	282	0.01	458		-9			-3	
Cabernet Mitos	R							282	0.01	459		282				
Aleksandrouli	R				219	0.00	474	281	0.01	460		62			28	
Raboso Veronese	R				307	0.01	433	277	0.01	461		-30			-10	
Dona Branca	W				296	0.01	439	276	0.01	462		-20			-7	
Maticha	W							275	0.01	463		275				
Manto Negro	R				470	0.01	385	273	0.01	464		-197			-42	
Vernaccia di Oristano	W				565	0.01	365	272	0.01	465		-293			-52	
Vidvizhenets	O							271	0.01	466		271				
Busuioaca de Bohotin	O							268	0.01	467		268				
Aurore	W				299	0.01	437	268	0.01	468		-31			-10	
Casculho	R						437	267		469		267				

Table 6 (cont.) Ranking of prime varieties by global grape area, and decadal changes, 1990, 2000 and 2010

Prime variety	Col	1990 Global area (ha)	1990 Global share %	1990 Global rank	2000 Global area (ha)	2000 Global share %	2000 Global rank	2010 Global area (ha)	2010 Global share %	2010 Global rank	Change (ha) 2000-1990	Change (ha) 2010-2000	Change (ha) 2010-1990	Changes % 2000-1990	Changes % 2010-2000	Changes % 2010-1990
Zengo	W							264	0.01	470		264				
Elvira	W				344	0.01	420	263	0.01	471		-81			-23	
Fokiano	R				162	0.00	504	262	0.01	472		100			62	
Clairette Rose	W				356	0.01	414	260	0.01	473		-96			-27	
Riton	W				2	0.00	911	257	0.01	474		255			12750	
Cornalin	R				93	0.00	568	256	0.01	475		163			175	
Mustoasa de Maderat	W							255	0.01	476		255				
Vignoles	W				68	0.00	613	254	0.01	477		186			272	
Danlas	W							254	0.01	478		254				
Posip Bijeli	W				6539	0.13	100	253	0.01	479		-6287			-96	
California	O							252	0.01	480		252				
Bouvier	W				365	0.01	412	250	0.01	481		-115			-32	
Ranna Melnishka Loza	R							249	0.01	482		249				
Trebbiano	W				685	0.01	330	248	0.01	483		-438			-64	
Telti Kyryk	W				172	0.00	495	246	0.01	484		74			43	
Triplett Blanc	W							244	0.01	485		244				
Lambrusco Viadanese	R				277	0.01	449	240	0.01	486		-37			-13	
Red Globe	R				2068	0.04	205	240	0.01	487		-1828			-88	
Traminette	W				5	0.00	850	240	0.01	488		235			4839	
Debina	W				455	0.01	388	239	0.01	489		-216			-48	
Trincadeira das Pratas	W				216	0.00	476	239	0.01	490		23			11	
Gouveio Roxo	R							238	0.01	491		238				
Trbljan	W							231	0.01	492		231				
Fiesta	W				161	0.00	505	230	0.00	493		69			43	
Palava	O							230	0.00	494		230				
Perricone	R				580	0.01	360	228	0.00	495		-351			-61	
Reichensteiner	W				319	0.01	428	228	0.00	496		-92			-29	
Muscat Rose	O				159	0.00	507	227	0.00	497		69			43	
Doina	R							227	0.00	498		227				
Viosinho	W				17	0.00	758	225	0.00	499		209			1251	
Gamay de Teinturier Bouze	R				318	0.01	429	225	0.00	500		-93			-29	
Cabernet Dorsa	R				43	0.00	656	223	0.00	501		180			418	
Refosco di Faedis	R				256	0.01	458	217	0.00	502		-38			-15	
Garanoir	R				76	0.00	593	216	0.00	503		140			185	

Table 6 (cont.) Ranking of prime varieties by global grape area, and decadal changes, 1990, 2000 and 2010

Prime vairiety	Col	1990 Global area (ha)	1990 Global share %	1990 Global rank	2000 Global area (ha)	2000 Global share %	2000 Global rank	2010 Global area (ha)	2010 Global share %	2010 Global rank	2000-1990 Change (ha)	2010-2000 Change (ha)	2010-1990 Change (ha)	2000-1990 Changes %	2010-2000 Changes %	2010-1990 Changes %
Lairen	W				298	0.01	438	214	0.00	504		-84			-28	
Cabernet Moravia	R							212	0.00	505		212				
Cayuga White	W				108	0.00	549	212	0.00	506		104			97	
Menu Pineau	W				380	0.01	407	212	0.00	507		-168			-44	
Malbo Gentile	R				106	0.00	552	211	0.00	508		105			99	
Malvasia Bianca di Basilicata	W				875	0.02	306	210	0.00	509		-665			-76	
Vermentino Nero	R				143	0.00	516	210	0.00	510		67			46	
Pinot Noir Precoce	R				86	0.00	577	209	0.00	511		123			144	
Forastera	W				543	0.01	368	208	0.00	512		-334			-62	
Kujundzusa	W							206	0.00	513		206				
Carricante	W				252	0.01	460	205	0.00	514		-47			-19	
Trebbiano Spoletino	W				242	0.00	467	200	0.00	515		-42			-17	
Giro	R				537	0.01	371	200	0.00	516		-338			-63	
Roter Veltliner	O				258	0.01	456	199	0.00	517		-59			-23	
Tsulukidzis Tetra	W				152	0.00	509	195	0.00	518		43			28	
Tinta de Pegoes	R							195	0.00	519		195				
Jubileum 75	R							194	0.00	520		194				
Bonamico	R				83	0.00	580	193	0.00	521		110			133	
San Giuseppe Nero	R				348	0.01	419	192	0.00	522		-156			-45	
Viktoria Gyongye	W							190	0.00	523		190				
Rossignola	R				295	0.01	441	188	0.00	524		-107			-36	
Juhfark	W							186	0.00	525		186				
Fintendo	R							183	0.00	526		183				
Malagousia	W				23	0.00	724	182	0.00	527		160			700	
Folgasao	W				409	0.01	399	182	0.00	528		-227			-56	
Barbera Bianca	W				251	0.01	461	181	0.00	529		-70			-28	
Alvarelhao	R				159	0.00	506	180	0.00	530		21			13	
Turan	R							177	0.00	531		177				
Maceratino	W				122	0.00	530	177	0.00	532		55			45	
Papazkarasi	R				122	0.00	529	175	0.00	533		53			43	
Crystal	W				1	0.00	930	175	0.00	534		173			12393	
Arvine	W				61	0.00	622	172	0.00			111			183	
Levokumski Sustainable	O							170	0.00	536		170				
Pallagrello Nero	R							169	0.00	537		169				

Table 6 (cont.) Ranking of prime varieties by global grape area, and decadal changes, 1990, 2000 and 2010

Prime variety	Col	1990 Global area (ha)	1990 Global share %	1990 Global rank	2000 Global area (ha)	2000 Global share %	2000 Global rank	2010 Global area (ha)	2010 Global share %	2010 Global rank	2000-1990 Change (ha)	2010-2000 Change (ha)	2010-1990 Change (ha)	2000-1990 Changes %	2010-2000 Changes %	2010-1990 Changes %
Koshu	O				118	0.00	537	168	0.00	538		51			43	
Praca	W							166	0.00	539		166				
Valbom	R							166	0.00	540		166				
Emerald Riesling	W				593	0.01	356	164	0.00	541		-428			-72	
Biancolella	W				385	0.01	405	164	0.00	542		-222			-58	
Preto Martinho	R				428	0.01	394	163	0.00	543		-265			-62	
Roesler	R							160	0.00	544		160				
Medina	R							159	0.00	545		159				
Greco	W				1325	0.03	251	158	0.00	546		-1167			-88	
Callet	R				151	0.00	510	154	0.00	547		3			2	
Schioppettino	R				93	0.00	567	154	0.00	548		61			65	
Canari Noir	R							152	0.00	549		152				
Maratheftiko	R							152	0.00	550		152				
Pedral	R				179	0.00	488	151	0.00	551		-28			-15	
Vranac	R							149	0.00	552		149				
Castelino	R							147	0.00	553		147				
Amur	R							146	0.00	554		146				
Stepnyak	W							144	0.00	555		144				
Chardonel	W							144	0.00	556		144				
Negoska	R				96	0.00	564	143	0.00	557		46			48	
Nasco	W				166	0.00	502	141	0.00	558		-25			-15	
Ofthalmo	R							141	0.00	559		141				
Goldburger	W				309	0.01	431	140	0.00	560		-168			-55	
Heroldrebe	R				199	0.00	479	140	0.00	561		-59			-30	
Roobernet	R				78	0.00	589	139	0.00	562		61			79	
Moscato di Terracina	W				229	0.00	471	138	0.00	563		-91			-40	
Valdiguie	R				79	0.00	586	138	0.00	564		59			75	
Lambrusca di Alessandria	R				888	0.02	304	137	0.00	565		-751			-85	
Casavecchia	R							136	0.00	566		136				
Biborkadarka	R				202	0.00	478	136	0.00	567		-67			-33	
Frontenac	R							135	0.00	568		135				
Nero Buono di Cori	R				114	0.00	541	135	0.00	569		21			19	
Zlahtina	W							135	0.00	570		135				
Vespolina	R				103	0.00	557	134	0.00	571		31			30	

Table 6 (cont.) Ranking of prime varieties by global grape area, and decadal changes, 1990, 2000 and 2010

		1990			2000			2010			2000-1990	2010-2000	2010-1990	2000-1990	2010-2000	2010-1990
Prime variety	Col	Global area (ha)	Global share %	Global rank	Global area (ha)	Global share %	Global rank	Global area (ha)	Global share %	Global rank	Change (ha)	Change (ha)	Change (ha)	Changes %	Changes %	Changes %
Ranfol	W							134	0.00	572		134				
Devin	W							133	0.00	573		133				
Neretta Cuneese	R				374	0.01	409	132	0.00	574		-242			-65	
Timorasso	W				19	0.00	751	129	0.00	575		111			597	
Trebbianina	W							128	0.00	576		128				
Picolit	W				93	0.00	570	128	0.00	577		35			37	
Rieslina	W							127	0.00	578		127				
Delaware	O				134	0.00	518	127	0.00	579		-7			-5	
Muscat Bailey A	R				72	0.00	602	122	0.00	580		50			70	
Caino Blanco	W				69	0.00	611	121	0.00	581		52			75	
Rebo	R				37	0.00	675	120	0.00	582		83			224	
Siegerrebe	O				167	0.00	499	120	0.00	583		-48			-29	
Zeta	W							118	0.00	584		118				
Zierfandler	O				98	0.00	562	117	0.00	585		19			19	
Hrvatica	R				245	0.01	465	116	0.00	586		-129			-53	
Riesus	W							115	0.00	587		115				
Dorinto	W							115	0.00	588		115				
Malvasia Nera di Basilicata	R				754	0.02	320	114	0.00	589		-639			-85	
Diolinoir	R				31	0.00	690	114	0.00	590		83			266	
Asprouda	W				433	0.01	391	113	0.00	591		-320			-74	
Moristel	R							112	0.00	592		112				
Lambrusco Oliva	R							112	0.00	593		112				
Tintilia del Molise	R							111	0.00	594		111				
Fonte Cal	W				355	0.01	416	111	0.00	595		-244			-69	
Malvasia Branca de Sao Jorge	W				55	0.00	634	110	0.00	596		56			102	
Spergola	W							110	0.00	597		110				
Maiskii Chernyi	R				77	0.00	590	110	0.00	598		33			43	
Caloria	R				129	0.00	524	108	0.00	599		-21			-16	
Muscat a Petits Grains Noirs	R							108	0.00	600		108				
Malvasia di Casorzo	R				98	0.00	563	107	0.00	601		10			10	
Nieddera	R				58	0.00	629	107	0.00	602		49			83	
Generosa	W				9	0.00	815	107	0.00	603		97			1053	
Sercial	W				306	0.01	434	106	0.00	604		-200			-65	
Geisenheim	R							106	0.00	605		106				

Table 6 (cont.) Ranking of prime varieties by global grape area, and decadal changes, 1990, 2000 and 2010

Prime variety	Col	1990 Global area (ha)	1990 Global share %	1990 Global rank	2000 Global area (ha)	2000 Global share %	2000 Global rank	2010 Global area (ha)	2010 Global share %	2010 Global rank	2000-1990 Change (ha)	2010-2000 Change (ha)	2010-1990 Change (ha)	2000-1990 Changes %	2010-2000 Changes %	2010-1990 Changes %
Rotgipfler	W				118	0.00	535	105	0.00	606		-13			-11	
Prensal	W				114	0.00	542	105	0.00	607		-9			-8	
Kakotrygis	W							103	0.00	608		103				
Poeloeske Muskotaly	W							103	0.00	609		103				
Complexa	R				6	0.00	838	103	0.00	610		96			1506	
Foglia Tonda	R				40	0.00	664	101	0.00	611		61			153	
Ruche	R				46	0.00	650	100	0.00	612		54			118	
Misket	W				3764	0.08	135									
Superior Seedless	W				2842	0.06	163	9	0.00	975		-2833			-100	
Tinto Basto	R				2331	0.05	187	62	0.00	688		-2269			-97	
Moscatel Branco	W				1419	0.03	241	30	0.00	808		-1389			-98	
Sumoll	R				1401	0.03	246	83	0.00	642		-1318			-94	
Agadai	W				1265	0.03	262									
Montu	W				1091	0.02	281									
Korinthiaki	R	28126	0.53	41	834	0.02	312	54	0.00	711	-27292	-780	-28071		-93	-100
Koenigin der Weingaerten	W				750	0.02	321	61	0.00	691		-689			-92	
Abbuoto	R				696	0.01	328	37	0.00	767		-659			-95	
Panse Valenciano	W				649	0.01	336	1	0.00	1160		-648				
Amaral	R				582	0.01	359	92	0.00	623		-490			-84	
Flame Seedless	R	20194	0.38	46	541	0.01	369	42	0.00	754	-19653	-499	-20152		-92	-100
Bonarda Grande	R				538	0.01	370									
Servant	W				530	0.01	374	54	0.00	715		-477			-90	
Terret Noir	R				370	0.01	410									
Chenel	W				339	0.01	422	79	0.00	653		-260			-77	
Royalty	R				338	0.01	423	97	0.00	619		-241			-71	
Fino de Ribera del Fresno	W				332	0.01	424	45	0.00	746		-287			-86	
Afus Ali	W				328	0.01	426	8	0.00	980		-320			-98	
Barbera Sarda	R				326	0.01	427	84	0.00	639		-242			-74	
Carica l'Asino	W				299	0.01	436	17	0.00	887		-282			-94	
Ehrenfelser	W				289	0.01	444	79	0.00	654		-210			-73	
Bukettraube	W				280	0.01	445	71	0.00	670		-210			-75	
Negretto	R				280	0.01	446	75	0.00	660		-204			-73	
Gamay Teinturier de Chaudenay	R				267	0.01	451	24	0.00	846		-243			-73	
Terret Gris	W				262	0.01	452								-91	

Table 6 (cont.) Ranking of prime varieties by global grape area, and decadal changes, 1990, 2000 and 2010

		1990			2000			2010			2000-1990	2010-2000	2010-1990	2000-1990	2010-2000	2010-1990
Prime vairiety	Col	Global area (ha)	Global share %	Global rank	Global area (ha)	Global share %	Global rank	Global area (ha)	Global share %	Global rank	Change (ha)	Change (ha)	Change (ha)	Changes %	Changes %	Changes %
Lambrusco Montericco	R				262	0.01	453	70	0.00	671		-191			-73	
Mandon	R				261	0.01	454									
Sciascinoso	R				253	0.01	459	94	0.00	621		-159			-63	
Fileri	W				249	0.01	462	97	0.00	618		-152			-61	
Doradillo	W				249	0.01	464									
Magliocco Dolce	R				243	0.00	466	87	0.00	633		-157			-64	
Optima	W				239	0.00	468	37	0.00	770		-203			-85	
Nosiola	W				191	0.00	481	79	0.00	652		-112			-59	
De Chaunac	R				186	0.00	484	91	0.00	625		-95			-51	
Therona	W				185	0.00	485	99	0.00	614		-86			-47	
Malvasia di Schierano	R				181	0.00	487	89	0.00	629		-92			-51	
Merlot Blanc	W				176	0.00	490	31	0.00	801		-145			-82	
Garrido Fino	W				174	0.00	492	59	0.00	700		-115			-66	
Kanaan	W				172	0.00	494	25	0.00	835		-147			-86	
Baroque	W				169	0.00	496	90	0.00	627		-79			-47	
Torbato	W				168	0.00	497	19	0.00	874		-149			-88	
Guardavalle	W				168	0.00	498	33	0.00	788		-134			-80	
Incrocio Manzoni 2.15	R				166	0.00	503	86	0.00	636		-80			-48	
Canorroyo	W				157	0.00	508									
Regner	W				150	0.00	511	44	0.00	748		-106			-71	
Arinarnoa	R				149	0.00	512	32	0.00	793		-116			-78	
Aglianicone	R				148	0.00	513	62	0.00	687		-86			-58	
Arvesiniadu	W				147	0.00	515	30	0.00	809		-117			-80	
Centurian	R				134	0.00	517	34	0.00	784		-100			-75	
Gamay Teinturier Freaux	R				132	0.00	519	55	0.00	706		-77			-58	
Montils	W				131	0.00	520									
Merille	R					0.00	521									
Verdil	W				131	0.00	522	57	0.00	702		-74			-56	
Rose du Var	O				129	0.00	523									
Jampal	W				127	0.00	525	71	0.00	668		-57			-44	
Colombana Nera	R				126	0.00	526	38	0.00	764		-88			-70	
Piculit Neri	R				126	0.00	527	22	0.00	857		-104			-83	
Arrufiac	W				126	0.00	528									
Perle	O				121	0.00	531	21	0.00	862		-100			-83	

Table 6 (cont.) Ranking of prime varieties by global grape area, and decadal changes, 1990, 2000 and 2010

Prime variety	Col	1990 Global area (ha)	1990 Global share %	1990 Global rank	2000 Global area (ha)	2000 Global share %	2000 Global rank	2010 Global area (ha)	2010 Global share %	2010 Global rank	2000-1990 Change (ha)	2010-2000 Change (ha)	2010-1990 Change (ha)	2000-1990 Changes %	2010-2000 Changes %	2010-1990 Changes %
San Michele	R				120	0.00	532	57	0.00	703		-63			-53	
Tarrango	R				120	0.00	533	72	0.00	663		-48			-40	
Groppello di Mocasina	R				120	0.00	534	81	0.00	648		-39			-32	
Sugra Five	W				118	0.00	536	2	0.00	1104		-116				
Rollo	W				117	0.00	538	51	0.00	727		-67			-57	
Albanello	W				117	0.00	539	18	0.00	885		-99			-85	
Muscat a Petits Grains Roses	R				116	0.00	540									
Canaiolo Rosa	W				114	0.00	543	1	0.00	1187		-113			-40	
Goustolidi	W				112	0.00	544	68	0.00	675		-44			-40	
Grechetto Rosso	R				111	0.00	545	49	0.00	737		-62			-56	
Malvasia Rosa	R				111	0.00	546	32	0.00	799		-79			-72	
Lumassina	W				111	0.00	547	98	0.00	617		-13			-12	
Bouchales	R				108	0.00	548									
Verdea	W				107	0.00	550	83	0.00	641		-24			-22	
Blanca Ovoide	W				107	0.00	551	40	0.00	756		-67			-63	
Moscatello Selvatico	W				105	0.00	553	35	0.00	780		-71			-67	
Vespaiola	W				105	0.00	554	94	0.00	620		-10			-10	
Stavroto	R				104	0.00	555	11	0.00	942		-93			-89	
Piquepoul Noir	R				103	0.00	556	10	0.00	964		-94			-91	
Rossola Nera	R				102	0.00	558	86	0.00	634		-16			-16	
Nobling	W				102	0.00	559	50	0.00	730		-52			-51	
Petit Rouge	R				100	0.00	560	84	0.00	640		-16			-16	
Dalkauer	W				100	0.00	561									
Drenak Crven	R	20275	0.38	45												
Other varieties		1321510	24.98		577964	11.85		270521	5.88							
Total		**5290000**	**100.00**		**4878176**	**100.00**		**4601445**	**100.00**		**-411824**	**-276731**	**-688555**	**-8**	**-6**	

Table 7: Red winegrape area and share of all varieties, by country, 2000 and 2010

Country	Area (ha) of red varieties		Changes in red varieties		National share (%) of red varieties	
	2000	2010	Hectares	%	2000	2010
Algeria	30200	30200	0	0	100	100
Argentina	102809	120556	17747	17	51	60
Armenia						
Australia	77752	92430	14678	19	60	61
Austria	12977	16137	3159	24	27	35
Brazil	31721	40041	8321	26	60	81
Bulgaria	58273	35543	-22730	-39	61	63
Canada	4740	4654	-87	-2	56	46
Chile	86936	81115	-5821	-7	76	73
Croatia	15084	7085	-7999	-53	25	34
Cyprus	14625	5707	-8918	-61	80	66
Czech Rep.	3399	5817	2418	71	30	36
France	594692	576972	-17720	-3	69	68
Georgia	4563	5853	1290	28	12	12
Germany	7067	15726	8658	123	7	15
Greece	26254	29384	3129	12	52	54
Hungary	20939	21087	148	1	24	30
Italy	328933	356121	27189	8	52	57
Luxembourg	67	101	34	51	5	8
Moldova	35741	35741	0	0	40	40
Morocco	44187	43653	-535	-1	89	89
New Zealand	2825	7688	4864	172	28	24
Portugal	118336	108396	-9939	-8	58	67
Romania	61576	26482	-35094	-57	28	16
Russia	10706	9625	-1081	-10	19	38
Serbia	21390	21390	0	0	31	31
Slovakia	2649	3934	1286	49	17	31
Slovenia	6103	5282	-820	-13	26	32
South Africa	33846	44429	10583	31	36	44
Spain	456322	552696	96374	21	39	54
Switzerland	7913	8574	661	8	53	58
Tunisia	16836	16836	0	0	100	100
United Kingdom	200	405	205	102	23	34
United States	96126	141834	45709	48	55	62
Uruguay	8555	6152	-2403	-28	96	80
China		28350	28350			96
Japan		2213	2213			60
Kazakhstan		982	982			14
Mexico		3409	3409			62
Myanmar		44	44			59
Peru		2292	2292			60
Thailand		99	99			66
Turkey		8677	8677			67
Ukraine		16149	16149			31
Missing 9	43608	(62215)	(18607)	(43)	(54)	(54)
Old World subtotal	**1825698**	**1873462**	**47764**	**2.6**	**46.2**	**52.5**
New World subtotal	**562252**	**666402**	**104150**	**18.5**	**60.9**	**64.5**
World total	**2387950**	**2539864**	**195522**	**8.2**	**49.0**	**55.2**

Table 8: White winegrape area and share of all varieties, by country, 2000 and 2010

Country	Area (ha) of white varieties		Changes in white varieties		National share (%) of white varieties	
	2000	2010	Hectares	%	2000	2010
Algeria						
Argentina	55983	43488	-12495	-22	28	22
Armenia	11206	11206	0	0	100	100
Australia	52850	56062	3212	6	40	37
Austria	34870	28903	-5967	-17	72	63
Brazil	21119	9357	-11762	-56	40	19
Bulgaria	37724	16431	-21293	-56	39	29
Canada	3548	4865	1318	37	42	48
Chile	27021	30240	3220	12	24	27
Croatia	44364	13394	-30971	-70	75	65
Cyprus	3656	2901	-755	-21	20	34
Czech Rep.	7932	9521	1589	20	70	59
France	267941	267290	-651	0	31	32
Georgia	32836	42122	9286	28	88	88
Germany	94175	81764	-12411	-13	90	80
Greece	24279	20265	-4014	-17	48	37
Hungary	63842	45947	-17896	-28	73	66
Italy	301104	252229	-48875	-16	47	40
Luxembourg	1126	1057	-69	-6	84	81
Moldova	52061	52061	0	0	58	58
Morocco	5413	5347	-65	-1	11	11
New Zealand	6984	22772	15788	226	70	71
Portugal	86667	55119	-31548	-36	42	34
Romania	158209	142241	-15968	-10	71	84
Russia	45626	15463	-30164	-66	81	60
Serbia	47609	47609	0	0	69	69
Slovakia	12932	8460	-4472	-35	83	67
Slovenia	17369	10571	-6798	-39	74	65
South Africa	59706	56326	-3380	-6	64	56
Spain	725484	475562	-249922	-34	61	46
Switzerland	6979	6029	-950	-14	46	41
Tunisia						
United Kingdom	673	734	61	9	77	61
United States	78616	79168	552	1	45	35
Uruguay	325	1493	1168	359	4	19
China		1193	1193			4
Japan		1282	1282			35
Kazakhstan		5343	5343			77
Mexico		2056	2056			38
Myanmar		31	31			41
Peru		1532	1532			40
Thailand		50	50			34
Turkey		4179	4179			33
Ukraine		35458	35458			68
Missing 9	35547	(51125)	(15578)	(44)	(44)	(44)
Old World subtotal	**2077993**	**1651125**	**-426868**	**-20.5**	**53.3**	**46.3**
New World subtotal	**312237**	**315997**	**3760**	**1.2**	**34.3**	**30.6**
World total	**2425777**	**1967122**	**-458655**	**-18.9**	**49.7**	**42.8**

Table Section II: Regional coverage of each country

Table 9: Winegrape area by region for each country, 2000

Region	Area (hectares)	National share (%)	Region	Area (hectares)	National share (%)
Algeria	**30200**	**100.00**	**Australia (cont.)**		
			Kangaroo Island	34	0.03
Argentina			Langhorne Creek	3737	2.86
Mendoza	141081	70.15	Limestone C. Other	7529	5.76
San Juan	45285	22.52	Lower Murray Other	145	0.11
Other AR	14746	7.33	Margaret River	3401	2.60
Total	**201113**	**100.00**	Mclaren Vale	4695	3.59
			Mornington Peninsula	402	0.31
Armenia	**11206**	**100.00**	Mount Benson	299	0.23
			Mt Lofty Rgs Other	488	0.37
Australia			Mudgee	2152	1.65
Adelaide Hills	1811	1.39	Murray Darling NSW	5576	4.27
Alpine/Bchworth	803	0.61	Murray Darling Vic	15663	11.99
Aus. Capital Terr.	15	0.01	N. E. Vic Other	1254	0.96
Barossa Other	249	0.19	N. W. Vic Other	3177	2.43
Barossa Valley	7673	5.88	Nthn Rivers Other	12	0.01
Beechworth	35	0.03	Nthn Slopes Other	174	0.13
Bendigo	607	0.46	Nthn Territory	302	0.23
Big Rivers Other	1015	0.78	Orange	995	0.76
Blackwood Valley	501	0.38	Padthaway	3226	2.47
Canberra District	110	0.08	Perricoota	153	0.12
C. Ranges Other	302	0.23	Perth Hills	316	0.24
Central Vic Other	876	0.67	Pt Phillip Other	129	0.10
Central WA	70	0.05	Pyrenees	428	0.33
Clare Valley	3617	2.77	Queensland Other	1207	0.92
Cowra	1533	1.17	Riverina	12398	9.49
Currency Creek	940	0.72	Riverland	18336	14.04
Eastern Plain etc.	39	0.03	Rutherglen	793	0.61
Eden Valley	1224	0.94	South Burnett	344	0.26
Far North Other	107	0.08	South Coast Other	112	0.09
Fleurieu Other	510	0.39	SW Australia Other	802	0.61
Geelong	322	0.25	Southern Fleurieu	328	0.25
Geographe	480	0.37	Sthn NSW Other	914	0.70
Gippsland	174	0.13	Sunbury	79	0.06
Goulburn Valley	1090	0.83	Swan District	812	0.62
Grampians	424	0.32	Swan Hill NSW	544	0.42
Granite Belt	433	0.33	Swan Hill Vic.	3725	2.85
Great Southern	2391	1.83	Tasmania	680	0.52
Greater Perth Other	395	0.30	The Peninsulas	50	0.04
Hastings River	118	0.09	Tumbarumba	278	0.21
Henty	183	0.14	SE Coastal WA	65	0.05
Hilltops	383	0.29	West Plains Other	328	0.25
Hunter	3669	2.81	West Vic Other	110	0.08
Hunter Valley Other	278	0.21	Yarra Valley	2038	1.56
			Total	**130602**	**100.00**

Table 9 (cont.) Winegrape area by region for each country, 2000

Region	Area (hectares)	National share (%)	Region	Area (hectares)	National share (%)
Austria			**France**		
Burgenland	14540	29.98	Correze, Haute-Vienne	50	0.01
Niederosterreich	29975	61.81	Aisne	2340	0.27
Steiermark	3283	6.77	Alpes de Haute	1082	0.13
Wien and Other	699	1.44	Alsace	15128	1.75
Total	**48496**	**100.00**	Aquitaine Other	25732	2.98
			Ardeche	12295	1.42
Brazil	**52840**	**100.00**	Aude	85270	9.86
			Auvergne	1096	0.13
Bulgaria	**95997**	**100.00**	Bouches-du-Rhone	11089	1.28
			Bourgogne	29941	3.46
Canada	**8498**	**100.00**	Centre	22316	2.58
			Champagne-Ardenne	28671	3.32
Chile			Charente	38514	4.45
Araucania	5	0.00	Charente-Maritime	40321	4.66
Atacama	797	0.70	Corse	6992	0.81
Coquimbo	11083	9.72	Deux-Sevres, Vienne	1973	0.23
Del Bio Bio	13747	12.06	France2	2020	0.23
Del Maule	45053	39.53	Gard	67133	7.76
Metropolitana	9453	8.29	Gers	19913	2.30
O'Higgins	29044	25.48	Gironde	124617	14.41
Valparaiso	4783	4.20	Herault	105647	12.22
Total	**113966**	**100.00**	Lorraine	184	0.02
			Midi-Pyrenees Other	18872	2.18
Croatia	**59448**	**100.00**	Pays de la Loire Other	37882	4.38
			Pyrenees-Orientales	37659	4.35
Cyprus	**18282**	**100.00**	Rhone Alpes Other	44861	5.19
			Seine-Et-Marne	26	0.00
Czech Republic	**11331**	**100.00**	Var	31420	3.63
			Vaucluse	51801	5.99
			Total	**864846**	**100.00**
			Georgia Total	**37419**	**100.00**

Table 9 (cont.) Winegrape area by region for each country, 2000

Region	Area (hectares)	National share (%)	Region	Area (hectares)	National share (%)
Germany			**Italy (cont.)**		
Ahr	520	0.50	Benevento	10291	1.62
Baden	15551	14.92	Bergamo	881	0.14
Franken	5992	5.75	Biella	289	0.05
Hessische Bergstrasse	456	0.44	Bologna	7049	1.11
Mittelrhein	572	0.55	Bolzano-Bozen	4781	0.75
Mosel-Saar-Ruwer	11520	11.05	Brescia	3904	0.61
Nahe	4603	4.42	Brindisi	13498	2.12
Rheingau	3216	3.09	Cagliari	8398	1.32
Rheinhessen	26381	25.32	Caltanissetta	5526	0.87
Rhein-Pfalz	23338	22.40	Campobasso	4858	0.76
Saale-Unstrut	616	0.59	Caserta	2964	0.47
Sachsen	409	0.39	Catania	3875	0.61
Wurttemberg	11033	10.59	Catanzaro	1336	0.21
Total	**104207**	**100.00**	Chieti	25986	4.08
			Como	18	0.00
Greece			Cosenza	5107	0.80
Anatoliki Mak., Thraki	384	0.76	Cremona	39	0.01
Attiki	6113	12.02	Crotone	3266	0.51
Dytiki Ellada	8031	15.78	Cuneo	16272	2.56
Dytiki Makedonia	1690	3.32	Enna	586	0.09
Ionia Nisia	2707	5.32	Ferrara	569	0.09
Ipeiros	632	1.24	Firenze	15940	2.50
Kentriki Makedonia	2494	4.90	Foggia	28797	4.52
Kriti	5312	10.44	Forli-Cesena	6746	1.06
Notio Aigaio	5313	10.44	Frosinone	4162	0.65
Peloponnisos	8197	16.11	Genova	147	0.02
Sterea Ellada	5991	11.78	Gorizia	3474	0.55
Thessalia	3043	5.98	Grosseto	3843	0.60
Voreio Aigaio	2196	4.32	Imperia	454	0.07
Total	**50878**	**100.00**	Isernia	563	0.09
			La Spezia	833	0.13
Hungary	**86886**	**100.00**	L'Aquila	855	0.13
			Latina	6045	0.95
			Lecce	10021	1.57
Italy			Lecco	44	0.01
Agrigento	19624	3.08	Livorno	1214	0.19
Alessandria	14873	2.34	Lodi	22	0.00
Ancona	4591	0.72	Lucca	728	0.11
Arezzo	4887	0.77	Macerata	1482	0.23
Ascoli Piceno	8211	1.29	Mantova	1830	0.29
Asti	18016	2.83	Massa-Carrara	275	0.04
Avellino	6287	0.99	Matera	1645	0.26
Bari	16954	2.66	Messina	2253	0.35
Belluno	9	0.00	Milano	238	0.04

Table 9 (cont.) Winegrape area by region for each country, 2000

Region	Area (hectares)	National share (%)	Region	Area (hectares)	National share (%)
Italy (cont.)			**Italy (cont.)**		
Modena	7585	1.19	Verbano-Cusio-Ossola	29	0.00
Napoli	1956	0.31	Vercelli	169	0.03
Novara	575	0.09	Verona	23359	3.67
Nuoro	7208	1.13	Vibo Valentia	845	0.13
Oristano	3250	0.51	Vicenza	6898	1.08
Padova	6313	0.99	Viterbo	4628	0.73
Palermo	16515	2.59	**Total**	**636662**	**100.00**
Parma	574	0.09			
Pavia	13734	2.16	**Luxembourg Total**	**1348**	**100.00**
Perugia	8040	1.26			
Pesaro E Urbino	1391	0.22	**Moldova Total**	**89844**	**100.00**
Pescara	3146	0.49			
Piacenza	5568	0.87	**Morocco Total**	**49600**	**100.00**
Pisa	2386	0.37			
Pistoia	633	0.10	**New Zealand**		
Pordenone	6671	1.05	Auckland	392	3.95
Potenza	5431	0.85	Canterbury	232	2.33
Prato	335	0.05	Central Otago	280	2.81
Ragusa	1520	0.24	Gisborne	1681	16.91
Ravenna	16910	2.66	Hawkes Bay	2443	24.57
Reggio Di Calabria	2101	0.33	Marlborough	4054	40.77
Reggio Nell'Emilia	8263	1.30	Nelson	203	2.04
Rieti	1490	0.23	Waikato	119	1.20
Rimini	2653	0.42	Waipara	210	2.11
Roma	10519	1.65	Wairarapa	328	3.30
Rovigo	258	0.04	**Total**	**9942**	**100.00**
Salerno	5222	0.82			
Sassari	6232	0.98	**Portugal**		
Savona	399	0.06	Alentejo	14905	7.27
Siena	15718	2.47	Algarve	1900	0.93
Siracusa	1583	0.25	Alto Tras-Os-Montes	63371	30.91
Sondrio	987	0.16	Beira Interior	20851	10.17
Taranto	15156	2.38	Beira Litoral	23921	11.67
Teramo	2785	0.44	Entre Douro e Minho	29678	14.48
Terni	5548	0.87	Madeira	1513	0.74
Torino	1777	0.28	Acores	1689	0.82
Trapani	59078	9.28	Ribatejo e Oeste	47173	23.01
Trento	8844	1.39	**Total**	**205003**	**100.00**
Treviso	24008	3.77			
Trieste	182	0.03	**Romania**	**222173**	
Udine	7171	1.13			
Valle D'Aosta	424	0.07	**Russia**	**56332**	**100.00**
Varese	19	0.00			
Venezia	6018	0.95			

Table 9 (cont.) Winegrape area by region for each country, 2000

Region	Area (hectares)	National share (%)	Region	Area (hectares)	National share (%)
Serbia	**68999**	**100.00**	**Spain (cont.)**		
			Malaga	6467	0.55
Slovakia	**15580**	**100.00**	Murcia	45058	3.81
			Navarra	23619	2.00
Slovenia	**23472**	**100.00**	Rioja	39459	3.34
			Tarragona	32839	2.78
South Africa			Toledo	172334	14.58
Breedekloof	10385	11.09	Valencia	64216	5.43
Little Karoo	3168	3.38	Valladolid	15837	1.34
Malmesbury	13670	14.60	Zamora	15883	1.34
Olifants River	9015	9.63	Zaragoza	41546	3.52
Orange River	5025	5.36	**Total**	**1181805.76**	**100.00**
Paarl	17249	18.42			
Robertson	12227	13.06	**Switzerland**		
Stellenbosch	16112	17.20	Aargau	395	2.62
Worcester	6805	7.27	Basel-Landschaft	99	0.66
Total	**93656**	**100.00**	Bern	257	1.71
			Fribourg	116	0.77
Spain			Geneva	1355	9.01
Alava	11338	0.96	Graubunden	414	2.75
Albacete	107563	9.10	Jura	7	0.05
Alicante	25466	2.15	Lucerne	19	0.12
Almeria, Granada, Jaen, S	9635	0.82	Neuchÿtel	605	4.02
Asturias	84	0.01	Schaffhausen	500	3.32
Avila, Palencia, Salamanca	13995	1.18	Schwyz	30	0.20
Badajoz	81209	6.87	St. Gallen	217	1.44
Barcelona	24223	2.05	Thurgau	274	1.82
Burgos	13264	1.12	Ticino	961	6.39
Caceres	4310	0.36	Valais	5255	34.94
Cadiz	9931	0.84	Vaud	3879	25.79
Canarias	13727	1.16	Zurich	645	4.29
Cantabria	39	0.00	Other CH	14	0.10
Castellon	1190	0.10	**Total**	**15042**	**100.00**
Ciudad Real	206366	17.46			
Cordoba	12777	1.08	**Tunisia**	**16836**	**100.00**
Cuenca	97721	8.27			
Galicia	31747	2.69	**United Kingdom**	**873**	**100.00**
Girona, Lleida	7390	0.63			
Guadalajara	2827	0.24			
Guipuzcoa, Vizcaya	243	0.02			
Huelva	6747	0.57			
Huesca, Teruel	7599	0.64			
Illes Balears	1718	0.15			
Leon	15964	1.35			
Madrid	17475	1.48			

Table 9 (cont.) winegrape area by region for each country, 2000

Region	Area (hectares)	National share (%)	Region	Area (hectares)	National share (%)
United States			**United States (cont.)**		
Alameda	546	0.31	San Mateo	19	0.01
Amador	1014	0.58	Santa Barbara	4043	2.30
Benton Co.	88	0.05	Santa Clara	443	0.25
Butte	58	0.03	Santa Cruz	68	0.04
Calavaras	114	0.06	Shasta	15	0.01
Chautauqua-Erie	8116	4.62	Solano	698	0.40
Columbia River	293	0.17	Sonoma	14708	8.37
Colusa	539	0.31	Stanislaus	5358	3.05
Contra Costa	397	0.23	Sutter	32	0.02
Douglas Co.	190	0.11	Tehama	53	0.03
El Dorado	338	0.19	Trinity	15	0.01
Finger Lakes	3692	2.10	Tulare	4602	2.62
Fresno	17606	10.02	Ventura	3	0.00
Glenn	580	0.33	Washington	6880	3.92
Humboldt	4	0.00	Washington Co.	393	0.22
Josephine Co.	117	0.07	Yamhill Co.	1016	0.58
Kern	11198	6.37	Yolo	2446	1.39
Kings	949	0.54	Yuba	126	0.07
Lake	1444	0.82	**United States**	**175693**	**100.00**
Lane Co.	254	0.14			
Los Angeles	12	0.01	**Uruguay**	**8880**	**100.00**
Madera	17427	9.92			
Marin	33	0.02	**Missing 9**	**80221**	**100.00**
Marion Co.	221	0.13			
Mariposa	23	0.01			
Mendocino	5050	2.87			
Merced	5901	3.36			
Michigan	526	0.30			
Monterey	11688	6.65			
Napa	12258	6.98			
Nevada	76	0.04			
Oregon-Other	216	0.12			
Other New York	1544	0.88			
Other Valley	106	0.06			
Placer	37	0.02			
Polk Co.	383	0.22			
Riverside	845	0.48			
Sacramento	3611	2.06			
San Benito	720	0.41			
San Bernardino	558	0.32			
San Diego	25	0.01			
San Joaquin	20930	11.91			
San Luis Obispo	5047	2.87			

Table 10: Winegrape area by region for each country, 2010

Region	Area (hectares)	National share (%)	Region	Area (hectares)	National share(%)
Algeria	**30200**	**100.00**	**Australia**		
			Adelaide Hills	3861	2.54
Argentina			Adelaide Plains	880	0.58
Albardon	701	0.35	Alpine Valleys	705	0.46
Angaco	1756	0.87	Aus. Capital Terr.	4	0.00
Catamarca	2253	1.12	Barossa Other	91	0.06
Caucete	5769	2.87	Barossa Valley	9763	6.43
Julio	2161	1.07	Beechworth	57	0.04
Junin	11571	5.76	Bendigo	771	0.51
La Rioja	6420	3.19	Big Rivers Other	629	0.41
Lavalle	13238	6.58	Blackwood Valley	249	0.16
Lujan De Cuyo	13525	6.73	Canberra ACT	105	0.07
Maipu	13349	6.64	Canberra NSW	378	0.25
Mayo	6566	3.27	C. Ranges Other	227	0.15
Neuquen	1653	0.82	Central Vic Other	56	0.04
Pocito	2323	1.16	Central WA	62	0.04
Rawson	1277	0.64	Clare Valley	4801	3.16
Rio Negro	1643	0.82	Coonawarra	5985	3.94
Rivadavia	15699	7.81	Cowra	1427	0.94
Salta	2549	1.27	Currency Creek	871	0.57
San Martin M	29738	14.79	Eastern Plain ect.	25	0.02
San Martin S	2809	1.40	Eden Valley	1933	1.27
San Rafael	14088	7.01	Far North Other	11	0.01
Santa Rosa	9499	4.72	Fleurieu Other	187	0.12
Sarmiento	6984	3.47	Geelong	515	0.34
Tunuyan	7881	3.92	Geographe	1181	0.78
Tupungato	8676	4.32	Gippsland	236	0.16
Ullum	529	0.26	Glenrowan	203	0.13
Other-Mendoza	14357	7.14	Goulburn Valley	1612	1.06
Other-San Juan	3095	1.54	Grampians	506	0.33
Other-AR	677	0.34	Granite Belt	331	0.22
Total	**201060**	**100.00**	Great Southern	2804	1.85
			Greater Perth Other	36	0.02
Armenia	**11206**	**100.00**	Gundagai	408	0.27
			Hastings River	18	0.01
			Heathcote	1245	0.82
			Henty	183	0.12
			Hilltops	484	0.32
			Hunter	3450	2.27
			Hunter Valley Other	24	0.02
			Kangaroo Island	89	0.06
			King Valley	1320	0.87
			Langhorne Creek	5957	3.92

Table 10 (cont.) Winegrape area by region for each country, 2010

Region	Area (hectares)	National share (%)	Region	Area (hectares)	National share (%)
Australia (cont.)			**Australia (cont.)**		
Limestone C. Other	476	0.31	Tasmania	1251	0.82
Lower Murray Other	260	0.17	The Peninsulas	93	0.06
Macedon Ranges	224	0.15	Tumbarumba	254	0.17
Manjimup	179	0.12	Upper Goulburn	245	0.16
Margaret River	4894	3.22	SE Coastal WA	19	0.01
Mclaren Vale	6490	4.28	West Plains Other	236	0.16
Mornington Peninsula	752	0.50	West Vic Other	73	0.05
Mount Benson	233	0.15	Wrattonbully	2818	1.86
Mt Lofty Rgs Other	468	0.31	Yarra Valley	2440	1.61
Mudgee	3414	2.25	**Total**	**151788**	**100.00**
Murray Darling NSW	6533	4.30			
Murray Darling Vic	8339	5.49	**Austria**		
New England	123	0.08	Burgenland	13842	30.40
N. E. Vic Other	74	0.05	Niederosterreich	27184	59.70
N. W. Vic Other	121	0.08	Steiermark	3867	8.49
Nthn Rivers other	41	0.03	Wien and Other	640	1.40
Nthn Slopes Other	145	0.10	**Total**	**45533**	**100.00**
Orange	1546	1.02			
Padthaway	5028	3.31	**Brazil**	**49412**	**100.00**
Peel	96	0.06			
Pemberton	622	0.41	**Bulgaria**		
Perricoota	671	0.44	Severen Tsentralen	3868	6.89
Perth Hills	295	0.19	Severoiztochen	5837	10.40
Pt Phillip Other	68	0.04	Severozapaden	5830	10.39
Pyrenees	874	0.58	Yugoiztochen	19533	34.80
Queensland Other	187	0.12	Yugozapaden	3599	6.41
Riverina	20154	13.28	Yuzhen Tsentralen	17466	31.12
Riverland	20009	13.18	**Total**	**56133**	**100.00**
Robe	644	0.42			
Rutherglen	853	0.56	**Canada**		
Shoalhaven Coast	40	0.03	British Colombia	3995	39.56
South Burnett	240	0.16	Ontario	6102	60.44
South Coast Other	113	0.07	**Total**	**10096**	**100.00**
SW Australia Other	101	0.07			
Southern Fleurieu	414	0.27			
Sthn Flinders	180	0.12			
Southern Highlands	202	0.13			
Sthn NSW Other	119	0.08			
Strathbogie Ranges	369	0.24			
Sunbury	129	0.09			
Swan District	784	0.52			
Swan Hill NSW	308	0.20			
Swan Hill Vic	3869	2.55			

Table 10 (cont.) Winegrape area by region for each country, 2010

Region	Area (hectares)	National share (%)	Region	Area (hectares)	National share (%)
Chile			**Czech Republic**		
Araucania	12	0.01	Cechy	785	4.83
Atacama	12	0.01	Morava	15457	95.17
Coquimbo	2155	1.93	**Total**	**16242**	**100.00**
De Los Lagos	6	0.01			
Del Bio Bio	3420	3.07	**France**		
Del Maule	49014	43.95	Aquitaine-Other	2644	0.31
Metropolitana	12214	10.95	Ardeche	12025	1.42
O'Higgins	36170	32.43	Aude	74965	8.85
Valparaiso	8522	7.64	Bas Rhin	6965	0.82
Total	**111525**	**100.00**	Bouches du Rhone	11866	1.40
			Centre-Other	501	0.06
China			Champagne-Viticole	32478	3.84
Beijing	3067	10.38	Charente	40571	4.79
Gansu	4987	16.88	Charente Maritime	40483	4.78
Ningxia	11152	37.74	Cher	4027	0.48
Shandong	67	0.23	Corse	7013	0.83
Shanxi	547	1.85	Cote d'Or	9665	1.14
Sichuan	533	1.81	Dordogne	13293	1.57
Tianjin	400	1.35	Drome	19129	2.26
Xinjiang	3133	10.61	Gard	61678	7.28
Yantai	4373	14.80	Gers	18976	2.24
Other CN	1287	4.35	Gironde	123889	14.63
Total	**29545**	**100.00**	Herault	96973	11.45
			Haut Rhin	9190	1.09
Croatia			Indre	424	0.05
Dalmatinska Zagora	602	2.90	Indre et Loire	10443	1.23
Hrvatsko Primorje	210	1.01	Landes	2147	0.25
Istra	3083	14.85	Loir et Cher	7432	0.88
Moslavina	228	1.10	Loire Atlantique	15569	1.84
Plesivica	452	2.18	Lot	5365	0.63
Podunavlje	3206	15.45	Lot et Garonne	6941	0.82
Pokuplje	41	0.20	Maine et Loire	20759	2.45
Prigorje - Bilogora	791	3.81	Midi Pyrenees-Other	3694	0.44
Sjeverna Dalmacija	2333	11.24	Nievre	1611	0.19
Slavonija	3307	15.94	Pays de Loire-Other	647	0.08
Srednja Juzna Dalm.	2972	14.32	Poitou-Charentes-Other	1818	0.21
Zagorje-Medimurje	1266	6.10	Prov.-C. d'AOther	1235	0.15
Other HR	2263	10.90	Pyrenees Orientales	29945	3.54
Total	**20754**	**100.00**	Rhone	18682	2.21
			Rhone-Alpes-Other	4119	0.49
			Saone et Loire	13486	1.59
Cyprus	**8608**	**100.00**	Savoie	1323	0.16

Table 10 (cont.) Winegrape area by region for each country, 2010

Region	Area (hectares)	National share (%)	Region	Area (hectares)	National share (%)
France (cont.)			**Hungary**		
Tarn	7248	0.86	Badacsony	1618	2.32
Tarn Et Garonne	3894	0.46	Balatonboglar	3305	4.74
Var	32160	3.80	Balatonfelvidek	1025	1.47
Vaucluse	55270	6.53	Balatonfured-Csopak	2180	3.13
Vendee	1318	0.16	Bukk	1055	1.51
Vienne	1091	0.13	Csongrad	1513	2.17
Yonne	7131	0.84	Eger	5509	7.90
Other FR	6796	0.80	Etyek-Budai	1717	2.46
Total	**846880**	**100.00**	Hajos-Bajai	1982	2.84
			Kunsag	22263	31.93
Georgia	**48001**	**100.00**	Matra	6294	9.03
			Mor	730	1.05
Germany			Nagy-Somlo	598	0.86
Ahr	550	0.54	Neszmely	1587	2.28
Baden	15830	15.51	Pannonhalma	615	0.88
Franken	6100	5.98	Pecs	777	1.11
Hessische Bergstra E	420	0.41	Sopron	1919	2.75
Mittelrhein	450	0.44	Szekszard	2333	3.35
Mosel-Saar-Ruwer	8970	8.79	Tokaj	5994	8.60
Nahe	4160	4.08	Tolna	2526	3.62
Rheingau	3060	3.00	Villany	2582	3.70
Rheinhessen	26470	25.94	Zala	1592	2.28
Rhein-Pfalz	23460	22.99	**Total**	**69715**	**100.00**
Saale-Unstrut	700	0.69			
Sachsen	460	0.45			
Wurttemberg	11430	11.20			
Total	**102060**	**100.00**			
Greece					
Anatoliki Mak., Thraki	1234	2.27			
Attiki	5599	10.29			
Dytiki Ellada	6484	11.92			
Dytiki Makedonia	2083	3.83			
Ionia Nisia	2422	4.45			
Ipeiros	559	1.03			
Kentriki Makedonia	4256	7.83			
Kriti	7863	14.46			
Notio Aigaio	3547	6.52			
Peloponissos	8134	14.96			
Sterea Ellada	6457	11.87			
Thessalia	3415	6.28			
Vorreio Aigaio	2337	4.30			
Total	**54389**	**100.00**			

Table 10 (cont.) Winegrape area by region for each country, 2010

Region	Area (hectares)	National share (%)	Region	Area (hectares)	National share (%)
Italy			**Mexico**		
Abruzzo	32189	5.14	Aguascalientes	850	15.55
Basilicata	4863	0.78	Sonora	1164	21.30
Calabria	9785	1.56	Suma Baja California	2863	52.39
Campania	23185	3.71	Suma Coahuila	279	5.11
Emilia-Romagna	55796	8.92	Zacatecas	309	5.65
Friuli-Venezia Giulia	19250	3.08	Total	5465	100.00
Lazio	16401	2.62			
Liguria	1538	0.25	**Moldova**	89844	100.00
Lombardia	23089	3.69			
Marche	16745	2.68	**Morocco**	49000	100.00
Molise	5154	0.82			
Piemonte	46317	7.40	**Myanmar**	75	100.00
Puglia	82760	13.23			
Sardegna	18465	2.95	**New Zealand**		
Sicilia	104068	16.63	Auckland	543	1.70
Toscana	59839	9.56	Canterbury	320	1.00
Trentino Alto Adige	15658	2.50	Gisborne	2149	6.72
Umbria	12491	2.00	Hawkes Bay	4921	15.40
Valle D'Aosta	463	0.07	Marlborough	18401	57.57
Veneto	77644	12.41	Nelson	813	2.54
Total	**625700**	**100.00**	Otago	1532	4.79
			Waikato	147	0.46
Japan			Waipara	1442	4.51
Hokkaido	835	22.47	Wairarapa	859	2.69
Nagano	754	20.30	Other NZ	836	2.62
Yamagata	392	10.56	**Total**	**31964**	**100.00**
Yamanashi	632	17.01			
Other JP	1102	29.66	**Peru**		
Total	**3715**	**100.00**	Arequipa	1356	35.40
			Lima	783	20.44
Kazakhstan			Moquegua	877	22.89
Almaty	4553	65.62	Tacna	815	21.27
East Kazakhstan	3	0.04	**Total**	**3831**	**100.00**
South Kazakhstan	2162	31.16			
West Kazakhstan	2	0.03			
Zhambyl	217	3.12			
Other KZ	2	0.03			
Total	**6938**	**100**			
Luxembourg	1304	100.00			

Table 10 (cont.) Winegrape area by region for each country, 2010

Region	Area (hectares)	National share (%)	Region	Area (hectares)	National share (%)
Portugal			**Slovenia**		
Acores	176	0.11	Bela Krajina	365	2.23
Alentejo	21892	13.39	Bizeljsko Sremic	907	5.54
Algarve	1078	0.66	Dolenjska	1476	9.02
Alto Tras-Os-Montes	59112	36.15	Goriska Brda	1898	11.61
Beira Interior	15968	9.76	Kras	593	3.62
Beira Litoral	15241	9.32	Prekmurje	564	3.45
Entre Douro e Minho	14288	8.74	Slovenska Istra	1626	9.94
Madeira	847	0.52	Stajerska Slovenija	6374	38.97
Ribatejo e Oeste	34920	21.36	Vipavska Dolina	2526	15.44
Total	**163522**	**100.00**	Other SI	26	0.16
			Total	**16354**	**100.00**
Romania					
Bucuresti - Ilfov	443	0.26	**South Africa**		
Centru	5349	3.14	Breedekloof	12568	12.44
Nord-Est	28072	16.48	Little Karoo	2822	2.79
Nord-Vest	6667	3.92	Malmesbury	14224	14.08
Sud - Muntenia	27069	15.90	Olifants River	9997	9.90
Sud-Est	68081	39.98	Orange River	5078	5.03
Sud-Vest Oltenia	31966	18.77	Paarl	16568	16.40
Vest	2645	1.55	Robertson	14004	13.86
Total	**170292**	**100.00**	Stellenbosch	17107	16.93
			Worcester	8649	8.56
Russia			**Total**	**101016**	**100.00**
Krasnodar Krai	21224	82.82			
Rostov Oblast	4404	17.18			
Total	**25628**	**100.00**			
Serbia	**68999**	**100.00**			
Slovakia					
Juznoslovenska	4141	32.77			
Malokarpatska	3683	29.14			
Nitrianska	2652	20.98			
Stredoslovenska	1155	9.14			
Tokajska	453	3.59			
Vychodoslovenska	553	4.38			
Total	**12637**	**100.00**			

Table 10 (cont.) Winegrape area by region for each country, 2010

Region	Area (hectares)	National share (%)	Region	Area (hectares)	National share (%)
Spain			**Switzerland**		
Alava	13040	1.27	Aargau	399	2.69
Albacete	96745	9.41	Basel-Landschaft	114	0.77
Alicante	14661	1.43	Bern	242	1.63
Almeria, Granada, Jaen, S	6950	0.68	Fribourg	117	0.79
Asturias	95	0.01	Geneva	1292	8.72
Avila, Palencia, Salamanc	9154	0.89	Graubünden	421	2.84
Badajoz	82749	8.05	Jura	14	0.09
Barcelona	22339	2.17	Lucerne	41	0.28
Burgos	16276	1.58	Neuchytel	591	3.99
Caceres	3857	0.38	Schaffhausen	478	3.22
Cadiz	10156	0.99	Schwyz	38	0.26
Canarias	8653	0.84	St. Gallen	215	1.45
Cantabria	50	0.00	Thurgau	263	1.78
Castellon	1214	0.12	Ticino	1069	7.21
Ciudad Real	175764	17.09	Valais	5070	34.21
Cordoba	8278	0.81	Vaud	3819	25.77
Cuenca	94883	9.23	Zurich	614	4.14
Galicia	25457	2.48	Other CH	25	0.17
Girona, Lleida	7560	0.74	**Total**	**14820**	**100.00**
Guadalajara	2149	0.21			
Guipuzcoa, Vizcaya	736	0.07	**Thailand**	**149**	**100.00**
Huelva	4230	0.41			
Huesca, Teruel	9277	0.90	**Tunisia Total**	**16836**	**100.00**
Illes Balears	1544	0.15			
Leon	12149	1.18	**Turkey**		
Madrid	12576	1.22	Akdeniz	28	0.21
Malaga	2079	0.20	Ege	6770	52.66
Murcia	35437	3.45	Guney Dogu	438	3.40
Navarra	22411	2.18	Marmara	1745	13.57
Rioja	44576	4.34	Orta Dogu	1895	14.74
Tarragona	29617	2.88	Orta Guney	1553	12.08
Toledo	125760	12.23	Orta Kuzey	428	3.33
Valencia	57559	5.60	**Total**	**12856**	**100.00**
Valladolid	22081	2.15			
Zamora	12906	1.26	**Ukraine Total**	**52293**	**100.00**
Zaragoza	35294	3.43			
Total	**1028258**	**100.00**	**United Kingdom**	**1198**	**100.00**
			United States		
			Alameda	1145	0.50
			Amador	1255	0.55
			Arizona	101	0.04
			Arkansas	243	0.11

Table 10 (cont.) Winegrape area by region for each country, 2010

Region	Area (hectares)	National share (%)	Region	Area (hectares)	National share (%)
United States (cont.)			**United States (cont.)**		
Benton Co.	155	0.07	Orange	0	0.00
Butte	58	0.03	Other New York	1508	0.66
Calaveras	253	0.11	Other W. Valley	154	0.07
Chautauqua-Erie	7561	3.32	Pennsylvania	1004	0.44
Colorado	271	0.12	Placer	70	0.03
Columbia Gorge	159	0.07	Polk Co.	928	0.41
Columbia River 2	610	0.27	Puget Sound	72	0.03
Columbia Valley	3023	1.33	Rattlesnake Hills	647	0.28
Colusa	646	0.28	Red Mountain	515	0.23
Contra Costa	675	0.30	Riverside	333	0.15
Douglas Co.	350	0.15	Sacramento	7406	3.25
El Dorado	660	0.29	San Benito	959	0.42
Finger Lakes	3801	1.67	San Bernardino	209	0.09
Fresno	16010	7.02	San Diego	78	0.03
Georgia	567	0.25	San Joaquin	27146	11.91
Glenn	329	0.14	San Luis Obispo	11484	5.04
Horse Heaven Hills	4283	1.88	San Mateo	29	0.01
Humboldt	36	0.02	Santa Barbara	6512	2.86
Illinois	373	0.16	Santa Clara	609	0.27
Indiana	263	0.12	Santa Cruz	160	0.07
Iowa	194	0.09	Shasta	41	0.02
Jackson Co.	536	0.24	Siskiyou	8	0.00
Josephine Co.	162	0.07	Snipes Mountain	285	0.12
Kentucky	210	0.09	Solano	1231	0.54
Kern	8422	3.69	Sonoma	22265	9.77
Kings	615	0.27	Stanislaus	3079	1.35
Lake	3122	1.37	Sutter	54	0.02
Lake Chelan	100	0.04	Tehama	59	0.03
Lane Co.	341	0.15	Texas	1214	0.53
Los Angeles	53	0.02	Trinity	49	0.02
Madera	14273	6.26	Tulare	3432	1.51
Marin	62	0.03	Tuolumne	12	0.01
Marion Co.	660	0.29	Ventura	21	0.01
Mariposa	24	0.01	Virginia	1065	0.47
Mendocino	6555	2.88	Wahluke Slope	2689	1.18
Merced	4418	1.94	Walla Walla Valley	528	0.23
Michigan	1072	0.47	Washington Co.	670	0.29
Minnesota	418	0.18	Yakima Valley	5444	2.39
Missouri	647	0.28	Yamhill Co.	2273	1.00
Monterey	15600	6.84	Yolo	4263	1.87
Napa	17768	7.79	Yuba	39	0.02
Nevada	159	0.07	**Total**	**227948**	**100.00**
North Carolina	728	0.32			
Ohio	436	0.19	**Uruguay**	**7657**	**100.00**

Table 11: Winegrape area by region for the United States, 1990, 2000 and 2010

Region	1990 Hectares	Share %	2000 Hectares	Share %	2010 Hectares	Share %
California	**132174**	**88.12**	**151657**	**86.32**	**181687**	**79.71**
Alameda	680	0.45	546	0.31	1145	0.50
Amador	689	0.46	1014	0.58	1255	0.55
Butte	36	0.02	58	0.03	58	0.03
Calaveras	86	0.06	114	0.06	253	0.11
Colusa	509	0.34	539	0.31	646	0.28
Contra Costa	293	0.20	397	0.23	675	0.30
El Dorado	194	0.13	338	0.19	660	0.29
Fresno	13181	8.79	17606	10.02	16010	7.02
Glenn	579	0.39	580	0.33	329	0.14
Humboldt		0.00	4	0.00	36	0.02
Kern	10241	6.83	11198	6.37	8422	3.69
Kings	570	0.38	949	0.54	615	0.27
Lake	1383	0.92	1444	0.82	3122	1.37
Los Angeles	10	0.01	12	0.01	53	0.02
Madera	15459	10.31	17427	9.92	14273	6.26
Mariposa	16	0.01	23	0.01	24	0.01
Marin	4	0.00	33	0.02	62	0.03
Mendocino	5003	3.34	5050	2.87	6555	2.88
Merced	5518	3.68	5901	3.36	4418	1.94
Monterey	11458	7.64	11688	6.65	15600	6.84
Napa	13888	9.26	12258	6.98	17768	7.79
Nevada	52	0.03	76	0.04	159	0.07
Orange		0.00		0.00	0	0.00
Placer	29	0.02	37	0.02	70	0.03
Riverside	934	0.62	845	0.48	333	0.15
Sacramento	1622	1.08	3611	2.06	7406	3.25
San Benito	704	0.47	720	0.41	959	0.42
San Bernardino	448	0.30	558	0.32	209	0.09
San Diego	30	0.02	25	0.01	78	0.03
San Joaquin	15632	10.42	20930	11.91	27146	11.91
San Mateo	18	0.01	19	0.01	29	0.01
San Luis Obispo	3571	2.38	5047	2.87	11484	5.04
Santa Barbara	3706	2.47	4043	2.30	6512	2.86
Santa Clara	402	0.27	443	0.25	609	0.27
Santa Cruz	43	0.03	68	0.04	160	0.07
Shasta	6	0.00	15	0.01	41	0.02
Siskiyou		0.00		0.00	8	0.00
Solano	500	0.33	698	0.40	1231	0.54
Stanislaus	6103	4.07	5358	3.05	3079	1.35
Sutter		0.00	32	0.02	54	0.02
Sonoma	13751	9.17	14708	8.37	22265	9.77
Tehama	57	0.04	53	0.03	59	0.03
Trinity	2	0.00	15	0.01	49	0.02
Tulare	3880	2.59	4602	2.62	3432	1.51
Tuolumne		0.00		0.00	12	0.01
Ventura		0.00	3	0.00	21	0.01
Yolo	762	0.51	2446	1.39	4263	1.87
Yuba	125	0.08	126	0.07	39	0.02

Table 11 (cont.) Winegrape area by region for the United States, 1990, 2000 and 2010

Region	1990 Hectares	Share %	2000 Hectares	Share %	2010 Hectares	Share %
Washington	**2889**	**1.93**	**6880**	**3.92**	**17745**	**7.78**
Columbia Gorge					159	0.07
Columbia Valley					3023	1.33
Horse Heaven Hills					4283	1.88
Lake Chelan					100	0.04
Puget Sound					72	0.03
Rattlesnake Hills					647	0.28
Red Mountain					515	0.23
Snipes Mountain					285	0.12
Wahluke Slope					2689	1.18
Walla Walla Valley					528	0.23
Yakima Valley					5444	2.39
New York	**13355**	**8.90**	**13352**	**7.60**	**12870**	**5.65**
Chautauqua-Erie			8116	4.62	7561	3.32
Finger Lakes			3692	2.10	3801	1.67
Other New York			1544	0.88	1508	0.66
Oregon	**1578**	**1.05**	**3278**	**1.87**	**6839**	**3.00**
Benton Co.			88	0.05	155	0.07
Columbia River			293	0.17	610	0.27
Douglas Co.			190	0.11	350	0.15
Jackson Co.					536	0.24
Josephine Co.			117	0.07	162	0.07
Lane Co.			254	0.14	341	0.15
Marion Co.			221	0.13	660	0.29
Other W. Valley					154	0.07
Other Valley			106	0.06		
Polk Co.			383	0.22	928	0.41
Washington Co.			393	0.22	670	0.29
Yamhill Co.			1016	0.58	2273	1.00
Oregon-Other			216	0.12		0.00
Arizona					101	0.04
Arkansas					243	0.11
Colorado					271	0.12
Georgia					567	0.25
Illinois					373	0.16
Indiana					263	0.12
Iowa					194	0.09
Kentucky					210	0.09
Michigan			526	0.30	1072	0.47
Minnesota					418	0.18
Missouri					647	0.28
North Carolina					728	0.32
Ohio					436	0.19
Pennsylvania					1004	0.44
Texas					1214	0.53
Virginia					1065	0.47
Total	**149996**	**100**	**175693**	**100**	**227948**	**100**

Table 12: Large regions or regions within each state in Australia and Italy, 2010

Australia			Italy		
Aus. Capital Terr.	Far North Other	***Western Australia***	***Abruzzo***	La Spezia	Caltanissetta
Aus. Capital Terr.	Fleurieu other	Blackwood Valley	Chieti	Savona	Catania
Canberra ACT	Kangaroo Island	Central WA	L'Aquila	***Lombardia***	Enna
New South Wales	Langhorne Creek	Eastern Plain ect.	Pescara	Bergamo	Messina
Big Rivers Other	Limestone C. other	Geographe	Teramo	Brescia	Palermo
Canberra NSW	Lower Murray Other	Great Southern	***Basilicata***	Como	Ragusa
Central Ranges other	McLaren Vale	Greater Perth Other	Matera	Cremona	Siracusa
Cowra	Mount Benson	Manjimup	Potenza	Lecco	Trapani
Gundagai	Mt Lofty Rgs Other	Margaret River	***Calabria***	Lodi	***Toscana***
Hastings River	Padthaway	Peel	Catanzaro	Mantova	Arezzo
Hilltops	Riverland	Pemberton	Cosenza	Milano	Firenze
Hunter	Robe	Perth Hills	Crotone	Pavia	Grosseto
Hunter Valley Other	SA - other	SE Coastal WA	Reggio di Calabria	Sondrio	Livorno
Mudgee	Southern Fleurieu	SW Australia Other	Vibo Valentia	Varese	Lucca
Murray Darling NSW	Sthn Flinders	Swan District	***Campania***	***Marche***	Massa-Carrara
New England	The Peninsulas	WA other	Avellino	Ancona	Pisa
NSW other	Wrattonbully	***Tasmania***	Benevento	Ascoli Piceno	Pistoia
Nthn Rivers other	***Victoria***		Caserta	Macerata	Prato
Nthn Slopes Other	Central Victoria		Napoli	Pesaro e Urbino	Siena
Orange	Alpine Valleys		Salerno	***Molise***	***Trentino AA***
Perricoota	Beechworth		***Emilia R.***	Campobasso	Bolzano-Bozen
Riverina	Bendigo		Bologna	Isernia	Trento
Shoalhaven Coast	Central Vic Other		Ferrara	***Piemonte***	***Umbria***
South Coast Other	Geelong		Forli-Cesena	Alessandria	Perugia
Southern Highlands	Gippsland		Modena	Asti	Terni
Southern NSW other	Glenrowan		Parma	Biella	***Valle d'Aosta***
Swan Hill NSW	Heathcote		Piacenza	Cuneo	***Veneto***
Tumbarumba	Henty		Ravenna	Novara	Belluno
Upper Goulburn	King Valley		Reggio nell'Emilia	Verbano-C.-Oss.	Padova
West Plains Other	Macedon Ranges		Rimini	Torino	Rovigo
Queensland	Mornington Peninsula		***Friuli VG***	Vercelli	Treviso
Granite Belt	Murray Darling Vic		Gorizia	***Puglia***	Venezia
Queensland Other	N. E. Vic Other		Pordenone	Bari	Verona
South Burnett	N. W. Vic Other		Trieste	Brindisi	Vicenza
South Australia	Port Phillip - other		Udine	Foggia	
Adelaide Hills	Pyrenees		***Lazio***	Lecce	
Adelaide Plains	Rutherglen		Frosinone	Taranto	
Barossa Other	Strathbogie Ranges		Latina	***Sardegna***	
Barossa Valley	Sunbury		Rieti	Cagliari	
Bordertown	Swan Hill Vic		Roma	Nuoro	
Clare Valley	West Vic Other		Viterbo	Oristano	
Coonawarra	Western Victoria		***Liguria***	Sassari	
Currency Creek	Yarra Valley		Genova	***Sicilia***	
Eden Valley			Imperia	Agrigento	

Table Section III: Winegrape varietal coverage globally

Table 13: Prime varieties' colour, country of origin, synonyms, and 2010 global area, share and rank

Prime variety	Col.	Synonyms	Country of origin	2010 Area (hectares)	Share (%)	Rank
Abbo	R	Abbou(MA)	Morocco	2375	0.05	167
Abbuoto	R		Italy	37	0.00	767
Abondant	W		France			
Abouriou	R		France	364	0.01	414
Abrusco	R	Colorino(IT)	Italy	423	0.01	393
Acolon	R		Germany	449	0.01	388
Adakarasi	R		Turkey	69	0.00	674
Afus Ali	W	Roseti (ES),Waltham Cross(AU)	Lebanon	8	0.00	980
Agadai	W		Russia			
Agiorgitiko	R		Greece	2905	0.06	149
Aglianico	R	Aglianico del Vulture(IT), Aglianco(AR)	Italy	9963	0.22	69
Aglianicone	R		Italy	62	0.00	687
Agni	R		Czech Rep	6	0.00	1012
Agronomica	R		Portugal	327	0.01	436
Agua Santa	R		Portugal	78	0.00	657
Airen	W	Airen (ES),Forcallat Blanca(ES),Burra Blanca(ES)	Spain	252364	5.48	3
Aladasturi	R		Georgia	59	0.00	699
Alarije	W	Malfar(ES)	Spain	1726	0.04	195
Alb de Ialoveni	W		Moldova	2	0.00	1104
Albalonga	W		Germany			
Albana	W		Italy	1523	0.03	206
Albanello	W		Italy	18	0.00	885
Albaranzeuli Bianco	W		Italy	7	0.00	999
Albaranzeuli Nero	R		Italy	49	0.00	735
Albarin Blanco	W		Spain	23	0.00	851
Albarola	W	Bianchetta Genovese(AT)	Italy	1453	0.03	213
Albarossa	R		Italy	80	0.00	649
Albillo Mayor	W	Albilla(CL,PE)	Spain	1319	0.03	229
Albillo Real	W	Albillo(CL,ES)	Spain	861	0.02	290
Alcanon	W		Spain	60	0.00	695
Aleatico	R		Italy	333	0.01	432
Aledo	W		Spain	7	0.00	995
Aleksandrouli	R		Georgia	281	0.01	460
Aletta	W		Hungary	723	0.02	313
Alfrocheiro	R	Tinta Bastardinha(PT),Bastarda Negra(SP)	Portugal	1188	0.03	244
Alicante Henri Bouschet	R	Alicante(IT),Alicante Bouchet(IT,MA,TR,AM),Garnacha Tintorera(ES,EL),Tintoreras(CL),Alicante Bouschet(BR,CL,HU,PT,ZA,MM), Alikante Mouse(EL)	France	38985	0.85	23
Aligote	W		France	36119	0.78	24
Alionza	W		Italy	11	0.00	947
Almafre	W	Almafra(PT)	Portugal	0	0.00	1242
Alminhaca	W	Almenhaca(PT)	Portugal	1	0.00	1184
Alphonse Lavallee	R	Ribier(FR),Alfonso Lavalle(PE,ES)	France	883	0.02	287
Altesse	W		France	356	0.01	419
Alvar Branco	W	Alvar(PT)	Portugal	0	0.00	1239
Alvar Roxo	O		Portugal	2	0.00	1123
Alvarelhao	R	Brancellao(ES), Pilongo(IT),Brancelho(PT)	Portugal	180	0.00	530
Alvarelhao Ceitao	R			0	0.00	1266

Table 13 (cont.) Prime varieties' colour, country of origin, synonyms, and 2010 global area, share and rank

Prime variety	Col.	Synonyms	Country of origin	2010 Area (hectares)	Share (%)	Rank
Alvarinho	W	Albarino (CL,US,ES),Albarino Blanco(ES)	Portugal	5523	0.12	103
Amaral	R	Asal Tinto(PT)	Portugal	92	0.00	623
Amigne	W		Switzerland	43	0.00	750
Amur	R		Moldova	146	0.00	554
Ancellotta	R	Ancelota(BR)	Italy	4774	0.10	111
Andre	R		Czech Rep	472	0.01	378
Antao Vaz	W		Portugal	1252	0.03	234
AR110	O			1	0.00	1160
AR99	O			5	0.00	1028
Aramon Bouschet	R					
Aramon Gris	W		France			
Aramon Noir	R	Amor-Nao-Me-Deixes(PT),Aramon(PT,FR)	France	2892	0.06	151
Aramont	W					
Aranel	W		France			
Arany Sarfeher	W	Sarfeher(HU), Izsaki(HU)	Hungary	1133	0.02	250
Arbane	W		France			
Argelina	R			1	0.00	1161
Ariana	R		Czech Rep	3	0.00	1071
Arinarnoa	R		France	32	0.00	793
Arinto de Bucelas	W	Arinto(PT),Pederna(PT)	Portugal	4446	0.10	118
Arinto Roxo	R			36	0.00	771
Arjuncao	R		Portugal	1	0.00	1177
Arneis	W		Italy	1122	0.02	252
Arnsburger	W		Germany	30	0.00	804
Aromon Blanc	W					
Arriloba	W		France	7	0.00	997
Arrufiac	W		France			
Arvesiniadu	W		Italy	30	0.00	809
Arvine	W	Petite Arvine(CH,IT)	Switzerland	172	0.00	535
Asirtiko red	R		Greece	5	0.00	1036
Aspiran Bouschet	R		France	3042	0.07	144
Asprouda	W	Asproudi(EL)		113	0.00	591
Assaraky	W			1	0.00	1159
Assyrtiko	W	Asirtiko(EL)	Greece	902	0.02	282
Athiri	W		Greece	748	0.02	308
Athiri (red)	R					
Aubin Blanc	W	Aubin(FR)	France			
Aubun	R		France	648	0.01	330
Aurelius	W		Czech Rep	70	0.00	672
Aurore	W	Aurora(US)	France	268	0.01	468
Auxerrois	W		France	2741	0.06	154
Avana	R		Italy	28	0.00	819
Avarengo	R		Italy	987	0.02	268
Avesso	W		Portugal	685	0.01	326
Azal	W	Azal Branco(PT)	Portugal	1072	0.02	262
Babeasca Gris	W	Babeasca Gri(RO)	Romania	328	0.01	435
Babeasca Neagra	R	Rara Neagra(MD)	Romania	3122	0.07	141
Babic	R		Croatia	359	0.01	418
Babica	R		Croatia	18	0.00	884
	W	Babosa(PT)	Spain	2	0.00	1103
Bacchus	W		Germany	2047	0.04	180
Baco Blanc	W	Baco Divers(FR)	France	773	0.02	303

Table 13 (cont.) Prime varieties' colour, country of origin, synonyms, and 2010 global area, share and rank

Prime variety	Col.	Synonyms	Country of origin	2010 Area (hectares)	Share (%)	Rank
Baco Noir	R	Baco(US),Baco Divers(FR)	France	467	0.01	382
Baga	R	Carrasquenho(PT),Carrega Burros(PT)	Portugal	4108	0.09	122
Bailey	R		USA	34	0.00	783
Bakator Roz	R	Piros Bakator(HU)	Hungary	2	0.00	1118
Baleille	W		France			
Baratuciat	W		Italy	2	0.00	1124
Barbarossa	O		Italy			
Barbaroux	O		France			
Barbera	R	Barbera Nera(IT)	Italy	24178	0.53	36
Barbera Bianca	W		Italy	181	0.00	529
Barbera Sarda	R		Italy	84	0.00	639
Barcelo	W		Portugal	23	0.00	853
Bariadorgia	W	Carcajolo Blanc(FR)	Italy			
Barkhatnyi	W	Barkhatny(RU)	Russia	30	0.00	807
Baroque	W		France	90	0.00	627
Barreto de Semente	R	Barreto(PT)	Portugal	3	0.00	1090
Barsaglina	R		Italy	17	0.00	890
Bastardillo	R					
Bastardo Branco	W			15	0.00	908
Bastardo Magarachsky	R	Bastardo Magaraceskii(MD),Bastardo Magarachskiy(UA)	Ukraine	2370	0.05	168
Batili	W					
Batily	R			54	0.00	713
Batoca	W		Portugal	11	0.00	937
Bayanshira	W	Bayan-shirey(KZ)	Azerbaijan	645	0.01	331
Beba	W	Breval(FR),Teta de Vaca (CA),Iso(ES)	Spain	3036	0.07	146
Beclan	R	Petit Beclan(FR)	France			
Bellandais	R		France			
Bellone	W		Italy	511	0.01	364
Bequignol Noir	R	Bequignol(FR)	France	698	0.02	321
Bianca	W		Hungary	6450	0.14	92
Biancame	W		Italy	2599	0.06	161
Bianchetta Trevigiana	W		Italy	13	0.00	916
Bianco d'Alessano	W		Italy	419	0.01	396
Biancolella	W		Italy	164	0.00	542
Biancone di Portoferraio	W	Biancone(IT)	Italy	78	0.00	656
Biancu Gentile	W		France			
Biborkadarka	R	Bibor Kadarka(HU)	Hungary	136	0.00	567
Bical	W		Portugal	924	0.02	275
Black Queen	R		Japan	486	0.01	374
Blanc Dame	W		France			
Blanc du Bois	W		USA	28	0.00	816
Blanca Ovoide	W			40	0.00	756
Blanqueiro	W	Blanqueiron(FR)	France			
Blattner Reds	R		Switzerland	39	0.00	761
Blattner Whites	W		Switzerland	25	0.00	831
Blauburger	R		Austria	1337	0.03	226
Blauer Portugieser	R	Modry Portugal(CZ,SI,AT),Portugais Blue (CL),Portugues Azul(PT), Portoghese(IT),Portugizac(HR)	Austria	3798	0.08	128
Blauer Wildbacher	R	Wildbacher(IT)	Austria	368	0.01	412

Table 13 (cont.) Prime varieties' colour, country of origin, synonyms, and 2010 global area, share and rank

Prime variety	Col.	Synonyms	Country of origin	2010 Area (hectares)	Share (%)	Rank
Blaufrankisch	R	Burgund Mare (RO), Franconia(IT), Frankovka (CZ,SI,HR), Frankovka Modra(SK), Lemberger(CA,US), Modra Frankinja(SI), Borgonja(HR), Borgona(PE)	Austria	16141	0.35	48
Blush Seedless	R		USA			
Boal Barreiro	W			1	0.00	1198
Boal Vencedor	W	Vencedor(PT)	Portugal	2	0.00	1095
Bobal	R		Spain	80120	1.74	12
Bogazkere	R		Turkey	1106	0.02	253
Bogdanusa	W		Croatia	48	0.00	739
Boiziau	R		France			
Bombino Bianco	W		Italy	1239	0.03	235
Bombino Nero	R		Italy	1201	0.03	243
Bonamico	R	Buonamico(AR)	Italy	193	0.00	521
Bonarda Grande	R					
Bonda	R		Italy	7	0.00	1000
Bondola	R		Switzerland	13	0.00	923
Bordo	R		USA	8287	0.18	80
Borracal	R	Caino Tinto(ES)	Portugal	683	0.01	327
Bosco	W		Italy	82	0.00	644
Bouchales	R		France			
Bouillet	R		France			
Bourboulenc	W		France	597	0.01	344
Bousquet Precoce	W	Precoce Bousquet(FR)	France			
Bouvier	W	Bouvierovo Hrozno(SK)	Slovenia	250	0.01	481
Bracciola Nera	R	Bracciola(IT)	Italy	26	0.00	827
Brachetto del Piemonte	R	Brachetto(IT)	Italy	1460	0.03	211
Branco Especial	W		Portugal	3	0.00	1069
Branco Sr. Joao	W	Branco Joao(PT)	Portugal	0	0.00	1213
Branco Valente	W	Valente(PT)	Portugal	0	0.00	1240
Brandam	W	Branda(PT)	Portugal	312	0.01	444
Braquet Noir	R	Brachet(FR)	France			
Breidecker	W		Germany	7	0.00	996
Brianna	W		USA	12	0.00	928
Bric	R		Italy	2	0.00	1099
Brocada	W					
Bronner	W		Germany	6	0.00	1014
Brun Argente	R		France			
Budai Zold	W		Hungary	6	0.00	1007
Bukettraube	W		Germany	71	0.00	670
Burdin	W	Burdin Divers(FR)				
Bussanello	W		Italy	12	0.00	936
Busuioaca de Bohotin	O		Romania	268	0.01	467
Caberinta	R		Argentina	47	0.00	742
Cabernet Cortis	R		Germany	20	0.00	867
Cabernet Cubin	R		Germany	40	0.00	757
Cabernet Diane	R			0	0.00	1215
Cabernet Dore	W			1	0.00	1141
Cabernet Dorio	R		Germany	20	0.00	868
Cabernet Dorsa	R		Germany	223	0.00	501
Cabernet Franc	R	Kamberne Fran(EL)	Spain	53599	1.16	17
Cabernet Jura	R		Switzerland	19	0.00	876
Cabernet Malbec	R		France			

Table 13 (cont.) Prime varieties' colour, country of origin, synonyms, and 2010 global area, share and rank

Prime variety	Col.	Synonyms	Country of origin	2010 Area (hectares)	Share (%)	Rank
Cabernet Mitos	R		Germany	282	0.01	459
Cabernet Moravia	R		Czech Rep	212	0.00	505
Cabernet Sauvignon	R	Cabernet(PE,TN,AM), Burdeos(PE),Kamberne Sovinion(EL)	France	290091	6.30	1
Cabinda	R		Portugal	362	0.01	416
Cabral	R	Malvasia Cabral(PT)	Portugal	2	0.00	1119
Caddiu	R		Italy	309	0.01	448
Cainho de Moreira	W	Cainho(PT)	Portugal	7	0.00	988
Caino Blanco	W		Portugal	121	0.00	581
Caladoc	R		France	3675	0.08	129
Calagrano	W		Spain	4794	0.10	110
California	O		USA	252	0.01	480
Calitor Blanc	W		France			
Calitor Gris	W		France			
Calitor Noir	R		France			
Calkarasi	R		Turkey	625	0.01	339
Callet	R		Spain	154	0.00	547
Caloria	R		Italy	108	0.00	599
Calrao	R			1	0.00	1156
Camaralet de Lasseube	W	Camarate(PT)	France	515	0.01	361
Campanario	R		Portugal	2	0.00	1117
Campbell Early	R		USA	61	0.00	692
Canada Muscat	W		USA			
Canadice	R		USA	0	0.00	1235
Canaiolo Nero	R		Italy	1068	0.02	263
Canaiolo Rosa	W		Italy	1	0.00	1187
Canari Noir	R	Canari(AR), Folle Noire(UY)	France	152	0.00	549
Canela	R		Spain	2	0.00	1122
Canelon	O			8	0.00	981
Canorroyo	W		Spain			
Capolongo	W			5	0.00	1027
Caracol	W		Portugal	33	0.00	792
Caramela	W			0	0.00	1207
Cardinal	R	Kardinal Crveni(HR),Cardenal(MX)	USA	545	0.01	354
Carica l'Asino	W		Italy	17	0.00	887
Carignan Blanc	W	Carinena Blanco (ES),Carinena Blanca(FR)	France	3061	0.07	143
Carignan Bouschet	R		France			
Carignan Gris	W		Spain			
Carmenere	R	Carmenere(US,CA,HU,IT,BR),Cabernet Gernischt(CN),Carmenere Crni(HR)	France	11360	0.25	62
Carmine	R		USA			
Carminoir	R		Switzerland	10	0.00	951
Carnelian	R		USA	316	0.01	442
Carrega Branco	W		Portugal	507	0.01	367
Carrega Tinto	R		Portugal	17	0.00	889
Carricante	W		Italy	205	0.00	514
Cartouche	W					
Casavecchia	R		Italy	136	0.00	566
Casculho	R		Portugal	267	0.01	469
Casetta	R		Italy	12	0.00	926
Castalia	W		Portugal	0	0.00	1243
Castel	R	Castel Divers(FR)	France	2	0.00	1102

Table 13 (cont.) Prime varieties' colour, country of origin, synonyms, and 2010 global area, share and rank

Prime variety	Col.	Synonyms	Country of origin	2010 Area (hectares)	Share (%)	Rank
Castela	R		Portugal	8	0.00	983
Castelao	R	Periquita(PT),Casteloa(PT)	Portugal	11088	0.24	64
Castelao Branco	W		Portugal	37	0.00	765
Castelino	R		Portugal	147	0.00	553
Castelo Branco	W		Portugal	5	0.00	1042
Castets	R		France			
Castiglione	R		Italy	18	0.00	881
Castonotal	W					
Catalanesca	W		Italy	54	0.00	714
Catanese Nero	R		Italy	15	0.00	907
Catarratto Bianco	W	Catarratto Bianco Comune(IT),Catarratto Bianco Lucido(IT),Catarratto(US)	Italy	34863	0.76	28
Catawba	R		USA	633	0.01	337
Cavrara	R		Italy	23	0.00	850
Cavus	W		Turkey	3	0.00	1091
Cayetana Blanca	W	Pardina (ES),Robal(ES), Sarigo(PT),Blanca Cayetana(ES),Mourisco Branco(PT),Baladi Verdejo(ES)	Spain	39741	0.86	22
Cayuga White	W	Cayuga(US)	USA	212	0.00	506
Cellerina	R	Slarina (IT)	Italy	2	0.00	1127
Centenial Seedless	W		USA			
Centesimino	R		Italy	24	0.00	841
Centurian	R		USA	34	0.00	784
Cep Rouge	R		France			
Cerceal Branco	W	Cercial(PT)	Portugal	379	0.01	404
Cereza	O		Argentina	29189	0.63	34
Cesanese	R	Cesanese Comune(IT),Cesanese d'Affile(IT)	Italy	679	0.01	329
Cesar	R		France			
Cetinka	W		Croatia	35	0.00	782
Chambourcin	R		France	1130	0.02	251
Chancellor	R		France	49	0.00	734
Chardonel	W		USA	144	0.00	556
Chardonnay	W	Chardonnay Blanc(BG),Sardone(EL)	France	198793	4.32	5
Charmont	W		Switzerland	10	0.00	966
Chasan	W		France	801	0.02	301
Chasselas	W	Chasselas Dorato(IT), Chaslas(RU),Chaselas Dorada(ES),Weißer Gutedel(DE),Plemenka Bijela(HR)	Switzerland	13186	0.29	54
Chasselas Rouge	R	Chasselas Roxo(PT),Chasselas Rose(FR)		7	0.00	1001
Chasselas Sabor	W		Portugal	0	0.00	1262
Chatus	R		France	13	0.00	917
Chelois	R		France	1	0.00	1179
Chelva	W	Uva Rey(ES)	Spain	6168	0.13	97
Chenanson	R		France	506	0.01	368
Chenel	W		S. Africa	79	0.00	653
Chenin Blanc	W	Chenin(FR,MM,IT,UY)	France	35164	0.76	26
Chenivesse	R		France			
Chinuri	W		Georgia	1225	0.03	239
Chkhaveri	O		Georgia	26	0.00	829
Cianorie	R	Cjanorie(IT)	Italy	2	0.00	1093

Table 13 (cont.) Prime varieties' colour, country of origin, synonyms, and 2010 global area, share and rank

Prime variety	Col.	Synonyms	Country of origin	2010 Area (hectares)	Share (%)	Rank
Cidreiro	R		Portugal	0	0.00	1250
Ciliegiolo	R		Italy	1830	0.04	189
Cinsaut	R	Ottavianello(IT), Cinsault(MA,CL,CN,TR),Black Malvoisie(US),Senso(EL), Cargadora(CL)	France	36040	0.78	25
Cinsaut Blanc	W		France	7	0.00	994
Cinsaut Seedless	R			13	0.00	920
Citronny Magarach	W	Citronny of Magarach (RU)	Ukraine	307	0.01	449
Cividin	W		Italy	4	0.00	1048
Clairette	W	Clairet (RU),Clairette Blanche(ZA)	France	2900	0.06	150
Clairette Rose	W		France	260	0.01	473
Clarin	W		France			
Claverie	W		France			
Cococciola	W		Italy	983	0.02	269
Coda di Volpe Bianca	W	Guarnaccia(IT)	Italy	586	0.01	347
Codega de Larinho	W	Codega do Larinho(PT)	Portugal	629	0.01	338
Codivarta	W		France			
Codrinski	R			5	0.00	1029
Colgadero	R			5	0.00	1030
Colobel	R		France	0	0.00	1236
Colombana Nera	R	Colombana Nero(IT)	Italy	38	0.00	764
Colombard	W	French Colombard (US),Colombar(ZA)	France	32076	0.70	32
Colomino	W		S. Africa	5	0.00	1040
Coloraillo	R		Spain	374	0.01	407
Completer	W		Switzerland	3	0.00	1074
Complexa	R		Portugal	103	0.00	610
Concieira	R		Portugal	52	0.00	722
Concord	R	Concord Clone 30(BR)	USA	12238	0.27	58
Coracao de Galo	R		Portugal	1	0.00	1182
Corbina Vicentina	R	Corbina(IT)	Italy	12	0.00	929
Cordenossa	R		Italy	5	0.00	1025
Cornalin	R	Humagne Rouge(CH)	Italy	256	0.01	475
Cornarea	R		Italy	13	0.00	918
Cornifesto	R		Portugal	499	0.01	372
Corot Noir	R		USA	27	0.00	826
Corropio	R		Spain	1	0.00	1143
Cortese	W		Italy	2953	0.06	148
Corvina Veronese	R	Corvina(IT)	Italy	7496	0.16	87
Corvinone	R		Italy	930	0.02	274
Corvo	R		Portugal	0	0.00	1208
Cot	R	Malbec(PE,ZA,BR,US,TR,AU,MD,CA, ES,AR,CL,NZ),Malbech(IT), Mancin(FR)	France	40688	0.88	21
Couderc	W	Couderc Divers(FR),Couderc 13(BR)	France	834	0.02	297
Couderc Noir	R	Couderc(FR,BR)	France	2691	0.06	157
Counoise	R		France	443	0.01	391
Courbu Blanc	W	Courbu(FR)	France			
Courbu Noir	R		France			
Cove	W		Italy	6	0.00	1003
Cramposie Selectionata	W		Romania	409	0.01	397
Crimson Cabernet	R			1	0.00	1142
Crimson Seedless	R		USA	2	0.00	1105

Table 13 (cont.) Prime varieties' colour, country of origin, synonyms, and 2010 global area, share and rank

Prime variety	Col.	Synonyms	Country of origin	2010 Area (hectares)	Share (%)	Rank
Criolla Grande	R		Argentina	17080	0.37	44
Criolla Mediana	R		Argentina	9	0.00	975
Croatina	R		Croatia	5700	0.12	102
Crouchen	W		France	724	0.02	312
Crovassa	R		Italy	0	0.00	1234
Crystal	W	Cristal(PE,CL)	China	175	0.00	534
Cs.2	R			0	0.00	1260
Csaba Gyongye	W	Csabagyongye(HU)	Hungary	89	0.00	630
Cserszegi Fuszeres	W		Hungary	3609	0.08	131
Csillam	W		Hungary	20	0.00	872
Csokaszolo	R		Hungary	2	0.00	1100
Csomorika	W		Hungary	0	0.00	1210
Dakapo	R		Germany	53	0.00	720
Dalkauer	W		Germany			
Damaschino	W	Alicante Branco(PT),Planta Fina (ES),Faranah(FR),Valenci(AR)	Italy	2083	0.05	178
Danlas	W		France	254	0.01	478
Dawn Seedless	W		USA			
De Chaunac	R		France	91	0.00	625
De Cilindro	W		Spain			
Debina	W	Dempina(EL)	Greece	239	0.01	489
Debit	W		Croatia	403	0.01	398
Deckrot	R		Germany	10	0.00	953
Decuerno	R					
Dekabrskii	R	Dekabrsky(RU)	Moldova	78	0.00	655
Delaware	O		USA	127	0.00	579
Deliciosa	R		Portugal	0	0.00	1257
Devin	W		Slovakia	133	0.00	573
Diagalves	W		Portugal	1156	0.03	248
Dimrit	R		Turkey	863	0.02	288
Dimyat	W	Zoumiatiko(EL),Smederevka(HR),Dimiat(BG)	Bulgaria	2401	0.05	166
Dindarella	R		Italy	7	0.00	998
Diolinoir	R		Switzerland	114	0.00	590
Diseca Ranina	W		Croatia	2	0.00	1120
Docal	R		Portugal	0	0.00	1246
Doina	R		Moldova	227	0.00	498
Dolcetto	R		Italy	6333	0.14	94
Dolciame	W		Italy	11	0.00	948
Domina	R		Germany	361	0.01	417
Dominga	W		Spain	1	0.00	1162
Dona Branca	W		Portugal	276	0.01	462
Dona Joaquina	W		Portugal	24	0.00	844
Donzelinho Branco	W		Portugal	65	0.00	682
Donzelinho Roxo	R		Portugal	0	0.00	1255
Donzelinho Tinto	R		Portugal	33	0.00	789
Doradilla	W		Spain	40	0.00	758
Doradillo	W		Spain			
Doral	W		Switzerland	27	0.00	824
Dorinto	W	Arinto do Interior(PT)	Portugal	115	0.00	588
Dornfelder	R		Germany	8101	0.18	84
Dostoinyi	R		Russia	65	0.00	683
Douce Noire	R	Bonarda(AR,IT,BR),Turca(IT),Charbono(US),Corbeau(FR)	France	18976	0.41	40

Table 13 (cont.) Prime varieties' colour, country of origin, synonyms, and 2010 global area, share and rank

Prime variety	Col.	Synonyms	Country of origin	2010 Area (hectares)	Share (%)	Rank
Doukkali	R			16557	0.36	47
Doux d'Henry	R		Italy	9	0.00	967
Droujba	W	Drujba(MD)	Bulgaria	3	0.00	1072
Drupeggio	W	Canaiolo Bianco(IT)	Italy	286	0.01	456
Duna Gyongye	R		Hungary	63	0.00	685
Dunaj	R		Slovakia	46	0.00	744
Dunavski Lazur	W		Bulgaria	483	0.01	375
Dunkelfelder	R		Germany	329	0.01	434
Dunze	R					
Duras	R		France	923	0.02	276
Durasa	R		Italy	6	0.00	1015
Durella	W		Italy	470	0.01	379
Durif	R	Petite Syrah (CL),Petite Sirah(US,BR)	France	3557	0.08	133
Edelweiss	W		USA	32	0.00	798
Ederena	R		France			
Egiodola	R		France	372	0.01	408
Ehrenbreitsteiner	W		Germany			
Ehrenfelser	W		Germany	79	0.00	654
Ekigaina	R		France	1	0.00	1151
Ekim Kara	R		Ukraine	27	0.00	825
Elbling	W	Burger (US),Elbling Weisser(DE)	Germany	1418	0.03	217
Elbling Rot	R	Elbling Roter(DE)	Germany			
Elvira	W		USA	263	0.01	471
Emerald Riesling	W		USA	164	0.00	541
Emerald seedless	W		USA			
Emir	W		Turkey	688	0.01	324
Enantio	R	Lambrusco a Foglia Frastagliata(IT)	Italy	724	0.02	311
Encruzado	W		Portugal	282	0.01	458
Ensanyo Tintas	R			27	0.00	822
Ensayo Blancas	W			1	0.00	1163
Erbaluce	W		Italy	319	0.01	441
Erbamat	W		Italy	24	0.00	843
Erbanno	R			0	0.00	1259
Ervi	R		Italy	4	0.00	1045
Esganacao Preto	R	Esgana Cao Tinto(PT)	Portugal	0	0.00	1267
Esganinho	W		Portugal	0	0.00	1252
Espadeiro	R		Portugal	469	0.01	380
Espadeiro Mole	R		Portugal	0	0.00	1221
Estreito Macio	W		Portugal	3	0.00	1083
Etraire de l'Adui	R		France			
Ezerfurtu	W		Hungary	377	0.01	405
Ezerjo	W		Hungary	1074	0.02	261
Faberrebe	W	Faber(UK)	Germany	524	0.01	356
Falanghina	W		Italy	3037	0.07	145
Famoso	W		Italy	6	0.00	1009
Farinheira	R		Portugal	3	0.00	1075
Fenile	W		Italy	5	0.00	1022
Fepiro	R		Portugal	0	0.00	1268
Fer	R		France	1817	0.04	190
Fernao Pires	W	Molinha(PT)	Portugal	9511	0.21	74
Fernao Pires Rosado	R		Portugal	98	0.00	615
Fertilia	R		Italy	3	0.00	1064
Feteasca Alba	W	Dievcie Hrozno(SK)	Moldova	17469	0.38	43
Feteasca Neagra	R		Moldova	1719	0.04	196

Table 13 (cont.) Prime varieties' colour, country of origin, synonyms, and 2010 global area, share and rank

Prime variety	Col.	Synonyms	Country of origin	2010 Area (hectares)	Share (%)	Rank
Feteasca Regala	W		Romania	13136	0.29	55
Feunate	R		France			
Fiano	W		Italy	1377	0.03	222
Fiesta	W		USA	230	0.00	493
Fileri	W			97	0.00	618
Fino de Ribera del Fresno	W			45	0.00	746
Fintendo	R		Spain	183	0.00	526
Fioletovy Ranny	R		Russia	50	0.00	730
Flame Seedless	R		USA	42	0.00	754
Flavis	W		Italy	3	0.00	1067
Flora	O		USA	8	0.00	985
Florental	R		France			
Fogarina	R		Italy	5	0.00	1026
Foglia Tonda	R		Italy	101	0.00	611
Fogoneu	R		Spain	35	0.00	778
Fokiano	R		Greece	262	0.01	472
Fokiano (white)	W		Greece			
Folgasao	W		Portugal	182	0.00	528
Folgasao Roxo	R		Portugal	18	0.00	879
Folha de Figueira	W		Portugal	3	0.00	1062
Folle Blanche	W		France	1845	0.04	188
Fontan	R		France			
Fontanara	W		Germany			
Fonte Cal	W		Portugal	111	0.00	595
Forastera	W		Italy	208	0.00	512
Forcallat Tinta	R		Spain	1163	0.03	247
Forgiarin	R		Italy	4	0.00	1051
Forsellina	R		Italy	7	0.00	992
Fortana	R	Canina Nera(IT)	Italy	642	0.01	334
Francavidda	W		Italy	13	0.00	924
Francusa	W		Romania	621	0.01	340
Frappato	R		Italy	752	0.02	307
Fredonia	R		USA	37	0.00	769
Freisa	R		Italy	1049	0.02	264
Freisamer	W		Germany	4	0.00	1044
Frontenac	R		USA	135	0.00	568
Frontenac gris	W		USA	59	0.00	701
Fruhroter Veltliner	R	Korai Piros Veltelini (HU),Malvasier(AT), Veltlinske Cervene Rane (CZ),Veltlinske Cervene Skore(SK),Velteliner Rouge Precoce(FR),Veltliner Fruehrot(FR)	Austria	846	0.02	294
Fubiano	W		Italy	9	0.00	970
	R		France			
Fumin	R		Italy	31	0.00	800
Furmint	W	Šipon(SI),Moslavac(HR),Sipelj(HR),Malvasia Verde(BR)	Hungary	5259	0.11	104
Gaglioppo	R		Italy	4214	0.09	120
Gaillard	R	Gaillard Divers(FR)	France			
Galbena de Odobesti	W		Romania	385	0.01	402
Galego Dourado	W	Galego(PT) ,Pedro Luis(ES,ZA)	Portugal	16	0.00	897
Galotta	R		Switzerland	13	0.00	919
Gamaret	R		Switzerland	399	0.01	399

Table 13 (cont.) Prime varieties' colour, country of origin, synonyms, and 2010 global area, share and rank

Prime variety	Col.	Synonyms	Country of origin	2010 Area (hectares)	Share (%)	Rank
Gamay de Teinturier Bouze	R	Gammay de Bouze(MD),Gamays Teinturiers(FR)	France	225	0.00	500
Gamay Noir	R	Gamay Beaujolais(BR), Gamay(FR,PT,CL,UK,UY),Gamay Precoce(FR),Plant Robert(CH),Gamay St Romain(BR)	France	32671	0.71	30
Gamay Teinturier de Chaudenay	R	Gamay de Chaudenay(FR)	Germany	24	0.00	846
Gamay Teinturier Freaux	R	Gammay Freaux(MD)	Germany	55	0.00	706
Gamba Rossa	R		Italy	0	0.00	1232
Ganson	R		France			
Garandmak	W		Armenia	931	0.02	273
Garanoir	R	Granoir(IT)	Switzerland	216	0.00	503
Garganega	W	Grecanico Dorato(IT)	Italy	15402	0.33	50
Gargiulo	R	c g 45803(AR),c.g.2539(AR), c.g.4113(AR)	Argentina	47	0.00	741
Garnacha Blanca	W	Grenache Blanc(SZ,FR,US,HR)	Spain	7370	0.16	88
Garnacha Peluda	R	Lledoner Pelut (FR)	Spain	1232	0.03	236
Garnacha Roja	W	Grenache Gris(FR,TH), Grenas Rose(EL)	Spain	1784	0.04	192
Garnacha Tinta	R	Tocai Rosso(IT),Cannonao(IT), Grenache Noir(HR),Cannonau(IT), Vernaccia Nera (IT), Garnacha(ES,AR,BR,CL), Grenache(FR,MA,CN, AU,US,TR,CY,PE,ZA,NZ,BR,PT,TN,AM,DZ,CA,MX),Vernaccia Nera Grossa(IT),Vernaccina Nero(IT)	Spain	184735	4.01	7
Garonnet	R		France			
Garrido Fino	W		Spain	59	0.00	700
Gascon	R		France			
Gateta	R		Spain	2	0.00	1106
Gegic	W		Croatia	11	0.00	941
Geisenheim	R	Geisenheim Hybrids (CA)	Germany	106	0.00	605
Generosa	W		Portugal	107	0.00	603
Gesztus	W		Hungary	0	0.00	1230
Gewurztraminer	W	Tramin Cerveny(SI,CZ), Traminer Aromatico(IT),Traminer Rose(MA,UA),Traminer Rot(BG),Traminer Roz(RO),Traminac Crveni(HR), Traminer(AU,AT)		14269	0.31	53
Gibi	W		Spain	917	0.02	278
Ginestra	W		Italy	4	0.00	1054
Giro	R		Italy	200	0.00	516
GM 322	R			17	0.00	891
Godello	W	Agudello (ES),Godelho(PT),Gouveio(PT,BR)	Spain	1094	0.02	255
Goecseji Zamatos	W	Gocseji Zamatos(HU),Gecsei Zamatos(RU)	Hungary	55	0.00	705
Goher	W		Hungary	1	0.00	1194
Goldburger	W		Austria	140	0.00	560
Golden Muscat	W		USA	1	0.00	1183
Goldriesling	W		France	20	0.00	869
Goldtraminer	W		Italy	9	0.00	973
Golubok	R	Goluboc(MD)	Ukraine	87	0.00	632

Table 13 (cont.) Prime varieties' colour, country of origin, synonyms, and 2010 global area, share and rank

Prime variety	Col.	Synonyms	Country of origin	2010 Area (hectares)	Share (%)	Rank
Goncalo Pires	R		Portugal	1	0.00	1189
Goruli Mtsvane	W		Georgia	287	0.01	454
Gosen	R		Italy	1	0.00	1138
Gouais Blanc	W	Gouais(CH)	France			
Gouget Noir	R	Gouget(FR)	France			
Goustolidi	W		Greece	68	0.00	675
Gouveio Preto	R		Portugal	0	0.00	1226
Gouveio Real	W	Gouveio Estimado(PT)	Portugal	582	0.01	348
Gouveio Roxo	R		Portugal	238	0.01	491
GR 7	R		USA	32	0.00	796
Grachen	W		S. Africa	2	0.00	1098
Graciano	R	Tinta Miuda(PT),Cagnulari(IT), Morrastel(FR), Graciana(AR), Bovale(IT),Tintilla de Rota(ES),Tinta Fontes(PT)	Spain	3102	0.07	142
Graisse	W		France			
Gramon	R		France			
Grand Manchen	W			8	0.00	982
Grand Noir	R	Gran Negro(ES),Grand Noir de la Calmette(FR)	France	955	0.02	271
Grangeal	R		Portugal	1	0.00	1150
Granho	W		Portugal	0	0.00	1233
Grapariol	W		Italy	2	0.00	1101
Grasa de Cotnari	W	Koverszolo(HU)	Romania	685	0.01	325
Grasevina	W	Borba(ES),Ryzlink Vlaƙy(CZ), Welschriesling(HU,AT,BR,BG,CZ,PT,SI,SK),Riesling Italian(RO),Riesling Italico(IT),Laƙi Rizling(SI),Rizling Vlašky(SK), Italian Riesling(HU,RS), Grasevina Bijela(HR),	Croatia	61200	1.33	15
Grassen	R		France			
Grechetto di Orvieto	W	Grechetto(IT)	Italy	1501	0.03	208
Grechetto Rosso	R		Italy	49	0.00	737
Greco	W	Asprinio(IT),Grec(EL),Greco di Tufo(AR)	Italy	158	0.00	546
Greco Bianco	W		Italy	1604	0.03	202
Greco Nero	R		Italy	1223	0.03	240
Grenache Rose	R	Grenas Rose(EL)		645	0.01	332
Grignolino	R		Italy	915	0.02	279
Grillo	W		Italy	6295	0.14	95
Gringet	W		France			
Grolleau Gris	W		France	454	0.01	386
Grolleau Noir	R	Grolleau(FR)	France	2350	0.05	170
Groppello di Mocasina	R	Groppello di Santo Stefano(IT)	Italy	81	0.00	648
Groppello di Revo	R		Italy	12	0.00	931
Groppello Gentile	R		Italy	326	0.01	437
Gros bec	R					
Gros Manseng	W		France	4995	0.11	108
Grossa	R		Portugal	73	0.00	662
Gruner Veltliner	W	Veltliner(IT),Veltlinske Zelene(SI,CZ)	Austria	18842	0.41	41
Guardavalle	W		Italy	33	0.00	788
Guillemot	W		France			
Gutenborner	W		Germany	2	0.00	1107

Table 13 (cont.) Prime varieties' colour, country of origin, synonyms, and 2010 global area, share and rank

Prime variety	Col.	Synonyms	Country of origin	2010 Area (hectares)	Share (%)	Rank
Gyongyrizling	W		Hungary	23	0.00	848
Hajnalka	W		Hungary	0	0.00	1264
Harslevelu	W	Lipovina(SK) Feuille de Tilleul(HU)	Hungary	1856	0.04	187
Hegel	R		Germany			
Helfensteiner	R		Germany	10	0.00	954
Herbemont	R		USA	764	0.02	306
Heroldrebe	R		Germany	140	0.00	561
Himbertscha	W		Switzerland			
Himrod	W		USA	0	0.00	1209
Holder	W		Germany			
Hondarrabi Beltza	R	Ondarrabi Beltza(ES),Beltza(CL)	Spain	53	0.00	716
Hrvatica	R	Negrara(IT)	Croatia	116	0.00	586
Huerta del Rey	W		Spain	2	0.00	1108
Humagne	W	Humagne Blanc(CH)	Switzerland	30	0.00	805
Huxelrebe	W		Germany	607	0.01	343
Ilichevskii Rannii	R	Iliciovski Ciornai Rannii(MD)	Ukraine	5	0.00	1031
Imperial Napoleon	R		Spain	12	0.00	935
Imperial Seedless	O			1	0.00	1164
Impigno	W		Italy	7	0.00	993
Incrocio Bianco Fedit 51	W		Italy	5	0.00	1037
Incrocio Bruni 54	W		Italy	12	0.00	932
Incrocio Manzoni 2.15	R		Italy	86	0.00	636
Incrocio Terzi 1	R		Italy	44	0.00	749
Invernenga	W		Italy	7	0.00	1002
Inzolia	W	Ansonica(IT)	Italy	6133	0.13	98
Irsai Oliver	W	Muskat Oliver(CH)	Hungary	1414	0.03	218
Isabella	R	Lidia(MD,UA), Isabel(BR),Isabel Precoce(BR), Frutilla(UY)	USA	32494	0.71	31
Italia	W		Italy	1145	0.02	249
Italica	W		Italy	367	0.01	413
Ives	R		USA	16	0.00	896
J ibanez	R			35	0.00	779
Jacquere	W		France	1028	0.02	265
Jacquez	R	Lenoir(MX),Black Spanish(US)	USA	2368	0.05	169
Jampal	W	Pinheira Branca(PT)	Portugal	71	0.00	668
Joannes Seyve	R	Johan.Seyve D.(FR)	France			
Johanniter	W		Germany	51	0.00	725
Joubertin	R		France			
Juan Garcia	R	Tinta Gorda(ES),Mouraton(ES),Gorda(PT)	Spain	1707	0.04	198
Jubilaumsrebe	W		Austria	14	0.00	914
Jubileum 75	R		Hungary	194	0.00	520
Juhfark	W		Hungary	186	0.00	525
Juliana	W			0	0.00	1237
Jurancon Blanc	W		France			
Jurancon Noir	R		France	706	0.02	319
Jurie	W	Jurie Divers(FR)	France			
Juwel	W		Germany	10	0.00	955
K.35	W			0	0.00	1245
Kabar	W		Hungary	18	0.00	883
Kadarka	R	Gamza(BG)	Hungary	1087	0.02	258
Kakotrygis	W		Greece	103	0.00	608
Kalecik Karasi	R		Turkey	861	0.02	291
Kanaan	W			25	0.00	835
Kangun	W		Armenia	850	0.02	293

Table 13 (cont.) Prime varieties' colour, country of origin, synonyms, and 2010 global area, share and rank

Prime variety	Col.	Synonyms	Country of origin	2010 Area (hectares)	Share (%)	Rank
Kanzler	W		Germany	10	0.00	956
Karalahna	R		Turkey	4	0.00	1055
Karasakiz	R	Kuntra(TR)	Turkey	4	0.00	1056
Karat	W		Hungary	50	0.00	729
Karinian	W					
Karmin	R		Hungary	36	0.00	774
Kay Gray	W		USA	1	0.00	1140
Kek Bakator	W			3	0.00	1088
Keknyelu	W		Hungary	43	0.00	751
Kerner	W	Kerner Bijeli(HR)	Germany	3994	0.09	125
Kernling	W		Germany	15	0.00	901
Khikhvi	W		Georgia	6	0.00	1004
Kiralyleanyka	W		Hungary	855	0.02	292
Kisi	W		Georgia	26	0.00	830
Knipperle	W		France			
Koenigin der Weingaerten	W	Regina dei Vigneti(IT),Tzaritza Na	Hungary	61	0.00	691
Koksis Irma	W	Kocsis Irma(HU)		11	0.00	945
Kokur Bely	W	Cokur white(UA)	Ukraine	918	0.02	277
Kolor	R		Germany	2	0.00	1109
Korinthiaki	R	Corinto Nero(IT),Corinto(PE), Currant(AU),Black Corinth(US)	Greece	54	0.00	711
Korona	W		Hungary	1	0.00	1200
Koshu	O		Japan	168	0.00	538
Kotsifali	R		Greece	2330	0.05	171
Kovidinka	O	Ruzica Crvena(HR)	Hungary	1075	0.02	260
Krakhuna	W		Georgia	46	0.00	743
Kraljevina	W		Croatia	447	0.01	389
Krasnostop Zolotovsky	R	Krasnostop Anapsky(RU)	Russia	562	0.01	352
Krassato	R		Greece	52	0.00	723
Kreaca	W	Banati Rizling(HU)	Serbia	3	0.00	1081
Kujundzusa	W		Croatia	206	0.00	513
Kuldzhinskii	O	Kuldzhinskiy(KZ)	Kazakhstan	385	0.01	401
Kunbarat	W		Hungary	9	0.00	979
Kunleany	W		Hungary	1211	0.03	242
Kurucver	R		Hungary	0	0.00	1249
La Crescent	W		USA	77	0.00	658
La Crosse	W		USA	25	0.00	832
Labrusco	R		Portugal	81	0.00	647
Lacoste	R	Auxerrois Rupes(FR)	France			
Lacrima Christi	R		Italy	85	0.00	637
Lacrima di Morro d'Alba	R	Lacrima(IT)	Italy	421	0.01	395
Lado	W		Spain	1	0.00	1165
Lafnetscha	W		Switzerland			
Lagarino Bianco	W		Italy	23	0.00	855
Lagrein	R		Italy	717	0.02	315
Lairen	W	Malvar(ES)	Spain	214	0.00	504
Lakhegyi Mezes	W		Hungary	306	0.01	451
Lambrusca di Alessandria	R		Italy	137	0.00	565
Lambrusco	R		Italy	45	0.00	745
Lambrusco Barghi	R		Italy	18	0.00	
Lambrusco di Sorbara	R		Italy	1606	0.03	201
Lambrusco Grasparossa	R		Italy	2738	0.06	156
Lambrusco Maestri	R		Italy	2272	0.05	172
Lambrusco Marani	R		Italy	1394	0.03	221

Table 13 (cont.) Prime varieties' colour, country of origin, synonyms, and 2010 global area, share and rank

Prime variety	Col.	Synonyms	Country of origin	2010 Area (hectares)	Share (%)	Rank
Lambrusco Montericco	R		Italy	70	0.00	671
Lambrusco Oliva	R		Italy	112	0.00	593
Lambrusco Salamino	R		Italy	5003	0.11	107
Lambrusco Viadanese	R		Italy	240	0.01	486
Lameiro	W		Portugal	0	0.00	1218
Landal	R		France			
Landot	W	Landot Divers(FR)	France			
Landot Noir	R	Landot(US, FR)	France	2	0.00	1094
Lariao	W		Portugal	4	0.00	1059
Lasina	R		Croatia	14	0.00	910
Laska	R	Lasca(FR)	Austria			
Laurot	R		Czech Rep	6	0.00	1013
Lauzet	W		France			
Leanyka	W		Hungary	838	0.02	296
Lecinaro	R			1	0.00	1192
Leira	W		Portugal	1	0.00	1197
Len de l'El	W		France	640	0.01	335
Leon Millot	R		France	23	0.00	849
Leopoldo III	R					
Levokumski Sustainable	O			170	0.00	536
Levokumsky	R			720	0.02	314
Liatiko	R		Greece	1211	0.03	241
Liatiko(white)	W		Greece			
Liliorila	W		France			
Limnio	R		Greece	372	0.01	409
Limnio(white)	W					
Listain de Huelva	W	Manteudo(PT)	Spain	350	0.01	422
Listan Negro	R	Almuneco(ES),Negra Commun (ES)	Spain	2666	0.06	160
Listan Prieto	R	Mission(US),Pais (CL),Moscatel Negra(CL),Moscatel Negro(ES),Criolla Chica(AR)	Spain	4564	0.10	115
Listrao Roxo	R	Listrao(PT)	Portugal			
Lorena	W		Brazil	519	0.01	359
Louise Swenson	W		USA	3	0.00	1076
Loureiro	W	Loureiro Blanca(ES),	Portugal	4054	0.09	124
Lourela	R		Portugal	0	0.00	1238
Lumassina	W		Italy	98	0.00	617
Lusitano	R		Portugal	0	0.00	1256
Luzidio	W		Portugal	0	0.00	1231
Macabeo	W	Macabeu(FR)	Spain	41046	0.89	20
Maceratino	W		Italy	177	0.00	532
Madeleine Angevine	W		France	52	0.00	724
Madeleine Sylvaner	W		Portugal	7	0.00	991
Magliocco Canino	R		Italy	539	0.01	355
Magliocco Dolce	R	Marsigliana Nera(IT)	Italy	87	0.00	633
Magyarfrankos	R	Magyar Frankos (HU)	Hungary	0	0.00	1216
Maiolica	R		Italy	26	0.00	828
Maiolina	R		Italy	1	0.00	1131
Maiskii Chernyi	R	Mayskiy(KZ)	Moldova	110	0.00	598
Malaga Blanc	W		Thailand	16	0.00	894
Malagousia	W	Malagouzia(EL)	Greece	182	0.00	527
Malbo Gentile	R		Italy	211	0.00	508
Malegue	R	Malegue Divers(FR)	France			
Maliverne	W					

Table 13 (cont.) Prime varieties' colour, country of origin, synonyms, and 2010 global area, share and rank

Prime variety	Col.	Synonyms	Country of origin	2010 Area (hectares)	Share (%)	Rank
Malvarisco	R		Portugal	3	0.00	1066
Malvasia Amarela	W			14	0.00	911
Malvasia Bianca di Basilicata	W		Italy	210	0.00	509
Malvasia Bianca di Candia	W	Malvasia Bianca(PT,US,BR,IT)	Italy	9891	0.21	71
Malvasia Bianca Lunga	W	Malvasia del Chianti(BR), Marastina(HR)	Italy	2544	0.06	163
Malvasia Branca de Sao Jorge	W		Portugal	110	0.00	596
Malvasia Candida Roxa	R			3	0.00	1079
Malvasia del Lazio	W		Italy	590	0.01	346
Malvasia di Candia Aromatica	W		Italy	895	0.02	284
Malvasia di Casorzo	R		Italy	107	0.00	601
Malvasia di Lipari	W	Malvasia di Sardegna(IT),Malvasia Candida(PT),Malvasia de Sitges(ES),Malvasia Dubrovacka Bijela(HR)	Italy	310	0.01	447
Malvasia di Schierano	R		Italy	89	0.00	629
Malvasia Fina	W	Gual(ES) ,Boal(PT),Boal Branco(PT), Torrontes(ES,AR,CL,UY),Assario Branco(PT), Boal Espinho(PT)	Portugal	3416	0.07	137
Malvasia Fina Roxa	R		Portugal	25	0.00	833
Malvasia Nera di Basilicata	R		Italy	114	0.00	589
Malvasia Nera di Brindisi	R	Malvasia Negra(ES),Malvasia Nera di Lecce(IT),Malvasia Nera(AR)	Italy	1314	0.03	230
Malvasia Nera Lunga	R		Italy	38	0.00	763
Malvasia Parda	W			1	0.00	1132
Malvasia Preta	R	Pinheira Roxa(PT)	Portugal	1003	0.02	266
Malvasia Romana	W			0	0.00	1247
Malvasia Rosa	R		Italy	32	0.00	799
Malvasia Trigueira	R	Trigueira(PT)	Portugal	12	0.00	930
Malvazija Istarska	W	Malvazija(SI),Malvasia Istriana(IT),Malvasija Istarska(HR)	Croatia	2740	0.06	155
Malvia	W		Portugal	0	0.00	1241
Mammolo	R	Sciaccarello (FR)	Italy	825	0.02	298
Mandilaria	R		Greece	885	0.02	286
Mandon	R		Spain			
Manseng Noir	R	Ferrol(PT),Ferron(ES),	France	56	0.00	704
Manteudo Preto	R		Portugal	16	0.00	893
Manto Negro	R		Spain	273	0.01	464
Manzoni Bianco	W	Manzoni(PT)	Italy	382	0.01	403
Manzoni Moscato	R		Italy	20	0.00	871
Manzoni Rosa	O		Italy	29	0.00	811
Maratheftiko	R		Cyprus	152	0.00	550
Marechal Foch	R	Foch(US)	France	344	0.01	428
Mariensteiner	W		Germany			
Mario Feld	R			0	0.00	1263
Marmajuelo	W	Vermejuela(ES)	Spain	24	0.00	838
Marquette	R		USA	88	0.00	631
Marquinhas	W		Portugal	11	0.00	944
Mars	R			2	0.00	1114
Marsanne	W	Marsanne Blanche (CH)	France	1742	0.04	194
Marselan	R		France	2497	0.05	164
Marufo	R	Mourisco(PT),Moravia Dulce (ES),Mourisco Roxo(PT)	Portugal	6579	0.14	91
Marzemina Bianca	W			54	0.00	712

Table 13 (cont.) Prime varieties' colour, country of origin, synonyms, and 2010 global area, share and rank

Prime variety	Col.	Synonyms	Country of origin	2010 Area (hectares)	Share (%)	Rank
Marzemino	R	Marzemina Grossa(IT)	Italy	1091	0.02	257
Maticha	W		Morocco	275	0.01	463
Matrai Muskotaly	W		Hungary	67	0.00	678
Matrasa	R		Azerbaijan	28	0.00	818
Maturana Blanca	W	Maturano Bianco(ES)	Spain	18	0.00	886
Mauzac Blanc	W	Mauzac (FR)	France	1991	0.04	182
Mauzac Noir	R		France			
Mauzac Rose	W		France			
Mavro	R		Cyprus	3575	0.08	132
Mavro Messenikola	R	Messenikola(EL)	Greece			
Mavrodafni	R		Greece	345	0.01	427
Mavrouda	R	Mavroudi(EL)	Greece	520	0.01	358
Mavrud	R		Bulgaria	1296	0.03	232
Mayolet	R		Italy	7	0.00	990
Mazuelo	R	Bovale Grande(IT),Carignane(US, ES),Carinena(ES),Mazuela(ES), Carignan(FR,MA,CL,TR,ZA,EL,MM), Carignan Noir(CY),Carignano(IT)	Spain	80178	1.74	11
Mazzese	R		Italy	76	0.00	659
Mecle de Bourgoin	R		France			
Medina	R		Hungary	159	0.00	545
Melara	W		Italy	3	0.00	1084
Melhorio	R		Portugal	0	0.00	1261
Melon	W		France	12365	0.27	56
Mencia	R	Loureiro Tinto(ES) ,Jaen (PT,BR),Jaen Tinto(ES)	Spain	10658	0.23	65
Menoir	R	Menoire(HU)	Hungary	65	0.00	680
Menu Pineau	W	Orbois(FR)	France	212	0.00	507
Merille	R		France			
Merlese	R		Italy	14	0.00	909
Merlo	W					
Merlot	R		France	267169	5.81	2
Merlot Blanc	W		France	31	0.00	801
Merseguera	W		Spain	3946	0.09	126
Merzling	W		Germany			
Meslier Saint-François	W		France			
Mezes Feher	W	Mezes(HU)	Hungary	2	0.00	1097
Michele Parlieri	W			1	0.00	1166
Michurinetz	R			0	0.00	1214
Miguel del Arco	R	Vidau(ES),Miguel de Arco(ES)	Spain	468	0.01	381
Milgranet	R		France			
Milia	R		Slovakia	1	0.00	1135
Mindelo	R		Portugal	1	0.00	1202
Minella Bianca	W		Italy	65	0.00	681
Misket	W		Ukraine			
Misket Cherven	O		Bulgaria	4159	0.09	121
Misket Varnenski	W		Bulgaria	336	0.01	430
Molette	W		France			
Molinara	R	Molinera(ES,BR)	Italy	717	0.02	316
Mollard	R		France			
Monastrell	R	Garrut(CL),Mataro(US,CY,AU,ZA), Mourvedre(CA,TR,CL)	Spain	69850	1.52	14
Monbadon	W		France			
Mondet	R		Portugal	0	0.00	1227

Table 13 (cont.) Prime varieties' colour, country of origin, synonyms, and 2010 global area, share and rank

Prime variety	Col.	Synonyms	Country of origin	2010 Area (hectares)	Share (%)	Rank
Mondeuse Blanche	W		France			
Mondeuse Grise	W		France			
Mondeuse Noire	R	Mondeuse(FR,HR),Mondeuse Rouge(CH)	France	306	0.01	450
Monemvassia	W	Monemvasia(EL)	Greece	481	0.01	377
Monerac	R		France			
Monica Nera	R	Monica(IT)	Italy	1404	0.03	219
Monstruosa	W	Monstruosa de Monterrei(ES)		1	0.00	1167
Montepulciano	R	Cordisco(AR)	Italy	34947	0.76	27
Montils	W		France			
Montonico Bianco	W	Montonico(US)	Italy	734	0.02	310
Montu	W		Italy			
Monvedro	R		Portugal	6	0.00	1020
Moore's Diamond	W	Moores Diamond(US)	USA	42	0.00	753
Moradella	R		Italy	6	0.00	1019
Moravia Agria	R		Spain	550	0.01	353
Morenillo	R		Spain			
Moreto	R		Portugal	900	0.02	283
Morio-Muskat	W	Morio Muscat(PT)	Germany	509	0.01	365
Moristel	R		Spain	112	0.00	592
Mornen Noir	R	Mornen(FR)	France			
Morone	R		Italy	13	0.00	922
Morrastel Bouschet	R	Gros Morras.Bous.(FR)	France			
Moscadet	W		Portugal	4	0.00	1058
Moscargo	R		Portugal	0	0.00	1253
Moscatel Branco	W	Moscatel Nunes(PT)	Portugal		0.00	808
Moscatel Lilaz	W	Lilas(PT)	Portugal	0	0.00	1269
Moscatel Rosada	O	Moscatel Rosado(AR)	Portugal	7329	0.16	89
Moscatello Selvatico	W		Italy	35	0.00	780
Moscato di Scanzo	R		Italy	53	0.00	717
Moscato di Terracina	W		Italy	138	0.00	563
Moscato Embrapa	W		Brazil	862	0.02	289
Moscato Giallo	W	Moscatel Amarilla (CL),Muskat Zuti(HR), Moscatel Amarillo(AR)	Italy	1470	0.03	210
Moscato Nazareno	W			68	0.00	677
Moscato Rosa del Trentino	R	Muskat RuZa Crni(HR),Moscato Rosado(BR),Moscato Rosa(IT)	Italy	81	0.00	646
Moscatuel	R		Argentina	61	0.00	689
Moschofilero	R	Fileri(EL)	Greece	934	0.02	272
Moschofilero	O		Greece	80	0.00	651
Moschomavro	R	Moschato(EL)	Greece	1428	0.03	215
Mostosa	W		Italy	24	0.00	842
Mourisco de Semente	R		Portugal	60	0.00	694
Mourisco de Trevoes	R		Portugal	2	0.00	1115
Mourvaison	R		France			
Mouyssagues	R		France			
Mskhali	W		Armenia	1093	0.02	256
Mtsvane Kakhuri	W	Mtsvane (GE)	Georgia	319	0.01	440
Müller Thurgau	W	Rivaner(LU),Rizvanac(HR), Findling(UK)	Germany	22753	0.49	37
Muscadel (red)	R			371	0.01	410
Muscadelle	W		France	1656	0.04	199
Muscardin	R		France			
Muscat a Petits Grains Noirs	R	Moscatel Galego Tinto(PT)	Greece	108	0.00	600

Table 13 (cont.) Prime varieties' colour, country of origin, synonyms, and 2010 global area, share and rank

Prime variety	Col.	Synonyms	Country of origin	2010 Area (hectares)	Share (%)	Rank
Muscat a Petits Grains Roses	R	Muskateller Roter(DE)	Greece			
Muscat a Petits Grains Rouge	R	Moscatel Galego Roxo(PT)	Greece	613	0.01	341
Muscat Amber	O			21	0.00	862
Muscat Bailey A	R	Muscat Bailey(BR)	Japan	122	0.00	580
Muscat Blanc a Petits Grains	W	Bornova Misketi(TR),Moscato Bianco(IT,BR),Moscatel Frontignan(ES),Moscatel de Grano Menudo(ES),Moscatel Galego Branco(PT), Muscat Frontignan(MD), Muskateller(DE,AT),Muscat Blanc(US,HU,CH),Tamaioasa Romaneasca(RO),Muscat de Frontignan(ZA,UY),Moscato Canelli(BR),Muscat Canelli(US), Muskat Bijeli(HR), Moscatel de Grano Menudo(ES),Muskat Zlty(SK), Muscat a Petits Grains Blanc(AU), Muscat Petits Grains(FR,MM), Rumeni Muskat(SI), Moscato(IT), Moscatel, Muskat(DE), Moschato (EL),Muscat White(UA,RU), Muskateller Gelber(DE),Muscat de Colmar(FR),Tamianka(RO)	Italy	31112	0.68	33
Muscat de Ialoveni	W			20	0.00	870
Muscat Fleur d'Oranger	W	Muscat Orange(US)	France	91	0.00	626
Muscat of Alexandria	W	Moscatel Graudo(PT),Muscat d'Alexandrie (ZA),Zibibbo (BR,IT),Muscat Gordo Blanco(AU),Malaga (CY,HU),Moscatel de Malaga (ES),Moscato de Alexandria(IT),Moscatel Graudo(PT),Moscatel de Alejandria(AR,ES)	Greece	26336	0.57	35
Muscat of Alexandria Red	R	Red Hanepoot (ZA)	S. Africa	6	0.00	1017
Muscat of Hamburg	R	Moscatel de Hamburg(UY,ES), Moscato Nero di Acqui(IT), Muskat Hungarian(UK), Moscatel Hamburt(ES),Hamburgii Muskotaly(HU),Muskat Hamburg(HR),Muscat Hambourg(FR,RU,US)	United Kin	8137	0.18	81
Muscat Ottonel	W	Muskat Otonel(HR),Muskat Ottonel(AT,CZ,DE,SK),Moscato Ottonel(IT)	France	10234	0.22	68
Muscat Rose	O			227	0.00	497
Muscat Swenson	W	Muscats(CA)	USA	24	0.00	836
Muscat Violet	R			27	0.00	821
Muskat Moravsky	W		Czech Rep	514	0.01	362
Mustoasa de Maderat	W		Romania	255	0.01	476
Naia	W		Portugal	0	0.00	1211
Naparo	R		Spain	1	0.00	1168
Narince	W		Turkey	769	0.02	305
Nascetta	W		Italy	21	0.00	860
Nasco	W		Italy	141	0.00	558

Table 13 (cont.) Prime varieties' colour, country of origin, synonyms, and 2010 global area, share and rank

Prime variety	Col.	Synonyms	Country of origin	2010 Area (hectares)	Share (%)	Rank
Nebbiera	R		Italy	12	0.00	934
Nebbiolo	R		Italy	5992	0.13	99
Negoska	R	Negkoska(EL)	Greece	143	0.00	557
Negramoll	R	Negra Mole(PT),Negra Criolla (PE), Saborinho(PT,IT),Tinta Negra(PT), Mulata(PT),Rabo de Ovelha Tinto(PT,IT),Molar(PT),Mollar(PE,ES)	Spain	3193	0.07	139
Negrette	R	Pinot St George(BR)	France	1228	0.03	237
Negretto	R		Italy	75	0.00	660
Negroamaro	R	Negro Amaro(IT)	Italy	11460	0.25	60
Negroamaro Precoce	R		Italy	32	0.00	797
Negru de Ialoveni	R		Moldova	15	0.00	902
Nektar	W		Hungary	21	0.00	859
Ner d'Ala	R		Italy	30	0.00	806
Nerello Cappuccio	R		Italy	508	0.01	366
Nerello Mascalese	R		Italy	2883	0.06	152
Neretta Cuneese	R		Italy	132	0.00	574
Neretto di Bairo	R		Italy	34	0.00	785
Nero	R		Hungary	50	0.00	728
Nero Buono di Cori	R	Nero Buono(IT)	Italy	135	0.00	569
Nero d'Avola	R	Calabrese (IT)	Italy	16596	0.36	45
Nero di Troia	R	Uva di Troia(IT)	Italy	2572	0.06	162
Neronet	R		Czech Rep	72	0.00	664
Neuburger	W	Neuburske(CZ,SI)	Austria	964	0.02	270
Nevoeira	R		Portugal	0	0.00	1220
New York Muscat	R		USA	5	0.00	1035
Neyret	R		Italy	41	0.00	755
Niagara	W		USA	4670	0.10	112
Nieddera	R		Italy	107	0.00	602
Nigra	R		Italy	3	0.00	1092
Nincusa	R		Croatia	17	0.00	892
Noah	W		USA	71	0.00	666
Nobling	W		Germany	50	0.00	731
Nocera	R		Italy	15	0.00	904
Noir Fleurien	R		France			
Noiret	R		USA	33	0.00	791
Noria	W		Slovakia	1	0.00	1136
Norton	R	Cynthiana(US)	USA	329	0.01	433
Nosiola	W		Italy	79	0.00	652
Nosztori Rizling	W		Hungary	1	0.00	1193
Notardomenico	R		Italy	10	0.00	963
Noual	W		France			
Nouvelle	W		S. Africa	422	0.01	394
Nuragus	W		Italy	1345	0.03	225
Oberlin	R		France			
Oberlin White	W	Oberlin Divers(FR)	France			
Odessky Cherny	R	Odessa Black(UA), Alibernet(CZ,HU,SK)	Ukraine	2686	0.06	158
Odola	R		France			
Odysseus	W		Hungary	4	0.00	1043
Oeillade Bousche	R		France			
Ofthalmo	R		Cyprus	141	0.00	559
Ohanes	W		Spain		0.00	1169
Ojaleshi	R		Georgia	32	0.00	794
Okuzgozu	R		Turkey	1479	0.03	209

Table 13 (cont.) Prime varieties' colour, country of origin, synonyms, and 2010 global area, share and rank

Prime variety	Col.	Synonyms	Country of origin	2010 Area (hectares)	Share (%)	Rank
Olivette Noire	R	Cornichon Violet(FR)	France			
Ondarrabi Zuri	W		Spain	492	0.01	373
Ondenc	W		France			
Onitskanskii Belyi	W	Alb de Onitcani(MD),Onitcani(RU)	Moldova	71	0.00	667
Optima	W		Germany	37	0.00	770
Ora	W		France	0	0.00	1225
Oraniensteiner	W		Germany	3	0.00	1086
Orion	W		Germany	10	0.00	957
Orpheus	W		Hungary	0	0.00	1228
Orpicchio	W		Italy	1	0.00	1205
Ortega	W		Germany	637	0.01	336
Ortrugo	W		Italy	611	0.01	342
Oseleta	R		Italy	15	0.00	906
Osteiner	W		Germany	1	0.00	1170
Otskhanuri Sapere	R		Georgia	6	0.00	1005
Padeiro	R		Portugal	86	0.00	635
Palatina	W		Hungary	6	0.00	1016
Palava	O		Czech Rep	230	0.00	494
Pallagrello Bianco	W		Italy	55	0.00	709
Pallagrello Nero	R		Italy	169	0.00	537
Palomino Fino	W	Listan(FR), Palomino(US,NZ,ZA),Malvasia Rei(PT),Palomino Superior(ES)	Spain	22510	0.49	38
Palot	W		Spain			
Pamid	R	Rosioara(RO),Piros Szlanka(HU),Pamitis(EL)	Bulgaria	9827	0.21	73
Pampanaro	W			5	0.00	1041
Pampanuto	W		Italy	356	0.01	420
Pannon Frankos	R		Hungary	16	0.00	895
Panse Valenciano	W	Panse Valenciana(ES)	Spain	1	0.00	1171
Paolina	W		Italy	1	0.00	1134
Papazkarasi	R		Turkey	175	0.00	533
Pardillo	W	Marisancho(ES)	Spain	4364	0.09	119
Parellada	W		Spain	8847	0.19	77
Parraleta	R	Caricagiola(IT),Pau Ferro (PT),Tinta Caiada(PT),Tinta Lameira(PT), Bonvedro(PT),Carcajolo Noir(FR)	Spain	346	0.01	424
Parreira Matias	R		Portugal	1	0.00	1188
Pascal Blanc	W	Pascal(FR)	France			
Pascale	R	Nieddu Mannu(IT)	Italy	375	0.01	406
Passau	R		Italy	5	0.00	1024
Passerina	W		Italy	894	0.02	285
Patagonia	W			24	0.00	847
Patorra	R		Portugal	10	0.00	960
Patria	W		Hungary	3	0.00	1077
Patricia	R		Brazil	1	0.00	1180
Pavana	R		Italy	32	0.00	795
Pe Comprido	W		Portugal	1	0.00	1153
Pecorello	R		Italy	34	0.00	786
Pecorino	W	Uvina(PE)	Italy	1228	0.03	238
Pecsi Szagos	W	Zold Szagos(HU)	Hungary	1	0.00	1154
Pedral	R		Portugal	151	0.00	551

Table 13 (cont.) Prime varieties' colour, country of origin, synonyms, and 2010 global area, share and rank

				2010		
Prime variety	*Col.*	*Synonyms*	*Country of origin*	*Area (hectares)*	*Share (%)*	*Rank*
Pedro Gimenez	W	Pedro Jimenez (CL)	Argentina	12250	0.27	57
Pedro Ximenez	W	Perrum(PT),Pedro Gimenez Rio Colorado(AR)	Spain	9243	0.20	76
Pelaverga	R		Italy	55	0.00	708
Pelaverga Piccolo	R		Italy	6	0.00	1018
Peloursin	R		France			
Pelso	W			1	0.00	1191
Pepella	W		Italy	3	0.00	1078
Perdea	W		France			
Perera	W		Italy	4	0.00	1052
Perigo	W		Portugal	4	0.00	1050
Perla dei Vivi	R		Italy	1	0.00	1186
Perle	O		Germany	21	0.00	863
Perlette	W		USA	1	0.00	1172
Perlita	W			1	0.00	1173
Perola	W		Portugal			
Perricone	R		Italy	228	0.00	495
Perruno	W	Royal(ES)	Spain	1509	0.03	207
Persan	R	Becuet (IT)	France	3	0.00	1073
Pervenets Magaracha	W	Pervenec Magaracha(UA), Pervenets of Magarach(RU),Early Magaratch(RU), Magaracha's Firstborn(RU)	Ukraine	2881	0.06	153
Pervomaisky	R	Pervomaiskii(MD)	Uzbekishta	64	0.00	684
Petit Bouschet	R	Tintinha(PT), Bouschet Petit(PT)	France	15	0.00	899
Petit Courbu	W	Petit Courbou Ondarrzurizerrat(ES)	France	36	0.00	776
Petit Manseng	W	Pt. Manseng Blanc(FR)	France	1327	0.03	228
Petit Meslier	W		France			
Petit Rouge	R		Italy	84	0.00	640
Petit Verdot	R	Verdot(AR)	France	7202	0.16	90
Pexem	R		Portugal	3	0.00	1089
Phoenix	W		Germany	51	0.00	726
Picapoll Blanco	W		Spain	37	0.00	768
Piccola Nera	O		Italy	17	0.00	888
Picolit	W		Italy	128	0.00	577
Piculit Neri	R		Italy	22	0.00	857
Piedirosso	R		Italy	699	0.02	320
Pignola Valtellinese	R	Pignola(IT)	Italy	49	0.00	738
Pignoletto	W		Italy	1707	0.04	197
Pignolo	R		Italy	93	0.00	622
Pineau d'Aunis	R		France	435	0.01	392
Pinella	W		Italy	72	0.00	665
Pinot Blanc	W	Pinot Bianco(IT),Pinot Blanco(AR,UY), Weißer Burgunder(AT, DE),Beli Pinot(SI),Rulandske Bile (CZ),Pinot White(UA),Pinot Bijeli(HR)	France	14724	0.32	52
Pinot Gris	O	Pinot Grigio(IT),Rulander(UK),Sivi Pinot(SI),Grauer Burgunder(DE,AT), Pinot Grey(UA),Pinot Sivi(HR), Rulandske sede(CZ,SK)	France	43563	0.95	19
Pinot Meunier	R	Meunier(IT)	France	11267	0.24	63

Table 13 (cont.) Prime varieties' colour, country of origin, synonyms, and 2010 global area, share and rank

Prime variety	Col.	Synonyms	Country of origin	2010 Area (hectares)	Share (%)	Rank
Pinot Noir	R	Pinot Nero(IT),Blauer Burgunder(AT), Rulandske Modre (CZ),Pinot Negro(AR), Pinot Crni(HR)	France	86662	1.88	10
Pinot Noir Precoce	R	Fruhburgunder(DE),Pinot Precoce(FR)	France	209	0.00	511
Pinotage	R		S. Africa	6404	0.14	93
Pintes	W		Hungary	3	0.00	1085
Pintosa	W		Portugal	2	0.00	1121
Piquepoul Blanc	W		France	1455	0.03	212
Piquepoul Bousch	R		France			
Piquepoul Gris	W		France			
Piquepoul Noir	R	Pical(PT),Picapoll Negro(ES)	France	10	0.00	964
Plant Droit	R	Espanenc(FR)	France			
Planta Mula	R		Spain	24	0.00	839
Planta Nova	W	Alvarelhao Branco(PT)	Spain	1395	0.03	220
Plantet	R		France	1105	0.02	254
Plassa	R		Italy	91	0.00	624
Plavac Mali	R	Plavac Mali Crni(HR)	Croatia	1569	0.03	205
Plavay	W	Rumeni Plavec(SI)	Moldova	60	0.00	693
Plavec Zuti	W	Plavac Zuti(HU)	Croatia	13	0.00	921
Plavina	R	Plavina Crna(HR)	Croatia	643	0.01	333
Podarok Magaracha	W	Podarok of Magarach (RU),Magaracha's Gift(RU)	Ukraine	504	0.01	369
Poeloeske Muskotaly	W	Poloskei Muskotaly(HU)	Hungary	103	0.00	609
Pollera Nera	R		Italy	54	0.00	710
Portan	R		France	311	0.01	445
Portland	W		USA	12	0.00	927
Posip Bijeli	W	Posip(HR)	Croatia	253	0.01	479
Pougnet	R		France			
Poulsard	R		France	311	0.01	446
Poulsard Blanc	W		France			
Pozsonyi	W	Pozsonyi Feher(HU)	Hungary	10	0.00	949
Praca	W		Portugal	166	0.00	539
Prairie Star	W		USA	21	0.00	861
Precoce de Malingre	W					
Prensal	W	Pensal Blanco(ES)	Spain	105	0.00	607
Preto Cardana	R		Portugal	5	0.00	1038
Preto Martinho	R	Amostrinha(PT)	Portugal	163	0.00	543
Prie	W	Prie Blanc(IT)	Italy	33	0.00	790
Prieto Picudo	R		Spain	4587	0.10	114
Primavera	R		Portugal	40	0.00	760
Primetta	R	Prie Rouge(IT)	Italy	24	0.00	845
Prodest	R		Italy			
Prokupac	R		Serbia	15180	0.33	51
Promissao	W		Portugal	6	0.00	1008
Prosecco	W		Italy	18437	0.40	42
Prosecco Lungo	W		Italy	1367	0.03	223
Provareau	R		France			
Prunelard	R		France			
Prunesta	R		Italy	36	0.00	775
Pugnitello	R		Italy	28	0.00	814
Putzscheere	W		Hungary			
Quagliano	R		Italy	9	0.00	971

Table 13 (cont.) Prime varieties' colour, country of origin, synonyms, and 2010 global area, share and rank

Prime variety	Col.	Synonyms	Country of origin	2010 Area (hectares)	Share (%)	Rank
Quebranta	R		Peru	345	0.01	425
Rabigato	W	Rabigato Franco(PT)	Portugal	1273	0.03	233
Rabigato Moreno	W		Portugal	1	0.00	1181
Rabo de Anho	R		Portugal	99	0.00	613
Rabo de Lobo	R		Portugal	3	0.00	1065
Rabo de Ovelha	W		Portugal	908	0.02	281
Raboso Piave	R	Raboso(AR)	Italy	771	0.02	304
Raboso Veronese	R		Italy	277	0.01	461
Raffiat de Moncade	W		France			
Raisaine	W		France			
Ramisco	R	Ramisco Tinto(PT)	Portugal	34	0.00	787
Ranfol	W		Slovenia	134	0.00	572
Ranna Melnishka Loza	R		Bulgaria	249	0.01	482
Rathay	R		Austria	9	0.00	977
Ratinho	W		Portugal	84	0.00	638
Rauschling	W		Germany	23	0.00	854
Ravat	R	Ravat Divers(FR)	France			
Ravat Blanc	W		France			
Rayon d'Or	W		France			
Rebo	R		Italy	120	0.00	582
Recantina	R		Italy	9	0.00	968
Red Globe	R		USA	240	0.01	487
Red Semillon	R			10	0.00	958
Refosco	R	Refosk(SI,HR)	Italy	1420	0.03	216
Refosco dal Peduncolo Rosso	R		Italy	1076	0.02	259
Refosco di Faedis	R	Refosco Nostrano(IT)	Italy	217	0.00	502
Refren	W		Hungary	0	0.00	1217
Regent	R		Germany	69	0.00	673
Regina	W		Lebanon	321	0.01	439
Regner	W		Germany	44	0.00	748
Reichensteiner	W		Germany	228	0.00	496
Reliance	R		USA	4	0.00	1061
Retagliado Bianco	W		Italy	28	0.00	815
Reze	W		Switzerland			
Ribolla Gialla	W	Rebula(HU,SI)	Italy	1178	0.03	246
Rieslaner	W		Germany	60	0.00	696
Rieslina	W		Argentina	127	0.00	578
Riesling	W	Ryzlink Rynsky(CZ),Weißer Riesling(AT), Weisser Riesling(ZA),White Riesling (US,BG,CA),Renski Rizling(SI), Rajinski Rizling(HR),J. Riesling(CA), Riesling de Rhin(MD),Riesling Renan(EL),Riesling-Lion(JP),Rizling Rynsky(SI),Rynsky Riesling(CZ)	Germany	50060	1.09	18
Riesus	W		Ukraine	115	0.00	587
Rio Grande	W		Portugal	1	0.00	1203
Ripolo	W		Italy	1	0.00	1149
Riton	W		Moldova	257	0.01	474
Rkatsiteli	W	Rkatiteli(BR),Rkaciteli(HR), Rkaziteli(BG)	Georgia	58641	1.27	16
Robola	W	Rombola(EL)	Greece	465	0.01	383

Table 13 (cont.) Prime varieties' colour, country of origin, synonyms, and 2010 global area, share and rank

Prime variety	Col.	Synonyms	Country of origin	2010 Area (hectares)	Share (%)	Rank
Roditis	O		Greece	4661	0.10	113
Roditis(Red)	R			3834	0.08	127
Roesler	R		Austria	160	0.00	544
Rojal Tinta	R		Spain	1801	0.04	191
Rollo	W	Livornese Bianca(IT)	Italy	51	0.00	727
Rombola Red	R			6	0.00	1021
Rome	R		Spain	297	0.01	452
Romeiko	R		Greece	1597	0.03	203
Romorantin	W		France			
Rondinella	R		Italy	2481	0.05	165
Rondo	R		Germany	40	0.00	759
Roobernet	R			139	0.00	562
Rosa Arica	R			1	0.00	1174
Rosciola rose	O			2	0.00	1096
Rose du Var	O	Roussanne du Var(FR)	France			
Rossara Trentina	R	Rossara(IT)	Italy	8	0.00	984
Rossese	R		Italy	312	0.01	443
Rossese Bianco	W		Italy	7	0.00	987
Rossignola	R		Italy	188	0.00	524
Rossola Nera	R		Italy	86	0.00	634
Rotberger	R		Germany	1	0.00	1145
Roter Veltliner	O	Piros Veltelini (HU)	Austria	199	0.00	517
Rotgipfler	W		Austria	105	0.00	606
Roublot	W		France			
Rougeon	R		France	42	0.00	752
Roussanne	W		France	1746	0.04	193
Roussette d'Ayze	W		France			
Roussin	R		Italy	3	0.00	1068
Roviello Bianco	W		Italy	2	0.00	1130
Roxo de Vila Flor	R	Roxo Flor(PT)	Portugal	0	0.00	1244
Roxo Rei	R		Portugal	0	0.00	1223
Royal de Alloza	R	Derechero(ES)	Spain	29	0.00	812
Royalty	R		USA	97	0.00	619
Rozala Bianca	W	Rozalia(HU)		2	0.00	1129
Rozsakoe	W			19	0.00	878
Rual	R	Roal(PT)	Portugal	1	0.00	1146
Rubea	R		Brazil	81	0.00	645
Rubilande	R		France			
Rubin Golodrigi	R	Ruby of Golodryga(RU)	Ukraine	82	0.00	643
Rubin Tairovsky	R	Rubin Tairovski(MD)	Ukraine	2	0.00	1110
Rubinovy Magaracha	R	Ruby Magaracha(KZ)	Ukraine	0	0.00	1251
Rubintos	R		Hungary	18	0.00	882
Rubired	R		USA	4556	0.10	116
Ruby	R		USA	9	0.00	969
Ruby Cabernet	R	Rubi Cabernet(ES)	USA	5730	0.12	101
Ruby Seedless	R		USA			
Ruche	R		Italy	100	0.00	612
Rufete	R	Castellana(ES),Tinta Pinheira(PT)	Portugal	4833	0.11	109
Ruggine	W		Italy	1	0.00	1133
S. Mamede	W	Sao Mamede(PT)	Portugal	1	0.00	1195
S.V. 23-512	R			29	0.00	813
Sabrevois	R		USA	10	0.00	959
Sacy	W		France			
Sagrantino	R		Italy	995	0.02	267

Table 13 (cont.) Prime varieties' colour, country of origin, synonyms, and 2010 global area, share and rank

Prime variety	Col.	Synonyms	Country of origin	2010 Area (hectares)	Share (%)	Rank
Saint Jeannet	R		Argentina	44	0.00	747
Saint Macaire	R		France			
Saint-Pierre Doré	W		France			
Salvador	R		France	394	0.01	400
Samarrinho	W		Portugal	1	0.00	1139
San Giuseppe Nero	R		Italy	192	0.00	522
San Lunardo	W		Italy	10	0.00	965
San Martino	R		Italy	21	0.00	865
San Michele	R		Italy	57	0.00	703
Sanforte	R		Italy	1	0.00	1204
Sangiovese	R	Nielluccio(FR),Prugnolo Gentile(IT), Sangioveto (US)	Italy	77709	1.69	13
Sankt Laurent	R	Svatovavrinecke (PT),Saint Laurent(FR,CA),Szentlorinc(HU)	Austria	3007	0.07	147
Santa Maria	W		Italy	3	0.00	1080
Santarena	R	Santareno(PT)	Portugal	739	0.02	309
Santoal	W		Portugal	9	0.00	972
Sao Saul	R			1	0.00	1178
Saperavi	R		Georgia	8126	0.18	82
Saperavi Severny	R	Saperavi Severnii(MD),Saperavi Nothern(RU)	Russia	350	0.01	421
Sauvignon Blanc	W	Sauvignon(TR,SI,HU,EL,UK,IT,PT,MD,RO,RU,FR,CZ,AR,UA),Sauvignon Musque(US),Sauvignon Blanca(ES), Sovinion(EL)	France	110138	2.39	8
Sauvignon Gris	W		France	483	0.01	376
Sauvignon Rose	O		France			
Sauvignonasse	W	Sauvignon Vert(CL),Tocai Friulano(IT,US),Zeleni Sauvignon(SI)	France	4449	0.10	117
Savagnin Blanc	W	Savagnin(AU),Traminer(RU,HU,CA,RO),Traminac Bijeli(HR),Traminec(SI)	France	1898	0.04	186
Savagnin Rose	W		France			
Savatiano	W	Savvatiano(EL)	Greece	9920	0.22	70
Scheurebe	W		Germany	1984	0.04	183
Schiava	R		Italy	517	0.01	360
Schiava Gentile	R		Italy	694	0.02	322
Schiava Grigia	R		Italy	66	0.00	679
Schiava Grossa	R	Tschaggele(IT)	Italy	580	0.01	350
Schioppettino	R		Italy	154	0.00	548
Schonburger	O		Germany	59	0.00	698
Sciaglin	W		Italy	6	0.00	1006
Sciascinoso	R	Olivella Nera(IT)	Italy	94	0.00	621
Scimiscia	W		Italy	5	0.00	1034
Seara Nova	W		Portugal	681	0.01	328
Segalin	R		France			
Seibel	R	Seibel Divers(FR),Seibel Hybrids(BR)		591	0.01	345
Seibel white	W	Seibel Divers(FR)				
Seinoir	R		France			
Select	W		France			
Semebat	R		France			

Table 13 (cont.) Prime varieties' colour, country of origin, synonyms, and 2010 global area, share and rank

Prime variety	Col.	Synonyms	Country of origin	2010 Area (hectares)	Share (%)	Rank
Semidano	W		Italy	36	0.00	772
Semillon	W	Semilion(RU),Semilao(PT), Semigion(EL)	France	22156	0.48	39
Sennen	R		Italy	10	0.00	952
Serbina	R			6	0.00	1011
Sercial	W	Esganoso(PT)	Portugal	106	0.00	604
Sercialinho	W		Portugal	9	0.00	978
Serna	O		Argentina	10	0.00	961
Servanin	R		France			
Servant	W	Raisin Blanc(ZA)	France	54	0.00	715
Sevilhao	R		Portugal	14	0.00	912
Seyval Blanc	W	Seyval(FR,US)	France	464	0.01	384
Sgavetta	R		Italy	47	0.00	740
Shiroka Melnishka	R	Shiroka Melnishka Loza(BG)	Bulgaria	1580	0.03	204
Siegerrebe	O		Germany	120	0.00	583
Silcher	W		Germany			
Silvaner	W	Sylvaner(AT,NZ,FR,AU,EL,CH,UK,BR,CA),Sylvaner Verde(IT),Silvanac Zeleni(HR),Zold Szilvani (HU), Rhin(ES),Silvanske Zelene(SK), Sylvanske Zelene(CZ)	Austria	2255	0.05	173
Siria	W	Ciguente(ES),Roupeiro Branco(PT), Sabro(ES,PT),Alvadurao(PT),Dona Blanca(ES),Malvasia Branca(PT), Valenciana Blanca(ES), Codega(PT), Crato Espanhol(PT)	Portugal	7898	0.17	86
Sirio	W		Italy	14	0.00	913
Skrlet	W		Croatia	61	0.00	690
Slankamenka	W		Serbia	31	0.00	803
Solaris	W		Germany	20	0.00	873
Soperga	R		Italy	22	0.00	856
Sovereign Opal	W		Canada	3	0.00	1082
Spergola	W		Italy	110	0.00	597
St Croix	R		USA	25	0.00	834
St Pepin	W		USA	19	0.00	875
St Vincent	R		USA	23	0.00	852
Stavroto	R		Greece	11	0.00	942
Stepnyak	W	Stepniak(RU)	Russia	144	0.00	555
Steuben	R		USA	39	0.00	762
Storgozia	R		Bulgaria	295	0.01	453
Sugra Five	W		USA	2	0.00	1111
Sukholimanskiy Bely	W	Suholimanskiy White(UA),Suholimenschii Belii (MD),Sukholimansky (RU)	Ukraine	2156	0.05	175
Sultaniye	W	Sultana(AU),Soultanina(CY),Thompson Seedless(PE, ES),Thompson(PT)	Turkey	3407	0.07	138
Sumoll	R	Vijiriego Negro(ES)	Spain	83	0.00	642
Superior Seedless	W			9	0.00	976
Suscan	R	Brajda Crna(HR)	Croatia	5	0.00	1023
Susumaniello	R		Italy	50	0.00	733
Swenson Red	R		USA	11	0.00	940
Symphony	W		USA	324	0.01	438
Syrah	R	Shiraz(AU,TR,ZA,CY,TH), Syrach(ES), Sirach(EL),Chirac(MX)	France	185568	4.03	6

Table 13 (cont.) Prime varieties' colour, country of origin, synonyms, and 2010 global area, share and rank

Prime variety	Col.	Synonyms	Country of origin	2010 Area (hectares)	Share (%)	Rank
Szeremi Zold	W			0	0.00	1219
Taltos	W		Hungary	1	0.00	1158
Tamarez	W		Portugal	343	0.01	429
Taminga	W		Australia			
Tannat	R		France	5940	0.13	100
Tarrango	R		Australia	72	0.00	663
Tavkveri	R		Georgia	37	0.00	766
Taylor	R					
Tazzelenghe	R		Italy	55	0.00	707
Teinturier	R		France	7	0.00	986
Telti Kyryk	W			246	0.01	484
Tempranillo	R	Aragonez(PT),Tinta Roriz(PT),Tinto de Toro(ES),Valdepenas(US),Negra de Mesa(ES)	Spain	232561	5.05	4
Tempranillo Blanco	W		Spain	5	0.00	1032
Teneron	R	Valency(MA)	Spain	3488	0.08	135
Teoulier Noir	R	Teoulier(FR)	France			
Termarina Rossa	O	Termarina(IT)	Italy	20	0.00	866
Teroldego	R		Italy	839	0.02	295
Terrano	R	Teran(HR,SI)	Italy	500	0.01	371
Terrantez	W		Portugal	12	0.00	933
Terrantez do Pico	W		Portugal	0	0.00	1224
Terras 20	R	Alicante Terras 20(FR)	France			
Terret Blanc	W		France	1451	0.03	214
Terret Gris	W		France			
Terret Noir	R		France			
Therona	W		S. Africa	99	0.00	614
Thrapsathiri	W		Greece	31	0.00	802
Tibouren	R		France	445	0.01	390
Timorasso	W		Italy	129	0.00	575
Tinta Aguiar	R		Portugal	75	0.00	661
Tinta Barroca	R	Barroco(CL),Tinta Barocca (ZA)	Portugal	6172	0.13	96
Tinta Bragao	R	Bragao(PT)	Portugal	63	0.00	686
Tinta Carvalha	R		Portugal	1311	0.03	231
Tinta da Barca	R	Barca(PT)	Portugal	345	0.01	426
Tinta da Melra	R	Melra(PT)	Portugal	1	0.00	1199
Tinta de Alcoa	R	Alcoa(PT)	Portugal	24	0.00	840
Tinta de Cidadelhe	R	Cidadelhe(PT)	Portugal	1	0.00	1190
Tinta de Pegoes	R	Tinto Pegoes(PT)	Portugal	195	0.00	519
Tinta de Porto Santo	R	Tinta Porto Santo(PT)	Portugal	2	0.00	1125
Tinta do Rodo	R	Rodo(PT)	Portugal	3	0.00	1063
Tinta Engomada	R	Engomada(PT)	Portugal	4	0.00	1053
Tinta Francisca	R		Portugal	53	0.00	718
Tinta Malandra	R	Malandra(PT)	Portugal	0	0.00	1270
Tinta Martins	R		Portugal	11	0.00	946
Tinta Mesquita	R		Portugal	1	0.00	1147
Tinta Penajoia	R		Portugal	53	0.00	
Tinta Pereira	R		Portugal	1	0.00	1155
Tinta Pomar	R		Portugal	30	0.00	810
Tinta Roseira	R	Roseira(PT)	Portugal	4	0.00	1060
Tinta Valdosa	R	Valdosa(PT)	Portugal	1	0.00	1201
Tinta Varejoa	R	Varejoa(PT)	Portugal	1	0.00	1157
Tintem	R			9	0.00	974
Tintilia del Molise	R	Tintilia(IT)	Italy	111	0.00	594

Table 13 (cont.) Prime varieties' colour, country of origin, synonyms, and 2010 global area, share and rank

Prime variety	Col.	Synonyms	Country of origin	2010 Area (hectares)	Share (%)	Rank
Tinto Basto	R			62	0.00	688
Tinto Cao	R		Portugal	369	0.01	411
Tinto de la Pampana Blanca	R		Spain	5145	0.11	105
Tinto de Zafra	R			2	0.00	1112
Tinto do Aurelio	R	Tinta Aurelio(PT)	Portugal	0	0.00	1271
Tinto Jeroma	R					
Tinto Velasco	R		Spain	2684	0.06	159
Torbato	W	Tourbat(FR)	Italy	19	0.00	874
Torrontes Mendocino	W		Argentina	713	0.02	317
Torrontes Riojano	W	Torontel(PE,CL)	Argentina	8115	0.18	83
Torrontes Sanjuanino	W	Moscatel Austria(CL)	Argentina	2052	0.04	179
Tortosina	W		Spain	503	0.01	370
Touriga Branca	W		Portugal	36	0.00	773
Touriga Femea	R		Portugal	15	0.00	905
Touriga Franca	R	Touriga Francesa(AR)	Portugal	11586	0.25	59
Touriga Nacional	R	Touriga(AU),Tourigo(PT)	Portugal	10435	0.23	67
Trajadura	W	Treixadura (ES)	Portugal	2169	0.05	174
Traminette	W		USA	240	0.01	488
Trbljan	W	Trbljan Bijeli(HR)	Croatia	231	0.01	492
Trebbianina	W			128	0.00	576
Trebbiano	W		Italy	248	0.01	483
Trebbiano d'Abruzzo	W	Trebbiano Abruzzese(IT)	Italy	5091	0.11	106
Trebbiano Giallo	W		Italy	10609	0.23	66
Trebbiano Modenese	W		Italy	363	0.01	415
Trebbiano Romagnolo	W		Italy	15893	0.35	49
Trebbiano Spoletino	W		Italy	200	0.00	515
Trebbiano Toscano	W	St Emilion (US), Ugni Blanc(FR,BG,UY), Talia(PT,BR,PE),Uni Blance(EL),Uni Blan (EL)	Italy	109772	2.39	9
Trepat	R	Bonicaire(ES),Parrel Verdal (ES)	Spain	1358	0.03	224
Tressot	R		France			
Trevisana Nera	R		Italy	15	0.00	898
Tribidrag	R	Zinfandel(PT,US,CL,AU,NZ,CA,ZA,BR),Primitivo(IT,US),Crljenak Kastelanski(HR)	Croatia	32745	0.71	29
Trilla	W		Hungary	1	0.00	1152
Trincadeira	R	Tinta Amarela(ZA),Crato Preto(PT),Trincadeira Preta(AR)	Portugal	9270	0.20	75
Trincadeira das Pratas	W		Portugal	239	0.01	490
Trincadeiro Branco	W	Trincadeira Branca(PT)	Portugal	59	0.00	697
Triomphe	R		France	15	0.00	903
Triplett Blanc	W			244	0.01	485
Triunfo	R		Portugal	2	0.00	1116
Trnjak	R		Croatia	15	0.00	900
Trobat	R	Panse Negro(ES)	Spain	1	0.00	1175
Tronto	R		Italy	2	0.00	1126
Trousseau	R	Bastardo(PT),Tinta(PT),Tinta Lisboa(PT), Verdejo Negro(ES),Bastarda (ES), Maturana Tinta(ES),Bastardo Rouge(PT),Bastardo Roxo(PT),Bastardo Tinto(PT)	France	3431	0.07	136
Trousseau Gris	O	Gray Riesling(US)	France			

Table 13 (cont.) Prime varieties' colour, country of origin, synonyms, and 2010 global area, share and rank

Prime variety	Col.	Synonyms	Country of origin	2010 Area (hectares)	Share (%)	Rank
Tsimlyansky Cherny	R	Tsymlansky Black(RU)	Russia	451	0.01	387
Tsitska	W		Georgia	3642	0.08	130
Tsolikouri	W		Georgia	7903	0.17	85
Tsulukidzis Tetra	W		Georgia	195	0.00	518
Tsvetochny (Floral)	W			89	0.00	628
Tsvetochny (Flowery)	W			80	0.00	650
Turan	R	Agria(CA)	Hungary	177	0.00	531
Turchetta	R			3	0.00	1070
Ucelut	W		Italy	10	0.00	962
Uni Blan	R			1	0.00	1144
Urreti	W		Hungary	0	0.00	1258
Usakhelouri	R		Georgia	10	0.00	950
Uva Cao	W		Portugal	1	0.00	1185
Uva del Fantini	R		Italy	0	0.00	1254
Uva del Tunde	R		Italy	2	0.00	1128
Uva Longanesi	R		Italy	512	0.01	363
Uva Rara	R		Italy	460	0.01	385
Uva Tosca	R		Italy	71	0.00	669
Uvalino	R		Italy	1	0.00	1137
Valais Noir	R		France			
Valbom	R		Portugal	166	0.00	540
Valdiguie	R	Napa Gamay(US)	France	138	0.00	564
Valenci Tinto	R	Grumier Tinto(FR)	Spain	27	0.00	823
Valentino Nero	R	Valentino(IT)	Italy	21	0.00	864
Valerien	W		France			
Valiant	R		USA	11	0.00	943
Valveirinha	W	Valveirinho(PT)	Portugal	0	0.00	1229
Valvin Muscat	W		USA	6	0.00	1010
Varousset	R		France			
Vasilaki	W		Turkey	4	0.00	1057
Vega	W		Italy	35	0.00	781
Ventura	W		Canada	24	0.00	837
Venus	R		USA	1	0.00	1148
Verdea	W		Italy	83	0.00	641
Verdealbara	W			0	0.00	1212
Verdeca	W	Lagorthi(EL)	Italy	796	0.02	302
Verdejo	W	Verdejo Blanco (ES)	Spain	16578	0.36	46
Verdelet	W		France	1	0.00	1196
Verdelho	W		Portugal	2005	0.04	181
Verdelho Roxo	R		Portugal	4	0.00	1047
Verdelho Tinto	R		Portugal	28	0.00	817
Verdello	W		Italy	287	0.01	455
Verdesse	W		France	7	0.00	989
Verdial	W	Verdial Branco(PT)	Portugal	1	0.00	1206
Verdial Tinto	R			3	0.00	1087
Verdicchio Bianco	W	Boschera(IT),Peverella(BR),Trebbiano di Soave(IT),Verdicchio(AR)	Italy	3532	0.08	134
Verdil	W		Spain	57	0.00	702
Verdiso	W	Pedevenda (IT)	Italy	68	0.00	676
Verdoncho	W		Spain	2124	0.05	176
Verduschia	W		Italy	11	0.00	938
	W	Verduzzo(AR)	Italy	812	0.02	299
Verduzzo Trevigiano	W		Italy	708	0.02	318

Table 13 (cont.) Prime varieties' colour, country of origin, synonyms, and 2010 global area, share and rank

Prime variety	Col.	Synonyms	Country of origin	Area (hectares)	Share (%)	Rank
Vermentino	W	Pigato(IT),Favorita(IT),Favorita Diaz(AR)	Italy	8617	0.19	78
Vermentino Nero	R		Italy	210	0.00	510
Vernaccia di Oristano	W		Italy	272	0.01	465
Vernaccia di San Gimignano	W	Bervedino(IT)	Italy	522	0.01	357
Vertes Csillaga	W		Hungary	21	0.00	858
Vertzami	R	Lefkada (CY)	Greece	335	0.01	431
Veruccese	R			0	0.00	1222
Vespaiola	W		Italy	94	0.00	620
Vespolina	R		Italy	134	0.00	571
Victoria	W			52	0.00	721
Vidal	W	Vidal Blanc(US),Vidal 256(CA),Vidal Divers(FR)	France	1644	0.04	200
Vidal Red	R	Vidal divers(FR)				
Vidvizhenets	O			271	0.01	466
Vien de Nus	R		Italy	13	0.00	925
Vignoles	W	Ravat 51(US)	France	254	0.01	477
Vijariego	W	Diego(ES) ,Vijiriego(ES)	Spain	285	0.01	457
Viktor	W		Hungary	0	0.00	1248
Viktoria Gyongye	W			190	0.00	523
Vilana	W		Greece	579	0.01	351
Vilana(Red)	R					
Villard Blanc	W		France	689	0.01	323
Villard Noir	R		France	1328	0.03	227
Vincent	R		Canada	11	0.00	939
Vineti	W					
Vinhao	R	Sousao(PT),Souson(ES),Souzao(US,ZA)	Portugal	3160	0.07	140
Viognier	W	Viogner(BR,IT,UY)	France	11400	0.25	61
Violeta	R		Brazil	98	0.00	616
Viorica	W		Moldova	347	0.01	423
Viosinho	W		Portugal	225	0.00	499
Vital	W		Portugal	1182	0.03	245
Vitovska	W	Vitouska(IT)	Italy	50	0.00	732
Voskeat	W	Voskehat(AM)	Armenia	809	0.02	300
Vranac	R		Montenegr	149	0.00	552
Vugava	W		Croatia	36	0.00	777
Vuillermin	R		Italy	4	0.00	1046
Vulcanus	W			5	0.00	1039
Weldra	W		S. Africa	14	0.00	915
Wurzer	W		Germany	5	0.00	1033
Xara	R			0	0.00	1265
Xarello	W	Xarello Blanco(ES)	Spain	8393	0.18	79
Xarello Rosado	W	Pansa Rosada(ES)	Spain	1	0.00	1176
Xinomavro	R		Greece	1971	0.04	184
Xinomavro (White)	W					
Xynisteri	W		Cyprus	2092	0.05	177
Yaqui	R			2	0.00	1113
Zalagyongye	W	Zala Dende(RU)	Hungary	1948	0.04	185
Zalema	W		Spain	4097	0.09	123
Zametovka	R	Kavcina Crna(HR)	Slovenia	914	0.02	280
Zefir	W		Hungary	49	0.00	736
Zengo	W		Hungary	264	0.01	470

Table 13 (cont.) Prime varieties' colour, country of origin, synonyms, and 2010 global area, share and rank

Prime variety	Col.	Synonyms	Country of origin	Area (hectares)	Share (%)	Rank
Zenit	W	Zenith(RU)	Hungary	580	0.01	349
Zeta	W		Hungary	118	0.00	584
Zeusz	W		Hungary	28	0.00	820
Zierfandler	O	Cirfandli (HU)	Austria	117	0.00	585
Zlahtina	W		Croatia	135	0.00	570
Zlatarica Vrgorska	W	Zlatarica(HR)	Croatia	19	0.00	877
Zoumiatiko Red	R					
Zupljanka	W		Serbia	4	0.00	1049
Zweigelt	R	Zweigeltrebe(UK,CA,SK,NZ)	Austria	9847	0.21	72

Table 14: Prime varieties' global area and share of each synonym, and synonym's share of each prime variety, 2000

Prime variety	Col	Synonym	Area (hectares)	Share (%) of global area	Synonym's share (%) of prime variety
Abbo	R	Abbou	2375	0.05	100
Abrusco	R	Colorino	394	0.01	99
		Abrusco	5	0.00	1
Afus Ali	W	Waltham Cross	328	0.01	100
		Roseti	0	0.00	0
Aglianico	R	Aglianico	7015	0.14	76
		Aglianico del Vulture	2250	0.05	24
Airen	W	Airen	387525	7.94	100
		Forcallat Blanca	435	0.01	0.1
		Burra Blanca	18	0.00	0.0
Alarije	W	Alarije	1665	0.03	99
		Malfar	21	0.00	1
Albarola	W	Albarola	4011	0.08	98
		Bianchetta Genovese	79	0.00	2
Albillo Mayor	W	Albilla	5	0.00	100
Albillo Real	W	Albillo	3368	0.07	100
Alfrocheiro	R	Alfrocheiro	518	0.01	99
		Bastarda Negra	5	0.00	1
Alicante Henri Bouschet	R	Garnacha Tintorera	18321	0.38	49
		Alicante Henri Bouschet	9105	0.19	25
		Alicante Bouschet	5470	0.11	15
		Tintorera	2519	0.05	7
		Alicante Bouchet	1169	0.02	3
		Alicante	440	0.01	1
		Alikante Mouse	21	0.00	0
Alphonse Lavallee	R	Alphonse Lavallee	13	0.00	83
		Ribier	2	0.00	16
		Alfonso Lavalle	0	0.00	1
Alvarelhao	R	Brancelho	99	0.00	62
		Alvarelhao	46	0.00	29
		Brancellao	14	0.00	9
Alvarinho	W	Albarino	4149	0.09	81
		Alvarinho	964	0.02	19
Aramon Noir	R	Aramon	9084	0.19	100
Arany Sarfeher	W	Izsaki	2914	0.06	100
Arinto de Bucelas	W	Pederna	2782	0.06	70
		Arinto	1184	0.02	30
Arvine	W	Arvine	57	0.00	93
		Petite Arvine	4	0.00	7
Asprouda	W	Asproudi	433	0.01	100
Assyrtiko	W	Asirtiko	1128	0.02	100
Aubin Blanc	W	Aubin	2	0.00	100
Aurore	W	Aurora	299	0.01	100
Babeasca Neagra	R	Babeasca Neagra	3642	0.07	98
		Rara Neagra	80	0.00	2
Baco Blanc	W	Baco Blanc	2103	0.04	98
		Baco Divers	34	0.00	2
Baco Noir	R	Baco Noir	397	0.01	100
		Baco Divers	1	0.00	0

Table 14 (cont.) Prime varieties' global area and share of each synonym, and synonym's share of each prime variety, 2000

Prime variety	Col	Synonym	Area (hectares)	Share (%) of global area	Synonym's share (%) of prime variety
Barbera	R	Barbera Nera	27175	0.56	82
		Barbera	5872	0.12	18
Bariadorgia	W	Carcajolo Blanc	0	0.00	100
Bastardo Magarachsky	R	Bastardo Magaraceskii	1040	0.02	53
		Bastardo Magarachsky	929	0.02	47
Beba	W	Beba	4748	0.10	100
		Breval	9	0.00	0
		Iso	5	0.00	0
Beclan	R	Petit Beclan	0	0.00	100
Bequignol Noir	R	Bequignol	1	0.00	100
Biancone di Portoferraio	W	Biancone	67	0.00	100
Biborkadarka	R	Bibor Kadarka	202	0.00	100
Blanqueiro	W	Blanqueiron	1	0.00	100
Blauer Portugieser	R	Blauer Portugieser	3953	0.08	92
		Portugais Bleu	232	0.00	5
		Portoghese	94	0.00	2
Blauer Wildbacher	R	Blauer Wildbacher	464	0.01	98
		Wildbacher	8	0.00	2
Blaufrankisch	R	Blaufrankisch	12723	0.26	99
		Franconia	111	0.00	1
		Lemberger	45	0.00	0
Borracal	R	Borracal	2035	0.04	77
		Caino Tinto	619	0.01	23
Bousquet Precoce	W	Precoce Bousquet	16	0.00	100
Bracciola Nera	R	Bracciola	89	0.00	100
Brachetto del Piemonte	R	Brachetto	1534	0.03	100
Braquet Noir	R	Brachet	8	0.00	100
Burdin	W	Burdin Divers	0	0.00	100
Cabernet Franc	R	Cabernet Franc	48147	0.99	100
		Kamberne Fran	40	0.00	0
Cabernet Sauvignon	R	Cabernet Sauvignon	220202	4.51	100
		Kamberne Sovinion	688	0.01	0
Camaralet de Lasseube	W	Camarate	690	0.01	100
		Camaralet Lasseu	0	0.00	0
Carignan Blanc	W	Carignan Blanc	976	0.02	94
		Carinena Blanco	58	0.00	6
Castel	R	Castel Divers	0	0.00	100
Castelao	R	Periquita	14424	0.30	100
Catarratto Bianco	W	Catarratto Bianco Comune	43176	0.89	85
		Catarratto Bianco Lucido	7535	0.15	15
Cayetana Blanca	W	Blanca Cayetana	48138	0.99	87
		Pardina	6797	0.14	12
		Robal	567	0.01	1
Cayuga White	W	Cayuga	108	0.00	100
Cerceal Branco	W	Cercial	597	0.01	100
Cesanese	R	Cesanese d'Affile	577	0.01	56
		Cesanese Comune	447	0.01	44
Chardonnay	W		145308	2.98	100
		Sardone	36	0.00	0

Table 14 (cont.) Prime varieties' global area and share of each synonym, and synonym's share of each prime variety, 2000

Prime variety	Col	Synonym	Area (hectares)	Share (%) of global area	Synonym's share (%) of prime variety
Chasselas	W	Chasselas	12097	0.25	91
		Weisser Gutedel	1198	0.02	9
		Chasselas Dorato	22	0.00	0
		Chaselas Dorada	1	0.00	0
Chasselas Rouge	R	Chasselas Rose	11	0.00	100
Chelva	W	Chelva	10875	0.22	100
		Uva Rey	2	0.00	0
Chenin Blanc	W	Chenin Blanc	32273	0.66	70
		Chenin	13533	0.28	30
Cinsaut	R	Cinsaut	35672	0.73	74
		Cinsault	12343	0.25	25
		Ottavianello	274	0.01	1
		Senso	108	0.00	0
		Black Malvoisie	22	0.00	0
Clairette	W	Clairette	3065	0.06	77
		Clairette Blanche	938	0.02	23
Coda di Volpe Bianca	W	Coda di Volpe Bianca	951	0.02	97
		Guarnaccia	29	0.00	3
Codega de Larinho	W	Codega do Larinho	4058	0.08	100
Colombana Nera	R	Colombana Nero	126	0.00	100
Colombard	W	French Colombard	18010	0.37	47
		Colombar	11432	0.23	30
		Colombard	8705	0.18	23
Cornalin	R	Humagne Rouge	60	0.00	64
		Cornalin	33	0.00	36
Corvina Veronese	R	Corvina	4781	0.10	100
Cot	R	Malbec	18006	0.37	74
		Cot	6145	0.13	25
		Malbech	251	0.01	1
		Mancin	0	0.00	0
Couderc	W	Couderc Divers	4	0.00	100
Couderc Noir	R	Coudrec	305	0.01	50
		Couderc 13	299	0.01	49
		Coudrec Divers	5	0.00	1
Courbu Blanc	W	Courbu	47	0.00	100
Damaschino	W	Alicante Branco	1530	0.03	65
		Planta Fina	449	0.01	19
		Damaschino	380	0.01	16
		Faranah	1	0.00	0
Debina	W	Dembina	455	0.01	100
Dimyat	W	Dimiat	7649	0.16	99
		Zoumiatiko	91	0.00	1
Douce Noire	R	Bonarda	17533	0.36	99
		Turca	99	0.00	1
		Charbono	21	0.00	0
		Corbeau	1	0.00	0
Droujba	W	Drujba	3	0.00	100
Drupeggio	W	Canaiolo Bianco	617	0.01	100
Durif	R	Petite Sirah	923	0.02	77
		Durif	274	0.01	23

Table 14 (cont.) Prime varieties' global area and share of each synonym, and synonym's share of each prime variety, 2000

Prime variety	Col	Synonym	Area (hectares)	Share (%) of global area	Synonym's share (%) of prime variety
Elbling	W	Elbling Weisser	1042	0.02	56
		Burger	656	0.01	35
		Elbling	165	0.00	9
Elbling Rot	W	Elbling Roter	4	0.00	100
Enantio	R	Lambrusco A Foglia Frastagliata	1062	0.02	100
Fortana	R	Fortana	948	0.02	76
		Canina Nera	304	0.01	24
Fruhroter Veltliner	R	Fruhroter Veltliner	626	0.01	99
		Malvasier	6	0.00	1
		Velteliner Rouge Precoce	0	0.00	0
Gaillard	R	Gaillard Divers	0	0.00	100
Galego Dourado	W	Pedro Luis	51	0.00	100
Gamay de Teinturier Bouze	R	Gamay de Teinturier Bouze	282	0.01	89
		Gamays Teinturiers	26	0.00	8
		Gammay de Bouze	10	0.00	3
Gamay Noir	R	Gamay	37261	0.76	99
		Gamay Beaujolais	352	0.01	1
		Gamay Noir	181	0.00	0
		Gamay Precoce	2	0.00	0
Gamay Teinturier de Chaudenay	R	Gamay Chaudenay	267	0.01	100
Gamay Teinturier Freaux	R	Gamay Teinturier Freaux	77	0.00	58
		Gammay Freaux	55	0.00	42
Garanoir	R	Garanoir	50	0.00	66
		Granoir	26	0.00	34
Garganega	W	Garganega	11379	0.23	69
		Grecanico Dorato	5170	0.11	31
Garnacha Blanca	W	Grenache Blanc	6488	0.13	60
		Garnacha Blanca	4333	0.09	40
Garnacha Peluda	R	Garnacha Peluda	1460	0.03	72
		Lledoner Pelut	564	0.01	28
Garnacha Roja	W	Grenache Gris	2635	0.05	95
		Garnacha Roja	126	0.00	5
		Grenas Rose	1	0.00	0
Garnacha Tinta	R	Grenache	111277	2.28	52
		Garnacha	95800	1.96	45
		Cannonao	6197	0.13	3
		Tocai Rosso	356	0.01	0
		Vernaccia Nera	228	0.00	0
		Garnacha Tinta	129	0.00	0
Gewurztraminer	W	Gewurztraminer	6514	0.13	61
		Traminer Rose	2731	0.06	26
		Traminer	884	0.02	8
		Traminer Aromatico	541	0.01	5
Godello	W	Gouveio	929	0.02	62
		Godello	461	0.01	31
		Agudello	99	0.00	7
Golubok	R	Goluboc	50	0.00	100
Gouais Blanc	W	Gouais	1	0.00	100
Gouget Noir	R	Gouget	1	0.00	100

Table 14 (cont.) Prime varieties' global area and share of each synonym, and synonym's share of each prime variety, 2000

Prime variety	Col	Synonym	Area (hectares)	Share (%) of global area	Synonym's share (%) of prime variety
Graciano	R	Tinta Miuda	584	0.01	31
		Bovale	573	0.01	30
		Graciano	435	0.01	23
		Cagnulari	311	0.01	16
		Morrastel	7	0.00	0
Grand Noir	R	Gran Negro	895	0.02	95
		Grand Noir	47	0.00	5
		Grand Noir De La Calmette	4	0.00	0
Grasevina	W	Italian Riesling	39797	0.82	43
		Welschriesling	32528	0.67	35
		Grasevina Bijela	16051	0.33	17
		Riesling Italico	2007	0.04	2
		Borba	1923	0.04	2
Grechetto di Orvieto	W	Grechetto	1177	0.02	100
Greco	W	Greco	920	0.02	69
		Asprinio	405	0.01	31
		Grec	1	0.00	0
Grenache Rose	R	Grenas Rose	22	0.00	100
Grolleau Noir	R	Grolleau	2201	0.05	100
Groppello di Mocasina	R	Groppello di Santo Stefano	66	0.00	56
		Groppello di Mocasina	53	0.00	44
Gruner Veltliner	W	Gruner Veltliner	23475	0.48	99
		Veltliner	129	0.00	1
Hondarrabi Beltza	R	Ondarrabi Beltza	11	0.00	100
Hrvatica	R	Negrara	245	0.01	100
Humagne	W	Humagne Blanc	9	0.00	100
Ilichevskii Rannii	R	Iliciovski Ciornai Rannii	5	0.00	100
Inzolia	W	Ansonica	9259	0.19	100
Isabella	R	Isabel	14285	0.29	52
		Isabella	12491	0.26	46
		Lidia	599	0.01	2
Jacquez	R	Jacquez	170	0.00	75
		Lenoir	56	0.00	25
Joannes Seyve	R	Johan.Seyve D.	3	0.00	100
Juan Garcia	R	Juan Garcia	1673	0.03	81
		Mouraton	224	0.00	11
		Tinta Gorda	179	0.00	9
Jurie	W	Jurie Divers	0	0.00	100
Kadarka	R	Gamza	1619	0.03	62
		Kadarka	1012	0.02	38
Koenigin der Weingaerten	W	Tzaritza Na Loziata	567	0.01	76
		Regina dei Vigneti	184	0.00	24
Korinthiaki	R	Currant	778	0.02	93
		Corinto Nero	56	0.00	7
Lacoste	R	Auxerrois Rupes	1	0.00	100
Lacrima di Morro d'Alba	R	Lacrima	652	0.01	100
Lairen	W	Malvar	298	0.01	100
Landot	W	Landot Divers	0	0.00	100
Landot Noir	R	Landot Divers	0	0.00	100

Table 14 (cont.) Prime varieties' global area and share of each synonym, and synonym's share of each prime variety, 2000

Prime variety	Col	Synonym	Area (hectares)	Share (%) of global area	Synonym's share (%) of prime variety
Laska	R	Lasca	1	0.00	100
Listain de Huelva	W	Manteudo	596	0.01	100
Listan Negro	R	Listan Negro	3250	0.07	99
		Negra Comun	25	0.00	1
		Almuneco	17	0.00	1
Listan Prieto	R	Pais	15181	0.31	98
		Mission	340	0.01	2
		Moscatel Negro	11	0.00	0
Listrao Roxo	R	Listrao	10	0.00	100
Loureiro	W	Loureiro	3939	0.08	90
		Loureiro Blanca	454	0.01	10
Macabeo	W	Macabeo	42902	0.88	89
		Macabeu	5223	0.11	11
Magliocco Dolce	R	Marsigliana Nera	243	0.00	100
Maiskii Chernyi	R	Mayskiy	77	0.00	100
Malagousia	W	Malagouzia	23	0.00	100
Malegue	R	Malegue Divers	1	0.00	100
Malvasia Bianca di Candia	W	Malvasia Bianca di Candia	8244	0.17	64
		Malvasia Bianca	4645	0.10	36
Malvasia di Lipari	W	Malvasia di Sardegna	367	0.01	71
		Malvasia di Lipari	127	0.00	25
		Malvasia Sitges	21	0.00	4
Malvasia Fina	W	Torrontes	4751	0.10	67
		Boal	1549	0.03	22
		Assario Branco	778	0.02	11
		Gual	23	0.00	0
Malvasia Nera di Brindisi	R	Malvasia Nera di Brindisi	2178	0.04	69
		Malvasia Nera di Lecce	648	0.01	20
		Malvasia Negra	348	0.01	11
Malvazija Istarska	W	Malvasija Istarska	7134	0.15	94
		Malvasia Istriana	425	0.01	6
Mammolo	R	Sciaccarello	639	0.01	82
		Mammolo	138	0.00	18
Manseng Noir	R	Manseng Noir	5	0.00	52
		Ferron	5	0.00	48
Manzoni Bianco	W	Manzoni	8290	0.17	100
Marechal Foch	R	Marechal Foch	151	0.00	87
		Foch	22	0.00	13
Marmajuelo	W	Vermejuela	37	0.00	100
Marsanne	W	Marsanne	1479	0.03	98
		Marsanne Blanche	33	0.00	2
Marufo	R	Moravia Dulce	2827	0.06	45
		Mourisco	2633	0.05	42
		Marufo	879	0.02	14
Mauzac Blanc	W	Mauzac	3251	0.07	100
Mavro Messenikola	R	Messenikola	3	0.00	100
Mavrouda	R	Mavroudi	349	0.01	100

Table 14 (cont.) Prime varieties' global area and share of each synonym, and synonym's share of each prime variety, 2000

Prime variety	Col	Synonym	Area (hectares)	Share (%) of global area	Synonym's share (%) of prime variety
Mazuelo	R	Carignan	98238	2.01	78
		Carignane	18214	0.37	14
		Mazuela	8103	0.17	6
		Carignano	1721	0.04	1
		Mazuelo	374	0.01	0
Mencia	R	Mencia	10077	0.21	77
		Jaen	1971	0.04	15
		Jaen Tinto	1068	0.02	8
		Loureiro Tinto	21	0.00	0
Molinara	R	Molinara	1301	0.03	80
		Molinera	334	0.01	20
Monastrell	R	Monastrell	67163	1.38	88
		Mourvedre	8006	0.16	10
		Mataro	1135	0.02	1
Mondeuse Noire	R	Mondeuse	1404	0.03	100
Monemvassia	W	Monemvasia	418	0.01	100
Monica Nera	R	Monica	2835	0.06	100
Monstruosa	W	Monstruosa de Monterrei	2	0.00	100
Montonico Bianco	W	Montonico Bianco	647	0.01	99
		Montonico	10	0.00	1
Moore's Diamond	W	Moores Diamond	19	0.00	100
Morio-Muskat	W	Morio Muscat	1188	0.02	100
Mornen Noir	R	Mornen	1	0.00	100
Morrastel Bouschet	R	Gros Morras.Bous.	1	0.00	100
Moscatel Branco	W	Moscatel Nunes	1419	0.03	100
Moscato Giallo	W	Moscato Giallo	345	0.01	84
		Moscatel Amarilla	65	0.00	16
Moscato Rosa del Trentino	R	Moscato Rosa	93	0.00	100
Moschofilero	R	Moschofilero	293	0.01	69
		Fileri	130	0.00	31
Moschomavro	R	Moschato	2305	0.05	100
Mtsvane Kakhuri	W	Mtsvane	249	0.01	100
Muller Thurgau	W	Muller Thurgau	33074	0.68	99
		Rivaner	459	0.01	1
		Findling	39	0.00	0
Muscat Blanc a Petits Grains	W	Moscato Bianco	13016	0.27	46
		Muscat Petits Grains	6934	0.14	24
		Moschato	2222	0.05	8
		Muscat Blanc	2052	0.04	7
		Tamianka	1012	0.02	4
		Muscat Blanc a Petits Grains	981	0.02	3
		Muscat de Frontignan	773	0.02	3
		Muskat	526	0.01	2
		Muscat a Petits Grains Blanc	214	0.00	1
		Moscatel de Grano Menudo	200	0.00	1
		Muscat Frontignan	172	0.00	1
		Muskateller	143	0.00	1
		Muskateller Gelber	87	0.00	0
		Muscat Canelli	45	0.00	0
		Moscatel Fontinan	23	0.00	0
		Muscat de Colmar	1	0.00	0

Table 14 (cont.) Prime varieties' global area and share of each synonym, and synonym's share of each prime variety, 2000

Prime variety	Col	Synonym	Area (hectares)	Share (%) of global area	Synonym's share (%) of prime variety
Muscat Fleur d'Oranger	W	Muscat Orange	36	0.00	100
Muscat of Alexandria	W	Muscat of Alexandria	12030	0.25	41
		Moscatel de Malaga	6144	0.13	21
		Muscat d'Alexandrie	4047	0.08	14
		Muscat Alexandr.	3027	0.06	10
		Muscat Gordo Blanco	2495	0.05	8
		Zibibbo	1157	0.02	4
		Moscatel Graudo	510	0.01	2
Muscat of Alexandria Red	R	Red Hanepoot	11	0.00	100
Muscat of Hamburg	R	Muscat of Hamburg	3205	0.07	45
		Moscatel Hambourg	2886	0.06	41
		Muscat Hambourg	769	0.02	11
		Moscato Nero Di Acqui	199	0.00	3
		Moscatel Hamburt	6	0.00	0
Negoska	R	Negkoska	96	0.00	100
Negramoll	R	Negramoll	1674	0.03	47
		Mollar	842	0.02	24
		Negra Mole	509	0.01	14
		Rabo de Ovelha Tinto	318	0.01	9
		Tinta Negra	212	0.00	6
		Mulata	1	0.00	0
		Saborinho	0	0.00	0
Negroamaro	R	Negro Amaro	16619	0.34	100
Nero Buono di Cori	R	Nero Buono	114	0.00	100
Nero d'Avola	R	Calabrese	11318	0.23	100
Norton	R	Cynthiana	0	0.00	100
Oberlin White	W	Oberlin Divers	1	0.00	100
Olivette Noire	R	Cornichon Violet	0	0.00	100
Onitskanskii Belyi	W	Alb de Onitcani	5	0.00	100
Palomino Fino	W	Palomino Fino	20884	0.43	69
		Listan	7261	0.15	24
		Palomino	2096	0.04	7
		Palomino Superior	56	0.00	0
Pamid	R	Pamid	22703	0.47	100
		Pamiti	15	0.00	0
Panse Valenciano	W	Panse Valenciana	649	0.01	100
Pardillo	W	Marisancho	7272	0.15	100
Parraleta	R	Caricagiola	141	0.00	84
		Parraleta	15	0.00	9
		Carcajolo Noir	11	0.00	6
Pascal Blanc	W	Pascal	0	0.00	100
Pascale	R	Pascale	1229	0.03	78
		Nieddu Mannu	344	0.01	22
Perruno	W	Perruno	1756	0.04	62
		Royal	1075	0.02	38
Pervenets Magaracha	W	Pervenetz Magaratcha	1295	0.03	46
		Early Magaratch	1093	0.02	39
		Pervenets Magaracha	449	0.01	16
Pervomaisky	R	Pervomaiskii	64	0.00	100

Table 14 (cont.) Prime varieties' global area and share of each synonym, and synonym's share of each prime variety, 2000

Prime variety	Col	Synonym	Area (hectares)	Share (%) of global area	Synonym's share (%) of prime variety
Petit Manseng	W	Pt.Manseng Blanc	613	0.01	100
Pignola Valtellinese	R	Pignola	70	0.00	100
Pinot Blanc	W	Pinot Blanc	6618	0.14	39
		Pinot Bianco	4993	0.10	29
		Weisser Burgunder	2936	0.06	17
		Burgunder	2396	0.05	14
		Pinot Blanco	48	0.00	0
Pinot Gris	O	Pinot Gris	9338	0.19	49
		Pinot Grigio	6612	0.14	35
		Rulander	2636	0.05	14
		Grauer Burgunder	293	0.01	2
Pinot Meunier	R	Meunier	10825	0.22	100
		Pinot Menier	7	0.00	0
Pinot Noir	R	Pinot Noir	55357	1.13	92
		Pinot Nero	3287	0.07	5
		Pinot Negro	1047	0.02	2
		Blauer Burgunder	409	0.01	1
Pinot Noir Precoce	R	Fruhburgunder	84	0.00	98
		Pinot Precoce	1	0.00	2
Piquepoul Noir	R	Piquepoul Noir	94	0.00	91
		Picapoll Negro	10	0.00	9
Plant Droit	R	Plant Droit	35	0.00	87
		Espanenc	5	0.00	13
Posip Bijeli	W	Posip	6539	0.13	100
Prensal	W	Pensal Blanco	114	0.00	100
Prie	W	Prie Blanc	36	0.00	100
Primetta	R	Prie Rouge	17	0.00	100
Ravat	R	Ravat Divers	1	0.00	100
Refosco di Faedis	R	Refosco Nostrano	256	0.01	100
Ribolla Gialla	W	Rebula	1127	0.02	80
		Ribolla Gialla	280	0.01	20
Riesling	W	Riesling Weisser	22350	0.46	52
		Riesling	7146	0.15	17
		White Riesling	6006	0.12	14
		Riesling	3407	0.07	8
		Weisser Riesling	2120	0.04	5
		Riesling de Rhin	1343	0.03	3
		Rynsky Riesling	793	0.02	2
Rkatsiteli	W	Rkatsiteli	46417	0.95	69
		Rkatiteli	11508	0.24	17
		Rkaziteli	9429	0.19	14
Robola	W	Rombola	359	0.01	100
Rollo	W	Rollo	108	0.00	92
		Livornese Bianca	9	0.00	8
Rose du Var	O	Roussanne Var	129	0.00	100
Rossara Trentina	R	Rossara	29	0.00	100
Rubin Tairovsky	R	Rubin Tairovski	2	0.00	100
Ruby Cabernet	R	Ruby Cabernet	7397	0.15	100
		Rubi Cabernet	22	0.00	0

Prime variety	Col	Synonym	Area (hectares)	Share (%) of global area	Synonym's share (%) of prime variety
Rufete	R	Rufete	2985	0.06	88
		Tinta Pinheira	412	0.01	12
		Castellana	1	0.00	0
Sangiovese	R	Sangiovese	66501	1.36	97
		Nielluccio	1564	0.03	2
		Sangioveto	666	0.01	1
		Prugnolo Gentile	146	0.00	0
Sankt Laurent	R	St. Laurent	2370	0.05	100
Saperavi Severny	R	Saperavi Severnii	25	0.00	100
Sauvignon Blanc	W	Sauvignon	34444	0.71	53
		Sauvignon Blanc	29787	0.61	46
		Sauvignon Blanca	467	0.01	1
		Sovinion	158	0.00	0
		Sauvignon Musque	33	0.00	0
Sauvignonasse	W	Tocai Friulano	4564	0.09	83
		Sauvignonasse	798	0.02	15
		Sauvignon Vert	132	0.00	2
Savatiano	W	Savvatiano	12747	0.26	100
Schiava Grossa	R	Schiava Grossa	1240	0.03	99
		Tschaggele	18	0.00	1
Sciascinoso	R	Sciascinoso	136	0.00	54
		Olivella Nera	116	0.00	46
seibel	R	Seibel Hybrids	1967	0.04	99
		Seibel Divers	24	0.00	1
Seibel white	W	Seibel Divers	15	0.00	100
Semillon	W	Semillon	26209	0.54	100
		Semigion	21	0.00	0
Sercial	W	Esganoso	282	0.01	92
		Sercial	24	0.00	8
Servant	W	Raisin Blanc	432	0.01	81
		Servant	98	0.00	19
Seyval Blanc	W	Seyval Blanc	352	0.01	91
		Seyval	36	0.00	9
Silvaner	W	Sylvaner	2196	0.05	52
		Silvaner	1877	0.04	45
		Sylvaner Verde	112	0.00	3
		Rhin	0	0.00	0
Siria	W	Roupeiro Branco	1527	0.03	55
		Dona Blanca	758	0.02	27
		Ciguente	268	0.01	10
		Crato Espanhol	155	0.00	6
		Valenciana Blanca	76	0.00	3
		Sabro	6	0.00	0
Sukholimanskiy Bely	W	Sukholimanskiy Bely	1032	0.02	63
		Suholimenschii Belii	599	0.01	37
Sultaniye	W	Sultana	10298	0.21	72
		Sultaniye	4049	0.08	28
		Thompson	4	0.00	0
Sumoll	R	Sumoll	1390	0.03	99
		Vijiriego Negro	11	0.00	1

Table 14 (cont.) Prime varieties' global area and share of each synonym, and synonym's share of each prime variety, 2000

Prime variety	Col	Synonym	Area (hectares)	Share (%) of global area	Synonym's share (%) of prime variety
Syrah	R	Syrah	66455	1.36	65
		Shiraz	34926	0.72	34
		Syrach	86	0.00	0
		Sirach	39	0.00	0
		Chirac	10	0.00	0
Tempranillo	R	Tempranillo	81710	1.68	88
		Tinta Roriz	5764	0.12	6
		Tinto de Toro	3723	0.08	4
		Aragonez	1592	0.03	2
		Valdepenas	194	0.00	0
		Negra de Mesa	2	0.00	0
Teneron	R	Valency	3488	0.07	100
Teoulier Noir	R	Teoulier	1	0.00	100
Terras 20	R	Alicante Terras 20	13	0.00	100
Tinta Barroca	R	Tinta Barroca	5657	0.12	93
		Tinta Barocca	395	0.01	7
Torbato	W	Torbato	139	0.00	83
		Tourbat	29	0.00	17
Touriga Nacional	R	Touriga Nacional	4041	0.08	95
		Tourigo	149	0.00	3
		Touriga	73	0.00	2
Trajadura	W	Trajadura	1788	0.04	74
		Treixadura	628	0.01	26
Trebbiano d'Abruzzo	W	Trebbiano Abruzzese	8435	0.17	100
Trebbiano Toscano	W	Ugni Blanc	95872	1.97	70
		Trebbiano Toscano	39447	0.81	29
		Uni Blance	720	0.01	1
		Talia	382	0.01	0
		St Emilion	151	0.00	0
Trepat	R	Trepat	1159	0.02	66
		Bonicaire	539	0.01	31
		Parrel Verdal	65	0.00	4
Tribidrag	R	Zinfandel	19077	0.39	71
		Primitivo	7838	0.16	29
Trincadeira	R	Trincadeira	7062	0.14	97
		Tinta Amarela	164	0.00	2
		Crato Preto	39	0.00	1
Trobat	R	Panse Negro	83	0.00	100
Trousseau	R	Bastardo	1754	0.04	83
		Verdejo Negro	227	0.00	11
		Trousseau	126	0.00	6
		Bastarda	13	0.00	1
Trousseau Gris	O	Gray Riesling	28	0.00	100
Valenci Tinto	R	Grumier Tinto	5	0.00	100
Valentino Nero	R	Valentino	56	0.00	100
Verdejo	W	Verdejo Blanco	4453	0.09	100
Verdicchio Bianco	W	Verdicchio Bianco	3330	0.07	66
		Trebbiano di Soave	1710	0.04	34
		Boschera	3	0.00	0

Table 14 (cont.) Prime varieties' global area and share of each synonym, and synonym's share of each prime variety, 2000

Prime variety	Col	Synonym	Area (hectares)	Share (%) of global area	Synonym's share (%) of prime variety
Verdiso	W	Verdiso	65	0.00	91
		Pedevenda	6	0.00	9
Vermentino	W	Vermentino	5330	0.11	91
		Favorita	273	0.01	5
		Pigato	232	0.00	4
Vernaccia di San Gimignano	W	Vernaccia di San Gimignano	772	0.02	90
		Bervedino	82	0.00	10
Vidal	W	Vidal Blanc	611	0.01	100
		Vidal Divers	0	0.00	0
Vidal Red	R	Vidal Divers	0	0.00	100
Vignoles	W	Vignoles	35	0.00	51
		Ravat 51	34	0.00	49
Vijariego	W	Vijiriego	509	0.01	100
		Diego	0	0.00	0
Vinhao	R	Vinhao	5296	0.11	89
		Souson	590	0.01	10
		Souzao	51	0.00	1
Viognier	W	Viognier	3133	0.06	99
		Viogner	27	0.00	1
Vitovska	W	Vitouska	42	0.00	100
Voskeat	W	Voskehat	809	0.02	100
Xarello	W	Xarello Blanco	10288	0.21	100
Xarello Rosado	W	Pansa Rosada	10	0.00	100
Other primes with no synonyms			1104536	22.64	
Other Varieties			569508	11.67	
Total			**4878176**	**100**	

Table 15: Prime varieties' global area and share of each synonym, and synonym's share of each prime variety, 2010

Prime variety	Col	Synonym	Area (hectares)	Share (%) of global area	Synonym's share (%) of prime variety
Abbo	R	Abbou	2375	0.05	100
Abrusco	R	Colorino	421	0.01	100
		Abrusco	2	0.00	0
Afus Ali	W	Roseti	8	0.00	100
Aglianico	R	Aglianico	7551	0.16	76
		Aglianico del Vulture	2413	0.05	24
Airen	W	Airen	252180	5.48	100
		Forcallat Blanca	166	0.00	0
		Burra Blanca	18	0.00	0
Alarije	W	Alarije	1722	0.04	100
		Malfar	4	0.00	0
Albarola	W	Albarola	1406	0.03	97
		Bianchetta Genovese	48	0.00	3
Albillo Mayor	W	Albillo Mayor	1312	0.03	99
		Albilla	7	0.00	1
Albillo Real	W	Albillo	861	0.02	100
Alfrocheiro	R	Alfrocheiro	1180	0.03	99
		Bastarda Negra	7	0.00	1
		Tinta Bastardinha	1	0.00	0
Alicante Henri Bouschet	R	Garnacha Tintorera	19551	0.42	50
		Alicante Bouschet	8427	0.18	22
		Alicante Henri Bouschet	5086	0.11	13
		Tintoreras	3887	0.08	10
		Alicante Bouchet	1608	0.03	4
		Alicante	370	0.01	1
		Alikante Mouse	56	0.00	0
Almafre	W	Almafra	0	0.00	100
Alminhaca	W	Almenhaca	1	0.00	100
Alphonse Lavallee	R	Alphonse Lavallee	829	0.02	94
		Alfonso Lavalle	54	0.00	6
Alvar Branco	W	Alvar	0	0.00	100
Alvarelhao	R	Pilongo	106	0.00	59
		Alvarelhao	53	0.00	30
		Brancellao	21	0.00	12
Alvarinho	W	Albarino	3530	0.08	64
		Alvarinho	1993	0.04	36
Aramon Noir	R	Aramon	2891	0.06	100
		Amor-Nao-Me-Deixes	1	0.00	0
Arany Sarfeher	W	Arany Sarfeher	1130	0.02	100
		Sarfeher	3	0.00	0
Arinto de Bucelas	W	Arinto	4446	0.10	100
Arvine	W	Arvine	154	0.00	89
		Petite Arvine	19	0.00	11

Table 15 (cont.) Prime varieties' global area and share of each synonym, and synonym's share of each prime variety, 2010

Prime variety	Col	Synonym	Area (hectares)	Share (%) of global area	Synonym's share (%) of prime variety
Asprouda	W	Asproudi	113	0.00	100
Assyrtiko	W	Asirtiko	902	0.02	100
Aurore	W	Aurora	268	0.01	100
Babeasca Gris	W	Babeasca Gri	328	0.01	100
Babeasca Neagra	R	Babeasca Neagra	3042	0.07	97
		Rara Neagra	80	0.00	3
Babosa de Madere	W	Babosa	2	0.00	100
Baco Noir	R	Baco Noir	465	0.01	99
		Baco	2	0.00	1
Baga	R	Baga	4102	0.09	100
		Carrega Burros	4	0.00	0
		Carrasquenho	2	0.00	0
Bakator Roz	R	Piros Bakator	2	0.00	100
Barkhatnyi	W	Barkhatny	30	0.00	100
Barreto de Semente	R	Barreto	3	0.00	100
Bastardo Magarachsky	R	Bastardo Magarachskiy	1330	0.03	56
		Bastardo Magaraceskii	1040	0.02	44
Bayanshira	W	Bayan-Shirey	645	0.01	100
Beba	W	Beba	2949	0.06	97
		Teta de Vaca	64	0.00	2
		Breval	19	0.00	1
		Iso	4	0.00	0
Bequignol Noir	R	Bequignol	698	0.02	100
Biancone di Portoferraio	W	Biancone	78	0.00	100
Biborkadarka	R	Bibor Kadarka	136	0.00	100
Blauer Portugieser	R	Blauer Portugieser	2838	0.06	75
		Modry Portugal	714	0.02	19
		Portoghese	167	0.00	4
		Portugizac	42	0.00	1
		Portugues Azul	36	0.00	1
		Portugais Blue	2	0.00	0
Blauer Wildbacher	R	Blauer Wildbacher	365	0.01	99
		Wildbacher	3	0.00	1
Blaufrankisch	R	Blaufrankisch	11229	0.24	70
		Frankovka	1668	0.04	10
		Frankovka Modra	1378	0.03	9
		Burgund Mare	760	0.02	5
		Modra Frankinja	680	0.01	4
		Borgona	290	0.01	2
		Franconia	59	0.00	0
		Borgonja	50	0.00	0
		Lemberger	26	0.00	0
Boal Vencedor	W	Vencedor	2	0.00	100

Table 15 (cont.) Prime varieties' global area and share of each synonym, and synonym's share of each prime variety, 2010

Prime variety	Col	Synonym	Area (hectares)	Share (%) of global area	Synonym's share (%) of prime variety
Bonamico	R	Buonamico	167	0.00	86
		Bonamico	26	0.00	14
Borracal	R	Caino Tinto	523	0.01	77
		Borracal	160	0.00	23
Bouvier	W	Bouvier	244	0.01	98
		Bouvierovo Hrozno	6	0.00	2
Brachetto del Piemonte	R	Brachetto	1460	0.03	100
Branco Sr. Joao	W	Branco Joao	0	0.00	100
Branco Valente	W	Valente	0	0.00	100
Brandam	W	Branda	312	0.01	100
Cabernet Sauvignon	R	Cabernet Sauvignon	290058	6.30	100
		Burdeos	33	0.00	0
Cabral	R	Malvasia Cabral	2	0.00	100
Cainho de Moreira	W	Cainho	7	0.00	100
Camaralet de Lasseube	W	Camarate	515	0.01	100
Canari Noir	R	Canari	139	0.00	91
		Folle Noire	13	0.00	9
Cardinal	R	Cardinal	286	0.01	52
		Cardenal	168	0.00	31
		Kardinal Crveni	91	0.00	17
Carignan Blanc	W	Carinena Blanco	2650	0.06	87
		Carignan Blanc	411	0.01	13
Carmenere	R	Carmenere	9988	0.22	88
		Cabernet Gernischt	1353	0.03	12
		Carmenere Crni	19	0.00	0
Castelao	R	Castelao	11065	0.24	100
		Casteloa	11	0.00	0
		Periquita	11	0.00	0
Catarratto Bianco	W	Catarratto Bianco Comune	25935	0.56	74
		Catarratto Bianco Lucido	8859	0.19	25
		Catarratto	68	0.00	0
Cayetana Blanca	W	Pardina	26767	0.58	67
		Blanca Cayetana	12280	0.27	31
		Robal	303	0.01	1
		Baladi Verdejo	243	0.01	1
		Mourisco Branco	141	0.00	0
		Sarigo	7	0.00	0
Cayuga White	W	Cayuga White	167	0.00	79
		Cayuga	45	0.00	21
Cellerina	R	Slarina	2	0.00	100
Cerceal Branco	W	Cercial	311	0.01	100
Cesanese	R	Cesanese d'Affile	372	0.01	55
		Cesanese Comune	307	0.01	45

Table 15 (cont.) Prime varieties' global area and share of each synonym, and synonym's share of each prime variety, 2010

Prime variety	Col	Synonym	Area (hectares)	Share (%) of global area	Synonym's share (%) of prime variety
Chardonnay	W	Chardonnay	196336	4.27	99
		Chardonnay Blanc	2457	0.05	1
Chasselas	W	Chasselas	11971	0.26	91
		Gutedel Weisser	1120	0.02	8
		Chasselas Dorato	34	0.00	0
		Plemenka Bijela	21	0.00	0
		Chaslas	21	0.00	0
		Chaselas Dorada	20	0.00	0
Chasselas Rouge	W	Chasselas Roxo	7	0.00	100
Chenin Blanc	W	Chenin Blanc	22720	0.49	65
		Chenin	12443	0.27	35
Cianorie	R	Cjanorie	2	0.00	100
Cinsaut	R	Cinsaut	22913	0.50	64
		Cinsault	13011	0.28	36
		Ottavianello	51	0.00	0
		Senso	43	0.00	0
		Cargadora	22	0.00	0
Citronny Magarach	W	Citronny of Magarach	307	0.01	100
Clairette	W	Clairette	2588	0.06	89
		Clairette Blanche	290	0.01	10
		Clairet	22	0.00	1
Coda di Volpe Bianca	W	Coda di Volpe Bianca	555	0.01	95
		Guarnaccia	32	0.00	5
Codega de Larinho	W	Codega do Larinho	629	0.01	100
Colombard	W	Colombar	11990	0.26	37
		Colombard	10060	0.22	31
		French Colombard	10025	0.22	31
Concord	R	Concord	12164	0.26	99
		Concord Clone 30	74	0.00	1
Corbina Vicentina	R	Corbina	12	0.00	100
Cornalin	R	Humagne Rouge	128	0.00	50
		Cornalin	128	0.00	50
Corvina Veronese	R	Corvina	7496	0.16	100
		Corvina Veronese	0	0.00	0
Cot	R	Malbec	34193	0.74	84
		Cot	6234	0.14	15
		Malbech	260	0.01	1
Couderc Noir	R	Couderc Noir	2477	0.05	92
		Couderc	214	0.00	8
Couderc	W	Couderc 13	834	0.02	100
Crystal	W	Crystal	171	0.00	98
		Cristal	4	0.00	2
	W	Csabagyongye	89	0.00	100

Table 15 (cont.) Prime varieties' global area and share of each synonym, and synonym's share of each prime variety, 2010

Prime variety	Col	Synonym	Area (hectares)	Share (%) of global area	Synonym's share (%) of prime variety
Damaschino	W	Alicante Branco	1037	0.02	50
		Valenci	586	0.01	28
		Planta Fina	239	0.01	11
		Damaschino	221	0.00	11
Debina	W	Dembina	239	0.01	100
Dekabrskii	R	Dekabrsky	78	0.00	100
Dimyat	W	Dimyat	2386	0.05	99
		Zoumiatiko	9	0.00	0
		Smederevka	6	0.00	0
Dorinto	W	Arinto do Interior	14	0.00	100
Douce Noire	R	Bonarda	18877	0.41	99
		Turca	65	0.00	0
		Charbono	34	0.00	0
		Douce Noire	0	0.00	0
Droujba	W	Drujba	3	0.00	100
Drupeggio	W	Canaiolo Bianco	286	0.01	100
Durif	R	Petite Sirah	2863	0.06	80
		Durif	455	0.01	13
		Petit Syrah	135	0.00	4
		Petite Syrah	104	0.00	3
Elbling	W	Elbling Weisser	550	0.01	39
		Burger	498	0.01	35
		Elbling	370	0.01	26
Enantio	R	Lambrusco a Foglia Frastagliata	724	0.02	100
Esganacao Preto	R	Esgana Cao Tinto	0	0.00	100
Faberrebe	W	Faberrebe	520	0.01	99
		Faber	4	0.00	1
Fernao Pires	W	Fernao Pires	9504	0.21	100
		Molinha	7	0.00	0
Feteasca Alba	W	Feteasca Alba	17250	0.37	99
		Dievcie Hrozno	219	0.00	1
Fortana	R	Fortana	402	0.01	63
		Canina Nera	240	0.01	37
Fruhroter Veltliner	R	Fruhroter Veltliner	424	0.01	50
		Veltlinske Cervene Rane	217	0.00	26
		Veltlinske Cervene Skore	195	0.00	23
		Korai Piros Veltelini	10	0.00	1
		Malvasier	0	0.00	0
Furmint	W	Furmint	4435	0.10	84
		Sipon	651	0.01	12
		Moslavac	161	0.00	3
		Sipelj	11	0.00	0

Table 15 (cont.) Prime varieties' global area and share of each synonym, and synonym's share of each prime variety, 2010

Prime variety	Col	Synonym	Area (hectares)	Share (%) of global area	Synonym's share (%) of prime variety
Galego Dourado	W	Galego Dourado	12	0.00	76
		Pedro Luis	3	0.00	19
		Galego	1	0.00	6
Gamay de Teinturier Bouze	R	Gamay de Teinturier Bouze	215	0.00	96
		Gammay de Bouze	10	0.00	4
Gamay Noir	R	Gamay	32455	0.71	99
		Gamay Noir	207	0.00	1
		Plant Robert	6	0.00	0
		Gamay St Romain	3	0.00	0
Gamay Teinturier de Chaudenay	R	Gamay de Chaudenay	24	0.00	100
Gamay Teinturier Freaux	R	Gammay Freaux	55	0.00	100
Garanoir	R	Garanoir	203	0.00	94
		Granoir	13	0.00	6
Garganega	W	Garganega	11292	0.25	73
		Grecanico Dorato	4110	0.09	27
Gargiulo	R	C.G.2539	34	0.00	75
		C G 45803	10	0.00	23
		C.G.4113	1	0.00	2
Garnacha Blanca	W	Grenache Blanc	5107	0.11	69
		Garnacha Blanca	2263	0.05	31
Garnacha Peluda	R	Garnacha Peluda	799	0.02	65
		Lledoner Pelut	433	0.01	35
Garnacha Roja	W	Grenache Gris	1707	0.04	96
		Garnacha Roja	77	0.00	4
Garnacha Tinta	R	Grenache	108061	2.35	58
		Garnacha	58811	1.28	32
		Garnacha Tinta	11389	0.25	6
		Cannonau	5422	0.12	3
		Tocai Rosso	655	0.01	0
		Vernaccia Nera	280	0.01	0
		Grenache Noir	103	0.00	0
		Vernaccina Nero	9	0.00	0
		Vernaccia Nera Grossa	7	0.00	0
Gewurztraminer	W	Gewurztraminer	5793	0.13	41
		Traminer Rose	3692	0.08	26
		Traminer Aromatico	1408	0.03	10
		Traminer	1143	0.02	8
		Tramin Cerveny	866	0.02	6
		Traminer Rot	747	0.02	5
		Traminer Roz	385	0.01	3
		Traminac Crveni	234	0.01	2

Table 15 (cont.) Prime varieties' global area and share of each synonym, and synonym's share of each prime variety, 2010

Prime variety	Col	Synonym	Area (hectares)	Share (%) of global area	Synonym's share (%) of prime variety
Godello	W	Godello	579	0.01	53
		Gouveio	489	0.01	45
		Agudello	26	0.00	2
		Godelho	1	0.00	0
Goecseji Zamatos	W	Gecsei Zamatos	40	0.00	72
		Gocseji Zamatos	15	0.00	28
Golubok	R	Goluboc	50	0.00	57
		Golubok	37	0.00	43
Gouveio Real	W	Gouveio Real	582	0.01	100
		Gouveio Estimado	0	0.00	0
Graciano	R	Graciano	2269	0.05	73
		Tinta Miuda	332	0.01	11
		Cagnulari	260	0.01	8
		Bovale	209	0.00	7
		Graciana	19	0.00	1
		Tintilla de Rota	12	0.00	0
		Tinta Fontes	0	0.00	0
Grand Noir	R	Gran Negro	774	0.02	81
		Grand Noir	181	0.00	19
Grasa de Cotnari	W	Grasa de Cotnari	640	0.01	93
		Koverszolo	45	0.00	7
Grasevina	W	Italian Riesling	33120	0.72	54
		Welschriesling	8126	0.18	13
		Riesling Italian	7530	0.16	12
		Grasevina	4901	0.11	8
		Laki Rizling	2360	0.05	4
		Rizling Vlasky	1655	0.04	3
		Riesling Italico	1568	0.03	3
		Ryzlink VlaKy	1148	0.02	2
		Borba	791	0.02	1
Grechetto di Orvieto	W	Grechetto	1501	0.03	100
Greco	W	Asprinio	158	0.00	100
		Greco di Tufo	0	0.00	0
Grolleau Noir	R	Grolleau	2350	0.05	100
Groppello di Mocasina	R	Groppello di Mocasina	51	0.00	62
		Groppello di Santo Stefano	30	0.00	38
Gruner Veltliner	W	Gruner Veltliner	15059	0.33	80
		Veltlinske Zelene	3618	0.08	19
		Veltliner	165	0.00	1
Harslevelu	W	Feuille de Tilleul	1659	0.04	89
		Lipovina	141	0.00	8
		Harslevelu	56	0.00	3

Table 15 (cont.) Prime varieties' global area and share of each synonym, and synonym's share of each prime variety, 2010

Prime variety	Col	Synonym	Area (hectares)	Share (%) of global area	Synonym's share (%) of prime variety
Hondarrabi Beltza	R	Ondarrabi Beltza	53	0.00	99
		Beltza	0	0.00	1
Hrvatica	R	Negrara	116	0.00	100
Humagne	W	Humagne Blanc	30	0.00	100
Ilichevskii Rannii	R	Iliciovski Ciornai Rannii	5	0.00	100
Inzolia	W	Ansonica	6133	0.13	100
Irsai Oliver	W	Irsai Oliver	1410	0.03	100
		Muskat Oliver	5	0.00	0
Isabella	R	Isabella	30959	0.67	95
		Lidia	869	0.02	3
		Isabel Precoce	410	0.01	1
		Frutilla	256	0.01	1
Jacquez	R	Jacquez	2252	0.05	95
		Lenoir	80	0.00	3
		Black Spanish	36	0.00	2
Jampal	W	Jampal	71	0.00	100
		Pinheira Branca	0	0.00	0
Juan Garcia	R	Juan Garcia	1290	0.03	76
		Tinta Gorda	142	0.00	8
		Mouraton	140	0.00	8
		Gorda	135	0.00	8
Kadarka	R	Gamza	550	0.01	51
		Kadarka	537	0.01	49
Karasakiz	R	Kuntra	4	0.00	100
Kerner	W	Kerner	3989	0.09	100
		Kerner Bijeli	4	0.00	0
Koenigin der Weingaerten	W	Regina dei Vigneti	61	0.00	100
Koksis Irma	W	Kocsis Irma	11	0.00	100
Kokur Bely	W	Cokur White	918	0.02	100
Korinthiaki	R	Corinto Nero	50	0.00	92
		Corinto	4	0.00	8
Kovidinka	O	Kovidinka	1020	0.02	95
		Ruzica Crvena	56	0.00	5
Krasnostop Zolotovsky	R	Krasnostop Anapsky	211	0.00	100
Kreaca	W	Banati Rizling	3	0.00	100
Kuldzhinskii	O	Kuldzhinskiy	385	0.01	100
Lacrima di Morro d'Alba	R	Lacrima	421	0.01	100
Lairen	W	Malvar	214	0.00	100
Landot Noir	R	Landot	2	0.00	100
	W	Manteudo	350	0.01	100
Listan Negro	R	Listan Negro	2624	0.06	98
		Negra Commun	26	0.00	1
		Almuneco	16	0.00	1

Table 15 (cont.) Prime varieties' global area and share of each synonym, and synonym's share of each prime variety, 2010

Prime variety	Col	Synonym	Area (hectares)	Share (%) of global area	Synonym's share (%) of prime variety
Listan Prieto	R	Pais	3868	0.08	85
		Criolla Chica	423	0.01	9
		Mission	265	0.01	6
		Moscatel Negro	6	0.00	0
		Moscatel Negra	1	0.00	0
Loureiro	W	Loureiro	3469	0.08	86
		Loureiro Blanca	585	0.01	14
Macabeo	W	Macabeo	38419	0.83	94
		Macabeu	2628	0.06	6
Magliocco Dolce	R	Marsigliana Nera	87	0.00	100
Magyarfrankos	R	Magyar Frankos	0	0.00	100
Maiskii Chernyi	R	Mayskiy	110	0.00	100
Malagousia	W	Malagouzia	182	0.00	100
Malvasia Bianca di Candia	W	Malvasia Bianca di Candia	4976	0.11	50
		Malvasia Bianca	4915	0.11	50
Malvasia Bianca Lunga	W	Malvasia Bianca Lunga	2259	0.05	89
		Marastina	285	0.01	11
Malvasia di Lipari	W	Malvasia di Sardegna	114	0.00	37
		Malvasia Sitges	112	0.00	36
		Malvasia di Lipari	53	0.00	17
		Malvasia Dubrovacka Bijela	24	0.00	8
		Malvasia Candida	7	0.00	2
Malvasia Fina	W	Malvasia Fina	2719	0.06	80
		Torrontes	464	0.01	14
		Boal Branco	190	0.00	6
		Gual	22	0.00	1
		Boal Espinho	21	0.00	1
		Boal	0	0.00	0
Malvasia Nera di Brindisi	R	Malvasia Nera di Brindisi	879	0.02	67
		Malvasia Nera di Lecce	402	0.01	31
		Malvasia Negra	33	0.00	3
		Malvasia Nera	0	0.00	0
Malvasia Preta	R	Malvasia Preta	1003	0.02	100
		Pinheira Roxa	0	0.00	0
Malvasia Trigueira	R	Trigueira	12	0.00	100
Malvazija Istarska	W	Malvazija Istarska	1705	0.04	62
		Malvazija	740	0.02	27
		Malvasia Istriana	296	0.01	11
Mammolo	R	Sciaccarello	773	0.02	94
		Mammolo	52	0.00	6
Manseng Noir	R	Ferrol	50	0.00	89
		Ferron	6	0.00	11

Table 15 (cont.) Prime varieties' global area and share of each synonym, and synonym's share of each prime variety, 2010

Prime variety	Col	Synonym	Area (hectares)	Share (%) of global area	Synonym's share (%) of prime variety
Marechal Foch	R	Marechal Foch	277	0.01	81
		Foch	67	0.00	19
Marmajuelo	W	Vermejuela	24	0.00	100
Marsanne	W	Marsanne	1694	0.04	97
		Marsanne Blanche	48	0.00	3
Marufo	R	Marufo	3020	0.07	46
		Moravia Dulce	2571	0.06	39
		Mourisco	958	0.02	15
		Mourisco Roxo	31	0.00	0
Marzemino	R	Marzemino	1085	0.02	99
		Marzemina Grossa	5	0.00	1
Maturana Blanca	W	Maturana Blanca	8	0.00	45
		Maturano Bianco	10	0.00	55
Mauzac Blanc	W	Mauzac	1991	0.04	100
Mavrouda	R	Mavroudi	520	0.01	100
Mazuelo	R	Carignan	55910	1.22	70
		Carignane	17015	0.37	21
		Mazuela	4749	0.10	6
		Carignano	1645	0.04	2
		Carignan Noir	481	0.01	1
		Bovale Grande	378	0.01	0
Mencia	R	Mencia	7888	0.17	74
		Jaen	2454	0.05	23
		Jaen Tinto	295	0.01	3
		Loureiro Tinto	22	0.00	0
Menoir	R	Menoire	65		100
Menu Pineau	W	Orbois	212	0.00	100
Mezes Feher	W	Mezes	2	0.00	100
Miguel del Arco	R	Miguel del Arco	429	0.01	92
		Vidau	39	0.00	8
Molinara	R	Molinara	595	0.01	83
		Molinera	122	0.00	17
Monastrell	R	Monastrell	58414	1.27	84
		Mourvedre	9832	0.21	14
		Mataro	1603	0.03	2
		Garrut	1	0.00	0
Mondeuse Noire	R	Mondeuse	302	0.01	99
		Mondeuse Rouge	4	0.00	1
Monemvassia	W	Monemvasia	481	0.01	100
Monstruosa	W	Monstruosa de Monterrei	1	0.00	100
Montepulciano	R	Montepulciano	34862	0.76	100
		Cordisco	85	0.00	0
Moore's Diamond	W	Moores Diamond	42	0.00	100

Table 15 (cont.) Prime varieties' global area and share of each synonym, and synonym's share of each prime variety, 2010

Prime variety	Col	Synonym	Area (hectares)	Share (%) of global area	Synonym's share (%) of prime variety
Morio-Muskat	W	Morio Muscat	39	0.00	100
Moscatel Branco	W	Moscatel Nunes	30	0.00	100
Moscatel Lilaz	W	Lilas	0	0.00	100
Moscatel Rosada	O	Moscatel Rosado	7259	0.16	99
		Moscatel Rosada	70	0.00	1
Moscato Giallo	W	Moscato Giallo	1256	0.03	85
		Moscatel Amarillo	131	0.00	9
		Muskat Zuti	59	0.00	4
		Moscatel Amarilla	25	0.00	2
Moscato Rosa del Trentino	R	Moscato Rosa	66	0.00	82
		Muskat Ruza Crni	14	0.00	18
		Moscato Rosado	0	0.00	1
Moschofilero	R	Moschofilero	613	0.01	66
		Fileri	321	0.01	34
Moschomavro	R	Moschato	1428	0.03	100
Mtsvane Kakhuri	W	Mtsvane	319	0.01	100
Muller Thurgau	W	Muller Thurgau	22488	0.49	99
		Rivaner	184	0.00	1
		Rizvanac	60	0.00	0
		Findling	21	0.00	0
Muscat a Petits Grains Noirs	R	Moscatel Galego Tinto	108	0.00	100
Muscat a Petits Grains Rouge	R	Moscatel Galego Roxo	68	0.00	100
Muscat Bailey A	R	Muscat Bailey A	103	0.00	84
		Muscat Bailey	19	0.00	16

Table 15 (cont.) Prime varieties' global area and share of each synonym, and synonym's share of each prime variety, 2010

Prime variety	Col	Synonym	Area (hectares)	Share (%) of global area	Synonym's share (%) of prime variety
Muscat Blanc a Petits Grains	W	Moscato Bianco	11600	0.25	37
		Muscat Petits Grains	7620	0.17	24
		Moschato	2162	0.05	7
		Muscat Blanc	1388	0.03	4
		Moscatel de Grano Menudo	996	0.02	3
		Muscat	957	0.02	3
		Tamaioasa Romaneasca	840	0.02	3
		Muscat White	819	0.02	3
		Moscatel	740	0.02	2
		Muscat de Frontignan	689	0.01	2
		Muscat a Petits Grains Blanc	533	0.01	2
		Muskat	526	0.01	2
		Moscatel Galego Branco	505	0.01	2
		Muskateller	492	0.01	2
		Rumeni Muskat	353	0.01	1
		Muscat Frontignan	172	0.00	1
		Muskateller Gelber	170	0.00	1
		Moscatel Frontignan	162	0.00	1
		Bornova Misketi	114	0.00	0
		Muscat Canelli	103	0.00	0
		Muskat Bijeli	56	0.00	0
		Muscat Blanc a Petits Grains	51	0.00	0
		Muskat Zlty	48	0.00	0
		Muscat de Frontignan	10	0.00	0
		Muscat Petit Grain	7	0.00	0
Muscat Fleur d'Oranger	W	Muscat Orange	91	0.00	100
Muscat of Alexandria	W	Muscat of Alexandria	7571	0.16	29
		Moscatel de Malaga	5470	0.12	21
		Moscatel de Alejandria	4029	0.09	15
		Moscatel de Alejandrja	2767	0.06	11
		Muscat d'Alexandrie	2167	0.05	8
		Muscat Gordo Blanco	2043	0.04	8
		Zibibbo	1521	0.03	6
		Moscatel Graudo	647	0.01	2
		Malaga	120	0.00	0
Muscat of Alexandria Red	R	Red Hanepoot	6	0.00	100
Muscat of Hamburg	R	Muscat Hambourg	3706	0.08	46
		Muscat of Hamburg	2760	0.06	34
		Moscatel Hamburg	1500	0.03	18
		Moscato Nero di Acqui	73	0.00	1
		Muskat Hungarian	70	0.00	1
		Muskat Hamburg	14	0.00	0
		Hamburgi Muskotaly	12	0.00	0
		Moscatel de Hamburg	2	0.00	0

Table 15 (cont.) Prime varieties' global area and share of each synonym, and synonym's share of each prime variety, 2010

Prime variety	Col	Synonym	Area (hectares)	Share (%) of global area	Synonym's share (%) of prime variety
Muscat Ottonel	W	Muscat Ottonel	9707	0.21	95
		Muskat-Ottonel	527	0.01	5
		Moscato Ottonel	0	0.00	0
Muscat Swenson	W	Muscats	24	0.00	100
Negoska	R	Negkoska	143	0.00	100
Negramoll	R	Negra Criolla	1250	0.03	39
		Mollar	677	0.01	21
		Negramoll	590	0.01	18
		Tinta Negra	400	0.01	13
		Negra Mole	270	0.01	8
		Rabo de Ovelha Tinto	4	0.00	0
		Molar	2	0.00	0
		Saborinho	0	0.00	0
		Mulata	0	0.00	0
Nero Buono di Cori	R	Nero Buono	135	0.00	100
Nero d'Avola	R	Calabrese	16595	0.36	100
		Nero d'Avola	1	0.00	0
Neuburger	W	Neuburske	312	0.01	100
Norton	R	Norton	227	0.00	69
		Cynthiana	102	0.00	31
Odessky Cherny	R	Odessa Black	2426	0.05	90
		Alibernet	260	0.01	10
Onitskanskii Belyi	W	Onitcani	66	0.00	93
		Alb de Onitcani	5	0.00	7
Palomino Fino	W	Palomino Fino	12562	0.27	56
		Listan	3329	0.07	15
		Malvasia Rei	3033	0.07	13
		Palomino Superior	2945	0.06	13
		Palomino	642	0.01	3
Pamid	R	Pamid	6792	0.15	69
		Rosioara	2930	0.06	30
		Piros Szlanka	82	0.00	1
		Pamiti	22	0.00	0
Panse Valenciano	W	Panse Valenciana	1	0.00	100
Pardillo	W	Marisancho	4364	0.09	100
Parraleta	R	Tinta Caiada	162	0.00	47
		Caricagiola	119	0.00	34
		Parraleta	56	0.00	16
		Tinta Lameira	5	0.00	1
		Bonvedro	3	0.00	1
		Pau Ferro	1	0.00	0
Pascale	R	Pascale	341	0.01	91
		Nieddu Mannu	35	0.00	9

Table 15 (cont.) Prime varieties' global area and share of each synonym, and synonym's share of each prime variety, 2010

Prime variety	Col	Synonym	Area (hectares)	Share (%) of global area	Synonym's share (%) of prime variety
Pecorino	W	Pecorino	1114	0.02	91
		Uvina	114	0.00	9
Pecsi Szagos	W	Zold Szagos	1	0.00	100
Pedro Gimenez	W	Pedro Gimenez	12132	0.26	99
		Pedro Jimenez	118	0.00	1
Pedro Ximenez	W	Pedro Ximenez	9038	0.20	98
		Perrum	197	0.00	2
		Pedro Gimenez Rio Colorado	8	0.00	0
Perruno	W	Perruno	1054	0.02	70
		Royal	455	0.01	30
Persan	R	Becuet	3	0.00	100
Pervenets Magaracha	W	Pervenets of Magarach	1915	0.04	66
		Pervenec Magaracha	643	0.01	22
		Magaracha's Firstborn	323	0.01	11
Pervomaisky	R	Pervomaiskii	64	0.00	100
Petit Bouschet	R	Tintinha	11	0.00	72
		Petit Bouschet	4	0.00	28
Petit Courbu	W	Petit Courbou Ondarrzurizerrat	36	0.00	100
Petit Verdot	R	Petit Verdot	6696	0.15	93
		Verdot	507	0.01	7
Pignola Valtellinese	R	Pignola	49	0.00	100
Pinot Blanc	W	Burgunder	3870	0.08	26
		Pinot Blanc	3534	0.08	24
		Pinot Bianco	3086	0.07	21
		Weisser Burgunder	1914	0.04	13
		Rulandske Bile	1255	0.03	9
		Beli Pinot	525	0.01	4
		Pinot White	338	0.01	2
		Pinot Bijeli	188	0.00	1
		Pinot Blanco	15	0.00	0
Pinot Gris	O	Pinot Gris	19333	0.42	44
		Pinot Grigio	17281	0.38	40
		Rulander	4459	0.10	10
		Rulandske Sede	917	0.02	2
		Pinot Grey	638	0.01	1
		Sivi Pinot	501	0.01	1
		Pinot Sivi	219	0.00	1
		Grauer Burgunder	215	0.00	0
Pinot Meunier	R	Meunier	11192	0.24	99
		Pinot Meunier	74		1
		Pinot Menier	1	0.00	0

Table 15 (cont.) Prime varieties' global area and share of each synonym, and synonym's share of each prime variety, 2010

Prime variety	Col	Synonym	Area (hectares)	Share (%) of global area	Synonym's share (%) of prime variety
Pinot Noir	R	Pinot Noir	78302	1.70	90
		Pinot Nero	5046	0.11	6
		Pinot Negro	1802	0.04	2
		Rulandske Modre	688	0.01	1
		Blauer Burgunder	646	0.01	1
		Pinot Crni	180	0.00	0
Pinot Noir Precoce	R	Fruhburgunder	209	0.00	100
Piquepoul Noir	R	Pical	6	0.00	58
		Picapoll Negro	4	0.00	42
Planta Nova	W	Planta Nova	1366	0.03	98
		Alvarelhao Branco	29	0.00	2
Plavac Mali	R	Plavac Mali Crni	1569	0.03	100
Plavay	W	Rumeni Plavec	60	0.00	100
Plavec Zuti	W	Plavac Zuti	13	0.00	100
Plavina	R	Plavina Crna	643	0.01	100
Podarok Magaracha	W	Podarok Magaracha	212	0.00	42
		Magaracha's Gift	162	0.00	32
		Podarok of Magarach	130	0.00	26
Poeloeske Muskotaly	W	Poloskei Muskotaly	103	0.00	100
Pozsonyi	W	Pozsonyi Feher	10	0.00	100
Prensal	W	Pensal Blanco	105	0.00	100
Preto Martinho	R	Preto Martinho	162	0.00	99
		Amostrinha	1	0.00	1
Prie	W	Prie Blanc	33	0.00	100
Primetta	R	Prie Rouge	24	0.00	100
Rabigato	W	Rabigato	1235	0.03	97
		Rabigato Franco	38	0.00	3
Raboso Piave	R	Raboso Piave	728	0.02	94
		Raboso	43	0.00	6
Ramisco	R	Ramisco Tinto	32	0.00	95
		Ramisco	2	0.00	5
Refosco	R	Refosk	1414	0.03	100
		Refosco	6	0.00	0
Refosco di Faedis	R	Refosco Nostrano	217	0.00	100
Ribolla Gialla	W	Rebula	743	0.02	63
		Ribolla Gialla	435	0.01	37

Table 15 (cont.) Prime varieties' global area and share of each synonym, and synonym's share of each prime variety, 2010

Prime variety	Col	Synonym	Area (hectares)	Share (%) of global area	Synonym's share (%) of prime variety
Riesling	W	Riesling Weisser	22520	0.49	45
		Riesling	15802	0.34	32
		White Riesling	4488	0.10	9
		Weisser Riesling	2063	0.04	4
		Riesling de Rhin	1343	0.03	3
		Ryzlink Rynsky	1181	0.03	2
		J. Riesling	693	0.02	1
		Rajinski Rizling	676	0.01	1
		Renski Rizling	676	0.01	1
		Rizling Rynsky	605	0.01	1
		Riesling-Lion	11	0.00	0
		Riesling Renan	2	0.00	0
Rkatsiteli	W	Rkatsiteli	46720	1.02	80
		Rkatiteli	11864	0.26	20
		Rkaciteli	57	0.00	0
Robola	W	Rombola	465	0.01	100
Rollo	W	Rollo	38	0.00	75
		Livornese Bianca	13	0.00	25
Rossara Trentina	R	Rossara	8	0.00	100
Roter Veltliner	O	Roter Veltliner	193	0.00	97
		Piros Veltelini	5	0.00	3
Roxo de Vila Flor	R	Roxo Flor	0	0.00	100
Royal de Alloza	R	Derechero	29	0.00	100
Rozala Bianca	W	Rozalia	2	0.00	100
Rual	R	Roal	1	0.00	100
Rubin Golodrigi	R	Ruby of Golodryga	82	0.00	100
Rubin Tairovsky	R	Rubin Tairovski	2	0.00	100
Rubinovy Magaracha	R	Ruby Magaracha	0	0.00	100
Ruby Cabernet	R	Ruby Cabernet	5701	0.12	99
		Rubi Cabernet	29	0.00	1
Rufete	R	Rufete	4815	0.10	100
		Castellana	18	0.00	0
S. Mamede	W	Sao Mamede	1	0.00	100
Sangiovese	R	Sangiovese	76059	1.65	98
		Nielluccio	1589	0.03	2
		Prugnolo Gentile	61	0.00	0
Sankt Laurent	R	Svatovavrinecke	2230	0.05	74
		Sankt Laurent	775	0.02	26
		Szentlorinc	1	0.00	0
		St.Laurent	0	0.00	0
Santarena	R	Santareno	739		100
Saperavi Severny	R	Saperavi Nothern	325	0.01	93
		Saperavi Severnii	25	0.00	7

Table 15 (cont.) Prime varieties' global area and share of each synonym, and synonym's share of each prime variety, 2010

Prime variety	Col	Synonym	Area (hectares)	Share (%) of global area	Synonym's share (%) of prime variety
Sauvignon Blanc	W	Sauvignon Blanc	55859	1.21	51
		Sauvignon	50179	1.09	46
		Sauvignon Blanca	4011	0.09	4
		Sauvignon Musque	89	0.00	0
Sauvignonasse	W	Tocai Friulano	2959	0.06	66
		Sauvignon Vert	785	0.02	18
		Sauvignonasse	515	0.01	12
		Zeleni Sauvignon	190	0.00	4
Savagnin Blanc	W	Traminer	1006	0.02	53
		Savagnin Blanc	564	0.01	30
		Traminec	215	0.00	11
		Savagnin	94	0.00	5
		Traminac Bijeli	18	0.00	1
Savatiano	W	Savvatiano	9920	0.22	100
Schiava Grossa	R	Schiava Grossa	559	0.01	96
		Tschaggele	21	0.00	4
Sciascinoso	R	Sciascinoso	50	0.00	54
		Olivella Nera	43	0.00	46
Semillon	W	Semillon	22142	0.48	100
		Semigion	8	0.00	0
		Semilao	6	0.00	0
Sercial	W	Sercial	106	0.00	100
		Esganoso	0	0.00	0
Servant	W	Raisin Blanc	54	0.00	100
Seyval Blanc	W	Seyval Blanc	370	0.01	80
		Seyval	93	0.00	20
Shiroka Melnishka	R	Shiroka Melnishka Loza	1580	0.03	100
Silvaner	W	Sylvaner	1690	0.04	75
		Silvanac Zeleni	139	0.00	6
		Sylvanske Zelene	122	0.00	5
		Silvanske Zelene	117	0.00	5
		Silvaner	98	0.00	4
		Sylvaner Verde	80	0.00	4
		Zold Szilvani	8	0.00	0
Siria	W	Siria	5828	0.13	74
		Malvasia Branca	967	0.02	12
		Dona Blanca	508	0.01	6
		Roupeiro Branco	279	0.01	4
		Ciguente	236	0.01	3
		Crato Espanhol	36	0.00	0
		Alvadurao	34	0.00	0
		Sabro	9	0.00	0
		Valenciana Blanca	2	0.00	0

Table 15 (cont.) Prime varieties' global area and share of each synonym, and synonym's share of each prime variety, 2010

Prime variety	Col	Synonym	Area (hectares)	Share (%) of global area	Synonym's share (%) of prime variety
Stepnyak	W	Stepniak	144	0.00	100
Sukholimanskiy Bely	W	Suholimanskiy White	1477	0.03	69
		Suholimenschii Belii	599	0.01	28
		Sukholimansky	80	0.00	4
Sultaniye	W	Sultaniye	1750	0.04	51
		Thompson Seedless	856	0.02	25
		Sultana	430	0.01	13
		Soultanina	371	0.01	11
Sumoll	R	Sumoll	75	0.00	90
		Vijiriego Negro	8	0.00	10
Suscan	R	Brajda Crna	3	0.00	100
Syrah	R	Syrah	111079	2.41	60
		Shiraz	54474	1.18	29
		Syrach	20000	0.43	11
		Chirac	15	0.00	0
Tempranillo	R	Tempranillo	209412	4.55	90
		Aragonez	16706	0.36	7
		Tinto de Toro	6443	0.14	3
Teneron	R	Valency	3488	0.08	100
Termarina Rossa	O	Termarina	20	0.00	100
Terrano	R	Teran	228	0.00	100
Tinta Barroca	R	Tinta Barroca	6171	0.13	100
		Barroco	1	0.00	0
Tinta Bragao	R	Bragao	63	0.00	100
Tinta da Barca	R	Barca	345	0.01	100
Tinta da Melra	R	Melra	1	0.00	100
Tinta de Alcoa	R	Alcoa	24	0.00	100
Tinta de Cidadelhe	R	Cidadelhe	1	0.00	100
Tinta de Pegoes	R	Tinto Pegoes	195	0.00	100
Tinta de Porto Santo	R	Tinta Porto Santo	2	0.00	100
Tinta do Rodo	R	Rodo	3	0.00	100
Tinta Engomada	R	Engomada	4	0.00	100
Tinta Malandra	R	Malandra	0	0.00	100
Tinta Roseira	R	Roseira	4	0.00	100
Tinta Valdosa	R	Valdosa	1	0.00	100
Tinta Varejoa	R	Varejoa	1	0.00	100
Tintilia del Molise	R	Tintilia	111	0.00	100
Tinto do Aurelio	R	Tinta Aurelio	0		100
Torrontes Riojano	W	Torrontes Riojano	7683	0.17	95
		Torontel	433	0.01	5
Torrontes Sanjuanino	W	Torrontes Sanjuanino	2048	0.04	100
		Moscatel Austria	4	0.00	0
Touriga Franca	R	Touriga Francesa	0	0.00	100

Table 15 (cont.) Prime varieties' global area and share of each synonym, and synonym's share of each prime variety, 2010

Prime variety	Col	Synonym	Area (hectares)	Share (%) of global area	Synonym's share (%) of prime variety
Touriga Nacional	R	Touriga Nacional	10388	0.23	100
		Touriga	48	0.00	0
Trajadura	W	Trajadura	1171	0.03	54
		Treixadura	998	0.02	46
Trbljan	W	Trbljan Bijeli	231	0.01	100
Trebbiano d'Abruzzo	W	Trebbiano Abruzzese	5091	0.11	100
Trebbiano Toscano	W	Ugni Blanc	87473	1.90	80
		Trebbiano Toscano	21711	0.47	20
		Uni Blan	297	0.01	0
		Talia	212	0.00	0
		St. Emilion	80	0.00	0
Trepat	R	Trepat	1083	0.02	80
		Bonicaire	263	0.01	19
		Parrel Verdal	12	0.00	1
Tribidrag	R	Zinfandel	20399	0.44	62
		Primitivo	12281	0.27	38
		Crljenak Kastelanski	65	0.00	0
		Tribidrag	0	0.00	0
Trincadeira	R	Trincadeira	9246	0.20	100
		Tinta Amarela	24	0.00	0
		Trincadeira Preta	0	0.00	0
Trincadeiro Branco	W	Trincadeira Branca	59	0.00	100
Trobat	R	Panse Negro	1	0.00	100
Trousseau	R	Bastardo	1487	0.03	43
		Tinta	1359	0.03	40
		Bastardo Tinto	311	0.01	9
		Trousseau	172	0.00	5
		Verdejo Negro	62	0.00	2
		Bastardo Roxo	28	0.00	1
		Bastarda	10	0.00	0
		Maturana Tinta	3	0.00	0
		Tinta Lisboa	0	0.00	0
Tsimlyansky Cherny	R	Tsymlansky Black	281	0.01	100
Turan	R	Turan	175	0.00	99
		Agria	2	0.00	1
Valdiguie	R	Napa Gamay	134	0.00	97
		Valdiguie	4	0.00	3
Valveirinha	W	Valveirinho	0	0.00	100
Verdeca	W	Lagorthi	0	0.00	100
Verdejo	W	Verdejo Blanco	6034	0.13	100
Verdial	W	Verdial Branco	1	0.00	100

Table 15 (cont.) Prime varieties' global area and share of each synonym, and synonym's share of each prime variety, 2010

Prime variety	Col	Synonym	Area (hectares)	Share (%) of global area	Synonym's share (%) of prime variety
Verdicchio Bianco	W	Verdicchio Bianco	2389	0.05	68
		Trebbiano di Soave	1135	0.02	32
		Boschera	6	0.00	0
		Verdicchio	2	0.00	0
Verdiso	W	Verdiso	50	0.00	74
		Pedevenda	18	0.00	26
Verduzzo Friulano	W	Verduzzo Friulano	808	0.02	99
		Verduzzo	5	0.00	1
Vermentino	W	Vermentino	8131	0.18	94
		Pigato	264	0.01	3
		Favorita	220	0.00	3
		Favorita Diaz	2	0.00	0
Vernaccia di San Gimignano	W	Vernaccia di San Gimignano	512	0.01	98
		Bervedino	10	0.00	2
Vertzami	R	Vertzami	239	0.01	71
		Lefkada	96	0.00	29
Vidal	W	Vidal 256	1270	0.03	77
		Vidal Blanc	333	0.01	20
		Vidal	41	0.00	2
Vijariego	W	Vijiriego	283	0.01	99
		Diego	2	0.00	1
Vinhao	R	Vinhao	2422	0.05	77
		Souson	610	0.01	19
		Souzao	68	0.00	2
		Sousao	61	0.00	2
Viognier	W	Viognier	10145	0.22	89
		Viogner	1255	0.03	11
Vitovska	W	Vitouska	50	0.00	100
Voskeat	W	Voskehat	809	0.02	100
Xarello	W	Xarello Blanco	8326	0.18	100
Xarello Rosado	W	Pansa Rosada	1	0.00	100
Zalagyongye	W	Zalagyongye	1870	0.04	96
		Zala Dende	78	0.00	4
Zametovka	R	Zametovka	913	0.02	100
		Kavcina Crna	0	0.00	0
Zenit	W	Zenit	559	0.01	96
		Zenith	21	0.00	4
Zierfandler	O	Zierfandler	85	0.00	73
		Cirfandli	32	0.00	27
Zlatarica Vrgorska	W	Zlatarica	19	0.00	100
Zweigelt	R	Zweigelt	8885	0.19	90
		Zweigeltrebe	962	0.02	10
Other primes with no synonyms			1032842	22.45	
Other varieties			259169	5.63	
Total			**4601445**	**100**	

Table 16: Synonyms' global area and share of each prime variety, 2000

Synonym	Col	Prime variety	Area (hectares)	Share (%) of global area	Synonym's share (%) of prime variety
Abbou	R	Abbo	2375	0.05	100
Abrusco	R	Abrusco	5	0.00	1
Aglianico	R	Aglianico	7015	0.14	1
Aglianico del Vulture	R	Aglianico	2250	0.05	0
Agudello	W	Godello	99	0.00	7
Airen	W	Airen	387525	7.94	100
Alarije	W	Alarije	1665	0.03	99
Alb de Onitcani	W	Onitskanskii Belyi	5	0.00	100
Albarino	W	Alvarinho	4149	0.09	81
Albarola	W	Albarola	4011	0.08	1
Albilla	W	Albillo Mayor	5	0.00	100
Albillo	W	Albillo Real	3368	0.07	100
Alfonso Lavalle	R	Alphonse Lavallee	0	0.00	1
Alfrocheiro	R	Alfrocheiro	518	0.01	99
Alicante	R	Alicante Henri Bouschet	440	0.01	1
Alicante Bouchet	R	Alicante Henri Bouschet	1169	0.02	3
Alicante Bouschet	R	Alicante Henri Bouschet	5470	0.11	15
Alicante Branco	W	Damaschino	1530	0.03	65
Alicante Henri Bouschet	R	Alicante Henri Bouschet	9105	0.19	25
Alicante Terras 20	R	Terras 20	13	0.00	100
Alikante Mouse	R	Alicante Henri Bouschet	21	0.00	0
Almuneco	R	Listan Negro	17	0.00	1
Alphonse Lavallee	R	Alphonse Lavallee	13	0.00	83
Alvarelhao	R	Alvarelhao	46	0.00	29
Alvarinho	W	Alvarinho	964	0.02	19
Ansonica	W	Inzolia	9259	0.19	100
Aragonez	R	Tempranillo	1592	0.03	2
Aramon	R	Aramon Noir	9084	0.19	100
Arinto	W	Arinto de Bucelas	1184	0.02	30
Arvine	W	Arvine	57	0.00	93
Asirtiko	W	Assyrtiko	1128	0.02	100
Asprinio	W	Greco	405	0.01	31
Asproudi	W	Asprouda	433	0.01	100
Assario Branco	W	Malvasia Fina	778	0.02	11
Aubin	W	Aubin Blanc	2	0.00	100
Aurora	W	Aurore	299	0.01	100
Auxerrois Rupes	R	Lacoste	1	0.00	100
Babeasca Neagra	R	Babeasca Neagra	3642	0.07	98
Baco Blanc	W	Baco Blanc	2103	0.04	98
Baco Divers	W	Baco Blanc	34	0.00	2
Baco Divers N	R	Baco Noir	1	0.00	0
Baco Noir	R	Baco Noir	397	0.01	100
Barbera	R	Barbera	5872	0.12	18
Barbera Nera	R	Barbera	27175	0.56	82
Bastarda	R	Trousseau	13	0.00	1

Table 16 (cont.) Synonyms' global area and share of each prime variety, 2000

Synonym	Col	Prime variety	Area (hectares)	Share (%) of global area	Synonym's share (%) of prime variety
Bastarda Negra	R	Alfrocheiro	5	0.00	1
Bastardo	R	Trousseau	1754	0.04	83
Bastardo Magaraceskii	R	Bastardo Magarachsky	1040	0.02	53
Bastardo Magarachsky	R	Bastardo Magarachsky	929	0.02	47
Beba	W	Beba	4748	0.10	100
Bequignol	R	Bequignol Noir	1	0.00	100
Bervedino	W	Vernaccia di San Gimignano	82	0.00	10
Bianchetta Genovese	W	Albarola	79	0.00	0
Biancone	W	Biancone di Portoferraio	67	0.00	100
Biborkadarka	R	Biborkadarka	202	0.00	100
Black Malvoisie	R	Cinsaut	22	0.00	0
Blanca Cayetana	W	Cayetana Blanca	6797	0.14	12
Blanqueiron	W	Blanqueiro	1	0.00	100
Blauer Burgunder	R	Pinot Noir	409	0.01	1
Blauer Portugieser	R	Blauer Portugieser	3953	0.08	92
Blauer Wildbacher	R	Blauer Wildbacher	464	0.01	98
Blaufrankisch	R	Blaufrankisch	12723	0.26	99
Boal	W	Malvasia Fina	1549	0.03	22
Bonarda	R	Douce Noire	17533	0.36	99
Bonicaire	R	Trepat	539	0.01	31
Borba	W	Grasevina	1923	0.04	2
Borracal	R	Borracal	2035	0.04	77
Boschera	W	Verdicchio Bianco	3	0.00	0
Bovale	R	Graciano	573	0.01	30
Bracciola	R	Bracciola Nera	89	0.00	100
Brachet	R	Braquet Noir	8	0.00	100
Brachetto	R	Brachetto del Piemonte	1534	0.03	100
Brancelho	R	Alvarelhao	99	0.00	62
Brancellao	R	Alvarelhao	14	0.00	9
Breval	W	Beba	9	0.00	0
Burdin Divers	W	Burdin	0	0.00	100
Burger	W	Elbling	656	0.01	35
Burgunder	W	Pinot Blanc	2396	0.05	14
Burra Blanca	W	Airen	18	0.00	0
Cabernet Franc	R	Cabernet Franc	48147	0.99	100
Cabernet Sauvignon	R	Cabernet Sauvignon	220202	4.51	100
Cagnulari	R	Graciano	311	0.01	16
Caino Tinto	R	Borracal	619	0.01	23
Calabrese	R	Nero d'Avola	11318	0.23	100
Camaralet Lasseu	W	Camaralet de Lasseube	0	0.00	0
Camarate	W	Camaralet de Lasseube	690	0.01	100
Canaiolo Bianco	W	Drupeggio	617	0.01	100
Canina Nera	R	Fortana	304	0.01	24
Cannonao	R	Garnacha Tinta	6197	0.13	3
Carcajolo Blanc	W		0	0.00	100

Table 16 (cont.) Synonyms' global area and share of each prime variety, 2000

Synonym	Col	Prime variety	Area (hectares)	Share (%) of global area	Synonym's share (%) of prime variety
Carcajolo Noir	R	Parraleta	11	0.00	6
Caricagiola	R	Parraleta	141	0.00	84
Carignan	R	Mazuelo	98238	2.01	78
Carignan Blanc	W	Carignan Blanc	976	0.02	94
Carignane	R	Mazuelo	18214	0.37	14
Carignano	R	Mazuelo	1721	0.04	1
Carinena Blanco	W	Carignan Blanc	58	0.00	6
Castel Divers	R	Castel	0	0.00	100
Castellana	R	Rufete	1	0.00	0
Catarratto Bianco Comune	W	Catarratto Bianco	43176	0.89	85
Catarratto Bianco Lucido	W	Catarratto Bianco	7535	0.15	15
Cayuga	W	Cayuga White	108	0.00	100
Cercial	W	Cerceal Branco	597	0.01	100
Cesanese Comune	R	Cesanese	447	0.01	44
Cesanese d'Affile	R	Cesanese	577	0.01	56
Charbono	R	Douce Noire	21	0.00	0
Chardonnay	W	Chardonnay	145308	2.98	100
Chaselas Dorada	W	Chasselas	1	0.00	0
Chasselas	W	Chasselas	12097	0.25	91
Chasselas Dorato	W	Chasselas	22	0.00	0
Chasselas Rose	R	Chasselas Rouge	11	0.00	100
Chelva	W	Chelva	10875	0.22	100
Chenin	W	Chenin Blanc	13533	0.28	30
Chenin Blanc	W	Chenin Blanc	32273	0.66	70
Chirac	R	Syrah	10	0.00	0
Ciguente	W	Siria	268	0.01	10
Cinsault	R	Cinsaut	12343	0.25	25
Cinsaut	R	Cinsaut	35672	0.73	74
Clairette	W	Clairette	3065	0.06	77
Clairette Blanche	W	Clairette	938	0.02	23
Coda di Volpe Bianca	W	Coda di Volpe Bianca	951	0.02	97
Codega do Larinho	W	Codega de Larinho	4058	0.08	100
Colombana Nero	R	Colombana Nera	126	0.00	100
Colombar	W	Colombard	11432	0.23	30
Colombard	W	Colombard	8705	0.18	23
Colorino	R	Abrusco	394	0.01	99
Corbeau	R	Douce Noire	1	0.00	0
Corinto Nero	R	Korinthiaki	56	0.00	7
Cornalin	R	Cornalin	33	0.00	36
Cornichon Violet	R	Olivette Noire	0	0.00	100
Corvina	R	Corvina Veronese	4781	0.10	100
Cot	R	Cot	6145	0.13	25
Couderc 13	R	Couderc Noir	299	0.01	49
Couderc Divers	W	Couderc	4	0.00	100

Table 16 (cont.) Synonyms' global area and share of each prime variety, 2000

Synonym	Col	Prime variety	Area (hectares)	Share (%) of global area	Synonym's share (%) of prime variety
Coudrec	R	Couderc Noir	305	0.01	50
Coudrec Divers	R	Couderc Noir	5	0.00	1
Courbu	W	Courbu Blanc	47	0.00	100
Crato Espanhol	W	Siria	155	0.00	6
Crato Preto	R	Trincadeira	39	0.00	1
Currant	R	Korinthiaki	778	0.02	93
Cynthiana	R	Norton	0	0.00	100
Damaschino	W	Damaschino	380	0.01	16
Dembina	W	Debina	455	0.01	100
Diego	W	Vijariego	0	0.00	0
Dimiat	W	Dimyat	7649	0.16	99
Dona Blanca	W	Siria	758	0.02	27
Drujba	W	Droujba	3	0.00	100
Durif	R	Durif	274	0.01	23
Early Magaratch	W	Pervenets Magaracha	1093	0.02	39
Elbling	W	Elbling	165	0.00	9
Elbling Roter	W	Elbling Rot	4	0.00	100
Elbling Weisser	W	Elbling	1042	0.02	56
Esganoso	W	Sercial	282	0.01	92
Espanenc	R	Plant Droit	5	0.00	13
Faranah	W	Damaschino	1	0.00	0
Favorita	W	Vermentino	273	0.01	5
Ferron	R	Manseng Noir	5	0.00	48
Fileri	R	Moschofilero	130	0.00	31
Findling	W	Muller Thurgau	39	0.00	0
Foch	R	Marechal Foch	22	0.00	13
Forcallat Blanca	W	Airen	435	0.01	0
Fortana	R	Fortana	948	0.02	76
Franconia	R	Blaufrankisch	111	0.00	1
French Colombard	W	Colombard	18010	0.37	47
Fruhburgunder	R	Pinot Noir Precoce	84	0.00	98
Fruhroter Veltliner	R	Fruhroter Veltliner	626	0.01	99
Gaillard Divers	R	Gaillard	0	0.00	100
Gamay	R	Gamay Noir	37261	0.76	99
Gamay Beaujolais	R	Gamay Noir	352	0.01	1
Gamay Chaudenay	R	Gamay Teinturier de Chaudenay	267	0.01	100
Gamay de Teinturier Bouze	R	Gamay de Teinturier Bouze	282	0.01	89
Gamay Noir	R	Gamay Noir	181	0.00	0
Gamay Precoce	R	Gamay Noir	2	0.00	0
Gamay Teinturier Freaux	R	Gamay Teinturier Freaux	77	0.00	58
Gamays Teinturiers	R	Gamay de Teinturier Bouze	26	0.00	8
Gammay de Bouze	R	Gamay de Teinturier Bouze	10	0.00	3
Gammay Freaux	R	Gamay Teinturier Freaux	55	0.00	42
Gamza	R	Kadarka	1619	0.03	62

Table 16 (cont.) Synonyms' global area and share of each prime variety, 2000

Synonym	Col	Prime variety	Area (hectares)	Share (%) of global area	Synonym's share (%) of prime variety
Garanoir	R	Garanoir	50	0.00	66
Garganega	W	Garganega	11379	0.23	69
Garnacha	R	Garnacha Tinta	95800	1.96	45
Garnacha Blanca	W	Garnacha Blanca	4333	0.09	40
Garnacha Peluda	R	Garnacha Peluda	1460	0.03	72
Garnacha Roja	W	Garnacha Roja	126	0.00	5
Garnacha Tinta	R	Garnacha Tinta	129	0.00	0
Garnacha Tintorera	R	Alicante Henri Bouschet	18321	0.38	49
Gewurztraminer	W	Gewurztraminer	6514	0.13	61
Godello	W	Godello	461	0.01	31
Goluboc	R	Golubok	50	0.00	100
Gouais	W	Gouais Blanc	1	0.00	100
Gouget	R	Gouget Noir	1	0.00	100
Gouveio	W	Godello	929	0.02	62
Graciano	R	Graciano	435	0.01	23
Gran Negro	R	Grand Noir	895	0.02	95
Grand Noir	R	Grand Noir	47	0.00	5
Grand Noir De La Calmette	R	Grand Noir	4	0.00	0
Granoir	R	Garanoir	26	0.00	34
Grasevina Bijela	W	Grasevina	16051	0.33	17
Grauer Burgunder	O	Pinot Gris	293	0.01	2
Gray Riesling	O	Trousseau Gris	28	0.00	100
Grec	W	Greco	1	0.00	0
Grecanico Dorato	W	Garganega	5170	0.11	31
Grechetto	W	Grechetto di Orvieto	1177	0.02	100
Greco	W	Greco	920	0.02	69
Grenache	R	Garnacha Tinta	111277	2.28	52
Grenache Blanc	W	Garnacha Blanca	6488	0.13	60
Grenache Gris	W	Garnacha Roja	2635	0.05	95
Grenas Rose	R	Grenache Rose	22	0.00	100
Grenas Rose	W	Garnacha Roja	1	0.00	0
Grolleau	R	Grolleau Noir	2201	0.05	100
Groppello di Mocasina	R	Groppello di Mocasina	53	0.00	44
Groppello di Santo Stefano	R	Groppello di Mocasina	66	0.00	56
Gros Morras.Bous.	R	Morrastel Bouschet	1	0.00	100
Grumier Tinto	R	Valenci Tinto	5	0.00	100
Gruner Veltliner	W	Gruner Veltliner	23475	0.48	99
Gual	W	Malvasia Fina	23	0.00	0
Guarnaccia	W	Coda di Volpe Bianca	29	0.00	3
Humagne Blanc	W	Humagne	9	0.00	100
Humagne Rouge	R	Cornalin	60	0.00	64
Iliciovski Ciornai Rannii	R	Ilichevskii Rannii	5	0.00	100
Isabel	R	Isabella	14285	0.29	52
Isabella	R	Isabella	12491	0.26	46

Table 16 (cont.) Synonyms' global area and share of each prime variety, 2000

Synonym	Col	Prime variety	Area (hectares)	Share (%) of global area	Synonym's share (%) of prime variety
Iso	W	Beba	5	0.00	0
Italian Riesling	W	Grasevina	39797	0.82	43
Izsaki	W	Arany Sarfeher	2914	0.06	100
Jacquez	R	Jacquez	170	0.00	75
Jaen	R	Mencia	1971	0.04	15
Jaen Tinto	R	Mencia	1068	0.02	8
Johan.Seyve D.	R	Joannes Seyve	3	0.00	100
Juan Garcia	R	Juan Garcia	1673	0.03	81
Jurie Divers	W	Jurie	0	0.00	100
Kadarka	R	Kadarka	1012	0.02	38
Kamberne Fran	R	Cabernet Franc	40	0.00	0
Kamberne Sovinion	R	Cabernet Sauvignon	688	0.01	0
Lacrima	R	Lacrima di Morro d'Alba	652	0.01	100
Lambrusco A Foglia Frastagliata	R	Enantio	1062	0.02	100
Landot Divers	W	Landot	0	0.00	100
Landot Divers	R	Landot Noir	0	0.00	100
Lasca	R	Laska	1	0.00	100
Lemberger	R	Blaufrankisch	45	0.00	0
Lenoir	R	Jacquez	56	0.00	25
Lidia	R	Isabella	599	0.01	2
Listan	W	Palomino Fino	7261	0.15	24
Listan Negro	R	Listan Negro	3250	0.07	99
Listrao	R	Listrao Roxo	10	0.00	100
Livornese Bianca	W	Rollo	9	0.00	8
Lledoner Pelut	R	Garnacha Peluda	564	0.01	28
Loureiro	W	Loureiro	3939	0.08	90
Loureiro Blanca	W	Loureiro	454	0.01	10
Loureiro Tinto	R	Mencia	21	0.00	0
Macabeo	W	Macabeo	42902	0.88	89
Macabeu	W	Macabeo	5223	0.11	11
Malagouzia	W	Malagousia	23	0.00	100
Malbec	R	Cot	18006	0.37	74
Malbech	R	Cot	251	0.01	1
Malegue Divers	R	Malegue	1	0.00	100
Malfar	W	Alarije	21	0.00	1
Malvar	W	Lairen	298	0.01	100
Malvasia Bianca	W	Malvasia Bianca di Candia	4645	0.10	36
Malvasia Bianca di Candia	W	Malvasia Bianca di Candia	8244	0.17	64
Malvasia di Lipari	W	Malvasia di Lipari	127	0.00	25
Malvasia di Sardegna	W	Malvasia di Lipari	367	0.01	71
Malvasia Istriana	W	Malvazija Istarska	425	0.01	6
Malvasia Negra	R	Malvasia Nera di Brindisi	348	0.01	11
Malvasia Nera di Brindisi	R	Malvasia Nera di Brindisi	2178	0.04	69
Malvasia Nera di Lecce	R	Malvasia Nera di Brindisi	648	0.01	20

Table 16 (cont.) Synonyms' global area and share of each prime variety, 2000

Synonym	Col	Prime variety	Area (hectares)	Share (%) of global area	Synonym's share (%) of prime variety
Malvasia Sitges	W	Malvasia di Lipari	21	0.00	4
Malvasier	R	Fruhroter Veltliner	6	0.00	1
Malvasija Istarska	W	Malvazija Istarska	7134	0.15	94
Mammolo	R	Mammolo	138	0.00	18
Mancin	R	Cot	0	0.00	0
Manseng Noir	R	Manseng Noir	5	0.00	52
Manteudo	W	Listain de Huelva	596	0.01	100
Manzoni	W	Manzoni Bianco	8290	0.17	100
Marechal Foch	R	Marechal Foch	151	0.00	87
Marisancho	W	Pardillo	7272	0.15	100
Marsanne	W	Marsanne	1479	0.03	98
Marsanne Blanche	W	Marsanne	33	0.00	2
Marsigliana Nera	R	Magliocco Dolce	243	0.00	100
Marufo	R	Marufo	879	0.02	14
Mataro	R	Monastrell	1135	0.02	1
Mauzac	W	Mauzac Blanc	3251	0.07	100
Mavroudi	R	Mavrouda	349	0.01	100
Mayskiy	R	Maiskii Chernyi	77	0.00	100
Mazuela	R	Mazuelo	8103	0.17	6
Mazuelo	R	Mazuelo	374	0.01	0
Mencia	R	Mencia	10077	0.21	77
Messenikola	R	Mavro Messenikola	3	0.00	100
Meunier	R	Pinot Meunier	10825	0.22	100
Mission	R	Listan Prieto	340	0.01	2
Molinara	R	Molinara	1301	0.03	80
Molinera	R	Molinara	334	0.01	20
Mollar	R	Negramoll	842	0.02	24
Monastrell	R	Monastrell	67163	1.38	88
Mondeuse	R	Mondeuse Noire	1404	0.03	100
Monemvasia	W	Monemvassia	418	0.01	100
Monica	R	Monica Nera	2835	0.06	100
Monstruosa de Monterrei	W	Monstruosa	2	0.00	100
Montonico	W	Montonico Bianco	10	0.00	1
Montonico Bianco	W	Montonico Bianco	647	0.01	99
Moores Diamond	W	Moore's Diamond	19	0.00	100
Moravia Dulce	R	Marufo	2827	0.06	45
Morio Muscat	W	Morio-Muskat	1188	0.02	100
Mornen	R	Mornen Noir	1	0.00	100
Morrastel	R	Graciano	7	0.00	0
Moscatel Amarilla	W	Moscato Giallo	65	0.00	16
Moscatel de Grano Menudo	W	Muscat Blanc a Petits Grains	200	0.00	1
Moscatel de Malaga	W	Muscat of Alexandria	6144	0.13	21
Moscatel Fontinan	W	Muscat Blanc a Petits Grains	23	0.00	0
Moscatel Graudo	W	Muscat of Alexandria	510	0.01	2

Table 16 (cont.) Synonyms' global area and share of each prime variety, 2000

Synonym	Col	Prime variety	Area (hectares)	Share (%) of global area	Synonym's share (%) of prime variety
Moscatel Hambourg	R	Muscat of Hamburg	2886	0.06	41
Moscatel Hamburt	R	Muscat of Hamburg	6	0.00	0
Moscatel Negro	R	Listan Prieto	11	0.00	0
Moscatel Nunes	W	Moscatel Branco	1419	0.03	100
Moscato Bianco	W	Muscat Blanc a Petits Grains	13016	0.27	46
Moscato Giallo	W	Moscato Giallo	345	0.01	84
Moscato Nero Di Acqui	R	Muscat of Hamburg	199	0.00	3
Moscato Rosa	R	Moscato Rosa del Trentino	93	0.00	100
Moschato	W	Muscat Blanc a Petits Grains	2222	0.05	8
Moschato	R	Moschomavro	2305	0.05	100
Moschofilero	R	Moschofilero	293	0.01	69
Mouraton	R	Juan Garcia	224	0.00	11
Mourisco	R	Marufo	2633	0.05	42
Mourvedre	R	Monastrell	8006	0.16	10
Mtsvane	W	Mtsvane Kakhuri	249	0.01	100
Muller Thurgau	W	Muller Thurgau	33074	0.68	99
Mulata	R	Negramoll	1	0.00	0
Muscat a Petits Grains Blanc	W	Muscat Blanc a Petits Grains	214	0.00	1
Muscat Alexandr.	W	Muscat of Alexandria	3027	0.06	10
Muscat Blanc	W	Muscat Blanc a Petits Grains	2052	0.04	7
Muscat Blanc a Petits Grains	W	Muscat Blanc a Petits Grains	981	0.02	3
Muscat Canelli	W	Muscat Blanc a Petits Grains	45	0.00	0
Muscat d'Alexandrie	W	Muscat of Alexandria	4047	0.08	14
Muscat de Colmar	W	Muscat Blanc a Petits Grains	1	0.00	0
Muscat de Frontignan	W	Muscat Blanc a Petits Grains	773	0.02	3
Muscat Frontignan	W	Muscat Blanc a Petits Grains	172	0.00	1
Muscat Gordo Blanco	W	Muscat of Alexandria	2495	0.05	8
Muscat Hambourg	R	Muscat of Hamburg	769	0.02	11
Muscat of Alexandria	W	Muscat of Alexandria	12030	0.25	41
Muscat of Hamburg	R	Muscat of Hamburg	3205	0.07	45
Muscat Orange	W	Muscat Fleur d'Oranger	36	0.00	100
Muscat Petits Grains	W	Muscat Blanc a Petits Grains	6934	0.14	24
Muskat	W	Muscat Blanc a Petits Grains	526	0.01	2
Muskateller	W	Muscat Blanc a Petits Grains	143	0.00	1
Muskateller Gelber	W	Muscat Blanc a Petits Grains	87	0.00	0
Negkoska	R	Negoska	96	0.00	100
Negra Comun	R	Listan Negro	25	0.00	1
Negra de Mesa	R	Tempranillo	2	0.00	0
Negra Mole	R	Negramoll	509	0.01	14
Negramoll	R	Negramoll	1674	0.03	47
Negrara	R	Hrvatica	245	0.01	100
Negro Amaro	R	Negroamaro	16619	0.34	100
Nero Buono	R	Nero Buono di Cori	114	0.00	100

Table 16 (cont.) Synonyms' global area and share of each prime variety, 2000

Synonym	Col	Prime variety	Area (hectares)	Share (%) of global area	Synonym's share (%) of prime variety
Nieddu Mannu	R	Pascale	344	0.01	22
Nielluccio	R	Sangiovese	1564	0.03	2
Oberlin Divers	W	Oberlin White	1	0.00	100
Olivella Nera	R	Sciascinoso	116	0.00	46
Ondarrabi Beltza	R	Hondarrabi Beltza	11	0.00	100
Ottavianello	R	Cinsaut	274	0.01	1
Pais	R	Listan Prieto	15181	0.31	98
Palomino	W	Palomino Fino	2096	0.04	7
Palomino Fino	W	Palomino Fino	20884	0.43	69
Palomino Superior	W	Palomino Fino	56	0.00	0
Pamid	R	Pamid	22703	0.47	100
Pamiti	R	Pamid	15	0.00	0
Pansa Rosada	W	Xarello Rosado	10	0.00	100
Panse Negro	R	Trobat	83	0.00	100
Panse Valenciana	W	Panse Valenciano	649	0.01	100
Pardina	W	Cayetana Blanca	48138	0.99	87
Parraleta	R	Parraleta	15	0.00	9
Parrel Verdal	R	Trepat	65	0.00	4
Pascal	W	Pascal Blanc	0	0.00	100
Pascale	R	Pascale	1229	0.03	78
Pederna	W	Arinto de Bucelas	2782	0.06	70
Pedevenda	W	Verdiso	6	0.00	9
Pedro Luis	W	Galego Dourado	51	0.00	100
Pensal Blanco	W	Prensal	114	0.00	100
Periquita	R	Castelao	14424	0.30	100
Perruno	W	Perruno	1756	0.04	62
Pervenets Magaracha	W	Pervenets Magaracha	449	0.01	16
Pervenetz Magaratcha	W	Pervenets Magaracha	1295	0.03	46
Pervomaiskii	R	Pervomaisky	64	0.00	100
Petit Beclan	R	Beclan	0	0.00	100
Petite Arvine	W	Arvine	4	0.00	7
Petite Sirah	R	Durif	923	0.02	77
Picapoll Negro	R	Piquepoul Noir	10	0.00	9
Pigato	W	Vermentino	232	0.00	4
Pignola	R	Pignola Valtellinese	70	0.00	100
Pinot Bianco	W	Pinot Blanc	4993	0.10	29
Pinot Blanc	W	Pinot Blanc	6618	0.14	39
Pinot Blanco	W	Pinot Blanc	48	0.00	0
Pinot Grigio	O	Pinot Gris	6612	0.14	35
Pinot Gris	O	Pinot Gris	9338	0.19	49
Pinot Menier	R	Pinot Meunier	7	0.00	0
Pinot Negro	R	Pinot Noir	1047	0.02	2
Pinot Nero	R	Pinot Noir	3287	0.07	5
Pinot Noir	R	Pinot Noir	55357	1.13	92

Table 16 (cont.) Synonyms' global area and share of each prime variety, 2000

Synonym	Col	Prime variety	Area (hectares)	Share (%) of global area	Synonym's share (%) of prime variety
Pinot Precoce	R	Pinot Noir Precoce	1	0.00	2
Piquepoul Noir	R	Piquepoul Noir	94	0.00	91
Plant Droit	R	Plant Droit	35	0.00	87
Planta Fina	W	Damaschino	449	0.01	19
Portoghese	R	Blauer Portugieser	94	0.00	2
Portugais Bleu	R	Blauer Portugieser	232	0.00	5
Posip	W	Posip Bijeli	6539	0.13	100
Precoce Bousquet	W	Bousquet Precoce	16	0.00	100
Prie Blanc	W	Prie	36	0.00	100
Prie Rouge	R	Primetta	17	0.00	100
Primitivo	R	Tribidrag	7838	0.16	29
Prugnolo Gentile	R	Sangiovese	146	0.00	0
Pt.Manseng Blanc	W	Petit Manseng	613	0.01	100
Rabo de Ovelha Tinto	R	Negramoll	318	0.01	9
Raisin Blanc	W	Servant	432	0.01	81
Rara Neagra	R	Babeasca Neagra	80	0.00	2
Ravat 51	W	Vignoles	34	0.00	49
Ravat Divers	R	Ravat	1	0.00	100
Rebula	W	Ribolla Gialla	1127	0.02	80
Red Hanepoot	R	Muscat of Alexandria Red	11	0.00	100
Refosco Nostrano	R	Refosco di Faedis	256	0.01	100
Regina dei Vigneti	W	Koenigin der Weingaerten	184	0.00	24
Rhin	W	Silvaner	0	0.00	0
Ribier	R	Alphonse Lavallee	2	0.00	16
Ribolla Gialla	W	Ribolla Gialla	280	0.01	20
Riesling	W	Riesling	7146	0.15	17
Riesling	W	Riesling	3407	0.07	8
Riesling de Rhin	W	Riesling	1343	0.03	3
Riesling Italico	W	Grasevina	2007	0.04	2
Riesling Weisser	W	Riesling	22350	0.46	52
Rivaner	W	Muller Thurgau	459	0.01	1
Rkatiteli	W	Rkatsiteli	11508	0.24	17
Rkatsiteli	W	Rkatsiteli	46417	0.95	69
Rkaziteli	W	Rkatsiteli	9429	0.19	14
Robal	W	Cayetana Blanca	567	0.01	1
Rollo	W	Rollo	108	0.00	92
Rombola	W	Robola	359	0.01	100
Roseti	W	Afus Ali	0	0.00	0
Rossara	R	Rossara Trentina	29	0.00	100
Roupeiro Branco	W	Siria	1527	0.03	55
Roussanne Var	O	Rose du Var	129	0.00	100
Royal	W	Perruno	1075	0.02	38
Rubi Cabernet	R	Ruby Cabernet	22	0.00	0
Rubin Tairovski	R		2	0.00	100
Ruby Cabernet	R	Ruby Cabernet	7397	0.15	100

Table 16 (cont.) Synonyms' global area and share of each prime variety, 2000

Synonym	Col	Prime variety	Area (hectares)	Share (%) of global area	Synonym's share (%) of prime variety
Rufete	R	Rufete	2985	0.06	88
Rulander	O	Pinot Gris	2636	0.05	14
Rynsky Riesling	W	Riesling	793	0.02	2
Saborinho	R	Negramoll	0	0.00	0
Sabro	W	Siria	6	0.00	0
Sangiovese	R	Sangiovese	66501	1.36	97
Sangioveto	R	Sangiovese	666	0.01	1
Saperavi Severnii	R	Saperavi Severny	25	0.00	100
Sardone	W	Chardonnay	36	0.00	0
Sauvignon	W	Sauvignon Blanc	34444	0.71	53
Sauvignon Blanc	W	Sauvignon Blanc	29787	0.61	46
Sauvignon Blanca	W	Sauvignon Blanc	467	0.01	1
Sauvignon Musque	W	Sauvignon Blanc	33	0.00	0
Sauvignon Vert	W	Sauvignonasse	132	0.00	2
Sauvignonasse	W	Sauvignonasse	798	0.02	15
Savvatiano	W	Savatiano	12747	0.26	100
Schiava Grossa	R	Schiava Grossa	1240	0.03	99
Sciaccarello	R	Mammolo	639	0.01	82
Sciascinoso	R	Sciascinoso	136	0.00	54
Seibel Divers	W	Seibel white	15	0.00	100
Seibel Divers	R	seibel	24	0.00	1
Seibel Hybrids	R	seibel	1967	0.04	99
Semigion	W	Semillon	21	0.00	0
Semillon	W	Semillon	26209	0.54	100
Senso	R	Cinsaut	108	0.00	0
Sercial	W	Sercial	24	0.00	8
Servant	W	Servant	98	0.00	19
Seyval	W	Seyval Blanc	36	0.00	9
Seyval Blanc	W	Seyval Blanc	352	0.01	91
Shiraz	R	Syrah	34926	0.72	34
Silvaner	W	Silvaner	1877	0.04	45
Sirach	R	Syrah	39	0.00	0
Souson	R	Vinhao	590	0.01	10
Souzao	R	Vinhao	51	0.00	1
Sovinion	W	Sauvignon Blanc	158	0.00	0
St Emilion	W	Trebbiano Toscano	151	0.00	0
St. Laurent	R	Sankt Laurent	2370	0.05	100
Suholimenschii Belii	W	Sukholimanskiy Bely	599	0.01	37
Sukholimanskiy Bely	W	Sukholimanskiy Bely	1032	0.02	63
Sultana	W	Sultaniye	10298	0.21	72
Sultaniye	W	Sultaniye	4049	0.08	28
Sumoll	R	Sumoll	1390	0.03	99
Sylvaner	W	Silvaner	2196	0.05	52

Table 16 (cont.) Synonyms' global area and share of each prime variety, 2000

Synonym	Col	Prime variety	Area (hectares)	Share (%) of global area	Synonym's share (%) of prime variety
Sylvaner Verde	W	Silvaner	112	0.00	3
Syrach	R	Syrah	86	0.00	0
Syrah	R	Syrah	66455	1.36	65
Talia	W	Trebbiano Toscano	382	0.01	0
Tamianka	W	Muscat Blanc a Petits Grains	1012	0.02	4
Tempranillo	R	Tempranillo	81710	1.68	88
Teoulier	R	Teoulier Noir	1	0.00	100
Thompson	W	Sultaniye	4	0.00	0
Tinta Amarela	R	Trincadeira	164	0.00	2
Tinta Barocca	R	Tinta Barroca	395	0.01	7
Tinta Barroca	R	Tinta Barroca	5657	0.12	93
Tinta Gorda	R	Juan Garcia	179	0.00	9
Tinta Miuda	R	Graciano	584	0.01	31
Tinta Negra	R	Negramoll	212	0.00	6
Tinta Pinheira	R	Rufete	412	0.01	12
Tinta Roriz	R	Tempranillo	5764	0.12	6
Tinto de Toro	R	Tempranillo	3723	0.08	4
Tintorera	R	Alicante Henri Bouschet	2519	0.05	7
Tocai Friulano	W	Sauvignonasse	4564	0.09	83
Tocai Rosso	R	Garnacha Tinta	356	0.01	0
Torbato	W	Torbato	139	0.00	83
Torrontes	W	Malvasia Fina	4751	0.10	67
Tourbat	W	Torbato	29	0.00	17
Touriga	R	Touriga Nacional	73	0.00	2
Touriga Nacional	R	Touriga Nacional	4041	0.08	95
Tourigo	R	Touriga Nacional	149	0.00	3
Trajadura	W	Trajadura	1788	0.04	74
Traminer	W	Gewurztraminer	884	0.02	8
Traminer Aromatico	W	Gewurztraminer	541	0.01	5
Traminer Rose	W	Gewurztraminer	2731	0.06	26
Trebbiano Abruzzese	W	Trebbiano d'Abruzzo	8435	0.17	100
Trebbiano di Soave	W	Verdicchio Bianco	1710	0.04	34
Trebbiano Toscano	W	Trebbiano Toscano	39447	0.81	29
Treixadura	W	Trajadura	628	0.01	26
Trepat	R	Trepat	1159	0.02	66
Trincadeira	R	Trincadeira	7062	0.14	97
Trousseau	R	Trousseau	126	0.00	6
Tschaggele	R	Schiava Grossa	18	0.00	1
Turca	R	Douce Noire	99	0.00	
Tzaritza Na Loziata	W	Koenigin der Weingaerten	567	0.01	76
Ugni Blanc	W	Trebbiano Toscano	95872	1.97	70
Uni Blance	W	Trebbiano Toscano	720	0.01	1
Uva Rey	W	Chelva	2	0.00	0
Valdepenas	R	Tempranillo	194	0.00	0

Table 16 (cont.) Synonyms' global area and share of each prime variety, 2000

Synonym	Col	Prime variety	Area (hectares)	Share (%) of global area	Synonym's share (%) of prime variety
Valenciana Blanca	W	Siria	76	0.00	3
Valency	R	Teneron	3488	0.07	100
Valentino	R	Valentino Nero	56	0.00	100
Velteliner Rouge Precoce	R	Fruhroter Veltliner	0	0.00	0
Veltliner	W	Gruner Veltliner	129	0.00	1
Verdejo Blanco	W	Verdejo	4453	0.09	100
Verdejo Negro	R	Trousseau	227	0.00	11
Verdicchio Bianco	W	Verdicchio Bianco	3330	0.07	66
Verdiso	W	Verdiso	65	0.00	91
Vermejuela	W	Marmajuelo	37	0.00	100
Vermentino	W	Vermentino	5330	0.11	91
Vernaccia di San Gimignano	W	Vernaccia di San Gimignano	772	0.02	90
Vernaccia Nera	R	Garnacha Tinta	228	0.00	0
Vidal Blanc	W	Vidal	611	0.01	100
Vidal Divers	W	Vidal	0	0.00	0
Vidal Divers	R	Vidal Red	0	0.00	100
Vignoles	W	Vignoles	35	0.00	51
Vijiriego	W	Vijariego	509	0.01	100
Vijiriego Negro	R	Sumoll	11	0.00	1
Vinhao	R	Vinhao	5296	0.11	89
Viogner	W	Viognier	27	0.00	1
Viognier	W	Viognier	3133	0.06	99
Vitouska	W	Vitovska	42	0.00	100
Voskehat	W	Voskeat	809	0.02	100
Waltham Cross	W	Afus Ali	328	0.01	100
Weisser Burgunder	W	Pinot Blanc	2936	0.06	17
Weisser Gutedel	W	Chasselas	1198	0.02	9
Weisser Riesling	W	Riesling	2120	0.04	5
Welschriesling	W	Grasevina	32528	0.67	35
White Riesling	W	Riesling	6006	0.12	14
Wildbacher	R	Blauer Wildbacher	8	0.00	2
Xarello Blanco	W	Xarello	10288	0.21	100
Zibibbo	W	Muscat of Alexandria	1157	0.02	4
Zinfandel	R	Tribidrag	19077	0.39	71
Zoumiatiko	W	Dimyat	91	0.00	1
		Other primes with no synonyms	1104536	22.64	
Other varieties			569508	11.67	
Total			**4878176**	**100**	
Prime total			2897798	59	
Synonym total			1410870	29	
Other varieties			569508	12	
Total			**4878176**	**100**	

Table 17: Synonyms' global area and share of each prime variety, 2010

Synonym	Col	Prime variety	Area (hectares)	Share (%) of global area	Synonym's share (%) of prime variety
Abbou	R	Abbo	2375	0.05	100
Abrusco	R	Abrusco	2	0.00	0
Aglianico	R	Aglianico	7551	0.16	76
Aglianico del Vulture	R	Aglianico	2413	0.05	24
Agria	R	Turan	2	0.00	1
Agudello	W	Godello	26	0.00	2
Airen	W	Airen	252180	5.48	100
Alarije	W	Alarije	1722	0.04	100
Alb de Onitcani	W	Onitskanskii Belyi	5	0.00	7
Albarino	W	Alvarinho	3530	0.08	64
Albarola	W	Albarola	1406	0.03	97
Albilla	W	Albillo Mayor	7	0.00	1
Albillo	W	Albillo Real	861	0.02	100
Albillo Mayor	W	Albillo Mayor	1312	0.03	99
Alcoa	R	Tinta de Alcoa	24	0.00	100
Alfonso Lavalle	R	Alphonse Lavallee	54	0.00	6
Alfrocheiro	R	Alfrocheiro	1180	0.03	99
Alibernet	R	Odessky Cherny	260	0.01	10
Alicante	R	Alicante Henri Bouschet	370	0.01	1
Alicante Bouchet	R	Alicante Henri Bouschet	1608	0.03	4
Alicante Bouschet	R	Alicante Henri Bouschet	8427	0.18	22
Alicante Branco	W	Damaschino	1037	0.02	50
Alicante Henri Bouschet	R	Alicante Henri Bouschet	5086	0.11	13
Alikante Mouse	R	Alicante Henri Bouschet	56	0.00	0
Almafra	W	Almafre	0	0.00	100
Almenhaca	W	Alminhaca	1	0.00	100
Almuneco	R	Listan Negro	16	0.00	1
Alphonse Lavallee	R	Alphonse Lavallee	829	0.02	94
Alvadurao	W	Siria	34	0.00	0
Alvar	W	Alvar Branco	0	0.00	100
Alvarelhao	R	Alvarelhao	53	0.00	30
Alvarelhao Branco	W	Planta Nova	29	0.00	2
Alvarinho	W	Alvarinho	1993	0.04	36
Zametovka	R	Zametovka	913	0.02	100
Amor-Nao-Me-Deixes	R	Aramon Noir	1	0.00	0
Amostrinha	R	Preto Martinho	1	0.00	1
Ansonica	W	Inzolia	6133	0.13	100
Aragonez	R	Tempranillo	16706	0.36	7
Aramon	R	Aramon Noir	2891	0.06	100
Arany Sarfeher	W	Arany Sarfeher	1130	0.02	100
Arinto	W	Arinto de Bucelas	4446	0.10	100
Arinto do Interior	W	Dorinto	14	0.00	100
Arvine	W	Arvine	154	0.00	89
Asirtiko	W	Assyrtiko	902	0.02	100

Table 17 (cont.) Synonyms' global area and share of each prime variety, 2010

Synonym	Col	Prime variety	Area (hectares)	Share (%) of global area	Synonym's share (%) of prime variety
Asprinio	W	Greco	158	0.00	100
Asproudi	W	Asprouda	113	0.00	100
Aurora	W	Aurore	268	0.01	100
Babeasca Gri	W	Babeasca Gris	328	0.01	100
Babeasca Neagra	R	Babeasca Neagra	3042	0.07	97
Babosa	W	Babosa de Madere	2	0.00	100
Baco	R	Baco Noir	2	0.00	1
Baco Noir	R	Baco Noir	465	0.01	99
Baga	R	Baga	4102	0.09	100
Baladi Verdejo	W	Cayetana Blanca	243	0.01	1
Banati Rizling	W	Kreaca	3	0.00	100
Barca	R	Tinta da Barca	345	0.01	100
Barkhatny	W	Barkhatnyi	30	0.00	100
Barreto	R	Barreto de Semente	3	0.00	100
Barroco	R	Tinta Barroca	1	0.00	0
Bastarda	R	Trousseau	10	0.00	0
Bastarda Negra	R	Alfrocheiro	7	0.00	1
Bastardo	R	Trousseau	1487	0.03	43
Bastardo Magaraceskii	R	Bastardo Magarachsky	1040	0.02	44
Bastardo Magarachskiy	R	Bastardo Magarachsky	1330	0.03	56
Bastardo Roxo	R	Trousseau	28	0.00	1
Bastardo Tinto	R	Trousseau	311	0.01	9
Bayan-Shirey	W	Bayanshira	645	0.01	100
Beba	W	Beba	2949	0.06	97
Becuet	R	Persan	3	0.00	100
Beli Pinot	W	Pinot Blanc	525	0.01	4
Beltza	R	Hondarrabi Beltza	0	0.00	1
Bequignol	R	Bequignol Noir	698	0.02	100
Bervedino	W	Vernaccia di San Gimignano	10	0.00	2
Bianchetta Genovese	W	Albarola	48	0.00	3
Biancone	W	Biancone di Portoferraio	78	0.00	100
Bibor Kadarka	R	Biborkadarka	136	0.00	100
Black Spanish	R	Jacquez	36	0.00	2
Blanca Cayetana	W	Cayetana Blanca	12280	0.27	31
Blauer Burgunder	R	Pinot Noir	646	0.01	1
Blauer Portugieser	R	Blauer Portugieser	2838	0.06	75
Blauer Wildbacher	R	Blauer Wildbacher	365	0.01	99
Blaufrankisch	R	Blaufrankisch	11229	0.24	70
Boal	W	Malvasia Fina	0	0.00	0
Boal Branco	W	Malvasia Fina	190	0.00	6
Boal Espinho	W	Malvasia Fina	21	0.00	1
Bonamico	R	Bonamico	26	0.00	14
Bonarda	R	Douce Noire	18877	0.41	99
Bonicaire	R	Trepat	263	0.01	19
Bonvedro	R	Parraleta	3	0.00	1

Table 17 (cont.) Synonyms' global area and share of each prime variety, 2010

Synonym	Col	Prime variety	Area (hectares)	Share (%) of global area	Synonym's share (%) of prime variety
Borba	W	Grasevina	791	0.02	1
Borgona	R	Blaufrankisch	290	0.01	2
Borgonja	R	Blaufrankisch	50	0.00	0
Bornova Misketi	W	Muscat Blanc a Petits Grains	114	0.00	0
Borracal	R	Borracal	160	0.00	23
Boschera	W	Verdicchio Bianco	6	0.00	0
Bouvier	W	Bouvier	244	0.01	98
Bouvierovo Hrozno	W	Bouvier	6	0.00	2
Bovale	R	Graciano	209	0.00	7
Bovale Grande	R	Mazuelo	378	0.01	0
Brachetto	R	Brachetto del Piemonte	1460	0.03	100
Bragao	R	Tinta Bragao	63	0.00	100
Brajda Crna	R	Suscan	3	0.00	100
Brancellao	R	Alvarelhao	21	0.00	12
Branco Joao	W	Branco Sr. Joao	0	0.00	100
Branda	W	Brandam	312	0.01	100
Breval	W	Beba	19	0.00	1
Buonamico	R	Bonamico	167	0.00	86
Burdeos	R	Cabernet Sauvignon	33	0.00	0
Burger	W	Elbling	498	0.01	35
Burgund Mare	R	Blaufrankisch	760	0.02	5
Burgunder	W	Pinot Blanc	3870	0.08	26
Burra Blanca	W	Airen	18	0.00	0
C G 45803	R	Gargiulo	10	0.00	23
C.G.2539	R	Gargiulo	34	0.00	75
C.G.4113	R	Gargiulo	1	0.00	2
Cabernet Gernischt	R	Carmenere	1353	0.03	12
Cabernet Sauvignon	R	Cabernet Sauvignon	290058	6.30	100
Cagnulari	R	Graciano	260	0.01	8
Cainho	W	Cainho de Moreira	7	0.00	100
Caino Tinto	R	Borracal	523	0.01	77
Calabrese	R	Nero d'Avola	16595	0.36	100
Camarate	W	Camaralet de Lasseube	515	0.01	100
Canaiolo Bianco	W	Drupeggio	286	0.01	100
Canari	R	Canari Noir	139	0.00	91
Canina Nera	R	Fortana	240	0.01	37
Cannonau	R	Garnacha Tinta	5422	0.12	3
Cardenal	R	Cardinal	168	0.00	31
Cardinal	R	Cardinal	286	0.01	52
Cargadora	R	Cinsaut	22	0.00	0
Caricagiola	R	Parraleta	119	0.00	34
Carignan	R	Mazuelo	55910	1.22	70
Carignan Blanc	W	Carignan Blanc	411	0.01	13

Table 17 (cont.) Synonyms' global area and share of each prime variety, 2010

Synonym	Col	Prime variety	Area (hectares)	Share (%) of global area	Synonym's share (%) of prime variety
Carignan Noir	R	Mazuelo	481	0.01	1
Carignane	R	Mazuelo	17015	0.37	21
Carignano	R	Mazuelo	1645	0.04	2
Carinena Blanco	W	Carignan Blanc	2650	0.06	87
Carmenere	R	Carmenere	9988	0.22	88
Carmenere Crni	R	Carmenere	19	0.00	0
Carrasquenho	R	Baga	2	0.00	0
Carrega Burros	R	Baga	4	0.00	0
Castelao	R	Castelao	11065	0.24	100
Castellana	R	Rufete	18	0.00	0
Casteloa	R	Castelao	11	0.00	0
Catarratto	W	Catarratto Bianco	68	0.00	0
Catarratto Bianco Comune	W	Catarratto Bianco	25935	0.56	74
Catarratto Bianco Lucido	W	Catarratto Bianco	8859	0.19	25
Cayuga	W	Cayuga White	45	0.00	21
Cayuga White	W	Cayuga White	167	0.00	79
Cercial	W	Cerceal Branco	311	0.01	100
Cesanese Comune	R	Cesanese	307	0.01	45
Cesanese d'Affile	R	Cesanese	372	0.01	55
Charbono	R	Douce Noire	34	0.00	0
Chardonnay	W	Chardonnay	196336	4.27	99
Chardonnay Blanc	W	Chardonnay	2457	0.05	1
Chaselas Dorada	W	Chasselas	20	0.00	0
Chaslas	W	Chasselas	21	0.00	0
Chasselas	W	Chasselas	11971	0.26	91
Chasselas Dorato	W	Chasselas	34	0.00	0
Chasselas Roxo	W	Chasselas Rouge	7	0.00	100
Chenin	W	Chenin Blanc	12443	0.27	35
Chenin Blanc	W	Chenin Blanc	22720	0.49	65
Chirac	R	Syrah	15	0.00	0
Cidadelhe	R	Tinta de Cidadelhe	1	0.00	100
Ciguente	W	Siria	236	0.01	3
Cinsault	R	Cinsaut	13011	0.28	36
Cinsaut	R	Cinsaut	22913	0.50	64
Cirfandli	O	Zierfandler	32	0.00	27
Citronny of Magarach	W	Citronny Magarach	307	0.01	100
Cjanorie	R	Cianorie	2	0.00	100
Clairet	W	Clairette	22	0.00	1
Clairette	W	Clairette	2588	0.06	89
Clairette Blanche	W	Clairette	290	0.01	10
Coda di Volpe Bianca	W	Coda di Volpe Bianca	555	0.01	95
Codega do Larinho	W	Codega de Larinho	629	0.01	100
Cokur White	W	Kokur Bely	918	0.02	100
Colombar	W	Colombard	11990	0.26	37

Table 17 (cont.) Synonyms' global area and share of each prime variety, 2010

Synonym	Col	Prime variety	Area (hectares)	Share (%) of global area	Synonym's share (%) of prime variety
Colombard	W	Colombard	10060	0.22	31
Colorino	R	Abrusco	421	0.01	100
Concord	R	Concord	12164	0.26	99
Concord Clone 30	R	Concord	74	0.00	1
Corbina	R	Corbina Vicentina	12	0.00	100
Cordisco	R	Montepulciano	85	0.00	0
Corinto	R	Korinthiaki	4	0.00	8
Corinto Nero	R	Korinthiaki	50	0.00	92
Cornalin	R	Cornalin	128	0.00	50
Corvina	R	Corvina Veronese	7496	0.16	100
Corvina Veronese	R	Corvina Veronese	0	0.00	0
Cot	R	Cot	6234	0.14	15
Couderc	R	Couderc Noir	214	0.00	8
Couderc 13	W	Couderc	834	0.02	100
Couderc Noir	R	Couderc Noir	2477	0.05	92
Crato Espanhol	W	Siria	36	0.00	0
Criolla Chica	R	Listan Prieto	423	0.01	9
Cristal	W	Crystal	4	0.00	2
Crljenak Kastelanski	R	Tribidrag	65	0.00	0
Crystal	W	Crystal	171	0.00	98
Csabagyongye	W	Csaba Gyongye	89	0.00	100
Cynthiana	R	Norton	102	0.00	31
Damaschino	W	Damaschino	221	0.00	11
Dekabrsky	R	Dekabrskii	78	0.00	100
Dembina	W	Debina	239	0.01	100
Derechero	R	Royal de Alloza	29	0.00	100
Diego	W	Vijariego	2	0.00	1
Dievcie Hrozno	W	Feteasca Alba	219	0.00	1
Dimyat	W	Dimyat	2386	0.05	99
Dona Blanca	W	Siria	508	0.01	6
Douce Noire	R	Douce Noire	0	0.00	0
Drujba	W	Droujba	3	0.00	100
Durif	R	Durif	455	0.01	13
Elbling	W	Elbling	370	0.01	26
Elbling Weisser	W	Elbling	550	0.01	39
Engomada	R	Tinta Engomada	4	0.00	100
Esgana Cao Tinto	R	Esganacao Preto	0	0.00	100
Esganoso	W	Sercial	0	0.00	0
Faber	W	Faberrebe	4	0.00	1
Faberrebe	W	Faberrebe	520	0.01	99
Favorita	W	Vermentino	220	0.00	3
Favorita Diaz	W	Vermentino	2	0.00	0
Fernao Pires	W	Fernao Pires	9504	0.21	100
Ferrol	R		50	0.00	89
Ferron	R	Manseng Noir	6	0.00	11

Table 17 (cont.) Synonyms' global area and share of each prime variety, 2010

Synonym	Col	Prime variety	Area (hectares)	Share (%) of global area	Synonym's share (%) of prime variety
Feteasca Alba	W	Feteasca Alba	17250	0.37	99
Feuille de Tilleul	W	Harslevelu	1659	0.04	89
Fileri	R	Moschofilero	321	0.01	34
Findling	W	Muller Thurgau	21	0.00	0
Foch	R	Marechal Foch	67	0.00	19
Folle Noire	R	Canari Noir	13	0.00	9
Forcallat Blanca	W	Airen	166	0.00	0
Fortana	R	Fortana	402	0.01	63
Franconia	R	Blaufrankisch	59	0.00	0
Frankovka	R	Blaufrankisch	1668	0.04	10
Frankovka Modra	R	Blaufrankisch	1378	0.03	9
French Colombard	W	Colombard	10025	0.22	31
Fruhburgunder	R	Pinot Noir Precoce	209	0.00	100
Fruhroter Veltliner	R	Fruhroter Veltliner	424	0.01	50
Frutilla	R	Isabella	256	0.01	1
Furmint	W	Furmint	4435	0.10	84
Galego	W	Galego Dourado	1	0.00	6
Galego Dourado	W	Galego Dourado	12	0.00	76
Gamay	R	Gamay Noir	32455	0.71	99
Gamay de Chaudenay	R	Gamay Teinturier de Chaudenay	24	0.00	100
Gamay de Teinturier Bouze	R	Gamay de Teinturier Bouze	215	0.00	96
Gamay Noir	R	Gamay Noir	207	0.00	1
Gamay St Romain	R	Gamay Noir	3	0.00	0
Gammay de Bouze	R	Gamay de Teinturier Bouze	10	0.00	4
Gammay Freaux	R	Gamay Teinturier Freaux	55	0.00	100
Gamza	R	Kadarka	550	0.01	51
Garanoir	R	Garanoir	203	0.00	94
Garganega	W	Garganega	11292	0.25	73
Garnacha	R	Garnacha Tinta	58811	1.28	32
Garnacha Blanca	W	Garnacha Blanca	2263	0.05	31
Garnacha Peluda	R	Garnacha Peluda	799	0.02	65
Garnacha Roja	W	Garnacha Roja	77	0.00	4
Garnacha Tinta	R	Garnacha Tinta	11389	0.25	6
Garnacha Tintorera	R	Alicante Henri Bouschet	19551	0.42	50
Garrut	R	Monastrell	1	0.00	0
Gecsei Zamatos	W	Goecseji Zamatos	40	0.00	72
Gewurztraminer	W	Gewurztraminer	5793	0.13	41
Gocseji Zamatos	W	Goecseji Zamatos	15	0.00	28
Godelho	W	Godello	1	0.00	0
Godello	W	Godello	579	0.01	53
Goluboc	R	Golubok	50	0.00	57
Golubok	R	Golubok	37	0.00	43
Gorda	R	Juan Garcia	135	0.00	8

Table 17 (cont.) Synonyms' global area and share of each prime variety, 2010

Synonym	Col	Prime variety	Area (hectares)	Share (%) of global area	Synonym's share (%) of prime variety
Gouveio	W	Godello	489	0.01	45
Gouveio Estimado	W	Gouveio Real	0	0.00	0
Gouveio Real	W	Gouveio Real	582	0.01	100
Graciana	R	Graciano	19	0.00	1
Graciano	R	Graciano	2269	0.05	73
Gran Negro	R	Grand Noir	774	0.02	81
Grand Noir	R	Grand Noir	181	0.00	19
Granoir	R	Garanoir	13	0.00	6
Grasa de Cotnari	W	Grasa de Cotnari	640	0.01	93
Grasevina	W	Grasevina	4901	0.11	8
Grauer Burgunder	O	Pinot Gris	215	0.00	0
Grecanico Dorato	W	Garganega	4110	0.09	27
Grechetto	W	Grechetto di Orvieto	1501	0.03	100
Greco di Tufo	W	Greco	0	0.00	0
Grenache	R	Garnacha Tinta	108061	2.35	58
Grenache Blanc	W	Garnacha Blanca	5107	0.11	69
Grenache Gris	W	Garnacha Roja	1707	0.04	96
Grenache Noir	R	Garnacha Tinta	103	0.00	0
Grolleau	R	Grolleau Noir	2350	0.05	100
Groppello di Mocasina	R	Groppello di Mocasina	51	0.00	62
Groppello di Santo Stefano	R	Groppello di Mocasina	30	0.00	38
Gruner Veltliner	W	Gruner Veltliner	15059	0.33	80
Gual	W	Malvasia Fina	22	0.00	1
Guarnaccia	W	Coda di Volpe Bianca	32	0.00	5
Gutedel Weisser	W	Chasselas	1120	0.02	8
Hamburgi Muskotaly	R	Muscat of Hamburg	12	0.00	0
Harslevelu	W	Harslevelu	56	0.00	3
Humagne Blanc	W	Humagne	30	0.00	100
Humagne Rouge	R	Cornalin	128	0.00	50
Iliciovski Ciornai Rannii	R	Ilichevskii Rannii	5	0.00	100
Irsai Oliver	W	Irsai Oliver	1410	0.03	100
Isabel Precoce	R	Isabella	410	0.01	1
Isabella	R	Isabella	30959	0.67	95
Iso	W	Beba	4	0.00	0
Italian Riesling	W	Grasevina	33120	0.72	54
J. Riesling	W	Riesling	693	0.02	1
Jacquez	R	Jacquez	2252	0.05	95
Jaen	R	Mencia	2454	0.05	23
Jaen Tinto	R	Mencia	295	0.01	3
Jampal	W	Jampal	71	0.00	100
Juan Garcia	R	Juan Garcia	1290	0.03	76
Kadarka	R	Kadarka	537	0.01	49
Kardinal Crveni	R	Cardinal	91	0.00	17
Kavcina Crna	R	Zametovka	0	0.00	0

Table 17 (cont.) Synonyms' global area and share of each prime variety, 2010

Synonym	Col	Prime variety	Area (hectares)	Share (%) of global area	Synonym's share (%) of prime variety
Kerner	W	Kerner	3989	0.09	100
Kerner Bijeli	W	Kerner	4	0.00	0
Kocsis Irma	W	Koksis Irma	11	0.00	100
Korai Piros Veltelini	R	Fruhroter Veltliner	10	0.00	1
Koverszolo	W	Grasa de Cotnari	45	0.00	7
Kovidinka	O	Kovidinka	1020	0.02	95
Krasnostop Anapsky	R	Krasnostop Zolotovsky	211	0.00	100
Kuldzhinskiy	O	Kuldzhinskii	385	0.01	100
Kuntra	R	Karasakiz	4	0.00	100
Lacrima	R	Lacrima di Morro d'Alba	421	0.01	100
Lagorthi	W	Verdeca	0	0.00	100
Laki Rizling	W	Grasevina	2360	0.05	4
Lambrusco a Foglia Frastaglia	R	Enantio	724	0.02	100
Landot	R	Landot Noir	2	0.00	100
Lefkada	R	Vertzami	96	0.00	29
Lemberger	R	Blaufrankisch	26	0.00	0
Lenoir	R	Jacquez	80	0.00	3
Lidia	R	Isabella	869	0.02	3
Lilas	W	Moscatel Lilaz	0	0.00	100
Lipovina	W	Harslevelu	141	0.00	8
Listan	W	Palomino Fino	3329	0.07	15
Listan Negro	R	Listan Negro	2624	0.06	98
Livornese Bianca	W	Rollo	13	0.00	25
Lledoner Pelut	R	Garnacha Peluda	433	0.01	35
Loureiro	W	Loureiro	3469	0.08	86
Loureiro Blanca	W	Loureiro	585	0.01	14
Loureiro Tinto	R	Mencia	22	0.00	0
Macabeo	W	Macabeo	38419	0.83	94
Macabeu	W	Macabeo	2628	0.06	6
Magaracha's Firstborn	W	Pervenets Magaracha	323	0.01	11
Magaracha's Gift	W	Podarok Magaracha	162	0.00	32
Magyar Frankos	R	Magyarfrankos	0	0.00	100
Malaga	W	Muscat of Alexandria	120	0.00	0
Malagouzia	W	Malagousia	182	0.00	100
Malandra	R	Tinta Malandra	0	0.00	100
Malbec	R	Cot	34193	0.74	84
Malbech	R	Cot	260	0.01	1
Malfar	W	Alarije	4	0.00	0
Malvar	W	Lairen	214	0.00	100
Malvasia Bianca	W	Malvasia Bianca di Candia	4915	0.11	50
Malvasia Bianca di Candia	W	Malvasia Bianca di Candia	4976	0.11	50
Malvasia Bianca Lunga	W	Malvasia Bianca Lunga	2259	0.05	89
Malvasia Branca	W	Siria	967	0.02	12
Malvasia Cabral	R	Cabral	2	0.00	100

Table 17 (cont.) Synonyms' global area and share of each prime variety, 2010

Synonym	Col	Prime variety	Area (hectares)	Share (%) of global area	Synonym's share (%) of prime variety
Malvasia Candida	W	Malvasia di Lipari	7	0.00	2
Malvasia di Lipari	W	Malvasia di Lipari	53	0.00	17
Malvasia di Sardegna	W	Malvasia di Lipari	114	0.00	37
Malvasia Dubrovacka Bijela	W	Malvasia di Lipari	24	0.00	8
Malvasia Fina	W	Malvasia Fina	2719	0.06	80
Malvasia Istriana	W	Malvazija Istarska	296	0.01	11
Malvasia Negra	R	Malvasia Nera di Brindisi	33	0.00	3
Malvasia Nera	R	Malvasia Nera di Brindisi	0	0.00	0
Malvasia Nera di Brindisi	R	Malvasia Nera di Brindisi	879	0.02	67
Malvasia Nera di Lecce	R	Malvasia Nera di Brindisi	402	0.01	31
Malvasia Preta	R	Malvasia Preta	1003	0.02	100
Malvasia Rei	W	Palomino Fino	3033	0.07	13
Malvasia Sitges	W	Malvasia di Lipari	112	0.00	36
Malvasier	R	Fruhroter Veltliner	0	0.00	0
Malvazija	W	Malvazija Istarska	740	0.02	27
Malvazija Istarska	W	Malvazija Istarska	1705	0.04	62
Mammolo	R	Mammolo	52	0.00	6
Manteudo	W	Listain de Huelva	350	0.01	100
Marastina	W	Malvasia Bianca Lunga	285	0.01	11
Marechal Foch	R	Marechal Foch	277	0.01	81
Marisancho	W	Pardillo	4364	0.09	100
Marsanne	W	Marsanne	1694	0.04	97
Marsanne Blanche	W	Marsanne	48	0.00	3
Marsigliana Nera	R	Magliocco Dolce	87	0.00	100
Marufo	R	Marufo	3020	0.07	46
Marzemina Grossa	R	Marzemino	5	0.00	1
Marzemino	R	Marzemino	1085	0.02	99
Mataro	R	Monastrell	1603	0.03	2
Maturana Blanca	W	Maturana Blanca	8	0.00	45
Maturana Tinta	R	Trousseau	3	0.00	0
Maturano Bianco	W	Maturana Blanca	10	0.00	55
Mauzac	W	Mauzac Blanc	1991	0.04	100
Mavroudi	R	Mavrouda	520	0.01	100
Mayskiy	R	Maiskii Chernyi	110	0.00	100
Mazuela	R	Mazuelo	4749	0.10	6
Melra	R	Tinta da Melra	1	0.00	100
Mencia	R	Mencia	7888	0.17	74
Menoire	R	Menoir	65	0.00	100
Meunier	R	Pinot Meunier	11192	0.24	99
Mezes	W	Mezes Feher	2	0.00	100
Miguel del Arco	R	Miguel del Arco	429	0.01	92
Mission	R	Listan Prieto	265	0.01	6
Modra Frankinja	R	Blaufrankisch	680	0.01	4
Modry Portugal	R	Blauer Portugieser	714	0.02	19
Molar	R		2	0.00	0

Table 17 (cont.) Synonyms' global area and share of each prime variety, 2010

Synonym	Col	Prime variety	Area (hectares)	Share (%) of global area	Synonym's share (%) of prime variety
Molinara	R	Molinara	595	0.01	83
Molinera	R	Molinara	122	0.00	17
Molinha	W	Fernao Pires	7	0.00	0
Mollar	R	Negramoll	677	0.01	21
Monastrell	R	Monastrell	58414	1.27	84
Mondeuse	R	Mondeuse Noire	302	0.01	99
Mondeuse Rouge	R	Mondeuse Noire	4	0.00	1
Monemvasia	W	Monemvassia	481	0.01	100
Monstruosa de Monterrei	W	Monstruosa	1	0.00	100
Montepulciano	R	Montepulciano	34862	0.76	100
Moores Diamond	W	Moore's Diamond	42	0.00	100
Moravia Dulce	R	Marufo	2571	0.06	39
Morio Muscat	W	Morio-Muskat	39	0.00	100
Moscatel	W	Muscat Blanc a Petits Grains	740	0.02	2
Moscatel Amarilla	W	Moscato Giallo	25	0.00	2
Moscatel Amarillo	W	Moscato Giallo	131	0.00	9
Moscatel Austria	W	Torrontes Sanjuanino	4	0.00	0
Moscatel de Alejandria	W	Muscat of Alexandria	2767	0.06	11
Moscatel de Alejandria	W	Muscat of Alexandria	4029	0.09	15
Moscatel de Grano Menudo	W	Muscat Blanc a Petits Grains	996	0.02	3
Moscatel de Hamburg	R	Muscat of Hamburg	2	0.00	0
Moscatel de Malaga	W	Muscat of Alexandria	5470	0.12	21
Moscatel Frontignan	W	Muscat Blanc a Petits Grains	162	0.00	1
Moscatel Galego Branco	W	Muscat Blanc a Petits Grains	505	0.01	2
Moscatel Galego Roxo	R	Muscat a Petits Grains Rouge	68	0.00	100
Moscatel Galego Tinto	R	Muscat a Petits Grains Noirs	108	0.00	100
Moscatel Graudo	W	Muscat of Alexandria	647	0.01	2
Moscatel Hamburg	R	Muscat of Hamburg	1500	0.03	18
Moscatel Negra	R	Listan Prieto	1	0.00	0
Moscatel Negro	R	Listan Prieto	6	0.00	0
Moscatel Nunes	W	Moscatel Branco	30	0.00	100
Moscatel Rosada	O	Moscatel Rosada	70	0.00	1
Moscatel Rosado	O	Moscatel Rosada	7259	0.16	99
Moscato Bianco	W	Muscat Blanc a Petits Grains	11600	0.25	37
Moscato Giallo	W	Moscato Giallo	1256	0.03	85
Moscato Nero di Acqui	R	Muscat of Hamburg	73	0.00	1
Moscato Ottonel	W	Muscat Ottonel	0	0.00	0
Moscato Rosa	R	Moscato Rosa del Trentino	66	0.00	82
Moscato Rosado	R	Moscato Rosa del Trentino	0	0.00	1
Moschato	W	Muscat Blanc a Petits Grains	2162	0.05	7
Moschato R	R	Moschomavro	1428	0.03	100
Moschofilero	R	Moschofilero	613	0.01	66
Moslavac	W	Furmint	161	0.00	3
Mouraton	R	Juan Garcia	140	0.00	8

Table 17 (cont.) Synonyms' global area and share of each prime variety, 2010

Synonym	Col	Prime variety	Area (hectares)	Share (%) of global area	Synonym's share (%) of prime variety
Mourisco	R	Marufo	958	0.02	15
Mourisco Branco	W	Cayetana Blanca	141	0.00	0
Mourisco Roxo	R	Marufo	31	0.00	0
Mourvedre	R	Monastrell	9832	0.21	14
Mtsvane	W	Mtsvane Kakhuri	319	0.01	100
Mulata	R	Negramoll	0	0.00	0
Muller Thurgau	W	Muller Thurgau	22488	0.49	99
Muscat	W	Muscat Blanc a Petits Grains	957	0.02	3
Muscat a Petits Grains Blanc	W	Muscat Blanc a Petits Grains	533	0.01	2
Muscat Bailey	R	Muscat Bailey A	19	0.00	16
Muscat Bailey A	R	Muscat Bailey A	103	0.00	84
Muscat Blanc	W	Muscat Blanc a Petits Grains	1388	0.03	4
Muscat Blanc a Petits Grains	W	Muscat Blanc a Petits Grains	51	0.00	0
Muscat Canelli	W	Muscat Blanc a Petits Grains	103	0.00	0
Muscat d'Alexandrie	W	Muscat of Alexandria	2167	0.05	8
Muscat de Frontignan	W	Muscat Blanc a Petits Grains	10	0.00	0
Muscat de Frontignan	W	Muscat Blanc a Petits Grains	689	0.01	2
Muscat Frontignan	W	Muscat Blanc a Petits Grains	172	0.00	1
Muscat Gordo Blanco	W	Muscat of Alexandria	2043	0.04	8
Muscat Hambourg	R	Muscat of Hamburg	3706	0.08	46
Muscat of Alexandria	W	Muscat of Alexandria	7571	0.16	29
Muscat of Hamburg	R	Muscat of Hamburg	2760	0.06	34
Muscat Orange	W	Muscat Fleur d'Oranger	91	0.00	100
Muscat Ottonel	W	Muscat Ottonel	9707	0.21	95
Muscat Petit Grain	W	Muscat Blanc a Petits Grains	7	0.00	0
Muscat Petits Grains	W	Muscat Blanc a Petits Grains	7620	0.17	24
Muscat White	W	Muscat Blanc a Petits Grains	819	0.02	3
Muscats	W	Muscat Swenson	24	0.00	100
Muskat	W	Muscat Blanc a Petits Grains	526	0.01	2
Muskat Bijeli	W	Muscat Blanc a Petits Grains	56	0.00	0
Muskat Hamburg	R	Muscat of Hamburg	14	0.00	0
Muskat Hungarian	R	Muscat of Hamburg	70	0.00	1
Muskat Oliver	W	Irsai Oliver	5	0.00	0
Muskat Ruza Crni	R	Moscato Rosa del Trentino	14	0.00	18
Muskat Zlty	W	Muscat Blanc a Petits Grains	48	0.00	0
Muskat Zuti	W	Moscato Giallo	59	0.00	4
Muskateller	W	Muscat Blanc a Petits Grains	492	0.01	2
Muskateller Gelber	W	Muscat Blanc a Petits Grains	170	0.00	1
Muskat-Ottonel	W	Muscat Ottonel	527	0.01	5
Napa Gamay	R	Valdiguie	134	0.00	97
Negkoska	R	Negoska	143	0.00	100
Negra Commun	R	Listan Negro	26	0.00	1
Negra Criolla	R	Negramoll	1250	0.03	39
Negra Mole	R	Negramoll	270	0.01	8

Table 17 (cont.) Synonyms' global area and share of each prime variety, 2010

Synonym	Col	Prime variety	Area (hectares)	Share (%) of global area	Synonym's share (%) of prime variety
Negramoll	R	Negramoll	590	0.01	18
Negrara	R	Hrvatica	116	0.00	100
Nero Buono	R	Nero Buono di Cori	135	0.00	100
Nero d'Avola	R	Nero d'Avola	1	0.00	0
Neuburske	W	Neuburger	312	0.01	100
Nieddu Mannu	R	Pascale	35	0.00	9
Nielluccio	R	Sangiovese	1589	0.03	2
Norton	R	Norton	227	0.00	69
Odessa Black	R	Odessky Cherny	2426	0.05	90
Olivella Nera	R	Sciascinoso	43	0.00	46
Ondarrabi Beltza	R	Hondarrabi Beltza	53	0.00	99
Onitcani	W	Onitskanskii Belyi	66	0.00	93
Orbois	W	Menu Pineau	212	0.00	100
Ottavianello	R	Cinsaut	51	0.00	0
Pais	R	Listan Prieto	3868	0.08	85
Palomino	W	Palomino Fino	642	0.01	3
Palomino Fino	W	Palomino Fino	12562	0.27	56
Palomino Superior	W	Palomino Fino	2945	0.06	13
Pamid	R	Pamid	6792	0.15	69
Pamiti	R	Pamid	22	0.00	0
Pansa Rosada	W	Xarello Rosado	1	0.00	100
Panse Negro	R	Trobat	1	0.00	100
Panse Valenciana	W	Panse Valenciano	1	0.00	100
Pardina	W	Cayetana Blanca	26767	0.58	67
Parraleta	R	Parraleta	56	0.00	16
Parrel Verdal	R	Trepat	12	0.00	1
Pascale	R	Pascale	341	0.01	91
Pau Ferro	R	Parraleta	1	0.00	0
Pecorino	W	Pecorino	1114	0.02	91
Pedevenda	W	Verdiso	18	0.00	26
Pedro Gimenez	W	Pedro Gimenez	12132	0.26	99
Pedro Gimenez Rio Colorado	W	Pedro Ximenez	8	0.00	0
Pedro Jimenez	W	Pedro Gimenez	118	0.00	1
Pedro Luis	W	Galego Dourado	3	0.00	19
Pedro Ximenez	W	Pedro Ximenez	9038	0.20	98
Pensal Blanco	W	Prensal	105	0.00	100
Periquita	R	Castelao	11	0.00	0
Perrum	W	Pedro Ximenez	197	0.00	2
Perruno	W	Perruno	1054	0.02	70
Pervenec Magaracha	W	Pervenets Magaracha	643	0.01	22
Pervenets of Magarach	W	Pervenets Magaracha	1915	0.04	66
Pervomaiskii	R	Pervomaisky	64	0.00	100
Petit Bouschet	R	Petit Bouschet	4	0.00	28
Petit Courbou Ondarrzurizerra	W	Petit Courbu	36	0.00	100
Petit Syrah	R	Durif	135	0.00	4

Table 17 (cont.) Synonyms' global area and share of each prime variety, 2010

Synonym	Col	Prime variety	Area (hectares)	Share (%) of global area	Synonym's share (%) of prime variety
Petit Verdot	R	Petit Verdot	6696	0.15	93
Petite Arvine	W	Arvine	19	0.00	11
Petite Sirah	R	Durif	2863	0.06	80
Petite Syrah	R	Durif	104	0.00	3
Pical	R	Piquepoul Noir	6	0.00	58
Picapoll Negro	R	Piquepoul Noir	4	0.00	42
Pigato	W	Vermentino	264	0.01	3
Pignola	R	Pignola Valtellinese	49	0.00	100
Pilongo	R	Alvarelhao	106	0.00	59
Pinheira Branca	W	Jampal	0	0.00	0
Pinheira Roxa	R	Malvasia Preta	0	0.00	0
Pinot Bianco	W	Pinot Blanc	3086	0.07	21
Pinot Bijeli	W	Pinot Blanc	188	0.00	1
Pinot Blanc	W	Pinot Blanc	3534	0.08	24
Pinot Blanco	W	Pinot Blanc	15	0.00	0
Pinot Crni	R	Pinot Noir	180	0.00	0
Pinot Grey	O	Pinot Gris	638	0.01	1
Pinot Grigio	O	Pinot Gris	17281	0.38	40
Pinot Gris	O	Pinot Gris	19333	0.42	44
Pinot Menier	R	Pinot Meunier	1	0.00	0
Pinot Meunier	R	Pinot Meunier	74	0.00	1
Pinot Negro	R	Pinot Noir	1802	0.04	2
Pinot Nero	R	Pinot Noir	5046	0.11	6
Pinot Noir	R	Pinot Noir	78302	1.70	90
Pinot Sivi	O	Pinot Gris	219	0.00	1
Pinot White	W	Pinot Blanc	338	0.01	2
Piros Bakator	R	Bakator Roz	2	0.00	100
Piros Szlanka	R	Pamid	82	0.00	1
Piros Veltelini	O	Roter Veltliner	5	0.00	3
Plant Robert	R	Gamay Noir	6	0.00	0
Planta Fina	W	Damaschino	239	0.01	11
Planta Nova	W	Planta Nova	1366	0.03	98
Plavac Mali Crni	R	Plavac Mali	1569	0.03	100
Plavac Zuti	W	Plavec Zuti	13	0.00	100
Plavina Crna	R	Plavina	643	0.01	100
Plemenka Bijela	W	Chasselas	21	0.00	0
Podarok Magaracha	W	Podarok Magaracha	212	0.00	42
Podarok of Magarach	W	Podarok Magaracha	130	0.00	26
Poloskei Muskotaly	W	Poeloeske Muskotaly	103	0.00	100
Portoghese	R	Blauer Portugieser	167	0.00	4
Portugais Blue	R	Blauer Portugieser	2	0.00	0
Portugizac	R	Blauer Portugieser	42	0.00	1
Portugues Azul	R	Blauer Portugieser	36	0.00	1
Pozsonyi Feher	W	Pozsonyi	10	0.00	100

Table 17 (cont.) Synonyms' global area and share of each prime variety, 2010

Synonym	Col	Prime variety	Area (hectares)	Share (%) of global area	Synonym's share (%) of prime variety
Preto Martinho	R	Preto Martinho	162	0.00	99
Prie Blanc	W	Prie	33	0.00	100
Prie Rouge	R	Primetta	24	0.00	100
Primitivo	R	Tribidrag	12281	0.27	38
Prugnolo Gentile	R	Sangiovese	61	0.00	0
Rabigato	W	Rabigato	1235	0.03	97
Rabigato Franco	W	Rabigato	38	0.00	3
Rabo de Ovelha Tinto	R	Negramoll	4	0.00	0
Raboso	R	Raboso Piave	43	0.00	6
Raboso Piave	R	Raboso Piave	728	0.02	94
Raisin Blanc	W	Servant	54	0.00	100
Rajinski Rizling	W	Riesling	676	0.01	1
Ramisco	R	Ramisco	2	0.00	5
Ramisco Tinto	R	Ramisco	32	0.00	95
Rara Neagra	R	Babeasca Neagra	80	0.00	3
Rebula	W	Ribolla Gialla	743	0.02	63
Red Hanepoot	R	Muscat of Alexandria Red	6	0.00	100
Refosco	R	Refosco	6	0.00	0
Refosco Nostrano	R	Refosco di Faedis	217	0.00	100
Refosk	R	Refosco	1414	0.03	100
Regina dei Vigneti	W	Koenigin der Weingaerten	61	0.00	100
Renski Rizling	W	Riesling	676	0.01	1
Ribolla Gialla	W	Ribolla Gialla	435	0.01	37
Riesling	W	Riesling	15802	0.34	32
Riesling de Rhin	W	Riesling	1343	0.03	3
Riesling Italian	W	Grasevina	7530	0.16	12
Riesling Italico	W	Grasevina	1568	0.03	3
Riesling Renan	W	Riesling	2	0.00	0
Riesling Weisser	W	Riesling	22520	0.49	45
Riesling-Lion	W	Riesling	11	0.00	0
Rivaner	W	Muller Thurgau	184	0.00	1
Rizling Rynsky	W	Riesling	605	0.01	1
Rizling Vlasky	W	Grasevina	1655	0.04	3
Rizvanac	W	Muller Thurgau	60	0.00	0
Rkaciteli	W	Rkatsiteli	57	0.00	0
Rkatiteli	W	Rkatsiteli	11864	0.26	20
Rkatsiteli	W	Rkatsiteli	46720	1.02	80
Roal	R	Rual	1	0.00	100
Robal	W	Cayetana Blanca	303	0.01	1
Rodo	R	Tinta do Rodo	3	0.00	100
Rollo	W	Rollo	38	0.00	75
Rombola	W	Robola	465	0.01	100
Roseira	R	Tinta Roseira	4	0.00	100
Roseti	W	Afus Ali	8	0.00	100

Table 17 (cont.) Synonyms' global area and share of each prime variety, 2010

Synonym	Col	Prime variety	Area (hectares)	Share (%) of global area	Synonym's share (%) of prime variety
Rosioara	R	Pamid	2930	0.06	30
Rossara	R	Rossara Trentina	8	0.00	100
Roter Veltliner	O	Roter Veltliner	193	0.00	97
Roupeiro Branco	W	Siria	279	0.01	4
Roxo Flor	R	Roxo de Vila Flor	0	0.00	100
Royal	W	Perruno	455	0.01	30
Rozalia	W	Rozala Bianca	2	0.00	100
Rubi Cabernet	R	Ruby Cabernet	29	0.00	1
Rubin Tairovski	R	Rubin Tairovsky	2	0.00	100
Ruby Cabernet	R	Ruby Cabernet	5701	0.12	99
Ruby Magaracha	R	Rubinovy Magaracha	0	0.00	100
Ruby of Golodryga	R	Rubin Golodrigi	82	0.00	100
Rufete	R	Rufete	4815	0.10	100
Rulander	O	Pinot Gris	4459	0.10	10
Rulandske Sede	O	Pinot Gris	917	0.02	2
Rulandske Bile	W	Pinot Blanc	1255	0.03	9
Rulandske Modre	R	Pinot Noir	688	0.01	1
Rumeni Muskat	W	Muscat Blanc a Petits Grains	353	0.01	1
Rumeni Plavec	W	Plavay	60	0.00	100
Ruzica Crvena	O	Kovidinka	56	0.00	5
Ryzlink Rynsky	W	Riesling	1181	0.03	2
Ryzlink Vlaky	W	Grasevina	1148	0.02	2
Saborinho	R	Negramoll	0	0.00	0
Sabro	W	Siria	9	0.00	0
Sangiovese	R	Sangiovese	76059	1.65	98
Sankt Laurent	R	Sankt Laurent	775	0.02	26
Santareno	R	Santarena	739	0.02	100
Sao Mamede	W	S. Mamede	1	0.00	100
Saperavi Nothern	R	Saperavi Severny	325	0.01	93
Saperavi Severnii	R	Saperavi Severny	25	0.00	7
Sarfeher	W	Arany Sarfeher	3	0.00	0
Sarigo	W	Cayetana Blanca	7	0.00	0
Sauvignon	W	Sauvignon Blanc	50179	1.09	46
Sauvignon Blanc	W	Sauvignon Blanc	55859	1.21	51
Sauvignon Blanca	W	Sauvignon Blanc	4011	0.09	4
Sauvignon Musque	W	Sauvignon Blanc	89	0.00	0
Sauvignon Vert	W	Sauvignonasse	785	0.02	18
Sauvignonasse	W	Sauvignonasse	515	0.01	12
Savagnin	W	Savagnin Blanc	94	0.00	5
Savagnin Blanc	W	Savagnin Blanc	564	0.01	30
Savvatiano	W	Savatiano	9920	0.22	100
Schiava Grossa	R	Schiava Grossa	559	0.01	96
Sciaccarello	R	Mammolo	773	0.02	94
Sciascinoso	R	Sciascinoso	50	0.00	54

Table 17 (cont.) Synonyms' global area and share of each prime variety, 2010

Synonym	Col	Prime variety	Area (hectares)	Share (%) of global area	Synonym's share (%) of prime variety
Semigion	W	Semillon	8	0.00	0
Semilao	W	Semillon	6	0.00	0
Semillon	W	Semillon	22142	0.48	100
Senso	R	Cinsaut	43	0.00	0
Sercial	W	Sercial	106	0.00	100
Seyval	W	Seyval Blanc	93	0.00	20
Seyval Blanc	W	Seyval Blanc	370	0.01	80
Shiraz	R	Syrah	54474	1.18	29
Shiroka Melnishka Loza	R	Shiroka Melnishka	1580	0.03	100
Silvanac Zeleni	W	Silvaner	139	0.00	6
Silvaner	W	Silvaner	98	0.00	4
Silvanske Zelene	W	Silvaner	117	0.00	5
Sipelj	W	Furmint	11	0.00	0
Sipon	W	Furmint	651	0.01	12
Siria	W	Siria	5828	0.13	74
Sivi Pinot	O	Pinot Gris	501	0.01	1
Slarina	R	Cellerina	2	0.00	100
Smederevka	W	Dimyat	6	0.00	0
Soultanina	W	Sultaniye	371	0.01	11
Sousao	R	Vinhao	61	0.00	2
Souson	R	Vinhao	610	0.01	19
Souzao	R	Vinhao	68	0.00	2
St. Emilion	W	Trebbiano Toscano	80	0.00	0
St.Laurent	R	Sankt Laurent	0	0.00	0
Stepniak	W	Stepnyak	144	0.00	100
Suholimanskiy White	W	Sukholimanskiy Bely	1477	0.03	69
Suholimenschii Belii	W	Sukholimanskiy Bely	599	0.01	28
Sukholimansky	W	Sukholimanskiy Bely	80	0.00	4
Sultana	W	Sultaniye	430	0.01	13
Sultaniye	W	Sultaniye	1750	0.04	51
Sumoll	R	Sumoll	75	0.00	90
Svatovavrinecke	R	Sankt Laurent	2230	0.05	74
Sylvaner	W	Silvaner	1690	0.04	75
Sylvaner Verde	W	Silvaner	80	0.00	4
Sylvanske Zelene	W	Silvaner	122	0.00	5
Syrach	R	Syrah	20000	0.43	11
Syrah	R	Syrah	111079	2.41	60
Szentlorinc	R	Sankt Laurent	1	0.00	0
Talia	W	Trebbiano Toscano	212	0.00	0
Tamaioasa Romaneasca	W	Muscat Blanc a Petits Grains	840	0.02	3
Tempranillo	R	Tempranillo	209412	4.55	90
Teran	R	Terrano	228	0.00	100
Termarina	O	Termarina Rossa	20	0.00	100
Teta de Vaca	W	Beba	64	0.00	2

Table 17 (cont.) Synonyms' global area and share of each prime variety, 2010

Synonym	Col	Prime variety	Area (hectares)	Share (%) of global area	Synonym's share (%) of prime variety
Thompson Seedless	W	Sultaniye	856	0.02	25
Tinta	R	Trousseau	1359	0.03	40
Tinta Amarela	R	Trincadeira	24	0.00	0
Tinta Aurelio	R	Tinto do Aurelio	0	0.00	100
Tinta Barroca	R	Tinta Barroca	6171	0.13	100
Tinta Bastardinha	R	Alfrocheiro	1	0.00	0
Tinta Caiada	R	Parraleta	162	0.00	47
Tinta Fontes	R	Graciano	0	0.00	0
Tinta Gorda	R	Juan Garcia	142	0.00	8
Tinta Lameira	R	Parraleta	5	0.00	1
Tinta Lisboa	R	Trousseau	0	0.00	0
Tinta Miuda	R	Graciano	332	0.01	11
Tinta Negra	R	Negramoll	400	0.01	13
Tinta Porto Santo	R	Tinta de Porto Santo	2	0.00	100
Tintilia	R	Tintilia del Molise	111	0.00	100
Tintilla de Rota	R	Graciano	12	0.00	0
Tintinha	R	Petit Bouschet	11	0.00	72
Tinto de Toro	R	Tempranillo	6443	0.14	3
Tinto Pegoes	R	Tinta de Pegoes	195	0.00	100
Tintoreras	R	Alicante Henri Bouschet	3887	0.08	10
Tocai Friulano	W	Sauvignonasse	2959	0.06	66
Tocai Rosso	R	Garnacha Tinta	655	0.01	0
Torontel	W	Torrontes Riojano	433	0.01	5
Torrontes	W	Malvasia Fina	464	0.01	14
Torrontes Riojano	W	Torrontes Riojano	7683	0.17	95
Torrontes Sanjuanino	W	Torrontes Sanjuanino	2048	0.04	100
Touriga	R	Touriga Nacional	48	0.00	0
Touriga Francesa	R	Touriga Franca	0	0.00	100
Touriga Nacional	R	Touriga Nacional	10388	0.23	100
Trajadura	W	Trajadura	1171	0.03	54
Tramin Cerveny	W	Gewurztraminer	866	0.02	6
Traminac Bijeli	W	Savagnin Blanc	18	0.00	1
Traminac Crveni	W	Gewurztraminer	234	0.01	2
Traminec	W	Savagnin Blanc	215	0.00	11
Traminer	W	Savagnin Blanc	1006	0.02	53
Traminer	W	Gewurztraminer	1143	0.02	8
Traminer Aromatico	W	Gewurztraminer	1408	0.03	10
Traminer Rose	W	Gewurztraminer	3692	0.08	26
Traminer Rot	W	Gewurztraminer	747	0.02	5
Traminer Roz	W	Gewurztraminer	385	0.01	3
Trbljan Bijeli	W	Trbljan	231	0.01	100
Trebbiano Abruzzese	W	Trebbiano d'Abruzzo	5091	0.11	100
Trebbiano di Soave	W	Verdicchio Bianco	1135	0.02	32
Trebbiano Toscano	W	Trebbiano Toscano	21711	0.47	20

Table 17 (cont.) Synonyms' global area and share of each prime variety, 2010

Synonym	Col	Prime variety	Area (hectares)	Share (%) of global area	Synonym's share (%) of prime variety
Treixadura	W	Trajadura	998	0.02	46
Trepat	R	Trepat	1083	0.02	80
Tribidrag	R	Tribidrag	0	0.00	0
Trigueira	R	Malvasia Trigueira	12	0.00	100
Trincadeira	R	Trincadeira	9246	0.20	100
Trincadeira Branca	W	Trincadeiro Branco	59	0.00	100
Trincadeira Preta	R	Trincadeira	0	0.00	0
Trousseau	R	Trousseau	172	0.00	5
Tschaggele	R	Schiava Grossa	21	0.00	4
Tsymlansky Black	R	Tsimlyansky Cherny	281	0.01	100
Turan	R	Turan	175	0.00	99
Turca	R	Douce Noire	65	0.00	0
Ugni Blanc	W	Trebbiano Toscano	87473	1.90	80
Uni Blan	W	Trebbiano Toscano	297	0.01	0
Uvina	W	Pecorino	114	0.00	9
Valdiguie	R	Valdiguie	4	0.00	3
Valdosa	R	Tinta Valdosa	1	0.00	100
Valenci	W	Damaschino	586	0.01	28
Valenciana Blanca	W	Siria	2	0.00	0
Valency	R	Teneron	3488	0.08	100
Valente	W	Branco Valente	0	0.00	100
Valveirinho	W	Valveirinha	0	0.00	100
Varejoa	R	Tinta Varejoa	1	0.00	100
Veltliner	W	Gruner Veltliner	165	0.00	1
Veltlinske Cervene Rane	R	Fruhroter Veltliner	217	0.00	26
Veltlinske Cervene Skore	R	Fruhroter Veltliner	195	0.00	23
Veltlinske Zelene	W	Gruner Veltliner	3618	0.08	19
Vencedor	W	Boal Vencedor	2	0.00	100
Verdejo Blanco	W	Verdejo	6034	0.13	100
Verdejo Negro	R	Trousseau	62	0.00	2
Verdial Branco	W	Verdial	1	0.00	100
Verdicchio	W	Verdicchio Bianco	2	0.00	0
Verdicchio Bianco	W	Verdicchio Bianco	2389	0.05	68
Verdiso	W	Verdiso	50	0.00	74
Verdot	R	Petit Verdot	507	0.01	7
Verduzzo	W	Verduzzo Friulano	5	0.00	1
Verduzzo Friulano	W	Verduzzo Friulano	808	0.02	99
Vermejuela	W	Marmajuelo	24	0.00	100
Vermentino	W	Vermentino	8131	0.18	94
Vernaccia di San Gimignano	W	Vernaccia di San Gimignano	512	0.01	98
Vernaccia Nera	R	Garnacha Tinta	280	0.01	0
Vernaccia Nera Grossa	R	Garnacha Tinta	7	0.00	0
Vernaccina Nero	R	Garnacha Tinta	9	0.00	0
Vertzami	R	Vertzami	239	0.01	71
Vidal	W	Vidal	41	0.00	2

Table 17 (cont.) Synonyms' global area and share of each prime variety, 2010

Synonym	Col	Prime variety	Area (hectares)	Share (%) of global area	Synonym's share (%) of prime variety
Vidal 256	W	Vidal	1270	0.03	77
Vidal Blanc	W	Vidal	333	0.01	20
Vidau	R	Miguel del Arco	39	0.00	8
Vijiriego	W	Vijariego	283	0.01	99
Vijiriego Negro	R	Sumoll	8	0.00	10
Vinhao	R	Vinhao	2422	0.05	77
Viogner	W	Viognier	1255	0.03	11
Viognier	W	Viognier	10145	0.22	89
Vitouska	W	Vitovska	50	0.00	100
Voskehat	W	Voskeat	809	0.02	100
Weisser Burgunder	W	Pinot Blanc	1914	0.04	13
Weisser Riesling	W	Riesling	2063	0.04	4
Welschriesling	W	Grasevina	8126	0.18	13
White Riesling	W	Riesling	4488	0.10	9
Wildbacher	R	Blauer Wildbacher	3	0.00	1
Xarello Blanco	W	Xarello	8326	0.18	100
Zala Dende	W	Zalagyongye	78	0.00	4
Zalagyongye	W	Zalagyongye	1870	0.04	96
Zeleni Sauvignon	W	Sauvignonasse	190	0.00	4
Zenit	W	Zenit	559	0.01	96
Zenith	W	Zenit	21	0.00	4
Zibibbo	W	Muscat of Alexandria	1521	0.03	6
Zierfandler	O	Zierfandler	85	0.00	73
Zinfandel	R	Tribidrag	20399	0.44	62
Zlatarica	W	Zlatarica Vrgorska	19	0.00	100
Zold Szagos	W	Pecsi Szagos	1	0.00	100
Zold Szilvani	W	Silvaner	8	0.00	0
Zoumiatiko	W	Dimyat	9	0.00	0
Zweigelt	R	Zweigelt	8885	0.19	90
Zweigeltrebe	R	Zweigelt	962	0.02	10
		Other primes with no synonyms	1032842	22.45	
Other varieties			259169	5.63	
Total			**4601445**	**100**	
Prime total			3074456	67	
Synonym total			1267819	28	
Other varieties			259169	6	
Total			**4601445**	**100**	

Table 18: Share of number of prime varieties and global winegrape area, by country of origin, 2000 and 2010

Country	Share (%) of number of prime variety		Share (%) of global area	
	2000	2010	2000	2010
France	23.8	9.4	26.3	35.8
Spain	8.2	6.9	28.1	26.1
Italy	27.1	25.8	13.3	12.8
Portugal	6.8	15.4	3.0	3.0
Croatia	0.8	2.1	3.0	2.3
Germany	4.9	4.4	2.2	2.1
Georgia	1.8	1.4	1.7	1.8
United States	4.1	5.3	1.7	1.7
Argentina	0.5	1.0	1.7	1.5
Greece	3.5	2.7	1.3	1.3
Austria	1.6	1.3	1.2	1.3
Hungary	1.6	5.4	0.6	0.7
Bulgaria	0.5	0.8	0.7	0.4
Moldova	0.8	0.9	0.5	0.4
Romania	0.4	0.7	0.2	0.4
Serbia	0.1	0.3	0.3	0.3
Switzerland	1.4	1.3	0.3	0.3
Ukraine	1.2	1.1	0.3	0.3
Turkey	1.4	1.1	0.4	0.2
United Kingdom	0.1	0.1	0.1	0.2
South Africa	0.8	0.6	0.1	0.2
Cyprus	0.2	0.3	0.3	0.1
Armenia	0.4	0.3	0.1	0.1
Morocco	0.1	0.2	0.0	0.1
Russia	0.2	0.6	0.0	0.0
Czech Rep.	0.0	0.7		0.0
Brazil	0.0	0.4		0.0
Slovenia	0.1	0.2	0.0	0.0
Japan	0.3	0.2	0.0	0.0
Azerbaijan	0.2	0.2	0.0	0.0
Kazakhstan	0.2	0.1	0.0	0.0
Peru	0.1	0.1	0.0	0.0
Lebanon	0.1	0.2	0.0	0.0
Slovakia	0.0	0.3		0.0
China	0.1	0.1	0.0	0.0
Montenegro	0.0	0.1		0.0
Australia	0.2	0.1	0.0	0.0
Uzbekistan	0.1	0.1	0.0	0.0
Canada	0.1	0.2	0.0	0.0
Thailand	0.1	0.1	0.0	0.0
Other	6.3	7.5	12.6	6.5
Old world subtotal	**87.3**	**84.2**	**83.7**	**90.0**
New world subtotal	**6.4**	**8.3**	**3.7**	**3.5**
Total	**100**	**100**	**100**	**100**

Table 19 : Prime varieties' global area and share of all varieties globally, by prime's country of origin, 2000

	Hectares	Share (%)		Hectares	Share (%)
Spain			**Spain(continued)**		
Airen	387978	7.95	Mazuelo	126650	2.60
Alarije	1686	0.03	Mencia	13138	0.27
Albillo Mayor	5	0.00	Merseguera	7460	0.15
Albillo Real	3368	0.07	Miguel del Arco	1267	0.03
Alcanon	54	0.00	Monastrell	76304	1.56
Beba	4762	0.10	Moravia Agria	1092	0.02
Bobal	100128	2.05	Morenillo	39	0.00
Cabernet Franc	48551	1.00	Naparo	0	0.00
Calagrano	8229	0.17	Negramoll	3557	0.07
Callet	151	0.00	Ohanes	0	0.00
Canorroyo	157	0.00	Ondarrabi Zuri	189	0.00
Carignan Gris	25	0.00	Palomino Fino	30297	0.62
Cayetana Blanca	55502	1.14	Palot	4	0.00
Chelva	10877	0.22	Panse Valenciano	649	0.01
Coloraillo	614	0.01	Pardillo	7272	0.15
De Cilindro	15	0.00	Parellada	11188	0.23
Dominga	0	0.00	Parraleta	167	0.00
Doradilla	24	0.00	Pedro Ximenez	17272	0.35
Doradillo	249	0.01	Perruno	2831	0.06
Fogoneu	36	0.00	Picapoll Blanco	34	0.00
Forcallat Tinta	2690	0.06	Planta Mula	1	0.00
Garnacha Blanca	10821	0.22	Planta Nova	2029	0.04
Garnacha Peluda	2024	0.04	Prensal	114	0.00
Garnacha Roja	2761	0.06	Prieto Picudo	3256	0.07
Garnacha Tinta	213987	4.39	Rojal Tinta	2845	0.06
Garrido Fino	174	0.00	Rome	2	0.00
Gateta	7	0.00	Sumoll	1401	0.03
Godello	1489	0.03	Tempranillo	92985	1.91
Graciano	1910	0.04	Teneron	3488	0.07
Hondarrabi Beltza	11	0.00	Tinto de la Pampana Blanca	4726	0.10
Huerta del Rey	35	0.00	Tinto Velasco	3272	0.07
Juan Garcia	2077	0.04	Tortosina	930	0.02
Lado	1	0.00	Trepat	1763	0.04
Lairen	298	0.01	Trobat	83	0.00
Listain de Huelva	596	0.01	Valenci Tinto	5	0.00
Listan Negro	3291	0.07	Verdejo	4453	0.09
Listan Prieto	15532	0.32	Verdil	131	0.00
Macabeo	48125	0.99	Verdoncho	3092	0.06
Mandon	261	0.01	Vijariego	510	0.01
Manto Negro	470	0.01	Xarello	10288	0.21
Marmajuelo	37	0.00	Xarello Rosado	10	0.00
			Zalema	5969	0.12
			Total (84 varieties)	**1369767**	**28.08**

Table 19 (cont.) Prime varieties' global area and share of all varieties globally, by prime's country of origin, 2000

	Hectares	Share (%)		Hectares	Share (%)
France			**France (continued)**		
Abondant	0	0.00	Camaralet de Lasseube	691	0.01
Abouriou	419	0.01	Carignan Blanc	1035	0.02
Alicante Henri Bouschet	37043	0.76	Carignan Bouschet	16	0.00
Aligote	35668	0.73	Carmenere	5711	0.12
Alphonse Lavallee	15	0.00	Castel	0	0.00
Altesse	294	0.01	Castets	0	0.00
Aramon Gris	72	0.00	Cep Rouge	0	0.00
Aramon Noir	9084	0.19	Cesar	8	0.00
Aranel	22	0.00	Chambourcin	257	0.01
Arbane	1	0.00	Chancellor	27	0.00
Arinarnoa	149	0.00	Chardonnay	145344	2.98
Arriloba	59	0.00	Chasan	914	0.02
Arrufiac	126	0.00	Chatus	15	0.00
Aspiran Bouschet	308	0.01	Chenanson	636	0.01
Aubin Blanc	2	0.00	Chenin Blanc	45806	0.94
Aubun	1411	0.03	Chenivesse	1	0.00
Aurore	299	0.01	Cinsaut	48419	0.99
Auxerrois	2302	0.05	Cinsaut Blanc	41	0.00
Baco Blanc	2137	0.04	Clairette	4003	0.08
Baco Noir	397	0.01	Clairette Rose	356	0.01
Baleille	1	0.00	Clarin	11	0.00
Barbaroux	79	0.00	Claverie	3	0.00
Baroque	169	0.00	Codivarta	3	0.00
Beclan	0	0.00	Colobel	3	0.00
Bellandais	2	0.00	Colombard	38146	0.78
Bequignol Noir	1	0.00	Cot	24402	0.50
Biancu Gentile	1	0.00	Couderc	4	0.00
Blanc Dame	0	0.00	Couderc Noir	610	0.01
Blanqueiro	1	0.00	Counoise	638	0.01
Boiziau	1	0.00	Courbu Blanc	47	0.00
Bouchales	108	0.00	Courbu Noir	2	0.00
Bouillet	2	0.00	Crouchen	2259	0.05
Bourboulenc	772	0.02	De Chaunac	186	0.00
Bousquet Precoce	16	0.00	Douce Noire	17653	0.36
Braquet Noir	8	0.00	Duras	972	0.02
Brun Argente	14	0.00	Durif	1197	0.02
Cabernet Malbec	34	0.00	Ederena	0	0.00
Cabernet Sauvignon	220890	4.53	Egiodola	315	0.01
Caladoc	1427	0.03	Ekigaina	5	0.00
Calitor Blanc	8	0.00	Etraire de l'Adui	8	0.00
Calitor Gris	2	0.00	Fer	1278	0.03
Calitor Noir	75	0.00	Feunate	0	0.00
			Florental	1	0.00

Table 19 (cont.) Prime varieties' global area and share of all varieties globally, by prime's country of origin, 2000

	Hectares	Share (%)		Hectares	Share (%)
France (continued)			**France (continued)**		
Folle Blanche	2648	0.05	Mauzac Noir	10	0.00
Fontan	0	0.00	Mauzac Rose	59	0.00
Fuella Nera	4	0.00	Mecle de Bourgoin	2	0.00
Gaillard	0	0.00	Melon	13253	0.27
Gamay de Teinturier Bouze	318	0.01	Menu Pineau	380	0.01
Gamay Noir	37796	0.77	Merille	131	0.00
Ganson	28	0.00	Merlot	211967	4.35
Garonnet	7	0.00	Merlot Blanc	176	0.00
Gascon	0	0.00	Meslier Saint-Francois	55	0.00
Goldriesling	10	0.00	Milgranet	2	0.00
Gouais Blanc	1	0.00	Molette	30	0.00
Gouget Noir	1	0.00	Mollard	23	0.00
Graisse	22	0.00	Monbadon	0	0.00
Gramon	14	0.00	Mondeuse Blanche	22	0.00
Grand Noir	945	0.02	Mondeuse Grise	0	0.00
Grassen	1	0.00	Mondeuse Noire	1404	0.03
Gringet	74	0.00	Monerac	2	0.00
Grolleau Gris	806	0.02	Montils	131	0.00
Grolleau Noir	2201	0.05	Mornen Noir	1	0.00
Gros Manseng	2160	0.04	Morrastel Bouschet	1	0.00
Guillemot	0	0.00	Mourvaison	9	0.00
Jacquere	1086	0.02	Mouyssagues	0	0.00
Joannes Seyve	3	0.00	Muscadelle	2207	0.05
Joubertin	0	0.00	Muscardin	19	0.00
Jurancon Blanc	24	0.00	Muscat Fleur d'Oranger	36	0.00
Jurancon Noir	1294	0.03	Muscat Ottonel	12259	0.25
Jurie	0	0.00	Negrette	1319	0.03
Knipperle	2	0.00	Noir Fleurien	0	0.00
Lacoste	1	0.00	Noual	1	0.00
Landal	16	0.00	Oberlin	0	0.00
Landot	0	0.00	Oberlin White	1	0.00
Landot Noir	0	0.00	Odola	1	0.00
Lauzet	1	0.00	Oeillade Bousche	10	0.00
Len de l'El	734	0.02	Olivette Noire	0	0.00
Leon Millot	17	0.00	Ondenc	12	0.00
Liliorila	3	0.00	Pascal Blanc	0	0.00
Malegue	1		Peloursin	0	0.00
Manseng Noir	10	0.00	Perdea	13	0.00
Marechal Foch	173	0.00	Persan	3	0.00
Marsanne	1512	0.03	Petit Bouschet	1	0.00
Marselan	176	0.00	Petit Courbu	75	0.00
Mauzac Blanc	3251	0.07	Petit Manseng	613	0.01
			Petit Meslier	3	0.00

Table 19 (cont.) Prime varieties' global area and share of all varieties globally, by prime's country of origin, 2000

	Hectares	Share (%)		Hectares	Share (%)
France (continued)			**France (continued)**		
Petit Verdot	1481	0.03	Select	8	0.00
Pineau d'Aunis	430	0.01	Semebat	2	0.00
Pinot Blanc	16990	0.35	Semillon	26230	0.54
Pinot Gris	18879	0.39	Servanin	0	0.00
Pinot Meunier	10832	0.22	Servant	530	0.01
Pinot Noir	60099	1.23	Seyval Blanc	389	0.01
Pinot Noir Precoce	86	0.00	Syrah	101516	2.08
Piquepoul Blanc	975	0.02	Tannat	5557	0.11
Piquepoul Bousch	0	0.00	Teinturier	1	0.00
Piquepoul Gris	9	0.00	Teoulier Noir	1	0.00
Piquepoul Noir	103	0.00	Terras 20	13	0.00
Plant Droit	40	0.00	Terret Blanc	2703	0.06
Plantet	209	0.00	Terret Gris	262	0.01
Portan	368	0.01	Terret Noir	370	0.01
Pougnet	0	0.00	Tibouren	457	0.01
Poulsard	295	0.01	Tressot	0	0.00
Poulsard Blanc	14	0.00	Trousseau	2120	0.04
Provareau	2	0.00	Trousseau Gris	28	0.00
Prunelard	2	0.00	Valais Noir	4	0.00
Raffiat de Moncade	16	0.00	Valdiguie	79	0.00
Raisaine	1	0.00	Valerien	2	0.00
Ravat	1	0.00	Varousset	12	0.00
Ravat Blanc	2	0.00	Verdesse	8	0.00
Rayon d'Or	1	0.00	Vidal	611	0.01
Romorantin	81	0.00	Vignoles	68	0.00
Rose du Var	129	0.00	Villard Blanc	746	0.02
Roublot	0	0.00	Villard Noir	601	0.01
Rougeon	36	0.00	Viognier	3160	0.06
Roussanne	874	0.02	**Total (241 varieties)**	**1283077**	**26.30**
Roussette d'Ayze	3	0.00			
Rubilande	3	0.00			
Sacy	63	0.00			
Saint Macaire	1	0.00			
Saint-Pierre Dore	1	0.00			
Salvador	572	0.01			
Sauvignon Blanc	64889	1.33			
Sauvignon Gris	44	0.00			
Sauvignon Rose	26	0.00			
Sauvignonasse	5494	0.11			
Savagnin Blanc	430	0.01			
Savagnin Rose	35	0.00			
Segalin	54	0.00			
Seinoir	15	0.00			

Table 19 (cont.) Prime varieties' global area and share of all varieties globally, by prime's country of origin, 2000

	Hectares	Share (%)		Hectares	Share (%)
Italy			**Italy (continued)**		
Abbuoto	696	0.01	Carica l'Asino	299	0.01
Abrusco	399	0.01	Carricante	252	0.01
Aglianico	9264	0.19	Castiglione	83	0.00
Aglianicone	148	0.00	Catanese Nero	76	0.00
Albana	2487	0.05	Catarratto Bianco	50711	1.04
Albanello	117	0.00	Cesanese	1024	0.02
Albaranzeuli Bianco	72	0.00	Ciliegiolo	2527	0.05
Albaranzeuli Nero	40	0.00	Cococciola	887	0.02
Albarola	4090	0.08	Coda di Volpe Bianca	980	0.02
Albarossa	5	0.00	Colombana Nera	126	0.00
Aleatico	458	0.01	Cornalin	93	0.00
Alionza	41	0.00	Cornarea	22	0.00
Ancellotta	4391	0.09	Cortese	3113	0.06
Arneis	738	0.02	Corvina Veronese	4781	0.10
Arvesiniadu	147	0.00	Corvinone	88	0.00
Avana	53	0.00	Cove	56	0.00
Avarengo	1453	0.03	Crovassa	2	0.00
Barbarossa	16	0.00	Damaschino	2360	0.05
Barbera	33048	0.68	Dindarella	9	0.00
Barbera Bianca	251	0.01	Dolcetto	7191	0.15
Barbera Sarda	326	0.01	Dolciame	6	0.00
Bariadorgia	0	0.00	Doux d'Henry	26	0.00
Barsaglina	20	0.00	Drupeggio	617	0.01
Bellone	1315	0.03	Durasa	23	0.00
Biancame	1330	0.03	Durella	599	0.01
Bianchetta Trevigiana	53	0.00	Enantio	1062	0.02
Bianco d'Alessano	941	0.02	Erbaluce	329	0.01
Biancolella	385	0.01	Ervi	5	0.00
Biancone di Portoferraio	67	0.00	Falanghina	1658	0.03
Bombino Bianco	2893	0.06	Fertilia	13	0.00
Bombino Nero	1156	0.02	Fiano	758	0.02
Bonamico	83	0.00	Flavis	12	0.00
Bonda	3	0.00	Foglia Tonda	40	0.00
Bosco	88	0.00	Forastera	543	0.01
Bracciola Nera	89	0.00	Forgiarin	2	0.00
Brachetto del Piemonte	1534	0.03	Forsellina	9	0.00
Bric	21	0.00	Fortana	1252	0.03
Bussanello	8	0.00	Francavidda	86	0.00
Caddiu	978	0.02	Frappato	784	0.02
Caloria	129	0.00	Freisa	1436	0.03
Canaiolo Nero	2304	0.05	Fubiano	2	0.00
Canaiolo Rosa	114	0.00	Fumin	73	0.00

Table 19 (cont.) Prime varieties' global area and share of all varieties globally, by prime's country of origin, 2000

	Hectares	Share (%)		Hectares	Share (%)
Italy (continued)			**Italy (continued)**		
Gaglioppo	3592	0.07	Malvasia di Candia Aromatica	1643	0.03
Garganega	16549	0.34	Malvasia di Casorzo	98	0.00
Giro	537	0.01	Malvasia di Lipari	516	0.01
Grechetto di Orvieto	1177	0.02	Malvasia di Schierano	181	0.00
Grechetto Rosso	111	0.00	Malvasia Nera di Basilicata	754	0.02
Greco	1325	0.03	Malvasia Nera di Brindisi	3174	0.07
Greco Bianco	660	0.01	Malvasia Rosa	111	0.00
Greco Nero	2715	0.06	Mammolo	777	0.02
Grignolino	1353	0.03	Manzoni Bianco	8290	0.17
Grillo	1803	0.04	Marzemina Bianca	78	0.00
Groppello di Mocasina	120	0.00	Marzemino	994	0.02
Groppello Gentile	219	0.00	Mayolet	4	0.00
Guardavalle	168	0.00	Mazzese	80	0.00
Impigno	60	0.00	Melara	13	0.00
Incrocio Bianco Fedit 51	11	0.00	Minella Bianca	73	0.00
Incrocio Bruni 54	12	0.00	Molinara	1634	0.03
Incrocio Manzoni 2.15	166	0.00	Monica Nera	2835	0.06
Incrocio Terzi 1	65	0.00	Montepulciano	28679	0.59
Invernenga	32	0.00	Montonico Bianco	656	0.01
Inzolia	9259	0.19	Montu	1091	0.02
Italia	706	0.01	Morone	22	0.00
Italica	178	0.00	Moscatello Selvatico	105	0.00
Lacrima di Morro d'Alba	652	0.01	Moscato di Scanzo	73	0.00
Lagrein	471	0.01	Moscato di Terracina	229	0.00
Lambrusca di Alessandria	888	0.02	Moscato Giallo	410	0.01
Lambrusco	42	0.00	Moscato Rosa del Trentino	93	0.00
Lambrusco di Sorbara	1409	0.03	Mostosa	95	0.00
Lambrusco Grasparossa	1720	0.04	Muscat Blanc a Petits Grains	28401	0.58
Lambrusco Maestri	1362	0.03	Nasco	166	0.00
Lambrusco Marani	2280	0.05	Nebbiera	20	0.00
Lambrusco Montericco	262	0.01	Nebbiolo	5047	0.10
Lambrusco Salamino	4147	0.09	Negretto	280	0.01
Lambrusco Viadanese	277	0.01	Negroamaro	16619	0.34
Lumassina	111	0.00	Ner d'Ala	8	0.00
Maceratino	122	0.00	Nerello Cappuccio	1501	0.03
Magliocco Canino	579	0.01	Nerello Mascalese	4167	0.09
Magliocco Dolce	243	0.00	Neretta Cuneese	374	0.01
Maiolica	70	0.00	Neretto di Bairo	53	0.00
Malbo Gentile	106	0.00	Nero Buono di Cori	114	0.00
Malvasia Bianca di Basilicata	875	0.02	Nero d'Avola	11318	0.23
Malvasia Bianca di Candia	12889	0.26	Nero di Troia	1765	0.04
Malvasia Bianca Lunga	3937	0.08	Neyret	76	0.00
Malvasia del Lazio	2366	0.05	Nieddera	58	0.00

Table 19 (cont.) Prime varieties' global area and share of all varieties globally, by prime's country of origin, 2000

	Hectares	Share (%)		Hectares	Share (%)
Italy (continued)			**Italy (continued)**		
Nigra	7	0.00	Rondinella	2797	0.06
Nocera	27	0.00	Rossara Trentina	29	0.00
Nosiola	191	0.00	Rossese	232	0.00
Notardomenico	13	0.00	Rossignola	295	0.01
Nuragus	3186	0.07	Rossola Nera	102	0.00
Ortrugo	485	0.01	Roussin	3	0.00
Pampanuto	277	0.01	Ruche	46	0.00
Pascale	1573	0.03	Sagrantino	351	0.01
Passau	12	0.00	San Giuseppe Nero	348	0.01
Passerina	715		San Lunardo	22	0.00
Pavana	69	0.00	San Martino	44	0.00
Pecorello	16	0.00	San Michele	120	0.00
Pecorino	166	0.00	Sangiovese	68877	1.41
Pelaverga	28	0.00	Santa Maria	15	0.00
Pelaverga Piccolo	24	0.00	Schiava	1231	0.03
Perera	25	0.00	Schiava Gentile	1158	0.02
Perricone	580	0.01	Schiava Grigia	79	0.00
Petit Rouge	100	0.00	Schiava Grossa	1259	0.03
Piccola Nera	17	0.00	Schioppettino	93	0.00
Picolit	93	0.00	Sciaglin	4	0.00
Piculit Neri	126	0.00	Sciascinoso	253	0.01
Piedirosso	896	0.02	Semidano	48	0.00
Pignola Valtellinese	70	0.00	Sgavetta	61	0.00
Pignoletto	6009	0.12	Sirio	23	0.00
Pignolo	18	0.00	Soperga	32	0.00
Pinella	66	0.00	Susumaniello	62	0.00
Plassa	41	0.00	Tazzelenghe	68	0.00
Pollera Nera	19	0.00	Teroldego	682	0.01
Prie	36	0.00	Terrano	194	0.00
Primetta	17	0.00	Timorasso	19	0.00
Prodest	2	0.00	Torbato	168	0.00
Prosecco	7498	0.15	Trebbiano	685	0.01
Prunesta	92	0.00	Trebbiano d'Abruzzo	8435	0.17
Quagliano	8	0.00	Trebbiano Giallo	3984	0.08
Raboso Piave	1270	0.03	Trebbiano Modenese	583	0.01
Raboso Veronese	307	0.01	Trebbiano Romagnolo	19492	0.40
Rebo	37	0.00	Trebbiano Spoletino	242	0.00
Refosco	1267	0.03	Trebbiano Toscano	136572	2.80
Refosco dal Peduncolo Rosso	711	0.01	Trevisana Nera	33	0.00
Refosco di Faedis	256	0.01	Ucelut	10	0.00
Retagliado Bianco	26	0.00	Uva Rara	570	0.01
Ribolla Gialla	1406	0.03	Uva Tosca	84	0.00
Rollo	117	0.00	Valentino Nero	56	0.00

Table 19 (cont.) Prime varieties' global area and share of all varieties globally, by prime's country of origin, 2000

	Hectares	Share (%)
Italy (continued)		
Vega	27	0.00
Verdea	107	0.00
Verdeca	2208	0.05
Verdello	662	0.01
Verdicchio Bianco	5043	0.10
Verdiso	71	0.00
Verduschia	15	0.00
Verduzzo Friulano	1592	0.03
Verduzzo Trevigiano	1657	0.03
Vermentino	5835	0.12
Vermentino Nero	143	0.00
Vernaccia di Oristano	565	0.01
Vernaccia di San Gimignano	854	0.02
Vespaiola	105	0.00
Vespolina	103	0.00
Vien de Nus	25	0.00
Vitovska	42	0.00
Vuillermin	0	0.00
Total (274 varieties)	**650480**	**13.33**

Table 19 (cont.) Prime varieties' global area and share of all varieties globally, by prime's country of origin, 2000

	Hectares	Share (%)		Hectares	Share (%)
Portugal			**Portugal (continued)**		
Agronomica	19	0.00	Pedral	179	0.00
Alfrocheiro	523	0.01	Perola	68	0.00
Alvarelhao	159	0.00	Preto Martinho	428	0.01
Alvarinho	5113	0.10	Rabigato	1133	0.02
Amaral	582	0.01	Rabo de Ovelha	2330	0.05
Antao Vaz	376	0.01	Ramisco	72	0.00
Arinto de Bucelas	3966	0.08	Rio Grande	4	0.00
Avesso	636	0.01	Rufete	3397	0.07
Azal	3302	0.07	Seara Nova	1213	0.02
Baga	6730	0.14	Sercial	306	0.01
Barcelo	34	0.00	Siria	2791	0.06
Batoca	80	0.00	Tamarez	585	0.01
Bical	912	0.02	Terrantez	27	0.00
Borracal	2654	0.05	Tinta Barroca	6052	0.12
Caino Blanco	69	0.00	Tinta Carvalha	1920	0.04
Caracol	14	0.00	Tinto Cao	556	0.01
Castelao	14424	0.30	Touriga Franca	6674	0.14
Cerceal Branco	597	0.01	Touriga Nacional	4263	0.09
Codega de Larinho	4058	0.08	Trajadura	2416	0.05
Complexa	6	0.00	Trincadeira	7265	0.15
Cornifesto	259	0.01	Trincadeira das Pratas	216	0.00
Diagalves	1088	0.02	Uva Cao	33	0.00
Dona Branca	296	0.01	Verdelho	1639	0.03
Donzelinho Branco	59	0.00	Verdelho Tinto	1	0.00
Encruzado	291	0.01	Vinhao	5937	0.12
Espadeiro	1682	0.03	Viosinho	17	0.00
Fernao Pires	14545	0.30	Vital	2246	0.05
Folgasao	409	0.01	**Total (69 varieties)**	**147389**	**3.02**
Fonte Cal	355	0.01			
Galego Dourado	51	0.00			
Generosa	9	0.00			
Jampal	127	0.00			
Listrao Roxo	10	0.00			
Loureiro	4392	0.09			
Malvasia Branca de Sao Jorge	55	0.00			
Malvasia Fina	7102	0.15			
Malvasia Preta	1157	0.02			
Marufo	6339	0.13			
Monvedro	14	0.00			
Moreto	1053	0.02			
Moscatel Branco	1419	0.03			
Moscatel Rosada	10656	0.22			

Table 19 (cont.) Prime varieties' global area and share of all varieties globally, by prime's country of origin, 2000

	Hectares	Share (%)		Hectares	Share (%)
Croatia			**Germany (continued)**		
Babic	1189	0.02	Morio-Muskat	1188	0.02
Croatina	3116	0.06	Muller Thurgau	33572	0.69
Grasevina	92306	1.89	Nobling	102	0.00
Hrvatica	245	0.01	Optima	239	0.00
Malvazija Istarska	7559	0.15	Orion	8	0.00
Plavac Mali	6539	0.13	Ortega	1054	0.02
Posip Bijeli	6539	0.13	Osteiner	3	0.00
Tribidrag	26915	0.55	Perle	121	0.00
Total (10 varieties)	**144408**	**2.96**	Phoenix	24	0.00
			Rauschling	23	0.00
Germany			Regent	16	0.00
Albalonga	57	0.00	Regner	150	0.00
Arnsburger	3	0.00	Reichensteiner	319	0.01
Bacchus	3392	0.07	Rieslaner	70	0.00
Breidecker	28	0.00	Riesling	43166	0.88
Bukettraube	280	0.01	Scheurebe	3655	0.07
Cabernet Dorsa	43	0.00	Schonburger	39	0.00
Dalkauer	100	0.00	Siegerrebe	167	0.00
Deckrot	30	0.00	Silcher	7	0.00
Domina	187	0.00	**Total (50 varieties)**	**105040**	**2.15**
Dornfelder	3766	0.08			
Dunkelfelder	280	0.01	**Georgia**		
Ehrenbreitsteiner	13	0.00	Aladasturi	46	0.00
Ehrenfelser	289	0.01	Aleksandrouli	219	0.00
Elbling	1864	0.04	Chinuri	955	0.02
Elbling Rot	4	0.00	Chkhaveri	20	0.00
Faberrebe	1586	0.03	Goruli Mtsvane	224	0.00
Fontanara	2	0.00	Khikhvi	5	0.00
Freisamer	17	0.00	Kisi	20	0.00
Gamay Teinturier de Chaudenay	267	0.01	Krakhuna	36	0.00
Gamay Teinturier Freaux	132	0.00	Mtsvane Kakhuri	249	0.01
Hegel	10	0.00	Ojaleshi	25	0.00
Helfensteiner	26	0.00	Otskhanuri Sapere	5	0.00
Heroldrebe	199	0.00	Rkatsiteli	67354	1.38
Holder	13	0.00	Saperavi	6707	0.14
Huxelrebe	1289	0.03	Tavkveri	29	0.00
Juwel	42	0.00	Tsitska	2839	0.06
Kanzler	53	0.00	Tsolikouri	6161	0.13
Kerner	7111	0.15	Tsulukidzis Tetra	152	0.00
Kernling	18	0.00	Usakhelouri	8	0.00
Mariensteiner	9	0.00	**Total (18 varieties)**	**85054**	**1.74**
Merzling	5	0.00			

Table 19 (cont.) Prime varieties' global area and share of all varieties globally, by prime's country of origin, 2000

	Hectares	Share (%)		Hectares	Share (%)
Argentina			**United States (continued)**		
Cereza	31666	0.65	Ruby Cabernet	7419	0.15
Criolla Grande	24641	0.51	Ruby Seedless	0	0.00
Pedro Gimenez	15101	0.31	Sugra Five	118	0.00
Torrontes Riojano	8187	0.17	Symphony	184	0.00
Torrontes Sanjuanino	3166	0.06	Traminette	5	0.00
Total (5 varieties)	**82760**	**1.70**	**Total (41 varieties)**	**80698**	**1.65**
United States			**Greece**		
Blush Seedless	10	0.00	Agiorgitiko	2320	0.05
Bordo	3379	0.07	Asirtiko Red	22	0.00
Campbell Early	43	0.00	Assyrtiko	1106	0.02
Canada Muscat	49	0.00	Athiri	1273	0.03
Cardinal	3190	0.07	Debina	455	0.01
Carmine	10	0.00	Fokiano	162	0.00
Carnelian	625	0.01	Fokiano (White)	57	0.00
Catawba	635	0.01	Goustolidi	112	0.00
Cayuga White	108	0.00	Korinthiaki	834	0.02
Centenial Seedless	2	0.00	Kotsifali	1148	0.02
Centurian	134	0.00	Krassato	38	0.00
Concord	11816	0.24	Liatiko	2476	0.05
Crimson Seedless	1	0.00	Liatiko(White)	70	0.00
Dawn Seedless	5	0.00	Limnio	95	0.00
Delaware	134	0.00	Malagousia	23	0.00
Elvira	344	0.01	Mandilaria	845	0.02
Emerald Riesling	593	0.01	Mavro Messenikola	3	0.00
Emerald Seedless	16	0.00	Mavrodafni	537	0.01
Fiesta	161	0.00	Mavrouda	349	0.01
Flame Seedless	541	0.01	Monemvassia	418	0.01
Flora	6	0.00	Moschofilero	423	0.01
Fredonia	86	0.00	Moschofilero	46	0.00
Herbemont	1453	0.03	Moschomavro	2305	0.05
Isabella	27376	0.56	Muscat a Petits Grains Roses	116	0.00
Ives	23	0.00	Muscat a Petits Grains Rouge	500	0.01
Jacquez	226	0.00	Muscat of Alexandria	29411	0.60
Moore's Diamond	19	0.00	Negoska	96	0.00
Niagara	15343	0.31	Robola	356	0.01
Noah	71	0.00	Roditis	299	0.01
Norton	0		Romeiko	382	0.01
Perlette	1	0.00	Savatiano	12747	0.26
Portland	9	0.00	Stavroto	104	0.00
Red Globe	2068	0.04	Vertzami	491	0.01
Royalty	338	0.01	Vilana	506	0.01
Rubired	4153	0.09	Xinomavro	1816	0.04
Ruby	6	0.00	**Total (35 varieties)**	**61942**	**1.27**

Table 19 (cont.) Prime varieties' global area and share of all varieties globally, by prime's country of origin, 2000

	Hectares	Share (%)		Hectares	Share (%)
Austria			**Moldova**		
Blauburger	1002	0.02	Alb de Ialoveni	2	0.00
Blauer Portugieser	4278	0.09	Feteasca Alba	23828	0.49
Blauer Wildbacher	472	0.01	Feteasca Neagra	1214	0.02
Blaufrankisch	12879	0.26	Maiskii Chernyi	77	0.00
FruHroter Veltliner	632	0.01	Negru de Ialoveni	15	0.00
Goldburger	309	0.01	Onitskanskii Belyi	5	0.00
Gruner Veltliner	23604	0.48	Riton	2	0.00
Jubilaumsrebe	30	0.00	Viorica	40	0.00
Laska	1	0.00	**Total (7 varieties)**	**25183**	**0.52**
Neuburger	1434	0.03			
Roter Veltliner	258	0.01	**Turkey**		
Rotgipfler	118	0.00	Adakarasi	48	0.00
Sankt Laurent	2370	0.05	Bogazkere	773	0.02
Silvaner	4185	0.09	Calkarasi	436	0.01
Zierfandler	98	0.00	Cavus	2	0.00
Zweigelt	7230	0.15	Dimrit	602	0.01
Total (16 varieties)	**58900**	**1.21**	Emir	480	0.01
			Kalecik Karasi	601	0.01
Bulgaria			Karalahna	3	0.00
Dimyat	7718	0.16	Karasakiz	3	0.00
Droujba	3	0.00	Narince	537	0.01
Mavrud	647	0.01	Okuzgozu	1033	0.02
Pamid	22718	0.47	Papazkarasi	122	0.00
Shiroka Melnishka	3804	0.08	Sultaniye	14351	0.29
Total (5 varieties)	**34891**	**0.72**	Vasilaki	3	0.00
Hungary			**Total (14 varieties)**	**18993**	**0.39**
Arany Sarfeher	2914	0.06			
Bianca	2180	0.04	**Serbia**		
Biborkadarka	202	0.00	Prokupac	15180	0.31
Cserszegi Fuszeres	2185	0.04	**Total (1 variety)**	**15180**	**0.31**
Ezerfurtu	405	0.01			
Ezerjo	3157	0.06	**Cyprus**		
Furmint	3481	0.07	Mavro	10969	0.22
Harslevelu	1296	0.03	Xynisteri	2742	0.06
Kadarka	2630	0.05	**Total (2 varieties)**	**13711**	**0.28**
Koenigin der Weingaerten	750	0.02			
Kovidinka	1214	0.02			
Kunleany	1376	0.03			
Lakhegyi Mezes	567	0.01			
Putzscheere	0	0.00			
Zalagyongye	4330	0.09			
Zenit	405	0.01			
Total (16 varieties)	**27093**	**0.56**			

Table 19 (cont.) Prime varieties' global area and share of all varieties globally, by prime's country of origin, 2000

	Hectares	Share (%)		Hectares	Share (%)
Switzerland			**South Africa**		
Amigne	21	0.00	Chenel	339	0.01
Arvine	61	0.00	Colomino	16	0.00
Bondola	17	0.00	Grachen	3	0.00
Charmont	7	0.00	Muscat of Alexandria Red	11	0.00
Chasselas	13318	0.27	Nouvelle	2	0.00
Completer	2	0.00	Pinotage	6574	0.13
Diolinoir	31	0.00	Therona	185	0.00
Doral	3	0.00	Weldra	54	0.00
Gamaret	71	0.00	**Total (8 varieties)**	**7184**	**0.15**
Garanoir	76	0.00			
Himbertscha	0	0.00	**United Kingdom**		
Humagne	9	0.00	Muscat of Hamburg	7066	0.14
Lafnetscha	1	0.00	**Total (1 variety)**	**7066**	**0.14**
	1	0.00			
Total (14 varieties)	**13617**	**0.28**	**Armenia**		
			Garandmak	931	0.02
Ukraine			Kangun	850	0.02
Bastardo Magarachsky	1969	0.04	Mskhali	1093	0.02
Ekim Kara	19	0.00	Voskeat	809	0.02
Golubok	50	0.00	**Total (4 varieties)**	**3683**	**0.08**
Ilichevskii Rannii	5	0.00			
Kokur Bely	641	0.01	**Morocco**		
Misket	3764	0.08	Abbo	2375	0.05
Odessky Cherny	1694	0.03	**Total (1 variety)**	**2375**	**0.05**
Pervenets Magaracha	2837	0.06			
Podarok Magaracha	148	0.00	**Lebanon**		
Rubin Tairovsky	2	0.00	Afus Ali	328	0.01
Rubinovy Magaracha	0	0.00	Regina	1509	0.03
Sukholimanskiy Bely	1631	0.03	**Total (2 varieties)**	**1837**	**0.04**
Total (13 varieties)	**12760**	**0.26**			
			Russia		
Romania			Agadai	1265	0.03
Babeasca Neagra	3722	0.08	Saperavi Severny	25	0.00
Feteasca Regala	2578	0.05	**Total (2 varieties)**	**1290**	**0.03**
Galbena de Odobesti	546	0.01			
Grasa de Cotnari	850	0.02	**Japan**		
Total (4 varieties)	**7696**	**0.16**	Black Queen	340	0.01
			Koshu	118	0.00
			Muscat Bailey A	72	0.00
			Total (3 varieties)	**529**	**0.01**

Table 19 (cont.) Prime varieties' global area and share of all varieties globally, by prime's country of origin, 2000

	Hectares	Share (%)
Azerbaijan		
Bayanshira	451	0.01
Matrasa	20	0.00
Total (2 varieties)	**470**	**0.01**
Slovenia		
Bouvier	365	0.01
Total (1 variety)	**366**	**0.01**
Kazakhstan		
Kuldzhinskii	269	0.01
Total (1 variety)	**269**	**0.01**
Peru		
Quebranta	230	0.00
Total (1 variety)	**230**	**0.00**
Australia		
Taminga	46	0.00
Tarrango	120	0.00
Total (2 varieties)	**166**	**0.00**
Uzbekishtan		
Pervomaisky	64	0.00
Total (1 variety)	**64**	**0.00**
Canada		
Ventura	39	0.00
Total (1 variety)	**39**	**0.00**
Thailand		
Malaga Blanc	11	0.00
Total (1 variety)	**11**	**0.00**
China		
Crystal	1	0.00
Total (1 variety)	**1**	**0.00**
Unknown origin & other	613961.5	12.59
Total (1012 varieties)	**4878176**	**100**

Table 20 : Prime varieties' global area and share of all varieties globally, by prime's country of origin, 2010

	Hectares	Share (%)		Hectares	Share (%)
France			**France (continued)**		
Abouriou	364	0.01	Crouchen	724	0.02
Alicante Henri Bouschet	38985	0.85	Danlas	254	0.01
Aligote	36119	0.78	De Chaunac	91	0.00
Alphonse Lavallee	883	0.02	Douce Noire	18976	0.41
Altesse	356	0.01	Duras	923	0.02
Aramon Noir	2892	0.06	Durif	3557	0.08
Arinarnoa	32	0.00	Egiodola	372	0.01
Arriloba	7	0.00	Ekigaina	1	0.00
Aspiran Bouschet	3042	0.07	Fer	1817	0.04
Aubun	648	0.01	Folle Blanche	1845	0.04
Aurore	268	0.01	Gamay de Teinturier Bouze	225	0.00
Auxerrois	2741	0.06	Gamay Noir	32671	0.71
Baco Blanc	773	0.02	Goldriesling	20	0.00
Baco Noir	467	0.01	Grand Noir	955	0.02
Baroque	90	0.00	Grolleau Gris	454	0.01
Bequignol Noir	698	0.02	Grolleau Noir	2350	0.05
Bourboulenc	597	0.01	Gros Manseng	4995	0.11
Cabernet Sauvignon	290091	6.30	Jacquere	1028	0.02
Caladoc	3675	0.08	Jurancon Noir	706	
Camaralet de Lasseube	515	0.01	Landot Noir	2	0.00
Canari Noir	152	0.00	Len de l'El	640	0.01
Carignan Blanc	3061	0.07	Leon Millot	23	0.00
Carmenere	11360	0.25	Madeleine Angevine	52	0.00
Castel	2	0.00	Manseng Noir	56	0.00
Chambourcin	1130	0.02	Marechal Foch	344	0.01
Chancellor	49	0.00	Marsanne	1742	0.04
Chardonnay	198793	4.32	Marselan	2497	0.05
Chasan	801	0.02	Mauzac Blanc	1991	0.04
Chatus	13	0.00	Melon	12365	0.27
Chelois	1	0.00	Menu Pineau	212	0.00
Chenanson	506	0.01	Merlot	267169	5.81
Chenin Blanc	35164	0.76	Merlot Blanc	31	0.00
Cinsaut	36040	0.78	Mondeuse Noire	306	0.01
Cinsaut Blanc	7	0.00	Muscadelle	1656	0.04
Clairette	2900	0.06	Muscat Fleur d'Oranger	91	0.00
Clairette Rose	260	0.01	Muscat Ottonel	10234	0.22
Colobel	0	0.00	Negrette	1228	0.03
Colombard	32076	0.70	Ora	0	0.00
Cot	40688	0.88	Persan	3	0.00
Couderc Noir	3525	0.08	Petit Bouschet	15	0.00
Counoise	443	0.01	Petit Courbu	36	0.00
			Petit Manseng	1327	0.03

Table 20 (cont.) Prime varieties' global area and share of all varieties globally, by prime's country of origin, 2010

	Hectares	Share (%)
France (continued)		
Petit Verdot	7202	0.16
Pineau d'Aunis	435	0.01
Pinot Blanc	14724	0.32
Pinot Gris	43563	0.95
Pinot Meunier	11267	0.24
Pinot Noir	86662	1.88
Pinot Noir Precoce	209	0.00
Piquepoul Blanc	1455	0.03
Piquepoul Noir	10	0.00
Plantet	1105	0.02
Portan	311	0.01
Poulsard	311	0.01
Rougeon	42	0.00
Roussanne	1746	0.04
Salvador	394	0.01
Sauvignon Blanc	110138	2.39
Sauvignon Gris	483	0.01
Sauvignonasse	4449	0.10
Savagnin Blanc	1898	0.04
Semillon	22156	0.48
Servant	54	0.00
Seyval Blanc	464	0.01
Syrah	185568	4.03
Tannat	5940	0.13
Teinturier	7	0.00
Terret Blanc	1451	0.03
Tibouren	445	0.01
Triomphe	15	0.00
Trousseau	3431	0.07
Valdiguie	138	0.00
Verdelet	1	0.00
Verdesse	7	0.00
Vidal	1644	0.04
Vignoles	254	0.01
Villard Blanc	689	0.01
Villard Noir	1328	0.03
Viognier	11400	0.25
Total (120 varieties)	**1645594**	**35.76**

Table 20 (cont.) Prime varieties' global area and share of all varieties globally, by prime's country of origin, 2010

	Hectares	Share (%)		Hectares	Share (%)
Spain			**Spain (continued)**		
Airen	252364	5.48	Maturana Blanca	18	0.00
Alarije	1726	0.04	Mazuelo	80178	1.74
Albarin Blanco	23	0.00	Mencia	10658	0.23
Albillo Mayor	1319	0.03	Merseguera	3946	0.09
Albillo Real	861	0.02	Miguel del Arco	468	0.01
Alcanon	60	0.00	Monastrell	69850	1.52
Aledo	7	0.00	Moravia Agria	550	0.01
Babosa de Madere	2	0.00	Moristel	112	0.00
Beba	3036	0.07	Naparo	1	0.00
Bobal	80120	1.74	Negramoll	3193	0.07
Cabernet Franc	53599	1.16	Ohanes	1	0.00
Calagrano	4794	0.10	Ondarrabi Zuri	492	0.01
Callet	154	0.00	Palomino Fino	22510	0.49
Canela	2	0.00	Panse Valenciano	1	0.00
Cayetana Blanca	39741	0.86	Pardillo	4364	0.09
Chelva	6168	0.13	Parellada	8847	0.19
Coloraillo	374	0.01	Parraleta	346	0.01
Corropio	1	0.00	Pedro Ximenez	9243	0.20
Dominga	1	0.00	Perruno	1509	0.03
Doradilla	40	0.00	Picapoll Blanco	37	0.00
Fintendo	183	0.00	Planta Mula	24	0.00
Fogoneu	35	0.00	Planta Nova	1395	0.03
Forcallat Tinta	1163	0.03	Prensal	105	0.00
Garnacha Blanca	7370	0.16	Prieto Picudo	4587	0.10
Garnacha Peluda	1232	0.03	Rojal Tinta	1801	0.04
Garnacha Roja	1784	0.04	Rome	297	0.01
Garnacha Tinta	184735	4.01	Royal de Alloza	29	0.00
Garrido Fino	59	0.00	Sumoll	83	0.00
Gateta	2	0.00	Tempranillo	232561	5.05
Gibi	917	0.02	Tempranillo Blanco	5	0.00
Godello	1094	0.02	Teneron	3488	0.08
Graciano	3102	0.07	Tinto de la Pampana Blanca	5145	0.11
Hondarrabi Beltza	53	0.00	Tinto Velasco	2684	0.06
Huerta del Rey	2	0.00	Tortosina	503	0.01
Imperial Napoleon	12	0.00	Trepat	1358	0.03
Juan Garcia	1707	0.04	Trobat	1	0.00
Lado	1	0.00	Valenci Tinto	27	0.00
Lairen	214	0.00	Verdejo	16578	0.36
Listain de Huelva	350	0.01	Verdil	57	0.00
Listan Negro	2666	0.06	Verdoncho	2124	0.05
Listan Prieto	4564	0.10	Vijariego	285	0.01
Macabeo	41046	0.89	Xarello	8393	0.18
Manto Negro	273	0.01	Xarello Rosado	1	0.00
Marmajuelo	24	0.00	Zalema	4097	
			Total (88 varieties)	**1198931**	**26.06**

Table 20 (cont.) Prime varieties' global area and share of all varieties globally, by prime's country of origin, 2010

	Hectares	Share (%)		Hectares	Share (%)
Italy			**Italy (continued)**		
Abbuoto	37	0.00	Casavecchia	136	0.00
Abrusco	423	0.01	Casetta	12	0.00
Aglianico	9963	0.22	Castiglione	18	0.00
Aglianicone	62	0.00	Catalanesca	54	0.00
Albana	1523	0.03	Catanese Nero	15	0.00
Albanello	18	0.00	Catarratto Bianco	34863	0.76
Albaranzeuli Bianco	7	0.00	Cavrara	23	0.00
Albaranzeuli Nero	49	0.00	Cellerina	2	0.00
Albarola	1453	0.03	Centesimino	24	0.00
Albarossa	80	0.00	Cesanese	679	0.01
Aleatico	333	0.01	Cianorie	2	0.00
Alionza	11	0.00	Ciliegiolo	1830	0.04
Ancellotta	4774	0.10	Cividin	4	0.00
Arneis	1122	0.02	Cococciola	983	0.02
Arvesiniadu	30	0.00	Coda di Volpe Bianca	586	0.01
Avana	28	0.00	Colombana Nera	38	0.00
Avarengo	987	0.02	Corbina Vicentina	12	0.00
Baratuciat	2	0.00	Cordenossa	5	0.00
Barbera	24178	0.53	Cornalin	256	0.01
Barbera Bianca	181	0.00	Cornarea	13	0.00
Barbera Sarda	84	0.00	Cortese	2953	0.06
Barsaglina	17	0.00	Corvina Veronese	7496	0.16
Bellone	511	0.01	Corvinone	930	0.02
Biancame	2599	0.06	Cove	6	0.00
Bianchetta Trevigiana	13	0.00	Crovassa	0	0.00
Bianco d'Alessano	419	0.01	Damaschino	2083	0.05
Biancolella	164	0.00	Dindarella	7	0.00
Biancone Di Portoferraio	78	0.00	Dolcetto	6333	0.14
Bombino Bianco	1239	0.03	Dolciame	11	0.00
Bombino Nero	1201	0.03	Doux d'Henry	9	0.00
Bonamico	193	0.00	Drupeggio	286	0.01
Bonda	7	0.00	Durasa	6	0.00
Bosco	82	0.00	Durella	470	0.01
Bracciola Nera	26	0.00	Enantio	724	0.02
Brachetto del Piemonte	1460	0.03	Erbaluce	319	0.01
Bric	2	0.00	Erbamat	24	0.00
Bussanello	12	0.00	Ervi	4	0.00
Caddiu	309	0.01	Falanghina	3037	0.07
Caloria	108	0.00	Famoso	6	0.00
Canaiolo Nero	1068	0.02	Fenile	5	0.00
Canaiolo Rosa	1	0.00	Fertilia	3	0.00
Carica l'Asino	17	0.00	Fiano	1377	0.03
Carricante	205	0.00	Flavis	3	0.00
			Fogarina	5	0.00

Table 20 (cont.) Prime varieties' global area and share of all varieties globally, by prime's country of origin, 2010

	Hectares	Share (%)		Hectares	Share (%)
Italy (continued)			**Italy (continued)**		
Foglia Tonda	101	0.00	Lambrusca di Alessandria	137	0.00
Forastera	208	0.00	Lambrusco	45	0.00
Forgiarin	4	0.00	Lambrusco Barghi	18	0.00
Forsellina	7	0.00	Lambrusco di Sorbara	1606	0.03
Fortana	642	0.01	Lambrusco Grasparossa	2738	0.06
Francavidda	13	0.00	Lambrusco Maestri	2272	0.05
Frappato	752	0.02	Lambrusco Marani	1394	0.03
Freisa	1049	0.02	Lambrusco Montericco	70	0.00
Fubiano	9	0.00	Lambrusco Oliva	112	0.00
Fumin	31	0.00	Lambrusco Salamino	5003	0.11
Gaglioppo	4214	0.09	Lambrusco Viadanese	240	0.01
Gamba Rossa	0	0.00	Lumassina	98	0.00
Garganega	15402	0.33	Maceratino	177	0.00
Ginestra	4	0.00	Magliocco Canino	539	0.01
Giro	200	0.00	Magliocco Dolce	87	0.00
Goldtraminer	9	0.00	Maiolica	26	0.00
Gosen	1	0.00	Maiolina	1	0.00
Grapariol	2	0.00	Malbo Gentile	211	0.00
Grechetto di Orvieto	1501	0.03	Malvasia Bianca di Basilicata	210	0.00
Grechetto Rosso	49	0.00	Malvasia Bianca di Candia	9891	0.21
Greco	158	0.00	Malvasia Bianca Lunga	2544	0.06
Greco Bianco	1604	0.03	Malvasia del Lazio	590	0.01
Greco Nero	1223	0.03	Malvasia di Candia Aromatica	895	0.02
Grignolino	915	0.02	Malvasia di Casorzo	107	0.00
Grillo	6295	0.14	Malvasia di Lipari	310	0.01
Groppello di Mocasina	81	0.00	Malvasia di Schierano	89	0.00
Groppello di Revo	12	0.00	Malvasia Nera di Basilicata	114	0.00
Groppello Gentile	326	0.01	Malvasia Nera di Brindisi	1314	0.03
Guardavalle	33	0.00	Malvasia Nera Lunga	38	0.00
Impigno	7	0.00	Malvasia Rosa	32	0.00
Incrocio Bianco Fedit 51	5	0.00	Mammolo	825	0.02
Incrocio Bruni 54	12	0.00	Manzoni Bianco	382	0.01
Incrocio Manzoni 2.15	86	0.00	Manzoni Moscato	20	0.00
Incrocio Terzi 1	44	0.00	Manzoni Rosa	29	0.00
Invernenga	7	0.00	Marzemina Bianca	54	0.00
Inzolia	6133	0.13	Marzemino	1091	0.02
Italia	1145	0.02	Mayolet	7	0.00
Italica	367	0.01	Mazzese	76	0.00
Lacrima Christi	85	0.00	Melara	3	0.00
Lacrima di Morro d'Alba	421	0.01	Merlese	14	0.00
Lagarino Bianco	23	0.00	Minella Bianca	65	0.00
Lagrein	717	0.02	Molinara	717	0.02

Table 20 (cont.) Prime varieties' global area and share of all varieties globally, by prime's country of origin, 2010

	Hectares	Share (%)		Hectares	Share (%)
Italy (continued)			**Italy (continued)**		
Monica Nera	1404	0.03	Passau	5	0.00
Montepulciano	34947	0.76	Passerina	894	0.02
Montonico Bianco	734	0.02	Pavana	32	0.00
Moradella	6	0.00	Pecorello	34	0.00
Morone	13	0.00	Pecorino	1228	0.03
Moscatello Selvatico	35	0.00	Pelaverga	55	0.00
Moscato di Scanzo	53	0.00	Pelaverga Piccolo	6	0.00
Moscato di Terracina	138	0.00	Pepella	3	0.00
Moscato Giallo	1470	0.03	Perera	4	0.00
Moscato Rosa del Trentino	81	0.00	Perla dei Vivi	1	0.00
Mostosa	24	0.00	Perricone	228	0.00
Muscat Blanc a Petits Grains	31112	0.68	Petit Rouge	84	0.00
Nascetta	21	0.00	Piccola Nera	17	0.00
Nasco	141	0.00	Picolit	128	0.00
Nebbiera	12	0.00	Piculit Neri	22	0.00
Nebbiolo	5992	0.13	Piedirosso	699	0.02
Negretto	75	0.00	Pignola Valtellinese	49	0.00
Negroamaro	11460	0.25	Pignoletto	1707	0.04
Negroamaro Precoce	32	0.00	Pignolo	93	0.00
Ner d'Ala	30	0.00	Pinella	72	0.00
Nerello Cappuccio	508	0.01	Plassa	91	0.00
Nerello Mascalese	2883	0.06	Pollera Nera	54	0.00
Neretta Cuneese	132	0.00	Prie	33	0.00
Neretto di Bairo	34	0.00	Primetta	24	0.00
Nero Buono di Cori	135	0.00	Prosecco	18437	0.40
Nero d'Avola	16596	0.36	Prosecco Lungo	1367	0.03
Nero di Troia	2572	0.06	Prunesta	36	0.00
Neyret	41	0.00	Pugnitello	28	0.00
Nieddera	107	0.00	Quagliano	9	0.00
Nigra	3	0.00	Raboso Piave	771	0.02
Nocera	15	0.00	Raboso Veronese	277	0.01
Nosiola	79	0.00	Rebo	120	0.00
Notardomenico	10	0.00	Recantina	9	0.00
Nuragus	1345	0.03	Refosco	1420	0.03
Orpicchio	1	0.00	Refosco dal Peduncolo Rosso	1076	0.02
Ortrugo	611	0.01	Refosco di Faedis	217	0.00
Oseleta	15	0.00	Retagliado Bianco	28	0.00
Pallagrello Bianco	55	0.00	Ribolla Gialla	1178	0.03
Pallagrello Nero	169	0.00	Ripolo	1	0.00
Pampanuto	356	0.01	Rollo	51	0.00
Paolina	1	0.00	Rondinella	2481	0.05
Pascale	375	0.01	Rossara Trentina	8	0.00

Table 20 (cont.) Prime varieties' global area and share of all varieties globally, by prime's country of origin, 2010

	Hectares	Share (%)		Hectares	Share (%)
Italy (continued)			**Italy (continued)**		
Rossese	312	0.01	Trebbiano Spoletino	200	0.00
Rossese Bianco	7	0.00	Trebbiano Toscano	109772	2.39
Rossignola	188	0.00	Trevisana Nera	15	0.00
Rossola Nera	86	0.00	Tronto	2	0.00
Roussin	3	0.00	Ucelut	10	0.00
Roviello Bianco	2	0.00	Uva del Fantini	0	0.00
Ruche	100	0.00	Uva del Tunde	2	0.00
Ruggine	1	0.00	Uva Longanesi	512	0.01
Sagrantino	995	0.02	Uva Rara	460	0.01
San Giuseppe Nero	192	0.00	Uva Tosca	71	0.00
San Lunardo	10	0.00	Uvalino	1	0.00
San Martino	21	0.00	Valentino Nero	21	0.00
San Michele	57	0.00	Vega	35	0.00
Sanforte	1	0.00	Verdea	83	0.00
Sangiovese	77709	1.69	Verdeca	796	0.02
Santa Maria	3	0.00	Verdello	287	0.01
Schiava	517	0.01	Verdicchio Bianco	3532	0.08
Schiava Gentile	694	0.02	Verdiso	68	0.00
Schiava Grigia	66	0.00	Verduschia	11	0.00
Schiava Grossa	580	0.01	Verduzzo Friulano	812	0.02
Schioppettino	154	0.00	Verduzzo Trevigiano	708	0.02
Sciaglin	6	0.00	Vermentino	8617	0.19
Sciascinoso	94	0.00	Vermentino Nero	210	0.00
Scimiscia	5	0.00	Vernaccia di Oristano	272	0.01
Semidano	36	0.00	Vernaccia di San Gimignano	522	0.01
Sennen	10	0.00	Vespaiola	94	0.00
Sgavetta	47	0.00	Vespolina	134	0.00
Sirio	14	0.00	Vien de Nus	13	0.00
Soperga	22	0.00	Vitovska	50	0.00
Spergola	110	0.00	Vuillermin	4	0.00
Susumaniello	50	0.00	**Total (328 varieties)**	**588999**	**12.80**
Tazzelenghe	55	0.00			
Termarina Rossa	20	0.00			
Teroldego	839	0.02			
Terrano	500	0.01			
Timorasso	129	0.00			
Tintilia del Molise	111	0.00			
Torbato	19	0.00			
Trebbiano	248	0.01			
Trebbiano d'Abruzzo	5091	0.11			
Trebbiano Giallo	10609	0.23			
Trebbiano Modenese	363	0.01			
Trebbiano Romagnolo	15893	0.35			

Table 20 (cont.) Prime varieties' global area and share of all varieties globally, by prime's country of origin, 2010

	Hectares	Share (%)		Hectares	Share (%)
Portugal			**Portugal (continued)**		
Agronomica	327	0.01	Chasselas Sabor	0	0.00
Agua Santa	78	0.00	Cidreiro	0	0.00
Alfrocheiro	1188	0.03	Codega de Larinho	629	0.01
Almafre	0	0.00	Complexa	103	0.00
Alminhaca	1	0.00	Concieira	52	0.00
Alvar Branco	0	0.00	Coracao de Galo	1	0.00
Alvar Roxo	2	0.00	Cornifesto	499	0.01
Alvarelhao	180	0.00	Corvo	0	0.00
Alvarinho	5523	0.12	Deliciosa	0	0.00
Amaral	92	0.00	Diagalves	1156	0.03
Antao Vaz	1252	0.03	Docal	0	0.00
Arinto de Bucelas	4446	0.10	Dona Branca	276	0.01
Arjuncao	1	0.00	Dona Joaquina	24	0.00
Avesso	685	0.01	Donzelinho Branco	65	0.00
Azal	1072	0.02	Donzelinho Roxo	0	0.00
Baga	4108	0.09	Donzelinho Tinto	33	0.00
Barcelo	23	0.00	Dorinto	115	0.00
Barreto de Semente	3	0.00	Encruzado	282	0.01
Batoca	11	0.00	Esganacao Preto	0	0.00
Bical	924	0.02	Esganinho	0	0.00
Boal Vencedor	2	0.00	Espadeiro	469	0.01
Borracal	683	0.01	Espadeiro Mole	0	0.00
Branco Especial	3	0.00	Estreito Macio	3	0.00
Branco Sr. Joao	0	0.00	Farinheira	3	0.00
Branco Valente	0	0.00	Fepiro	0	0.00
Brandam	312	0.01	Fernao Pires	9511	0.21
Cabinda	362	0.01	Fernao Pires Rosado	98	0.00
Cabral	2	0.00	Folgasao	182	0.00
Cainho de Moreira	7	0.00	Folgasao Roxo	18	0.00
Caino Blanco	121	0.00	Folha de Figueira	3	0.00
Campanario	2	0.00	Fonte Cal	111	0.00
Caracol	33	0.00	Galego Dourado	16	0.00
Carrega Branco	507	0.01	Generosa	107	0.00
Carrega Tinto	17	0.00	Goncalo Pires	1	0.00
Casculho	267	0.01	Gouveio Preto	0	0.00
Castalia	0	0.00	Gouveio Real	582	0.01
Castela	8	0.00	Gouveio Roxo	238	0.01
Castelao	11088	0.24	Grangeal	1	0.00
Castelao Branco	37	0.00	Granho	0	0.00
Castelino	147	0.00	Grossa	73	0.00
Castelo Branco	5	0.00	Jampal	71	0.00
Cerceal Branco	379	0.01	Labrusco	81	0.00
			Lameiro	0	0.00

Table 20 (cont.) Prime varieties' global area and share of all varieties globally, by prime's country of origin, 2010

	Hectares	Share (%)		Hectares	Share (%)
Portugal (continued)			**Portugal (continued)**		
Lariao	4	0.00	Promissao	6	0.00
Leira	1	0.00	Rabigato	1273	0.03
Loureiro	4054	0.09	Rabigato Moreno	1	0.00
Lourela	0	0.00	Rabo de Anho	99	0.00
Lusitano	0	0.00	Rabo de Lobo	3	0.00
Luzidio	0	0.00	Rabo de Ovelha	908	0.02
Madeleine Sylvaner	7	0.00	Ramisco	34	0.00
Malvarisco	3	0.00	Ratinho	84	0.00
Malvasia Branca de Sao Jorge	110	0.00	Rio Grande	1	0.00
Malvasia Fina	3416	0.07	Roxo de Vila Flor	0	0.00
Malvasia Fina Roxa	25	0.00	Roxo Rei	0	0.00
Malvasia Preta	1003	0.02	Rual	1	0.00
Malvasia Trigueira	12	0.00	Rufete	4833	0.11
Malvia	0	0.00	S. Mamede	1	0.00
Manteudo Preto	16	0.00	Samarrinho	1	0.00
Marquinhas	11	0.00	Santarena	739	0.02
Marufo	6579	0.14	Santoal	9	0.00
Melhorio	0	0.00	Seara Nova	681	0.01
Mindelo	1	0.00	Sercial	106	0.00
Mondet	0	0.00	Sercialinho	9	0.00
Monvedro	6	0.00	Sevilhao	14	0.00
Moreto	900	0.02	Siria	7898	0.17
Moscadet	4	0.00	Tamarez	343	0.01
Moscargo	0	0.00	Terrantez	12	0.00
Moscatel Branco	30	0.00	Terrantez do Pico	0	0.00
Moscatel Lilaz	0	0.00	Tinta Aguiar	75	0.00
Moscatel Rosada	7329	0.16	Tinta Barroca	6172	0.13
Mourisco de Semente	60		Tinta Bragao	63	0.00
Mourisco de Trevoes	2	0.00	Tinta Carvalha	1311	0.03
Naia	0	0.00	Tinta da Barca	345	0.01
Nevoeira	0	0.00	Tinta da Melra	1	0.00
Padeiro	86	0.00	Tinta de Alcoa	24	0.00
Parreira Matias	1	0.00	Tinta de Cidadelhe	1	0.00
Patorra	10	0.00	Tinta de Pegoes	195	0.00
Pe Comprido	1	0.00	Tinta de Porto Santo	2	0.00
Pedral	151	0.00	Tinta do Rodo	3	0.00
Perigo	4	0.00	Tinta Engomada	4	0.00
Pexem	3	0.00	Tinta Francisca	53	0.00
Pintosa	2	0.00	Tinta Malandra	0	0.00
Praca	166	0.00	Tinta Martins	11	0.00
Preto Cardana	5	0.00	Tinta Mesquita	1	0.00
Preto Martinho	163	0.00	Tinta Penajoia	53	0.00
Primavera	40	0.00	Tinta Pereira	1	0.00

Table 20 (cont.) Prime varieties' global area and share of all varieties globally, by prime's country of origin, 2010

	Hectares	Share (%)		Hectares	Share (%)
Portugal (continued)			**Croatia**		
Tinta Pomar	30	0.00	Babic	359	0.01
Tinta Roseira	4	0.00	Babica	18	0.00
Tinta Valdosa	1	0.00	Bogdanusa	48	0.00
Tinta Varejoa	1	0.00	Cetinka	35	0.00
Tinto Cao	369	0.01	Croatina	5700	0.12
Tinto do Aurelio	0	0.00	Debit	403	0.01
Touriga Branca	36	0.00	Diseca Ranina	2	0.00
Touriga Femea	15	0.00	Gegic	11	0.00
Touriga Franca	11586	0.25	Grasevina	61200	1.33
Touriga Nacional	10435	0.23	Hrvatica	116	0.00
Trajadura	2169	0.05	Kraljevina	447	0.01
Trincadeira	9270	0.20	Kujundzusa	206	0.00
Trincadeira das Pratas	239	0.01	Lasina	14	0.00
Trincadeiro Branco	59	0.00	Malvazija Istarska	2740	0.06
Triunfo	2	0.00	Nincusa	17	0.00
Uva Cao	1	0.00	Plavac Mali	1569	0.03
Valbom	166	0.00	Plavec Zuti	13	0.00
Valveirinha	0	0.00	Plavina	643	0.01
Verdelho	2005	0.04	Posip Bijeli	253	0.01
Verdelho Roxo	4	0.00	Skrlet	61	0.00
Verdelho Tinto	28	0.00	Suscan	5	0.00
Verdial	1	0.00	Trbljan	231	0.01
Vinhao	3160	0.07	Tribidrag	32745	0.71
Viosinho	225	0.00	Trnjak	15	0.00
Vital	1182	0.03	Vugava	36	0.00
Total (196 varieties)	**139264**	**3.03**	Zlahtina	135	0.00
			Zlatarica Vrgorska	19	0.00
			Total (27 varieties)	**107039**	**2.33**

Table 20 (cont.) Prime varieties' global area and share of all varieties globally, by prime's country of origin, 2010

	Hectares	Share (%)		Hectares	Share (%)
Germany			**Germany (continued)**		
Acolon	449	0.01	Perle	21	0.00
Arnsburger	30	0.00	Phoenix	51	0.00
Bacchus	2047	0.04	Rauschling	23	0.00
Breidecker	7	0.00	Regent	69	0.00
Bronner	6	0.00	Regner	44	0.00
Bukettraube	71	0.00	Reichensteiner	228	0.00
Cabernet Cortis	20	0.00	Rieslaner	60	0.00
Cabernet Cubin	40	0.00	Riesling	50060	1.09
Cabernet Dorio	20	0.00	Rondo	40	0.00
Cabernet Dorsa	223	0.00	Rotberger	1	0.00
Cabernet Mitos	282	0.01	Scheurebe	1984	0.04
Dakapo	53	0.00	Schonburger	59	0.00
Deckrot	10	0.00	Siegerrebe	120	0.00
Domina	361	0.01	Solaris	20	0.00
Dornfelder	8101	0.18	Wurzer	5	0.00
Dunkelfelder	329	0.01	**Total (56 varieties)**	**95882**	**2.08**
Ehrenfelser	79	0.00			
Elbling	1418	0.03			
Faberrebe	524	0.01			
Freisamer	4	0.00			
Gamay Teinturier de Chaudenay	24	0.00			
Gamay Teinturier Freaux	55	0.00			
Geisenheim	106	0.00			
Gutenborner	2	0.00			
Helfensteiner	10	0.00			
Heroldrebe	140	0.00			
Huxelrebe	607	0.01			
Johanniter	51	0.00			
Juwel	10	0.00			
Kanzler	10	0.00			
Kerner	3994	0.09			
Kernling	15	0.00			
Kolor	2	0.00			
Morio-Muskat	509	0.01			
Muller Thurgau	22753	0.49			
Nobling	50	0.00			
Optima	37	0.00			
Oraniensteiner	3	0.00			
Orion	10	0.00			
Ortega	637	0.01			
Osteiner	1	0.00			

Table 20 (cont.) Prime varieties' global area and share of all varieties globally, by prime's country of origin, 2010

	Hectares	Share (%)		Hectares	Share (%)
Georgia			**United States**		
Aladasturi	59	0.00	Bailey	34	0.00
Aleksandrouli	281	0.01	Blanc du Bois	28	0.00
Chinuri	1225	0.03	Bordo	8287	0.18
Chkhaveri	26	0.00	Brianna	12	0.00
Goruli Mtsvane	287	0.01	California	252	0.01
Khikhvi	6	0.00	Campbell Early	61	0.00
Kisi	26	0.00	Canadice	0	0.00
Krakhuna	46	0.00	Cardinal	545	0.01
Mtsvane Kakhuri	319	0.01	Carnelian	316	0.01
Ojaleshi	32	0.00	Catawba	633	0.01
Otskhanuri Sapere	6	0.00	Cayuga White	212	0.00
Rkatsiteli	58641	1.27	Centurian	34	0.00
Saperavi	8126	0.18	Chardonel	144	0.00
Tavkveri	37	0.00	Concord	12238	0.27
Tsitska	3642	0.08	Corot Noir	27	0.00
Tsolikouri	7903	0.17	Crimson Seedless	2	0.00
Tsulukidzis Tetra	195	0.00	Delaware	127	0.00
Usakhelouri	10	0.00	Edelweiss	32	0.00
Total (18 varieties)	**80868**	**1.76**	Elvira	263	0.01
			Emerald Riesling	164	0.00
			Fiesta	230	0.00
			Flame Seedless	42	0.00
			Flora	8	0.00
			Fredonia	37	0.00
			Frontenac	135	0.00
			Frontenac Gris	59	0.00
			Golden Muscat	1	0.00
			Gr 7	32	0.00
			Herbemont	764	0.02
			Himrod	0	0.00
			Isabella	32494	0.71
			Ives	16	0.00
			Jacquez	2368	0.05
			Kay Gray	1	0.00
			La Crescent	77	0.00
			La Crosse	25	0.00
			Louise Swenson	3	0.00
			Marquette	88	0.00
			Moore's Diamond	42	0.00
			Muscat Swenson	24	0.00
			New York Muscat	5	0.00

Table 20 (cont.) Prime varieties' global area and share of all varieties globally, by prime's country of origin, 2010

	Hectares	Share (%)		Hectares	Share (%)
United States (continued)			**Greece**		
Niagara	4670	0.10	Agiorgitiko	2905	0.06
Noah	71	0.00	Asirtiko Red	5	0.00
Noiret	33	0.00	Assyrtiko	902	0.02
Norton	329	0.01	Athiri	748	0.02
Perlette	1	0.00	Debina	239	0.01
Portland	12	0.00	Fokiano	262	0.01
Prairie Star	21	0.00	Goustolidi	68	0.00
Red Globe	240	0.01	Kakotrygis	103	0.00
Reliance	4	0.00	Korinthiaki	54	0.00
Royalty	97	0.00	Kotsifali	2330	0.05
Rubired	4556	0.10	Krassato	52	0.00
Ruby	9	0.00	Liatiko	1211	0.03
Ruby Cabernet	5730	0.12	Limnio	372	0.01
Sabrevois	10	0.00	Malagousia	182	0.00
St Croix	25	0.00	Mandilaria	885	0.02
St Pepin	19	0.00	Mavrodafni	345	0.01
St Vincent	23	0.00	Mavrouda	520	0.01
Steuben	39	0.00	Monemvassia	481	0.01
Sugra Five	2	0.00	Moschofilero	934	0.02
Swenson Red	11	0.00	Moschofilero	80	0.00
Symphony	324	0.01	Moschomavro	1428	0.03
Traminette	240	0.01	Muscat a Petits Grains Noirs	108	0.00
Valiant	11	0.00	Muscat a Petits Grains Rouge	613	0.01
Valvin Muscat	6	0.00	Muscat of Alexandria	26336	0.57
Venus	1	0.00	Negoska	143	0.00
Total (66 varieties)	**76349**	**1.66**	Robola	465	0.01
			Roditis	4661	0.10
Argentina			Romeiko	1597	0.03
Moscatuel	61	0.00	Savatiano	9920	0.22
Pedro Gimenez	12250	0.27	Stavroto	11	0.00
Rieslina	127	0.00	Thrapsathiri	31	0.00
Saint Jeannet	44	0.00	Vertzami	335	0.01
Serna	10	0.00	Vilana	579	0.01
Torrontes Mendocino	713	0.02	Xinomavro	1971	0.04
Torrontes Riojano	8115	0.18	**Total (34 varieties)**	**60873**	**1.32**
Torrontes Sanjuanino	2052	0.04			
Total (13 varieties)	**69743**	**1.52**			

Table 20 (cont.) Prime varieties' global area and share of all varieties globally, by prime's country of origin, 2010

	Hectares	Share (%)		Hectares	Share (%)
Austria			**Hungary (continued)**		
Blauburger	1337	0.03	Kadarka	1087	0.02
Blauer Portugieser	3798	0.08	Karat	50	0.00
Blauer Wildbacher	368	0.01	Karmin	36	0.00
Blaufrankisch	16141	0.35	Keknyelu	43	0.00
FruHroter Veltliner	846	0.02	Kiralyleanyka	855	0.02
Goldburger	140	0.00	Koenigin der Weingaerten	61	0.00
Gruner Veltliner	18842	0.41	Korona	1	0.00
Jubilaumsrebe	14	0.00	Kovidinka	1075	0.02
Neuburger	964	0.02	Kunbarat	9	0.00
Rathay	9	0.00	Kunleany	1211	0.03
Roesler	160	0.00	Kurucver	0	0.00
Roter Veltliner	199	0.00	Lakhegyi Mezes	306	0.01
Rotgipfler	105	0.00	Leanyka	838	0.02
Sankt Laurent	3007	0.07	Magyarfrankos	0	0.00
Silvaner	2255	0.05	Matrai Muskotaly	67	0.00
Zierfandler	117	0.00	Medina	159	0.00
Zweigelt	9847	0.21	Menoir	65	0.00
Total (17 varieties)	**58150**	**1.26**	Mezes Feher	2	0.00
			Nektar	21	0.00
Hungary			Nero	50	0.00
Aletta	723	0.02	Nosztori Rizling	1	0.00
Arany Sarfeher	1133	0.02	Odysseus	4	0.00
Bakator Roz	2	0.00	Orpheus	0	0.00
Bianca	6450	0.14	Palatina	6	0.00
Biborkadarka	136	0.00	Pannon Frankos	16	0.00
Budai Zold	6	0.00	Patria	3	0.00
Csaba Gyongye	89	0.00	Pccsi Szagos	1	0.00
Cserszegi Fuszeres	3609	0.08	Pintes	3	0.00
Csillam	20	0.00	Poeloeske Muskotaly	103	0.00
Csokaszolo	2	0.00	Pozsonyi	10	0.00
Csomorika	0	0.00	Refren	0	0.00
Duna Gyongye	63	0.00	Rubintos	18	0.00
Ezerfurtu	377	0.01	Taltos	1	0.00
Ezerjo	1074	0.02	Trilla	1	0.00
Furmint	5259	0.11	Turan	177	0.00
Gesztus	0	0.00	Urreti	0	0.00
Goecseji Zamatos	55	0.00	Vertes Csillaga	21	0.00
Goher	1	0.00	Viktor	0	0.00
Gyongyrizling	23	0.00	Zalagyongye	1948	0.04
Hajnalka	0	0.00	Zefir	49	0.00
Harslevelu	1856	0.04	Zengo	264	0.01
Irsai Oliver	1414	0.03	Zenit	580	0.01
Jubileum 75	194	0.00	Zeta	118	0.00
Juhfark	186	0.00	Zeusz	28	0.00
Kabar	18	0.00	**Total (69 varieties)**	**31983**	**0.70**

Table 20 (cont.) Prime varieties' global area and share of all varieties globally, by prime's country of origin, 2010

	Hectares	Share (%)		Hectares	Share (%)
Bulgaria			**Serbia**		
Dimyat	2401	0.05	Kreaca	3	0.00
Droujba	3	0.00	Prokupac	15180	0.33
Dunavski Lazur	483	0.01	Slankamenka	31	0.00
Mavrud	1296	0.03	Zupljanka	4	0.00
Misket Cherven	4159	0.09	**Total (4 varieties)**	**15217**	**0.33**
Misket Varnenski	336	0.01			
Pamid	9827	0.21	**Switzerland**		
Ranna Melnishka Loza	249	0.01	Amigne	43	0.00
Shiroka Melnishka	1580	0.03	Arvine	172	0.00
Storgozia	295	0.01	Blattner Reds	39	0.00
Total (10 varieties)	**20628**	**0.45**	Blattner Whites	25	0.00
			Bondola	13	0.00
Moldova			Cabernet Jura	19	0.00
Alb de Ialoveni	2	0.00	Carminoir	10	0.00
Amur	146	0.00	Charmont	10	0.00
Dekabrskii	78	0.00	Chasselas	13186	0.29
Doina	227	0.00	Completer	3	0.00
Feteasca Alba	17469	0.38	Diolinoir	114	0.00
Feteasca Neagra	1719	0.04	Doral	27	0.00
Maiskii Chernyi	110	0.00	Galotta	13	0.00
Negru de Ialoveni	15	0.00	Gamaret	399	0.01
Onitskanskii Belyi	71	0.00	Garanoir	216	0.00
Plavay	60	0.00	Humagne	30	0.00
Riton	257	0.01	**Total (16 varieties)**	**14321**	**0.31**
Viorica	347	0.01			
Total (12 varieties)	**20501**	**0.45**	**Ukraine**		
			Bastardo Magarachsky	2370	0.05
Romania			Citronny Magarach	307	0.01
Babeasca Gris	328	0.01	Ekim Kara	27	0.00
Babeasca Neagra	3122	0.07	Golubok	87	0.00
Busuioaca de Bohotin	268	0.01	Ilichevskii Rannii	5	0.00
Cramposie Selectionata	409	0.01	Kokur Bely	918	0.02
Feteasca Regala	13136	0.29	Odessky Cherny	2686	0.06
Francusa	621	0.01	Pervenets Magaracha	2881	0.06
Galbena de Odobesti	385	0.01	Podarok Magaracha	504	0.01
Grasa de Cotnari	685	0.01	Riesus	115	0.00
Mustoasa de Maderat	255		Rubin Golodrigi	82	0.00
Total (9 varieties)	**19209**	**0.42**	Rubin Tairovsky	2	0.00
			Rubinovy Magaracha	0	0.00
			Sukholimanskiy Bely	2156	0.05
			Total (14 varieties)	**12141**	**0.26**

Table 20 (cont.) Prime varieties' global area and share of all varieties globally, by prime's country of origin, 2010

	Hectares	Share (%)		Hectares	Share (%)
Turkey			**Armenia**		
Adakarasi	69	0.00	Garandmak	931	0.02
Bogazkere	1106	0.02	Kangun	850	0.02
Calkarasi	625	0.01	Mskhali	1093	0.02
Cavus	3	0.00	Voskeat	809	0.02
Dimrit	863	0.02	**Total (4 varieties)**	**3683**	**0.08**
Emir	688	0.01			
Kalecik Karasi	861	0.02	**Morocco**		
Karalahna	4	0.00	Abbo	2375	0.05
Karasakiz	4	0.00	Maticha	275	0.01
Narince	769	0.02	**Total (2 varieties)**	**2650**	**0.06**
Okuzgozu	1479	0.03			
Papazkarasi	175	0.00	**Russia**		
Sultaniye	3407	0.07	Barkhatnyi	30	0.00
Vasilaki	4	0.00	Dostoinyi	65	0.00
Total (14 varieties)	**10054**	**0.22**	Fioletovy Ranny	50	0.00
			Krasnostop Zolotovsky	562	0.01
United Kingdom			Saperavi Severny	350	0.01
Muscat of Hamburg	8137	0.18	Stepnyak	144	0.00
Total (1 variety)	**8137**	**0.18**	Tsimlyansky Cherny	451	0.01
			Total (7 varieties)	**1652**	**0.04**
South Africa					
Chenel	79	0.00	**Czech Rep.**		
Colomino	5	0.00	Agni	6	0.00
Grachen	2	0.00	Andre	472	0.01
Muscat of Alexandria Red	6	0.00	Ariana	3	0.00
Nouvelle	422	0.01	Aurelius	70	0.00
Pinotage	6404	0.14	Cabernet Moravia	212	0.00
Therona	99	0.00	Laurot	6	0.00
Weldra	14	0.00	Muskat Moravsky	514	0.01
Total (8 varieties)	**7031**	**0.15**	Neronet	72	0.00
			Palava	230	0.00
Cyprus			**Total (9 varieties)**	**1584**	**0.03**
Maratheftiko	152	0.00			
Mavro	3575	0.08	**Brazil**		
Ofthalmo	141	0.00	Lorena	519	0.01
Xynisteri	2092	0.05	Moscato Embrapa	862	0.02
Total (4 varieties)	**5960**	**0.13**	Patricia	1	0.00
			Rubea	81	0.00
			Violeta	98	0.00
			Total (5 varieties)	**1561**	**0.03**

Table 20 (cont.) Prime varieties' global area and share of all varieties globally, by prime's country of origin, 2010

	Hectares	Share (%)		Hectares	Share (%)
Slovenia			**Australia**		
Bouvier	250	0.01	Tarrango	72	0.00
Ranfol	134	0.00	**Total (1 variety)**	**72**	**0.00**
Zametovka	914	0.02			
Total (3 varieties)	**1297**	**0.03**	**Uzbekishtan**		
			Pervomaisky	64	0.00
Japan			**Total (1 variety)**	**64**	**0.00**
Black Queen	486	0.01			
Koshu	168	0.00	**Canada**		
Muscat Bailey A	122	0.00	Sovereign Opal	3	0.00
Total (3 varieties)	**777**	**0.02**	Ventura	24	0.00
			Vincent	11	0.00
Azerbaijan			**Total (3 varieties)**	**38**	**0.00**
Bayanshira	645	0.01			
Matrasa	28	0.00	**Thailand**		
Total (2 varieties)	**673**	**0.01**	Malaga Blanc	16	0.00
			Total (1 variety)	**16**	**0.00**
Kazakhstan					
Kuldzhinskii	385	0.01	**Unknown origin & other varieties**	298938	6.50
Total (1 variety)	**385**	**0.01**			
			Total (1271 varieties)	**4601445**	**100.00**
Peru					
Quebranta	345	0.01			
Total (1 variety)	**345**	**0.01**			
Lebanon					
Afus Ali	8	0.00			
Regina	321	0.01			
Total (2 varieties)	**329**	**0.01**			
Slovakia					
Devin	133	0.00			
Dunaj	46	0.00			
Milia	1	0.00			
Noria	1	0.00			
Total (4 varieties)	**182**	**0.00**			
China					
Crystal	175	0.00			
Total (1 variety)	**175**	**0.00**			
Montenegro					
Vranac	149	0.00			
Total (1 variety)	**149**	**0.00**			

Table 21: Shares (%) of national winegrape area by varietal country of origin, 2000

Country of planting →	Algeria	Argentina	Armenia	Australia	Austria	Brazil	Bulgaria	Canada	Chile
Country of origin									
Spain	45.0	2.3		3.4	0.1	0.8		6.7	16.6
France	55.0	34.6		73.7	9.9	4.5	30.4	54.0	68.3
Italy		3.2	4.7	1.1	0.3	1.3	1.9		0.2
Portugal		5.3		1.0					3.8
Croatia					8.9	1.7	3.8		0.1
Germany				2.4	11.3		0.7	5.7	0.3
Georgia			22.0				9.8		
Argentina		41.1							
USA		1.2		1.9		66.7	3.2	18.6	
Greece		2.8		2.8		1.5			
Austria					64.3				
Bulgaria							36.1		
Hungary					0.0		2.3		
Moldova									
Turkey		1.1		7.9					
Serbia									
Cyprus									
Switzerland									0.4
Ukraine							3.9		
Romania									
S. Africa									
UK							0.5		
Armenia			32.9						
Morocco									
Lebanon				0.3					
Russia									
Japan									
Azerbaijan									
Slovenia						0.8			
Kazakhstan									
Peru									
Australia				0.1					
Uzbekishtan									
Canada									
Thailand									
China									
Unknown origin & other varieties		8.5	40.4	5.4	4.5	23.5	7.5	15.0	10.5
Old World subtotal	**100.0**	**49.2**	**59.6**	**92.6**	**95.5**	**9.8**	**88.9**	**66.4**	**89.5**
New World subtotal		**42.3**		**2.0**		**66.7**	**3.6**	**18.6**	
World total	**100**	**100**	**100**	**100**	**100**	**100**	**100**	**100**	**100**

Table 21 (cont.) Shares (%) of national winegrape area by varietal country of origin, 2000

Country of planting → Country of origin	Croatia	Cyprus	Czech Rep.	France	Georgia	Germany	Greece	Hungary	Italy
Spain				29.2			0.1	0.6	2.5
France	2.0		5.0	57.2	1.3	5.5	2.5	8.5	10.9
Italy				11.8		0.1	5.8	1.8	80.8
Portugal									
Croatia	63.0		11.0	0.0				7.7	2.1
Germany			21.0	0.4		65.8		5.6	0.3
Georgia					92.0				
Argentina									
USA				0.0					
Greece				0.4			61.1		0.2
Austria	2.0		40.0	0.3		0.0		15.4	0.1
Bulgaria							0.2	0.1	
Hungary				0.0				23.6	0.0
Moldova								1.1	
Turkey									
Serbia									
Cyprus		75.0							
Switzerland				0.1		1.1		2.2	0.0
Ukraine									
Romania								0.7	
S. Africa									
UK				0.1					0.0
Armenia									
Morocco									
Lebanon									0.2
Russia									
Japan									
Azerbaijan									
Slovenia									
Kazakhstan									
Peru									
Australia									
Uzbekishtan									
Canada									
Thailand									
China									
Unknown origin & other varieties	33.0	25.0	23.0	0.6	6.7	27.5	30.4	32.7	2.9
Old World subtotal	**67.0**	**75.0**	**77.0**	**99.4**	**93.3**	**72.5**	**69.6**	**67.3**	**97.1**
New World subtotal				**0.1**					**0.0**
World total	**100**	**100**	**100**	**100**	**100**	**100**	**100**	**100**	**100**

Table 21 (cont.) Shares (%) of national winegrape area by varietal country of origin, 2000

Country of planting →	Luxem bourg	Moldova	Morocco	N. Zealand	Portugal	Romania	Russia	Serbia	Slovakia	Slovenia
Country of origin										
Spain			12.1	1.4	6.1					
France	39.8	61.5	10.2	83.0	1.7	18.0	14.3		9.0	16.9
Italy		0.2			0.9	0.5				10.2
Portugal					57.5					
Croatia						6.8		48.0	25.0	15.2
Germany	59.2	1.7		10.0			2.4		12.0	
Georgia		13.6					0.2	25.0		
Argentina										
USA		12.8		0.1						
Greece			7.4		0.2					
Austria	0.1	0.1		0.2					33.0	
Bulgaria		0.0								
Hungary		0.0					7.0			
Moldova		4.9				8.7			2.0	
Turkey										
Serbia								22.0		
Cyprus										
Switzerland				0.3				5.0		
Ukraine		1.9					4.2			
Romania		0.1				3.0			2.0	
S. Africa				0.7						
UK								4.0		
Armenia										
Morocco			4.8							
Lebanon										
Russia		0.0					2.2			
Japan										
Azerbaijan										
Slovenia										
Kazakhstan										
Peru										
Australia										
Uzbekishtan		0.1								
Canada										
Thailand										
China										
Unknown origin & other varieties	0.9	3.1	65.6	4.4	33.5	62.8	44.8	21.0	17.0	57.7
Old World subtotal	**99.1**	**84.2**	**29.6**	**94.8**	**66.5**	**37.2**	**55.2**	**75.0**	**83.0**	**42.3**
New World subtotal		**12.8**	**4.8**	**0.8**				**4.0**		
World total	**100**	**100**	**100**	**100**	**100**	**100**	**100**	**100**	**100**	**100**

Table 21 (cont.) Shares (%) of national winegrape area by varietal country of origin, 2000

Country of planting →	S. Africa	Spain	Switzerland	Tunisia	UK	USA	Uruguay	Missing 9	*Old World*	*New World*	*World*
Country of origin											
Spain	2.4	85.9	0.1	59.0		5.6	4.1	2.6	**33.0**	**7.6**	**28.1**
France	78.9	2.4	53.7	14.0	24.2	64.9	50.8	54.7	**19.8**	**53.4**	**26.3**
Italy	1.0	0.2	0.9	5.0		4.1		2.4	**16.0**	**2.0**	**13.3**
Portugal	0.9	1.0				0.0			**3.3**	**1.8**	**3.0**
Croatia	0.0	0.2		2.0		10.6			**3.2**	**2.1**	**3.0**
Germany	0.8	0.0	4.9		37.8	1.5		3.3	**2.4**	**1.2**	**2.2**
Georgia								14.8	**1.9**	**1.3**	**1.7**
Argentina								0.0		**8.8**	**1.7**
USA	2.6	0.0				11.1		3.1	**0.4**	**6.8**	**1.7**
Greece	4.3	0.5				1.1			**1.1**	**2.1**	**1.3**
Austria		0.0	1.4		12.0	0.0		0.5	**1.5**	**0.1**	**1.2**
Bulgaria									**0.9**		**0.7**
Hungary	0.3								**0.7**	**0.0**	**0.6**
Moldova								0.1	**0.6**	**0.0**	**0.5**
Turkey		0.0						8.1	**0.1**	**1.4**	**0.4**
Serbia									**0.4**		**0.3**
Cyprus									**0.3**		**0.3**
Switzerland		0.0	37.4						**0.3**	**0.0**	**0.3**
Ukraine								6.1	**0.3**		**0.3**
Romania									**0.2**		**0.2**
S. Africa	7.6									**0.8**	**0.1**
UK		0.0				0.0	32.5		**0.1**	**0.3**	**0.1**
Armenia									**0.1**		**0.1**
Morocco										**0.3**	**0.0**
Lebanon		0.0							**0.0**	**0.0**	
Russia									**0.0**		**0.0**
Japan								0.7		**0.1**	**0.0**
Azerbaijan								0.6	**0.0**		**0.0**
Slovenia									**0.0**		**0.0**
Kazakhstan								0.3	**0.0**		**0.0**
Peru								0.3		**0.0**	**0.0**
Australia										**0.0**	**0.0**
Uzbekishtan									**0.0**		**0.0**
Canada						0.0				**0.0**	**0.0**
Thailand								0.0		**0.0**	**0.0**
China								0.0		**0.0**	**0.0**
Unknown origin & other varieties	1.0	9.8	1.5	20.0	26.0	1.0	12.6	2.6	**13.4**	**9.4**	**12.6**
Old World subtotal	**88.8**	**90.2**	**98.5**	**80.0**	**74.0**	**87.8**	**54.9**	**93.4**	**86.3**	**73.1**	**83.7**
New World subtotal	**10.1**	**0.0**				**11.1**	**32.5**	**4.0**	**0.5**	**17.0**	**3.7**
World total	**100**	**100**	**100**	**100**	**100**	**100**	**100**	**100**	**100**	**100**	**100**

Table 22: Shares (%) of national winegrape area by varietal country of origin, 2010

Country of planting →	Algeria	Argentina	Armenia	Australia	Austria	Brazil	Bulgaria	Canada	Chile
Country of origin									
France	55.0	52.6		88.1	14.8	12.7	44.0	70.5	92.1
Spain	45.0	4.2		2.3	0.1	0.5		6.7	5.2
Italy		3.3	4.7	1.1	1.1	3.5	1.3	0.1	0.2
Portugal		3.6		1.0		0.0		0.1	0.1
Croatia		0.0		0.1	7.6	0.4		0.1	0.1
Germany		0.0		2.7	9.4	0.0		11.1	0.3
Georgia			22.0				5.6		
USA		0.1		0.6		73.8		4.4	
Argentina		34.4							0.5
Greece		1.5		1.5		0.0			1.0
Austria		0.0			62.9	0.0		0.5	0.0
Hungary					0.0	0.0	1.0	0.0	
Bulgaria							30.5		
Moldova									
Romania									
Serbia									
Switzerland						0.0		0.7	0.1
Ukraine									
Turkey				0.3					
UK									
S. Africa						0.2		0.1	
Cyprus									
Armenia			32.9						
Morocco		0.1							
Russia									
Czech Rep.									
Brazil						3.2			
Slovakia						0.5			
Japan						0.0			
Azerbaijan									
Kazakhstan									
Peru									
Lebanon									
China									0.0
Montenegro									
Australia				0.0					
Uzbekishtan									
Canada								0.0	
Thailand									
Unknown origin & other varieties		0.0	40.4	2.1	3.6	5.6	17.7	5.8	0.5
Old World subtotal	100.0	65.3	59.6	97.2	96.4	17.2	82.3	89.7	99.0
New World subtotal		34.7		0.7		77.2		4.5	0.5
World total	100	100	100	100	100	100	100	100	100

Table 22 (cont.) Shares (%) of national winegrape area by varietal country of origin, 2010

Country of planting →	China	Croatia	Cyprus	Czech Rep.	France	Georgia	Germany	Greece	Hungary
Country of origin									
France	96.6	15.3	9.3	25.1	61.8	1.3	10.4	8.1	19.9
Spain	1.8	1.2	10.9		24.1			0.1	1.9
Italy		4.9			11.5		0.2	4.5	1.0
Portugal									0.1
Croatia		52.2		7.1					6.7
Germany	1.5	3.6		17.7	0.4		54.9	0.0	4.9
Georgia		0.3				92.0			
USA	0.1	0.4			0.0				
Argentina									
Greece			2.5		0.3			61.9	
Austria		4.2		37.3	0.2			0.0	19.1
Hungary		1.2		0.4					37.2
Bulgaria		0.0						0.1	0.1
Moldova									
Romania									0.1
Serbia		0.2							0.0
Switzerland		0.1			0.3		1.1		2.7
Ukraine				0.1					0.0
Turkey			4.3						
UK		0.1			0.4				0.0
S. Africa									
Cyprus			69.2						
Armenia									
Morocco									
Russia									
Czech Rep.				6.9					
Brazil									
Slovakia		0.6							0.0
Japan									
Azerbaijan									
Kazakhstan									
Peru									
Lebanon									
China									
Montenegro		0.7							
Australia									
Uzbekishtan									
Canada									
Thailand									
Unknown origin & other varieties	0.0	15.1	3.7	5.5	0.9	6.7	33.4	25.3	6.2
Old World subtotal	**99.8**	**84.4**	**96.3**	**94.5**	**98.6**	**93.3**	**66.6**	**74.7**	**93.8**
New World subtotal	**0.1**	**0.5**			**0.4**				**0.0**
World total	**100**	**100**	**100**	**100**	**100**	**100**		**100**	**100**

Table 22 (cont.) Shares (%) of national winegrape area by varietal country of origin, 2010

Country of planting → Country of origin	Italy	Japan	Kazakhstan	Luxembourg	Mexico	Moldova	Morocco	Myanmar	N. Zealand
France	16.9	52.5	6.9	46.6	39.7	61.5	10.3	80.2	91.4
Spain	2.5		0.8		16.9		12.2	10.3	0.6
Italy	73.0				7.8	0.2		9.5	0.1
Portugal									0.0
Croatia	3.2								0.0
Germany	0.3	14.5	1.6	51.8		1.7			3.6
Georgia			57.4			13.6			
USA		6.8	0.1		8.7	12.8			0.0
Argentina									
Greece	0.3						7.5		
Austria	0.1	6.2				0.1			0.0
Hungary	0.0					0.0			
Bulgaria						0.0			
Moldova			1.6			4.9			
Romania						0.1			
Serbia									
Switzerland	0.0								0.0
Ukraine			0.0			1.9			
Turkey					15.4				
UK	0.0								
S. Africa									0.2
Cyprus									
Armenia									
Morocco							4.8		
Russia						0.0			
Czech Rep.									
Brazil									
Slovakia									
Japan		19.9							
Azerbaijan			9.7						
Kazakhstan			5.6						
Peru									
Lebanon	0.1								
China									
Montenegro									
Australia									
Uzbekishtan						0.1			
Canada									
Thailand									
Unknown origin & other varieties	3.8		16.4	1.6	11.4	3.1	65.2		4.1
Old World subtotal	**96.2**	**73.3**	**83.5**	**98.4**	**79.8**	**84.2**	**30.0**	**100.0**	**95.6**
New World subtota	**0.0**	**26.7**	**0.1**		**8.7**	**12.8**	**4.8**		**0.2**
World total	**100**	**100**	**100**	**100**	**100**	**100**	**100**	**100**	**100**

Table 22 (cont.) Shares (%) of national winegrape area by varietal country of origin, 2010

Country of planting →	Peru	Portugal	Romania	Russia	Serbia	Slovakia	Slovenia	S. Africa	Spain	Switzerland
Country of origin										
France	2.2	9.7	19.5	41.9		14.8	31.5	84.3	9.3	55.5
Spain	32.9	15.4		0.1				1.9	86.6	0.4
Italy	38.8	1.1	0.5	0.8		0.4	15.4	0.9	0.2	2.1
Portugal		72.3						0.6	1.1	
Croatia			4.4		48.0	13.1	20.0	0.0	0.1	
Germany		0.0		3.9		12.2	4.1	0.3	0.0	4.7
Georgia			0.2	5.5						
USA	8.8			0.6				2.3	0.0	
Argentina	0.2									
Greece		0.5						2.1	0.8	
Austria	7.6	0.0	0.4			39.1	4.2			1.8
Hungary				14.8		4.9	4.0	0.1		0.0
Bulgaria			1.7	1.9						
Moldova			8.6	4.2		1.7	0.4			
Romania			11.1			1.8				
Serbia					22.0					
Switzerland		0.0		0.1	5.0				0.0	33.9
Ukraine				12.3		1.9				
Turkey	0.4									
UK				0.7	4.0				0.0	
S. Africa								6.8		
Cyprus										
Armenia										
Morocco										
Russia				6.3						
Czech Rep.						3.7				
Brazil										
Slovakia						1.5	5.6			
Japan										
Azerbaijan										
Kazakhstan										
Peru	8.6								0.0	
Lebanon									0.0	
China	0.1			0.7						
Montenegro										
Australia										
Uzbekishtan										
Canada										
Thailand										
Unknown origin & other varieties	0.4	0.9	53.5	6.2	21.0	5.0	14.8	0.7	1.9	1.6
Old World subtotal	**81.9**	**99.1**	**46.5**	**91.8**	**75.0**	**95.0**	**85.2**	**90.2**	**98.1**	**98.4**
New World subtotal	**17.7**			**2.0**	**4.0**			**9.1**	**0.0**	
World total	**100**	**100**	**100**	**100**	**100**	**100**	**100**	**100**	**100**	**100**

Table 22 (cont.) Shares (%) of national winegrape area by varietal country of origin, 2010

Country of planting → / Country of origin	Thailand	Tunisia	Turkey	Ukraine	UK	USA	Uruguay	*Old World*	*New World*	*World*
France	66.2	14.0	32.5	48.2	61.2	69.7	54.5	**26.8**	**66.9**	**35.8**
Spain	6.7	59.0	1.2		0.1	3.3	4.5	**31.9**	**5.9**	**26.1**
Italy	3.6	5.0	1.0	1.3		2.4	10.4	**15.9**	**2.0**	**12.8**
Portugal					0.1	0.1	0.1	**3.6**	**0.9**	**3.0**
Croatia		2.0				8.7		**2.4**	**2.0**	**2.3**
Germany	1.3		0.0	5.2	38.5	2.3	0.2	**2.3**	**1.4**	**2.1**
Georgia				25.0				**2.3**		**1.8**
USA				4.6		8.8	3.7	**0.4**	**6.0**	**1.7**
Argentina									**6.8**	**1.5**
Greece						0.6		**1.3**	**1.3**	**1.3**
Austria					0.1	0.0		**1.6**	**0.1**	**1.3**
Hungary								**0.9**	**0.0**	**0.7**
Bulgaria								**0.6**		**0.4**
Moldova								**0.6**		**0.4**
Romania								**0.5**		**0.4**
Serbia								**0.4**		**0.3**
Switzerland								**0.4**	**0.0**	**0.3**
Ukraine				13.5				**0.3**		**0.3**
Turkey			65.3					**0.2**	**0.1**	**0.2**
UK						0.0	19.6	**0.2**	**0.2**	**0.2**
S. Africa						0.0			**0.7**	**0.2**
Cyprus								**0.2**		**0.1**
Armenia								**0.1**		**0.1**
Morocco									**0.3**	**0.1**
Russia								**0.0**		**0.0**
Czech Rep.								**0.0**		**0.0**
Brazil									**0.2**	**0.0**
Slovakia								**0.0**		**0.0**
Japan	11.4								**0.1**	**0.0**
Azerbaijan								**0.0**		**0.0**
Kazakhstan								**0.0**		**0.0**
Peru								**0.0**	**0.0**	**0.0**
Lebanon								**0.0**		**0.0**
China								**0.0**	**0.0**	**0.0**
Montenegro								**0.0**		**0.0**
Australia									**0.0**	**0.0**
Uzbekishtan								**0.0**		**0.0**
Canada						0.0			**0.0**	**0.0**
Thailand	10.9								**0.0**	**0.0**
Unknown origin & other varieties		20.0		2.3	0.1	4.0	7.1	**6.8**	**5.3**	**6.5**
Old World subtotal	**77.7**	**80.0**	**100.0**	**93.1**	**99.9**	**87.1**	**69.7**	**92.6**	**80.6**	**89.9**
New World subtotal	**22.3**			**4.6**		**8.9**	**23.2**	**0.6**	**14.1**	**3.6**
World total	**100**	**100**	**100**	**100**	**100**	**100**	**100**	**100**	**100**	**100**

Table 23: National shares (%) of top, top 3, top 5, top 10 and top 20 varieties by winegrape area, 2000

Country	Top variety	Top 3	Top 5	Top 10	Top 20
Algeria	25.0	70.0	85.0		
Argentina	15.7	36.1	51.1	73.2	99.8
Armenia	22.0	40.1	54.9		
Australia	22.4	54.8	68.5	82.3	91.8
Austria	36.0	53.9	66.8	84.5	93.2
Brazil	27.0	58.9	67.3	75.7	100.0
Bulgaria	23.5	46.0	63.8	81.7	93.1
Canada	11.5	30.9	44.2	70.0	87.8
Chile	31.6	56.1	68.7	83.0	89.1
Croatia	27.0	50.0	63.0		
Cyprus	60.0				
Czech Rep.	15.0	40.0	56.0	77.0	
France	11.7	33.9	50.5	72.4	87.1
Georgia	52.8	79.1	89.3	92.2	93.3
Germany	21.4	47.9	54.6	65.2	71.2
Greece	25.1	43.6	52.7	67.5	78.4
Hungary	8.0	19.7	27.1	41.9	58.4
Italy	9.9	24.0	32.8	46.5	61.2
Luxembourg	34.1	59.6	83.2	99.9	
Moldova	17.6	43.1	61.2	90.5	99.4
Morocco	33.4	48.7	60.5		
New Zealand	28.0	63.4	76.6	91.0	96.9
Portugal	7.0	17.6	24.4	37.0	50.6
Romania	8.2	18.8	25.8	34.0	
Russia	23.3	32.9	40.0	53.5	
Serbia	48.0	75.0			
Slovakia	25.0	56.0	69.0	82.0	
Slovenia	15.2	27.2	37.5		
South Africa	24.1	45.7	59.1	84.3	95.4
Spain	32.8	49.4	61.8	75.3	82.6
Switzerland	35.7	79.5	89.7	94.7	97.5
Tunisia	45.0	62.0	72.0		
United Kingdom	12.8	36.3	53.8		
United States	20.4	41.2	60.8	78.7	91.9
Uruguay	32.5	71.8	83.5		
"Missing 9"	25.4	47.2	58.0	70.3	82.6
Old World subtotal	**9.8**	**18.8**	**24.8**	**36.3**	**49.9**
New World subtotal	**13.1**	**27.4**	**36.6**	**50.8**	**68.7**
World total	**8.0**	**16.9**	**24.2**	**35.6**	**48.6**

Table 24: National shares (%) of top, top 3, top 5, top 10 and top 20 varieties, by winegrape area, 2010

Country	Top variety	Top 3	Top 5	Top 10	Top 20
Algeria	25.0	70.0	85.0		
Argentina	15.4	39.0	55.6	78.7	94.0
Armenia	22.0	40.1	54.9		
Australia	28.1	63.5	74.4	87.8	95.5
Austria	29.7	51.4	63.0	79.8	92.5
Brazil	37.0	60.9	74.1	85.8	92.7
Bulgaria	18.8	46.0	59.1	78.4	
Canada	12.7	34.3	49.5	74.3	92.2
Chile	36.5	59.2	76.1	92.5	98.7
China	76.5	93.2	97.4	99.9	
Croatia	22.6	38.4	45.4	59.5	71.7
Cyprus	41.5	71.4	80.0	90.6	
Czech Rep.	9.7	27.0	41.4	67.7	93.5
France	13.7	34.7	49.5	72.5	87.1
Georgia	52.8	79.1	89.3	92.2	93.3
Germany	22.1	43.0	51.2	60.3	64.8
Greece	18.2	33.9	43.5	59.5	74.9
Hungary	11.5	24.1	33.5	50.3	71.5
Italy	11.4	22.6	30.5	45.3	64.0
Japan	22.0	50.8	73.1	94.6	
Kazakhstan	51.2	66.7	76.2	86.1	
Luxembourg	28.4	56.5	80.1	99.9	
Mexico	15.4	37.4	51.0	72.2	
Moldova	17.6	43.1	61.2	90.5	99.4
Morocco	33.8	49.3	61.3		
Myanmar	35.8	74.5	89.4	99.7	
New Zealand	50.7	77.9	86.9	94.1	96.6
Peru	32.7	68.5	84.7	97.7	99.7
Portugal	10.2	24.1	36.0	55.0	74.8
Romania	7.6	21.6	30.3	40.6	45.8
Russia	14.0	36.5	50.4	67.2	85.3
Serbia	48.0	75.0			
Slovakia	16.5	40.6	55.4	73.3	90.3
Slovenia	14.4	29.7	42.3	65.2	85.2
South Africa	18.3	42.4	61.9	87.0	95.8
Spain	24.5	52.5	65.0	78.7	89.1
Switzerland	29.7	67.0	77.3	86.8	94.4
Thailand	44.5	66.8	83.1	98.0	
Tunisia	45.0	62.0	72.0		
Turkey	13.6	35.7	51.1	78.2	98.4
Ukraine	22.1	49.8	61.5	84.2	99.5
United Kingdom	19.6	48.7	61.8	79.7	93.7
United States	17.9	43.2	59.2	76.5	89.0
Uruguay	23.7	54.7	73.4	86.2	91.2
Old World subtotal	**7.1**	**19.0**	**27.5**	**40.3**	**54.9**
New World subtotal	**15.4**	**33.5**	**45.1**	**59.4**	**75.3**
World total	**6.3**	**17.6**	**27.0**	**41.7**	**55.1**

Table 25: Source of prime varietal name and its main synonym, and their shares of prime variety's global area, 2000

Summary of data in this table				
Source*	of varieties	Share (%) of no. of varieties	Area (hectares)	Share (%) of global area
RHV	795	79	4214540	86.4
VIVC	171	17	80056	1.6
Unknown	46	4	583579	12.0
Total	**1012**	**100**	**4878176**	**100**

*RHV = Jancis Robinson, Julia Harding, Josê Vouillamoz, *Wine Grapes*, London Allen Lane, 2012
VIVC = *Vitis International Variety Catalogue*, http://www.vivc.de

Prime variety	Source of prime name	Share (%) of prime variety's total area	Name of main synonym	Share (%) of prime variety's total area
Abbo	VIVC	0	Abbou	100
Abbuoto	RHV	100		
Abondant	VIVC	100		
Abouriou	RHV	100		
Abrusco	RHV	1	Colorino	99
Adakarasi	RHV	100		
Afus Ali	VIVC	0	Waltham Cross	100
Agadai	VIVC	100		
Agiorgitiko	RHV	100		
Aglianico	RHV	76	Aglianico del Vulture	24
Aglianicone	RHV	100		
Agronomica	RHV	100		
Airen	RHV	100	Forcallat Blanca	0
Aladasturi	RHV	100		
Alarije	RHV	99	Malfar	1
Alb de Ialoveni	VIVC	100		
Albalonga	RHV	100		
Albana	RHV	100		
Albanello	RHV	100		
Albaranzeuli Bianco	RHV	100		
Albaranzeuli Nero	RHV	100		
Albarola	RHV	98	Bianchetta Genovese	2
Albarossa	RHV	100		
Albillo Mayor	RHV	0	Albilla	100
Albillo Real	RHV	0	Albillo	100
Alcanon	RHV	100		

Table 25 (cont.) Source of prime varietal name and its main synonym, and their shares of prime variety's global area, 2000

Prime variety	Source of prime name	Share (%) of prime variety's total area	Name of main synonym	Share (%) of prime variety's total area
Aleatico	RHV	100		
Aleksandrouli	RHV	100		
Alfrocheiro	RHV	99	Bastarda Negra	1
Alicante Henri Bouschet	RHV	25	Garnacha Tintorera	49
Aligote	RHV	100		
Alionza	RHV	100		
Alphonse Lavallee	VIVC	83	Ribier	16
Altesse	RHV	100		
Alvarelhao	RHV	29	Brancelho	62
Alvarinho	RHV	19	Albarino	81
Amaral	RHV	100		
Amigne	RHV	100		
Ancellotta	RHV	100		
Antao Vaz	RHV	100		
Ar110		100		
Ar99		100		
Aramon Bouschet		100		
Aramon Gris	VIVC	100		
Aramon Noir	RHV	0	Aramon	100
Aramont	VIVC	0		
Aranel	RHV	100		
Arany Sarfeher	RHV	0	Izsaki	100
Arbane	RHV	100		
Argelina	VIVC	100		
Arinarnoa	RHV	100		
Arinto de Bucelas	RHV	0	Pederna	70
Arneis	RHV	100		
Arnsburger	RHV	100		
Aromon Blanc		100		
Arriloba	RHV	100		
Arrufiac	RHV	100		
Arvesiniadu	RHV	100		
Arvine	RHV	93	Petite Arvine	7
Asirtiko Red		100		
Aspiran Bouschet	RHV	100		
Asprouda		0	Asproudi	100
Assyrtiko	RHV	0	Asirtiko	100
Athiri	RHV	100		
Athiri (Red)		100		
Aubin Blanc	RHV	0	Aubin	100
Aubun	RHV	100		
Aurore	RHV	0	Aurora	100
Auxerrois	RHV	100		

Table 25 (cont.) Source of prime varietal name and its main synonym, and their shares of prime variety's global area, 2000

Prime variety	Source of prime name	Share (%) of prime variety's total area	Name of main synonym	Share (%) of prime variety's total area
Avana	RHV	100		
Avarengo	RHV	100		
Avesso	RHV	100		
Azal	RHV	100		
Babeasca Neagra	RHV	98	Rara Neagra	2
Babic	RHV	100		
Bacchus	RHV	100		
Baco Blanc	RHV	98	Baco Divers	2
Baco Noir	RHV	100	Baco Divers	0
Baga	RHV	100		
Baleille	VIVC	100		
Barbarossa	RHV	100		
Barbaroux	RHV	100		
Barbera	RHV	18	Barbera Nera	82
Barbera Bianca	RHV	100		
Barbera Sarda	RHV	100		
Barcelo	RHV	100		
Bariadorgia	RHV	0	Carcajolo Blanc	100
Baroque	RHV	100		
Barsaglina	RHV	100		
Bastardillo		100		
Bastardo Magarachsky	RHV	47	Bastardo Magaraceskii	53
Batili		100		
Batily		100		
Batoca	RHV	100		
Bayanshira	RHV	100		
Beba	RHV	100	Breval	0
Beclan	RHV	0	Petit Beclan	100
Bellandais	VIVC	100		
Bellone	RHV	100		
Bequignol Noir	RHV	0	Bequignol	100
Bianca	RHV	100		
Biancame	RHV	100		
Bianchetta Trevigiana	RHV	100		
Bianco d'Alessano	RHV	100		
Biancolella	RHV	100		
Biancone di Portoferraio	RHV	0	Biancone	100
Biancu Gentile	RHV	100		
Biborkadarka	RHV	0	Bibor Kadarka	100
Bical	RHV	100		
Black Queen	RHV	100		
Blanc Dame	RHV	100		
Blanca Ovoide		100		

Table 25 (cont.) Source of prime varietal name and its main synonym, and their shares of prime variety's global area, 2000

Prime variety	Source of prime name	Share (%) of prime variety's total area	Name of main synonym	Share (%) of prime variety's total area
Blanqueiro	RHV	0	Blanqueiron	100
Blauburger	RHV	100		
Blauer Portugieser	RHV	92	Portugais Bleu	5
Blauer Wildbacher	RHV	98	Wildbacher	2
Blaufrankisch	RHV	99	Franconia	1
Blush Seedless	VIVC	100		
Bobal	RHV	100		
Bogazkere	RHV	100		
Boiziau	VIVC	100		
Bombino Bianco	RHV	100		
Bombino Nero	RHV	100		
Bonamico	RHV	100		
Bonarda Grande		100		
Bonda	RHV	100		
Bondola	RHV	100		
Bordo	RHV	100		
Borracal	RHV	77	Caino Tinto	23
Bosco	RHV	100		
Bouchales	RHV	100		
Bouillet	VIVC	100		
Bourboulenc	RHV	100		
Bousquet Precoce	VIVC	0	Precoce Bousquet	100
Bouvier	RHV	100		
Bracciola Nera	RHV	0	Bracciola	100
Brachetto del Piemonte	RHV	0	Brachetto	100
Braquet Noir	RHV	0	Brachet	100
Breidecker	RHV	100		
Bric	VIVC	100		
Brocada		100		
Brun Argente	RHV	100		
Bukettraube	RHV	100		
Burdin		0	Burdin Divers	100
Bussanello	RHV	100		
Cabernet Dorsa	RHV	100		
Cabernet Franc	RHV	100	Kamberne Fran	0
Cabernet Malbec	VIVC	100		
Cabernet Sauvignon	RHV	99	Kamberne Sovinion	0
Caddiu	RHV	100		
Caino Blanco	RHV	100		
Caladoc	RHV	100		
Calagrano	RHV	100		
Calitor Blanc	VIVC	100		
Calitor Gris	VIVC	100		

Table 25 (cont.) Source of prime varietal name and its main synonym, and their shares of prime variety's global area, 2000

Prime variety	Source of prime name	Share (%) of prime variety's total area	Name of main synonym	Share (%) of prime variety's total area
Calitor Noir	RHV	100		
Calkarasi	RHV	100		
Callet	RHV	100		
Caloria	RHV	100		
Camaralet de Lasseube	RHV	0	Camarate	100
Campbell Early	RHV	100		
Canada Muscat	RHV	100		
Canaiolo Nero	RHV	100		
Canaiolo Rosa	VIVC	100		
Canorroyo	VIVC	100		
Caracol	RHV	100		
Cardinal	RHV	100		
Carica l'Asino	RHV	100		
Carignan Blanc	VIVC	94	Carinena Blanco	6
Carignan Bouschet	VIVC	100		
Carignan Gris	VIVC	100		
Carmenere	RHV	100		
Carmine	RHV	100		
Carnelian	RHV	100		
Carricante	RHV	100		
Cartouche		100		
Castel	VIVC	0	Castel Divers	100
Castelao	RHV	0	Periquita	100
Castets	RHV	100		
Castiglione	RHV	100		
Castonotal		100		
Catanese Nero	RHV	100		
Catarratto Bianco	RHV	0	Catarratto Bianco Comune	85
Catawba	RHV	100		
Cavus	RHV	100		
Cayetana Blanca	RHV	87	Pardina	12
Cayuga White	RHV	0	Cayuga	100
Centenial Seedless	VIVC	100		
Centurian	RHV	100		
Cep Rouge	VIVC	100		
Cerceal Branco	RHV	0	Cercial	100
Cereza	RHV	100		
Cesanese	RHV	0	Cesanese d'Affile	56
Cesar	RHV	100		
Chambourcin	RHV	100		
Chancellor	RHV	100		
Chardonnay	RHV	100	Sardone	0
Charmont	RHV	100		

Table 25 (cont.) Source of prime varietal name and its main synonym, and their shares of prime variety's global area, 2000

Prime variety	Source of prime name	Share (%) of prime variety's total area	Name of main synonym	Share (%) of prime variety's total area
Chasan	RHV	100		
Chasselas	RHV	91	Weisser Gutedel	9
Chasselas Rouge	VIVC	0	Chasselas Rose	100
Chatus	RHV	100		
Chelva	RHV	100	Uva Rey	0
Chenanson	RHV	100		
Chenel	RHV	100		
Chenin Blanc	RHV	70	Chenin	30
Chenivesse	VIVC	100		
Chinuri	RHV	100		
Chkhaveri	RHV	100		
Ciliegiolo	RHV	100		
Cinsaut	RHV	74	Cinsault	25
Cinsaut Blanc	VIVC	100		
Cinsaut Seedless		100		
Clairette	RHV	77	Clairette Blanche	23
Clairette Rose	VIVC	100		
Clarin	VIVC	100		
Claverie	RHV	100		
Cococciola	RHV	100		
Coda di Volpe Bianca	RHV	97	Guarnaccia	3
Codega de Larinho	RHV	0	Codega do Larinho	100
Codivarta	RHV	100		
Codrinski	VIVC	100		
Colgadero	VIVC	100		
Colobel	RHV	100		
Colombana Nera	RHV	0	Colombana Nero	100
Colombard	RHV	23	French Colombard	47
Colomino	RHV	100		
Coloraillo	RHV	100		
Completer	RHV	100		
Complexa	RHV	100		
Concord	RHV	100		
Cornalin	RHV	36	Humagne Rouge	64
Cornarea	RHV	100		
Cornifesto	RHV	100		
Cortese	RHV	100		
Corvina Veronese	RHV	0	Corvina	100
Corvinone	RHV	100		
Cot	RHV	25	Malbec	74
Couderc	VIVC	0	Couderc Divers	100
Couderc Noir	RHV	0	Coudrec	50
Counoise	RHV	100		

Table 25 (cont.) Source of prime varietal name and its main synonym, and their shares of prime variety's global area, 2000

Prime variety	Source of prime name	Share (%) of prime variety's total area	Name of main synonym	Share (%) of prime variety's total area
Courbu Blanc	RHV	0	Courbu	100
Courbu Noir	RHV	100		
Cove	VIVC	100		
Crimson Seedless	VIVC	100		
Criolla Grande	RHV	100		
Croatina	RHV	100		
Crouchen	RHV	100		
Crovassa	RHV	100		
Crystal	RHV	100		
Cserszegi Fuszeres	RHV	100		
Dalkauer	RHV	100		
Damaschino	RHV	16	Alicante Branco	65
Dawn Seedless	VIVC	100		
De Chaunac	RHV	100		
De Cilindro	VIVC	100		
Debina	RHV	0	Dempina	100
Deckrot	RHV	100		
Decuerno		100		
Delaware	RHV	100		
Diagalves	RHV	100		
Dimrit	RHV	100		
Dimyat	RHV	0	Dimiat	99
Dindarella	RHV	100		
Diolinoir	RHV	100		
Dolcetto	RHV	100		
Dolciame	RHV	100		
Domina	RHV	100		
Dominga	VIVC	100		
Dona Branca	RHV	100		
Donzelinho Branco	RHV	100		
Doradilla	RHV	100		
Doradillo	VIVC	100		
Doral	RHV	100		
Dornfelder	RHV	100		
Douce Noire	RHV	0	Bonarda	99
Doukkali	VIVC	100		
Doux d'Henry	RHV	100		
Droujba	VIVC	0	Drujba	100
Drupeggio	RHV	100	Canaiolo Bianco	100
Dunkelfelder	RHV	100		
Dunze		100		
Duras	RHV			
Durasa	VIVC	100		

Table 25 (cont.) Source of prime varietal name and its main synonym, and their shares of prime variety's global area, 2000

Prime variety	Source of prime name	Share (%) of prime variety's total area	Name of main synonym	Share (%) of prime variety's total area
Durella	RHV	100		
Durif	RHV	23	Petite Sirah	77
Ederena	RHV	100		
Egiodola	RHV	100		
Ehrenbreitsteiner	VIVC	100		
Ehrenfelser	RHV	100		
Ekigaina	RHV	100		
Ekim Kara	RHV	100		
Elbling	RHV	9	Elbling Weisser	56
Elbling Rot	VIVC	0	Elbling Roter	100
Elvira	RHV	100		
Emerald Riesling	RHV	100		
Emerald Seedless	VIVC	100		
Emir	RHV	100		
Enantio	RHV	0	Lambrusco a Foglia Frastagliata	100
Encruzado	RHV	100		
Erbaluce	RHV	100		
Ervi	RHV	100		
Espadeiro	RHV	100		
Etraire de l'Adui	RHV	100		
Ezerfurtu	RHV	100		
Ezerjo	RHV	100		
Faberrebe	RHV	100		
Falanghina	VIVC	100		
Fer	RHV	100		
Fernao Pires	RHV	100		
Fertilia	RHV	100		
Feteasca Alba	RHV	100		
Feteasca Neagra	RHV	100		
Feteasca Regala	RHV	100		
Feunate	VIVC	100		
Fiano	RHV	100		
Fiesta	VIVC	100		
Fileri		100		
Fino de Ribera del Fresno		100		
Flame Seedless	VIVC	100		
Flavis	RHV	100		
Flora	RHV	100		
Florental	RHV	100		
Foglia Tonda	RHV	100		
Fogoneu	RHV	100		
Fokiano	RHV	100		
Fokiano (White)	VIVC	100		

Table 25 (cont.) Source of prime varietal name and its main synonym, and their shares of prime variety's global area, 2000

Prime variety	Source of prime name	Share (%) of prime variety's total area	Name of main synonym	Share (%) of prime variety's total area
Folgasao	RHV	100		
Folle Blanche	RHV	100		
Fontan	VIVC	100		
Fontanara	VIVC	100		
Fonte Cal	RHV	100		
Forastera	RHV	100		
Forcallat Tinta	RHV	100		
Forgiarin	RHV	100		
Forsellina	RHV	100		
Fortana	RHV	76	Canina Nera	24
Francavidda	RHV	100		
Frappato	RHV	100		
Fredonia	RHV	100		
Freisa	RHV	100		
Freisamer	RHV	100		
Fruhroter Veltliner	RHV	99	Malvasier	1
Fubiano	RHV	100		
Fuella Nera	RHV	100		
Fumin	RHV	100		
Furmint	RHV	100		
Gaglioppo	RHV	100		
Gaillard	RHV	0	Gaillard Divers	100
Galbena de Odobesti	RHV	100		
Galego Dourado	RHV	0	Pedro Luis	100
Gamaret	RHV	100		
Gamay de Teinturier Bouze	RHV	89	Gamays Teinturiers	8
Gamay Noir	RHV	0	Gamay	99
Gamay Teinturier de Chaudenay	VIVC	0	Gamay de Chaudenay	100
Gamay Teinturier Freaux	VIVC	58	Gammay Freaux	42
Ganson	RHV	100		
Garandmak	RHV	100		
Garanoir	RHV	66	Granoir	34
Garganega	RHV	69	Grecanico Dorato	31
Garnacha Blanca	VIVC	40	Grenache Blanc	60
Garnacha Peluda	RHV	72	Lledoner Pelut	28
Garnacha Roja	RHV	5	Grenache Gris	95
Garnacha Tinta	RHV	0	Grenache	52
Garonnet	VIVC	100		
Garrido Fino	RHV	100		
Gascon	RHV	100		
Gateta	VIVC	100		
Generosa	RHV	100		
Gewurztraminer	RHV	61		26

Table 25 (cont.) Source of prime varietal name and its main synonym, and their shares of prime variety's global area, 2000

Prime variety	Source of prime name	Share (%) of prime variety's total area	Name of main synonym	Share (%) of prime variety's total area
Giro	RHV	100		
Godello	RHV	31	Gouveio	62
Goldburger	RHV	100		
Goldriesling	RHV	100		
Golubok	RHV	0	Goluboc	100
Goruli Mtsvane	RHV	100		
Gouais Blanc	RHV	0	Gouais	100
Gouget Noir	RHV	0	Gouget	100
Goustolidi	RHV	100		
Grachen	VIVC	100		
Graciano	RHV	23	Tinta Miuda	31
Graisse	RHV	100		
Gramon	RHV	100		
Grand Noir	RHV	5	Gran Negro	95
Grasa de Cotnari	RHV	100		
Grasevina	RHV	0	Italian Riesling	43
Grassen	VIVC	100		
Grechetto di Orvieto	RHV	0	Grechetto	100
Grechetto Rosso	VIVC	100		
Greco	RHV	69	Asprinio	31
Greco Bianco	RHV	100		
Greco Nero	RHV	100		
Grenache Rose		0	Grenas Rose	100
Grignolino	RHV	100		
Grillo	RHV	100		
Gringet	RHV	100		
Grolleau Gris	VIVC	100		
Grolleau Noir	RHV	0	Grolleau	100
Groppello di Mocasina	RHV	44	Groppello di Santo Stefano	56
Groppello Gentile	RHV	100		
Gros Bec		100		
Gros Manseng	RHV	100		
Gruner Veltliner	RHV	99	Veltliner	1
Guardavalle	RHV	100		
Guillemot	VIVC	100		
Harslevelu	RHV	100		
Hegel	VIVC	100		
Helfensteiner	RHV	100		
Herbemont	RHV	100		
Heroldrebe	RHV	100		
Himbertscha	RHV	100		
Holder	RHV	100		
Hondarrabi Beltza	RHV	0	Ondarrabi Beltza	100

Table 25 (cont.) Source of prime varietal name and its main synonym, and their shares of prime variety's global area, 2000

Prime variety	Source of prime name	Share (%) of prime variety's total area	Name of main synonym	Share (%) of prime variety's total area
Hrvatica	RHV	0	Negrara	100
Huerta del Rey	VIVC	100		
Humagne	RHV	0	Humagne Blanc	100
Huxelrebe	RHV	100		
Ilichevskii Rannii	VIVC	0	Iliciovski Ciornai Rannii	100
Imperial Seedless		100		
Impigno	RHV	100		
Incrocio Bianco Fedit 51	RHV	100		
Incrocio Bruni 54	RHV	100		
Incrocio Manzoni 2.15	RHV	100		
Incrocio Terzi 1	RHV	100		
Invernenga	RHV	100		
Inzolia	RHV	0	Ansonica	100
Isabella	RHV	46	Isabel	52
Italia	RHV	100		
Italica	RHV	100		
Ives	RHV	100		
Jacquere	RHV	100		
Jacquez	RHV	75	Lenoir	25
Jampal	RHV	100		
Joannes Seyve	VIVC	0	Johan.Seyve D.	100
Joubertin	VIVC	100		
Juan Garcia	RHV	81	Mouraton	11
Jubilaumsrebe	RHV	100		
Jurancon Blanc	RHV	100		
Jurancon Noir	RHV	100		
Jurie	VIVC	0	Jurie Divers	100
Juwel	RHV	100		
Kadarka	RHV	38	Gamza	62
Kalecik Karasi	RHV	100		
Kanaan	VIVC	100		
Kangun	VIVC	100		
Kanzler	RHV	100		
Karalahna	RHV	100		
Karasakiz	RHV	100		
Karinian		100		
Kerner	RHV	100		
Kernling	VIVC	100		
Khikhvi	RHV	100		
Kisi	RHV	100		
Knipperle	RHV	100		
Koenigin der Weingaerten	VIVC	0	Tzaritza Na Loziata	76
Kokur Bely	RHV	100		

Table 25 (cont.) Source of prime varietal name and its main synonym, and their shares of prime variety's global area, 2000

Prime variety	Source of prime name	Share (%) of prime variety's total area	Name of main synonym	Share (%) of prime variety's total area
Korinthiaki	RHV	0	Currant	93
Koshu	RHV	100		
Kotsifali	RHV	100		
Kovidinka	RHV	100		
Krakhuna	RHV	100		
Krassato	RHV	100		
Kuldzhinskii	VIVC	100		
Kunleany	RHV	100		
Lacoste	VIVC	0	Auxerrois Rupes	100
Lacrima di Morro d'Alba	RHV	0	Lacrima	100
Lado	RHV	100		
Lafnetscha	RHV	100		
Lagrein	RHV	100		
Lairen	RHV	0	Malvar	100
Lakhegyi Mezes	VIVC	100		
Lambrusca di Alessandria	RHV	100		
Lambrusco	RHV	100		
Lambrusco di Sorbara	RHV	100		
Lambrusco Grasparossa	RHV	100		
Lambrusco Maestri	RHV	100		
Lambrusco Marani	RHV	100		
Lambrusco Montericco	RHV	100		
Lambrusco Salamino	RHV	100		
Lambrusco Viadanese	RHV	100		
Landal	RHV	100		
Landot	VIVC	0	Landot Divers	100
Landot Noir	RHV	0	Landot Divers	100
Laska	VIVC	0	Lasca	100
Lauzet	RHV	100		
Len de l'El	RHV	100		
Leon Millot	RHV	100		
Leopoldo III	VIVC	100		
Liatiko	RHV	100		
Liatiko(White)	VIVC	100		
Liliorila	RHV	100		
Limnio	RHV	100		
Limnio(White)		100		
Listain de Huelva	RHV	0	Manteudo	100
Listan Negro	RHV	99	Negra Comun	1
Listan Prieto	RHV	0	Pais	98
Listrao Roxo	VIVC	0	Listrao	100
Loureiro	RHV	90	Loureiro Blanca	10
Lumassina	RHV	100		

Table 25 (cont.) Source of prime varietal name and its main synonym, and their shares of prime variety's global area, 2000

Prime variety	Source of prime name	Share (%) of prime variety's total area	Name of main synonym	Share (%) of prime variety's total area
Macabeo	RHV	89	Macabeu	11
Maceratino	RHV	100		
Magliocco Canino	RHV	100		
Magliocco Dolce	RHV	0	Marsigliana Nera	100
Maiolica	RHV	100		
Maiskii Chernyi	VIVC	0	Mayskiy	100
Malaga Blanc	RHV	100		
Malagousia	RHV	0	Malagouzia	100
Malbo Gentile	RHV	100		
Malegue	VIVC	0	Malegue Divers	100
Maliverne		100		
Malvasia Bianca di Basilicata	RHV	100		
Malvasia Bianca di Candia	RHV	64	Malvasia Bianca	36
Malvasia Bianca Lunga	RHV	100		
Malvasia Branca de Sao Jorge	RHV	100		
Malvasia del Lazio	RHV	100		
Malvasia di Candia Aromatica	RHV	100		
Malvasia di Casorzo	RHV	100		
Malvasia di Lipari	RHV	25	Malvasia di Sardegna	71
Malvasia di Schierano	RHV	100		
Malvasia Fina	RHV	0	Torrontes	67
Malvasia Nera di Basilicata	RHV	100		
Malvasia Nera di Brindisi	RHV	69	Malvasia Nera di Lecce	20
Malvasia Preta	RHV	100		
Malvasia Rosa	VIVC	100		
Malvazija Istarska	RHV	94	Malvasia Istriana	6
Mammolo	RHV	18	Sciaccarello	82
Mandilaria	RHV	100		
Mandon	RHV	100		
Manseng Noir	RHV	52	Ferron	48
Manto Negro	RHV	100		
Manzoni Bianco	RHV	0	Manzoni	100
Marechal Foch	RHV	87	Foch	13
Mariensteiner	VIVC	100		
Marmajuelo	RHV	0	Vermejuela	100
Marsanne	RHV	98	Marsanne Blanche	2
Marselan	RHV	100		
Marufo	RHV	14	Moravia Dulce	45
Marzemina Bianca	RHV	100		
Marzemino	RHV			
Matrasa	RHV	100		
Mauzac Blanc	RHV	0	Mauzac	100
Mauzac Noir	RHV	100		

Table 25 (cont.) Source of prime varietal name and its main synonym, and their shares of prime variety's global area, 2000

Prime variety	Source of prime name	Share (%) of prime variety's total area	Name of main synonym	Share (%) of prime variety's total area
Mauzac Rose	VIVC	100		
Mavro	RHV	100		
Mavro Messenikola	RHV	0	Messenikola	100
Mavrodafni	RHV	100		
Mavrouda	RHV	0	Mavroudi	100
Mavrud	RHV	100		
Mayolet	VIVC	100		
Mazuelo	RHV	0	Carignan	78
Mazzese	RHV	100		
Mecle de Bourgoin	RHV	100		
Melara	RHV	100		
Melon	RHV	100		
Mencia	RHV	77	Jaen	15
Menu Pineau	RHV	100		
Merille	RHV	100		
Merlo		100		
Merlot	RHV	100		
Merlot Blanc	VIVC	100		
Merseguera	RHV	100		
Merzling	RHV	100		
Meslier Saint-Francois	RHV	100		
Michele Parlieri	VIVC	100		
Miguel del Arco	VIVC	100		
Milgranet	RHV	100		
Minella Bianca	RHV	100		
Misket	VIVC	100		
Molette	RHV	100		
Molinara	RHV	80	Molinera	20
Mollard	RHV	100		
Monastrell	RHV	88	Mourvedre	10
Monbadon	RHV	100		
Mondeuse Blanche	RHV	100		
Mondeuse Grise	VIVC	100		
Mondeuse Noire	RHV	0	Mondeuse	100
Monemvassia	RHV	0	Monemvasia	100
Monerac	RHV	100		
Monica Nera	RHV	0	Monica	100
Monstruosa	RHV	0	Monstruosa de Monterrei	100
Montepulciano	RHV	100		
Montils	RHV	100		
Montonico Bianco	RHV	99	Montonico	1
Montu	RHV	100		
Monvedro	RHV	100		

Table 25 (cont.) Source of prime varietal name and its main synonym, and their shares of prime variety's global area, 2000

Prime variety	Source of prime name	Share (%) of prime variety's total area	Name of main synonym	Share (%) of prime variety's total area
Moore's Diamond	RHV	0	Moores Diamond	100
Moravia Agria	RHV	100		
Morenillo	VIVC	100		
Moreto	VIVC	100		
Morio-Muskat	RHV	0	Morio Muscat	100
Mornen Noir	RHV	0	Mornen	100
Morone	RHV	100		
Morrastel Bouschet	RHV	0	Gros Morras.Bous.	100
Moscatel Branco	VIVC	0	Moscatel Nunes	100
Moscatel Rosada	VIVC	100		
Moscatello Selvatico	RHV	100		
Moscato di Scanzo	RHV	100		
Moscato di Terracina	RHV	100		
Moscato Giallo	RHV	84	Moscatel Amarilla	16
Moscato Rosa del Trentino	RHV	0	Moscato Rosa	100
Moschofilero	RHV	69	Fileri	31
Moschofilero	VIVC	100		
Moschomavro	RHV	0	Moschato	100
Mostosa	RHV	100		
Mourvaison	VIVC	100		
Mouyssagues	RHV	100		
Mskhali	RHV	100		
Mtsvane Kakhuri	RHV	0	Mtsvane	100
Muller Thurgau	RHV	99	Rivaner	1
Muscadel (Red)	RHV	100		
Muscadelle	RHV	100		
Muscardin	RHV	100		
Muscat a Petits Grains Roses	VIVC	100		
Muscat a Petits Grains Rouge	VIVC	100		
Muscat Bailey A	RHV	100		
Muscat Blanc a Petits Grains	RHV	3	Moscato Bianco	46
Muscat de Ialoveni		100		
Muscat Fleur d'Oranger	RHV	0	Muscat Orange	100
Muscat of Alexandria	RHV	41	Moscatel de Malaga	21
Muscat of Alexandria Red	VIVC	0	Red Hanepoot	100
Muscat of Hamburg	RHV	45	Moscatel Hambourg	41
Muscat Ottonel	RHV	100		
Muscat Rose	VIVC	100		
Muscat Violet	VIVC	100		
Naparo		100		
Narince	RHV	100		
Nasco	RHV	100		
Nebbiera	RHV	100		

Table 25 (cont.) Source of prime varietal name and its main synonym, and their shares of prime variety's global area, 2000

Prime variety	Source of prime name	Share (%) of prime variety's total area	Name of main synonym	Share (%) of prime variety's total area
Nebbiolo	RHV	100		
Negoska	RHV	0	Negkoska	100
Negramoll	RHV	47	Mollar	24
Negrette	RHV	100		
Negretto	RHV	100		
Negroamaro	RHV	0	Negro Amaro	100
Negru de Ialoveni	VIVC	100		
Ner d'Ala	RHV	100		
Nerello Cappuccio	RHV	100		
Nerello Mascalese	RHV	100		
Neretta Cuneese	RHV	100		
Neretto di Bairo	RHV	100		
Nero Buono di Cori	RHV	0	Nero Buono	100
Nero d'Avola	RHV	0	Calabrese	100
Nero di Troia	RHV	100		
Neuburger	RHV	100		
Neyret	RHV	100		
Niagara	RHV	100		
Nieddera	RHV	100		
Nigra	RHV	100		
Noah	RHV	100		
Nobling	RHV	100		
Nocera	RHV	100		
Noir Fleurien	RHV	100		
Nosiola	RHV	100		
Notardomenico	RHV	100		
Noual	VIVC	100		
Nouvelle	RHV	100		
Nuragus	RHV	100		
Norton	RHV	0	Cynthiana	100
Oberlin	VIVC	100		
Oberlin White	VIVC	0	Oberlin Divers	100
Odessky Cherny	RHV	100		
Odola	VIVC	100		
Oeillade Bousche	VIVC	100		
Ohanes	VIVC	100		
Ojaleshi	RHV	100		
Okuzgozu	RHV	100		
Olivette Noire	VIVC	0	Cornichon Violet	100
Ondarrabi Zuri	VIVC	100		
Ondenc	RHV	100		
Onitskanskii Belyi	VIVC	0	Alb de Onitcani	100
Optima	RHV	100		

Table 25 (cont.) Source of prime varietal name and its main synonym, and their shares of prime variety's global area, 2000

Prime variety	Source of prime name	Share (%) of prime variety's total area	Name of main synonym	Share (%) of prime variety's total area
Orion	RHV	100		
Ortega	RHV	100		
Ortrugo	RHV	100		
Osteiner	RHV	100		
Otskhanuri Sapere	RHV	100		
Palomino Fino	RHV	69	Listan	24
Palot	VIVC	100		
Pamid	RHV	100	Pamiti	0
Pampanuto	RHV	100		
Panse Valenciano	VIVC	0	Panse Valenciana	100
Papazkarasi	RHV	100		
Pardillo	RHV	0	Marisancho	100
Parellada	RHV	100		
Parraleta	RHV	9	Caricagiola	84
Pascal Blanc	RHV	0	Pascal	100
Pascale	RHV	78	Nieddu Mannu	22
Passau	RHV	100		
Passerina	RHV	100		
Pavana	RHV	100		
Pecorello	VIVC	100		
Pecorino	RHV	100		
Pedral	RHV	100		
Pedro Gimenez	RHV	100		
Pedro Ximenez	RHV	100		
Pelaverga	RHV	100		
Pelaverga Piccolo	RHV	100		
Peloursin	RHV	100		
Perdea	VIVC	100		
Perera	RHV	100		
Perle	RHV	100		
Perlette	VIVC	100		
Perlita		100		
Perola	VIVC	100		
Perricone	RHV	100		
Perruno	RHV	62	Royal	38
Persan	RHV	100		
Pervenets Magaracha	RHV	16	Pervenetz Magaratcha	46
Pervomaisky	RHV	0	Pervomaiskii	100
Petit Bouschet	RHV	100		
Petit Courbu	RHV	100		
Petit Manseng	RHV	0	Pt. Manseng Blanc	100
Petit Meslier	RHV	100		
Petit Rouge	RHV	100		

Table 25 (cont.) Source of prime varietal name and its main synonym, and their shares of prime variety's global area, 2000

Prime variety	Source of prime name	Share (%) of prime variety's total area	Name of main synonym	Share (%) of prime variety's total area
Petit Verdot	RHV	100		
Phoenix	RHV	100		
Picapoll Blanco	RHV	100		
Piccola Nera	RHV	100		
Picolit	RHV	100		
Piculit Neri	RHV	100		
Piedirosso	RHV	100		
Pignola Valtellinese	RHV	0	Pignola	100
Pignoletto	RHV	100		
Pignolo	RHV	100		
Pineau d'Aunis	RHV	100		
Pinella	RHV	100		
Pinot Blanc	RHV	39	Pinot Bianco	29
Pinot Gris	RHV	49	Pinot Grigio	35
Pinot Meunier	RHV	0	Meunier	100
Pinot Noir	RHV	92	Pinot Nero	5
Pinot Noir Precoce	RHV	0	Frühburgunder	98
Pinotage	RHV	100		
Piquepoul Blanc	RHV	100		
Piquepoul Bousch	VIVC	100		
Piquepoul Gris	VIVC	100		
Piquepoul Noir	RHV	91	Picapoll Negro	9
Plant Droit	RHV	87	Espanenc	13
Planta Mula	VIVC	100		
Planta Nova	RHV	100		
Plantet	RHV	100		
Plassa	RHV	100		
Plavac Mali	RHV	100		
Podarok Magaracha	RHV	100		
Pollera Nera	RHV	100		
Portan	RHV	100		
Portland	VIVC	100		
Posip Bijeli	RHV	0	Posip	100
Pougnet	VIVC	100		
Poulsard	RHV	100		
Poulsard Blanc	RHV	100		
Precoce de Malingre	RHV	100		
Prensal	RHV	0	Pensal Blanco	100
Preto Martinho	RHV	100		
Prie	RHV	0	Prie Blanc	100
Prieto Picudo	RHV	100		
Primetta	RHV	0	Prie Rouge	100
Prodest	RHV	100		

Table 25 (cont.) Source of prime varietal name and its main synonym, and their shares of prime variety's global area, 2000

Prime variety	Source of prime name	Share (%) of prime variety's total area	Name of main synonym	Share (%) of prime variety's total area
Prokupac	RHV	100		
Prosecco	RHV	100		
Provareau	VIVC	100		
Prunelard	RHV	100		
Prunesta	RHV	100		
Putzscheere	VIVC	100		
Quagliano	RHV	100		
Quebranta	RHV	100		
Rabigato	RHV	100		
Rabo de Ovelha	RHV	100		
Raboso Piave	RHV	100		
Raboso Veronese	RHV	100		
Raffiat de Moncade	RHV	100		
Raisaine	VIVC	100		
Ramisco	RHV	100		
Rauschling	RHV	100		
Ravat	VIVC	0	Ravat Divers	100
Ravat Blanc	RHV	100		
Rayon d'Or	RHV	100		
Rebo	RHV	100		
Red Globe	VIVC	100		
Red Semillon		100		
Refosco	RHV	100		
Refosco dal Peduncolo Rosso	RHV	100		
Refosco di Faedis	RHV	0	Refosco Nostrano	100
Regent	RHV	100		
Regina	VIVC	100		
Regner	RHV	100		
Reichensteiner	RHV	100		
Retagliado Bianco	RHV	100		
Reze	RHV	100		
Ribolla Gialla	RHV	20	Rebula	80
Rieslaner	RHV	100		
Riesling	RHV	17	Riesling Weisser	52
Rio Grande	RHV	100		
Riton	VIVC	100		
Rkatsiteli	RHV	69	Rkatiteli	17
Robola	RHV	0	Rombola	100
Roditis	RHV	100		
Roditis(Red)		100		
Rojal Tinta	VIVC	100		
Rollo	RHV	92	Livornese Bianca	8
Rombola Red		100		

Table 25 (cont.) Source of prime varietal name and its main synonym, and their shares of prime variety's global area, 2000

Prime variety	Source of prime name	Share (%) of prime variety's total area	Name of main synonym	Share (%) of prime variety's total area
Rome	RHV	100		
Romeiko	RHV	100		
Romorantin	RHV	100		
Rondinella	RHV	100		
Roobernet	VIVC	100		
Rosa Arica		100		
Rose du Var	RHV	0	Roussanne du Var	100
Rossara Trentina	RHV	0	Rossara	100
Rossese	RHV	100		
Rossignola	RHV	100		
Rossola Nera	RHV	100		
Roter Veltliner	RHV	100		
Rotgipfler	RHV	100		
Roublot	VIVC	100		
Rougeon	VIVC	100		
Roussanne	RHV	100		
Roussette d'Ayze	RHV	100		
Roussin	RHV	100		
Royalty	RHV	100		
Rubilande	VIVC	100		
Rubin Tairovsky	RHV	0	Rubin Tairovski	100
Rubinovy Magaracha	RHV	100		
Rubired	RHV	100		
Ruby	VIVC	100		
Ruby Cabernet	RHV	100	Rubi Cabernet	0
Ruby Seedless	VIVC	100		
Ruche	RHV	100		
Rufete	RHV	88	Tinta Pinheira	12
Sacy	RHV	100		
Sagrantino	RHV	100		
Saint Macaire	RHV	100		
Saint-Pierre Dore	VIVC	100		
Salvador	RHV	100		
San Giuseppe Nero	RHV	100		
San Lunardo	RHV	100		
San Martino	RHV	100		
San Michele	RHV	100		
Sangiovese	RHV	97	Nielluccio	2
Sankt Laurent	RHV	0	St. Laurent	100
Santa Maria	RHV	100		
Saperavi	RHV	100		
Saperavi Severny	RHV	0	Saperavi Severnii	100
Sauvignon Blanc	RHV	46	Sauvignon	53

Table 25 (cont.) Source of prime varietal name and its main synonym, and their shares of prime variety's global area, 2000

Prime variety	Source of prime name	Share (%) of prime variety's total area	Name of main synonym	Share (%) of prime variety's total area
Sauvignon Gris	RHV	100		
Sauvignon Rose	RHV	100		
Sauvignonasse	RHV	15	Tocai Friulano	83
Savagnin Blanc	RHV	100		
Savagnin Rose	RHV	100		
Savatiano	RHV	0	Savvatiano	100
Scheurebe	RHV	100		
Schiava	RHV	100		
Schiava Gentile	RHV	100		
Schiava Grigia	RHV	100		
Schiava Grossa	RHV	99	Tschaggele	1
Schioppettino	RHV	100		
Schonburger	RHV	100		
Sciaglin	RHV	100		
Sciascinoso	RHV	54	Olivella Nera	46
Seara Nova	RHV	100		
Segalin	RHV	100		
Seibel		0	Seibel Hybrids	99
Seibel White		0	Seibel Divers	100
Seinoir	VIVC	100		
Select	VIVC	100		
Semebat	VIVC	100		
Semidano	RHV	100		
Semillon	RHV	100	Semigion	0
Sercial	RHV	8	Esganoso	92
Servanin	VIVC	100		
Servant	RHV	19	Raisin Blanc	81
Seyval Blanc	RHV	91	Seyval	9
Sgavetta	RHV	100		
Shiroka Melnishka	RHV	100		
Siegerrebe	RHV	100		
Silcher	VIVC	100		
Silvaner	RHV	45	Sylvaner	52
Siria	RHV	0	Roupeiro Branco	55
Sirio	VIVC	100		
Soperga	RHV	100		
Stavroto	RHV	100		
Sugra Five	VIVC	100		
Sukholimanskiy Bely	RHV	63	Suholimenschii Belii	37
Sultaniye	RHV	28	Sultana	72
Sumoll	RHV		Vijiriego Negro	1
Superior Seedless		100		
Susumaniello	RHV	100		

Table 25 (cont.) Source of prime varietal name and its main synonym, and their shares of prime variety's global area, 2000

Prime variety	Source of prime name	Share (%) of prime variety's total area	Name of main synonym	Share (%) of prime variety's total area
Symphony	RHV	100		
Syrah	RHV	65	Shiraz	34
Tamarez	RHV	100		
Taminga	RHV	100		
Tannat	RHV	100		
Tarrango	RHV	100		
Tavkveri	RHV	100		
Taylor	VIVC	100		
Tazzelenghe	RHV	100		
Teinturier	RHV	100		
Telti Kyryk		100		
Tempranillo	RHV	88	Tinta Roriz	6
Teneron	VIVC	0	Valency	100
Teoulier Noir	RHV	0	Teoulier	100
Teroldego	RHV	100		
Terrano	RHV	100		
Terrantez	RHV	100		
Terras 20	VIVC	0	Alicante Terras 20	100
Terret Blanc	RHV	100		
Terret Gris	RHV	100		
Terret Noir	RHV	100		
Therona	VIVC	100		
Tibouren	RHV	100		
Timorasso	RHV	100		
Tinta Barroca	RHV	93	Tinta Barocca	7
Tinta Carvalha	RHV	100		
Tinto Basto	VIVC	100		
Tinto Cao	RHV	100		
Tinto de la Pampana Blanca	VIVC	100		
Tinto de Zafra		100		
Tinto Jeroma		100		
Tinto Velasco	RHV	100		
Torbato	RHV	83	Tourbat	17
Torrontes Riojano	RHV	100		
Torrontes Sanjuanino	RHV	100		
Tortosina	VIVC	100		
Touriga Franca	RHV	100		
Touriga Nacional	RHV	95	Tourigo	3
Trajadura	RHV	74	Treixadura	26
Traminette	RHV	100		
Trebbiano	RHV	100		
Trebbiano d'Abruzzo	RHV	0	Trebbiano Abruzzese	100
Trebbiano Giallo	RHV	100		

Table 25 (cont.) Source of prime varietal name and its main synonym, and their shares of prime variety's global area, 2000

Prime variety	Source of prime name	Share (%) of prime variety's total area	Name of main synonym	Share (%) of prime variety's total area
Trebbiano Modenese	RHV	100		
Trebbiano Romagnolo	RHV	100		
Trebbiano Spoletino	RHV	100		
Trebbiano Toscano	RHV	29	Ugni Blanc	70
Trepat	RHV	66	Bonicaire	31
Tressot	RHV	100		
Trevisana Nera	RHV	100		
Tribidrag	RHV	0	Zinfandel	71
Trincadeira	RHV	97	Tinta Amarela	2
Trincadeira das Pratas	RHV	100		
Trobat	VIVC	0	Panse Negro	100
Trousseau	RHV	6	Bastardo	83
Trousseau Gris	VIVC	0	Gray Riesling	100
Tsitska	RHV	100		
Tsolikouri	RHV	100		
Tsulukidzis Tetra	RHV	100		
Ucelut	RHV	100		
Uni Blan		100		
Usakhelouri	RHV	100		
Uva Cao	VIVC	100		
Uva Rara	RHV	100		
Uva Tosca	RHV	100		
Valais Noir	VIVC	100		
Valdiguie	RHV	100		
Valenci Tinto	VIVC	0	Grumier Tinto	100
Valentino Nero	RHV	0	Valentino	100
Valerien	VIVC	100		
Varousset	VIVC	100		
Vasilaki	RHV	100		
Vega	RHV	100		
Ventura	VIVC	100		
Verdea	RHV	100		
Verdeca	RHV	100		
Verdejo	RHV	0	Verdejo Blanco	100
Verdelho	RHV	100		
Verdelho Tinto	VIVC	100		
Verdello	RHV	100		
Verdesse	RHV	100		
Verdicchio Bianco	RHV	66	Trebbiano di Soave	34
Verdil	RHV	100		
	RHV	91	Pedevenda	9
Verdoncho	RHV	100		
Verduschia	VIVC	100		

Table 25 (cont.) Source of prime varietal name and its main synonym, and their shares of prime variety's global area, 2000

Prime variety	Source of prime name	Share (%) of prime variety's total area	Name of main synonym	Share (%) of prime variety's total area
Verduzzo Friulano	RHV	100		
Verduzzo Trevigiano	RHV	100		
Vermentino	RHV	91	Favorita	5
Vermentino Nero	RHV	100		
Vernaccia di Oristano	RHV	100		
Vernaccia di San Gimignano	RHV	90	Bervedino	10
Vertzami	RHV	100		
Vespaiola	RHV	100		
Vespolina	RHV	100		
Vidal	RHV	0	Vidal Blanc	100
Vidal Red		0	Vidal Divers	100
Vien de Nus	RHV	100		
Vignoles	RHV	51	Ravat 51	49
Vijariego	RHV	100	Diego	0
Vilana	RHV	100		
Vilana(Red)		100		
Villard Blanc	RHV	100		
Villard Noir	VIVC	100		
Vineti		100		
Vinhao	RHV	89	Souson	10
Viognier	RHV	99	Viogner	1
Viorica	VIVC	100		
Viosinho	RHV	100		
Vital	RHV	100		
Vitovska	RHV	0	Vitouska	100
Voskeat	RHV	0	Voskehat	100
Vuillermin	RHV	100		
Weldra	VIVC	100		
Xarello	RHV	0	Xarello Blanco	100
Xarello Rosado	VIVC	0	Pansa Rosada	100
Xinomavro	RHV	100		
Xinomavro (White)		100		
Xynisteri	RHV	100		
Yaqui	VIVC	100		
Zalagyongye	RHV	100		
Zalema	RHV	100		
Zenit	RHV	100		
Zierfandler	RHV	100		
Zoumiatiko Red		100		
Zweigelt	RHV	100		

Table 26: Source of prime varietal name and its main synonym, and their shares of prime variety's global area, 2010

Summary of data in this table				
Source*	Number of varieties	Share (%) of no. of varieties	Area (hectares)	Share (%) of global area
RHV	891	70	4262462	92.6
VIVC	334	26	72986	1.6
Unknown	46	4	265997	5.8
Total	**1271**	**100**	**4601445**	**100**

*RHV = Jancis Robinson, Julia Harding, Josê Vouillamoz, *Wine Grapes*, London Allen Lane, 2012
VIVC = *Vitis International Variety Catalogue*, http://www.vivc.de

Prime variety	Source of prime name	Share (%) of prime variety's total area	Name of main synonym	Share (%) of prime variety's total area
Abbo	VIVC	0	Abbou	100
Abbuoto	RHV	100		
Abouriou	RHV	100		
Abrusco	RHV	100	Colorino	0
Acolon	RHV	100		
Adakarasi	RHV	100		
Afus Ali	VIVC	0	Roseti	100
Agiorgitiko	RHV	100		
Aglianico	RHV	76	Aglianico del Vulture	24
Aglianicone	RHV	100		
Agni	RHV	100		
Agronomica	RHV	100		
Agua Santa	RHV	100		
Airen	RHV	100	Forcallat Blanca	0
Aladasturi	RHV	100		
Alarije	RHV	100	Malfar	0
Alb de Ialoveni	VIVC	100		
Albana	RHV	100		
Albanello	RHV	100		
Albaranzeuli Bianco	RHV	100		
Albaranzeuli Nero	RHV	100		
Albarin Blanco	RHV	100		
Albarola	RHV	97	Bianchetta Genovese	3
Albarossa	RHV	100		
Albillo Mayor	RHV	99	Albilla	1
Albillo Real	RHV	0	Albillo	100

Table 26 (cont.) Source of prime varietal name and its main synonym, and their shares of prime variety's global area, 2010

Prime variety	Source of prime name	Share (%) of prime variety's total area	Name of main synonym	Share (%) of prime variety's total area
Alcanon	RHV	100		
Aleatico	RHV	100		
Aledo	VIVC	100		
Aleksandrouli	RHV	100		
Aletta	VIVC	100		
Alfrocheiro	RHV	99	Bastarda Negra	1
Alicante Henri Bouschet	RHV	13	Garnacha Tintorera	50
Aligote	RHV	100		
Alionza	RHV	100		
Almafre	VIVC	0	Almafra	100
Alminhaca	VIVC	0	Almenhaca	100
Alphonse Lavallee	VIVC	94	Alfonso Lavalle	6
Altesse	RHV	100		
Alvar Branco	VIVC	0	Alvar	100
Alvar Roxo	VIVC	100		
Alvarelhao	RHV	30	Pilongo	59
Alvarelhao Ceitao	VIVC	100		
Alvarinho	RHV	36	Albarino	64
Amaral	RHV	100		
Amigne	RHV	100		
Amur	VIVC	100		
Ancellotta	RHV	100		
Andre	RHV	100		
Antao Vaz	RHV	100		
Ar110		100		
Ar99		100		
Aramon Noir	RHV	0	Aramon	100
Arany Sarfeher	RHV	100	Sarfeher	0
Argelina	VIVC	100		
Ariana	VIVC	100		
Arinarnoa	RHV	100		
Arinto de Bucelas	RHV	0	Arinto	100
Arinto Roxo	VIVC	100		
Arjuncao	VIVC	100		
Arneis	RHV	100		
Arnsburger	RHV	100		
Arriloba	RHV	100		
Arvesiniadu	RHV	100		
Arvine	RHV	89	Petite Arvine	11
Asirtiko Red		100		
Aspiran Bouschet	RHV	100		
Asprouda		0	Asproudi	100
Assaraky	VIVC	100		

Prime variety	Source of prime name	Share (%) of prime variety's total area	Name of main synonym	Share (%) of prime variety's total area
Assyrtiko	RHV	0	Asirtiko	100
Athiri	RHV	100		
Aubun	RHV	100		
Aurelius	RHV	100		
Aurore	RHV	0	Aurora	100
Auxerrois	RHV	100		
Avana	RHV	100		
Avarengo	RHV	100		
Avesso	RHV	100		
Azal	RHV	100		
Babeasca Gris	VIVC	0	Babeasca Gri	100
Babeasca Neagra	RHV	97	Rara Neagra	3
Babic	RHV	100		
Babica	RHV	100		
Babosa de Madere	VIVC	0	Babosa	100
Bacchus	RHV	100		
Baco Blanc	RHV	100		
Baco Noir	RHV	99	Baco	1
Baga	RHV	100	Carrega Burros	0
Bailey	VIVC	100		
Bakator Roz	VIVC	0	Piros Bakator	100
Baratuciat	RHV	100		
Barbera	RHV	100		
Barbera Bianca	RHV	100		
Barbera Sarda	RHV	100		
Barcelo	RHV	100		
Barkhatnyi	VIVC	0	Barkhatny	100
Baroque	RHV	100		
Barreto de Semente	VIVC	0	Barreto	100
Barsaglina	RHV	100		
Bastardo Branco	VIVC	100		
Bastardo Magarachsky	RHV	0	Bastardo Magarachskiy	56
Batily		100		
Batoca	RHV	100		
Bayanshira	RHV	0	Bayan-shirey	100
Beba	RHV	97	Teta de Vaca	2
Bellone	RHV	100		
Bequignol Noir	RHV	0	Bequignol	100
Bianca	RHV	100		
Biancame	RHV	100		
Bianchetta Trevigiana	RHV	100		
Bianco d'Alessano	RHV	100		
Biancolella	RHV	100		

Table 26 (cont.) Source of prime varietal name and its main synonym, and their shares of prime variety's global area, 2010

Prime variety	Source of prime name	Share (%) of prime variety's total area	Name of main synonym	Share (%) of prime variety's total area
Biancone Di Portoferraio	RHV	0	Biancone	100
Biborkadarka	RHV	0	Bibor Kadarka	100
Bical	RHV	100		
Black Queen	RHV	100		
Blanc du Bois	RHV	100		
Blanca Ovoide		100		
Blattner Reds	VIVC	100		
Blattner Whites	VIVC	100		
Blauburger	RHV	100		
Blauer Portugieser	RHV	75	Modry Portugal	19
Blauer Wildbacher	RHV	99	Wildbacher	1
Blaufrankisch	RHV	70	Frankovka	10
Boal Barreiro	VIVC	100		
Boal Vencedor	VIVC	0	Vencedor	100
Bobal	RHV	100		
Bogazkere	RHV	100		
Bogdanusa	RHV	100		
Bombino Bianco	RHV	100		
Bombino Nero	RHV	100		
Bonamico	RHV	14	Buonamico	86
Bonda	RHV	100		
Bondola	RHV	100		
Bordo	RHV	100		
Borracal	RHV	23	Caino Tinto	77
Bosco	RHV	100		
Bourboulenc	RHV	100		
Bouvier	RHV	98	Bouvierovo Hrozno	2
Bracciola Nera	RHV	100		
Brachetto del Piemonte	RHV	0	Brachetto	100
Branco Especial	VIVC	100		
Branco Sr. Joao	VIVC	0	Branco Joao	100
Branco Valente	VIVC	0	Valente	100
Brandam	VIVC	0	Branda	100
Breidecker	RHV	100		
Brianna	RHV	100		
Bric	VIVC	100		
Bronner	RHV	100		
Budai Zold	RHV	100		
Bukettraube	RHV	100		
Bussanello	RHV	100		
Busuioaca de Bohotin	RHV	100		
Caberinta	RHV	100		
Cabernet Cortis	RHV	100		

Table 26 (cont.) Source of prime varietal name and its main synonym, and their shares of prime variety's global area, 2010

Prime variety	Source of prime name	Share (%) of prime variety's total area	Name of main synonym	Share (%) of prime variety's total area
Cabernet Cubin	RHV	100		
Cabernet Diane		100		
Cabernet Dore		100		
Cabernet Dorio	RHV	100		
Cabernet Dorsa	RHV	100		
Cabernet Franc	RHV	100		
Cabernet Jura	RHV	100		
Cabernet Mitos	RHV	100		
Cabernet Moravia	RHV	100		
Cabernet Sauvignon	RHV	100	Burdeos	0
Cabinda	VIVC	100		
Cabral	VIVC	0	Malvasia Cabral	100
Caddiu	RHV	100		
Cainho de Moreira	VIVC	0	Cainho	100
Caino Blanco	RHV	100		
Caladoc	RHV	100		
Calagrano	RHV	100		
California	VIVC	100		
Calkarasi	RHV	100		
Callet	RHV	100		
Caloria	RHV	100		
Calrao	VIVC	100		
Camaralet de Lasseube	RHV	0	Camarate	100
Campanario	VIVC	100		
Campbell Early	RHV	100		
Canadice	VIVC	100		
Canaiolo Nero	RHV	100		
Canaiolo Rosa	VIVC	100		
Canari Noir	RHV	0	Canari	91
Canela	VIVC	100		
Canelon	VIVC	100		
Capolongo		100		
Caracol	RHV	100		
Caramela	VIVC	100		
Cardinal	RHV	52	Cardenal	31
Carica l'Asino	RHV	100		
Carignan Blanc	VIVC	13	Carinena Blanco	87
Carmenere	RHV	88	Cabernet Gernischt	12
Carminoir	RHV	100		
Carnelian	RHV	100		
Carrega Branco	RHV	100		
Carrega Tinto	VIVC	100		
Carricante	RHV	100		

Table 26 (cont.) Source of prime varietal name and its main synonym, and their shares of prime variety's global area, 2010

Prime variety	Source of prime name	Share (%) of prime variety's total area	Name of main synonym	Share (%) of prime variety's total area
Casavecchia	RHV	100		
Casculho	VIVC	100		
Casetta	RHV	100		
Castalia	VIVC	100		
Castel	VIVC	100		
Castela	VIVC	100		
Castelao	RHV	100	Periquita	0
Castelao Branco	VIVC	100		
Castelino	VIVC	100		
Castelo Branco	VIVC	100		
Castiglione	RHV	100		
Catalanesca	RHV	100		
Catanese Nero	RHV	100		
Catarratto Bianco	RHV	0	Catarratto Bianco Comune	74
Catawba	RHV	100		
Cavrara	RHV	100		
Cavus	RHV	100		
Cayetana Blanca	RHV	0	Pardina	67
Cayuga White	RHV	79	Cayuga	21
Cellerina	VIVC	0	Slarina	100
Centesimino	RHV	100		
Centurian	RHV	100		
Cerceal Branco	RHV	0	Cercial	100
Cereza	RHV	100		
Cesanese	RHV	0	Cesanese d'Affile	55
Cetinka	RHV	100		
Chambourcin	RHV	100		
Chancellor	RHV	100		
Chardonel	RHV	100		
Chardonnay	RHV	99	Chardonnay Blanc	1
Charmont	RHV	100		
Chasan	RHV	100		
Chasselas	RHV	91	Gutedel Weisser	8
Chasselas Rouge	VIVC	0	Chasselas Roxo	100
Chasselas Sabor	VIVC	100		
Chatus	RHV	100		
Chelois	RHV	100		
Chelva	RHV	100		
Chenanson	RHV	100		
Chenel	RHV	100		
Chenin Blanc	RHV	65	Chenin	35
Chinuri	RHV	100		
Chkhaveri	RHV	100		

Table 26 (cont.) Source of prime varietal name and its main synonym, and their shares of prime variety's global area, 2010

Prime variety	Source of prime name	Share (%) of prime variety's total area	Name of main synonym	Share (%) of prime variety's total area
Cianorie	RHV	0	Cjanorie	100
Cidreiro	VIVC	100		
Ciliegiolo	RHV	100		
Cinsaut	RHV	64	Cinsault	36
Cinsaut Blanc	VIVC	100		
Cinsaut Seedless		100		
Citronny Magarach	RHV	0	Citronny of Magarach	100
Cividin	RHV	100		
Clairette	RHV	89	Clairette Blanche	10
Clairette Rose	VIVC	100		
Cococciola	RHV	100		
Coda di Volpe Bianca	RHV	95	Guarnaccia	5
Codega de Larinho	RHV	0	Codega do Larinho	100
Codrinski	VIVC	100		
Colgadero	VIVC	100		
Colobel	RHV	100		
Colombana Nera	RHV	100		
Colombard	RHV	31	Colombar	37
Colomino	RHV	100		
Coloraillo	RHV	100		
Completer	RHV	100		
Complexa	RHV	100		
Concieira	VIVC	100		
Concord	RHV	99	Concord Clone 3	1
Coracao de Galo	VIVC	100		
Corbina Vicentina	VIVC	0	Corbina	100
Cordenossa	RHV	100		
Cornalin	RHV	50	Humagne Rouge	50
Cornarea	RHV	100		
Cornifesto	RHV	100		
Corot Noir	RHV	100		
Corropio	VIVC	100		
Cortese	RHV	100		
Corvina Veronese	RHV	0	Corvina	100
Corvinone	RHV	100		
Corvo	VIVC	100		
Cot	RHV	15	Malbec	84
Couderc Noir	RHV	92	Couderc	8
Couderc	VIVC	0		100
Counoise	RHV	100		
Cove	VIVC	100		
Cramposie Selectionata	RHV	100		
Crimson Cabernet		100		

Table 26 (cont.) Source of prime varietal name and its main synonym, and their shares of prime variety's global area, 2010

Prime variety	Source of prime name	Share (%) of prime variety's total area	Name of main synonym	Share (%) of prime variety's total area
Crimson Seedless	VIVC	100		
Criolla Grande	RHV	100		
Criolla Mediana	VIVC	100		
Croatina	RHV	100		
Crouchen	RHV	100		
Crovassa	RHV	100		
Crystal	RHV	98	Cristal	2
Cs.2		100		
Csaba Gyongye	RHV	0	Csabagyongye	100
Cserszegi Fuszeres	RHV	100		
Csillam	VIVC	100		
Csokaszolo	RHV	100		
Csomorika	VIVC	100		
Dakapo	RHV	100		
Damaschino	RHV	11	Alicante Branco	50
Danlas	VIVC	100		
De Chaunac	RHV	100		
Debina	RHV	0	Dempina	100
Debit	RHV	100		
Deckrot	RHV	100		
Dekabrskii	VIVC	0	Dekabrsky	100
Delaware	RHV	100		
Deliciosa	VIVC	100		
Devin	RHV	100		
Diagalves	RHV	100		
Dimrit	RHV	100		
Dimyat	RHV	99	Zoumiatiko	0
Dindarella	RHV	100		
Diolinoir	RHV	100		
Diseca Ranina	RHV	100		
Docal	VIVC	100		
Doina	RHV	100		
Dolcetto	RHV	100		
Dolciame	RHV	100		
Domina	RHV	100		
Dominga	VIVC	100		
Dona Branca	RHV	100		
Dona Joaquina	VIVC	100		
Donzelinho Branco	RHV	100		
Donzelinho Roxo	VIVC	100		
Donzelinho Tinto	RHV	100		
Doradilla	RHV	100		
Doral	RHV	100		

Table 26 (cont.) Source of prime varietal name and its main synonym, and their shares of prime variety's global area, 2010

Prime variety	Source of prime name	Share (%) of prime variety's total area	Name of main synonym	Share (%) of prime variety's total area
Dorinto	RHV	0	Arinto do Interior	100
Dornfelder	RHV	100		
Dostoinyi	VIVC	100		
Douce Noire	RHV	0	Bonarda	99
Doukkali	VIVC	100		
Doux d'Henry	RHV	100		
Droujba	VIVC	0	Drujba	100
Drupeggio	RHV	0	Canaiolo Bianco	100
Duna Gyongye	VIVC	100		
Dunaj	RHV	100		
Dunavski Lazur	VIVC	100		
Dunkelfelder	RHV	100		
Duras	RHV	100		
Durasa	VIVC	100		
Durella	RHV	100		
Durif	RHV	13	Petite Sirah	80
Edelweiss	RHV	100		
Egiodola	RHV	100		
Ehrenfelser	RHV	100		
Ekigaina	RHV	100		
Ekim Kara	RHV	100		
Elbling	RHV	26	Elbling Weisser	39
Elvira	RHV	100		
Emerald Riesling	RHV	100		
Emir	RHV	100		
Enantio	RHV	0	Lambrusco a Foglia Frastagliata	100
Encruzado	RHV	100		
Ensanyo Tintas		100		
Ensayo Blancas		100		
Erbaluce	RHV	100		
Erbamat	RHV	100		
Erbanno	VIVC	100		
Ervi	RHV	100		
Esganacao Preto	VIVC	0	Esgana Cao Tinto	100
Esganinho	VIVC	100		
Espadeiro	RHV	100		
Espadeiro Mole	VIVC	100		
Estreito Macio	VIVC	100		
Ezerfurtu	RHV	100		
Ezerjo	RHV	100		
Faberrebe	RHV	99		1
Falanghina	VIVC	100		
Famoso	VIVC	100		

Table 26 (cont.) Source of prime varietal name and its main synonym, and their shares of prime variety's global area, 2010

Prime variety	Source of prime name	Share (%) of prime variety's total area	Name of main synonym	Share (%) of prime variety's total area
Farinheira	VIVC	100		
Fenile	RHV	100		
Fepiro	VIVC	100		
Fer	RHV	100		
Fernao Pires	RHV	100	Molinha	0
Fernao Pires Rosado	VIVC	100		
Fertilia	RHV	100		
Feteasca Alba	RHV	99	Dievcie Hrozno	1
Feteasca Neagra	RHV	100		
Feteasca Regala	RHV	100		
Fiano	RHV	100		
Fiesta	VIVC	100		
Fileri		100		
Fino de Ribera del Fresno		100		
Fintendo	VIVC	100		
Fioletovy Ranny	RHV	100		
Flame Seedless	VIVC	100		
Flavis	RHV	100		
Flora	RHV	100		
Fogarina	RHV	100		
Foglia Tonda	RHV	100		
Fogoneu	RHV	100		
Fokiano	RHV	100		
Folgasao	RHV	100		
Folgasao Roxo	VIVC	100		
Folha de Figueira	VIVC	100		
Folle Blanche	RHV	100		
Fonte Cal	RHV	100		
Forastera	RHV	100		
Forcallat Tinta	RHV	100		
Forgiarin	RHV	100		
Forsellina	RHV	100		
Fortana	RHV	63	Canina Nera	37
Francavidda	RHV	100		
Francusa	RHV	100		
Frappato	RHV	100		
Fredonia	RHV	100		
Freisa	RHV	100		
Freisamer	RHV	100		
Frontenac	RHV	100		
Frontenac Gris	VIVC	100		
Fruhroter Veltliner	RHV	50	Veltlinske Cervene Rane	26
Fubiano	RHV	100		

Table 26 (cont.) Source of prime varietal name and its main synonym, and their shares of prime variety's global area, 2010

Prime variety	Source of prime name	Share (%) of prime variety's total area	Name of main synonym	Share (%) of prime variety's total area
Fumin	RHV	100		
Furmint	RHV	84	Sipon	12
Gaglioppo	RHV	100		
Galbena de Odobesti	RHV	100		
Galego Dourado	RHV	76	Pedro Luis	19
Galotta	RHV	100		
Gamaret	RHV	100		
Gamay de Teinturier Bouze	RHV	96	Gammay de Bouze	4
Gamay Noir	RHV	1	Gamay	99
Gamay Teinturier de Chaudenay	VIVC	0	Gamay de Chaudenay	100
Gamay Teinturier Freaux	VIVC	0	Gammay Freaux	100
Gamba Rossa	VIVC	100		
Garandmak	RHV	100		
Garanoir	RHV	94	Granoir	6
Garganega	RHV	73	Grecanico Dorato	27
Gargiulo	VIVC	0	C.G.2539	75
Garnacha Blanca	VIVC	31	Grenache Blanc	69
Garnacha Peluda	RHV	65	Lledoner Pelut	35
Garnacha Roja	RHV	4	Grenache Gris	96
Garnacha Tinta	RHV	6	Grenache	58
Garrido Fino	RHV	100		
Gateta	VIVC	100		
Gegic	RHV	100		
Geisenheim	VIVC	100		
Generosa	RHV	100		
Gesztus	VIVC	100		
Gewurztraminer	RHV	41	Traminer Rose	26
Gibi	RHV	100		
Ginestra	RHV	100		
Giro	RHV	100		
Gm 322		100		
Godello	RHV	53	Gouveio	45
Goecseji Zamatos	VIVC	28	Gecsei Zamatos	72
Goher	VIVC	100		
Goldburger	RHV	100		
Golden Muscat	RHV	100		
Goldriesling	RHV	100		
Goldtraminer	VIVC	100		
Golubok	RHV	43	Goluboc	57
Goncalo Pires	VIVC	100		
Goruli Mtsvane	RHV	100		
Gosen		100		
Goustolidi	RHV	100		

Table 26 (cont.) Source of prime varietal name and its main synonym, and their shares of prime variety's global area, 2010

Prime variety	Source of prime name	Share (%) of prime variety's total area	Name of main synonym	Share (%) of prime variety's total area
Gouveio Preto	VIVC	100		
Gouveio Real	RHV	100	Gouveio Estimado	0
Gouveio Roxo	VIVC	100		
Gr 7	RHV	100		
Grachen	VIVC	100		
Graciano	RHV	73	Tinta Miuda	11
Grand Manchen		100		
Grand Noir	RHV	19	Gran Negro	81
Grangeal	VIVC	100		
Granho	VIVC	100		
Grapariol	RHV	100		
Grasa de Cotnari	RHV	93	Koverszolo	7
Grasevina	RHV	8	Italian Riesling	54
Grechetto di Orvieto	RHV	0	Grechetto	100
Grechetto Rosso	VIVC	100		
Greco	RHV	0	Asprinio	100
Greco Bianco	RHV	100		
Greco Nero	RHV	100		
Grenache Rose		100		
Grignolino	RHV	100		
Grillo	RHV	100		
Grolleau Gris	VIVC	100		
Grolleau Noir	RHV	0	Grolleau	100
Groppello di Mocasina	RHV	62	Groppello di Santo Stefano	38
Groppello di Revo	RHV	100		
Groppello Gentile	RHV	100		
Gros Manseng	RHV	100		
Grossa	RHV	100		
Gruner Veltliner	RHV	80	Veltlinske Zelene	19
Guardavalle	RHV	100		
Gutenborner	RHV	100		
Gyongyrizling	VIVC	100		
Hajnalka	VIVC	100		
Harslevelu	RHV	3	Feuille de Tilleul	89
Helfensteiner	RHV	100		
Herbemont	RHV	100		
Heroldrebe	RHV	100		
Himrod	VIVC	100		
Hondarrabi Beltza	RHV	0	Ondarrabi Beltza	99
Hrvatica	RHV	0	Negrara	100
Huerta del Rey	VIVC	100		
Humagne	RHV	0	Humagne Blanc	100
Huxelrebe	RHV	100		

Table 26 (cont.) Source of prime varietal name and its main synonym, and their shares of prime variety's global area, 2010

Prime variety	Source of prime name	Share (%) of prime variety's total area	Name of main synonym	Share (%) of prime variety's total area
Ilichevskii Rannii	VIVC	0	Iliciovski Ciornai Rannii	100
Imperial Napoleon	VIVC	100		
Imperial Seedless		100		
Impigno	RHV	100		
Incrocio Bianco Fedit 51	RHV	100		
Incrocio Bruni 54	RHV	100		
Incrocio Manzoni 2.15	RHV	100		
Incrocio Terzi 1	RHV	100		
Invernenga	RHV	100		
Inzolia	RHV	0	Ansonica	100
Irsai Oliver	RHV	100	Muskat Oliver	0
Isabella	RHV	95	Lidia	3
Italia	RHV	100		
Italica	RHV	100		
Ives	RHV	100		
J Ibanez		100		
Jacquere	RHV	100		
Jacquez	RHV	95	Lenoir	3
Jampal	RHV	100	Pinheira Branca	0
Johanniter	RHV	100		
Juan Garcia	RHV	76	Tinta Gorda	8
Jubilaumsrebe	RHV	100		
Jubileum 75	VIVC	100		
Juhfark	RHV	100		
Juliana	VIVC	100		
Jurancon Noir	RHV	100		
Juwel	RHV	100		
K.35		100		
Kabar	RHV	100		
Kadarka	RHV	49	Gamza	51
Kakotrygis	RHV	100		
Kalecik Karasi	RHV	100		
Kanaan	VIVC	100		
Kangun	VIVC	100		
Kanzler	RHV	100		
Karalahna	RHV	100		
Karasakiz	RHV	0	Kuntra	100
Karat	RHV	100		
Karmin	VIVC	100		
Kay Gray	RHV	100		
Kek Bakator		100		
Keknyelu	RHV	100		
Kerner	RHV	100	Kerner Bijeli	0

Table 26 (cont.) Source of prime varietal name and its main synonym, and their shares of prime variety's global area, 2010

Prime variety	Source of prime name	Share (%) of prime variety's total area	Name of main synonym	Share (%) of prime variety's total area
Kernling	VIVC	100		
Khikhvi	RHV	100		
Kiralyleanyka	RHV	100		
Kisi	RHV	100		
Koenigin der Weingaerten	VIVC	0	Regina dei Vigneti	100
Koksis Irma	VIVC	0	Kocsis Irma	100
Kokur Bely	RHV	0	Cokur white	100
Kolor	VIVC	100		
Korinthiaki	RHV	0	Corinto Nero	92
Korona	VIVC	100		
Koshu	RHV	100		
Kotsifali	RHV	100		
Kovidinka	RHV	95	Ruzica Crvena	5
Krakhuna	RHV	100		
Kraljevina	RHV	100		
Krasnostop Zolotovsky	RHV	0	Krasnostop Anapsky	100
Krassato	RHV	100		
Kreaca	RHV	0	Banati Rizling	100
Kujundzusa	RHV	100		
Kuldzhinskii	VIVC	0	Kuldzhinskiy	100
Kunbarat	VIVC	100		
Kunleany	RHV	100		
Kurucver	VIVC	100		
La Crescent	RHV	100		
La Crosse	RHV	100		
Labrusco	VIVC	100		
Lacrima Christi	VIVC	100		
Lacrima di Morro d'Alba	RHV	0	Lacrima	100
Lado	RHV	100		
Lagarino Bianco	RHV	100		
Lagrein	RHV	100		
Lairen	RHV	0	Malvar	100
Lakhegyi Mezes	VIVC	100		
Lambrusca di Alessandria	RHV	100		
Lambrusco	RHV	100		
Lambrusco Barghi	RHV	100		
Lambrusco di Sorbara	RHV	100		
Lambrusco Grasparossa	RHV	100		
Lambrusco Maestri	RHV	100		
Lambrusco Marani	RHV	100		
Lambrusco Montericco	RHV	100		
Lambrusco Oliva	RHV	100		
Lambrusco Salamino	RHV	100		

Table 26 (cont.) Source of prime varietal name and its main synonym, and their shares of prime variety's global area, 2010

Prime variety	Source of prime name	Share (%) of prime variety's total area	Name of main synonym	Share (%) of prime variety's total area
Lambrusco Viadanese	RHV	100		
Lameiro	VIVC	100		
Landot Noir	RHV	0	Landot	100
Lariao	VIVC	100		
Lasina	RHV	100		
Laurot	RHV	100		
Leanyka	RHV	100		
Lecinaro		100		
Leira	VIVC	100		
Len de l'El	RHV	100		
Leon Millot	RHV	100		
Levokumski Sustainable		100		
Levokumsky	VIVC	100		
Liatiko	RHV	100		
Limnio	RHV	100		
Listain de Huelva	RHV	0	Manteudo	100
Listan Negro	RHV	98	Negra Commun	1
Listan Prieto	RHV	0	Pais	85
Lorena	VIVC	100		
Louise Swenson	RHV	100		
Loureiro	RHV	86	Loureiro Blanca	14
Lourela	VIVC	100		
Lumassina	RHV	100		
Lusitano	VIVC	100		
Luzidio	VIVC	100		
Macabeo	RHV	94	Macabeu	6
Maceratino	RHV	100		
Madeleine Angevine	RHV	100		
Madeleine Sylvaner	VIVC	100		
Magliocco Canino	RHV	100		
Magliocco Dolce	RHV	0	Marsigliana Nera	100
Magyarfrankos	RHV	0	Magyar Frankos	100
Maiolica	RHV	100		
Maiolina	RHV	100		
Maiskii Chernyi	VIVC	0	Mayskiy	100
Malaga Blanc	RHV	100		
Malagousia	RHV	0	Malagouzia	100
Malbo Gentile	RHV	100		
Malvarisco	VIVC	100		
Malvasia Amarela		100		
Malvasia Bianca di Basilicata	RHV	100		
Malvasia Bianca di Candia	RHV	50	Malvasia Bianca	50
Malvasia Bianca Lunga	RHV	89	Marastina	11

Table 26 (cont.) Source of prime varietal name and its main synonym, and their shares of prime variety's global area, 2010

Prime variety	Source of prime name	Share (%) of prime variety's total area	Name of main synonym	Share (%) of prime variety's total area
Malvasia Branca de Sao Jorge	RHV	100		
Malvasia Candida Roxa	VIVC	100		
Malvasia del Lazio	RHV	100		
Malvasia di Candia Aromatica	RHV	100		
Malvasia di Casorzo	RHV	100		
Malvasia di Lipari	RHV	17	Malvasia di Sardegna	37
Malvasia di Schierano	RHV	100		
Malvasia Fina	RHV	80	Torrontes	14
Malvasia Fina Roxa	VIVC	100		
Malvasia Nera di Basilicata	RHV	100		
Malvasia Nera di Brindisi	RHV	67	Malvasia Nera di Lecce	31
Malvasia Nera Lunga	RHV	100		
Malvasia Parda	VIVC	100		
Malvasia Preta	RHV	100	Pinheira Roxa	0
Malvasia Romana	VIVC	100		
Malvasia Rosa	VIVC	100		
Malvasia Trigueira	VIVC	0	Trigueira	100
Malvazija Istarska	RHV	62	Malvazija	27
Malvia	VIVC	100		
Mammolo	RHV	6	Sciaccarello	94
Mandilaria	RHV	100		
Manseng Noir	RHV	0	Ferrol	89
Manteudo Preto	VIVC	100		
Manto Negro	RHV	100		
Manzoni Bianco	RHV	100		
Manzoni Moscato	RHV	100		
Manzoni Rosa	RHV	100		
Maratheftiko	RHV	100		
Marechal Foch	RHV	81	Foch	19
Mario Feld	VIVC	100		
Marmajuelo	RHV	0	Vermejuela	100
Marquette	RHV	100		
Marquinhas	VIVC	100		
Mars	VIVC	100		
Marsanne	RHV	97	Marsanne Blanche	3
Marselan	RHV	100		
Marufo	RHV	46	Moravia Dulce	39
Marzemina Bianca	RHV	100		
Marzemino	RHV	99	Marzemina Grossa	1
Maticha	VIVC	100		
Matrai Muskotaly	RHV	100		
Matrasa	RHV	100		
Maturana Blanca	RHV	45	Maturano Bianco	55

Table 26 (cont.) Source of prime varietal name and its main synonym, and their shares of prime variety's global area, 2010

Prime variety	Source of prime name	Share (%) of prime variety's total area	Name of main synonym	Share (%) of prime variety's total area
Mauzac Blanc	RHV	0	Mauzac	100
Mavro	RHV	100		
Mavrodafni	RHV	100		
Mavrouda	RHV	0	Mavroudi	100
Mavrud	RHV	100		
Mayolet	VIVC	100		
Mazuelo	RHV	0	Carignan	70
Mazzese	RHV	100		
Medina	VIVC	100		
Melara	RHV	100		
Melhorio	VIVC	100		
Melon	RHV	100		
Mencia	RHV	74	Jaen	23
Menoir	RHV	0	Menoire	100
Menu Pineau	RHV	0	Orbois	100
Merlese	VIVC	100		
Merlot	RHV	100		
Merlot Blanc	VIVC	100		
Merseguera	RHV	100		
Mezes Feher	RHV	0	Mezes	100
Michele Parlieri	VIVC	100		
Michurinetz	VIVC	100		
Miguel del Arco	VIVC	92	Vidau	8
Milia	RHV	100		
Mindelo	VIVC	100		
Minella Bianca	RHV	100		
Misket Cherven	RHV	100		
Misket Varnenski	RHV	100		
Molinara	RHV	83	Molinera	17
Monastrell	RHV	84	Mourvedre	14
Mondet	VIVC	100		
Mondeuse Noire	RHV	0	Mondeuse	99
Monemvassia	RHV	0	Monemvasia	100
Monica Nera	RHV	100		
Monstruosa	RHV	0	Monstruosa de Monterrei	100
Montepulciano	RHV	100	Cordisco	0
Montonico Bianco	RHV	100		
Monvedro	RHV	100		
Moore's Diamond	RHV	0	Moores Diamond	100
Moradella	RHV	100		
Moravia Agria	RHV	100		
Moreto	VIVC	100		
Morio-Muskat	RHV	0	Morio Muscat	100

Table 26 (cont.) Source of prime varietal name and its main synonym, and their shares of prime variety's global area, 2010

Prime variety	Source of prime name	Share (%) of prime variety's total area	Name of main synonym	Share (%) of prime variety's total area
Moristel	RHV	100		
Morone	RHV	100		
Moscadet	VIVC	100		
Moscargo	VIVC	100		
Moscatel Branco	VIVC	0	Moscatel Nunes	100
Moscatel Lilaz	VIVC	0	Lilas	100
Moscatel Rosada	VIVC	1	Moscatel Rosado	99
Moscatello Selvatico	RHV	100		
Moscato di Scanzo	RHV	100		
Moscato di Terracina	RHV	100		
Moscato Embrapa	VIVC	100		
Moscato Giallo	RHV	85	Moscatel Amarillo	9
Moscato Nazareno		100		
Moscato Rosa del Trentino	RHV	0	Moscato Rosa	82
Moscatuel	VIVC	100		
Moschofilero	RHV	66	Fileri	34
Moschofilero	VIVC	100		
Moschomavro	RHV	0	Moschato	100
Mostosa	RHV	100		
Mourisco de Semente	VIVC	100		
Mourisco de Trevoes	VIVC	100		
Mskhali	RHV	100		
Mtsvane Kakhuri	RHV	0	Mtsvane	100
Muller Thurgau	RHV	99	Rivaner	1
Muscadel (Red)	RHV	100		
Muscadelle	RHV	100		
Muscat a Petits Grains Noirs	VIVC	0	Moscatel Galego Tinto	100
Muscat a Petits Grains Rouge	VIVC	0	Moscatel Galego Roxo	100
Muscat Amber		100		
Muscat Bailey A	RHV	84	Muscat Bailey	16
Muscat Blanc a Petits Grains	RHV	0	Moscato Bianco	37
Muscat de Ialoveni		100		
Muscat Fleur d'Oranger	RHV	0	Muscat Orange	100
Muscat of Alexandria	RHV	29	Moscatel de Malaga	21
Muscat of Alexandria Red	VIVC	0	Red Hanepoot	100
Muscat of Hamburg	RHV	34	Muscat Hambourg	46
Muscat Ottonel	RHV	95	Muskat-Ottonel	5
Muscat Rose	VIVC	100		
Muscat Swenson	RHV	0	Muscats	100
Muscat Violet	VIVC	100		
Muskat Moravsky	RHV	100		
Mustoasa de Maderat	RHV	100		
Naia	VIVC	100		

Table 26 (cont.) Source of prime varietal name and its main synonym, and their shares of prime variety's global area, 2010

Prime variety	Source of prime name	Share (%) of prime variety's total area	Name of main synonym	Share (%) of prime variety's total area
Naparo	VIVC	100		
Narince	RHV	100		
Nascetta	RHV	100		
Nasco	RHV	100		
Nebbiera	RHV	100		
Nebbiolo	RHV	100		
Negoska	RHV	0	Negkoska	100
Negramoll	RHV	18	Negra Criolla	39
Negrette	RHV	100		
Negretto	RHV	100		
Negroamaro	RHV	100		
Negroamaro Precoce	VIVC	100		
Negru de Ialoveni	VIVC	100		
Nektar	VIVC	100		
Ner d'Ala	RHV	100		
Nerello Cappuccio	RHV	100		
Nerello Mascalese	RHV	100		
Neretta Cuneese	RHV	100		
Neretto di Bairo	RHV	100		
Nero	VIVC	100		
Nero Buono di Cori	RHV	0	Nero Buono	100
Nero d'Avola	RHV	0	Calabrese	100
Nero di Troia	RHV	100		
Neronet	RHV	100		
Neuburger	RHV	0	Neuburske	100
Nevoeira	VIVC	100		
New York Muscat	RHV	100		
Neyret	RHV	100		
Niagara	RHV	100		
Nieddera	RHV	100		
Nigra	RHV	100		
Nincusa	RHV	100		
Noah	RHV	100		
Nobling	RHV	100		
Nocera	RHV	100		
Noiret	RHV	100		
Noria	RHV	100		
Norton	RHV	69	Cynthiana	31
Nosiola	RHV	100		
Nosztori Rizling	VIVC	100		
Notardomenico	RHV	100		
Nouvelle	RHV	100		
Nuragus	RHV	100		

Table 26 (cont.) Source of prime varietal name and its main synonym, and their shares of prime variety's global area, 2010

Prime variety	Source of prime name	Share (%) of prime variety's total area	Name of main synonym	Share (%) of prime variety's total area
Odessky Cherny	RHV	0	Odessa Black	90
Odysseus	VIVC	100		
Ofthalmo	RHV	100		
Ohanes	VIVC	100		
Ojaleshi	RHV	100		
Okuzgozu	RHV	100		
Ondarrabi Zuri	VIVC	100		
Onitskanskii Belyi	VIVC	0	Onitcani	93
Optima	RHV	100		
Ora	VIVC	100		
Oraniensteiner	RHV	100		
Orion	RHV	100		
Orpheus	VIVC	100		
Orpicchio	VIVC	100		
Ortega	RHV	100		
Ortrugo	RHV	100		
Oseleta	RHV	100		
Osteiner	RHV	100		
Otskhanuri Sapere	RHV	100		
Padeiro	RHV	100		
Palatina	VIVC	100		
Palava	RHV	100		
Pallagrello Bianco	RHV	100		
Pallagrello Nero	RHV	100		
Palomino Fino	RHV	56	Listan	15
Pamid	RHV	69	Rosioara	30
Pampanaro	VIVC	100		
Pampanuto	RHV	100		
Pannon Frankos	VIVC	100		
Panse Valenciano	VIVC	0	Panse Valenciana	100
Paolina	RHV	100		
Papazkarasi	RHV	100		
Pardillo	RHV	0	Marisancho	100
Parellada	RHV	100		
Parraleta	RHV	16	Tinta Caiada	47
Parreira Matias	VIVC	100		
Pascale	RHV	91	Nieddu Mannu	9
Passau	RHV	100		
Passerina	RHV	100		
Patagonia	VIVC	100		
Patorra	VIVC	100		
Patria	VIVC	100		
Patricia	VIVC	100		

Table 26 (cont.) Source of prime varietal name and its main synonym, and their shares of prime variety's global area, 2010

Prime variety	Source of prime name	Share (%) of prime variety's total area	Name of main synonym	Share (%) of prime variety's total area
Pavana	RHV	100		
Pe Comprido	VIVC	100		
Pecorello	VIVC	100		
Pecorino	RHV	91	Uvina	9
Pecsi Szagos	VIVC	0	Zold Szagos	100
Pedral	RHV	100		
Pedro Gimenez	RHV	99	Pedro Jimenez	1
Pedro Ximenez	RHV	98	Perrum	2
Pelaverga	RHV	100		
Pelaverga Piccolo	RHV	100		
Pelso	VIVC	100		
Pepella	RHV	100		
Perera	RHV	100		
Perigo	VIVC	100		
Perla dei Vivi	VIVC	100		
Perle	RHV	100		
Perlette	VIVC	100		
Perlita		100		
Perricone	RHV	100		
Perruno	RHV	70	Royal	30
Persan	RHV	0	Becuet	100
Pervenets Magaracha	RHV	0	Pervenets of Magarach	66
Pervomaisky	RHV	0	Pervomaiskii	100
Petit Bouschet	RHV	28	Tintinha	72
Petit Courbu	RHV	100	Petit Courbou Ondarrzurizerra	100
Petit Manseng	RHV	100		
Petit Rouge	RHV	100		
Petit Verdot	RHV	93	Verdot	7
Pexem	VIVC	100		
Phoenix	RHV	100		
Picapoll Blanco	RHV	100		
Piccola Nera	RHV	100		
Picolit	RHV	100		
Piculit Neri	RHV	100		
Piedirosso	RHV	100		
Pignola Valtellinese	RHV	0	Pignola	100
Pignoletto	RHV	100		
Pignolo	RHV	100		
Pineau d'Aunis	RHV	100		
Pinella	RHV	100		
Pinot Blanc	RHV	24	Burgunder	26
Pinot Gris	RHV	44	Pinot Grigio	40
Pinot Meunier	RHV	1	Meunier	99

Table 26 (cont.) Source of prime varietal name and its main synonym, and their shares of prime variety's global area, 2010

Prime variety	Source of prime name	Share (%) of prime variety's total area	Name of main synonym	Share (%) of prime variety's total area
Pinot Noir	RHV	90	Pinot Nero	6
Pinot Noir Precoce	RHV	0	Fruhburgunder	100
Pinotage	RHV	100		
Pintes	VIVC	100		
Pintosa	VIVC	100		
Piquepoul Blanc	RHV	100		
Piquepoul Noir	RHV	0	Pical	58
Planta Mula	VIVC	100		
Planta Nova	RHV	98	Alvarelhao Branco	2
Plantet	RHV	100		
Plassa	RHV	100		
Plavac Mali	RHV	0	Plavac Mali Crni	100
Plavay	VIVC	0	Rumeni Plavec	100
Plavec Zuti	RHV	0	Plavac Zuti	100
Plavina	RHV	0	Plavina Crna	100
Podarok Magaracha	RHV	42	Magaracha's Gift	32
Poeloeske Muskotaly	VIVC	0	Poloskei Muskotaly	100
Pollera Nera	RHV	100		
Portan	RHV	100		
Portland	VIVC	100		
Posip Bijeli	RHV	100		
Poulsard	RHV	100		
Pozsonyi	VIVC	0	Pozsonyi Feher	100
Praca	VIVC	100		
Prairie Star	RHV	100		
Prensal	RHV	0	Pensal Blanco	100
Preto Cardana	VIVC	100		
Preto Martinho	RHV	99	Amostrinha	1
Prie	RHV	0	Prie Blanc	100
Prieto Picudo	RHV	100		
Primavera	VIVC	100		
Primetta	RHV	0	Prie Rouge	100
Prokupac	RHV	100		
Promissao	VIVC	100		
Prosecco	RHV	100		
Prosecco Lungo	RHV	100		
Prunesta	RHV	100		
Pugnitello	RHV	100		
Quagliano	RHV	100		
Quebranta	RHV	100		
Rabigato	RHV	97	Rabigato Franco	3
Rabigato Moreno	VIVC	100		

Table 26 (cont.) Source of prime varietal name and its main synonym, and their shares of prime variety's global area, 2010

Prime variety	Source of prime name	Share (%) of prime variety's total area	Name of main synonym	Share (%) of prime variety's total area
Rabo de Anho	VIVC	100		
Rabo de Lobo	VIVC	100		
Rabo de Ovelha	RHV	100		
Raboso Piave	RHV	94	Raboso	6
Raboso Veronese	RHV	100		
Ramisco	RHV	5	Ramisco Tinto	95
Ranfol	RHV	100		
Ranna Melnishka Loza	RHV	100		
Rathay	RHV	100		
Ratinho	VIVC	100		
Rauschling	RHV	100		
Rebo	RHV	100		
Recantina	RHV	100		
Red Globe	VIVC	100		
Red Semillon		100		
Refosco	RHV	0	Refosk	100
Refosco dal Peduncolo Rosso	RHV	100		
Refosco di Faedis	RHV	0	Refosco Nostrano	100
Refren	VIVC	100		
Regent	RHV	100		
Regina	VIVC	100		
Regner	RHV	100		
Reichensteiner	RHV	100		
Reliance	VIVC	100		
Retagliado Bianco	RHV	100		
Ribolla Gialla	RHV	37	Rebula	63
Rieslaner	RHV	100		
Rieslina	VIVC	100		
Riesling	RHV	32	Riesling Weisser	45
Riesus	RHV	100		
Rio Grande	RHV	100		
Ripolo	RHV	100		
Riton	VIVC	100		
Rkatsiteli	RHV	80	Rkatiteli	20
Robola	RHV	0	Rombola	100
Roditis	RHV	100		
Roditis(Red)		100		
Roesler	RHV	100		
Rojal Tinta	VIVC	100		
Rollo	RHV	75	Livornese Bianca	25
Rombola Red		100		
Rome	RHV	100		
Romeiko	RHV	100		

Table 26 (cont.) Source of prime varietal name and its main synonym, and their shares of prime variety's global area, 2010

Prime variety	Source of prime name	Share (%) of prime variety's total area	Name of main synonym	Share (%) of prime variety's total area
Rondinella	RHV	100		
Rondo	RHV	100		
Roobernet	VIVC	100		
Rosa Arica		100		
Rosciola Rose		100		
Rossara Trentina	RHV	0	Rossara	100
Rossese	RHV	100		
Rossese Bianco	RHV	100		
Rossignola	RHV	100		
Rossola Nera	RHV	100		
Rotberger	RHV	100		
Roter Veltliner	RHV	3	Piros Veltelini	97
Rotgipfler	RHV	100		
Rougeon	VIVC	100		
Roussanne	RHV	100		
Roussin	RHV	100		
Roviello Bianco	RHV	0		
Roxo de Vila Flor	VIVC	100	Roxo Flor	100
Roxo Rei	VIVC	100		
Royal de Alloza	RHV	0	Derechero	100
Royalty	RHV	100		
Rozala Bianca	VIVC	0	Rozalia	100
Rozsakoe	VIVC	100		
Rual	VIVC	0	Roal	100
Rubea	VIVC	100		
Rubin Golodrigi	RHV	0	Ruby of Golodryga	100
Rubin Tairovsky	RHV	0	Rubin Tairovski	100
Rubinovy Magaracha	RHV	0	Ruby Magaracha	100
Rubintos	RHV	100		
Rubired	RHV	100		
Ruby	VIVC	100		
Ruby Cabernet	RHV	99	Rubi Cabernet	1
Ruche	RHV	100		
Rufete	RHV	100	Castellana	0
Ruggine	RHV	100		
S. Mamede	VIVC	0	Sao Mamede	100
S.V. 23-512		100		
Sabrevois	RHV	100		
Sagrantino	RHV	100		
Saint Jeannet	VIVC	100		
Salvador	RHV	100		
Samarrinho	VIVC	100		
San Giuseppe Nero	RHV	100		

Table 26 (cont.) Source of prime varietal name and its main synonym, and their shares of prime variety's global area, 2010

Prime variety	Source of prime name	Share (%) of prime variety's total area	Name of main synonym	Share (%) of prime variety's total area
San Lunardo	RHV	100		
San Martino	RHV	100		
San Michele	RHV	100		
Sanforte	VIVC	100		
Sangiovese	RHV	98	Nielluccio	2
Sankt Laurent	RHV	26	Svatovavrinecke	74
Santa Maria	RHV	100		
Santarena	VIVC	0	Santareno	100
Santoal	VIVC	100		
Sao Saul	VIVC	100		
Saperavi	RHV	100		
Saperavi Severny	RHV	0	Saperavi Nothern	93
Sauvignon Blanc	RHV	51	Sauvignon	46
Sauvignon Gris	RHV	100		
Sauvignonasse	RHV	12	Tocai Friulano	66
Savagnin Blanc	RHV	30	Traminer	53
Savatiano	RHV	0	Savvatiano	100
Scheurebe	RHV	100		
Schiava	RHV	100		
Schiava Gentile	RHV	100		
Schiava Grigia	RHV	100		
Schiava Grossa	RHV	96	Tschaggele	4
Schioppettino	RHV	100		
Schonburger	RHV	100		
Sciaglin	RHV	100		
Sciascinoso	RHV	54	Olivella Nera	46
Scimiscia	RHV	100		
Seara Nova	RHV	100		
Seibel		100		
Semidano	RHV	100		
Semillon	RHV	100	Semigion	0
Sennen	VIVC	100		
Serbina	VIVC	100		
Sercial	RHV	100	Esganoso	0
Sercialinho	RHV	100		
Serna	VIVC	100		
Servant	RHV	0	Raisin Blanc	100
Sevilhao	VIVC	100		
Seyval Blanc	RHV	80	Seyval	20
Sgavetta	RHV	100		
Shiroka Melnishka	RHV	0		100
Siegerrebe	RHV	100		
Silvaner	RHV	4	Sylvaner	75

Table 26 (cont.) Source of prime varietal name and its main synonym, and their shares of prime variety's global area, 2010

Prime variety	Source of prime name	Share (%) of prime variety's total area	Name of main synonym	Share (%) of prime variety's total area
Siria	RHV	74	Malvasia Branca	12
Sirio	VIVC	100		
Skrlet	RHV	100		
Slankamenka	RHV	100		
Solaris	RHV	100		
Soperga	RHV	100		
Sovereign Opal	VIVC	100		
Spergola	RHV	100		
St Croix	RHV	100		
St Pepin	RHV	100		
St Vincent	RHV	100		
Stavroto	RHV	100		
Stepnyak	VIVC	0	Stepniak	100
Steuben	RHV	100		
Storgozia	RHV	100		
Sugra Five	VIVC	100		
Sukholimanskiy Bely	RHV	0	Suholimanskiy White	69
Sultaniye	RHV	51	Thompson Seedless	25
Sumoll	RHV	90	Vijiriego Negro	10
Superior Seedless		100		
Suscan	RHV	0	Brajda Crna	100
Susumaniello	RHV	100		
Swenson Red	RHV	100		
Symphony	RHV	100		
Syrah	RHV	60	Shiraz	29
Szeremi Zold		100		
Taltos	VIVC	100		
Tamarez	RHV	100		
Tannat	RHV	100		
Tarrango	RHV	100		
Tavkveri	RHV	100		
Tazzelenghe	RHV	100		
Teinturier	RHV	100		
Telti Kyryk		100		
Tempranillo	RHV	90	Aragonez	7
Tempranillo Blanco	RHV	100		
Teneron	VIVC	0	Valency	100
Termarina Rossa	RHV	0	Termarina	100
Teroldego	RHV	100		
Terrano	RHV	0	Teran	100
Terrantez	RHV	100		
Terrantez do Pico	RHV	100		
Terret Blanc	RHV	100		

Table 26 (cont.) Source of prime varietal name and its main synonym, and their shares of prime variety's global area, 2010

Prime variety	Source of prime name	Share (%) of prime variety's total area	Name of main synonym	Share (%) of prime variety's total area
Therona	VIVC	100		
Thrapsathiri	RHV	100		
Tibouren	RHV	100		
Timorasso	RHV	100		
Tinta Aguiar	VIVC	100		
Tinta Barroca	RHV	100	Barroco	0
Tinta Bragao	VIVC	0	Bragao	100
Tinta Carvalha	RHV	100		
Tinta da Barca	VIVC	0	Barca	100
Tinta da Melra	VIVC	0	Melra	100
Tinta de Alcoa	VIVC	0	Alcoa	100
Tinta de Cidadelhe	VIVC	0	Cidadelhe	100
Tinta de Pegoes	VIVC	0	Tinto Pegoes	100
Tinta de Porto Santo	VIVC	0	Tinta Porto Santo	100
Tinta do Rodo	VIVC	0	Rodo	100
Tinta Engomada	VIVC	0	Engomada	100
Tinta Francisca	RHV	100		
Tinta Malandra	VIVC	0	Malandra	100
Tinta Martins	VIVC	100		
Tinta Mesquita	VIVC	100		
Tinta Penajoia	VIVC	100		
Tinta Pereira	VIVC	100		
Tinta Pomar	VIVC	100		
Tinta Roseira	VIVC	0	Roseira	100
Tinta Valdosa	VIVC	0	Valdosa	100
Tinta Varejoa	VIVC	0	Varejoa	100
Tintem	VIVC	100		
Tintilia del Molise	RHV	0	Tintilia	100
Tinto Basto	VIVC	100		
Tinto Cao	RHV	100		
Tinto de la Pampana Blanca	VIVC	100		
Tinto de Zafra		100		
Tinto do Aurelio	VIVC	0	Tinta Aurelio	100
Tinto Velasco	RHV	100		
Torbato	RHV	100		
Torrontes Mendocino	VIVC	100		
Torrontes Riojano	RHV	95	Torontel	5
Torrontes Sanjuanino	RHV	100	Moscatel Austria	0
Tortosina	VIVC			
Touriga Branca	VIVC	100		
Touriga Femea	RHV	100		
Touriga Franca	RHV	0	Touriga Francesa	100
Touriga Nacional	RHV	100	Touriga	0

Table 26 (cont.) Source of prime varietal name and its main synonym, and their shares of prime variety's global area, 2010

Prime variety	Source of prime name	Share (%) of prime variety's total area	Name of main synonym	Share (%) of prime variety's total area
Trajadura	RHV	54	Treixadura	46
Traminette	RHV	100		
Trbljan	RHV	0	Trbljan Bijeli	100
Trebbianina	VIVC	100		
Trebbiano	RHV	100		
Trebbiano d'Abruzzo	RHV	0	Trebbiano Abruzzese	100
Trebbiano Giallo	RHV	100		
Trebbiano Modenese	RHV	100		
Trebbiano Romagnolo	RHV	100		
Trebbiano Spoletino	RHV	100		
Trebbiano Toscano	RHV	20	Ugni Blanc	80
Trepat	RHV	80	Bonicaire	19
Trevisana Nera	RHV	100		
Tribidrag	RHV	0	Zinfandel	62
Trilla	VIVC	100		
Trincadeira	RHV	100	Tinta Amarela	0
Trincadeira das Pratas	RHV	100		
Trincadeiro Branco	VIVC	0	Trincadeira Branca	100
Triomphe	RHV	100		
Triplett Blanc		100		
Triunfo	VIVC	100		
Trnjak	RHV	100		
Trobat	VIVC	0	Panse Negro	100
Tronto	RHV	100		
Trousseau	RHV	5	Bastardo	43
Tsimlyansky Cherny	RHV	0	Tsymlansky Black	100
Tsitska	RHV	100		
Tsolikouri	RHV	100		
Tsulukidzis Tetra	RHV	100		
Tsvetochny (Floral)		100		
Tsvetochny (Flowery)		100		
Turan	RHV	99	Agria	1
Turchetta	VIVC	100		
Ucelut	RHV	100		
Uni Blan		100		
Urreti	VIVC	100		
Usakhelouri	RHV	100		
Uva Cao	VIVC	100		
Uva del Fantini	VIVC	100		
Uva del Tunde	VIVC	100		
Uva Longanesi	RHV	100		
Uva Rara	RHV	100		
Uva Tosca	RHV	100		

Table 26 (cont.) Source of prime varietal name and its main synonym, and their shares of prime variety's global area, 2010

Prime variety	Source of prime name	Share (%) of prime variety's total area	Name of main synonym	Share (%) of prime variety's total area
Uvalino	RHV	100		
Valbom	VIVC	100		
Valdiguie	RHV	3	Napa Gamay	97
Valenci Tinto	VIVC	100		
Valentino Nero	RHV	100		
Valiant	RHV	100		
Valveirinha	VIVC	0	Valveirinho	100
Valvin Muscat	RHV	100		
Vasilaki	RHV	100		
Vega	RHV	100		
Ventura	VIVC	100		
Venus	VIVC	100		
Verdea	RHV	100		
Verdealbara	VIVC	100		
Verdeca	RHV	0	Lagorthi	100
Verdejo	RHV	0	Verdejo Blanco	100
Verdelet	VIVC	100		
Verdelho	RHV	100		
Verdelho Roxo	VIVC	100		
Verdelho Tinto	VIVC	100		
Verdello	RHV	100		
Verdesse	RHV	100		
Verdial	VIVC	0	Verdial Branco	100
Verdial Tinto	VIVC	100		
Verdicchio Bianco	RHV	68	Trebbiano di Soave	32
Verdil	RHV	100		
Verdiso	RHV	74	Pedevenda	26
Verdoncho	RHV	100		
Verduschia	VIVC	100		
Verduzzo Friulano	RHV	99	Verduzzo	1
Verduzzo Trevigiano	RHV	100		
Vermentino	RHV	94	Pigato	3
Vermentino Nero	RHV	100		
Vernaccia di Oristano	RHV	100		
Vernaccia di San Gimignano	RHV	98	Bervedino	2
Vertes Csillaga	VIVC	100		
Vertzami	RHV	71	Lefkada	29
Veruccese	VIVC	100		
Vespaiola	RHV	100		
Vespolina	RHV	100		
Victoria	VIVC	100		
Vidal	RHV	2	Vidal 256	77
Vidvizhenets				
Vien de Nus	RHV	100		

Table 26 (cont.) Source of prime varietal name and its main synonym, and their shares of prime variety's global area, 2010

Prime variety	Source of prime name	Share (%) of prime variety's total area	Name of main synonym	Share (%) of prime variety's total area
Vignoles	RHV	100		
Vijariego	RHV	99	Diego	1
Viktor	VIVC	100		
Viktoria Gyongye	VIVC	100		
Vilana	RHV	100		
Villard Blanc	RHV	100		
Villard Noir	VIVC	100		
Vincent	RHV	100		
Vinhao	RHV	77	Souson	19
Viognier	RHV	89	Viogner	11
Violeta	VIVC	100		
Viorica	VIVC	100		
Viosinho	RHV	100		
Vital	RHV	100		
Vitovska	RHV	0	Vitouska	100
Voskeat	RHV	0	Voskehat	100
Vranac	RHV	100		
Vugava	RHV	100		
Vuillermin	RHV	100		
Vulcanus	VIVC	100		
Weldra	VIVC	100		
Wurzer	RHV	100		
Xara	VIVC	100		
Xarello	RHV	0	Xarello Blanco	100
Xarello Rosado	VIVC	0	Pansa Rosada	100
Xinomavro	RHV	100		
Xynisteri	RHV	100		
Yaqui	VIVC	100		
Zalagyongye	RHV	96	Zala Dende	4
Zalema	RHV	100		
Zametovka	RHV	0	Kavcina Crna	100
Zefir	RHV	100		
Zengo	RHV	100		
Zenit	RHV	96	Zenith	4
Zeta	RHV	100		
Zeusz	RHV	100		
Zierfandler	RHV	73	Cirfandli	27
Zlahtina	RHV	100		
Zlatarica Vrgorska	RHV	0	Zlatarica	100
Zupljanka	RHV	100		
Zweigelt	RHV	90	Zweigeltrebe	10

Table Section IV: Winegrape areas for world's top varieties, by country

Table 27: National winegrape area (hectares) for world's top 30 red varieties, 2000

Country	Cabernet Sauvignon	Garnacha Tinta	Merlot	Mazuelo	Syrah	Bobal	Tempranillo	Monastrell
Algeria	1510	6040	1510	7550	1510			
Argentina	12199		5513		7915		4335	
Armenia								
Australia	24997	2139	7669	90	29295		41	948
Austria	312		112					
Brazil	587		469					
Bulgaria	10441		11169					
Canada	569		674					
Chile	35967		12825	641	2040		1	22
Croatia								
Cyprus								
Czech Rep.								
France	53413	95717	101309	95745	50676		1549	7634
Georgia	223							
Germany								
Greece	688		180		39			
Hungary	1052		486					
Italy	7682	6781	21861	1721	1025		7	
Luxembourg								
Moldova	7590		8123					
Morocco		802		1692				
N. Zealand	654		657		60			
Portugal	318						7356	
Romania	8620		7810					
Russia	1578							
Serbia								
Slovakia	156							
Slovenia			1197					
S. Africa	8824	40	4888	71	5631		14	13
Spain	4519	95800	1186	8103	86	100128	79310	67160
Switzerland	34		848		54			
Tunisia	337	2020		7576	337			337
UK								
USA	17573	4519	16875	3088	1509		201	187
Uruguay	675		1057		62			
"Missing 9"	20373	129	5549	374	1278		171	3
Total	**220890**	**213987**	**211967**	**126650**	**101516**	**100128**	**92985**	**76304**

Table 27 (cont.) National winegrape area (hectares) for world's top 30 red varieties, 2000

Country	Sangiovese	Pinot Noir	Cabernet Franc	Cinsaut	Gamay Noir	Alicante Henri Bouschet	Barbera	Montepulciano
Algeria		1510		7550		3020		
Argentina	2491	1047	207				1061	
Armenia								
Australia	372	3223	744				103	
Austria		409	27					
Brazil			405					
Bulgaria		769						
Canada		457	567		263			
Chile	123	1614	689	195		2882		
Croatia								
Cyprus								
Czech Rep.								
France	1564	26525	36094	31593	34537	8764		
Georgia								
Germany								
Greece			40	108		21		
Hungary		243	526					
Italy	62761	3287	6639	274	152	510	27175	28679
Luxembourg		66			1			
Moldova		6521						
Morocco				3940		1098		
N. Zealand		1098	118					
Portugal						675		
Romania		1740						
Russia								
Serbia								
Slovakia								
Slovenia								
	35	487	488	3533	36	8	15	
Spain		417	30		1	18321		
Switzerland		4601	16		1977			
Tunisia	842			842		842		
UK								
USA	682	5343	1189	33	684	563	4693	
Uruguay			364					
"Missing 9"	8	741	409	351	144	341		
Total	**68877**	**60099**	**48551**	**48419**	**37796**	**37043**	**33048**	**28679**

Table 27 (cont.) National winegrape area (hectares) for world's top 30 red varieties, 2000

Country	Isabella	Tribidrag	Criolla Grande	Cot	Pamid	Douce Noire	Negroamaro	Doukkali
Algeria								
Argentina			24641	16347		14989		
Armenia								
Australia				429				
Austria								
Brazil	14285							
Bulgaria					22581			
Canada								
Chile		91		929				
Croatia								
Cyprus								
Czech Rep.								
France		1		6129		1		
Georgia								
Germany								
Greece					15			
Hungary					121			
Italy		7828		251		2642	16619	
Luxembourg								
Moldova	11401			39				
Morocco								16557
N. Zealand				67				
Portugal								
Romania								
Russia								
Serbia								
Slovakia								
Slovenia								
S. Africa		28		76				
Spain				23				
Switzerland				0				
Tunisia		337						
UK								
USA	16	18630		97		21		
Uruguay								
"Missing 9"	1673			16				
Total	**27376**	**26915**	**24641**	**24402**	**22718**	**17653**	**16619**	**16557**

Table 27 (cont.) National winegrape area (hectares) for world's top 30 red varieties, 2000

Country	Listan Prieto	Prokupac	Castelao	Mencia	Blaufrankisch	Concord	Other Red	Total Red
Algeria								30200
Argentina							12064	102809
Armenia								
Australia							7703	77752
Austria						2641	9477	12977
Brazil						2509	13465	31721
Bulgaria							13313	58273
Canada						977	1234	4740
Chile	15181						13736	86936
Croatia					1189		13895	15084
Cyprus							14625	14625
Czech Rep.					680		2719	3399
France							43439	594692
Georgia							4340	4563
Germany							7067	7067
Greece							25164	26254
Hungary					6920		11591	20939
Italy					111		132926	328933
Luxembourg								67
Moldova							2067	35741
Morocco							20098	44187
N. Zealand							171	2825
Portugal			14424	1971			93592	118336
Romania							43406	61576
Russia							9128	10706
Serbia		15180					6210	21390
Slovakia					1091		1402	2649
Slovenia							4906	6103
S. Africa							9659	33846
Spain	11			11166			70061	456322
Switzerland							382	7913
Tunisia							3367	16836
UK							200	200
USA	340				45	8330	11510	96126
Uruguay							6397	8555
"Missing 9"					203		11844	43608
Total	**15532**	**15180**	**14424**	**13138**	**12879**	**11816**	**621159**	**2387950**

Table 28: National shares (%) of global winegrape area for world's top 30 red varieties, 2000

Country	Cabernet Sauvignon	Garnacha Tinta	Merlot	Mazuelo	Syrah	Bobal	Tempranillo	Monastrell
Algeria	0.68	2.82	0.71	5.96	1.49			
Argentina	5.52		2.60		7.80		4.66	
Armenia								
Australia	11.32	1.00	3.62	0.07	28.86		0.04	1.24
Austria	0.14		0.05					
Brazil	0.27		0.22					
Bulgaria	4.73		5.27					
Canada	0.26		0.32					
Chile	16.28		6.05	0.51	2.01		0.00	0.03
Croatia								
Cyprus								
Czech Rep.								
France	24.18	44.73	47.79	75.60	49.92		1.67	10.00
Georgia	0.10							
Germany								
Greece	0.31		0.08		0.04			
Hungary	0.48		0.23					
Italy	3.48	3.17	10.31	1.36	1.01		0.01	
Luxembourg								
Moldova	3.44		3.83					
Morocco		0.37		1.34				
N. Zealand	0.30		0.31		0.06			
Portugal	0.14						7.91	
Romania	3.90		3.68					
Russia	0.71							
Serbia								
Slovakia	0.07							
Slovenia			0.56					
S. Africa	3.99	0.02	2.31	0.06	5.55		0.01	0.02
Spain	2.05	44.77	0.56	6.40	0.09	100.00	85.29	88.02
Switzerland	0.02		0.40		0.05			
Tunisia	0.15	0.94		5.98	0.33			0.44
UK								
USA	7.96	2.11	7.96	2.44	1.49		0.22	0.25
Uruguay	0.31		0.50		0.06			
"Missing 9"	9.22	0.06	2.62	0.30	1.26		0.18	0.00
Total	**100**	**100**	**100**	**100**	**100**	**100**	**100**	**100**

Table 28 (cont.) National shares (%) of global winegrape area for world's top 30 red varieties, 2000

Country	Sangiovese	Pinot Noir	Cabernet Franc	Cinsaut	Gamay Noir	Alicante Henri Bouschet	Barbera	Montepulciano
Algeria		2.51		15.59		8.15		
Argentina	3.62	1.74	0.43				3.21	
Armenia								
Australia	0.54	5.36	1.53				0.31	
Austria		0.68	0.06					
Brazil			0.83					
Bulgaria		1.28						
Canada		0.76	1.17		0.70			
Chile	0.18	2.69	1.42	0.40		7.78		
Croatia								
Cyprus								
Czech Rep.								
France	2.27	44.14	74.34	65.25	91.38	23.66		
Georgia								
Germany								
Greece			0.08	0.22		0.06		
Hungary		0.40	1.08					
Italy	91.12	5.47	13.67	0.57	0.40	1.38	82.23	100.00
Luxembourg		0.11			0.00			
Moldova		10.85						
Morocco				8.14		2.96		
N. Zealand		1.83	0.24					
Portugal						1.82		
Romania		2.90						
Russia								
Serbia								
Slovakia								
Slovenia								
	0.05	0.81	1.01	7.30	0.10	0.02	0.05	
Spain		0.69	0.06		0.00	49.46		
Switzerland		7.66	0.03		5.23			
Tunisia	1.22			1.74		2.27		
UK								
USA	0.99	8.89	2.45	0.07	1.81	1.52	14.20	
Uruguay			0.75					
"Missing 9"	0.01	1.23	0.84	0.73	0.38	0.92		
Total	**100**	**100**	**100**	**100**	**100**	**100**	**100**	**100**

Table 28 (cont.) National shares (%) of global winegrape area for world's top 30 red varieties, 2000

Country	Isabella	Tribidrag	Criolla Grande	Cot	Pamid	Douce Noire	Negroamaro	Doukkali
Algeria								
Argentina			100.00	66.99		84.91		
Armenia								
Australia				1.76				
Austria								
Brazil	52.18							
Bulgaria					99.40			
Canada								
Chile		0.34		3.81				
Croatia								
Cyprus								
Czech Rep.								
France		0.01		25.12		0.00		
Georgia								
Germany								
Greece					0.07			
Hungary					0.53			
Italy		29.08		1.03		14.97	100.00	
Luxembourg								
Moldova	41.65			0.16				
Morocco								100.00
N. Zealand				0.27				
Portugal								
Romania								
Russia								
Serbia								
Slovakia								
Slovenia								
S. Africa		0.10		0.31				
Spain				0.09				
Switzerland				0.00				
Tunisia		1.25						
UK								
USA	0.06	69.22		0.40		0.12		
Uruguay								
"Missing 9"	6.11			0.07				
Total	**100**	**100**	**100**	**100**	**100**	**100**	**100**	**100**

Table 28 (cont.) National shares (%) of global winegrape area for world's top 30 red varieties, 2000

Country	Listan Prieto	Prokupac	Castelao	Mencia	Blaufrankisch	Concord	Other Red	Total Red
Algeria								1.26
Argentina							1.94	4.31
Armenia								
Australia							1.24	3.26
Austria					20.50		1.53	0.54
Brazil						21.23	2.17	1.33
Bulgaria							2.14	2.44
Canada						8.27	0.20	0.20
Chile	97.74						2.21	3.64
Croatia					9.23		2.24	0.63
Cyprus							2.35	0.61
Czech Rep.					5.28		0.44	0.14
France							6.99	24.90
Georgia							0.70	0.19
Germany							1.14	0.30
Greece							4.05	1.10
Hungary					53.73		1.87	0.88
Italy					0.86		21.40	13.77
Luxembourg								0.00
Moldova							0.33	1.50
Morocco							3.24	1.85
N. Zealand							0.03	0.12
Portugal			100.00	15.01			15.07	4.96
Romania							6.99	2.58
Russia							1.47	0.45
Serbia		100.00					1.00	0.90
Slovakia					8.47		0.23	0.11
Slovenia							0.79	0.26
S. Africa							1.56	1.42
Spain	0.07			84.99			11.28	19.11
Switzerland							0.06	0.33
Tunisia							0.54	0.71
UK							0.03	0.01
USA	2.19				0.35	70.50	1.85	4.03
Uruguay							1.03	0.36
"Missing 9"					1.57		1.91	1.83
Total	**100**	**100**	**100**	**100**	**100**	**100**	**100**	**100**

Table 29: Shares (%) of world's top 30 red varieties in national winegrape area, by country, 2000

Country	Cabernet Sauvignon	Garnacha Tinta	Merlot	Mazuelo	Syrah	Bobal	Tempranillo	Monastrell
Algeria	5.00	20.00	5.00	25.00	5.00			
Argentina	6.07		2.74		3.94		2.16	
Armenia								
Australia	19.14	1.64	5.87	0.07	22.43		0.03	0.73
Austria	0.64		0.23					
Brazil	1.11		0.89					
Bulgaria	10.88		11.64					
Canada	6.69		7.93					
Chile	31.56		11.25	0.56	1.79		0.00	0.02
Croatia								
Cyprus								
Czech Rep.								
France	6.18	11.07	11.71	11.07	5.86		0.18	0.88
Georgia	0.60							
Germany								
Greece	1.35		0.35		0.08			
Hungary	1.21		0.56					
Italy	1.21	1.07	3.43	0.27	0.16		0.00	
Luxembourg								
Moldova	8.45		9.04					
Morocco		1.62		3.41				
N. Zealand	6.58		6.61		0.60			
Portugal	0.16						3.59	
Romania	3.88		3.52					
Russia	2.80							
Serbia								
Slovakia	1.00							
Slovenia			5.10					
S. Africa	9.42	0.04	5.22	0.08	6.01		0.01	0.01
Spain	0.38	8.11	0.10	0.69	0.01	8.47	6.71	5.68
Switzerland	0.23		5.64		0.36			
Tunisia	2.00	12.00		45.00	2.00			2.00
UK								
USA	10.00	2.57	9.60	1.76	0.86		0.11	0.11
Uruguay	7.60		11.90		0.70			
"Missing 9"	25.40	0.16	6.92	0.47	1.59		0.21	0.00
World	**4.53**	**4.39**	**4.35**	**2.60**	**2.08**	**2.05**	**1.91**	**1.56**

Table 29 (cont.) Shares (%) of world's top 30 red varieties in national winegrape area, by country, 2000

Country	Sangiovese	Pinot Noir	Cabernet Franc	Cinsaut	Gamay Noir	Alicante Henri Bouschet	Barbera	Montepulciano
Algeria		5.00		25.00		10.00		
Argentina	1.24	0.52	0.10				0.53	
Armenia								
Australia	0.28	2.47	0.57				0.08	
Austria		0.84	0.06					
Brazil			0.77					
Bulgaria		0.80						
Canada		5.38	6.67		3.10			
Chile	0.11	1.42	0.60	0.17		2.53		
Croatia								
Cyprus								
Czech Rep.								
France	0.18	3.07	4.17	3.65	3.99	1.01		
Georgia								
Germany								
Greece			0.08	0.21		0.04		
Hungary		0.28	0.61					
Italy	9.86	0.52	1.04	0.04	0.02	0.08	4.27	4.50
Luxembourg		4.90			0.07			
Moldova		7.26						
Morocco				7.94		2.21		
N. Zealand		11.04	1.19					
Portugal						0.33		
Romania		0.78						
Russia								
Serbia								
Slovakia								
Slovenia								
	0.04	0.52	0.52	3.77	0.04	0.01	0.02	
Spain		0.04	0.00		0.00	1.55		
Switzerland		30.59	0.10		13.14			
Tunisia	5.00			5.00		5.00		
UK								
USA	0.39	3.04	0.68	0.02	0.39	0.32	2.67	
Uruguay			4.10					
"Missing 9"	0.01	0.92	0.51	0.44	0.18	0.42		
World	**1.41**	**1.23**	**1.00**	**0.99**	**0.77**	**0.76**	**0.68**	**0.59**

Table 29 (cont.) Shares (%) of world's top 30 red varieties in national winegrape area, by country, 2000

Country	Isabella	Tribidrag	Criolla Grande	Cot	Pamid	Douce Noire	Negroamaro	Doukkali
Algeria								
Argentina			12.25	8.13		7.45		
Armenia								
Australia				0.33				
Austria								
Brazil	27.04							
Bulgaria					23.52			
Canada								
Chile		0.08		0.82				
Croatia								
Cyprus								
Czech Rep.								
France		0.00		0.71		0.00		
Georgia								
Germany								
Greece					0.03			
Hungary					0.14			
Italy		1.23		0.04		0.42	2.61	
Luxembourg								
Moldova	12.69			0.04				
Morocco								33.38
N. Zealand				0.67				
Portugal								
Romania								
Russia								
Serbia								
Slovakia								
Slovenia								
S. Africa		0.03		0.08				
Spain				0.00				
Switzerland				0.00				
Tunisia		2.00						
UK								
USA	0.01	10.60		0.06		0.01		
Uruguay								
"Missing 9"	2.09			0.02				
World	**0.56**	**0.55**	**0.51**	**0.50**	**0.47**	**0.36**	**0.34**	**0.34**

Table 29 (cont.) Shares (%) of world's top 30 red varieties in national winegrape area, by country, 2000

Country	Listan Prieto	Prokupac	Castelao	Mencia	Blaufrankisch	Concord	Other Red	Other varieties	Total
Algeria									100
Argentina							6.00	48.88	100
Armenia								100.00	100
Australia							5.90	40.47	100
Austria					5.44		19.54	73.24	100
Brazil						4.75	25.48	39.97	100
Bulgaria							13.87	39.30	100
Canada						11.50	14.52	44.22	100
Chile	13.32						12.05	23.72	100
Croatia					2.00		23.37	74.63	100
Cyprus							80.00	20.00	100
Czech Rep.					6.00		24.00	70.00	100
France							5.02	31.24	100
Georgia							11.60	87.81	100
Germany							6.78	93.22	100
Greece							49.46	48.40	100
Hungary					7.96		13.34	75.90	100
Italy					0.02		20.88	48.33	100
Luxembourg								95.03	100
Moldova							2.30	60.22	100
Morocco							40.52	10.91	100
N. Zealand							1.72	71.59	100
Portugal			7.04	0.96			45.65	42.28	100
Romania							19.54	72.28	100
Russia							16.20	81.00	100
Serbia		22.00					9.00	69.00	100
Slovakia					7.00		9.00	83.00	100
Slovenia							20.90	74.00	100
S. Africa							10.31	63.86	100
Spain	0.00			0.94			5.93	61.39	100
Switzerland							2.54	47.39	100
Tunisia							20.00		100
UK							22.91	77.09	100
USA	0.19				0.03	4.74	6.55	45.29	100
Uruguay							72.04	3.66	100
"Missing 9"					0.25		14.76	45.64	100
World	**0.32**	**0.31**	**0.30**	**0.27**	**0.26**	**0.24**	**12.73**	**51.05**	**100**

Table 30: National winegrape area (hectares) for world's top 30 red varieties, 2010

Country	Cabernet Sauvignon	Merlot	Tempranillo	Syrah	Garnacha Tinta	Pinot Noir	Mazuelo	Bobal
Algeria	1510	1510		1510	6040	1510	7550	
Argentina	16372	6282	6120	12810	16	1802	29	
Armenia								
Australia	25967	10028	476	42675	1748	4690		
Austria	592	644		137		646		
Brazil	914	766	16		1	145		
Bulgaria	8436	10573						
Canada	542	999	6	274	2	640		
Chile	40728	10041	48	6027	37	2884	477	
China	22612	3560		223	11	40		
Croatia	646	780		187	103	180	34	
Cyprus	369	63		244	84		481	
Czech Rep.	230	90				688		
France	56386	115746	766	68587	94240	29738	53155	
Georgia	286							
Germany	260							
Greece	1550	1248	19	641			16	
Hungary	2863	1907		177		1091		
Italy	13724	28042	23	6739	6372	5046	2023	
Japan	469	817				64		
Kazakhstan	20					180		
Luxembourg						3		
Mexico	756	391	229	145	140		448	
Moldova	7590	8123				6521		
Morocco					802		1692	
Myanmar	1		3	27		7	4	
N. Zealand	517	1369	7	293	2	4776		
Peru	48	2		2	1	1		
Portugal	1671	772	16706	3501	84	148	338	
Romania	3718	10988				1089		
Russia	3593	1588				533		
Serbia								
Slovakia	570							
Slovenia	453	996						
S. Africa	12325	6497	38	10136	187	962	81	
Spain	23237	15540	207677	20000	70140	1044	4749	80120
Switzerland	63	1028		181		4402		
Thailand	7		4	66		1		
Tunisia	337			337	2020		7576	
Turkey	391	355	9	1367	33	3	84	
Ukraine	4869	2820				767		
UK	1	2				233		
USA	34788	22729	414	9197	2666	16776	1441	
Uruguay	682	875		87	5	55		
Total	**290091**	**267169**	**232561**	**185568**	**184735**	**86662**	**80178**	**80120**

Table 30 (cont.) National winegrape area (hectares) for world's top 30 red varieties, 2010

Country	Sangiovese	Monastrell	Cabernet Franc	Cot	Alicante Henri Bouschet	Cinsaut	Montepulciano	Tribidrag
Algeria					3020	7550		
Argentina	2011	8	626	31047	166	1	85	0
Armenia								
Australia	589	692	591	356				149
Austria			56					
Brazil	26		229	37	129		2	0
Bulgaria								
Canada	3	2	664	39				8
Chile	100	59	1321	1264	4228	198		58
China			507			3		
Croatia			95					65
Cyprus		172	203					
Czech Rep.								
France	1589	9363	36948	6155	4957	20800		
Georgia								
Germany								
Greece			23		56	43		
Hungary	1		1352	0	21			
Italy	71619		6314	260	645	51	34824	12234
Japan								
Kazakhstan			56					
Luxembourg								
Mexico								
Moldova				39				
Morocco					1098	3940		
Myanmar					0			
N. Zealand	6		163	156			7	4
Peru				10				
Portugal			24		3322	16		
Romania			20					
Serbia								
Slovakia								
Slovenia								
S. Africa	61	403	934	450	10	2052		34
Spain		58406	849	93	19551			
Switzerland			54	10				
Thailand	2							
Tunisia	842	337			842	842		337
Turkey	9	4	23	13	488	500		
Ukraine								
UK			1					
USA	852	404	2215	717	431	45	29	19857
Uruguay		1	334	41	22			
Total	**77709**	**69850**	**53599**	**40688**	**38985**	**36040**	**34947**	**32745**

Table 30 (cont.) National winegrape area (hectares) for world's top 30 red varieties, 2010

Country	Gamay Noir	Isabella	Barbera	Douce Noire	Criolla Grande	Nero d'Avola	Doukkali	Blaufrankisch
Algeria								
Argentina	1		546	18127	17080	1		
Armenia								
Australia			116					
Austria								3228
Brazil	16	18279	5	0				
Bulgaria								
Canada	220		1					4
Chile	0		4					
China								
Croatia								558
Cyprus								
Czech Rep.								1160
France	30443							
Georgia								
Germany								
Greece								
Hungary	3							7998
Italy	122		20524	815		16595		59
Japan								
Kazakhstan								
Luxembourg	98							
Mexico								
Moldova		11401						
Morocco							16557	
Myanmar								
N. Zealand	12							
Peru								290
Portugal	0							
Romania								760
Russia		162						
Serbia								
Slovakia								1378
Slovenia			134					680
S. Africa	19		51					
Spain								
Switzerland	1521							3
Thailand								
Tunisia								
Turkey	206							
Ukraine		2396						
UK	1							
USA			2798	34				22
Uruguay	9	256						
Total	**32671**	**32494**	**24178**	**18976**	**17080**	**16596**	**16557**	**16141**

Table 30 (cont.) National winegrape area (hectares) for world's top 30 red varieties, 2010

Country	Prokupac	Concord	Touriga Franca	Negroamaro	Carmenere	Pinot Meunier	Other Red	Total Red
Algeria								30200
Argentina			0		56	12	7360	120556
Armenia								
Australia							4354	92430
Austria							10835	16137
Brazil		3543			7		15929	40041
Bulgaria							16534	35543
Canada		252			2	5	993	4654
Chile					8827		4816	81115
China					1353		40	28350
Croatia					19		4418	7085
Cyprus							4091	5707
Czech Rep.							3649	5817
France						11088	37011	576972
Georgia							5567	5853
Germany							15466	15726
Greece							25788	29384
Hungary						0	5673	21087
Italy				11460	1074	14	117543	356121
Japan							864	2213
Kazakhstan							726	982
Luxembourg							0	101
Mexico							1300	3409
Moldova							2067	35741
Morocco							19564	43653
Myanmar							2	44
N. Zealand						19	357	7688
Peru							1938	2292
Portugal			11582				70234	108396
Romania							9927	26482
Russia							3729	9625
Serbia	15180						6210	21390
Slovakia							1987	3934
Slovenia							3019	5282
S. Africa			3			13	10174	44429
Spain						1	51289	552696
Switzerland							1312	8574
Thailand							19	99
Tunisia							3367	16836
Turkey							5194	8677
Ukraine							5297	16149
UK						50	117	405
USA		8421			22	66	17911	141834
Uruguay		22					3763	6152
Total	**15180**	**12238**	**11586**	**11460**	**11360**	**11267**	**500434**	**2539864**

Table 31: National shares (%) of global winegrape area for world's top 30 red varieties, 2010

Country	Cabernet Sauvignon	Merlot	Tempranillo	Syrah	Garnacha Tinta	Pinot Noir	Mazuelo	Bobal
Algeria	0.52	0.57		0.81	3.27	1.74	9.42	
Argentina	5.64	2.35	2.63	6.90	0.01	2.08	0.04	
Armenia								
Australia	8.95	3.75	0.20	23.00	0.95	5.41		
Austria	0.20	0.24		0.07		0.75		
Brazil	0.31	0.29	0.01		0.00	0.17		
Bulgaria	2.91	3.96						
Canada	0.19	0.37	0.00	0.15	0.00	0.74		
Chile	14.04	3.76	0.02	3.25	0.02	3.33	0.60	
China	7.79	1.33		0.12	0.01	0.05		
Croatia	0.22	0.29		0.10	0.06	0.21	0.04	
Cyprus	0.13	0.02		0.13	0.05		0.60	
Czech Rep.	0.08	0.03				0.79		
France	19.44	43.32	0.33	36.96	51.01	34.31	66.30	
Georgia	0.10							
Germany	0.09							
Greece	0.53	0.47	0.01	0.35			0.02	
Hungary	0.99	0.71		0.10		1.26		
Italy	4.73	10.50	0.01	3.63	3.45	5.82	2.52	
Japan	0.16	0.31				0.07		
Kazakhstan	0.01					0.21		
Luxembourg						0.00		
Mexico	0.26	0.15	0.10	0.08	0.08		0.56	
Moldova	2.62	3.04				7.52		
Morocco					0.43		2.11	
Myanmar	0.00		0.00	0.01		0.01	0.01	
N. Zealand	0.18	0.51	0.00	0.16	0.00	5.51		
Peru	0.02	0.00		0.00	0.00	0.00		
Portugal	0.58	0.29	7.18	1.89	0.05	0.17	0.42	
Romania	1.28	4.11				1.26		
Russia	1.24	0.59				0.62		
Serbia								
Slovakia	0.20							
Slovenia	0.16	0.37						
S. Africa	4.25	2.43	0.02	5.46	0.10	1.11	0.10	
Spain	8.01	5.82	89.30	10.78	37.97	1.20	5.92	100.00
Switzerland	0.02	0.38		0.10		5.08		
Thailand	0.00		0.00	0.04		0.00		
Tunisia	0.12			0.18	1.09		9.45	
Turkey	0.13	0.13	0.00	0.74	0.02	0.00	0.10	
Ukraine	1.68	1.06				0.89		
UK	0.00	0.00				0.27		
USA	11.99	8.51	0.18	4.96	1.44	19.36	1.80	
Uruguay	0.24	0.33		0.05	0.00	0.06		
Total	**100**	**100**	**100**	**100**	**100**	**100**	**100**	**100**

Table 31 (cont.) National shares (%) of global winegrape area for world's top 30 red varieties, 2010

Country	Sangiovese	Monastrell	Cabernet Franc	Cot	Alicante Henri Bouschet	Cinsaut	Montepulciano	Tribidrag
Algeria					7.75	20.95		
Argentina	2.59	0.01	1.17	76.31	0.43	0.00	0.24	0.00
Armenia								
Australia	0.76	0.99	1.10	0.87				0.46
Austria			0.10					
Brazil	0.03		0.43	0.09	0.33		0.00	0.00
Bulgaria								
Canada	0.00	0.00	1.24	0.10				0.02
Chile	0.13	0.08	2.46	3.11	10.84	0.55		0.18
China			0.95			0.01		
Croatia			0.18					0.20
Cyprus		0.25	0.38					
Czech Rep.								
France	2.05	13.40	68.93	15.13	12.71	57.71		
Georgia								
Germany								
Greece			0.04		0.14	0.12		
Hungary	0.00		2.52	0.00	0.05			
Italy	92.16		11.78	0.64	1.66	0.14	99.65	37.36
Japan								
Kazakhstan			0.11					
Luxembourg								
Mexico								
Moldova				0.10				
Morocco					2.82	10.93		
Myanmar				0.00				
N. Zealand	0.01		0.30	0.38			0.02	0.01
Peru				0.02				
Portugal			0.04		8.52	0.04		
Romania			0.04					
Serbia								
Slovakia								
Slovenia								
S. Africa	0.08	0.58	1.74	1.10	0.03	5.69		0.10
Spain		83.62	1.58	0.23	50.15			
Switzerland			0.10	0.03				
Thailand	0.00							
Tunisia	1.08	0.48			2.16	2.34		1.03
Turkey	0.01	0.01	0.04	0.03	1.25	1.39		
Ukraine								
UK			0.00					
USA	1.10	0.58	4.13	1.76	1.10	0.12	0.08	60.64
Uruguay		0.00	0.62	0.10	0.06			
Total	**100**	**100**	**100**	**100**	**100**	**100**	**100**	**100**

Table 31 (cont.) National shares (%) of global winegrape area for world's top 30 red varieties, 2010

Country	Gamay Noir	Isabella	Barbera	Douce Noire	Criolla Grande	Nero d'Avola	Doukkali	Blaufrankisch
Algeria								
Argentina	0.00		2.26	95.53	100.00	0.00		
Armenia								
Australia			0.48					
Austria								20.00
Brazil	0.05	56.25	0.02	0.00				
Bulgaria								
Canada	0.67		0.01					0.03
Chile	0.00		0.01					
China								
Croatia								3.46
Cyprus								
Czech Rep.								7.19
France	93.18							
Georgia								
Germany								
Greece								
Hungary	0.01							49.55
Italy	0.37		84.89	4.29		100.00		0.37
Japan								
Kazakhstan								
Luxembourg	0.30							
Mexico								
Moldova		35.09						
Morocco							100.00	
Myanmar								
N. Zealand	0.04							
Peru								1.80
Portugal	0.00							
Romania								4.71
Russia		0.50						
Serbia								
Slovakia								8.54
Slovenia			0.55					4.21
S. Africa	0.06		0.21					
Spain								
Switzerland	4.65							0.02
Thailand								
Tunisia								
Turkey	0.63							
Ukraine		7.37						
UK	0.00							
USA			11.57	0.18				0.14
Uruguay	0.03	0.79						
Total	**100**	**100**	**100**	**100**	**100**	**100**	**100**	**100**

Table 31 (cont.) National shares (%) of global winegrape area for world's top 30 red varieties, 2010

Country	Prokupac	Concord	Touriga Franca	Negroamaro	Carmenere	Pinot Meunier	Other Red	Total Red
Algeria								1.19
Argentina			0.00		0.49	0.10	1.47	4.75
Armenia								
Australia							0.87	3.64
Austria							2.16	0.64
Brazil		28.95			0.06		3.18	1.58
Bulgaria							3.30	1.40
Canada		2.06			0.02	0.04	0.20	0.18
Chile					77.70		0.96	3.19
China					11.91		0.01	1.12
Croatia					0.16		0.88	0.28
Cyprus							0.82	0.22
Czech Rep.							0.73	0.23
France						98.42	7.40	22.72
Georgia							1.11	0.23
Germany							3.09	0.62
Greece							5.14	1.16
Hungary					0.00		1.13	0.83
Italy				100.00	9.45	0.13	23.49	14.02
Japan							0.17	0.09
Kazakhstan							0.14	0.04
Luxembourg							0.00	0.00
Mexico							0.26	0.13
Moldova							0.41	1.41
Morocco							3.91	1.72
Myanmar							0.00	0.00
N. Zealand						0.17	0.07	0.30
Peru							0.39	0.09
Portugal			99.97				14.03	4.27
Romania							1.98	1.04
Russia							0.74	0.38
Serbia	100.00						1.24	0.84
Slovakia							0.40	0.15
Slovenia							0.60	0.21
S. Africa			0.03			0.11	2.03	1.75
Spain						0.01	10.25	21.75
Switzerland							0.26	0.34
Thailand							0.00	0.00
Tunisia							0.67	0.66
Turkey							1.04	0.34
Ukraine							1.06	0.64
UK						0.44	0.02	0.02
USA		68.81			0.20	0.58	3.58	5.58
Uruguay		0.18					0.75	0.24
Total	**100**	**100**	**100**	**100**	**100**	**100**	**100**	**100**

Table 32: Shares (%) of world's top 30 red varieties in national winegrape area, by country, 2010

Country	Cabernet Sauvignon	Merlot	Tempranillo	Syrah	Garnacha Tinta	Pinot Noir	Mazuelo	Bobal
Algeria	5.00	5.00		5.00	20.00	5.00	25.00	
Argentina	8.14	3.12	3.04	6.37	0.01	0.90	0.01	
Armenia								
Australia	17.11	6.61	0.31	28.12	1.15	3.09		
Austria	1.30	1.41		0.30		1.42		
Brazil	1.85	1.55	0.03		0.00	0.29		
Bulgaria	15.03	18.84						
Canada	5.37	9.89	0.06	2.71	0.02	6.34		
Chile	36.52	9.00	0.04	5.40	0.03	2.59	0.43	
China	76.54	12.05		0.75	0.04	0.14		
Croatia	3.11	3.76		0.90	0.50	0.87	0.17	
Cyprus	4.29	0.73		2.83	0.98		5.59	
Czech Rep.	1.42	0.55				4.24		
France	6.66	13.67	0.09	8.10	11.13	3.51	6.28	
Georgia	0.60							
Germany	0.25							
Greece	2.85	2.29	0.03	1.18			0.03	
Hungary	4.11	2.74		0.25		1.56		
Italy	2.19	4.48	0.00	1.08	1.02	0.81	0.32	
Japan	12.63	21.98				1.71		
Kazakhstan	0.28					2.59		
Luxembourg						0.23		
Mexico	13.83	7.15	4.19	2.65	2.56		8.20	
Moldova	8.45	9.04				7.26		
Morocco					1.64		3.45	
Myanmar	0.97		4.46	35.83		8.98	5.87	
N. Zealand	1.62	4.28	0.02	0.92	0.01	14.94		
Peru	1.25	0.05		0.05	0.03	0.03		
Portugal	1.02	0.47	10.22	2.14	0.05	0.09	0.21	
Romania	2.18	6.45				0.64		
Russia	14.02	6.20				2.08		
Serbia								
Slovakia	4.51							
Slovenia	2.77	6.09						
S. Africa	12.20	6.43	0.04	10.03	0.19	0.95	0.08	
Spain	2.26	1.51	20.20	1.95	6.82	0.10	0.46	7.79
Switzerland	0.42	6.94		1.22		29.71		
Thailand	4.65		2.85	44.46		0.35		
Tunisia	2.00			2.00	12.00		45.00	
Turkey	3.04	2.76	0.07	10.63	0.25	0.02	0.65	
Ukraine	9.31	5.39				1.47		
UK	0.08	0.17				19.45		
USA	15.26	9.97	0.18	4.03	1.17	7.36	0.63	
Uruguay	8.91	11.43		1.14	0.07	0.72		
World	**6.30**	**5.81**	**5.05**	**4.03**	**4.01**	**1.88**	**1.74**	**1.74**

Table 32 (cont.) Shares (%) of world's top 30 red varieties in national winegrape area, by country, 2010

Country	Sangiovese	Monastrell	Cabernet Franc	Cot	Alicante Henri Bouschet	Cinsaut	Montepulciano	Tribidrag
Algeria					10.00	25.00		
Argentina	1.00	0.00	0.31	15.44	0.08	0.00	0.04	0.00
Armenia								
Australia	0.39	0.46	0.39	0.23				0.10
Austria			0.12					
Brazil	0.05		0.46	0.08	0.26		0.00	0.00
Bulgaria								
Canada	0.03	0.02	6.58	0.38				0.08
Chile	0.09	0.05	1.18	1.13	3.79	0.18		0.05
China			1.71			0.01		
Croatia			0.46					0.31
Cyprus		2.00	2.36					
Czech Rep.								
France	0.19	1.11	4.36	0.73	0.59	2.46		
Georgia								
Germany								
Greece			0.04		0.10	0.08		
Hungary	0.00		1.94	0.00	0.03			
Italy	11.45		1.01	0.04	0.10	0.01	5.57	1.96
Japan								
Kazakhstan			0.81					
Luxembourg								
Mexico								
Moldova				0.04				
Morocco					2.24	8.04		
Myanmar					0.31			
N. Zealand	0.02		0.51	0.49			0.02	0.01
Peru				0.26				
Portugal			0.01		2.03	0.01		
Romania				0.08				
Serbia								
Slovakia								
Slovenia								
S. Africa	0.06	0.40	0.92	0.45	0.01	2.03		0.03
Spain		5.68	0.08	0.01	1.90			
Switzerland			0.36	0.07				
Thailand	1.41							
Tunisia	5.00	2.00			5.00	5.00		2.00
Turkey	0.07	0.03	0.18	0.10	3.79	3.89		
Ukraine								
UK			0.08					
USA	0.37	0.18	0.97	0.31	0.19	0.02	0.01	8.71
Uruguay		0.01	4.36	0.54	0.29			
World	**1.69**	**1.52**	**1.16**	**0.88**	**0.85**	**0.78**	**0.76**	**0.71**

Table 32 (cont.) Shares (%) of world's top 30 red varieties in national winegrape area, by country, 2010

Country	Gamay Noir	Isabella	Barbera	Douce Noire	Criolla Grande	Nero d'Avola	Doukkali	Blaufrankisch
Algeria								
Argentina	0.00		0.27	9.02	8.49	0.00		
Armenia								
Australia			0.08					
Austria								7.09
Brazil	0.03	36.99	0.01	0.00				
Bulgaria								
Canada	2.18		0.01					0.04
Chile	0.00		0.00					
China								
Croatia								2.69
Cyprus								
Czech Rep.								7.14
France	3.59							
Georgia								
Germany								
Greece								
Hungary	0.00							11.47
Italy	0.02		3.28	0.13		2.65		0.01
Japan								
Kazakhstan								
Luxembourg	7.52							
Mexico								
Moldova		12.69						
Morocco							33.79	
Myanmar								
N. Zealand	0.04							
Peru								7.57
Portugal	0.00							
Romania								0.45
Russia		0.63						
Serbia								
Slovakia								10.91
Slovenia			0.82					4.16
S. Africa	0.02		0.05					
Spain								
Switzerland	10.26							0.02
Thailand								
Tunisia								
Turkey	1.60							
Ukraine		4.58						
UK	0.08							
USA			1.23	0.01				0.01
Uruguay	0.12	3.34						
World	**0.71**	**0.71**	**0.53**	**0.41**	**0.37**	**0.36**	**0.36**	**0.35**

Table 32 (cont.) Shares (%) of world's top 30 red varieties in national winegrape area, by country, 2010

Country	Prokupac	Concord	Touriga Franca	Negroamaro	Carmenere	Pinot Meunier	Other Red	Non-Red varieties	Total
Algeria									100
Argentina		0.00			0.03	0.01	3.66	40.04	100
Armenia								100.00	100
Australia							2.87	39.11	100
Austria							23.79	64.56	100
Brazil		7.17			0.01		32.24	18.96	100
Bulgaria							29.46	36.68	100
Canada		2.50			0.02	0.05	9.83	53.91	100
Chile					7.91		4.32	27.27	100
China					4.58		0.14	4.05	100
Croatia					0.09		21.29	65.86	100
Cyprus							47.53	33.70	100
Czech Rep.							22.47	64.19	100
France						1.31	4.37	31.87	100
Georgia							11.60	87.81	100
Germany							15.15	84.59	100
Greece							47.41	45.98	100
Hungary					0.00		8.14	69.75	100
Italy				1.83	0.17	0.00	18.79	43.08	100
Japan							23.25	40.42	100
Kazakhstan							10.47	85.84	100
Luxembourg							0.01	92.25	100
Mexico							23.79	37.62	100
Moldova							2.30	60.22	100
Morocco							39.93	10.91	100
Myanmar							2.57	41.01	100
N. Zealand						0.06	1.12	75.95	100
Peru							50.59	40.17	
Portugal			7.08				42.95	33.71	100
Romania							5.83	84.45	100
Russia							14.55	62.44	100
Serbia	22.00						9.00	69.00	100
Slovakia							15.72	68.87	100
Slovenia							18.46	67.70	100
S. Africa			0.00			0.01	10.07	56.02	100
Spain						0.00	4.99	46.25	100
Switzerland							8.86	42.14	100
Thailand							12.67	33.60	100
Tunisia							20.00		100
Turkey							40.40	32.51	100
Ukraine							10.13	69.12	100
UK						4.17	9.77	66.19	100
USA		3.69			0.01	0.03	7.86	37.78	100
Uruguay		0.29					49.14	19.66	100
World	**0.33**	**0.27**	**0.25**	**0.25**	**0.25**	**0.24**	**10.88**	**44.80**	**100**

Table 33: National winegrape area (hectares) for world's top 30 white varieties, 2000

Country	Airen	Chardonnay	Trebbiano Toscano	Grasevina	Rkatsiteli	Sauvignon Blanc	Cayetana Blanca	Catarratto Bianco
Algeria								
Argentina		4625	2846			827		
Armenia					2469			
Australia		17266				2602		
Austria				4323		314		
Brazil		330	688	880		140		
Bulgaria		1862	1821	3602	9429	405		
Canada		973				148		
Chile		7672				6662		
Croatia				16051				
Cyprus								
Czech Rep.		567		1246				
France		36496	90341			20933		
Georgia					19741			
Germany		531						
Greece		36	720			158		
Hungary		2954		6677		324		
Italy		11687	39447	2007		3312		50711
Luxembourg		8						
Moldova		5134			11508	8151		
Morocco								
N. Zealand		2787				2423		
Portugal			382					
Romania		1376		15014	506	4613		
Russia		1639			13152			
Serbia				33120				
Slovakia		623		3895				
Slovenia		1549		3568		1221		
S. Africa		6067	147			5436		
Spain	387978	1814	28	1923		467	55502	
Switzerland		226				38		
Tunisia								
UK		68						
USA		35791	151			4191		
Uruguay		142				142		
"Missing 9"		3120			10549	2383		
Total	**387978**	**145344**	**136572**	**92306**	**67354**	**64889**	**55502**	**50711**

Table 33 (cont.) National winegrape area (hectares) for world's top 30 white varieties, 2000

Country	Macabeo	Chenin Blanc	Riesling	Colombard	Aligote	Müller Thurgau	Palomino Fino	Muscat of Alexandria
Algeria								
Argentina		3591						5539
Armenia								
Australia		841	3129	1801			124	2495
Austria			1643			3289		
Brazil								809
Bulgaria			647		1659			
Canada			482					
Chile		76	286					
Croatia								
Cyprus								
Czech Rep.			793			1586		
France	5223	9837	3407	6896	1756	5	440	3027
Georgia					97			
Germany			22350			20691		
Greece								
Hungary			1619			3278		
Italy			599			996		1157
Luxembourg			175			459		
Moldova			1343		15790	173		
Morocco								3669
N. Zealand		146	490			419	21	
Portugal								510
Romania					7608			
Russia			1376		1821			
Serbia								
Slovakia						1870		
Slovenia								
S. Africa		22566	477	11432			1632	4047
Spain	42902	105	97				27685	6144
Switzerland		1	8		20	686		
Tunisia								
UK								
USA		8433	1965	18010			319	2013
Uruguay								
"Missing 9"		210	2279		6916	120	76	
Total	**48125**	**45806**	**43166**	**38146**	**35668**	**33572**	**30297**	**29411**

Table 33 (cont.) National winegrape area (hectares) for world's top 30 white varieties, 2000

Country	Muscat Blanc a Petits Grains	Semillon	Feteasca Alba	Gruner Veltliner	Trebbiano Romagnolo	Pedro Ximenez	Pinot Blanc	Garganega
Algeria								
Argentina		1028					48	
Armenia	526							
Australia	214	6528				89		
Austria	143			17479			2936	
Brazil		384						
Bulgaria								
Canada							146	
Chile		1893				2379	14	
Croatia								
Cyprus								
Czech Rep.				1700				
France	6935	14015					1401	
Georgia							171	
Germany	87						2396	
Greece	2222	21						
Hungary	1538		971	1335				
Italy	13016	8		129	19492		4993	16549
Luxembourg							138	
Moldova	172		4334				350	
Morocco								
N. Zealand		229						
Portugal								
Romania	1012		18211					
Russia							2995	
Serbia								
Slovakia			312	2960			623	
Slovenia								
S. Africa	773	1029					35	
Spain	223					14803		
Switzerland	44	3					77	
Tunisia								
UK								
USA	515	709					431	
Uruguay								
"Missing 9"	981	382				1	238	
Total	**28401**	**26230**	**23828**	**23604**	**19492**	**17272**	**16990**	**16549**

Table 33 (cont.) National winegrape area (hectares) for world's top 30 white varieties, 2000

Country	Niagara	Pedro Gimenez	Fernao Pires	Sultaniye	Chasselas	Melon	Other White	Total White
Algeria								
Argentina		15101		2229			20150	55983
Armenia							8211	11206
Australia				10298			7462	52850
Austria							4742	34870
Brazil	13436						4452	21119
Bulgaria							18299	37724
Canada	461						1338	3548
Chile					404		7635	27021
Croatia							28313	44364
Cyprus							3656	3656
Czech Rep.							2040	7932
France					943	13253	53032	267941
Georgia							12827	32836
Germany					1198		46923	94175
Greece							21121	24279
Hungary					1902		43244	63842
Italy					22		136979	301104
Luxembourg							346	1126
Moldova							5106	52061
Morocco							1744	5413
N. Zealand					25		444	6984
Portugal			14206				71569	86667
Romania							109869	158209
Russia							24643	45626
Serbia					3450		11040	47609
Slovakia							2649	12932
Slovenia							11032	17369
S. Africa			339				5728	59706
Spain				4	1		185808	725484
Switzerland					5373		503	6979
Tunisia								
UK							605	673
USA	1357						4731	78616
Uruguay							41	325
"Missing 9"	89			1820			6374	35547
Total		15101	14545	14351	13318	13253	862657	2425777

Table 34: National shares (%) of global winegrape area for world's top 30 white varieties, 2000

Country	Airen	Chardonnay	Trebbiano Toscano	Grasevina	Rkatsiteli	Sauvignon Blanc	Cayetana Blanca	Catarratto Bianco
Algeria								
Argentina		3.18	2.08			1.27		
Armenia					3.67			
Australia		11.88				4.01		
Austria				4.68		0.48		
Brazil		0.23	0.50	0.95		0.22		
Bulgaria		1.28	1.33	3.90	14.00	0.62		
Canada		0.67				0.23		
Chile		5.28				10.27		
Croatia				17.39				
Cyprus								
Czech Rep.		0.39		1.35				
France		25.11	66.15			32.26		
Georgia					29.31			
Germany		0.37						
Greece		0.02	0.53			0.24		
Hungary		2.03		7.23		0.50		
Italy		8.04	28.88	2.17		5.10		100.00
Luxembourg		0.01						
Moldova		3.53			17.09	12.56		
Morocco								
N. Zealand		1.92				3.73		
Portugal			0.28					
Romania		0.95		16.27	0.75	7.11		
Russia		1.13			19.53			
Serbia				35.88				
Slovakia		0.43		4.22				
Slovenia		1.07		3.87		1.88		
S. Africa		4.17	0.11			8.38		
Spain	100.00	1.25	0.02	2.08		0.72	100.00	
Switzerland		0.16				0.06		
Tunisia								
UK		0.05						
USA		24.62	0.11			6.46		
Uruguay		0.10				0.22		
"Missing 9"		2.15			15.66	3.67		
Total	**100**	**100**	**100**	**100**	**100**	**100**	**100**	**100**

Table 34 (cont.) National shares (%) of global winegrape area for world's top 30 white varieties, 2000

Country	Macabeo	Chenin Blanc	Riesling	Colombard	Aligote	Müller Thurgau	Palomino Fino	Muscat of Alexandria
Algeria								
Argentina		7.84						18.83
Armenia								
Australia		1.84	7.25	4.72			0.41	8.48
Austria			3.81			9.80		
Brazil								2.75
Bulgaria			1.50		4.65			
Canada			1.12					
Chile		0.17	0.66					
Croatia								
Cyprus								
Czech Rep.			1.84			4.73		
France	10.85	21.48	7.89	18.08	4.92	0.01	1.45	10.29
Georgia					0.27			
Germany			51.78			61.63		
Greece								
Hungary			3.75			9.76		
Italy			1.39			2.97		3.93
Luxembourg			0.41			1.37		
Moldova			3.11		44.27	0.52		
Morocco								12.48
N. Zealand		0.32	1.14			1.25	0.07	
Portugal								1.73
Romania					21.33			
Russia			3.19		5.11			
Serbia								
Slovakia						5.57		
Slovenia								
S. Africa		49.26	1.10	29.97			5.39	13.76
Spain	89.15	0.23	0.23				91.38	20.89
Switzerland		0.00	0.02		0.06	2.04		
Tunisia								
UK								
USA		18.41	4.55	47.21			1.05	6.84
Uruguay								
"Missing 9"		0.46	5.28		19.39	0.36	0.25	
Total	**100**	**100**	**100**	**100**	**100**	**100**	**100**	**100**

Table 34 (cont.) National shares (%) of global winegrape area for world's top 30 white varieties, 2000

Country	Muscat Blanc a Petits Grains	Semillon	Feteasca Alba	Gruner Veltliner	Trebbiano Romagnolo	Pedro Ximenez	Pinot Blanc	Garganega
Algeria								
Argentina		3.92					0.28	
Armenia	1.85							
Australia	0.75	24.89					0.52	
Austria	0.50			74.05			17.28	
Brazil		1.47						
Bulgaria								
Canada							0.86	
Chile		7.22				13.77	0.08	
Croatia								
Cyprus								
Czech Rep.				7.20				
France	24.42	53.43					8.24	
Georgia							1.01	
Germany	0.31						14.10	
Greece	7.83	0.08						
Hungary	5.41		4.08	5.66				
Italy	45.83	0.03		0.55	100.00		29.39	100.00
Luxembourg							0.81	
Moldova	0.61		18.19				2.06	
Morocco								
N. Zealand		0.87						
Portugal								
Romania	3.56		76.43					
Russia							17.63	
Serbia								
Slovakia			1.31	12.54			3.67	
Slovenia								
S. Africa	2.72	3.92					0.20	
Spain	0.79					85.71		
Switzerland	0.15	0.01					0.46	
Tunisia								
UK								
USA	1.81	2.70					2.54	
Uruguay								
"Missing 9"	3.45	1.46				0.00	1.40	
Total	**100**	**100**	**100**	**100**	**100**	**100**	**100**	**100**

Table 34 (cont.) National shares (%) of global winegrape area for world's top 30 white varieties, 2000

Country	Niagara	Pedro Gimenez	Fernao Pires	Sultaniye	Chasselas	Melon	Other White	Total White
Algeria								
Argentina		100.00		15.53			2.34	2.31
Armenia							0.95	0.46
Australia				71.76			0.87	2.18
Austria							0.55	1.44
Brazil	87.57						0.52	0.87
Bulgaria							2.12	1.56
Canada	3.01						0.16	0.15
Chile					3.03		0.88	1.11
Croatia							3.28	1.83
Cyprus							0.42	0.15
Czech Rep.							0.24	0.33
France					7.08	100.00	6.15	11.05
Georgia							1.49	1.35
Germany					8.99		5.44	3.88
Greece							2.45	1.00
Hungary					14.28		5.01	2.63
Italy					0.16		15.88	12.41
Luxembourg							0.04	0.05
Moldova							0.59	2.15
Morocco							0.20	0.22
N. Zealand					0.19		0.05	0.29
Portugal			97.67				8.30	3.57
Romania							12.74	6.52
Russia							2.86	1.88
Serbia					25.91		1.28	1.96
Slovakia							0.31	0.53
Slovenia							1.28	0.72
S. Africa			2.33				0.66	2.46
Spain				0.03	0.01		21.54	29.91
Switzerland					40.34		0.06	0.29
Tunisia								
UK							0.07	0.03
USA	8.84						0.55	3.24
Uruguay							0.00	0.01
"Missing 9"	0.58			12.68			0.74	1.47
Total		100	100	100	100	100	100	100

Table 35: Shares (%) of world's top 30 white varieties in national winegrape winegrape area, by country, 2000

Country	Airen	Chardonnay	Trebbiano Toscano	Grasevina	Rkatsiteli	Sauvignon Blanc	Cayetana Blanca	Catarratto Bianco
Algeria								
Argentina		2.30	1.42			0.41		
Armenia					22.03			
Australia		13.22				1.99		
Austria				8.91		0.65		
Brazil		0.62	1.30	1.67		0.26		
Bulgaria		1.94	1.90	3.75	9.82	0.42		
Canada		11.45				1.74		
Chile		6.73				5.85		
Croatia				27.00				
Cyprus								
Czech Rep.		5.00		11.00				
France		4.22	10.45			2.42		
Georgia					52.76			
Germany		0.51						
Greece		0.07	1.42			0.31		
Hungary		3.40		7.69		0.37		
Italy		1.84	6.20	0.32		0.52		7.97
Luxembourg		0.59						
Moldova		5.71			12.81	9.07		
Morocco								
N. Zealand		28.03				24.37		
Portugal			0.19					
Romania		0.62		6.76	0.23	2.08		
Russia		2.91			23.35			
Serbia				48.00				
Slovakia		4.00		25.00				
Slovenia		6.60		15.20		5.20		
S. Africa		6.48	0.16			5.80		
Spain	32.83	0.15	0.00	0.16		0.04	4.70	
Switzerland		1.50				0.25		
Tunisia								
UK		7.79						
USA		20.37	0.09			2.39		
Uruguay		1.60				1.60		
"Missing 9"		3.89			13.15	2.97		
World	**7.95**	**2.98**	**2.80**	**1.89**	**1.38**	**1.33**	**1.14**	**1.04**

Table 35 (cont.) Shares (%) of world's top 30 white varieties in national winegrape winegrape area, by country, 2000

Country	Macabeo	Chenin Blanc	Riesling	Colombard	Aligote	Müller Thurgau	Palomino Fino	Muscat of Alexandria
Algeria								
Argentina		1.79						2.75
Armenia								
Australia		0.64	2.40	1.38			0.10	1.91
Austria			3.39			6.78		
Brazil								1.53
Bulgaria			0.67		1.73			
Canada			5.67					
Chile		0.07	0.25					
Croatia								
Cyprus								
Czech Rep.			7.00			14.00		
France	0.60	1.14	0.39	0.80	0.20	0.00	0.05	0.35
Georgia					0.26			
Germany			21.45			19.86		
Greece								
Hungary			1.86			3.77		
Italy			0.09			0.16		0.18
Luxembourg			12.98			34.05		
Moldova			1.49		17.57	0.19		
Morocco								7.40
N. Zealand		1.47	4.93			4.21	0.21	
Portugal								0.25
Romania					3.42			
Russia			2.44		3.23			
Serbia								
Slovakia						12.00		
Slovenia								
S. Africa		24.09	0.51	12.21			1.74	4.32
Spain	3.63	0.01	0.01				2.34	0.52
Switzerland		0.01	0.05		0.13	4.56		
Tunisia								
UK								
USA		4.80	1.12	10.25			0.18	1.15
Uruguay								
"Missing 9"		0.26	2.84		8.62	0.15	0.09	
World	**0.99**	**0.94**	**0.88**	**0.78**	**0.73**	**0.69**	**0.62**	**0.60**

Table 35 (cont.) Shares (%) of world's top 30 white varieties in national winegrape winegrape area, by country, 2000

Country	Muscat Blanc a Petits Grains	Semillon	Feteasca Alba	Gruner Veltliner	Trebbiano Romagnolo	Pedro Ximenez	Pinot Blanc	Garganega
Algeria								
Argentina		0.51					0.02	
Armenia	4.69							
Australia	0.16	5.00				0.07		
Austria	0.30			36.04			6.05	
Brazil		0.73						
Bulgaria								
Canada							1.71	
Chile		1.66				2.09	0.01	
Croatia								
Cyprus								
Czech Rep.				15.00				
France	0.80	1.62					0.16	
Georgia							0.46	
Germany	0.08						2.30	
Greece	4.37	0.04						
Hungary	1.77		1.12	1.54				
Italy	2.04	0.00		0.02	3.06		0.78	2.60
Luxembourg							10.24	
Moldova	0.19		4.82				0.39	
Morocco								
N. Zealand		2.30						
Portugal								
Romania	0.46		8.20					
Russia							5.32	
Serbia								
Slovakia			2.00	19.00			4.00	
Slovenia								
S. Africa	0.83	1.10					0.04	
Spain	0.02					1.25		
Switzerland	0.29	0.02					0.51	
Tunisia								
UK								
USA	0.29	0.40					0.25	
Uruguay								
"Missing 9"	1.22	0.48				0.00	0.30	
World	**0.58**	**0.54**	**0.49**	**0.48**	**0.40**	**0.35**	**0.35**	**0.34**

Table 35 (cont.) Shares (%) of world's top 30 white varieties in national winegrape winegrape area, by country, 2000

Country	Niagara	Pedro Gimenez	Fernao Pires	Sultaniye	Chasselas	Melon	Other White	Other varieties	National Total
Algeria								100.00	100
Argentina		7.51		1.11			10.02	72.16	100
Armenia							73.28		100
Australia				7.88			5.71	59.53	100
Austria							9.78	28.10	100
Brazil	25.43						8.43	60.03	100
Bulgaria							19.06	60.70	100
Canada	5.43						15.74	58.26	100
Chile					0.35		6.70	76.29	100
Croatia							47.63	25.37	100
Cyprus							20.00	80.00	100
Czech Rep.							18.00	30.00	100
France					0.11	1.53	6.13	69.02	100
Georgia							34.28	12.25	100
Germany					1.15		45.03	9.63	100
Greece							41.51	52.28	100
Hungary					2.19		49.77	26.52	100
Italy					0.00		21.52	52.71	100
Luxembourg							25.67	16.47	100
Moldova							5.68	42.05	100
Morocco							3.52	89.09	100
N. Zealand					0.25		4.47	29.75	100
Portugal			6.93				34.91	57.72	100
Romania							49.45	28.79	100
Russia							43.75	19.00	100
Serbia					5.00		16.00	31.00	100
Slovakia							17.00	17.00	100
Slovenia							47.00	26.00	100
S. Africa			0.36				6.12	36.25	100
Spain				0.00	0.00		15.72	38.61	100
Switzerland					35.72		3.34	53.60	100
Tunisia								100.00	100
UK							69.30	22.91	100
USA	0.77						2.69	55.25	100
Uruguay							0.46	96.34	100
"Missing 9"	0.11			2.27			7.95	55.69	100
World	**0.31**	**0.31**	**0.30**	**0.29**	**0.27**	**0.27**	**17.68**	**50.27**	**100**

Table 36: National winegrape area (hectares) for world's top 30 white varieties, 2010

Country	Airen	Chardonnay	Sauvignon Blanc	Trebbiano Toscano	Grasevina	Rkatsiteli	Riesling	Macabeo
Algeria								
Argentina		6473	2296	1922			89	2
Armenia						2469		
Australia		27773	6467				4114	
Austria		1380	845		3462		1852	
Brazil		377	45		200		9	
Bulgaria		2457		723		3121		
Canada		1178	320				871	
Chile		13082	12159				367	
China		738	1				437	
Croatia		668	249	210	4701	57	676	
Cyprus		128						
Czech Rep.		766	804		1148		1181	
France		44593	26839	83892			3490	2628
Georgia						25324		
Germany		1180	460				22520	
Greece		586	256	297			2	
Hungary		2757	907		4664		1304	
Italy		19709	3744	21501	1568		446	
Japan		602					11	
Kazakhstan						3552	111	
Luxembourg		16					121	
Mexico			120					
Moldova		5134	8151			11508	1343	
Morocco								
Myanmar		1	22					
N. Zealand		3911	16205				979	
Peru		1						
Portugal		803	171	212			18	
Romania		1067	4157		7530	356		
Russia		1981	951	66		702	882	
Serbia					33120			
Slovakia		310	208		1655		605	
Slovenia		1208	1061		2360		676	
S. Africa		8278	9551	74			211	
Spain	252364	6958	4011	45	791		161	38417
Switzerland		321	134				12	
Thailand								
Tunisia								
Turkey		142	146				3	
Ukraine		2985	3123			11552	2702	
UK		235	3				1	
USA		40846	6584	80			4852	
Uruguay		149	147	751			15	
Total	**252364**	**198793**	**110138**	**109772**	**61200**	**58641**	**50060**	**41046**

Table 36 (cont.) National winegrape area (hectares) for world's top 30 white varieties, 2010

Country	Cayetana Blanca	Aligote	Chenin Blanc	Catarratto Bianco	Colombard	Muscat Blanc a Petits Grains	Muscat of Alexandria	Müller Thurgau
Algeria								
Argentina			2462			94	2939	
Armenia						526		
Australia			541		2205	533	2043	
Austria						492		2044
Brazil		0	18		46	1005	7	
Bulgaria								
Canada			7					7
Chile			57				1090	
China			10					
Croatia						56		60
Cyprus							120	
Czech Rep.								1572
France		1952	9828		7790	7620	2610	
Georgia		124						
Germany						170		13480
Greece						2162		
Hungary		0	6			709		2098
Italy			45	34794		11506	1521	1312
Japan								172
Kazakhstan		277						
Luxembourg								184
Mexico			275			246		
Moldova		15790				172		173
Morocco							3669	
Myanmar			1			7		
N. Zealand			50					79
Peru			2			361		
Portugal	148		0			505	647	
Romania		7297				840		
Russia		1029				145		106
Slovakia						48		932
Slovenia						353		
S. Africa			18515		11990	689	2167	
Spain	39593		100		4	1291	8237	
Switzerland		23	6			49		493
Thailand			13		11	3		
Tunisia								
Turkey						114		
Ukraine		9627				674		
UK								43
USA			3221	68	10025	733	1285	
Uruguay			7		4	10		
Total	**39741**	**36119**	**35164**	**34863**	**32076**	**31112**	**26336**	**22753**

Table 36 (cont.) National winegrape area (hectares) for world's top 30 white varieties, 2010

Country	Palomino Fino	Semillon	Gruner Veltliner	Prosecco	Feteasca Alba	Verdejo	Trebbiano Romagnolo	Garganega
Algeria								
Argentina	115	855	8	10				27
Armenia								
Australia		6112						
Austria			13519					
Brazil		24		173				0
Bulgaria								
Canada		19						
Chile		846						
China		1						
Croatia								
Cyprus								
Czech Rep.			1527					
France		11693						
Georgia								
Germany								
Greece		8						
Hungary		58	1533					
Italy		31	165	18255			15893	15375
Japan								
Kazakhstan								
Luxembourg								
Mexico	109							
Moldova					4334			
Morocco								
Myanmar								
N. Zealand	14	201						
Peru								
Portugal	3033	89						
Romania					12916			
Russia		25						
Serbia								
Slovakia			2091		219			
Slovenia								
S. Africa	270	1182						
Spain	18836					16578		
Switzerland		5						
Thailand								
Tunisia								
Turkey		547						
Ukraine								
UK								
USA	135	436						
Uruguay		24						
Total	22510	22156	18842	18437	17469	16578	15893	15402

Table 36 (cont.) National winegrape area (hectares) for world's top 30 white varieties, 2010

Country	Pinot Blanc	Gewurztraminer	Chasselas	Feteasca Regala	Melon	Pedro Gimenez	Other White	Total White
Algeria								
Argentina	6				1	12132	14060	43488
Armenia							8211	11206
Australia		834					5439	56062
Austria	1914	309					3087	28903
Brazil	1	13	3				7437	9357
Bulgaria		747					9383	16431
Canada	125	404	5				1929	4865
Chile		316	88			118	2117	30240
China	2	5						1193
Croatia	188	234	21				6273	13394
Cyprus							2653	2901
Czech Rep.	732	601					1190	9521
France	1292	3083	2441		12364		45174	267290
Georgia	219						16455	42122
Germany	3870		1120				38964	81764
Greece							16954	20265
Hungary	237		1892				29782	45947
Italy	3086	1408	34				101835	252229
Japan							498	1282
Kazakhstan							1404	5343
Luxembourg	162	20					554	1057
Mexico							1306	2056
Moldova	350	2731					2375	52061
Morocco							1678	5347
Myanmar								31
N. Zealand	16	311	2				1004	22772
Peru							1168	1532
Portugal	22	0	76				49396	55119
Romania		385		12905			94788	142241
Russia	695		21				8860	15463
Serbia			3450				11040	47609
Slovakia	523	265		231			1374	8460
Slovenia	525						4388	10571
S. Africa	14	122					3261	56326
Spain		301	20				87855	475562
Switzerland	105	49	4013				819	6029
Thailand							22	50
Tunisia								
Turkey							3229	4179
Ukraine	338	961					3496	35458
UK	23	1					428	734
USA	269	1144						79168
Uruguay	9	24					353	1493
Total	**14724**	**14269**	**13186**	**13136**	**12365**	**12250**	**599727**	**1967122**

Table 37: National shares (%) of global winegrape area for world's top 30 white, 2010

Country	Airen	Chardonnay	Sauvignon Blanc	Trebbiano Toscano	Grasevina	Rkatsiteli	Riesling	Macabeo
Algeria								
Argentina		3.26	2.08	1.75			0.18	0.00
Armenia						4.21		
Australia		13.97	5.87				8.22	
Austria		0.69	0.77		5.66		3.70	
Brazil		0.19	0.04		0.33		0.02	
Bulgaria		1.24		0.66		5.32		
Canada		0.59	0.29				1.74	
Chile		6.58	11.04				0.73	
China		0.37	0.00				0.87	
Croatia		0.34	0.23	0.19	7.68	0.10	1.35	
Cyprus		0.06						
Czech Rep.		0.39	0.73		1.88		2.36	
France		22.43	24.37	76.42			6.97	6.40
Georgia						43.18		
Germany		0.59	0.42				44.99	
Greece		0.29	0.23	0.27			0.00	
Hungary		1.39	0.82		7.62		2.60	
Italy		9.91	3.40	19.59	2.56		0.89	
Japan		0.30					0.02	
Kazakhstan						6.06	0.22	
Luxembourg		0.01					0.24	
Mexico			0.11					
Moldova		2.58	7.40			19.62	2.68	
Morocco								
Myanmar		0.00	0.02					
N. Zealand		1.97	14.71				1.96	
Peru		0.00						
Portugal		0.40	0.16	0.19			0.04	
Romania		0.54	3.77		12.30	0.61		
Russia		1.00	0.86	0.06		1.20	1.76	
Serbia					54.12			
Slovakia		0.16	0.19		2.70		1.21	
Slovenia		0.61	0.96		3.86		1.35	
S. Africa		4.16	8.67	0.07			0.42	
Spain	100.00	3.50	3.64	0.04	1.29		0.32	93.59
Switzerland		0.16	0.12				0.02	
Thailand								
Tunisia								
Turkey		0.07	0.13				0.00	
Ukraine		1.50	2.84			19.70	5.40	
UK		0.12	0.00				0.00	
USA		20.55	5.98	0.07			9.69	
Uruguay		0.07	0.13	0.68			0.03	
Total	**100**	**100**	**100**	**100**	**100**	**100**	**100**	**100**

Table 37 (cont.) National shares (%) of global winegrape area for world's top 30 white, 2010

Country	Cayetana Blanca	Aligote	Chenin Blanc	Catarratto Bianco	Colombard	Muscat Blanc a Petits Grains	Muscat of Alexandria	Muller Thurgau
Algeria								
Argentina			7.00			0.30	11.16	
Armenia						1.69		
Australia			1.54		6.87	1.71	7.76	
Austria						1.58		8.98
Brazil		0.00	0.05		0.14	3.23	0.02	
Bulgaria								
Canada			0.02					0.03
Chile			0.16				4.14	
China			0.03					
Croatia						0.18		0.26
Cyprus							0.46	
Czech Rep.								6.91
France		5.40	27.95		24.29	24.49	9.91	
Georgia		0.34						
Germany						0.55		59.24
Greece						6.95		
Hungary		0.00	0.02			2.28		9.22
Italy			0.13	99.80		36.98	5.77	5.77
Japan								0.75
Kazakhstan		0.77						
Luxembourg								0.81
Mexico			0.78			0.79		
Moldova		43.72				0.55		0.76
Morocco							13.93	
Myanmar			0.00			0.02		
N. Zealand			0.14					0.35
Peru			0.01			1.16		
Portugal	0.37		0.00			1.62	2.46	
Romania		20.20				2.70		
Russia		2.85				0.47		0.47
Slovakia						0.15		4.09
Slovenia						1.13		
S. Africa			52.66		37.38	2.22	8.23	
Spain	99.63		0.28		0.01	4.15	31.28	
Switzerland		0.06	0.02			0.16		2.16
Thailand			0.04		0.03	0.01		
Tunisia								
Turkey						0.37		
Ukraine		26.65				2.17		
UK								0.19
USA			9.16	0.20	31.25	2.36	4.88	
Uruguay			0.02		0.01	0.03		
Total	**100**	**100**	**100**	**100**	**100**	**100**	**100**	**100**

Table 37 (cont.) National shares (%) of global winegrape area for world's top 30 white, 2010

Country	Palomino Fino	Semillon	Gruner Veltliner	Prosecco	Feteasca Alba	Verdejo	Trebbiano Romagnolo	Garganega
Algeria								
Argentina	0.51	3.86	0.04	0.05				0.17
Armenia								
Australia		27.59						
Austria			71.75					
Brazil		0.11		0.94				0.00
Bulgaria								
Canada		0.09						
Chile		3.82						
China		0.00						
Croatia								
Cyprus								
Czech Rep.			8.10					
France		52.78						
Georgia								
Germany								
Greece		0.04						
Hungary		0.26	8.13					
Italy		0.14	0.88	99.01			100.00	99.82
Japan								
Kazakhstan								
Luxembourg								
Mexico	0.48							
Moldova						24.81		
Morocco								
Myanmar								
N. Zealand	0.06	0.91						
Peru								
Portugal	13.47	0.40						
Romania					73.94			
Russia		0.11						
Serbia								
Slovakia			11.10		1.25			
Slovenia								
S. Africa	1.20	5.34						
Spain	83.68					100.00		
Switzerland		0.02						
Thailand								
Tunisia								
Turkey		2.47						
Ukraine								
UK								
USA	0.60	1.97						
Uruguay		0.11						
Total	**100**	**100**	**100**	**100**	**100**	**100**	**100**	**100**

Table 37 (cont.) National shares (%) of global winegrape area for world's top 30 white, 2010

Country	Pinot Blanc	Gewurztraminer	Chasselas	Feteasca Regala	Melon	Pedro Gimenez	Other White	Total White
Algeria								
Argentina	0.04				0.01	99.04	2.34	2.21
Armenia							1.37	0.57
Australia		5.85					0.91	2.85
Austria	13.00	2.17					0.51	1.47
Brazil	0.01	0.09	0.02				1.24	0.48
Bulgaria		5.23					1.56	0.84
Canada	0.85	2.83	0.04				0.32	0.25
Chile		2.21	0.67			0.96	0.35	1.54
China	0.01	0.04					0.00	0.06
Croatia	1.27	1.64	0.16				1.05	0.68
Cyprus							0.44	0.15
Czech Rep.	4.97	4.21					0.20	0.48
France	8.78	21.60	18.51		99.99		7.53	13.59
Georgia	1.49						2.74	2.14
Germany	26.28		8.49				6.50	4.16
Greece							2.83	1.03
Hungary	1.61		14.35				4.97	2.34
Italy	20.96	9.87	0.25				16.98	12.82
Japan							0.08	0.07
Kazakhstan							0.23	0.27
Luxembourg	1.10	0.14					0.09	0.05
Mexico							0.22	0.10
Moldova	2.38	19.14					0.40	2.65
Morocco							0.28	0.27
Myanmar								
N. Zealand	0.11	2.18	0.02				0.17	1.16
Peru							0.19	0.08
Portugal	0.15	0.00	0.57				8.24	2.80
Romania		2.70		98.24			15.81	7.23
Russia	4.72		0.16				1.48	0.79
Serbia			26.16				1.84	2.42
Slovakia	3.55	1.86		1.76			0.23	0.43
Slovenia	3.57						0.73	0.54
S. Africa	0.10	0.86					0.54	2.86
Spain		2.11	0.15				14.65	24.18
Switzerland	0.71	0.35	30.44				0.14	0.31
Thailand							0.00	0.00
Tunisia							0.00	0.00
Turkey							0.54	0.21
Ukraine	2.30	6.74					0.58	1.80
UK	0.16	0.01					0.07	0.04
USA		8.01					1.58	4.02
Uruguay	0.06	0.17					0.06	0.08
Total	**100**	**100**	**100**	**100**	**100**	**100**	**100**	**100**

Table 38: Shares (%) of world's top 30 white varieties in national winegrape area, by country, 2010

Country	Airen	Chardonnay	Sauvignon Blanc	Trebbiano Toscano	Grasevina	Rkatsiteli	Riesling	Macabeo
Algeria								
Argentina		3.22	1.14	0.96			0.04	0.00
Armenia						22.03		
Australia		18.30	4.26				2.71	
Austria		3.03	1.86		7.60		4.07	
Brazil		0.76	0.09		0.41		0.02	
Bulgaria		4.38		1.29		5.56		
Canada		11.67	3.17				8.63	
Chile		11.73	10.90				0.33	
China		2.50	0.00				1.48	
Croatia		3.22	1.20	1.01	22.65	0.27	3.26	
Cyprus		1.49						
Czech Rep.		4.72	4.95		7.07		7.27	
France		5.27	3.17	9.91			0.41	0.31
Georgia						52.76		
Germany		1.16	0.45				22.07	
Greece		1.08	0.47	0.55			0.00	
Hungary		3.95	1.30		6.69		1.87	
Italy		3.15	0.60	3.44	0.25		0.07	
Japan		16.19					0.30	
Kazakhstan						51.20	1.60	
Luxembourg		1.23					9.28	
Mexico			2.20					
Moldova		5.71	9.07			12.81	1.49	
Morocco								
Myanmar		1.50	29.23					
N. Zealand		12.24	50.70				3.06	
Peru		0.03						
Portugal		0.49	0.10	0.13			0.01	
Romania		0.63	2.44		4.42	0.21		
Russia		7.73	3.71	0.26		2.74	3.44	
Serbia					48.00			
Slovakia		2.45	1.65		13.10		4.79	
Slovenia		7.39	6.49		14.43		4.13	
S. Africa		8.20	9.45	0.07			0.21	
Spain	24.54	0.68	0.39	0.00	0.08		0.02	3.74
Switzerland		2.17	0.90				0.08	
Thailand								
Tunisia								
Turkey		1.10	1.13				0.02	
Ukraine		5.71	5.97			22.09	5.17	
UK		19.62	0.25				0.08	
USA		17.92	2.89	0.03			2.13	
Uruguay		1.95	1.92	9.81			0.20	
World	**5.48**	**4.32**	**2.39**	**2.39**	**1.33**	**1.27**	**1.09**	**0.89**

Table 38 (cont.) Shares (%) of world's top 30 white varieties in national winegrape area, by country, 2010

Country	Cayetana Blanca	Aligote	Chenin Blanc	Catarratto Bianco	Colombard	Muscat Blanc a Petits Grains	Muscat of Alexandria	Muller Thurgau
Algeria								
Argentina			1.22			0.05	1.46	
Armenia						4.69		
Australia			0.36		1.45	0.35	1.35	
Austria						1.08		4.49
Brazil		0.00	0.04		0.09	2.03	0.01	
Bulgaria								
Canada			0.07					0.07
Chile			0.05				0.98	
China			0.03					
Croatia						0.27		0.29
Cyprus							1.39	
Czech Rep.								9.68
France		0.23	1.16		0.92	0.90	0.31	
Georgia		0.26						
Germany						0.17		13.21
Greece						3.97		
Hungary		0.00	0.01			1.02		3.01
Italy			0.01	5.56		1.84	0.24	0.21
Japan								4.62
Kazakhstan		3.99						
Luxembourg								14.11
Mexico			5.03			4.50		
Moldova		17.57				0.19		0.19
Morocco							7.49	
Myanmar			0.81			9.46		
N. Zealand			0.16					0.25
Peru			0.05			9.42		
Portugal	0.09		0.00			0.31	0.40	
Romania		4.28				0.49		
Russia		4.02				0.57		0.41
Slovakia						0.38		7.37
Slovenia						2.16		
S. Africa			18.33		11.87	0.68	2.15	
Spain	3.85		0.01		0.00	0.13	0.80	
Switzerland		0.15	0.04			0.33		3.32
Thailand			8.86		7.48	2.19		
Tunisia								
Turkey						0.88		
Ukraine		18.41				1.29		
UK								3.59
USA			1.41	0.03	4.40	0.32	0.56	
Uruguay			0.09		0.05	0.13		
World	**0.86**	**0.78**	**0.76**	**0.76**	**0.70**	**0.68**	**0.57**	**0.49**

Table 38 (cont.) Shares (%) of world's top 30 white varieties in national winegrape area, by country, 2010

Country	Palomino Fino	Semillon	Gruner Veltliner	Prosecco	Feteasca Alba	Verdejo	Trebbiano Romagnolo	Garganega
Algeria								
Argentina	0.06	0.43	0.00	0.00				0.01
Armenia								
Australia		4.03						
Austria			29.69					
Brazil		0.05		0.35				0.00
Bulgaria								
Canada		0.19						
Chile		0.76						
China		0.00						
Croatia								
Cyprus								
Czech Rep.			9.40					
France		1.38						
Georgia								
Germany								
Greece		0.01						
Hungary		0.08	2.20					
Italy		0.00	0.03	2.92			2.54	2.46
Japan								
Kazakhstan								
Luxembourg								
Mexico	1.99							
Moldova					4.82			
Morocco								
Myanmar								
N. Zealand	0.04	0.63						
Peru								
Portugal	1.85	0.05						
Romania					7.58			
Russia		0.10						
Serbia								
Slovakia			16.54		1.73			
Slovenia								
S. Africa	0.27	1.17						
Spain	1.83					1.61		
Switzerland		0.03						
Thailand								
Tunisia								
Turkey		4.25						
Ukraine								
UK								
USA	0.06	0.19						
Uruguay		0.31						
World	**0.49**	**0.48**	**0.41**	**0.40**	**0.38**	**0.36**	**0.35**	**0.33**

Table 38 (cont.) Shares (%) of world's top 30 white varieties in national winegrape area, by country, 2010

Country	Pinot Blanc	Gewurztraminer	Chasselas	Feteasca Regala	Melon	Pedro Gimenez	Other White	Non-white Varieties	Total
Algeria								100.00	100
Argentina	0.00				0.00	6.03	6.99	78.37	100
Armenia							73.28		100
Australia		0.55					3.58	63.07	100
Austria	4.20	0.68					6.78	36.52	100
Brazil	0.00	0.03	0.01				15.05	81.06	100
Bulgaria		1.33					16.72	70.73	100
Canada	1.24	4.00	0.05				19.10	51.81	100
Chile		0.28	0.08			0.11	1.90	72.88	100
China	0.01	0.02						95.96	100
Croatia	0.90	1.13	0.10				30.23	35.46	100
Cyprus							30.82	66.30	100
Czech Rep.	4.51	3.70					7.33	41.38	100
France	0.15	0.36	0.29		1.46		5.33	68.44	100
Georgia	0.46						34.28	12.25	100
Germany	3.79		1.10				38.18	19.89	100
Greece							31.17	62.74	100
Hungary	0.34		2.71				42.72	34.09	100
Italy	0.49	0.23	0.01				16.28	59.69	100
Japan							13.39	65.49	100
Kazakhstan							20.23		100
Luxembourg	12.42	1.53					42.48	18.95	100
Mexico							23.89	62.38	100
Moldova	0.39	3.04					2.64	42.05	100
Morocco							3.43	89.09	100
Myanmar								58.99	100
N. Zealand	0.05	0.97	0.01				3.14	28.76	100
Peru							30.49	60.01	100
Portugal	0.01	0.00	0.05				30.21	66.29	100
Romania		0.23		7.58			55.66	16.47	100
Russia	2.71		0.08				34.57	39.66	100
Serbia			5.00				16.00	31.00	100
Slovakia	4.14	2.10		1.83			10.87	33.05	100
Slovenia	3.21						26.83	35.36	100
S. Africa	0.01	0.12					3.23	44.24	100
Spain		0.03	0.00				8.54	53.75	100
Switzerland	0.71	0.33	27.08				5.53	59.32	100
Thailand							15.06	66.40	100
Tunisia								100.00	100
Turkey							25.11	67.49	100
Ukraine	0.65	1.84					6.69	32.19	100
UK	1.92	0.08					35.73	38.73	100
USA	0.12	0.50					4.16	65.27	100
Uruguay	0.12	0.31					4.61	80.50	100
World	**0.32**	**0.31**	**0.29**	**0.29**	**0.27**	**0.27**	**13.03**	**57.25**	**100**

Table 39: National winegrape areas (hectares) for world's top 6 non-red/white varieties, 2000

Country	Cereza	Pinot Gris	Moscatel Rosada	Kovidinka	Roditis	Kuldzhinskii	Other	Non-Red/White Total	% of all winegrapes
Algeria									
Argentina	31666		10656					42321	0.87
Armenia									
Australia									
Austria		293					356	648	0.01
Brazil									
Bulgaria									
Canada		210						210	0.00
Chile		2					7	9	0.00
Croatia									
Cyprus									
Czech Rep.									
France		1969					244	2213	0.05
Georgia							20	20	0.00
Germany		2636					328	2965	0.06
Greece					299		46	345	0.01
Hungary		890		1214				2104	0.04
Italy		6608					17	6626	0.14
Luxembourg		155						155	0.00
Moldova		2042						2042	0.04
Morocco									
N. Zealand		127					6	133	0.00
Portugal									
Romania		2388						2388	0.05
Russia									
Serbia									
Slovakia									
Slovenia									
S. Africa		104						104	0.00
Spain									
Switzerland		149						149	0.00
Tunisia									
UK									
USA		826					125	951	0.02
Uruguay									
"Missing 9"		480				269	317	1066	0.02
Total	**31666**	**18879**	**10656**	**1214**	**299**	**269**	**1466**	**64449**	**1.32**

Table 40: National shares (%) of global winegrape area for world's top 6 non-red/white varieties, 2000

Country	Cereza	Pinot Gris	Moscatel Rosada	Kovidinka	Roditis	kuldzhinskii	Other	Non-Red/White Total
Algeria								
Argentina	100.00		100.00					65.67
Armenia								
Australia								
Austria		1.55					24.27	1.01
Brazil								
Bulgaria								
Canada		1.11						0.33
Chile		0.01					0.48	0.01
Croatia								
Cyprus								
Czech Rep.								
France		10.43					16.63	3.43
Georgia							1.36	0.03
Germany		13.97					22.38	4.60
Greece					100.00		3.11	0.53
Hungary		4.72		100.00				3.27
Italy		35.00					1.17	10.28
Luxembourg		0.82						0.24
Moldova		10.82						3.17
Morocco								
N. Zealand		0.67					0.41	0.21
Portugal								
Romania		12.65						3.70
Russia								
Serbia								
Slovakia								
Slovenia								
S. Africa		0.55						0.16
Spain								
Switzerland		0.79						0.23
Tunisia								
UK								
USA		4.37					8.56	1.48
Uruguay								
"Missing 9"		2.54				100	22	1.65
Total	**100**	**100**	**100**	**100**	**100**	**100**	**100**	**100**

Table 41: National winegrape area (hectares) for world's top 6 non-red/white varieties, 2010

Country	Pinot Gris	Cereza	Moscatel Rosada	Roditis	Misket Cherven	Kovidinka	Other	Non-Red/White Total	% of all winegrapes
Algeria									
Argentina	297	29189	7259				269	37015	0.80
Armenia									
Australia	3296							3296	0.07
Austria	215						279	493	0.01
Brazil	7						7	14	0.00
Bulgaria					4159			4159	0.09
Canada	549						28	578	0.01
Chile	100		70					169	0.00
China	2							2	0.00
Croatia	219					56		275	0.01
Cyprus									
Czech Rep.	706						198	904	0.02
France	2617							2617	0.06
Georgia							26	26	0.00
Germany	4450						120	4570	0.10
Greece				4661			80	4741	0.10
Hungary	1624					1020	37	2681	0.06
Italy	17281						69	17350	0.38
Japan							220	220	0.00
Kazakhstan							613	613	0.01
Luxembourg	146							146	0.00
Mexico									
Moldova	2042							2042	0.04
Morocco									
Myanmar									
N. Zealand	1501						2	1503	0.03
Peru							7	7	0.00
Portugal	5						2	6	0.00
Romania	1301						268	1569	0.03
Russia	78						462	540	0.01
Serbia									
Slovakia	211						32	242	0.01
Slovenia	501							501	0.01
S. Africa	261							261	0.01
Spain									
Switzerland	216							216	0.00
Thailand									
Tunisia									
Turkey									
Ukraine	685							685	0.01
UK	9						50	59	0.00
USA	5231						1714	6946	0.15
Uruguay	12							12	0.00
Total	**43563**	**29189**	**7329**	**4661**	**4159**	**1075**	**4482**	**94459**	**2.05**

Table 42: National shares (%) of global winegrape area for world's top 6 non-red/white varieties, 2010

Country	Cereza	Moscatel Rosada	Roditis	Misket Cherven	Kovidinka	Other	Non-Red/White Total
Algeria							
Argentina	0.68	100.00	99.05			6.01	39.19
Armenia							
Australia	7.57						3.49
Austria	0.49					6.22	0.52
Brazil	0.02					0.16	0.01
Bulgaria				100.00			4.40
Canada	1.26					0.63	0.61
Chile	0.23	0.95					0.18
China	0.00						0.00
Croatia	0.50				5.19		0.29
Cyprus							
Czech Rep.	1.62					4.42	0.96
France	6.01						2.77
Georgia						0.57	0.03
Germany	10.22					2.68	4.84
Greece			100.00			1.78	5.02
Hungary	3.73				94.81	0.84	2.84
Italy	39.67					1.54	18.37
Japan						4.90	0.23
Kazakhstan						13.67	0.65
Luxembourg	0.34						0.15
Mexico							
Moldova	4.69						2.16
Morocco							
Myanmar							
N. Zealand	3.45					0.04	1.59
Peru						0.16	0.01
Portugal	0.01					0.04	0.01
Romania	2.99					5.98	1.66
Russia	0.18					10.31	0.57
Serbia							
Slovakia	0.48					0.70	0.26
Slovenia	1.15						0.53
S. Africa	0.60						0.28
Spain							
Switzerland	0.50						0.23
Thailand							
Tunisia							
Turkey							
Ukraine	1.57						0.73
UK	0.02					1.12	0.06
USA	12.01					38.25	7.35
Uruguay	0.03						0.01
Total	**100**	**100**	**100**	**100**	**100**	**100**	**100**

Table Section V: Winegrape areas and Varietal Intensity Indexes for national top 45 varieties

Table 43: Winegrape areas, national and global shares (and Varietal Intensity Indexes) for national top 45 varieties, 2000

	Algeria					Argentina				
Prime variety	Col	Area	Nat'l share	Glob'l share	VII*	Prime variety	Col	Area	Nat'l share	Glob'l share	VII*
Cinsaut	R	7550	25.0	15.6	25.2	Cereza	O	31665.5	15.7	100.0	24.3
Mazuelo	R	7550	25.0	6.0	9.6	Criolla Grande	R	24641	12.3	100.0	24.3
Garnacha Tinta	R	6040	20.0	2.8	4.6	Cot	R	16347	8.1	67.0	16.2
Alicante Henri Bouschet	R	3020	10.0	8.2	13.2	Pedro Gimenez	W	15101	7.5	100.0	24.3
Cabernet Sauvignon	R	1510	5.0	0.7	1.1	Douce Noire	R	14989	7.5	84.9	20.6
Merlot	R	1510	5.0	0.7	1.2	Cabernet Sauvignon	R	12199	6.1	5.5	1.3
Pinot Noir	R	1510	5.0	2.5	4.1	Moscatel Rosada	O	10655.6	5.3	100.0	24.3
Syrah	R	1510	5.0	1.5	2.4	Torrontes Riojano	W	8181	4.1	99.9	24.2
Total		30200	100			Syrah	R	7915	3.9	7.8	1.9
						Muscat of Alexandria	W	5538.5	2.8	18.8	4.6
						Merlot	R	5513	2.7	2.6	0.6
						Chardonnay	W	4625	2.3	3.2	0.8
						Tempranillo	R	4335	2.2	4.7	1.1
						Chenin Blanc	W	3591	1.8	7.8	1.9
						Torrontes Sanjuanino	W	3165.6	1.6	100.0	24.3
						Trebbiano Toscano	W	2846	1.4	2.1	0.5
						Superior Seedless	W	2835.4	1.4	99.8	24.2
						Sangiovese	R	2491	1.2	3.6	0.9
						Sultaniye	W	2229	1.1	15.5	3.8
						Red Globe	R	1895.1	0.9	91.6	22.2
						Barbera	R	1061	0.5	3.2	0.8
						Pinot Noir	R	1047	0.5	1.7	0.4
						Semillon	W	1028	0.5	3.9	1.0
						Sauvignon Blanc	W	827	0.4	1.3	0.3
						Sauvignonasse	W	798	0.4	14.5	3.5
						Flame Seedless	R	508.9	0.3	94.0	22.8
						Aspiran Bouschet	R	307.9	0.2	99.9	24.2
						Cabernet Franc	R	207	0.1	0.4	0.1
						Viognier	W	151	0.1	4.8	1.2
						Tannat	R	136	0.1	2.4	0.6
						Pinot Blanc	W	48	0.0	0.3	0.1
						Other varieties		14235	7.1		
						Total		201113	100		

Note: VII* indicates Varital Intensity Indexes relative to the world, as defined in the introduction.

Table 43 (cont.) Winegrape areas, national and global shares (and Varietal Intensity Indexes) for national top 45 varieties, 2000

	Armenia					Australia				
Prime variety	Col	Area	Nat'l share	Glob'l share	VII*	Prime variety	Col	Area	Nat'l share	Glob'l share	VII*
Rkatsiteli	W	2469	22.0	3.7	16.0	Syrah	R	29295	22.4	28.9	10.8
Mskhali	W	1093	9.8	100.0	435.3	Cabernet Sauvignon	R	24997	19.1	11.3	4.2
Garandmak	W	931	8.3	100.0	435.3	Chardonnay	W	17266	13.2	11.9	4.4
Kangun	W	850	7.6	100.0	435.3	Sultaniye	W	10298	7.9	71.8	26.8
Voskeat	W	809	7.2	100.0	435.3	Merlot	R	7669	5.9	3.6	1.4
Muscat Blanc a Petits Grains	W	526	4.7	1.9	8.1	Semillon	W	6528	5.0	24.9	9.3
Other varieties		4528	40.4			Pinot Noir	R	3223	2.5	5.4	2.0
Total		11206	100			Riesling	W	3129	2.4	7.2	2.7
						Sauvignon Blanc	W	2602	2.0	4.0	1.5
						Muscat of Alexandria	W	2495	1.9	8.5	3.2
						Ruby Cabernet	R	2424	1.9	32.7	12.2
						Garnacha Tinta	R	2139	1.6	1.0	0.4
						Colombard	W	1801	1.4	4.7	1.8
						Verdelho	W	1293	1.0	78.9	29.5
						Monastrell	R	948	0.7	1.2	0.5
						Chenin Blanc	W	841	0.6	1.8	0.7
						Korinthiaki	R	778	0.6	93.3	34.9
						Cabernet Franc	R	744	0.6	1.5	0.6
						Petit Verdot	R	721	0.6	48.7	18.2
						Trebbiano	W	685	0.5	100.0	37.4
						Gewurztraminer	W	521	0.4	4.9	1.8
						Cot	R	429	0.3	1.8	0.7
						Muscat a Petits Grains I	R	380	0.3	76.0	28.4
						Sangiovese	R	372	0.3	0.5	0.2
						Afus Ali	W	328	0.3	100.0	37.3
						Doradillo	W	249	0.2	100.0	37.4
						Marsanne	W	216	0.2	14.3	5.3
						Muscat Blanc a Petits G	W	214	0.2	0.8	0.3
						Muscadelle	W	198	0.2	9.0	3.4
						Durif	R	181	0.1	15.1	5.6
						Palomino Fino	W	124	0.1	0.4	0.2
						Tarrango	R	120	0.1	100.0	37.4
						Viognier	W	117	0.1	3.7	1.4
						Pinot Meunier	R	107	0.1	1.0	0.4
						Barbera	R	103	0.1	0.3	0.1
						Crouchen	W	98	0.1	4.3	1.6
						Mazuelo	R	90	0.1	0.1	0.0
						Pedro Ximenez	W	89	0.1	0.5	0.2
						Touriga Nacional	R	73	0.1	1.7	0.6
						Nebbiolo	R	50	0.0	1.0	0.4
						Canada Muscat	W	49	0.0	100.0	37.4
						Taminga	W	46	0.0	100.0	37.4
						Tempranillo	R	41	0.0	0.0	0.0
						Other varieties		6532	5.0		
						Total		130602	100		

Table 43 (cont.) Winegrape areas, national and global shares (and Varietal Intensity Indexes) for national top 45 varieties, 2000

	Austria					Brazil				
Prime variety	Col	Area	Nat'l share	Glob'l share	VII*	Prime variety	Col	Area	Nat'l share	Glob'l share	VII*
Gruner Veltliner	W	17479	36.0	74.1	74.5	Isabella	R	14285	27.0	52.2	48.2
Zweigelt	R	4350	9.0	60.2	60.5	Niagara	W	13436	25.4	87.6	80.8
Grasevina	W	4323	8.9	4.7	4.7	Bordo	R	3379	6.4	100.0	92.3
Muller Thurgau	W	3289	6.8	9.8	9.9	Concord	R	2509	4.7	21.2	19.6
Pinot Blanc	W	2936	6.1	17.3	17.4	Seibel	R	1967	3.7	99	91.2
Blaufrankisch	R	2641	5.4	20.5	20.6	Herbemont	R	1453	2.7	100	92.3
Blauer Portugieser	R	2358	4.9	55.1	55.4	Grasevina	W	880	1.7	1.0	0.9
Riesling	W	1643	3.4	3.8	3.8	Muscat of Alexandria	W	809	1.5	2.8	2.5
Neuburger	W	1094	2.3	76.3	76.7	Trebbiano Toscano	W	688	1.3	0.5	0.5
Blauburger	R	884	1.8	88.2	88.7	Cabernet Sauvignon	R	587	1.1	0.3	0.2
Fruhroter Veltliner	R	626	1.3	99.0	99.6	Merlot	R	469	0.9	0.2	0.2
Scheurebe	W	529	1.1	14.5	14.6	Cabernet Franc	R	405	0.8	0.8	0.8
Blauer Wildbacher	R	464	1.0	98.3	98.8	Semillon	W	384	0.7	1.5	1.4
Muscat Ottonel	W	418	0.9	3.4	3.4	Chardonnay	W	330	0.6	0.2	0.2
Sankt Laurent	R	415	0.9	17.5	17.6	Couderc Noir	R	299	0.6	49.1	45.3
Pinot Noir	R	409	0.8	0.7	0.7	Tannat	R	182	0.3	3.3	3.0
Bouvier	W	365	0.8	100	101	Jacquez	R	170	0.3	75.3	69.5
Gewurztraminer	W	363	0.7	3.4	3.4	Gewurztraminer	W	140	0.3	1	1.2
Sauvignon Blanc	W	314	0.6	0.5	0.5	Sauvignon Blanc	W	140	0.3	0.2	0.2
Cabernet Sauvignon	R	312	0.6	0.1	0.1	Other varieties		10328	19.5		
Goldburger	W	309	0.6	100	101	Total		52840	100.0		
Pinot Gris	O	293	0.6	1.5	1.6						
Roter Veltliner	O	258	0.5	100	101						
Muscat Blanc a Petits Grains	W	143	0.3		0.5						
Rotgipfler	W	118	0.2	100	101						
Merlot	R	112	0.2	0.1	0.1						
Zierfandler	O	98	0.2	100	101						
Silvaner	W	53	0.1	1.3	1.3						
Jubilaumsrebe	W	30	0.1	100	101						
Cabernet Franc	R	27	0.1	0.1	0.1						
Furmint	W	1	0.0	0.0	0.0						
Other varieties		1843	3.8								
Total		48496	100								

Table 43 (cont.) Winegrape areas, national and global shares (and Varietal Intensity Indexes) for national top 45 varieties, 2000

	Bulgaria					Canada				
Prime variety	Col	Area	Nat'l share	Glob'l share	VII* Prime variety	Col	Area	Nat'l share	Glob'l share	VII*
Pamid	R	22581	23.5	99.4	50.5 Concord	R	977	11.5	8.3	47.5
Merlot	R	11169	11.6	5.3	2.7 Chardonnay	W	973	11.5	0.7	3.8
Cabernet Sauvignon	R	10441	10.9	4.7	2.4 Merlot	R	674	7.9	0.3	1.8
Rkatsiteli	W	9429	9.8	14.0	7.1 Cabernet Sauvignon	R	569	6.7	0.3	1.5
Dimyat	W	7649	8.0	99.1	50.4 Cabernet Franc	R	567	6.7	1.2	6.7
Shiroka Melnishka	R	3804	4.0	100.0	50.8 Vidal	W	514	6.0	84.1	482.9
Misket	W	3764	3.9	100.0	50.8 Riesling	W	482	5.7	1.1	6.4
Grasevina	W	3602	3.8	3.9	2.0 Niagara	W	461	5.4	3.0	17.3
Cardinal	R	3035	3.2	95.1	48.3 Pinot Noir	R	457	5.4	0.8	4.4
Muscat Ottonel	W	2914	3.0	23.8	12.1 Baco Noir	R	279	3.3	70.3	403
Chardonnay	W	1862	1.9	1.3	0.7 Gamay Noir	R	263	3.1	0.7	4.0
Trebbiano Toscano	W	1821	1.9	1.3	0.7 Gewurztraminer	W	237	2.8	2.2	12.7
Aligote	W	1659	1.7	4.7	2.4 Pinot Gris	O	210	2.5	1.1	6.4
Kadarka	R	1619	1.7	61.5	31.3 Sauvignon Blanc	W	148	1.7	0.2	1.3
Gewurztraminer	W	971	1.0	9.1	4.6 Pinot Blanc	W	146	1.7	0.9	4.9
Pinot Noir	R	769	0.8	1.3	0.7 Seyval Blanc	W	132	1.5	33.8	194.2
Mavrud	R	647	0.7	100.0	50.8 De Chaunac	R	119	1.4	64.1	368
Riesling	W	647	0.7	1.5	0.8 Marechal Foch	R	109	1.3	63.1	362
Koenigin der Weingaerten	W	567	0.6	75.5	38.4 Fredonia	R	73	0.9	84.9	487
Muscat of Hamburg	R	445	0.5	6.3	3.2 Elvira	W	69	0.8	20.0	114.9
Sauvignon Blanc	W	405	0.4	0.6	0.3 Other varieties		1040	12.2		
Other varieties		6197	6.5		Total		8498	100		
Total		95997	100							

Table 43 (cont.) Winegrape areas, national and global shares (and Varietal Intensity Indexes) for national top 45 varieties, 2000

	Chile					Croatia				
Prime variety	Col	Area	Nat'l share	Glob'l share	VII*	Prime variety	Col	Area	Nat'l share	Glob'l share	VII*
Cabernet Sauvignon	R	35967	31.6	16.3	7.0	Grasevina	W	16051	27.0	17.4	14.3
Listan Prieto	R	15181	13.3	97.7	41.8	Malvazija Istarska	W	7134	12.0	94.4	77.4
Merlot	R	12825	11.3	6.1	2.6	Plavac Mali	R	6539	11.0	100.0	82.1
Chardonnay	W	7672	6.7	5.3	2.3	Posip Bijeli	W	6539	11.0	100.0	82.1
Sauvignon Blanc	W	6662	5.8	10.3	4.4	Babic	R	1189	2.0	100.0	82.1
Carmenere	R	4719	4.1	82.6	35.4	Blaufrankisch	R	1189	2.0	9.2	7.6
Malvasia Fina	W	4305	3.8	60.6	25.9	Mondeuse Noire	R	1189	2.0	84.7	69.5
Alicante Henri Bouschet	R	2882	2.5		3.3	Other varieties		19618	33.0		
Pedro Ximenez	W	2379	2.1	13.8	5.9	Total		59448	100		
Syrah	R	2040	1.8	2.0	0.9						
Semillon	W	1893	1.7	7.2	3.1						
Pinot Noir	R	1614	1.4	2.7	1.1						
Cot	R	929	0.8	3.8	1.6						
Cabernet Franc	R	689	0.6	1.4	0.6						
Mazuelo	R	641	0.6	0.5	0.2						
Chasselas	W	404	0.4	3.0	1.3						
Riesling	W	286	0.3	0.7	0.3						
Cinsaut	R	195	0.2	0.4	0.2						
Sauvignonasse	W	132	0.1	2.4	1.0						
Viognier	W	128	0.1	4.1	1.7						
Sangiovese	R	123	0.1	0.2	0.1						
Gewurztraminer	W	121	0.1	1.1	0.5						
Blanca Ovoide	W	107	0.1	100.0	42.8						
Tribidrag	R	91	0.1	0.3	0.1						
Petit Verdot	R	84	0.1	5.7	2.4						
Chenin Blanc	W	76	0.1	0.2	0.1						
Moscato Giallo	W	65	0.1	15.9	6.8						
Monastrell	R	22	0.0	0.0	0.0						
Pinot Blanc	W	14	0.0	0.1	0.0						
Nebbiolo	R	10	0.0	0.2	0.1						
Sauvignon Rose	O	7	0.0	26.8	11.5						
Albillo Real	W	2	0.0	0.1	0.0						
Pinot Gris	O	2	0.0	0.0	0.0						
Marsanne	W	1	0.0	0.1	0.0						
Tempranillo	R	1	0.0	0.0	0.0						
Other varieties		11697	10.3								
Total		113966	100								

Table 43 (cont.) Winegrape areas, national and global shares (and Varietal Intensity Indexes) for national top 45 varieties, 2000

	Cyprus					Czech Republic					
Prime variety	Col	Area	Nat'l share	Glob'l share	VII*	Prime variety	Col	Area	Nat'l share	Glob'l share	VII*
Mavro	R	10969	60	100	266.8	Gruner Veltliner	W	1699.7	15.0	7.2	31.0
Xynisteri	W	2742	15	100	266.8	Muller Thurgau	W	1586.4	14.0	4.7	20.3
Other varieties		4570	25			Grasevina	W	1246.4	11.0	1.4	5.8
Total		18282	100			Sankt Laurent	R	1019.8	9.0	43.0	185.3
						Riesling	W	793	7.0	1.8	7.9
						Blaufrankisch	R	680	6.0	5.3	22.7
						Chardonnay	W	567	5.0	0.4	1.7
						Zweigelt	R	453	4.0	6.3	27.0
						Blauer Portugieser	R	340	3.0	7.9	34.2
						Neuburger	W	340	3.0	23.7	102.1
						Other varieties		2606.2	23.0		
						Total		11331	100		

Table 43 (cont.) Winegrape areas, national and global shares (and Varietal Intensity Indexes) for national top 45 varieties, 2000

	France						Georgia				
Prime variety	Col	Area	Nat'l share	Glob'l share	VII*	Prime variety	Col	Area	Nat'l share	Glob'l share	VII*
Merlot	R	101309	11.7	47.8	2.7	Rkatsiteli	W	19741	52.8	29.3	38.2
Mazuelo	R	95745	11.1	75.6	4.3	Tsolikouri	W	6161	16.5	100.0	130.4
Garnacha Tinta	R	95717	11.1	44.7	2.5	Saperavi	R	3704	9.9	55.2	72.0
Trebbiano Toscano	W	90341	10.4	66.1	3.7	Tsitska	W	2839	7.6	100.0	130.4
Cabernet Sauvignon	R	53413	6.2	24.2	1.4	Chinuri	W	955	2.6	100.0	130.4
Syrah	R	50676	5.9	49.9	2.8	Mtsvane Kakhuri	W	249	0.7	100.0	130.4
Chardonnay	W	36496	4.2	25.1	1.4	Goruli Mtsvane	W	224	0.6	100.0	130.4
Cabernet Franc	R	36094	4.2	74.3	4.2	Cabernet Sauvignon	R	223	0.6	0.1	0.1
Gamay Noir	R	34537	4.0	91.4	5.2	Aleksandrouli	R	219	0.6	100.0	130.4
Cinsaut	R	31593	3.7	65.2	3.7	Pinot Blanc	W	171	0.5	1.0	1.3
Pinot Noir	R	26525	3.1	44.1	2.5	Tsulukidzis Tetra	W	152	0.4	100.0	130.4
Sauvignon Blanc	W	20933	2.4	32.3	1.8	Aligote	W	97	0.3	0.3	0.4
Semillon	W	14015	1.6	53.4	3.0	Aladasturi	R	46	0.1	100.0	130.4
Melon	W	13253	1.5	100.0	5.6	Krakhuna	W	36	0.1	100.0	130.4
Pinot Meunier	R	10621	1.2	98.1	5.5	Tavkveri	R	29	0.1	100.0	130.4
Chenin Blanc	W	9837	1.1	21.5	1.2	Ojaleshi	R	25	0.1	100.0	130.4
Aramon Noir	R	9084	1.1	100.0	5.6	Chkhaveri	O	20	0.1	100.0	130.4
Alicante Henri Bouschet	R	8764	1.0	23.7	1.3	Kisi	W	20	0.1	100.0	130.4
Monastrell	R	7634	0.9	10.0	0.6	Usakhelouri	R	8	0.02	100.0	130.4
Muscat Blanc a Petits Grains	W	6935	0.8	24.4	1.4	Khikhvi	W	5	0.01	100.0	130.4
Colombard	W	6896	0.8	18.1	1.0	Otskhanuri Sapere	R	5	0.01	100.0	130.4
Garnacha Blanca	W	6461	0.7	59.7	3.4	Other varieties		2490	6.7		
Cot	R	6129	0.7	25.1	1.4	Total		37419	100		
Macabeo	W	5223	0.6	10.9	0.6						
Riesling	W	3407	0.4	7.9	0.4						
Mauzac Blanc	W	3251	0.4	100.0	5.6						
Muscat of Alexandria	W	3027	0.4	10.3	0.6						
Clairette	W	2918	0.3	72.9	4.1						
Tannat	R	2760	0.3	49.7	2.8						
Gewurztraminer	W	2758	0.3	25.8	1.5						
Terret Blanc	W	2703	0.3	100.0	5.6						
Garnacha Roja	W	2635	0.3	95.4	5.4						
Vermentino	W	2634	0.3	45.1	2.5						
Folle Blanche	W	2605	0.3	98.4	5.5						
Viognier	W	2360	0.3	74.7	4.2						
Grolleau Noir	R	2201	0.3	100.0	5.6						
Gros Manseng	W	2160	0.2	100.0	5.6						
Baco Blanc	W	2137	0.2	100.0	5.6						
Muscadelle	W	2009	0.2	91.0	5.1						
Auxerrois	W	1997	0.2	86.8	4.9						
Pinot Gris	O	1969	0.2	10.4	0.6						
Silvaner	W	1934	0.2	46.2	2.6						
Aligote	W	1756	0.2	4.9	0.3						
Sangiovese	R	1564	0.2	2.3	0.1						
Tempranillo	R	1549	0.2	1.7	0.1						
Other varieties		36279	4.2								
Total		864846	100								

Table 43 (cont.) Winegrape areas, national and global shares (and Varietal Intensity Indexes) for national top 45 varieties, 2000

	Germany					Greece				
Prime variety	Col	Area	Nat'l share	Glob'l share	VII*	Prime variety	Col	Area	Nat'l share	Glob'l share	VII*
Riesling	W	22350	21.4	51.8	24.2	Savatiano	W	12747	25.1	100.0	95.9
Muller Thurgau	W	20691	19.9	61.6	28.9	Roditis(Red)	R	6945	13.7	100.0	95.9
Kerner	W	6828	6.6	96.0	44.9	Liatiko	R	2476	4.9	100.0	95.9
Dornfelder	R	3765	3.6	100.0	46.8	Agiorgitiko	R	2320	4.6	100.0	95.9
Bacchus	W	3279	3.1	96.7	45.3	Moschomavro	R	2305	4.5	100.0	95.9
Scheurebe	W	3126	3.0	85.5	40.0	Muscat Blanc a Petits Grains	W	2222	4.4	7.8	7.5
Pinot Gris	O	2636	2.5	14.0	6.5	Xinomavro	R	1816	3.6	100.0	95.9
Pinot Blanc	W	2396	2.3	14.1	6.6	Athiri	W	1273	2.5	100.0	95.9
Faberrebe	W	1586	1.5	100.0	46.8	Kotsifali	R	1148	2.3	100.0	95.9
Huxelrebe	W	1289	1.2	100.0	46.8	Assyrtiko	W	1106	2.2	100.0	95.9
Chasselas	W	1198	1.1	9.0	4.2	Mandilaria	R	845	1.7	100.0	95.9
Morio-Muskat	W	1167	1.1	98.2	46.0	Trebbiano Toscano	W	720	1.4	0.5	0.51
Ortega	W	1054	1.0	100.0	46.8	Cabernet Sauvignon	R	688	1.4	0.3	0.3
Elbling	W	1042	1.0	55.9	26.2	Mavrodafni	R	537	1.1	100.0	95.9
Chardonnay	W	531	0.5	0.4	0.2	Vilana	W	506	1.0	100.0	95.9
Dunkelfelder	R	280	0.3	100.0	46.8	Vertzami	R	491	1.0	100.0	95.9
Reichensteiner	W	257	0.2	80.6	37.7	Debina	W	455	0.9	100.0	95.9
Ehrenfelser	W	255	0.2	88.2	41.3	Asprouda	W	433	0.9	100.0	95.9
Optima	W	239	0.2	100.0	46.8	Moschofilero	W	423	0.8	100.0	95.9
Heroldrebe	R	199	0.2	100.0	46.8	Monemvassia	W	418	0.8	100.0	95.9
Domina	R	187	0.2	100.0	46.8	Romeiko	R	382	0.8	100.0	95.9
Siegerrebe	O	167	0.2	100.0	46.8	Robola	W	356	0.7	100.0	95.9
Regner	W	150	0.1	100.0	46.8	Mavrouda	R	349	0.7	100.0	95.9
Perle	O	121	0.1	100.0	46.8	Roditis	O	299	0.6	100.0	95.9
Nobling	W	102	0.1	99.9	46.7	Fileri	W	249	0.5	100.0	95.9
Muscat Blanc a Petits Grains	W	87	0.1	0.3	0.1	Merlot	R	180	0.4	0.1	0.08
Pinot Noir Precoce	R	84	0.1	98.5	46.1	Fokiano	R	162	0.3	100.0	95.9
Auxerrois	W	77	0.1	3.4	1.6	Sauvignon Blanc	W	158	0.3	0.2	0.23
Rieslaner	W	70	0.1	100.0	46.8	Goustolidi	W	112	0.2	100.0	95.9
Kanzler	W	53	0.1	100.0	46.8	Cinsaut	R	108	0.2	0.2	0.21
Juwel	W	42	0.0	100.0	46.8	Stavroto	R	104	0.2	100.0	95.9
Schonburger	O	39	0.0	100.0	46.8	Negoska	R	96	0.2	100.0	95.9
Deckrot	R	30	0.0	100.0	46.8	Limnio	R	95	0.2	100.0	95.9
Helfensteiner	R	26	0.0	100.0	46.8	Dimyat	W	70	0.1	0.9	0.87
Phoenix	W	24	0.0	100.0	46.8	Liatiko(White)	W	70	0.1	100.0	95.9
Kernling	W	18	0.0	100.0	46.8	Vilana(Red)	R	60	0.1	100.0	95.9
Freisamer	W	16	0.0	96.6	45.2	Fokiano (White)	W	57	0.1	100.0	95.9
Albalonga	W	16	0.0	27.8	13.0	Moschofilero	O	46	0.1	100.0	95.9
Ehrenbreitsteiner	W	13	0.0	100.0	46.8	Cabernet Franc	R	40	0.1	0.1	0.08
Holder	W	13	0.0	100.0	46.8	Athiri (Red)	R	40	0.1	100.0	95.9
Hegel	R	10	0.0	100.0	46.8	Syrah	R	39	0.1	0.0	0.04
Goldriesling	W	10	0.0	99.6	46.6	Krassato	R	38	0.1	100.0	95.9
Mariensteiner	W	9	0.0	100.0	46.8	Batily	R	38	0.1	100.0	95.9
Orion	W	8	0.0	100.0	46.8	Chardonnay	W	36	0.1	0.0	0.02
Muscat Ottonel	W	7	0.0	0.1	0.0	Limnio(White)	W	27	0.1	100.0	95.9
Other varieties		28657	27.5			Other varieties		7791	15.3		
Total		104207	100			Total		50878	100		

Table 43 (cont.) Winegrape areas, national and global shares (and Varietal Intensity Indexes) for national top 45 varieties, 2000

	Hungary					Italy				
Prime variety	Col	Area	Nat'l share	Glob'l share	VII*	Prime variety	Col	Area	Nat'l share	Glob'l share	VII*
Blaufrankisch	R	6920	8.0	53.7	30.2	Sangiovese	R	62761	9.9	91.1	7.0
Grasevina	W	6677	7.7	7.2	4.1	Catarratto Bianco	W	50711	8.0	100.0	7.7
Furmint	W	3480	4.0	100.0	56.1	Trebbiano Toscano	W	39447	6.2	28.9	2.2
Mutler Thurgau	W	3278	3.8	9.8	5.5	Montepulciano	R	28679	4.5	100.0	7.7
Ezerjo	W	3157	3.6	100.0	56.1	Barbera	R	27175	4.3	82.2	6.3
Chardonnay	W	2954	3.4	2.0	1.1	Merlot	R	21861	3.4	10.3	0.8
Arany Sarfeher	W	2914	3.4	100.0	56.1	Trebbiano Romagnolo	W	19492	3.1	100.0	7.7
Zalagyongye	W	2550	2.9	58.9	33.1	Negroamaro	R	16619	2.6	100.0	7.7
Zweigelt	R	2266	2.6	31.3	17.6	Garganega	W	16549	2.6	100.0	7.7
Cserszegi Fuszeres	W	2185	2.5	100.0	56.1	Muscat Blanc a Petits Grains	W	13016	2.0	45.8	3.5
Chasselas	W	1902	2.2	14.3	8.0	Malvasia Bianca di Candia	W	11921	1.9	92.5	7.1
Riesling	W	1619	1.9	3.8	2.1	Chardonnay	W	11687	1.8	8.0	0.6
Silvaner	W	1619	1.9	38.7	21.7	Nero d'Avola	R	11318	1.8	100.0	7.7
Muscat Blanc a Petits Grains	W	1538	1.8	5.4	3.0	Aglianico	R	9264	1.5	100.0	7.7
Muscat Ottonel	W	1416	1.6	11.6	6.5	Inzolia	W	9259	1.5	100.0	7.7
Kunleany	W	1376	1.6	100.0	56.1	Trebbiano d'Abruzzo	W	8435	1.3	100.0	7.7
Gruner Veltliner	W	1335	1.5	5.7	3.2	Manzoni Bianco	W	8290	1.3	100.0	7.7
Blauer Portugieser	R	1255	1.4	29.3	16.5	Tribidrag	R	7828	1.2	29.1	2.2
Kovidinka	O	1214	1.4	100.0	56.1	Cabernet Sauvignon	R	7682	1.2	3.5	0.3
Cabernet Sauvignon	R	1052	1.2	0.5	0.3	Prosecco	W	7498	1.2	100.0	7.7
Harslevelu	W	1012	1.2	78.1	43.8	Dolcetto	R	7156	1.1	99.5	7.6
Kadarka	R	1012	1.2	38.5	21.6	Garnacha Tinta	R	6781	1.1	3.2	0.2
Feteasca Alba	W	971	1.1	4.1	2.3	Cabernet Franc	R	6639	1.0	13.7	1.0
Pinot Gris	O	890	1.0	4.7	2.6	Pinot Gris	O	6608	1.0	35.0	2.7
Feteasca Regala	W	567	0.7	22.0	12.3	Pignoletto	W	6009	0.9	100.0	7.7
Lakhegyi Mezes	W	567	0.7	100.0	56.1	Verdicchio Bianco	W	5043	0.8		7.7
Cabernet Franc	R	526	0.6	1.1	0.6	Pinot Blanc	W	4993	0.8	29.4	2.3
Merlot	R	486	0.6	0.2	0.1	Corvina Veronese	R	4781	0.8	100.0	7.7
Ezerfurtu	W	405	0.5	100.0	56.1	Nebbiolo	R	4778	0.8	94.7	7.3
Zenit	W	405	0.5	100.0	56.1	Sauvignonasse	W	4517	0.7	82.2	6.3
Sauvignon Blanc	W	324	0.4	0.5	0.3	Ancellotta	R	4389	0.7	100.0	7.7
Pinot Noir	R	243	0.3	0.4	0.2	Nerello Mascalese	R	4167	0.7	100.0	7.7
Biborkadarka	R	202	0.2	100.0	56.1	Lambrusco Salamino	R	4147	0.7	100.0	7.7
Pamid	R	121	0.1	0.5	0.3	Albarola	W	4090	0.6	100.0	7.7
Other varieties		28449	32.7			Trebbiano Giallo	W	3984	0.6	100.0	7.7
Total		86886	100			Malvasia Bianca Lunga	W	3937	0.6	100.0	7.7
						Gaglioppo	R	3592	0.6	100.0	7.7
						Sauvignon Blanc	W	3312	0.5	5.1	0.4
						Pinot Noir	R	3287	0.5	5.5	0.4
						Vermentino	W	3201	0.5	54.9	4.2
						Nuragus	W	3186	0.5	100.0	7.7
						Croatina	R	3116	0.5	100.0	7.7
						Cortese	W	3113	0.5	100.0	7.7
						Bombino Bianco	W	2893	0.5	100.0	7.7
						Monica Nera	R	2835	0.4	100.0	7.7
						Other varieties		136615	21.5		
						Total		636662	100		

Table 43 (cont.) Winegrape areas, national and global shares (and Varietal Intensity Indexes) for national top 45 varieties, 2000

	Luxembourg						Moldova				
Prime variety	Col	Area	Nat'l share	Glob'l share	VII*	Prime variety	Col	Area	Nat'l share	Glob'l share	VII*
Müller Thurgau	W	459	34.1	1.4	49.5	Aligote	W	15790	17.6	44.3	24.0
Riesling	W	175	13.0	0.4	14.7	Rkatsiteli	W	11508	12.8	17.1	9.3
Auxerrois	W	169	12.5	7.3	265.7	Isabella	R	11401	12.7	41.6	22.6
Elbling	W	164	12.2	8.8	318.4	Sauvignon Blanc	W	8151	9.1	12.6	6.8
Pinot Gris	O	155	11.5	0.8	29.7	Merlot	R	8123	9.0	3.8	2.1
Pinot Blanc	W	138	10.2	0.8	29.4	Cabernet Sauvignon	R	7590	8.4	3.4	1.9
Pinot Noir	R	66	4.9	0.1	4.0	Pinot Noir	R	6521	7.3	10.9	5.9
Gewurztraminer	W	12	0.9	0.1	4.1	Chardonnay	W	5134	5.7	3.5	1.9
Chardonnay	W	8	0.6	0.0	0.2	Feteasca Alba	W	4334	4.8	18.2	9.9
Gamay Noir	R	1	0.1	0.0	0.1	Gewurztraminer	W	2731	3.0	25.6	13.9
Silvaner	W	1	0.1	0.0	0.9	Pinot Gris	O	2042	2.3	10.8	5.9
Total		1348	100			Muscat Ottonel	W	1520	1.7	12.4	6.7
						Riesling	W	1343	1.5	3.1	1.7
						Bastardo Magarachsky	R	1040	1.2	52.8	28.7
						Saperavi	R	716	0.8	10.7	5.8
						Sukholimanskiy Bely	W	599	0.7	36.7	19.9
						Pinot Blanc	W	350	0.4	2.1	1.1
						Müller Thurgau	W	173	0.2	0.5	0.3
						Muscat Blanc a Petits Grains	W	172	0.2	0.6	0.3
						Silvaner	W	98	0.1	2.3	1.3
						Babeasca Neagra	R	80	0.1	2.1	1.2
						Noah	W	71	0.1	100	54.3
						Pervomaisky	R	64	0.1	100	54.3
						Gamay Teinturier Freaux	R	55	0.1	41.8	22.7
						Golubok	R	50	0.1	100	54.3
						Viorica	W	40	0.0	100	54.3
						Cot	R	39	0.0	0.2	0.1
						Saperavi Severny	R	25	0.0	100	54.3
						Muscat de Ialoveni	W	20	0.0	100	54.3
						Bianca	W	15	0.0	0.7	0.4
						Negru de Ialoveni	R	15	0.0	100	54.3
						Gamay de Teinturier Bouze	R	10	0.0	3.1	1.7
						Codrinski	R	5	0.0	100	54.3
						Ilichevskii Rannii	R	5	0.0	100	54.3
						Onitskanskii Belyi	W	5	0.0	100	54.3
						Droujba	W	3	0.0	100	54.3
						Alb de Ialoveni	W	2	0.0	100	54.3
						Riton	W	2	0.0	100	54.3
						Rubin Tairovsky	R	2	0.0	100	54.3
						Total		89844	100		

Table 43 (cont.) Winegrape areas, national and global shares (and Varietal Intensity Indexes) for national top 45 varieties, 2000

	Morocco					New Zealand				
Prime variety	Col	Area	Nat'l share	Glob'l share	VII* Prime variety	Col	Area	Nat'l share	Glob'l share	VII*
Doukkali	R	16557	33.4	100	98.4 Chardonnay	W	2787	28.0	1.9	9.4
Cinsaut	R	3940	7.9	8.1	8.0 Sauvignon Blanc	W	2423	24.4	3.7	18.3
Muscat of Alexandria	W	3669	7.4	12.5	12.3 Pinot Noir	R	1098	11.0	1.8	9.0
Teneron	R	3488	7.0	100	98.4 Merlot	R	657	6.6	0.3	1.5
Abbo	R	2375	4.8	100	98.4 Cabernet Sauvignon	R	654	6.6	0.3	1.5
Mazuelo	R	1692	3.4	1.3	1.3 Riesling	W	490	4.9	1.1	5.6
Alicante Henri Bouschet	R	1098	2.2	3.0	2.9 Müller Thurgau	W	419	4.2	1.2	6.1
Garnacha Tinta	R	802	1.6	0.4	0.4 Semillon	W	229	2.3	0.9	4.3
Other varieties		15979	32.2		Chenin Blanc	W	146	1.5	0.3	1.6
Total		49600	100		Gewurztraminer	W	141	1.4	1.3	6.5
					Pinot Gris	O	127	1.3	0.7	3.3
					Cabernet Franc	R	118	1.2	0.2	1.2
					Pinotage	R	73	0.7	1.1	5.4
					Cot	R	67	0.7	0.3	1.3
					Reichensteiner	W	62	0.6	19.4	95.2
					Syrah	R	60	0.6	0.1	0.3
					Breidecker	W	28	0.3	100.0	490.7
					Chasselas	W	25	0.3	0.2	0.9
					Palomino Fino	W	21	0.2	0.1	0.3
					Blauburger	R	13	0.1	1.3	6.4
					Flora	O	6	0.1	100.0	490.7
					Silvaner	W	4	0.0	0.1	0.5
					Other varieties		294	3.0		
					Total		9942	100		

Table 43 (cont.) Winegrape areas, national and global shares (and Varietal Intensity Indexes) for national top 45 varieties, 2000

Portugal						Romania					
Prime variety	Col	Area	Nat'l share	Glob'l share	VII*	Prime variety	Col	Area	Nat'l share	Glob'l share	VII*
Castelao	R	14424	7.0	100.0	23.8	Feteasca Alba	W	18211	8.2	76.4	16.8
Fernao Pires	W	14206	6.9	97.7	23.2	Grasevina	W	15014	6.8	16.3	3.6
Tempranillo	R	7356	3.6	7.9	1.9	Cabernet Sauvignon	R	8620	3.9	3.9	0.9
Trincadeira	R	7264	3.5	100.0	23.8	Merlot	R	7810	3.5	3.7	0.8
Baga	R	6730	3.3	100.0	23.8	Aligote	W	7608	3.4	21.3	4.7
Touriga Franca	R	6671	3.3	100.0	23.8	Muscat Ottonel	W	5787	2.6	47.2	10.4
Tinta Barroca	R	5657	2.8	93.5	22.2	Sauvignon Blanc	W	4613	2.1	7.1	1.6
Vinhao	R	5296	2.6	89.2	21.2	Babeasca Neagra	R	3642	1.6	97.9	21.5
Touriga Nacional	R	4149	2.0	97.3	23.2	Pinot Gris	O	2388	1.1	12.6	2.8
Codega de Larinho	W	4058	2.0	100.0	23.8	Pinot Noir	R	1740	0.8	2.9	0.6
Arinto de Bucelas	W	3966	1.9	100.0	23.8	Feteasca Regala	W	1700	0.8	65.9	14.5
Loureiro	W	3939	1.9	89.7	21.3	Chardonnay	W	1376	0.6	0.9	0.2
Marufo	R	3512	1.7	55.4	13.2	Feteasca Neagra	R	1214	0.5	100.0	22.0
Azal	W	3302	1.6	100.0	23.8	Muscat Blanc a Petits Grains	W	1012	0.5	3.6	0.8
Rufete	R	2338	1.1	68.8	16.4	Grasa de Cotnari	W	850	0.4	100.0	22.0
Rabo de Ovelha	W	2330	1.1	100.0	23.8	Galbena de Odobesti	W	546	0.2	100.0	22.0
Malvasia Fina	W	2328	1.1	32.8	7.8	Rkatsiteli	W	506	0.2	0.8	0.2
Vital	W	2246	1.1	100.0	23.8	Gewurztraminer	W	445	0.2	4.2	0.9
Borracal	R	2035	1.0	76.7	18.2	Other varieties		139091	62.6		
Mencia	R	1971	1.0	15.0	3.6	Total		222173	100		
Tinta Carvalha	R	1920	0.9	100.0	23.8						
Trajadura	W	1788	0.9	74.0	17.6						
Trousseau	R	1754	0.9	82.7	19.7						
Siria	W	1682	0.8	60.3	14.3						
Damaschino	W	1530	0.7	64.8	15.4						
Espadeiro	R	1478	0.7	87.9	20.9						
Moscatel Branco	W	1419	0.7	100.0	23.8						
Seara Nova	W	1213	0.6	100.0	23.8						
Malvasia Preta	R	1157	0.6	100.0	23.8						
Rabigato	W	1133	0.6	100.0	23.8						
Diagalves	W	1088	0.5	100.0	23.8						
Moreto	R	1053	0.5	100.0	23.8						
Negramoll	R	1040	0.5	29.2	7.0						
Alvarinho	W	964	0.5	18.9	4.5						
Godello	W	929	0.5	62.4	14.8						
Bical	W	912	0.4	100.0	23.8						
Camaralet de Lasseube	W	690	0.3	99.9	23.8						
Alicante Henri Bouschet	R	675	0.3	1.8	0.4						
Avesso	W	636	0.3	100.0	23.8						
Cerceal Branco	W	597	0.3	100.0	23.8						
Listain de Huelva	W	596	0.3	100.0	23.8						
Tamarez	W	585	0.3	100.0	23.8						
Graciano	R	584	0.3	30.6	7.3						
Amaral	R	582	0.3	100.0	23.8						
Tinto Cao	R	556	0.3	100.0	23.8						
Other varieties		74664	36.4								
Total		205003	100								

Table 43 (cont.) Winegrape areas, national and global shares (and Varietal Intensity Indexes) for national top 45 varieties, 2000

	Russia					Serbia				
Prime variety	Col	Area	Nat'l share	Glob'l share	VII* Prime variety	Col	Area	Nat'l share	Glob'l share	VII*
Rkatsiteli	W	13152	23.3	19.5	16.9 Grasevina	W	33120	48.0	35.9	25.4
Pinot Blanc	W	2995	5.3	17.6	15.3 Prokupac	R	15180	22.0	100.0	70.7
Pervenets Magaracha	W	2388	4.2	84.2	72.9 Chasselas	W	3449.9	5.0	25.9	18.3
Bianca	W	2165	3.8	99.3	86.0 Muscat of Hamburg	R	2760	4.0	39.1	27.6
Aligote	W	1821	3.2	5.1	4.4 Other varieties		14490	21.0		
Zalagyongye	W	1781	3.2	41.1	35.6 Total		68999	100		
Chardonnay	W	1639	2.9	1.1	1.0					
Cabernet Sauvignon	R	1578	2.8	0.7	0.6					
Riesling	W	1376	2.4	3.2	2.8					
Agadai	W	1265	2.2	100	86.6					
Saperavi	R	931	1.7	14	12.0					
Other varieties	R	25242	44.8							
Total	R	56332	100							

Table 43 (cont.) Winegrape areas, national and global shares (and Varietal Intensity Indexes) for national top 45 varieties, 2000

	Slovakia						Slovenia					
Prime variety	Col	Area	Nat'l share	Glob'l share	VII*	Prime variety	Col	Area	Nat'l share	Glob'l share	VII*
Grasevina	W	3895	25	4.2	13.2	Grasevina	W	3567.7	15.2	3.9	8.0
Gruner Veltliner	W	2960	19	12.5	39.3	Chardonnay	W	1549.1	6.6	1.1	2.2
Muller Thurgau	W	1870	12	5.6	17.4	Refosco	R	1267.5	5.4	100	207.8
Blaufrankisch	R	1091	7	8.5	26.5	Sauvignon Blanc	W	1220.5	5.2	1.9	3.9
Sankt Laurent	R	935	6	39.4	123.5	Merlot	R	1197.1	5.1	0.6	1.2
Chardonnay	W	623	4	0.4	1.3	Ribolla Gialla	W	1126.6	4.8	80.1	166.5
Pinot Blanc	W	623	4	3.7	11.5	Other varieties	R	13543	57.7		
Feteasca Alba	W	312	2	1.3	4.1	Total	R	23472	100		
Feteasca Regala	W	312	2	12.1	37.8						
Cabernet Sauvignon	R	156	1	0.1	0.2						
Silvaner	W	156	1	3.7	11.7						
Other varieties		2649	17								
Total		15580	100								

Table 43 (cont.) Winegrape areas, national and global shares (and Varietal Intensity Indexes) for national top 45 varieties, 2000

	South Africa					Spain				
Prime variety	Col	Area	Nat'l share	Glob'l share	VII*	Prime variety	Col	Area	Nat'l share	Glob'l share	VII*
Chenin Blanc	W	22566	24.1	49.3	25.7	Airen	W	387978	32.8	100.0	4.1
Colombard	W	11432	12.2	30.0	15.6	Bobal	R	100128	8.5	100.0	4.1
Cabernet Sauvignon	R	8824	9.4	4.0	2.1	Garnacha Tinta	R	95800	8.1	44.8	1.8
Pinotage	R	6501	6.9	98.9	51.5	Tempranillo	R	79310	6.7	85.3	3.5
Chardonnay	W	6067	6.5	4.2	2.2	Monastrell	R	67160	5.7	88.0	3.6
Syrah	R	5631	6.0	5.5	2.9	Cayetana Blanca	W	55502	4.7	100.0	4.1
Sauvignon Blanc	W	5436	5.8	8.4	4.4	Macabeo	W	42902	3.6	89.1	3.7
Merlot	R	4888	5.2	2.3	1.2	Palomino Fino	W	27685	2.3	91.4	3.8
Muscat of Alexandria	W	4047	4.3	13.8	7.2	Alicante Henri Bouschet	R	18321	1.6	49.5	2.0
Cinsaut	R	3533	3.8	7.3	3.8	Pedro Ximenez	W	14803	1.3	85.7	3.5
Crouchen	W	2161	2.3	95.7	49.8	Parellada	W	11188	0.9	100.0	4.1
Ruby Cabernet	R	2050	2.2	27.6	14.4	Mencia	R	11166	0.9	85.0	3.5
Palomino Fino	W	1632	1.7	5.4	2.8	Chelva	W	10877	0.9	100.0	4.1
Semillon	W	1029	1.1	3.9	2.0	Xarello	W	10288	0.9	100.0	4.1
Clairette	W	938	1.0	23.4	12.2	Calagrano	W	8229	0.7	100.0	4.1
Muscat Blanc a Petits Grains	W	773	0.8	2.7	1.4	Mazuelo	R	8103	0.7	6.4	0.3
Cabernet Franc	R	488	0.5	1.0	0.5	Merseguera	W	7460	0.6	100.0	4.1
Pinot Noir	R	487	0.5	0.8	0.4	Pardillo	W	7272	0.6	100.0	4.1
Riesling	W	477	0.5	1.1	0.6	Muscat of Alexandria	W	6144	0.5	20.9	0.9
Servant	W	432	0.5	81.5	42.4	Zalema	W	5969	0.5	100.0	4.1
Tinta Barroca	R	395	0.4	6.5	3.4	Beba	W	4762	0.4	100.0	4.1
Muscadel (Red)	R	360	0.4	100.0	52.1	Tinto de la Pampana Blanc	R	4726	0.4	100.0	4.1
Emerald Riesling	W	340	0.4	57.4	29.9	Cabernet Sauvignon	R	4519	0.4	2.0	0.1
Chenel	W	339	0.4	100.0	52.1	Verdejo	W	4453	0.4	100.0	4.1
Fernao Pires	W	339	0.4	2.3	1.2	Garnacha Blanca	W	4333	0.4	40.0	1.7
Harslevelu	W	284	0.3	21.9	11.4	Alvarinho	W	4149	0.4	81.1	3.3
Bukettraube	W	280	0.3	100.0	52.1	Albillo Real	W	3366	0.3	99.9	4.1
Gewurztraminer	W	210	0.2	2.0	1.0	Listan Negro	R	3291	0.3	100.0	4.1
Therona	W	185	0.2		52.1	Tinto Velasco	R	3272	0.3	100.0	4.1
Kanaan	W	172	0.2	100.0	52.1	Prieto Picudo	R	3256	0.3	100.0	4.1
Trebbiano Toscano	W	147	0.2	0.1	0.1	Verdoncho	W	3092	0.3	100.0	4.1
Petit Verdot	R	109	0.1	7.4	3.8	Rojal Tinta	R	2845	0.2	100.0	4.1
Pinot Gris	O	104	0.1	0.5	0.3	Perruno	W	2831	0.2	100.0	4.1
Roobernet	R	78	0.1	100.0	52.1	Marufo	R	2827	0.2	44.6	1.8
Cot	R	76	0.1	0.3	0.2	Forcallat Tinta	R	2690	0.2	100.0	4.1
Mazuelo	R	71	0.1	0.1	0.0	Tinto Basto	R	2331	0.2	100.0	4.1
Weldra	W	54	0.1	100.0	52.1	Juan Garcia	R	2077	0.2	100.0	4.1
Viognier	W	50	0.1	1.6	0.8	Planta Nova	W	2029	0.2	100.0	4.1
Galego Dourado	W	46	0.0	89.5	46.6	Grasevina	W	1923	0.2	2.1	0.1
Touriga Nacional	R	41	0.0	1.0	0.5	Chardonnay	W	1814	0.2	1.2	0.1
Cinsaut Blanc	W	41	0.0	100.0	52.1	Trepat	R	1763	0.1	100.0	4.1
Garnacha Tinta	R	40	0.0	0.0	0.0	Alarije	W	1686	0.1	100.0	4.1
Vinhao	R	36	0.0	0.6	0.3	Negramoll	R	1642	0.1	46.2	1.9
Gamay Noir	R	36	0.0	0.1	0.1	Garnacha Peluda	R	1460	0.1	72.1	3.0
Sangiovese	R	35	0.0	0.1	0.0	Sumoll	R	1401	0.1	100.0	4.1
Other varieties		395	0.4			Other varieties		132982.3	11.3		
Total		93656	100			Total		1181806	100		

Table 43 (cont.) Winegrape areas, national and global shares (and Varietal Intensity Indexes) for national top 45 varieties, 2000

Switzerland						Tunisia					
Prime variety	Col	Area	Nat'l share	Glob'l share	VII*	Prime variety	Col	Area	Nat'l share	Glob'l share	VII*
Chasselas	W	5373	35.7	40.3	130.8	Mazuelo	R	7576	45.0	6.0	17.3
Pinot Noir	R	4601	30.6	7.7	24.8	Garnacha Tinta	R	2020	12.0	0.9	2.7
Gamay Noir	R	1977	13.1	5.2	17.0	Alicante Henri Bouschet	R	842	5.0	2.3	6.6
Merlot	R	848	5.6	0.4	1.3	Cinsaut	R	842	5.0	1.7	5.0
Muller Thurgau	W	686	4.6	2.0	6.6	Sangiovese	R	842	5.0	1.2	3.5
Chardonnay	W	226	1.5	0.2	0.5	Cabernet Sauvignon	R	337	2.0	0.2	0.4
Silvaner	W	208	1.4	5.0	16.2	Monastrell	R	337	2.0	0.4	1.3
Pinot Gris	O	149	1.0	0.8	2.6	Syrah	R	337	2.0	0.3	1.0
Cornalin	R	92	0.6	98.7	320.1	Tribidrag	R	337	2.0	1.3	3.6
Pinot Blanc	W	77	0.5	0.5	1.5	Other varieties		3367	20.0		
Gamaret	R	60	0.4	84.8	274.9	Total		16836	100		
Arvine	W	57	0.4	93.0	301.6						
Syrah	R	54	0.4	0.1	0.2						
Garanoir	R	50	0.3	65.8	213.6						
Muscat Blanc a Petits Grains	W	44	0.3	0.2	0.5						
Sauvignon Blanc	W	38	0.2	0.1	0.2						
Cabernet Sauvignon	R	34	0.2	0.0	0.1						
Marsanne	W	33	0.2	2.2	7.1						
Gewurztraminer	W	31	0.2	0.3	0.9						
Diolinoir	R	25	0.2	79.6	258.0						
Rauschling	W	23	0.2	100.0	324.3						
Amigne	W	21	0.1	100.0	324.3						
Aligote	W	20	0.1	0.1	0.2						
Savagnin Blanc	W	17	0.1	3.9	12.7						
Bondola	R	17	0.1	100.0	324.3						
Regent	R	16	0.1	100.0	324.3						
Cabernet Franc	R	16	0.1	0.0	0.1						
Humagne	W	9	0.1	100.0	324.3						
Kerner	W	8	0.1	0.1	0.4						
Riesling	W	8	0.1	0.0	0.1						
Charmont	W	7	0.0	100.0	324.3						
Semillon	W	3	0.0	0.0	0.0						
Doral	W	3	0.0	100.0	324.3						
Completer	W	2	0.0	100.0	324.3						
Seyval Blanc	W	2	0.0	0.5	1.6						
Ancellotta	R	2	0.0	0.0	0.1						
Lafnetscha	W	1	0.0	100.0	324.3						
Gouais Blanc	W	1	0.0	100.0	324.3						
Plantet	R	1	0.0	0.5	1.6						
Chenin Blanc	W	1	0.0	0.0	0.0						
Auxerrois	W	1	0.0	0.0	0.1						
Reze	W	1	0.0	100.0	324.3						
Dunze	R	1	0.0	100.0	324.3						
Freisamer	W	1	0.0	3.4	10.9						
Bacchus	W	0	0.0	0.0	0.0						
Other varieties		196	1.3								
Total		15042	100								

Table 43 (cont.) Winegrape areas, national and global shares (and Varietal Intensity Indexes) for national top 45 varieties, 2000

	United Kingdom					United States					
Prime variety	Col	Area	Nat'l share	Glob'l share	VII*	Prime variety	Col	Area	Nat'l share	Glob'l share	VII*
Bacchus	W	112	12.8	3.3	184.5	Chardonnay	W	35791	20.4	24.6	6.8
Blauburger	R	105	12.0	10.5	585.6	Tribidrag	R	18630	10.6	69.2	19.2
Dalkauer	W	100	11.5	100.0	5587.8	Colombard	W	18010	10.3	47.2	13.1
Seyval Blanc	W	85	9.7	21.9	1222.0	Cabernet Sauvignon	R	17573	10.0	8.0	2.2
Chardonnay	W	68	7.8	0.0	2.6	Merlot	R	16875	9.6	8.0	2.2
Auxerrois	W	58	6.6	2.5	140.8	Chenin Blanc	W	8433	4.8	18.4	5.1
Cabernet Dorsa	R	43	4.9	100.0	5587.8	Concord	R	8330	4.7	70.5	19.6
Albalonga	W	41	4.7	72.2	4034.9	Pinot Noir	R	5343	3.0	8.9	2.5
Ehrenfelser	W	34	3.9	11.8	658.2	Barbera	R	4693	2.7	14.2	3.9
Other varieties		227	26.0			Garnacha Tinta	R	4519	2.6	2.1	0.6
Total		873	100			Sauvignon Blanc	W	4191	2.4	6.5	1.8
						Rubired	R	4153	2.4	100	27.8
						Mazuelo	R	3088	1.8	2.4	0.7
						Ruby Cabernet	R	2895	1.6	39.0	10.8
						Muscat of Alexandria	W	2013	1.1	6.8	1.9
						Riesling	W	1965	1.1	4.6	1.3
						Syrah	R	1509	0.9	1.5	0.4
						Niagara	W	1357	0.8	8.8	2.5
						Cabernet Franc	R	1189	0.7	2.4	0.7
						Malvasia Bianca di Candia	W	968	0.6	7.5	2.1
						Durif	R	923	0.5	77.1	21.4
						Pinot Gris	O	826	0.5	4.4	1.2
						Gewurztraminer	W	728	0.4	6.8	1.9
						Semillon	W	709	0.4	2.7	0.8
						Gamay Noir	R	684	0.4	1.8	0.5
						Sangiovese	R	682	0.4	1.0	0.3
						Elbling	W	656	0.4	35.2	9.8
						Catawba	R	635	0.4	100	27.8
						Carnelian	R	625	0.4	100	27.8
						Alicante Henri Bouschet	R	563	0.3	1.5	0.4
						Muscat Blanc a Petits Grains	W	515	0.3	1.8	0.5
						Pinot Blanc	W	431	0.2	2.5	0.7
						Listan Prieto	R	340	0.2	2.2	0.6
						Royalty	R	338	0.2	100	27.8
						Salvador	R	320	0.2	55.9	15.5
						Palomino Fino	W	319	0.2	1.1	0.3
						Viognier	W	314	0.2	10.0	2.8
						Aurore	W	299	0.2	100	27.8
						Elvira	W	275	0.2	80.0	22.2
						Emerald Riesling	W	253	0.1	42.6	11.8
						Tempranillo	R	201	0.1	0.2	0.1
						Monastrell	R	187	0.1	0.2	0.1
						Symphony	W	184	0.1	100	27.8
						Seyval Blanc	W	166	0.1	42.8	11.9
						Trebbiano Toscano	W	151	0.1	0.1	0.0
						Other varieties		2844	1.6		
						Total			100		

Table 43 (cont.) Winegrape areas, national and global shares (and Varietal Intensity Indexes) for national top 45 varieties, 2000

	Uruguay						Missing 9				
Prime variety	Col	Area	Nat'l share	Glob'l share	VII*	Prime variety	Col	Area	Nat'l share	Glob'l share	VII*
Muscat of Hamburg	R	2886	32.5	40.9	224.4	Cabernet Sauvignon	R	20373	25.4	9.2	5.6
Tannat	R	2433	27.4	43.8	240.6	Rkatsiteli	W	10549	13.1	15.7	9.5
Merlot	R	1057	11.9	0.5	2.7	Aligote	W	6916	8.6	19.4	11.8
Cabernet Sauvignon	R	675	7.6	0.3	1.7	Merlot	R	5549	6.9	2.6	1.6
Cabernet Franc	R	364	4.1	0.7	4.1	Chardonnay	W	3120	3.9	2.1	1.3
Chardonnay	W	142	1.6	0.1	0.5	Sauvignon Blanc	W	2383	3.0	3.7	2.2
Sauvignon Blanc	W	142	1.6	0.2	1.2	Riesling	W	2279	2.8	5.3	3.2
Syrah	R	62	0.7	0.1	0.3	Sultaniye	W	1820	2.3	12.7	7.7
Other varieties		1118	12.6			Odessky Cherny	R	1694	2.1	100	60.8
Total		8880	100			Isabella	R	1673	2.1	6.1	3.7
						Saperavi	R	1356	1.7	20.2	12.3
						Syrah	R	1278	1.6	1.3	0.8
						Okuzgozu	R	1033	1.3	100	60.8
						Sukholimanskiy Bely	W	1032	1.3	63.3	38.5
						Muscat Blanc a Petits Grains	W	981	1.2	3.5	2.1
						Carmenere	R	945	1.2	16.5	10.1
						Bastardo Magarachsky	R	929	1.2	47.2	28.7
						Negramoll	R	874	1.1	24.6	14.9
						Bogazkere	R	773	1.0	100	60.8
						Pinot Noir	R	741	0.9	1.2	0.8
						Italia	W	706	0.9	100	60.8
						Gewurztraminer	W	675	0.8	6.3	3.8
						Kokur Bely	W	641	0.8	100	60.8
						Dimrit	R	602	0.8	100	60.8
						Kalecik Karasi	R	601	0.7	100	60.8
						Narince	W	537	0.7	100	60.8
						Emir	W	480	0.6	100	60.8
						Pinot Gris	O	480	0.6	2.5	1.5
						Bayanshira	W	451	0.6	100	60.8
						Pervenets Magaracha	W	449	0.6	15.8	9.6
						Calkarasi	R	436	0.5	100	60.8
						Cabernet Franc	R	409	0.5	0.8	0.5
						Semillon	W	382	0.5	1.5	0.9
						Mazuelo	R	374	0.5	0.3	0.2
						Cinsaut	R	351	0.4	0.7	0.4
						Alicante Henri Bouschet	R	341	0.4	0.9	0.6
						Black Queen	R	340	0.4	100	60.8
						Kuldzhinskii	O	269	0.3	100	60.8
						Kerner	W	249	0.3	3.5	2.1
						Salvador	R	244	0.3	42.7	26.0
						Pinot Blanc	W	238	0.3	1.4	0.9
						Quebranta	R	230	0.3	100	60.8
						Chenin Blanc	W	210	0.3	0.5	0.3
						Blaufrankisch	R	203	0.3	1.6	1.0
						Telti Kyryk	W	172	0.2	100	60.8
						Other varieties		3850	4.8		
						Total		80221	100		

Table 44: Winegrape areas, national and global shares (and Varietal Intensity Indexes) for national top 45 varieties, 2010

	Algeria						Argentina				
Prime variety	Col	Area	Nat'l share	Glob'l share	VII*	Prime variety	Col	Area	Nat'l share	Glob'l share	VII*
Cinsaut	R	7550	25.0	20.9	31.9	Cot	R	31047	15.4	76.3	17.5
Mazuelo	R	7550	25.0	9.4	14.3	Cereza	O	29189	14.5	100	22.9
Garnacha Tinta	R	6040	20.0	3.3	5.0	Douce Noire	R	18127	9.0	95.5	21.9
Alicante Henri Bouschet	R	3020	10.0	7.7	11.8	Criolla Grande	R	17080	8.5	100	22.9
Pinot Noir	R	1510	5.0	1.7	2.7	Cabernet Sauvignon	R	16372	8.1	5.6	1.3
Syrah	R	1510	5.0	0.8	1.2	Syrah	R	12810	6.4	6.9	1.6
Merlot	R	1510	5.0	0.6	0.9	Pedro Gimenez	W	12132	6.0	99.0	22.7
Cabernet Sauvignon	R	1510	5.0	0.5	0.8	Torrontes Riojano	W	7683	3.8	94.7	21.7
Total		30200	100			Moscatel Rosada	O	7259	3.6	99.0	22.7
						Chardonnay	W	6473	3.2	3.3	0.7
						Merlot	R	6282	3.1	2.4	0.5
						Tempranillo	R	6120	3.0	2.6	0.6
						Aspiran Bouschet	R	3042	1.5	100	22.9
						Muscat of Alexandria	W	2939	1.5	11.2	2.6
						Chenin Blanc	W	2462	1.2	7.0	1.6
						Sauvignon Blanc	W	2296	1.1	2.1	0.5
						Torrontes Sanjuanino	W	2048	1.0	99.8	22.8
						Sangiovese	R	2011	1.0	2.6	0.6
						Trebbiano Toscano	W	1922	1.0	1.8	0.4
						Pinot Noir	R	1802	0.9	2.1	0.5
						Gibi	W	917	0.5	100	22.9
						Semillon	W	855	0.4	3.9	0.9
						Viognier	W	816	0.4	7.2	1.6
						Torrontes Mendocino	W	713	0.4	100	22.9
						Tannat	R	705	0.4	11.9	2.7
						Bequignol Noir	R	698	0.3	100	22.9
						Cabernet Franc	R	626	0.3	1.2	0.3
						Damaschino	W	586	0.3	28.1	6.4
						Barbera	R	546	0.3	2.3	0.5
						Sauvignonasse	W	515	0.3	11.6	2.6
						Petit Verdot	R	501	0.2	7.0	1.6
						Listan Prieto	R	423	0.2	9	2.1
						Greco Nero	R	396	0.2	32.4	7.4
						Ancellotta	R	302	0.2	6.3	1.4
						Pinot Gris	O	297	0.1	0.7	0.2
						Maticha	W	275	0.1	100	22.9
						California	O	252	0.1	100	22.9
						Fer	R	207	0.1	11.4	2.6
						Fintendo	R	183	0.1	100	22.9
						Bonamico	R	167	0.1	86	19.8
						Alicante Henri Bouschet		166	0.1	0.4	0.1
						Canari Noir	R	139	0.1	91	20.9
						Moscato Giallo	W	133	0.1	9.0	2.1
						Rieslina	W	127	0.1	100	22.9
						Italia	W	126	0.1	11.0	2.5
						Other varieties		1296	0.6		
						Total		201060	100		

Note: VII* indicates Varital Intensity Indexes relative to the world, as defined in the introduction.

Table 44 (cont.) Winegrape areas, national and global shares (and Varietal Intensity Indexes) for national top 45 varieties, 2010

	Armenia					Australia				
Prime variety	Col	Area	Nat'l share	Glob'l share	VII*	Prime variety	Col	Area	Nat'l share	Glob'l share	VII*
Rkatsiteli	W	2469	22.0	4.2	17.3	Syrah	R	42675	28.1	23.0	7.0
Mskhali	W	1093	9.8	100.0	410.6	Chardonnay	W	27773	18.3	14.0	4.2
Garandmak	W	931	8.3	100.0	410.6	Cabernet Sauvignon	R	25967	17.1	9.0	2.7
Kangun	W	850	7.6	100.0	410.6	Merlot	R	10028	6.6	3.8	1.1
Voskeat	W	809	7.2	100.0	410.6	Sauvignon Blanc	W	6467	4.3	5.9	1.8
Muscat Blanc a Petits Grains	W	526	4.7	1.7	6.9	Semillon	W	6112	4.0	27.6	8.4
Other varieties		4528	40.4			Pinot Noir	R	4690	3.1	5.4	1.6
Total		11206	100			Riesling	W	4114	2.7	8.2	2.5
						Pinot Gris	O	3296	2.2	7.6	2.3
						Colombard	W	2205	1.5	6.9	2.1
						Muscat of Alexandria	W	2043	1.3	7.8	2.4
						Garnacha Tinta	R	1748	1.2	0.9	0.3
						Verdelho	W	1535	1.0	76.6	23.2
						Viognier	W	1402	0.9	12.3	3.7
						Petit Verdot	R	1223	0.8	17.0	5.1
						Ruby Cabernet	R	962	0.6	16.8	5.1
						Gewurztraminer	W	834	0.5	5.8	1.8
						Monastrell	R	692	0.5	1.0	0.3
						Cabernet Franc	R	591	0.4	1.1	0.3
						Sangiovese	R	589	0.4	0.8	0.2
						Chenin Blanc	W	541	0.4	1.5	0.5
						Muscat Blanc a Petits Grains	W	533	0.4	1.7	0.5
						Tempranillo	R	476	0.3	0.2	0.1
						Sultaniye	W	430	0.3	12.6	3.8
						Durif	R	417	0.3	11.7	3.6
						Cot	R	356	0.2	0.9	0.3
						Marsanne	W	238	0.2	13.7	4.1
						Muscat a Petits Grains Rouge	R	230	0.2	37.5	11.4
						Dolcetto	R	154	0.1	2.4	0.7
						Arneis	W	153	0.1	13.6	4.1
						Tribidrag	R	149	0.1	0.5	0.1
						Barbera	R	116	0.1	0.5	0.1
						Nebbiolo	R	98	0.1	1.6	0.5
						Crouchen	W	95	0.1	13.1	4.0
						Savagnin Blanc	W	94	0.1	5.0	1.5
						Trebbiano	W	86	0.1	34.7	10.5
						Roussanne	W	83	0.1	4.8	1.4
						Tarrango	R	72	0.0	100.0	30.3
						Muscadelle	W	67	0.0	4.1	1.2
						Touriga Nacional	R	48	0.0	0.5	0.1
						Other varieties		2406	1.6		
						Total		151788	100		

Table 44 (cont.) Winegrape areas, national and global shares (and Varietal Intensity Indexes) for national top 45 varieties, 2010

	Austria						Brazil				
Prime variety	Col	Area	Nat'l share	Glob'l share	VII*	Prime variety	Col	Area	Nat'l share	Glob'l share	VII*
Gruner Veltliner	W	13519	29.7	71.7	72.5	Isabella	R	18279	37.0	56.3	52.4
Zweigelt	R	6412	14.1	65.1	65.8	Bordo	R	8287	16.8	100.0	93.1
Grasevina	W	3462	7.6	5.7	5.7	Concord	R	3543	7.2	28.9	27.0
Blaufrankisch	R	3228	7.1	20.0	20.2	Niagara	W	3177	6.4	68.0	63.4
Mutler Thurgau	W	2044	4.5	9.0	9.1	Couderc Noir	R	2477	5.0	92	93.12
Pinot Blanc	W	1914	4.2	13.0	13.1	Jacquez	R	2252	4.6	95.1	88.5
Riesling	W	1852	4.1	3.7	3.7	Muscat Blanc a Petits Grains	W	1005	2.0	3.2	3.0
Blauer Portugieser	R	1621	3.6	42.7	43.1	Cabernet Sauvignon	R	914	1.8	0.3	0.3
Chardonnay	W	1380	3.0	0.7	0.7	Moscato Embrapa	W	862	1.7	100.0	93.1
Blauburger	R	897	2.0	67.1	67.8	Couderc	W	833.5	1.7	100.0	93.12
Sauvignon Blanc	W	845	1.9	0.8	0.8	Merlot	R	766	1.5	0.3	0.3
Sankt Laurent	R	775	1.7	25.8	26.1	Herbemont	R	764	1.5	100.0	93.1
Neuburger	W	652	1.4	67.6	68.4	Seibel	R	581	1.2	98.3	91.5
Pinot Noir	R	646	1.4	0.7	0.8	Lorena	W	519	1.1	100.0	93.1
Merlot	R	644	1.4	0.2	0.2	Chardonnay	W	377	0.8	0.2	0.2
Cabernet Sauvignon	R	592	1.3	0.2	0.2	Tannat	R	295	0.6	5.0	4.6
Muscat Blanc a Petits Grains	W	492	1.1	1.6	1.6	Cabernet Franc	R	229	0.5	0.4	0.4
FruHroter Veltliner	R	424	0.9	50.1	50.6	Grasevina	W	200	0.4	0.3	0.3
Scheurebe	W	376	0.8	18.9	19.1	Prosecco	W	173	0.4	0.9	0.9
Blauer Wildbacher	R	365	0.8	99.3	100	Trebbiano	W	149	0.3	60.1	56.0
Muscat Ottonel	W	359	0.8	3.5	3.5	Pinot Noir	R	145	0.3	0.2	0.2
Gewurztraminer	W	309	0.7	2.2	2.2	Alicante Henri Bouschet	R	129	0.3	0.3	0.3
Bouvier	W	234	0.5	93.9	94.9	Moscato Giallo	W	126	0.3	8.6	8.0
Pinot Gris	O	215	0.5	0.5	0.5	Cynthiana	R	102	0.2	100.0	93.1
Roter Veltliner	O	193	0.4	97.2	98.3	Malvasia Bianca di Candia	W	100	0.2	1.0	0.9
Roesler	R	160	0.4	100.0	101	Ancellotta	R	99	0.2	2.1	1.9
Goldburger	W	140	0.3	99.8	101	Egiodola	R	99	0.2	26.5	24.6
Syrah	R	137	0.3	0.1	0.1	Violeta	R	98	0.2	100.0	93.1
Rotgipfler	W	105	0.2	100.0	101	Rubea	R	81	0.2	100.0	93.1
Zierfandler	O	85	0.2	72.8	73.5	Pinotage	R	75	0.2	1.2	1.1
Cabernet Franc	R	56	0.1	0.1	0.1	Moscato Nazareno	W	68	0.1	100.0	93.1
Silvaner	W	42	0.1	1.9	1.9	Colombard	W	46	0.1		0.1
Jubilaumsrebe	W	13	0.0	96.8	97.9	Sauvignon Blanc	W	45	0.1	0.0	0.0
Furmint	W	9	0.0	0.2	0.2	Ruby Cabernet	R	42	0.1	0.7	0.7
Rathay	R	9	0.0	100.0	101	Cot	R	37	0.1	0.1	0.1
Other varieties		1326	2.9			Bailey	R	34	0.1	100.0	93.1
Total		45533	100			Sangiovese	R	26	0.1	0.0	0.0
						Semillon	W	24	0.0	0.1	0.1
						Marselan	R	21	0.0	0.9	0.8
						Muscat Bailey A	R	19	0.0	15.9	14.8
						Chenin Blanc	W	18	0.0	0.1	0.0
						Tempranillo	R	16	0.0	0.0	0.0
						Gamay Noir	R	16	0.0	0.0	0.0
						Malvasia Amarela	W	14	0.0	100.0	93.1
						Furmint	W	13	0.0	0.3	0.2
						Other varieties		2226	4.5		
						Total		49412	100		

Table 44 (cont.) Winegrape areas, national and global shares (and Varietal Intensity Indexes) for national top 45 varieties, 2010

Bulgaria						Canada				
Prime variety	Col	Area	Nat'l share	Glob'l share	VII*	Prime variety	Col	Area	Nat'l share	Glob'l share	VII*
Merlot	R	10573	18.8	4.0	3.2	Vidal	W	1284	12.7	78.1	356.1
Cabernet Sauvignon	R	8436	15.0	2.9	2.4	Chardonnay	W	1178	11.7	0.6	2.7
Pamid	R	6792	12.1	69.1	56.7	Merlot	R	999	9.9	0.4	1.7
Misket Cherven	O	4159	7.4	100	82.0	Riesling	W	871	8.6	1.7	7.9
Muscat Ottonel	W	3236	5.8	31.6	25.9	Cabernet Franc	R	664	6.6	1.2	5.6
Rkatsiteli	W	3121	5.6	5.3	4.4	Pinot Noir	R	640	6.3	0.7	3.4
Chardonnay	W	2457	4.4	1.2	1.0	Pinot Gris	O	549	5.4	1.3	5.7
Dimyat	W	2386	4.3	99.4	81.5	Cabernet Sauvignon	R	542	5.4	0.2	0.9
Shiroka Melnishka	R	1580	2.8	100	82.0	Gewurztraminer	W	404	4.0	2.8	12.9
Mavrud	R	1296	2.3	100	82.0	Baco Noir	R	373	3.7	79.7	363
Gewurztraminer	W	747	1.3	5.2	4.3	Sauvignon Blanc	W	320	3.2	0.3	1.3
Trebbiano Toscano	W	723	1.3	0.7	0.5	Syrah	R	274	2.7	0.1	0.7
Kadarka	R	550	1.0	50.6	41.5	Concord	R	252	2.5	2.1	9.4
Misket Varnenski	W	336	0.6	100	81.974	Gamay Noir	R	220	2.2	0.7	3.1
Storgozia	R	295	0.5	100	81.974	Marechal Foch	R	158	1.6	46.1	210
Ranna Melnishka Loza	R	249	0.4	100	81.974	Niagara	W	155	1.5	3.3	15.1
Other varieties		9197	16.4			Pinot Blanc	W	125	1.2	0.9	3.9
Total		56133	100			Seyval Blanc	W	112	1.1	24.2	110
						Geisenheim	R	106	1.0	100.0	456
						Viognier	W	83	0.8	0.7	3.3
						Chambourcin	R	54	0.5	4.8	21.8
						Zweigelt	R	48	0.5	0.5	2.2
						Blattner Reds	R	39	0.4	100.0	456
						De Chaunac	R	39	0.4	42.7	195
						Cot	R	39	0.4	0.1	0.4
						Auxerrois	W	38	0.4	1.4	6.2
						Ortega	W	29	0.3	4.5	20.5
						S.V. 23-512	R	29	0.3	100.0	456
						Ehrenfelser	W	29	0.3	36.3	166
						Petit Verdot	R	27	0.3	0.4	1.7
						Blattner Whites	W	25	0.3	100.0	456
						Muscat Swenson	W	24	0.2	98.3	448.2
						Bacchus	W	21	0.2	1.0	4.7
						Semillon	W	19	0.2	0.1	0.4
						Siegerrebe	O	18	0.2	14.7	66.8
						Gm 322	R	17	0.2	100.0	456
						Kerner	W	11	0.1	0.3	1.3
						Schonburger	O	11	0.1	18.2	83.0
						Villard Noir	R	8	0.1	0.6	2.8
						Elvira	W	8	0.1	2.9	13.3
						Tribidrag	R	8	0.1	0.0	0.1
						Chenin Blanc	W	7	0.1	0.0	0.1
						Muller Thurgau	W	7	0.1	0.0	0.1
						Madeleine Angevine	W	7	0.1	12.8	58.4
						Madeleine Sylvaner	W	6	0.1	86.2	393
						Other varieties		222	2.2		
						Total		10096	100		

Table 44 (cont.) Winegrape areas, national and global shares (and Varietal Intensity Indexes) for national top 45 varieties, 2010

	Chile					China					
Prime variety	Col	Area	Nat'l share	Glob'l share	VII*	Prime variety	Col	Area	Nat'l share	Glob'l share	VII*
Cabernet Sauvignon	R	40728	36.5	14.0	5.8	Cabernet Sauvignon	R	22612	76.5	7.8	12.1
Chardonnay	W	13082	11.7	6.6	2.7	Merlot	R	3560	12.1	1.3	2.1
Sauvignon Blanc	W	12159	10.9	11.0	4.6	Carmenere	R	1353	4.6	11.9	18.5
Merlot	R	10041	9.0	3.8	1.6	Chardonnay	W	738	2.5	0.4	0.6
Carmenere	R	8827	7.9	77.7	32.1	Cabernet Franc	R	507	1.7	0.9	1.5
Syrah	R	6027	5.4	3.2	1.3	Riesling	W	437	1.5	0.9	1.4
Alicante Henri Bouschet	R	4228	3.8	10.8	4.5	Syrah	R	223	0.8	0.1	0.2
Listan Prieto	R	3869	3.5	84.8	35.0	Ruby Cabernet	R	40	0.1	0.7	1.1
Pinot Noir	R	2884	2.6	3.3	1.4	Pinot Noir	R	40	0.1	0.0	0.1
Cabernet Franc	R	1321	1.2	2.5	1.0	Garnacha Tinta	R	11	0.0	0.0	0.0
Cot	R	1264	1.1	3.1	1.3	Chenin Blanc	W	10	0.0	0.0	0.0
Muscat of Alexandria	W	1090	1.0	4.1	1.7	Gewurztraminer	W	5	0.0	0.0	0.1
Semillon	W	846	0.8	3.8	1.6	Cinsaut	R	3	0.0	0.0	0.0
Sauvignonasse	W	785	0.7	17.6	7.3	Pinot Blanc	W	2	0.0	0.0	0.0
Viognier	W	753	0.7	6.6	2.7	Pinot Gris	O	2	0.0	0.0	0.0
Petit Verdot	R	576	0.5	8.0	3.3	Sauvignon Blanc	W	1	0.0	0.0	0.0
Mazuelo	R	477	0.4	0.6	0.2	Semillon	W	1	0.0	0.0	0.0
Torrontes Riojano	W	425	0.4	5.2	2.2	Total		29545	100		
Riesling	W	367	0.3	0.7	0.3						
Gewurztraminer	W	316	0.3	2.2	0.9						
Cinsaut	R	198	0.2	0.5	0.2						
Pedro Gimenez	W	118	0.1	1.0	0.4						
Durif	R	104	0.1	2.9	1.2						
Sangiovese	R	100	0.1	0.1	0.1						
Pinot Gris	O	100	0.1	0.2	0.1						
Chasselas	W	88	0.1	0.7	0.3						
Lacrima Christi	R	85	0.1	100	41.3						
Moscatel Rosada	O	70	0.1	1.0	0.4						
Monastrell	R	59	0.1	0.1	0.0						
Tribidrag	R	58	0.1	0.2	0.1						
Chenin Blanc	W	57	0.1	0.2	0.1						
Tempranillo	R	48	0.0	0.0	0.0						
Blanca Ovoide	W	40	0.0	100	41.3						
Garnacha Tinta	R	37	0.0	0.0	0.0						
Moscato Giallo	W	25	0.0	1.7	0.7						
Marsanne	W	17	0.0	1.0	0.4						
Nebbiolo	R	11	0.0	0.2	0.1						
Roussanne	W	6	0.0	0.3	0.1						
Korinthiaki	R	4	0.0	7.6	3.1						
Torrontes Sanjuanino	W	4	0.0	0.2	0.1						
Barbera	R	4	0.0	0.0	0.0						
Tannat	R	2	0.0	0.0	0.0						
Blauer Portugieser	R	2	0.0	0.0	0.0						
Crystal	W	2	0.0	0.9	0.4						
Tinta Barroca	R	1	0.0	0.0	0.0						
Other varieties			0.2								
Total		111525	100								

Table 44 (cont.) Winegrape areas, national and global shares (and Varietal Intensity Indexes) for national top 45 varieties, 2010

	Croatia					Cyprus				
Prime variety	Col	Area	Nat'l share	Glob'l share	VII*	Prime variety	Col	Area	Nat'l share	Glob'l share	VII*
Grasevina	W	4701	22.6	7.7	17.0	Mavro	R	3575	41.5	100.0	534.6
Malvazija Istarska	W	1705	8.2	62.2	137.9	Xynisteri	W	2092	24.3	100.0	534.6
Plavac Mali	R	1569	7.6	100.0	221.7	Mazuelo	R	481	5.6	0.6	3.2
Merlot	R	780	3.8	0.3	0.6	Sultaniye	W	371	4.3	10.9	58.2
Riesling	W	676	3.3	1.4	3.0	Cabernet Sauvignon	R	369	4.3	0.1	0.7
Chardonnay	W	668	3.2	0.3	0.7	Syrah	R	244	2.8	0.1	0.7
Cabernet Sauvignon	R	646	3.1	0.2	0.5	Cabernet Franc	R	203	2.4	0.4	2.0
Plavina	R	643	3.1	100.0	221.7	Monastrell	R	172	2.0	0.2	1.3
Blaufrankisch	R	558	2.7	3.5	7.7	Maratheftiko	R	152	1.8	100	535
Debit	W	403	1.9	100.0	221.7	Ofthalmo	R	141	1.6	100	535
Babic	R	359	1.7	100.0	221.7	Chardonnay	W	128	1.5	0.1	0.3
Malvasia Bianca Lunga	W	285	1.4	11.2	24.8	Muscat of Alexandria	W	120	1.4	0.5	2.4
Kraljevina	W	268	1.3	59.9	132.9	Vertzami	R	96	1.1	28.6	153
Posip Bijeli	W	253	1.2	100.0	221.7	Garnacha Tinta	R	84	1.0	0.0	0.2
Sauvignon Blanc	W	249	1.2	0.2	0.5	Merlot	R	63	0.7	0.0	0.1
Gewurztraminer	W	234	1.1	1.6	3.6	Other varieties		317	3.7		
Trbljan	W	231	1.1	100.0	221.7	Total		8608	100		
Terrano	R	228	1.1	45.6	101.1						
Pinot Gris	O	219	1.1	0.5	1.1						
Trebbiano Toscano	W	210	1.0	0.2	0.4						
Kujundzusa	W	206	1.0	100.0	221.7						
Pinot Blanc	W	188	0.9	1.3	2.8						
Syrah	R	187	0.9	0.1	0.2						
Pinot Noir	R	180	0.9	0.2	0.5						
Furmint	W	172	0.8	3.3	7.3						
Vranac	R	149	0.7	100.0	221.7						
Silvaner	W	139	0.7	6.2	13.7						
Zlahtina	W	135	0.6	100.0	221.7						
Ranfol	W	134	0.6	100.0	221.7						
Zweigelt	R	123	0.6	1.3	2.8						
Refosco	R	122	0.6	8.6	19.1						
Garnacha Tinta	R	103	0.5	0.1	0.1						
Cabernet Franc	R	95	0.5	0.2	0.4						
Cardinal	R	91	0.4	16.7	37.0						
Tribidrag	R	65	0.3	0.2	0.4						
Skrlet	W	61	0.3	100.0	221.7						
Muller Thurgau	W	60	0.3	0.3	0.6						
Moscato Giallo	W	59	0.3	4.0	8.8						
Rkatsiteli	W	57	0.3	0.1	0.2						
Muscat Blanc a Petits Gr	W	56	0.3	0.2	0.4						
Kovidinka	O	56	0.3	5.2	11.5						
Victoria	W	52	0.3	100.0	221.7						
Bogdanusa	W	48	0.2	100.0	221.7						
Blauer Portugieser	R	42	0.2	1.1	2.4						
Vugava	W	36	0.2	100.0	221.7						
Other varieties		3255	15.7								
Total		20754	100								

Table 44 (cont.) Winegrape areas, national and global shares (and Varietal Intensity Indexes) for national top 45 varieties, 2010

	Czech Republic						France				
Prime variety	Col	Area	Nat'l share	Glob'l share	VII*	Prime variety	Col	Area	Nat'l share	Glob'l share	VII*
Muller Thurgau	W	1572	9.7	6.9	19.6	Merlot	R	115746	13.7	43.3	2.4
Gruner Veltliner	W	1527	9.4	8.1	23.0	Garnacha Tinta	R	94240	11.1	51.0	2.8
Sankt Laurent	R	1291	7.9	42.9	121.6	Trebbiano Toscano	W	83892	9.9	76.4	4.2
Riesling	W	1181	7.3	2.4	6.7	Syrah	R	68587	8.1	37.0	2.0
Blaufrankisch	R	1160	7.1	7.2	20.4	Cabernet Sauvignon	R	56386	6.7	19.4	1.1
Grasevina	W	1148	7.1	1.9	5.3	Mazuelo	R	53155	6.3	66.3	3.6
Zweigelt	R	811	5.0	8.2	23.3	Chardonnay	W	44593	5.3	22.4	1.2
Sauvignon Blanc	W	804	5.0	0.7	2.1	Cabernet Franc	R	36948	4.4	68.9	3.7
Chardonnay	W	766	4.7	0.4	1.1	Gamay Noir	R	30443	3.6	93.2	5.1
Pinot Blanc	W	732	4.5	5.0	14.1	Pinot Noir	R	29738	3.5	34.3	1.9
Pinot Gris	O	706	4.3	1.6	4.6	Sauvignon Blanc	W	26839	3.2	24.4	1.3
Pinot Noir	R	688	4.2	0.8	2.2	Cinsaut	R	20800	2.5	57.7	3.1
Blauer Portugieser	R	622	3.8	16.4	46.4	Melon	W	12364	1.5	100.0	5.4
Gewurztraminer	W	601	3.7	4.2	11.9	Semillon	W	11693	1.4	52.8	2.9
Muskat Moravsky	W	351	2.2	68.3	193.6	Pinot Meunier	R	11088	1.3	98.4	5.3
Neuburger	W	303	1.9	31.4	89.1	Chenin Blanc	W	9828	1.2	28.0	1.5
Andre	R	261	1.6	55.3	156.6	Monastrell	R	9363	1.1	13.4	0.7
Cabernet Sauvignon	R	230	1.4	0.1	0.2	Colombard	W	7790	0.9	24.3	1.3
Fruhroter Veltliner	R	217	1.3	25.6	72.6	Muscat Blanc a Petits Grains	W	7620	0.9	24.5	1.3
Cabernet Moravia	R	212	1.3	100.0	283.3	Cot	R	6155	0.7	15.1	0.8
Palava	O	198	1.2	86.3	244.4	Gros Manseng	W	4995	0.6	100.0	5.4
Silvaner	W	122	0.8	5.4	15.3	Garnacha Blanca	W	4976	0.6	67.5	3.7
Dornfelder	R	119	0.7	1.5	4.2	Alicante Henri Bouschet	R	4957	0.6	12.7	0.7
Merlot	R	90	0.6	0.0	0.1	Viognier	W	4395	0.5	38.6	2.1
Irsai Oliver	W	69	0.4	4.9	13.8	Vermentino	W	3569	0.4	41.4	2.3
Muscat Ottonel	W	60	0.4	0.6	1.7	Muscat of Hamburg	R	3504	0.4	43.1	2.3
Aurelius	W	44	0.3	63.3	179.3	Riesling	W	3490	0.4	7.0	0.4
Neronet	R	33	0.2	45.8	129.8	Gewurztraminer	W	3083	0.4	21.6	1.2
Odessky Cherny	R	17	0.1	0.6	1.8	Tannat	R	2914	0.3	49.1	2.7
Agni	R	6	0.0	100.0	283.3	Aramon Noir	R	2877	0.3	99.5	5.4
Laurot	R	6	0.0	100.0	283.3	Macabeo	W	2628	0.3	6.4	0.3
Ariana	R	3	0.0	100.0	283.3	Pinot Gris	O	2617	0.3	6.0	0.3
Other varieties		292	1.8			Muscat of Alexandria	W	2610	0.3	9.9	0.5
Total		16242	100			Caladoc	R	2464	0.3	67.0	3.6
						Chasselas	W	2441	0.3	18.5	1.0
						Clairette	W	2405	0.3		4.5
						Marselan	R	2375	0.3	95.1	5.2
						Auxerrois	W	2351	0.3	85.8	4.7
						Grolleau Noir	R	2350	0.3	100.0	5.4
						Mauzac Blanc	W	1991	0.2	100.0	5.4
						Aligote	W	1952	0.2	5.4	0.3
						Folle Blanche	W	1770	0.2	95.9	5.2
						Garnacha Roja	W	1699	0.2	95.2	5.2
						Fer	R	1610	0.2	88.6	4.8
						Sangiovese	R	1589	0.2	2.0	0.1
						Other varieties		38000	4.5		
						Total		846880	100		

Table 44 (cont.) Winegrape areas, national and global shares (and Varietal Intensity Indexes) for national top 45 varieties, 2010

	Georgia					Germany				
Prime variety	Col	Area	Nat'l share	Glob'l share	VII* Prime variety	Col	Area	Nat'l share	Glob'l share	VII*
Rkatsiteli	W	25324	52.8	43.2	41.4 Riesling	W	22520	22.1	45.0	20.3
Tsolikouri	W	7903	16.5	100.0	95.9 Müller Thurgau	W	13480	13.2	59.2	26.7
Saperavi	R	4751	9.9	58.5	56.1 Dornfelder	R	7920	7.8	97.8	44.1
Tsitska	W	3642	7.6	100	95.9 Pinot Gris	O	4450	4.4	10.2	4.6
Chinuri	W	1225	2.6	100	95.9 Pinot Blanc	W	3870	3.8	26.3	11.9
Mtsvane Kakhuri	W	319	0.7	100	95.9 Kerner	W	3510	3.4	87.9	39.6
Goruli Mtsvane	W	287	0.6	100	95.9 Bacchus	W	1910	1.9	93.3	42.1
Cabernet Sauvignon	R	286	0.6	0.1	0.1 Scheurebe	W	1600	1.6	80.7	36.4
Aleksandrouli	R	281	0.6	100	95.9 Chardonnay	W	1180	1.2	0.6	0.3
Pinot Blanc	W	219	0.5	1.5	1.4 Chasselas	W	1120	1.1	8.5	3.8
Tsulukidzis Tetra	W	195	0.4	100	95.9 Huxelrebe	W	590	0.6	97.2	43.8
Aligote	W	124	0.3	0.3	0.3 Ortega	W	590	0.6	92.7	41.8
Aladasturi	R	59	0.1	100	95.9 Elbling	W	550	0.5	38.8	17.5
Krakhuna	W	46	0.1	100	95.9 Faberrebe	W	520	0.5	99.2	44.7
Tavkveri	R	37	0.1	100	95.9 Morio-Muskat	W	470	0.5	92.3	41.6
Ojaleshi	R	32	0.1	100	95.9 Sauvignon Blanc	W	460	0.5	0.4	0.2
Chkhaveri	O	26	0.1	100	95.9 Acolon	R	440	0.4	97.9	44.1
Kisi	W	26	0.1	100	95.9 Domina	R	360	0.4	99.8	45.0
Usakhelouri	R	10	0.0	100	95.9 Dunkelfelder	R	300	0.3	91.2	41.1
Khikhvi	W	6	0.0	100	95.9 Cabernet Mitos	R	280	0.3	99.3	44.8
Otskhanuri Sapere	R	6	0.0	100	95.9 Cabernet Sauvignon	R	260	0.3	0.1	0.0
Other varieties		3194	6.7		Cabernet Dorsa	R	200	0.2	89.8	40.5
Total		48001	100		Pinot Noir Precoce	R	190	0.2	90.9	41.0
					Muscat Blanc a Petits Grains	W	170	0.2	0.5	0.2
					Auxerrois	W	160	0.2	5.8	2.6
					Heroldrebe	R	140	0.1	100.0	45.1
					Siegerrebe	O	90	0.1	75.3	33.9
					Reichensteiner	W	80	0.1	35.1	15.8
					Rieslaner	W	60	0.1	100.0	45.1
					Muscat Ottonel	W	60	0.1	0.6	0.3
					Nobling	W	50	0.0	100.0	45.1
					Ehrenfelser	W	50	0.0	63.7	28.7
					Cabernet Cubin	R	40	0.0	100.0	45.1
					Regner	W	40	0.0	90.9	41.0
					Johanniter	W	40	0.0	78.4	35.4
					Dakapo	R	40	0.0	75.9	34.2
					Optima	W	30	0.0	81.8	36.9
					Phoenix	W	30	0.0	58.8	26.5
					Cabernet Cortis	R	20	0.0	100.0	45.1
					Cabernet Dorio	R	20	0.0	100.0	45.1
					Goldriesling	W	20	0.0	100.0	45.1
					Perle	O	20	0.0	95.2	42.9
					Deckrot	R	10	0.0	100.0	45.1
					Helfensteiner	R	10	0.0	100.0	45.1
					Juwel	W	10	0.0	100.0	45.1
					Other varieties		34100	33.4		
					Total		102060	100		

Table 44 (cont.) Winegrape areas, national and global shares (and Varietal Intensity Indexes) for national top 45 varieties, 2010

	Greece						Hungary				
Prime variety	Col	Area	Nat'l share	Glob'l share	VII*	Prime variety	Col	Area	Nat'l share	Glob'l share	VII*
Savatiano	W	9920	18.2	100.0	84.6	Blaufrankisch	R	7998	11.5	49.6	32.7
Roditis	O	4661	8.6	100.0	84.6	Grasevina	W	4664	6.7	7.6	5.0
Roditis(Red)	R	3834	7.0	100.0	84.6	Furmint	W	4165	6.0	79.2	52.3
Agiorgitiko	R	2905	5.3	100.0	84.6	Cserszegi Fuszeres	W	3609	5.2	100	66.0
Kotsifali	R	2330	4.3	100.0	84.6	Bianca	W	2922	4.2	45.3	29.9
Muscat Blanc a Petits Grains	W	2162	4.0	6.9	5.9	Cabernet Sauvignon	R	2863	4.1	1.0	0.7
Xinomavro	R	1971	3.6	100.0	84.6	Chardonnay	W	2757	4.0	1.4	0.9
Romeiko	R	1597	2.9	100.0	84.6	Muller Thurgau	W	2098	3.0	9.2	6.1
Cabernet Sauvignon	R	1550	2.8	0.5	0.5	Zweigelt	R	2050	2.9	20.8	13.7
Moschomavro	R	1428	2.6	100.0	84.6	Merlot	R	1907	2.7	0.7	0.5
Merlot	R	1248	2.3	0.5	0.4	Chasselas	W	1892	2.7	14.3	9.5
Liatiko	R	1211	2.2	100.0	84.6	Zalagyongye	W	1755	2.5	90.1	59.5
Moschofilero	R	934	1.7	100.0	84.6	Harslevelu	W	1659	2.4	89.4	59.0
Assyrtiko	W	902	1.7	100.0	84.6	Pinot Gris	O	1624	2.3	3.7	2.5
Mandilaria	R	885	1.6	100.0	84.6	Gruner Veltliner	W	1533	2.2	8.1	5.4
Athiri	W	748	1.4	100.0	84.6	Cabernet Franc	R	1352	1.9	2.5	1.7
Grenache Rose	R	645	1.2	100.0	84.6	Riesling	W	1304	1.9	2.6	1.7
Syrah	R	641	1.2	0.3	0.3	Muscat Ottonel	W	1232	1.8	12.0	7.9
Chardonnay	W	586	1.1	0.3	0.2	Blauer Portugieser	R	1216	1.7	32.0	21.1
Vilana	W	579	1.1	100.0	84.6	Kunleany	W	1211	1.7	100	66.0
Mavrouda	R	520	1.0	100.0	84.6	Arany Sarfeher	W	1133	1.6	100	66.0
Monemvassia	W	481	0.9	100.0	84.6	Pinot Noir	R	1091	1.6	1.3	0.8
Robola	W	465	0.9	100.0	84.6	Irsai Oliver	W	1090	1.6	77.1	50.9
Limnio	R	372	0.7	100.0	84.6	Ezerjo	W	1074	1.5	100	66.0
Mavrodafni	R	345	0.6	100.0	84.6	Kovidinka	O	1020	1.5	94.8	62.6
Trebbiano Toscano	W	297	0.5	0.3	0.2	Sauvignon Blanc	W	907	1.3	0.8	0.5
Fokiano	R	262	0.5	100.0	84.6	Kiralyleanyka	W	855	1.2	100	66.0
Sauvignon Blanc	W	256	0.5	0.2	0.2	Leanyka	W	838	1.2	100	66.0
Vertzami	R	239	0.4	71.4	60.4	Savagnin Blanc	W	772	1.1	40.7	26.9
Debina	W	239	0.4	100.0	84.6	Aletta	W	723	1.0	100	66.0
Malagousia	W	182	0.3	100.0	84.6	Muscat Blanc a Petits Grains	W	709	1.0	2.3	1.5
Negoska		143	0.3	100.0	84.6	Zenit	W	559	0.8	96.4	63.6
Asprouda	W	113	0.2	100.0	84.6	Kadarka	R	532	0.8	48.9	32.3
Kakotrygis	W	103	0.2	100.0	84.6	Blauburger	R	435	0.6	32.6	21.5
Fileri	W	97	0.2	100.0	84.6	Ezerfurtu	W	377	0.5	100	66.0
Moschofilero	O	80	0.1	100.0	84.6	Lakhegyi Mezes	W	306	0.4	100	66.0
Goustolidi	W	68	0.1	100.0	84.6	Zengo	W	264	0.4	100	66.0
Alicante Henri Bouschet	R	56	0.1	0.1	0.1	Pinot Blanc	W	237	0.3	1.6	1.1
Batily	R	54	0.1	100.0	84.6	Jubileum 75	R	194	0.3	100	66.0
Krassato	R	52	0.1	100.0	84.6	Villard Blanc	W	192	0.3	27.9	18.4
Cinsaut	R	43	0.1	0.1	0.1	Viktoria Gyongye	W	190	0.3	100	66.0
Thrapsathiri	W	31	0.1	100.0	84.6	Juhfark	W	186	0.3	100	66.0
Cabernet Franc	R	23	0.0	0.0	0.0	Syrah	R	177	0.3	0.1	0.1
Pamid	R	22	0.0	0.2	0.2	Turan	R	175	0.3	98.7	65.1
Tempranillo	R	19	0.0	0.0	0.0	Medina	R	151	0.2	94.7	62.5
Other varieties		9092	16.7			Other varieties		5715	8.2		
Total		54389	100			Total		69715	100		

Table 44 (cont.) Winegrape areas, national and global shares (and Varietal Intensity Indexes) for national top 45 varieties, 2010

	Italy					Japan				
Prime variety	Col	Area	Nat'l share	Glob'l share	VII*	Prime variety	Col	Area	Nat'l share	Glob'l share	VII*
Sangiovese	R	71619	11.4	92.2	6.8	Merlot	R	817	22.0	0.3	3.8
Montepulciano	R	34824	5.6	99.6	7.3	Chardonnay	W	602	16.2	0.3	3.7
Catarratto Bianco	W	34794	5.6	99.8	7.3	Black Queen	R	469	12.6	96.5	1195.3
Merlot	R	28042	4.5	10.5	0.8	Cabernet Sauvignon	R	469	12.6	0.2	2.0
Trebbiano Toscano	W	21501	3.4	19.6	1.4	Kerner	W	357	9.6	8.9	110.8
Barbera	R	20524	3.3	84.9	6.2	Zweigelt	R	231	6.2	2.3	29.0
Chardonnay	W	19709	3.1	9.9	0.7	Müller Thurgau	W	172	4.6	0.8	9.3
Prosecco	W	18255	2.9	99.0	7.3	Koshu	O	168	4.5	100.0	1238.6
Pinot Gris	O	17281	2.8	39.7	2.9	Niagara	W	128	3.4	2.7	34.0
Nero d'Avola	R	16595	2.7	100.0	7.4	Muscat Bailey A	R	103	2.8	84.1	1042.3
Trebbiano Romagnolo	W	15893	2.5	100.0	7.4	Pinot Noir	R	64	1.7	0.1	0.9
Garganega	W	15375	2.5	99.8	7.3	Campbell Early	R	61	1.6	100.0	1238.6
Cabernet Sauvignon	R	13724	2.2	4.7	0.3	Delaware	O	51	1.4	40.5	502.0
Tribidrag	R	12234	2.0	37.4	2.7	Portland	W	12	0.3	100.0	1238.6
Muscat Blanc a Petits Grains	W	11506	1.8	37.0	2.7	Riesling	W	11	0.3	0.0	0.3
Negroamaro	R	11460	1.8	100.0	7.4	Total		3715	100		
Trebbiano Giallo	W	10609	1.7	100.0	7.4						
Aglianico	R	9910	1.6	99.5	7.3						
Malvasia Bianca di Candia	W	9231	1.5	93.3	6.9						
Corvina Veronese	R	7477	1.2	99.7	7.3						
Syrah	R	6739	1.1	3.6	0.3						
Garnacha Tinta	R	6372	1.0	3.4	0.3						
Cabernet Franc	R	6314	1.0	11.8	0.9						
Grillo	W	6295	1.0	100.0	7.4						
Inzolia	W	6133	1.0	100.0	7.4						
Dolcetto	R	6128	1.0	96.8	7.1						
Croatina	R	5684	0.9	99.7	7.3						
Nebbiolo	R	5536	0.9	92.4	6.8						
Trebbiano d'Abruzzo	W	5091	0.8	100.0	7.4						
Vermentino	W	5046	0.8	58.6	4.3						
Pinot Noir	R	5046	0.8	5.8	0.4						
Lambrusco Salamino	R	5003	0.8	100.0	7.4						
Ancellotta	R	4343	0.7	91.0	6.7						
Gaglioppo	R	4214	0.7	100.0	7.4						
Sauvignon Blanc	W	3744	0.6	3.4	0.2						
Verdicchio Bianco	W	3526	0.6	99.8	7.3						
Pinot Blanc	W	3086	0.5	21.0	1.5						
Falanghina	W	3037	0.5	100.0	7.4						
Cortese	W	2953	0.5	100.0	7.4						
Sauvignonasse	W	2911	0.5	65.4	4.8						
Nerello Mascalese	R	2883	0.5	100.0	7.4						
Lambrusco Grasparossa	R	2726	0.4	99.6	7.3						
Biancame	W	2599	0.4	100.0	7.4						
Nero di Troia	R	2572	0.4	100.0	7.4						
Rondinella	R	2479	0.4	99.9	7.3						
Other varieties		114678	18.3								
Total		625700	100								

Table 44 (cont.) Winegrape areas, national and global shares (and Varietal Intensity Indexes) for national top 45 varieties, 2010

	Kazakhstan					Luxembourg					
Prime variety	Col	Area	Nat'l share	Glob'l share	VII*	Prime variety	Col	Area	Nat'l share	Glob'l share	VII*
Rkatsiteli	W	3552	51.2	6.1	40.2	Elbling	W	370	28.4	26.1	920.9
Bayanshira	W	645	9.3	100.0	663.2	Muller Thurgau	W	184	14.1	0.8	28.5
Saperavi	R	428	6.2	5.3	34.9	Auxerrois	W	183	14.0	6.7	235.6
Kuldzhinskii	O	385	5.6	100.0	663.2	Pinot Blanc	W	162	12.4	1.1	38.8
Aligote	W	277	4.0	0.8	5.1	Pinot Gris	O	146	11.2	0.3	11.8
Muscat Rose	O	227	3.3	100.0	663.2	Riesling	W	121	9.3	0.2	8.5
Pinot Noir	R	180	2.6	0.2	1.4	Gamay Noir	R	98	7.5	0.3	10.6
Riesling	W	111	1.6	0.2	1.5	Gewurztraminer	W	20	1.5	0.1	4.9
Maiskii Chernyi	R	110	1.6	100.0	663.2	Chardonnay	W	16	1.2	0.0	0.3
Cabernet Franc	R	56	0.8	0.1	0.7	Pinot Noir	R	3	0.2	0.0	0.1
Matrasa	R	28	0.4	100.0	663.2	Other varieties		1	0.1		
Muscat Violet	R	27	0.4	100.0	663.2	Total		1304	100		
Cabernet Sauvignon	R	20	0.3	0.0	0.0						
Ruby	R	9	0.1	100.0	663.2						
Rubinovy Magaracha	R	0	0.0	100.0	663.2						
Other varieties		882	12.7								
Total		6938	100								

Table 44 (cont.) Winegrape areas, national and global shares (and Varietal Intensity Indexes) for national top 45 varieties, 2010

	Mexico					Moldova				
Prime variety	Col	Area	Nat'l share	Glob'l share	VII* Prime variety	Col	Area	Nat'l share	Glob'l share	VII*
Sultaniye	W	841	15.4	24.7	207.8 Aligote	W	15790	17.6	43.7	22.4
Cabernet Sauvignon	R	756	13.8	0.3	2.2 Rkatsiteli	W	11508	12.8	19.6	10.1
Mazuelo	R	448	8.2	0.6	4.7 Isabella	R	11401	12.7	35.1	18.0
Merlot	R	391	7.2	0.1	1.2 Sauvignon Blanc	W	8151	9.1	7.4	3.8
Salvador	R	350	6.4	88.9	748.2 Merlot	R	8123	9.0	3.0	1.6
Chenin Blanc	W	275	5.0	0.8	6.6 Cabernet Sauvignon	R	7590	8.4	2.6	1.3
Muscat Blanc a Petits Grains	W	246	4.5	0.8	6.7 Pinot Noir	R	6521	7.3	7.5	3.9
Fiesta	W	230	4.2	100.0	842.0 Chardonnay	W	5134	5.7	2.6	1.3
Tempranillo	R	229	4.2	0.1	0.8 Feteasca Alba	W	4334	4.8	24.8	12.7
Nebbiolo	R	180	3.3	3.0	25.3 Gewurztraminer	W	2731	3.0	19.1	9.8
Cardinal	R	168	3.1	30.8	259.6 Pinot Gris	O	2042	2.3	4.7	2.4
Syrah	R	145	2.7	0.1	0.7 Muscat Ottonel	W	1520	1.7	14.9	7.6
Garnacha Tinta	R	140	2.6	0.1	0.6 Riesling	W	1343	1.5	2.7	1.4
Durif	R	133	2.4	3.7	31.5 Bastardo Magarachsky	R	1040	1.2	43.9	22.5
Sauvignon Blanc	W	120	2.2	0.1	0.9 Saperavi	R	716	0.8	8.8	4.5
Palomino Fino	W	109	2.0	0.5	4.1 Sukholimanskiy Bely	W	599	0.7	27.8	14.2
Jacquez	R	80	1.5	3.4	28.4 Pinot Blanc	W	350	0.4	2.4	1.2
Other varieties		624	11.4		Muller Thurgau	W	173	0.2	0.8	0.4
Total		5465	100		Muscat Blanc a Petits Grains	W	172	0.2	0.6	0.3
					Silvaner	W	98	0.1	4.3	2.2
					Babeasca Neagra	R	80	0.1	2.6	1.3
					Noah	W	71	0.1	100.0	51.2
					Pervomaisky	R	64	0.1	100.0	51.2
					Gamay Teinturier Freaux	R	55	0.1	100.0	51.2
					Golubok	R	50	0.1	57.5	29.4
					Viorica	W	40	0.0	11.5	5.9
					Cot	R	39	0.0	0.1	0.0
					Saperavi Severny	R	25	0.0	7.1	3.7
					Muscat de Ialoveni	W	20	0.0	100.0	51.2
					Negru de Ialoveni	R	15	0.0	100.0	51.2
					Bianca	W	15	0.0	0.2	0.1
					Gamay de Teinturier Bouze	R	10	0.0	4.4	2.3
					Codrinski	R	5	0.0	100.0	51.2
					Ilichevskii Rannii	R	5	0.0	100.0	51.2
					Onitskanskii Belyi	W	5	0.0	7.0	3.6
					Droujba	W	3	0.0	100.0	51.2
					Alb de Ialoveni	W	2	0.0	100.0	51.2
					Rubin Tairovsky	R	2	0.0	100.0	51.2
					Riton	W	2	0.0	0.8	0.4
					Total		89844	100		

Table 44 (cont.) Winegrape areas, national and global shares (and Varietal Intensity Indexes) for national top 45 varieties, 2010

	Morocco					Myanmar				
Prime variety	Col	Area	Nat'l share	Glob'l share	VII* Prime variety	Col	Area	Nat'l share	Glob'l share	VII*
Doukkali	R	16557	33.8	100.0	93.9 Syrah	R	27	35.8	0.0	8.9
Cinsaut	R	3940	8.0	10.9	10.3 Sauvignon Blanc	W	22	29.2	0.0	12.2
Muscat of Alexandria	W	3669	7.5	13.9	13.1 Muscat Blanc a Petits Grains	W	7	9.5	0.0	14.0
Teneron	R	3488	7.1	100.0	93.9 Pinot Noir	R	7	9.0	0.0	4.8
Abbo	R	2375	4.8	100.0	93.9 Mazuelo	R	4	5.9	0.0	3.4
Mazuelo	R	1692	3.5	2.1	2.0 Tempranillo	R	3	4.5	0.0	0.9
Alicante Henri Bouschet	R	1098	2.2	2.8	2.6 Petit Verdot	R	2	2.6	0.0	16.4
Garnacha Tinta	R	802	1.6	0.4	0.4 Chardonnay	W	1	1.5	0.0	0.3
Other varieties		15379	31.4		Cabernet Sauvignon	R	1	1.0	0.0	0.2
Total		49000	100		Chenin Blanc	W	1	0.8	0.0	1.1
					Alicante Henri Bouschet	R	0	0.3	0.0	0.4
					Total		75	100		

Table 44 (cont.) Winegrape areas, national and global shares (and Varietal Intensity Indexes) for national top 45 varieties, 2010

	New Zealand					Peru				
Prime variety	Col	Area	Nat'l share	Glob'l share	VII*	Prime variety	Col	Area	Nat'l share	Glob'l share	VII*
Sauvignon Blanc	W	16205	50.7	14.7	21.2	Negramoll	R	1252	32.7	39.2	471.0
Pinot Noir	R	4776	14.9	5.5	7.9	Italia	W	1011	26.4	88.3	1060.7
Chardonnay	W	3911	12.2	2.0	2.8	Muscat Blanc a Petits Grains	W	361	9.4	1.2	13.9
Pinot Gris	O	1501	4.7	3.4	5.0	Quebranta	R	330	8.6	95.7	1148.9
Merlot	R	1369	4.3	0.5	0.7	Blaufrankisch	R	290	7.6	1.8	21.6
Riesling	W	979	3.1	2.0	2.8	Red Globe	R	240	6.3	100.0	1201.1
Cabernet Sauvignon	R	517	1.6	0.2	0.3	Pecorino	W	114	3.0	9.3	111.5
Gewurztraminer	W	311	1.0	2.2	3.1	Cardinal	R	53	1.4	9.7	116.8
Syrah	R	293	0.9	0.2	0.2	Cabernet Sauvignon	R	48	1.3	0.0	0.2
Semillon	W	201	0.6	0.9	1.3	Flame Seedless	R	42	1.1	100.0	1201.1
Viognier	W	163	0.5	1.4	2.1	Alphonse Lavallee	R	18	0.5	2.0	24.5
Cabernet Franc	R	163	0.5	0.3	0.4	Sultaniye	W	15	0.4	0.4	5.3
Cot	R	156	0.5	0.4	0.6	Cot	R	10	0.3	0.0	0.3
Muller Thurgau	W	79	0.2	0.3	0.5	Superior Seedless	W	9	0.2	100.0	1201.1
Pinotage	R	74	0.2	1.2	1.7	Torrontes Riojano	W	8	0.2	0.1	1.2
Reichensteiner	W	72	0.2	31.6	45.5	Albillo Mayor	W	7	0.2	0.5	6.4
Chenin Blanc	W	50	0.2	0.1	0.2	Ar99	O	5	0.1	100.0	1201.1
Pinot Meunier	R	19	0.1	0.2	0.2	Crimson Seedless	R	2	0.1	100.0	1201.1
Pinot Blanc	W	16	0.1	0.1	0.2	Crystal	W	2	0.1	1.1	13.8
Palomino Fino	W	14	0.0	0.1	0.1	Chenin Blanc	W	2	0.1	0.0	0.1
Gamay Noir	R	12	0.0	0.0	0.1	Syrah	R	2	0.1	0.0	0.0
Seibel	R	10	0.0	1.7	2.4	Merlot	R	2	0.1	0.0	0.0
Breidecker	W	7	0.0	100	144	Ar110	O	1	0.0	100.0	1201.1
Montepulciano	R	7	0.0	0.0	0.0	Imperial Seedless	O	1	0.0	100.0	1201.1
Tempranillo	R	7	0.0	0.0	0.0	Perlette	W	1	0.0	100.0	1201.1
Sangiovese	R	6	0.0	0.0	0.0	Rosa Arica	R	1	0.0	100.0	1201.1
Blauburger	R	5	0.0	0.4	0.5	Pedro Ximenez	W	1	0.0	0.0	0.1
Verdelho	W	5	0.0	0.2	0.4	Pinot Noir	R	1	0.0	0.0	0.0
Petit Verdot	R	5	0.0	0.1	0.1	Garnacha Tinta	R	1	0.0	0.0	0.0
Chambourcin	R	4	0.0	0.4	0.5	Chardonnay	W	1	0.0	0.0	0.0
Silvaner	W	4	0.0	0.2	0.3	Total		3831	100		
Tribidrag	R	4	0.0	0.0	0.0						
Zweigelt	R	3	0.0	0.0	0.0						
Kolor	R	2	0.0	100.0	144.0						
Flora	O	2	0.0	26.0	37.4						
Arnsburger	W	2	0.0	6.6	9.5						
Roussanne	W	2	0.0	0.1	0.2						
Dolcetto	R	2	0.0	0.0	0.0						
Chasselas	W	2	0.0	0	0						
Garnacha Tinta	R	2	0.0	0.0	0.0						
Osteiner	W	1	0.0	100.0	144.0						
Wurzer	W	1	0.0	20	29						
Scheurebe	W	1	0.0	0.1	0.1						
Nebbiolo	R	1	0.0	0.0	0.0						
Other varieties		998	3.1								
Total		31964	100								

Table 44 (cont.) Winegrape areas, national and global shares (and Varietal Intensity Indexes) for national top 45 varieties, 2010

	Portugal					Romania				
Prime variety	Col	Area	Nat'l share	Glob'l share	VII*	Prime variety	Col	Area	Nat'l share	Glob'l share	VII*
Tempranillo	R	16706	10.2	7.2	2.0	Feteasca Alba	W	12916	7.6	73.9	20.0
Touriga Franca	R	11582	7.1	100.0	28.1	Feteasca Regala	W	12905	7.6	98.2	26.5
Castelao	R	11086	6.8	100.0	28.1	Merlot	R	10988	6.5	4.1	1.1
Touriga Nacional	R	10175	6.2	97.5	27.4	Grasevina	W	7530	4.4	12.3	3.3
Fernao Pires	W	9376	5.7	98.6	27.7	Aligote	W	7297	4.3	20.2	5.5
Trincadeira	R	9246	5.7	99.7	28.1	Sauvignon Blanc	W	4157	2.4	3.8	1.0
Siria	W	7145	4.4	90.5	25.5	Cabernet Sauvignon	R	3718	2.2	1.3	0.3
Tinta Barroca	R	5939	3.6	96.2	27.1	Muscat Ottonel	W	3641	2.1	35.6	9.6
Arinto de Bucelas	W	4446	2.7	100.0	28.1	Babeasca Neagra	R	3042	1.8	97.4	26.3
Rufete	R	4183	2.6	86.6	24.4	Pamid	R	2930	1.7	29.8	8.1
Baga	R	4108	2.5	100.0	28.1	Feteasca Neagra	R	1719	1.0	100.0	27.0
Marufo	R	4008	2.5	60.9	17.1	Pinot Gris	O	1301	0.8	3.0	0.8
Syrah	R	3501	2.1	1.9	0.5	Pinot Noir	R	1089	0.6	1.3	0.3
Loureiro	W	3469	2.1	85.6	24.1	Chardonnay	W	1067	0.6	0.5	0.1
Alicante Henri Bouschet	R	3322	2.0	8.5	2.4	Muscat Blanc a Petits Grains	W	840	0.5	2.7	0.7
Trousseau	R	3149	1.9	91.8	25.8	Blaufrankisch	R	760	0.4	4.7	1.3
Palomino Fino	W	3033	1.9	13.5	3.8	Grasa de Cotnari	W	640	0.4	93.4	25.2
Malvasia Fina	W	2930	1.8	85.8	24.1	Francusa	W	621	0.4	100.0	27.0
Vinhao	R	2482	1.5	78.5	22.1	Cramposie Selectionata	W	409	0.2	100.0	27.0
Mencia	R	2454	1.5	23.0	6.5	Galbena de Odobesti	W	385	0.2	100.0	27.0
Alvarinho	W	1989	1.2	36.0	10.1	Gewurztraminer	W	385	0.2	2.7	0.7
Cabernet Sauvignon	R	1671	1.0	0.6	0.2	Rkatsiteli	W	356	0.2	0.6	0.2
Tinta Carvalha	R	1311	0.8	100.0	28.1	Babeasca Gris	W	328	0.2	100.0	27.0
Rabigato	W	1273	0.8	100.0	28.1	Busuioaca de Bohotin	O	268	0.2	100.0	27.0
Antao Vaz	W	1252	0.8	100.0	28.1	Mustoasa de Maderat	W	255	0.1	100.0	27.0
Caladoc	R	1197	0.7	32.6	9.2	Other varieties		90745	53.3		
Vital		1182	0.7	100.0	28.1	Total		170292	100		
Alfrocheiro	R	1180	0.7	99.3	28.0						
Trajadura	W	1171	0.7	54.0	15.2						
Diagalves	W	1156	0.7	100.0	28.1						
Azal	W	1072	0.7	100.0	28.1						
Damaschino	W	1037	0.6	49.8	14.0						
Malvasia Preta	R	1003	0.6	100.0	28.1						
Bical	W	924	0.6	100.0	28.1						
Rabo de Ovelha	W	908	0.6	100.0	28.1						
Moreto	R	900	0.6	100.0	28.1						
Chardonnay	W	803	0.5	0.4	0.1						
Merlot	R	772	0.5	0.3	0.1						
Santarena	R	739	0.5	100.0	28.1						
Avesso	W	685	0.4	100.0	28.1						
Seara Nova	W	681	0.4	100.0	28.1						
Negramoll	R	676	0.4	21.2	6.0						
Muscat of Alexandria	W	647	0.4	2.5	0.7						
Codega de Larinho	W	629	0.4	100.0	28.1						
Gouveio Real	W	582	0.4	100.0	28.14						
Other varieties		15744	9.6								
Total		163522	100								

Table 44 (cont.) Winegrape areas, national and global shares (and Varietal Intensity Indexes) for national top 45 varieties, 2010

	Russia						Serbia				
Prime variety	Col	Area	Nat'l share	Glob'l share	VII*	Prime variety	Col	Area	Nat'l share	Glob'l share	VII*
Cabernet Sauvignon	R	3593	14.0	1.2	2.2	Grasevina	W	33120	48.0	54.1	36.1
Bianca	W	3513	13.7	54.5	97.8	Prokupac	R	15180	22.0	100.0	66.7
Pervenets Magaracha	W	2238	8.7	77.7	139.5	Chasselas	W	3450	5.0	26.2	17.4
Chardonnay	W	1981	7.7	1.0	1.8	Muscat of Hamburg	R	2760	4.0	33.9	22.6
Merlot	R	1588	6.2	0.6	1.1	Other varieties		14490	21.0		
Aligote	W	1029	4.0	2.8	5.1	Total		68999	100		
Sauvignon Blanc	W	951	3.7	0.9	1.6						
Riesling	W	882	3.4	1.8	3.2						
Levokumsky	R	720	2.8	100.0	179.5						
Saperavi	R	716	2.8	8.8	15.8						
Rkatsiteli	W	702	2.7	1.2	2.1						
Pinot Blanc	W	695	2.7	4.7	8.5						
Krasnostop Zolotovsky	R	562	2.2	100.0	179.5						
Pinot Noir	R	533	2.1	0.6	1.1						
Dunavski Lazur	W	483	1.9	100.0	179.5						
Tsimlyansky Cherny	R	451	1.8	100.0	179.5						
Saperavi Severny	R	325	1.3	92.9	166.7						
Citronny Magarach	W	307	1.2	100.0	179.5						
Viorica	W	307	1.2	88.5	158.9						
Podarok Magaracha	W	292	1.1	57.9	104.0						
Vidvizhenets	O	271	1.1	100.0	179.5						
Riton	W	255	1.0	99.2	178.2						
Doina	R	227	0.9	100.0	179.5						
Savagnin Blanc	W	214	0.8	11.3	20.2						
Zalagyongye	W	193	0.8	9.9	17.8						
Muscat of Hamburg	R	180	0.7	2.2	4.0						
Crystal	W	171	0.7	98.0	175.9						
Levokumski Sustainable	O	170	0.7	100.0	179.5						
Isabella	R	162	0.6	0.5	0.9						
Amur	R	146	0.6	100.0	179.5						
Muscat Blanc a Petits Grains	W	145	0.6	0.5	0.8						
Stepnyak	W	144	0.6	100.0	179.5						
Riesus	W	115	0.4	100.0	179.5						
Muller Thurgau	W	106	0.4	0.5	0.8						
Tsvetochny (Floral)	W	89	0.3	100.0	179.5						
Rubin Golodrigi	R	82	0.3	100.0	179.5						
Tsvetochny (Flowery)	W	80	0.3	100.0	179.5						
Sukholimanskiy Bely	W	80	0.3	3.7	6.7						
Dekabrskii	R	78	0.3	100.0	179.5						
Pinot Gris	O	78	0.3	0.2	0.3						
Onitskanskii Belyi	W	66	0.3	93.0	166.9						
Trebbiano Toscano	W	66	0.3	0.1	0.1						
Dostoinyi	R	65	0.3	100.0	179.5						
Fioletovy Ranny	R	50	0.2	100.0	179.5						
Goecseji Zamatos	W	40	0.2	72.3	129.9						
Other varieties		487	1.9								
Total		25628	100								

Table 44 (cont.) Winegrape areas, national and global shares (and Varietal Intensity Indexes) for national top 45 varieties, 2010

	Slovakia					Slovenia				
Prime variety	Col	Area	Nat'l share	Glob'l share	VII*	Prime variety	Col	Area	Nat'l share	Glob'l share	VII*
Gruner Veltliner	W	2091	16.5	11.1	40.4	Grasevina	W	2360	14.4	3.9	10.9
Grasevina	W	1655	13.1	2.7	9.8	Refosco	R	1292	7.9	91.0	256
Blaufrankisch	R	1378	10.9	8.5	31.1	Chardonnay	W	1208	7.4	0.6	1.7
Sankt Laurent	R	939	7.4	31.2	114	Sauvignon Blanc	W	1061	6.5	1.0	2.7
Muller Thurgau	W	932	7.4	4.1	14.9	Merlot	R	996	6.1	0.4	1.0
Riesling	W	605	4.8	1.2	4.4	Zametovka	R	913	5.6	100	281
Cabernet Sauvignon	R	570	4.5	0.2	0.7	Ribolla Gialla	W	743	4.5	63.0	177
Pinot Blanc	W	523	4.1	3.5	12.9	Malvazija Istarska	W	740	4.5	27.0	75.9
Chardonnay	W	310	2.5	0.2	0.6	Blaufrankisch	R	680	4.2	4.2	11.9
Gewurztraminer	W	265	2.1	1.9	6.8	Riesling	W	676	4.1	1.4	3.8
Furmint	W	248	2.0	4.7	17.2	Furmint	W	651	4.0	12.4	34.8
Odessky Cherny	R	236	1.9	8.8	31.9	Pinot Blanc	W	525	3.2	3.6	10.0
Feteasca Regala	W	231	1.8	1.8	6.4	Pinot Gris	O	501	3.1	1.1	3.2
Irsai Oliver	W	227	1.8	16.0	58.4	Cabernet Sauvignon	R	453	2.8	0.2	0.4
Feteasca Alba	W	219	1.7	1.3	4.6	Muscat Blanc a Petits Grains	W	353	2.2	1.1	3.2
Andre	R	211	1.7	44.7	163	Savagnin Blanc	W	215	1.3	11	32
Pinot Gris	O	211	1.7	0.5	1.8	Sauvignonasse	W	190	1.2	4.3	12.0
Sauvignon Blanc	W	208	1.6	0.2	0.7	Kraljevina	W	179	1.1	40.1	113
Fruhroter Veltliner	R	195	1.5	23.0	83.9	Barbera	R	134	0.8	0.6	1.6
Muskat Moravsky	W	163	1.3	31.7	115	Plavay	W	60	0.4	100	281
Harslevelu	W	141	1.1	7.6	27.6	Kerner	W	2	0.0	0	0
Devin	W	133	1.1	100	364	Other varieties		2422	14.8		
Silvaner	W	117	0.9	5.2	19.0	Total		16354	100		
Zweigelt	R	116	0.9	1.2	4.3						
Blauer Portugieser	R	92	0.7	2.4	8.8						
Muscat Ottonel	W	48	0.4	0.5	1.7						
Muscat Blanc a Petits Grains	W	48	0.4	0.2	0.6						
Dunaj	R	46	0.4	100	364						
Neronet	R	39	0.3	54.2	197.3						
Palava	O	32	0.2	13.7	50.0						
Aurelius	W	26	0.2	36.7	134						
Neuburger	W	9	0.1	0.9	3.4						
Bouvier	W	6	0.0	2.2	8.2						
Milia	R	1	0.0	100	364						
Noria	W	1	0.0	100	364						
Other varieties		367	2.9								
Total		12637	100								

Table 44 (cont.) Winegrape areas, national and global shares (and Varietal Intensity Indexes) for national top 45 varieties, 2010

	South Africa						Spain				
Prime variety	Col	Area	Nat'l share	Glob'l share	VII*	Prime variety	Col	Area	Nat'l share	Glob'l share	VII*
Chenin Blanc	W	18515	18.3	52.7	24.0	Airen	W	252364	24.5	100	4.5
Cabernet Sauvignon	R	12325	12.2	4.2	1.9	Tempranillo	R	207677	20.2	89.3	4.0
Colombard	W	11990	11.9	37.4	17.0	Bobal	R	80120	7.8	100	4.5
Syrah	R	10136	10.0	5.5	2.5	Garnacha Tinta	R	70140	6.8	38.0	1.7
Sauvignon Blanc	W	9551	9.5	8.7	3.9	Monastrell	R	58406	5.7	83.6	3.7
Chardonnay	W	8278	8.2	4.2	1.9	Cayetana Blanca	W	39593	3.9	99.6	4.5
Merlot	R	6497	6.4	2.4	1.1	Macabeo	W	38417	3.7	93.6	4.2
Pinotage	R	6240	6.2	97.4	44.4	Cabernet Sauvignon	R	23237	2.3	8.0	0.4
Ruby Cabernet	R	2220	2.2	38.7	17.6	Syrah	R	20000	1.9	10.8	0.5
Muscat of Alexandria	W	2167	2.1	8.2	3.7	Alicante Henri Bouschet	R	19551	1.9	50.1	2.2
Cinsaut	R	2052	2.0	5.7	2.6	Palomino Fino	W	18836	1.8	83.7	3.7
Semillon	W	1182	1.2	5.3	2.4	Verdejo	W	16578	1.6	100	4.5
Pinot Noir	R	962	1.0	1.1	0.5	Merlot	R	15540	1.5	5.8	0.3
Cabernet Franc	R	934	0.9	1.7	0.8	Pedro Ximenez	W	9036	0.9	97.8	4.4
Viognier	W	892	0.9	7.8	3.6	Parellada	W	8847	0.9	100.0	4.5
Muscat Blanc a Petits Grains	W	689	0.7	2.2	1.0	Xarello	W	8393	0.8	100	4.5
Petit Verdot	R	648	0.6	9.0	4.1	Muscat of Alexandria	W	8237	0.8	31	1.4
Crouchen	W	629	0.6	86.9	39.6	Mencia	R	8204	0.8	77.0	3.4
Cot	R	450	0.4	1.1	0.5	Chardonnay	W	6958	0.7	3.5	0.2
Nouvelle	W	422	0.4	100.0	45.6	Chelva	W	6168	0.6	100.0	4.5
Monastrell	R	403	0.4	0.6	0.3	Tinto de la Pampana Blanca	R	5145	0.5	100	4.5
Muscadel (Red)	R	371	0.4	100.0	45.6	Calagrano	W	4794	0.5	100	4.5
Clairette	W	290	0.3	10.0	4.6	Mazuelo	R	4749	0.5	6	0.3
Palomino Fino	W	270	0.3	1.2	0.5	Prieto Picudo	R	4587	0.4	100.0	4.5
Pinot Gris	O	261	0.3	0.6	0.3	Pardillo	W	4364	0.4	100.0	4.5
Tinta Barroca	R	231	0.2	3.8	1.7	Zalema	W	4097	0.4	100	4.5
Riesling	W	211	0.2	0.4	0.2	Sauvignon Blanc	W	4011	0.4	4	0.2
Villard Blanc	W	188	0.2	27.3	12.4	Merseguera	W	3946	0.4	100	4.5
Garnacha Tinta	R	187	0.2	0.1	0.0	Alvarinho	W	3507	0.3	63.5	2.8
Roobernet	R	139	0.1	100.0	45.6	Beba	W	3036	0.3	100.0	4.5
Fernao Pires	W	135	0.1	1.4	0.6	Tinto Velasco	R	2684	0.3	100.0	4.5
Gewurztraminer	W	122	0.1	0.9	0.4	Listan Negro	R	2666	0.3	100	4.5
Emerald Riesling	W	104	0.1	63.3	28.9	Carignan Blanc	W	2650	0.3	87	3.9
Touriga Nacional	R	101	0.1	1.0	0.4	Marufo	R	2571	0.3	39	1.7
Therona	W	99	0.1	100.0	45.6	Graciano	R	2281	0.2	73.5	3.3
Mazuelo	R	81	0.1	0.1	0.0	Garnacha Blanca	W	2263	0.2	30.7	1.4
Chenel	W	79	0.1	100.0	45.6	Verdoncho	W	2124	0.2	100.0	4.5
Trebbiano Toscano	W	74	0.1	0.1	0.0	Rojal Tinta	R	1801	0.2	100.0	4.5
Bukettraube	W	71	0.1	100.0	45.6	Alarije	W	1726	0.2	100	4.5
Tannat	R	67	0.1	1.1	0.5	Petit Verdot	R	1661	0.2	23	1.0
Sangiovese	R	61	0.1	0.1	0.0	Juan Garcia	R	1572	0.2	92	4.1
Harslevelu	W	56	0.1	3.0	1.4	Perruno	W	1509	0.1	100.0	4.5
Servant	W	54	0.1	100.0	45.6	Planta Nova	W	1366	0.1	97.9	4.4
Barbera	R	51	0.1	0.2	0.1	Trepat	R	1358	0.1	100	4.5
Vinhao	R	47	0.0	1.5	0.7	Albillo Mayor	W	1312	0.1	99.45	4.5
Other varieties		483	0.5			Other varieties		40176	3.9		
Total		101016	100			Total		1028258	100		

Table 44 (cont.) Winegrape areas, national and global shares (and Varietal Intensity Indexes) for national top 45 varieties, 2010

	Switzerland						Thailand				
Prime variety	Col	Area	Nat'l share	Glob'l share	VII*	Prime variety	Col	Area	Nat'l share	Glob'l share	VII*
Pinot Noir	R	4402	29.7	5.1	15.8	Syrah	R	66	44.5	0.0	11.0
Chasselas	W	4013	27.1	30.4	94.5	Black Queen	R	17	11.4	3.5	1081
Gamay Noir	R	1521	10.3	4.7	14.5	Malaga Blanc	W	16	10.9	100.0	30920
Merlot	R	1028	6.9	0.4	1.2	Chenin Blanc	W	13	8.9	0.0	11.6
Müller Thurgau	W	493	3.3	2.2	6.7	Colombard	W	11	7.5	0.0	10.7
Gamaret	R	380	2.6	95.0	295	Cabernet Sauvignon	R	7	4.7	0.0	0.7
Chardonnay	W	321	2.2	0.2	0.5	Garnacha Roja	W	6	3.8	0.3	98.2
Cornalin	R	244	1.6	95.6	297	Tempranillo	R	4	2.9	0.0	0.6
Silvaner	W	241	1.6	10.7	33.2	Muscat Blanc a Petits Grains	W	3	2.2	0.0	3.2
Pinot Gris	O	216	1.5	0.5	1.5	Sangiovese	R	2	1.4	0.0	0.8
Garanoir	R	203	1.4	93.9	292	Dornfelder	R	2	1.3	0.0	7.1
Syrah	R	181	1.2	0.1	0.3	Viognier	W	1	0.4	0.0	1.5
Arvine	W	154	1.0	89.2	277	Pinot Noir	R	1	0.4	0.0	0.2
Sauvignon Blanc	W	134	0.9	0.1	0.4	Total		149	100		
Diolinoir	R	112	0.8	98.0	304						
Pinot Blanc	W	105	0.7	0.7	2.2						
Savagnin Blanc	W	83	0.6	4.4	13.6						
Cabernet Sauvignon	R	63	0.4	0.0	0.1						
Cabernet Franc	R	54	0.4	0.1	0.3						
Gewurztraminer	W	49	0.3	0.3	1.1						
Muscat Blanc a Petits Grains	W	49	0.3	0.2	0.5						
Marsanne	W	48	0.3	2.7	8.5						
Amigne	W	43	0.3	100	310						
Regent	R	41	0.3	59.0	183						
Viognier	W	31	0.2	0.3	0.8						
Humagne	W	30	0.2	100	310						
Doral	W	27	0.2	100	310						
Dunkelfelder	R	24	0.2	7.4	23.0						
Rauschling	W	23	0.2	100	310						
Aligote	W	23	0.2	0.1	0.2						
Cabernet Dorsa	R	22	0.1	9.8	30.4						
Dornfelder	R	21	0.1	0.3	0.8						
Cabernet Jura	R	19	0.1		310						
Ancellotta	R	19	0.1	0.4	1.2						
Kerner	W	19	0.1	0.5	1.5						
Zweigelt	R	15	0.1	0.2	0.5						
Galotta	R	13	0.1	100	310						
Bondola	R	13	0.1	100	310						
Solaris	W	13	0.1	64.5	200.3						
Marechal Foch	R	13	0.1	3.7	11						
Dakapo	R	13	0.1	24.1	74.8						
Riesling	W	12	0.1	0.0	0.1						
Johanniter	W	11	0.1	21.6	67.0						
Cot	R	10	0.1	0.0	0.1						
Carminoir	R	10	0.1	100	310.5						
Other varieties		261	1.8								
Total		14820	100								

Table 44 (cont.) Winegrape areas, national and global shares (and Varietal Intensity Indexes) for national top 45 varieties, 2010

	Tunisia						Turkey				
Prime variety	Col	Area	Nat'l share	Glob'l share	VII*	Prime variety	Col	Area	Nat'l share	Glob'l share	VII*
Mazuelo	R	7576	45.0	9.4	25.8	Sultaniye	W	1750	13.6	51.4	184
Garnacha Tinta	R	2020	12.0	1.1	3.0	Okuzgozu	R	1479	11.5	100	358
Cinsaut	R	842	5.0	2.3	6.4	Syrah	R	1367	10.6	0.7	2.6
Alicante Henri Bouschet	R	842	5.0	2.2	5.9	Bogazkere	R	1106	8.6	100	358
Sangiovese	R	842	5.0	1.1	3.0	Dimrit	R	863	6.7	100	358
Tribidrag	R	337	2.0	1.0	2.8	Kalecik Karasi	R	861	6.7	100	358
Monastrell	R	337	2.0	0.5	1.3	Narince	W	769	6.0	100	358
Syrah	R	337	2.0	0.2	0.5	Emir	W	688	5.3	100	358
Cabernet Sauvignon	R	337	2.0	0.1	0.3	Calkarasi	R	625	4.9	100	358
Other varieties		3367	20.0			Semillon	W	547	4.3	2.5	8.8
Total		16836	100			Cinsaut	R	500	3.9	1.4	5.0
						Alicante Henri Bouschet	R	488	3.8	1.3	4.5
						Cabernet Sauvignon	R	391	3.0	0.1	0.5
						Merlot	R	355	2.8	0.1	0.5
						Gamay Noir	R	206	1.6	0.6	2.3
						Papazkarasi	R	175	1.4	100	358
						Sauvignon Blanc	W	146	1.1	0.1	0.5
						Chardonnay	W	142	1.1	0.1	0.3
						Muscat Blanc a Petits Grains	W	114	0.9	0.4	1.3
						Mazuelo	R	84	0.7	0.1	0.4
						Adakarasi	R	69	0.5	100	358
						Garnacha Tinta	R	33	0.3	0.0	0.1
						Cabernet Franc	R	23	0.2	0.0	0.2
						Viognier	W	16	0.1	0.1	0.5
						Cot	R	13	0.1	0.0	0.1
						Petit Verdot	R	10	0.1	0.1	0.5
						Sangiovese	R	9	0.1	0.0	0.0
						Tempranillo	R	9	0.1	0.0	0.0
						Monastrell	R	4	0.0	0.0	0.0
						Karalahna	R	4	0.0	100	358
						Karasakiz	R	4	0.0	100	358
						Vasilaki	W	4	0.0	100	358
						Pinot Noir	R	3	0.0	0.0	0.0
						Cavus	W	3	0.0	100	358
						Riesling	W	3	0.0	0.0	0.0
						Total		12856	100		

Table 44 (cont.) Winegrape areas, national and global shares (and Varietal Intensity Indexes) for national top 45 varieties, 2010

	Ukraine					United Kingdom				
Prime variety	Col	Area	Nat'l share	Glob'l share	VII*	Prime variety	Col	Area	Nat'l share	Glob'l share	VII*
Rkatsiteli	W	11552	22.1	19.7	17.3	Chardonnay	W	235	19.6	0.1	4.5
Aligote	W	9627	18.4	26.7	23.5	Pinot Noir	R	233	19.4	0.3	10.3
Cabernet Sauvignon	R	4869	9.3	1.7	1.5	Bacchus	W	116	9.7	5.7	217.6
Sauvignon Blanc	W	3123	6.0	2.8	2.5	Seyval Blanc	W	85	7.1	18.3	704.2
Chardonnay	W	2985	5.7	1.5	1.3	Reichensteiner	W	71	5.9	31.2	1197.9
Merlot	R	2820	5.4	1.1	0.9	Pinot Meunier	R	50	4.2	0.4	17.0
Riesling	W	2702	5.2	5.4	4.7	Madeleine Angevine	W	45	3.8	87.2	3348.4
Odessky Cherny	R	2426	4.6	90.3	79.5	Müller Thurgau	W	43	3.6	0.2	7.3
Isabella	R	2396	4.6	7.4	6.5	Rondo	R	40	3.3	100.0	3840.9
Saperavi	R	1514	2.9	18.6	16.4	Schonburger	O	37	3.1	62.6	2405.9
Sukholimanskiy Bely	W	1477	2.8	68.5	60.3	Pinot Blanc	W	23	1.9	0.2	6.0
Bastardo Magarachsky	R	1330	2.5	56.1	49.4	Phoenix	W	21	1.8	41.2	1581.6
Gewurztraminer	W	961	1.8	6.7	5.9	Regent	R	19	1.6	27.4	1052.3
Kokur Bely	W	918	1.8	100	88.0	Pinot Noir Precoce	R	19	1.6	9.1	349.2
Pinot Noir	R	767	1.5	0.9	0.8	Ortega	W	18	1.5	2.8	108.6
Pinot Gris	O	685	1.3	1.6	1.4	Huxelrebe	W	17	1.4	2.8	107.6
Muscat Blanc a Petits Grains	W	674	1.3	2.2	1.9	Triomphe	R	15	1.3	100.0	3840.9
Pervenets Magaracha	W	643	1.2	22.3	19.6	Dornfelder	R	14	1.2	0.2	6.6
Pinot Blanc	W	338	0.6	2.3	2.0	Siegerrebe	O	12	1.0	10.0	385.6
Telti Kyryk	W	246	0.5	100	88.0	Orion	W	10	0.8	100.0	3840.9
Podarok Magaracha	W	212	0.4	42.1	37.0	Auxerrois	W	9	0.8	0.3	12.6
Ekim Kara	R	26.6	0.1	100	87.994	Pinot Gris	O	9	0.8	0.0	0.8
Total		52293	100			Solaris	W	7	0.6	35.5	1363.4
						Kerner	W	6	0.5	0.2	5.8
						Kernling	W	5	0.4	33.3	1280.3
						Wurzer	W	4	0.3	80.0	3072.8
						Regner	W	4	0.3	9.1	349.2
						Acolon	R	4	0.3	0.9	34.2
						Faberrebe	W	4	0.3	0.8	29.3
						Leon Millot	R	3	0.3	12.9	495.0
						Sauvignon Blanc	W	3	0.3	0.0	0.1
						Gutenborner	W	2	0.2	100.0	3840.9
						Dunkelfelder	R	2	0.2	0.6	23.4
						Scheurebe	W	2	0.2	0.1	3.9
						Merlot	R	2	0.2	0.0	0.0
						Madeleine Sylvaner	W	1	0.1	13.8	530.9
						Perle	O	1	0.1	4.8	182.9
						Optima	W	1	0.1	2.7	104.7
						Zweigelt	R	1	0.1	0.0	0.4
						Gewurztraminer	W	1	0.1	0.0	0.3
						Gamay Noir	R	1	0.1	0.0	0.1
						Riesling	W	1	0.1	0.0	0.1
						Cabernet Franc	R	1	0.1	0.0	0.1
						Cabernet Sauvignon	R	1	0.1	0.0	0.0
						Total		1198	100		

Table 44 (cont.) Winegrape areas, national and global shares (and Varietal Intensity Indexes) for national top 45 varieties, 2010

	United States						Uruguay				
Prime variety	Col	Area	Nat'l share	Glob'l share	VII*	Prime variety	Col	Area	Nat'l share	Glob'l share	VII*
Chardonnay	W	40846	17.9	20.5	4.1	Tannat	R	1815	23.7	30.6	183.6
Cabernet Sauvignon	R	34788	15.3	12.0	2.4	Muscat of Hamburg	R	1500	19.6	18.4	110.8
Merlot	R	22729	10.0	8.5	1.7	Merlot	R	875	11.4	0.3	2.0
Tribidrag	R	19857	8.7	60.6	12.2	Trebbiano Toscano	W	751	9.8	0.7	4.1
Pinot Noir	R	16776	7.4	19.4	3.9	Cabernet Sauvignon	R	682	8.9	0.2	1.4
Colombard	W	10025	4.4	31.3	6.3	Cabernet Franc	R	334	4.4	0.6	3.7
Syrah	R	9197	4.0	5.0	1.0	Isabella	R	256	3.3	0.8	4.7
Concord	R	8421	3.7	68.8	13.9	Chardonnay	W	149	1.9	0.1	0.5
Sauvignon Blanc	W	6584	2.9	6.0	1.2	Sauvignon Blanc	W	147	1.9	0.1	0.8
Pinot Gris	O	5231	2.3	12.0	2.4	Marselan	R	91	1.2	3.6	21.9
Riesling	W	4852	2.1	9.7	2.0	Syrah	R	87	1.1	0.0	0.3
Rubired	R	4556	2.0	100	20.2	Pinot Noir	R	55	0.7	0.1	0.4
Chenin Blanc	W	3221	1.4	9.2	1.8	Viognier	W	45	0.6	0.4	2.4
Durif	R	2865	1.3	80.6	16.3	Cot	R	41	0.5	0.1	0.6
Barbera	R	2798	1.2	11.6	2.3	Petit Verdot	R	32	0.4	0.4	2.7
Garnacha Tinta	R	2666	1.2	1.4	0.3	Arinarnoa	R	28	0.4	86.2	518.3
Ruby Cabernet	R	2431	1.1	42.4	8.6	Nebbiolo	R	26	0.3	0.4	2.6
Cabernet Franc	R	2215	1.0	4.1	0.8	Gewurztraminer	W	24	0.3	0.2	1.0
Mazuelo	R	1441	0.6	1.8	0.4	Semillon	W	24	0.3	0.1	0.7
Viognier	W	1374	0.6	12.1	2.4	Concord	R	22	0.3	0.2	1.1
Muscat of Alexandria	W	1285	0.6	4.9	1.0	Alicante Henri Bouschet	R	22	0.3	0.1	0.3
Niagara	W	1210	0.5	25.9	5.2	Riesling	W	15	0.2	0.0	0.2
Gewurztraminer	W	1144	0.5	8.0	1.6	Canari Noir	R	13	0.2	8.5	51.3
Petit Verdot	R	853	0.4	11.8	2.4	Pinot Gris	O	12	0.2	0.0	0.2
Sangiovese	R	852	0.4	1.1	0.2	Trebbiano	W	11	0.1	4.4	26.7
Muscat Blanc a Petits Grains	W	733	0.3	2.4	0.5	Muscat Blanc a Petits Grains	W	10	0.1	0.0	0.2
Cot	R	717	0.3	1.8	0.4	Pinot Blanc	W	9	0.1	0.1	0.4
Catawba	R	633	0.3	100	20.2	Gamay Noir	R	9	0.1	0.0	0.2
Malvasia Bianca di Candia	W	554	0.2	5.6	1.1	Sauvignon Gris	W	8	0.1	1.7	10.0
Elbling	W	498	0.2	35.1	7.1	Malvasia Fina	W	8	0.1	0.2	1.4
Semillon	W	436	0.2	2.0	0.4	Muscat Ottonel	W	7	0.1	0.1	0.4
Alicante Henri Bouschet	R	431	0.2	1.1	0.2	Chenin Blanc	W	7	0.1	0.0	0.1
Tempranillo	R	414	0.2	0.2	0.0	Garnacha Tinta	R	5	0.1	0.0	0.0
Monastrell	R	404	0.2	0.6	0.1	Arriloba	W	4	0.1	57.3	344.1
Vidal	W	360	0.2	22	4.4	Colombard	W	4	0.1	0.0	0.1
Symphony	W	324	0.1	100	20.2	Egiodola	R	3	0.0	0.8	4.8
Carnelian	R	316	0.1	100.0	20.2	Roussanne	W	3	0.0	0.2	1.0
Chambourcin	R	311	0.1	27.5	5.6	Marsanne	W	2	0.0	0.1	0.7
Pinot Blanc	W	269	0.1	1.8	0.4	Ruby Cabernet	R	2	0.0	0.0	0.2
Aurore	W	268	0.1	100.0	20.2	Pedro Ximenez	W	1	0.0	0.0	0.1
Listan Prieto	R	265	0.1	5.8	1.2	Monastrell	R	1	0.0	0.0	0.0
Seyval Blanc	W	259	0.1	56	11.3	Other varieties		517	6.8		
Elvira	W	255	0.1	97	19.6	Total		7657	100		
Vignoles	W	254	0.1	100	20.2						
Triplett Blanc	W	244	0.1	100.0	20.2						
Other varieties		11784	5.2								
Total		227948	100								

Table 45: Varietal Intensity Indexes (and winegrape areas, national and global shares) for national top 45 varieties, 2000

Algeria						Argentina					
Prime variety	Col	Area	Nat'l share	Glob'l share	VII*	Prime variety	Col	Area	Nat'l share	Glob'l share	VII*
Cinsaut	R	7550	25.0	15.6	25.2	Cereza	O	31666	15.7	100.0	24.3
Alicante Henri Bouschet	R	3020	10.0	8.2	13.2	Criolla Grande	R	24641	12.3	100.0	24.3
Mazuelo	R	7550	25.0	6.0	9.6	Pedro Gimenez	W	15101	7.5	100.0	24.3
Garnacha Tinta	R	6040	20.0	2.8	4.6	Moscatel Rosada	O	10656	5.3	100.0	24.3
Pinot Noir	R	1510	5.0	2.5	4.1	Torrontes Sanjuanino	W	3166	1.6	100.0	24.3
Syrah	R	1510	5.0	1.5	2.4	Torrontes Riojano	W	8181	4.1	99.9	24.2
Merlot	R	1510	5.0	0.7	1.2	Aspiran Bouschet	R	308	0.2	99.9	24.2
Cabernet Sauvignon	R	1510	5.0	0.7	1.1	Superior Seedless	W	2835	1.4	99.8	24.2
Total		30200	100			Flame Seedless	R	509	0.3	94.0	22.8
						Red Globe	R	1895	0.9	91.6	22.2
						Douce Noire	R	14989	7.5	84.9	20.6
						Cot	R	16347	8.1	67.0	16.2
						Muscat of Alexandria	W	5539	2.8	18.8	4.6
						Sultaniye	W	2229	1.1	15.5	3.8
						Sauvignonasse	W	798	0.4	14.5	3.5
						Chenin Blanc	W	3591	1.8	7.8	1.9
						Syrah	R	7915	3.9	7.8	1.9
						Cabernet Sauvignon	R	12199	6.1	5.5	1.3
						Viognier	W	151	0.1	4.8	1.2
						Tempranillo	R	4335	2.2	4.7	1.1
						Semillon	W	1028	0.5	3.9	1.0
						Sangiovese	R	2491	1.2	3.6	0.9
						Barbera	R	1061	0.5	3.2	0.8
						Chardonnay	W	4625	2.3	3.2	0.8
						Merlot	R	5513	2.7	2.6	0.6
						Tannat	R	136	0.1	2.4	0.6
						Trebbiano Toscano	W	2846	1.4	2.1	0.5
						Pinot Noir	R	1047	0.5	1.7	0.4
						Sauvignon Blanc	W	827	0.4	1.3	0.3
						Cabernet Franc	R	207	0.1	0.4	0.1
						Pinot Blanc	W	48	0.0	0.3	0.1
						Other varieties		14235	7.1		
						Total		201113	100		

Note: VII* indicates Varital intensity indexes relative to the world, as defined in the introduction.

Table 45 (cont.) Varietal Intensity Indexes (and winegrape areas, national and global shares) for national top 45 varieties, 2000

	Armenia						Australia				
Prime variety	Col	Area	Nat'l share	Glob'l share	VII*	Prime variety	Col	Area	Nat'l share	Glob'l share	VII*
Mskhali	W	1093	9.8	100.0	435.3	Trebbiano	W	685	0.5	100.0	37.4
Garandmak	W	931	8.3	100.0	435.3	Afus Ali	W	328	0.3	100.0	37.3
Kangun	W	850	7.6	100.0	435.3	Doradillo	W	249	0.2	100.0	37.4
Voskeat	W	809	7.2	100.0	435.3	Tarrango	R	120	0.1	100.0	37.4
Rkatsiteli	W	2469	22.0	3.7	16.0	Canada Muscat	W	49	0.0	100.0	37.4
Muscat Blanc a Petits Grains	W	526	4.7	1.9	8.1	Taminga	W	46	0.0	100.0	37.4
Other varieties		4528	40.4			Korinthiaki	R	778	0.6	93.3	34.9
Total		11206	100			Verdelho	W	1293	1.0	78.9	29.5
						Muscat a Petits Grains Rouge	R	380	0.3	76.0	28.4
						Sultaniye	W	10298	7.9	71.8	26.8
						Petit Verdot	R	721	0.6	48.7	18.2
						Ruby Cabernet	R	2424	1.9	32.7	12.2
						Syrah	R	29295	22.4	28.9	10.8
						Semillon	W	6528	5.0	24.9	9.3
						Durif	R	181	0.1	15.1	5.6
						Marsanne	W	216	0.2	14.3	5.3
						Chardonnay	W	17266	13.2	11.9	4.4
						Cabernet Sauvignon	R	24997	19.1	11.3	4.2
						Muscadelle	W	198	0.2	9.0	3.4
						Muscat of Alexandria	W	2495	1.9	8.5	3.2
						Riesling	W	3129	2.4	7.2	2.7
						Pinot Noir	R	3223	2.5	5.4	2.0
						Gewurztraminer	W	521	0.4	4.9	1.8
						Colombard	W	1801	1.4	4.7	1.8
						Crouchen	W	98	0.1	4.3	1.6
						Sauvignon Blanc	W	2602	2.0	4.0	1.5
						Viognier	W	117	0.1	3.7	1.4
						Merlot	R	7669	5.9	3.6	1.4
						Chenin Blanc	W	841	0.6	1.8	0.7
						Cot	R	429	0.3	1.8	0.7
						Touriga Nacional	R	73	0.1	1.7	0.6
						Cabernet Franc	R	744	0.6	1.5	0.6
						Monastrell	R	948	0.7	1.2	0.5
						Garnacha Tinta	R	2139	1.6	1.0	0.4
						Nebbiolo	R	50	0.0	1.0	0.4
						Pinot Meunier	R	107	0.1	1.0	0.4
						Muscat Blanc a Petits Grains	W	214	0.2	0.8	0.3
						Sangiovese	R	372	0.3	0.5	0.2
						Pedro Ximenez	W	89	0.1	0.5	0.2
						Palomino Fino	W	124	0.1	0.4	0.2
						Barbera	R	103	0.1	0.3	0.1
						Mazuelo	R	90	0.1	0.1	0.0
						Tempranillo	R	41	0.0	0.0	0.0
						Other varieties		6532	5.0		
						Total		130602	100		

Table 45 (cont.) Varietal Intensity Indexes (and winegrape areas, national and global shares) for national top 45 varieties, 2000

	Austria					Brazil				
Prime variety	Col	Area	Nat'l share	Glob'l share	VII*	Prime variety	Col	Area	Nat'l share	Glob'l share	VII*
Bouvier	W	365	0.8	100.0	100.6	Bordo	R	3379	6.4	100.0	92.3
Goldburger	W	309	0.6	100.0	100.6	Herbemont	R	1453	2.7	100.0	92.3
Roter Veltliner	O	258	0.5	100.0	100.6	Seibel	R	1967	3.7	98.8	91.2
Rotgipfler	W	118	0.2	100.0	100.6	Niagara	W	13436	25.4	87.6	80.8
Zierfandler	O	98	0.2	100.0	100.6	Jacquez	R	170	0.3	75.3	69.5
Jubilaumsrebe	W	30	0.1	100.0	100.6	Isabella	R	14285	27.0	52.2	48.2
FruHroter Veltliner	R	626	1.3	99.0	99.6	Couderc Noir	R	299	0.6	49.1	45.3
Blauer Wildbacher	R	464	1.0	98.3	98.8	Concord	R	2509	4.7	21.2	19.6
Blauburger	R	884	1.8	88.2	88.7	Tannat	R	182	0.3	3.3	3.0
Neuburger	W	1094	2.3	76.3	76.7	Muscat of Alexandria	W	809	1.5	2.8	2.5
Gruner Veltliner	W	17479	36.0	74.1	74.5	Semillon	W	384	0.7	1.5	1.4
Zweigelt	R	4350	9.0	60.2	60.5	Gewurztraminer	W	140	0.3	1.3	1.2
Blauer Portugieser	R	2358	4.9	55.1	55.4	Grasevina	W	880	1.7	1.0	0.9
Blaufrankisch	R	2641	5.4	20.5	20.6	Cabernet Franc	R	405	0.8	0.8	0.8
Sankt Laurent	R	415	0.9	17.5	17.6	Trebbiano Toscano	W	688	1.3	0.5	0.5
Pinot Blanc	W	2936	6.1	17.3	17.4	Cabernet Sauvignon	R	587	1.1	0.3	0.2
Scheurebe	W	529	1.1	14.5	14.6	Chardonnay	W	330	0.6	0.2	0.2
Muller Thurgau	W	3289	6.8	9.8	9.9	Merlot	R	469	0.9	0.2	0.2
Grasevina	W	4323	8.9	4.7	4.7	Sauvignon Blanc	W	140	0.3	0.2	0.2
Riesling	W	1643	3.4	3.8	3.8	Other varieties		10328	19.5		
Muscat Ottonel	W	418	0.9	3.4	3.4	Total		52840	100		
Gewurztraminer	W	363	0.7	3.4	3.4						
Pinot Gris	O	293	0.6	1.5	1.6						
Silvaner	W	53	0.1		1.3						
Pinot Noir	R	409	0.8	0.7	0.7						
Muscat Blanc a Petits Grains	W	143	0.3	0.5	0.5						
Sauvignon Blanc	W	314	0.6	0.5	0.5						
Cabernet Sauvignon	R	312	0.6	0.1	0.1						
Cabernet Franc	R	27	0.1	0.1	0.1						
Merlot	R	112	0.2	0.1	0.1						
Furmint	W	1	0.0	0.0	0.0						
Other varieties		1843	3.8								
Total		48496	100								

Table 45 (cont.) Varietal Intensity Indexes (and winegrape areas, national and global shares) for national top 45 varieties, 2000

	Bulgaria					Canada				
Prime variety	Col	Area	Nat'l share	Glob'l share	VII*	Prime variety	Col	Area	Nat'l share	Glob'l share	VII*
Shiroka Melnishka	R	3804	4.0	100.0	50.8	Fredonia	R	73	0.9	84.9	487.4
Misket	W	3764	3.9	100.0	50.8	Vidal	W	514	6.0	84.1	482.9
Mavrud	R	647	0.7	100.0	50.8	Baco Noir	R	279	3.3	70.3	403.3
Pamid	R	22581	23.5	99.4	50.5	De Chaunac	R	119	1.4	64.1	368.1
Dimyat	W	7649	8.0	99.1	50.4	Marechal Foch	R	109	1.3	63.1	362.1
Cardinal	R	3035	3.2	95.1	48.3	Seyval Blanc	W	132	1.5	33.8	194.2
Koenigin der Weingaerten	W	567	0.6	75.5	38.4	Elvira	W	69	0.8	20.0	114.9
Kadarka	R	1619	1.7	61.5	31.3	Concord	R	977	11.5	8.3	47.5
Muscat Ottonel	W	2914	3.0	23.8	12.1	Niagara	W	461	5.4	3.0	17.3
Rkatsiteli	W	9429	9.8	14.0	7.1	Gewurztraminer	W	237	2.8	2.2	12.7
Gewurztraminer	W	971	1.0	9.1	4.6	Cabernet Franc	R	567	6.7	1.2	6.7
Muscat of Hamburg	R	445	0.5	6.3	3.2	Riesling	W	482	5.7	1.1	6.4
Merlot	R	11169	11.6	5.3	2.7	Pinot Gris	O	210	2.5	1.1	6.4
Cabernet Sauvignon	R	10441	10.9	4.7	2.4	Pinot Blanc	W	146	1.7	0.9	4.9
Aligote	W	1659	1.7	4.7	2.4	Pinot Noir	R	457	5.4	0.8	4.4
Grasevina	W	3602	3.8	3.9	2.0	Gamay Noir	R	263	3.1	0.7	4.0
Riesling	W	647	0.7	1.5	0.8	Chardonnay	W	973	11.5	0.7	3.8
Trebbiano Toscano	W	1821	1.9	1.3	0.7	Merlot	R	674	7.9	0.3	1.8
Chardonnay	W	1862	1.9	1.3	0.7	Cabernet Sauvignon	R	569	6.7	0.3	1.5
Pinot Noir	R	769	0.8	1.3	0.7	Sauvignon Blanc	W	148	1.7	0.2	1.3
Sauvignon Blanc	W	405	0.4	0.6	0.3	Other varieties		1040	12.2		
Other varieties		6197	6.5			Total		8498	100		
Total		95997	100								

Table 45 (cont.) Varietal Intensity Indexes (and winegrape areas, national and global shares) for national top 45 varieties, 2000

	Chile					Croatia					
Prime variety	Col	Area	Nat'l share	Glob'l share	VII*	Prime variety	Col	Area	Nat'l share	Glob'l share	VII*
Blanca Ovoide	W	107	0.1	100.0	42.8	Plavac Mali	R	6539	11.0	100.0	82.1
Listan Prieto	R	15181	13.3	97.7	41.8	Posip Bijeli	W	6539	11.0	100.0	82.1
Carmenere	R	4719	4.1	82.6	35.4	Babic	R	1189	2.0	100.0	82.1
Malvasia Fina	W	4305	3.8	60.6	25.9	Malvazija Istarska	W	7134	12.0	94.4	77.4
Sauvignon Rose	O	7	0.0	26.8	11.5	Mondeuse Noire	R	1189	2.0	84.7	69.5
Cabernet Sauvignon	R	35967	31.6	16.3	7.0	Grasevina	W	16051	27.0	17.4	14.3
Moscato Giallo	W	65	0.1	15.9	6.8	Blaufrankisch	R	1189	2.0	9.2	7.6
Pedro Ximenez	W	2379	2.1		5.9	Other varieties		19618	33.0		
Sauvignon Blanc	W	6662	5.8	10.3	4.4	Total		59448	100		
Alicante Henri Bouschet	R	2882	2.5	7.8	3.3						
Semillon	W	1893	1.7	7.2	3.1						
Merlot	R	12825	11.3	6.1	2.6						
Petit Verdot	R	84	0.1	5.7	2.4						
Chardonnay	W	7672	6.7	5.3	2.3						
Viognier	W	128	0.1	4.1	1.7						
Cot	R	929	0.8	3.8	1.6						
Chasselas	W	404	0.4	3.0	1.3						
Pinot Noir	R	1614	1.4	2.7	1.1						
Sauvignonasse	W	132	0.1	2.4	1.0						
Syrah	R	2040	1.8	2.0	0.9						
Cabernet Franc	R	689	0.6	1.4	0.6						
Gewurztraminer	W	121	0.1	1.1	0.5						
Riesling	W	286	0.3	0.7	0.3						
Mazuelo	R	641	0.6	0.5	0.2						
Cinsaut	R	195	0.2	0.4	0.2						
Tribidrag	R	91	0.1	0.3	0.1						
Nebbiolo	R	9.5	0.0	0.2	0.1						
Sangiovese	R	123	0.1	0.2	0.1						
Chenin Blanc	W	76	0.1	0.2	0.1						
Pinot Blanc	W	14	0.0	0.1	0.0						
Marsanne	W	1	0.0	0.1	0.0						
Albillo Real	W	2	0.0	0.1	0.0						
Monastrell	R	22	0.0	0.0	0.0						
Pinot Gris	O	2	0.0	0.0	0.0						
Tempranillo	R	1	0.0	0.0	0.0						
Other varieties		11697	10.3								
Total		113966	100								

Table 45 (cont.) Varietal Intensity Indexes (and winegrape areas, national and global shares) for national top 45 varieties, 2000

	Cyprus					Czech Republic					
Prime variety	Col	Area	Nat'l share	Glob'l share	VII*	Prime variety	Col	Area	Nat'l share	Glob'l share	VII*
Mavro	R	10969	60.0	100	266.8	Sankt Laurent	R	1020	9.0	43.0	185.3
Xynisteri	W	2742	15.0	100	266.8	Neuburger	W	340	3.0	23.7	102.1
Other varieties		4570	25.0			Blauer Portugieser	R	340	3.0	7.9	34.2
Total		18282	100			Gruner Veltliner	W	1700	15.0	7.2	31.0
						Zweigelt	R	453	4.0	6.3	27.0
						Blaufrankisch	R	680	6.0	5.3	22.7
						Muller Thurgau	W	1586	14.0	4.7	20.3
						Riesling	W	793	7.0	1.8	7.9
						Grasevina	W	1246	11.0	1.4	5.8
						Chardonnay	W	567	5.0	0.4	1.7
						Other varieties		2606	23.0		
						Total		11331	100		

Table 45 (cont.) Varietal Intensity Indexes (and winegrape areas, national and global shares) for national top 45 varieties, 2000

	France					Georgia				
Prime variety	Col	Area	Nat'l share	Glob'l share	VII*	Prime variety	Col	Area	Nat'l share	Glob'l share	VII*
Baco Blanc	W	2137	0.2	100	5.6	Tsolikouri	W	6161	16.5	100.0	130.4
Aubun	R	1411	0.2	100	5.6	Tsitska	W	2839	7.6	100.0	130.4
Negrette	R	1319	0.2	100	5.6	Chinuri	W	955	2.6	100.0	130.4
Chasan	W	914	0.1	100	5.6	Mtsvane Kakhuri	W	249	0.7	100.0	130.4
Counoise	R	638	0.1	100	5.6	Goruli Mtsvane	W	224	0.6	100.0	130.4
Abouriou	R	419	0.0	100	5.6	Aleksandrouli	R	219	0.6	100.0	130.4
Terret Noir	R	370	0.0	100	5.6	Tsulukidzis Tetra	W	152	0.4	100.0	130.4
Clairette Rose	W	356	0.0	100	5.6	Aladasturi	R	46	0.1	100.0	130.4
Egiodola	R	315	0.0	100	5.6	Krakhuna	W	36	0.1	100.0	130.4
Marselan	R	176	0.0	100	5.6	Tavkveri	R	29	0.1	100.0	130.4
Baroque	W	169	0.0	100	5.6	Ojaleshi	R	25	0.1	100.0	130.4
Calitor Noir	R	75	0.0	100	5.6	Chkhaveri	O	20	0.1	100.0	130.4
Petit Courbu	W	75	0.0	100	5.6	Kisi	W	20	0.1	100.0	130.4
Aramon Gris	W	72	0.0	100	5.6	Usakhelouri	R	8	0.0	100.0	130.4
Arriloba	W	59	0.0	100	5.6	Khikhvi	W	5	0.0	100.0	130.4
Segalin	R	54	0.0	100	5.6	Otskhanuri Sapere	R	5	0.0	100.0	130.4
Mollard	R	23	0.0	100	5.6	Saperavi	R	3704	9.9	55.2	72.0
Barbarossa	O	16	0.0	100	5.6	Rkatsiteli	W	19741	52.8	29.3	38.2
Bousquet Precoce	W	16	0.0	100	5.6	Pinot Blanc	W	171	0.5	1.0	1.3
Carignan Bouschet	R	16	0.0	100	5.6	Aligote	W	97	0.3	0.3	0.4
Seinoir	R	15	0.0	100	5.6	Cabernet Sauvignon	R	223	0.6	0.1	0.1
Brun Argente	R	14	0.0	100	5.6	Other varieties		2490	6.7		
Poulsard Blanc	W	14	0.0	100	5.6	Total		37419	100		
Gramon	R	14	0.0	100	5.6						
Oeillade Bousche	R	10	0.0	100	5.6						
Mourvaison	R	9	0.0	100	5.6						
Cesar	R	8	0.0	100	5.6						
Select	W	8	0.0	100	5.6						
Couderc	W	4	0.0	100	5.6						
Fuella Nera	R	4	0.0	100	5.6						
Petit Meslier	W	3	0.0	100	5.6						
Roussette d'Ayze	W	3	0.0	100	5.6						
Liliorila	W	3	0.0	100	5.6						
Codivarta	W	3	0.0	100	5.6						
Joannes Seyve	R	3	0.0	100	5.6						
Calitor Gris	W	2	0.0	100	5.6						
Milgranet	R	2	0.0	100	5.6						
Chenivesse	R	1	0.0	100	5.6						
Baleille	W	1	0.0	100	5.6						
Biancu Gentile	W	1	0.0	100	5.6						
Noual	W	1	0.0	100	5.6						
Saint-Pierre Dore	W	1	0.0	100	5.6						
Pougnet	R	0	0.0	100	5.6						
Cynthiana	R	0	0.0	100	5.6						
Monbadon	W	0	0.0	100	5.6						
Other varieties		856094	99.0								
Total		864846	100								

Table 45 (cont.) Varietal Intensity Indexes (and winegrape areas, national and global shares) for national top 45 varieties, 2000

	Germany					Greece				
Prime variety	Col	Area	Nat'l share	Glob'l share	VII* Prime variety	Col	Area	Nat'l share	Glob'l share	VII*
Dornfelder	R	3765	3.6	100.0	46.8 Savatiano	W	12747	25.1	100	95.9
Faberrebe	W	1586	1.5	100.0	46.8 Roditis(Red)	R	6945	13.7	100	95.9
Huxelrebe	W	1289	1.2	100.0	46.8 Liatiko	R	2476	4.9	100	95.9
Ortega	W	1054	1.0	100.0	46.8 Agiorgitiko	R	2320	4.6	100	95.9
Dunkelfelder	R	280	0.3	100.0	46.8 Moschomavro	R	2305	4.5	100	95.9
Optima	W	239	0.2	100.0	46.8 Xinomavro	R	1816	3.6	100	95.9
Heroldrebe	R	199	0.2	100.0	46.8 Athiri	W	1273	2.5	100	95.9
Domina	R	187	0.2	100.0	46.8 Kotsifali	R	1148	2.3	100	95.9
Siegerrebe	O	167	0.2	100.0	46.8 Assyrtiko	W	1106	2.2	100	95.9
Regner	W	150	0.1	100.0	46.8 Mandilaria	R	845	1.7	100	95.9
Perle	O	121	0.1	100.0	46.8 Mavrodafni	R	537	1.1	100	95.9
Rieslaner	W	70	0.1	100.0	46.8 Vilana	W	506	1.0	100	95.9
Kanzler	W	53	0.1	100.0	46.8 Vertzami	R	491	1.0	100	95.9
Juwel	W	42	0.0	100.0	46.8 Debina	W	455	0.9	100	95.9
Schonburger	O	39	0.0	100.0	46.8 Asprouda	W	433	0.9	100	95.9
Deckrot	R	30	0.0	100.0	46.8 Moschofilero	R	423	0.8	100	95.9
Helfensteiner	R	26	0.0	100.0	46.8 Monemvassia	W	418	0.8	100	95.9
Phoenix	W	24	0.0	100.0	46.8 Romeiko	R	382	0.8	100	95.9
Kernling	W	18	0.0	100.0	46.8 Robola	W	356	0.7	100	95.9
Ehrenbreitsteiner	W	13	0.0	100.0	46.8 Mavrouda	R	349	0.7	100	95.9
Holder	W	13	0.0	100.0	46.8 Roditis	O	299	0.6	100	95.9
Hegel	R	10	0.0	100.0	46.8 Fileri	W	249	0.5	100	95.9
Mariensteiner	W	9	0.0	100.0	46.8 Fokiano	R	162	0.3	100	95.9
Orion	W	8	0.0	100.0	46.8 Goustolidi	W	112	0.2	100	95.9
Silcher	W	7	0.0	100.0	46.8 Stavroto	R	104	0.2	100	95.9
Merzling	W	5	0.0	100.0	46.8 Negoska	R	96	0.2	100	95.9
Elbling Rot	R	4	0.0	100.0	46.8 Limnio	R	95	0.2	100	95.9
Osteiner	W	3	0.0	100.0	46.8 Liatiko(White)	W	70	0.1	100	95.9
Arnsburger	W	3	0.0	100.0	46.8 Vilana(Red)	R	60	0.1	100	95.9
Fontanara	W	2	0.0	100.0	46.8 Fokiano (White)	W	57	0.1	100	95.9
Nobling	W	102	0.1	99.9	46.7 Athiri (Red)	R	40	0.1	100	95.9
Goldriesling	W	10	0.0	99.6	46.6 Krassato	R	38	0.1	100	95.9
Pinot Noir Precoce	R	84	0.1	98.5	46.1 Batily	R	38	0.1	100	95.9
Morio-Muskat	W	1167	1.1	98.2	46.0 Limnio(White)	W	27	0.1	100	95.9
Bacchus	W	3279	3.1	96.7	45.3 Batili	W	27	0.1	100	95.9
Freisamer	W	16	0.0	96.6	45.2 Uni Blan	R	26	0.1	100	95.9
Kerner	W	6828	6.6	96.0	44.9 Malagousia	W	23	0.0	100	95.9
Ehrenfelser	W	255	0.2	88.2	41.3 Grenache Rose	R	22	0.0	100	95.9
Scheurebe	W	3126	3.0	85.5	40.0 Asirtiko Red	R	22	0.0	100	95.9
Reichensteiner	W	257	0.2	80.6	37.7 Zoumiatiko Red	R	22	0.0	100	95.9
Muller Thurgau	W	20691	19.9	61.6	28.9 Karinian	W	14	0.0	100	95.9
Elbling	W	1042	1.0	55.9	26.2 Rombola Red	R	3	0.0	100	95.9
Riesling	W	22350	21.4	51.8	24.2 Merlo	W	3	0.0	100	95.9
Albalonga	W	16	0.0	27.8	13.0 Mavro Messenikola	R	3	0.0	100	95.9
Pinot Blanc	W	2396	2.3	14.1	6.6 Xinomavro (White)	W	3	0.0	100	95.9
Other varieties		33170	31.8		Other varieties		11932	23.5		
Total		104207	100		Total		50878	100		

Table 45 (cont.) Varietal Intensity Indexes (and winegrape areas, national and global shares) for national top 45 varieties, 2000

	Hungary					Italy				
Prime variety	Col	Area	Nat'l share	Glob'l share	VII*	Prime variety	Col	Area	Nat'l share	Glob'l share	VII*
Furmint	W	3480	4.0	100.0	56.1	Catarratto Bianco	W	50711	8.0	100	7.7
Ezerjo	W	3157	3.6	100.0	56.1	Montepulciano	R	28679	4.5	100	7.7
Arany Sarfeher	W	2914	3.4	100.0	56.1	Trebbiano Romagnolo	W	19492	3.1	100	7.7
Cserszegi Fuszeres	W	2185	2.5	100.0	56.1	Nero d'Avola	R	11318	1.8	100	7.7
Kunleany	W	1376	1.6	100.0	56.1	Inzolia	W	9259	1.5	100	7.7
Kovidinka	O	1214	1.4	100.0	56.1	Manzoni Bianco	W	8290	1.3	100	7.7
Lakhegyi Mezes	W	567	0.7	100.0	56.1	Nerello Mascalese	R	4167	0.7	100	7.7
Ezerfurtu	W	405	0.5	100.0	56.1	Lambrusco Salamino	R	4147	0.7	100	7.7
Zenit	W	405	0.5	100.0	56.1	Albarola	W	4090	0.6	100	7.7
Biborkadarka	R	202	0.2	100.0	56.1	Trebbiano Giallo	W	3984	0.6	100	7.7
Harslevelu	W	1012	1.2	78.1	43.8	Malvasia Bianca Lunga	W	3937	0.6	100	7.7
Zalagyongye	W	2550	2.9	58.9	33.1	Nuragus	W	3186	0.5	100	7.7
Blaufrankisch	R	6920	8.0	53.7	30.2	Cortese	W	3113	0.5	100	7.7
Silvaner	W	1619	1.9	38.7	21.7	Monica Nera	R	2835	0.4	100	7.7
Kadarka	R	1012	1.2	38.5	21.6	Greco Nero	R	2715	0.4	100	7.7
Zweigelt	R	2266	2.6	31.3	17.6	Ciliegiolo	R	2527	0.4	100	7.7
Blauer Portugieser	R	1255	1.4	29.3	16.5	Albana	W	2487	0.4	100	7.7
Feteasca Regala	W	567	0.7	22.0	12.3	Verdeca	W	2208	0.3	100	7.7
Chasselas	W	1902	2.2	14.3	8.0	Grillo	W	1803	0.3	100	7.7
Muscat Ottonel	W	1416	1.6	11.6	6.5	Nero di Troia	R	1765	0.3	100	7.7
Muller Thurgau	W	3278	3.8	9.8	5.5	Lambrusco Grasparossa	R	1720	0.3	100	7.7
Grasevina	W	6677	7.7	7.2	4.1	Verduzzo Trevigiano	W	1657	0.3	100	7.7
Gruner Veltliner	W	1335	1.5	5.7	3.2	Malvasia di Candia Aromat	W	1643	0.3	100	7.7
Muscat Blanc a Petits Grains	W	1538	1.8	5.4	3.0	Regina	W	1509	0.2	100	7.7
Pinot Gris	O	890	1.0	4.7	2.6	Avarengo	R	1453	0.2	100	7.7
Feteasca Alba	W	971	1.1	4.1	2.3	Biancame	W	1330	0.2		7.7
Riesling	W	1619	1.9	3.8	2.1	Raboso Piave	R	1270	0.2	100	7.7
Chardonnay	W	2954	3.4	2.0	1.1	Fortana	R	1252	0.2	100	7.7
Cabernet Franc	R	526	0.6	1.1	0.6	Schiava	R	1231	0.2	100	7.7
Pamid	R	121	0.1	0.5	0.3	Schiava Gentile	R	1158	0.2	100	7.7
Sauvignon Blanc	W	324	0.4	0.5	0.3	Montu	W	1091	0.2	100	7.7
Cabernet Sauvignon	R	1052	1.2	0.5	0.3	Caddiu	R	978	0.2	100	7.7
Pinot Noir	R	243	0.3	0.4	0.2	Piedirosso	R	896	0.1	100	7.7
Merlot	R	486	0.6	0.2	0.1	Cocacciola	W	887	0.1	100	7.7
Other varieties		28449	32.7			Refosco di Faedis	R	256	0.0	100	7.7
Total		86886	100			Tazzelenghe	R	68	0.0	100	7.7
						Neretto di Bairo	R	53	0.0	100	7.7
						Soperga	R	32	0.0	100	7.7
						Vien de Nus	R	25	0.0	100	7.7
						Nebbiera	R	20	0.0	100	7.7
						Pignolo	R	18	0.0	100	7.7
						Verduschia	W	15	0.0	100	7.7
						Bussanello	W	8	0.0	100	7.7
						Dolciame	W	6	0.0	100	7.7
						Mayolet	R	4	0.0	100	7.7
						Other varieties		447369	70.3		
						Total		636662	100		

Table 45 (cont.) Varietal Intensity Indexes (and winegrape areas, national and global shares) for national top 45 varieties, 2000

	Luxembourg					Moldova				
Prime variety	Col	Area	Nat'l share	Glob'l share	VII*	Prime variety	Col	Area	Nat'l share	Glob'l share	VII*
Elbling	W	164	12.2	8.8	318.4	Noah	W	71	0.1	100.0	54.3
Auxerrois	W	169	12.5	7.3	265.7	Pervomaisky	R	64	0.1	100.0	54.3
Muller Thurgau	W	459	34.1	1.4	49.5	Golubok	R	50	0.1	100.0	54.3
Pinot Gris	O	155	11.5	0.8	29.7	Viorica	W	40	0.0	100.0	54.3
Pinot Blanc	W	138	10.2	0.8	29.4	Saperavi Severny	R	25	0.0	100.0	54.3
Riesling	W	175	13.0	0.4	14.7	Muscat de Ialoveni	W	20	0.0	100.0	54.3
Gewurztraminer	W	12	0.9	0.1	4.1	Negru de Ialoveni	R	15	0.0	100.0	54.3
Pinot Noir	R	66	4.9	0.1	4.0	Codrinski	R	5	0.0	100.0	54.3
Silvaner	W	1	0.1	0.0	0.9	Ilichevskii Rannii	R	5	0.0	100.0	54.3
Chardonnay	W	8	0.6	0.0	0.2	Onitskanskii Belyi	W	5	0.0	100.0	54.3
Gamay Noir	R	1	0.1	0.0	0.1	Droujba	W	3	0.0	100.0	54.3
Total		1348	100			Alb de Ialoveni	W	2	0.0	100.0	54.3
						Riton	W	2	0.0	100.0	54.3
						Rubin Tairovsky	R	2	0.0	100.0	54.3
						Bastardo Magarachsky	R	1040	1.2	52.8	28.7
						Aligote	W	15790	17.6	44.3	24.0
						Gamay Teinturier Freaux	R	55	0.1	41.8	22.7
						Isabella	R	11401	12.7	41.6	22.6
						Sukholimanskiy Bely	W	599	0.7	36.7	19.9
						Gewurztraminer	W	2731	3.0	25.6	13.9
						Feteasca Alba	W	4334	4.8	18.2	9.9
						Rkatsiteli	W	11508	12.8	17.1	9.3
						Sauvignon Blanc	W	8151	9.1	12.6	6.8
						Muscat Ottonel	W	1520	1.7	12.4	6.7
						Pinot Noir	R	6521	7.3	10.9	5.9
						Pinot Gris	O	2042	2.3	10.8	5.9
						Saperavi	R	716	0.8	10.7	5.8
						Merlot	R	8123	9.0	3.8	2.1
						Chardonnay	W	5134	5.7	3.5	1.9
						Cabernet Sauvignon	R	7590	8.4	3.4	1.9
						Gamay de Teinturier Bouze	R	10	0.0	3.1	1.7
						Riesling	W	1343	1.5	3.1	1.7
						Silvaner	W	98	0.1	2.3	1.3
						Babeasca Neagra	R	80	0.1	2.1	1.2
						Pinot Blanc	W	350	0.4	2.1	1.1
						Bianca	W	15	0.0	0.7	0.4
						Muscat Blanc a Petits Grains	W	172	0.2	0.6	0.3
						Muller Thurgau	W	173	0.2	0.5	0.3
						Cot	R	39	0.0	0.2	0.1
						Total		89844	100		

Table 45 (cont.) Varietal Intensity Indexes (and winegrape areas, national and global shares) for national top 45 varieties, 2000

	Morocco					New Zealand				
Prime variety	Col	Area	Nat'l share	Glob'l share	VII* Prime variety	Col	Area	Nat'l share	Glob'l share	VII*
Doukkali	R	16557	33.4	100.0	98.4 Breidecker	W	28	0.3	100.0	490.7
Teneron	R	3488	7.0	100.0	98.4 Flora	O	6	0.1	100.0	490.7
Abbo	R	2375	4.8	100.0	98.4 Reichensteiner	W	62	0.6	19.4	95.2
Muscat of Alexandria	W	3669	7.4	12.5	12.3 Sauvignon Blanc	W	2423	24.4	3.7	18.3
Cinsaut	R	3940	7.9	8.1	8.0 Chardonnay	W	2787	28.0	1.9	9.4
Alicante Henri Bouschet	R	1098	2.2	3.0	2.9 Pinot Noir	R	1098	11.0	1.8	9.0
Mazuelo	R	1692	3.4	1.3	1.3 Gewurztraminer	W	141	1.4	1.3	6.5
Garnacha Tinta	R	802	1.6	0.4	0.4 Blauburger	R	13	0.1	1.3	6.4
Other varieties		15979	32.2		Muller Thurgau	W	419	4.2	1.2	6.1
Total		49600	100		Riesling	W	490	4.9	1.1	5.6
					Pinotage	R	73	0.7	1.1	5.4
					Semillon	W	229	2.3	0.9	4.3
					Pinot Gris	O	127	1.3	0.7	3.3
					Chenin Blanc	W	146	1.5	0.3	1.6
					Merlot	R	657	6.6	0.3	1.5
					Cabernet Sauvignon	R	654	6.6	0.3	1.5
					Cot	R	67	0.7	0.3	1.3
					Cabernet Franc	R	118	1.2	0.2	1.2
					Chasselas	W	25	0.3	0.2	0.9
					Silvaner	W	4	0.0	0.1	0.5
					Palomino Fino	W	21	0.2	0.1	0.3
					Syrah	R	60	0.6	0.1	0.3
					Other varieties		294	3.0		
					Total		9942	100		

Table 45 (cont.) Varietal Intensity Indexes (and winegrape areas, national and global shares) for national top 45 varieties, 2000

	Portugal						Romania				
Prime variety	Col	Area	Nat'l share	Glob'l share	VII*	Prime variety	Col	Area	Nat'l share	Glob'l share	VII*
Castelao	R	14424	7.0	100	23.8	Feteasca Neagra	R	1214	0.5	100.0	22.0
Codega de Larinho	W	4058	2.0	100	23.8	Grasa de Cotnari	W	850	0.4	100.0	22.0
Arinto de Bucelas	W	3966	1.9	100	23.8	Galbena de Odobesti	W	546	0.2	100.0	22.0
Azal	W	3302	1.6	100	23.8	Babeasca Neagra	R	3642	1.6	97.9	21.5
Rabo de Ovelha	W	2330	1.1	100	23.8	Feteasca Alba	W	18211	8.2	76.4	16.8
Vital	W	2246	1.1	100	23.8	Feteasca Regala	W	1700	0.8	65.9	14.5
Tinta Carvalha	R	1920	0.9	100	23.8	Muscat Ottonel	W	5787	2.6	47.2	10.4
Moscatel Branco	W	1419	0.7	100	23.8	Aligote	W	7608	3.4	21.3	4.7
Seara Nova	W	1213	0.6	100	23.8	Grasevina	W	15014	6.8	16.3	3.6
Malvasia Preta	R	1157	0.6	100	23.8	Pinot Gris	O	2388	1.1	12.6	2.8
Rabigato	W	1133	0.6	100	23.8	Sauvignon Blanc	W	4613	2.1	7.1	1.6
Diagalves	W	1088	0.5	100	23.8	Gewurztraminer	W	445	0.2	4.2	0.9
Moreto	R	1053	0.5	100	23.8	Cabernet Sauvignon	R	8620	3.9	3.9	0.9
Bical	W	912	0.4	100	23.8	Merlot	R	7810	3.5	3.7	0.8
Avesso	W	636	0.3	100	23.8	Muscat Blanc a Petits Grains	W	1012	0.5	3.6	0.8
Cerceal Branco	W	597	0.3	100	23.8	Pinot Noir	R	1740	0.8	2.9	0.6
Listain de Huelva	W	596	0.3	100	23.8	Chardonnay	W	1376	0.6	0.9	0.2
Tamarez	W	585	0.3	100	23.8	Rkatsiteli	W	506	0.2	0.8	0.2
Amaral	R	582	0.3	100	23.8	Other varieties		139091	62.6		
Tinto Cao	R	556	0.3	100	23.8	Total		222173	100		
Preto Martinho	R	428	0.2	100	23.8						
Folgasao	W	409	0.2	100	23.8						
Antao Vaz	W	376	0.2	100	23.8						
Fonte Cal	W	355	0.2	100	23.8						
Sercial	W	306	0.1	100	23.8						
Dona Branca	W	296	0.1	100	23.8						
Encruzado	W	291	0.1	100	23.8						
Cornifesto	R	259	0.1	100	23.8						
Jampal	W	127	0.1	100	23.8						
Batoca	W	80	0.0	100	23.8						
Ramisco	R	72	0.0	100	23.8						
Perola	W	68	0.0	100	23.8						
Donzelinho Branco	W	59	0.0	100	23.8						
Malvasia Branca de Sao Jorg	W	55	0.0	100	23.8						
Barcelo	W	34	0.0	100	23.8						
Uva Cao	W	33	0.0	100	23.8						
Terrantez	W	27	0.0	100	23.8						
Agronomica	R	19	0.0	100	23.8						
Viosinho	W	17	0.0	100	23.8						
Caracol	W	14	0.0	100	23.8						
Monvedro	R	14	0.0	100	23.8						
Listrao Roxo	R	10	0.0	100	23.8						
Generosa	W	9	0.0	100	23.8						
Complexa	R	6	0.0	100	23.8						
Verdelho Tinto	R	1	0.0	100	23.8						
Other varieties		157865	77.0								
Total		205003	100								

Table 45 (cont.) Varietal Intensity Indexes (and winegrape areas, national and global shares) for national top 45 varieties, 2000

	Russia						Serbia				
Prime variety	Col	Area	Nat'l share	Glob'l share	VII*	Prime variety	Col	Area	Nat'l share	Glob'l share	VII*
Bianca	W	2165	3.8	99.3	86.0	Prokupac	R	15180	22.0	100.0	70.7
Agadai	W	1265	2.2	100.0	86.6	Muscat of Hamburg	R	2760	4.0	39.1	27.6
Pervenets Magaracha	W	2388	4.2	84.2	72.9	Grasevina	W	33120	48.0	35.9	25.4
Zalagyongye	W	1781	3.2	41.1	35.6	Chasselas	W	3449.9	5.0	25.9	18.3
Rkatsiteli	W	13152	23.3	19.5	16.9	Other varieties		14490	21.0		
Pinot Blanc	W	2995	5.3	17.6	15.3	Total		68999	100		
Saperavi	R	931	1.7	13.9	12.0						
Aligote	W	1821	3.2	5.1	4.4						
Riesling	W	1376	2.4	3.2	2.8						
Chardonnay	W	1639	2.9	1.1	1.0						
Cabernet Sauvignon	R	1578	2.8	0.7	0.6						
Other varieties		25242	44.8								
Total		56332	100								

Table 45 (cont.) Varietal Intensity Indexes (and winegrape areas, national and global shares) for national top 45 varieties, 2000

	Slovakia						Slovenia				
Prime variety	Col	Area	Nat'l share	Glob'l share	VII*	Prime variety	Col	Area	Nat'l share	Glob'l share	VII*
Sankt Laurent	R	935	6.0	39.4	123.5	Refosco	R	1267	5.4	100.0	207.8
Gruner Veltliner	W	2960	19.0	12.5	39.3	Ribolla Gialla	W	1127	4.8	80.1	166.5
Feteasca Regala	W	312	2.0	12.1	37.8	Grasevina	W	3568	15.2	3.9	8.0
Blaufrankisch	R	1091	7.0	8.5	26.5	Sauvignon Blanc	W	1221	5.2	1.9	3.9
Muller Thurgau	W	1870	12.0	5.6	17.4	Chardonnay	W	1549	6.6	1.1	2.2
Grasevina	W	3895	25.0	4.2	13.2	Merlot	R	1197	5.1	0.6	1.2
Silvaner	W	156	1.0	3.7	11.7	Other varieties		13543	57.7		
Pinot Blanc	W	623	4.0	3.7	11.5	Total		23472	100		
Feteasca Alba	W	312	2.0	1.3	4.1						
Chardonnay	W	623	4.0	0.4	1.3						
Cabernet Sauvignon	R	156	1.0	0.1	0.2						
Other varieties		2649	17.0								
Total		15580	100								

Table 45 (cont.) Varietal Intensity Indexes (and winegrape areas, national and global shares) for national top 45 varieties, 2000

	South Africa					Spain				
Prime variety	Col	Area	Nat'l share	Glob'l share	VII*	Prime variety	Col	Area	Nat'l share	Glob'l share	VII*
Muscadel (Red)	R	360	0.4	100.0	52.1	Airen	W	387978	32.8	100	4.1
Chenel	W	339	0.4	100.0	52.1	Bobal	R	100128	8.5	100	4.1
Bukettraube	W	280	0.3	100.0	52.1	Cayetana Blanca	W	55502	4.7	100	4.1
Therona	W	185	0.2	100.0	52.1	Parellada	W	11188	0.9	100	4.1
Kanaan	W	172	0.2	100.0	52.1	Chelva	W	10877	0.9	100	4.1
Roobernet	R	78	0.1	100.0	52.1	Xarello	W	10288	0.9	100	4.1
Weldra	W	54	0.1	100.0	52.1	Pardillo	W	7272	0.6	100	4.1
Cinsaut Blanc	W	41	0.0	100.0	52.1	Zalema	W	5969	0.5	100	4.1
Colomino	W	16	0.0	100.0	52.1	Beba	W	4762	0.4	100	4.1
Muscat of Alexandria Red	R	11	0.0	100.0	52.1	Listan Negro	R	3291	0.3	100	4.1
Red Semillon	R	4	0.0	100.0	52.1	Tinto Velasco	R	3272	0.3	100	4.1
Grachen	W	3	0.0	100.0	52.1	Prieto Picudo	R	3256	0.3	100	4.1
Nouvelle	W	2	0.0	100.0	52.1	Perruno	W	2831	0.2	100	4.1
Pinotage	R	6501	6.9	98.9	51.5	Forcallat Tinta	R	2690	0.2	100	4.1
Crouchen	W	2161	2.3	95.7	49.8	Tinto Basto	R	2331	0.2	100	4.1
Galego Dourado	W	46	0.0	89.5	46.6	Juan Garcia	R	2077	0.2	100	4.1
Servant	W	432	0.5	81.5	42.4	Planta Nova	W	2029	0.2	100	4.1
Emerald Riesling	W	340	0.4	57.4	29.9	Sumoll	R	1401	0.1	100	4.1
Chenin Blanc	W	22566	24.1	49.3	25.7	Miguel del Arco	R	1267	0.1	100	4.1
Colombard	W	11432	12.2	30.0	15.6	Tortosina	W	930	0.1	100	4.1
Ruby Cabernet	R	2050	2.2	27.6	14.4	Coloraillo	R	614	0.1	100	4.1
Clairette	W	938	1.0	23.4	12.2	Vijariego	W	510	0.0	100	4.1
Harslevelu	W	284	0.3	21.9	11.4	Fino de Ribera del Fresn	W	332	0.0	100	4.1
Muscat of Alexandria	W	4047	4.3	13.8	7.2	Lairen	W	298	0.0	100	4.1
Sauvignon Blanc	W	5436	5.8	8.4	4.4	Mandon	R	261	0.0	100	4.1
Petit Verdot	R	109	0.1	7.4	3.8	Garrido Fino	W	174	0.0	100	4.1
Cinsaut	R	3533	3.8	7.3	3.8	Canorroyo	W	157	0.0	100	4.1
Tinta Barroca	R	395	0.4	6.5	3.4	Sugra Five	W	118	0.0	100	4.1
Syrah	R	5631	6.0		2.9	Prensal	W	114	0.0	100	4.1
Palomino Fino	W	1632	1.7	5.4	2.8	Marmajuelo	W	37	0.0	100	4.1
Chardonnay	W	6067	6.5	4.2	2.2	Picapoll Blanco	W	34	0.0	100	4.1
Cabernet Sauvignon	R	8824	9.4	4.0	2.1	Doradilla	W	24	0.0	100	4.1
Semillon	W	1029	1.1	3.9	2.0	Yaqui	R	22	0.0	100	4.1
Muscat Blanc a Petits Grains	W	773	0.8	2.7	1.4	De Cilindro	W	15	0.0	100	4.1
Fernao Pires	W	339	0.4	2.3	1.2	Xarello Rosado	W	10	0.0	100	4.1
Merlot	R	4888	5.2	2.3	1.2	Blush Seedless	R	10	0.0	100	4.1
Gewurztraminer	W	210	0.2	2.0	1.0	Colgadero	R	6	0.0	100	4.1
Morio-Muskat	W	21	0.0	1.8	0.9	Valenci Tinto	R	5	0.0	100	4.1
Viognier	W	50	0.1	1.6	0.8	Decuerno	R	4	0.0	100	4.1
Riesling	W	477	0.5	1.1	0.6	Bastardillo	R	3	0.0	100	4.1
Cabernet Franc	R	488	0.5	1.0	0.5	Michele Parlieri	W	3	0.0	100	4.1
Touriga Nacional	R	41	0.0	1.0	0.5	Centenial Seedless	W	2	0.0	100	4.1
Villard Blanc	W	7	0.0	0.9	0.5	Leopoldo III	R	2	0.0	100	4.1
Pinot Noir	R	487	0.5	0.8	0.4	Tinto Jeroma	R	1	0.0	100	4.1
Vinhao	R	36	0.0	0.6	0.3	Perlita	W	1	0.0	100	4.1
Other varieties		841	0.9			Other varieties		559708	47.4		
Total		93656	100			Total		1181806	100		

Table 45 (cont.) Varietal Intensity Indexes (and winegrape areas, national and global shares) for national top 45 varieties, 2000

	Switzerland					Tunisia				
Prime variety	Col	Area	Nat'l share	Glob'l share	VII*	Prime variety	Col	Area	Nat'l share	Glob'l share	VII*
Rauschling	W	23	0.2	100.0	324.3	Mazuelo	R	7576	45.0	6.0	17.3
Amigne	W	21	0.1	100.0	324.3	Alicante Henri Bouschet	R	842	5.0	2.3	6.6
Bondola	R	17	0.1	100.0	324.3	Cinsaut	R	842	5.0	1.7	5.0
Regent	R	16	0.1	100.0	324.3	Tribidrag	R	337	2.0	1.3	3.6
Humagne	W	9	0.1	100.0	324.3	Sangiovese	R	842	5.0	1.2	3.5
Charmont	W	7	0.0	100.0	324.3	Garnacha Tinta	R	2020	12.0	0.9	2.7
Doral	W	3	0.0	100.0	324.3	Monastrell	R	337	2.0	0.4	1.3
Completer	W	2	0.0	100.0	324.3	Syrah	R	337	2.0	0.3	1.0
Lafnetscha	W	1	0.0	100.0	324.3	Cabernet Sauvignon	R	337	2.0	0.2	0.4
Gouais Blanc	W	1	0.0	100.0	324.3	Other varieties		3367	20.0		
Reze	W	1	0.0	100.0	324.3	Total		16836	100		
Dunze	R	1	0.0	100.0	324.3						
Himbertscha	W	0	0.0	100.0	324.3						
Cornalin	R	92	0.6	98.7	320.1						
Arvine	W	57	0.4	93.0	301.6						
Gamaret	R	60	0.4	84.8	274.9						
Diolinoir	R	25	0.2	79.6	258.0						
Garanoir	R	50	0.3	65.8	213.6						
Chasselas	W	5373	35.7	40.3	130.8						
Pinot Noir	R	4601	30.6	7.7	24.8						
Gamay Noir	R	1977	13.1	5.2	17.0						
Silvaner	W	208	1.4	5.0	16.2						
Savagnin Blanc	W	17	0.1	3.9	12.7						
Freisamer	W	1	0.0	3.4	10.9						
Marsanne	W	33	0.2	2.2	7.1						
Mutler Thurgau	W	686	4.6	2.0	6.6						
Pinot Gris	O	149	1.0	0.8	2.6						
Plantet	R	1	0.0	0.5	1.6						
Seyval Blanc	W	2	0.0	0.5	1.6						
Pinot Blanc	W	77	0.5	0.5	1.5						
Merlot	R	848	5.6	0.4	1.3						
Gewurztraminer	W	31	0.2	0.3	0.9						
Chardonnay	W	226	1.5	0.2	0.5						
Muscat Blanc a Petits Grains	W	44	0.3	0.2	0.5						
Nobling	W	0	0.0	0.1	0.5						
Altesse	W	0	0.0	0.1	0.4						
Kerner	W	8	0.1	0.1	0.4						
Sauvignon Blanc	W	38	0.2	0.1	0.2						
Aligote	W	20	0.1	0.1	0.2						
Syrah	R	54	0.4	0.1	0.2						
Ancellotta	R	2	0.0	0.0	0.1						
Cabernet Franc	R	16	0.1	0.0	0.1						
Auxerrois	W	1	0.0	0.0	0.1						
Riesling	W	8	0.1	0.0	0.1						
Cabernet Sauvignon	R	34	0.2	0.0	0.1						
Other varieties		200	1.3								
Total		15042	100								

Table 45 (cont.) Varietal Intensity Indexes (and winegrape areas, national and global shares) for national top 45 varieties, 2000

United Kingdom						United States					
Prime variety	Col	Area	Nat'l share	Glob'l share	VII*	Prime variety	Col	Area	Nat'l share	Glob'l share	VII*
Dalkauer	W	100	11.5	100.0	5587.8	Rubired	R	4153	2.4	100.0	27.8
Cabernet Dorsa	R	43	4.9	100.0	5587.8	Catawba	R	635	0.4	100.0	27.8
Albalonga	W	41	4.7	72.2	4034.9	Carnelian	R	625	0.4	100.0	27.8
Seyval Blanc	W	85	9.7	21.9	1222.0	Royalty	R	338	0.2	100.0	27.8
Ehrenfelser	W	34		11.8	658.2	Aurore	W	299	0.2	100.0	27.8
Blauburger	R	105	12.0	10.5	585.6	Symphony	W	184	0.1	100.0	27.8
Bacchus	W	112	12.8	3.3	184.5	Centurian	R	134	0.1	100.0	27.8
Auxerrois	W	58	6.6	2.5	140.8	Cayuga White	W	108	0.1	100.0	27.8
Chardonnay	W	68	7.8	0.0	2.6	Vignoles	W	68	0.0	100.0	27.8
Other varieties		227	26.0			Lambrusco	R	42	0.0	100.0	27.8
Total		873	100			Ventura	W	39	0.0	100.0	27.8
						Muscat Fleur d'Oranger	W	36	0.0	100.0	27.8
						Rougeon	R	36	0.0	100.0	27.8
						Trousseau Gris	O	28	0.0	100.0	27.8
						Chancellor	R	27	0.0	100.0	27.8
						Ives	R	23	0.0	100.0	27.8
						Moore's Diamond	W	19	0.0	100.0	27.8
						Carmine	R	10	0.0	100.0	27.8
						Traminette	W	5	0.0	100.0	27.8
						Elvira	W	275	0.2	80.0	22.2
						Durif	R	923	0.5	77.1	21.4
						Delaware	O	98	0.1	73.2	20.3
						Leon Millot	R	12	0.0	72.4	20.1
						Concord	R	8330	4.7	70.5	19.6
						Tribidrag	R	18630	10.6	69.2	19.2
						Salvador	R	320	0.2	55.9	15.5
						Colombard	W	18010	10.3	47.2	13.1
						Seyval Blanc	W	166	0.1	42.8	11.9
						Emerald Riesling	W	253	0.1	42.6	11.8
						Ruby Cabernet	R	2895	1.6	39.0	10.8
						Marechal Foch	R	64	0.0	36.7	10.2
						De Chaunac	R	67	0.0	35.9	10.0
						Elbling	W	656	0.4	35.2	9.8
						Baco Noir	R	112	0.1	28.1	7.8
						Chardonnay	W	35791	20.4	24.6	6.8
						Chenin Blanc	W	8433	4.8	18.4	5.1
						Vidal	W	97	0.1	15.8	4.4
						Fredonia	R	13	0.0	15.1	4.2
						Barbera	R	4693	2.7	14.2	3.9
						Chambourcin	R	28	0.0	11.0	3.1
						Viognier	W	314	0.2	10.0	2.8
						Pinot Noir	R	5343	3.0	8.9	2.5
						Niagara	W	1357	0.8	8.8	2.5
						Merlot	R	16875	9.6	8.0	2.2
						Cabernet Sauvignon	R	17573	10.0	8.0	2.2
						Other varieties		27557	15.7		
						Total		175693	100		

Table 45 (cont.) Varietal Intensity Indexes (and winegrape areas, national and global shares) for national top 45 varieties, 2000

	Uruguay				
Prime variety	Col	Area	Nat'l share	Glob'l share	VII*
Tannat	R	2433	27.4	43.8	240.6
Muscat of Hamburg	R	2886	32.5	40.9	224.4
Cabernet Franc	R	364	4.1	0.7	4.1
Merlot	R	1057	11.9	0.5	2.7
Cabernet Sauvignon	R	675	7.6	0.3	1.7
Sauvignon Blanc	W	142	1.6	0.2	1.2
Chardonnay	W	142	1.6	0.1	0.5
Syrah	R	62	0.7	0.1	0.3
Other varieties		1118	12.6		
Total		8880	100		

Table 46: Varietal Intensity Indexes (and winegrape areas, national and global shares) for national top 45 varieties, 2010

Algeria						Argentina					
Prime variety	Col	Area	Nat'l share	Glob'l share	VII*	Prime variety	Col	Area	Nat'l share	Glob'l share	VII*
Cinsaut	R	7550	25.0	20.9	31.9	Cereza	O	29189	14.5	100.0	22.9
Mazuelo	R	7550	25.0	9.4	14.3	Criolla Grande	R	17080	8.5	100.0	22.9
Alicante Henri Bouschet	R	3020	10.0	7.7	11.8	Aspiran Bouschet	R	3042	1.5	100.0	22.9
Garnacha Tinta	R	6040	20.0	3.3	5.0	Gibi	W	917	0.5	100.0	22.9
Pinot Noir	R	1510	5.0	1.7	2.7	Torrontes Mendocino	W	713	0.4	100.0	22.9
Syrah	R	1510	5.0	0.8	1.2	Bequignol Noir	R	698	0.3	100.0	22.9
Merlot	R	1510	5.0	0.6	0.9	Maticha	W	275	0.1	100.0	22.9
Cabernet Sauvignon	R	1510	5.0	0.5	0.8	California	O	252	0.1	100.0	22.9
Total		30200	100			Fintendo	R	183	0.1	100.0	22.9
						Rieslina	W	127	0.1	100.0	22.9
						Moscatuel	R	61	0.0	100.0	22.9
						Gargiulo	R	47	0.0	100.0	22.9
						Caberinta	R	47	0.0	100.0	22.9
						Saint Jeannet	R	44	0.0	100.0	22.9
						Patagonia	W	24	0.0	100.0	22.9
						Serna	O	10	0.0	100.0	22.9
						Criolla Mediana	R	9	0.0	100.0	22.9
						Canelon	O	8	0.0	100.0	22.9
						Canela	R	2	0.0	100.0	22.9
						Torrontes Sanjuanino	W	2048	1.0	99.8	22.8
						Moscatel Rosada	O	7259	3.6	99.0	22.7
						Pedro Gimenez	W	12132	6.0	99.0	22.7
						Douce Noire	R	18127	9.0	95.5	21.9
						Torrontes Riojano	W	7683	3.8	94.7	21.7
						Canari Noir	R	139	0.1	91.5	20.9
						Ekigaina	R	1	0.0	89.9	20.6
						Bonamico	R	167	0.1	86.4	19.8
						Cot	R	31047	15.4	76.3	17.5
						Manseng Noir	R	29	0.0	50.7	11.6
						Greco Nero	R	396	0.2	32.4	7.4
						Damaschino	W	586	0.3	28.1	6.4
						Tannat	R	705	0.4	11.9	2.7
						Sauvignonasse	W	515	0.3	11.6	2.6
						Fer	R	207	0.1	11.4	2.6
						Muscat of Alexandria	W	2939	1.5	11.2	2.6
						Italia	W	126	0.1	11.0	2.5
						Listan Prieto	R	423	0.2	9.3	2.1
						Moscato Giallo	W	133	0.1	9.0	2.1
						Viognier	W	816	0.4	7.2	1.6
						Chenin Blanc	W	2462	1.2	7.0	1.6
						Petit Verdot	R		0.2	7.0	1.6
						Syrah	R	12810	6.4	6.9	1.6
						Ancellotta	R	302	0.2	6.3	1.4
						Cabernet Sauvignon	R	16372	8.1	5.6	1.3
						Raboso Piave	R	43	0.0	5.6	1.3
						Other varieties		30367	15.1		
						Total		201060	100		

Note: VII* indicates Varital intensity indexes relative to the world, as defined in the introduction.

Table 46 (cont.) Varietal Intensity Indexes (and winegrape areas, national and global shares) for national top 45 varieties, 2010

Armenia						Australia					
Prime variety	Col	Area	Nat'l share	Glob'l share	VII*	Prime variety	Col	Area	Nat'l share	Glob'l share	VII*
Mskhali	W	1093	9.8	100.0	410.6	Tarrango	R	72	0.0	100.0	30.3
Garandmak	W	931	8.3	100.0	410.6	Verdelho	W	1535	1.0	76.6	23.2
Kangun	W	850	7.6	100.0	410.6	Muscat a Petits Grains Rouge	R	230	0.2	37.5	11.4
Voskeat	W	809	7.2	100.0	410.6	Trebbiano	W	86	0.1	34.7	10.5
Rkatsiteli	W	2469	22.0	4.2	17.3	Semillon	W	6112	4.0	27.6	8.4
Muscat Blanc a Petits Grains	W	526	4.7	1.7	6.9	Syrah	R	42675	28.1	23.0	7.0
Other varieties		4528	40.4			Petit Verdot	R	1223	0.8	17.0	5.1
Total		11206	100			Ruby Cabernet	R	962	0.6	16.8	5.1
						Chardonnay	W	27773	18.3	14.0	4.2
						Marsanne	W	238	0.2	13.7	4.1
						Arneis	W	153	0.1	13.6	4.1
						Crouchen	W	95	0.1	13.1	4.0
						Sultaniye	W	430	0.3	12.6	3.8
						Viognier	W	1402	0.9	12.3	3.7
						Durif	R	417	0.3	11.7	3.6
						Cabernet Sauvignon	R	25967	17.1	9.0	2.7
						Riesling	W	4114	2.7	8.2	2.5
						Muscat of Alexandria	W	2043	1.3	7.8	2.4
						Pinot Gris	O	3296	2.2	7.6	2.3
						Colombard	W	2205	1.5	6.9	2.1
						Sauvignon Blanc	W	6467	4.3	5.9	1.8
						Gewurztraminer	W	834	0.5	5.8	1.8
						Pinot Noir	R	4690	3.1	5.4	1.6
						Savagnin Blanc	W	94	0.1	5.0	1.5
						Roussanne	W	83	0.1	4.8	1.4
						Muscadelle	W	67	0.0	4.1	1.2
						Merlot	R	10028	6.6	3.8	1.1
						Dolcetto	R	154	0.1	2.4	0.7
						Muscat Blanc a Petits Grains	W	533	0.4	1.7	0.5
						Nebbiolo	R	98	0.1	1.6	0.5
						Chenin Blanc	W	541	0.4	1.5	0.5
						Cabernet Franc	R	591	0.4	1.1	0.3
						Monastrell	R	692	0.5	1.0	0.3
						Garnacha Tinta	R	1748	1.2	0.9	0.3
						Cot	R	356	0.2	0.9	0.3
						Sangiovese	R	589	0.4	0.8	0.2
						Barbera	R	116	0.1	0.5	0.1
						Touriga Nacional	R	48	0.0	0.5	0.1
						Tribidrag	R	149	0.1	0.5	0.1
						Tempranillo	R	476	0.3	0.2	0.1
						Other varieties		2406	1.6		
						Total		151788	100		

Table 46 (cont.) Varietal Intensity Indexes (and winegrape areas, national and global shares) for national top 45 varieties, 2010

	Austria					Brazil				
Prime variety	Col	Area	Nat'l share	Glob'l share	VII*	Prime variety	Col	Area	Nat'l share	Glob'l share	VII*
Roesler	R	160	0.4	100.0	101.1	Bordo	R	8287	16.8	100.0	93.1
Rotgipfler	W	105	0.2	100.0	101.1	Moscato Embrapa	W	862	1.7	100.0	93.1
Rathay	R	9	0.0	100.0	101.1	Couderc	W	834	1.7	100.0	93.1
Goldburger	W	140	0.3	99.8	100.9	Herbemont	R	764	1.5	100.0	93.1
Blauer Wildbacher	R	365	0.8	99.3	100.3	Lorena	W	519	1.1	100.0	93.1
Roter Veltliner	O	193	0.4	97.2	98.3	Cynthiana	R	102	0.2	100.0	93.1
Jubilaumsrebe	W	13	0.0	96.8	97.9	Violeta	R	98	0.2	100.0	93.1
Bouvier	W	234	0.5	93.9	94.9	Rubea	R	81	0.2	100.0	93.1
Zierfandler	O	85	0.2	72.8	73.5	Moscato Nazareno	W	68	0.1	100.0	93.1
Gruner Veltliner	W	13519	29.7	71.7	72.5	Bailey	R	34	0.1	100.0	93.1
Neuburger	W	652	1.4	67.6	68.4	Malvasia Amarela	W	14	0.0	100.0	93.1
Blauburger	R	897	2.0	67.1	67.8	Venus	R	1	0.0	100.0	93.1
Zweigelt	R	6412	14.1	65.1	65.8	Patricia	R	1	0.0	100.0	93.1
Fruhroter Veltliner	R	424	0.9	50.1	50.6	Ora	W	0	0.0	100.0	93.1
Blauer Portugieser	R	1621	3.6	42.7	43.1	Juliana	W	0	0.0	100.0	93.1
Sankt Laurent	R	775	1.7	25.8	26.1	Couderc Noir	R	2477	5.0	92.0	93.1
Blaufrankisch	R	3228	7.1	20.0	20.2	Seibel	R	581	1.2	98.3	91.5
Scheurebe	W	376	0.8	18.9	19.1	Jacquez	R	2252	4.6	95.1	88.5
Pinot Blanc	W	1914	4.2	13.0	13.1	Flora	O	6	0.0	74.0	68.9
Muller Thurgau	W	2044	4.5	9.0	9.1	Niagara	W	3177	6.4	68.0	63.4
Grasevina	W	3462	7.6	5.7	5.7	Trebbiano	W	149	0.3	60.1	56.0
Riesling	W	1852	4.1	3.7	3.7	Isabella	R	18279	37.0	56.3	52.4
Muscat Ottonel	W	359	0.8	3.5	3.5	Arriloba	W	3	0.0	42.7	39.8
Gewurztraminer	W	309	0.7	2.2	2.2	Concord	R	3543	7.2	28.9	27.0
Silvaner	W	42	0.1	1.9	1.9	Egiodola	R	99	0.2	26.5	24.6
Muscat Blanc a Petits Grains	W	492	1.1	1.6	1.6	Lambrusco	R	8	0.0	16.8	15.7
Sauvignon Blanc	W	845	1.9	0.8	0.8	Muscat Bailey A	R	19	0.0	15.9	14.8
Pinot Noir	R	646	1.4	0.7	0.8	Arinarnoa	R	3	0.0	10.7	9.9
Chardonnay	W	1380	3.0	0.7	0.7	Ekigaina	R	0	0.0	10.1	9.4
Pinot Gris	O	215	0.5	0.5	0.5	Moscato Giallo	W	126	0.3	8.6	8.0
Merlot	R	644	1.4	0.2	0.2	Tannat	R	295	0.6	5.0	4.6
Cabernet Sauvignon	R	592	1.3	0.2	0.2	Muscat Blanc a Petits Grair	W	1005	2.0		3.0
Furmint	W	9	0.0	0.2	0.2	Valdiguie	R	4	0.0	3.2	3.0
Cabernet Franc	R	56	0.1	0.1	0.1	Schonburger	O	1	0.0	2.2	2.1
Syrah	R	137	0.3	0.1	0.1	Ancellotta	R	99	0.2	2.1	1.9
Other varieties		1326	2.9			Pinotage	R	75	0.2	1.2	1.1
Total		45533	100			Teroldego	R	10	0.0	1.2	1.1
						Malvasia Bianca di Candia	W	100	0.2	1.0	0.9
						Prosecco	W	173	0.4	0.9	0.9
						Marselan	R	21	0.0	0.9	0.8
						Rebo	R	1	0.0	0.8	0.7
						Ruby Cabernet	R	42	0.1	0.7	0.7
						Moscato Rosa del Trentino	R	0	0.0	0.5	0.5
						Cabernet Franc	R	229	0.5	0.4	0.4
						Alicante Henri Bouschet	R	129	0.3	0.3	0.3
						Other varieties		4640	9.4		
						Total		49412	100		

Table 46 (cont.) Varietal Intensity Indexes (and winegrape areas, national and global shares) for national top 45 varieties, 2010

Bulgaria						Canada					
Prime variety	Col	Area	Nat'l share	Glob'l share	VII*	Prime variety	Col	Area	Nat'l share	Glob'l share	VII*
Misket Cherven	O	4159	7.4	100.0	82.0	Geisenheim Hybrids	R	106	1.0	100.0	455.7
Shiroka Melnishka	R	1580	2.8	100.0	82.0	Blattner Reds	R	39	0.4	100.0	455.7
Mavrud	R	1296	2.3	100.0	82.0	S.V. 23-512	R	29	0.3	100.0	455.7
Misket Varnenski	W	336	0.6	100.0	82.0	Blattner Whites	W	25	0.3	100.0	455.7
Storgozia	R	295	0.5	100.0	82.0	Muscat Swenson	W	24	0.2	98.3	448.2
Ranna Melnishka Loza	R	249	0.4	100.0	82.0	Gm 322	R	17	0.2	100.0	455.7
Dimyat	W	2386	4.3	99.4	81.5	New York Muscat	R	5	0.0	100.0	455.7
Pamid	R	6792	12.1	69.1	56.7	Sovereign Opal	W	3	0.0	100.0	455.7
Kadarka	R	550	1.0	50.6	41.5	Castel	R	2	0.0	100.0	455.7
Muscat Ottonel	W	3236	5.8	31.6	25.9	Rotberger	R	1	0.0	100.0	455.7
Rkatsiteli	W	3121	5.6	5.3	4.4	Verdelet	W	1	0.0	100.0	455.7
Gewurztraminer	W	747	1.3	5.2	4.3	Michurinetz	R	0	0.0	100.0	455.7
Merlot	R	10573	18.8	4.0	3.2	Madeleine Sylvaner	W	6	0.1	86.2	392.8
Cabernet Sauvignon	R	8436	15.0	2.9	2.4	Baco Noir	R	373	3.7	79.7	363.5
Chardonnay	W	2457	4.4	1.2	1.0	Vidal	W	1284	12.7	78.1	356.1
Trebbiano Toscano	W	723	1.3	0.7	0.5	Oraniensteiner	W	2	0.0	61.8	281.8
Other varieties		9197	16.4			Marechal Foch	R	158	1.6	46.1	210.1
Total		56133	100			De Chaunac	R	39	0.4	42.7	194.8
						Ehrenfelser	W	29	0.3	36.3	165.6
						Seyval Blanc	W	112	1.1	24.2	110.1
						Schonburger	O	11	0.1	18.2	83.0
						Optima	W	6	0.1	15.5	70.5
						Siegerrebe	O	18	0.2	14.7	66.8
						Madeleine Angevine	W	7	0.1	12.8	58.4
						Leon Millot	R	3	0.0	12.5	57.1
						Chancellor	R	3	0.0	5.8	26.5
						Chambourcin	R	54	0.5	4.8	21.8
						Ortega	W	29	0.3	4.5	20.5
						Niagara	W	155	1.5	3.3	15.1
						Elvira	W	8	0.1	2.9	13.3
						Gewurztraminer	W	404	4.0	2.8	12.9
						Concord	R	252	2.5	2.1	9.4
						Reichensteiner	W	5	0.0	2.0	9.3
						Riesling	W	871	8.6	1.7	7.9
						Auxerrois	W	38	0.4	1.4	6.2
						Turan	R	2	0.0	1.3	5.9
						Pinot Gris	O	549	5.4	1.3	5.7
						Cabernet Franc	R	664	6.6	1.2	5.6
						Bacchus	W	21	0.2	1.0	4.7
						Pinot Blanc	W	125	1.2	0.9	3.9
						Trebbiano	W	2	0.0	0.8	3.7
						Dunkelfelder	R	2	0.0	0.8	3.5
						Pinot Noir	R	640	6.3	0.7	3.4
						Viognier	W	83	0.8	0.7	3.3
						Gamay Noir	R	220	2.2	0.7	3.1
						Other varieties		3671	36.4		
						Total		10096	100		

Table 46 (cont.) Varietal Intensity Indexes (and winegrape areas, national and global shares) for national top 45 varieties, 2010

	Chile					China				
Prime variety	Col	Area	Nat'l share	Glob'l share	VII* Prime variety	Col	Area	Nat'l share	Glob'l share	VII*
Lacrima Christi	R	85	0.1	100.0	41.3 Carmenere	R	1353	4.6	11.9	18.5
Blanca Ovoide	W	40	0.0	100.0	41.3 Cabernet Sauvignon	R	22612	76.5	7.8	12.1
Listan Prieto	R	3869	3.5	84.8	35.0 Merlot	R	3560	12.1	1.3	2.1
Carmenere	R	8827	7.9	77.7	32.1 Cabernet Franc	R	507	1.7	0.9	1.5
Sauvignonasse	W	785	0.7	17.6	7.3 Riesling	W	437	1.5	0.9	1.4
Cabernet Sauvignon	R	40728	36.5	14.0	5.8 Ruby Cabernet	R	40	0.1	0.7	1.1
Sauvignon Blanc	W	12159	10.9	11.0	4.6 Chardonnay	W	738	2.5	0.4	0.6
Alicante Henri Bouschet	R	4228	3.8	10.8	4.5 Syrah	R	223	0.8	0.1	0.2
Petit Verdot	R	576	0.5	8.0	3.3 Pinot Noir	R	40	0.1	0.0	0.1
Korinthiaki	R	4	0.0	7.6	3.1 Gewurztraminer	W	5	0.0	0.0	0.1
Viognier	W	753	0.7	6.6	2.7 Chenin Blanc	W	10	0.0	0.0	0.0
Chardonnay	W	13082	11.7	6.6	2.7 Pinot Blanc	W	2	0.0	0.0	0.0
Torrontes Riojano	W	425	0.4	5.2	2.2 Cinsaut	R	3	0.0	0.0	0.0
Muscat of Alexandria	W	1090	1.0	4.1	1.7 Garnacha Tinta	R	11	0.0	0.0	0.0
Semillon	W	846	0.8	3.8	1.6 Pinot Gris	O	2	0.0	0.0	0.0
Merlot	R	10041	9.0	3.8	1.6 Semillon	W	1	0.0	0.0	0.0
Pinot Noir	R	2884	2.6	3.3	1.4 Sauvignon Blanc	W	1	0.0	0.0	0.0
Syrah	R	6027	5.4	3.2	1.3 Total		29545	100		
Cot	R	1264	1.1	3.1	1.3					
Durif	R	104	0.1	2.9	1.2					
Cabernet Franc	R	1321	1.2	2.5	1.0					
Gewurztraminer	W	316	0.3	2.2	0.9					
Moscato Giallo	W	25	0.0	1.7	0.7					
Marsanne	W	17	0.0	1.0	0.4					
Pedro Gimenez	W	118	0.1	1.0	0.4					
Moscatel Rosada	O	70	0.1	1.0	0.4					
Hondarrabi Beltza	R	0	0.0	0.9	0.4					
Crystal	W	2	0.0	0.9	0.4					
Riesling	W	367	0.3	0.7	0.3					
Chasselas	W	88	0.1	0.7	0.3					
Mazuelo	R	477	0.4	0.6	0.2					
Cinsaut	R	198	0.2	0.5	0.2					
Roussanne	W	6	0.0	0.3	0.1					
Pinot Gris	O	100	0.1	0.2	0.1					
Torrontes Sanjuanino	W	4	0.0	0.2	0.1					
Nebbiolo	R	11	0.0	0.2	0.1					
Tribidrag	R	58	0.1	0.2	0.1					
Chenin Blanc	W	57	0.1	0.2	0.1					
Sangiovese	R	100	0.1	0.1	0.1					
Monastrell	R	59	0.1	0.1	0.0					
Blauer Portugieser	R	2	0.0	0.0	0.0					
Tannat	R	2	0.0	0.0	0.0					
Tempranillo	R	48	0.0	0.0	0.0					
Garnacha Tinta	R	37	0.0	0.0	0.0					
Albillo Mayor	W	0	0.0	0.0	0.0					
Other varieties				0.2						
Total		111525	100							

Table 46 (cont.) Varietal Intensity Indexes (and winegrape areas, national and global shares) for national top 45 varieties, 2010

	Croatia						Cyprus				
Prime variety	Col	Area	Nat'l share	Glob'l share	VII*	Prime variety	Col	Area	Nat'l share	Glob'l share	VII*
Plavac Mali	R	1569	7.6	100.0	221.7	Mavro	R	3575	41.5	100	534.6
Plavina	R	643	3.1	100.0	221.7	Xynisteri	W	2092	24.3	100	535
Debit	W	403	1.9	100.0	221.7	Maratheftiko	R	152	1.8	100	534.6
Babic	R	359	1.7	100.0	221.7	Ofthalmo	R	141	1.6	100	535
Posip Bijeli	W	253	1.2	100.0	221.7	Vertzami	R	96	1.1	28.6	153
Trbljan	W	231	1.1	100.0	221.7	Sultaniye	W	371	4.3	10.9	58.2
Kujundzusa	W	206	1.0	100.0	221.7	Mazuelo	R	481	5.6	0.5999	3.2
Vranac	R	149	0.7	100.0	221.7	Muscat of Alexandria	W	120	1.4	0.5	2.4
Zlahtina	W	135	0.6	100.0	221.7	Cabernet Franc	R	203	2.4	0.4	2.0
Ranfol	W	134	0.6	100.0	221.7	Monastrell	R	172	2.0	0.2	1.3
Skrlet	W	61	0.3	100.0	221.7	Syrah	R	244	2.8	0.1	0.7
Victoria	W	52	0.3	100.0	221.7	Cabernet Sauvignon	R	369	4.3	0.1	0.7
Bogdanusa	W	48	0.2	100.0	221.7	Chardonnay	W	128	1.5	0.1	0.3
Vugava	W	36	0.2	100.0	221.7	Garnacha Tinta	R	84	1.0	0.0	0.2
Cetinka	W	35	0.2	100.0	221.7	Merlot	R	63	0.7	0.0	0.1
Slankamenka	W	31	0.1	100.0	221.7	Other varieties		317	3.7		
Zlatarica Vrgorska	W	19	0.1	100.0	221.7	Total		8608	100		
Babica	R	18	0.1	100.0	221.7						
Nincusa	R	17	0.1	100.0	221.7						
Trnjak	R	15	0.1	100.0	221.7						
Lasina	R	14	0.1	100.0	221.7						
Plavec Zuti	W	13	0.1	100.0	221.7						
Gegic	W	11	0.1	100.0	221.7						
Suscan	R	5	0.0	100.0	221.7						
Zupljanka	W	4	0.0	100.0	221.7						
Diseca Ranina	W	2	0.0	100.0	221.7						
Malvazija Istarska	W	1705	8.2	62.2	137.9						
Kraljevina	W	268	1.3	59.9	132.9						
Terrano	R	228	1.1	45.6	101.1						
Moscato Rosa del Trentino	R	14	0.1	17.7	39.3						
Cardinal	R	91	0.4	16.7	37.0						
Malvasia Bianca Lunga	W	285	1.4	11.2	24.8						
Refosco	R	122	0.6	8.6	19.1						
Malvasia di Lipari	W	24	0.1	7.8	17.4						
Grasevina	W	4701	22.6	7.7	17.0						
Silvaner	W	139	0.7	6.2	13.7						
Medina	R	8	0.0	5.3	11.7						
Kovidinka	O	56	0.3	5.2	11.5						
Moscato Giallo	W	59	0.3	4.0	8.8						
Blaufrankisch	R	558	2.7	3.5	7.7						
Furmint	W	172	0.8	3.3	7.3						
Gewurztraminer	W	234	1.1	1.6	3.6						
Riesling	W	676	3.3	1.4	3.0						
Pinot Blanc	W	188	0.9	1.3	2.8						
Zweigelt	R	123	0.6	1.3	2.8						
Other varieties		6641	32.0								
Total		20754	100								

Table 46 (cont.) Varietal Intensity Indexes (and winegrape areas, national and global shares) for national top 45 varieties, 2010

Czech Republic						France				
Prime variety	Col	Area	Nat'l share	Glob'l share	VII* Prime variety	Col	Area	Nat'l share	Glob'l share	VII*
Cabernet Moravia	R	212	1.3	100.0	283.3 Melon	W	12364	1.5	100.0	5.4
Agni	R	6	0.0	100.0	283.3 Gros Manseng	W	4995	0.6	100.0	5.4
Laurot	R	6	0.0	100.0	283.3 Grolleau Noir	R	2350	0.3	100.0	5.4
Ariana	R	3	0.0	100.0	283.3 Mauzac Blanc	W	1991	0.2	100.0	5.4
Palava	O	198	1.2	86.3	244.4 Piquepoul Blanc	W	1455	0.2	100.0	5.4
Muskat Moravsky	W	351	2.2	68.3	193.6 Terret Blanc	W	1451	0.2	100.0	5.4
Aurelius	W	44	0.3	63.3	179.3 Plantet	R	1105	0.1	100.0	5.4
Andre	R	261	1.6	55.3	156.6 Duras	R	923	0.1	100.0	5.4
Neronet	R	33	0.2	45.8	129.8 Chasan	W	801	0.1	100.0	5.4
Sankt Laurent	R	1291	7.9	42.9	121.6 Baco Blanc	W	773	0.1	100.0	5.4
Neuburger	W	303	1.9	31.4	89.1 Jurancon Noir	R	706	0.1	100.0	5.4
FruHroter Veltliner	R	217	1.3	25.6	72.6 Aubun	R	648	0.1	100.0	5.4
Blauer Portugieser	R	622	3.8	16.4	46.4 Len de l'El	W	640	0.1	100.0	5.4
Zweigelt	R	811	5.0	8.2	23.3 Chenanson	R	506	0.1	100.0	5.4
Gruner Veltliner	W	1527	9.4	8.1	23.0 Grolleau Gris	W	454	0.1	100.0	5.4
Blaufrankisch	R	1160	7.1	7.2	20.4 Tibouren	R	445	0.1	100.0	5.4
Muller Thurgau	W	1572	9.7	6.9	19.6 Counoise	R	443	0.1	100.0	5.4
Silvaner	W	122	0.8	5.4	15.3 Pineau d'Aunis	R	435	0.1	100.0	5.4
Pinot Blanc	W	732	4.5	5.0	14.1 Abouriou	R	364	0.0	100.0	5.4
Irsai Oliver	W	69	0.4	4.9	13.8 Altesse	W	356	0.0	100.0	5.4
Gewurztraminer	W	601	3.7	4.2	11.9 Portan	R	311	0.0	100.0	5.4
Riesling	W	1181	7.3	2.4	6.7 Poulsard	R	311	0.0	100.0	5.4
Grasevina	W	1148	7.1	1.9	5.3 Clairette Rose	W	260	0.0	100.0	5.4
Pinot Gris	O	706	4.3	1.6	4.6 Danlas	W	254	0.0	100.0	5.4
Dornfelder	R	119	0.7	1.5	4.2 Menu Pineau	W	212	0.0	100.0	5.4
Pinot Noir	R	688	4.2	0.8	2.2 Baroque	W	90	0.0	100.0	5.4
Sauvignon Blanc	W	804	5.0	0.7	2.1 Merlot Blanc	W	31	0.0	100.0	5.4
Odessky Cherny	R	17	0.1	0.6	1.8 Gamay Teinturier de Chaudenay	R	24	0.0	100.0	5.4
Muscat Ottonel	W	60	0.4	0.6	1.7 Jacquere	W	1027	0.1	99.9	5.4
Chardonnay	W	766	4.7	0.4	1.1 Negrette	R	1227	0.1	99.9	5.4
Cabernet Sauvignon	R	230	1.4	0.1	0.2 Bourboulenc	W	596	0.1	99.8	5.4
Merlot	R	90	0.6	0.0	0.1 Aramon Noir	R	2877	0.3	99.5	5.4
Other varieties		292	1.8		Villard Noir	R	1320	0.2	99.4	5.4
Total		16242	100		Pinot Meunier	R	11088	1.3	98.4	5.3
					Mondeuse Noire	R	299	0.0	97.6	5.3
					Petit Manseng	W	1280	0.2		5.2
					Sauvignon Gris	W	463	0.1	96.0	5.2
					Muscadelle	W	1589	0.2	95.9	5.2
					Folle Blanche	W	1770	0.2	95.9	5.2
					Gamay de Teinturier Bouze	R	215	0.0	95.6	5.2
					Garnacha Roja	W	1699	0.2	95.2	5.2
					Marselan	R	2375	0.3	95.1	5.2
					Alphonse Lavallee	R	829	0.1	93.9	5.1
					Mammolo	R	773	0.1	93.7	5.1
					Gamay Noir	R	30443	3.6	93.2	5.1
					Other varieties		752317	88.8		
					Total		846880	100		

Table 46 (cont.) Varietal Intensity Indexes (and winegrape areas, national and global shares) for national top 45 varieties, 2010

Georgia						Germany				
Prime variety	Col	Area	Nat'l share	Glob'l share	VII*	Prime variety	Col	Area	Nat'l share	Glob'l share	VII*
Tsolikouri	W	7903	16.5	100.0	95.9	Heroldrebe	R	140	0.1	100.0	45.1
Tsitska	W	3642	7.6	100.0	95.9	Rieslaner	W	60	0.1	100.0	45.1
Chinuri	W	1225	2.6	100.0	95.9	Nobling	W	50	0.0	100.0	45.1
Mtsvane Kakhuri	W	319	0.7	100.0	95.9	Cabernet Cubin	R	40	0.0	100.0	45.1
Goruli Mtsvane	W	287	0.6	100.0	95.9	Cabernet Cortis	R	20	0.0	100.0	45.1
Aleksandrouli	R	281	0.6	100.0	95.9	Cabernet Dorio	R	20	0.0	100.0	45.1
Tsulukidzis Tetra	W	195	0.4	100.0	95.9	Goldriesling	W	20	0.0	100.0	45.1
Aladasturi	R	59	0.1	100.0	95.9	Deckrot	R	10	0.0	100.0	45.1
Krakhuna	W	46	0.1	100.0	95.9	Helfensteiner	R	10	0.0	100.0	45.1
Tavkveri	R	37	0.1	100.0	95.9	Juwel	W	10	0.0	100.0	45.1
Ojaleshi	R	32	0.1	100.0	95.9	Kanzler	W	10	0.0	100.0	45.1
Chkhaveri	O	26	0.1	100.0	95.9	Domina	R	360	0.4	99.8	45.0
Kisi	W	26	0.1	100.0	95.9	Cabernet Mitos	R	280	0.3	99.3	44.8
Usakhelouri	R	10	0.0	100.0	95.9	Faberrebe	W	520	0.5	99.2	44.7
Khikhvi	W	6	0.0	100.0	95.9	Acolon	R	440	0.4	97.9	44.1
Otskhanuri Sapere	R	6	0.0	100.0	95.9	Dornfelder	R	7920	7.8	97.8	44.1
Saperavi	R	4751	9.9	58.5	56.1	Huxelrebe	W	590	0.6	97.2	43.8
Rkatsiteli	W	25324	52.8	43.2	41.4	Perle	O	20	0.0	95.2	42.9
Pinot Blanc	W	219	0.5	1.5	1.4	Bacchus	W	1910	1.9	93.3	42.1
Aligote	W	124	0.3	0.3	0.3	Ortega	W	590	0.6	92.7	41.8
Cabernet Sauvignon	R	286	0.6	0.1	0.1	Morio-Muskat	W	470	0.5	92.3	41.6
Other varieties		3194	6.7			Dunkelfelder	R	300	0.3	91.2	41.1
Total		48001	100			Pinot Noir Precoce	R	190	0.2	90.9	41.0
						Regner	W	40	0.0	90.9	41.0
						Cabernet Dorsa	R	200	0.2	89.8	40.5
						Kerner	W	3510	3.4	87.9	39.6
						Optima	W	30	0.0	81.8	36.9
						Scheurebe	W	1600	1.6	80.7	36.4
						Johanniter	W	40	0.0	78.4	35.4
						Dakapo	R	40	0.0	75.9	34.2
						Siegerrebe	O	90	0.1	75.3	33.9
						Kernling	W	10	0.0	66.7	30.1
						Ehrenfelser	W	50	0.0	63.7	28.7
						Mutler Thurgau	W	13480	13.2	59.2	26.7
						Phoenix	W	30	0.0	58.8	26.5
						Riesling	W	22520	22.1	45.0	20.3
						Elbling	W	550	0.5	38.8	17.5
						Reichensteiner	W	80	0.1	35.1	15.8
						Pinot Blanc	W	3870	3.8	26.3	11.9
						Schonburger	O	10	0.0	16.9	7.6
						Pinot Gris	O	4450	4.4	10.2	4.6
						Chasselas	W	1120	1.1	8.5	3.8
						Auxerrois	W	160	0.2	5.8	2.6
						Chardonnay	W	1180	1.2	0.6	0.3
						Muscat Ottonel	W	60	0.1	0.6	0.3
						Other varieties		34960	34.3		
						Total		102060	100		

Table 46 (cont.) Varietal Intensity Indexes (and winegrape areas, national and global shares) for national top 45 varieties, 2010

	Greece					Hungary				
Prime variety	Col	Area	Nat'l share	Glob'l share	VII*	Prime variety	Col	Area	Nat'l share	Glob'l share	VII*
Savatiano	W	9920	18.2	100.0	84.6	Cserszegi Fuszeres	W	3609	5.2	100.0	66.0
Roditis	O	4661	8.6	100.0	84.6	Kunleany	W	1211	1.7	100.0	66.0
Roditis(Red)	R	3834	7.0	100.0	84.6	Arany Sarfeher	W	1133	1.6	100.0	66.0
Agiorgitiko	R	2905	5.3	100.0	84.6	Ezerjo	W	1074	1.5	100.0	66.0
Kotsifali	R	2330	4.3	100.0	84.6	Kiralyleanyka	W	855	1.2	100.0	66.0
Xinomavro	R	1971	3.6	100.0	84.6	Leanyka	W	838	1.2	100.0	66.0
Romeiko	R	1597	2.9	100.0	84.6	Aletta	W	723	1.0	100.0	66.0
Moschomavro	R	1428	2.6	100.0	84.6	Ezerfurtu	W	377	0.5	100.0	66.0
Liatiko	R	1211	2.2	100.0	84.6	Lakhegyi Mezes	W	306	0.4	100.0	66.0
Moschofilero	R	934	1.7	100.0	84.6	Jubileum 75	R	194	0.3	100.0	66.0
Assyrtiko	W	902	1.7	100.0	84.6	Juhfark	W	186	0.3	100.0	66.0
Mandilaria	R	885	1.6	100.0	84.6	Biborkadarka	R	136	0.2	100.0	66.0
Athiri	W	748	1.4	100.0	84.6	Csaba Gyongye	W	89	0.1	100.0	66.0
Grenache Rose	R	645	1.2	100.0	84.6	Matrai Muskotaly	W	67	0.1	100.0	66.0
Vilana	W	579	1.1	100.0	84.6	Menoir	R	65	0.1	100.0	66.0
Mavrouda	R	520	1.0	100.0	84.6	Duna Gyongye	R	63	0.1	100.0	66.0
Monemvassia	W	481	0.9	100.0	84.6	Nero	R	50	0.1	100.0	66.0
Robola	W	465	0.9	100.0	84.6	Karat	W	50	0.1	100.0	66.0
Limnio	R	372	0.7	100.0	84.6	Keknyelu	W	43	0.1	100.0	66.0
Mavrodafni	R	345	0.6	100.0	84.6	Karmin	R	36	0.1	100.0	66.0
Fokiano	R	262	0.5	100.0	84.6	Gyongyrizling	W	23	0.0	100.0	66.0
Debina	W	239	0.4	100.0	84.6	Nektar	W	21	0.0	100.0	66.0
Malagousia	W	182	0.3	100.0	84.6	Rozsakoe	W	19	0.0	100.0	66.0
Negoska	R	143	0.3	100.0	84.6	Kabar	W	18	0.0	100.0	66.0
Asprouda	W	113	0.2	100.0	84.6	Koksis Irma	W	11	0.0	100.0	66.0
Kakotrygis	W	103	0.2	100.0	84.6	Kunbarat	W	9	0.0	100.0	66.0
Fileri	W	97	0.2	100.0	84.6	Budai Zold	W	6	0.0	100.0	66.0
Moschofilero	O	80	0.1	100.0	84.6	Palatina	W	6	0.0	100.0	66.0
Goustolidi	W	68	0.1	100.0	84.6	Vulcanus	W	5	0.0	100.0	66.0
Batily	R	54	0.1	100.0	84.6	Odysseus	W	4	0.0	100.0	66.0
Krassato	R	52	0.1	100.0	84.6	Pintes	W	3	0.0	100.0	66.0
Thrapsathiri		31	0.1	100.0	84.6	Kek Bakator	W	3	0.0	100.0	66.0
Stavroto	R	11	0.0	100.0	84.6	Mezes Feher	W	2	0.0	100.0	66.0
Rombola Red	R	6	0.0	100.0	84.6	Csokaszolo	R	2	0.0	100.0	66.0
Asirtiko Red	R	5	0.0	100.0	84.6	Bakator Roz	R	2	0.0	100.0	66.0
Uni Blan	R	1	0.0	100.0	84.6	Nosztori Rizling	W	1	0.0	100.0	66.0
Vertzami	R	239	0.4	71.4	60.4	Goher	W	1	0.0	100.0	66.0
Muscat Blanc a Petits Grains	W	2162	4.0	6.9	5.9	Korona	W	1	0.0	100.0	66.0
Cabernet Sauvignon	R	1550	2.8	0.5	0.5	Csomorika	W	0	0.0	100.0	66.0
Merlot	R	1248	2.3	0.5	0.4	Magyarfrankos	R	0	0.0	100.0	66.0
Dimyat	W	9	0.0	0.4	0.3	Orpheus	W	0	0.0	100.0	66.0
Refosco	R	5	0.0	0.4	0.3	K.35	W	0	0.0	100.0	66.0
Syrah	R	641	1.2	0.3	0.3	Kurucver	R	0	0.0	100.0	66.0
Chardonnay	W	586	1.1	0.3	0.2	Cs.2	R	0	0.0	100.0	66.0
Trebbiano Toscano	W	297	0.5	0.3	0.2	Hajnalka	W	0	0.0	100.0	66.0
Other varieties		9474	17.4			Other varieties		58473	83.9		
Total		54389	100			Total		69715	100		

Table 46 (cont.) Varietal Intensity Indexes (and winegrape areas, national and global shares) for national top 45 varieties, 2010

	Italy					Japan				
Prime variety	Col	Area	Nat'l share	Glob'l share	VII*	Prime variety	Col	Area	Nat'l share	Glob'l share	VII*
Grillo	W	6295	1.0	100	7.4	Koshu	O	168	4.5	100.0	1238.6
Trebbiano d'Abruzzo	W	5091	0.8	100	7.4	Campbell Early	R	61	1.6	100.0	1238.6
Grechetto di Orvieto	W	1501	0.2	100	7.4	Portland	W	12	0.3	100.0	1238.6
Brachetto del Piemonte	R	1460	0.2	100	7.4	Black Queen	R	469	12.6	96.5	1195.3
Fiano	W	1377	0.2	100	7.4	Muscat Bailey A	R	103	2.8	84.1	1042.3
Bombino Nero	R	1201	0.2	100	7.4	Delaware	O	51	1.4	40.5	502.0
Canaiolo Nero	R	1068	0.2	100	7.4	Kerner	W	357	9.6	8.9	110.8
Avarengo	R	987	0.2	100	7.4	Niagara	W	128	3.4	2.7	34.0
Enantio	R	724	0.1	100	7.4	Zweigelt	R	231	6.2	2.3	29.0
Piedirosso	R	699	0.1	100	7.4	Müller Thurgau	W	172	4.6	0.8	9.3
Bellone	W	511	0.1	100	7.4	Merlot	R	817	22.0	0.3	3.8
Durella	W	470	0.1	100	7.4	Chardonnay	W	602	16.2	0.3	3.7
Bianco d'Alessano	W	419	0.1	100	7.4	Cabernet Sauvignon	R	469	12.6	0.2	2.0
Erbaluce	W	319	0.1	100	7.4	Pinot Noir	R	64	1.7	0.1	0.9
Caddiu	R	309	0.0	100	7.4	Riesling	W	11	0.3	0.0	0.3
Drupeggio	W	286	0.0	100	7.4	Total		3715	100		
Giro	R	200	0.0	100	7.4						
Casavecchia	R	136	0.0	100	7.4						
Vespolina	R	134	0.0	100	7.4						
Barbera Sarda	R	84	0.0	100	7.4						
Uva Tosca	R	71	0.0	100	7.4						
Susumaniello	R	50	0.0	100	7.4						
Albaranzeuli Nero	R	49	0.0	100	7.4						
Avana	R	28	0.0	100	7.4						
Centesimino	R	24	0.0	100	7.4						
Cavrara	R	23	0.0	100	7.4						
Piculit Neri	R	22	0.0	100	7.4						
Carica l'Asino	W	17	0.0	100	7.4						
Vien de Nus	R	13	0.0	100	7.4						
Bussanello	W	12	0.0	100	7.4						
Alionza	W	11	0.0	100	7.4						
Dolciame	W	11	0.0	100	7.4						
Sennen	R	10	0.0	100	7.4						
San Lunardo	W	10	0.0	100	7.4						
Fubiano	W	9	0.0	100	7.4						
Verdesse	W	7	0.0	100	7.4						
Dindarella	R	7	0.0	100	7.4						
Bonda	R	7	0.0	100	7.4						
Moradella	R	6	0.0	100	7.4						
Fogarina	R	5	0.0	100	7.4						
Ginestra	W	4	0.0	100	7.4						
Fertilia	R	3	0.0	100	7.4						
Cianorie	R	2	0.0	100	7.4						
Baratuciat	W	2	0.0	100	7.4						
Gamba Rossa	R	0	0.0	100	7.4						
Other varieties		602029	96.2								
Total		625700	100								

Table 46 (cont.) Varietal Intensity Indexes (and winegrape areas, national and global shares) for national top 45 varieties, 2010

	Kazakhstan					Luxembourg				
Prime variety	Col	Area	Nat'l share	Glob'l share	VII* Prime variety	Col	Area	Nat'l share	Glob'l share	VII*
Bayanshira	W	645	9.3	100.0	663.2 Elbling	W	370	28.4	26.1	920.9
Kuldzhinskii	O	385	5.6	100.0	663.2 Auxerrois	W	183	14.0	6.7	235.6
Muscat Rose	O	227	3.3	100.0	663.2 Pinot Blanc	W	162	12.4	1.1	38.8
Maiskii Chernyi	R	110	1.6	100.0	663.2 Mutler Thurgau	W	184	14.1	0.8	28.5
Matrasa	R	28	0.4	100.0	663.2 Pinot Gris	O	146	11.2	0.3	11.8
Muscat Violet	R	27	0.4	100.0	663.2 Gamay Noir	R	98	7.5	0.3	10.6
Ruby	R	9	0.1	100.0	663.2 Riesling	W	121	9.3	0.2	8.5
Rubinovy Magaracha	R	0	0.0	100.0	663.2 Gewurztraminer	W	20	1.5	0.1	4.9
Rkatsiteli	W	3552	51.2	6.1	40.2 Chardonnay	W	16	1.2	0.0	0.3
Saperavi	R	428	6.2	5.3	34.9 Pinot Noir	R	3	0.2	0.0	0.1
Aligote	W	277	4.0	0.8	5.1 Other varieties		1	0.1		
Riesling	W	111	1.6	0.2	1.5 Total		1304	100		
Pinot Noir	R	180	2.6	0.2	1.4					
Cabernet Franc	R	56	0.8	0.1	0.7					
Cabernet Sauvignon	R	20	0.3	0.0	0.0					
Other varieties		882	12.7							
Total		6938	100							

Table 46 (cont.) Varietal Intensity Indexes (and winegrape areas, national and global shares) for national top 45 varieties, 2010

	Mexico						Moldova				
Prime variety	Col	Area	Nat'l share	Glob'l share	VII*	Prime variety	Col	Area	Nat'l share	Glob'l share	VII*
Fiesta	W	230	4.2	100.0	842.0	Noah	W	71	0.1	100.0	51.2
Salvador	R	350	6.4	88.9	748.2	Pervomaisky	R	64	0.1	100.0	51.2
Cardinal	R	168	3.1	30.8	259.6	Gamay Teinturier Freaux	R	55	0.1	100.0	51.2
Sultaniye	W	841	15.4	24.7	207.8	Muscat de Ialoveni	W	20	0.0	100.0	51.2
Durif	R	133	2.4	3.7	31.5	Negru de Ialoveni	R	15	0.0	100.0	51.2
Jacquez	R	80	1.5	3.4	28.4	Codrinski	R	5	0.0	100.0	51.2
Nebbiolo	R	180	3.3	3.0	25.3	Ilichevskii Rannii	R	5	0.0	100.0	51.2
Muscat Blanc a Petits Grains	W	246	4.5	0.8	6.7	Droujba	W	3	0.0	100.0	51.2
Chenin Blanc	W	275	5.0	0.8	6.6	Alb de Ialoveni	W	2	0.0	100.0	51.2
Mazuelo	R	448	8.2	0.6	4.7	Rubin Tairovsky	R	2	0.0	100.0	51.2
Palomino Fino	W	109	2.0	0.5	4.1	Golubok	R	50	0.1	57.5	29.4
Cabernet Sauvignon	R	756	13.8	0.3	2.2	Bastardo Magarachsky	R	1040	1.2	43.9	22.5
Merlot	R	391	7.2	0.1	1.2	Aligote	W	15790	17.6	43.7	22.4
Sauvignon Blanc	W	120	2.2	0.1	0.9	Isabella	R	11401	12.7	35.1	18.0
Tempranillo	R	229	4.2	0.1	0.8	Sukholimanskiy Bely	W	599	0.7	27.8	14.2
Syrah	R	145	2.7	0.1	0.7	Feteasca Alba	W	4334	4.8	24.8	12.7
Garnacha Tinta	R	140	2.6	0.1	0.6	Rkatsiteli	W	11508	12.8	19.6	10.1
Other varieties		624	11.4			Gewurztraminer	W	2731	3.0	19.1	9.8
Total		5465	100			Muscat Ottonel	W	1520	1.7	14.9	7.6
						Viorica	W	40	0.0	11.5	5.9
						Saperavi	R	716	0.8	8.8	4.5
						Pinot Noir	R	6521	7.3	7.5	3.9
						Sauvignon Blanc	W	8151	9.1	7.4	3.8
						Saperavi Severny	R	25	0.0	7.1	3.7
						Onitskanskii Belyi	W	5	0.0	7.0	3.6
						Pinot Gris	O	2042	2.3	4.7	2.4
						Gamay de Teinturier Bouze	R	10	0.0	4.4	2.3
						Silvaner	W	98	0.1	4.3	2.2
						Merlot	R	8123	9.0	3.0	1.6
						Riesling	W	1343	1.5	2.7	1.4
						Cabernet Sauvignon	R	7590	8.4	2.6	1.3
						Chardonnay	W	5134	5.7	2.6	1.3
						Babeasca Neagra	R	80	0.1	2.6	1.3
						Pinot Blanc	W	350	0.4	2.4	1.2
						Riton	W	2	0.0	0.8	0.4
						Muller Thurgau	W	173	0.2	0.8	0.4
						Muscat Blanc a Petits Grains	W	172	0.2	0.6	0.3
						Bianca	W	15	0.0	0.2	0.1
						Cot	R	39	0.0	0.1	0.0
						Total		89844	100		

Table 46 (cont.) Varietal Intensity Indexes (and winegrape areas, national and global shares) for national top 45 varieties, 2010

	Morocco					Myanmar				
Prime variety	Col	Area	Nat'l share	Glob'l share	VII* Prime variety	Col	Area	Nat'l share	Glob'l share	VII*
Doukkali	R	16557	33.8	100.0	93.9 Petit Verdot	R	2	2.6	0.0	16.4
Teneron	R	3488	7.1	100.0	93.9 Muscat Blanc a Petits Grains	W	7	9.5	0.0	14.0
Abbo	R	2375	4.8	100.0	93.9 Sauvignon Blanc	W	22	29.2	0.0	12.2
Muscat of Alexandria	W	3669	7.5	13.9	13.1 Syrah	R	27	35.8	0.0	8.9
Cinsaut	R	3940	8.0	10.9	10.3 Pinot Noir	R	7	9.0	0.0	4.8
Alicante Henri Bouschet	R	1098	2.2	2.8	2.6 Mazuelo	R	4	5.9	0.0	3.4
Mazuelo	R	1692	3.5	2.1	2.0 Chenin Blanc	W	1	0.8	0.0	1.1
Garnacha Tinta	R	802	1.6	0.4	0.4 Tempranillo	R	3	4.5	0.0	0.9
Other varieties		15379	31.4		Alicante Henri Bouschet	R	0	0.3	0.0	0.4
Total		49000	100		Chardonnay	W	1	1.5	0.0	0.3
					Cabernet Sauvignon	R	1	1.0	0.0	0.2
					Total		75	100		

Table 46 (cont.) Varietal Intensity Indexes (and winegrape areas, national and global shares) for national top 45 varieties, 2010

	New Zealand						Peru				
Prime variety	Col	Area	Nat'l share	Glob'l share	VII*	Prime variety	Col	Area	Nat'l share	Glob'l share	VII*
Breidecker	W	7	0.0	100.0	144.0	Red Globe	R	240	6.3	100.0	1201.1
Kolor	R	2	0.0	100.0	144.0	Flame Seedless	R	42	1.1	100.0	1201.1
Osteiner	W	1	0.0	100.0	144.0	Superior Seedless	W	9	0.2	100.0	1201.1
Reichensteiner	W	72	0.2	31.6	45.5	Ar99	O	5	0.1	100.0	1201.1
Flora	O	2	0.0	26.0	37.4	Crimson Seedless	R	2	0.1	100.0	1201.1
Wurzer	W	1	0.0	20.0	28.8	Ar110	O	1	0.0	100.0	1201.1
Sauvignon Blanc	W	16205	50.7	14.7	21.2	Imperial Seedless	O	1	0.0	100.0	1201.1
Arnsburger	W	2	0.0	6.6	9.5	Perlette	W	1	0.0	100.0	1201.1
Pinot Noir	R	4776	14.9	5.5	7.9	Rosa Arica	R	1	0.0	100.0	1201.1
Pinot Gris	O	1501	4.7	3.4	5.0	Quebranta	R	330	8.6	95.7	1148.9
Gewurztraminer	W	311	1.0	2.2	3.1	Italia	W	1011	26.4	88.3	1060.7
Chardonnay	W	3911	12.2	2.0	2.8	Negramoll	R	1252	32.7	39.2	471.0
Riesling	W	979	3.1	2.0	2.8	Cardinal	R	53	1.4	9.7	116.8
Seibel	R	10	0.0	1.7	2.4	Pecorino	W	114	3.0	9.3	111.5
Viognier	W	163	0.5	1.4	2.1	Alphonse Lavallee	R	18	0.5	2.0	24.5
Pinotage	R	74	0.2	1.2	1.7	Blaufrankisch	R	290	7.6	1.8	21.6
Semillon	W	201	0.6	0.9	1.3	Muscat Blanc a Petits Grains	W	361	9.4	1.2	13.9
Merlot	R	1369	4.3	0.5	0.7	Crystal	W	2	0.1	1.1	13.8
Cot	R	156	0.5	0.4	0.6	Albillo Mayor	W	7	0.2	0.5	6.4
Blauburger	R	5	0.0	0.4	0.5	Sultaniye	W	15	0.4	0.4	5.3
Chambourcin	R	4	0.0	0.4	0.5	Torrontes Riojano	W	8	0.2	0.1	1.2
Muller Thurgau	W	79	0.2	0.3	0.5	Cot	R	10	0.3	0.0	0.3
Cabernet Franc	R	163	0.5	0.3	0.4	Cabernet Sauvignon	R	48	1.3	0.0	0.2
Verdelho	W	5	0.0	0.2	0.4	Pedro Ximenez	W	1	0.0	0.0	0.1
Cabernet Sauvignon	R	517	1.6	0.2	0.3	Chenin Blanc	W	2	0.1	0.0	0.1
Silvaner	W	4	0.0	0.2	0.3	Pinot Noir	R	1	0.0	0.0	0.0
Pinot Meunier	R	19	0.1	0.2	0.2	Syrah	R	2	0.1	0.0	0.0
Syrah	R	293	0.9	0.2	0.2	Merlot	R	2	0.1	0.0	0.0
Chenin Blanc	W	50	0.2	0.1	0.2	Garnacha Tinta	R	1	0.0	0.0	0.0
Roussanne	W	2	0.0	0.1	0.2	Chardonnay	W	1	0.0	0.0	0.0
Pinot Blanc	W	16	0.1	0.1	0.2	Total		3831	100		
Petit Verdot	R	5	0.0	0.1	0.1						
Palomino Fino	W	14	0.0	0.1	0.1						
Scheurebe	W	1	0.0	0.1	0.1						
Gamay Noir	R	12	0.0	0.0	0.1						
Dolcetto	R	2	0.0	0.0	0.0						
Zweigelt	R	3	0.0	0.0	0.0						
Montepulciano	R	7	0.0	0.0	0.0						
Nebbiolo	R	1	0.0	0.0	0.0						
Chasselas	W	2	0.0	0.0	0.0						
Tribidrag	R	4	0.0	0.0	0.0						
Sangiovese	R	6	0.0	0.0	0.0						
Tempranillo	R	7	0.0	0.0	0.0						
Garnacha Tinta	R	2	0.0	0.0	0.0						
Other varieties		998	3.1								
Total		31964	100								

Table 46 (cont.) Varietal Intensity Indexes (and winegrape areas, national and global shares) for national top 45 varieties, 2010

	Portugal					Romania				
Prime variety	Col	Area	Nat'l share	Glob'l share	VII*	Prime variety	Col	Area	Nat'l share	Glob'l share	VII*
Arinto de Bucelas	W	4446	2.7	100.0	28.1	Mustoasa de Maderat	W	255	0.1	100.0	27.0
Antao Vaz	W	1252	0.8	100.0	28.1	Babeasca Gris	W	328	0.2	100.0	27.0
Azal	W	1072	0.7	100.0	28.1	Busuioaca de Bohotin	O	268	0.2	100.0	27.0
Bical	W	924	0.6	100.0	28.1	Francusa	W	621	0.4	100.0	27.0
Santarena	R	739	0.5	100.0	28.1	Cramposie Selectionata	W	409	0.2	100.0	27.0
Gouveio Real	W	582	0.4	100.0	28.1	Feteasca Neagra	R	1719	1.0	100.0	27.0
Cerceal Branco	W	379	0.2	100.0	28.1	Galbena de Odobesti	W	385	0.2	100.0	27.0
Cabinda	R	362	0.2	100.0	28.1	Feteasca Regala	W	12905	7.6	98.2	26.5
Brandam	W	312	0.2	100.0	28.1	Babeasca Neagra	R	3042	1.8	97.4	26.3
Trincadeira das Pratas	W	239	0.1	100.0	28.1	Grasa de Cotnari	W	640	0.4	93.4	25.2
Fernao Pires Rosado	R	98	0.1	100.0	28.1	Feteasca Alba	W	12916	7.6	73.9	20.0
Amaral	R	92	0.1	100.0	28.1	Muscat Ottonel	W	3641	2.1	35.6	9.6
Padeiro	R	86	0.1	100.0	28.1	Pamid	R	2930	1.7	29.8	8.1
Agua Santa	R	78	0.0	100.0	28.1	Aligote	W	7297	4.3	20.2	5.5
Tinta Aguiar	R	75	0.0	100.0	28.1	Grasevina	W	7530	4.4	12.3	3.3
Tinta Penajoia	R	53	0.0	100.0	28.1	Blaufrankisch	R	760	0.4	4.7	1.3
Primavera	R	40	0.0	100.0	28.1	Merlot	R	10988	6.5	4.1	1.1
Castelao Branco	W	37	0.0	100.0	28.1	Sauvignon Blanc	W	4157	2.4	3.8	1.0
Arinto Roxo	R	36	0.0	100.0	28.1	Pinot Gris	O	1301	0.8	3.0	0.8
Moscatel Branco	W	30	0.0	100.0	28.1	Muscat Blanc a Petits Grains	W	840	0.5	2.7	0.7
Folgasao Roxo	R	18	0.0	100.0	28.1	Gewurztraminer	W	385	0.2	2.7	0.7
Carrega Tinto	R	17	0.0	100.0	28.1	Cabernet Sauvignon	R	3718	2.2	1.3	0.3
Batoca	W	11	0.0	100.0	28.1	Pinot Noir	R	1089	0.6	1.3	0.3
Marquinhas	W	11	0.0	100.0	28.1	Rkatsiteli	W	356	0.2	0.6	0.2
Tinta Martins	R	11	0.0	100.0	28.1	Chardonnay	W	1067	0.6	0.5	0.1
Cainho de Moreira	W	7	0.0	100.0	28.1	Other varieties		90745	53.3		
Verdelho Roxo		4	0.0	100.0	28.1	Total		170292	100		
Branco Especial	W	3	0.0	100.0	28.1						
Boal Vencedor	W	2	0.0	100.0	28.1						
Campanario	R	2	0.0	100.0	28.1						
Cabral	R	2	0.0	100.0	28.1						
Alvar Roxo	O	2	0.0	100.0	28.1						
Tinta de Porto Santo	R	2	0.0	100.0	28.1						
Arjuncao	R	1	0.0	100.0	28.1						
Rabigato Moreno	W	1	0.0	100.0	28.1						
Alminhaca	W	1	0.0	100.0	28.1						
S. Mamede	W	1	0.0	100.0	28.1						
Branco Sr. Joao	W	0	0.0	100.0	28.1						
Gouveio Preto	R	0	0.0	100.0	28.1						
Mondet	R	0	0.0	100.0	28.1						
Alvar Branco	W	0	0.0	100.0	28.1						
Branco Valente	W	0	0.0	100.0	28.1						
Malvia	W	0	0.0	100.0	28.1						
Deliciosa	R	0	0.0	100.0	28.1						
Melhorio	R	0	0.0	100.0	28.1						
Other varieties		152492	93.3								
Total		163522	100								

Table 46 (cont.) Varietal Intensity Indexes (and winegrape areas, national and global shares) for national top 45 varieties, 2010

Russia						Serbia					
Prime variety	Col	Area	Nat'l share	Glob'l share	VII*	Prime variety	Col	Area	Nat'l share	Glob'l share	VII*
Levokumsky	R	720	2.8	100.0	179.5	Prokupac	R	15180	22.0	100.0	66.7
Krasnostop Zolotovsky	R	562	2.2	100.0	179.5	Grasevina	W	33120	48.0	54.1	36.1
Dunavski Lazur	W	483	1.9	100.0	179.5	Muscat of Hamburg	R	2760	4.0	33.9	22.6
Tsimlyansky Cherny	R	451	1.8	100.0	179.5	Chasselas	W	3449.9	5.0	26.2	17.4
Citronny Magarach	W	307	1.2	100.0	179.5	Other varieties		14490	21.0		
Vidvizhenets	O	271	1.1	100.0	179.5	Total		68999	100		
Doina	R	227	0.9	100.0	179.5						
Levokumski Sustainable	O	170	0.7	100.0	179.5						
Amur	R	146	0.6	100.0	179.5						
Stepnyak	W	144	0.6	100.0	179.5						
Riesus	W	115	0.4	100.0	179.5						
Tsvetochny (Floral)	W	89	0.3	100.0	179.5						
Rubin Golodrigi	R	82	0.3	100.0	179.5						
Tsvetochny (Flowery)	W	80	0.3	100.0	179.5						
Dekabrskii	R	78	0.3	100.0	179.5						
Dostoinyi	R	65	0.3	100.0	179.5						
Fioletovy Ranny	R	50	0.2	100.0	179.5						
Barkhatnyi	W	30	0.1	100.0	179.5						
Muscat Amber	O	21	0.1	100.0	179.5						
Riton	W	255	1.0	99.2	178.2						
Crystal	W	171	0.7	98.0	175.9						
Onitskanskii Belyi	W	66	0.3	93.0	166.9						
Saperavi Severny	R	325	1.3	92.9	166.7						
Viorica	W	307	1.2	88.5	158.9						
Pervenets Magaracha	W	2238	8.7	77.7	139.5						
Goecseji Zamatos	W	40	0.2	72.3	129.9						
Podarok Magaracha	W	292	1.1	57.9	104.0						
Bianca	W	3513	13.7	54.5	97.8						
Golubok	R	37	0.1	42.5	76.4						
Savagnin Blanc	W	214	0.8	11.3	20.2						
Zalagyongye	W	193	0.8	9.9	17.8						
Saperavi	R	716	2.8	8.8	15.8						
Pinot Blanc	W	695	2.7	4.7	8.5						
Sukholimanskiy Bely	W	80	0.3	3.7	6.7						
Zenit	W	21	0.1	3.6	6.5						
Aligote	W	1029	4.0	2.8	5.1						
Muscat of Hamburg	R	180	0.7	2.2	4.0						
Riesling	W	882	3.4	1.8	3.2						
Irsai Oliver	W	24	0.1	1.7	3.0						
Cabernet Sauvignon	R	3593	14.0	1.2	2.2						
Rkatsiteli	W	702	2.7	1.2	2.1						
Chardonnay	W	1981	7.7	1.0	1.8						
Sauvignon Blanc	W	951	3.7	0.9	1.6						
Clairette	W	22	0.1	0.8	1.4						
Pinot Noir	R	533	2.1	0.6	1.1						
Other varieties		2477	9.7								
Total		25628	100								

Table 46 (cont.) Varietal Intensity Indexes (and winegrape areas, national and global shares) for national top 45 varieties, 2010

	Slovakia					Slovenia				
Prime variety	Col	Area	Nat'l share	Glob'l share	VII*	Prime variety	Col	Area	Nat'l share	Glob'l share	VII*
Devin	W	133	1.1	100.0	364.1	Zametovka	R	913	5.6	100.0	281.3
Dunaj	R	46	0.4	100.0	364.1	Plavay	W	60	0.4	100.0	281.4
Milia	R	1	0.0	100.0	364.1	Refosco	R	1292	7.9	91.0	255.9
Noria	W	1	0.0	100.0	364.1	Ribolla Gialla	W	743	4.5	63.0	177.4
Neronet	R	39	0.3	54.2	197.3	Kraljevina	W	179	1.1	40.1	112.7
Andre	R	211	1.7	44.7	162.9	Malvazija Istarska	W	740	4.5	27.0	75.9
Aurelius	W	26	0.2	36.7	133.7	Furmint	W	651	4.0	12.4	34.8
Muskat Moravsky	W	163	1.3	31.7	115.3	Savagnin Blanc	W	215	1.3	11.3	31.9
Sankt Laurent	R	939	7.4	31.2	113.7	Sauvignonasse	W	190	1.2	4.3	12.0
Fruhroter Veltliner	R	195	1.5	23.0	83.9	Blaufrankisch	R	680	4.2	4.2	11.9
Irsai Oliver	W	227	1.8	16.0	58.4	Grasevina	W	2360	14.4	3.9	10.9
Palava	O	32	0.2	13.7	50.0	Pinot Blanc	W	525	3.2	3.6	10.0
Gruner Veltliner	W	2091	16.5	11.1	40.4	Riesling	W	676	4.1	1.4	3.8
Odessky Cherny	R	236	1.9	8.8	31.9	Pinot Gris	O	501	3.1	1.1	3.2
Blaufrankisch	R	1378	10.9	8.5	31.1	Muscat Blanc a Petits Grains	W	353	2.2	1.1	3.2
Harslevelu	W	141	1.1	7.6	27.6	Sauvignon Blanc	W	1061	6.5	1.0	2.7
Silvaner	W	117	0.9	5.2	19.0	Chardonnay	W	1208	7.4	0.6	1.7
Furmint	W	248	2.0	4.7	17.2	Barbera	R	134	0.8	0.6	1.6
Muller Thurgau	W	932	7.4	4.1	14.9	Merlot	R	996	6.1	0.4	1.0
Pinot Blanc	W	523	4.1	3.5	12.9	Cabernet Sauvignon	R	453	2.8	0.2	0.4
Grasevina	W	1655	13.1	2.7	9.8	Kerner	W	2	0.0	0.0	0.1
Blauer Portugieser	R	92	0.7	2.4	8.8	Other varieties		2422	14.8		
Bouvier	W	6	0.0	2.2	8.2	Total		16354	100		
Gewurztraminer	W	265	2.1	1.9	6.8						
Feteasca Regala	W	231	1.8	1.8	6.4						
Feteasca Alba	W	219	1.7	1.3	4.6						
Riesling	W	605	4.8	1.2	4.4						
Zweigelt	R	116	0.9	1.2	4.3						
Neuburger	W	9	0.1	0.9	3.4						
Pinot Gris	O	211	1.7	0.5	1.8						
Muscat Ottonel	W	48	0.4	0.5	1.7						
Cabernet Sauvignon	R	570	4.5	0.2	0.7						
Sauvignon Blanc	W	208	1.6	0.2	0.7						
Chardonnay	W	310	2.5	0.2	0.6						
Muscat Blanc a Petits Grains	W	48	0.4	0.2	0.6						
Other varieties		367	2.9								
Total		12637	100								

Table 46 (cont.) Varietal Intensity Indexes (and winegrape areas, national and global shares) for national top 45 varieties, 2010

	South Africa						Spain				
Prime variety	Col	Area	Nat'l share	Glob'l share	VII*	Prime variety	Col	Area	Nat'l share	Glob'l share	VII*
Nouvelle	W	422	0.4	100.0	45.6	Airen	W	252364	24.5	100	4.5
Muscadel (Red)	R	371	0.4	100.0	45.6	Bobal	R	80120	7.8	100	4.5
Roobernet	R	139	0.1	100.0	45.6	Verdejo	W	16578	1.6	100	4.5
Therona	W	99	0.1	100.0	45.6	Parellada	W	8847	0.9	100	4.5
Chenel	W	79	0.1	100.0	45.6	Chelva	W	6168	0.6	100	4.5
Bukettraube	W	71	0.1	100.0	45.6	Calagrano	W	4794	0.5	100	4.5
Servant	W	54	0.1	100.0	45.6	Zalema	W	4097	0.4	100	4.5
Kanaan	W	25	0.0	100.0	45.6	Merseguera	W	3946	0.4	100	4.5
Weldra	W	14	0.0	100.0	45.6	Tinto Velasco	R	2684	0.3	100	4.5
Red Semillon	R	10	0.0	100.0	45.6	Listan Negro	R	2666	0.3	100	4.5
Cinsaut Blanc	W	7	0.0	100.0	45.6	Alarije	W	1726	0.2	100	4.5
Muscat of Alexandria Red	R	6	0.0	100.0	45.6	Forcallat Tinta	R	1163	0.1	100	4.5
Colomino	W	5	0.0	100.0	45.6	Albillo Real	W	861	0.1	100	4.5
Grachen	W	2	0.0	100.0	45.6	Miguel del Arco	R	468	0.0	100	4.5
Pinotage	R	6240	6.2	97.4	44.4	Coloraillo	R	374	0.0	100	4.5
Crouchen	W	629	0.6	86.9	39.6	Vijariego	W	285	0.0	100	4.5
Emerald Riesling	W	104	0.1	63.3	28.9	Manto Negro	R	273	0.0	100	4.5
Chenin Blanc	W	18515	18.3	52.7	24.0	Lairen	W	214	0.0	100	4.5
Ruby Cabernet	R	2220	2.2	38.7	17.6	Callet	R	154	0.0	100	4.5
Colombard	W	11990	11.9	37.4	17.0	Caino Blanco	W	121	0.0	100	4.5
Villard Blanc	W	188	0.2	27.3	12.4	Moristel	R	112	0.0	100	4.5
Galego Dourado	W	3	0.0	18.8	8.6	Tinto Basto	R	62	0.0	100	4.5
Clairette	W	290	0.3	10.0	4.6	Alcanon	W	60	0.0	100	4.5
Petit Verdot	R	648	0.6	9.0	4.1	Garrido Fino	W	59	0.0	100	4.5
Sauvignon Blanc	W	9551	9.5	8.7	3.9	Fino de Ribera del Fresno	W	45	0.0	100	4.5
Muscat of Alexandria	W	2167	2.1	8.2	3.7	Doradilla	W	40	0.0	100	4.5
Viognier	W	892	0.9	7.8	3.6	Fogoneu	R	35	0.0	100	4.5
Morio-Muskat	W	39	0.0	7.7	3.5	J Ibanez	R	35	0.0	100	4.5
Cinsaut	R	2052	2.0	5.7	2.6	Royal de Alloza	R	29	0.0	100	4.5
Syrah	R	10136	10.0	5.5	2.5	Ensanyo Tintas	R	27	0.0	100	4.5
Semillon	W	1182	1.2	5.3	2.4	Marmajuelo	W	24	0.0	100	4.5
Cabernet Sauvignon	R	12325	12.2	4.2	1.9	Planta Mula	R	24	0.0	100	4.5
Chardonnay	W	8278	8.2	4.2	1.9	Cinsaut Seedless	R	13	0.0	100	4.5
Tinta Barroca	R	231	0.2	3.8	1.7	Imperial Napoleon	R	12	0.0	100	4.5
Harslevelu	W	56	0.1	3.0	1.4	Afus Ali	W	8	0.0	100	4.5
Roussanne	W	45	0.0	2.6	1.2	Grand Manchen	W	8	0.0	100	4.5
Merlot	R	6497	6.4	2.4	1.1	Aledo	W	7	0.0	100	4.5
Muscat Blanc a Petits Grain	W	689	0.7	2.2	1.0	Colgadero	R	5	0.0	100	4.5
Cabernet Franc	R	934	0.9	1.7	0.8	Gateta	R	2	0.0	100	4.5
Vinhao	R	47	0.0	1.5	0.7	Huerta del Rey	W	2	0.0	100	4.5
Fernao Pires	W	135	0.1	1.4	0.6	Argelina	R	1	0.0	100	4.5
Verdelho	W	25	0.0	1.2	0.6	Dominga	W	1	0.0	100	4.5
Palomino Fino	W	270	0.3	1.2	0.5	Ensayo Blancas	W	1	0.0	100	4.5
Tannat	R	67	0.1	1.1	0.5	Lado	W	1	0.0	100	4.5
Pinot Noir	R	962	1.0	1.1	0.5	Michele Parlieri	W	1	0.0	100	4.5
Other varieties		2306	2.3			Other varieties		639741	62.2		
Total		101016	100			Total		1028258	100		

Table 46 (cont.) Varietal Intensity Indexes (and winegrape areas, national and global shares) for national top 45 varieties, 2010

	Switzerland						Thailand				
Prime variety	Col	Area	Nat'l share	Glob'l share	VII*	Prime variety	Col	Area	Nat'l share	Glob'l share	VII*
Amigne	W	43	0.3	100.0	310.5	Malaga Blanc	W	16	10.9	100.0	30919.7
Humagne	W	30	0.2	100.0	310.5	Black Queen	R	17	11.4	3.5	1080.7
Doral	W	27	0.2	100.0	310.5	Garnacha Roja	W	6	3.8	0.3	98.2
Rauschling	W	23	0.2	100.0	310.5	Chenin Blanc	W	13	8.9	0.0	11.6
Cabernet Jura	R	19	0.1	100.0	310.5	Syrah	R	66	44.5	0.0	11.0
Galotta	R	13	0.1	100.0	310.5	Colombard	W	11	7.5	0.0	10.7
Bondola	R	13	0.1	100.0	310.5	Dornfelder	R	2	1.3	0.0	7.1
Carminoir	R	10	0.1	100.0	310.5	Muscat Blanc a Petits Grains	W	3	2.2	0.0	3.2
Charmont	W	10	0.1	100.0	310.5	Viognier	W	1	0.4	0.0	1.5
Freisamer	W	4	0.0	100.0	310.5	Sangiovese	R	2	1.4	0.0	0.8
Completer	W	3	0.0	100.0	310.5	Cabernet Sauvignon	R	7	4.7	0.0	0.7
Diolinoir	R	112	0.8	98.0	304.2	Tempranillo	R	4	2.9	0.0	0.6
Cornalin	R	244	1.6	95.6	296.8	Pinot Noir	R	1	0.4	0.0	0.2
Gamaret	R	380	2.6	95.0	295.0	Total		149	100		
Garanoir	R	203	1.4	93.9	291.5						
Arvine	W	154	1.0	89.2	276.9						
Solaris	W	13	0.1	64.5	200.3						
Regent	R	41	0.3	59.0	183.1						
Leon Millot	R	9	0.1	40.2	124.7						
Chasselas	W	4013	27.1	30.4	94.5						
Dakapo	R	13	0.1	24.1	74.8						
Johanniter	W	11	0.1	21.6	67.0						
Silvaner	W	241	1.6	10.7	33.2						
Cabernet Dorsa	R	22	0.1	9.8	30.4						
Dunkelfelder	R	24	0.2	7.4	23.0						
Pinot Noir	R	4402	29.7	5.1	15.8						
Gamay Noir	R	1521	10.3	4.7	14.5						
Savagnin Blanc	W	83	0.6	4.4	13.6						
Marechal Foch	R	13	0.1	3.7	11.5						
Marsanne	W	48	0.3	2.7	8.5						
Muller Thurgau	W	493	3.3	2.2	6.7						
Seyval Blanc	W	8	0.1	1.7	5.2						
Mondeuse Noire	R	4	0.0		3.7						
Sauvignon Gris	W	5	0.0	1.1	3.5						
Pinot Blanc	W	105	0.7	0.7	2.2						
Pinot Gris	O	216	1.5	0.5	1.5						
Kerner	W	19	0.1	0.5	1.5						
Ancellotta	R	19	0.1	0.4	1.2						
Merlot	R	1028	6.9	0.4	1.2						
Gewurztraminer	W	49	0.3	0.3	1.1						
Irsai Oliver	W	5	0.0	0.3	1.0						
Viognier	W	31	0.2	0.3	0.8						
Dornfelder	R	21	0.1	0.3	0.8						
Scheurebe	W	5	0.0	0.2	0.8						
Chambourcin	R	3	0.0	0.2	0.7						
Other varieties		1068	7.2								
Total		14820	100								

Table 46 (cont.) Varietal Intensity Indexes (and winegrape areas, national and global shares) for national top 45 varieties, 2010

Tunisia						Turkey					
Prime variety	Col	Area	Nat'l share	Glob'l share	VII*	Prime variety	Col	Area	Nat'l share	Glob'l share	VII*
Mazuelo	R	7576	45.0	9.4	25.8	Okuzgozu	R	1479	11.5	100.0	357.9
Cinsaut	R	842	5.0	2.3	6.4	Bogazkere	R	1106	8.6	100.0	357.9
Alicante Henri Bouschet	R	842	5.0	2.2	5.9	Dimrit	R	863	6.7	100.0	357.9
Garnacha Tinta	R	2020	12.0	1.1	3.0	Kalecik Karasi	R	861	6.7	100.0	357.9
Sangiovese	R	842	5.0	1.1	3.0	Narince	W	769	6.0	100.0	357.9
Tribidrag	R	337	2.0	1.0	2.8	Emir	W	688	5.3	100.0	357.9
Monastrell	R	337	2.0	0.5	1.3	Calkarasi	R	625	4.9	100.0	357.9
Syrah	R	337	2.0	0.2	0.5	Papazkarasi	R	175	1.4	100.0	357.9
Cabernet Sauvignon	R	337	2.0	0.1	0.3	Adakarasi	R	69	0.5	100.0	357.9
Other varieties		3367	20.0			Karalahna	R	4	0.0	100.0	357.9
Total		16836	100			Karasakiz	R	4	0.0	100.0	357.9
						Vasilaki	W	4	0.0	100.0	357.9
						Cavus	W	3	0.0	100.0	357.9
						Sultaniye	W	1750	13.6	51.4	183.8
						Semillon	W	547	4.3	2.5	8.8
						Cinsaut	R	500	3.9	1.4	5.0
						Alicante Henri Bouschet	R	488	3.8	1.3	4.5
						Syrah	R	1367	10.6	0.7	2.6
						Gamay Noir	R	206	1.6	0.6	2.3
						Muscat Blanc a Petits Grains	W	114	0.9	0.4	1.3
						Viognier	W	16	0.1	0.1	0.5
						Petit Verdot	R	10	0.1	0.1	0.5
						Cabernet Sauvignon	R	391	3.0	0.1	0.5
						Merlot	R	355	2.8	0.1	0.5
						Sauvignon Blanc	W	146	1.1	0.1	0.5
						Mazuelo	R	84	0.7	0.1	0.4
						Chardonnay	W	142	1.1	0.1	0.3
						Cabernet Franc	R	23	0.2	0.0	0.2
						Cot	R	13	0.1	0.0	0.1
						Garnacha Tinta	R	33	0.3	0.0	0.1
						Sangiovese	R	9	0.1	0.0	0.0
						Monastrell	R	4	0.0	0.0	0.0
						Riesling	W	3	0.0	0.0	0.0
						Tempranillo	R	9	0.1	0.0	0.0
						Pinot Noir	R	3	0.0	0.0	0.0
						Total		12856	100		

Table 46 (cont.) Varietal Intensity Indexes (and winegrape areas, national and global shares) for national top 45 varieties, 2010

Ukraine						United Kingdom					
Prime variety	Col	Area	Nat'l share	Glob'l share	VII*	Prime variety	Col	Area	Nat'l share	Glob'l share	VII*
Kokur Bely	W	918	1.8	100.0	88.0	Rondo	R	40	3.3	100.0	3840.9
Telti Kyryk	W	246	0.5	100.0	88.0	Triomphe	R	15	1.3	100.0	3840.9
Ekim Kara	R	27	0.1	100.0	88.0	Orion	W	10	0.8	100.0	3840.9
Odessky Cherny	R	2426	4.6	90.3	79.5	Gutenborner	W	2	0.2	100.0	3840.9
Sukholimanskiy Bely	W	1477	2.8	68.5	60.3	Madeleine Angevine	W	45	3.8	87.2	3348.4
Bastardo Magarachsky	R	1330	2.5	56.1	49.4	Wurzer	W	4	0.3	80.0	3072.8
Podarok Magaracha	W	212	0.4	42.1	37.0	Schonburger	O	37	3.1	62.6	2405.9
Aligote	W	9627	18.4	26.7	23.5	Phoenix	W	21	1.8	41.2	1581.6
Pervenets Magaracha	W	643	1.2	22.3	19.6	Solaris	W	7	0.6	35.5	1363.4
Rkatsiteli	W	11552	22.1	19.7	17.3	Kernling	W	5	0.4	33.3	1280.3
Saperavi	R	1514	2.9	18.6	16.4	Reichensteiner	W	71	5.9	31.2	1197.9
Isabella	R	2396	4.6	7.4	6.5	Regent	R	19	1.6	27.4	1052.3
Gewurztraminer	W	961	1.8	6.7	5.9	Seyval Blanc	W	85	7.1	18.3	704.2
Riesling	W	2702	5.2	5.4	4.7	Madeleine Sylvaner	W	1	0.1	13.8	530.9
Sauvignon Blanc	W	3123	6.0	2.8	2.5	Leon Millot	R	3	0.3	12.9	495.0
Pinot Blanc	W	338	0.6	2.3	2.0	Siegerrebe	O	12	1.0	10.0	385.6
Muscat Blanc a Petits Grains	W	674	1.3	2.2	1.9	Pinot Noir Precoce	R	19	1.6	9.1	349.2
Cabernet Sauvignon	R	4869	9.3	1.7	1.5	Regner	W	4	0.3	9.1	349.2
Pinot Gris	O	685	1.3	1.6	1.4	Bacchus	W	116	9.7	5.7	217.6
Chardonnay	W	2985	5.7	1.5	1.3	Perle	O	1	0.1	4.8	182.9
Merlot	R	2820	5.4	1.1	0.9	Ortega	W	18	1.5	2.8	108.6
Pinot Noir	R	767	1.5	0.9	0.8	Huxelrebe	W	17	1.4	2.8	107.6
Total		52293	100			Optima	W	1	0.1	2.7	104.7
						Acolon	R	4	0.3	0.9	34.2
						Faberrebe	W	4	0.3	0.8	29.3
						Dunkelfelder	R	2	0.2	0.6	23.4
						Pinot Meunier	R	50	4.2	0.4	17.0
						Auxerrois	W	9	0.8	0.3	12.6
						Pinot Noir	R	233	19.4	0.3	10.3
						Muller Thurgau	W	43	3.6	0.2	7.3
						Dornfelder	R	14	1.2	0.2	6.6
						Pinot Blanc	W	23	1.9	0.2	6.0
						Kerner	W	6	0.5	0.2	5.8
						Chardonnay	W	235	19.6	0.1	4.5
						Scheurebe	W	2	0.2	0.1	3.9
						Pinot Gris	O	9	0.8	0.0	0.8
						Zweigelt	R	1	0.1	0.0	0.4
						Gewurztraminer	W	1	0.1	0.0	0.3
						Gamay Noir	R	1	0.1	0.0	0.1
						Sauvignon Blanc	W	3	0.3	0.0	0.1
						Riesling	W	1	0.1	0.0	0.1
						Cabernet Franc	R	1	0.1	0.0	0.1
						Merlot	R	2	0.2	0.0	0.0
						Cabernet Sauvignon	R	1	0.1	0.0	0.0
						Total		1198	100		

Table 46 (cont.) Varietal Intensity Indexes (and winegrape areas, national and global shares) for national top 45 varieties, 2010

	United States						Uruguay				
Prime variety	Col	Area	Nat'l share	Glob'l share	VII*	Prime variety	Col	Area	Nat'l share	Glob'l share	VII*
Rubired	R	4556	2.0	100.0	20.2	Arinarnoa	R	28	0.4	86.2	518.3
Catawba	R	633	0.3	100.0	20.2	Arriloba	W	4	0.1	57.3	344.1
Symphony	W	324	0.1	100.0	20.2	Tannat	R	1815	23.7	30.6	183.6
Carnelian	R	316	0.1	100.0	20.2	Muscat of Hamburg	R	1500	19.6	18.4	110.8
Aurore	W	268	0.1	100.0	20.2	Canari Noir	R	13	0.2	8.5	51.3
Triplett Blanc	W	244	0.1	100.0	20.2	Trebbiano	W	11	0.1	4.4	26.7
Norton	R	227	0.1	100.0	20.2	Marselan	R	91	1.2	3.6	21.9
Cayuga White	W	212	0.1	100.0	20.2	Sauvignon Gris	W	8	0.1	1.7	10.0
Chardonel	W	144	0.1	100.0	20.2	Egiodola	R	3	0.0	0.8	4.8
Frontenac	R	135	0.1	100.0	20.2	Isabella	R	256	3.3	0.8	4.7
Muscat Fleur d'Oranger	W	91	0.0	100.0	20.2	Trebbiano Toscano	W	751	9.8	0.7	4.1
Marquette	R	88	0.0	100.0	20.2	Cabernet Franc	R	334	4.4	0.6	3.7
La Crescent	W	77	0.0	100.0	20.2	Petit Verdot	R	32	0.4	0.4	2.7
Frontenac Gris	W	59	0.0	100.0	20.2	Nebbiolo	R	26	0.3	0.4	2.6
Rougeon	R	42	0.0	100.0	20.2	Viognier	W	45	0.6	0.4	2.4
Moore's Diamond	W	42	0.0	100.0	20.2	Merlot	R	875	11.4	0.3	2.0
Steuben	R	39	0.0	100.0	20.2	Cabernet Sauvignon	R	682	8.9	0.2	1.4
Fredonia	R	37	0.0	100.0	20.2	Malvasia Fina	W	8	0.1	0.2	1.4
Centurian	R	34	0.0	100.0	20.2	Concord	R	22	0.3	0.2	1.1
Noiret	R	33	0.0	100.0	20.2	Roussanne	W	3	0.0	0.2	1.0
Gr 7	R	32	0.0	100.0	20.2	Gewurztraminer	W	24	0.3	0.2	1.0
Edelweiss	W	32	0.0	100.0	20.2	Sauvignon Blanc	W	147	1.9	0.1	0.8
Blanc du Bois	W	28	0.0	100.0	20.2	Marsanne	W	2	0.0	0.1	0.7
Corot Noir	R	27	0.0	100.0	20.2	Semillon	W	24	0.3	0.1	0.7
La Crosse	W	25	0.0	100.0	20.2	Cot	R	41	0.5	0.1	0.6
St Croix	R	25	0.0	100.0	20.2	Chardonnay	W	149	1.9	0.1	0.5
St Vincent	R	23	0.0	100.0	20.2	Muscat Ottonel	W	7	0.1	0.1	0.4
Prairie Star	W	21	0.0	100.0	20.2	Pinot Noir	R	55	0.7	0.1	0.4
St Pepin	W	19	0.0	100.0	20.2	Pinot Blanc	W	9	0.1	0.1	0.4
Ives	R	16	0.0	100.0	20.2	Alicante Henri Bouschet	R	22	0.3	0.1	0.3
Brianna	W	12	0.0	100.0	20.2	Syrah	R	87	1.1	0.0	0.3
Sabrevois	R	10	0.0	100.0	20.2	Ruby Cabernet	R	2	0.0	0.0	0.2
Reliance	R	4	0.0	100.0	20.2	Muscat Blanc a Petits Grains	W	10	0.1	0.0	0.2
Louise Swenson	W	3	0.0	100.0	20.2	Riesling	W	15	0.2	0.0	0.2
Landot Noir	R	2	0.0	100.0	20.2	Gamay Noir	R	9	0.1	0.0	0.2
Mars	R	2	0.0	100.0	20.2	Pinot Gris	O	12	0.2	0.0	0.2
Kay Gray	W	1	0.0	100.0	20.2	Chenin Blanc	W	7	0.1	0.0	0.1
Cabernet Dore	W	1	0.0	100.0	20.2	Colombard	W	4	0.1	0.0	0.1
Crimson Cabernet	R	1	0.0	100.0	20.2	Pedro Ximenez	W	1	0.0	0.0	0.1
Chelois	R	1	0.0	100.0	20.2	Garnacha Tinta	R	5	0.1	0.0	0.0
Golden Muscat	W	1	0.0	100.0	20.2	Monastrell	R	1	0.0	0.0	0.0
Himrod	W	0	0.0	100.0	20.2	Other varieties		517	6.8		
Cabernet Diane	R	0	0.0	100.0	20.2	Total		7657	100		
Canadice	R	0	0.0	100.0	20.2						
Colobel	R	0	0.0	100.0	20.2						
Other varieties		220059	96.5								
Total		227948	100								

Table Section VI: Regional Varietal Intensity Indexes for world's top varieties

Table 47: Varietal Intensity Indexes for the top 25 regions for world's top 30 red varieties, 2000

Cabernet Sauvignon			Garnacha Tinta			Merlot			Mazuelo		
	Region	Varietal Intensity Indexes		Region	Varietal Intensity Indexes		Region	Varietal Intensity Indexes		Region	Varietal Intensity Indexes
CL	Metropolitana	12.61	IT	Nuoro	14.29	CH	Ticino	19.27	TN	Tunisia	17.33
AU	Limestone C.Other	11.47	ES	Zaragoza	13.63	IT	Rovigo	13.13	FR	Aude	14.54
CL	O'Higgins	11.07	FR	Vaucluse	12.72	FR	Gironde	11.49	FR	Herault	10.93
US	Yuba	10.90	ES	Madrid	9.91	US	Oregon-Other	9.40	DZ	Algeria	9.63
US	Butte	10.12	ES	Huesca, Teruel	9.19	US	Marin	8.70	FR	Pyrenees-Orientales	7.83
AU	Currency Creek	9.30	ES	Avila, Palencia, Salama	9.08	IT	Padova	8.64	FR	Var	7.59
AU	Langhorne Creek	8.80	ES	Navarra	8.40	IT	Venezia	7.26	ES	Girona, Lleida	7.31
AU	Lower Murray Other	8.40	US	Glenn	7.99	IT	Pordenone	7.13	IT	Cagliari	6.77
AU	Kangaroo Island	8.02	FR	Bouches-du-Rhone	6.85	US	Trinity	7.03	FR	Gard	6.20
AU	Hilltops	7.52	FR	Gard	6.05	US	Mariposa	6.58	FR	Bouches-du-Rhone	5.51
AU	Mount Benson	7.20	ES	La Rioja	5.19	IT	Bergamo	5.83	FR	Vaucluse	3.77
CL	Del Maule	7.04	FR	Var	4.99	US	Sacramento	5.69	ES	Tarragona	3.69
AU	West Victoria Other	6.85	FR	Rhone Alpes Other	4.98	FR	Aquitaine Other	5.64	US	Contra Costa	3.50
AU	Beechworth	6.73	FR	Pyrenees-Orientales	4.65	US	Columbia River	5.52	US	Placer	2.54
US	Napa	6.73	DZ	Algeria	4.56	US	Washington	5.47	US	Madera	2.46
AU	Mudgee	6.17	FR	Ardeche	4.53	IT	Udine	5.02	FR	Alpes de Haute	2.16
AU	Orange	6.14	US	San Bernardino	4.14	AU	Alpine/Bchworth	4.74	US	Mendocino	2.08
US	San Luis Obispo	5.95	FR	Alpes de Haute	4.09	IT	Treviso	4.51	FR	Ardeche	2.05
AU	Margaret River	5.84	ES	Toledo	3.84	US	Tehama	4.43	US	Santa Clara	1.76
AU	Clare Valley	5.78	ES	Castellon	2.81	US	San Diego	4.15	US	San Joaquin	1.42
M9	Missing 9	5.61	IT	Sassari	2.80	US	Napa	4.04	MA	Morocco	1.31
AU	Perricoota	5.53	TN	Tunisia	2.74	IT	Vicenza	4.01	US	Stanislaus	1.26
AU	The Peninsulas	5.47	US	Kings	2.63	CL	O'Higgins	3.95	ES	Navarra	1.21
US	San Benito	5.46	FR	Corse	2.47	NZ	Auckland	3.94	FR	Rhone Alpes Other	1.14
AU	Padthaway	5.45	FR	Aude	2.24	US	Solano	3.82	ES	La Rioja	1.14

Table 47 (cont.) Varietal Intensity Indexes for the top 25 regions for world's top 30 red varieties, 2000

	Syrah			Bobal			Tempranillo			Monastrell	
	Region	Varietal Intensity Indexes		Region	Varietal Intensity Indexes		Region	Varietal Intensity Indexes		Region	Varietal Intensity Indexes
US	Ventura	30.03	ES	Valencia	28.70	ES	Alava	39.31	ES	Region De Murcia	48.48
AU	Far North - Other	29.12	ES	Cuenca	20.67	ES	Burgos	31.06	ES	Alicante	23.29
AU	Bendigo	25.88	ES	Albacete	8.83	ES	Guadalajara	27.54	US	Contra Costa	15.40
AU	Grampians	21.75	ES	Caceres	0.92	ES	La Rioja	25.77	ES	Albacete	13.10
AU	Kangaroo Island	20.59	ES	Avila, Palencia, Sal	0.80	ES	Valladolid	12.54	AU	Perricoota	9.61
US	Shasta	20.02	ES	Huesca, Teruel	0.52	ES	Zamora	12.42	US	Placer	7.73
AU	Barossa - Other	19.77	ES	Zaragoza	0.52	ES	Navarra	12.09	FR	Var	4.36
AU	Mclaren Vale	19.12	ES	Almeria, Granada, J	0.48	ES	Castellon	10.41	ES	Illes Balears	4.25
AU	Pyrenees	18.19	ES	Alicante	0.21	ES	Avila, Palencia, Salai	6.42	AU	Barossa - Other	3.16
AU	Rutherglen	18.06	ES	Illes Balears	0.19	PT	AltoTras-os-Mont.	4.46	US	San Diego	2.10
AU	Aus. Capital Terr.	17.90	ES	Castellon	0.19	PT	Alentejo	4.27	AU	Alpine/Bchworth	2.09
AU	Barossa Valley	17.80	ES	Tarragona	0.08	ES	Madrid	3.45	AU	Riverland	1.69
AU	Sthn NSW Other	17.77	ES	Madrid	0.04	ES	Huesca, Teruel	3.29	ES	Castellon	1.63
AU	Nthn Slopes Other	17.30	ES	Guadalajara	0.04	ES	Ciudad Real	3.03	AU	Eastern Plain etc.	1.63
AU	Southern Fleurieu	17.10	ES	Girona, Lleida	0.04	ES	Zaragoza	2.95	ES	Girona, Lleida	1.53
AU	Mudgee	16.45	ES	Region De Murcia	0.03	ES	Girona, Lleida	2.69	FR	Vaucluse	1.48
AU	Currency Creek	16.26	ES	Toledo	0.02	ES	Illes Balears	2.61	AU	Lower Murray Other	1.45
AU	Langhorne Creek	16.04	ES	Alava	0.02	ES	Valencia	1.61	TN	Tunisia	1.28
AU	Sunbury	15.47	ES	Zamora	0.02	AR	Mendoza	1.58	FR	Pyrenees-Orientales	1.16
AU	Orange	15.26	ES	Ciudad Real	0.02	ES	Cuenca	1.41	ES	Almeria, Granada, Jaen, St	1.14
AU	The Peninsulas	15.25	ES	Navarra	0.01	ES	Barcelona	1.37	FR	Bouches-du-Rhone	1.07
AU	Mt Lofty Rgs Other	15.05	ES	Valladolid	0.01	ES	Tarragona	1.03	FR	Aude	1.00
AU	Hilltops	14.94	ES	Badajoz	0.00	ES	Almeria, Granada, Ja	0.96	US	Riverside	0.98
AU	Clare Valley	14.81	ES	Burgos	0.00	ES	Badajoz	0.89	AU	Barossa Valley	0.97
AU	Central Vic Other	14.73	ES	Canarias	0.00	US	Stanislaus	0.84	US	San Bernardino	0.93

Table 47 (cont.) Varietal Intensity Indexes for the top 25 regions for world's top 30 red varieties, 2000

Sangiovese		Varietal Intensity Indexes	Pinot Noir		Varietal Intensity Indexes	Cabernet Franc		Varietal Intensity Indexes	Cinsaut		Varietal Intensity Indexes
	Region			Region			Region			Varietal Intensity Indexes	
IT	Siena	49.22	CH	Graubünden	62.36	FR	Deux-Sevres, Vienne	30.31	DZ	Algeria	25.19
IT	Firenze	46.65	CH	Schaffhausen	62.24	FR	Centre	24.46	FR	Var	16.63
IT	Rimini	45.73	CH	St. Gallen	60.31	FR	Pays de la Loire Other	22.29	FR	Bouches-du-Rhone	9.88
IT	Arezzo	44.18	US	Benton Co.	54.36	FR	Correze, Haute-Vienne	20.74	FR	Herault	9.84
IT	Prato	37.01	CH	Thurgau	52.86	IT	Venezia	13.98	FR	Alpes de Haute	9.76
IT	Pistoia	36.61	CH	Basel-Landschaft	51.52	FR	Aquitaine Other	13.50	ZA	Paarl	8.61
IT	Forli-Cesena	34.69	US	Yamhill Co.	49.12	FR	Gironde	11.45	FR	Gard	8.56
IT	Grosseto	27.56	CH	Zurich	48.79	IT	Udine	8.65	MA	Morocco	8.00
IT	Pisa	27.20	CH	Aargau	48.38	US	Nevada	8.06	ZA	Breedekloof	7.91
IT	Ascoli Piceno	25.61	US	Polk Co.	45.08	IT	Treviso	7.93	FR	Ardeche	6.67
IT	Pesaro e Urbino	21.76	CH	Other Region	42.57	IT	Gorizia	7.77	FR	Aude	5.68
IT	Lucca	19.41	US	Humboldt	40.58	IT	Pordenone	7.61	FR	Corse	5.26
IT	Matera	19.07	NZ	Central Otago	39.55	NZ	Auckland	7.58	TN	Tunisia	5.04
IT	Foggia	16.90	CH	Schwyz	36.71	IT	Padova	7.13	ZA	Malmesbury	5.03
IT	Isernia	16.08	US	Marion Co.	36.27	CA	Canada	6.70	FR	Vaucluse	4.77
IT	Bari	16.07	US	Other Valley	35.01	FR	Midi Pyren. Other	5.96	EL	Dytiki Makedonia	1.97
IT	Livorno	16.02	CH	Neuchÿtel	34.87	AU	Aus. Capital Terr.	5.91	IT	Brindisi	1.93
FR	Corse	15.84	US	Washington Co.	32.77	IT	Brescia	5.82	ZA	Worcester	1.93
IT	Perugia	15.12	FR	Champagne Ardenne	32.67	IT	Vicenza	5.47	EL	Thessalia	1.54
IT	Macerata	10.71	AU	Mornington Peninsula	31.37	US	Other New York	5.40	ZA	Stellenbosch	1.53
IT	Caserta	9.71	CH	Lucerne	30.30	IT	Lecco	5.37	FR	Rhone Alpes Other	1.17
IT	Rieti	8.99	US	Lane Co.	29.34	IT	Bergamo	4.70	EL	Kentriki Makedonia	1.15
IT	Taranto	8.77	US	Josephine Co.	28.65	AU	Hastings River	4.61	ZA	Robertson	1.03
US	San Diego	8.13	CH	Bern	28.54	US	Michigan	4.17	CL	Del Bio Bio	0.85
IT	Caltanissetta	7.45	CH	Valais	28.53	IT	Rovigo	4.17	ZA	Olifants River	0.66

Table 47 (cont.) Varietal Intensity Indexes for the top 25 regions for world's top 30 red varieties, 2000

	Gamay Noir	Varietal Intensity Indexes		Alicante Henri Bouschet	Region	Varietal Intensity Indexes		Barbera	Region	Varietal Intensity Indexes		Montepulciano	Region	Varietal Intensity Indexes
	Varietal Intensity Indexes													
FR	Auvergne	85.05	ES	Galicia	32.07	IT	Asti	72.50	IT	L'Aquila	114.15
FR	Rhone Alpes Other	64.82	DZ	Algeria	13.17	IT	Verbano-C.-Ossola	56.93	IT	Pescara	113.91
FR	Lorraine	49.82	IT	Reggio di Calabria	9.93	IT	Alessandria	52.37	IT	Teramo	98.20
CH	Geneva	44.88	ES	Albacete	7.46	IT	Piacenza	42.96	IT	Campobasso	80.91
CH	Valais	23.57	TU	Tunisia	6.58	IT	Salerno	42.76	IT	Chieti	73.93
FR	Centre	18.57	ES	Huesca, Teruel	5.81	IT	Torino	42.27	IT	Ascoli Piceno	36.75
CH	Vaud	18.10	ES	Leon	5.25	IT	Milano	39.79	IT	Isernia	35.84
FR	Correze, Haute-Vienne	15.27	CL	O'Higgins	5.17	IT	Pavia	36.55	IT	Bari	22.42
FR	Bourgogne	14.72	US	San Bernardino	4.87	IT	Lodi	36.35	IT	Ancona	17.63
FR	Deux-Sevres, Vienne	14.66	FR	Herault	4.48	IT	Biella	33.62	IT	Foggia	16.57
US	San Benito	9.58	IT	Catania	3.93	IT	Varese	26.12	IT	Macerata	16.37
FR	Midi Pyren. Other	8.79	CL	Del Maule	3.93	IT	Cuneo	22.27	IT	Rieti	10.78
FR	Pays de la Loire Other	7.45	US	Tulare	3.75	US	Fresno	21.50	IT	Caserta	9.84
FR	Ardeche	7.10	FR	Aude	3.54	IT	Lecco	20.13	IT	Taranto	8.93
US	Solano	5.84	PT	Alentejo	3.12	IT	Parma	15.86	IT	Pesaro e Urbino	7.62
IT	Valle d'Aosta	5.56	FR	Gard	3.02	IT	Vercelli	14.55	IT	Benevento	6.87
CA	Canada	3.99	CL	Metropolitana	2.97	IT	Brescia	13.33	IT	Matera	6.16
US	Monterey	2.41	MA	Morocco	2.92	IT	Caserta	11.81	IT	Viterbo	5.35
US	San Diego	2.12	FR	Bouches-du-Rhone	2.89	AU	The Peninsulas	11.79	IT	Frosinone	4.51
US	Tehama	1.99	ES	Alicante	2.82	IT	Como	10.98	IT	Brindisi	4.43
	Lake	1.92	ES	Castellon	2.73	IT	Cremona	10.06	IT	Avellino	3.61
CH	Fribourg	1.83	US	Kings	2.30	US	Stanislaus	8.91	IT	Roma	3.23
IT	Perugia	1.12	ES	Zamora	2.09	IT	Benevento	8.61	IT	Terni	2.55
US	Mendocino	1.11	CL	Coquimbo	1.84	US	Merced	6.98	IT	Salerno	2.31
FR	France2	1.09	US	Fresno	1.69	US	Amador	6.83	IT	Grosseto	2.29

Table 47 (cont.) Varietal Intensity Indexes for the top 25 regions for world's top 30 red varieties, 2000

Isabella			Tribidrag			Criolla Grande			Cot		
	Region	Varietal Intensity Indexes		Region	Varietal Intensity Indexes		Region	Varietal Intensity Indexes		Region	Varietal Intensity Indexes
BR	Brazil	48.18	US	Colusa	154.46	AR	Mendoza	33.24	FR	Midi Pyren. Other	40.41
MD	Moldova	22.61	US	Amador	130.61	AR	San Juan	3.85	AR	Mendoza	20.32
M9	Missing 9	3.72	US	San Bernardino	92.33	AR	Other Regions	0.94	AR	Other Regions	12.44
US	Finger Lakes	0.76	US	Butte	81.81				AU	Perricoota	6.92
DZ	Algeria	0.00	US	San Joaquin	64.59				NZ	Auckland	5.15
AR	Mendoza	0.00	IT	Taranto	62.27				AR	San Juan	4.82
AR	San Juan	0.00	US	Placer	61.74				FR	Centre	4.26
AR	Other Regions	0.00	US	Contra Costa	54.00				AU	Bendigo	3.56
AM	Armenia	0.00	US	El Dorado	46.83				IT	Belluno	3.47
AU	Adelaide Hills	0.00	US	Sutter	45.31				AU	Great Southern	3.44
AU	Alpine/Bchworth	0.00	US	Glenn	44.39				CL	O'Higgins	3.39
AU	Aus. Capital Terr.	0.00	US	Mariposa	35.60				AU	Mt Lofty Rgs Other	3.28
AU	Barossa - Other	0.00	US	Calavaras	28.38				FR	Aquitaine Other	3.25
AU	Barossa Valley	0.00	US	Mendocino	25.24				NZ	Hawkes Bay	3.05
AU	Beechworth	0.00	US	Ventura	22.66				AU	Barossa - Other	2.41
AU	Bendigo	0.00	US	San Luis Obispo	21.52				AU	Padthaway	2.41
AU	Big Rivers - Other	0.00	US	Lake	21.38				NZ	Waikato	2.34
AU	Blackwood Valley	0.00	US	Kings	19.40				AU	Pyrenees	2.33
AU	Canberra District	0.00	US	Sonoma	19.37				AU	Clare Valley	2.07
AU	C. Ranges Other	0.00	US	Sacramento	16.41				IT	Venezia	2.05
AU	Central Vic Other	0.00	US	Stanislaus	15.47				AU	Langhorne Creek	1.87
AU	Central WA	0.00	US	Merced	15.19				AU	Nthn Slopes Other	1.84
AU	Clare Valley	0.00	US	Alameda	14.92				AU	Swan District	1.80
AU	Cowra	0.00	IT	Bari	14.89				NZ	Wairarapa	1.71
AU	Currency Creek	0.00	US	Kern	14.62				FR	Gironde	1.64

Table 47 (cont.) Varietal Intensity Indexes for the top 25 regions for world's top 30 red varieties, 2000

	Pamid			Douce Noire			Negroamaro			Doukkali	
	Region	Varietal Intensity Indexes		Region	Varietal Intensity Indexes		Region	Varietal Intensity Indexes		Region	Varietal Intensity Indexes
BG	Bulgaria	50.51	IT	Varese	45.72	IT	Lecce	242.24	MA	Morocco	98.35
EL	Dytiki Makedonia	1.92	IT	Pavia	41.59	IT	Brindisi	161.74			
HU	Hungary	0.30	AR	Mendoza	25.08	IT	Taranto	15.83			
			IT	Biella	22.33	IT	Matera	1.99			
			IT	Parma	19.04	IT	Reggio di Calabria	1.05			
			IT	Lodi	17.42	IT	Cosenza	0.52			
			AR	Other Regions	12.86	IT	Potenza	0.40			
			IT	Vercelli	12.24	IT	Enna	0.28			
			IT	Torino	9.59	IT	Agrigento	0.25			
			AR	San Juan	9.14	IT	Messina	0.22			
			IT	Lecco	3.74	IT	Asti	0.18			
			IT	Piacenza	3.16	IT	Cuneo	0.15			
			US	Nevada	2.96	IT	Catania	0.13			
			IT	Asti	2.06	IT	Bari	0.10			
			IT	Novara	1.80	IT	Salerno	0.08			
			IT	Cuneo	0.77	IT	Valle d'Aosta	0.06			
			IT	Massa-Carrara	0.75	IT	Foggia	0.05			
			IT	Terni	0.65	IT	Catanzaro	0.04			
			IT	Genova	0.56	IT	Pavia	0.04			
			US	Santa Clara	0.51	IT	Torino	0.03			
			IT	Bergamo	0.51	IT	Pordenone	0.03			
			IT	Messina	0.45	IT	Caserta	0.02			
			IT	Rovigo	0.43	IT	Nuoro	0.02			
			IT	Nell'Emilia	0.41		Campobasso	0.02			
			IT	Mantova	0.39	IT	Trento	0.02			

Table 47 (cont.) Varietal Intensity Indexes for the top 25 regions for world's top 30 red varieties, 2000

Listan Prieto			Prokupac			Castelao			Mencia		
	Region	Varietal Intensity Indexes		Region	Varietal Intensity Indexes		Region	Varietal Intensity Indexes		Region	Varietal Intensity Indexes
CL	Del Bio Bio	129.36	RS	Serbia	70.70	PT	Ribatejo E Oeste	81.30	ES	Cantabria	181.47
US	Placer	82.83				PT	Algarve	54.66	ES	Principado de Asturias	154.78
CL	Del Maule	63.29				PT	Alentejo	53.53	ES	Leon	138.72
US	San Bernardino	52.65				PT	Beira Litoral	4.12	ES	Galicia	30.63
US	Kings	5.36				PT	Acores	2.19	ES	Almeria, Granada, Jaen, Sev	29.79
CL	Valparaiso	3.81				PT	Beira Interior	1.88	ES	Zamora	25.91
US	Stanislaus	3.77							PT	Beira Litoral	22.81
CL	O'Higgins	3.42							PT	Beira Interior	8.94
CL	Coquimbo	1.73							ES	Avila, Palencia, Salamanca,	4.38
US	Santa Clara	1.44							ES	Burgos	3.39
US	Amador	1.25							ES	Valladolid	1.45
US	Riverside	1.05							ES	Badajoz	1.31
US	Tulare	1.02							ES	Caceres	0.09
US	San Joaquin	0.99							ES	Albacete	0.04
US	Fresno	0.84							ES	Guadalajara	0.03
ES	Illes Balears	0.83							ES	Huesca, Teruel	0.01
US	Merced	0.39							ES	Barcelona	0.00
ES	Cantabria	0.32							ES	Cuenca	0.00
US	Madera	0.20							ES	Valencia	0.00
CL	Metropolitana	0.17									
ES	Canarias	0.11									
US	Sonoma	0.03									
ES	Galicia	0.01									

Table 47 (cont.) Varietal Intensity Indexes for the top 25 regions for world's top 30 red varieties, 2000

	Blaufrankisch			Concord	
	Region	Varietal Intensity Indexes		Region	Varietal Intensity Indexes
AT	Burgenland	64.95	AT	Burgenland	64.95
HU	Hungary	30.17	HU	Hungary	30.17
SK	Slovakia	26.51	SK	Slovakia	26.51
CZ	Czechrepublic	22.73	CZ	Czechrepubl	22.73
IT	Bergamo	13.90	IT	Bergamo	13.90
HR	Croatia	7.58	HR	Croatia	7.58
IT	Varese	4.94	IT	Varese	4.94
AT	Wien and other	3.15	AT	Wien and c	3.15
IT	Udine	2.80	IT	Udine	2.80
US	Washington	2.45	US	Washington	2.45
AT	Steiermark	2.00	AT	Steiermark	2.00
AT	Niederosterreich	1.57	AT	Niederoste	1.57
IT	Valle d'Aosta	1.38	IT	Valle d'Ao	1.38
M9	Missing 9	0.96	M9	Missing 9	0.96
IT	Gorizia	0.86	IT	Gorizia	0.86
IT	Trieste	0.73	IT	Trieste	0.73
IT	Genova	0.52	IT	Genova	0.52
IT	Salerno	0.19	IT	Salerno	0.19
IT	Venezia	0.15	IT	Venezia	0.15
IT	Biella	0.14	IT	Biella	0.14
IT	Potenza	0.13	IT	Potenza	0.13
IT	Torino	0.09	IT	Torino	0.09
IT	Cosenza	0.08	IT	Cosenza	0.08
IT	Terni	0.05	IT	Terni	0.05
IT	Lucca	0.04	IT	Lucca	0.04

Table 48: Varietal Intensity Indexes for top 25 regions for world's top 30 red varieties, 2010

Cabernet Sauvignon			Merlot			Tempranillo			Syrah		
	Region	Varietal Intensity Indexes		Region	Varietal Intensity Indexes		Region	Varietal Intensity Indexes		Region	Varietal Intensity Indexes
CN	Beijing	15.86	CN	Other Region	14.55	ES	Burgos	18.66	AU	Sthn Flinders	20.15
CN	Shandong	15.86	CH	Ticino	13.79	ES	Rioja	14.09	AU	Barossa Other	18.95
CN	Sichuan	15.86	JP	Nagano	10.09	ES	Alava	11.95	US	Ventura	17.17
CN	Tianjin	15.86	FR	Gironde	9.60	ES	Zamora	11.53	AU	Grampians	15.82
CN	Yantai	15.72	US	Shasta	8.61	ES	Guadalajara	10.62	AU	Far North Other	14.43
CN	Ningxia	12.22	JP	Yamagata	8.50	ES	Navarra	9.81	AU	Heathcote	14.40
CN	Gansu	10.18	FR	Lot Et Garonne	6.04	ES	Valladolid	8.39	US	Tuolumne	14.05
CN	Xinjiang	10.12	FR	Dordogne	5.58	ES	Avila, Palencia, Salaman	5.83	AU	Gundagai	13.39
AU	Coonawarra	9.07	BG	Yuzhen Tsentralen	5.46	ES	Badajoz	5.12	AU	Bendigo	13.36
US	Red Mountain	8.37	US	Wahluke Slope	3.99	ES	Castellon	4.83	AU	Central Vic Other	13.28
CL	Metropolitana	8.35	US	Rattlesnake Hills	3.95	ES	Ciudad Real	3.90	AU	Barossa Valley	13.24
US	Butte	7.71	AU	N. E. Vic Other	3.88	PT	Alentejo	3.77	AU	Mt Lofty Rgs Other	12.84
AU	Wrattonbully	7.07	US	Humboldt	3.85	ES	Zaragoza	3.44	AU	Mclaren Vale	12.76
US	Napa	6.69	AU	C. Ranges Other	3.80	ES	Caceres	3.41	AU	Fleurieu Other	11.24
CL	O'Higgins	6.57	CN	Xinjiang	3.66	ES	Cuenca	3.40	AU	Pyrenees	11.15
US	Los Angeles	6.56	SI	Vipavska Dolina	3.61	ES	Albacete	2.85	TH	Thailand	11.02
AU	Far North Other	6.49	AU	Alpine Valleys	3.57	AU	Southern Highlands	2.62	AU	Rutherglen	10.81
CN	Shanxi	6.38	NZ	Hawkes Bay	3.56	PT	Alto Tras-Os-Montes	2.59	AU	Greater Perth Other	10.81
US	Walla Walla Valley	6.37	EL	Anatoliki Mak., Thraki	3.51	ES	Valencia	2.55	AU	SE Coastal WA	10.74
AU	Limestone C.Other	6.19	US	Columbia Valley	3.34	FR	Other Regions	2.23	AU	West Plains Other	10.55
CL	Del Maule	5.93	US	Horse Heaven Hills	3.33	ES	Huesca, Teruel	2.13	AU	Glenrowan	10.30
US	Lake	5.91	SI	Goriska Brda	3.26	ES	Girona, Lleida	1.93	AU	Kangaroo Island	10.00
AU	Hilltops	5.72	CN	Gansu	3.22	PT	Beira Litoral	1.90	AU	Lower Murray Other	9.74
JP	Yamanashi	5.54	US	Merced	3.19	ES	Toledo	1.72	AU	Central WA	9.52
AU	Fleurieu Other	5.31	US	Mariposa	3.18	ES	Madrid	1.62	AU	Southern Fleurieu	9.51

Table 48 (cont.) Varietal Intensity Indexes for top 25 regions for world's top 30 red varieties, 2010

Garnacha Tinta		Varietal Intensity Indexes	Pinot Noir		Varietal Intensity Indexes	Mazuelo		Varietal Intensity Indexes	Bobal		Varietal Intensity Indexes
Region				Region			Region			Region	
FR	Vaucluse	12.37	US	Marin	43.38	TN	Tunisia	25.83	ES	Valencia	32.77
ES	Zaragoza	11.73	US	Yamhill Co.	42.44	MX	Aguascalientes	25.32	ES	Cuenca	19.45
FR	Drome	11.63	US	Polk Co.	41.82	DZ	Algeria	14.35	ES	Albacete	8.48
ES	Madrid	10.59	NZ	Otago	41.66	FR	Aude	12.34	ES	Caceres	1.31
FR	Bouches Du Rhone	7.71	CH	Graubünden	40.97	FR	Herault	9.62	ES	Zaragoza	0.62
ES	Avila, Palencia, Salam	7.64	US	Benton Co.	39.93	FR	Pyrenees Orientales	8.25	ES	Castellon	0.28
IT	Sardegna	7.34	CH	Schaffhausen	37.04	FR	Var	7.73	ES	Huesca, Teruel	0.28
FR	Gard	6.86	FR	Cote D'Or	36.14	IT	Sardegna	5.80	ES	Alicante	0.19
FR	Var	6.47	US	Washington Co.	35.37	FR	Bouches Du Rhone	5.25	ES	Madrid	0.13
ES	Huesca, Teruel	6.35	CH	St. Gallen	34.89	FR	Gard	5.00	ES	Almeria, Granada, J	0.11
FR	Pyrenees Orientales	5.63	FR	Other Regions	34.72	FR	Vaucluse	4.17	ES	Avila, Palencia, Sal:	0.06
DZ	Algeria	4.98	US	Other W. Valley	32.98	MX	Zacatecas	3.71	ES	Badajoz	0.05
FR	Ardeche	4.82	CH	Thurgau	31.36	FR	Drome	3.40	ES	Toledo	0.04
US	Glenn	4.80	CH	Basel-Landschaft	31.31	MM	Myanmar	3.37	ES	Guadalajara	0.03
ES	Navarra	4.23	CH	Aargau	30.36	CY	Cyprus	3.21	ES	Ciudad Real	0.02
ES	Asturias	3.95	CH	Zurich	29.00	US	San Diego	2.97	ES	Murcia	0.01
US	Kings	3.92	NZ	Wairarapa	28.74	MX	Sonora	2.61	ES	Navarra	0.01
ES	Alava	3.69	US	Marion Co.	27.96	US	Madera	2.07	ES	Canarias	0.01
ES	Toledo	3.56	US	Douglas Co.	27.62	US	San Bernardino	2.00	ES	Alava	0.00
ES	Castellon	3.45	CH	Neuchytel	26.95	MA	Morocco	1.98			
ES	Zamora	3.27	US	Puget Sound	24.76	ES	Rioja	1.94			
ES	Rioja	3.15	US	Santa Cruz	24.46	FR	Provence-C. D'Azur-Other	1.80			
FR	Provence-C. D'Azur-Ot	3.01	US	Josephine Co.	23.44	US	Contra Costa	1.79			
TN	Tunisia	2.99	AU	Mornington Penin:	22.98	FR	Ardeche	1.72			
ES	Tarragona	2.96	US	San Mateo	22.86	ES	Alava	1.50			

Table 48 (cont.) Varietal Intensity Indexes for top 25 regions for world's top 30 red varieties, 2010

	Sangiovese	Varietal Intensity Indexes		Monastrell	Varietal Intensity Indexes		Cabernet Franc	Varietal Intensity Indexes		Cot	Varietal Intensity Indexes
	Region			Region			Region			Region	
IT	Toscana	37.85	ES	Murcia	54.38	FR	Indre Et Loire	44.03	FR	Lot	76.32
FR	Corse	13.41	ES	Alicante	36.31	FR	Maine Et Loire	35.86	AR	Lujan De Cuyo	54.33
IT	Marche	12.60	FR	Other Regions	16.58	FR	Vienne	24.81	AR	Tunuyan	46.54
IT	Umbria	11.68	ES	Albacete	12.48	FR	Other Regions	21.68	AR	Neuquen	40.23
IT	Emilia-Romagna	9.08	US	Contra Costa	6.67	FR	Poitou-Charentes-Other	19.34	AR	Tupungato	37.22
IT	Puglia	8.95	FR	Var	4.50	CN	Shanxi	18.84	AR	Other-Mendoza	35.73
US	Tuolumne	7.90	ES	Illes Balears	3.50	FR	Lot Et Garonne	12.96	AR	Salta	31.15
IT	Basilicata	4.67	ES	Castellon	2.23	AU	Pyrenees	11.95	AR	Maipu	28.69
US	Mariposa	3.98	FR	Pyrenees Orientales	2.14	FR	Aquitaine-Other	10.81	AR	Rio Negro	22.81
IT	Campania	3.26	AU	Lower Murray Other	2.10	HU	Villany	10.59	AR	Other-Argentinan	22.55
IT	Molise	3.14	US	Placer	1.91	US	Nevada	10.46	AR	Junin	13.69
US	San Diego	3.07	FR	Vaucluse	1.78	FR	Landes	10.38	AR	San Rafael	12.35
TN	Tunisiatotal	2.96	US	El Dorado	1.57	FR	Midi Pyrenees-Other	10.27	AR	Rivadavia	12.22
IT	Lazio	2.95	FR	Aude	1.50	FR	Dordogne	9.29	AR	Catamarca	10.23
AU	Central WA	2.89	ES	Valencia	1.47	US	Virginia	9.20	AR	Sarmiento	10.08
AU	Limestone C.Other	2.86	CL	Atacama	1.42	FR	Tarn Et Garonne	8.89	AR	Ullum	9.73
IT	Liguria	2.82	TN	Tunisia	1.32	FR	Gironde	8.59	AR	La Rioja	9.23
US	Riverside	2.59	CY	Cyprus	1.32	HU	Szekszard	8.59	FR	Indre	8.65
CL	Atacama	2.55	AU	Barossa Valley	1.29	US	Kentucky	6.63	FR	Other Regions	7.60
AU	Kangaroo Island	2.53	US	Mariposa	1.11	CA	Ontario	6.40	NZ	Waikato	7.37
US	Trinity	2.45	FR	Gard	0.96	FR	Loir Et Cher	6.24	CL	Atacama	7.31
AU	Alpine Valleys	2.12	FR	Bouches Du Rhone	0.92	FR	Pays De Loire-Other	6.00	AR	San Martin S	7.13
US	Nevada	2.10	AU	Greater Perth Other	0.92	US	Placer	5.99	AR	Other-San Juan	6.72
US	Amador	2.06	AU	Padthaway	0.90	US	Other New Yorkn	5.97	AR	Rawson	6.39
AR	Maipu	1.92	AU	Heathcote	0.85	IT	Friuli Venezia Giul.	5.66	AR	25 De Mayo	6.33

Table 48 (cont.) Varietal Intensity Indexes for top 25 regions for world's top 30 red varieties, 2010

Alicante Henri Bouschet		Cinsaut		Montepulciano		Tribidrag	
Region	Varietal Intensity Indexes	Region	Varietal Intensity Indexes	Region	Varietal Intensity Indexes	Region	Varietal Intensity Indexes
FR Other Regions	30.93	TU Marmara	36.58	IT Abruzzo	72.99	US San Bernardino	107.64
ES Galicia	22.12	DZ Algeria	31.92	IT Molise	64.54	US Amador	86.49
CL Atacama	15.25	FR Var	20.92	IT Marche	25.27	US Colusa	72.73
DZ Algeria	11.80	FR Bouches Du Rhone	10.54	IT Puglia	14.45	US San Joaquin	41.26
ES Albacete	10.71	MA Morocco	10.27	IT Lazio	4.78	US Sutter	37.75
TU Ege	8.50	FR Provence-C. D'Azur-Other	8.98	IT Basilicata	3.92	US Butte	37.08
PT Alentejo	8.26	FR Herault	7.91	IT Campania	3.62	US Placer	35.95
TN Tunisia	5.90	FR Other Regions	7.21	AR Ullum	3.14	US Glenn	34.53
CL Del Maule	5.48	FR Gard	6.76	IT Umbria	2.09	US Contra Costa	31.34
PT Ribatejo E Oeste	4.99	TN Tunisia	6.38	IT Sardegna	1.06	US Mariposa	28.34
CL O'Higgins	4.85	ZA Paarl	5.95	IT Calabria	0.74	US El Dorado	27.48
ES Avila, Palencia, Salama	4.37	ZA Breedekloof	5.66	AR 25 De Mayo	0.60	US Kings	23.20
ES Alicante	4.07	CL Del Bio Bio	5.60	IT Liguria	0.58	US Stanislaus	20.09
CL Coquimbo	3.77	FR Vaucluse	4.32	IT Toscana	0.57	IT Puglia	19.98
CL Metropolitana	3.65	FR Ardeche	3.83	AR San Martin S	0.52	US Merced	18.36
MA Morocco	2.64	FR Aude	3.78	IT Valle D'Aosta	0.46	US Mendocino	16.88
FR Herault	2.57	ZA Malmesbury	3.33	US Contra Costa	0.39	US Tulare	15.88
ES Castellon	2.53	FR Drome	2.37	AR 9 De Julio	0.38	US San Luis Obispo	14.77
US Tulare	2.46	ZA Worcester	1.38	AR Caucete	0.34	US Calaveras	14.16
ES Murcia	2.12	EL Kentriki Makedonia	1.28	US Tulare	0.30	US Siskiyou	14.05
ES Cuenca	1.96	ZA Stellenbosch	1.06	Amador	0.25	US Sonoma	13.00
ES Huesca, Teruel	1.76	US Riverside	0.93	US Calaveras	0.21	US Madera	12.30
ES Caceres	1.71	ZA Robertson	0.73	AR Other-Argentinan	0.19	US Sacramento	11.69
FR Bouches Du Rhone	1.66	ZA Olifants River	0.47	IT Emilia-Romagna	0.15	US Trinity	11.61
FR Gard	1.43	US Contra Costa	0.23	US Mendocino	0.09	US Lake	11.35

Table 48 (cont.) Varietal Intensity Indexes for top 25 regions for world's top 30 red varieties, 2010

Gamay Noir			Isabella			Barbera			Douce Noire		
	Region	Varietal Intensity Indexes		Region	Varietal Intensity Indexes		Region	Varietal Intensity Indexes		Region	Varietal Intensity Indexes
FR	Rhone	138.26	BR	Brazil	52.38	IT	Piemonte	57.15	AR	Lavalle	37.28
FR	Indre	59.10	MD	Moldova	17.97	US	Fresno	20.99	AR	Santa Rosa	34.57
FR	Rhone-Alpes-Other	46.42	UA	Ukraine	6.49	IT	Lombardia	20.85	AR	San Martin	30.63
CH	Geneva	40.41	UY	Uruguay	4.73	US	Placer	11.07	AR	Rivadavia	29.96
FR	Loir Et Cher	32.36	RU	Krasnodar Krai	1.08	IT	Campania	10.97	AR	San Rafael	28.36
FR	Other Regions	31.00				SI	Vipavska Dolina	10.07	AR	Sarmiento	23.59
FR	Vendee	27.36				US	Amador	9.52	AR	Junin	23.37
FR	Saone Et Loire	24.97				AU	Sunbury	7.81	AR	Tupungato	22.67
FR	Vienne	22.84				US	Tulare	7.43	AR	La Rioja	20.47
CH	Valais	19.59				IT	Emilia-Romagna	7.39	AR	9 De Julio	18.63
TU	Marmara	16.65				US	El Dorado	7.35	AR	Caucete	18.23
CH	Vaud	16.33				US	Madera	7.19	AR	Maipu	18.15
FR	Tarn	13.97				US	Kings	4.76	AR	San Martin S	15.05
LU	Luxembourg	10.58				AR	La Rioja	3.78	AR	25 De Mayo	13.85
FR	Ardeche	8.02				US	Ventura	3.66	AR	Other-Mendoza	13.45
FR	Indre Et Loire	7.74				US	Nevada	3.38	AR	Ullum	13.20
FR	Maine Et Loire	6.87				AU	Perricoota	2.84	AR	Other-San Juan	12.54
FR	Loire Atlantique	6.65				US	Butte	2.64	AR	Catamarca	11.16
FR	Tarn Et Garonne	5.95				AU	South Burnett	2.54	AR	Pocito	10.00
IT	Valle D'Aosta	5.15				US	Alameda	2.29	AR	Lujan De Cuyo	9.99
FR	Centre-Other	5.15				AU	South Coast - Other	2.19	AR	Albardon	7.68
FR	Lot	5.11				IT	Basilicata	2.00	AR	Angaco	7.68
FR	Nievre	4.47				AR	Other-Argentinan	2.00	AR	Tunuyan	5.76
FR	Cher	4.13				AU	Geographe	1.93	AR	Rawson	4.99
CA	Ontario	3.65				US	Shasta	1.87	AR	Salta	4.46

Table 48 (cont.) Varietal Intensity Indexes for top 25 regions for world's top 30 red varieties, 2010

Criolla Grande			Nero d'Avola			Doukkali			Blaufrankisch		
	Region	Varietal Intensity Indexes		Region	Varietal Intensity Indexes		Region	Varietal Intensity Indexes		Region	Varietal Intensity Indexes
AR	San Martin	54.19	IT	Sicilia	43.54	MA	Morocco	93.91	HU	Sopron	164.64
AR	Junin	51.76	IT	Calabria	4.26				PE	Lima	93.21
AR	Rivadavia	49.03	IT	Basilicata	0.17				HU	Szekszard	82.30
AR	Santa Rosa	32.61	IT	Lazio	0.13				HU	Csongrad	76.09
AR	San Rafael	31.44	IT	Toscana	0.12				AT	Burgenland	62.88
AR	Lavalle	21.27	IT	Veneto	0.11				HU	Hajos-Bajai	58.93
AR	Other-Mendoza	18.64	IT	Puglia	0.08				SI	Bela Krajina	57.92
AR	Maipu	8.48	IT	Campania	0.05				SI	Bizeljsko Sremic	54.52
AR	25 De Mayo	6.04	IT	Umbria	0.04				HU	Eger	52.06
AR	Sarmiento	5.61	IT	Marche	0.02				SI	Dolenjska	50.99
AR	Caucete	4.29	IT	Molise	0.01				HU	Bukk	50.93
AR	Albardon	4.11	IT	Sardegna	0.01				SK	Vychodoslovenska	46.23
AR	Lujan De Cuyo	3.46	IT	Friuli Venezia Giul.	0.00					Stredoslovenska	42.26
AR	Angaco	3.30	IT	Abruzzo	0.00				HU	Tolna	39.14
AR	Other-San Juan	3.05							SK	Juznoslovenska	38.15
AR	San Martin S	2.96							SI	Other	36.16
AR	9 De Julio	2.92							HU	Kunsag	35.00
AR	Rawson	2.00							HR	Moslavina	28.82
AR	Rio Negro	1.16							HU	Villany	27.14
AR	Catamarca	1.05							SK	Malokarpatska	25.59
AR	Tupungato	0.84							SK	Nitrianska	24.23
AR	La Rioja	0.71							HU	Matra	22.33
AR	Other-Argentinan	0.48							CZ	Morava	21.12
AR	Tunuyan	0.38							HR	Slavonija	20.57
AR	Pocito	0.35							HR	Podunavlje	17.16

Table 48 (cont.) Varietal Intensity Indexes for top 25 regions for world's top 30 red varieties, 2010

Prokupac			Concord			Touriga Franca			Negroamaro		
	Region	Varietal Intensity Indexes		Region	Varietal Intensity Indexes		Region	Varietal Intensity Indexes		Region	Varietal Intensity Indexes
SR	Serbia	66.69	US	Chautauqua-Erien	325.32	PT	Alto Tras-Os-Montes	71.16	IT	Puglia	55.27
			US	Ohio	231.95	PT	Beira Interior	11.78	IT	Liguria	1.56
			US	Pennsylvania	159.72	PT	Ribatejo E Oeste	4.53	IT	Valle D'Aosta	0.65
			US	Finger Lakesn	88.87	PT	Alentejo	1.38	IT	Basilicata	0.65
			US	Other New Yorkn	50.15	PT	Entre Douro E Minho	0.83	IT	Molise	0.38
			US	Missouri	32.88	PT	Algarve	0.36	IT	Lombardia	0.19
			BR	Brazil	26.96	PT	Beira Litoral	0.31	IT	Calabria	0.19
			US	Iowa	16.82				IT	Piemonte	0.09
			CA	Ontario	15.53				IT	Umbria	0.08
			US	Kentucky	6.53				IT	Campania	0.07
			US	Virginia	5.21				IT	Sicilia	0.04
			UY	Uruguay	1.08				IT	Emilia-Romagna	0.02
									IT	Veneto	0.01
									IT	Marche	0.01
									IT	Friuli Venezia Giul.	0.01
									IT	Sardegna	0.00
									IT	Toscana	0.00

Table 48 (cont.) Varietal Intensity Indexes for top 25 regions for world's top 30 red varieties, 2010

Carmenere			Pinot Meunier		
	Region	Varietal Intensity Indexes		Region	Varietal Intensity Indexes
CL	O'Higgins	52.72	FR	Champagne-Viticole	139.44
CN	Ningxia	45.99	UK	Uk	17.05
CL	Coquimbo	29.49	US	Riverside	2.48
CL	Metropolitana	26.85	US	Sonoma	0.85
CL	Del Maule	24.70	ES	Guipuzcoa, Vizcaya	0.55
CL	Atacama	17.44	CA	British Colombia	0.47
CL	Del Bio Bio	7.93	US	Napa	0.28
CN	Gansu	7.04	AR	Salta	0.18
CL	Valparaiso	4.56	US	Mendocino	0.13
HR	Istra	2.44	US	San Luis Obispo	0.10
IT	Lazio	2.02	IT	Lombardia	0.06
IT	Basilicata	1.88	IT	Molise	0.03
IT	Friuli Venezia Giul.	1.88	IT	Sicilia	0.03
IT	Sardegna	1.65	IT	Toscana	0.01
AR	La Rioja	1.39	IT	Trentino Alto Adige	0.00
IT	Molise	1.32	IT	Marche	0.00
IT	Veneto	1.15	IT	Veneto	0.00
IT	Lombardia	0.89	IT	Emilia-Romagna	0.00
IT	Calabria	0.82	IT	Puglia	0.00
IT	Umbria	0.68			
IT	Sicilia	0.65			
IT	Puglia	0.62			
AR	Lujan De Cuyo	0.53			
IT	Toscana	0.48			
US	Madera	0.42			

Table 49: Varietal Intensity Indexes for the top 25 regions for world's top 30 white varieties, 2000

	Airen			Chardonnay			Trebbiano Toscano			Grasevina	
	Region	Varietal Intensity Indexes		Region	Varietal Intensity Indexes		Region	Varietal Intensity Indexes		Region	Varietal Intensity Indexes
ES	Ciudad Real	10.38	CL	Araucania	33.56	FR	Charente	34.42	SR	Serbia	25.37
ES	Toledo	9.25	US	Santa Barbara	21.10	FR	Charente-Maritime	33.00	ES	Caceres	16.31
ES	Cuenca	5.44	US	Santa Cruz	20.85	US	Los Angeles	15.48	HR	Croatia	14.27
ES	Madrid	4.73	US	Riverside	19.82	FR	Gers	12.66	SK	Slovakia	13.21
ES	Albacete	4.36	US	Tehama	19.62	IT	Pisa	10.04	AT	Steiermark	11.21
ES	Guadalajara	4.31	US	Shasta	19.58	IT	Terni	9.64	SI	Slovenia	8.03
ES	Almeria, Granada, Jaen, S	0.65	US	Yolo	19.17	IT	Latina	9.38	AT	Burgenland	7.17
ES	Region De Murcia	0.63	US	San Mateo	17.85	IT	Chieti	9.00	IT	Pavia	6.54
ES	Malaga	0.45	US	Sutter	16.78	IT	Viterbo	8.95	CZ	Czechrepublic	5.81
ES	Cordoba	0.34	US	Monterey	16.73	IT	Roma	8.45	HU	Hungary	4.06
ES	Alicante	0.09	NZ	Gisborne	16.24	IT	Foggia	8.22	RO	Romania	3.57
ES	Huelva	0.02	AU	Tumbarumba	15.49	IT	Livorno	8.19	AT	Niederosterreich	2.85
ES	Caceres	0.02	FR	France2	15.24	IT	Lucca	7.10	AT	Wien and other	2.54
ES	Badajoz	0.02	FR	Bourgogne	14.62	IT	Pistoia	7.04	BG	Bulgaria	1.98
ES	Canarias	0.01	CL	Valparaiso	14.01	IT	Grosseto	6.92	IT	Lecco	1.49
ES	Valencia	0.01	US	Alameda	12.97	IT	Perugia	6.43	IT	Milano	1.14
ES	Zamora	0.01	US	Santa Clara	12.64	IT	Prato	6.12	BR	Brazil	0.88
ES	Zaragoza	0.01	AU	Hunter Valley Othe	12.52	IT	Arezzo	5.05	IT	Rovigo	0.40
ES	Valladolid	0.00	AU	Cowra	11.91	IT	Agrigento	4.96	ES	Badajoz	0.37
ES	Castellon	0.00	AU	Hunter	11.78	IT	Firenze	4.22	IT	Gorizia	0.37
ES	Burgos	0.00	US	Sacramento	11.78	IT	Frosinone	3.86	IT	Bologna	0.26
ES	Avila, Palencia, Salamanc	0.00	US	Nevada	11.49	IT	Ascoli Piceno	3.81	IT	Piacenza	0.24
ES	Girona, Lleida	0.00	US	Sonoma	11.39	IT	Benevento	3.71	IT	Venezia	0.23
ES	Navarra	0.00	US	Mendocino	11.25	IT	Palermo	3.52	IT	Pordenone	0.16
ES	Rioja	0.00	US	Solano	11.14	IT	Campobasso	3.36	IT	Padova	0.15

Table 49 (cont.) Varietal Intensity Indexes for the top 25 regions for world's top 30 white varieties, 2000

Rkatsiteli			Sauvignon Blanc			Cayetana Blanca			Catarratto Bianco		
	Region	Varietal Intensity Indexes		Region	Varietal Intensity Indexes		Region	Varietal Intensity Indexes		Region	Varietal Intensity Indexes
GE	Georgia	38.21	NZ	Marlborough	35.23	ES	Badajoz	59.36	IT	Trapani	61.18
RU	Russia	16.91	EL	Anatoliki Mak.Thraki	23.43	ES	Caceres	1.48	IT	Palermo	53.63
AM	Armenia	15.96	FR	Centre	19.16	ES	Zaragoza	1.16	IT	Agrigento	17.26
M9	Missing 9	9.52	NZ	Nelson	17.46	ES	Valladolid	0.07	IT	Catania	3.12
MD	Moldova	9.28	US	Yuba	16.14	ES	Guadalajara	0.04	IT	Messina	2.66
BG	Bulgaria	7.11	US	Lake	16.03	ES	Zamora	0.01	IT	La Spezia	1.64
RO	Romania	0.16	NZ	Waipara Valley	14.40	ES	Avila, Palencia, Salama	0.01	IT	Caltanissetta	1.63
			AU	SE Coastal WA	12.68	ES	Ciudad Real	0.00	IT	Sassari	0.62
			NZ	Wairarapa	11.73	ES	Cuenca	0.00	IT	Genova	0.62
			NZ	Waikato	10.07	ES	Canarias	0.00	IT	Imperia	0.48
			US	Calavaras	9.63	ES	Galicia	0.00	IT	Massa-Carrara	0.24
			IT	Gorizia	9.54	ES	Burgos	0.00	IT	Savona	0.22
			FR	Deux-Sevres, Vienne	9.27	ES	Alava	0.00	IT	Napoli	0.12
			AU	Adelaide Hills	8.94	ES	Leon	0.00	IT	Valle D'Aosta	0.08
			AU	Mount Benson	8.56				IT	Oristano	0.08
			NZ	Hawkes Bay	8.49				IT	Cagliari	0.08
			IT	Lecco	8.27				IT	Brescia	0.07
			US	Mariposa	8.05				IT	Caserta	0.06
			AU	Margaret River	7.94				IT	Pistoia	0.06
			CL	Valparaiso	7.91				IT	Campobasso	0.06
			CL	Del Maule	7.85				IT	Torino	0.06
			AU	Greater Perth Other	7.67				IT	Pisa	0.06
			ZA	Stellenbosch	7.61				IT	Lucca	0.05
			AU	Pyrenees	7.32				IT	Cosenza	0.05
			MD	Moldova	6.82				IT	Matera	0.05

Table 49 (cont.) Varietal Intensity Indexes for the top 25 regions for world's top 30 white varieties, 2000

Macabeo			Chenin Blanc			Riesling			Colombard		
	Region	Varietal Intensity Indexes		Region	Varietal Intensity Indexes		Region	Varietal Intensity Indexes		Region	Varietal Intensity Indexes
ES	Tarragona	33.35	ZA	Olifants River	37.32	DE	Rheingau	89.53	ZA	Orange River	66.92
ES	Girona, Lleida	24.47	ZA	Worcester	31.78	DE	Mittelrhein	82.68	US	Madera	40.40
ES	Barcelona	24.16	ZA	Malmesbury	30.45	DE	Hessische Bergs.	62.48	US	Kern	35.83
ES	Zaragoza	20.51	ZA	Breedekloof	30.08	DE	Mosel-Saar-Ruwer	61.26	US	Fresno	34.20
ES	Rioja	14.90	ZA	Orange River	28.70	DE	Nahe	28.85	US	Glenn	33.91
ES	Huesca, Teruel	14.88	ZA	Paarl	27.86	AU	Eden Valley	28.01	ZA	Little Karoo	32.31
ES	Alava	13.11	US	Sutter	26.62	DE	Wurttemberg	25.52	FR	Gers	32.01
FR	Pyrenees-Orientales	12.38	ZA	Little Karoo	22.76	FR	Alsace	25.44	ZA	Olifants River	30.81
ES	Castellon	9.33	FR	Deux-Sevres, Vienne	20.49	NZ	Canterbury	24.99	US	Tulare	30.42
ES	Valladolid	7.35	ZA	Robertson	17.69	DE	Rhein-Pfalz	23.90	US	Stanislaus	27.82
ES	Navarra	7.29	AU	Perth Hills	17.21	US	Columbia River	23.38	US	Merced	22.15
ES	Valencia	1.62	FR	Centre	16.81	NZ	Nelson	19.02	ZA	Robertson	21.52
ES	Illes Balears	1.57	FR	Pays de la Loire Other	15.09	DE	Sachsen	18.34	ZA	Breedekloof	19.71
ES	Badajoz	1.52	AU	Swan District	13.78	US	Michigan	17.73	US	Kings	17.29
ES	Albacete	1.31	US	Kern	13.01	NZ	Waipara Valley	17.02	ZA	Worcester	17.19
FR	Aude	0.63	US	Madera	12.49	US	Yuba	15.94	US	San Joaquin	5.05
ES	Burgos	0.62	ZA	Stellenbosch	11.93	AU	Clare Valley	15.75	AU	Riverina	4.61
ES	Cuenca	0.58	AU	Greater Perth Other	10.84	LU	Luxembourg	14.67	US	Calavaras	4.55
ES	Caceres	0.33	US	Fresno	10.61	US	Douglas Co.	14.43	AU	Riverland	4.40
ES	Guipuzcoa, Vizcaya	0.27	US	Stanislaus	10.52	AT	Wien and other	14.29	ZA	Paarl	4.24
ES	Avila, Palencia, Salam	0.21	US	Merced	9.58	AU	Henty	12.97	AU	Murray Darling NS'	3.57
ES	Region De Murcia	0.20	AU	Central WA	6.71	AU	Canberra District	12.45	AU	Murray Darling Vic	3.37
ES	Almeria, Granada, Jae	0.14	US	Tulare	6.47	US	Washington Co.	12.10	US	Alameda	3.32
ES	Ciudad Real	0.13	US	Kings	6.36	US	Washington	11.83	ZA	Malmesbury	3.21
ES	Zamora	0.11	NZ	Waikato	6.33	US	Humboldt	11.30	FR	Aquitaine Other	3.04

Table 49 (cont.) Varietal Intensity Indexes for the top 25 regions for world's top 30 white varieties, 2000

Aligote			Müller Thurgau			Palomino Fino			Muscat of Alexandria		
	Region	Varietal Intensity Indexes		Region	Varietal Intensity Indexes		Region	Varietal Intensity Indexes		Region	Varietal Intensity Indexes
MD	Moldova	24.04	CH	Lucerne	75.67	ES	Cadiz	153.67	US	Kings	32.75
M9	Missing 9	11.79	DE	Franken	58.91	ES	Canarias	79.22	ES	Malaga	24.53
FR	Bourgogne	7.77	CH	Other Region	57.76	ES	Cantabria	73.50	ZA	Little Karoo	23.31
RO	Romania	4.68	LU	Luxembourg	49.48	ES	Leon	27.31	ZA	Breedekloof	18.74
RU	Russia	4.42	CH	Aargau	47.21	ES	Galicia	21.65	AR	San Juan	16.14
BG	Bulgaria	2.36	CH	Schwyz	45.24	ES	Valladolid	19.01	ZA	Olifants River	15.64
CH	Geneva	1.81	CH	Zurich	40.25	ES	Zamora	18.26	US	Tulare	15.26
FR	Auvergne	0.76	CH	Thurgau	39.74	US	San Bernardino	7.36	ES	Alicante	14.87
GE	Georgia	0.35	DE	Baden	39.14	NZ	Waikato	6.20	ZA	Orange River	14.70
FR	Rhone Alpes Other	0.13	DE	Sachsen	33.66	ES	Almeria, Granada, Jaen,	6.07	MA	Morocco	12.27
CH	Vaud	0.04	DE	Saale-Unstrut	32.50	NZ	Auckland	5.25	FR	Pyrenees-Orientales	12.15
CH	Valais	0.03	DE	Rheinhessen	30.89	ES	Principado de Asturias	3.18	AU	Riverland	9.71
FR	Alpes de Haute	0.01	DE	Mosel-Saar-Ruwer	30.09	US	Riverside	3.16	US	Kern	8.64
FR	Gard	0.00	DE	Nahe	28.98	ES	Huelva	2.90	AU	Murray Darling NSW	8.17
FR	Bouches-du-Rhone	0.00	DE	Rhein-Pfalz	25.72	US	Contra Costa	2.30	ZA	Worcester	7.89
FR	Centre	0.00	CH	Schaffhausen	25.56	FR	Gers	2.25	AU	Swan Hill NSW	7.41
FR	Herault	0.00	CH	Jura	24.91	ES	Avila, Palencia, Salamar	1.71	AU	Swan Hill Vic	6.90
FR	Vaucluse	0.00	CH	Basel-Landschaft	24.05	US	Madera	1.26	US	Fresno	6.61
FR	Midi Pyren. Other	0.00	CH	St. Gallen	21.15	AU	Lower Murray Other	1.22	AU	Greater Perth Other	6.59
FR	Ardeche	0.00	CZ	Czechrepublic	20.34	ES	Malaga	1.08	AR	Other Regions	6.25
FR	Pays de la Loire Othe	0.00		Slovakia	17.44	AU	Beechworth	0.93	AU	Lower Murray Other	6.17
FR	Charente	0.00	NZ	Gisborne	16.89	US	Fresno	0.89	AU	N. W. Vic Other	5.70
			DE	Hessische Bergs.	16.00	AU	Rutherglen	0.69	ES	Valencia	5.70
			AT	Steiermark	15.52	AU	Riverland	0.53	US	San Diego	5.44
			CH	Graubünden	12.00	AU	Barossa Valley	0.52	AU	Murray Darling Vic	5.20

Table 49 (cont.) Varietal Intensity Indexes for the top 25 regions for world's top 30 white varieties, 2000

Muscat Blanc a Petits Grains			Semillon			Feteasca Alba			Gruner Veltliner		
	Region	Varietal Intensity Indexes		Region	Varietal Intensity Indexes		Region	Varietal Intensity Indexes		Region	Varietal Intensity Indexes
EL	Voreio Aigaio	147.75	AU	Nthn Rivers Other	33.81	RO	Romania	16.78	AT	Niederosterreich	100.24
IT	Cuneo	45.58	AU	Hunter	33.78	MD	Moldova	9.88	AT	Wien and other	58.97
IT	Asti	36.68	FR	Aquitaine Other	31.59	SK	Slovakia	4.09	SK	Slovakia	39.27
EL	Anatoliki Mak.Thraki	33.09	AU	Riverina	29.74	HU	Hungary	2.29	AT	Burgenland	38.89
US	Los Angeles	22.90	AU	Hunter Valley Other	28.39				CZ	Czechrepublic	31.00
IT	Alessandria	18.24	AU	Hastings River	27.52				HU	Hungary	3.18
FR	Pyrenees-Orientales	13.65	AU	Margaret River	23.50				IT	Pescara	3.01
IT	Padova	10.85	AU	Southern Fleurieu	20.53				IT	La Spezia	0.88
IT	Matera	9.66	AU	Barossa Valley	19.16				IT	Oristano	0.81
IT	Pavia	9.01	AU	Sthn NSW Other	16.97				IT	Bolzano-Bozen	0.56
US	San Diego	8.45	AU	South Coast - Other	15.00				AT	Steiermark	0.35
AM	Armenia	8.06	AU	Cowra	14.13				IT	Genova	0.21
IT	Sassari	6.55	AU	Nthn Slopes Other	14.12				IT	Sassari	0.19
IT	Potenza	5.72	FR	Gironde	13.85				IT	Cagliari	0.14
ZA	Robertson	5.54	AU	Fleurieu Other	13.59				IT	Chieti	0.14
FR	Corse	4.88	AU	Big Rivers Other	12.07				IT	Viterbo	0.11
AT	Steiermark	4.49	AU	South Burnett	11.51				IT	Frosinone	0.11
IT	Salerno	4.22	AU	Mudgee	11.03				IT	Latina	0.10
ZA	Little Karoo	4.19	AU	Hilltops	10.89				IT	Imperia	0.10
EL	Dytiki Ellada	3.92	AU	Clare Valley	10.36				IT	Foggia	0.05
IT	Bari	3.78	AU	Sunbury	10.17				IT	Teramo	0.05
FR	Rhone Alpes Other	3.62	AU	SW Australia Other	10.11				IT	Sondrio	0.03
IT	Bergamo	3.58	AU	Geographe	9.85				IT	Ancona	0.03
IT	Parma	3.49	US	Alameda	9.52				IT	Ascoli Piceno	0.02
IT	Piacenza	3.45	AU	Adelaide Hills	9.46				IT	Nuoro	0.02

Table 49 (cont.) Varietal Intensity Indexes for the top 25 regions for world's top 30 white varieties, 2000

Trebbiano Romagnolo			Pedro Ximenez			Pinot Blanc			Garganega		
	Region	Varietal Intensity Indexes		Region	Varietal Intensity Indexes		Region	Varietal Intensity Indexes		Region	Varietal Intensity Indexes
IT	Ravenna	190.42	ES	Cordoba	269.20	AT	Steiermark	49.61	IT	Verona	103.87
IT	Ferrara	128.33	CL	Coquimbo	56.60	DE	Sachsen	36.76	IT	Vicenza	97.36
IT	Bologna	91.89	CL	Atacama	55.99	AT	Wien and other	36.68	IT	Trapani	22.63
IT	Forli-Cesena	86.52	ES	Malaga	30.95	DE	Saale-Unstrut	31.56	IT	Padova	11.63
IT	Rimini	46.36	ES	Almeria, Granada, Jaen,	9.01	IT	Bolzano-Bozen	29.60	IT	Agrigento	5.26
IT	Rovigo	9.38	ES	Caceres	7.51	LU	Luxembourg	29.39	IT	Palermo	4.28
IT	Piacenza	6.29	ES	Badajoz	3.40	US	Oregon-Other	25.27	IT	Mantova	2.90
IT	Mantova	4.49	AU	Fleurieu Other	2.21	IT	Brescia	24.47	IT	Foggia	2.33
IT	Pesaro e Urbino	2.98	AU	Lower Murray Other	2.14	FR	Alsace	22.49	IT	Bari	1.79
IT	Parma	2.89	AU	Rutherglen	1.92	AT	Burgenland	20.61	IT	Matera	1.55
IT	Modena	2.17	AU	Swan District	1.81		Gorizia	19.33	IT	Taranto	1.23
IT	Macerata	2.07	AU	Greater Perth Other	1.79	IT	Lecco	17.37	IT	Perugia	1.19
IT	Rieti	1.73	ES	Valencia	1.49	DE	Baden	17.22	IT	Ascoli Piceno	1.09
IT	Padova	1.34	AU	Barossa Valley	1.07	IT	Pordenone	16.00	IT	Campobasso	0.92
IT	Agrigento	1.18	AU	Clare Valley	0.75	IT	Treviso	15.42	IT	Brindisi	0.76
IT	Terni	1.06	ES	Castellon	0.63	RU	Russia	15.26	IT	Brescia	0.75
IT	Taranto	0.80	ES	Avila, Palencia, Salamar	0.45	IT	Venezia	13.02	IT	Sassari	0.73
IT	Frosinone	0.76	ES	Principado de Asturias	0.41	IT	Udine	12.93	IT	Modena	0.61
IT	Salerno	0.72	AU	Sunbury	0.36	AT	Niederosterreich	11.83	IT	Lecce	0.54
IT	Cremona	0.70	AU	Currency Creek	0.33	SK	Slovakia	11.48	IT	Bergamo	0.40
IT	Savona	0.68	AU	Eden Valley	0.28	IT	Vicenza	11.13	IT	Udine	0.39
IT	Foggia	0.66	AU	Riverland	0.27	IT	Bergamo	10.94	IT	Rovigo	0.35
IT	Catania	0.65	ES	Tarragona	0.24	IT	Padova	9.66	IT	Benevento	0.26
IT	Ascoli Piceno	0.60	AU	Mclaren Vale	0.16	DE	Nahe	8.02	IT	Latina	0.20
IT	Caserta	0.59	ES	Cuenca	0.15	CH	Geneva	7.88	IT	Avellino	0.20

Table 49 (cont.) Varietal Intensity Indexes for the top 25 regions for world's top 30 white varieties, 2000

Niagara			Pedro Gimenez			Fernao Pires			Sultaniye		
	Region	Varietal Intensity Indexes		Region	Varietal Intensity Indexes		Region	Varietal Intensity Indexes		Region	Varietal Intensity Indexes
BR	Brazil	80.84	AR	Mendoza	26.80	PT	Ribatejo E Oeste	68.31	AU	N. W. Vic Other	139.17
US	Other New York	50.16	AR	San Juan	22.05	PT	Beira Litoral	50.81	AU	Murray Darling Vic	119.43
US	Chautauqua-Erie	30.60	AR	Other Regions	6.74	PT	Alentejo	7.19	AU	Swan Hill NSW	119.08
US	Finger Lakes	28.57				PT	Beira Interior	4.46	AU	Swan Hill Vic	97.24
CA	Canada	17.26				PT	AltoTras-os-Mont.	1.98	AU	Murray Darling NSW	81.09
M9	Missing 9	0.35				PT	Acores	0.71	AU	West Plains Other	30.54
									AU	Big Rivers Other	25.38
									AU	West Victoria Other	23.49
									AU	Swan District	21.59
									AU	Pt Phillip Other	20.24
									AU	Grampians	18.77
									AU	Queensland - Other	18.67
									AU	Nthn Territory	18.04
									AR	San Juan	11.24
									AU	N. E. Vic Other	11.04
									AU	Hilltops	8.97
									AU	Greater Perth Other	8.95
									AU	Sthn NSW Other	8.85
									AU	Riverland	8.59
									AU	Mt Lofty Rgs Other	8.50
									M9	Missing 9	7.71
									AR	Other Regions	6.40
									AU	Central WA	6.33
									AU	South Burnett	5.04
									AU	Central Vic Other	3.30

Table 49 (cont.) Varietal Intensity Indexes for the top 25 regions for world's top 30 white varieties, 2000

	Chasselas			Melon	
	Region	Varietal Intensity Indexes		Region	Varietal Intensity Indexes
CH	Vaud	252.22	FR	Pays de la Loire Other	128.62
CH	Fribourg	249.98	FR	France2	0.58
CH	Bern	185.32	FR	Auvergne	0.13
CH	Neuchŷtel	180.09	FR	Bourgogne	0.13
CH	Geneva	131.02	FR	Alsace	0.02
CH	Valais	117.97	FR	Centre	0.00
DE	Baden	27.65	FR	Champagne-Ardenne	0.00
CH	Basel-Landschaft	22.32			
SR	Serbia	18.31			
CH	Other Region	12.64			
DE	Saale-Unstrut	10.73			
CL	Del Bio Bio	9.97			
HU	Hungary	8.02			
FR	Alsace	4.61			
CH	Ticino	3.93			
DE	Sachsen	3.31			
NZ	Gisborne	2.40			
NZ	Auckland	1.87			
NZ	Hawkes Bay	1.83			
FR	Bouches-du-Rhone	1.60			
FR	Ardeche	1.39			
FR	Rhone Alpes Other	1.37			
FR	Herault	0.88			
CH	St. Gallen	0.84			
FR	Vaucluse	0.64			

Table 50: Varietal Intensity Indexes for top 25 regions for world's top 30 white varieties, 2010

	Airen			Chardonnay			Sauvignon Blanc			Trebbiano Toscano	
	Region	Varietal Intensity Indexes		Region	Varietal Intensity Indexes		Region	Varietal Intensity Indexes		Region	Varietal Intensity Indexes
ES	Ciudad Real	12.68	FR	Yonne	18.33	FR	Nievre	34.13	FR	Charente	39.94
ES	Toledo	11.39	US	Tehama	15.17	NZ	Marlborough	31.66	FR	Charente Maritime	37.97
ES	Madrid	6.49	AU	Hunter Valley Other	15.08	FR	Cher	30.73	IT	Abruzzo	7.58
ES	Cuenca	5.44	NZ	Gisborne	12.24	FR	Centre-Other	19.08	FR	Gers	7.55
ES	Guadalajara	5.23	AU	Cowra	11.89	NZ	Waipara	19.01	FR	Landes	6.82
ES	Albacete	3.07	FR	Saone Et Loire	11.89	NZ	Nelson	16.55	IT	Lazio	5.02
ES	Almeria, Granada, Ja	0.85	JP	Yamagata	10.72	FR	Loir Et Cher	16.54	IT	Umbria	4.88
ES	Malaga	0.78	US	Yolo	10.25	CL	Valparaiso	14.83	US	Los Angeles	4.18
ES	Murcia	0.60	AU	Nthn Rivers other	9.98	CL	De Los Lagos	13.93	UY	Uruguay	4.11
ES	Cordoba	0.21	US	Santa Barbara	9.50	AU	Pemberton	13.89	IT	Puglia	2.52
ES	Alicante	0.11	US	Monterey	9.30	MM	Myanmar	12.21	HR	Sjeverna Dalmacija	2.35
ES	Canarias	0.03	US	San Mateo	9.00	CL	Araucania	11.06	IT	Toscana	2.17
ES	Burgos	0.02	US	San Benito	8.85	AU	SW Australia Other	10.04	FR	Var	2.09
ES	Valencia	0.01	AU	Tumbarumba	8.47	NZ	Wairarapa	9.58	IT	Marche	1.90
ES	Badajoz	0.01	AU	Big Rivers Other	7.76	US	Lake	9.54	IT	Molise	1.72
ES	Zamora	0.01	CL	De Los Lagos	7.72	AU	Blackwood Valley	8.55	BG	Yugoiztochen	1.30
ES	Valladolid	0.01	AU	New England	7.55	AU	Adelaide Hills	8.52	FR	Bouches Du Rhone	1.30
ES	Caceres	0.00	AU	C. Ranges Other	7.36	NZ	Hawkes Bay	7.57	FR	Lot Et Garonne	1.25
ES	Huelva	0.00	US	Solano	7.30	ZA	Stellenbosch	6.94	EL	Thessalia	1.23
ES	Avila, Palencia, Sala	0.00	CL	Valparaiso	7.27	AU	Margaret River	6.81	EL	Anatoliki Mak., Thraki	1.21
ES	Leon	0.00	AU	Murray Darling Vic	7.06	FR	Poitou-Charentes-Othe	6.79	FR	Other Regions	1.15
ES	Zaragoza	0.00	US	Santa Cruz	7.03	AU	Great Southern	6.62	AR	Santa Rosa	0.98
			FR	Champagne-Viticole	6.96	AU	Mount Benson	6.43	IT	Campania	0.91
			US	Sutter	6.91	AU	Strathbogie Rgs	6.43	FR	Vaucluse	0.81
			US	Trinity	6.70	AU	Southern Highlands	6.16	IT	Sicilia	0.81

Table 50 (cont.) Varietal Intensity Indexes for top 25 regions for world's top 30 white varieties, 2010

Grasevina				Rkatsiteli				Riesling				Macabeo		
	Region	Varietal Intensity Indexes			Region	Varietal Intensity Indexes			Region	Varietal Intensity Indexes			Region	Varietal Intensity Indexes
HR	Podunavlje	45.55	KZ	Almaty	44.86	DE	Rheingau	72.69	ES	Tarragona	28.67
HR	Slavonija	45.20	GE	Georgia	41.40	DE	Mittelrhein	61.28	ES	Barcelona	25.34
HU	Balatonfelvidek	39.17	KZ	Zhambyl	31.92	DE	Mosel-Saar-Ruwer	55.13	ES	Girona, Lleida	15.67
SR	Serbia	36.09	KZ	South - Kazakhstan	31.25	DE	Hessische Bergstra E	43.77	ES	Zaragoza	12.28
HU	Badacsony	33.28	UA	Ukraine	17.34	US	Rattlesnake Hills	25.93	ES	Rioja	10.39
HU	Balatonfured-Cs.	29.62	AM	Armenia	17.29	AU	Eden Valley	25.41	ES	Castellon	9.70
SI	Prekmurje	29.61	RU	Rostov Oblast	10.14	DE	Nahe	24.97	FR	Pyrenees Orientales	8.49
HR	Prigorje - Bilogora	25.01	MD	Moldova	10.05	AU	Aus. Capital Terr.	22.98	ES	Huesca, Teruel	8.40
HU	Pannonhalma	20.93	BG	Severoiztochen	9.26	DE	Rhein-Pfalz	21.71	ES	Alava	6.38
HR	Pokuplje	20.20	KZ	Other-Region	8.94	FR	Bas Rhin	20.72	ES	Valladolid	5.57
HU	Nagy-Somlo	20.13	BG	Yugoiztochen	5.44	US	Michigan	20.64	ES	Caceres	4.94
HR	Zagorje-Medimur.	19.86	BG	Severen Tsentralen	4.65	AU	Clare Valley	19.61	ES	Badajoz	4.66
HR	Moslavina	18.63	BG	Severozapaden	3.06	US	Yakima Valley	19.53	ES	Valencia	4.47
SI	Stajerska Slovenija	18.37	BG	Yuzhen Tsentralen	2.61	FR	Haut Rhin	19.17	ES	Albacete	3.59
SK	Vychodoslovenska	17.70	HR	Dalmatinska Zagora	1.80	NZ	Waipara	18.17	ES	Navarra	2.38
HR	Plesivica	17.43	HR	Sjeverna Dalmacija	1.43	DE	Wurttemberg	16.65	ES	Alicante	1.66
SI	Bizeljsko Sremic	14.40	BG	Yugozapaden	0.87	US	Lake Chelan	16.00	ES	Ciudad Real	1.49
AT	Steiermark	12.80	RU	Krasnodar Krai	0.49	NZ	Canterbury	14.86	ES	Cuenca	1.43
SI	Bela Krajina	11.77	KZ	East - Kazakhstan	0.46	US	Columbia Valley	14.03	ES	Illes Balears	1.09
SK	Juznoslovenska	11.61	RO	Sud-Est	0.37	HR	Zagorje-Medimur.	13.89	FR	Other Regions	0.86
RO	Centru	10.53	RO	Sud-Vest Oltenia	0.07	AU	Canberra ACT	13.69	ES	Toledo	0.55
SK	Nitrianska	10.29	RO	Sud - Muntenia	0.02	DE	Rheinhessen	13.47	ES	Murcia	0.47
RO	Vest	9.84	RO	Nord-Est	0.01	HR	Plesivica	12.42	FR	Aude	0.46
SK	Malokarpatska	9.35				DE	Sachsen	11.99	ES	Cordoba	0.27
SI	Other	9.01				AT	Wien and other	11.80	ES	Almeria, Granada, Jae	0.16

Table 50 (cont.) Varietal Intensity Indexes for top 25 regions for world's top 30 white varieties, 2010

	Cayetana Blanca			Aligote			Chenin Blanc			Catarratto Bianco	
	Region	Varietal Intensity Indexes		Region	Varietal Intensity Indexes		Region	Varietal Intensity Indexes		Region	Varietal Intensity Indexes
ES	Badajoz	54.57	UA	Ukraine	23.45	FR	Pays De Loire-Other	41.50	IT	Sicilia	44.08
ES	Almeria, Granada, Jaen	4.01	MD	Moldova	22.39	FR	Indre Et Loire	40.14	US	San Luis Obispo	0.12
ES	Caceres	1.02	KZ	East - Kazakhstan	20.25	ZA	Olifants River	35.99	US	Sonoma	0.12
ES	Zaragoza	0.98	RU	Rostov Oblast	17.94	FR	Maine Et Loire	32.16	US	Napa	0.10
PT	Alto Tras-Os-Montes	0.21	KZ	Other-Region	14.94	ZA	Orange River	30.43	US	Monterey	0.08
PT	Ribatejo E Oeste	0.10	RO	Nord-Est	12.99	ZA	Worcester	30.14	US	San Joaquin	0.07
PT	Beira Interior	0.06	FR	Cote D'Or	8.92	ZA	Breedekloof	29.31	IT	Puglia	0.03
ES	Guadalajara	0.05	FR	Saone Et Loire	8.29	ZA	Malmesbury	27.57	IT	Toscana	0.02
PT	Alentejo	0.03	RO	Sud-Est	8.15	ZA	Paarl	24.82	IT	Friuli Venezia Giul.	0.02
ES	Cordoba	0.03	KZ	Almaty	7.08	ZA	Little Karoo	24.11	IT	Marche	0.01
ES	Huelva	0.03	FR	Yonne	6.06	AU	Perth Hills	20.73	IT	Veneto	0.01
ES	Avila, Palencia, Salama	0.01	KZ	West - Kazakhstan	5.48	AU	Greater Perth Other	18.64	IT	Calabria	0.01
ES	Huesca, Teruel	0.01	RU	Krasnodar Krai	2.46	AU	Eastern Plain ect.	18.16	IT	Piemonte	0.00
ES	Alicante	0.01	CH	Geneva	2.05	AU	Swan District	17.46	IT	Emilia-Romagna	0.00
PT	Entre Douro E Minho	0.01	KZ	South - Kazakhstan	1.30	ZA	Robertson	15.82	IT	Campania	0.00
ES	Cuenca	0.00	FR	Other Regions	1.10	US	Sutter	15.62	IT	Molise	0.00
PT	Algarve	0.00	KZ	Zhambyl	0.45	MX	Suma Baja Cali.	12.57			
ES	Albacete	0.00	GE	Georgia	0.33	US	Kings	12.05			
ES	Ciudad Real	0.00	RO	Sud - Muntenia	0.24	TH	Thailand	11.60			
PT	Beira Litoral	0.00	RO	Sud-Vest Oltenia	0.12	US	Texas	10.91			
			CH	Vaud	0.04	ZA	Stellenbosch	10.90			
			CH	Valais	0.02	FR	Other Regions	9.90			
			HU	Matra	0.00	US	Fresno	7.73			
			BR	Brazil	0.00	US	Madera	7.50			
						AU	Peel	6.40			

Table 50 (cont.) Varietal Intensity Indexes for top 25 regions for world's top 30 white varieties, 2010

Colombard			Muscat Blanc a Petits Grains			Muscat of Alexandria			Müller Thurgau		
	Region	Varietal Intensity Indexes		Region	Varietal Intensity Indexes		Region	Varietal Intensity Indexes		Region	Varietal Intensity Indexes
ZA	Orange River	75.80	EL	Vorreio Aigaio	107.48	ES	Malaga	131.61	DE	Franken	59.67
FR	Gers	42.08	MX	Zacatecas	57.91	CL	Del Bio Bio	49.76	CH	Other Region	49.18
ZA	Little Karoo	42.04	PE	Arequipa	37.74	CL	Atacama	46.65	CH	Thurgau	47.26
ZA	Olifants River	35.85	IT	Piemonte	31.14	US	Glenn	30.69	CH	Lucerne	44.10
US	Fresno	35.56	MX	Aguascalientes	21.75	AR	Albardon	26.64	CH	Aargau	42.99
US	Madera	30.97	FR	Pyrenees Orientales	15.03	AR	Other-San Juan	24.89	CH	Zurich	42.82
US	Kern	26.59	SK	Tokajska	14.86	ES	Alicante	24.36	JP	Hokkaido	38.48
FR	Landes	24.84	US	Siskiyou	14.79	AR	Ullum	24.18	CZ	Cechy	35.55
US	Tulare	24.16	MM	Myanmar	14.00	US	Colusa	21.90	DE	Sachsen	35.17
ZA	Robertson	22.97	HU	Tokaj	12.84	US	Kings	21.38	DE	Saale-Unstrut	34.67
ZA	Breedekloof	21.51	FR	Drome	8.97	AU	Greater Perth Other	18.55	DE	Baden	34.37
ZA	Worcester	18.09	AM	Armenia	6.94	AR	25 De Mayo	15.69	CH	Schwyz	33.92
US	Stanislaus	13.91	AT	Steiermark	6.94	AU	N. W. Vic Other	14.01	DE	Rheinhessen	33.08
AU	N. W. Vic Other	11.26	SI	Stajerska Slovenija	6.50	FR	Pyrenees Orientales	13.83	CH	Schaffhausen	28.83
TH	Thailand	10.73	IT	Valle D'Aosta	6.14	MA	Morocco	13.08	LU	Luxembourg	28.54
US	Kings	9.25	SI	Bela Krajina	5.69	ZA	Little Karoo	12.96	DE	Mosel-Saar-Ruwer	28.41
AU	Murray Darling Vic	7.84	US	Texas	5.42	US	Tulare	11.83	DE	Nahe	26.74
FR	Lot Et Garonne	6.58	SI	Slovenska Istra	5.32	AR	San Martin S	10.41	CH	Basel-Landschaft	26.12
FR	Other Regions	6.33	FR	Corse	4.85	ZA	Breedekloof	10.14	CH	St. Gallen	24.35
US	Merced	6.10	EL	Ionia Nisia	4.45	ES	Valencia	9.06	HU	Neszmely	23.05
AU	Riverland	5.62	FR	Other Regions	4.14	AR	La Rioja	9.03	HU	Matra	20.22
AU	Murray Darling NSW	4.55	EL	Dytiki Ellada	4.13	AR	Caucete	8.72	DE	Rhein-Pfalz	19.74
AU	Riverina	4.19	ZA	Robertson	4.04	AU	Murray Darling Vic	8.64	SK	Stredoslovenska	19.01
ZA	Paarl	4.09	US	Riverside	3.95	AU	Murray Darling NSW	8.39	SK	Malokarpatska	18.98
	Glenn	4.05	FR	Herault	3.41	AR	Sarmiento	8.16	CZ	Morava	18.76

Table 50 (cont.) Varietal Intensity Indexes for top 25 regions for world's top 30 white varieties, 2010

	Palomino Fino			Semillon			Gruner Veltliner			Prosecco	
	Region	Varietal Intensity Indexes		Region	Varietal Intensity Indexes		Region	Varietal Intensity Indexes		Region	Varietal Intensity Indexes
ES	Cadiz	186.18	AU	New England	80.88	AT	Niederosterreich	106.77	IT	Veneto	57.03
ES	Canarias	78.05	TU	Marmara	65.09	AT	Wien and other	59.19	IT	Friuli Venezia Giul.	5.06
MX	Suma Coahuila	50.55	FR	Dordogne	58.21	SK	Malokarpatska	50.27	BR	Brazil	0.87
ES	Cantabria	41.30	AU	Hunter	35.35	SK	Nitrianska	47.19	IT	Toscana	0.27
ES	Leon	28.07	AU	Hastings River	27.39	SK	Juznoslovenska	37.22	IT	Molise	0.10
ES	Galicia	26.51	AU	Margaret River	24.28	SK	Stredoslovenska	35.85	IT	Marche	0.10
ES	Almeria, Granada, Jaer	12.09	AU	South Burnett	22.54	AT	Burgenland	25.99	IT	Puglia	0.08
MX	Sonora	7.02	AU	Riverina	21.79	CZ	Morava	23.86	IT	Basilicata	0.07
PT	Ribatejo E Oeste	6.66	AU	Geographe	19.96	HU	Etyek-Budai	23.27	IT	Emilia-Romagna	0.03
PT	Alto Tras-Os-Montes	6.25	AU	Great Southern	18.56	HU	Balatonboglar	21.87	IT	Sicilia	0.02
NZ	Waikato	4.44	AU	Blackwood Valley	16.17	HU	Mor	20.32	IT	Trentino Alto Adige	0.02
ES	Zamora	4.15	AU	Swan Hill NSW	16.17	HU	Tolna	18.18	IT	Calabria	0.01
ES	Valladolid	3.45	AU	Shoalhaven Coast	15.73	HU	Pecs	12.59	IT	Umbria	0.01
AR	Other-Argentinan	3.05	AU	South Coast Other	15.25	HU	Sopron	11.91	IT	Abruzzo	0.00
ES	Asturias	2.16	AU	SW Australia Other	13.82	HU	Balatonfelvidek	8.67	IT	Piemonte	0.00
ES	Huelva	2.08	AU	Eastern Plain ect.	12.72	SK	Vychodoslovenska	8.59	IT	Lazio	0.00
ES	Avila, Palencia, Salam:	2.03	AU	Manjimup	12.64	HU	Csongrad	8.00	IT	Campania	0.00
US	Contra Costa	1.23	FR	Gironde	12.38	HU	Bukk	7.45	IT	Sardegna	0.00
US	Madera	1.08	AU	Pemberton	12.15	HU	Matra	7.03	IT	Lombardia	0.00
ES	Caceres	0.74	AU	Greater Perth Other	11.60	HU	Zala	5.64			
PT	Entre Douro E Minho	0.73	AU	Barossa Valley	11.41	CZ	Cechy	5.29			
US	Fresno	0.59	AU	Swan District	11.07	HU	Neszmely	3.76			
AR	San Rafael	0.57	AU	Cowra	10.91	HU	Villany	3.16			
US	Riverside	0.50	AU	Southern Fleurieu	10.32	HU	Badacsony	3.08			
AR	25 De Mayo	0.40	AU	Nthn Slopes Other	10.01	HU	Kunsag	2.38			

Table 50 (cont.) Varietal Intensity Indexes for top 25 regions for world's top 30 white varieties, 2010

Feteasca Alba		Varietal Intensity Indexes	Verdejo		Varietal Intensity Indexes	Trebbiano Romagnolo		Varietal Intensity Indexes	Garganega		Varietal Intensity Indexes
	Region			Region			Region			Region	
RO	Sud-Est	29.22	ES	Valladolid	116.61	IT	Emilia-Romagna	80.50	IT	Veneto	41.25
RO	Nord-Est	28.25	ES	Caceres	29.43	IT	Puglia	0.84	IT	Sicilia	11.49
RO	Centru	24.18	ES	Avila, Palencia, Salamanca, Seg	26.74	IT	Marche	0.70	IT	Puglia	1.58
RO	Nord-Vest	16.75	ES	Zamora	6.22	IT	Molise	0.26	IT	Marche	1.15
MD	Moldova	12.71	ES	Ciudad Real	4.04	IT	Lombardia	0.21	IT	Calabria	1.00
SK	Vychodoslovenska	8.61	ES	Cuenca	3.24	IT	Lazio	0.17	IT	Basilicata	0.44
SK	Nitrianska	8.60	ES	Albacete	3.15	IT	Umbria	0.14	IT	Lombardia	0.41
RO	Sud - Muntenia	7.65	ES	Leon	2.15	IT	Veneto	0.12	IT	Molise	0.23
RO	Sud-Vest Oltenia	5.20	ES	Toledo	1.46	IT	Toscana	0.09	IT	Umbria	0.19
SK	Juznoslovenska	4.11	ES	Badajoz	0.65	IT	Calabria	0.06	IT	Emilia-Romagna	0.15
SK	Malokarpatska	3.19	ES	Guadalajara	0.39	IT	Liguria	0.05	IT	Abruzzo	0.09
RO	Vest	2.09	ES	Huelva	0.07	IT	Abruzzo	0.04	IT	Campania	0.09
SK	Stredoslovenska	1.13	ES	Burgos	0.02	IT	Campania	0.02	IT	Toscana	0.07
			ES	Navarra	0.01	IT	Basilicata	0.02	IT	Lazio	0.05
			ES	Galicia	0.01	IT	Sicilia	0.00	IT	Friuli Venezia Giul.	0.03
			ES	Valencia	0.01	IT	Sardegna	0.00	IT	Sardegna	0.02
			ES	Murcia	0.01				IT	Piemonte	0.01
			ES	Rioja	0.01				BR	Brazil	0.00

469

Table 50 (cont.) Varietal Intensity Indexes for top 25 regions for world's top 30 white varieties, 2010

	Pinot Blanc				Gewurztraminer				Chasselas				Feteasca Regala	
	Region	Varietal Intensity Indexes			Region	Varietal Intensity Indexes			Region	Varietal Intensity Indexes			Region	Varietal Intensity Indexes
LU	Luxembourg	38.80	FR	Haut Rhin	71.59	CH	Vaud	214.36	RO	Centru	92.21
DE	Saale-Unstrut	35.69	US	Columbia Gorge	59.75	CH	Fribourg	169.28	RO	Vest	51.92
AT	Steiermark	34.91	FR	Bas Rhin	47.97	FR	Tarn Et Garonne	126.47	RO	Sud-Est	35.64
DE	Sachsen	33.95	US	Lake Chelan	36.56	CH	Bern	124.40	RO	Nord-Vest	20.86
SK	Stredoslovenska	30.03	CL	Araucania	29.27	CH	Neuchytel	120.45	RO	Nord-Est	17.93
HR	Moslavina	23.64	CA	British Colombia	23.10	CH	Valais	72.33	RO	Sud - Muntenia	15.96
DE	Baden	23.48	SK	Vychodoslovenska	20.74	CH	Geneva	70.23	SK	Nitrianska	13.96
DE	Hessische Bergstra E	22.31	RO	Centru	18.45	FR	Other Regions	48.58	RO	Sud-Vest Oltenia	12.17
FR	Haut Rhin	21.96	IT	Trentino Alto Adige	18.02	HU	Matra	31.62	SK	Stredoslovenska	6.97
FR	Bas Rhin	20.85	US	Colorado	17.81	DE	Baden	24.25	SK	Malokarpatska	6.72
AT	Wien and other	20.55	US	Josephine Co.	17.69	HU	Csongrad	22.70	SK	Juznoslovenska	2.67
DE	Nahe	17.27	HR	Podunavlje	16.32	SR	Serbia	17.45	SK	Vychodoslovenska	0.01
SI	Prekmurje	17.24	SK	Stredoslovenska	16.09	HU	Etyek-Budai	16.07			
SK	Malokarpatska	17.03	US	Santa Clara	15.01	HU	Neszmely	15.51			
CZ	Cechy	14.72	BG	Severoiztochen	13.87	HU	Kunsag	12.69			
CZ	Morava	14.04	AU	New England	13.11	CH	Basel-Landschaft	11.72			
SI	Stajerska Slovenija	13.44	US	San Benito	12.39	DE	Saale-Unstrut	9.97			
AT	Burgenland	12.44	CZ	Morava	12.00	CL	Del Bio Bio	9.00			
DE	Rhein-Pfalz	12.11	CZ	Cechy	10.68	HU	Hajos-Bajai	8.78			
SI	Goriska Brda	11.51	US	Trinity	10.66	HU	Zala	8.56			
IT	Trentino Alto Adige	11.44	MD	Moldova	9.80	HU	Balatonboglar	7.95			
HR	Zagorje-Medimur.	11.05	US	Yakima Valley	9.33	HU	Bukk	4.72			
SK	Nitrianska	10.78	SK	Tokajska	8.65	CH	Other Region	4.10			
HU	Bukk	10.77	AU	Mudgee	7.92	HU	Pecs	3.89			
DE	Rheinhessen	10.74	CH	Fribourg	7.84	FR	Lot Et Garonne	3.58			

Table 50 (cont.) Varietal Intensity Indexes for top 25 regions for world's top 30 white varieties, 2010

	Melon			Pedro Gimenez	
	Region	Varietal Intensity Indexes		Region	Varietal Intensity Indexes
FR	Loire Atlantique	273.02	AR	Lavalle	41.11
FR	Pays De Loire-Other	37.63	AR	Rawson	41.00
FR	Maine Et Loire	15.30	AR	25 De Mayo	39.44
FR	Other Regions	1.24	AR	San Martin S	37.79
			AR	9 De Julio	36.00
			AR	Rivadavia	35.81
			AR	Sarmiento	33.40
			AR	Junin	30.81
			AR	Angaco	28.41
			AR	San Martin	27.28
			AR	Santa Rosa	25.70
			AR	Maipu	24.47
			AR	Rio Negro	22.25
			AR	Caucete	21.56
			AR	San Rafael	21.24
			AR	Other-Mendoza	15.93
			AR	Pocito	13.10
			CL	Coquimbo	11.56
			AR	Ullum	8.66
			AR	Other-San Juan	8.36
			AR	Tunuyan	6.35
			AR	Lujan De Cuyo	6.16
			AR	Tupungato	3.52
			AR	Albardon	3.22
			AR	Other-Argentinan	2.39

Table 51: Varietal Intensity Indexes for the top 25 regions for world's top 6 non-red/white varieties, 2000

Cereza			Pinot Gris			Moscatel Rosada		
	Region	Varietal Intensity Indexes		Region	Varietal Intensity Indexes		Region	Varietal Intensity Indexes
AR	San Juan	41.87	US	Lane Co.	84.76	AR	Mendoza	33.76
AR	Other AR	20.30	US	Marion Co.	76.67	AR	Other AR	3.73
AR	Mendoza	19.01	US	Josephine Co.	50.96	AR	San Juan	1.34
			US	Other Valley	50.30			
			US	Washington Co.	47.63			
			IT	Gorizia	38.21			
			IT	Pordenone	35.29			
			US	Yamhill Co.	34.59			
			US	Benton Co.	34.37			
			US	Polk Co.	32.47			
			FR	Alsace	31.67			
			IT	Trento	30.56			
			LU	Luxembourg	29.71			
			US	Douglas Co.	28.04			
			US	Humboldt	25.84			
			IT	Udine	25.32			
			DE	Baden	23.28			
			NZ	Central Otago	22.54			
			IT	Venezia	21.02			
			DE	Sachsen	20.72			

Kovidinka			Roditis			Kuldzhinskii		
	Region	Varietal Intensity Indexes		Region	Varietal Intensity Indexes		Region	Varietal Intensity Indexes
HU	Hungary	56.14	EL	Peloponnisos	519.01	M9	Missing 9	60.81
			EL	Dytiki Ellada	77.65			

Table 52: Varietal Intensity Indexes for top 25 regions for world's top 6 non-red/white varieties, 2010

Pinot Gris			Cereza			Moscatel Rosada		
	Region	Varietal Intensity Indexes		Region	Varietal Intensity Indexes		Region	Varietal Intensity Indexes
US	Lane Co.	54.07	AR	Albardon	91.66	AR	San Rafael	70.88
US	Marion Co.	37.63	AR	Rawson	85.76	AR	San Martin	38.65
IT	Friuli Venezia Giul.	26.07	AR	Pocito	75.23	AR	Other-Mendoza	35.06
AU	Sthn NSW Other	24.79	AR	Angaco	69.55	AR	Santa Rosa	33.94
IT	Trentino Alto Adige	19.71	AR	Catamarca	64.69	AR	Junin	33.54
US	Benton Co.	18.75	AR	9 De Julio	59.58	AR	Rivadavia	26.54
US	Columbia Gorge	18.23	AR	Other-San Juan	58.46	AR	Lavalle	25.91
US	Washington Co.	17.80	AR	Caucete	47.88	AR	Maipu	19.98
FR	Haut Rhin	17.78	AR	25 De Mayo	43.46	AR	Rio Negro	18.38
AU	Big Rivers Other	16.23	AR	Sarmiento	41.09	AR	Ullum	13.53
US	Josephine Co.	14.22	AR	San Martin S	39.29	AR	Lujan De Cuyo	4.69
HU	Badacsony	13.25	AR	San Martin	29.35	AR	Sarmiento	4.51
FR	Bas Rhin	13.20	AR	Ullum	28.05	CL	Coquimbo	3.76
US	Solano	13.19	AR	Santa Rosa	26.62	AR	Other-Argentina	2.50
CH	Jura	12.96	AR	Lavalle	24.85	AR	Salta	2.14
AU	Mornington Peninsu	12.45	AR	Junin	24.09	AR	25 De Mayo	1.24
AU	King Valley	12.05	AR	Rivadavia	17.70	AR	Rawson	1.23
US	Polk Co.	11.88	AR	San Rafael	14.77	AR	Neuquen	1.10
LU	Luxembourg	11.83	AR	Other-Mendoza	14.48	AR	Pocito	1.03
CA	British Colombia	11.41	AR	La Rioja	11.72	AR	Catamarca	0.95
US	Other W. Valley	11.40	AR	Maipu	10.42	AR	La Rioja	0.75
DE	Baden	11.34	AR	Lujan De Cuyo	3.54	CL	Del Maule	0.72
HU	Balatonfelvidek	10.85	AR	Other-Argentinan	2.58	AR	Tunuyan	0.49
NZ	Canterbury	10.80	AR	Rio Negro	1.43	AR	Tupungato	0.37
US	Siskiyou	10.56	AR	Tunuyan	0.62	AR	Caucete	0.24

Roditis			Misket Cherven			Kovidinka		
	Region	Varietal Intensity Indexes		Region	Varietal Intensity Indexes		Region	Varietal Intensity Indexes
EL	Dytiki Ellada	416.40	BG	Yugoiztochen	149.02	HU	Csongrad	307.47
EL	Peloponissos	101.76	BG	Yuzhen Tsentralen	91.72	HU	Kunsag	170.77
EL	Thessalia	90.66	BG	Severoiztochen	7.20	HR	Slavonija	70.85
EL	Sterea Ellada	66.09	BG	Severen Tsentralen	4.58	HU	Hajos-Bajai	30.82
EL	Kentriki Makedonia	55.60	BG	Severozapaden	4.55	HU	Zala	20.67
EL	Attiki	15.84	BG	Yugozapaden	0.61	HR	Moslavina	19.90
EL	Dytiki Makedonia	9.48				HU		0.37
						HU	Sopron	0.20
						HU	Neszmely	0.08

Table 53: Winegrape areas and Varietal Intensity Indexes for each region's top 6 varieties, by region, 2010

Algeria

Prime variety	Col	Regional %	VII*
Cinsaut	R	25.0	
Mazuelo	R	25.0	
Garnacha Tinta	R	20.0	
Alicante Henri Bouschet	R	10.0	
Cabernet Sauvignon	R	5.0	
Merlot	R	5.0	
Other varieties		10.0	
Total		100.0	

Argentina

	25 De Mayo				9 De Julio		
Prime variety	Col	Regional %	VII*	Prime variety	Col	Regional %	VII*
Cereza	O	27.6	1.9	Cereza	O	37.8	2.6
Pedro Gimenez	W	10.5	1.7	Syrah	R	10.9	1.7
Muscat of Alexandria	W	9.0	6.1	Pedro Gimenez	W	9.6	1.6
Syrah	R	8.7	1.4	Douce Noire	R	7.7	0.9
Douce Noire	R	5.7	0.6	Cabernet Sauvignon	R	4.9	0.6
Cot	R	5.6	0.4	Cot	R	4.4	0.3
Other varieties		32.9		Other varieties		24.7	
Total		100.0		Total		100.0	

	Albardon				Angaco		
Prime variety	Col	Regional %	VII*	Prime variety	Col	Regional %	VII*
Cereza	O	58.1	4.0	Cereza	O	44.1	3.0
Muscat of Alexandria	W	15.2	10.4	Torrontes Sanjuanino	W	17.0	16.7
Syrah	R	7.8	1.2	Pedro Gimenez	W	7.6	1.3
Cabernet Sauvignon	R	3.3	0.4	Torrontes Riojano	W	4.5	1.2
Douce Noire	R	3.2	0.4	Syrah	R	4.2	0.7
Torrontes Sanjuanino	W	1.7	1.6	Muscat of Alexandria	W	4.1	2.8
Other varieties		10.7		Other varieties		18.5	
Total		100.0		Total		100.0	

	Catamarca				Caucete		
Prime variety	Col	Regional %	VII*	Prime variety	Col	Regional %	VII*
Cereza	O	41.0	2.8	Cereza	O	30.4	2.1
Torrontes Riojano	W	14.2	3.7	Syrah	R	11.5	1.8
Cabernet Sauvignon	R	14.0	1.7	Torrontes Sanjuanino	W	9.6	9.4
Syrah	R	10.1	1.6	Douce Noire	R	7.5	0.8
Cot	R	9.1	0.6	Pedro Gimenez	W	5.7	1.0
Douce Noire	R	4.6	0.5	Muscat of Alexandria	W	5.0	3.4
Other varieties		7.1		Other varieties		30.2	
Total		100.0		Total		100.0	

	Junin				La Rioja		
Prime variety	Col	Regional %	VII*	Prime variety	Col	Regional %	VII*
Criolla Grande	R	19.2	2.3	Torrontes Riojano	W	33.3	8.7
Cereza	O	15.3	1.1	Cabernet Sauvignon	R	12.9	1.6
Cot	R	12.1	0.8	Syrah	R	9.7	1.5
Douce Noire	R	9.6	1.1	Douce Noire	R	8.4	0.9
Pedro Gimenez	W	8.2	1.4	Cot	R	8.2	0.5
Moscatel Rosada	O	5.3	1.5	Cereza	O	7.4	0.5
Other varieties		30.2		Other varieties		20.1	
Total		100.0		Total		100.0	

Note: VII* indicates Varital Intensity Indexes relative to nation, as defined in the introduction.

Table 53 (cont.) Winegrape areas and Varietal Intensity Indexes for each region's top 6 varieties, by region, 2010

Argentina continued

Lavalle				Lujan De Cuyo			
Prime variety	*Col*	*Regional %*	*VII**	*Prime variety*	*Col*	*Regional %*	*VII**
Cereza	O	15.8	1.1	Cot	R	48.0	3.1
Douce Noire	R	15.4	1.7	Cabernet Sauvignon	R	17.1	2.1
Pedro Gimenez	W	10.9	1.8	Merlot	R	4.5	1.4
Syrah	R	10.6	1.7	Chardonnay	W	4.3	1.3
Criolla Grande	R	7.9	0.9	Douce Noire	R	4.1	0.5
Torrontes Riojano	W	5.2	1.4	Syrah	R	2.5	0.4
Other varieties		34.2		Other varieties		19.5	
Total		100.0		Total		100.0	

Maipu				Neuquen			
Prime variety	*Col*	*Regional %*	*VII**	*Prime variety*	*Col*	*Regional %*	*VII**
Cot	R	25.4	1.6	Cot	R	35.6	2.3
Cabernet Sauvignon	R	13.0	1.6	Cabernet Sauvignon	R	16.1	2.0
Douce Noire	R	7.5	0.8	Merlot	R	14.3	4.6
Cereza	O	6.6	0.5	Pinot Noir	R	13.6	15.2
Pedro Gimenez	W	6.5	1.1	Chardonnay	W	7.5	2.3
Chardonnay	W	4.8	1.5	Sauvignon Blanc	W	5.0	4.3
Other varieties		36.2		Other varieties		8.0	
Total		100.0		Total		100.0	

Other-Argentinan				Other-Mendoza			
Prime variety	*Col*	*Regional %*	*VII**	*Prime variety*	*Col*	*Regional %*	*VII**
Cot	R	19.9	1.3	Cot	R	31.6	2.0
Pinot Noir	R	14.4	16.1	Cabernet Sauvignon	R	10.1	1.2
Cabernet Sauvignon	R	14.0	1.7	Cereza	O	9.2	0.6
Merlot	R	12.7	4.1	Criolla Grande	R	6.9	0.8
Syrah	R	6.1	1.0	Tempranillo	R	6.5	2.1
Torrontes Riojano	W	5.0	1.3	Syrah	R	6.1	1.0
Other varieties		27.9		Other varieties		29.6	
Total		100.0		Total		100.0	

Other-San Juan				Pocito			
Prime variety	*Col*	*Regional %*	*VII**	*Prime variety*	*Col*	*Regional %*	*VII**
Cereza	O	37.1	2.6	Cereza	O	47.7	3.3
Muscat of Alexandria	W	14.2	9.7	Syrah	R	13.3	2.1
Syrah	R	8.3	1.3	Cabernet Sauvignon	R	4.9	0.6
Cot	R	5.9	0.4	Douce Noire	R	4.1	0.5
Douce Noire	R	5.2	0.6	Cot	R	3.6	0.2
Tannat	R	3.4	9.7	Pedro Gimenez	W	3.5	0.6
Other varieties		25.8		Other varieties		22.9	
Total		100.0		Total		100.0	

Rawson				Rio Negro			
Prime variety	*Col*	*Regional %*	*VII**	*Prime variety*	*Col*	*Regional %*	*VII**
Cereza	O	54.4	3.7	Cot	R	20.2	1.3
Pedro Gimenez	W	10.9	1.8	Merlot	R	16.8	5.4
Syrah	R	7.4	1.2	Torrontes Mendocino	W	7.4	20.8
Cot	R	5.7	0.4	Pinot Noir	R	7.3	8.2
Cabernet Sauvignon	R	3.4	0.4	Pedro Gimenez	W	5.9	1.0
Torrontes Riojano	W	3.0	0.8	Cabernet Sauvignon	R	5.7	0.7
Other varieties		15.3		Other varieties		36.7	
Total		100.0		Total		100.0	

Table 53 (cont.) Winegrape areas and Varietal Intensity Indexes for each region's top 6 varieties, by region, 2010

Argentina continued

Rivadavia				Salta			
Prime variety	*Col*	*Regional %*	*VII**	*Prime variety*	*Col*	*Regional %*	*VII**
Criolla Grande	R	18.2	2.1	Torrontes Riojano	W	34.4	9.0
Douce Noire	R	12.4	1.4	Cot	R	27.5	1.8
Cereza	O	11.2	0.8	Cabernet Sauvignon	R	18.8	2.3
Cot	R	10.8	0.7	Tannat	R	4.3	12.3
Pedro Gimenez	W	9.5	1.6	Merlot	R	2.1	0.7
Syrah	R	5.8	0.9	Douce Noire	R	1.8	0.2
Other varieties		32.1		Other varieties		11.1	
Total		100.0		Total		100.0	

San Martin M				San Martin S			
Prime variety	*Col*	*Regional %*	*VII**	*Prime variety*	*Col*	*Regional %*	*VII**
Criolla Grande	R	20.1	2.4	Cereza	O	24.9	1.7
Cereza	O	18.6	1.3	Torrontes Sanjuanino	W	11.1	10.9
Douce Noire	R	12.6	1.4	Pedro Gimenez	W	10.1	1.7
Pedro Gimenez	W	7.3	1.2	Syrah	R	7.6	1.2
Moscatel Rosada	O	6.2	1.7	Cot	R	6.3	0.4
Syrah	R	5.5	0.9	Douce Noire	R	6.2	0.7
Other varieties		29.7		Other varieties		33.9	
Total		100.0		Total		100.0	

San Rafael				Santa Rosa			
Prime variety	*Col*	*Regional %*	*VII**	*Prime variety*	*Col*	*Regional %*	*VII**
Douce Noire	R	11.7	1.3	Cereza	O	16.9	1.2
Criolla Grande	R	11.7	1.4	Douce Noire	R	14.3	1.6
Moscatel Rosada	O	11.3	3.1	Criolla Grande	R	12.1	1.4
Cot	R	10.9	0.7	Syrah	R	7.5	1.2
Cabernet Sauvignon	R	9.4	1.2	Pedro Gimenez	W	6.8	1.1
Cereza	O	9.4	0.6	Cabernet Sauvignon	R	6.5	0.8
Other varieties		35.7		Other varieties		35.9	
Total		100.0		Total		100.0	

Sarmiento				Tupungato			
Prime variety	*Col*	*Regional %*	*VII**	*Prime variety*	*Col*	*Regional %*	*VII**
Cereza	O	26.1	1.8	Cot	R	32.9	2.1
Douce Noire	R	9.7	1.1	Chardonnay	W	14.0	4.3
Cot	R	8.9	0.6	Cabernet Sauvignon	R	11.2	1.4
Pedro Gimenez	W	8.9	1.5	Douce Noire	R	9.3	1.0
Cabernet Sauvignon	R	8.8	1.1	Merlot	R	8.7	2.8
Syrah	R	8.4	1.3	Pinot Noir	R	5.9	6.6
Other varieties		29.2		Other varieties		17.9	
Total		100.0		Total		100.0	

Tunuyan				Ullum			
Prime variety	*Col*	*Regional %*	*VII**	*Prime variety*	*Col*	*Regional %*	*VII**
Cot	R	41.1	2.7	Cereza	O	17.8	1.2
Cabernet Sauvignon	R	15.7	1.9	Muscat of Alexandria	W	13.8	9.5
Merlot	R	7.7	2.5	Syrah	R	12.0	1.9
Chardonnay	W	7.0	2.2	Cot	R	8.6	0.6
Tempranillo	R	5.0	1.6	Cabernet Sauvignon	R	8.5	1.0
Syrah	R	4.9	0.8	Chardonnay	W	6.4	2.0
Other varieties		18.5		Other varieties		32.9	
Total		100.0		Total		100.0	

Table 53 (cont.) Winegrape areas and Varietal Intensity Indexes for each region's top 6 varieties, by region, 2010

Armenia

Armenia

Prime variety	Col	Regional %	VII*
Rkatsiteli	W	22.0	
Mskhali	W	9.8	
Garandmak	W	8.3	
Kangun	W	7.6	
Voskeat	W	7.2	
Muscat Blanc a Petits Grain	W	4.7	
Other varieties		40.4	
Total		100.0	

Australia

Adelaide Hills

Prime variety	Col	Regional %	VII*
Chardonnay	W	20.7	1.1
Sauvignon Blanc	W	20.4	4.8
Syrah	R	12.1	0.4
Pinot Noir	R	11.6	3.7
Cabernet Sauvignon	R	8.3	0.5
Merlot	R	4.7	0.7
Other varieties		22.2	
Total		100.0	

Adelaide Plains

Prime variety	Col	Regional %	VII*
Syrah	R	32.3	1.1
Chardonnay	W	13.8	0.8
Cabernet Sauvignon	R	12.8	0.8
Sauvignon Blanc	W	9.5	2.2
Merlot	R	6.9	1.0
Riesling	W	3.6	1.3
Other varieties		21.2	
Total		100.0	

Alpine Valleys

Prime variety	Col	Regional %	VII*
Merlot	R	20.7	3.1
Chardonnay	W	16.6	0.9
Syrah	R	14.6	0.5
Sauvignon Blanc	W	9.3	2.2
Cabernet Sauvignon	R	8.0	0.5
Pinot Noir	R	7.1	2.3
Other varieties		23.7	
Total		100.0	

Australian Capital Territory

Prime variety	Col	Regional %	VII*
Riesling	W	25.0	9.2
Syrah	R	12.5	0.4
Cabernet Sauvignon	R	12.5	0.7
Merlot	R	12.5	1.9
Chardonnay	W	0.0	0.0
Sauvignon Blanc	W	0.0	0.0
Other varieties		37.5	
Total		100.0	

Barossa - Other

Prime variety	Col	Regional %	VII*
Syrah	R	76.4	2.7
Cabernet Sauvignon	R	12.1	0.7
Riesling	W	4.7	1.7
Muscat of Alexandria	W	2.2	1.6
Chardonnay	W	2.1	0.1
Sauvignon Blanc	W	1.5	0.4
Other varieties		0.9	
Total		100.0	

Barossa Valley

Prime variety	Col	Regional %	VII*
Syrah	R	53.4	1.9
Cabernet Sauvignon	R	13.9	0.8
Chardonnay	W	5.9	0.3
Semillon	W	5.5	1.4
Garnacha Tinta	R	5.3	4.6
Merlot	R	4.0	0.6
Other varieties		12.0	
Total		100.0	

Beechworth

Prime variety	Col	Regional %	VII*
Syrah	R	26.7	0.9
Chardonnay	W	17.5	1.0
Cabernet Sauvignon	R	16.8	1.0
Merlot	R	14.4	2.2
Pinot Noir	R	4.7	1.5
Nebbiolo	R	3.0	46.3
Other varieties		16.8	
Total		100.0	

Bendigo

Prime variety	Col	Regional %	VII*
Syrah	R	53.9	1.9
Cabernet Sauvignon	R	17.6	1.0
Merlot	R	6.7	1.0
Chardonnay	W	6.7	0.4
Pinot Gris	O	2.8	1.3
Pinot Noir	R	2.0	0.7
Other varieties		10.2	
Total		100.0	

Table 53 (cont.) Winegrape areas and Varietal Intensity Indexes for each region's top 6 varieties, by region, 2010

Australia continued

Big Rivers - Other				Blackwood Valley			
Prime variety	Col	Regional %	VII*	Prime variety	Col	Regional %	VII*
Chardonnay	W	33.5	1.8	Cabernet Sauvignon	R	22.7	1.3
Syrah	R	19.5	0.7	Syrah	R	21.3	0.8
Pinot Gris	O	15.4	7.1	Sauvignon Blanc	W	20.5	4.8
Cabernet Sauvignon	R	9.6	0.6	Chardonnay	W	17.3	0.9
Merlot	R	8.2	1.2	Semillon	W	7.8	1.9
Pinot Noir	R	4.0	1.3	Merlot	R	5.3	0.8
Other varieties		9.7		Other varieties		5.1	
Total		100.0		Total		100.0	

Canberra District (Act)				Canberra District (NSW)			
Prime variety	Col	Regional %	VII*	Prime variety	Col	Regional %	VII*
Syrah	R	25.7	0.9	Syrah	R	32.2	1.1
Riesling	W	14.9	5.5	Cabernet Sauvignon	R	20.7	1.2
Viognier	W	14.2	15.4	Merlot	R	11.1	1.7
Cabernet Sauvignon	R	11.5	0.7	Riesling	W	9.2	3.4
Chardonnay	W	10.8	0.6	Chardonnay	W	5.6	0.3
Merlot	R	9.6	1.5	Pinot Noir	R	4.6	1.5
Other varieties		13.3		Other varieties		16.6	
Total		100.0		Total		100.0	

Central Ranges - Other				Central Victoria - Other			
Prime variety	Col	Regional %	VII*	Prime variety	Col	Regional %	VII*
Chardonnay	W	31.8	1.7	Syrah	R	53.5	1.9
Merlot	R	22.1	3.3	Cabernet Sauvignon	R	11.5	0.7
Syrah	R	20.8	0.7	Chardonnay	W	8.3	0.5
Cabernet Sauvignon	R	16.6	1.0	Merlot	R	5.9	0.9
Ruby Cabernet	R	2.5	3.9	Tarrango	R	5.3	111.7
Pinot Gris	O	1.5	0.7	Riesling	W	3.5	1.3
Other varieties		4.8		Other varieties		11.9	
Total		100.0		Total		100.0	

Central Western Australia				Clare Valley			
Prime variety	Col	Regional %	VII*	Prime variety	Col	Regional %	VII*
Syrah	R	38.4	1.4	Syrah	R	34.2	1.2
Cabernet Sauvignon	R	14.1	0.8	Riesling	W	21.3	7.9
Merlot	R	9.8	1.5	Cabernet Sauvignon	R	21.0	1.2
Sauvignon Blanc	W	9.8	2.3	Merlot	R	6.2	0.9
Garnacha Tinta	R	5.4	4.7	Chardonnay	W	4.9	0.3
Sangiovese	R	4.9	12.6	Semillon	W	2.7	0.7
Other varieties		17.7		Other varieties		9.7	
Total		100.0		Total		100.0	

Coonawarra				Cowra			
Prime variety	Col	Regional %	VII*	Prime variety	Col	Regional %	VII*
Cabernet Sauvignon	R	57.2	3.3	Chardonnay	W	51.4	2.8
Syrah	R	20.2	0.7	Syrah	R	20.5	0.7
Chardonnay	W	7.3	0.4	Cabernet Sauvignon	R	7.9	0.5
Merlot	R	6.8	1.0	Merlot	R	6.4	1.0
Sauvignon Blanc	W	2.8	0.7	Semillon	W	5.3	1.3
Riesling	W	1.8	0.7	Verdelho	W	3.5	3.4
Other varieties		4.0		Other varieties		5.2	
Total		100.0		Total		100.0	

Table 53 (cont.) Winegrape areas and Varietal Intensity Indexes for each region's top 6 varieties, by region, 2010

Australia continued

Currency Creek				Eastern Plains, Inland And North Of Wa			
Prime variety	*Col*	*Regional %*	*VII**	*Prime variety*	*Col*	*Regional %*	*VII**
Syrah	R	37.5	1.3	Verdelho	W	25.7	25.4
Cabernet Sauvignon	R	30.0	1.8	Chenin Blanc	W	13.9	38.9
Chardonnay	W	8.4	0.5	Syrah	R	13.5	0.5
Sauvignon Blanc	W	8.0	1.9	Cabernet Sauvignon	R	10.6	0.6
Merlot	R	6.6	1.0	Semillon	W	6.1	1.5
Pinot Gris	O	1.5	0.7	Garnacha Tinta	R	6.1	5.3
Other varieties		8.1		Other varieties		24.1	
Total		100.0		Total		100.0	

Eden Valley				Far North - Other			
Prime variety	*Col*	*Regional %*	*VII**	*Prime variety*	*Col*	*Regional %*	*VII**
Syrah	R	29.4	1.0	Syrah	R	58.2	2.1
Riesling	W	27.6	10.2	Cabernet Sauvignon	R	40.9	2.4
Chardonnay	W	13.7	0.7	Sangiovese	R	0.9	2.3
Cabernet Sauvignon	R	12.1	0.7	Total		100.0	
Sauvignon Blanc	W	2.8	0.7				
Merlot	R	2.6	0.4				
Other varieties		11.8					
Total		100.0					

Fleurieu - Other				Geelong			
Prime variety	*Col*	*Regional %*	*VII**	*Prime variety*	*Col*	*Regional %*	*VII**
Syrah	R	45.3	1.6	Pinot Noir	R	36.9	11.9
Cabernet Sauvignon	R	33.5	2.0	Syrah	R	20.9	0.7
Chardonnay	W	16.1	0.9	Chardonnay	W	16.5	0.9
Riesling	W	2.2	0.8	Sauvignon Blanc	W	6.5	1.5
Viognier	W	1.8	1.9	Cabernet Sauvignon	R	4.2	0.2
Garnacha Tinta	R	0.7	0.6	Viognier	W	2.4	2.6
Other varieties		0.4		Other varieties		12.6	
Total		100.0		Total		100.0	

Geographe				Gippsland			
Prime variety	*Col*	*Regional %*	*VII**	*Prime variety*	*Col*	*Regional %*	*VII**
Cabernet Sauvignon	R	20.7	1.2	Pinot Noir	R	35.6	11.5
Syrah	R	20.4	0.7	Chardonnay	W	24.7	1.4
Chardonnay	W	16.2	0.9	Syrah	R	10.1	0.4
Sauvignon Blanc	W	12.8	3.0	Cabernet Sauvignon	R	10.1	0.6
Merlot	R	9.9	1.5	Sauvignon Blanc	W	5.3	1.2
Semillon	W	9.6	2.4	Merlot	R	3.8	0.6
Other varieties		10.4		Other varieties		10.4	
Total		100.0		Total		100.0	

Glenrowan				Goulburn Valley			
Prime variety	*Col*	*Regional %*	*VII**	*Prime variety*	*Col*	*Regional %*	*VII**
Syrah	R	41.5	1.5	Syrah	R	30.5	1.1
Cabernet Sauvignon	R	31.6	1.8	Cabernet Sauvignon	R	15.5	0.9
Merlot	R	12.2	1.8	Chardonnay	W	14.5	0.8
Muscat of Alexandria	W	4.1	3.0	Merlot	R	9.1	1.4
Pinot Gris	O	2.3	1.0	Sauvignon Blanc	W	7.2	1.7
Muscadelle	W	1.9	43.4	Marsanne	W	3.6	23.1
Other varieties		6.4		Other varieties		19.6	
Total		100.0		Total		100.0	

Table 53 (cont.) Winegrape areas and Varietal Intensity Indexes for each region's top 6 varieties, by region, 2010

Australia continued

Grampians				Granite Belt			
Prime variety	*Col*	*Regional %*	*VII**	*Prime variety*	*Col*	*Regional %*	*VII**
Syrah	R	63.8	2.3	Syrah	R	21.6	0.8
Cabernet Sauvignon	R	11.5	0.7	Cabernet Sauvignon	R	15.6	0.9
Chardonnay	W	8.4	0.5	Merlot	R	10.6	1.6
Riesling	W	6.0	2.2	Chardonnay	W	9.2	0.5
Merlot	R	2.7	0.4	Sauvignon Blanc	W	6.8	1.6
Pinot Noir	R	2.0	0.7	Semillon	W	3.4	0.9
Other varieties		5.6		Other varieties		32.8	
Total		100.0		Total		100.0	

Great Southern				Greater Perth - Other			
Prime variety	*Col*	*Regional %*	*VII**	*Prime variety*	*Col*	*Regional %*	*VII**
Syrah	R	22.7	0.8	Syrah	R	43.6	1.5
Cabernet Sauvignon	R	18.3	1.1	Chenin Blanc	W	14.2	40.0
Chardonnay	W	16.2	0.9	Muscat of Alexandria	W	10.6	7.9
Sauvignon Blanc	W	15.8	3.7	Cabernet Sauvignon	R	8.4	0.5
Semillon	W	8.9	2.2	Garnacha Tinta	R	5.9	5.1
Riesling	W	7.2	2.7	Semillon	W	5.6	1.4
Other varieties		10.9		Other varieties		11.7	
Total		100.0		Total		100.0	

Gundagai				Hastings River			
Prime variety	*Col*	*Regional %*	*VII**	*Prime variety*	*Col*	*Regional %*	*VII**
Syrah	R	54.0	1.9	Chardonnay	W	20.3	1.1
Cabernet Sauvignon	R	19.4	1.1	Semillon	W	13.2	3.3
Chardonnay	W	18.1	1.0	Cabernet Sauvignon	R	10.4	0.6
Muscat of Alexandria	W	2.0	1.5	Verdelho	W	7.1	7.1
Pinot Noir	R	1.7	0.6	Viognier	W	4.4	4.8
Colombard	W	1.1	0.8	Syrah	R	3.8	0.1
Other varieties		3.6		Other varieties		40.7	
Total		100.0		Total		100.0	

Heathcote				Henty			
Prime variety	*Col*	*Regional %*	*VII**	*Prime variety*	*Col*	*Regional %*	*VII**
Syrah	R	58.1	2.1	Pinot Noir	R	39.2	12.7
Chardonnay	W	11.2	0.6	Chardonnay	W	21.4	1.2
Cabernet Sauvignon	R	6.7	0.4	Riesling	W	10.2	3.8
Merlot	R	3.7	0.6	Pinot Gris	O	7.1	3.3
Viognier	W	2.8	3.1	Syrah	R	6.0	0.2
Pinot Noir	R	2.5	0.8	Cabernet Sauvignon	R	3.9	0.2
Other varieties		15.0		Other varieties		12.2	
Total		100.0		Total		100.0	

Hilltops				Hunter			
Prime variety	*Col*	*Regional %*	*VII**	*Prime variety*	*Col*	*Regional %*	*VII**
Cabernet Sauvignon	R	36.1	2.1	Syrah	R	29.7	1.1
Syrah	R	33.5	1.2	Chardonnay	W	27.6	1.5
Chardonnay	W	11.2	0.6	Semillon	W	17.0	4.2
Merlot	R	4.3	0.7	Verdelho	W	8.7	8.6
Riesling	W	3.5	1.3	Cabernet Sauvignon	R	4.6	0.3
Semillon	W	2.1	0.5	Merlot	R	3.5	0.5
Other varieties		9.3		Other varieties		8.9	
Total		100.0		Total		100.0	

Table 53 (cont.) Winegrape areas and Varietal Intensity Indexes for each region's top 6 varieties, by region, 2010

Australia continued

Hunter Valley - Other				Kangaroo Island			
Prime variety	*Col*	*Regional %*	*VII**	*Prime variety*	*Col*	*Regional %*	*VII**
Chardonnay	W	65.1	3.6	Syrah	R	40.3	1.4
Syrah	R	19.6	0.7	Cabernet Sauvignon	R	31.2	1.8
Verdelho	W	3.8	3.7	Chardonnay	W	6.5	0.4
Merlot	R	3.3	0.5	Sauvignon Blanc	W	5.4	1.3
Semillon	W	3.3	0.8	Sangiovese	R	4.3	11.0
Other varieties		4.8		Cabernet Franc	R	3.6	9.3
Total		100.0		Other varieties		8.7	
				Total		100.0	

King Valley				Langhorne Creek			
Prime variety	*Col*	*Regional %*	*VII**	*Prime variety*	*Col*	*Regional %*	*VII**
Merlot	R	13.6	2.1	Syrah	R	34.8	1.2
Cabernet Sauvignon	R	13.3	0.8	Cabernet Sauvignon	R	31.5	1.8
Chardonnay	W	12.8	0.7	Chardonnay	W	12.9	0.7
Syrah	R	12.2	0.4	Merlot	R	6.8	1.0
Pinot Gris	O	11.4	5.3	Riesling	W	2.9	1.1
Sauvignon Blanc	W	9.1	2.1	Garnacha Tinta	R	2.0	1.8
Other varieties		27.6		Other varieties		9.2	
Total		100.0		Total		100.0	

Limestone Coast - Other				Lower Murray - Other			
Prime variety	*Col*	*Regional %*	*VII**	*Prime variety*	*Col*	*Regional %*	*VII**
Cabernet Sauvignon	R	39.0	2.3	Syrah	R	39.3	1.4
Syrah	R	19.6	0.7	Chardonnay	W	24.9	1.4
Chardonnay	W	10.9	0.6	Cabernet Sauvignon	R	19.2	1.1
Pinot Noir	R	10.0	3.2	Merlot	R	6.0	0.9
Merlot	R	8.1	1.2	Monastrell	R	3.2	7.0
Sangiovese	R	4.8	12.5	Garnacha Tinta	R	2.2	1.9
Other varieties		7.5		Other varieties		5.3	
Total		100.0		Total		100.0	

Macedon Ranges				Manjimup			
Prime variety	*Col*	*Regional %*	*VII**	*Prime variety*	*Col*	*Regional %*	*VII**
Pinot Noir	R	37.8	12.2	Cabernet Sauvignon	R	21.4	1.3
Chardonnay	W	23.6	1.3	Chardonnay	W	18.6	1.0
Syrah	R	13.2	0.5	Merlot	R	18.1	2.7
Cabernet Sauvignon	R	7.7	0.4	Sauvignon Blanc	W	14.0	3.3
Merlot	R	3.6	0.5	Verdelho	W	12.1	12.0
Sauvignon Blanc	W	3.4	0.8	Semillon	W	6.1	1.5
Other varieties		10.7		Other varieties		9.7	
Total		100.0		Total		100.0	

Margaret River				McLaren Vale			
Prime variety	*Col*	*Regional %*	*VII**	*Prime variety*	*Col*	*Regional %*	*VII**
Cabernet Sauvignon	R	22.9	1.3	Syrah	R	51.5	1.8
Sauvignon Blanc	W	16.3	3.8	Cabernet Sauvignon	R	17.5	1.0
Chardonnay	W	16.0	0.9	Chardonnay	W	7.5	0.4
Syrah	R	14.3	0.5	Garnacha Tinta	R	5.5	4.7
Semillon	W	11.7	2.9	Merlot	R	4.3	0.7
Merlot	R	8.5	1.3	Sauvignon Blanc	W	2.7	0.6
Other varieties		10.3		Other varieties		11.2	
Total		100.0		Total		100.0	

Table 53 (cont.) Winegrape areas and Varietal Intensity Indexes for each region's top 6 varieties, by region, 2010

Australia continued

Mornington Peninsula				Mount Benson			
Prime variety	*Col*	*Regional %*	*VII**	*Prime variety*	*Col*	*Regional %*	*VII**
Pinot Noir	R	43.3	14.0	Cabernet Sauvignon	R	27.1	1.6
Chardonnay	W	25.3	1.4	Syrah	R	25.0	0.9
Pinot Gris	O	11.8	5.4	Chardonnay	W	17.8	1.0
Syrah	R	5.6	0.2	Sauvignon Blanc	W	15.4	3.6
Sauvignon Blanc	W	3.3	0.8	Merlot	R	13.6	2.1
Cabernet Sauvignon	R	3.1	0.2	Semillon	W	1.1	0.3
Other varieties		7.5		Other varieties		0.0	
Total		100.0		Total		100.0	

Mount Lofty Ranges - Other				Mudgee			
Prime variety	*Col*	*Regional %*	*VII**	*Prime variety*	*Col*	*Regional %*	*VII**
Syrah	R	51.8	1.8	Syrah	R	32.5	1.2
Cabernet Sauvignon	R	15.5	0.9	Cabernet Sauvignon	R	23.6	1.4
Chardonnay	W	5.8	0.3	Chardonnay	W	16.3	0.9
Riesling	W	5.8	2.1	Merlot	R	10.4	1.6
Garnacha Tinta	R	4.1	3.5	Semillon	W	4.6	1.2
Merlot	R	3.0	0.5	Gewurztraminer	W	2.5	4.5
Other varieties		14.1		Other varieties		10.1	
Total		100.0		Total		100.0	

Murray Darling - NSW				Murray Darling - Vic			
Prime variety	*Col*	*Regional %*	*VII**	*Prime variety*	*Col*	*Regional %*	*VII**
Chardonnay	W	26.7	1.5	Chardonnay	W	30.5	1.7
Syrah	R	20.0	0.7	Syrah	R	18.8	0.7
Cabernet Sauvignon	R	12.1	0.7	Cabernet Sauvignon	R	14.8	0.9
Merlot	R	9.7	1.5	Merlot	R	7.9	1.2
Pinot Gris	O	8.6	4.0	Colombard	W	5.5	3.8
Sauvignon Blanc	W	4.8	1.1	Muscat of Alexandria	W	4.9	3.7
Other varieties		18.2		Other varieties		17.7	
Total		100.0		Total		100.0	

New England Australia				North East Victoria - Other			
Prime variety	*Col*	*Regional %*	*VII**	*Prime variety*	*Col*	*Regional %*	*VII**
Semillon	W	38.9	9.7	Cabernet Sauvignon	R	29.8	1.7
Chardonnay	W	32.6	1.8	Merlot	R	22.6	3.4
Syrah	R	8.1	0.3	Chardonnay	W	15.6	0.9
Cabernet Sauvignon	R	4.2	0.2	Syrah	R	11.8	0.4
Gewurztraminer	W	4.1	7.4	Pinot Noir	R	6.5	2.1
Merlot	R	2.8	0.4	Pinot Gris	O	3.4	1.6
Other varieties		9.2		Other varieties		10.3	
Total		100.0		Total		100.0	

North West Victoria - Other				Northern Rivers - Other			
Prime variety	*Col*	*Regional %*	*VII**	*Prime variety*	*Col*	*Regional %*	*VII**
Syrah	R	26.9	1.0	Chardonnay	W	43.1	2.4
Cabernet Sauvignon	R	14.6	0.9	Merlot	R	6.4	1.0
Chardonnay	W	14.2	0.8	Syrah	R	5.6	0.2
Merlot	R	12.4	1.9	Cabernet Sauvignon	R	3.2	0.2
Muscat of Alexandria	W	8.0	6.0	Pinot Gris	O	2.7	1.2
Colombard	W	7.9	5.4	Verdelho	W	1.7	1.7
Other varieties		16.0		Other varieties		37.3	
Total		100.0		Total		100.0	

Table 53 (cont.) Winegrape areas and Varietal Intensity Indexes for each region's top 6 varieties, by region, 2010

Australia continued

Northern Slopes - Other				Orange			
Prime variety	*Col*	*Regional %*	*VII** *Prime variety*		*Col*	*Regional %*	*VII**
Syrah	R	25.3	0.9 Syrah		R	28.4	1.0
Cabernet Sauvignon	R	25.1	1.5 Cabernet Sauvignon		R	19.4	1.1
Merlot	R	15.6	2.4 Chardonnay		W	18.7	1.0
Chardonnay	W	15.3	0.8 Merlot		R	12.4	1.9
Semillon	W	4.8	1.2 Sauvignon Blanc		W	6.5	1.5
Verdelho	W	2.9	2.9 Pinot Gris		O	3.0	1.4
Other varieties		11.0	Other varieties			11.7	
Total		100.0	Total			100.0	

Padthaway				Peel			
Prime variety	*Col*	*Regional %*	*VII** *Prime variety*		*Col*	*Regional %*	*VII**
Syrah	R	29.0	1.0 Cabernet Sauvignon		R	30.6	1.8
Cabernet Sauvignon	R	24.5	1.4 Syrah		R	22.1	0.8
Chardonnay	W	18.9	1.0 Chardonnay		W	17.2	0.9
Merlot	R	8.2	1.2 Merlot		R	5.1	0.8
Riesling	W	3.4	1.3 Chenin Blanc		W	4.9	13.7
Pinot Gris	O	3.4	1.5 Semillon		W	4.8	1.2
Other varieties		12.5	Other varieties			15.4	
Total		100.0	Total			100.0	

Pemberton				Perricoota			
Prime variety	*Col*	*Regional %*	*VII** *Prime variety*		*Col*	*Regional %*	*VII**
Sauvignon Blanc	W	33.2	7.8 Syrah		R	30.5	1.1
Chardonnay	W	21.7	1.2 Chardonnay		W	28.6	1.6
Pinot Noir	R	9.6	3.1 Cabernet Sauvignon		R	19.8	1.2
Cabernet Sauvignon	R	8.5	0.5 Merlot		R	5.8	0.9
Merlot	R	7.5	1.1 Garnacha Tinta		R	2.3	2.0
Semillon	W	5.9	1.5 Semillon		W	1.8	0.5
Other varieties		13.6	Other varieties			11.3	
Total		100.0	Total			100.0	

Perth Hills				Port Phillip - Other			
Prime variety	*Col*	*Regional %*	*VII** *Prime variety*		*Col*	*Regional %*	*VII**
Syrah	R	25.0	0.9 Pinot Noir		R	39.6	12.8
Chardonnay	W	20.4	1.1 Chardonnay		W	20.4	1.1
Chenin Blanc	W	15.8	44.4 Cabernet Sauvignon		R	13.0	0.8
Verdelho	W	11.2	11.0 Syrah		R	12.1	0.4
Cabernet Sauvignon	R	7.4	0.4 Merlot		R	5.2	0.8
Viognier	W	3.4	3.6 Riesling		W	2.5	0.9
Other varieties		16.9	Other varieties			7.2	
Total		100.0	Total			100.0	

Pyrenees				Queensland - Other			
Prime variety	*Col*	*Regional %*	*VII** *Prime variety*		*Col*	*Regional %*	*VII**
Syrah	R	45.0	1.6 Syrah		R	30.5	1.1
Cabernet Sauvignon	R	16.1	0.9 Cabernet Sauvignon		R	11.3	0.7
Cabernet Franc	R	13.9	35.8 Chardonnay		W	11.0	0.6
Merlot	R	8.2	1.2 Verdelho		W	7.9	7.8
Chardonnay	W	5.5	0.3 Merlot		R	7.1	1.1
Sauvignon Blanc	W	3.0	0.7 Semillon		W	4.0	1.0
Other varieties		8.4	Other varieties			28.2	
Total		100.0	Total			100.0	

Table 53 (cont.) Winegrape areas and Varietal Intensity Indexes for each region's top 6 varieties, by region, 2010

Australia continued

Riverina				Riverland			
Prime variety	*Col*	*Regional %*	*VII**	*Prime variety*	*Col*	*Regional %*	*VII**
Syrah	R	23.6	0.8	Syrah	R	28.1	1.0
Chardonnay	W	22.7	1.2	Chardonnay	W	23.4	1.3
Semillon	W	10.5	2.6	Cabernet Sauvignon	R	15.6	0.9
Cabernet Sauvignon	R	7.2	0.4	Merlot	R	5.5	0.8
Merlot	R	6.8	1.0	Muscat of Alexandria	W	4.1	3.1
Pinot Gris	O	5.2	2.4	Colombard	W	3.9	2.7
Other varieties		24.1		Other varieties		19.4	
Total		100.0		Total		100.0	

Robe				Rutherglen			
Prime variety	*Col*	*Regional %*	*VII**	*Prime variety*	*Col*	*Regional %*	*VII**
Syrah	R	27.8	1.0	Syrah	R	43.6	1.6
Cabernet Sauvignon	R	24.7	1.4	Cabernet Sauvignon	R	11.3	0.7
Chardonnay	W	24.0	1.3	Muscat a Petits Grains Rou	R	9.9	65.7
Pinot Noir	R	10.0	3.2	Durif	R	8.7	31.8
Merlot	R	5.4	0.8	Chardonnay	W	3.3	0.2
Sauvignon Blanc	W	3.6	0.8	Muscadelle	W	2.6	59.7
Other varieties		4.6		Other varieties		20.5	
Total		100.0		Total		100.0	

Shoalhaven Coast				South Burnett			
Prime variety	*Col*	*Regional %*	*VII**	*Prime variety*	*Col*	*Regional %*	*VII**
Chardonnay	W	16.4	0.9	Syrah	R	32.0	1.1
Cabernet Sauvignon	R	11.9	0.7	Cabernet Sauvignon	R	18.3	1.1
Verdelho	W	10.6	10.5	Chardonnay	W	13.6	0.7
Syrah	R	9.8	0.4	Semillon	W	10.9	2.7
Semillon	W	7.6	1.9	Merlot	R	7.6	1.2
Sauvignon Blanc	W	5.6	1.3	Verdelho	W	6.6	6.5
Other varieties		38.1		Other varieties		11.1	
Total		100.0		Total		100.0	

South Coast - Other				South West Australia - Other			
Prime variety	*Col*	*Regional %*	*VII**	*Prime variety*	*Col*	*Regional %*	*VII**
Chardonnay	W	21.8	1.2	Sauvignon Blanc	W	24.0	5.6
Syrah	R	19.5	0.7	Chardonnay	W	18.3	1.0
Cabernet Sauvignon	R	7.5	0.4	Merlot	R	14.3	2.2
Semillon	W	7.3	1.8	Cabernet Sauvignon	R	13.4	0.8
Verdelho	W	5.7	5.6	Syrah	R	12.8	0.5
Pinot Noir	R	5.0	1.6	Semillon	W	6.7	1.7
Other varieties		33.3		Other varieties		10.5	
Total		100.0		Total		100.0	

Southern Fleurieu				Southern Flinders Ranges			
Prime variety	*Col*	*Regional %*	*VII**	*Prime variety*	*Col*	*Regional %*	*VII**
Syrah	R	38.4	1.4	Syrah	R	81.3	2.9
Cabernet Sauvignon	R	18.6	1.1	Cabernet Sauvignon	R	10.8	0.6
Chardonnay	W	12.0	0.7	Riesling	W	2.4	0.9
Merlot	R	5.7	0.9	Merlot	R	1.7	0.3
Sauvignon Blanc	W	5.2	1.2	Sangiovese	R	1.3	3.4
Semillon	W	5.0	1.2	Garnacha Tinta	R	0.7	0.6
Other varieties		15.3		Other varieties		1.9	
Total		100.0		Total		100.0	

Table 53 (cont.) Winegrape areas and Varietal Intensity Indexes for each region's top 6 varieties, by region, 2010

Australia continued

Southern Highlands				Southern NSW - Other			
Prime variety	*Col*	*Regional %*	*VII**	*Prime variety*	*Col*	*Regional %*	*VII**
Chardonnay	W	16.2	0.9	Syrah	R	29.5	1.0
Sauvignon Blanc	W	14.7	3.5	Pinot Gris	O	23.5	10.8
Tempranillo	R	13.3	42.3	Cabernet Sauvignon	R	10.2	0.6
Pinot Noir	R	11.7	3.8	Chardonnay	W	9.7	0.5
Cabernet Sauvignon	R	10.7	0.6	Sauvignon Blanc	W	8.9	2.1
Syrah	R	10.2	0.4	Merlot	R	5.5	0.8
Other varieties		23.1		Other varieties		12.7	
Total		100.0		Total		100.0	

Strathbogie Ranges				Sunbury			
Prime variety	*Col*	*Regional %*	*VII**	*Prime variety*	*Col*	*Regional %*	*VII**
Chardonnay	W	23.1	1.3	Syrah	R	34.1	1.2
Sauvignon Blanc	W	15.4	3.6	Pinot Noir	R	15.1	4.9
Pinot Noir	R	14.4	4.7	Chardonnay	W	11.2	0.6
Syrah	R	12.1	0.4	Sauvignon Blanc	W	9.4	2.2
Merlot	R	11.2	1.7	Cabernet Sauvignon	R	9.3	0.5
Cabernet Sauvignon	R	9.8	0.6	Merlot	R	6.7	1.0
Other varieties		13.9		Other varieties		14.2	
Total		100.0		Total		100.0	

Swan District				Swan Hill NSW			
Prime variety	*Col*	*Regional %*	*VII**	*Prime variety*	*Col*	*Regional %*	*VII**
Syrah	R	17.9	0.6	Syrah	R	29.2	1.0
Chardonnay	W	14.0	0.8	Chardonnay	W	15.3	0.8
Chenin Blanc	W	13.3	37.4	Cabernet Sauvignon	R	14.5	0.8
Verdelho	W	12.3	12.1	Semillon	W	7.8	1.9
Cabernet Sauvignon	R	10.4	0.6	Merlot	R	5.9	0.9
Garnacha Tinta	R	7.2	6.3	Sauvignon Blanc	W	4.6	1.1
Other varieties		24.9		Other varieties		22.6	
Total		100.0		Total		100.0	

Swan Hill Vic				Tasmania			
Prime variety	*Col*	*Regional %*	*VII**	*Prime variety*	*Col*	*Regional %*	*VII**
Chardonnay	W	23.7	1.3	Pinot Noir	R	42.4	13.7
Syrah	R	23.3	0.8	Chardonnay	W	23.3	1.3
Cabernet Sauvignon	R	8.2	0.5	Sauvignon Blanc	W	11.4	2.7
Merlot	R	7.5	1.1	Riesling	W	8.5	3.1
Sauvignon Blanc	W	7.1	1.7	Pinot Gris	O	6.5	3.0
Muscat of Alexandria	W	3.8	2.8	Cabernet Sauvignon	R	2.6	0.2
Other varieties		26.4		Other varieties		5.3	
Total		100.0		Total		100.0	

The Peninsulas				Tumbarumba			
Prime variety	*Col*	*Regional %*	*VII**	*Prime variety*	*Col*	*Regional %*	*VII**
Syrah	R	37.4	1.3	Chardonnay	W	36.6	2.0
Cabernet Sauvignon	R	27.4	1.6	Pinot Noir	R	32.4	10.5
Merlot	R	10.5	1.6	Syrah	R	16.6	0.6
Chardonnay	W	7.6	0.4	Sauvignon Blanc	W	5.9	1.4
Viognier	W	6.8	7.3	Riesling	W	2.1	0.8
Riesling	W	4.2	1.5	Pinot Gris	O	1.8	0.8
Other varieties		6.0		Other varieties		4.5	
Total		100.0		Total		100.0	

Table 53 (cont.) Winegrape areas and Varietal Intensity Indexes for each region's top 6 varieties, by region, 2010

Australia continued

	Upper Goulburn				Western Australian South East Coastal		
Prime variety	*Col*	*Regional %*	*VII**	*Prime variety*	*Col*	*Regional %*	*VII**
Chardonnay	W	22.1	1.2	Syrah	R	43.3	1.5
Pinot Noir	R	20.5	6.6	Chardonnay	W	22.5	1.2
Cabernet Sauvignon	R	13.4	0.8	Sauvignon Blanc	W	11.8	2.8
Syrah	R	13.1	0.5	Cabernet Sauvignon	R	9.6	0.6
Sauvignon Blanc	W	10.7	2.5	Merlot	R	8.0	1.2
Merlot	R	7.3	1.1	Riesling	W	2.7	1.0
Other varieties		13.0		Other varieties		2.1	
Total		100.0		Total		100.0	

	Western Plains - Other				Western Victoria - Other		
Prime variety	*Col*	*Regional %*	*VII**	*Prime variety*	*Col*	*Regional %*	*VII**
Syrah	R	42.5	1.5	Syrah	R	28.4	1.0
Chardonnay	W	22.7	1.2	Cabernet Sauvignon	R	25.0	1.5
Cabernet Sauvignon	R	6.1	0.4	Pinot Noir	R	15.4	5.0
Merlot	R	6.1	0.9	Chardonnay	W	9.1	0.5
Verdelho	W	6.1	6.0	Merlot	R	8.6	1.3
Ruby Cabernet	R	3.4	5.4	Pinot Gris	O	3.4	1.6
Other varieties		13.2		Other varieties		10.2	
Total		100.0		Total		100.0	

	Wrattonbully				Yarra Valley		
Prime variety	*Col*	*Regional %*	*VII**	*Prime variety*	*Col*	*Regional %*	*VII**
Cabernet Sauvignon	R	44.6	2.6	Pinot Noir	R	28.9	9.4
Syrah	R	23.4	0.8	Chardonnay	W	27.2	1.5
Merlot	R	11.7	1.8	Cabernet Sauvignon	R	13.6	0.8
Chardonnay	W	9.9	0.5	Syrah	R	10.0	0.4
Pinot Gris	O	3.9	1.8	Sauvignon Blanc	W	7.4	1.7
Sauvignon Blanc	W	2.1	0.5	Merlot	R	4.9	0.7
Other varieties		4.4		Other varieties		8.1	
Total		100.0		Total		100.0	

Austria

	Burgenland				Niederosterreich		
Prime variety	*Col*	*Regional %*	*VII**	*Prime variety*	*Col*	*Regional %*	*VII**
Blaufrankisch	R	22.1	3.1	Gruner Veltliner	W	43.7	1.5
Zweigelt	R	19.1	1.4	Zweigelt	R	12.3	0.9
Gruner Veltliner	W	10.6	0.4	Blauer Portugieser	R	5.9	1.6
Grasevina	W	10.3	1.4	Riesling	W	5.7	1.4
Chardonnay	W	4.1	1.3	Muller Thurgau	W	5.1	1.1
Pinot Blanc	W	4.0	0.9	Grasevina	W	5.0	0.7
Other varieties		29.8		Other varieties		22.3	
Total		100.0		Total		100.0	

	Steiermark				Wien And Other Bundeslander		
Prime variety	*Col*	*Regional %*	*VII**	*Prime variety*	*Col*	*Regional %*	*VII**
Grasevina	W	17.0	2.2	Gruner Veltliner	W	24.2	0.8
Pinot Blanc	W	11.2	2.7	Riesling	W	12.8	3.2
Sauvignon Blanc	W	11.0	5.9	Chardonnay	W	8.2	2.7
Zweigelt	R	9.7	0.7	Zweigelt	R	7.9	0.6
Blauer Wildbacher	R	9.4	11.8	Pinot Blanc	W	6.6	1.6
Chardonnay	W	7.2	2.4	Grasevina	W	4.2	0.6
Other varieties		34.4		Other varieties		36.1	
Total		100.0		Total		100.0	

Table 53 (cont.) Winegrape areas and Varietal Intensity Indexes for each region's top 6 varieties, by region, 2010

Brazil

Prime variety	Col	Regional %	VII*
Isabella	R	37.0	
Bordo	R	16.8	
Concord	R	7.2	
Niagara	W	6.4	
Couderc Noir	R	5.0	
Jacquez	R	4.6	
Other varieties		23.0	
Total		100.0	

Bulgaria

	Severen Tsentralen				Severoiztochen		
Prime variety	Col	Regional %	VII*	Prime variety	Col	Regional %	VII*
Cabernet Sauvignon	R	22.7	1.5	Dimyat	W	12.9	3.0
Muscat Ottonel	W	14.1	2.4	Rkatsiteli	W	11.8	2.1
Merlot	R	9.4	0.5	Chardonnay	W	11.2	2.6
Chardonnay	W	5.9	1.4	Pamid	R	9.0	0.7
Rkatsiteli	W	5.9	1.1	Muscat Ottonel	W	8.7	1.5
Pamid	R	4.2	0.3	Misket Varnenski	W	5.8	9.6
Other varieties		37.7		Other varieties		40.7	
Total		100.0		Total		100.0	

	Severozapaden				Yugoiztochen		
Prime variety	Col	Regional %	VII*	Prime variety	Col	Regional %	VII*
Cabernet Sauvignon	R	17.0	1.1	Merlot	R	16.3	0.9
Merlot	R	12.1	0.6	Cabernet Sauvignon	R	15.0	1.0
Pamid	R	10.3	0.8	Misket Cherven	O	13.5	1.8
Kadarka	R	7.3	7.5	Pamid	R	12.1	1.0
Storgozia	R	5.1	9.6	Muscat Ottonel	W	9.2	1.6
Rkatsiteli	W	3.9	0.7	Rkatsiteli	W	6.9	1.2
Other varieties		44.3		Other varieties		26.9	
Total		100.0		Total		100.0	

	Yugozapaden				Yuzhen Tsentralen		
Prime variety	Col	Regional %	VII*	Prime variety	Col	Regional %	VII*
Shiroka Melnishka	R	43.8	15.6	Merlot	R	31.7	1.7
Merlot	R	12.7	0.7	Cabernet Sauvignon	R	17.3	1.1
Pamid	R	10.7	0.9	Pamid	R	15.7	1.3
Cabernet Sauvignon	R	10.3	0.7	Misket Cherven	O	8.3	1.1
Ranna Melnishka Loza	R	6.9	15.6	Mavrud	R	6.1	2.6
Chardonnay	W	1.1	0.3	Rkatsiteli	W	3.3	0.6
Other varieties		14.4		Other varieties		17.6	
Total		100.0		Total		100.0	

Canada

	British Colombia				Ontario		
Prime variety	Col	Regional %	VII*	Prime variety	Col	Regional %	VII*
Merlot	R	16.2	1.6	Vidal	W	20.8	1.6
Pinot Gris	O	10.8	2.0	Chardonnay	W	13.2	1.1
Pinot Noir	R	9.6	1.5	Riesling	W	11.4	1.3
Chardonnay	W	9.3	0.8	Cabernet Franc	R	7.5	1.1
Cabernet Sauvignon	R	7.7	1.4	Baco Noir	R	6.0	1.6
Gewurztraminer	W	7.2	1.8	Merlot	R	5.7	0.6
Other varieties		39.3		Other varieties			
Total		100.0		Total		100.0	

Table 53 (cont.) Winegrape areas and Varietal Intensity Indexes for each region's top 6 varieties, by region, 2010

Chile

Araucania				Atacama			
Prime variety	*Col*	*Regional %*	*VII**	*Prime variety*	*Col*	*Regional %*	*VII**
Pinot Noir	R	29.6	11.4	Muscat of Alexandria	W	26.7	27.3
Chardonnay	W	26.5	2.3	Alicante Henri Bouschet	R	12.9	3.4
Sauvignon Blanc	W	26.5	2.4	Cabernet Sauvignon	R	6.5	0.2
Gewurztraminer	W	9.1	32.0	Cot	R	6.5	5.7
Riesling	W	8.4	25.5	Viognier	W	6.5	9.6
Total		100.0		Chardonnay	W	4.8	0.4
				Other varieties		36.2	
				Total		100.0	

Coquimbo				De Los Lagos			
Prime variety	*Col*	*Regional %*	*VII**	*Prime variety*	*Col*	*Regional %*	*VII**
Chardonnay	W	26.4	2.2	Chardonnay	W	33.3	2.8
Syrah	R	20.3	3.8	Sauvignon Blanc	W	33.3	3.1
Cabernet Sauvignon	R	14.9	0.4	Pinot Noir	R	33.3	12.9
Sauvignon Blanc	W	11.1	1.0	Total		100.0	
Carmenere	R	7.3	0.9				
Pinot Noir	R	4.2	1.6				
Other varieties		15.8					
Total		100.0					

Del Bio Bio				Del Maule			
Prime variety	*Col*	*Regional %*	*VII**	*Prime variety*	*Col*	*Regional %*	*VII**
Muscat of Alexandria	W	28.5	29.1	Cabernet Sauvignon	R	37.4	1.0
Listan Prieto	R	11.8	3.4	Sauvignon Blanc	W	12.4	1.1
Chardonnay	W	10.6	0.9	Chardonnay	W	11.7	1.0
Pinot Noir	R	10.3	4.0	Merlot	R	7.7	0.9
Cabernet Sauvignon	R	9.9	0.3	Listan Prieto	R	7.0	2.0
Sauvignon Blanc	W	7.0	0.6	Carmenere	R	6.1	0.8
Other varieties		21.8		Other varieties		17.9	
Total		100.0		Total		100.0	

Metropolitana				O'Higgins			
Prime variety	*Col*	*Regional %*	*VII**	*Prime variety*	*Col*	*Regional %*	*VII**
Cabernet Sauvignon	R	52.7	1.4	Cabernet Sauvignon	R	41.4	1.1
Merlot	R	9.0	1.0	Carmenere	R	13.0	1.6
Chardonnay	W	8.6	0.7	Merlot	R	12.3	1.4
Syrah	R	8.0	1.5	Syrah	R	7.5	1.4
Carmenere	R	6.6	0.8	Chardonnay	W	7.4	0.6
Sauvignon Blanc	W	5.7	0.5	Sauvignon Blanc	W	5.2	0.5
Other varieties		9.4		Other varieties		13.1	
Total		100.0		Total		100.0	

Valparaiso			
Prime variety	*Col*	*Regional %*	*VII**
Sauvignon Blanc	W	35.5	3.3
Chardonnay	W	31.4	2.7
Pinot Noir	R	14.0	5.4
Merlot	R	5.7	0.6
Cabernet Sauvignon	R	3.9	0.1
Syrah	R	3.7	0.7
Other varieties		5.8	
Total		100.0	

Table 53 (cont.) Winegrape areas and Varietal Intensity Indexes for each region's top 6 varieties, by region, 2010

China

Beijing				Gansu			
Prime variety	*Col*	*Regional %*	*VII**	*Prime variety*	*Col*	*Regional %*	*VII**
Cabernet Sauvignon	R	100.0	1.3	Cabernet Sauvignon	R	64.2	0.8
Total		100.0		Merlot	R	18.7	1.6
				Chardonnay	W	5.3	2.1
				Cabernet Franc	R	4.7	2.7
				Riesling	W	2.7	1.8
				Syrah	R	2.7	3.5
				Other varieties		1.7	
				Total		100.0	

Ningxia				Shandong			
Prime variety	*Col*	*Regional %*	*VII**	*Prime variety*	*Col*	*Regional %*	*VII**
Cabernet Sauvignon	R	77.1	1.0	Cabernet Sauvignon	R	100.0	1.3
Carmenere	R	11.4	2.5	Total		100.0	
Merlot	R	7.1	0.6				
Chardonnay	W	1.7	0.7				
Cabernet Franc	R	1.4	0.8				
Syrah	R	0.6	0.8				
Other varieties		0.8					
Total		100.0					

Shanxi				Sichuan			
Prime variety	*Col*	*Regional %*	*VII**	*Prime variety*	*Col*	*Regional %*	*VII**
Cabernet Sauvignon	R	40.2	0.5	Cabernet Sauvignon	R	100.0	1.3
Cabernet Franc	R	22.0	12.8	Total		100.0	
Merlot	R	15.9	1.3				
Chardonnay	W	14.6	5.9				
Riesling	W	3.7	2.5				
Syrah	R	3.7	4.9				
Other varieties		0.0					
Total		100.0					

Tianjin				Xinjiang			
Prime variety	*Col*	*Regional %*	*VII**	*Prime variety*	*Col*	*Regional %*	*VII**
Cabernet Sauvignon	R	100.0	1.3	Cabernet Sauvignon	R	63.8	0.8
Total		100.0		Merlot	R	21.3	1.8
				Riesling	W	8.5	5.8
				Chardonnay	W	6.4	2.6
				Total		100.0	

Yantai				Other Regions			
Prime variety	*Col*	*Regional %*	*VII**	*Prime variety*	*Col*	*Regional %*	*VII**
Cabernet Sauvignon	R	99.1	1.3	Merlot	R	84.5	7.0
Ruby Cabernet	R	0.9	6.8	Cabernet Sauvignon	R	15.5	0.2
Total		100.0		Total		100.0	

Table 53 (cont.) Winegrape areas and Varietal Intensity Indexes for each region's top 6 varieties, by region, 2010

Croatia

Dalmatinska Zagora				Hrvatsko Primorje			
Prime variety	Col	Regional %	VII*	Prime variety	Col	Regional %	VII*
Kujundzusa	W	34.2	34.5	Zlahtina	W	58.5	90.2
Plavina	R	9.6	3.1	Cabernet Sauvignon	R	5.6	1.8
Vranac	R	8.1	11.4	Gegic	W	5.3	98.7
Merlot	R	7.1	1.9	Chardonnay	W	4.5	1.4
Cardinal	R	6.1	14.0	Trbljan	W	3.4	3.1
Trbljan	W	5.1	4.5	Plavina	R	2.9	0.9
Other varieties		29.7		Other varieties		19.9	
Total		100.0		Total		100.0	

Istra				Moslavina			
Prime variety	Col	Regional %	VII*	Prime variety	Col	Regional %	VII*
Malvazija Istarska	W	55.1	6.7	Grasevina	W	24.8	1.1
Merlot	R	10.2	2.7	Skrlet	W	21.8	74.0
Terrano	R	7.4	6.7	Blaufrankisch	R	10.1	3.8
Cabernet Sauvignon	R	6.2	2.0	Chardonnay	W	9.6	3.0
Chardonnay	W	4.6	1.4	Pinot Blanc	W	7.6	8.4
Refosco	R	4.0	6.7	Riesling	W	4.8	1.5
Other varieties		12.5		Other varieties		21.2	
Total		100.0		Total		100.0	

Plesivica				Podunavlje			
Prime variety	Col	Regional %	VII*	Prime variety	Col	Regional %	VII*
Grasevina	W	23.2	1.0	Grasevina	W	60.6	2.7
Riesling	W	13.5	4.1	Blaufrankisch	R	6.0	2.2
Kraljevina	W	8.2	6.4	Riesling	W	5.9	1.8
Chardonnay	W	8.0	2.5	Chardonnay	W	5.5	1.7
Blauer Portugieser	R	6.9	34.2	Cabernet Sauvignon	R	5.1	1.6
Ranfol	W	4.5	6.9	Gewurztraminer	W	5.1	4.5
Other varieties		35.8		Other varieties		11.8	
Total		100.0		Total		100.0	

Pokuplje				Prigorje - Bilogora			
Prime variety	Col	Regional %	VII*	Prime variety	Col	Regional %	VII*
Skrlet	W	27.7	93.9	Grasevina	W	33.3	1.5
Grasevina	W	26.9	1.2	Kraljevina	W	22.4	17.4
Chardonnay	W	8.8	2.7	Riesling	W	8.1	2.5
Kraljevina	W	6.7	5.2	Chardonnay	W	5.6	1.7
Riesling	W	5.8	1.8	Ranfol	W	3.1	4.9
Blaufrankisch	R	4.6	1.7	Blaufrankisch	R	3.1	1.1
Other varieties		19.6		Other varieties		24.5	
Total		100.0		Total		100.0	

Sjeverna Dalmacija				Slavonija			
Prime variety	Col	Regional %	VII*	Prime variety	Col	Regional %	VII*
Debit	W	16.8	8.7	Grasevina	W	60.1	2.7
Plavina	R	15.4	5.0	Blaufrankisch	R	7.2	2.7
Babic	R	11.9	6.9	Riesling	W	4.8	1.5
Merlot	R	9.0	2.4	Chardonnay	W	4.3	1.3
Syrah	R	5.8	6.4	Zweigelt	R	2.8	4.7
Trebbiano Toscano	W	5.6	5.5	Cabernet Sauvignon	R	2.6	0.8
Other varieties		35.4		Other varieties		18.2	
Total		100.0		Total		100.0	

Table 53 (cont.) Winegrape areas and Varietal Intensity Indexes for each region's top 6 varieties, by region, 2010

Croatia continued

Srednja I Juzna Dalmacija				Zagorje-Medimurje			
Prime variety	*Col*	*Regional %*	*VII**	*Prime variety*	*Col*	*Regional %*	*VII**
Plavac Mali	R	49.4	6.5	Grasevina	W	26.4	1.2
Plavina	R	7.4	2.4	Riesling	W	15.1	4.6
Posip Bijeli	W	6.9	5.7	Furmint	W	11.4	13.7
Trbljan	W	5.6	5.1	Sauvignon Blanc	W	7.8	6.5
Malvasia Bianca Lunga	W	5.0	3.6	Ranfol	W	6.9	10.8
Merlot	R	3.2	0.8	Chardonnay	W	5.2	1.6
Other varieties		22.6		Other varieties		27.2	
Total		100.0		Total		100.0	

Cyprus

Other Regions				Cyprus			
Prime variety	*Col*	*Regional %*	*VII**	*Prime variety*	*Col*	*Regional %*	*VII**
Other varieties		100.0		Mavro	R	41.5	
Total		100.0		Xynisteri	W	24.3	
				Mazuelo	R	5.6	
				Sultaniye	W	4.3	
				Cabernet Sauvignon	R	4.3	
				Syrah	R	2.8	
				Other varieties		17.1	
				Total		100.0	

Czech Republic

Cechy				Morava			
Prime variety	*Col*	*Regional %*	*VII**	*Prime variety*	*Col*	*Regional %*	*VII**
Muller Thurgau	W	17.6	1.8	Grasevina	W	14.4	1.0
Riesling	W	10.2	1.4	Gruner Veltliner	W	9.8	1.0
Pinot Noir	R	10.1	2.4	Muller Thurgau	W	9.3	1.0
Sankt Laurent	R	9.6	1.2	Sankt Laurent	R	7.9	1.0
Pinot Gris	O	7.3	1.7	Blaufrankisch	R	7.4	1.0
Blauer Portugieser	R	7.0	1.8	Sauvignon Blanc	W	5.1	1.0
Other varieties		38.3		Other varieties		46.2	
Total		100.0		Total		100.0	

France

Aquitaine-Other				Ardeche			
Prime variety	*Col*	*Regional %*	*VII**	*Prime variety*	*Col*	*Regional %*	*VII**
Tannat	R	27.3	79.2	Syrah	R	24.9	3.1
Petit Manseng	W	26.6	175.8	Garnacha Tinta	R	19.3	1.7
Gros Manseng	W	25.1	42.5	Merlot	R	12.5	0.9
Cabernet Franc	R	12.6	2.9	Cabernet Sauvignon	R	7.1	1.1
Cabernet Sauvignon	R	3.6	0.5	Gamay Noir	R	5.7	1.6
Muscadelle	W	0.8	4.5	Chardonnay	W	5.5	1.1
Other varieties		4.1		Other varieties		24.9	
Total		100.0		Total		100.0	

Aude				Bas Rhin			
Prime variety	*Col*	*Regional %*	*VII**	*Prime variety*	*Col*	*Regional %*	*VII**
Mazuelo	R	21.5	3.4	Riesling	W	22.5	54.7
Merlot	R	14.7	1.1	Gewurztraminer	W	14.9	40.9
Syrah	R	14.2	1.8	Auxerrois	W	14.6	52.6
Garnacha Tinta	R	11.3	1.0	Silvaner	W	13.9	84.2
Cabernet Sauvignon	R	7.0	1.1	Pinot Gris	O	12.5	40.4
Chardonnay	W	5.9	1.1	Pinot Noir	R	10.3	2.9
Other varieties		25.3		Other varieties		11.3	
Total		100.0		Total		100.0	

Table 53 (cont.) Winegrape areas and Varietal Intensity Indexes for each region's top 6 varieties, by region, 2010

France continued

Bouches Du Rhone				Centre-Other			
Prime variety	*Col*	*Regional %*	*VII**	*Prime variety*	*Col*	*Regional %*	*VII**
Garnacha Tinta	R	31.0	2.8	Sauvignon Blanc	W	45.7	14.4
Syrah	R	11.9	1.5	Cabernet Sauvignon	R	22.5	3.4
Cabernet Sauvignon	R	9.8	1.5	Chardonnay	W	14.1	2.7
Mazuelo	R	9.1	1.5	Pinot Noir	R	7.2	2.1
Cinsaut	R	8.3	3.4	Gamay Noir	R	3.7	1.0
Merlot	R	5.1	0.4	Menu Pineau	W	3.0	121.4
Other varieties		24.9		Other varieties		3.8	
Total		100.0		Total		100.0	

Champagne-Viticole				Charente			
Prime variety	*Col*	*Regional %*	*VII**	*Prime variety*	*Col*	*Regional %*	*VII**
Pinot Noir	R	35.5	10.1	Trebbiano Toscano	W	95.3	9.6
Pinot Meunier	R	34.1	26.1	Merlot	R	1.8	0.1
Chardonnay	W	30.1	5.7	Colombard	W	0.8	0.9
Other varieties		0.3		Cabernet Sauvignon	R	0.5	0.1
Total		100.0		Sauvignon Blanc	W	0.3	0.1
				Gamay Noir	R	0.2	0.0
				Other varieties		1.1	
				Total		100.0	

Charente Maritime				Cher			
Prime variety	*Col*	*Regional %*	*VII**	*Prime variety*	*Col*	*Regional %*	*VII**
Trebbiano Toscano	W	90.6	9.1	Sauvignon Blanc	W	73.5	23.2
Merlot	R	3.1	0.2	Pinot Noir	R	22.3	6.3
Colombard	W	1.9	2.1	Gamay Noir	R	2.9	0.8
Cabernet Sauvignon	R	1.0	0.1	Pinot Gris	O	0.2	0.5
Sauvignon Blanc	W	1.0	0.3	Plantet	R	0.0	0.2
Cabernet Franc	R	0.7	0.1	Other varieties		1.1	
Other varieties		1.8		Total		100.0	
Total		100.0					

Corse				Cote D'Or			
Prime variety	*Col*	*Regional %*	*VII**	*Prime variety*	*Col*	*Regional %*	*VII**
Sangiovese	R	22.6	120.7	Pinot Noir	R	68.1	19.4
Merlot	R	11.9	0.9	Chardonnay	W	21.9	4.2
Vermentino	W	11.4	27.2	Aligote	W	7.0	30.4
Mammolo	R	11.0	120.8	Gamay Noir	R	2.0	0.6
Chardonnay	W	6.8	1.3	Other varieties		1.0	
Muscat Blanc a Petits Grains	W	3.3	3.6	Total		100.0	
Other varieties		32.9					
Total		100.0					

Dordogne				Drome			
Prime variety	*Col*	*Regional %*	*VII**	*Prime variety*	*Col*	*Regional %*	*VII**
Merlot	R	32.4	2.4	Garnacha Tinta	R	46.7	4.2
Semillon	W	28.0	20.3	Syrah	R	25.7	3.2
Cabernet Sauvignon	R	11.9	1.8	Muscat Blanc a Petits Grains	W	6.1	6.7
Cabernet Franc	R	10.8	2.5	Mazuelo	R	5.9	0.9
Sauvignon Blanc	W	8.8	2.8	Merlot	R	2.4	0.2
Muscadelle	W	3.3	17.6	Clairette	W	2.2	7.9
Other varieties		4.8		Other varieties		11.0	
Total		100.0		Total		100.0	

Table 53 (cont.) Winegrape areas and Varietal Intensity Indexes for each region's top 6 varieties, by region, 2010

France continued

Gard				Gers			
Prime variety	*Col*	*Regional %*	*VII** *Prime variety*		*Col*	*Regional %*	*VII**
Garnacha Tinta	R	27.5	2.5	Colombard	W	29.3	31.9
Syrah	R	19.3	2.4	Trebbiano Toscano	W	18.0	1.8
Merlot	R	11.5	0.8	Gros Manseng	W	10.9	18.5
Mazuelo	R	8.7	1.4	Sauvignon Blanc	W	9.5	3.0
Cabernet Sauvignon	R	7.7	1.2	Tannat	R	7.6	22.2
Cinsaut	R	5.3	2.2	Merlot	R	4.4	0.3
Other varieties		20.0		Other varieties		20.2	
Total		100.0		Total		100.0	

Gironde				Herault			
Prime variety	*Col*	*Regional %*	*VII** *Prime variety*		*Col*	*Regional %*	*VII**
Merlot	R	55.7	4.1	Mazuelo	R	16.8	2.7
Cabernet Sauvignon	R	21.6	3.2	Syrah	R	16.2	2.0
Cabernet Franc	R	10.0	2.3	Merlot	R	11.5	0.8
Semillon	W	6.0	4.3	Garnacha Tinta	R	10.7	1.0
Sauvignon Blanc	W	4.2	1.3	Cabernet Sauvignon	R	8.4	1.3
Cot	R	0.8	1.0	Cinsaut	R	6.2	2.5
Other varieties		1.8		Other varieties		30.2	
Total		100.0		Total		100.0	

Haut Rhin				Indre			
Prime variety	*Col*	*Regional %*	*VII** *Prime variety*		*Col*	*Regional %*	*VII**
Gewurztraminer	W	22.2	61.0	Gamay Noir	R	42.0	11.7
Riesling	W	20.9	50.6	Pinot Noir	R	24.1	6.9
Pinot Gris	O	16.8	54.5	Cot	R	7.6	10.5
Auxerrois	W	13.8	49.8	Gamay Teinturier de Chaud	R	5.6	1996.3
Pinot Noir	R	9.4	2.7	Cabernet Franc	R	4.4	1.0
Pinot Blanc	W	7.0	46.1	Other varieties		16.3	
Other varieties		9.8		Total		100.0	
Total		100.0					

Indre Et Loire				Landes			
Prime variety	*Col*	*Regional %*	*VII** *Prime variety*		*Col*	*Regional %*	*VII**
Cabernet Franc	R	51.3	11.8	Colombard	W	17.3	18.8
Chenin Blanc	W	30.7	26.4	Trebbiano Toscano	W	16.3	1.6
Gamay Noir	R	5.5	1.5	Baco Blanc	W	12.6	137.9
Sauvignon Blanc	W	3.1	1.0	Cabernet Franc	R	12.1	2.8
Cot	R	1.9	2.7	Tannat	R	8.3	24.0
Grolleau Noir	R	1.8	6.5	Gros Manseng	W	6.7	11.4
Other varieties		5.7		Other varieties		26.8	
Total		100.0		Total		100.0	

				Loire Atlantique			
Prime variety	*Col*	*Regional %*	*VII** *Prime variety*		*Col*	*Regional %*	*VII**
Sauvignon Blanc	W	39.6	12.5	Melon	W	73.4	50.3
Gamay Noir	R	23.0	6.4	Folle Blanche	W	8.1	38.8
Cabernet Franc	R	7.3	1.7	Gamay Noir	R	4.7	1.3
Chardonnay	W	5.0	0.9	Chardonnay	W	3.8	0.7
Cot	R	4.4	6.1	Cabernet Franc	R	2.6	0.6
Pinot Noir	R	4.1	1.2	Sauvignon Blanc	W	1.2	0.4
Other varieties		16.7		Other varieties		6.2	
Total		100.0		Total		100.0	

Table 53 (cont.) Winegrape areas and Varietal Intensity Indexes for each region's top 6 varieties, by region, 2010

France continued

Lot				Lot Et Garonne			
Prime variety	*Col*	*Regional %*	*VII**	*Prime variety*	*Col*	*Regional %*	*VII**
Cot	R	67.5	92.8	Merlot	R	35.1	2.6
Merlot	R	15.3	1.1	Cabernet Franc	R	15.1	3.5
Gamay Noir	R	3.6	1.0	Cabernet Sauvignon	R	15.1	2.3
Villard Noir	R	3.2	20.7	Sauvignon Blanc	W	9.6	3.0
Cabernet Franc	R	2.8	0.7	Colombard	W	4.6	5.0
Tannat	R	2.4	7.0	Semillon	W	3.4	2.5
Other varieties		5.1		Other varieties		17.1	
Total		100.0		Total		100.0	

Maine Et Loire				Midi Pyrenees-Other			
Prime variety	*Col*	*Regional %*	*VII**	*Prime variety*	*Col*	*Regional %*	*VII**
Cabernet Franc	R	41.8	9.6	Cabernet Franc	R	12.0	2.7
Chenin Blanc	W	24.6	21.2	Syrah	R	9.8	1.2
Grolleau Noir	R	8.8	31.6	Fer	R	9.0	47.1
Gamay Noir	R	4.9	1.4	Cabernet Sauvignon	R	8.1	1.2
Cabernet Sauvignon	R	4.1	0.6	Tannat	R	7.4	21.6
Melon	W	4.1	2.8	Gros Manseng	W	7.3	12.3
Other varieties		11.8		Other varieties		46.4	
Total		100.0		Total		100.0	

Nievre				Pays De Loire-Other			
Prime variety	*Col*	*Regional %*	*VII**	*Prime variety*	*Col*	*Regional %*	*VII**
Sauvignon Blanc	W	81.7	25.8	Chenin Blanc	W	31.7	27.3
Pinot Noir	R	5.5	1.6	Chardonnay	W	16.0	3.0
Gamay Noir	R	3.2	0.9	Melon	W	10.1	6.9
Merlot	R	0.0	0.0	Cabernet Sauvignon	R	9.8	1.5
Garnacha Tinta	R	0.0	0.0	Chambourcin	R	7.0	78.2
Trebbiano Toscano	W	0.0	0.0	Cabernet Franc	R	7.0	1.6
Other varieties		9.6		Other varieties		18.4	
Total		100.0		Total		100.0	

Poitou-Charentes-Other				Provence-C. D'Azur-Other			
Prime variety	*Col*	*Regional %*	*VII**	*Prime variety*	*Col*	*Regional %*	*VII**
Cabernet Franc	R	22.5	5.2	Caladoc	R	23.5	80.8
Sauvignon Blanc	W	16.2	5.1	Muscat of Hamburg	R	14.7	35.6
Chardonnay	W	12.7	2.4	Syrah	R	13.8	1.7
Plantet	R	10.4	79.5	Garnacha Tinta	R	12.1	1.1
Cabernet Sauvignon	R	3.4	0.5	Vermentino	W	10.0	23.7
Merlot	R	0.8	0.1	Cinsaut	R	7.0	2.9
Other varieties		34.0		Other varieties		18.9	
Total		100.0		Total		100.0	

Pyrenees Orientales				Rhone			
Prime variety	*Col*	*Regional %*	*VII**	*Prime variety*	*Col*	*Regional %*	*VII**
Garnacha Tinta	R	22.6	2.0	Gamay Noir	R	98.2	27.3
Syrah	R	16.3	2.0	Syrah	R	1.7	0.2
Mazuelo	R	14.4	2.3	Other varieties		0.2	
Muscat Blanc a Petits Grains	W	10.2	11.3	Total		100.0	
Muscat of Alexandria	W	7.9	25.7				
Macabeo	W	7.6	24.4				
Other varieties		21.1					
Total		100.0					

Table 53 (cont.) Winegrape areas and Varietal Intensity Indexes for each region's top 6 varieties, by region, 2010

France continued

Rhone-Alpes-Other

Prime variety	Col	Regional %	VII*
Gamay Noir	R	33.0	9.2
Chardonnay	W	22.1	4.2
Syrah	R	6.7	0.8
Viognier	W	5.3	10.2
Jacquere	W	3.1	25.7
Clairette	W	1.5	5.2
Other varieties		28.4	
Total		100.0	

Saone Et Loire

Prime variety	Col	Regional %	VII*
Chardonnay	W	51.4	9.8
Pinot Noir	R	23.7	6.8
Gamay Noir	R	17.7	4.9
Aligote	W	6.5	28.2
Other varieties		0.7	
Total		100.0	

Savoie

Prime variety	Col	Regional %	VII*
Jacquere	W	68.0	560.3
Altesse	W	15.2	360.6
Chardonnay	W	8.7	1.6
Roussanne	W	7.3	45.7
Other varieties		0.9	
Total		100.0	

Tarn

Prime variety	Col	Regional %	VII*
Fer	R	14.2	74.5
Duras	R	12.7	116.3
Syrah	R	12.3	1.5
Mauzac Blanc	W	11.1	47.3
Gamay Noir	R	9.9	2.8
Len de l'El	W	8.8	116.6
Other varieties		31.0	
Total		100.0	

Tarn Et Garonne

Prime variety	Col	Regional %	VII*
Chasselas	W	36.2	125.7
Negrette	R	11.5	79.1
Cabernet Franc	R	10.4	2.4
Syrah	R	6.0	0.7
Muscat of Hamburg	R	5.7	13.7
Gamay Noir	R	4.2	1.2
Other varieties		26.1	
Total		100.0	

Var

Prime variety	Col	Regional %	VII*
Garnacha Tinta	R	26.0	2.3
Cinsaut	R	16.4	6.7
Mazuelo	R	13.5	2.1
Syrah	R	13.3	1.6
Monastrell	R	6.8	6.2
Cabernet Sauvignon	R	5.9	0.9
Other varieties		18.2	
Total		100.0	

Vaucluse

Prime variety	Col	Regional %	VII*
Garnacha Tinta	R	49.7	4.5
Syrah	R	16.4	2.0
Mazuelo	R	7.3	1.2
Muscat of Hamburg	R	4.7	11.4
Cinsaut	R	3.4	1.4
Monastrell	R	2.7	2.4
Other varieties		15.9	
Total		100.0	

Vendee

Prime variety	Col	Regional %	VII*
Gamay Noir	R	19.4	5.4
Chambourcin	R	18.5	206.5
Plantet	R	11.0	84.0
Pinot Noir	R	10.9	3.1
Villard Noir	R	8.2	52.7
Other varieties			
Total		100.0	

Vienne

Prime variety	Col	Regional %	VII*
Cabernet Franc	R	28.9	6.6
Villard Noir	R	17.1	109.5
Gamay Noir	R	16.2	4.5
Plantet	R	15.6	119.4
Other varieties		22.2	
Total		100.0	

Yonne

Prime variety	Col	Regional %	VII*
Chardonnay	W	79.2	15.0
Pinot Noir	R	11.5	3.3
Aligote	W	4.8	20.6
Sauvignon Blanc	W	2.0	0.6
Other varieties		2.5	
Total		100.0	

Table 53 (cont.) Winegrape areas and Varietal Intensity Indexes for each region's top 6 varieties, by region, 2010

	Georgia		
	Other Regions		
Prime variety	Col	Regional %	VII*
Rkatsiteli	W	52.8	
Tsolikouri	W	16.5	
Saperavi	R	9.9	
Tsitska	W	7.6	
Chinuri	W	2.6	
Mtsvane Kakhuri	W	0.7	
Other varieties		10.1	
Total		100.0	

Germany

	Ahr				Baden		
Prime variety	Col	Regional %	VII*	Prime variety	Col	Regional %	VII*
Riesling	W	7.3	0.3	Muller Thurgau	W	16.9	1.3
Pinot Noir Precoce	R	5.5	29.3	Pinot Gris	O	10.7	2.5
Muller Thurgau	W	1.8	0.1	Pinot Blanc	W	7.5	2.0
Dornfelder	R	1.8	0.2	Riesling	W	7.3	0.3
Pinot Gris	O	0.0	0.0	Chasselas	W	6.9	6.3
Pinot Blanc	W	0.0	0.0	Chardonnay	W	1.0	0.9
Other varieties		83.6		Other varieties		49.6	
Total		100.0		Total		100.0	

	Franken				Hessische Bergstra E		
Prime variety	Col	Regional %	VII*	Prime variety	Col	Regional %	VII*
Muller Thurgau	W	29.5	2.2	Riesling	W	47.6	2.2
Bacchus	W	12.1	6.5	Pinot Blanc	W	7.1	1.9
Domina	R	5.6	15.8	Muscat Ottonel	W	4.8	81.0
Riesling	W	4.9	0.2	Dornfelder	R	2.4	0.3
Kerner	W	3.6	1.0	Kerner	W	2.4	0.7
Dornfelder	R	2.5	0.3	Muller Thurgau	W	0.0	0.0
Other varieties		41.8		Other varieties		35.7	
Total		100.0		Total		100.0	

	Mittelrhein				Mosel-Saar-Ruwer		
Prime variety	Col	Regional %	VII*	Prime variety	Col	Regional %	VII*
Riesling	W	66.7	3.0	Riesling	W	60.0	2.7
Muller Thurgau	W	4.4	0.3	Muller Thurgau	W	13.9	1.1
Dornfelder	R	2.2	0.3	Elbling	W	6.1	11.4
Pinot Blanc	W	2.2	0.6	Kerner	W	3.9	1.1
Kerner	W	2.2	0.6	Dornfelder	R	3.6	0.5
Pinot Gris	O	0.0	0.0	Pinot Blanc	W	2.8	0.7
Other varieties		22.2		Other varieties		9.7	
Total		100.0		Total		100.0	

Table 53 (cont.) Winegrape areas and Varietal Intensity Indexes for each region's top 6 varieties, by region, 2010

Germany continued

Nahe

Prime variety	Col	Regional %	VII*
Riesling	W	27.2	1.2
Muller Thurgau	W	13.2	1.0
Dornfelder	R	10.6	1.4
Pinot Blanc	W	5.5	1.5
Pinot Gris	O	5.0	1.2
Kerner	W	4.3	1.3
Other varieties		34.1	
Total		100.0	

Rheingau

Prime variety	Col	Regional %	VII*
Riesling	W	79.1	3.6
Muscat Ottonel	W	1.3	22.2
Dornfelder	R	0.3	0.0
Pinot Blanc	W	0.3	0.1
Chardonnay	W	0.3	0.3
Dunkelfelder	R	0.3	1.1
Other varieties		18.3	
Total		100.0	

Rheinhessen

Prime variety	Col	Regional %	VII*
Muller Thurgau	W	16.4	1.2
Riesling	W	14.7	0.7
Dornfelder	R	12.8	1.7
Kerner	W	4.5	1.3
Pinot Gris	O	4.4	1.0
Pinot Blanc	W	3.4	0.9
Other varieties		43.8	
Total		100.0	

Rhein-Pfalz

Prime variety	Col	Regional %	VII*
Riesling	W	23.6	1.1
Dornfelder	R	13.3	1.7
Muller Thurgau	W	9.8	0.7
Kerner	W	4.7	1.4
Pinot Gris	O	4.5	1.0
Pinot Blanc	W	3.9	1.0
Other varieties		40.2	
Total		100.0	

Saale-Unstrut

Prime variety	Col	Regional %	VII*
Muller Thurgau	W	17.1	1.3
Pinot Blanc	W	11.4	3.0
Riesling	W	7.1	0.3
Dornfelder	R	5.7	0.7
Kerner	W	5.7	1.7
Pinot Gris	O	4.3	1.0
Other varieties		48.6	
Total		100.0	

Sachsen

Prime variety	Col	Regional %	VII*
Muller Thurgau	W	17.4	1.3
Riesling	W	13.0	0.6
Pinot Blanc	W	10.9	2.9
Pinot Gris	O	8.7	2.0
Dornfelder	R	4.3	0.6
Kerner	W	4.3	1.3
Other varieties		41.3	
Total		100.0	

Wurttemberg

Prime variety	Col	Regional %	VII*
Riesling	W	18.1	0.8
Dornfelder	R	3.0	0.4
Muller Thurgau	W	2.9	0.2
Kerner	W	2.9	0.8
Acolon	R	1.9	4.5
Pinot Gris	O	1.0	0.2
Other varieties		70.3	
Total		100.0	

Greece

Anatoliki Makedonia, Thraki

Prime variety	Col	Regional %	VII*
Merlot	R	20.4	8.9
Cabernet Sauvignon	R	12.4	4.3
Chardonnay	W	10.0	9.3
Sauvignon Blanc	W	9.3	19.7
Syrah	R	8.4	7.1
Limnio	R	4.3	6.3
Other varieties		35.2	
Total		100.0	

Attiki

Prime variety	Col	Regional %	VII*
Savatiano	W	88.6	4.9
Roditis	O	1.6	0.2
Agiorgitiko	R	1.3	0.2
Grenache Rose	R	1.0	0.8
Vilana	W	0.9	0.9
Roditis (red)	R	0.9	0.1
Other varieties		5.7	
Total		100.0	

Table 53 (cont.) Winegrape areas and Varietal Intensity Indexes for each region's top 6 varieties, by region, 2010

Greece continued

Dytiki Ellada				Dytiki Makedonia			
Prime variety	*Col*	*Regional %*	*VII**	*Prime variety*	*Col*	*Regional %*	*VII**
Roditis	O	42.2	4.9	Xinomavro	R	55.3	15.3
Roditis (red)	R	28.0	4.0	Moschomavro	R	12.5	4.8
Mavrodafni	R	4.4	6.9	Syrah	R	2.9	2.5
Muscat Blanc a Petits Grains	W	2.9	0.4	Merlot	R	2.9	1.3
Moschofilero	R	2.6	1.5	Negoska	R	1.0	3.8
Mavrouda	R	2.0	2.1	Roditis	O	1.0	0.1
Other varieties		17.9		Other varieties		24.4	
Total		100.0		Total		100.0	

Ionia Nisia				Ipeiros			
Prime variety	*Col*	*Regional %*	*VII**	*Prime variety*	*Col*	*Regional %*	*VII**
Robola	W	17.8	20.8	Debina	W	36.7	83.5
Vertzami	R	9.4	21.5	Cabernet Sauvignon	R	5.6	2.0
Kakotrygis	W	4.3	22.5	Roditis (red)	O	1.7	0.2
Muscat Blanc a Petits Grains	W	3.0	0.8	Vertzami	R	1.4	3.2
Goustolidi	W	2.8	22.5	Savatiano	W	1.2	0.1
Mavrodafni	R	2.5	4.0	Mavrouda	R	0.6	0.7
Other varieties		60.2		Other varieties		52.8	
Total		100.0		Total		100.0	

Kentriki Makedonia				Kriti			
Prime variety	*Col*	*Regional %*	*VII**	*Prime variety*	*Col*	*Regional %*	*VII**
Xinomavro	R	16.2	4.5	Kotsifali	R	29.6	6.9
Merlot	R	15.7	6.9	Romeiko	R	20.3	6.9
Cabernet Sauvignon	R	11.4	4.0	Liatiko	R	14.1	6.3
Roditis (red)	R	6.6	0.9	Vilana	W	5.4	5.1
Roditis	O	5.6	0.7	Mandilaria	R	5.3	3.3
Limnio	R	5.4	7.9	Cabernet Sauvignon	R	1.1	0.4
Other varieties		39.0		Other varieties		24.2	
Total		100.0		Total		100.0	

Notio Aigaio				Peloponissos			
Prime variety	*Col*	*Regional %*	*VII**	*Prime variety*	*Col*	*Regional %*	*VII**
Assyrtiko	W	19.0	11.4	Agiorgitiko	R	32.2	6.0
Athiri	W	17.6	12.8	Roditis (red)	R	10.5	1.5
Monemvassia	W	13.3	15.1	Roditis	O	10.3	1.2
Mandilaria	R	12.8	7.8	Moschofilero	R	8.8	5.1
Cabernet Sauvignon	R	3.6	1.3	Grenache Rose	R	4.8	4.0
Liatiko	R	2.9	1.3	Savatiano	W	4.1	0.2
Other varieties		30.9		Other varieties		29.3	
Total		100.0		Total		100.0	

Sterea Ellada				Thessalia			
Prime variety	*Col*	*Regional %*	*VII**	*Prime variety*	*Col*	*Regional %*	*VII**
Savatiano	W	69.0	3.8	Moschomavro	R	31.0	11.8
Roditis (red)	R	7.7	1.1	Roditis	O	9.2	1.1
Roditis	O	6.7	0.8	Roditis(red)	R	8.0	1.1
Cabernet Sauvignon	R	3.8	1.3	Xinomavro	R	3.4	0.9
Grenache Rose	R	2.1	1.8	Trebbiano Toscano	W	2.9	5.4
Syrah	R	1.8	1.6	Syrah	R	2.8	2.4
Other varieties		9.0		Other varieties		39.1	
Total		100.0		Total		100.0	

Table 53 (cont.) Winegrape areas and Varietal Intensity Indexes for each region's top 6 varieties, by region, 2010

Greece continued

	Vorreio Aigaio		
Prime variety	*Col*	*Regional %*	*VII**
Muscat Blanc a Petits Gra	W	72.7	18.3
Fokiano	R	5.6	11.7
Limnio	R	3.0	4.4
Cabernet Sauvignon	R	0.7	0.3
Savatiano	W	0.5	0.0
Chardonnay	W	0.1	0.1
Other varieties		17.3	
Total		100.0	

Hungary

	Badacsony				Balatonboglar		
Prime variety	*Col*	*Regional %*	*VII**	*Prime variety*	*Col*	*Regional %*	*VII**
Grasevina	W	44.3	6.6	Chardonnay	W	10.4	2.6
Pinot Gris	O	12.5	5.4	Gruner Veltliner	W	9.0	4.1
Pinot Noir	R	4.4	2.8	Kiralyleanyka	W	8.7	7.1
Muller Thurgau	W	4.2	1.4	Merlot	R	8.3	3.0
Muscat Ottonel	W	2.4	1.4	Grasevina	W	7.5	1.1
Riesling	W	2.4	1.3	Irsai Oliver	W	6.8	4.4
Other varieties		29.8		Other varieties		49.3	
Total		100.0		Total		100.0	

	Balatonfelvidek				Balatonfured-Csopak		
Prime variety	*Col*	*Regional %*	*VII**	*Prime variety*	*Col*	*Regional %*	*VII**
Grasevina	W	52.1	7.8	Grasevina	W	39.4	5.9
Chardonnay	W	11.1	2.8	Pinot Gris	O	6.7	2.9
Pinot Gris	O	10.3	4.4	Blaufrankisch	R	5.5	0.5
Gruner Veltliner	W	3.5	1.6	Zweigelt	R	4.9	1.7
Sauvignon Blanc	W	2.7	2.1	Chardonnay	W	4.8	1.2
Irsai Oliver	W	2.5	1.6	Cabernet Sauvignon	R	4.7	1.1
Other varieties		17.8		Other varieties		34.1	
Total		100.0		Total		100.0	

	Bukk				Csongrad		
Prime variety	*Col*	*Regional %*	*VII**	*Prime variety*	*Col*	*Regional %*	*VII**
Blaufrankisch	R	17.9	1.6	Blaufrankisch	R	26.7	2.3
Leanyka	W	15.9	13.2	Riesling	W	8.5	4.5
Grasevina	W	9.4	1.4	Kovidinka	O	7.2	4.9
Zweigelt	R	5.4	1.8	Kunleany	W	7.1	4.1
Chardonnay	W	5.2	1.3	Chasselas	W	6.5	2.4
Cserszegi Fuszeres	W	5.0	1.0	Grasevina	W	6.4	1.0
Other varieties		41.3		Other varieties		37.6	
Total		100.0		Total		100.0	

	Eger				Etyek-Budai		
Prime variety	*Col*	*Regional %*	*VII**	*Prime variety*	*Col*	*Regional %*	*VII**
Blaufrankisch	R	18.3	1.6	Chardonnay	W	14.7	3.7
Cabernet Sauvignon	R	8.8	2.1	Gruner Veltliner	W	9.5	4.3
Merlot	R	8.1	3.0	Sauvignon Blanc	W	6.4	4.9
Leanyka	W	5.6	4.7	Muller Thurgau	W	6.0	2.0
Blauburger	R	5.2	8.3	Pinot Gris	O	5.9	2.5
Harslevelu	W	4.9	2.1	Riesling	W	4.9	2.6
Other varieties		49.1		Other varieties		52.5	
Total		100.0		Total		100.0	

Table 53 (cont.) Winegrape areas and Varietal Intensity Indexes for each region's top 6 varieties, by region, 2010
Hungary continued

Hajos-Bajai				Kunsag			
Prime variety	*Col*	*Regional %*	*VII**	*Prime variety*	*Col*	*Regional %*	*VII**
Blaufrankisch	R	20.7	1.8	Bianca	W	12.3	2.9
Cabernet Sauvignon	R	16.2	3.9	Blaufrankisch	R	12.3	1.1
Cserszegi Fuszeres	W	12.8	2.5	Cserszegi Fuszeres	W	12.1	2.3
Zweigelt	R	7.3	2.5	Zalagyongye	W	6.8	2.7
Chardonnay	W	5.0	1.3	Arany Sarfeher	W	5.0	3.1
Kunleany	W	3.8	2.2	Kunleany	W	4.5	2.6
Other varieties		34.0		Other varieties		46.9	
Total		100.0		Total		100.0	

Matra				Mor			
Prime variety	*Col*	*Regional %*	*VII**	*Prime variety*	*Col*	*Regional %*	*VII**
Muller Thurgau	W	10.0	3.3	Ezerjo	W	18.4	11.9
Chasselas	W	9.1	3.3	Savagnin Blanc	W	18.3	16.5
Pinot Gris	O	7.9	3.4	Gruner Veltliner	W	8.3	3.8
Blaufrankisch	R	7.8	0.7	Chardonnay	W	6.8	1.7
Muscat Ottonel	W	7.5	4.2	Leanyka	W	5.1	4.2
Grasevina	W	6.5	1.0	Sauvignon Blanc	W	4.5	3.5
Other varieties		51.3		Other varieties		38.6	
Total		100.0		Total		100.0	

Nagy-Somlo				Neszmely			
Prime variety	*Col*	*Regional %*	*VII**	*Prime variety*	*Col*	*Regional %*	*VII**
Grasevina	W	26.8	4.0	Chardonnay	W	16.9	4.3
Juhfark	W	15.5	58.0	Muller Thurgau	W	11.4	3.8
Furmint	W	12.2	2.0	Pinot Gris	O	8.0	3.5
Harslevelu	W	5.7	2.4	Ezerjo	W	7.8	5.1
Savagnin Blanc	W	2.2	2.0	Irsai Oliver	W	7.0	4.5
Pinot Gris	O	1.9	0.8	Kiralyleanyka	W	5.9	4.8
Other varieties		35.7		Other varieties		43.0	
Total		100.0		Total		100.0	

Pannonhalma				Pecs			
Prime variety	*Col*	*Regional %*	*VII**	*Prime variety*	*Col*	*Regional %*	*VII**
Grasevina	W	27.8	4.2	Chardonnay	W	9.7	2.5
Riesling	W	9.2	4.9	Grasevina	W	9.3	1.4
Muller Thurgau	W	8.5	2.8	Kiralyleanyka	W	5.8	4.8
Chardonnay	W	8.1	2.0	Gruner Veltliner	W	5.2	2.3
Savagnin Blanc	W	6.9	6.3	Muller Thurgau	W	4.9	1.6
Irsai Oliver	W	4.5	2.9	Sauvignon Blanc	W	4.1	3.1
Other varieties		35.1		Other varieties		61.0	
Total		100.0		Total		100.0	

Sopron				Szekszard			
Prime variety	*Col*	*Regional %*	*VII**	*Prime variety*	*Col*	*Regional %*	*VII**
Blaufrankisch	R	57.8	5.0	Blaufrankisch	R	28.9	2.5
Zweigelt	R	7.4	2.5	Merlot	R	13.4	4.9
Cabernet Sauvignon	R	6.0	1.5	Cabernet Sauvignon	R	10.2	2.5
Gruner Veltliner	W	4.9	2.2	Cabernet Franc	R	10.0	5.2
Merlot	R	4.2	1.5	Zweigelt	R	5.4	1.8
Pinot Noir	R	3.6	2.3	Grasevina	W	5.1	0.8
Other varieties		16.1		Other varieties		27.0	
Total		100.0		Total		100.0	

Table 53 (cont.) Winegrape areas and Varietal Intensity Indexes for each region's top 6 varieties, by region, 2010
Hungary continued

Tokaj

Prime variety	Col	Regional %	VII*
Furmint	W	67.7	11.3
Harslevelu	W	18.8	7.9
Muscat Blanc a Petits Grains	W	8.7	8.5
Zeta	W	2.0	11.6
Grasa de Cotnari	W	0.7	11.5
Zenit	W	0.3	0.4
Other varieties		1.8	
Total		100.0	

Tolna

Prime variety	Col	Regional %	VII*
Blaufrankisch	R	13.7	1.2
Chardonnay	W	12.2	3.1
Zweigelt	R	8.5	2.9
Gruner Veltliner	W	7.4	3.4
Merlot	R	6.5	2.4
Cabernet Sauvignon	R	6.4	1.5
Other varieties		45.3	
Total		100.0	

Villany

Prime variety	Col	Regional %	VII*
Cabernet Sauvignon	R	16.8	4.1
Blauer Portugieser	R	16.5	9.5
Cabernet Franc	R	12.3	6.4
Merlot	R	10.6	3.9
Blaufrankisch	R	9.5	0.8
Grasevina	W	8.5	1.3
Other varieties		25.7	
Total		100.0	

Zala

Prime variety	Col	Regional %	VII*
Grasevina	W	4.5	0.7
Cabernet Sauvignon	R	3.7	0.9
Muller Thurgau	W	3.6	1.2
Chardonnay	W	3.0	0.8
Chasselas	W	2.5	0.9
Gruner Veltliner	W	2.3	1.1
Other varieties		80.4	
Total		100.0	

Italy

Abruzzo

Prime variety	Col	Regional %	VII*
Montepulciano	R	55.4	10.0
Trebbiano Toscano	W	18.1	5.3
Trebbiano d'Abruzzo	W	9.4	11.6
Chardonnay	W	2.4	0.8
Sangiovese	R	2.3	0.2
Pecorino	W	1.9	10.9
Other varieties		10.4	
Total		100.0	

Basilicata

Prime variety	Col	Regional %	VII*
Aglianico	R	47.5	30.0
Sangiovese	R	7.9	0.7
Tribidrag	R	3.8	1.9
Montepulciano	R	3.0	0.5
Italica	W	2.7	45.6
Malvasia Bianca di Candia	W	2.4	1.6
Other varieties		32.7	
Total		100.0	

Calabria

Prime variety	Col	Regional %	VII*
Gaglioppo	R	42.6	63.3
Greco Nero	R	6.5	49.2
Magliocco Canino	R	5.3	62.0
Greco Bianco	W	4.2	16.3
Malvasia Bianca di Candia	W	3.4	2.3
Sangiovese	R	3.0	0.3
Other varieties		34.9	
Total		100.0	

Campania

Prime variety	Col	Regional %	VII*
Aglianico	R	29.6	18.7
Falanghina	W	12.0	24.6
Barbera	R	5.8	1.8
Malvasia Bianca di Candia	W	5.5	3.7
Sangiovese	R	5.5	0.5
Greco Bianco	W	4.2	16.4
Other varieties		37.5	
Total		100.0	

Emilia-Romagna

Prime variety	Col	Regional %	VII*
Trebbiano Romagnolo	W	27.8	10.9
Sangiovese	R	15.3	1.3
Lambrusco Salamino	R	8.3	10.4
Ancellotta	R	7.3	10.5
Lambrusco Grasparossa	R	4.0	9.2
Barbera	R	3.9	1.2
Other varieties		33.3	
Total		100.0	

Friuli-Venezia Giulia

Prime variety	Col	Regional %	VII*
Pinot Gris	O	24.7	8.9
Merlot	R	14.7	3.3
Sauvignonasse	W	8.5	18.2
Chardonnay	W	7.0	2.2
Sauvignon Blanc	W	6.7	11.2
Cabernet Franc	R	6.6	6.5
Other varieties		31.9	
Total		100.0	

Table 53 (cont.) Winegrape areas and Varietal Intensity Indexes for each region's top 6 varieties, by region, 2010

Italy continued

Lazio				Liguria			
Prime variety	*Col*	*Regional %*	*VII** *Prime variety*	*Col*	*Regional %*	*VII**
Malvasia Bianca di Candia	W	21.7	14.7	Vermentino	W	35.7	44.3
Trebbiano Giallo	W	12.7	7.5	Rossese	R	9.9	198.3
Trebbiano Toscano	W	12.0	3.5	Albarola	W	7.6	32.9
Merlot	R	6.7	1.5	Dolcetto	R	5.0	5.1
Sangiovese	R	5.0	0.4	Sangiovese	R	4.8	0.4
Cesanese	R	4.0	36.5	Bosco	W	4.2	317.6
Other varieties		38.0		Other varieties		32.8	
Total		100.0		Total		100.0	

Lombardia				Marche			
Prime variety	*Col*	*Regional %*	*VII** *Prime variety*	*Col*	*Regional %*	*VII**
Croatina	R	16.2	17.8	Sangiovese	R	21.3	1.9
Pinot Noir	R	12.8	15.9	Montepulciano	R	19.2	3.4
Chardonnay	W	12.2	3.9	Verdicchio Bianco	W	13.7	24.3
Barbera	R	11.0	3.3	Biancame	W	6.4	15.5
Grasevina	W	5.7	22.7	Trebbiano Toscano	W	4.5	1.3
Pinot Gris	O	4.5	1.6	Passerina	W	3.9	27.1
Other varieties		37.7		Other varieties		31.0	
Total		100.0		Total		100.0	

Molise				Piemonte			
Prime variety	*Col*	*Regional %*	*VII** *Prime variety*	*Col*	*Regional %*	*VII**
Montepulciano	R	49.0	8.8	Barbera	R	30.0	9.2
Cabernet Sauvignon	R	8.4	3.8	Muscat Blanc a Petits Grain	W	21.1	11.4
Trebbiano d'Abruzzo	W	5.6	6.9	Dolcetto	R	12.9	13.2
Sangiovese	R	5.3	0.5	Nebbiolo	R	9.7	10.9
Trebbiano Toscano	W	4.1	1.2	Cortese	W	5.7	12.0
Tintilia del Molise	R	2.1	118.1	Brachetto del Piemonte	R	2.7	11.7
Other varieties		25.4		Other varieties		17.9	
Total		100.0		Total		100.0	

Puglia				Sardegna			
Prime variety	*Col*	*Regional %*	*VII** *Prime variety*	*Col*	*Regional %*	*VII**
Sangiovese	R	15.1	1.3	Garnacha Tinta	R	29.4	29.0
Tribidrag	R	14.2	7.3	Vermentino	W	17.0	21.1
Negroamaro	R	13.8	7.5	Mazuelo	R	10.1	31.3
Montepulciano	R	11.0	2.0	Monica Nera	R	7.3	32.7
Trebbiano Toscano	W	6.0	1.8	Nuragus	W	7.3	33.8
Trebbiano Giallo	W	4.4	2.6	Sangiovese	R	3.1	0.3
Other varieties		35.5		Other varieties		25.7	
Total		100.0		Total		100.0	

Sicilia				Toscana			
Prime variety	*Col*	*Regional %*	*VII** *Prime variety*	*Col*	*Regional %*	*VII**
Catarratto Bianco	W	33.4	6.0	Sangiovese	R	63.9	5.6
Nero d'Avola	R	15.7	5.9	Trebbiano Toscano	W	5.2	1.5
Grillo	W	6.0	6.0	Merlot	R	4.8	1.1
Inzolia	W	5.7	5.8	Cabernet Sauvignon	R	4.3	2.0
Syrah	R	5.1	4.7	Canaiolo Nero	R	1.6	9.3
Chardonnay	W	4.7	1.5	Syrah	R	1.2	1.1
Other varieties		29.4		Other varieties		18.2	
Total		100.0		Total		100.0	

Table 53 (cont.) Winegrape areas and Varietal Intensity Indexes for each region's top 6 varieties, by region, 2010

Italy continued

Trentino Alto Adige

Prime variety	Col	Regional %	VII*	Prime variety	Col	Regional %	VII*
Chardonnay	W	21.3	6.8	Sangiovese	R	19.7	1.7
Pinot Gris	O	18.7	6.8	Trebbiano Toscano	W	11.6	3.4
Muller Thurgau	W	7.0	33.4	Grechetto di Orvieto	W	10.9	45.3
Merlot	R	5.7	1.3	Merlot	R	10.4	2.3
Gewurztraminer	W	5.6	24.8	Sagrantino	R	7.3	45.7
Teroldego	R	4.3	33.4	Cabernet Sauvignon	R	4.5	2.1
Other varieties		37.4		Other varieties		35.6	
Total		100.0		Total		100.0	

Valle D'Aosta / Veneto

Prime variety	Col	Regional %	VII*	Prime variety	Col	Regional %	VII*
Petit Rouge	R	15.9	1186.2	Prosecco	W	22.9	7.8
Nebbiolo	R	9.4	10.6	Garganega	W	13.8	5.6
Pinot Noir	R	6.5	8.1	Merlot	R	12.4	2.8
Prie	W	6.3	1176.0	Corvina Veronese	R	9.6	8.0
Fumin	R	5.2	1036.1	Pinot Gris	O	8.5	3.1
Muscat Blanc a Petits Grain	W	4.1	2.3	Cabernet Sauvignon	R	3.9	1.8
Other varieties		52.6		Other varieties		28.8	
Total		100.0		Total		100.0	

Japan

Hokkaido / Nagano

Prime variety	Col	Regional %	VII*	Prime variety	Col	Regional %	VII*
Kerner	W	39.7	4.1	Merlot	R	58.6	2.7
Zweigelt	R	26.0	4.2	Chardonnay	W	27.8	1.7
Muller Thurgau	W	19.0	4.1	Niagara	W	9.2	2.7
Niagara	W	6.1	1.8	Pinot Noir	R	4.4	2.6
Campbell Early	R	4.9	3.0	Black Queen	R	0.0	0.0
Delaware	O	1.8	1.3	Cabernet Sauvignon	R	0.0	0.0
Other varieties		2.5		Other varieties		0.0	
Total		100.0		Total		100.0	

Other Region / Yamagata

Prime variety	Col	Regional %	VII*	Prime variety	Col	Regional %	VII*
Black Queen	R	22.6	1.8	Merlot	R	49.3	2.2
Cabernet Sauvignon	R	22.6	1.8	Chardonnay	W	46.3	2.9
Chardonnay	W	19.1	1.2	Muscat Bailey A	R	4.4	1.6
Merlot	R	16.4	0.7	Total		100.0	
Muscat Bailey A	R	4.6	1.7				
Delaware	O	3.3	2.4				
Other varieties		11.5					
Total		100.0					

Yamanashi

Prime variety	Col	Regional %	VII*
Black Queen	R	34.9	2.8
Cabernet Sauvignon	R	34.9	2.8
Koshu	O	24.6	5.4
Muscat Bailey A	R	5.6	2.0
Total		100.0	

Table 53 (cont.) Winegrape areas and Varietal Intensity Indexes for each region's top 6 varieties, by region, 2010

Kazakhstan

	Almaty				East - Kazakhstan		
Prime variety	Col	*Regional %*	*VII**	*Prime variety*	Col	*Regional %*	*VII**
Rkatsiteli	W	57.2	1.1	Aligote	W	15.9	4.0
Kuldzhinskii	O	6.9	1.2	Pinot Noir	R	11.1	4.3
Saperavi	R	6.1	1.0	Ruby	R	3.6	27.2
Aligote	W	5.6	1.4	Maiskii Chernyi	R	3.1	2.0
Pinot Noir	R	3.8	1.5	Muscat Violet	R	2.9	7.3
Maiskii Chernyi	R	1.8	1.2	Muscat Rose	O	2.5	0.8
Other varieties		18.7		Other varieties		60.9	
Total		100.0		Total		100.0	

	South - Kazakhstan				West - Kazakhstan		
Prime variety	Col	*Regional %*	*VII**	*Prime variety*	Col	*Regional %*	*VII**
Rkatsiteli	W	39.8	0.8	Pinot Noir	R	13.3	5.1
Bayanshira	W	26.9	2.9	Muscat Violet	R	7.9	20.2
Muscat Rose	O	9.0	2.8	Ruby	R	4.8	35.9
Saperavi	R	7.0	1.1	Aligote	W	4.3	1.1
Kuldzhinskii	O	3.3	0.6	Bayanshira	W	2.4	0.3
Riesling	W	1.8	1.1	Riesling	W	1.9	1.2
Other varieties		12.2		Other varieties		65.4	
Total		100.0		Total		100.0	

	Zhambyl				Other Regions		
Prime variety	Col	*Regional %*	*VII**	*Prime variety*	Col	*Regional %*	*VII**
Rkatsiteli	W	40.7	0.8	Bayanshira	W	14.3	1.5
Aligote	W	0.4	0.1	Aligote	W	11.7	2.9
Muscat Rose	O	0.2	0.1	Rkatsiteli	W	11.4	0.2
Bayanshira	W	0.2	0.0	Muscat Violet	R	10.4	26.5
Muscat Violet	R	0.2	0.4	Pinot Noir	R	8.5	3.3
Pinot Noir	R	0.1	0.0	Muscat Rose	O	1.9	0.6
Other varieties		58.2		Other varieties		41.7	
Total		100.0		Total		100.0	

Luxembourg

	Luxembourg		
Prime variety	Col	*Regional %*	*VII**
Elbling	W	28.4	
Muller Thurgau	W	14.1	
Auxerrois	W	14.0	
Pinot Blanc	W	12.4	
Pinot Gris	O	11.2	
Riesling	W	9.3	
Other varieties		10.6	
Total		100.0	

Mexico

	Aguascalientes				Sonora		
Prime variety	Col	*Regional %*	*VII**	*Prime variety*	Col	*Regional %*	*VII**
Mazuelo	R	44.1	5.4	Sultaniye	W	72.3	4.7
Salvador	R	41.2	6.4	Fiesta	W	19.8	4.7
Muscat Blanc a Petits Grains	W	14.7	3.3	Mazuelo	R	4.6	0.6
Total		100.0		Palomino Fino	W	3.4	1.7
				Total		100.0	

Table 53 (cont.) Winegrape areas and Varietal Intensity Indexes for each region's top 6 varieties, by region, 2010

Mexico continued

Suma Baja California				Suma Coahuila			
Prime variety	*Col*	*Regional %*	*VII**	*Prime variety*	*Col*	*Regional %*	*VII**
Cabernet Sauvignon	R	24.0	1.7	Jacquez	R	28.7	19.6
Merlot	R	12.0	1.7	Palomino Fino	W	24.7	12.4
Chenin Blanc	W	9.6	1.9	Cabernet Sauvignon	R	24.4	1.8
Tempranillo	R	8.0	1.9	Merlot	R	16.8	2.4
Nebbiolo	R	6.3	1.9	Syrah	R	5.4	2.0
Garnacha Tinta	R	4.9	1.9	Total		100.0	
Other varieties		35.2					
Total		100.0		Total		100.0	

Zacatecas			
Prime variety	*Col*	*Regional %*	*VII**
Cardinal	R	54.4	17.7
Muscat Blanc a Petits Gra	W	39.2	8.7
Mazuelo	R	6.5	0.8
Total		100.0	

Moldova

Moldova			
Prime variety	*Col*	*Regional %*	*VII**
Aligote	W	17.6	
Rkatsiteli	W	12.8	
Isabella	R	12.7	
Sauvignon Blanc	W	9.1	
Merlot	R	9.0	
Cabernet Sauvignon	R	8.4	
Other varieties		30.4	
Total		100.0	

Morocco

Morocco			
Prime variety	*Col*	*Regional %*	*VII**
Doukkali	R	33.8	
Cinsaut	R	8.0	
Muscat of Alexandria	W	7.5	
Teneron	R	7.1	
Abbo	R	4.8	
Mazuelo	R	3.5	
Other varieties		35.3	
Total		100.0	

Myanmar

Myanmar			
Prime variety	*Col*	*Regional %*	*VII**
Syrah	R	35.8	
Sauvignon Blanc	W	29.2	
Muscat Blanc a Petits Gra	W	9.5	
Pinot Noir	R	9.0	
Mazuelo	R	5.9	
Tempranillo	R	4.5	
Other varieties		6.2	
Total		100.0	

Table 53 (cont.) Winegrape areas and Varietal Intensity Indexes for each region's top 6 varieties, by region, 2010

New Zealand

	Auckland				Canterbury		
Prime variety	*Col*	*Regional %*	*VII**	*Prime variety*	*Col*	*Regional %*	*VII**
Chardonnay	W	22.3	1.8	Pinot Noir	R	39.0	2.6
Merlot	R	15.5	3.6	Chardonnay	W	17.7	1.4
Cabernet Sauvignon	R	11.2	6.9	Riesling	W	16.2	5.3
Pinot Gris	O	7.0	1.5	Sauvignon Blanc	W	11.3	0.2
Sauvignon Blanc	W	6.4	0.1	Pinot Gris	O	10.2	2.2
Pinot Noir	R	4.4	0.3	Gewurztraminer	W	1.5	1.6
Other varieties		33.2		Other varieties		4.1	
Total		100.0		Total		100.0	

	Gisborne				Hawkes Bay		
Prime variety	*Col*	*Regional %*	*VII**	*Prime variety*	*Col*	*Regional %*	*VII**
Chardonnay	W	52.9	4.3	Chardonnay	W	23.7	1.9
Pinot Gris	O	8.1	1.7	Merlot	R	20.7	4.8
Merlot	R	5.5	1.3	Sauvignon Blanc	W	18.1	0.4
Pinot Noir	R	3.8	0.3	Cabernet Sauvignon	R	7.9	4.9
Sauvignon Blanc	W	3.6	0.1	Pinot Noir	R	7.7	0.5
Riesling	W	0.3	0.1	Pinot Gris	O	7.2	1.5
Other varieties		25.7		Other varieties		14.8	
Total		100.0		Total		100.0	

	Marlborough				Nelson		
Prime variety	*Col*	*Regional %*	*VII**	*Prime variety*	*Col*	*Regional %*	*VII**
Sauvignon Blanc	W	75.8	1.5	Sauvignon Blanc	W	39.6	0.8
Pinot Noir	R	10.9	0.7	Pinot Noir	R	22.5	1.5
Chardonnay	W	5.9	0.5	Chardonnay	W	14.9	1.2
Pinot Gris	O	3.0	0.6	Pinot Gris	O	8.6	1.8
Riesling	W	2.4	0.8	Riesling	W	6.9	2.2
Merlot	R	0.5	0.1	Merlot	R	0.9	0.2
Other varieties		1.6		Other varieties		6.6	
Total		100.0		Total		100.0	

	Otago				Waikato		
Prime variety	*Col*	*Regional %*	*VII**	*Prime variety*	*Col*	*Regional %*	*VII**
Pinot Noir	R	78.5	5.3	Chardonnay	W	13.7	1.1
Pinot Gris	O	9.3	2.0	Cabernet Sauvignon	R	12.5	7.7
Chardonnay	W	4.4	0.4	Sauvignon Blanc	W	8.3	0.2
Riesling	W	4.0	1.3	Merlot	R	7.1	1.6
Sauvignon Blanc	W	2.2	0.0	Cot	R	6.5	13.3
Merlot	R	0.3	0.1	Seibel	W	5.4	173.5
Other varieties		1.4		Other varieties		46.5	
Total		100.0		Total		100.0	

	Waipara				Wairarapa		
Prime variety	*Col*	*Regional %*	*VII**	*Prime variety*	*Col*	*Regional %*	*VII**
Sauvignon Blanc	W	45.5	0.9	Pinot Noir	R	54.1	3.6
Pinot Noir	R	21.6	1.4	Sauvignon Blanc	W	22.9	0.5
Riesling	W	19.8	6.5	Chardonnay	W	8.1	0.7
Pinot Gris	O	5.7	1.2	Pinot Gris	O	5.5	1.2
Chardonnay	W	4.6	0.4	Riesling	W	3.6	1.2
Merlot	R	0.4	0.1	Cabernet Sauvignon	R	1.6	1.0
Other varieties		2.4		Other varieties		4.1	
Total		100.0		Total		100.0	

Table 53 (cont.) Winegrape areas and Varietal Intensity Indexes for each region's top 6 varieties, by region, 2010

New Zealand continued

Other Regions

Prime variety	Col	Regional %	VII*
Merlot	R	2.1	0.5
Pinot Gris	O	1.2	0.3
Chardonnay	W	0.4	0.0
Riesling	W	0.2	0.1
Pinot Noir	R	0.1	0.0
Sauvignon Blanc	W	0.1	0.0
Other varieties		96.0	
Total		100.0	

Peru

Arequipa				Lima			
Prime variety	Col	Regional %	VII*	Prime variety	Col	Regional %	VII*
Negramoll	R	48.2	1.5	Blaufrankisch	R	32.7	4.3
Muscat Blanc a Petits C	W	25.5	2.7	Quebranta	R	31.3	3.6
Pecorino	W	8.0	2.7	Italia	W	20.2	0.8
Red Globe	R	4.6	0.7	Red Globe	R	12.9	2.1
Italia	W	4.1	0.2	Negramoll	R	0.8	0.0
Flame Seedless	R	2.9	2.6	Pecorino	W	0.8	0.3
Other varieties		6.8		Other varieties		1.4	
Total		100.0		Total		100.0	

Moquegua				Tacna			
Prime variety	Col	Regional %	VII*	Prime variety	Col	Regional %	VII*
Negramoll	R	40.7	1.2	Italia	W	56.0	2.1
Italia	W	39.0	1.5	Negramoll	R	28.8	0.9
Quebranta	R	7.1	0.8	Cabernet Sauvignon	R	5.4	4.3
Red Globe	R	5.2	0.8	Red Globe	R	3.8	0.6
Cardinal	R	2.5	1.8	Blaufrankisch	R	1.5	0.2
Muscat Blanc a Petits C	W	1.4	0.1	Cardinal	R	1.1	0.8
Other varieties		4.1		Other varieties		3.4	
Total		100.0		Total		100.0	

Portugal

Alentejo				Algarve			
Prime variety	Col	Regional %	VII*	Prime variety	Col	Regional %	VII*
Tempranillo	R	19.0	1.9	Castelao	R	26.4	3.9
Trincadeira	R	17.1	3.0	Negramoll	R	25.0	60.4
Castelao	R	10.7	1.6	Siria	W	8.4	1.9
Alicante Henri Bousche	R	7.0	3.4	Malvasia Fina	W	5.8	3.3
Siria	W	5.8	1.3	Tempranillo	R	5.4	0.5
Antao Vaz	W	5.5	7.2	Listain de Huelva	W	5.2	24.4
Other varieties		34.8		Other varieties		24.6	
Total		100.0		Total		100.0	

Alto Tras-Os-Montes				Beira Interior			
Prime variety	Col	Regional %	VII*	Prime variety	Col	Regional %	VII*
Touriga Franca	R	17.9	2.5	Rufete	R	20.4	8.0
Tempranillo	R	13.1	1.3	Siria	W	14.2	3.3
Touriga Nacional	R	9.8	1.6	Marufo	R	12.7	5.2
Tinta Barroca	R	9.6	2.7	Tempranillo	R	7.1	0.7
Trincadeira	R	6.3	1.1	Touriga Nacional	R	5.2	0.8
Siria	W	5.8		Mencia	R	3.4	2.3
Other varieties		37.5		Other varieties		37.1	
Total		100.0		Total		100.0	

Table 53 (cont.) Winegrape areas and Varietal Intensity Indexes for each region's top 6 varieties, by region, 2010

Portugal continued

Beira Litoral				Entre Douro E Minho			
Prime variety	*Col*	*Regional %*	*VII**	*Prime variety*	*Col*	*Regional %*	*VII**
Baga	R	24.8	9.9	Loureiro	W	24.2	11.4
Fernao Pires	W	14.0	2.4	Arinto de Bucelas	W	18.3	6.7
Mencia	R	12.5	8.3	Vinhao	R	16.7	11.0
Touriga Nacional	R	11.4	1.8	Alvarinho	W	12.5	10.3
Tempranillo	R	9.6	0.9	Trajadura	W	8.2	11.4
Bical	W	4.4	7.7	Azal	W	7.5	11.4
Other varieties		23.4		Other varieties		12.7	
Total		100.0		Total		100.0	

Regiao Autonoma Da Madeira (Pt)				Regiao Autonoma Dos Acores			
Prime variety	*Col*	*Regional %*	*VII**	*Prime variety*	*Col*	*Regional %*	*VII**
Negramoll	R	46.6	112.7	Arinto de Bucelas	W	68.5	25.2
Malvasia Branca de Sao J	W	12.2	181.2	Agronomica	R	8.1	40.8
Complexa	R	12.1	193.1	Castelao	R	6.3	0.9
Verdelho	W	8.8	36.4	Seara Nova	W	6.1	14.7
Malvasia Fina	W	6.4	3.6	Verdelho	W	5.5	22.6
Caracol	W	3.9	191.0	Fernao Pires	W	1.9	0.3
Other varieties		10.0		Other varieties		3.5	
Total		100.0		Total		100.0	

Ribatejo E Oeste			
Prime variety	*Col*	*Regional %*	*VII**
Castelao	R	23.2	3.4
Fernao Pires	W	17.6	3.1
Syrah	R	6.4	3.0
Tempranillo	R	6.1	0.6
Alicante Henri Bouschet	R	4.2	2.1
Caladoc	R	3.4	4.7
Other varieties		39.1	
Total		100.0	

Romania

Bucuresti - Ilfov				Centru			
Prime variety	*Col*	*Regional %*	*VII**	*Prime variety*	*Col*	*Regional %*	*VII**
Other varieties		100.0		Feteasca Regala	W	26.3	3.5
Total		100.0		Grasevina	W	14.0	3.2
				Muscat Ottonel	W	11.7	5.5
				Sauvignon Blanc	W	11.3	4.6
				Feteasca Alba	W	9.2	1.2
				Gewurztraminer	W	5.7	25.3
				Other varieties		21.8	
				Total		100.0	

Nord-Est				Nord-Vest			
Prime variety	*Col*	*Regional %*	*VII**	*Prime variety*	*Col*	*Regional %*	*VII**
Feteasca Alba	W	10.7	1.4	Feteasca Alba	W	6.4	0.8
Aligote	W	10.2	2.4	Feteasca Regala	W	6.0	0.8
Feteasca Regala	W	5.1	0.7	Grasevina	W	5.7	1.3
Grasa de Cotnari	W	2.3	6.0	Muscat Ottonel	W	2.3	1.1
Merlot	R	1.9	0.3	Cabernet Sauvignon	R	1.0	0.4
Grasevina	W	1.9	0.4	Sauvignon Blanc	W	0.7	0.3
Other varieties		67.9		Other varieties		78.1	
Total		100.0		Total		100.0	

Table 53 (cont.) Winegrape areas and Varietal Intensity Indexes for each region's top 6 varieties, by region, 2010

Romania continued

Sud - Muntenia				Sud-Est			
Prime variety	*Col*	*Regional %*	*VII**	*Prime variety*	*Col*	*Regional %*	*VII**
Merlot	R	9.2	1.4	Feteasca Alba	W	11.1	1.5
Feteasca Regala	W	4.6	0.6	Merlot	R	10.4	1.6
Feteasca Alba	W	2.9	0.4	Feteasca Regala	W	10.2	1.3
Grasevina	W	2.1	0.5	Aligote	W	6.4	1.5
Blaufrankisch	R	1.6	3.5	Grasevina	W	6.4	1.4
Feteasca Neagra	R	1.5	1.4	Babeasca Neagra	R	4.1	2.3
Other varieties		78.2		Other varieties		51.5	
Total		100.0		Total		100.0	

Sud-Vest Oltenia				Vest			
Prime variety	*Col*	*Regional %*	*VII**	*Prime variety*	*Col*	*Regional %*	*VII**
Pamid	R	9.1	5.3	Feteasca Regala	W	14.8	2.0
Sauvignon Blanc	W	3.8	1.6	Grasevina	W	13.1	3.0
Feteasca Regala	W	3.5	0.5	Merlot	R	10.1	1.6
Cabernet Sauvignon	R	2.4	1.1	Cabernet Sauvignon	R	8.9	4.1
Feteasca Alba	W	2.0	0.3	Mustoasa de Maderat	W	7.9	52.8
Grasevina	W	1.9	0.4	Sauvignon Blanc	W	7.0	2.9
Other varieties		77.3		Other varieties		38.1	
Total		100.0		Total		100.0	

Russia

Krasnodar Krai				Rostov Oblast			
Prime variety	*Col*	*Regional %*	*VII**	*Prime variety*	*Col*	*Regional %*	*VII**
Cabernet Sauvignon	R	16.6	1.2	Bianca	W	17.8	1.3
Bianca	W	12.9	0.9	Aligote	W	14.1	3.5
Chardonnay	W	9.3	1.2	Rkatsiteli	W	12.9	4.7
Pervenets Magaracha	W	9.0	1.0	Saperavi Severny	R	7.4	5.8
Merlot	R	7.5	1.2	Pervenets Magaracha	W	7.3	0.8
Sauvignon Blanc	W	4.5	1.2	Vidvizhenets	O	6.2	5.8
Other varieties		40.2		Other varieties		34.4	
Total		100.0		Total		100.0	

Serbia

Serbia			
Prime variety	*Col*	*Regional %*	*VII**
Grasevina	W	48.0	
Prokupac	R	22.0	
Chasselas	W	5.0	
Muscat of Hamburg	R	4.0	
Other varieties		21.0	
Total		100.0	

Slovakia

Juznoslovenska				Malokarpatska			
Prime variety	*Col*	*Regional %*	*VII**	*Prime variety*	*Col*	*Regional %*	*VII**
Grasevina	W	15.4	1.2	Gruner Veltliner	W	20.6	1.2
Gruner Veltliner	W	15.2	0.9	Grasevina	W	12.4	0.9
Blaufrankisch	R	13.4	1.2	Muller Thurgau	W	9.4	1.3
Sankt Laurent	R	8.8	1.2	Blaufrankisch	R	9.0	0.8
Cabernet Sauvignon	R	8.4	1.9	Sankt Laurent	R	8.0	1.1
Muller Thurgau	W	5.4	0.7	Pinot Blanc	W	5.5	1.3
Other varieties		33.4		Other varieties		35.2	
Total		100.0		Total		100.0	

Table 53 (cont.) Winegrape areas and Varietal Intensity Indexes for each region's top 6 varieties, by region, 2010

Slovakia continued

Nitrianska				Stredoslovenska			
Prime variety	Col	Regional %	VII*	Prime variety	Col	Regional %	VII*
Gruner Veltliner	W	19.3	1.2	Blaufrankisch	R	14.8	1.4
Grasevina	W	13.7	1.0	Gruner Veltliner	W	14.7	0.9
Blaufrankisch	R	8.5	0.8	Pinot Blanc	W	9.6	2.3
Muller Thurgau	W	8.2	1.1	Muller Thurgau	W	9.4	1.3
Sankt Laurent	R	7.1	1.0	Riesling	W	8.0	1.7
Feteasca Regala	W	4.0	2.2	Sankt Laurent	R	7.1	1.0
Other varieties		39.2		Other varieties		36.3	
Total		100.0		Total		100.0	

Tokajska				Vychodoslovenska			
Prime variety	Col	Regional %	VII*	Prime variety	Col	Regional %	VII*
Furmint	W	52.1	26.5	Grasevina	W	23.5	1.8
Harslevelu	W	28.7	25.7	Blaufrankisch	R	16.2	1.5
Muscat Blanc a Petits Grai	W	10.0	26.6	Muller Thurgau	W	6.9	0.9
Gewurztraminer	W	2.7	1.3	Riesling	W	6.7	1.4
Cabernet Sauvignon	R	1.9	0.4	Gewurztraminer	W	6.4	3.1
Blaufrankisch	R	1.6	0.1	Pinot Gris	O	5.3	3.2
Other varieties		3.0		Other varieties		35.0	
Total		100.0		Total		100.0	

Slovenia

Outside Wine-Growing Districts				Podravje - Prekmurje			
Prime variety	Col	Regional %	VII*	Prime variety	Col	Regional %	VII*
Zametovka	R	23.6	4.2	Grasevina	W	39.4	2.7
Blaufrankisch	R	12.7	3.0	Chardonnay	W	11.2	1.5
Grasevina	W	12.0	0.8	Riesling	W	9.0	2.2
Mesano Belo In Rdece	W	9.1	12.1	Furmint	W	6.6	1.7
Kerner	W	7.0	636.3	Pinot Blanc	W	5.5	1.7
Kraljevina	W	5.2	4.7	Sauvignon Blanc	W	4.4	0.7
Other varieties		30.4		Other varieties		23.9	
Total		100.0		Total		100.0	

Podravje - Stajerska Slovenija				Posavje - Bela Krajina			
Prime variety	Col	Regional %	VII*	Prime variety	Col	Regional %	VII*
Grasevina	W	24.4	1.7	Blaufrankisch	R	20.3	4.9
Furmint	W	9.3	2.3	Grasevina	W	15.7	1.1
Riesling	W	9.3	2.2	Kraljevina	W	12.3	11.3
Sauvignon Blanc	W	9.1	1.4	Zametovka	R	9.2	1.7
Chardonnay	W	8.6	1.2	Muscat Blanc a Petits Grair	W	3.8	1.8
Muscat Blanc a Petits Grai	W	4.4	2.0	Sauvignon Blanc	W	3.8	0.6
Other varieties		35.0		Other varieties		34.8	
Total		100.0		Total		100.0	

Posavje - Bizeljsko Sremic				Posavje - Dolenjska			
Prime variety	Col	Regional %	VII*	Prime variety	Col	Regional %	VII*
Zametovka	R	21.4	3.8	Zametovka	R	41.2	7.4
Grasevina	W	19.1	1.3	Blaufrankisch	R	17.9	4.3
Blaufrankisch	R	19.1	4.6	Grasevina	W	9.2	0.6
Plavay	W	6.7	18.0	Kraljevina	W	9.0	8.2
Sauvignon Blanc	W	4.5	0.7	Mesano Belo In Rdece	W	8.2	10.9
Chardonnay	W	3.4	0.5	Other varieties		14.5	
Other varieties		25.7		Total		100.0	
Total		100.0					

Table 53 (cont.) Winegrape areas and Varietal Intensity Indexes for each region's top 6 varieties, by region, 2010

Slovenia continued

Primorje - Goriska Brda (Brda)				Primorje - Kras			
Prime variety	*Col*	*Regional %*	*VII**	*Prime variety*	*Col*	*Regional %*	*VII**
Ribolla Gialla	W	23.5	5.2	Refosco	R	76.1	9.6
Merlot	R	19.0	3.1	Malvazija Istarska	W	6.3	1.4
Chardonnay	W	16.7	2.3	Chardonnay	W	4.6	0.6
Sauvignonasse	W	10.0	8.6	Other varieties		13.0	
Pinot Gris	O	9.9	3.2	Total		100.0	
Cabernet Sauvignon	R	6.2	2.3				
Other varieties		14.6					
Total		100.0					

Primorje - Slovenska Istra				Primorje - Vipavska Dolina (Vipava)			
Prime variety	*Col*	*Regional %*	*VII**	*Prime variety*	*Col*	*Regional %*	*VII**
Refosco	R	48.5	6.1	Merlot	R	20.9	3.4
Malvazija Istarska	W	25.2	5.6	Ribolla Gialla	W	11.5	2.5
Cabernet Sauvignon	R	6.4	2.3	Sauvignon Blanc	W	11.2	1.7
Merlot	R	6.3	1.0	Malvazija Istarska	W	10.4	2.3
Muscat Blanc a Petits Gra	W	3.6	1.7	Cabernet Sauvignon	R	9.1	3.3
Chardonnay	W	3.2	0.4	Grasevina	W	8.1	0.6
Other varieties		6.8		Other varieties		28.7	
Total		100.0		Total		100.0	

South Africa

Breedekloof				Little Karoo			
Prime variety	*Col*	*Regional %*	*VII**	*Prime variety*	*Col*	*Regional %*	*VII**
Chenin Blanc	W	22.4	1.2	Colombard	W	29.3	2.5
Colombard	W	15.0	1.3	Chenin Blanc	W	18.4	1.0
Chardonnay	W	8.4	1.0	Muscat of Alexandria	W	7.4	3.5
Sauvignon Blanc	W	7.5	0.8	Chardonnay	W	6.8	0.8
Syrah	R	6.5	0.6	Syrah	R	4.5	0.4
Cabernet Sauvignon	R	6.5	0.5	Cabernet Sauvignon	R	4.3	0.4
Other varieties		33.8		Other varieties		29.3	
Total		100.0		Total		100.0	

Malmesbury				Olifants River			
Prime variety	*Col*	*Regional %*	*VII**	*Prime variety*	*Col*	*Regional %*	*VII**
Chenin Blanc	W	21.1	1.1	Chenin Blanc	W	27.5	1.5
Cabernet Sauvignon	R	15.8	1.3	Colombard	W	25.0	2.1
Syrah	R	13.7	1.4	Syrah	R	8.8	0.9
Pinotage	R	10.9	1.8	Sauvignon Blanc	W	5.7	0.6
Sauvignon Blanc	W	8.7	0.9	Pinotage	R	5.5	0.9
Chardonnay	W	6.5	0.8	Cabernet Sauvignon	R	5.3	0.4
Other varieties		23.4		Other varieties		22.1	
Total		100.0		Total		100.0	

Orange River				Paarl			
Prime variety	*Col*	*Regional %*	*VII**	*Prime variety*	*Col*	*Regional %*	*VII**
Colombard	W	52.8	4.5	Chenin Blanc	W	19.0	1.0
Chenin Blanc	W	23.3	1.3	Cabernet Sauvignon	R	17.2	1.4
Muscat of Alexandria	W	4.1	1.9	Syrah	R	13.5	1.3
Ruby Cabernet	R	2.5	1.1	Chardonnay	W	8.0	1.0
Cabernet Sauvignon	R	2.0	0.2	Pinotage	R	7.5	1.2
Syrah	R	1.6	0.2	Merlot	R	7.1	1.1
		13.8		Other varieties		27.8	
Total		100.0		Total		100.0	

Table 53 (cont.) Winegrape areas and Varietal Intensity Indexes for each region's top 6 varieties, by region, 2010

South Africa continued

Robertson				Stellenbosch			
Prime variety	Col	*Regional %*	VII*	*Prime variety*	Col	*Regional %*	VII*
Colombard	W	16.0	1.3	Cabernet Sauvignon	R	20.8	1.7
Chardonnay	W	15.9	1.9	Sauvignon Blanc	W	16.6	1.8
Sauvignon Blanc	W	12.3	1.3	Syrah	R	13.0	1.3
Chenin Blanc	W	12.1	0.7	Merlot	R	12.4	1.9
Cabernet Sauvignon	R	10.8	0.9	Chenin Blanc	W	8.3	0.5
Syrah	R	8.3	0.8	Chardonnay	W	6.9	0.8
Other varieties		24.6		Other varieties		21.9	
Total		100.0		Total		100.0	

Worcester			
Prime variety	Col	*Regional %*	VII*
Chenin Blanc	W	23.0	1.3
Colombard	W	12.6	1.1
Sauvignon Blanc	W	12.2	1.3
Chardonnay	W	10.1	1.2
Syrah	R	7.7	0.8
Cabernet Sauvignon	R	6.7	0.6
Other varieties		27.6	
Total		100.0	

Spain

Alava				Albacete			
Prime variety	Col	*Regional %*	VII*	*Prime variety*	Col	*Regional %*	VII*
Tempranillo	R	60.4	3.0	Monastrell	R	18.9	3.3
Garnacha Tinta	R	14.8	2.2	Airen	W	16.9	0.7
Cabernet Sauvignon	R	5.8	2.5	Bobal	R	14.8	1.9
Macabeo	W	5.7	1.5	Tempranillo	R	14.4	0.7
Merlot	R	5.3	3.5	Alicante Henri Bouschet	R	9.1	4.8
Mazuelo	R	2.6	5.7	Syrah	R	4.4	2.3
Other varieties		5.4		Other varieties		21.5	
Total		100.0		Total		100.0	

Alicante / Alacant				Almeria, Granada, Jaen, Sevilla			
Prime variety	Col	*Regional %*	VII*	*Prime variety*	Col	*Regional %*	VII*
Monastrell	R	55.1	9.7	Calagrano	W	16.4	35.2
Muscat of Alexandria	W	13.9	17.4	Tempranillo	R	7.9	0.4
Merseguera	W	5.5	14.4	Palomino Fino	W	5.9	3.2
Tempranillo	R	4.9	0.2	Pedro Ximenez	W	5.8	6.6
Cabernet Sauvignon	R	4.2	1.8	Garnacha Tinta	R	4.8	0.7
Garnacha Tinta	R	3.5	0.5	Airen	W	4.7	0.2
Other varieties		12.9		Other varieties		54.5	
Total		100.0		Total		100.0	

Avila, Palencia, Salamanca, Segovia, Soria				Badajoz			
Prime variety	Col	*Regional %*	VII*	*Prime variety*	Col	*Regional %*	VII*
Garnacha Tinta	R	30.7	4.5	Cayetana Blanca	W	47.1	12.2
Tempranillo	R	29.4	1.5	Tempranillo	R	25.9	1.3
Verdejo	W	9.6	6.0	Chelva	W	6.9	11.4
Albillo Mayor	W	6.4	50.1	Macabeo	W	4.2	1.1
Rufete	R	6.3	99.2	Beba	W	3.6	12.1
Juan Garcia	R	4.6	30.2	Cabernet Sauvignon	R	2.0	0.9
Other varieties		13.0		Other varieties		10.4	
Total		100.0		Total		100.0	

Table 53 (cont.) Winegrape areas and Varietal Intensity Indexes for each region's top 6 varieties, by region, 2010

Spain continued

	Barcelona				Burgos		
Prime variety	*Col*	*Regional %*	*VII**	*Prime variety*	*Col*	*Regional %*	*VII**
Xarello	W	28.9	35.4	Tempranillo	R	94.3	4.7
Macabeo	W	22.6	6.1	Albillo Mayor	W	2.9	22.8
Parellada	W	16.3	19.0	Garnacha Tinta	R	1.2	0.2
Merlot	R	7.7	5.1	Cabernet Sauvignon	R	0.5	0.2
Chardonnay	W	6.2	9.2	Mencia	R	0.3	0.4
Cabernet Sauvignon	R	5.4	2.4	Merlot	R	0.3	0.2
Other varieties		12.9		Other varieties		0.5	
Total		100.0		Total		100.0	

	Caceres						
Prime variety	*Col*	*Regional %*	*VII**	*Prime variety*	*Col*	*Regional %*	*VII**
Tempranillo	R	17.2	0.9	Palomino Fino	W	91.1	49.7
Alarije	W	14.1	83.9	Muscat of Alexandria	W	1.7	2.2
Cabernet Sauvignon	R	12.5	5.6	Tempranillo	R	0.9	0.0
Verdejo	W	10.6	6.6	Pedro Ximenez	W	0.7	0.8
Grasevina	W	7.4	95.7	Chardonnay	W	0.6	0.8
Syrah	R	6.2	3.2	Perruno	W	0.4	3.8
Other varieties		32.0		Other varieties		4.6	
Total		100.0		Total		100.0	

	Canarias				Cantabria		
Prime variety	*Col*	*Regional %*	*VII**	*Prime variety*	*Col*	*Regional %*	*VII**
Palomino Fino	W	38.2	20.8	Mencia	R	22.2	28.9
Listan Negro	R	30.7	118.4	Palomino Fino	W	20.2	11.0
Negramoll	R	6.8	55.4	Alvarinho	W	14.1	41.5
Vijariego	W	2.6	95.5	Godello	W	10.1	172.0
Muscat of Alexandria	W	2.0	2.5	Tempranillo	R	4.0	0.2
Forastera	W	1.8	118.8	Ondarrabi Zuri	W	4.0	84.4
Other varieties		17.9		Other varieties		25.3	
Total		100.0		Total		100.0	

	Castellon / Castello				Ciudad Real		
Prime variety	*Col*	*Regional %*	*VII**	*Prime variety*	*Col*	*Regional %*	*VII**
Tempranillo	R	24.4	1.2	Airen	W	69.5	2.8
Garnacha Tinta	R	13.8	2.0	Tempranillo	R	19.7	1.0
Trepat	R	12.1	91.7	Syrah	R	1.6	0.8
Macabeo	W	8.7	2.3	Verdejo	W	1.5	0.9
Merseguera	W	3.9	10.1	Macabeo	W	1.3	0.4
Monastrell	R	3.4	0.6	Cabernet Sauvignon	R	1.1	0.5
Other varieties		33.7		Other varieties		5.2	
Total		100.0		Total		100.0	

	Comunidad De Madrid				Comunidad Foral De Navarra		
Prime variety	*Col*	*Regional %*	*VII**	*Prime variety*	*Col*	*Regional %*	*VII**
Garnacha Tinta	R	42.5	6.2	Tempranillo	R	49.6	2.5
Airen	W	35.6	1.4	Garnacha Tinta	R	17.0	2.5
Tempranillo	R	8.2	0.4	Cabernet Sauvignon	R	11.4	5.0
Calagrano	W	6.6	14.2	Merlot	R	10.6	7.0
Albillo Real	W	4.0	47.8	Chardonnay	W	3.1	4.5
Alicante Henri Bouschet	R	0.8	0.4	Graciano	R	2.2	9.7
Other varieties		2.3		Other varieties		6.3	
Total		100.0		Total		100.0	

Table 53 (cont.) Winegrape areas and Varietal Intensity Indexes for each region's top 6 varieties, by region, 2010
Spain continued

	Cordoba				Cuenca		
Prime variety	*Col*	*Regional %*	*VII**	*Prime variety*	*Col*	*Regional %*	*VII**
Pedro Ximenez		87.6	99.7	Bobal	R	33.9	4.3
Syrah		2.6	1.3	Airen	W	29.8	1.2
Merlot		1.3	0.8	Tempranillo	R	17.2	0.9
Airen		1.2	0.0	Syrah	R	3.4	1.8
Tempranillo		0.8	0.0	Marufo	R	1.9	7.8
Cabernet Sauvignon		0.7	0.3	Cabernet Sauvignon	R	1.8	0.8
Other varieties		5.9		Other varieties		11.9	
Total		100.0		Total		100.0	

	Galicia				Girona, Lleida		
Prime variety	*Col*	*Regional %*	*VII**	*Prime variety*	*Col*	*Regional %*	*VII**
Alicante Henri Bouschet	R	18.7	9.9	Chardonnay	W	15.3	22.6
Alvarinho	W	13.6	40.0	Macabeo	W	14.0	3.7
Palomino Fino	W	13.0	7.1	Cabernet Sauvignon	R	13.1	5.8
Mencia	R	9.6	12.5	Tempranillo	R	9.7	0.5
Trajadura	W	3.9	40.3	Carignan Blanc	W	9.7	37.5
Grand Noir	R	3.0	40.2	Merlot	R	7.8	5.1
Other varieties		38.1		Other varieties		30.4	
Total		100.0		Total		100.0	

	Guadalajara				Guipuzcoa, Vizcaya		
Prime variety	*Col*	*Regional %*	*VII**	*Prime variety*	*Col*	*Regional %*	*VII**
Tempranillo	R	53.7	2.7	Ondarrabi Zuri	W	66.6	1391.4
Airen	W	28.7	1.2	Folle Blanche	W	9.9	1359.8
Lairen	W	5.5	263.8	Hondarrabi Beltza	R	7.2	1397.1
Pardillo	W	1.5	3.5	Petit Courbu	W	4.9	1397.1
Garnacha Tinta	R	1.4	0.2	Chardonnay	W	2.3	3.4
Marufo	R	1.0	4.1	Riesling	W	1.2	78.1
Other varieties		8.2		Other varieties		7.9	
Total		100.0		Total		100.0	

	Huelva				Huesca, Teruel		
Prime variety	*Col*	*Regional %*	*VII**	*Prime variety*	*Col*	*Regional %*	*VII**
Zalema	W	95.2	238.9	Garnacha Tinta	R	25.5	3.7
Syrah	R	1.3	0.7	Cabernet Sauvignon	R	17.2	7.6
Palomino Fino	W	1.0	0.6	Merlot	R	12.1	8.0
Garrido Fino	W	0.8	131.8	Tempranillo	R	10.8	0.5
Tempranillo	R	0.3	0.0	Macabeo	W	7.5	2.0
Calagrano	W	0.1	0.3	Chardonnay	W	6.0	8.8
Other varieties		1.3		Other varieties		21.0	
Total		100.0		Total		100.0	

	Illes Balears				Leon		
Prime variety	*Col*	*Regional %*	*VII**	*Prime variety*	*Col*	*Regional %*	*VII**
Manto Negro	R	17.7	666.0	Mencia	R	38.8	50.5
Cabernet Sauvignon	R	16.3	7.2	Prieto Picudo	R	34.4	77.2
Callet	R	10.0	666.0	Palomino Fino	W	13.7	7.5
Merlot	R	9.8	6.5	Tempranillo	R	5.7	0.3
Chardonnay	W	6.9	10.1	Verdejo	W	0.8	0.5
Pensal Blanca	W	6.8	666.0	Siria	W	0.5	7.3
Other varieties		32.5		Other varieties		5.9	
Total		100.0		Total		100.0	

Table 53 (cont.) Winegrape areas and Varietal Intensity Indexes for each region's top 6 varieties, by region, 2010

Spain continued

Malaga				Principado de Asturias			
Prime variety	*Col*	*Regional %*	*VII**	*Prime variety*	*Col*	*Regional %*	*VII**
Muscat of Alexandria	W	75.3	94.0	Mencia	R	38.1	49.5
Pedro Ximenez	W	11.6	13.2	Garnacha Tinta	R	15.9	2.3
Airen	W	4.3	0.2	Trousseau	R	6.3	870.5
Doradilla	W	1.9	494.6	Palomino Fino	W	1.1	0.6
Muscat Blanc a Petits Grain	W	1.7	13.8	Albillo Real	W	1.1	12.6
Cabernet Sauvignon	R	0.8	0.4	Picapoll Blanco	W	1.1	294.1
Other varieties		4.3		Other varieties		36.5	
Total		100.0		Total		100.0	

Region De Murcia				Rioja			
Prime variety	*Col*	*Regional %*	*VII**	*Prime variety*	*Col*	*Regional %*	*VII**
Monastrell	R	82.5	14.5	Tempranillo	R	71.2	3.5
Airen	W	3.3	0.1	Garnacha Tinta	R	12.6	1.9
Tempranillo	R	2.8	0.1	Macabeo	W	9.3	2.5
Syrah	R	2.3	1.2	Mazuelo	R	3.4	7.3
Forcallat Tinta	R	1.9	16.6	Graciano	R	1.9	8.4
Alicante Henri Bouschet	R	1.8	0.9	Muscat Blanc a Petits G	W	0.3	2.1
Other varieties		5.5		Other varieties		1.4	
Total		100.0		Total		100.0	

Tarragona				Toledo			
Prime variety	*Col*	*Regional %*	*VII**	*Prime variety*	*Col*	*Regional %*	*VII**
Macabeo	W	25.6	6.8	Airen	W	62.5	2.5
Parellada	W	15.3	17.8	Garnacha Tinta	R	14.3	2.1
Garnacha Tinta	R	11.9	1.7	Tempranillo	R	8.7	0.4
Tempranillo	R	7.1	0.4	Tinto de la Pampana Bl	R	4.0	8.0
Carignan Blanc	W	6.0	23.2	Syrah	R	2.1	1.1
Xarello	W	5.9	7.3	Tinto Velasco	R	1.6	6.0
Other varieties		28.2		Other varieties		6.9	
Total		100.0		Total		100.0	

Valencia / Valencia				Valladolid			
Prime variety	*Col*	*Regional %*	*VII**	*Prime variety*	*Col*	*Regional %*	*VII**
Bobal	R	57.1	7.3	Tempranillo	R	42.4	2.1
Tempranillo	R	12.9	0.6	Verdejo	W	42.0	26.1
Muscat of Alexandria	W	5.2	6.5	Macabeo	W	5.0	1.3
Merseguera	W	5.1	13.4	Sauvignon Blanc	W	2.7	7.0
Macabeo	W	4.0	1.1	Palomino Fino	W	1.7	0.9
Garnacha Tinta	R	2.5	0.4	Cabernet Sauvignon	R	1.2	0.6
Other varieties		13.3		Other varieties		4.9	
Total		100.0		Total		100.0	

Zamora				Zaragoza			
Prime variety	*Col*	*Regional %*	*VII**	*Prime variety*	*Col*	*Regional %*	*VII**
Tempranillo	R	58.3	2.9	Garnacha Tinta	R	47.1	6.9
Garnacha Tinta	R	13.1	1.9	Tempranillo	R	17.4	0.9
Juan Garcia	R	6.7	43.9	Macabeo	W	11.0	2.9
Mencia	R	4.0	5.2	Cabernet Sauvignon	R	6.6	2.9
Verdejo	W	2.2	1.4	Syrah	R	5.4	2.8
Palomino Fino	W	2.0	1.1	Merlot	R	3.6	2.4
Other varieties		13.7		Other varieties		9.0	
Total		100.0		Total		100.0	

Table 53 (cont.) Winegrape areas and Varietal Intensity Indexes for each region's top 6 varieties, by region, 2010

Switzerland

Aargau				Basel-Landschaft			
Prime variety	*Col*	*Regional %*	*VII**	*Prime variety*	*Col*	*Regional %*	*VII**
Pinot Noir	R	57.2	1.9	Pinot Noir	R	59.0	2.0
Muller Thurgau	W	21.3	6.4	Muller Thurgau	W	12.9	3.9
Sauvignon Blanc	W	2.3	2.6	Chasselas	W	3.4	0.1
Garanoir	R	1.7	1.3	Kerner	W	2.4	18.7
Pinot Gris	O	1.6	1.1	Regent	R	2.1	7.7
Chardonnay	W	1.5	0.7	Chardonnay	W	2.1	1.0
Other varieties		14.4		Other varieties		18.2	
Total		100.0		Total		100.0	

Bern				Fribourg			
Prime variety	*Col*	*Regional %*	*VII**	*Prime variety*	*Col*	*Regional %*	*VII**
Pinot Noir	R	37.4	1.3	Chasselas	W	48.5	1.8
Chasselas	W	35.6	1.3	Pinot Noir	R	27.8	0.9
Muller Thurgau	W	4.9	1.5	Gamaret	R	4.8	1.9
Chardonnay	W	4.4	2.0	Pinot Gris	O	3.7	2.5
Pinot Gris	O	3.6	2.5	Garanoir	R	2.8	2.1
Sauvignon Blanc	W	2.9	3.2	Gewurztraminer	W	2.4	7.3
Other varieties		11.2		Other varieties		9.9	
Total		100.0		Total		100.0	

Geneva				Graubunden			
Prime variety	*Col*	*Regional %*	*VII**	*Prime variety*	*Col*	*Regional %*	*VII**
Gamay Noir	R	28.7	2.8	Pinot Noir	R	77.2	2.6
Chasselas	W	20.1	0.7	Muller Thurgau	W	7.4	2.2
Pinot Noir	R	10.1	0.3	Chardonnay	W	3.3	1.5
Gamaret	R	8.9	3.5	Pinot Blanc	W	2.4	3.4
Chardonnay	W	6.7	3.1	Pinot Gris	O	2.4	1.7
Garanoir	R	3.2	2.3	Sauvignon Blanc	W	1.9	2.1
Other varieties		22.3		Other varieties		5.4	
Total		100.0		Total		100.0	

Jura				Lucerne			
Prime variety	*Col*	*Regional %*	*VII**	*Prime variety*	*Col*	*Regional %*	*VII**
Garanoir	R	16.2	11.8	Pinot Noir	R	29.7	1.0
Pinot Gris	O	12.3	8.4	Muller Thurgau	W	21.8	6.6
Riesling	W	10.7	127.9	Pinot Gris	O	5.3	3.7
Pinot Noir	R	9.2	0.3	Savagnin Blanc	W	5.2	9.3
Cabernet Jura	R	5.4	41.4	Solaris	W	5.1	59.0
Cabernet Franc	R	1.6	4.5	Zweigelt	R	4.5	44.1
Other varieties		44.7		Other varieties		28.3	
Total		100.0		Total		100.0	

Neuchytel				Schaffhausen			
Prime variety	*Col*	*Regional %*	*VII**	*Prime variety*	*Col*	*Regional %*	*VII**
Pinot Noir	R	50.8	1.7	Pinot Noir	R	69.8	2.3
Chasselas	W	34.5	1.3	Muller Thurgau	W	14.3	4.3
Pinot Gris	O	3.8	2.6	Regent	R	2.1	7.5
Chardonnay	W	3.4	1.5	Cabernet Dorsa	R	1.5	10.5
Gamaret	R	1.5	0.6	Pinot Gris	O	1.5	1.1
Garanoir	R	1.3	0.9	Chardonnay	W	1.3	0.6
Other varieties		4.8		Other varieties		9.5	
Total		100.0		Total		100.0	

Table 53 (cont.) Winegrape areas and Varietal Intensity Indexes for each region's top 6 varieties, by region, 2010

Switzerland continued

Schwyz

Prime variety	Col	Regional %	VII*
Pinot Noir	R	42.4	1.4
Muller Thurgau	W	16.8	5.0
Cabernet Jura	R	5.7	43.8
Chardonnay	W	5.5	2.5
Rauschling	W	3.4	22.1
Dornfelder	R	2.8	19.8
Other varieties		23.4	
Total		100.0	

St. Gallen

Prime variety	Col	Regional %	VII*
Pinot Noir	R	65.7	2.2
Muller Thurgau	W	12.0	3.6
Chardonnay	W	3.2	1.5
Sauvignon Blanc	W	2.1	2.3
Pinot Gris	O	1.9	1.3
Diolinoir	R	1.3	1.8
Other varieties		13.7	
Total		100.0	

Thurgau

Prime variety	Col	Regional %	VII*
Pinot Noir	R	59.1	2.0
Muller Thurgau	W	23.4	7.0
Garanoir	R	1.9	1.4
Regent	R	1.7	6.2
Pinot Gris	O	1.5	1.0
Sauvignon Blanc	W	1.0	1.1
Other varieties		11.5	
Total		100.0	

Ticino

Prime variety	Col	Regional %	VII*
Merlot	R	80.1	11.5
Chardonnay	W	3.8	1.7
Gamaret	R	1.7	0.7
Pinot Noir	R	1.5	0.0
Sauvignon Blanc	W	1.3	1.5
Bondola	R	1.2	13.9
Other varieties		10.5	
Total		100.0	

Valais

Prime variety	Col	Regional %	VII*
Pinot Noir	R	33.4	1.1
Chasselas	W	20.7	0.8
Gamay Noir	R	13.9	1.4
Cornalin	R	4.8	2.9
Silvaner	W	4.6	2.9
Syrah	R	3.1	2.6
Other varieties		19.4	
Total		100.0	

Vaud

Prime variety	Col	Regional %	VII*
Chasselas	W	61.4	2.3
Pinot Noir	R	13.4	0.5
Gamay Noir	R	11.6	1.1
Gamaret	R	3.3	1.3
Garanoir	R	2.7	2.0
Chardonnay	W	1.0	0.5
Other varieties		6.4	
Total		100.0	

Zurich

Prime variety	Col	Regional %	VII*
Pinot Noir	R	54.6	1.8
Muller Thurgau	W	21.2	6.4
Rauschling	W	2.9	18.7
	W	2.0	0.9
Pinot Gris	O	1.9	1.3
Regent	R	1.8	6.4
Other varieties		15.6	
Total		100.0	

Other Regions

Prime variety	Col	Regional %	VII*
Pinot Noir	R	42.2	1.4
Muller Thurgau	W	24.3	7.3
Marechal Foch	R	3.9	45.3
Pinot Gris	O	3.6	2.5
Regent	R	3.4	12.3
Merlot	R	2.3	0.3
Other varieties		20.3	
Total		100.0	

Thailand

Prime variety	Col	Regional %	VII*
Syrah	R	44.5	
Black Queen	R	11.4	
Malaga Blanc	W	10.9	
Chenin Blanc	W	8.9	
Colombard	W	7.5	
Cabernet Sauvignon	R	4.7	
Other varieties		12.2	
Total		100.0	

Table 53 (cont.) Winegrape areas and Varietal Intensity Indexes for each region's top 6 varieties, by region, 2010

Tunisia

	Tunisia		
Prime variety	*Col*	*Regional %*	*VII**
Mazuelo	R	45.0	
Garnacha Tinta	R	12.0	
Alicante Henri Bouschet	R	5.0	
Cinsaut	R	5.0	
Sangiovese	R	5.0	
Cabernet Sauvignon	R	2.0	
Other varieties		26.0	
Total		100.0	

Turkey

	Akdeniz				Ege		
Prime variety	*Col*	*Regional %*	*VII**	*Prime variety*	*Col*	*Regional %*	*VII**
Cabernet Sauvignon	R	15.9	5.2	Sultaniye	W	25.8	1.9
Sauvignon Blanc	W	13.6	12.0	Syrah	R	18.4	1.7
Chardonnay	W	13.6	12.4	Calkarasi	R	9.2	1.9
Kalecik Karasi	R	11.4	1.7	Bogazkere	R	8.2	1.0
Pinot Noir	R	10.5	467.5	Kalecik Karasi	R	7.3	1.1
Okuzgozu	R	9.1	0.8	Alicante Henri Bouschet	R	7.2	1.9
Other varieties		25.9		Other varieties		23.8	
Total		100.0		Total		0.0	100.0

	Guney Dogu				Marmara		
Prime variety	*Col*	*Regional %*	*VII**	*Prime variety*	*Col*	*Regional %*	*VII**
Bogazkere	R	100.0	11.6	Semillon	W	31.3	7.4
Total		100.0		Cinsaut	R	28.7	7.4
				Gamay Noir	R	11.8	7.4
				Papazkarasi	R	10.0	7.4
				Merlot	R	5.2	1.9
				Adakarasi	R	3.9	7.4
				Other varieties		9.1	
				Total		100.0	

	Orta Dogu				Orta Guney		
Prime variety	*Col*	*Regional %*	*VII**	*Prime variety*	*Col*	*Regional %*	*VII**
Okuzgozu	R	57.1	5.0	Dimrit	R	48.3	7.2
Narince	W	39.6	6.6	Emir	W	44.3	8.3
Bogazkere	R	3.3	0.4	Kalecik Karasi	R	4.7	0.7
Sultaniye	W	0.0	0.0	Okuzgozu	R	0.8	0.1
Syrah	R	0.0	0.0	Narince	W	0.6	0.1
Dimrit	R	0.0	0.0	Sauvignon Blanc	W	0.5	0.4
Other varieties		0.0		Other varieties		0.9	
Total		100.0		Total		100.0	

	Orta Kuzey		
Prime variety	*Col*	*Regional %*	*VII**
Kalecik Karasi	R	64.3	9.6
Syrah	R	19.6	1.8
Bogazkere	R	11.7	1.4
Okuzgozu	R	4.4	0.4
Total		100.0	

Table 53 (cont.) Winegrape areas and Varietal Intensity Indexes for each region's top 6 varieties, by region, 2010

Ukraine

	Ukraine		
Prime variety	*Col*	*Regional %*	*VII**
Rkatsiteli	W	22.1	
Aligote	W	18.4	
Cabernet Sauvignon	R	9.3	
Sauvignon Blanc	W	6.0	
Chardonnay	W	5.7	
Merlot	R	5.4	
Other varieties		33.1	
Total		100.0	

United Kingdom

	UK		
Prime variety	*Col*	*Regional %*	*VII**
Chardonnay	W	19.6	
Pinot Noir	R	19.4	
Bacchus	W	9.7	
Seyval Blanc	W	7.1	
Reichensteiner	W	5.9	
Pinot Meunier	R	4.2	
Other varieties		34.1	
Total		100.0	

United States

	Alameda				Amador			
Prime variety	*Col*	*Regional %*	*VII**	*Prime variety*	*Col*	*Regional %*	*VII**
Cabernet Sauvignon	R	29.5	1.9	Tribidrag	R	61.5	7.1
Chardonnay	W	21.6	1.2	Syrah	R	7.8	1.9
Merlot	R	12.0	1.2	Barbera	R	5.0	4.1
Durif	R	9.4	7.5	Cabernet Sauvignon	R	5.0	0.3
Syrah	R	6.2	1.5	Sangiovese	R	3.5	9.4
Tribidrag	R	4.8	0.6	Durif	R	2.5	2.0
Other varieties		16.6		Other varieties		14.6	
Total		100.0		Total		100.0	

	Arizona				Arkansas		
Prime variety	*Col*	*Regional %*	*VII**	*Prime variety*	*Col*	*Regional %*	*VII**
Other varieties		100.0		Other varieties		100.0	

	Benton Co.				Butte		
Prime variety	*Col*	*Regional %*	*VII**	*Prime variety*	*Col*	*Regional %*	*VII**
Pinot Noir	R	75.2	10.3	Cabernet Sauvignon	R	48.6	3.2
Pinot Gris	O	17.8	7.8	Tribidrag	R	26.4	3.0
Chardonnay	W	3.1	0.2	Syrah	R	13.2	3.3
Cabernet Sauvignon	R	1.6	0.1	Merlot	R	6.9	0.7
Gewurztraminer	W	1.0	2.1	Sangiovese	R	2.1	5.6
Pinot Blanc	W	0.5	4.4	Barbera	R	1.4	1.1
Other varieties		0.8		Other varieties		1.4	
Total		100.0		Total		100.0	

Table 53 (cont.) Winegrape areas and Varietal Intensity Indexes for each region's top 6 varieties, by region, 2010

United States continued

Calaveras				Chautauqua-Erie			
Prime variety	*Col*	*Regional %*	*VII**	*Prime variety*	*Col*	*Regional %*	*VII**
Cabernet Sauvignon	R	15.8	1.0	Concord	R	86.5	23.4
Syrah	R	15.8	3.9	Niagara	W	8.0	15.2
Merlot	R	11.7	1.2	Catawba	R	1.7	6.2
Chardonnay	W	11.0	0.6	Elvira	W	0.7	6.6
Sauvignon Blanc	W	11.0	3.8	Seyval Blanc	W	0.3	2.7
Tribidrag	R	10.1	1.2	Delaware	O	0.3	8.9
Other varieties		24.5		Other varieties		2.4	
Total		100.0		Total		100.0	

Colorado				Columbia Gorge			
Prime variety	*Col*	*Regional %*	*VII**	*Prime variety*	*Col*	*Regional %*	*VII**
Merlot	R	16.7	1.7	Chardonnay	W	20.8	1.2
Cabernet Sauvignon	R	13.1	0.9	Gewurztraminer	W	18.5	37.3
Riesling	W	12.7	6.2	Pinot Gris	O	17.3	7.6
Chardonnay	W	11.9	0.7	Pinot Noir	R	10.7	1.5
Syrah	R	7.2	1.8	Riesling	W	5.6	2.7
Pinot Noir	R	5.8	0.8	Merlot	R	5.1	0.5
Other varieties		32.5		Other varieties		22.1	
Total		100.0		Total		100.0	

Columbia River 2				Columbia Valley			
Prime variety	*Col*	*Regional %*	*VII**	*Prime variety*	*Col*	*Regional %*	*VII**
Cabernet Sauvignon	R	24.5	1.6	Cabernet Sauvignon	R	23.4	1.5
Merlot	R	12.9	1.3	Merlot	R	19.4	1.9
Syrah	R	12.5	3.1	Chardonnay	W	17.8	1.0
Riesling	W	10.0	4.9	Riesling	W	15.3	7.4
Pinot Noir	R	9.2	1.3	Syrah	R	8.5	2.1
Chardonnay	W	3.7	0.2	Pinot Gris	O	3.3	1.5
Other varieties		27.1		Other varieties		12.2	
Total		100.0		Total		100.0	

Colusa				Contra Costa			
Prime variety	*Col*	*Regional %*	*VII**	*Prime variety*	*Col*	*Regional %*	*VII**
Tribidrag	R	51.8	6.0	Chardonnay	W	27.8	1.6
Chardonnay	W	15.9	0.9	Tribidrag	R	22.3	2.6
Muscat of Alexandria	W	12.5	22.3	Monastrell	R	10.1	57.4
Syrah	R	8.6	2.2	Pinot Gris	O	7.9	3.5
Cabernet Sauvignon	R	5.0	0.3	Merlot	R	7.3	0.7
Pinot Noir	R	2.0	0.3	Sauvignon Blanc	W	5.4	1.9
Other varieties		4.1		Other varieties		19.2	
Total		100.0		Total		100.0	

Douglas Co.				El Dorado			
Prime variety	*Col*	*Regional %*	*VII**	*Prime variety*	*Col*	*Regional %*	*VII**
Pinot Noir	R	52.0	7.1	Tribidrag	R	19.6	2.3
Pinot Gris	O	8.6	3.8	Cabernet Sauvignon	R	16.9	1.1
Syrah	R	5.0	1.2	Syrah	R	11.3	2.8
Merlot	R	3.8	0.4	Merlot	R	8.3	0.8
Chardonnay	W	3.6	0.2	Durif	R	6.1	4.8
Cabernet Sauvignon	R	3.6	0.2	Chardonnay	W	5.5	0.3
Other varieties		23.5		Other varieties		32.5	
Total		100.0		Total		100.0	

Table 53 (cont.) Winegrape areas and Varietal Intensity Indexes for each region's top 6 varieties, by region, 2010

United States continued

Finger Lakes				Fresno			
Prime variety	*Col*	*Regional %*	*VII**	*Prime variety*	*Col*	*Regional %*	*VII**
Concord	R	23.6	6.4	Colombard	W	24.8	5.7
Niagara	W	9.5	17.8	Rubired	R	11.6	5.8
Catawba	R	9.2	33.1	Barbera	R	11.0	9.0
Riesling	W	9.0	4.2	Ruby Cabernet	R	6.9	6.5
Aurore	W	7.0	59.2	Tribidrag	R	6.8	0.8
Elvira	W	5.2	46.7	Chenin Blanc	W	5.9	4.2
Other varieties		36.5		Other varieties		32.9	
Total		100.0		Total		100.0	

Georgia				Glenn			
Prime variety	*Col*	*Regional %*	*VII**	*Prime variety*	*Col*	*Regional %*	*VII**
Other varieties		100.0		Tribidrag	R	24.6	2.8
Total		100.0		Garnacha Tinta	R	19.3	16.5
				Muscat of Alexandria	W	17.6	31.3
				Chardonnay	W	14.6	0.8
				Syrah	R	11.1	2.7
				Rubired	R	9.5	4.7
				Other varieties		3.4	
				Total		100.0	

Horse Heaven Hills				Humboldt			
Prime variety	*Col*	*Regional %*	*VII**	*Prime variety*	*Col*	*Regional %*	*VII**
Cabernet Sauvignon	R	31.4	2.1	Merlot	R	22.3	2.2
Merlot	R	19.3	1.9	Pinot Noir	R	22.3	3.0
Chardonnay	W	16.7	0.9	Cabernet Sauvignon	R	17.9	1.2
Riesling	W	8.3	4.0	Syrah	R	14.5	3.6
Syrah	R	7.1	1.8	Chardonnay	W	5.6	0.3
Sauvignon Blanc	W	4.6	1.6	Nebbiolo	R	3.4	112.1
Other varieties		12.5		Other varieties		14.0	
Total		100.0		Total		100.0	

Illinois				Indiana			
Prime variety	*Col*	*Regional %*	*VII**	*Prime variety*	*Col*	*Regional %*	*VII**
Chambourcin	R	12.8	99.4	Chambourcin	R	13.1	101.4
Norton	R	7.9	79.8	Traminette	W	11.5	143.7
Marechal Foch	R	7.5	94.5	Chardonel	W	10.8	171.1
Frontenac	R	7.4	124.7	Vidal	W	10.0	74.0
Chardonel	W	7.2	113.8	Vignoles	W	9.2	87.0
Vignoles	W	7.1	66.6	Catawba	R	3.8	13.5
Other varieties		50.2		Other varieties		41.5	
Total		100.0		Total		100.0	

Iowa				Jackson Co.			
Prime variety	*Col*	*Regional %*	*VII**	*Prime variety*	*Col*	*Regional %*	*VII**
Marechal Foch	R	19.4	244.8	Pinot Noir	R	15.5	2.1
Edelweiss	W	11.1	802.1	Syrah	R	15.2	3.8
Frontenac	R	9.8	164.9	Merlot	R	11.4	1.1
La Crosse	W	6.9	629.5	Cabernet Sauvignon	R	9.6	0.6
St Croix	R	6.1	563.4	Pinot Gris	O	9.1	4.0
Concord	R	4.5	1.1	Chardonnay	W	6.1	0.3
Other varieties		42.3		Other varieties		33.1	
Total		100.0		Total		100.0	

Table 53 (cont.) Winegrape areas and Varietal Intensity Indexes for each region's top 6 varieties, by region, 2010

United States continued

Josephine Co.				Kentucky			
Prime variety	*Col*	*Regional %*	*VII**	*Prime variety*	*Col*	*Regional %*	*VII**
Pinot Noir	R	44.1	6.0	Vidal	W	11.8	87.2
Pinot Gris	O	13.5	5.9	Chambourcin	R	11.2	86.8
Riesling	W	12.2	5.9	Norton	R	10.8	108.8
Gewurztraminer	W	5.5	11.1	Cabernet Sauvignon	R	10.0	0.7
Chardonnay	W	4.7	0.3	Cabernet Franc	R	7.7	8.0
Merlot	R	3.7	0.4	Traminette	W	6.8	84.2
Other varieties		16.2		Other varieties		41.7	
Total		100.0		Total		100.0	

Kern				Kings			
Prime variety	*Col*	*Regional %*	*VII**	*Prime variety*	*Col*	*Regional %*	*VII**
Colombard	W	18.5	4.2	Rubired	R	26.1	13.1
Rubired	R	11.9	6.0	Tribidrag	R	16.5	1.9
Cabernet Sauvignon	R	8.9	0.6	Garnacha Tinta	R	15.7	13.5
Chardonnay	W	6.5	0.4	Muscat of Alexandria	W	12.2	21.8
Tribidrag	R	4.7	0.5	Chenin Blanc	W	9.2	6.5
Chenin Blanc	W	4.1	2.9	Colombard	W	6.4	1.5
Other varieties		45.4		Other varieties		13.8	
Total		100.0		Total		100.0	

Lake				Lake Chelan			
Prime variety	*Col*	*Regional %*	*VII**	*Prime variety*	*Col*	*Regional %*	*VII**
Cabernet Sauvignon	R	37.2	2.4	Riesling	W	17.4	8.5
Sauvignon Blanc	W	22.8	7.9	Pinot Noir	R	17.0	2.3
Tribidrag	R	8.1	0.9	Syrah	R	14.6	3.6
Merlot	R	6.4	0.6	Gewurztraminer	W	11.3	22.8
Chardonnay	W	5.6	0.3	Viognier	W	6.1	10.1
Syrah	R	4.7	1.2	Chardonnay	W	5.3	0.3
Other varieties		15.3		Other varieties		28.3	
Total		100.0		Total		100.0	

Lane Co.				Los Angeles			
Prime variety	*Col*	*Regional %*	*VII**	*Prime variety*	*Col*	*Regional %*	*VII**
Pinot Gris	O	51.2	22.5	Cabernet Sauvignon	R	41.4	2.7
Pinot Noir	R	40.4	5.5	Syrah	R	10.7	2.7
Riesling	W	3.8	1.8	Merlot	R	10.0	1.0
Chardonnay	W	2.0	0.1	Trebbiano Toscano	W	10.0	285.8
Pinot Blanc	W	0.6	5.0	Tribidrag	R	6.1	0.7
Merlot	R	0.1	0.0	Chardonnay	W	4.6	0.3
Other varieties		1.9		Other varieties		17.2	
Total		100.0		Total		100.0	

Madera				Marin			
Prime variety	*Col*	*Regional %*	*VII**	*Prime variety*	*Col*	*Regional %*	*VII**
Colombard	W	21.6	4.9	Pinot Noir	R	81.7	11.1
Chardonnay	W	14.0	0.8	Chardonnay	W	9.2	0.5
Tribidrag	R	8.8	1.0	Cabernet Sauvignon	R	4.6	0.3
Merlot	R	8.6	0.9	Riesling	W	2.6	1.3
Cabernet Sauvignon	R	8.5	0.6	Cabernet Franc	R	2.0	2.0
Garnacha Tinta	R	5.9	5.1	Total		100.0	
Other varieties		32.6					
Total		100.0					

Table 53 (cont.) Winegrape areas and Varietal Intensity Indexes for each region's top 6 varieties, by region, 2010

United States continued

Marion Co.				Mariposa			
Prime variety	*Col*	*Regional %*	*VII**	*Prime variety*	*Col*	*Regional %*	*VII**
Pinot Noir	R	52.7	7.2	Cabernet Sauvignon	R	26.1	1.7
Pinot Gris	O	35.6	15.6	Tribidrag	R	20.2	2.3
Riesling	W	6.0	2.9	Merlot	R	18.5	1.9
Chardonnay	W	1.7	0.1	Chardonnay	W	13.4	0.8
Gewurztraminer	W	0.4	0.9	Sangiovese	R	6.7	18.0
Pinot Blanc	W	0.4	3.6	Syrah	R	3.4	0.8
Other varieties		3.2		Other varieties		11.8	
Total		100.0		Total		100.0	

Mendocino				Merced			
Prime variety	*Col*	*Regional %*	*VII**	*Prime variety*	*Col*	*Regional %*	*VII**
Chardonnay	W	26.2	1.5	Chardonnay	W	25.0	1.4
Cabernet Sauvignon	R	14.9	1.0	Merlot	R	18.6	1.9
Pinot Noir	R	13.9	1.9	Tribidrag	R	13.1	1.5
Tribidrag	R	12.0	1.4	Cabernet Sauvignon	R	10.5	0.7
Merlot	R	10.4	1.0	Rubired	R	5.1	2.5
Sauvignon Blanc	W	4.9	1.7	Syrah	R	5.0	1.2
Other varieties		17.6		Other varieties		22.9	
Total		100.0		Total		100.0	

Michigan				Minnesota			
Prime variety	*Col*	*Regional %*	*VII**	*Prime variety*	*Col*	*Regional %*	*VII**
Riesling	W	22.5	10.9	Frontenac	R	20.3	342.7
Pinot Noir	R	8.9	1.2	Marquette	R	19.7	515.4
Chardonnay	W	8.1	0.5	La Crescent	W	14.9	441.4
Pinot Gris	O	7.9	3.5	Frontenac Gris	W	13.2	510.0
Cabernet Franc	R	5.8	6.0	Marechal Foch	R	4.5	56.6
Vidal	W	4.9	36.3	Prairie Star	W	3.9	428.9
Other varieties		41.9		Other varieties		23.4	
Total		100.0		Total		100.0	

Missouri				Monterey			
Prime variety	*Col*	*Regional %*	*VII**	*Prime variety*	*Col*	*Regional %*	*VII**
Norton	R	19.2	193.7	Chardonnay	W	40.2	2.2
Vignoles	W	13.0	122.4	Pinot Noir	R	16.4	2.2
Chardonel	W	11.9	189.0	Merlot	R	12.6	1.3
Chambourcin	R	9.6	74.7	Cabernet Sauvignon	R	9.2	0.6
Concord	R	8.7	2.2	Riesling	W	4.8	2.3
Vidal	W	7.4	54.6	Syrah	R	4.4	1.1
Other varieties		30.1		Other varieties		12.4	
Total		100.0		Total		100.0	

Napa				Nevada			
Prime variety	*Col*	*Regional %*	*VII**	*Prime variety*	*Col*	*Regional %*	*VII**
Cabernet Sauvignon	R	42.2	2.8	Cabernet Sauvignon	R	24.9	
Chardonnay	W	15.6	0.9	Syrah	R	16.5	4.1
Merlot	R	15.2	1.5	Chardonnay	W	13.5	0.8
Pinot Noir	R	6.1	0.8	Cabernet Franc	R	12.2	12.6
Sauvignon Blanc	W	5.6	1.9	Merlot	R	8.6	0.9
Tribidrag	R	3.4	0.4	Tribidrag	R	6.1	0.7
Other varieties		11.9		Other varieties		18.3	
Total		100.0		Total		100.0	

Table 53 (cont.) Winegrape areas and Varietal Intensity Indexes for each region's top 6 varieties, by region, 2010

United States continued

North Carolina				Ohio			
Prime variety	*Col*	*Regional %*	*VII**	*Prime variety*	*Col*	*Regional %*	*VII**
Other varieties		100.0		Concord	R	61.7	15.7
Total		100.0		Riesling	W	4.0	1.9
				Vidal	W	3.9	28.8
				Catawba	R	3.6	12.7
				Niagara	W	3.1	4.8
				Cabernet Franc	R	2.1	2.2
				Other varieties		21.6	
				Total		100.0	

Orange				Other New York			
Prime variety	*Col*	*Regional %*	*VII**	*Prime variety*	*Col*	*Regional %*	*VII**
Other Varities		100		Merlot	R	18.1	1.8
				Chardonnay	W	13.8	0.8
				Concord	R	13.3	3.6
				Niagara	W	11.7	22.0
				Cabernet Franc	R	7.0	7.2
				Cabernet Sauvignon	R	4.4	0.3
				Other varieties		31.7	
				Total		100.0	

Other W. Valley And At Large 1				Pennsylvania			
Prime variety	*Col*	*Regional %*	*VII**	*Prime variety*	*Col*	*Regional %*	*VII**
Pinot Noir	R	62.1	8.5	Concord	R	42.5	10.8
Pinot Gris	O	10.8	4.7	Catawba	R	6.8	23.7
Chardonnay	W	7.9	0.4	Chambourcin	R	5.0	39.1
Riesling	W	5.0	2.4	Cabernet Franc	R	4.6	4.7
Gewurztraminer	W	2.1	4.2	Chardonnay	W	4.5	0.3
Syrah	R	1.8	0.5	Vidal	W	4.3	31.9
Other varieties		10.3		Other varieties		32.3	
Total		100.0		Total		100.0	

Placer				Polk Co.			
Prime variety	*Col*	*Regional %*	*VII**	*Prime variety*	*Col*	*Regional %*	*VII**
Tribidrag	R	25.6	2.9	Pinot Noir	R	78.8	10.7
Listan Prieto	R	13.4	115.2	Pinot Gris	O	11.3	4.9
Syrah	R	9.9	2.5	Chardonnay	W	4.8	0.3
Cabernet Franc	R	7.0	7.2	Gewurztraminer	W	1.0	1.9
Barbera	R	5.8	4.8	Riesling	W	0.7	0.4
Sauvignon Blanc	W	3.5	1.2	Pinot Blanc	W	0.7	5.9
Other varieties		34.9		Other varieties		2.8	
Total		100.0		Total		100.0	

Puget Sound				Rattlesnake Hills			
Prime variety	*Col*	*Regional %*	*VII**	*Prime variety*	*Col*	*Regional %*	*VII**
Pinot Noir	R	46.6	6.4	Riesling	W	28.2	13.7
Pinot Gris	O	5.1	2.2	Merlot	R	23.0	2.3
Riesling	W	2.2	1.1	Cabernet Sauvignon	R	18.3	1.2
Other varieties		46.1		Chardonnay	W	7.4	0.4
Total		100.0		Syrah	R	4.8	1.2
				Cabernet Franc	R	4.1	4.2
				Other varieties		14.4	
				Total		100.0	

Table 53 (cont.) Winegrape areas and Varietal Intensity Indexes for each region's top 6 varieties, by region, 2010

United States continued

Red Mountain

Prime variety	Col	Regional %	VII*
Cabernet Sauvignon	R	52.8	3.5
Merlot	R	14.5	1.5
Syrah	R	13.6	3.4
Cabernet Franc	R	3.3	3.4
Semillon	W	1.6	8.2
Petit Verdot	R	1.5	4.0
Other varieties		12.8	
Total		100.0	

Riverside

Prime variety	Col	Regional %	VII*
Cabernet Sauvignon	R	22.6	1.5
Chardonnay	W	15.8	0.9
Merlot	R	8.4	0.8
Sauvignon Blanc	W	6.2	2.2
Syrah	R	5.3	1.3
Tribidrag	R	4.6	0.5
Other varieties		37.1	
Total		100.0	

Sacramento

Prime variety	Col	Regional %	VII*
Chardonnay	W	23.9	1.3
Cabernet Sauvignon	R	17.8	1.2
Merlot	R	16.2	1.6
Sauvignon Blanc	W	8.7	3.0
Tribidrag	R	8.3	1.0
Syrah	R	6.4	1.6
Other varieties		18.7	
Total		100.0	

San Benito

Prime variety	Col	Regional %	VII*
Chardonnay	W	38.2	2.1
Pinot Noir	R	17.4	2.4
Merlot	R	11.1	1.1
Cabernet Sauvignon	R	8.3	0.5
Gewurztraminer	W	3.8	7.7
Riesling	W	3.0	1.4
Other varieties		18.1	
Total		100.0	

San Bernardino

Prime variety	Col	Regional %	VII*
Tribidrag	R	76.6	8.8
Listan Prieto	R	11.2	96.7
Garnacha Tinta	R	4.8	4.1
Mazuelo	R	3.5	5.5
Chardonnay	W	0.8	0.0
Cabernet Sauvignon	R	0.4	0.0
Other varieties		2.7	
Total		100.0	

San Diego

Prime variety	Col	Regional %	VII*
Syrah	R	23.3	5.8
Cabernet Sauvignon	R	15.5	1.0
Merlot	R	14.0	1.4
Viognier	W	6.7	11.2
Cabernet Franc	R	5.2	5.4
Mazuelo	R	5.2	8.2
Other varieties		30.1	
Total		100.0	

San Joaquin

Prime variety	Col	Regional %	VII*
Tribidrag	R	29.4	3.4
Chardonnay	W	20.5	1.1
Cabernet Sauvignon	R	15.5	1.0
Merlot	R	11.3	1.1
Pinot Gris	O	3.7	1.6
Sauvignon Blanc	W	2.9	1.0
Other varieties		16.6	
Total		100.0	

San Luis Obispo

Prime variety	Col	Regional %	VII*
Cabernet Sauvignon	R	31.0	2.0
Merlot	R	14.3	1.4
Tribidrag	R	10.5	1.2
Chardonnay	W	10.5	0.6
Syrah	R	9.7	2.4
Pinot Noir	R	5.1	0.7
Other varieties		18.9	
Total		100.0	

San Mateo

Prime variety	Col	Regional %	VII*
Pinot Noir	R	43.1	5.9
Chardonnay	W	38.9	2.2
Cabernet Sauvignon	R	8.3	0.5
Tribidrag	R	6.9	0.8
Merlot	R	1.4	0.1
Sauvignon Blanc	W	1.4	0.5
Other varieties		0.0	
Total		100.0	

Santa Barbara

Prime variety	Col	Regional %	VII*
Chardonnay	W	41.1	2.3
Pinot Noir	R	21.9	3.0
Syrah	R	8.5	2.1
Pinot Gris	O	5.6	2.5
Cabernet Sauvignon	R	4.4	0.3
Merlot	R	3.6	0.4
Other varieties		14.9	
Total		100.0	

Table 53 (cont.) Winegrape areas and Varietal Intensity Indexes for each region's top 6 varieties, by region, 2010

United States continued

Santa Clara				Santa Cruz			
Prime variety	*Col*	*Regional %*	*VII**	*Prime variety*	*Col*	*Regional %*	*VII**
Chardonnay	W	22.9	1.3	Pinot Noir	R	46.1	6.3
Cabernet Sauvignon	R	22.5	1.5	Chardonnay	W	30.4	1.7
Merlot	R	16.4	1.6	Syrah	R	7.8	2.0
Syrah	R	6.4	1.6	Merlot	R	5.6	0.6
Tribidrag	R	6.0	0.7	Cabernet Sauvignon	R	3.0	0.2
Pinot Noir	R	4.7	0.6	Tribidrag	R	2.8	0.3
Other varieties		21.1		Other varieties		4.3	
Total		100.0		Total		100.0	

Shasta				Siskiyou			
Prime variety	*Col*	*Regional %*	*VII**	*Prime variety*	*Col*	*Regional %*	*VII**
Merlot	R	50.0	5.0	Chardonnay	W	15.0	0.8
Chardonnay	W	21.6	1.2	Merlot	R	15.0	1.5
Syrah	R	14.7	3.7	Pinot Noir	R	15.0	2.0
Cabernet Sauvignon	R	3.9	0.3	Cabernet Sauvignon	R	10.0	0.7
Tribidrag	R	2.9	0.3	Tribidrag	R	10.0	1.2
Viognier	W	2.0	3.3	Pinot Gris	O	10.0	4.4
Other varieties		4.9		Other varieties		25.0	
Total		100.0		Total		100.0	

Snipes Mountain				Solano			
Prime variety	*Col*	*Regional %*	*VII**	*Prime variety*	*Col*	*Regional %*	*VII**
Chardonnay	W	21.0	1.2	Chardonnay	W	31.5	1.8
Cabernet Sauvignon	R	20.2	1.3	Pinot Gris	O	12.5	5.5
Merlot	R	15.8	1.6	Cabernet Sauvignon	R	11.1	0.7
Syrah	R	11.1	2.8	Pinot Noir	R	10.8	1.5
Riesling	W	9.9	4.8	Merlot	R	7.1	0.7
Tribidrag	R	0.0	0.0	Durif	R	4.0	3.2
Other varieties		22.0		Other varieties		23.0	
Total		100.0		Total		100.0	

Sonoma				Stanislaus			
Prime variety	*Col*	*Regional %*	*VII**	*Prime variety*	*Col*	*Regional %*	*VII**
Chardonnay	W	26.0	1.5	Chardonnay	W	16.3	0.9
Cabernet Sauvignon	R	19.4	1.3	Tribidrag	R	14.3	1.6
Pinot Noir	R	19.1	2.6	Cabernet Sauvignon	R	13.4	0.9
Merlot	R	11.3	1.1	Colombard	W	9.7	2.2
Tribidrag	R	9.3	1.1	Merlot	R	8.8	0.9
Sauvignon Blanc	W	4.3	1.5	Syrah	R	6.4	1.6
Other varieties		10.6		Other varieties		31.1	
Total		100.0		Total		100.0	

Sutter				Tehama			
Prime variety	*Col*	*Regional %*	*VII**	*Prime variety*	*Col*	*Regional %*	*VII**
Chardonnay	W	29.9	1.7	Chardonnay	W	65.5	3.7
Lagrein	R	29.9	1074.6	Syrah	R	9.7	2.4
Tribidrag	R	26.9	3.1	Durif	R	9.0	7.2
Chenin Blanc	W	11.9	8.5	Pinot Noir	R	3.4	0.5
Merlot	R	1.5	0.1	Cabernet Sauvignon	R	2.8	0.2
Cabernet Sauvignon	R	0.0	0.0	Muscat of Alexandria	W	2.1	3.7
Other varieties		0.0		Other varieties		7.6	
Total		100.0		Total		100.0	

Table 53 (cont.) Winegrape areas and Varietal Intensity Indexes for each region's top 6 varieties, by region, 2010

United States continued

Texas				Trinity			
Prime variety	*Col*	*Regional %*	*VII**	*Prime variety*	*Col*	*Regional %*	*VII**
Cabernet Sauvignon	R	19.3	1.3	Chardonnay	W	28.9	1.6
Chardonnay	W	12.0	0.7	Pinot Noir	R	20.7	2.8
Merlot	R	10.0	1.0	Merlot	R	13.2	1.3
Chenin Blanc	W	8.3	5.9	Syrah	R	12.4	3.1
Syrah	R	5.7	1.4	Tribidrag	R	8.3	1.0
Muscat Blanc a Petits Grains	W	3.7	11.4	Cabernet Sauvignon	R	4.1	0.3
Other varieties		41.0		Other varieties		12.4	
Total		100.0		Total		100.0	

Tulare				Tuolumne			
Prime variety	*Col*	*Regional %*	*VII**	*Prime variety*	*Col*	*Regional %*	*VII**
Colombard	W	16.8	3.8	Syrah	R	56.7	14.1
Rubired	R	12.6	6.3	Cabernet Sauvignon	R	20.0	1.3
Tribidrag	R	11.3	1.3	Sangiovese	R	13.3	35.8
Cabernet Sauvignon	R	8.3	0.5	Merlot	R	6.7	0.7
Chardonnay	W	8.2	0.5	Tribidrag	R	3.3	0.4
Ruby Cabernet	R	7.1	6.7	Chardonnay	W	0.0	0.0
Other varieties		35.7		Other varieties		0.0	
Total		100.0		Total		100.0	

Ventura				Virginia			
Prime variety		*Regional %*	*VII**	*Prime variety*	*Col*	*Regional %*	*VII**
Syrah	R	69.2	17.2	Chardonnay	W	16.8	0.9
Cabernet Sauvignon	R	5.8	0.4	Merlot	R	12.0	1.2
Viognier	W	3.8	6.4	Cabernet Franc	R	10.7	11.1
Chardonnay	W	1.9	0.1	Cabernet Sauvignon	R	8.8	0.6
Merlot	R	1.9	0.2	Viognier	W	7.0	11.7
Tribidrag	R	1.9	0.2	Chambourcin	R	4.8	37.6
Other varieties		15.4		Other varieties		39.8	
Total		100.0		Total		100.0	

Wahluke Slope				Walla Walla Valley			
Prime variety	*Col*	*Regional %*	*VII**	*Prime variety*	*Col*	*Regional %*	*VII**
Cabernet Sauvignon	R	28.6	1.9	Cabernet Sauvignon	R	40.2	2.6
Merlot	R	23.2	2.3	Merlot	R	15.4	1.5
Chardonnay	W	14.8	0.8	Syrah	R	12.7	3.1
Riesling	W	12.8	6.2	Cabernet Franc	R	5.8	6.0
Syrah	R	6.4	1.6	Petit Verdot	R	2.5	6.8
Cabernet Franc	R	2.1	2.2	Chardonnay	W	2.1	0.1
Other varieties		12.1		Other varieties		21.3	
Total		100.0		Total		100.0	

Washington Co.				Yakima Valley			
Prime variety	*Col*	*Regional %*	*VII**	*Prime variety*	*Col*	*Regional %*	*VII**
Pinot Noir	R	66.6	9.1	Chardonnay	W	23.5	1.3
Pinot Gris	O	16.8	7.4	Riesling	W	21.2	10.3
Riesling	W	5.1	2.5	Merlot	R	17.1	1.7
Chardonnay	W	3.9	0.2	Cabernet Sauvignon	R	12.5	0.8
Gewurztraminer	W	1.9	3.8	Pinot Gris	O	6.4	2.8
Pinot Blanc	W	1.3	10.8	Syrah	R	5.4	1.3
Other varieties		4.5		Other varieties		14.0	
Total		100.0		Total		100.0	

Table 53 (cont.) Winegrape areas and Varietal Intensity Indexes for each region's top 6 varieties, by region, 2010

United States continued

Yamhill Co.				Yolo			
Prime variety	*Col*	*Regional %*	*VII**	*Prime variety*	*Col*	*Regional %*	*VII**
Pinot Noir	R	79.9	10.9	Chardonnay	W	44.3	2.5
Pinot Gris	O	8.9	3.9	Merlot	R	10.1	1.0
Chardonnay	W	5.4	0.3	Pinot Gris	O	9.0	4.0
Riesling	W	2.0	1.0	Sauvignon Blanc	W	5.3	1.9
Pinot Blanc	W	1.8	15.1	Cabernet Sauvignon	R	5.2	0.3
Gewurztraminer	W	0.4	0.8	Syrah	R	4.3	1.1
Other varieties		1.6		Other varieties		21.8	
Total		100.0		Total		100.0	

Yuba			
Prime variety	*Col*	*Regional %*	*VII**
Cabernet Sauvignon	R	20.8	1.4
Roussanne	W	18.8	306.3
Durif	R	17.7	14.1
Syrah	R	15.6	3.9
Chardonnay	W	10.4	0.6
Sauvignon Blanc	W	5.2	1.8
Other varieties		11.5	
Total		100.0	

Uruguay

Prime variety	*Col*	*Regional %*	*VII**
Tannat	R	23.7	
Muscat of Hamburg	R	19.6	
Merlot	R	11.4	
Trebbiano Toscano	W	9.8	
Cabernet Sauvignon	R	8.9	
Cabernet Franc	R	4.4	
Other varieties		22.2	
Total		100.0	

Table Section VII: Index of Varietal Similarity, by region and country

Table 54: Varietal Similarity Index of each region and country relative to the world, 2000

Region	Varietal Similarity Index	Region	Varietal Similarity Index
Algeria	0.35	**Australia (continued)**	
		Limestone C. Other	0.37
Argentina	0.30	Currency Creek	0.37
Mendoza	0.27	Yarra Valley	0.37
Sanjuan	0.27	Hilltops	0.38
Other Regions	0.29	Mudgee	0.38
		SE Coastal WA	0.38
Armenia	0.42	Greater Perth Other	0.38
		Lower Murray Other	0.39
Australia	0.45	Eastern Plain ect.	0.39
Tumbarumba	0.25	Padthaway	0.39
Far North Other	0.26	Goulburn Valley	0.39
Rutherglen	0.26	Orange	0.39
Bendigo	0.29	Mt Lofty Rgs Other	0.40
Hunter	0.29	Central WA	0.40
N. W. Vic Other	0.29	Canberra District	0.40
Perth Hills	0.30	West Vic Other	0.40
Murray Darling VIC	0.30	Swan Hill VIC	0.41
Eden Valley	0.31	Murray Darling NSW	0.41
Geelong	0.31	Riverland	0.41
Grampians	0.32	Hastings River	0.41
Sthn NSW Other	0.32	Perricoota	0.41
Henty	0.32	Great Southern	0.42
Barossa other	0.32	Fleurieu other	0.42
Tasmania	0.33	Margaret River	0.42
Aus. Capital Terr.	0.33	Blackwood Valley	0.43
Riverina	0.33	Beechworth	0.43
Mornington Pen.	0.33	Geographe	0.43
Kangaroo Island	0.34	Mount Benson	0.43
Cowra	0.34	Adelaide Hills	0.43
Hunter Valley other	0.34	Nthn Rivers Other	0.44
Barossa Valley	0.35	South Coast Other	0.46
Sunbury	0.35	SW Australia Other	0.46
Nthn Slopes Other	0.35	Alpine/Bchworth	0.48
Gippsland	0.36	N. E. Vic Other	0.49
Pyrenees	0.36	Nthn Territory	0.50
Southern Fleurieu	0.36	Swan District	0.54
Swan Hill NSW	0.36	Queensland Other	0.55
Clare Valley	0.37	Big Rivers Other	0.56
Pt Phillip Other	0.37	Granite Belt	0.56
McLaren Vale	0.37	C. Ranges Other	0.58
Peninsulas	0.37	South Burnett	0.61
Central Vic Other	0.37	West Plains Other	0.61
Langhorne Creek	0.37		

Table 54 (cont.) Varietal Similarity Index of each region and country relative to the world, 2000

Region	Varietal Similarity Index	Region	Varietal Similarity Index
Austria	**0.12**	**France**	**0.57**
Niederosterreich	0.09	Aisne	0.05
Steiermark	0.15	Alsace	0.08
Burgenland	0.15	Paysdela Loire except Maye	0.10
Wien and other	0.24	Auvergne	0.10
		Lorraine	0.10
		Seineet Marne	0.11
Brazil	**0.23**	Champagne Ardenne	0.15
		Centre	0.17
		France2	0.18
Bulgaria	**0.35**	Charente	0.18
		Charente Maritime	0.19
Canada	**0.46**	Deux Sevres Vienne	0.19
		Rhone Alpes Other	0.20
Chile	**0.46**	Midi Pyrenees Other	0.20
Del Bio Bio	0.26	Gers	0.21
Valparaiso	0.36	Bourgogne	0.21
Metropolitana	0.38	Vaucluse	0.34
Del Maule	0.38	Pyrenees Orientales	0.35
O'Higgins	0.39	Aquitaine Other	0.36
Coquimbo	0.42	Aude	0.37
		Corse	0.37
Croatia	**0.40**	Gironde	0.38
		Herault	0.40
Cyprus	**0.13**	Var	0.42
		Corr., Haute-Vien.	0.42
Czech Rep.	**0.39**	Alpes de Haute	0.43
		Bouchesdu Rhone	0.45
		Gard	0.47
		Ardeche	0.48
		Georgia	**0.14**
		Germany	**0.36**
		Mosel-Saar-Ruwer	0.09
		Mittelrhein	0.11
		Rheingau	0.13
		Hessische Bergs.	0.17
		Sachsen	0.25
		Nahe	0.27
		Rhein Pfalz	0.35
		Rheinhessen	0.35
		Saale Unstrut	0.39
		Wurttemberg	0.47

Table 54 (cont.) Varietal Similarity Index of each region and country relative to the world, 2000

Region	Varietal Similarity Index	Region	Varietal Similarity Index
Greece	**0.19**	**Italy (continued)**	
Voreio Aigaio	0.01	Rimini	0.11
Sterea Ellada	0.02	Pesaroe Urbino	0.12
Attiki	0.02	Siena	0.13
Kriti	0.03	Matera	0.13
Thessalia	0.03	Pavia	0.13
Dytiki Makedonia	0.09	Macerata	0.14
Ipeiros	0.09	Roma	0.15
Peloponnisos	0.13	Salerno	0.15
Dytiki Ellada	0.14	Palermo	0.15
Anatoliki Makedonia, Thraki	0.18	Pistoia	0.15
Notio Aigaio	0.18	Napoli	0.15
Kentriki Makedonia	0.23	Varese	0.17
Ionia Nisia	0.45	Rieti	0.18
		Prato	0.19
Hungary	**0.53**	Massa Carrara	0.19
		Viterbo	0.20
		Taranto	0.22
Italy	**0.36**	Sassari	0.22
Sondrio	0.02	Pisa	0.22
Nell'Emilia	0.02	Calabria	0.23
Siracusa	0.02	Oristano	0.23
Vercelli	0.02	Treviso	0.25
Novara	0.02	Lucca	0.25
Lecce	0.03	Vibo Valentia	0.26
Modena	0.04	Messina	0.27
Ravenna	0.04	Nuoro	0.28
LAquila	0.05	Vicenza	0.28
Trieste	0.06	Latina	0.28
Piacenza	0.06	Mantova	0.29
Teramo	0.06	Rovigo	0.29
Pescara	0.06	Trento	0.30
Valle D'Aosta	0.07	Udine	0.31
Lodi	0.08	Padova	0.32
Ragusa	0.08	Venezia	0.34
Verbano-C.-Ossola	0.08	Pordenone	0.36
Verona	0.09	Terni	0.37
Trapani	0.09	Lecco	0.37
Savona	0.09	Livorno	0.38
Parma	0.09	LaSpezia	0.39
Torino	0.10	Perugia	0.39
Milano	0.10		
Potenza	0.11		

Table 54 (cont.) Varietal Similarity Index of each region and country relative to the world, 2000

Region	Varietal Similarity Index	Region	Varietal Similarity Index
Luxembourg	**0.07**	**Spain**	**0.69**
		Huelva	0.03
Moldova	**0.31**	Guipuzcoa Vizcaya	0.04
		Cordoba	0.04
Morocco	**0.25**	Cadiz	0.05
		Cantabria	0.05
New Zealand	**0.34**	Badajoz	0.10
Central Otago	0.18	Canarias	0.14
Marlborough	0.20	Leon	0.16
Canterbury	0.23	Alava	0.17
Nelson	0.26	Tarragona	0.19
Waipara	0.27	Murcia	0.19
Wairarapa	0.29	Barcelona	0.20
Gisborne	0.31	Caceres	0.20
Hawkes Bay	0.44	Asturias	0.21
Auckland	0.47	Valencia	0.23
Waikato	0.60	Burgos	0.24
		Rioja	0.29
Portugal	**0.46**	Galicia	0.29
Entre Douroe Minho	0.24	Zaragoza	0.33
Algarve	0.26	Illes Balears	0.34
Acores	0.27	Huesca Teruel	0.37
Madeira	0.27	Guadalajara	0.40
Ribatejoe Oeste	0.29	Girona Lleida	0.41
Beira Litoral	0.29	Avila Palencia S S Soria	0.41
Beira Interior	0.45	Alicante	0.43
Alto Trasos Montes	0.47	Valladolid	0.43
		Zamora	0.45
Romania	**0.58**	Navarra	0.46
Russia	**0.51**	Malaga	0.48
Serbia	**0.27**	Cuenca	0.48
Slovakia	**0.33**	Castellon	0.49
Slovenia	**0.58**	Almeria Granada Jaen S	0.51
		Ciudad Real	0.54
South Africa	**0.29**	Madrid	0.55
Orange River	0.11	Albacete	0.55
Olifants River	0.18	Toledo	0.55
Breedekloof	0.22		
Little Karoo	0.32		
Worcester	0.34		
Malmesbury	0.36		
Paarl	0.41		
Robertson	0.44		
Stellenbosch	0.60		

Table 54 (cont.) Varietal Similarity Index of each region and country relative to the world, 2000

Region	Varietal Similarity Index	Region	Varietal Similarity Index
Switzerland	**0.12**	**United States (continued)**	
Vaud	0.05	Shasta	0.22
Fribourg	0.05	Josephine Co.	0.23
Neuchatel	0.07	Contra Costa	0.24
Schaffhausen	0.09	Tulare	0.25
Other region	0.09	Los Angeles	0.25
Valais	0.09	Santa Barbara	0.25
Lucerne	0.09	Santa Cruz	0.25
Geneva	0.10	Butte	0.26
Thurgau	0.10	Madera	0.26
Aargau	0.10	Riverside	0.27
St Gallen	0.11	San Mateo	0.27
Graubunden	0.11	Tehama	0.28
Bern	0.11	San Joaquin	0.29
Zurich	0.11	Glenn	0.29
Basel Landschaft	0.13	Yolo	0.30
Schwyz	0.17	Other New York	0.30
Araucania	0.18	Monterey	0.32
Ticino	0.29	Stanislaus	0.32
Jura	0.31	Yuba	0.33
Atacama	0.37	Alameda	0.36
		Merced	0.36
Tunisia	**0.34**	Mendocino	0.37
		Calavaras	0.37
United Kingdom	**0.36**	El Dorado	0.38
United States	**0.41**	Lake	0.39
Chautauqua Erie	0.02	Sonoma	0.39
Colusa	0.06	Marin	0.39
Amador	0.08	Sacramento	0.40
Finger Lakes	0.11	Douglas Co.	0.40
Ventura	0.13	San Diego	0.40
Benton Co.	0.13	Nevada	0.41
San Bernardino	0.15	Solano	0.41
Yamhill Co.	0.15	Trinity	0.41
Placer	0.15	Santa Clara	0.41
Lane Co.	0.17	Oregon Other	0.41
Marion Co.	0.17	Mariposa	0.42
Polkco	0.17	San Luis Obispo	0.42
Other Valley	0.19	Michigan	0.42
Sutter	0.19	San Benito	0.42
Kings	0.19	Washington	0.43
Humboldt	0.19	Napa	0.44
Fresno	0.20	Columbia River	0.45
Kern	0.21		
Washington Co.	0.22	**Uruguay**	**0.21**

Table 55: Varietal Similarity Index of each region and country relative to the world, 2010

Region	Varietal Similarity Index	Region	Varietal Similarity Index
Algeria	**0.36**	**Australia (continued)**	**0.62**
		New England	0.30
Argentina	**0.38**	Tasmania	0.32
Angaco	0.12	Sthn Flinders	0.32
Albardon	0.12	Mornington Pen.	0.33
Rawson	0.13	Barossa Other	0.34
Other San Juan	0.18	Henty	0.34
Pocito	0.19	Hunter Valley Other	0.36
9 de Julio	0.21	Eastern Plain ect.	0.37
San Martin S	0.23	Tumbarumba	0.39
Caucete	0.24	Grampians	0.39
Salta	0.24	Geelong	0.39
San Martin M	0.24	Greater Perth Other	0.40
Catamarca	0.25	Heathcote	0.41
25 de Mayo	0.25	Rutherglen	0.41
Junin	0.27	Hastings River	0.41
Rivadavia	0.28	Macedon Ranges	0.43
Rioja	0.28	Central Vic Other	0.43
Lujande Cuyo	0.28	Nthn Rivers Other	0.43
Sarmiento	0.31	Hunter	0.44
Lavalle	0.32	FarNorth Other	0.44
Santa Rosa	0.32	Barossa Valley	0.44
Other Mendoza	0.33	Pt Phillip Other	0.44
San Rafael	0.38	Gippsland	0.44
Tunuyan	0.38	Cowra	0.45
Maipu	0.41	Mt Lofty Rgs Other	0.45
Tupungato	0.42	Eden Valley	0.46
Neuquen	0.42	Gundagai	0.46
RioNegro	0.43	Bendigo	0.47
Ullum	0.44	Pemberton	0.47
Other AR	0.53	West Plains Other	0.47
		Perth Hills	0.48
Armenia	**0.25**	McLaren Vale	0.48
		Sthn NSW Other	0.48
		Pyrenees	0.48
		Clare Valley	0.51
		SE Coastal WA	0.51
		Yarra Valley	0.51
		Fleurieu Other	0.51
		Aus. Capital Terr.	0.51
		Sunbury	0.52
		Big Rivers Other	0.53
		Shoalhaven Coast	0.53

Table 55 (cont.) Varietal Similarity Index of each region and country relative to the world, 2010

Region	Varietal Similarity Index	Region	Varietal Similarity Index
Australia (continued)		**Australia (continued)**	
Canberra ACT	0.53	Geographe	0.65
Riverina	0.54	Beechworth	0.65
Glenrowan	0.54	Nthn Slopes Other	0.66
KangarooIsland	0.54	Alpine Valleys	0.67
Coonawarra	0.54	Southern Highlands	0.68
SwanDistrict	0.55	N. E. Vic Other	0.69
Queensland Other	0.55	Granite Belt	0.70
Southern Fleurieu	0.56	King Valley	0.70
Lower Murray Other	0.56		
South Burnett	0.56	**Austria**	**0.15**
South Coast Other	0.56	Niederosterreich	0.09
Central WA	0.56	Burgenland	0.19
Perricoota	0.57	Wien and other	0.28
Currency Creek	0.57	Steiermark	0.29
Hilltops	0.57		
Peninsulas	0.57	**Brazil**	**0.11**
Adelaide Hills	0.58		
Upper Goulburn	0.58	**Bulgaria**	**0.55**
Murray Darling VIC	0.59	Yugozapaden	0.24
Riverland	0.59	Severoiztochen	0.40
Blackwood Valley	0.59	Yugoiztochen	0.50
Adelaide Plains	0.59	Yuzhentsentralen	0.52
Langhorne Creek	0.59	Severozapaden	0.52
SW Australia Other	0.59	Severentsentralen	0.53
Great Southern	0.59		
Swan Hill VIC	0.60	**Canada**	**0.50**
Goulburn Valley	0.60	British Colombia	0.60
Robe	0.60	Ontario	0.34
Western Victoria Other	0.60		
Strathbogie Rgs	0.60	**Chile**	**0.60**
Swan Hill NSW	0.60	Atacama	0.31
Wrattonbully	0.60	DeLos Lagos	0.32
Canberra NSW	0.61	Araucania	0.32
Murray Darling NSW	0.61	Del Bio Bio	0.36
Mudgee	0.61	Valparaiso	0.41
Padthaway	0.62	Metropolitana	0.55
Limestone C. Other	0.62	Coquimbo	0.56
N. W. Vic Other	0.62	Del Maule	0.57
Peel	0.62	O'Higgins	0.57
C. Ranges Other	0.63		
Margaret River	0.63		
Manjimup	0.63		
Orange	0.64		
Mount Benson	0.65		

Table 55 (cont.) Varietal Similarity Index of each region and country relative to the world, 2010

Region	Varietal Similarity Index	Region	Varietal Similarity Index
China	**0.47**	**France**	**0.72**
Beijing	0.40	Savoie	0.04
Shandong	0.40	Loire Atlantique	0.04
Sichuan	0.40	Rhone	0.05
Tianjin	0.40	Aquitaine Other	0.07
Yantai	0.40	Indreet Loire	0.11
Other Region	0.44	Vienne	0.12
Ningxia	0.44	Vendee	0.13
Gansu	0.53	Bas Rhin	0.13
Xinjiang	0.53	Tarnet Garonne	0.14
ShanXi	0.57	Haut Rhin	0.14
		Indre	0.14
Croatia	**0.33**	Lot	0.15
Srednja Juzna Dalm.	0.06	Maineet Loire	0.16
Hrvatsko Primorje	0.09	Charente	0.16
Dalm. Zagora	0.12	Charente Maritime	0.18
Istra	0.15	Cher	0.18
Slavonija	0.16	Nievre	0.18
Pokuplje	0.17	Coted Or	0.21
Podunavlje	0.17	Champagne Viticole	0.23
Prigorje-Bilogora	0.18	Loiret Cher	0.23
Moslavina	0.20	Gers	0.27
Zagorje-Medimurje	0.21	Landes	0.29
Plesivica	0.25	Corse	0.29
Sjeverna-Dalmacija	0.33	Rhonealpes Other	0.30
Other HR	0.27	Yonne	0.30
		Saoneet Loire	0.31
Cyprus	**0.11**		0.31
		Paysdeloire Other	0.31
Czech Rep.	**0.24**	Provence-C. d'A Other	0.32
Cechy	0.21	Tarn	0.33
Morava	0.24	Vaucluse	0.39
		Poitoucharentes Other	0.39
		Centre Other	0.40
		Drome	0.40
		Dordogne	0.43
		Pyrenees Orientales	0.43
		Var	0.47
		Gironde	0.51
		Bouchesdu Rhone	0.54
		Lotet Garonne	0.55
		Gard	0.60
		Aude	0.61
		Ardeche	0.62
		Herault	0.64

Table 55 (cont.) Varietal Similarity Index of each region and country relative to the world, 2010

Region	Varietal Similarity Index	Region	Varietal Similarity Index
Georgia	**0.11**	**Hungary**	**0.36**
		Tokaj	0.02
Germany	**0.26**	Csongrad	0.13
MoselSaar Ruwer	0.10	Sopron	0.13
Rheingau	0.12	Kunsag	0.15
Mittelrhein	0.14	Balatonfelvidek	0.18
Ahr	0.15	Bukk	0.20
Hessische Bergs.	0.20	Badacsony	0.21
Franken	0.21	Mor	0.23
Wurttemberg	0.21	Balatonfured Cs.	0.23
Nahe	0.22	Nagy Somlo	0.23
Rheinhessen	0.24	Pannonhalma	0.25
Rhein Pfalz	0.24	Matra	0.28
Sachsen	0.25	Zala	0.31
Saale Unstrut	0.26	Hajos-Bajai	0.33
Baden	0.27	Neszmely	0.34
		Szekszard	0.36
Greece	**0.21**	Eger	0.38
Attiki	0.02	Etyek Budai	0.41
Dytiki Ellada	0.05	Tolna	0.44
Sterea Ellada	0.06	Pecs	0.45
Dytiki Makedonia	0.09	Villany	0.48
Peloponissos	0.10	Balatonboglar	0.48
Vorreio Aigaio	0.10		
Kriti	0.12		
Thessalia	0.16		
Notio Aigaio	0.17		
Ipeiros	0.17		
Ionia Nisia	0.21		
Kentriki Makedonia	0.48		
Anatoliki Mak., Thraki	0.63		

Table 55 (cont.) Varietal Similarity Index of each region and country relative to the world, 2010

Region	Varietal Similarity Index	Region	Varietal Similarity Index
Italy	**0.44**	**Mexico**	**0.52**
Calabria	0.09	Sonora	0.01
Piemonte	0.09	Zacatecas	0.04
Basilicata	0.10	Aguascalientes	0.09
Liguria	0.11	Suma Coahuila	0.35
Campania	0.12	Suma Baja Cal.	0.63
Abruzzo	0.13		
Emilia Romagna	0.14	**New Zealand**	**0.30**
Molise	0.18	Otago	0.15
Valle D'Aosta	0.18	Marlborough	0.20
Toscana	0.19	Wairarapa	0.24
Puglia	0.20	Waipara	0.24
Marche	0.20	Canterbury	0.28
Sicilia	0.22	Nelson	0.32
Lazio	0.28	Gisborne	0.41
Veneto	0.29	Hawkes Bay	0.60
Sardegna	0.31	Auckland	0.62
Lombardia	0.35	Waikato	0.65
Trentino	0.37	Other NZ	0.40
Friuli Venezia Giul.	0.38		
Umbria	0.41	**Peru**	**0.03**
		Lima	0.00
			0.01
Japan	**0.51**	Arequipa	0.03
South Kazakhstan	0.11	Tacna	0.04
Almaty	0.14		
Kazakhstan	0.15	**Portugal**	**0.29**
West Kazakhstan	0.21	Madeira	0.01
Zhambyl	0.25	Acores	0.01
Yamanashi	0.25	EntreDouroe Minho	0.02
East Kazakhstan	0.28	Algarve	0.11
Nagano	0.46	Beira Litoral	0.14
Yamagata	0.46	Beira Interior	0.15
Other JP	0.50	AltoTrasos Montes	0.19
		Ribatejoe Oeste	0.21
		Alentejo	0.32
Luxembourg	**0.07**		
Moldova	**0.43**		
Morocco	**0.14**		
Myanmar	**0.37**		

Table 55 (cont.) Varietal Similarity Index of each region and country relative to the world, 2010

Region	Varietal Similarity Index	Region	Varietal Similarity Index
Romania	**0.33**	**South Africa**	**0.50**
Centru	0.22	Orange River	0.13
BucurestiIlfov	0.27	Olifants River	0.29
Nord Vest	0.27	Little Karoo	0.31
Nord Est	0.27	Breedekloof	0.39
Sud Vest Oltenia	0.29	Worcester	0.44
Sud Muntenia	0.31	Robertson	0.52
Sud Est	0.39	Malmesbury	0.53
Vest	0.48	Paarl	0.57
		Stellenbosch	0.65
Russia	**0.48**		
Rostov Oblast	0.12		
Krasnodar Krai	0.50		
Serbia	**0.17**		
Slovakia	**0.22**		
Tokajska	0.04		
Malokarpatska	0.16		
Nitrianska	0.20		
Vychodoslovenska	0.21		
Stredoslovenska	0.22		
Juznoslovenska	0.26		
Slovenia	**0.44**		
Kras	0.05		
Dolenjska	0.09		
Slovens kaIstra	0.13		
Bizeljsko Sremic	0.22		
Belakrajina	0.25		
Prekmurje	0.28		
Stajerska Slovenija	0.33		
Goriskabrda Brda	0.43		
VipavskadolinaV	0.55		
Other SI	0.20		

Table 55 (cont.) Varietal Similarity Index of each region and country relative to the world, 2010

Region	Varietal Similarity Index	Region	Varietal Similarity Index
Spain	**0.62**	**Switzerland**	**0.21**
Huelva	0.01	Vaud	0.07
Hokkaido	0.03	Fribourg	0.10
Guipuzcoa Vizcaya	0.03	Neuchatel	0.13
Cadiz	0.05	Schaffhausen	0.14
Cordoba	0.05	Thurgau	0.14
Leon	0.07	Bern	0.15
Malaga	0.07	Graubunden	0.15
Canarias	0.10	Zurich	0.15
Murcia	0.14	Aargau	0.15
Asturias	0.16	Basel Landschaft	0.15
Galicia	0.18	Lucerne	0.16
Cantabria	0.19	St Gallen	0.16
Alicante	0.21	Valais	0.17
Valencia	0.23	Schwyz	0.19
Badajoz	0.24	Geneva	0.19
Barcelona	0.26	Jura	0.28
Valladolid	0.28	Ticino	0.40
Burgos	0.33	Other CH	0.17
Tarragona	0.35		
Rioja	0.38	**Thailand**	**0.31**
Zamora	0.41		
Avila Palencia S S Soria	0.43	**Tunisia**	**0.25**
Ciudad Real	0.45		
Almeria GranadaJaen Sevi	0.46	**Turkey**	**0.23**
Alava	0.46	Guney Dogu	0.00
Toledo	0.46	Orta Dogu	0.00
Cuenca	0.46	Orta Guney	0.01
Madrid	0.46	Orta Kuzey	0.08
Zaragoza	0.47	Marmara	0.15
Guadalajara	0.47	Ege	0.27
Castellon	0.48	Akdeniz	0.54
Albacete	0.53		
Caceres	0.54	**Ukraine**	**0.36**
Navarra	0.55		
Illes Balears	0.55	**United Kingdom**	**0.26**
Girona Lleida	0.66		
Huesca Teruel	0.68		

Table 55 (cont.) Varietal Similarity Index of each region and country relative to the world, 2010

Region	Varietal Similarity Index	Region	Varietal Similarity Index
United States	**0.65**	**United States (continued)**	
Arizona	0.00	Santa Barbara	0.43
Arkansas	0.00	Yolo	0.45
Georgia	0.00	Butte	0.47
North Carolina	0.00	Yuba	0.47
Iowa	0.00	San Joaquin	0.48
Chautauqua Erie	0.02	Madera	0.49
Minnesota	0.03	San Benito	0.49
Missouri	0.05	Other New york	0.50
Ohio	0.06	Monterey	0.51
San Bernardino	0.08	Solano	0.51
Orange	0.11	Trinity	0.51
Pennsylvania	0.12	Siskiyou	0.53
Finger Lakes	0.13	Shasta	0.53
Lane Co.	0.14	Rattlesnake Hills	0.54
Illinois	0.14	Lake	0.54
Amador	0.15	Jackson Co.	0.54
Yamhill Co.	0.15	Virginia	0.55
Polk Co.	0.15	Red Mountain	0.56
Benton Co.	0.15	Yakima Valley	0.57
Marion Co.	0.15	El Dorado	0.57
Washington Co.	0.16	Merced	0.58
Marin	0.18	Mendocino	0.58
Indiana	0.18	Sonoma	0.58
Other W Valley	0.19	Stanislaus	0.59
Kings	0.20	Walla Walla Valley	0.60
Sutter	0.21	Los Angeles	0.60
Colusa	0.22	Mariposa	0.61
Placer	0.23	Napa	0.61
Fresno	0.25	Humboldt	0.62
Douglas Co.	0.26	Columbia River 2	0.62
Puget Sound	0.26	Alameda	0.63
Josephine Co.	0.27	San Diego	0.63
Kentucky	0.28	Nevada	0.64
Ventura	0.33	San Luis Obispo	0.65
Glenn	0.34	Sacramento	0.65
San Mateo	0.34	Columbia Valley	0.66
Tehama	0.35	Wahluke Slope	0.66
Santa Cruz	0.35	Colorado	0.66
Michigan	0.37	Santa Clara	0.67
Columbia Gorge	0.37	Horse Heaven Hills	0.68
Tulare	0.39	Snipes Mountain	0.68
Lake Chelan	0.40	Riverside	0.68
Kern	0.40	Calaveras	0.70
Contra Costa	0.42	Texas	0.71
Tuolumne	0.43		
		Uruguay	**0.23**

Table 56: Varietal Similarity Index of each region in 2010 relative to that region in 2000

Region	Varietal Similarity Index	Region	Varietal Similarity Index
Argentina	**0.92**	**Australia (continued)**	
San Juan	0.92	Tasmania	0.93
Mendoza	0.89	Nthn Slopes Other	0.93
Other AR	0.91	Barossa other	0.93
		SE Coastal WA	0.92
Australia	**0.95**	Blackwood Valley	0.92
Hilltops	0.99	Hunter Valley other	0.92
Bendigo	0.99	Sunbury	0.91
Mudgee	0.99	Riverina	0.91
Eden Valley	0.99	Alpine/Bchworth	0.91
Kangaroo Island	0.98	Adelaide Hills	0.89
Goulburn Valley	0.98	Henty	0.89
Langhorne Creek	0.98	Central Vic Other	0.87
Margaret River	0.98	Lower Murray other	0.85
YarraValley	0.98	Perricoota	0.84
McLaren Vale	0.98	Canberra District ACT	0.84
Southern Fleurieu	0.97	Granite Belt	0.84
Rutherglen	0.97	SW Australia Other	0.84
Limestone C. Other	0.97	South Coastother	0.82
Clare Valley	0.97	Beech worth	0.77
Padthaway	0.97	Sthn NSW Other	0.77
Cowra	0.97	Swan District	0.75
Barossa Valley	0.97	Big Rivers other	0.75
Geographe	0.96	Nthn Rivers Other	0.74
Hunter	0.96	Murray Darling NSW	0.66
Hastings River	0.96	South Burnett	0.62
Mount Benson	0.96	Murray Darling VIC	0.58
CurrencyCreek	0.96	Greater Perth other	0.57
Gippsland	0.96	Swan Hill NSW	0.54
Grampians	0.96	Swan Hill VIC	0.47
Great Southern	0.96	N. W. Vic Other	0.45
Orange	0.95	Aus. Capital Terr.	0.43
West Vic Other	0.95	West Plains Other	0.39
Fleurieu other		Central WA	0.39
Perth Hills	0.95	Queensland other	0.27
Pyrenees	0.95	C. Ranges Other	0.18
Mornington Pen.	0.95	Eastern Plain ect.	0.08
Riverland	0.95		
Tumbarumba	0.94	**Austria**	**0.97**
Geelong	0.94	Niederosterreich	0.99
Mt Lofty Rgs other	0.94	Wien and Other	0.95
Pt Phillip Other	0.94	Burgen Land	0.91
The Peninsulas	0.94	Steiermark	0.91
Far North Other	0.94		
N. E. Vic Other	0.94	**Brazil**	**0.72**

Table 56 (cont.) Varietal Similarity Index of each region in 2010 relative to that region in 2000

Region	Varietal Similarity Index	Region	Varietal Similarity Index
Bulgaria	**0.81**	**Germany**	**0.94**
		Rheingau	1.00
Canada	**0.82**	Mose Lsaar Ruwer	0.98
		Mitte Lrhein	0.98
Chile	**0.91**	Saale Unstrut	0.97
Metropolitana	0.99	Franken	0.97
O'Higgins	0.98	Nahe	0.95
Delmaule	0.92	Hessische Bergs.	0.92
Valparaiso	0.83	Rhein Pfalz	0.91
Araucania	0.46	Rheinhessen	0.91
Delbiobio	0.28	Sachsen	0.90
Coquimbo	0.10	Baden	0.86
Atacama	0.00	Ahr	0.67
		Wurttemberg	0.52
Croatia	**0.80**		
		Greece	**0.73**
Cyprus	**0.90**	Attiki	1.00
		Voreio Aigaio	0.98
Czech Rep.	**0.75**	Sterea Ellada	0.98
		Dytiki Makedonia	0.97
France	**0.97**	Ipeiros	0.85
Charente	1.00	Notio Aigaio	0.78
Charente Maritime	1.00	Peloponnisos	0.75
Champagne Viticole	1.00	Kriti	0.70
Bourgogne	1.00	Ionia Nisia	0.64
Aquitaine	1.00	Kentriki Makedonia	0.62
Rhonealpes	0.99	Anatoliki Mak., Thraki	0.35
Paysdeloire	0.99	Dytiki Ellada	0.08
Centre	0.99	Thessalia	0.02
Vaucluse	0.99		
Alsace-Lorraine	0.98	**Hungary**	**0.65**
Var	0.97		
Bouchesdu Rhone	0.96		
Gard	0.95		
Pyrenees Orientales	0.95		
Herault	0.89		
Aude	0.88		
Midi Pyrenees	0.86		
Poitou-Charentes Other	0.67		
Corse	0.64		
Other FR	0.11		

Table 56 (cont.) Varietal Similarity Index of each region in 2010 relative to that region in 2000

Region	Varietal Similarity Index	Region	Varietal Similarity Index
Italy	**0.93**	**Romania**	**0.93**
Toscana	0.99		
Piemonte	0.99	**Russia**	**0.24**
Abruzzo	0.99		
Emilia Romagna	0.98	**Slovenia**	**0.68**
Molise	0.97		
Marche	0.96	**Slovakia**	**0.86**
Sicilia	0.94		
Liguria	0.93	**South Africa**	**0.96**
Puglia	0.93	Orange River	0.99
Basilicata	0.93	Olifants River	0.98
Calabria	0.92	Little Karoo	0.97
Sardegna	0.91	Breedekloof	0.96
Trentino	0.91	Worcester	0.96
Campania	0.90	Malmesbury	0.96
Veneto	0.90	Paarl	0.94
Lazio	0.86	Robertson	0.94
Friuli Venezia Giul.	0.86	Stellenbosch	0.87
Umbria	0.86		
Lombardia	0.80		
Valle D'Aosta	0.58		
New Zealand	**0.82**		
Gisborne	0.94		
Marlborough	0.93		
Canterbury	0.92		
Wairarapa	0.89		
Waikato	0.89		
Hawkes Bay	0.88		
Nelson	0.84		
Waipara Valley	0.79		
Auckland	0.77		
Luxembourg	**0.79**		
Portugal	**0.46**		
Ribatejoe Oeste	0.83		
Alentejo	0.79		
Entre Douroe Minho	0.78		
Algarve	0.78		
Beira Litoral	0.74		
Alto Trasos Montes	0.51		
Beira Interior	0.34		
Madeira	0.19		
Acores	0.08		

Table 56 (cont.) Varietal Similarity Index of each region in 2010 relative to that region in 2000

Region	Varietal Similarity Index	Region	Varietal Similarity Index
Spain	**0.89**	**Switzerland**	**0.99**
Cadiz	1.00	Ticino	1.00
Madrid	1.00	Thurgau	1.00
Cordoba	1.00	Schaffhausen	1.00
Huelva	1.00	St Gallen	1.00
Guadalajara	0.99	Vaud	1.00
Murcia	0.99	Graubunden	1.00
Toledo	0.99	Zurich	1.00
Guipuzcoa Vizcaya	0.99	Basellandschaft	1.00
Galicia	0.99	Aargau	0.99
Canarias	0.97	Otherregion	0.98
Ciudad Real	0.97	Valais	0.98
Valencia	0.97	Fribourg	0.97
Alava	0.96	Bern	0.97
Barcelona	0.96	Neuchatel	0.97
Rioja	0.95	Schwyz	0.96
Asturias	0.95	Geneva	0.95
Zaragoza	0.95	Lucerne	0.91
Burgos	0.95	Jura	0.78
Castellon	0.94		
Cuenca	0.94	**United Kingdom**	**0.32**
Leon	0.93		
Illes Balears	0.91		
Tarragona	0.89		
Badajoz	0.89		
Avila Palencia Sss	0.87		
Almeria Granadaj Aen Sev	0.86		
Albacete	0.85		
Cantabria	0.82		
Huesca Teruel	0.81		
Zamora	0.79		
Valladolid	0.77		
Navarra	0.71		
Alicante	0.69		
Girona Lleida	0.62		
Caceres	0.58		
Malaga	0.26		

Table 56 (cont.) Varietal Similarity Index of each region in 2010 relative to that region in 2000

Region	Varietal Similarity Index	Region	Varietal Similarity Index
United States	**0.93**	**United States (continued)**	
Chautauqua Erie	1.00	Nevada	0.80
Amador	0.99	Sutter	0.78
Benton Co	0.99	Placer	0.78
Finger Lakes	0.99	Santa Cruz	0.76
Marionco	0.98	Trinity	0.74
Yamhill Co	0.98	Stanislaus	0.72
San Joaquin	0.98	San Diego	0.72
Yolo	0.97	Kern	0.70
Fresno	0.97	Glenn	0.68
Polkco	0.96	Humboldt	0.65
Tehama	0.95	Riverside	0.62
Sonoma	0.95	Yuba	0.60
Napa	0.95	Marin	0.55
Mendocino	0.95	Shasta	0.46
Lane Co	0.95	Los Angeles	0.44
Other Valley	0.95		
Monterey	0.95		
San Bernardino	0.95		
Sacramento	0.94		
Colusa	0.94		
Washington Co	0.94		
Butte	0.93		
Kings	0.93		
Santa Barbara	0.93		
Ventura	0.93		
El Dorado	0.92		
Other Newyork	0.92		
Josephine Co	0.92		
Michigan	0.92		
Mariposa	0.92		
Santa Clara	0.91		
Tulare	0.90		
Madera	0.90		
San Mateo	0.89		
Lake	0.88		
San Luisobispo	0.88		
San Benito	0.88		
Solano	0.88		
Columbia River	0.85		
Alameda	0.85		
Douglas Co	0.84		
Merced	0.84		
Calavaras	0.80		

Table 57: Each country's 10 most-similar winegrape countries in the world according to the Varietal Similarity Index, 2000

Country	1	2	3	4	5	6	7	8	9	10
Algeria	0.70 TN	0.66 FR	0.19 AU	0.17 MA	0.17 US	0.16 CL	0.15 ZA	0.12 ES	0.09 MD	0.09 CA
Argentina	0.31 AU	0.28 CL	0.20 CA	0.19 ZA	0.19 US	0.19 FR	0.18 PT	0.17 RO	0.16 SI	0.15 BG
Armenia	0.84 RU	0.74 RO	0.71 SI	0.68 HU	0.52 DE	0.50 GE	0.49 UK	0.48 HR	0.44 PT	0.38 CZ
Australia	0.63 CL	0.55 US	0.47 FR	0.47 NZ	0.44 ZA	0.43 CA	0.31 AR	0.30 MD	0.28 BG	0.19 DZ
Austria	0.71 SK	0.69 CZ	0.26 HU	0.21 RS	0.20 LU	0.19 DE	0.19 HR	0.19 SI	0.11 RO	0.08 RU
Brazil	0.33 CA	0.30 PT	0.29 RO	0.28 MD	0.28 SI	0.25 HU	0.24 RU	0.20 HR	0.19 MA	0.18 CZ
Bulgaria	0.42 CL	0.37 MD	0.29 RU	0.29 GE	0.28 AU	0.28 CA	0.28 FR	0.27 US	0.20 AM	0.19 UY
Canada	0.61 US	0.55 NZ	0.47 CL	0.43 AU	0.37 FR	0.34 SI	0.33 MD	0.33 BR	0.32 RO	0.31 HU
Chile	0.63 AU	0.50 US	0.47 CA	0.42 BG	0.41 NZ	0.40 FR	0.36 ZA	0.28 AR	0.27 UY	
Croatia	0.76 SI	0.73 RS	0.70 HU	0.68 RO	0.65 SK	0.54 CZ	0.48 AM	0.45 PT	0.38 UK	
Cyprus	0.25 PT	0.20 MA	0.18 RO	0.16 SI	0.16 RU	0.14 HU	0.12 TN	0.11 CZ	0.10 HR	0.10 CA
Czech Rep.	0.87 SK	0.70 HU	0.69 AT	0.64 DE	0.60 SI	0.55 RO	0.54 HR	0.45 RS	0.44 RU	0.41 PT
France	0.66 DZ	0.52 TN	0.47 AU	0.45 US	0.40 CL	0.37 CA	0.33 NZ	0.32 IT	0.31 ZA	0.29 MD
Georgia	0.60 RU	0.50 AM	0.38 MD	0.29 BG	0.10 RO	0.09 SI	0.09 HU	0.07 DE	0.06 PT	0.06 UK
Germany	0.64 CZ	0.63 HU	0.59 RO	0.59 LU	0.56 SI	0.52 AM	0.51 RU	0.42 UK	0.40 SK	0.38 PT
Greece	0.28 PT	0.27 RO	0.25 SI	0.24 HU	0.23 RU	0.18 MA	0.17 AM	0.16 HR	0.16 UK	0.15 CZ
Hungary	0.88 SI	0.88 RO	0.70 HR	0.70 CZ	0.70 RU	0.68 AM	0.63 DE	0.62 PT	0.61 SK	0.56 UK
Italy	0.32 FR	0.23 US	0.19 CA	0.16 CL	0.15 NZ	0.14 AU	0.14 BG	0.13 SI	0.13 SI	0.12 TN
Luxembourg	0.59 DE	0.40 CZ	0.27 SK	0.20 AT	0.17 NZ	0.15 CH	0.14 CA	0.13 HU	0.07 MD	0.06 UK
Moldova	0.46 NZ	0.38 CL	0.38 GE	0.37 BG	0.35 US	0.33 CA	0.30 RU	0.30 AU	0.29 FR	0.28 BR
Morocco	0.46 PT	0.33 TN	0.28 RO	0.27 RU	0.26 SI	0.22 HU	0.20 CA	0.20 CY	0.19 BR	0.19 CZ
New Zealand	0.66 US	0.55 CA	0.47 AU	0.46 MD	0.41 CL	0.36 ZA	0.33 FR	0.23 CH	0.22 SI	0.21 CZ
Portugal	0.719 RO	0.68 SI	0.62 RU	0.62 HU	0.46 MA	0.45 HR	0.44 AM	0.44 UK	0.41 CZ	0.38 DE
Romania	0.88 HU	0.78 RU	0.74 AM	0.72 PT	0.68 HR	0.68 PT	0.60 UK	0.59 DE	0.55 CZ	0.46 SK
Russia	0.84 AM	0.78 RO	0.74 SI	0.70 HU	0.60 GE	0.51 DE	0.50 UK	0.48 HR	0.44 CZ	
Serbia	0.73 HR	0.67 SK	0.54 SI	0.48 HU	0.45 CZ	0.41 RO	0.24 AM	0.24 RU	0.21 PT	0.21 AT
Slovakia	0.87 CZ	0.71 AT	0.67 RS	0.65 HR	0.62 HU	0.61 HU	0.56 SI	0.46 RO	0.40 DE	0.31 RU
Slovenia	0.94 RO	0.88 HU	0.78 RU	0.74 AM	0.70 HU	0.68 PT	0.60 UK	0.59 DE	0.56 DE	0.56 SK
South Africa	0.84 AM	0.44 AU	0.36 NZ	0.36 CL	0.31 FR	0.24 CA	0.22 MD	0.19 AR	0.17 BG	0.15 DZ
Spain	0.56 US	0.19 SI	0.18 HU	0.17 PT	0.16 RU	0.16 AM	0.13 HR	0.13 UK	0.13 DE	0.12 DZ
	0.20 RO									

Table 57 (cont.) Each country's 10 most-similar winegrape countries in the world according to the Varietal Similarity Index, 2000

Switzerland	0.23 NZ	0.22 CA	0.19 MD	0.18 FR	0.15 LU	0.13 US	0.09 HU	0.09 DZ	0.08 AU	0.08 DE
Tunisia	0.70 DZ	0.52 FR	0.33 MA	0.26 PT	0.14 RO	0.14 RU	0.13 CL	0.13 CA	0.12 SI	0.12 CY
United Kingdc	0.60 RO	0.60 SI	0.56 HU	0.50 RU	0.49 AM	0.44 PT	0.42 DE	0.38 HR	0.35 CZ	0.28 CA
UnitedStates	0.66 NZ	0.61 CA	0.56 ZA	0.55 AU	0.50 CL	0.45 FR	0.35 MD	0.27 BG	0.23 IT	0.19 AR
Uruguay	0.27 CL	0.24 CA	0.19 FR	0.19 BG	0.18 PT	0.18 AU	0.17 US	0.16 MA	0.13 MD	0.13 RO
Old World	0.77 ES	0.59 RO	0.59 SI	0.55 HU	0.52 RU	0.50 FR	0.46 PT	0.46 AM	0.43 HR	0.40 CZ
New World	0.79 CL	0.79 AU	0.75 US	0.61 ZA	0.60 CA	0.55 FR	0.54 NZ	0.54 AR	0.40 MD	0.38 BG
World	0.69 ES	0.58 RO	0.58 SI	0.57 FR	0.54 HU	0.51 RU	0.47 CA	0.46 PT	0.46 CL	0.45 AU

Algeria(DZ), Argentina(AR), Armenia(AM), Australia(AU), Austria(AT), Brazil(BR), Bulgaria(BG), Canada(CA), Chile(CL), China(CN), Croatia(HR), Cyprus(CY), Czech Rep.(CZ), France(FR), Georgia(GE), Germany(DE), Greece(EL), Hungary(HU), Italy(IT), Japan(JP), Kazakhstan(KZ), Luxembourg(LU), Mexico(MX), Moldova(MD), Morocco(MA), Myanmar(MM), New Zealand(NZ), Peru(PE), Portugal(PT), Romania(RO), Russia(RU), Serbia(RS), Slovakia(SK), Slovenia(SI), South Africa(ZA), Spain(ES), Switzerland(CH), Thailand(TH), Tunisia(TN), Turkey(TR), Ukraine(UA), United Kingdom(UK), United States(US), Uruguay(UY)

Table 58: Each country's 10 most-similar winegrape countries in the world according to the Varietal Similarity Index, 2010

Country	1	2	3	4	5	6	7	8	9	10
Algeria	0.70 TN	0.55 FR	0.31 MX	0.20 TR	0.18 MM	0.18 US	0.18 AU	0.18 CL	0.17 MA	0.15 ZA
Argentina	0.37 AU	0.36 CL	0.31 US	0.30 CN	0.29 ZA	0.27 FR	0.24 TH	0.22 RU	0.22 JP	0.22 MX
Armenia	0.79 RO	0.59 KZ	0.58 DE	0.50 GE	0.32 SI	0.30 UA	0.26 HR	0.24 RS	0.23 BG	0.22 HU
Australia	0.72 US	0.70 TH	0.67 CL	0.64 MM	0.62 ZA	0.58 FR	0.51 CA	0.48 CN	0.48 JP	0.45 RU
Austria	0.79 SK	0.71 CZ	0.43 HU	0.26 SI	0.26 HR	0.20 RS	0.17 DE	0.16 JP	0.14 CA	0.11 LU
Brazil	0.37 MD	0.14 UA	0.12 UY	0.08 RO	0.08 US	0.07 BG	0.07 AM	0.06 RU	0.06 CA	0.06 MX
Bulgaria	0.59 JP	0.56 CL	0.55 CN	0.54 US	0.49 MX	0.48 FR	0.46 RU	0.40 MD	0.40 CA	0.38 AU
Canada	0.66 US	0.54 JP	0.51 AU	0.49 FR	0.45 CL	0.45 UK	0.43 RU	0.40 BG	0.38 MD	0.37 ZA
Chile	0.90 CN	0.75 US	0.67 AU	0.65 RU	0.58 ZA	0.57 JP	0.56 BG	0.51 MX	0.49 FR	0.45 CA
China	0.90 CL	0.59 RU	0.59 US	0.55 BG	0.53 MX	0.48 AU	0.46 JP	0.43 ZA	0.35 FR	0.31 MD
Croatia	0.78 RS	0.77 SI	0.50 HU	0.50 SK	0.39 RO	0.39 CZ	0.32 DE	0.26 AM	0.26 AT	0.26 BG
Cyprus	0.15 MX	0.12 TN	0.10 FR	0.10 AU	0.10 CL	0.09 DZ	0.09 CN	0.35 CA	0.09 US	0.08 TR
Czech Rep.	0.85 SK	0.71 AT	0.56 HU	0.44 SI	0.40 DE	0.39 HR	0.35 CA	0.35 LU	0.33 NZ	0.07 BG
France	0.58 AU	0.57 US	0.55 DZ	0.52 JP	0.49 CA	0.49 CL	0.48 BG	0.47 ZA	0.43 MX	0.29 UK
Georgia	0.91 KZ	0.63 UA	0.50 AM	0.38 MD	0.19 BG	0.10 RO	0.07 DE	0.04 HR	0.04 HR	0.41 UY
Germany	0.68 RO	0.58 AM	0.50 AM	0.40 CZ	0.32 LU	0.32 HU	0.32 DE	0.26 SK	0.25 CA	0.04 SI
Greece	0.27 BG	0.26 MA	0.24 MX	0.22 RO	0.21 SI	0.20 DE	0.18 AM	0.17 TN	0.16 HR	0.22 RS
Hungary	0.61 SK	0.58 SI	0.56 CZ	0.50 HR	0.43 AT	0.37 RS	0.36 RU	0.33 US	0.32 RO	0.15 US
Italy	0.35 FR	0.35 US	0.29 BG	0.28 JP	0.27 CA	0.25 AU	0.23 CL	0.22 SI	0.21 MX	0.32 DE
Japan	0.68 US	0.59 BG	0.57 CL	0.54 CA	0.52 FR	0.49 RU	0.48 AU	0.46 CN	0.39 ZA	0.20 UY
Kazakhstan	0.91 GE	0.68 UA	0.59 AM	0.44 MD	0.21 BG	0.20 RO	0.16 DE	0.14 RU	0.09 SI	0.37 MD
Luxembourg	0.33 CZ	0.32 DE	0.20 SK	0.19 CA	0.12 HU	0.12 SI	0.11 AT	0.10 UK	0.09 CH	0.08 HR
Mexico	0.53 CN	0.51 CL	0.49 BG	0.43 FR	0.41 ZA	0.41 US	0.40 TR	0.40 TN	0.36 AU	0.08 RU
Moldova	0.86 UA	0.48 RU	0.44 US	0.44 KZ	0.43 CL	0.41 NZ	0.40 BG	0.38 GE	0.38 CA	0.35 RU
Morocco	0.33 TN	0.26 EL	0.21 BG	0.19 MX	0.17 DZ	0.14 SI	0.13 DE	0.12 HR	0.09 IT	0.37 BR
Myanmar	0.69 TH	0.64 AU	0.63 NZ	0.45 ZA	0.38 FR	0.32 TR	0.29 CL	0.24 US	0.23 MD	0.09 RO
New Zealand	0.63 MM	0.41 MD	0.38 ZA	0.36 CA	0.35 US	0.35 SI	0.35 SI	0.33 CZ	0.31 UK	0.21 AR
Peru	0.11 HU	0.07 SK	0.06 MX	0.05 CZ	0.05 SI	0.04 MM	0.04 AT	0.03 EL	0.03 CN	0.03 IT
Portugal	0.32 ES	0.14 MX	0.14 MM	0.13 TH	0.12 AU	0.10 AR	0.08 CL	0.08 FR	0.07 ZA	0.07 US

550

Table 58 (cont.) Each country's 10 most-similar winegrape countries in the world according to the Varietal Similarity Index, 2010

Romania	0.79 AM	0.68 DE	0.46 SI	0.39 HR	0.35 RS	0.32 HU	0.30 BG	0.22 EL	0.21 MX	0.20 KZ
Russia	0.65 CL	0.59 US	0.59 CN	0.49 JP	0.48 MD	0.48 UA	0.46 BG	0.45 AU	0.43 CA	0.39 ZA
Serbia	0.78 HR	0.60 SI	0.43 SK	0.37 HU	0.35 RO	0.27 CZ	0.24 AM	0.22 DE	0.20 AT	0.10 EL
Slovakia	0.85 CZ	0.79 AT	0.61 HU	0.50 HR	0.47 SI	0.43 RS	0.26 DE	0.20 LU	0.18 CL	0.17 CA
Slovenia	0.77 HR	0.60 RS	0.58 HU	0.47 SK	0.46 RO	0.44 CZ	0.41 DE	0.38 US	0.36 CA	0.35 BG
South Africa	0.62 AU	0.60 US	0.58 CL	0.49 TH	0.47 FR	0.45 MM	0.43 CN	0.41 MX	0.36 CA	0.39 JP
Spain	0.32 PT	0.17 MX	0.16 FR	0.13 DZ	0.11 MM	0.10 AR	0.10 AU	0.09 TH	0.09 CL	0.09 US
Switzerland	0.47 UK	0.30 CA	0.28 US	0.25 FR	0.24 NZ	0.23 MD	0.20 HU	0.19 CZ	0.17 JP	0.17 MM
Thailand	0.70 AU	0.69 MM	0.49 ZA	0.36 TR	0.33 FR	0.24 AR	0.21 US	0.20 CL	0.18 MX	0.13 PT
Tunisia	0.70 DZ	0.40 MX	0.36 FR	0.33 MA	0.17 EL	0.15 IT	0.14 MM	0.14 BG	0.12 CY	0.09 US
Turkey	0.40 MX	0.39 AU	0.36 TH	0.32 MM	0.26 FR	0.23 ZA	0.20 CL	0.20 DZ	0.18 US	0.14 AR
Ukraine	0.86 MD	0.68 KZ	0.63 GE	0.48 RU	0.37 CL	0.36 BG	0.35 US	0.31 CN	0.30 AM	0.30 CA
United Kingdom	0.53 US	0.47 CH	0.45 CA	0.34 AU	0.33 JP	0.31 NZ	0.29 CZ	0.26 MD	0.25 RU	0.22 FR
United States	0.75 CL	0.72 AU	0.68 JP	0.66 CA	0.60 ZA	0.59 RU	0.59 CN	0.57 FR	0.54 BG	0.53 UK
Uruguay	0.41 FR	0.36 BG	0.32 CL	0.31 JP	0.30 US	0.30 CN	0.26 RU	0.25 CA	0.25 MX	0.22 MD
New World	**0.87 US**	**0.87 CL**	**0.84 AU**	**0.72 ZA**	**0.70 CN**	**0.64 FR**	**0.60 RU**	**0.60 JP**	**0.58 CA**	**0.57 AR**
Old World	**0.74 ES**	**0.64**	**0.46 BG**	**0.46 US**	**0.43 IT**	**0.43 MX**	**0.42 AU**	**0.40 SI**	**0.39 JP**	**0.39 CL**
World	**0.72 FR**	**0.65 US**	**0.62 ES**	**0.60 CL**	**0.55 BG**	**0.52 MX**	**0.51 JP**	**0.50 ZA**	**0.50 CA**	

Algeria(DZ), Argentina(AR), Armenia(AM), Australia(AU), Austria(AT), Brazil(BR), Bulgaria(BG), Canada(CA), Chile(CL), China(CN), Croatia(HR), Cyprus(CY), Czech Rep.(CZ), France(FR), Georgia(GE), Germany(DE), Greece(EL), Hungary(HU), Italy(IT), Japan(JP), Kazakhstan(KZ), Luxembourg(LU), Mexico(MX), Moldova(MD), Morocco(MA), Myanmar(MM), New Zealand(NZ), Peru(PE), Portugal(PT), Romania(RO), Russia(RU), Serbia(RS), Slovakia(SK), Slovenia(SI), South Africa(ZA), Spain(ES), Switzerland(CH), Thailand(TH), Tunisia(TN), Turkey(TR), Ukraine(UA), United Kingdom(UK), United States(US), Uruguay(UY)

Table 59: Each region's 3 most similar winegrape regions in the world according to the Varietal Similarity Index, 2000

Algeria	0.89	FRVar	0.84	FRHerault	0.82	FRGard
Argentina						
ARSan Juan	0.58	ARMendoza	0.30	AUSouth Burnett	0.29	AUWest Plains Other
ARMendoza	0.58	ARSan Juan	0.33	FRMidi Pyrenees Other	0.30	AUN. E. Vic Other
Armenia	0.84	Russia	0.82	AUNthn Territory	0.80	ESMalaga
Australia						
Adelaide Hills	0.94	AUYarra Valley	0.93	AUGippsland	0.92	AUAlpine/Bchworth
Alpine/Bchworth	0.94	AUBlackwood Valley	0.93	AUSW Australia Other	0.93	AUN. E. Vic Other
Aus. Capital Terr.	0.94	AUPyrenees	0.93	AUBarossaother	0.90	AUCentral Vic Other
Barossaother	0.94	AUFar North Other	0.94	AUBarossaValley	0.93	AUAus. Capital Terr.
BarossaValley	0.97	AUMcLaren Vale	0.97	AUSthn NSW Other	0.96	AUMt LoftyRgsOther
Beechworth	0.95	AUWest Vic Other	0.88	AUYarra Valley	0.88	AUCanberra District
Bendigo	0.99	AUFar North Other	0.97	AUGrampians	0.97	AUMcLaren Vale
Big Rivers Other	0.85	AUSth Coast Other	0.84	AUHunter Vall.Other	0.84	AUGranite Belt
Blackwood Valley	0.98	AUSW Australia Other	0.97	AUGeographe	0.96	AUGreat Southern
Canberra District	0.95	AUPadthaway	0.95	AUSunbury	0.95	AUCentral Vic Other
C. Ranges Other	0.97	AUNthn Territory	0.97	AUQueensland Other	0.96	Romania
Central Vic Other	0.98	AUSunbury	0.96	AUGoulburnValley	0.96	AUPadthaway
Central WA	0.87	AUEastern Plains etc.	0.84	PTAcores	0.83	PTMadeira
ClareValley	0.96	AUHilltops	0.96	AUGreat Southern	0.95	AUMudgee
Cowra	0.96	AUHunter Vall.Other	0.96	AUHunter	0.92	USShasta
Currency Creek	0.99	AULanghorne Creek	0.98	AULower Murr.Other	0.97	AUHilltops
Eastern Plains etc.	0.99	ITBelluno	0.97	PTAcores	0.95	PTMadeira
Eden Valley	0.92	AUClareValley	0.89	AUCanberra District	0.88	AUSunbury
Far North Other	0.99	AUBendigo	0.97	AUGrampians	0.96	AUPyrenees
Fleurieuother	0.99	AUMudgee	0.98	AUSouthern Fleurieu	0.98	AUMt LoftyRgsOther
Geelong	0.97	AUGippsland	0.97	AUPt Phillip Other	0.96	AUMornington Pen.
Geographe	0.98	AUGreat Southern	0.97	AUMudgee	0.97	AUOrange
Gippsland	0.98	AUYarra Valley	0.97	AUGeelong	0.96	AUPt Phillip Other
GoulburnValley	0.96	AUOrange	0.96	AUMt LoftyRgsOther	0.96	AUCentral Vic Other
Grampians	0.97	AUMcLaren Vale	0.97	AUBendigo	0.97	AUMcLaren Vale
Granite Belt	0.92	AUSouth Burnett	0.87	AUNthn Rivers Other	0.87	AUSth Coast Other
Greater Per. Other	0.75	AUSwan District	0.69	AUPerth Hills	0.63	AUCentral WA
Great Southern	0.98	AUGeographe	0.97	AUSW Australia Other	0.97	AUPadthaway
Hastings River	0.91	AUNthn Rivers Other	0.89	AUSth Coast Other	0.82	AUGranite Belt
Henty	0.94	AUGippsland	0.92	AUTasmania	0.92	AUGeelong
Hilltops	0.98	AULanghorne Creek	0.98	AUKangaroo Island	0.98	AUMudgee
Hunter	0.98	AUHunter Vall.Other	0.96	AUCowra	0.88	USShasta
Hunter Vall.Other	0.98	AUHunter	0.96	AUCowra	0.87	USShasta
Kangaroo Island	0.98	AULanghorne Creek	0.98	AUMudgee	0.98	AUHilltops
Langhorne Creek	0.99	AUCurrency Creek	0.98	AUHilltops	0.98	AULower Murr.Other
Limestone C.Other	0.96	AULanghorne Creek	0.96	AULower Murr.Other	0.96	AUCurrency Creek
Lower Murr.Other	0.98	AUCurrency Creek	0.98	AULanghorne Creek	0.97	AUHilltops
Margaret River	0.95	AUGeographe	0.94	AUBlackwood Valley	0.94	AUSW Australia Other
McLaren Vale	0.99	AUMt LoftyRgsOther	0.98	AUFleurieuother	0.97	AUGrampians
Mornington Pen.	0.96	AUTasmania	0.96	AUGeelong	0.95	AUPt Phillip Other
Mount Benson	0.96	AUN. E. Vic Other	0.95	AUOrange	0.94	AUGeographe
Mt Lofty Rgs Other	0.99	AUMcLaren Vale	0.98	AUFleurieuother	0.98	AUMudgee
Mudgee	0.99	AUOrange	0.99	AUFleurieuother	0.98	AUKangaroo Island
Murray Dar. NSW	0.95	AUMurray Dar. VIC	0.89	AUSwan Hil lNSW	0.88	AUSwan Hill VIC

Table 59 (cont.) Each region's 3 most similar winegrape regions in the world according to the Varietal Similarity Index, 2000

Australia (continued)

Murray Dar. VIC	0.97	AUN. W. Vic Other	0.95	AUMurray Dar. NSW	0.93	AUSwan Hil lNSW
N. E. Vic Other	0.96	AUMount Benson	0.96	AUSW Australia Other	0.95	AUGreat Southern
Nthn Rivers Other	0.91	AUHastings River	0.89	AUSth Coast Other	0.87	AUGranite Belt
Nthn Slopes Other	0.96	AUMt LoftyRgsOther	0.96	AUSthn NSW Other	0.96	AUSouthern Fleurieu
Nthn Territory	0.97	AUC. Ranges Other	0.95	AUQueensland Other	0.95	Romania
N. W. Vic Other	0.97	AUSwan Hil lNSW	0.97	AUMurray Dar. VIC	0.95	AUSwan Hill VIC
Orange	0.99	AUMudgee	0.98	AUFleurieuother	0.98	AUKangaroo Island
Padthaway	0.97	AUGreat Southern	0.96	AUCentral Vic Other	0.96	AUBlackwood Valley
Perricoota	0.91	AULower Murr.Other	0.91	AUFleurieuother	0.91	AURiverland
Perth Hills	0.80	AUCowra	0.77	AUCentral Vic Other	0.77	AUHunter
Pt Phillip Other	0.97	AUGeelong	0.96	AUGippsland	0.95	AUMornington Pen.
Pyrenees	0.96	AUMt LoftyRgsOther	0.96	AUMcLaren Vale	0.96	AUFar North Other
Queensland Other	0.97	AUC. Ranges Other	0.96	DEAhr	0.95	AUNorthern Territory
Riverina	0.93	AUNthn Slopes Other	0.92	AUSthn NSW Other	0.90	AUSouthern Fleurieu
Riverland	0.97	AUMt LoftyRgsOther	0.96	AUMudgee	0.95	AUFleurieuother
Rutherglen	0.92	AUBendigo	0.91	AUFar North Other	0.90	AUGrampians
South Burnett	0.92	AUGranite Belt	0.82	AUBig Rivers Other	0.81	AUCentral WA
Sth Coast Other	0.89	AUNthn Rivers Other	0.89	AUHastings River	0.87	AUGranite Belt
Southern Fleurieu	0.98	AUFleurieuother	0.98	AUMudgee	0.98	AUMt LoftyRgsOther
Sthn NSW Other	0.98	AUMt LoftyRgsOther	0.98	AUSouthern Fleurieu	0.97	AUMcLaren Vale
SW Australia Other	0.98	AUBlackwood Valley	0.97	AUGeographe	0.97	AUGreat Southern
Sunbury	0.98	AUCentral Vic Other	0.96	AUMt LoftyRgsOther	0.96	AUMudgee
Swan District	0.80	AUSouth Burnett	0.76	AUCentral WA	0.75	AUGreater Per.Other
Swan Hil lNSW	0.97	AUSwan Hill VIC	0.97	AUN. W. Vic Other	0.93	AUMurray Dar. VIC
Swan Hill VIC	0.97	AUSwan Hil lNSW	0.95	AUN. W. Vic Other	0.90	AUMurray Dar. VIC
Tasmania	0.96	AUMornington Pen.	0.95	NZWairarapa	0.94	AUGippsland
ThePeninsulas	0.93	AUOrange	0.92	AUKangaroo Island	0.92	AUMudgee
Tumbarumba	0.96	USSan mateo	0.95	FRBourgogne	0.95	USSanta Cruz
SE Coastal WA	0.95	AUGeographe	0.94	AUSW Australia Other	0.94	AUBlackwood Valley
West Plains Other	0.88	AUC. Ranges Other	0.82	AUNthn Territory	0.81	AUQueensland Other
West Vic Other	0.95	AUBeechworth	0.94	AUN. E. Vic Other	0.93	AUHilltops
Yarra Valley	0.98	AUGippsland	0.94	AUAdelaide Hills	0.94	AUPt Phillip Other

Austria

Burgenland	0.70	ATWien and other	0.69	ATNiederosterreich	0.54	ATSteiermark
Wien and other	0.88	ATNiederosterreich	0.71	Czech Rep.	0.70	ATBurgenland
Steiermark	0.54	ATBurgenland	0.46	ESCaceres	0.44	DESachsen
Niederosterreich	0.88	ATWien and other	0.69	ATBurgenland	0.20	ATSteiermark

Brazil

	0.33	Canada	0.33	ITBelluno	0.32	AUEastern Plain ect.

Bulgaria

	0.45	FRGironde	0.44	ITBergamo	0.44	USColumbia River

Canada

	0.70	USMichigan	0.67	NZAuckland	0.66	USWashington

Table 59 (cont.) Each region's 3 most similar winegrape regions in the world according to the Varietal Similarity Index, 2000

Chile							
Araucania	0.98	USRiverside	0.98	USSanta Barbara	0.95	USSanta Cruz	
Valparaiso	0.96	USMonterey	0.94	USSan mateo	0.94	USSanta Barbara	
OHiggins	0.99	CLMetropolitana	0.91	AULimestone C.Other	0.86	USYuba	
Metropolitana	0.99	CLOHiggins	0.93	AULimestone C.Other	0.90	USYuba	
Del Maule	0.86	CLOHiggins	0.84	CLMetropolitana	0.79	USYuba	
Del Bio Bio	0.67	AUEastern Plains etc.	0.67	PTAcores	0.66	ITBelluno	
Coquimbo	0.95	CLAtacama	0.68	ESMalaga	0.67	AUC. Ranges Other	
Atacama	0.95	CLCoquimbo	0.81	ESMalaga	0.77	AUNthn Territory	
Croatia	0.76	Slovenia	0.73	Serbia	0.70	Hungary	
Cyprus	0.32	AUEastern Plain ect.	0.31	ITBelluno	0.31	PTAcores	
Czech Rep.	0.87	Slovakia	0.71	ATWien and other	0.70	Hungary	
France							
Aisne	0.95	FRSeineet Marne	0.68	FRChampagne Arden.	0.36	AUHenty	
Alpes de Haute	0.91	FRArdeche	0.87	FRGard	0.85	FRBouches du Rhone	
Alsace	0.60	DEHessische Bergs.	0.59	DEMittelrhein	0.58	DERheingau	
Aquitaine Other	0.88	FRGironde	0.75	ITVenezia	0.72	ITPadova	
Ardeche	0.91	FRAlpes de Haute	0.89	FRGard	0.82	FRBouches du Rhone	
Aude	0.97	FRHerault	0.86	Tunisia	0.75	FRVar	
Auvergne	0.87	FRRhone Alpes Other	0.83	FRLorraine	0.70	CHGeneva	
Bouches du Rhone	0.96	FRGard	0.93	FRVar	0.91	FRVaucluse	
Bourgogne	0.95	AUTumbarumba	0.91	AUMornington Pen.	0.91	AUTasmania	
Centre	0.90	FRDeux-Sevres Vien.	0.59	NZMarlborough	0.48	FRPays de Loire Other	
Champagne Arden.	0.82	AUMornington Pen.	0.82	FRSeineet Marne	0.81	AUHenty	
Charente	1.00	FRCharente Maritime	0.86	USLos Angeles	0.82	ITTerni	
Charente Maritime	1.00	FRCharente	0.87	USLos Angeles	0.82	ITTerni	
Corr., Haute-Vien.	0.77	AUEastern Plains etc.	0.77	PTAcores	0.76	PTMadeira	
Corse	0.69	ITSiena	0.67	ITFirenze	0.66	ITArezzo	
Deux-Sevres Vien.	0.90	FRCentre	0.59	FRPays de Loire Other	0.51	ZAWorcester	
France2	0.88	USSanta Cruz	0.87	USSanta Barbara	0.86	USSan mateo	
Gard	0.96	FRBouches du Rhone	0.90	FRVar	0.89	FRArdeche	
Gers	0.79	FRCharente Maritime	0.78	FRCharente	0.69	USLos Angeles	
Gironde	0.89	ITPadova	0.88	ITBergamo	0.88	CHTicino	
Herault	0.97	FRAude	0.84	Algeria	0.82	FRVar	
Lorraine	0.83	FRAuvergne	0.68	FRRhone Alpes Other	0.65	CHValais	
Midi Pyrenees Othe	0.35	FRAquitaine Other	0.35	AUPyrenees	0.35	AUAus. Capital Terr.	
Pays de Loire Other	0.59	FRDeux-Sevres Vien.	0.48	FRCentre	0.29	ZAWorcester	
Pyrenees Orient.	0.78	FRGard	0.75	FRBouches du Rhone	0.73	FRVar	
Rhone Alpes Other	0.87	FRAuvergne	0.68	FRLorraine	0.62	CHGeneva	
Seineet Marne	0.95	FRAisne	0.82	FRChampagne Arden.	0.54	AUHenty	
Var	0.93	FRBouches du Rhone	0.90	FRGard	0.82	FRAlpes de Haute	
Vaucluse	0.91	FRBouches du Rhone	0.90	ESZaragoza	0.87	FRGard	
Georgia	50	Armenia	0.38	Moldova	0.29	Bulgaria	

Table 59 (cont.) Each region's 3 most similar winegrape regions in the world according to the Varietal Similarity Index, 2000

Germany						
Ahr	0.96	AUQueensland Other	0.92	AUC. Ranges Other	0.90	AUNthn Territory
Baden	0.95	DESaale Unstrut	0.88	DERheinhessen	0.87	DEFranken
Franken	0.91	DERheinhessen	0.89	DESaale Unstrut	0.87	DEBaden
Hessische Bergs.	0.98	DEMittelrhein	0.97	DERheingau	0.95	DEMosel-Saa-Ruwer
Mittelrhein	0.99	DERheingau	0.98	DEHessische Bergs.	0.95	Mosel-Saa-Ruwer
Mosel-Saa-Ruwer	0.95	DEMittelrhein	0.95	DEHessische Bergs.	0.92	DERheingau
Nahe	0.97	DERhein Pfalz	0.90	DESachsen	0.89	DERheinhessen
Rheingau	0.99	DEMittelrhein	0.97	DEHessische Bergs.	0.92	DEMosel-Saa-Ruwer
Rheinhessen	0.93	DESaale Unstrut	0.93	DERhein Pfalz	0.91	DEFranken
Rhein Pfalz	0.97	DENahe	0.93	DERheinhessen	0.89	DESachsen
Saale Unstrut	0.95	DEBaden	0.93	DERheinhessen	0.89	DEFranken
Sachsen	0.90	DENahe	0.89	DERhein Pfalz	0.87	DESaale Unstrut
Wurttemberg	0.92	AUNthn Territory	0.89	ESMalaga	0.88	AUC. Ranges Other
Greece						
Anatol. Mak.,Thrak	0.46	ELVoreioAigaio	0.35	FRCorr., Haute-Vien.	0.34	AUEastern Plains etc.
Attiki	1.00	ELSterea Ellada	0.30	ELPeloponnisos	0.05	ELKentriki Mak.
DytikiEllada	0.55	ELKentriki Mak.	0.50	ELPeloponnisos	0.41	AUEastern Plains etc.
Dytiki Mak.	0.84	ELKentriki Mak.	0.27	PTAcores	0.26	AUEastern Plains etc.
IoniaNisia	0.92	AUNthn Territory	0.89	ESMalaga	0.89	AUC. Ranges Other
Ipeiros	0.35	PTAcores	0.35	PTMadeira	0.34	AUEastern Plains etc.
Kentriki Mak.	0.84	ELDytiki Mak.	0.55	ELDytikiEllada	0.49	AUEastern Plains etc.
Kriti	0.08	AUEastern Plains etc.	0.08	PTAcores	0.08	ITBelluno
NotioAigaio	0.37	AUNthn Territory	0.36	AUC. Ranges Other	0.36	ESMalaga
Peloponnisos	0.50	ELDytikiEllada	0.31	ELKentriki Mak.	0.30	ELSterea Ellada
Sterea Ellada	0.30	ELPeloponnisos	0.06	ELKentriki Mak.	0.04	ELThessalia
Thessalia	0.28	ELKentriki Mak.	0.21	ELDytikiEllada	0.11	ELPeloponnisos
VoreioAigaio	0.46	ELAnatoliki Mak,Thrak	0.05	ELKentriki Mak.	0.05	ELDytiki Ellada
Hungary	0.88	Slovenia	0.88	Romania	0.85	AUC. Ranges Other
Italy						
Agrigento	0.64	ITPalermo	0.60	ITCaltanissetta	0.60	ITTrapani
Alessandria	0.90	ITAsti	0.75	ITSalerno	0.69	ITTorino
Ancona	0.91	ITMacerata	0.34	ITBrescia	0.21	ITAscoli Piceno
Arezzo	1.00	ITFirenze	0.99	ITPrato	0.98	ITSiena
Ascoli Piceno	0.86	ITBari	0.85	ITIsernia	0.84	ITArezzo
Asti	0.90	ITAlessandria	0.81	ITSalerno	0.73	ITTorino
Avellino	0.94	ITPotenza	0.75	ITBenevento	0.42	ITSalerno
Bari	0.86	ITAscoli Piceno	0.76	ITIsernia	0.76	ITMatera
Belluno	0.99	AUEastern Plains etc.	0.94	PTAcores	0.93	PTMadeira
Benevento	0.77	ITPotenza	0.75	ITAvellino	0.55	ITRieti
Bergamo	0.88	FRGironde	0.87	USOregon Other	0.82	ITPadova
Biella	0.82	ITVerbano-C.-Ossola	0.81	ITTorino	0.77	ITVarese
Bologna	0.89	ITRavenna	0.83	ITFerrara	0.71	ITForli Cesena
Bolzano Bozen	0.43	ITTrento	0.35	USJosephine Co	0.34	USSanmateo
Brescia	0.69	USNevada	0.67	ITLecco	0.67	USSanta Clara
Brindisi	0.99	ITLecce	0.25	ITTaranto	0.09	ITBari
Cagliari	0.67	ITOristano	0.40	FRAude	0.37	FRHerault
Caltanissetta	0.96	ITSiracusa	0.95	ITRagusa	0.60	ITAgrigento
Campobasso	0.98	ITPescara	0.97	ITLAquila	0.96	ITTeramo
Caserta	0.70	ITIsernia	0.67	ITMatera	0.62	ITAscoli Piceno
Catania	0.61	ITMessina	0.45	ITEnna	0.20	ITCatanzaro

Table 59 (cont.) Each region's 3 most similar winegrape regions in the world according to the Varietal Similarity Index, 2000

Italy (continued)					
Catanzaro	0.67	ITCosenza	0.58	ITCalabria	0.48	ITVibo Valentia
Chieti	0.94	ITCampobasso	0.89	ITPescara	0.88	ITTeramo
Como	0.65	ITMessina	0.60	ITCalabria	0.48	ITValle D'Aosta
Cosenza	0.76	ITCrotone	0.67	ITCatanzaro	0.64	ITCalabria
Cremona	0.75	ITNell'Emilia	0.49	ITMantova	0.37	ITPotenza
Crotone	0.76	ITCosenza	0.31	ITCalabria	0.25	ITCatanzaro
Cuneo	0.66	ITAlessandria	0.60	ITAsti	0.53	ITBiella
Enna	0.81	ITMessina	0.81	ITBelluno	0.80	AUEastern Plains etc.
Ferrara	0.95	ITRavenna	0.83	ITBologna	0.55	ITForli Cesena
Firenze	1.00	ITArezzo	0.99	ITSiena	0.98	ITPrato
Foggia	0.89	ITPisa	0.87	ITLucca	0.86	ITGrosseto
Forli Cesena	0.94	ITRimini	0.81	ITSiena	0.80	ITFirenze
Frosinone	0.65	ITLatina	0.64	ITRieti	0.63	ITViterbo
Genova	0.78	ITLaSpezia	0.65	ITMassa Carrara	0.51	ITSavona
Gorizia	0.89	ITUdine	0.82	ITPordenone	0.75	ITVenezia
Grosseto	0.96	ITPisa	0.96	ITPistoia	0.95	ITPrato
Imperia	0.78	ITSavona	0.56	ITMassa Carrara	0.54	ITSassari
Isernia	0.85	ITAscoli Piceno	0.76	ITBari	0.73	ITMatera
LAquila	0.99	ITPescara	0.97	ITCampobasso	0.96	ITTeramo
LaSpezia	0.78	ITGenova	0.66	ITMassa Carrara	0.58	ITSavona
Latina	0.90	ITViterbo	0.86	ITRoma	0.77	FRCharente Maritime
Lecce	0.99	ITBrindisi	0.21	ARArgentinatotal	0.17	ITTaranto
Lecco	0.75	USLAKE	0.74	USnapa	0.72	NZHawkes Bay
Livorno	0.85	ITLucca	0.84	ITPisa	0.81	ITGrosseto
Lodi	0.81	ITMilano	0.74	ITPiacenza	0.69	ITPavia
Lucca	0.97	ITPisa	0.95	ITGrosseto	0.91	ITPistoia
Macerata	0.91	ITAncona	0.52	ITAscoliPiceno	0.45	ITBari
Mantova	0.49	ITCremona	0.48	USOregonOther	0.48	ITRovigo
Massa Carrara	0.72	ITSavona	0.66	ITLaSpezia	0.65	ITGenova
Matera	0.83	ITSiena	0.82	ITFirenze	0.82	ITArezzo
Messina	0.81	ITEnna	0.68	ITCalabria	0.65	ITComo
Milano	0.85	ITPiacenza	0.81	ITLodi	0.68	ITPavia
Modena	0.44	ITNell'Emilia	0.32	ITCremona	0.23	ITMantova
Napoli	0.35	ITCaserta	0.31	ITBenevento	0.26	AUNthn Territory
Novara	0.86	ITVercelli	0.80	ITSondrio	0.65	ITBiella
Nuoro	0.43	ITSassari	0.36	ITCagliari	0.25	ITOristano
Oristano	0.67	ITCagliari	0.44	ITBelluno	0.44	AUEastern Plains etc.
Padova	0.94	ITRovigo	0.91	CHTicino	0.90	ITVenezia
Palermo	0.98	ITTrapani	0.64	ITAgrigento	0.64	ITAgrigento
Parma	0.47	ITPiacenza	0.40	ITPavia	0.37	ITSalerno
Pavia	0.69	ITLodi	0.69	ITAsti	0.68	ITMilano
Perugia	0.88	ITPisa	0.86	ITLucca	0.86	ITGrosseto
Pesaroe Urbino	0.63	ITRimini	0.59	ITSiena	0.58	ITFirenze
Pescara	0.99	ITLAquila	0.99	ITTeramo	0.98	ITCampobasso
Piacenza	0.85	ITMilano	0.74	ITLodi	0.67	ITPavia
Pisa	0.97	ITLucca	0.96	ITGrosseto	0.95	ITPistoia
Pistoia	0.98	ITArezzo	0.98	ITPrato	0.97	ITFirenze
Pordenone	0.96	ITVenezia	0.95	ITUdine	0.86	ITPadova
Potenza	0.94	ITAvellino	0.77	ITBenevento	0.44	ITSalerno
Prato	0.99	ITArezzo	0.98	ITFirenze	0.98	ITPistoia
Ragusa	0.98	ITSiracusa	0.95	ITCaltanissetta	0.51	ITAgrigento
Ravenna	0.95	ITFerrara	0.89	ITBologna	0.66	ITForli Cesena

Table 59 (cont.) Each region's 3 most similar winegrape regions in the world according to the Varietal Similarity Index, 2000

Italy (continued)					
Calabria	0.68 ITMessina	0.66	ITEnna	0.64	ITCosenza
Nell'Emilia	0.75 ITCremona	0.46	ITMantova	0.44	ITModena
Rieti	0.82 ITRoma	0.79	ITViterbo	0.69	ITFoggia
Rimini	0.95 ITSiena	0.94	ITFirenze	0.94	ITForli Cesena
Roma	0.86 ITLatina	0.83	ITViterbo	0.82	ITRieti
Rovigo	0.98 CHTicino	0.94	ITPadova	0.88	ITVenezia
Salerno	0.81 ITAsti	0.75	ITAlessandria	0.71	ITVerbano-C.-Ossola
Sassari	0.68 ITSavona	0.61	ITMassa Carrara	0.54	ITImperia
Savona	0.78 ITImperia	0.72	ITMassa Carrara	0.68	ITSassari
Siena	0.99 ITFirenze	0.98	ITArezzo	0.96	ITPrato
Siracusa	0.98 ITRagusa	0.96	ITCaltanissetta	0.50	ITAgrigento
Sondrio	0.97 ITVercelli	0.80	ITNovara	0.57	ITVerbano-C.-Ossola
Taranto	0.88 USAmador	0.87	USColusa	0.78	USSan Bernardino
Teramo	0.99 ITPescara	0.96	ITLAquila	0.96	ITCampobasso
Terni	0.84 ITViterbo	0.83	ITPerugia	0.82	FRCharente Maritime
Torino	0.81 ITBiella	0.73	ITAsti	0.69	ITVerbano-C.-Ossola
Trapani	0.98 ITPalermo	0.60	ITAgrigento	0.60	ITAgrigento
Trento	0.85 USYolo	0.85	USMonterey	0.83	USRiverside
Treviso	0.67 ITPadova	0.64	ITVenezia	0.63	ITPordenone
Trieste	0.20 ITGorizia	0.13	NZMarlborough	0.12	ITUdine
Udine	0.95 ITPordenone	0.92	ITVenezia	0.89	ITGorizia
Valle D'Aosta	0.52 ITVercelli	0.51	ITNovara	0.48	ITComo
Varese	0.77 ITBiella	0.72	ITVerbano-C.-Ossola	0.61	ITVercelli
Venezia	0.96 ITPordenone	0.92	ITUdine	0.90	ITPadova
Verbano-C.-Ossola	0.82 ITBiella	0.73	ITAsti	0.72	ITVarese
Vercelli	0.97 ITSondrio	0.86	ITNovara	0.67	ITBiella
Verona	0.74 ITVicenza	0.14	ITPadova	0.12	ITMantova
ViboValentia	0.75 AUEastern Plains etc.	0.75	PTAcores	0.74	ITBelluno
Vicenza	0.74 ITVerona	0.56	ITPadova	0.50	ITVenezia
Viterbo	0.90 ITLatina	0.84	ITTerni	0.83	ITRoma
Luxembourg	0.80 DESachsen	0.71	CHLucerne	0.66	DEFranken
Moldova	0.51 AUAdelaide Hills	0.49	AUAlpine/Bchworth	0.48	NZHawkes Bay
Morocco	0.62 PTAcores	0.62	AUEastern Plains etc.	0.61	PTMadeira
New Zealand					
Auckland	0.94 USNapa	0.93	USNevada	0.93	NZHawkes Bay
Canterbury	0.91 NZWaipara	0.91	AUTasmania	0.88	NZCentral Otago
Central Otago	0.98 USPolk Co	0.98	USHumboldt	0.97	USYamhill Co
Gisborne	0.94 USRiverside	0.94	USSanta Barbara	0.94	CLAraucania
Hawkes Bay	0.96 USSoland	0.93	USNevada	0.93	NZAuckland
Marlborough	0.86 NZNelson	0.80	NZWaipara	0.73	NZWairarapa
Nelson	0.96 NZWaipara	0.88	NZWairarapa	0.86	AUTasmania
Waikato	0.81 ZAStellenbosch	0.74	AUBig Rivers Other	0.72	NZHawkes Bay
Waipara	0.97 NZWairarapa	0.96	NZNelson	0.92	AUTasmania
Wairarapa	0.97 NZWaipara	0.95	AUTasmania	0.92	NZCentral Otago

Table 59 (cont.) Each region's 3 most similar winegrape regions in the world according to the Varietal Similarity Index, 2000

Portugal						
Alentejo	0.63	PTRibatejo e Oeste	0.48	PTAlgarve	0.40	PTAltoTras-os-Mont.
Algarve	0.53	PTMadeira	0.52	PTRibatejo e Oeste	0.48	PTAlentejo
AltoTras-os-Mont.	0.81	PTBeira Interior	0.78	ITBelluno	0.76	AUEastern Plains etc.
Beira Interior	0.83	ITBelluno	0.81	AUEastern Plains etc.	0.81	PTAltoTras-os-Mont.
Beira Litoral	0.60	PTBeira Interior	0.57	ITBelluno	0.56	AUEastern Plains etc.
Douroe Minho	0.44	ITBelluno	0.44	AUEastern Plains etc.	0.41	PTBeira Interior
Madeira	0.98	PTAcores	0.95	AUEastern Plains etc.	0.93	ITBelluno
Acores	0.98	PTMadeira	0.97	AUEastern Plains etc.	0.94	ITBelluno
Ribatejo e Oeste	0.63	PTAlentejo	0.52	PTAlgarve	0.51	PTBeira Litoral
Romania	0.96	AUC. Ranges Other	0.95	AUQueensland Other	0.95	AUNthn Territory
Russia	0.84	Armenia	0.79	AUQueensland Other	0.78	AUC. Ranges Other
Serbia	0.73	Croatia	0.69	ESCaceres	0.67	Slovakia
Slovakia	0.87	Czech Rep.	0.75	ATBurgenland	0.67	Serbia
Slovenia	0.94	Romania	0.92	AUC. Ranges Other	0.91	AUQueensland Other
South Africa						
Breedekloof	0.96	ZAOlifants River	0.94	ZAWorcester	0.86	ZALittle Karoo
Little Karoo	0.90	ZAOlifants River	0.89	ZAOrange River	0.87	ZAWorcester
Malmesbury	0.99	ZAPaarl	0.88	ZAWorcester	0.83	ZABreedekloof
Olifants River	0.96	ZABreedekloof	0.94	ZAWorcester	0.90	ZALittle Karoo
Orange River	0.89	ZALittle Karoo	0.89	USKern	0.88	USMadera
Paarl	0.99	ZAMalmesbury	0.88	ZAWorcester	0.84	ZABreedekloof
Robertson	0.91	ZAWorcester	0.87	ZALittle Karoo	0.83	ZAOlifants River
Stellenbosch	0.81	NZWaikato	0.80	ZAPaarl	0.79	ZAMalmesbury
Worcester	0.94	ZAOlifants River	0.94	ZABreedekloof	0.91	ZARobertson
Spain						
Alava	0.95	ESBurgos	0.91	ESRioja	0.82	ESGuadalajara
Zaragoza	0.98	ESHuesca Teruel	0.90	FRVaucluse	0.88	ESAvila Palencia
Zamora	0.70	ESBurgos	0.69	ESValladolid	0.67	ESAlava
Valladolid	0.73	ESBurgos	0.73	ESCastellon	0.69	ESZamora
Valencia	0.69	ESCuenca	0.42	ESAlbacete	0.15	ESCastellon
Toledo	0.97	ESCiudad Real	0.80	ESMadrid	0.75	ESAlbacete
Tarragona	0.85	ESGirona Lleida	0.76	ESBarcelona	0.53	FRPyrenees Orient.
Murcia	0.74	ESAlicante	0.51	ESAlbacete	0.51	USContra Costa
Asturias	0.75	ESLeon	0.66	PTAcores	0.65	PTMadeira
Malaga	0.94	AUNthn Territory	0.90	AUC. Ranges Other	0.89	ELIoniaNisia
Leon	0.84	ESCantabria	0.75	ESAsturias	0.49	ESGalicia
Rioja	0.91	ESAlava	0.88	ESBurgos	0.81	ESNavarra
Illes Balears	0.40	ZAStellenbosch	0.39	AUSth Coast Other	0.39	AUGranite Belt
Huesca Teruel	0.98	ESZaragoza	0.87	FRVaucluse	0.86	SalamancaSS
Huelva	0.07	ESAlmeria Granada Jae	0.06	AUEastern Plains etc.	0.06	ITBelluno
Guipuzcoa,Vizc.	0.06	DEWurttemberg	0.06	AUNthn Territory	0.06	ESMalaga
Guadalajara	0.82	ESAlava	0.80	ESBurgos	0.74	ESRioja
Girona Lleida	0.85	ESTarragona	0.64	FRPyrenees Orient.	0.61	ESBarcelona
Galicia	0.49	ESLeon	0.44	DEAhr	0.44	ITBelluno
Cuenca	0.84	ESAlbacete	0.84	ESAlbacete	0.72	ESCiudad Real

Table 59 (cont.) Each region's 3 most similar winegrape regions in the world according to the Varietal Similarity Index, 2000

Spain (continued)						
Cordoba	0.44	CLCoquimbo	0.33	CLAtacama	0.16	ESMalaga
Navarra	0.88	ESAvila Palencia Salam	0.85	ESHuesca Teruel	0.83	ESZaragoza
Madrid	0.80	ESToledo	0.71	ESZaragoza	0.71	SalamancaSS
Ciudad Real	0.97	ESToledo	0.77	ESAlbacete	0.72	ESCuenca
Castellon	0.76	ESNavarra	0.75	ESRioja	0.73	ESValladolid
Cantabria	0.84	ESLeon	0.68	ESCadiz	0.60	ESCanarias
Canarias	0.88	ESCadiz	0.60	ESCantabria	0.37	ESZamora
Cadiz	0.88	ESCanarias	0.68	ESCantabria	0.38	ESGalicia
Caceres	0.69	Serbia	0.46	ATSteiermark	0.32	ATBurgenland
Burgos	0.95	ESAlava	0.88	ESRioja	0.80	ESGuadalajara
Barcelona	0.76	ESTarragona	0.61	ESGirona Lleida	0.26	ESCastellon
Badajoz	0.07	ESCaceres	0.06	ESAlmeriaGranadaJaen	0.04	ESValladolid
Avila Palencia Sala	0.88	ESZaragoza	0.88	ESNavarra	0.86	ESHuesca Teruel
Almeria Granada Ja	0.74	DEAhr	0.73	AUQueensland Other	0.71	ITBelluno
Alicante	0.74	ESMurcia	0.72	ESMalaga	0.70	AUNthn Territory
Albacete	0.84	ESCuenca	0.77	ESCiudad Real	0.75	ESToledo
Switzerland						
Aargau	1.00	CHZurich	1.00	CHThurgau	0.99	CHSchwyz
Basel Landschaft	0.99	CHSt Gallen	0.99	CHSchaffhausen	0.98	CHThurgau
Bern	0.98	CHNeuchtel	0.95	CHFribourg	0.90	CHValais
Fribourg	0.97	CHVaud	0.95	CHBern	0.92	CHNeuchtel
Geneva	0.84	CHVaud	0.81	CHValais	0.73	CHFribourg
Graubunden	0.99	CHSt Gallen	0.99	CHSchaffhausen	0.98	CHBasel Landschaft
Jura	0.61	CHSchwyz	0.59	CHLucerne	0.55	CHAargau
Lucerne	0.93	CHSchwyz	0.90	CHAargau	0.87	CHZurich
Neuchtel	0.98	CHBern	0.92	CHValais	0.92	CHFribourg
otherregion	0.99	CHAargau	0.98	CHSchwyz	0.97	CHZurich
Schaffhausen	1.00	CHSt Gallen	0.99	CHBasel Landschaft	0.99	CHGraubunden
Schwyz	0.98	CHAargau	0.98	CHZurich	0.97	CHThurgau
St Gallen	1.00	CHSchaffhausen	0.99	CHGraubunden	0.99	CHBasel Landschaft
Thurgau	1.00	CHZurich	0.99	CHAargau	0.98	CHSchaffhausen
Ticino	0.98	ITRovigo	0.91	ITPadova	0.88	FRGironde
Valais	0.92	CHNeuchtel	0.90	CHBern	0.82	CHFribourg
Vaud	0.97	CHFribourg	0.89	CHBern	0.84	CHNeuchtel
Zurich	1.00	CHThurgau	1.00	CHAargau	0.98	CHBasel Landschaft
Tunisia	0.86	FRAude	0.81	FRHerault	0.70	Algeria
United Kingdom	0.62	AUC. Ranges Other	0.62	AUNthn Territory	0.61	AUQueensland Other
United States						
Alameda	0.96	USSanta Clara	0.95	USSolano	0.95	USNevada
Amador	0.99	USColusa	0.89	USSan Bernardino	0.88	ITTaranto
Benton Co	0.99	USYamhill Co	0.98	USPolk Co	0.97	CHGraubunden
Butte	0.85	USEl Dorado	0.76	USSan Joaquin	0.72	USAmador
Calaveras	0.94	USMendocino	0.93	USSolano	0.92	USSacramento
Chautauqua Erie	0.85	USFinger Lakes	0.01	ITBelluno	0.01	PTAcores
Columbia River	0.82	AUN. E. Vic Other	0.82	USOregon Other	0.77	AUAlpine/Bchworth
Colusa	0.99	USAmador	0.89	USSan Bernardino	0.87	ITTaranto
Contra Costa	0.80	USSan Joaquin	0.72	USMendocino	0.71	USSutter
Douglas Co	0.92	USWashington Co	0.92	USJosephine Co	0.90	USOther Valley

Table 59 (cont.) Each region's 3 most similar winegrape regions in the world according to the Varietal Similarity Index, 2000

United States (continued)						
El Dorado	0.93	USSan Joaquin	0.91	USMariposa	0.85	USCalaveras
Finger Lakes	0.85	USChautauqua Erie	0.20	USMichigan	0.16	NZCanterbury
Fresno	0.93	USKern	0.91	USMadera	0.88	USStanislaus
Glenn	0.71	USMadera	0.68	USStanislaus	0.66	FRVaucluse
Humboldt	0.98	NZCentral Otago	0.97	USPolkCo	0.97	USYamhill Co
Josephine Co	0.97	USOther Valley	0.97	USWashington Co	0.95	USLane Co
Kern	0.95	USMadera	0.93	USTulare	0.93	USFresno
Kings	0.75	USTulare	0.72	USKern	0.64	USFresno
Lake	0.90	USSan Luis Obispo	0.88	USCalaveras	0.88	USNapa
Lane Co	0.98	USMarion Co	0.95	USJosephine Co	0.95	USWashington Co
Los Angeles	0.87	FRCharente Maritime	0.86	FRCharente	0.72	ITTerni
Madera	0.95	USKern	0.91	USFresno	0.91	USStanislaus
Marin	0.92	USOregon Other	0.86	USTrinity	0.79	AUAlpine/Bchworth
Marion Co	0.98	USLane Co	0.97	USWashington Co	0.94	USJosephine Co
Mariposa	0.91	USEl Dorado	0.86	USCalaveras	0.85	USSan Luis Obispo
Mendocino	0.97	USSonoma	0.96	USSanta Clara	0.95	USAlameda
Merced	0.85	USStanislaus	0.81	USTulare	0.79	USCalaveras
Michigan	0.73	NZCanterbury	0.71	USDouglas Co	0.70	Canada
Monterey	0.98	USYolo	0.98	USRiverside	0.98	USSanta Barbara
Napa	0.97	USSan Luis Obispo	0.94	USSan Benito	0.94	NZAuckland
Nevada	0.96	USSanta Clara	0.96	USSonoma	0.96	USSolano
Oregon Other	0.92	USMarin	0.90	USTrinity	0.88	FRGironde
Other Valley	0.98	USWashington Co	0.97	USJosephine Co	0.97	USMarionCo
Placer	0.86	USSan Bernardino	0.75	USAmador	0.74	USColusa
Polk Co	1.00	USYamhill Co	0.98	NZCentral Otago	0.98	USBenton Co
Riverside	0.98	USYolo	0.98	USSanta Barbara	0.98	CLAraucania
Sacramento	0.97	USSolano	0.96	USSanta Clara	0.95	USNevada
San Benito	0.95	USSonoma	0.94	USSan Luis Obispo	0.94	USNapa
San Bernardino	0.89	USAmador	0.89	USColusa	0.86	USPlacer
San Diego	0.71	AUAus. Capital Terr.	0.69	AUAlpine/Bchworth	0.69	USWashington
San Joaquin	0.93	USEl Dorado	0.84	USColusa	0.84	USCalaveras
San Luis Obispo	0.97	USNapa	0.95	USSonoma	0.94	USSan Benito
San mateo	0.98	USSanta Cruz	0.97	USSanta Barbara	0.96	AUTumbarumba
Santa Barbara	0.99	USSanta Cruz	0.98	USRiverside	0.98	USMonterey
Santa Clara	0.97	USSonoma	0.96	USNevada	0.96	USAlameda
Santa Cruz	0.99	USSanta Barbara	0.98	USSan mateo	0.96	USMonterey
Shasta	0.92	AUCowra	0.88	AUHunter	0.87	AUHunter Vall.Other
Solano	0.97	USSacramento	0.96	USSonoma	0.96	USSanta Clara
Sonoma	0.97	USSanta Clara	0.97	USMendocino	0.96	USSolano
Stanislaus	0.91	USMadera	0.88	USFresno	0.87	USKern
Sutter	0.83	USMendocino	0.82	USRiverside	0.82	USYolo
Tehama	0.98	USYolo	0.95	USRiverside	0.94	USMonterey
Trinity	0.94	USWashington	0.90	USSacramento	0.87	NZAuckland
Tulare	0.93	USKern	0.89	USMadera	0.88	USFresno
Ventura	0.86	AUFar North Other	0.83	AUBendigo	0.83	AUBarossa Other
Washington	0.95	USSacramento	0.94	USTrinity	0.92	USNevada
Washington Co	0.98	USOther Valley	0.97	USJosephine Co	0.97	USMarion Co
Yamhill Co	1.00	USPolk Co	0.99	USBenton Co	0.97	NZCentral Otago
Yolo	0.98	USMonterey	0.98	USRiverside	0.98	USTehama
Yuba	0.90	CLMetropolitana	0.86	CLOHiggins	0.82	AULimestone C.Other
Uruguay	0.34	FRCorr., Haute-Vien.	0.33	ITBergamo	0.32	FRAquitaine Other

Table 60: Each region's 3 most similar winegrape regions in the world according to the Varietal Similarity Index, 2010

Algeria	0.85	FRVar	0.73	FRBouches du Rhone	0.73	FRHerault
Argentina						
25 de Mayo	0.97	AR9de Julio	0.97	ARSan Martin S	0.97	ARSarmiento
9 de Julio	0.98	ARPocito	0.97	AR25 de Mayo	0.97	ARRawson
Albardon	0.97	ARPocito	0.95	ARRawson	0.94	AR9deJulio
Angaco	0.95	ARCaucete	0.94	ARRawson	0.94	ARSan Martin S
Catamarca	0.93	ARPocito	0.91	ARRawson	0.91	AR9 de Julio
Caucete	0.97	AR9 de Julio	0.97	ARSan Martin S	0.96	AR25 de Mayo
Junin	0.98	ARRivadavia	0.94	ARSan Martin	0.91	ARSanta Rosa
LaRioja	0.86	ARSalta	0.61	ARCatamarca	0.52	ARLavalle
Lavalle	0.96	ARSanta Rosa	0.90	ARSan Martin M	0.87	ARRivadavia
Lujande Cuyo	0.98	ARTunuyan	0.93	ARTupungato	0.92	ARMaipu
Maipu	0.92	ARLujande Cuyo	0.92	ARTunuyan	0.90	ARTupungato
Neuquen	0.95	ARTunuyan	0.93	ARTupungato	0.91	ARLujande Cuyo
Pocito	0.98	AR9deJulio	0.98	ARRawson	0.97	ARAlbardon
Rawson	0.98	ARPocito	0.97	AR9deJulio	0.95	ARAlbardon
Rio Negro	0.86	ARNeuquen	0.79	ARTunuyan	0.79	ARTupungato
Rivadavia	0.98	ARJunin	0.93	ARSan Martin	0.92	ARSanta Rosa
Salta	0.86	ARLa Rioja	0.68	ARLujan de Cuyo	0.67	ARTunuyan
San Martin M	0.96	ARSanta Rosa	0.94	ARJunin	0.93	ARRivadavia
San Martin S	0.97	ARCaucete	0.97	AR25 de Mayo	0.94	ARAngaco
San Rafael	0.91	ARRivadavia	0.89	ARJunin	0.88	ARSanta Rosa
Santa Rosa	0.96	ARSan Martin	0.96	ARLavalle	0.92	ARRivadavia
Sarmiento	0.97	AR25 de Mayo	0.96	AR9de Julio	0.93	ARCaucete
Tunuyan	0.98	ARLujan de Cuyo	0.95	ARTupungato	0.95	ARNeuquen
Tupungato	0.95	ARTunuyan	0.93	ARNeuquen	0.93	ARLujan de Cuyo
Ullum	0.86	AR25 de Mayo	0.86	ARSarmiento	0.81	ARCaucete
Armenia	0.93	KZZhambyl	0.81	HUZala	0.81	RONord Vest
Australia						
Adelaide Hills	0.96	AUStrathbogie Rgs	0.92	AUPemberton	0.92	CLValparaiso
Adelaide Plains	0.98	AUGoulburn Valley	0.97	AUSouthern Fleurieu	0.97	AUSE Coastal WA
Alpine Valleys	0.93	AUKing Valley	0.90	AUStrathbogie Rgs	0.89	AUC. Ranges Other
Aus. Capital Terr.	0.81	DEHessische Bergs.	0.77	DEGermany	0.76	USColorado
Barossa other	1.00	AUSthn Flinders	0.99	AUGrampians	0.99	USVentura
Barossa Valley	0.99	AUMt LoftyRgsOther	0.99	AUMcLaren Vale	0.99	AUBendigo
Beechworth	0.97	AUOrange	0.96	AUMudgee	0.96	AUNthn Slopes Other
Bendigo	0.99	AUMcLaren Vale	0.99	AUMt LoftyRgsOther	0.99	AUBarossa Valley
Big Rivers other	0.97	AUMurray Dar. NSW	0.92	AUMurray Dar. VIC	0.91	AUCowra
Blackwood Valley	0.97	AUGeographe	0.97	AUMargaret River	0.97	AUGreat Southern
C. Ranges Other	0.93	AUMurray Dar. VIC	0.93	AUMurray Dar. NSW	0.92	AUBeechworth
Canberra ACT	0.89	AUEden Valley	0.89	AUCanberra NSW	0.89	AUGoulburn Valley
Canberra NSW	0.97	AUThe Peninsulas	0.95	AUCurrency Creek	0.95	AUGlenrowan
Central Vic Other	0.99	AUGrampians	0.99	AUHeathcote	0.99	AUBendigo
Central WA	0.96	AUMcLaren Vale	0.95	AUBendigo	0.95	AUMt LoftyRgsOther
Clare Valley	0.95	AUCanberra NSW	0.94	AUEden Valley	0.91	AUThePeninsulas
Coonawarra	0.98	AUWrattonbully	0.97	USRed Mountain	0.97	CLMetropolitana
Cowra	0.98	AUHunter Vall.Other	0.95	USTehama	0.93	AUMurray Dar. VIC
Currency Creek	0.99	AUKangaroo Island	0.98	AULanghorne Creek	0.98	AUThe Peninsulas
Eastern Plain ect.	0.84	AUSwan District	0.75	AUPerth Hills	0.65	AUQueensland other
Eden Valley	0.94	AUClare Valley	0.89	AUCanberra ACT	0.85	AUCanberra NSW

Table 60 (cont.) Each region's 3 most similar winegrape regions in the world according to the Varietal Similarity Index, 2010

Australia (continued)			
Far North Other	0.98 AUKangaroo Island	0.97 AUGlenrowan	0.96 AUFleurieu other
Fleurieu other	0.98 AULanghorne Creek	0.98 AUHilltops	0.98 AUKangaroo Island
Geelong	0.97 AUMacedon Ranges	0.95 AUPort Phillip other	0.94 AUGippsland
Geographe	0.98 AUMargaret River	0.97 AUBlackwood Valley	0.97 AUGreat Southern
Gippsland	0.99 AUMacedon Ranges	0.99 AUPort Phillip other	0.98 AUYarra Valley
Glenrowan	0.97 AUThe Peninsulas	0.97 AUCurrency Creek	0.97 AUFar North Other
Goulburn Valley	0.98 AUAdelaidePlains	0.98 AUOrange	0.97 AUSouthern Fleurieu
Grampians	0.99 AUHeathcote	0.99 AUBarossa other	0.99 AUCentral Vic Other
Granite Belt	0.94 AUNthn Slopes Other	0.94 AUBeechworth	0.94 AUSwan Hill NSW
Great Southern	0.97 AUBlackwood Valley	0.97 AUGeographe	0.95 AUMargaret River
Greater Per. Other	0.92 AUBarossa Valley	0.92 AUMt LoftyRgsOther	0.92 AUBarossa other
Gundagai	0.98 AUMcLaren Vale	0.97 AUBendigo	0.97 AUSouthern Fleurieu
Hastings River	0.89 AUShoalhaven Coast	0.81 AUNthn Rivers other	0.72 NZAuckland
Heathcote	0.99 AUGrampians	0.99 AUCentral Vic Other	0.98 AUBarossa other
Henty	0.97 AUTasmania	0.96 AUMornington Pen.	0.95 NZCanterbury
Hilltops	0.99 AULanghorne Creek	0.98 AUFleurieu other	0.97 AUCurrency Creek
Hunter	0.96 AURiverina	0.94 AUSouth Coast other	0.91 AUWest Plains Other
Hunter Vall.Other	0.98 AUCowra	0.97 USTehama	0.94 FRYonne
Kangaroo Island	0.99 AUCurrency Creek	0.98 AUFar North Other	0.98 AUFleurieu other
KingValley	0.93 AUAlpine Valleys	0.89 AUStrathbogie Rgs	0.87 CABritish Colombia
Langhorne Creek	0.99 AUHilltops	0.98 AUFleurieu other	0.98 AUCurrency Creek
Limestone C.Other	0.97 AUWrattonbully	0.96 AUCoonawarra	0.94 AUHilltops
Lower Murr. Other	0.98 AUPerricoota	0.98 AURiverland	0.96 AUGundagai
Macedon Ranges	0.99 AUGippsland	0.99 AUPort Phillip other	0.98 USSanta Cruz
Manjimup	0.88 USSacramento	0.88 AUSW Australia Other	0.87 AUMargaret River
Margaret River	0.98 AUGeographe	0.97 AUBlackwood Valley	0.95 AUGreat Southern
McLaren Vale	0.99 AUMt LoftyRgsOther	0.99 AUBarossa Valley	0.99 AUBendigo
Mornington Pen.	0.97 USSanta Cruz	0.96 AUTasmania	0.96 AUHenty
Mount Benson	0.97 AUGeographe	0.96 AUOrange	0.96 AUBlackwood Valley
Mt Lofty Rgs Other	0.99 AUBarossa Valley	0.99 AUMcLaren Vale	0.99 AUBendigo
Mudgee	0.98 AUPadthaway	0.98 AUOrange	0.98 AULanghorne Creek
Murray Dar. NSW	0.97 AUMurray Dar. VIC	0.97 AUBig Rivers other	0.95 AUSwan Hill VIC
Murray Dar. VIC	0.97 AUMurray Dar. NSW	0.95 AURiverland	0.95 AUSwan Hill VIC
N. E. Vic Other	0.96 USHorse Heaven Hills	0.94 USWahluke Slope	0.93 USSan Luis Obispo
N. W. Vic Other	0.93 AUSwanHill NSW	0.93 AURiverland	0.92 AUMudgee
New England	0.79 AUHunter	0.74 AURiverina	0.72 AUCowra
Nthn Rivers other	0.87 NZGisborne	0.87 AUHunter Vall.Other	0.85 USTehama
Nthn Slopes Other	0.97 AUMudgee	0.96 AUOrange	0.96 AUPadthaway
Orange	0.98 AUPadthaway	0.98 AUGoulburn Valley	0.98 AUMudgee
Padthaway	0.98 AUMudgee	0.98 AUOrange	0.98 AULanghorne Creek
Peel	0.96 AUHilltops	0.95 AUPadthaway	0.95 AULanghorne Creek
Pemberton	0.96 CLValparaiso	0.92 AUAdelaide Hills	0.91 AUSW Australia Other
Perricoota	0.98 AURiverland	0.98 AULower Murr.Other	0.96 AUPadthaway
Perth Hills	0.95 AUSwan District	0.87 AUWest Plains Other	0.86 AUSouth Coast other
Pt Phillip Other	0.99 AUMacedon Ranges	0.99 AUGippsland	0.96 USSanta Cruz
Pyrenees	0.96 AUBendigo	0.95 AUMcLaren Vale	0.95 AUMt LoftyRgsOther
Queensland Other	0.95 AUSouth Burnett	0.94 AUSwan Hill NSW	0.94 AUSouthern Fleurieu
Riverina	0.96 AUHunter	0.94 AUSouth Coast other	0.94 AUSwan Hill VIC
Riverland	0.98 AUPerricoota	0.98 AULower Murr.Other	0.96 AUSwan Hill VIC
Robe	0.97 AUPadthaway	0.96 AUPerricoota	0.96 AURiverland
Rutherglen	0.95 AUMt LoftyRgsOther	0.95 AUGrampians	0.95 AUBendigo
Shoalhaven Coast	0.89 AUHastings River	0.81 AUSouth Coast other	0.77 AUNthn Rivers other

Table 60 (cont.) Each region's 3 most similar winegrape regions in the world according to the Varietal Similarity Index, 2010

Australia (continued)

South Burnett	0.97 AUMudgee	0.96 AUSouthern Fleurieu	0.95 AUQueensland other
South Coast other	0.94 AUHunter	0.94 AURiverina	0.91 AUSwan Hill VIC
Southern Fleurieu	0.97 AUAdelaidePlains	0.97 AUGundagai	0.97 AUMcLaren Vale
Southern Highlands	0.90 AUStrathbogie Rgs	0.89 AUAdelaide Hills	0.88 AUUpper Goulburn
Sthn NSW Other	0.86 AUAdelaide Plains	0.83 AUGoulburn Valley	0.82 AUSouthern Fleurieu
Sthn Flinders	1.00 AUBarossa other	0.99 USVentura	0.99 AUGrampians
Strathbogie Rgs	0.97 AUUpper Goulburn	0.96 AUAdelaide Hills	0.90 AUAlpine Valleys
Sunbury	0.94 AUAdelaidePlains	0.93 AUSouthern Fleurieu	0.92 AUSE Coastal WA
SW Australia Other	0.92 AUBlackwood Valley	0.92 AUMargaret River	0.91 AUPemberton
Swan District	0.95 AUPerthHills	0.84 AUEastern Plains Inland	0.82 AUQueensland other
Swan Hill NSW	0.96 AUSouthern Fleurieu	0.95 AUMudgee	0.95 AUSouth Burnett
Swan Hill VIC	0.96 AURiverland	0.95 AUMurray Dar. NSW	0.95 AUMurray Dar. VIC
Tasmania	0.98 NZCanterbury	0.97 AUHenty	0.96 AUMornington Pen.
The Peninsulas	0.98 AUCurrency Creek	0.98 AULanghorne Creek	0.97 AUGlenrowan
Tumbarumba	0.95 USSanta Barbara	0.94 AUMacedon Ranges	0.94 AUGippsland
Upper Goulburn	0.97 AUYarra Valley	0.97 AUStrathbogie Rgs	0.93 AUGippsland
SE Coastal WA	0.97 AUAdelaide Plains	0.96 AUGoulburn Valley	0.96 AUWest Plains Other
West Plains Other	0.96 AUSE Coastal WA	0.95 AULower Murr.Other	0.95 AUGundagai
West Vic Other	0.94 AUCanberra NSW	0.93 AULanghorne Creek	0.93 AUHilltops
Wrattonbully	0.98 AUCoonawarra	0.97 AULimestone C.Other	0.95 AUHilltops
Yarra Valley	0.98 AUGippsland	0.97 AUUpper Goulburn	0.96 AUMacedon Ranges

Austria

Burgenland	0.81 HUTolna	0.76 HUSopron	0.74 HUCsongrad
Niederosterreich	0.88 ATWien and Other	0.77 SKMalokarpatska	0.75 SKNitrianska
Steiermark	0.74 SIStajerska Slovenija	0.72 SIPrekmurje	0.67 CZMorava
Wien and Other	0.88 ATNiederosterreich	0.76 SKMalokarpatska	0.74 SKNitrianska

Brazil

Brazil	0.37 MDMoldova	0.20 USFinger Lakes	0.18 USChautauqua Erie

Bulgaria

Severentsentralen	0.90 BGSeverozapaden	0.77 USColumbia River 2	0.77 MXSuma Baja Cali.
Severoiztochen	0.73 BGSeverentsentralen	0.70 BGSeverozapaden	0.69 BGYugoiztochen
Severozapaden	0.90 BGSeverentsentralen	0.74 BGYugoiztochen	0.74 MXSuma Baja Cali.
Yugoiztochen	0.88 BGYuzhentsentralen	0.76 BGSeverentsentralen	0.74 BGSeverozapaden
Yugozapaden	0.40 BGYuzhentsentralen	0.38 BGSeverozapaden	0.36 BGYugoiztochen
Yuzhentsentralen	0.88 BGYugoiztochen	0.84 FRGironde	0.79 FRLot et Garonne

Canada

British Colombia	0.87 AUKing Valley	0.85 AUAlpine Valleys	0.82 USColorado
Ontario	0.63 USMichigan	0.63 USVirginia	0.61 USYakima Valley

Chile

Araucania	0.97 CLDe Los Lagos	0.90 AUTasmania	0.89 CLValparaiso
Valparaiso	0.96 AUPemberton	0.93 CLDe Los Lagos	0.92 AUAdelaide Hills
O'Higgins	0.98 CLMetropolitana	0.95 CLDel Maule	0.94 CNGansu
Metropolitana	0.98 CLO'Higgins	0.97 CNGansu	0.97 CNNingxia
Del Maule	0.95 CLMetropolitana	0.95 CLO'Higgins	0.94 USNapa
Del BioBio	0.77 CLAtacama	0.76 ESMalaga	0.53 ARUllum
De Los Lagos	0.97 CLAraucania	0.93 CLValparaiso	0.90 NZNelson
Coquimbo	0.92 AURobe	0.92 AURiverland	0.91 AUPerricoota
Atacama	0.77 ESMalaga	0.77 CLDel BioBio	0.58 ARUllum

Table 60 (cont.) Each region's 3 most similar winegrape regions in the world according to the Varietal Similarity Index, 2010

China

Beijing	1.00	CNShandong	1.00	CNSichuan	1.00 CNTianjin
Gansu	0.99	CNXinjiang	0.97	CLMetropolitana	0.97 CNNingxia
Ningxia	0.98	CNBeijing	0.98	CNShandong	0.98 CNSichuan
Shandong	1.00	CNSichuan	1.00	CNTianjin	1.00 CNBeijing
ShanXi	0.91	USNapa	0.90	CNGansu	0.89 USHorse Heaven Hills
Sichuan	1.00	CNShandong	1.00	CNBeijing	1.00 CNTianjin
Tianjin	1.00	CNShandong	1.00	CNSichuan	1.00 CNBeijing
Xinjiang	0.99	CNGansu	0.95	CLMetropolitana	0.95 CNNingxia
Yantai	1.00	CNBeijing	1.00	CNShandong	1.00 CNSichuan

Croatia

Dalm. Zagora	0.26	HRSjeverna-Dalm.	0.19	CHTicino	0.18 BGYuzhentsentralen
Hrvatsko Primorje	0.12	USAlameda	0.12	USHorse Heaven Hills	0.12 USSanta Clara
Istra	0.53	SIPrimorje SlovenskaIstr	0.46	SIVipavska Dolina	0.29 SISlovenia
Moslavina	0.95	HRPokuplje	0.72	HRSlavonija	0.72 HRPodunavlje
Plesivica	0.91	HRZagorje-Medimur.	0.89	HRPrigorje-Bilogora	0.84 SIPrekmurje
Podunavlje	0.99	HRSlavonija	0.96	HUBalatonfured-Cs.	0.96 HUBalatonfelvidek
Pokuplje	0.95	HRMoslavina	0.69	HRPodunavlje	0.69 HRSlavonija
Prigorje-Bilogora	0.89	HRPlesivica	0.82	HRSlavonija	0.82 HRPodunavlje
Sjeverna-Dalm.	0.36	FRArdeche	0.36	USSan Diego	0.35 FRGard
Slavonija	0.99	HRPodunavlje	0.97	HUBalatonfured-Cs.	0.96 HUBalatonfelvidek
Srednja Juzna Dalm.	0.27	HRSjeverna-Dalm.	0.16	HRDalm. Zagora	0.09 ELAnatol. Mak.,Thraki
Zagorje-Medimur.	0.91	HRPlesivica	0.85	SIPrekmurje	0.84 SIStajerska Slovenija

Cyprus   0.15 MXMexico   0.15 FRAude   0.14 FRHerault

Czech Rep.

Cechy	0.85	CZMorava	0.67	CHLucerne	0.61 HUMatra
Morava	0.87	SKSlovakia	0.86	SKNitrianska	0.86 SKJuznoslovenska

France

Aquitaine Other	0.39	UYUruguay	0.37	FRLandes	0.34 FRMidi Pyrenees Other
Ardeche	0.93	FRGard	0.83	FRHerault	0.82 AUCentral WA
Aude	0.96	FRHerault	0.82	FRGard	0.77 FRArdeche
Bas Rhin	0.94	FRHaut Rhin	0.64	USLake Chelan	0.64 USMichigan
Bouches du Rhone	0.95	FRGard	0.93	FRVar	0.92 FRVaucluse
Centre Other	0.90	AUPemberton	0.88	NZMarlborough	0.86 FRNievre
Champagne Viticole	0.79	USSan Mateo	0.79	USSanta Cruz	0.77 UKUK
Charente	1.00	FRCharentemaritime	0.50	FRLandes	0.47 FRGers
Charentemaritime	1.00	FRCharente	0.51	FRLandes	0.49 FRGers
Cher	0.98	NZMarlborough	0.97	FRNievre	0.96 NZNewzealand
Corse	0.70	USOrange	0.69	DEAhr	0.64 KZWest Kazakhstan
Cote d'Or	0.97	USMarin	0.96	USYamhill Co	0.95 NZOtago
Dordogne	0.83	FRGironde	0.83	FRLotet Garonne	0.70 CHTicino
Drome	0.97	FRVaucluse	0.91	FRGard	0.90 FRBouches du Rhone
Gard	0.95	FRBouches du Rhone	0.93	FRArdeche	0.91 FRDrome
Gers	0.85	FRLandes	0.69	ZAOrange River	0.65 ZALittle Karoo
Gironde	0.95	FRLotet Garonne	0.92	CHTicino	0.84 BGYuzhentsentralen
Haut Rhin	0.94	FRBas Rhin	0.66	USLake Chelan	0.63 USMichigan
Herault	0.96	FRAude	0.86	FRGard	0.83 FRArdeche
Indre	0.81	FRRhone	0.72	CHGeneva	0.71 FRRhone Alpes Other
Indreet Loire	0.98	FRMaineet Loire	0.59	FRVienne	0.56 FRPays de Loire Other

Table 60 (cont.) Each region's 3 most similar winegrape regions in the world according to the Varietal Similarity Index, 2010

France (continued)			
Landes	0.85 FRGers	0.51 FRCharentemaritime	0.50 ZAOrange River
Loire Atlantique	0.29 FRPays de Loire Other	0.13 FRMaineet Loire	0.09 FRRhone Alpes Other
Loiret Cher	0.86 FRNievre	0.84 NZMarlborough	0.84 FRCher
Lot	0.92 ARLujan de Cuyo	0.90 ARTunuyan	0.84 ARNeuquen
Lotet Garonne	0.95 FRGironde	0.83 CHTicino	0.83 FRDordogne
Maine et Loire	0.98 FRIndreet Loire	0.62 FRPays de Loire Other	0.58 FRVienne
Midi Pyrenees Other	0.83 USOrange	0.82 DEAhr	0.75 KZWest Kazakhstan
Nievre	0.99 NZMarlborough	0.97 FRCher	0.86 NZWaipara
Pays de Loire Other	0.75 ZAWorcester	0.71 ZABreedekloof	0.70 ZAPaarl
Poitou-Charen.Other	0.63 HUPecs	0.62 ROBucurestiIlfov	0.61 HUZala
Prov.-C. d'A Other	0.56 FRBouches du Rhone	0.54 FRGard	0.53 FRVar
Pyrenees Orient.	0.85 FRDrome	0.82 FRGard	0.80 FRVaucluse
Rhone	0.81 FRIndre	0.74 CHGeneva	0.73 FRRhone Alpes Other
Rhone Alpes Other	0.73 FRRhone	0.71 FRIndre	0.65 AUNthn Rivers other
Saoneet Loire	0.91 FRYonne	0.89 USSan Benito	0.88 USMonterey
Savoie	0.13 FRRhone Alpes Other	0.12 FRYonne	0.12 USTehama
Tarn	0.49 AUCentral WA	0.49 AUGraniteBelt	0.47 AUCanberra NSW
Tarnet Garonne	0.79 CHVaud	0.69 CHFribourg	0.55 CHBern
Var	0.93 FRBouches du Rhone	0.88 FRGard	0.85 DZAlgeria
Vaucluse	0.97 FRDrome	0.92 FRBouches du Rhone	0.89 FRGard
Vendee	0.71 USOrange	0.70 KZWest Kazakhstan	0.69 DEAhr
Vienne	0.64 FRVendee	0.59 FRIndreet Loire	0.58 FRMaine et Loire
Yonne	0.97 USTehama	0.94 AUHunter Vall.Other	0.93 USYolo
Georgia	0.93 KZAlmaty	0.91 KZKazakhstan	0.78 KZSouth Kazakhstan
Germany			
Ahr	0.98 USOrange	0.94 DEWurttemberg	0.93 KZWest Kazakhstan
Baden	0.91 DESachsen	0.89 DESaale Unstrut	0.82 DERheinhessen
Franken	0.88 DESaale Unstrut	0.84 DESachsen	0.83 DERheinhessen
Hessische Bergs.	0.95 DEMittelrhein	0.92 DERheingau	0.88 DENahe
Mittelrhein	0.99 DERheingau	0.97 DEMosel-Saa-Ruwer	0.95 DEHessische Bergs.
Mosel-Saa-Ruwer	0.97 DEMittelrhein	0.96 DERheingau	0.87 DEHessische Bergs.
Nahe	0.98 DERhein Pfalz	0.94 DERheinhessen	0.88 DEHessische Bergs.
Rhein Pfalz	0.98 DENahe	0.94 DERheinhessen	0.86 DEHessische Bergs.
Rheingau	0.99 DEMitte lrhein	0.96 DEMosel-Saa-Ruwer	0.92 DEHessische Bergs.
Rheinhessen	0.94 DERhein Pfalz	0.94 DENahe	0.92 DESachsen
Saale Unstrut	0.95 DESachsen	0.89 DEBaden	0.88 DEFranken
Sachsen	0.95 DESaale Unstrut	0.92 DERheinhessen	0.91 DEBaden
Wurttemberg	0.94 DEAhr	0.89 KZWest Kazakhstan	0.87 USOrange

Table 60 (cont.) Each region's 3 most similar winegrape regions in the world according to the Varietal Similarity Index, 2010

Greece

Anatol. Mak.,Thraki	0.81 USSnipes Mountain	0.78 NZAuckland	0.77 USColumbia River 2
Attiki	0.98 ELSterea Ellada	0.13 ELPeloponissos	0.06 ELIonia Nisia
Dytiki Iada	0.55 ELPeloponissos	0.49 ELThessalia	0.44 ELKentriki Mak.
Dytiki Mak.	0.61 ELKentriki Mak.	0.43 ELThessalia	0.33 USOrange
Ionia Nisia	0.81 DEWurttemberg	0.80 DEAhr	0.80 KZWest Kazakhstan
Ipeiros	0.74 DEAhr	0.72 USOrange	0.71 KZWest Kazakhstan
Kentriki Mak.	0.65 ELAnatol. Mak.,Thraki	0.61 ELDytiki Mak.	0.60 BGYuzhentsentralen
Kriti	0.34 ROBucurestiIlfov	0.31 ROSud Vest Oltenia	0.31 HUZala
Notio Aigaio	0.43 ROBucurestiIlfov	0.40 KZEast Kazakhstan	0.39 ELIonia Nisia
Poponissos	0.55 ELDytiki Ellada	0.39 ELKentriki Mak.	0.37 ELThessalia
Sterea Iada	0.98 ELAttiki	0.21 ELPeloponissos	0.21 ELDytiki Ellada
Thessalia	0.69 ELVorreio Aigaio	0.63 USOrange	0.62 DEAhr
Vorreio Aigaio	0.69 ELThessalia	0.57 MXZacatecas	0.51 ITPiemonte

Hungary

Badacsony	0.96 HUBalatonfelvidek	0.95 HUBalatonfured-Cs.	0.94 HRSlavonija
Balatonboglar	0.80 HUEtyek-Budai	0.77 HUTolna	0.71 HUPecs
Balatonfelvidek	0.97 HUBalatonfured-Cs.	0.96 HRSlavonija	0.96 HRPodunavlje
Balatonfured-Cs.	0.97 HRSlavonija	0.97 HUBalatonfelvidek	0.96 HRPodunavlje
Bukk	0.78 HUEger	0.70 ATBurgenland	0.70 HUTolna
Csongrad	0.83 HUSopron	0.77 HUHajos-Bajai	0.76 HUSzekszard
Eger	0.89 HUSzekszard	0.78 HUBukk	0.78 HUSopron
Etyek Budai	0.82 HUNeszmely	0.82 HUNeszmely	0.80 HUBalatonboglar
Hajos-Bajai	0.78 HUTolna	0.77 HUSzekszard	0.77 HUCsongrad
Kunsag	0.69 HUCsongrad	0.68 HUHajos-Bajai	0.50 HUSopron
Matra	0.70 HUNeszmely	0.67 HUEtyek-Budai	0.67 HUTolna
Mor	0.55 HUNeszmely	0.54 HUPecs	0.50 HUZala
Nagy Somlo	0.81 SIPrekmurje	0.79 SIStajerska Slovenija	0.72 HUBadacsony
Neszmely	0.82 HUEtyek-Budai	0.71 ITTrentino	0.70 HUMatra
Pannonhalma	0.90 HUBalatonfured-Cs.	0.88 HUBalatonfelvidek	0.87 HRSlavonija
Pecs	0.77 HUEtyek Budai	0.72 HUZala	0.72 SIStajerska Slovenija
Sopron	0.86 HUSzekszard	0.83 HUCsongrad	0.78 HUEger
Szekszard	0.89 HUEger	0.86 HUSopron	0.77 HUHajos-Bajai
Tokaj	0.97 SKTokajska	0.31 HRZagorje-Medimur.	0.31 HUNagy Somlo
Tolna	0.81 ATBurgenland	0.78 HUHajos-Bajai	0.77 HUBalatonboglar
Villany	0.73 HUSzekszard	0.72 HUEger	0.71 CNShan Xi

Italy

Abruzzo	0.96 ITMolise	0.61 ITMarche	0.46 ITPuglia
Basilicata	0.90 ITCampania	0.25 FRCorse	0.23 DEAhr
Calabria	0.24 DEAhr	0.24 USOrange	0.23 KZWest Kazakhstan
Campania	0.90 ITBasilicata	0.27 FRCorse	0.26 DEAhr
Emilia Romagna	0.45 ITToscana	0.34 ITUmbria	0.30 ITMarche
Friuli Venezia Giul.	0.74 CABritish Colombia	0.71 ITTrentino	0.66 AUKing Valley
Lazio	0.49 ITUmbria	0.40 FRCharentemaritime	0.39 FRCharente
Liguria	0.49 FRCorse	0.46 ITSardegna	0.27 DEAhr
Lombardia	0.62 AUMornington Pen.	0.62 AUHenty	0.62 USSanMateo
Marche	0.65 ITToscana	0.65 ITMolise	0.61 ITAbruzzo
Molise	0.96 ITAbruzzo	0.65 ITMarche	0.47 ITPuglia
Piemonte	0.51 ELVorreioaigaio	0.39 ITLombardia	0.38 ELThessalia
Puglia	0.60 ITMarche	0.55 ITToscana	0.52 USAmador
Sardegna	0.78 FRVaucluse	0.77 FRBouches du Rhone	0.72 ESZaragoza

Table 60 (cont.) Each region's 3 most similar winegrape regions in the world according to the Varietal Similarity Index, 2010

Italy (continued)
Sicilia	0.21	AUBeechworth	0.21 AUMurray Dar. NSW	0.21	AUOrange
Toscana	0.73	ITUmbria	0.65 ITMarche	0.57	FRCorse
Trentino	0.82	USSolano	0.79 USYolo	0.79	USColumbia Gorge
Umbria	0.73	ITToscana	0.58 FRCorse	0.57	ITMarche
Valle D'Aosta	0.68	USOrange	0.67 DEAhr	0.67	KZWest Kazakhstan
Veneto	0.48	ITFriuli Venezia Giul.	0.42 CABritish Colombia	0.40	FRGironde

Kazakhastan
Almaty	0.93	GEGeorgia	0.83 KZSouth Kazakhstan	0.83	KZSouthKazakhstan
East Kazakhstan	0.87	KZWest Kazakhstan	0.78 DEWurttemberg	0.75	ELIonia Nisia
South Kazakhstan	0.83	KZAlmaty	0.78 GEGeorgia	0.58	KZZhambyl
West Kazakhstan	0.93	DEAhr	0.90 USOrange	0.89	DEWurttemberg
Zhambyl	0.81	HUZala	0.81 RONordVest	0.81	ROSud Muntenia

Japan
Hokkaido	0.32	CZCechy	0.31 ATBurgenland	0.31	DEFranken
Nagano	0.95	USShasta	0.94 JPYamagata	0.91	CHTicino
Yamagata	0.94	JPNagano	0.90 USShasta	0.83	USMerced
Yamanashi	0.63	CNBeijing	0.63 CNShandong	0.63	CNSichuan

Luxembourg   0.44 FRHaut Rhin   0.43 FRBasRhin   0.39 DESachsen

Moldova   0.50 NZHawkesBay   0.48 CABritish Colombia   0.47 USSacramento

Morocco   0.60 USOrange   0.60 DEAhr   0.56 KZWest Kazakhstan

Myanmar   0.75 USVentura   0.69 THThailand   0.68 USTuolumne

Mexico
Aguascalientes	0.62	TNTunisia	0.45 FRAude	0.39	FRHerault
Sonora	0.68	TUEGE	0.09 CYCyprus	0.05	TNTunisia
Suma Coahuila	0.58	CNXinjiang	0.58 CNGansu	0.56	USRed Mountain
Suma Baja Cali.	0.85	USWalla Walla Valley	0.82 USTexas	0.81	USColumbia River 2
Zacatecas	0.57	ELVorreio Aigaio	0.39 ELThessalia	0.30	ITPiemonte

New Zealand
Auckland	0.88	NZHawkes Bay	0.85 USSnipes Mountain	0.84	AUNthn Rivers other
Canterbury	0.98	AUTasmania	0.95 AUHenty	0.92	AUMornington Pen.
Gisborne	0.91	FRYonne	0.90 USYolo	0.90	USTehama
Hawkes Bay	0.88	NZAuckland	0.87 AUStrathbogie Rgs	0.85	AUAlpine Valleys
Marlborough	0.99	FRNievre	0.98 FRCher	0.90	NZWaipara
Nelson	0.94	NZWaipara	0.90 CLDe Los Lagos	0.90	FRCher
Otago	1.00	USYamhill Co	1.00 USPolk Co	0.99	USBenton Co
Waikato	0.83	USTexas	0.81 NZAuckland	0.80	NZHawkesBay
Waipara	0.94	NZNelson	0.91 FRCher	0.90	NZMarlborough
Wairarapa	0.93	NZOtago	0.93 AUTasmania	0.92	USYamhill Co

Peru
Arequipa	0.79	PTMadeira PT	0.69 PEMoquegua	0.56	PTAlgarve
Lima	0.39	PEMoquegua	0.39 PETacna	0.09	PEArequipa
Moquegua		PETacna	0.69 PEArequipa	0.65	PTMadeiraPT
Tacna	0.94	PEMoquegua	0.47 PEArequipa	0.41	PTMadeiraPT

Table 60 (cont.) Each region's 3 most similar winegrape regions in the world according to the Varietal Similarity Index, 2010

Portugal
Alentejo	0.61 ESBurgos	0.60 ESAlava	0.60 ESLaRioja
Acores	0.46 PTDouroe Minho	0.13 PTRibatejo e Oeste	0.12 PTAlentejo
Algarve	0.60 PTMadeira PT	0.56 PTRibatejo e Oeste	0.56 PEArequipa
AltoTras-os-Mont.	0.49 PTAlentejo	0.46 ESBurgos	0.44 ESLaRioja
Beira Litoral	0.33 PTRibatejo e Oeste	0.28 ESZamora	0.28 ESLeon
Beira Interior	0.44 PTAltoTras-os-Mont.	0.32 PTAlentejo	0.26 ESAvila Palencia SS
Douroe Minho	0.46 PTAcores	0.24 ESGalicia	0.14 ESCantabria
Madeira	0.79 PEArequipa	0.65 PEMoquegua	0.60 PTAlgarve
Ribatejo e Oeste	0.56 PTAlgarve	0.53 PTAlentejo	0.33 PTBeiraLitoral

Romania
BucurestiIlfov	0.96 RONord Vest	0.96 ROSud Vest Oltenia	0.96 HUZala
Centru	0.76 ROVest	0.65 ROSud Est	0.51 SIStajerska Slovenija
Nord Est	0.98 RONord Vest	0.97 ROSud Muntenia	0.97 ROSud Vest Oltenia
Nord Vest	0.99 ROSud Muntenia	0.99 HUZala	0.99 ROSud Vest Oltenia
Sud Est	0.93 RONordEst	0.91 ROSud Muntenia	0.90 RONord Vest
Sud Muntenia	0.99 RONord Vest	0.98 HUZala	0.98 ROSud Vest Oltenia
Sud Vest Oltenia	0.99 RONordVest	0.98 ROSud Muntenia	0.98 HUZala
Vest	0.76 ROCentru	0.61 ROSudEst	0.60 SIVipavska Dolina

Russia
Krasnodar Krai	0.75 USHorse Heaven Hills	0.75 USNapa	0.72 USRiverside
Rostov Oblast	0.56 UAUkraine	0.48 KZAlmaty	0.45 MDMoldova

Serbia
	0.85 HUBadacsony	0.85 HRSlavonija	0.85 HRPodunavlje

Slovakia
Juznoslovenska	0.94 SKNitrianska	0.92 SKMalokarpatska	0.86 CZMorava
Malokarpatska	0.98 SKNitrianska	0.92 SKJuznoslovenska	0.89 SKStredoslovenska
Nitrianska	0.98 SKMalokarpatska	0.94 SKJuznoslovenska	0.86 SKStredoslovenska
Stredoslovenska	0.89 SKMalokarpatska	0.86 SKNitrianska	0.85 SKJuznoslovenska
Tokajska	0.97 HUTokaj	0.32 HUNagy Somlo	0.29 HRZagorje-Medimur.
Vychodoslovenska	0.83 HUBalatonfured-Cs.	0.83 SKJuznoslovenska	0.81 HRSlavonija

Slovenia
Belakrajina	0.87 SIBizeljsko Sremic	0.81 SIOther	0.67 SIDolenjska
Bizeljsko Sremic	0.90 SIOther	0.87 SIBelakrajina	0.82 SIDolenjska
Dolenjska	0.90 SIOther	0.82 SIBizeljsko Sremic	0.67 SIBelakrajina
Goriskabrda Brda	0.70 SIVipavska Dolina	0.67 NZHawkes Bay	0.65 JPYamagata
Prekmurje	0.94 SIStajerska Slovenija	0.88 HUBadacsony	0.87 HRSlavonija
Primorje Kras	0.91 SISlovens kaIstra	0.15 HRIstra	0.13 ROBucurestiIlfov
Slovens kaIstra	0.91 SIPrimorje Kras	0.53 HRIstra	0.27 SIVipavska Dolina
Stajerska Slovenija	0.94 SIPrekmurje	0.84 HRZagorje-Medimur.	0.80 HRPlesivica
Vipavska Dolina	0.70 SIGoriskabrda Brda	0.70 NZHawkesBay	0.69 FRLotet Garonne
Other	0.90 SIBizeljsko Sremic	0.90 SIDolenjska	0.81 SIBelakrajina

Table 60 (cont.) Each region's 3 most similar winegrape regions in the world according to the Varietal Similarity Index, 2010

South Africa

Breedekloof	0.97 ZAWorcester	0.95 ZAOlifants River	0.88 ZALittle Karoo
Little Karoo	0.94 ZAOrange River	0.94 ZAOlifants River	0.88 ZABreedekloof
Malmesbury	0.99 ZAPaarl	0.87 ZAStellenbosch	0.85 ZAWorcester
Olifants River	0.95 ZABreedekloof	0.94 ZALittle Karoo	0.92 ZAWorcester
Orange River	0.94 ZALittle Karoo	0.87 ZAOlifants River	0.77 USFresno
Paarl	0.99 ZAMalmesbury	0.88 ZAStellenbosch	0.85 ZAWorcester
Robertson	0.91 ZAWorcester	0.88 ZABreedekloof	0.81 ZAOlifants River
Stellenbosch	0.89 AUMount Benson	0.88 AUMargaret River	0.88 ZAPaarl
Worcester	0.97 ZABreedekloof	0.92 ZAOlifants River	0.91 ZARobertson

Spain

Alava	0.99 ESLaRioja	0.98 ESNavarra	0.97 ESZamora
Albacete	0.78 ESCuenca	0.60 ESGuadalajara	0.59 ESAlicanteAlacant
Alicante	0.96 ESMurcia	0.59 ESAlbacete	0.29 CLAtacama
Almeria Granada Jaen	0.62 ROBucurestiIlfov	0.57 ROSud Vest Oltenia	0.57 ROSud Muntenia
Avila Palencia SSSor	0.83 ESZaragoza	0.81 ESZamora	0.80 ESNavarra
Badajoz	0.48 ESLaRioja	0.47 ESBurgos	0.47 ESAlava
Barcelona	0.75 ESTarragona	0.53 ESGirona Lleida	0.30 ESHuescaTeruel
Burgos	0.98 ESLaRioja	0.96 ESAlava	0.96 ESZamora
Caceres	0.67 ESValladolid	0.67 ESNavarra	0.63 ESAlava
Cadiz	0.75 ESCanarias	0.56 ESCantabria	0.51 MXSuma Coahuila
Canarias	0.75 ESCadiz	0.47 ESCantabria	0.39 ESGalicia
Cantabria	0.69 ESGalicia	0.60 ESLeon	0.56 ESCadiz
Castellon	0.77 ESAlava	0.77 ESNavarra	0.76 ESLaRioja
Ciudad Real	0.97 ESToledo	0.69 ESCuenca	0.69 ESGuadalajara
Navarra	0.98 ESAlava	0.94 ESLaRioja	0.93 ESZamora
Madrid	0.79 ESToledo	0.73 ESZaragoza	0.70 FRVaucluse
Cordoba	0.23 ESAlmeria Granada Jaen	0.16 ESMalaga	0.06 ESCaceres
Cuenca	0.78 ESAlbacete	0.75 ESValencia Valencia	0.69 ESCiudad Real
Galicia	0.69 ESCantabria	0.44 ESAsturias	0.42 DEWurttemberg
Girona Lleida	0.73 ESHuesca Teruel	0.72 ESTarragona	0.71 USSanta Clara
Guadalajara	0.88 ESBurgos	0.86 ESLaRioja	0.85 ESZamora
Guipuzcoa Vizcaya	0.13 ESCantabria	0.08 HUZala	0.08 ROSud Vest Oltenia
Huelva	0.04 ESAlmeria Granada Jaen	0.01 AUSthn Flinders	0.01 USVentura
Huesca Teruel	0.87 ESZaragoza	0.77 FRBouches du Rhone	0.76 FRGard
Illes Balears	0.66 USHorse Heaven Hills	0.66 AUN. E. Vic Other	0.66 USWalla Walla Valley
LaRioja	0.99 ESAlava	0.98 ESBurgos	0.97 ESZamora
Leon	0.60 ESCantabria	0.54 ESAsturias	0.34 ESGalicia
Malaga	0.77 CLAtacama	0.76 CLDel BioBio	0.46 ARUllum
Asturias	0.64 USOrange	0.63 DEAhr	0.58 KZWest Kazakhstan
Murcia	0.96 ESAlicanteAlacant	0.59 ESAlbacete	0.26 USContra Costa
Tarragona	0.75 ESBarcelona	0.72 ESGirona Lleida	0.57 ESHuesca Teruel
Toledo	0.97 ESCiudad Real	0.79 ESMadrid	0.65 ESCuenca
Valencia Valencia	0.75 ESCuenca	0.54 ESAlbacete	0.23 ESAlava
Valladolid	0.71 ESBurgos	0.71 ESZamora	0.70 ESLaRioja
Zamora	0.97 ESLaRioja	ESAlava	0.96 ESBurgos
Zaragoza	0.87 ESHuesca Teruel	0.84 FRDrome	0.83 ESAvila Palencia

Table 60 (cont.) Each region's 3 most similar winegrape regions in the world according to the Varietal Similarity Index, 2010

Switzerland			
Aargau	1.00 CHThurgau	1.00 CHZurich	0.99 CHBasel Landschaft
Basel Landschaft	1.00 CHSchaffhausen	1.00 CHSt Gallen	0.99 CHGraubunden
Bern	0.98 CHNeuchatel	0.95 CHFribourg	0.90 CHValais
Fribourg	0.95 CHBern	0.94 CHVaud	0.90 CHNeuchatel
Geneva	0.74 FRRhone	0.72 FRIndre	0.72 CHValais
Graubunden	1.00 CHSt Gallen	0.99 CHSchaffhausen	0.99 USYamhill Co
Jura	0.76 DEBaden	0.74 ROBucurestiIlfov	0.73 KZEast Kazakhstan
Lucerne	0.93 CHSchwyz	0.93 CHThurgau	0.93 CHZurich
Neuchatel	0.98 CHBern	0.92 CHValais	0.90 CHFribourg
Schaffhausen	1.00 CHSt Gallen	1.00 CHBasel Landschaft	0.99 CHGraubunden
Schwyz	0.98 CHZurich	0.98 CHAargau	0.98 CHThurgau
St Gallen	1.00 CHSchaffhausen	1.00 CHBasel Landschaft	1.00 CHGraubunden
Thurgau	1.00 CHAargau	1.00 CHZurich	0.98 CHSchaffhausen
Ticino	0.92 FRGironde	0.91 JPNagano	0.90 USShasta
Valais	0.92 CHNeuchatel	0.90 CHBern	0.82 CHFribourg
Vaud	0.94 CHFribourg	0.81 CHBern	0.79 FRTarnet Garonne
Zurich	1.00 CHAargau	1.00 CHThurgau	0.98 CHBasel Landschaft
Thailand	0.91 AUSthn Flinders	0.91 USVentura	0.906 AUBarossa other
Tunisia	0.74 FRAude	0.70 DZAlgeria	0.67 FRHerault
Turkey			
Akdeniz	0.78 AUStrathbogie Rgs	0.77 AUUpper Goulburn	0.76 USSacramento
Ege	0.68 MXSonora	0.55 AUN. W. Vic Other	0.53 AUSwan Hill NSW
Guney Dogu	0.27 TUAkdeniz	0.22 TUEge	0.17 TUOrta Kuzey
Marmara	0.53 AUNew England	0.52 FRDordogne	0.39 DZAlgeria
Orta Dogu	0.23 TUAkdeniz	0.13 TUEge	0.06 TUOrta Kuzey
Orta Guney	0.07 TUOrta Kuzey	0.05 TUEge	0.03 TUAkdeniz
Orta Kuzey	0.42 TUAkdeniz	0.38 TUEge	0.28 AUSthn Flinders
Ukraine	0.86 MDMoldova	0.70 KZAlmaty	0.63 GEGeorgia
United Kingdom	0.84 USSan Mateo	0.83 USSanta Cruz	0.81 AUTumbarumba
United States			
Alameda	0.94 USSanta Clara	0.92 USRiverside	0.92 USNapa
Amador	0.97 USSan Bernardino	0.93 USColusa	0.76 USSan Joaquin
Benton Co	1.00 USWashington Co	1.00 USPolk Co	0.99 USYamhill Co
Butte	0.90 USLos Angeles	0.89 USSan Luis Obispo	0.88 AUCoonawarra
Calaveras	0.92 AUMount Benson	0.90 AUGeographe	0.90 USNevada
Chautauqua Erie	0.99 USOhio	0.96 USPennsylvania	0.84 USFinger Lakes
Colorado	0.91 USSnipes Mountain	0.89 USColumbia Valley	0.88 USWahlukeSlope
Columbia River 2	0.88 USWalla Walla Valley	0.87 USJackson Co	0.86 USColorado
Columbia Valley	0.98 USWahluke Slope	0.96 USHorse Heaven Hills	0.93 USYakima Valley
ColumbiaGorge	0.79 ITTrentino	0.70 NZAuckland	0.70 NZAuckland
Colusa	0.93 USAmador	0.91 USSan Bernardino	0.85 USSan Joaquin
Contra Costa	0.87 USSan Joaquin	0.81 USMerced	0.79 USYolo
Douglas Co	0.98 USOther W Valley	0.96 USWashington Co	0.96 USPolk Co
El Dorado	0.87 USMariposa	0.86 USCalaveras	0.86 USSan Luis Obispo
Finger Lakes	0.88 USPennsylvania	0.86 USOhio	0.84 USChautauqua Erie

Table 60 (cont.) Each region's 3 most similar winegrape regions in the world according to the Varietal Similarity Index, 2010

United States (continued)			
Fresno	0.87 USTulare	0.85 USMadera	0.77 ZAOrange River
Glenn	0.78 USColusa	0.74 USKings	0.63 USSan Joaquin
Horse Heaven Hills	0.98 USWahluke Slope	0.96 USColumbia Valley	0.96 AUN. E. Vic Other
Humboldt	0.85 AUWest Vic Other	0.85 AUN. E. Vic Other	0.80 AUAlpine Valleys
Illinois	0.81 USIndiana	0.81 USIndiana	0.70 USMissouri
Indiana	0.81 USIllinois	0.63 ROBucurestiIlfov	0.62 USMissouri
Iowa	0.44 USMinnesota	0.41 USIllinois	0.21 USFinger Lakes
Jackson Co	0.87 USColumbia River 2	0.76 USColorado	0.75 USHumboldt
Josephine Co	0.97 USWashington Co	0.95 USDouglas Co	0.95 USBenton Co
Kentucky	0.68 USMissouri	0.62 USVirginia	0.60 CAOntario
Kern	0.71 USTulare	0.71 ZALittle Karoo	0.69 USFresno
Kings	0.74 USGlenn	0.68 USTulare	0.61 USFresno
Lake	0.91 CLDel Maule	0.88 CLMetropolitana	0.87 USNapa
Lake Chelan	0.75 USMichigan	0.74 USJosephine Co	0.71 AUEden Valley
Lane Co	0.95 USMarion Co	0.79 USWashington Co	0.79 USJosephine Co
Los Angeles	0.95 AUCoonawarra	0.95 USRed Mountain	0.94 CLMetropolitana
Madera	0.87 USTulare	0.85 USFresno	0.82 USStanislaus
Marin	0.99 USYamhill Co	0.99 CHGraubunden	0.99 NZOtago
MarionCo	0.95	0.94 USWashington Co	0.93 USBenton Co
Mariposa	0.91 USSan Luis Obispo	0.88 USSan Joaquin	0.87 USEl Dorado
Mendocino	0.98 USSonoma	0.94 USSacramento	0.92 USSan Benito
Merced	0.92 USSacramento	0.89 USMendocino	0.88 USSanta Clara
Michigan	0.81 DEHessische Bergs.	0.79 DEMittelrhein	0.77 DERheingau
Minnesota	0.44 USIowa	0.31 USIllinois	0.12 DEWurttemberg
Missouri	0.70 USIllinois	0.68 USKentucky	0.62 USIndiana
Monterey	0.99 USSan Benito	0.96 USSanta Barbara	0.94 USSolano
Napa	0.95 USSan Luis Obispo	0.95 CLMetropolitana	0.95 CNGansu
Nevada	0.90 AUPeel	0.90 USSan Luis Obispo	0.90 USCalaveras
Ohio	0.99 USChautauqua Erie	0.97 USPennsylvania	0.86 USFinger Lakes
Orange	0.98 DEAhr	0.90 KZWest Kazakhstan	0.87 DEWurttemberg
Other W Valleyand a	0.99 USWashington Co	0.99 USPolk Co	0.99 NZOtago
Pennsylvania	0.97 USOhio	0.96 USChautauqua Erie	0.88 USFinger Lakes
Placer	0.76 USAmador	0.74 USSan Bernardino	0.69 USColusa
Polk Co	1.00 USYamhill Co	1.00 NZOtago	1.00 USBenton Co
Puget Sound	0.87 USDouglas Co	0.82 USWashington Co	0.82 USPolk Co
Rattlesnake Hills	0.90 USColumbia Valley	0.88 USWahluke Slope	0.87 USYakima Valley
Red Mountain	0.97 USWalla Walla Valley	0.97 AUCoonawarra	0.97 CNGansu
Riverside	0.93 USHorse Heaven Hills	0.92 USAlameda	0.92 USSanta Clara
Sacramento	0.95 USSanta Clara	0.94 USMendocino	0.92 USMerced
San Benito	0.99 USMonterey	0.96 USSanta Barbara	0.93 USTrinity
San Bernardino	0.97 USAmador	0.91 USColusa	0.74 USPlacer
San Diego	0.90 AUThe Peninsulas	0.90 AUGlenrowan	0.89 AUCanberra NSW
San Joaquin	0.88 USMariposa	0.87 USContra Costa	0.86 USStanislaus
San Luis Obispo	0.95 USNapa	0.93 AUN. E. Vic Other	0.92 USAlameda
San Mateo	0.97 USSanta Cruz	0.95 AUGippsland	0.94 AUMornington Pen.
Santa Barbara	0.96 USMonterey	0.96 USSan Benito	0.95 AUTumbarumba
Santa Clara	0.95 USSacramento	0.94 USAlameda	0.92 AUN. E. Vic Other
Santa Cruz	0.98 AUMacedon Ranges	0.97 AUGippsland	0.97 USSan Mateo
Shasta	0.95 JPNagano	0.90 JPYamagata	0.90 CHTicino
Siskiyou	0.83 USSonoma	0.83 USMendocino	0.79 USSolano
Snipes Mountain	0.91 USColorado	0.90 USColumbiaValley	0.89 USWahluke Slope
Solano	0.94 USYolo	0.94 USMonterey	0.93 USSan Benito

Table 60 (cont.) Each region's 3 most similar winegrape regions in the world according to the Varietal Similarity Index, 2010

United States (continued)						
Sonoma	0.98	USMendocino	0.92	USSacramento	0.91	AUYarra Valley
Stanislaus	0.88	USMerced	0.86	USSan Joaquin	0.83	USSacramento
Sutter	0.71	USContra Costa	0.71	USContra Costa	0.67	USSan Joaquin
Tehama	0.97	FRYonne	0.97	AUHunter Vall.Other	0.95	USYolo
Texas	0.88	USSnipes Mountain	0.87	USRiverside	0.86	USAlameda
Trinity	0.93	USSan Benito	0.92	USMonterey	0.91	USSanta Barbara
Tulare	0.87	USFresno	0.87	USMadera	0.73	USStanislaus
Tuolumne	0.97	AUBendigo	0.96	AUMcLaren Vale	0.96	AUMt LoftyRgsOther
Ventura	0.99	AUSthn Flinders	0.99	AUBarossa other	0.98	AUGrampians
Virginia	0.77	USSanta Clara	0.76	USColorado	0.75	USSacramento
Wahluke Slope	0.98	USHorse Heaven Hills	0.98	USColumbia Valley	0.94	AUN. E. Vic Other
Walla Walla Valley	0.97	USRed Mountain	0.92	CNGansu	0.92	AUCoonawarra
Washington Co	1.00	USBenton Co	0.99	USPolk Co	0.99	NZOtago
Yakima Valley	0.93	USColumbia Valley	0.87	USRattlesnake Hills	0.86	USColorado
Yamhill Co	1.00	USPolk Co	1.00	NZOtago	0.99	USBenton Co
Yolo	0.95	USTehama	0.94	USSolano	0.93	USMonterey
Yuba	0.74	USAlameda	0.74	USNevada	0.73	AUNthn Slopes Other
Uruguay	0.41	FRMidi Pyrenees Other	0.39	FRAquitaine Other	0.37	ELAnatol. Mak.,Thraki

Table Section VIII: Summary charts for each of the world's top 50 varieties

61. Airen (White)

Country of origin: **Spain**

1990		2000			2010			2000-1990	2010-2000
Global area	Global share	Global rank	Global area	Global share	Global rank	Global area	Global share	Global rank	Changes %	Changes %
476396		9	387978	8	1	252364	5	3	-19	-35

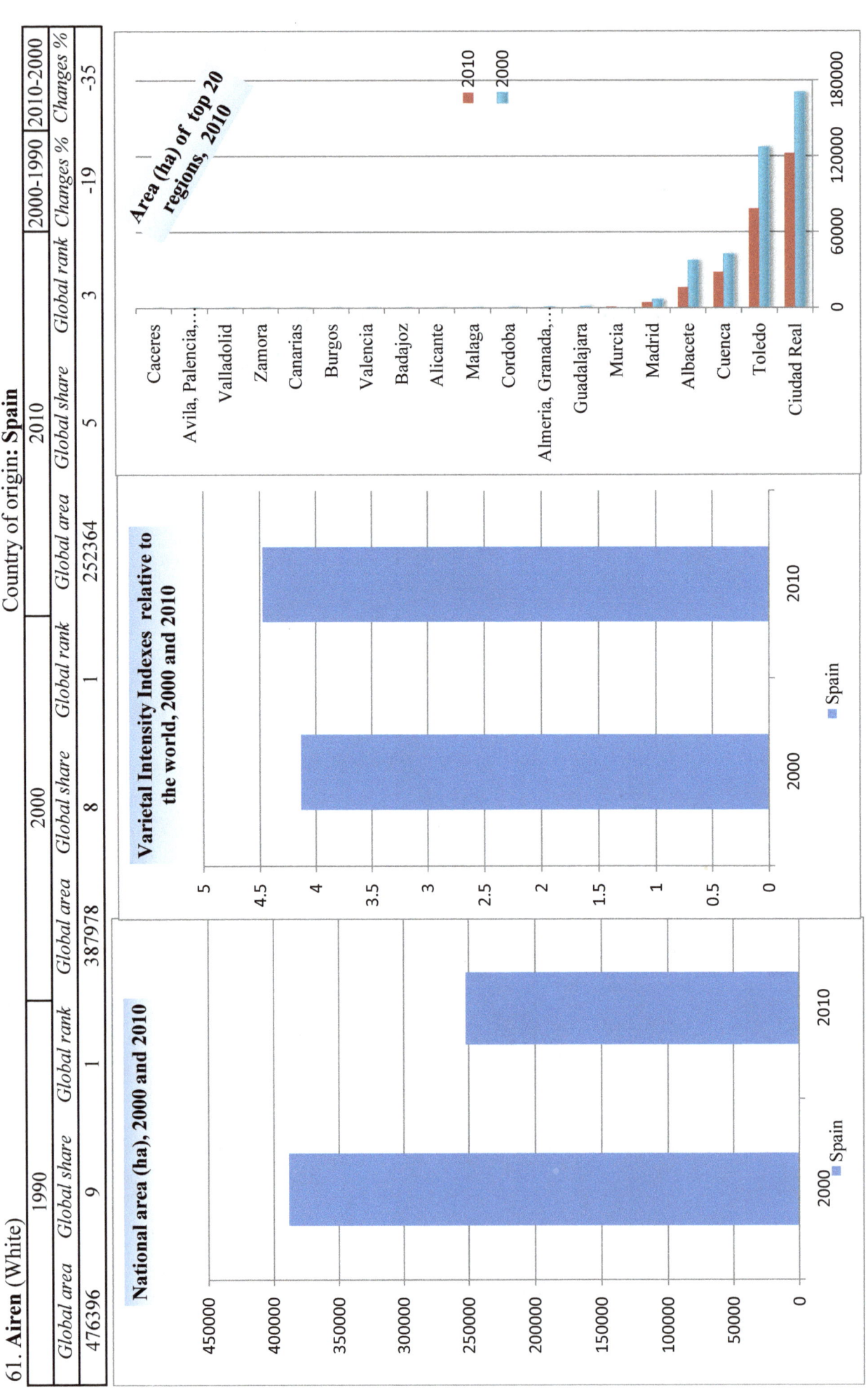

62. Alicante Henri Bouschet (Red)

Country of origin: **France**

	1990			2000			2010		2000-1990	2010-2000
Global area	Global share	Global rank	Global area	Global share	Global rank	Global area	Global share	Global rank	Changes %	Changes %
19587	0.4	47	37043	0.8	26	38985	0.8	23	89	5

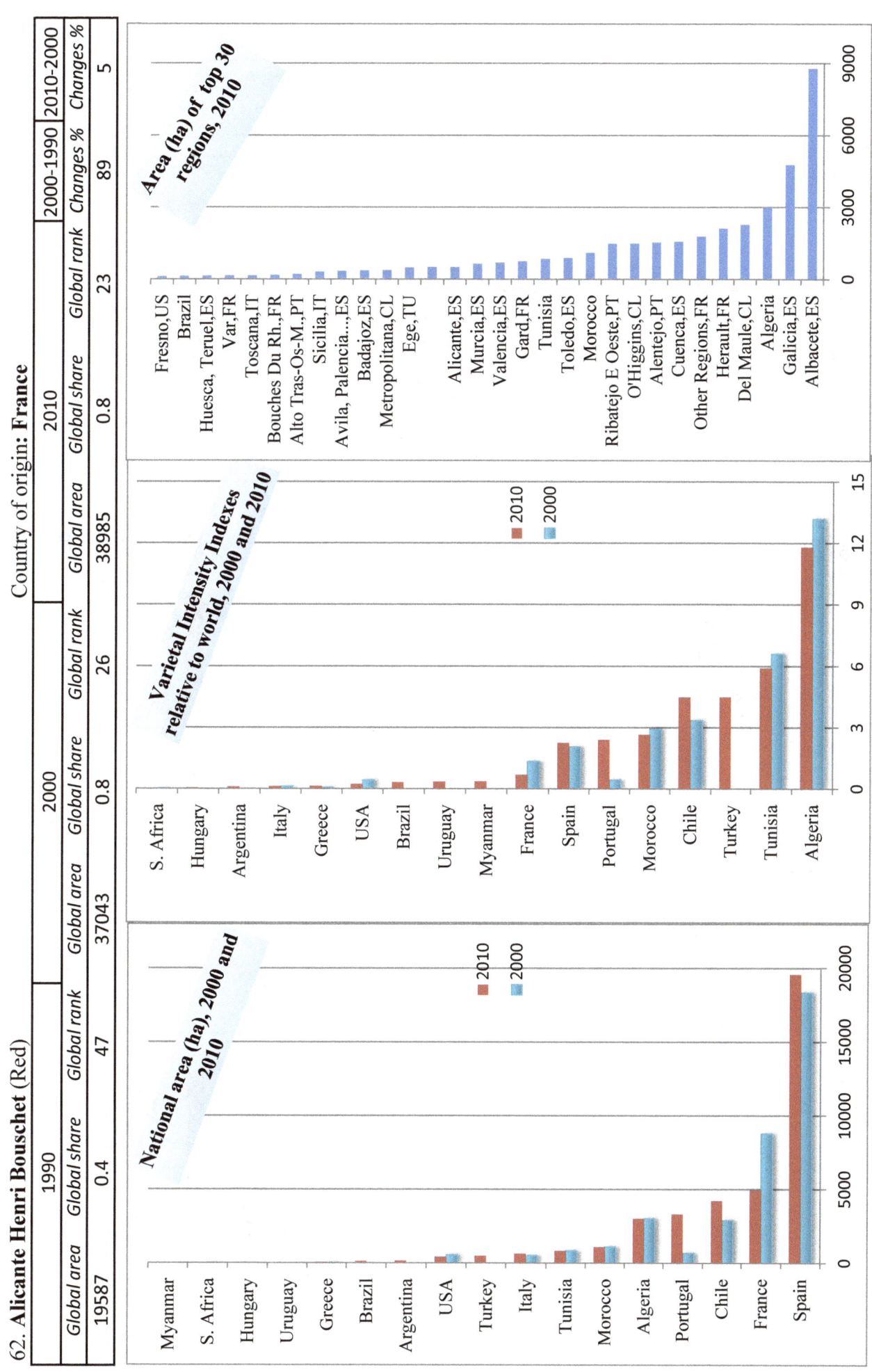

63. Aligoté (White)

Country of origin: France

	1990			2000			2010		2000-1990	2010-2000
Global area	Global share	Global rank	Global area	Global share	Global rank	Global area	Global share	Global rank	Changes %	Changes %
54430	1.0		35668	0.7	20	36119	0.8	27	-34	1	24

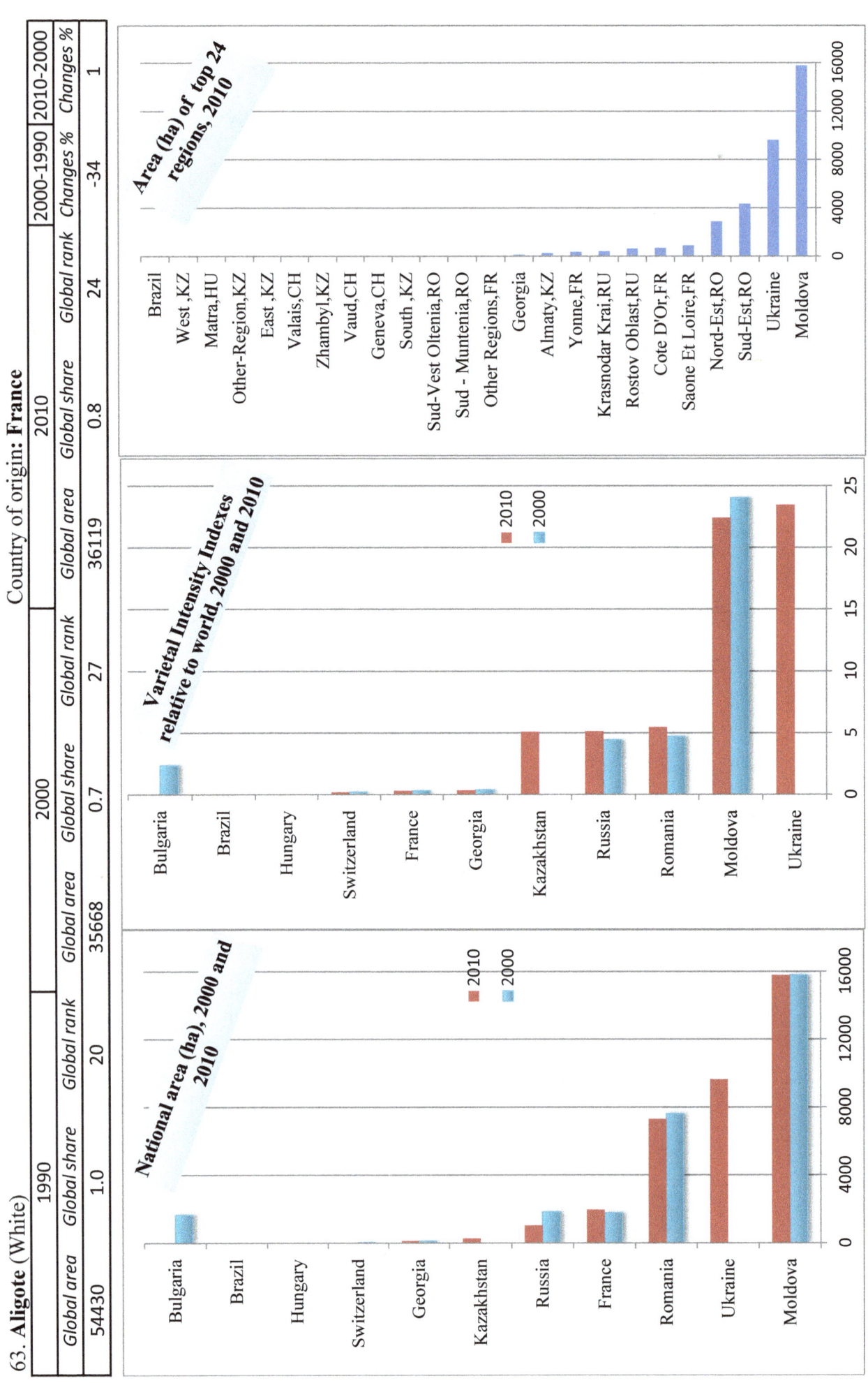

64. Barbera (Red)

Country of origin: Italy

	1990			2000			2010		2000-1990	2010-2000
Global area	Global share		Global area	Global rank	Global share	Global area	Global rank	Global share	Changes %	Changes %
67987	1.3		33048	15	0.7	24178	29	0.5	36	-51	-27

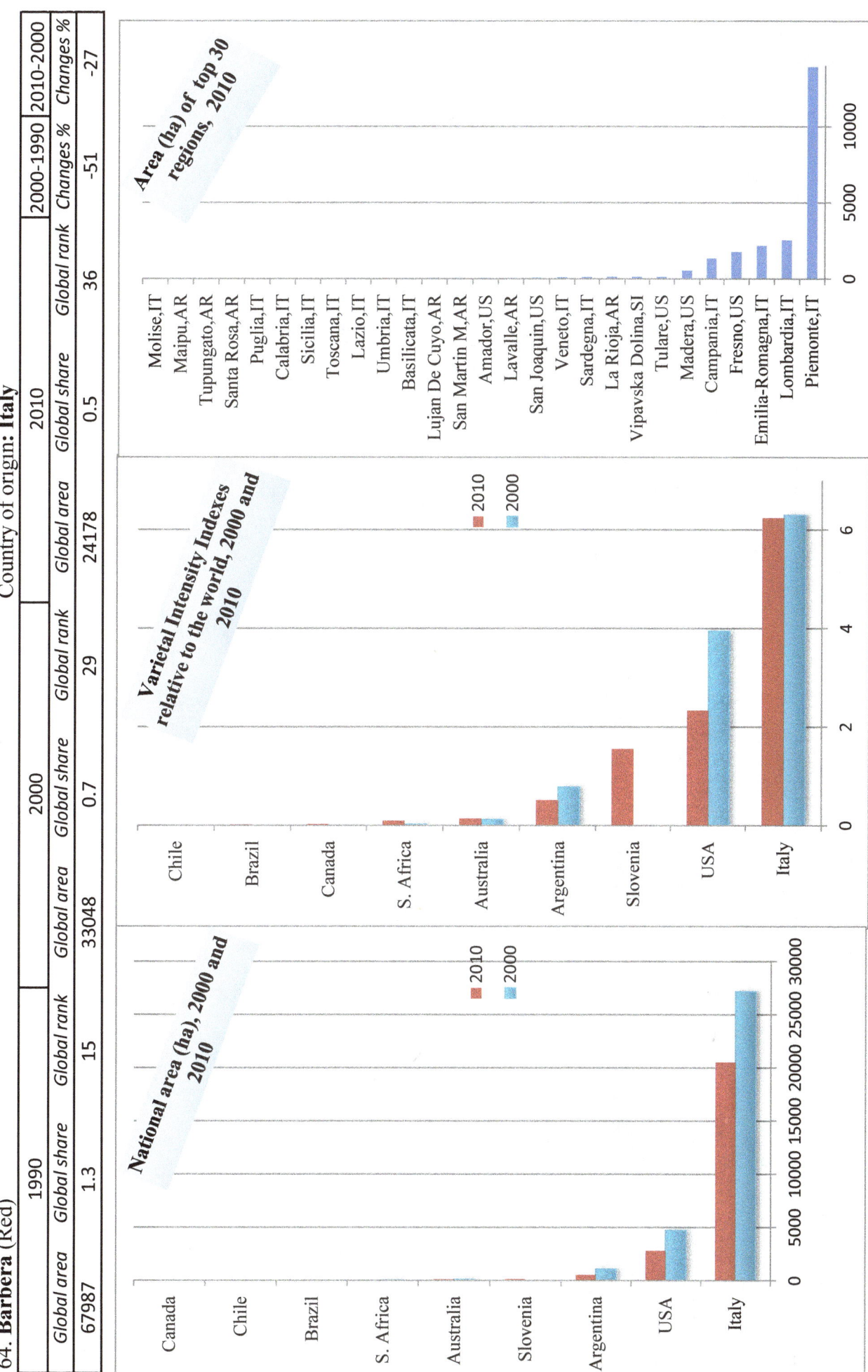

65. Blaufrankisch (Red)

Country of origin: Austria

	1990			2000			2010		2000-1990	2010-2000
	Global area	Global share	Global rank	Global area	Global share	Global rank	Global area	Global share	Global rank	Changes %	Changes %
	na	na	na	12879	0.3	62	16141	0.4	48		25

National area (ha), 2000 and 2010

Varietal Intensity Indexes relative to the world, 2000 and 2010

Area (ha) of top 30 regions, 2010

66. Bobal (Red)

Country of origin: **Spain**

	1990			2000			2010		2000-1990	2010-2000
Global area	Global share	Global rank	Global area	Global share	Global rank	Global area	Global share	Global rank	Changes %	Changes %
106149	2	10	100128	2	9	80120	2	12	-6	-20

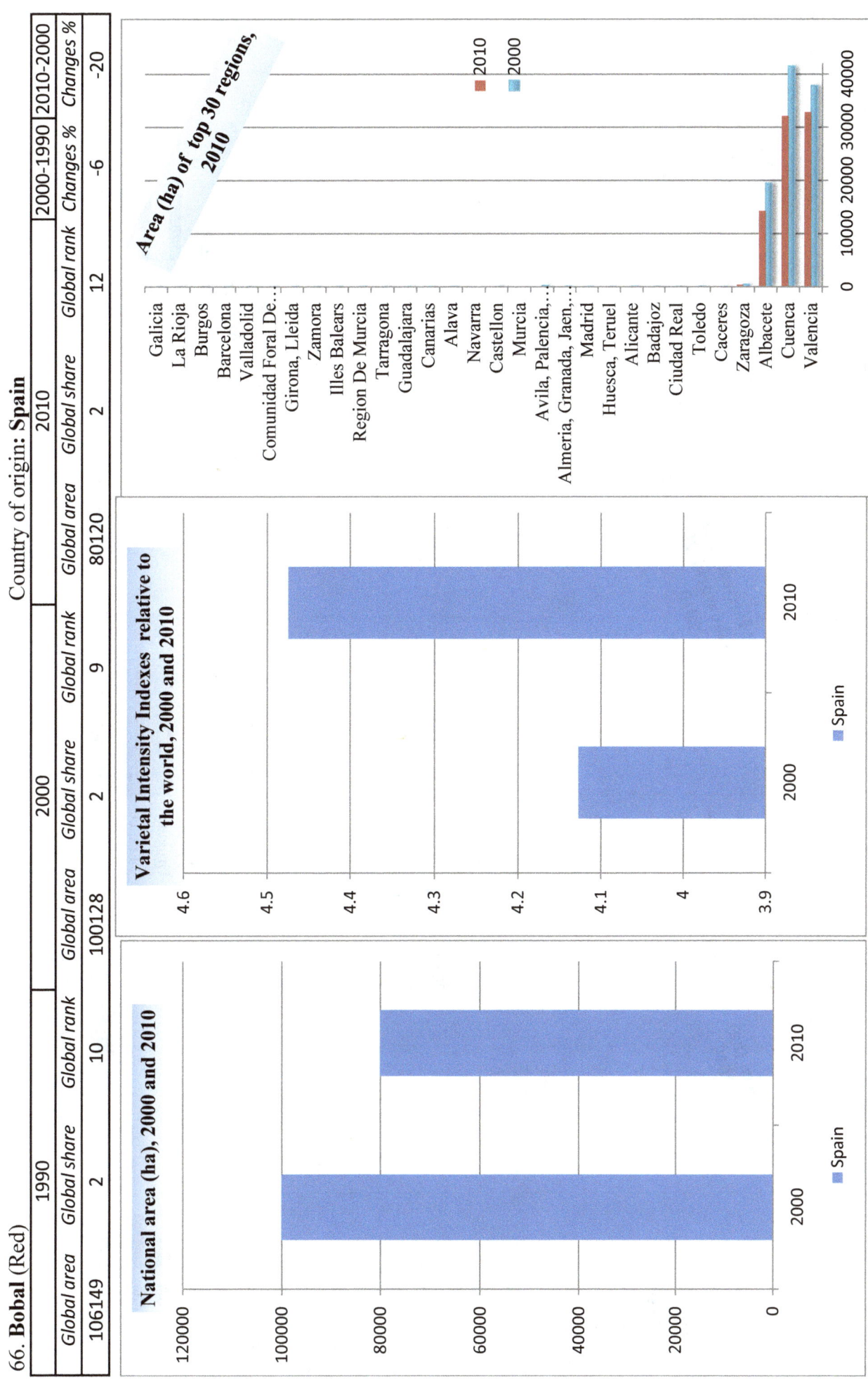

67. Cabernet Franc (Red)

Country of origin: **Spain**

	1990		2000			2010		2000-1990	2010-2000
	Global area	Global share	Global rank	Global area	Global share	Global rank	Global area	Global share	Global rank	Changes %	Changes %
	39619	0.7	32	48551	1.0	19	53599	1.2	17	23	10

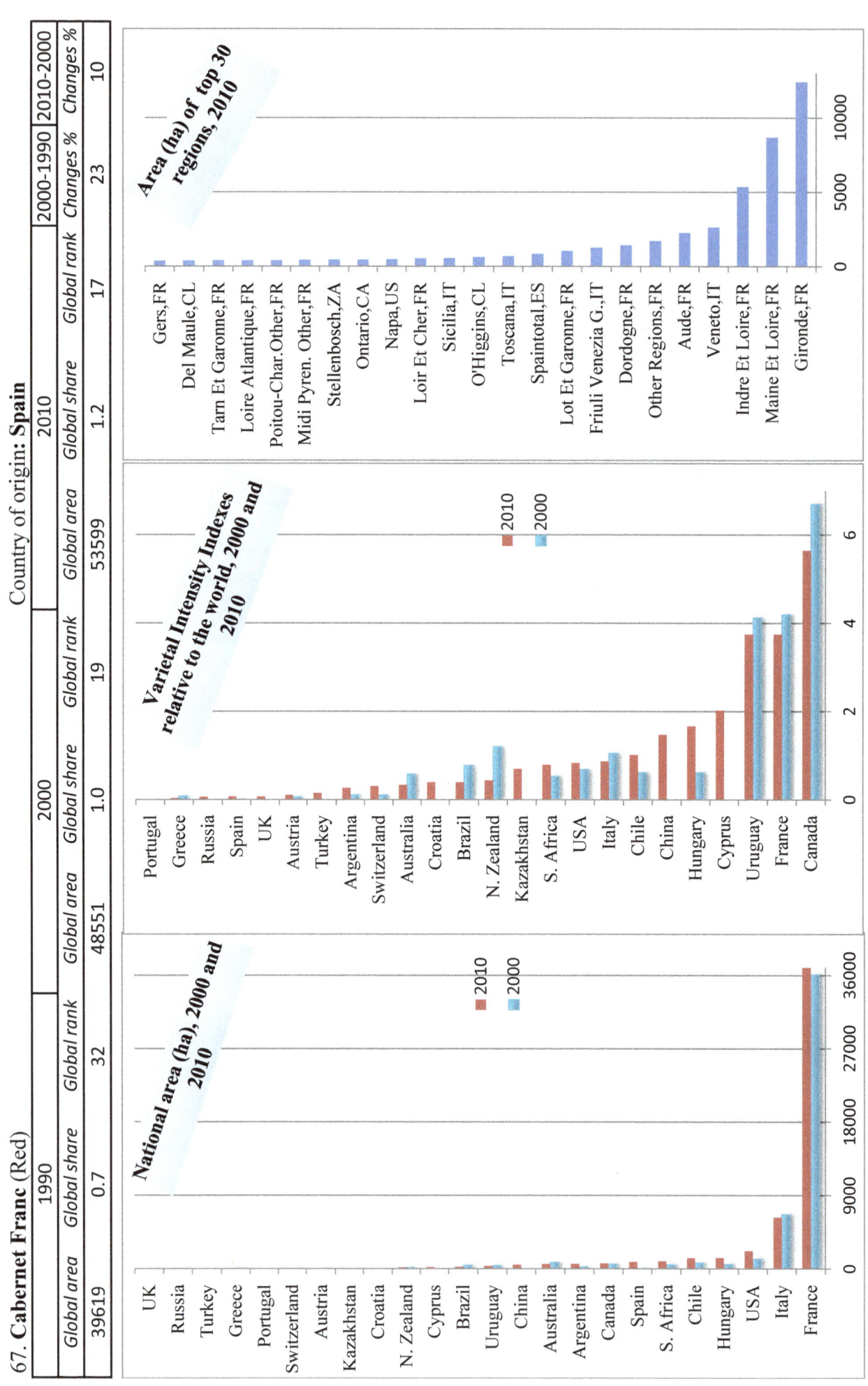

68. Cabernet Sauvignon (Red)

Country of origin: France

	1990			2000			2010			2000-1990	2010-2000
Global area	Global share	Global rank	Global area	Global share	Global rank	Global area	Global share	Global rank	Changes %	Changes %
127678	2	8	220890	5	2	290091	6	1	73	31

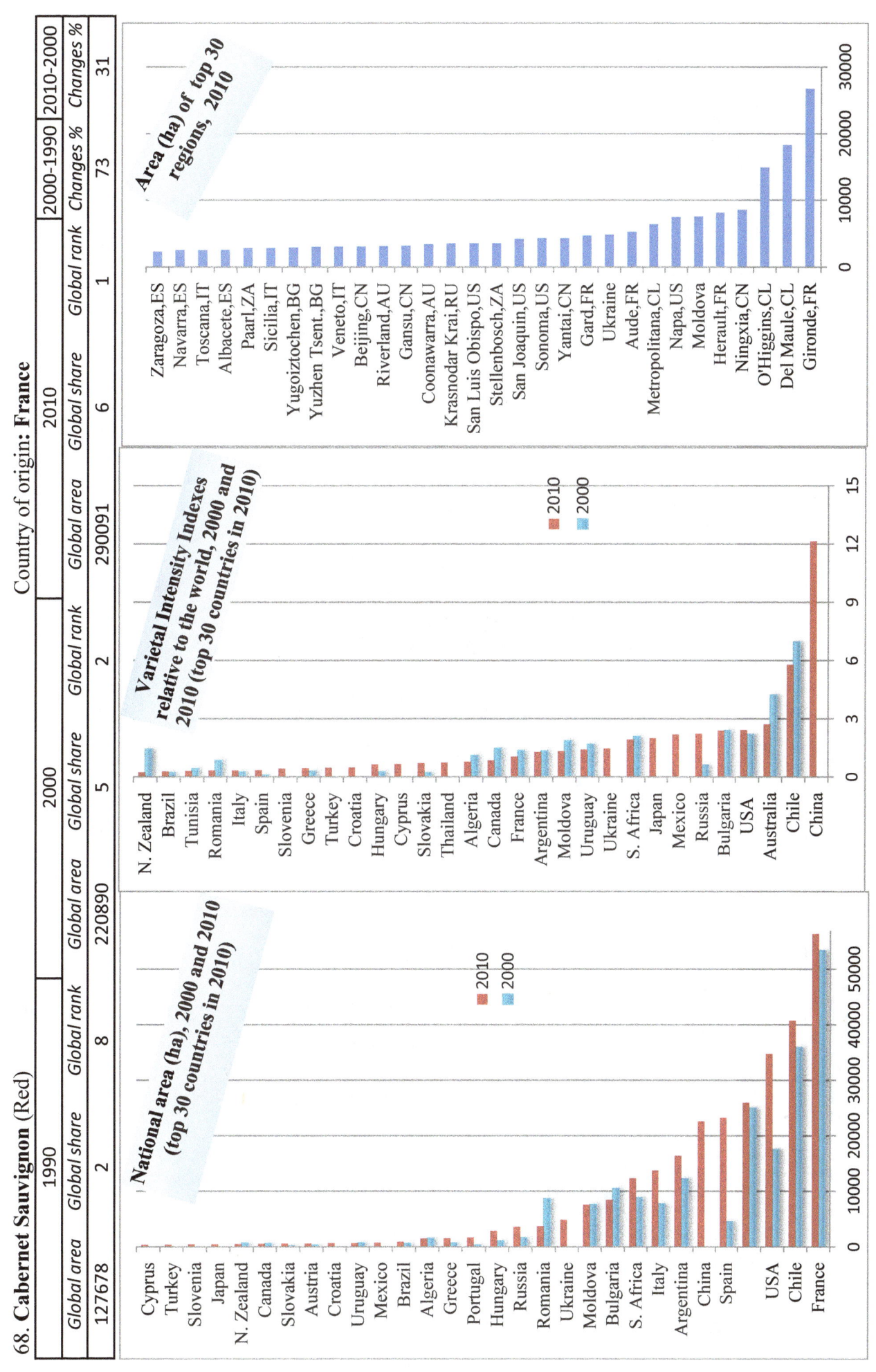

69. Catarratto Bianco (White)

Country of origin: Italy

	1990	2000			2010			2000-1990	2010-2000
Global area	Global share	Global area	Global rank	Global share	Global area	Global rank	Global share	Changes %	Changes %
80128	1.5	50711	12	1.0	34863	18	0.8	-37	-31

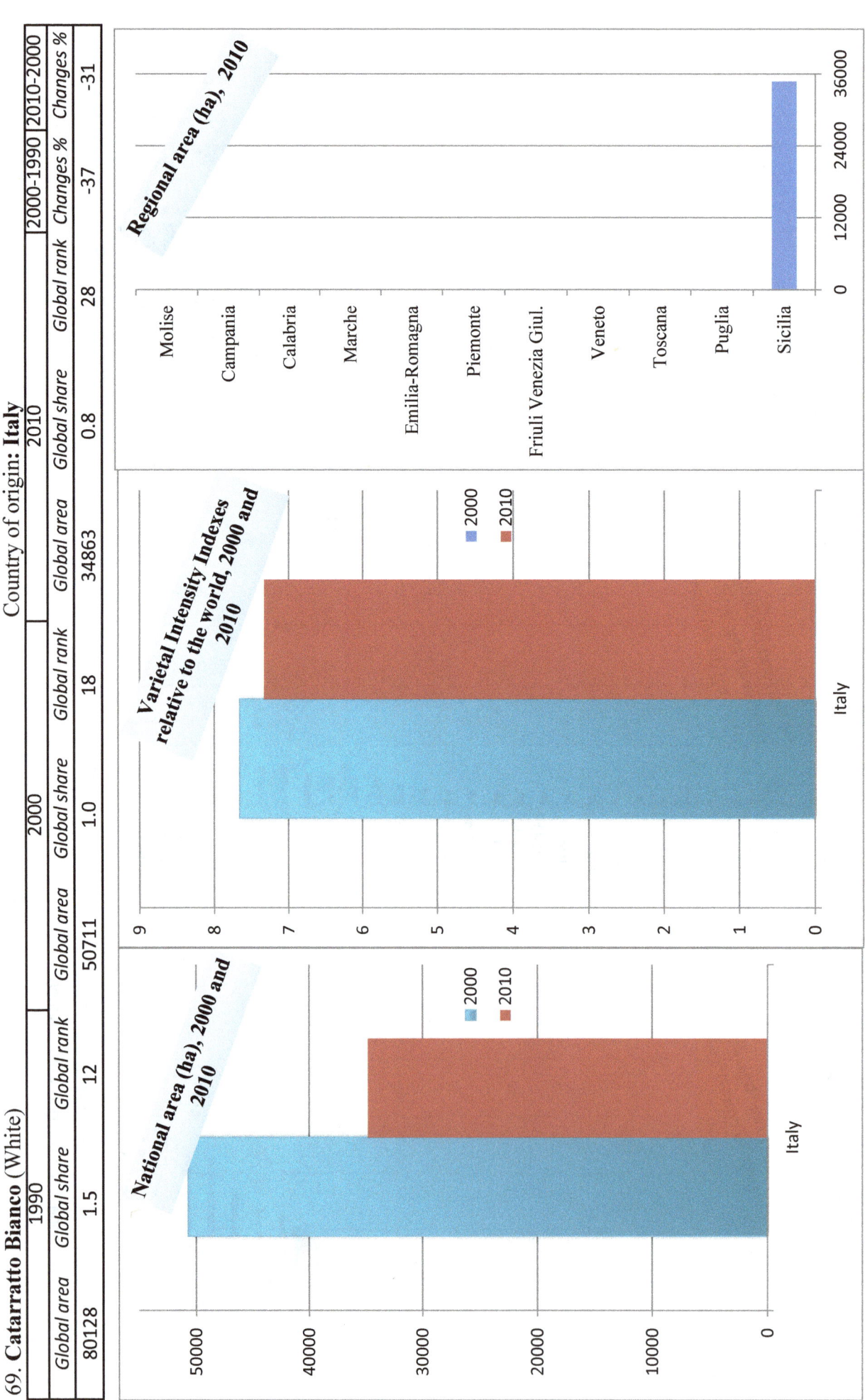

70. Cayetana Blanca (White)

Country of origin: **Spain**

	1990		2000			2010		2000-1990	2010-2000
Global area	Global share	Global rank	Global area	Global share	Global rank	Global area	Global share	Global rank	Changes %	Changes %
65276	1.2	16	55502	1.1	17	39741	0.9	22	-15	-28

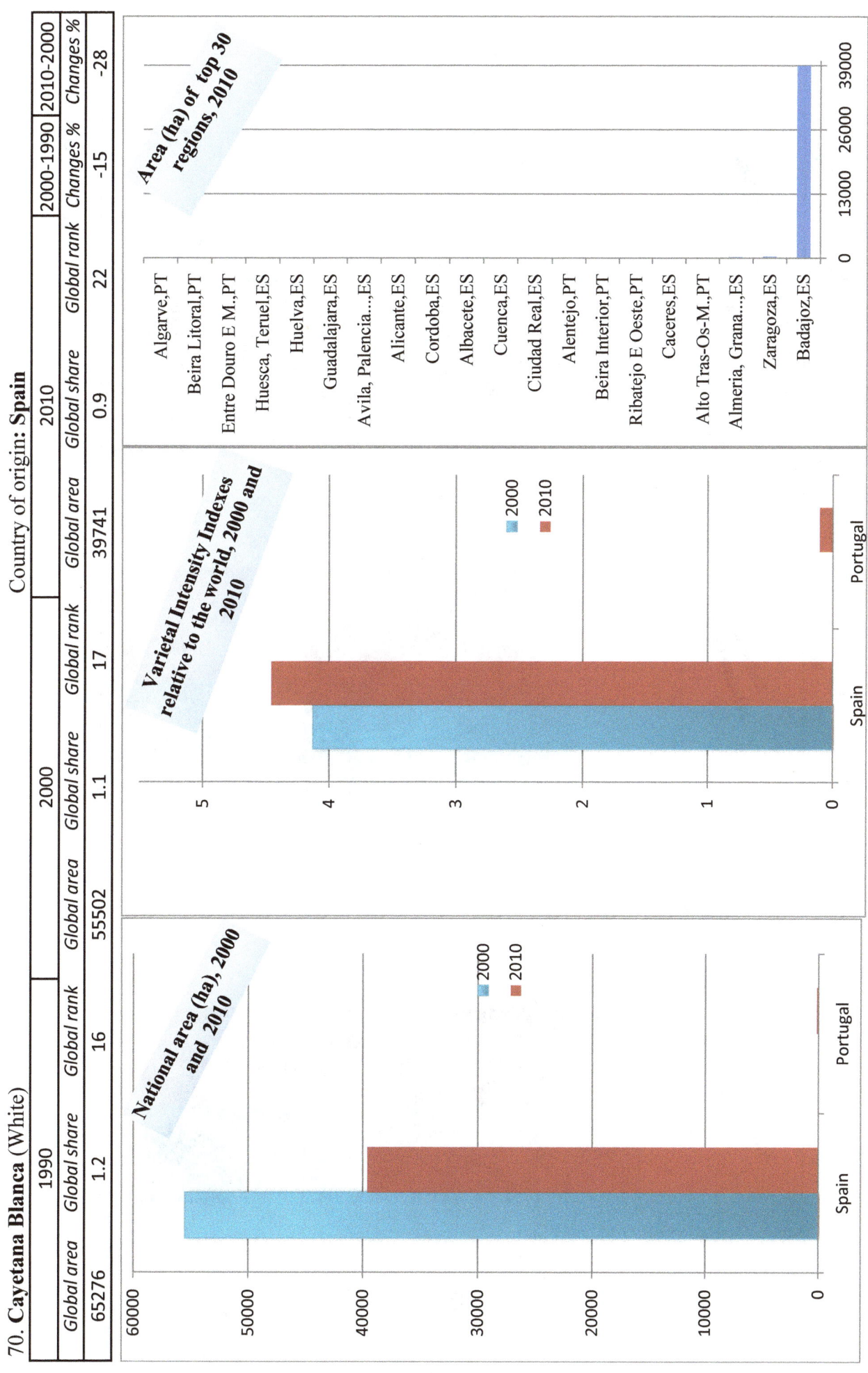

71. Cereza (Grey)

Country of origin: Argentina

	1990			2000			2010		2000-1990	2010-2000
Global area	Global share	Global rank	Global area	Global share	Global rank	Global area	Global share	Global rank	Changes %	Changes %
42937	0.8	27	31666	0.6	30	29189	0.6	34	-26	-8

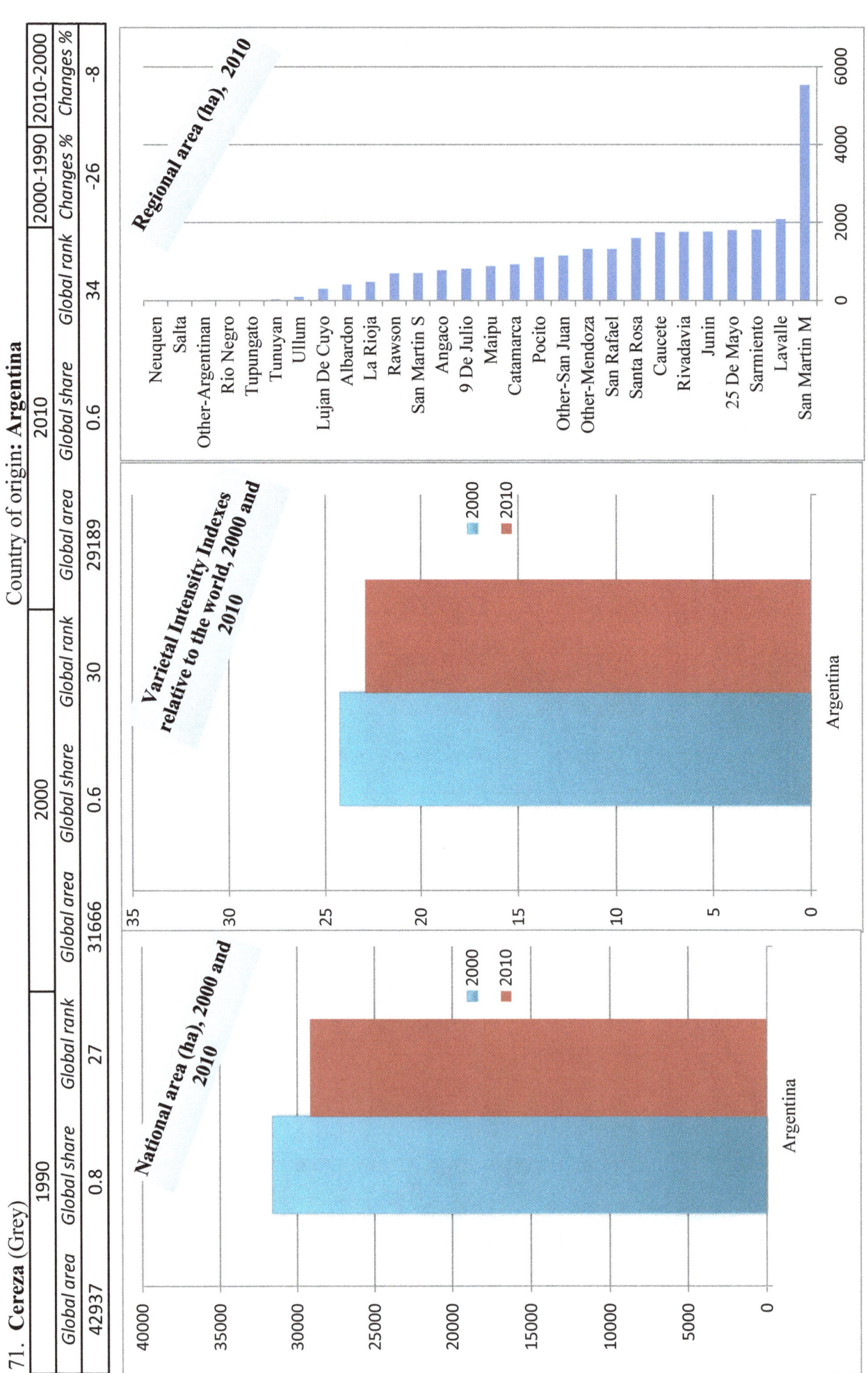

72. Chardonnay (White)

Country of origin: France

	1990		2000			2010		2000-1990	2010-2000
Global area	Global share	Global rank	Global area	Global share	Global rank	Global area	Global share	Global rank	Changes %	Changes %
69282	1	13	145344	3	5	198793	4	5	110	37

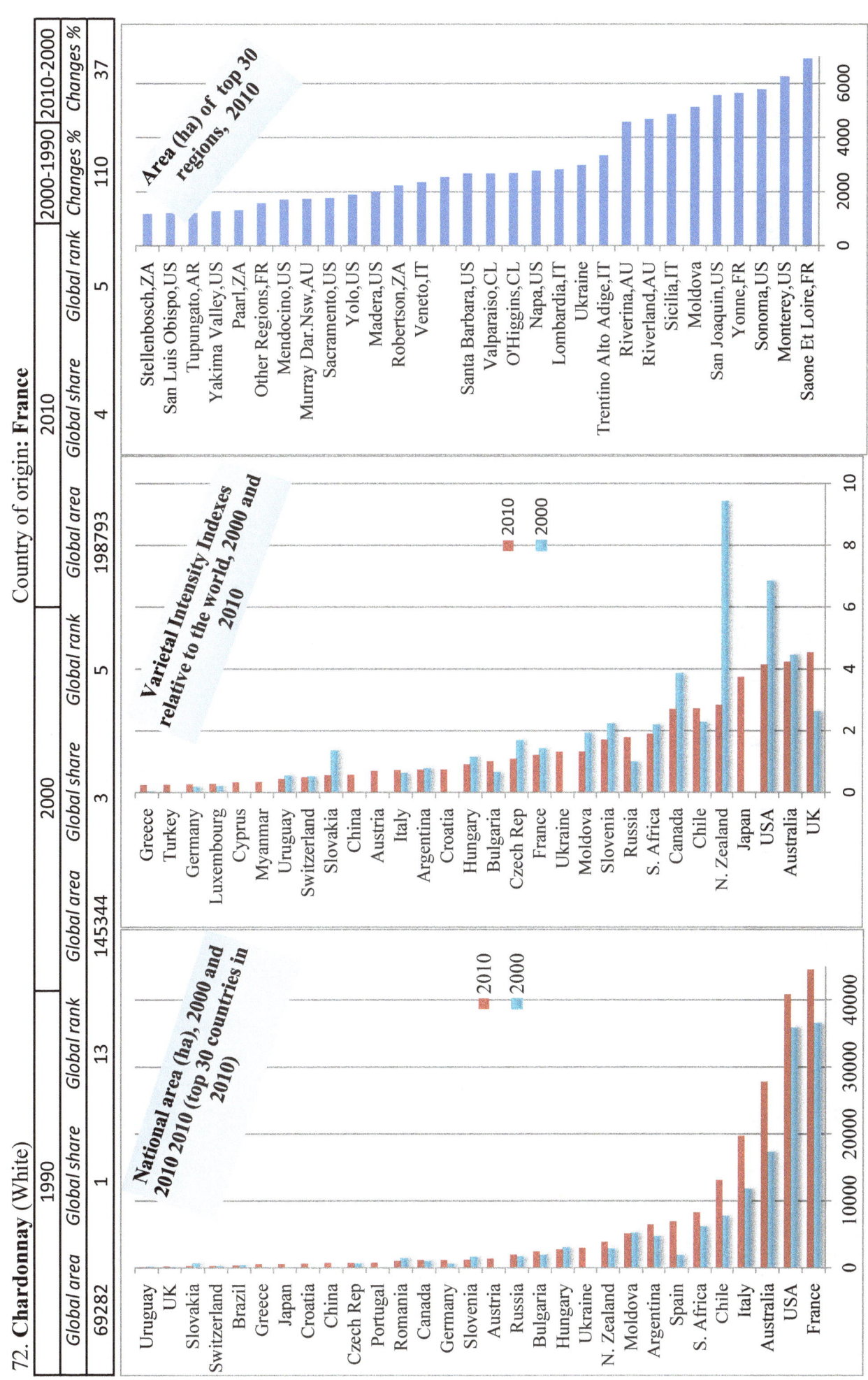

73. Chenin Blanc (White)

Country of origin: France

	1990			2000			2010		2000-1990	2010-2000
Global area	Global share	Global rank	Global area	Global share	Global rank	Global area	Global share	Global rank	Changes %	Changes %
59974	1.1		45806	0.9	19	35164	0.8	22	26	-24	-23

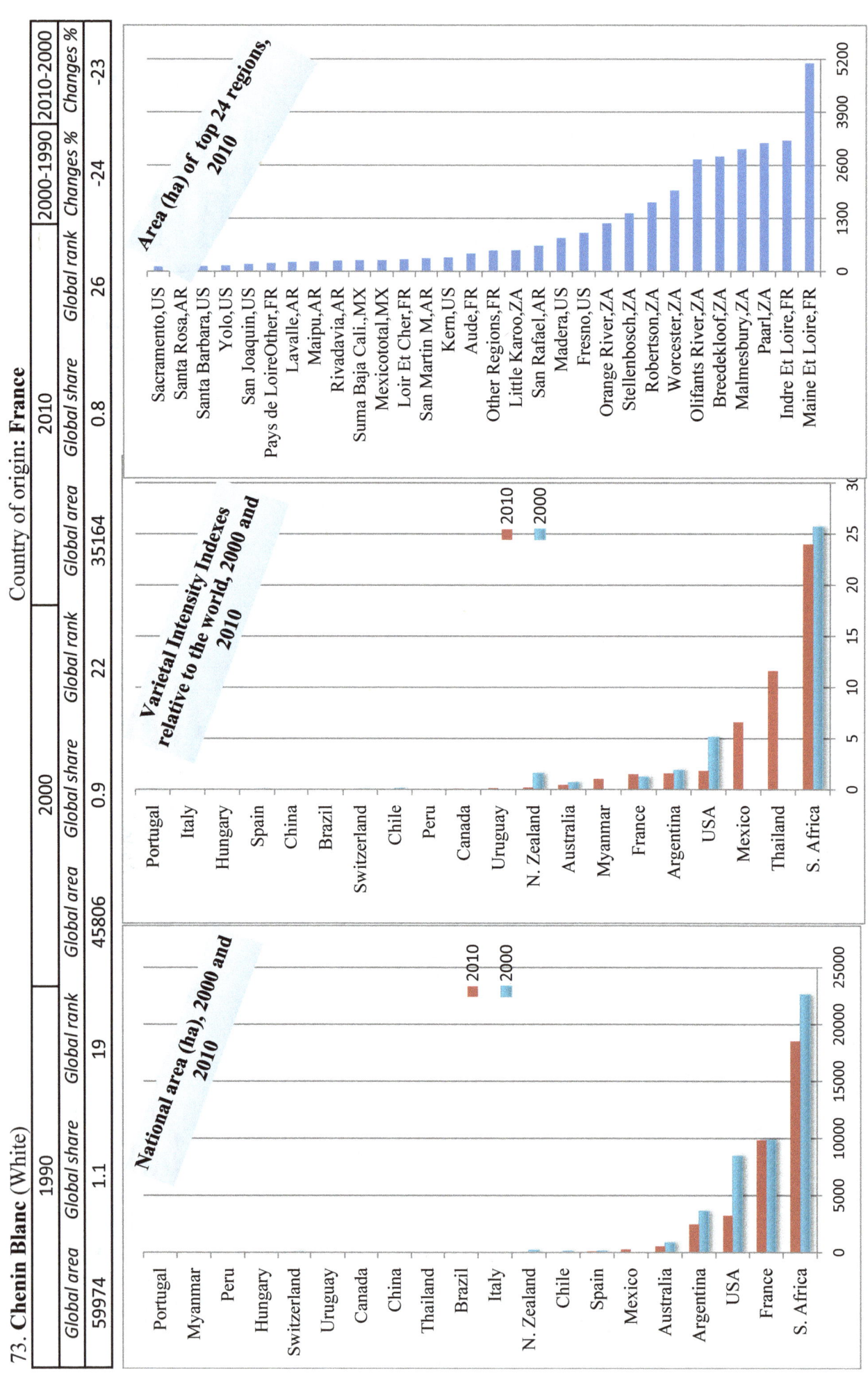

74. Cinsaut (Red)

Country of origin: France

	1990			2000			2010		2000-1990	2010-2000
	Global area	Global share	Global rank	Global area	Global share	Global rank	Global area	Global share	Global rank	Changes %	Changes %
	63171	1.2	18	48419	1.0	20	36040	0.8	25	-23	-26

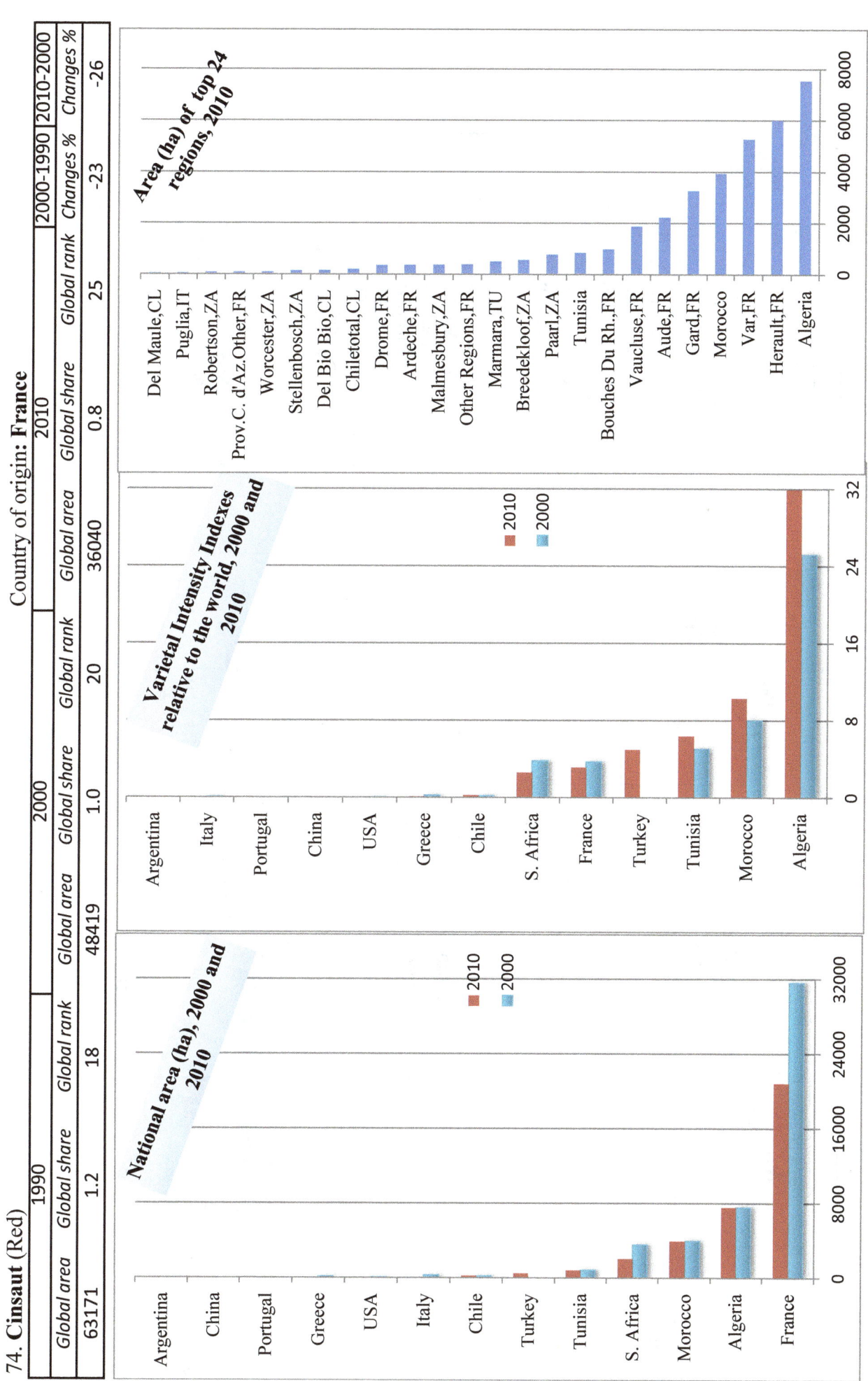

75. Colombard (White)

Country of origin: France

	1990		2000			2010			2000-1990	2010-2000
Global area	Global share	Global rank	Global area	Global share	Global rank	Global area	Global share	Global rank	Changes %	Changes %
36138	0.7	34	38146	0.8	24	32076	0.7	32	6	-16

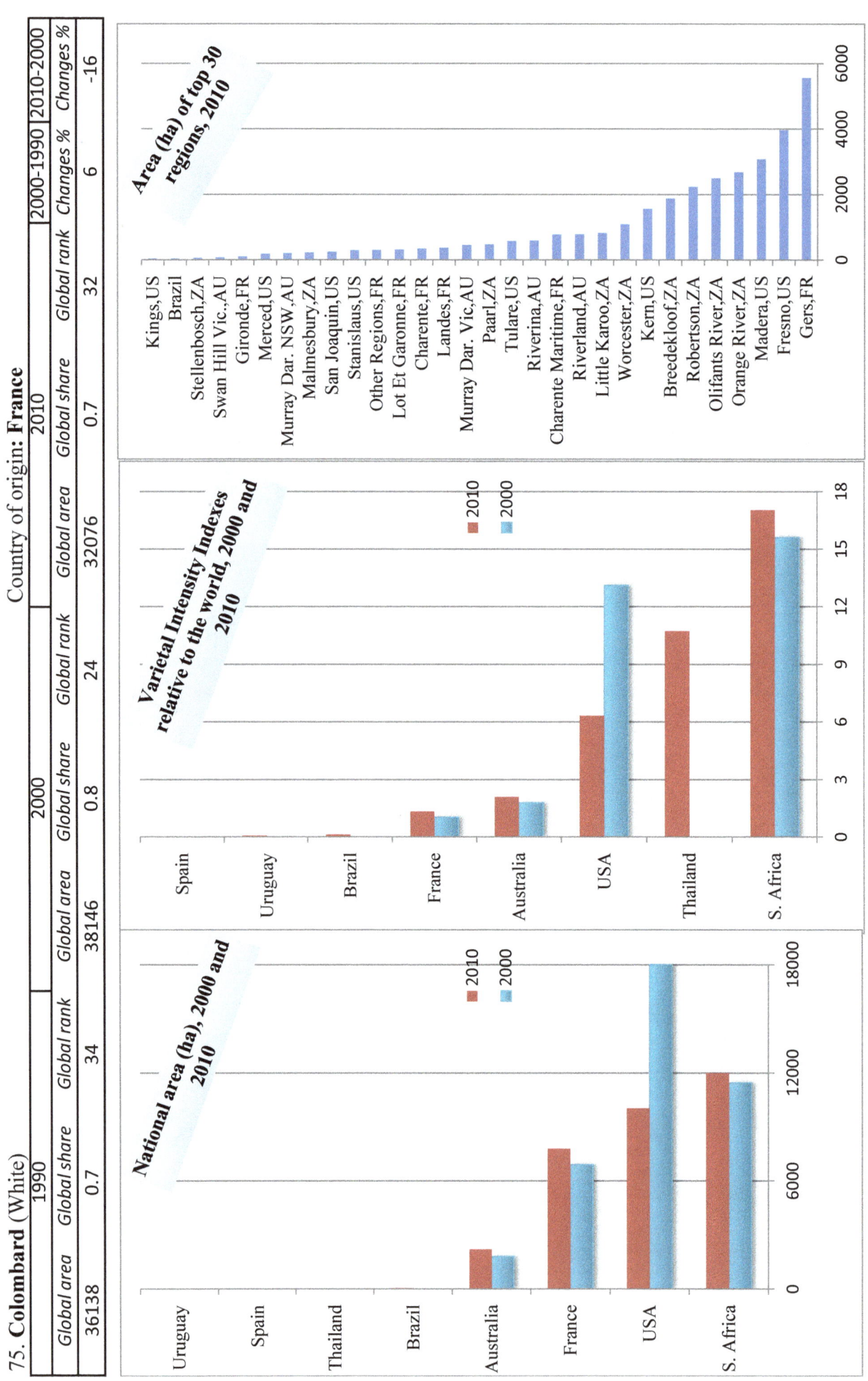

76. Cot (Red)

Country of origin: France

	1990			2000			2010		2000-1990	2010-2000
Global area	Global share	Global rank	Global area	Global share	Global rank	Global area	Global share	Global rank	Changes %	Changes %
16997	0.3	52	24402	0.5	39	40688	0.9	21	44	67

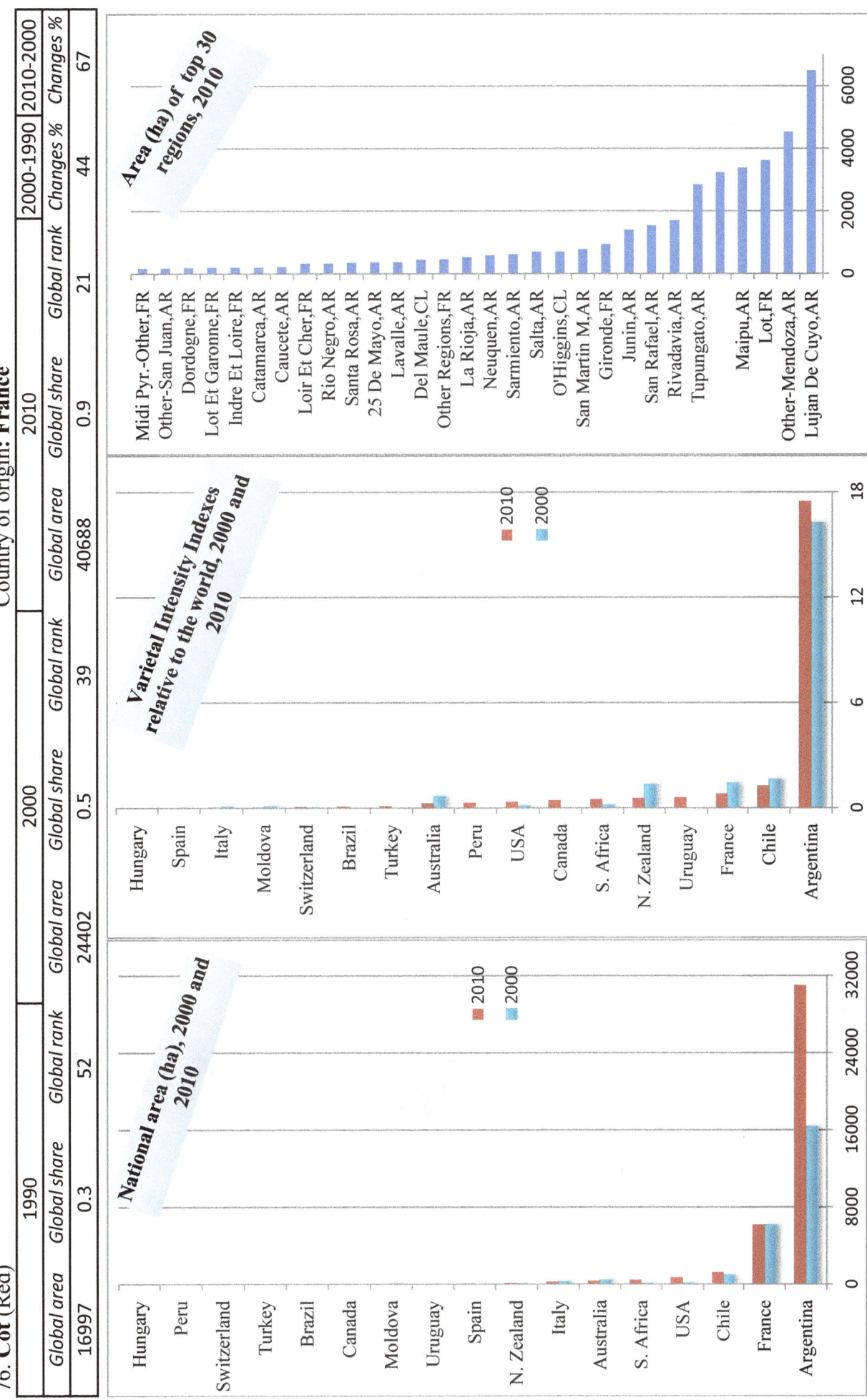

77. Criolla Grande (Red)

Country of origin: Argentina

	1990			2000			2010		2000-1990	2010-2000
Global area	Global share	Global rank	Global area	Global share	Global rank	Global area	Global share	Global rank	Changes %	Changes %
68513	1.3	14	24641	0.5	38	17080	0.4	44	-64	-31

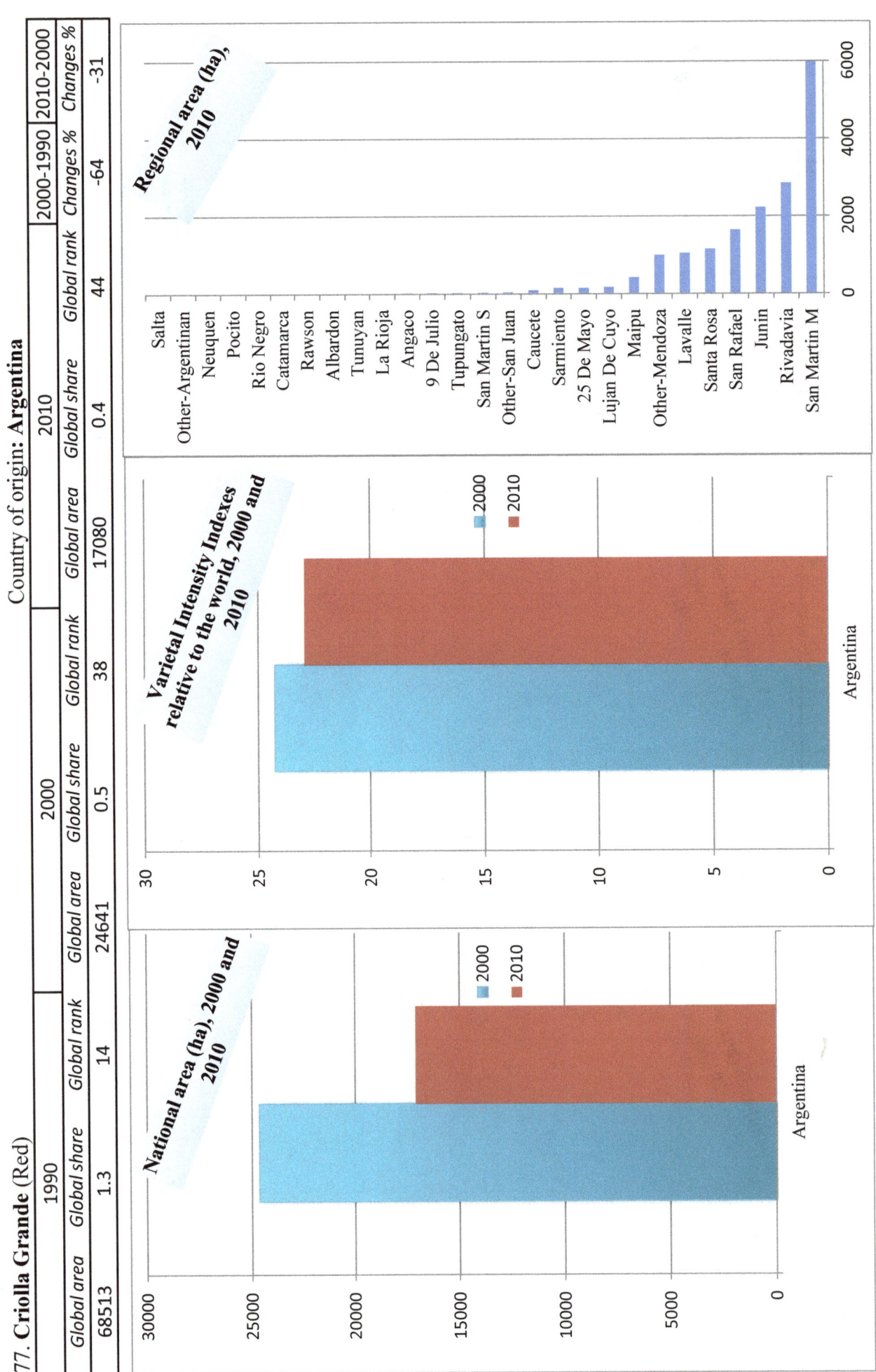

78. Douce Noire (White)

Country of origin: **France**

	1990		2000			2010		2000-1990	2010-2000
Global area	Global share	Global area	Global rank	Global share	Global area	Global rank	Global share	Changes %	Changes %
		17653	45	0.4	18976	40	0.4		7

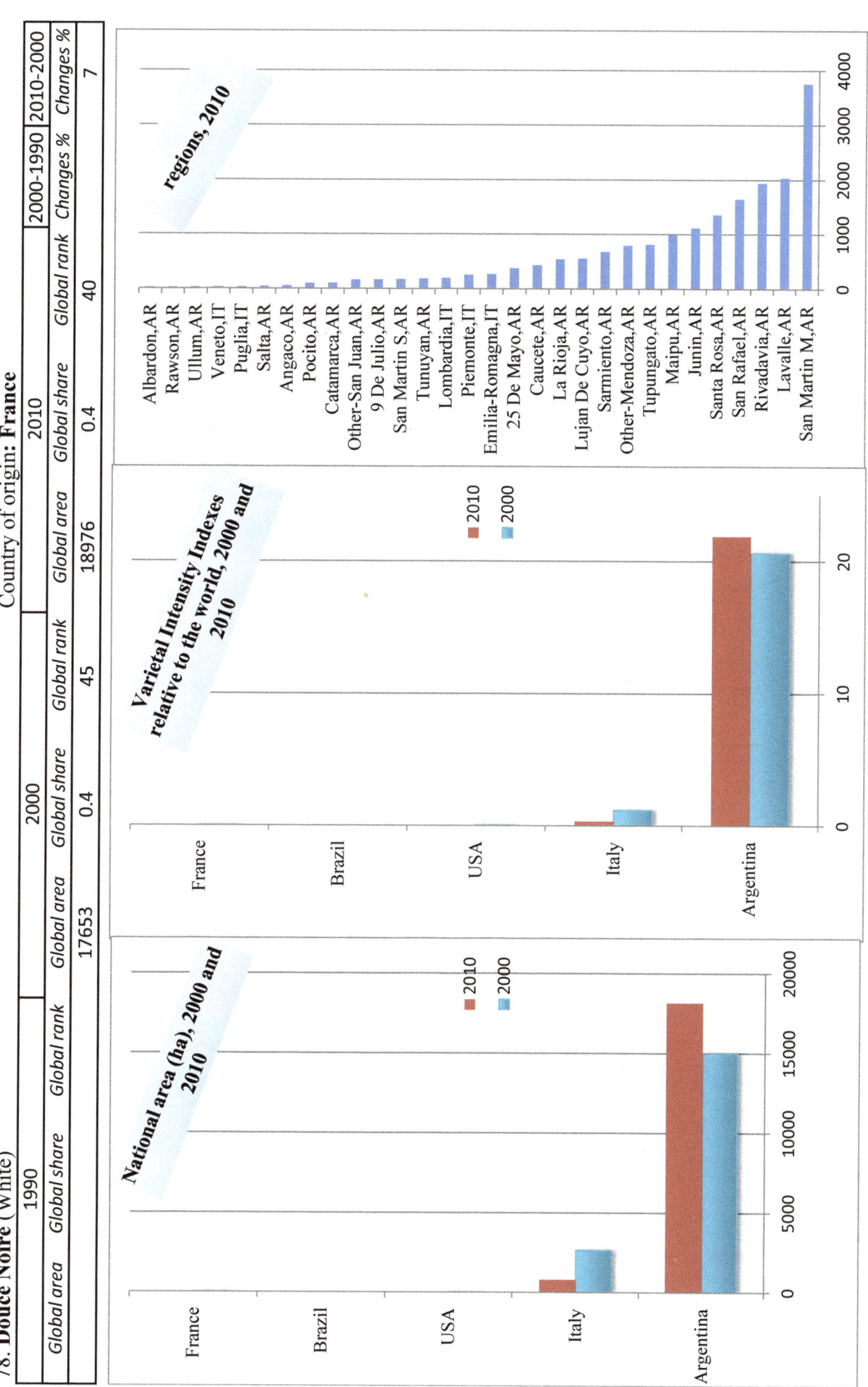

National area (ha), 2000 and 2010

Varietal Intensity Indexes relative to the world, 2000 and 2010

regions, 2010

79. Doukkali (Red)

	1990	2000			2010			2000-1990	2010-2000
Global area	Global share	Global area	Global share	Global rank	Global area	Global share	Global rank	Changes %	Changes %
na		16557	0.3	49	16557	0.4	47		0

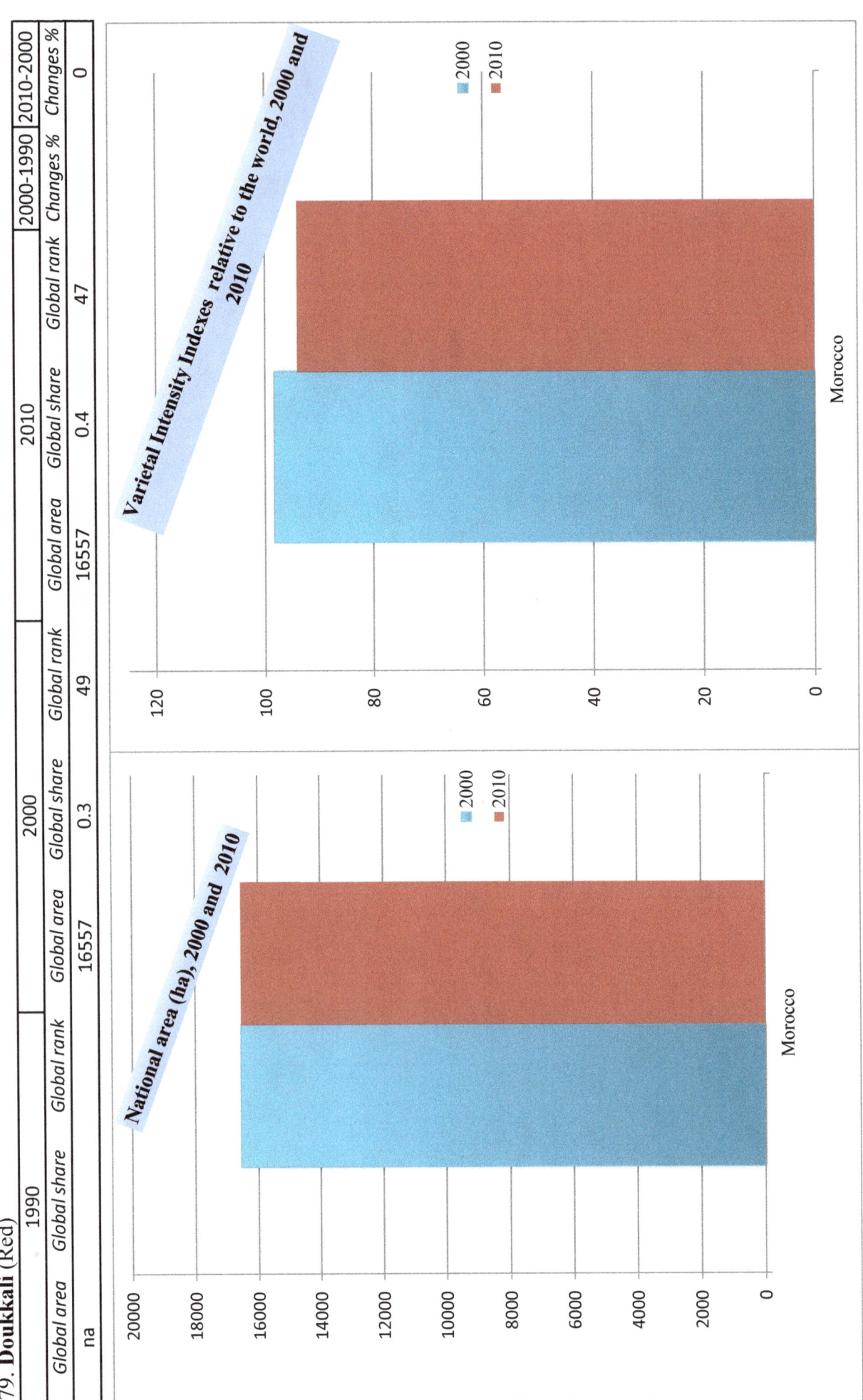

80. Feteasca Alba (White)

Country of origin: **Moldova**

	1990			2000			2010		2000-1990	2010-2000
Global area	Global share	Global rank	Global area	Global share	Global rank	Global area	Global share	Global rank	Changes %	Changes %
18373	0.3	49	23828	0.5	40	17469	0.4	43	30	-27

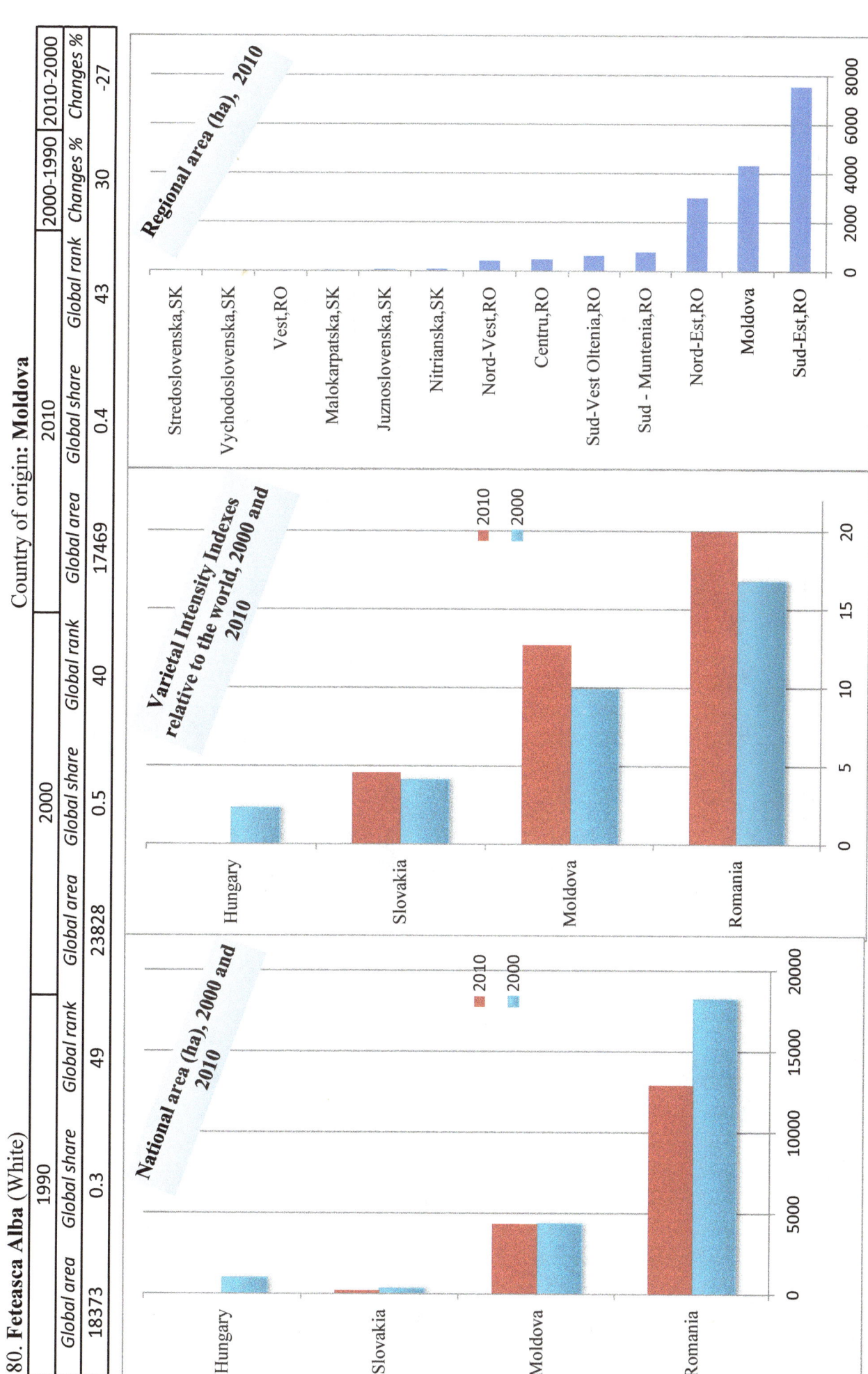

81. Gamay Noir (Red)

Country of origin: France

	1990		2000			2010			2000-1990	2010-2000
Global area	Global share	Global rank	Global area	Global share	Global rank	Global area	Global share	Global rank	Changes %	Changes %
35005	0.7	36	37796	0.8	25	32671	0.7	30	8	-14

National area (ha), 2000 and 2010

Varietal Intensity Indexes relative to the world, 2000 and 2010

Area (ha) of top 30 regions, 2010

82. Garganega (White)

Country of origin: **Italy**

	1990			2000			2010		2000-1990	2010-2000
Global area	Global share	Global rank	Global area	Global share	Global rank	Global area	Global share	Global rank	Changes %	Changes %
na			16549	0.3	50	15402	0.3	50		-7

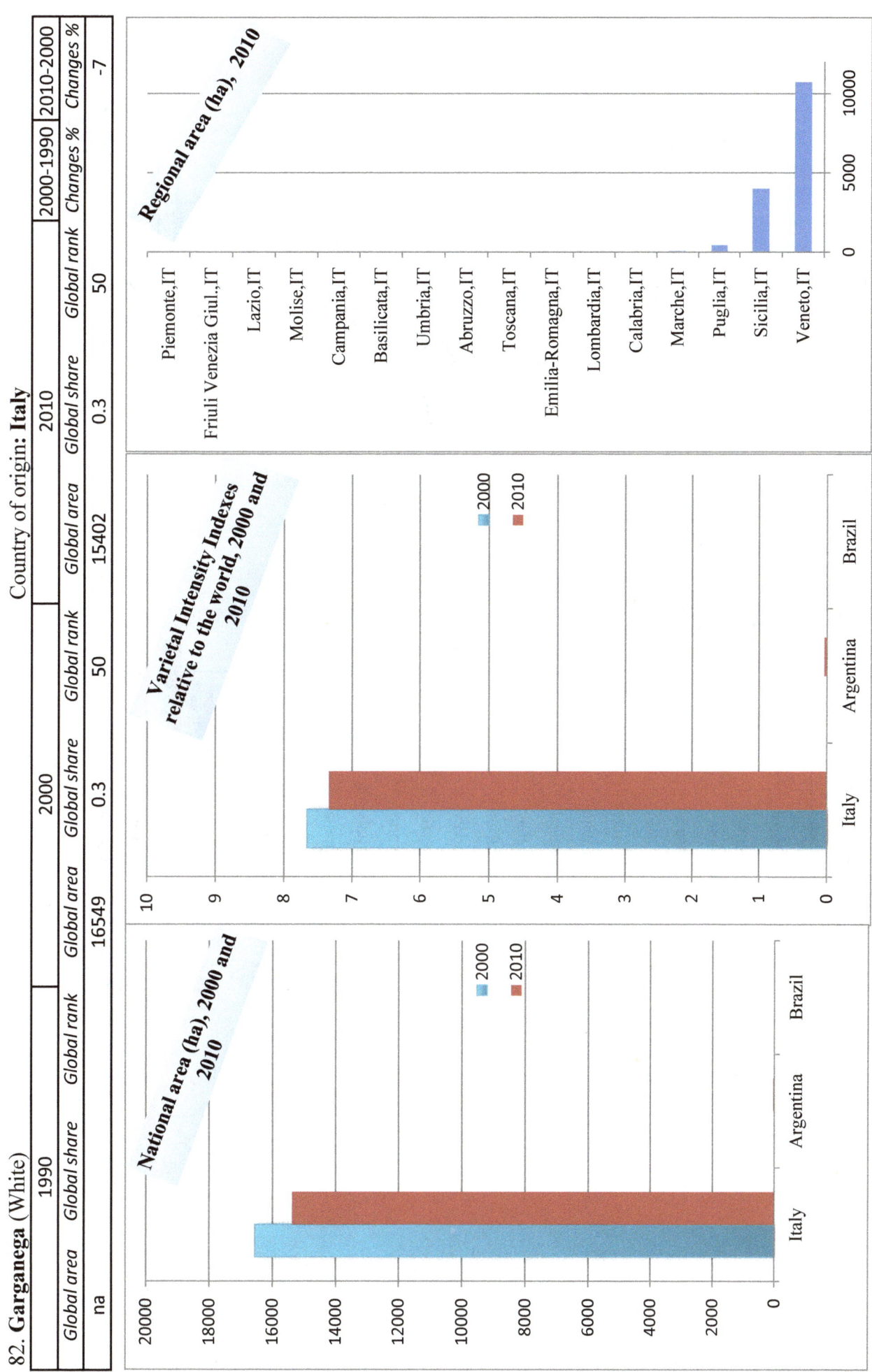

83. Garnacha Tinta (Red)

Country of origin: **Spain**

	1990			2000			2010		2000-1990	2010-2000
	Global area	Global share	Global rank	Global area	Global share	Global rank	Global area	Global share	Global rank	Changes %	Changes %
	282997	5	2	213987	4	3	184735	4	7	-24	-14

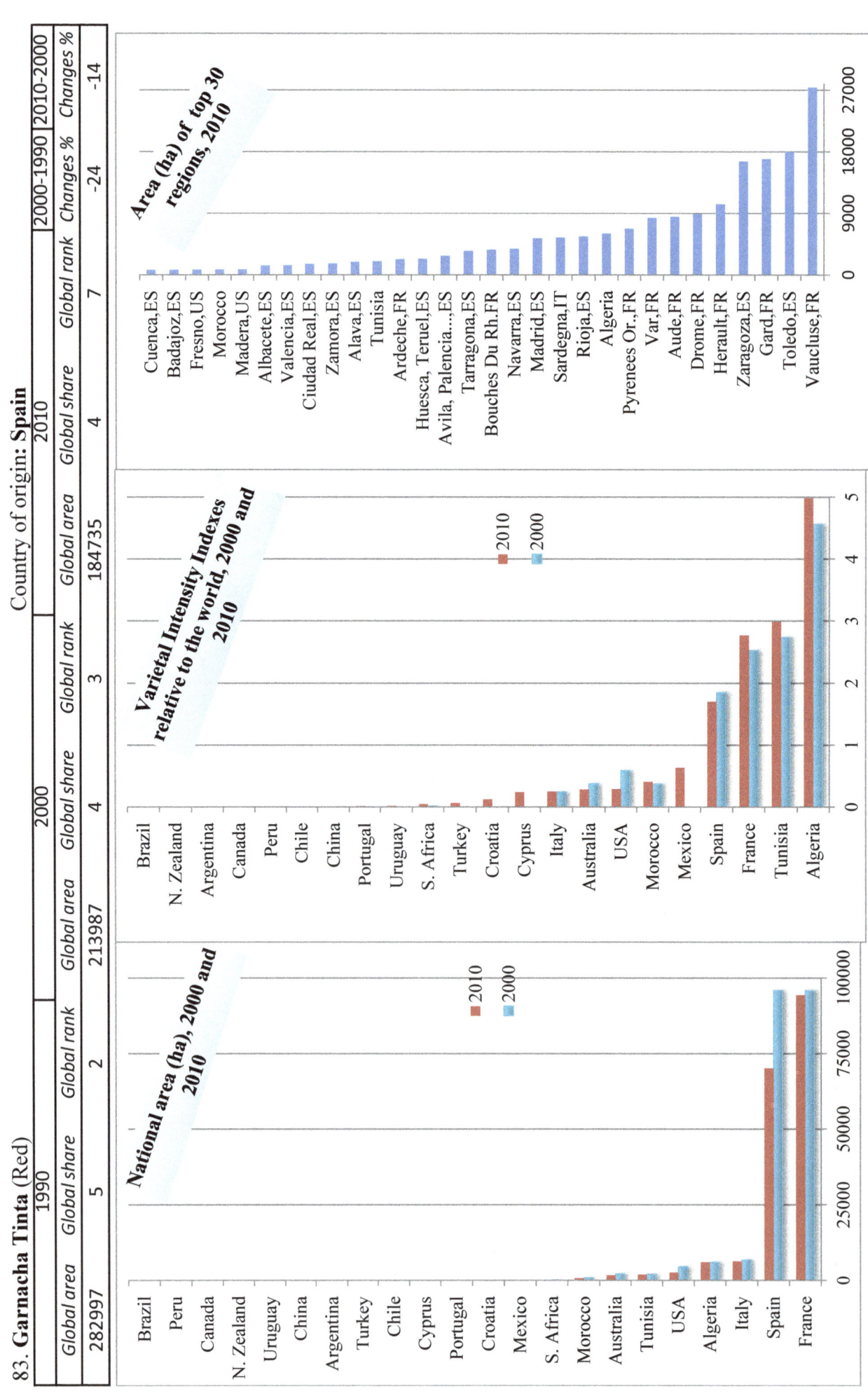

84. Graševina (White)

Country of origin: Croatia

	1990			2000			2010		2000-1990	2010-2000
Global area	Global share		Global area	Global share	Global rank	Global area	Global share	Global rank	Changes %	Changes %
19384	0.4		92306	1.9	48	61200	1.3	15	376	-34

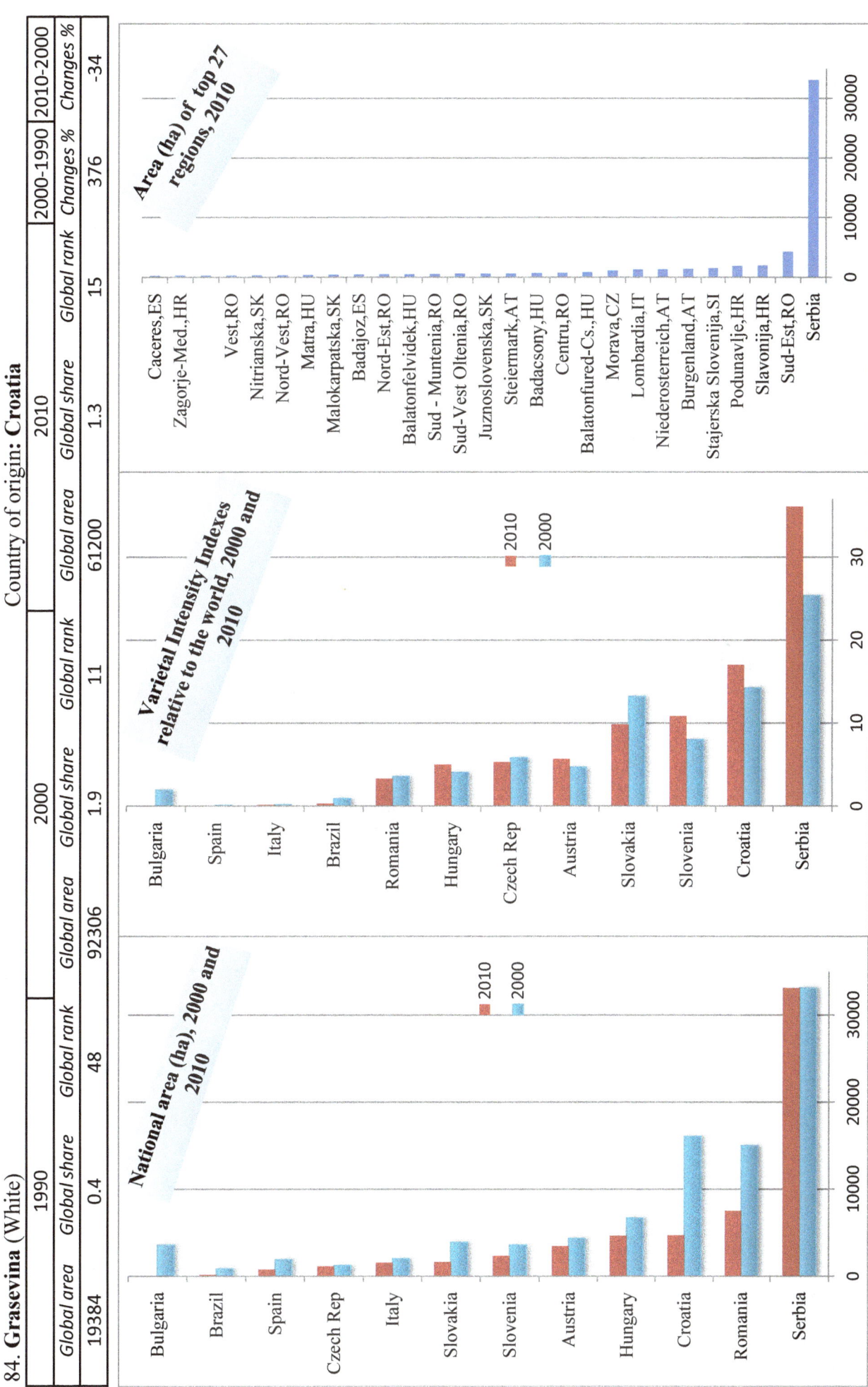

85. Gruner Veltliner (White)

Country of origin: Austria

	1990			2000			2010		2000-1990	2010-2000
	Global area	Global share	Global rank	Global area	Global share	Global rank	Global area	Global share	Global rank	Changes %	Changes %
	20760	0.4	43	23604	0.5	41	18842	0.4	41	14	-20

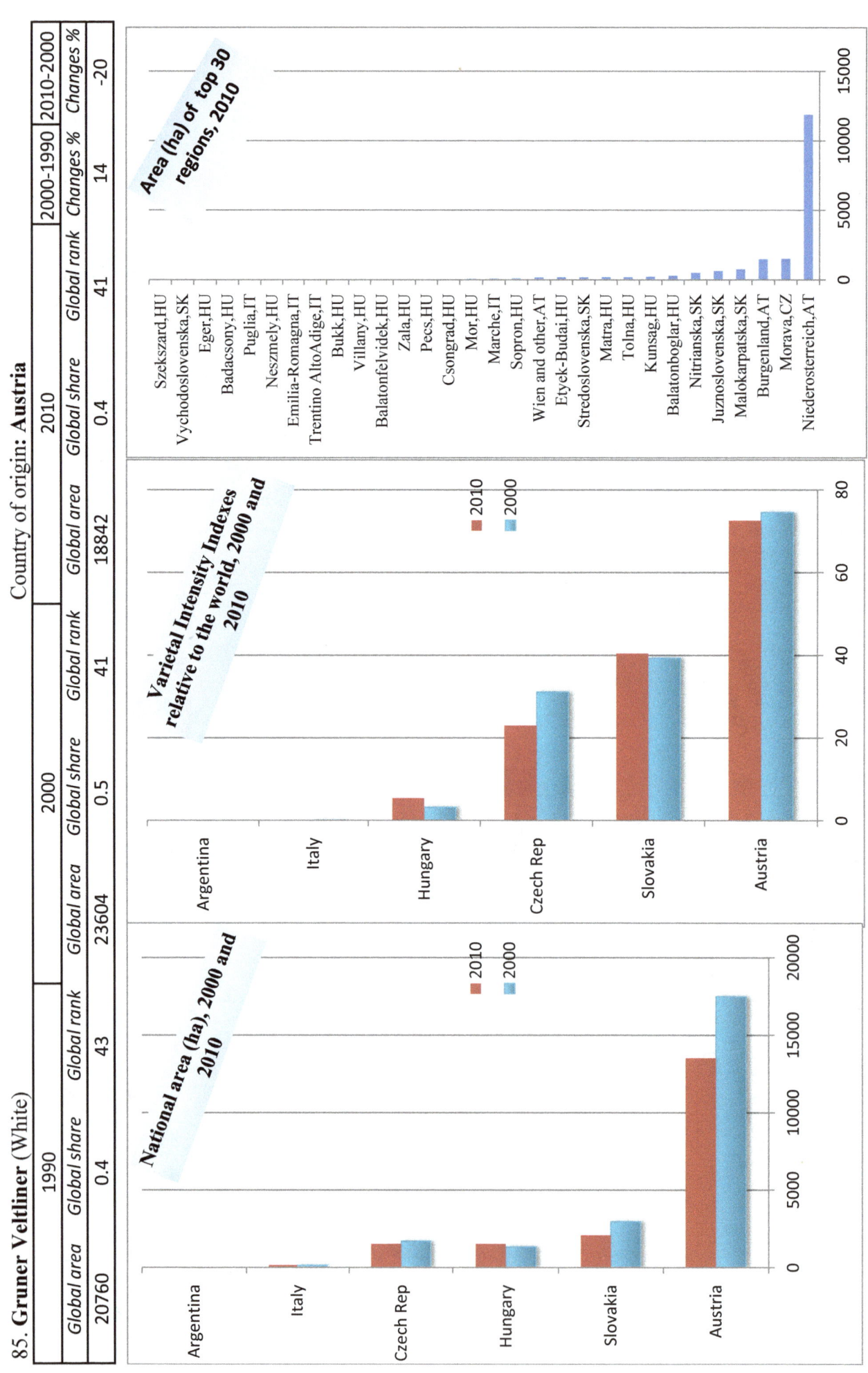

86. Isabella (Red)

Country of origin: **United States**

	1990			2000			2010			2000-1990	2010-2000
Global area	Global share	Global rank	Global area	Global share	Global rank	Global area	Global share	Global rank	Changes %	Changes %
21003	0.4	42	27376	0.6	35	32494	0.7	31	30	19

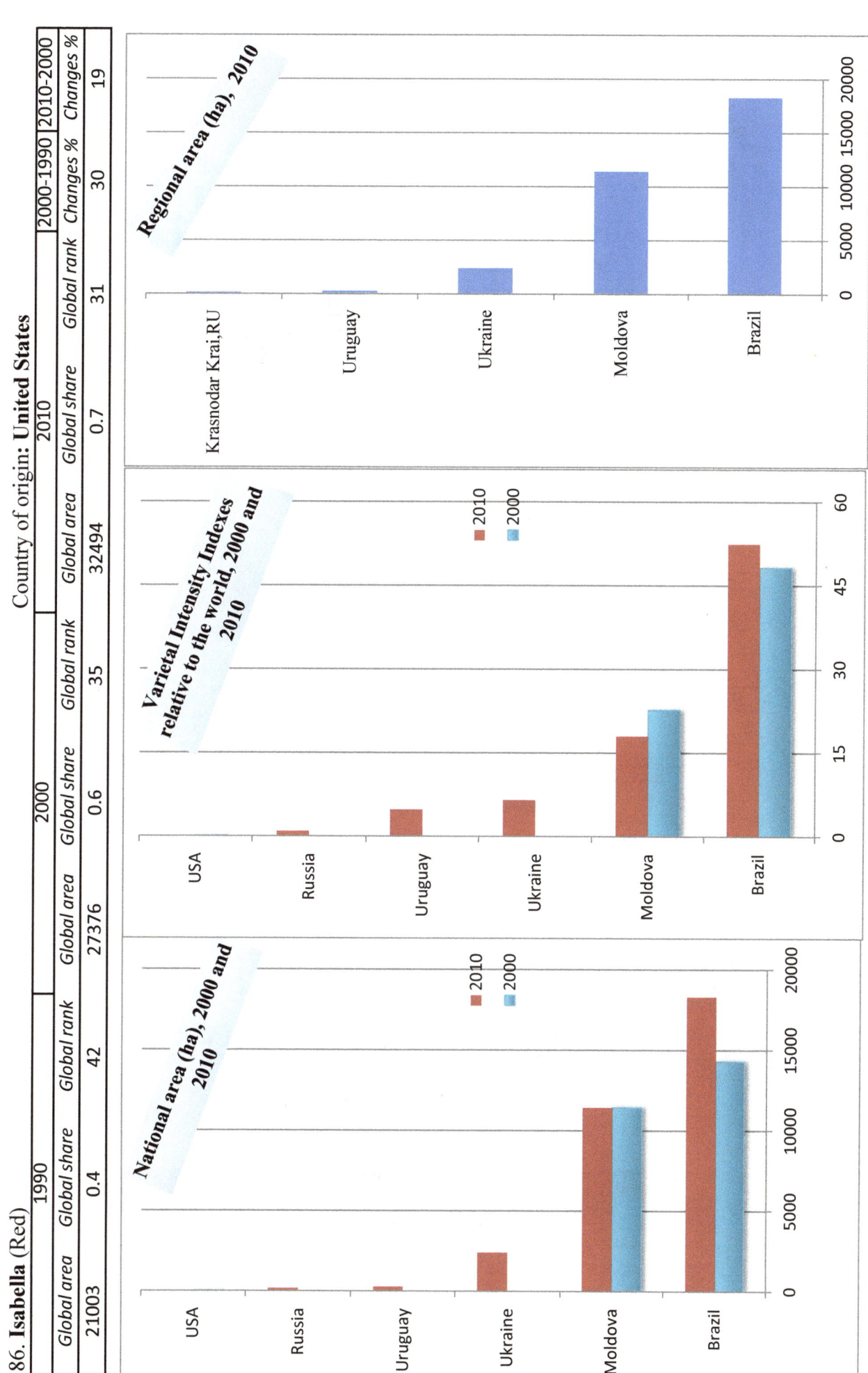

87. Macabeo (White)

Country of origin: **Spain**

	1990		2000			2010			2000-1990	2010-2000
Global area	Global share	Global area	Global share	Global rank	Global area	Global share	Global rank	Changes %	Changes %
43504	0.8	48125	1.0	21	41046	0.9	20	11	-15

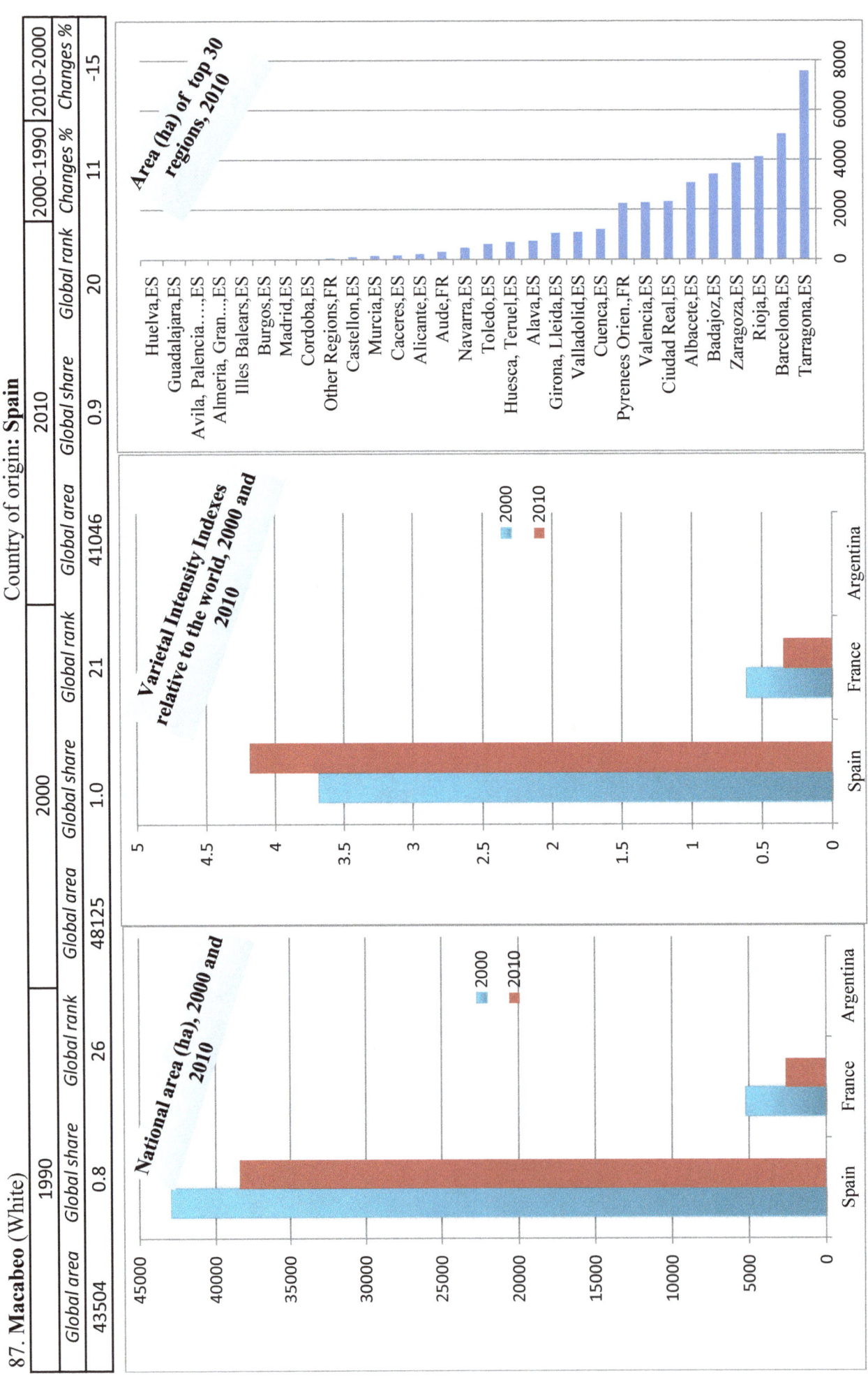

88. Merlot (Red)

Country of origin: France

	1990			2000			2010		2000-1990	2010-2000
	Global area	Global share	Global rank	Global area	Global share	Global rank	Global area	Global share	Global rank	Changes %	Changes %
	154752	3	7	211967	4	4	267169	6	2	37	26

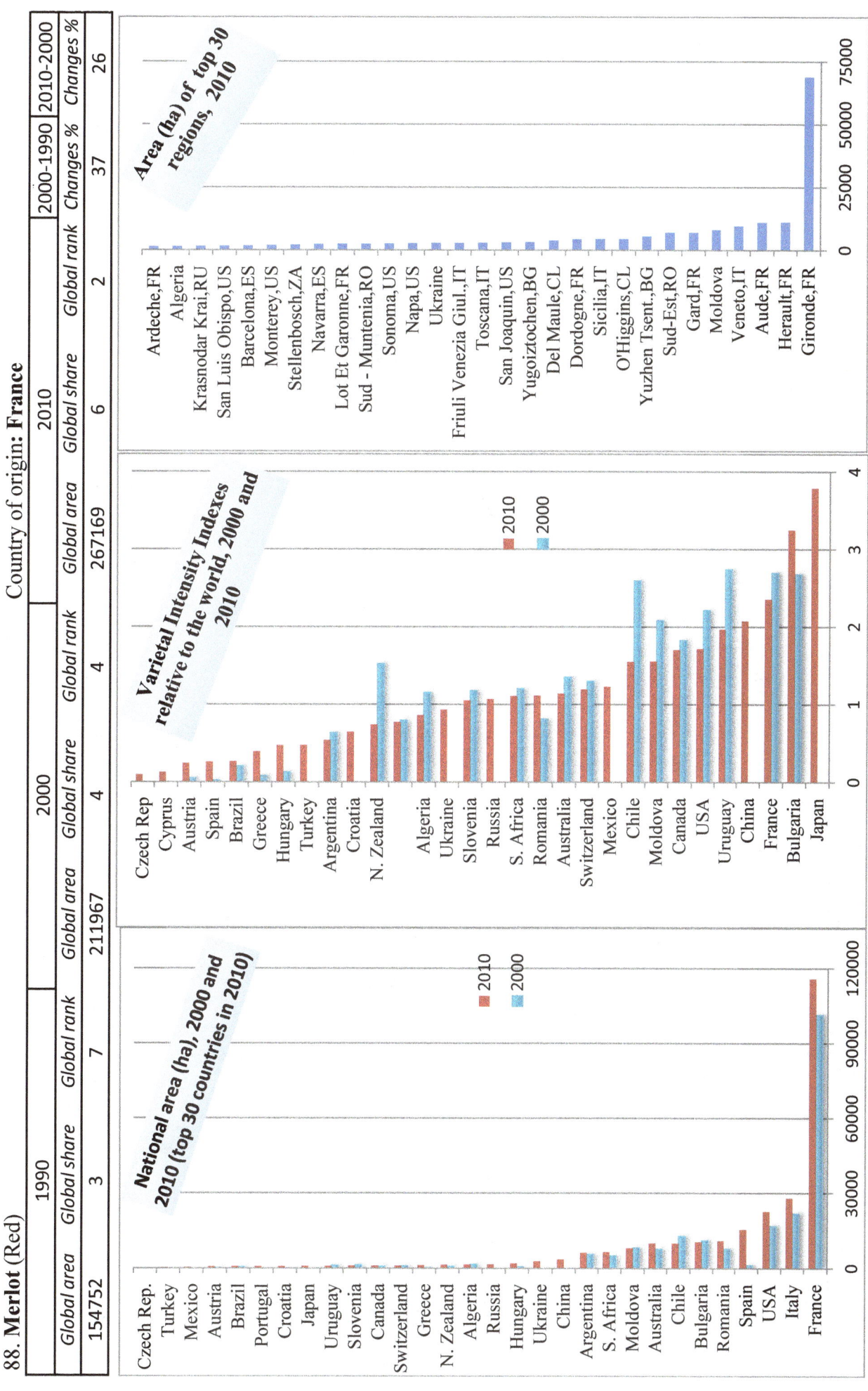

89. Mazuelo (Red)

Country of origin: **Spain**

	1990		2000			2010		2000-1990	2010-2000
Global area	Global share	Global rank	Global area	Global share	Global rank	Global area	Global share	Global rank	Changes %	Changes %
202869	4	6	126650	3	7	80178	2	11	-38	-37

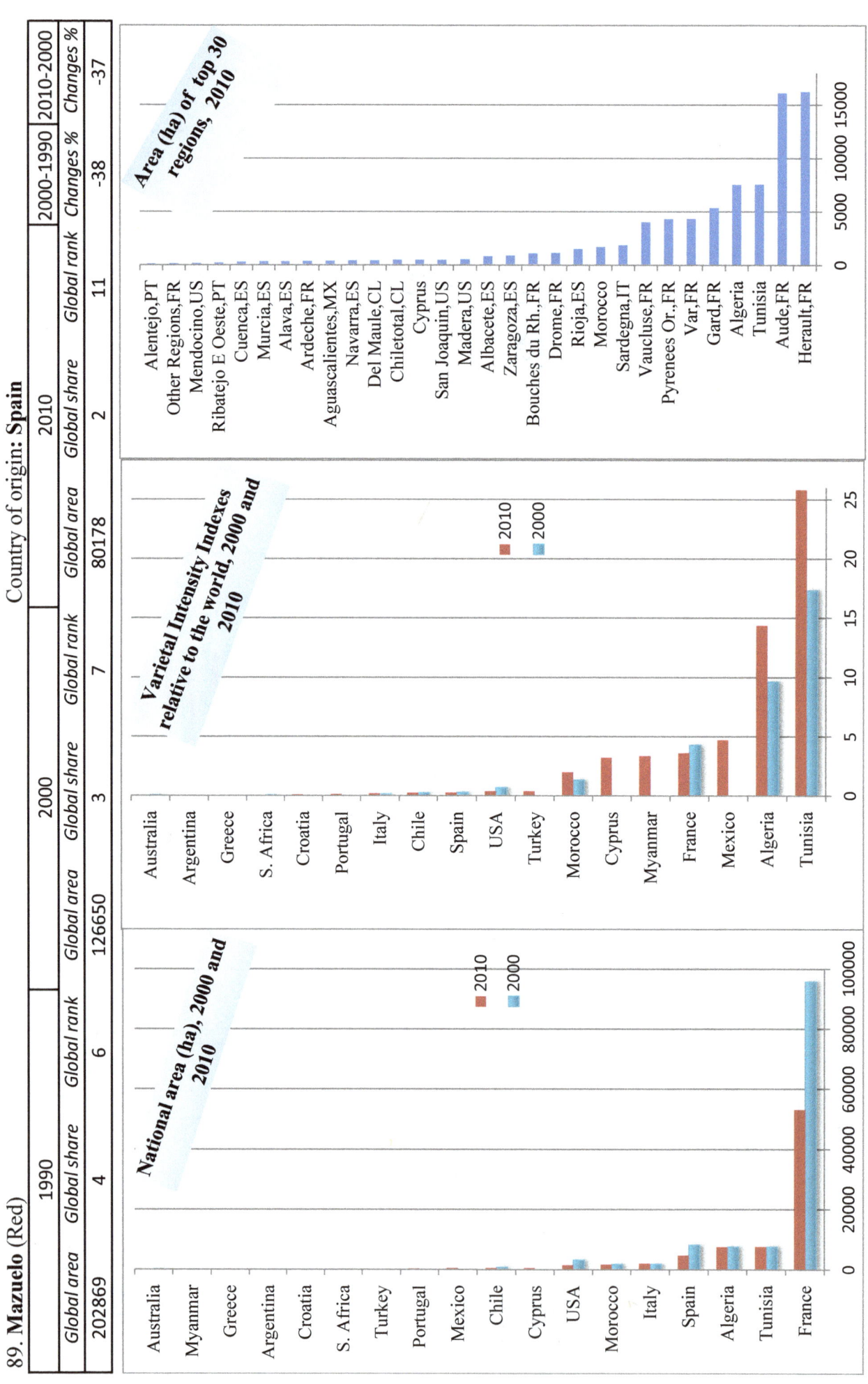

90. Monastrell (Red)

Country of origin: **Spain**

	1990			2000			2010		2000-1990	2010-2000
Global area	Global share	Global rank	Global area	Global share	Global rank	Global area	Global share	Global rank	Changes %	Changes %
108213	2		76304	2	9	69850	2	14	-29	-8

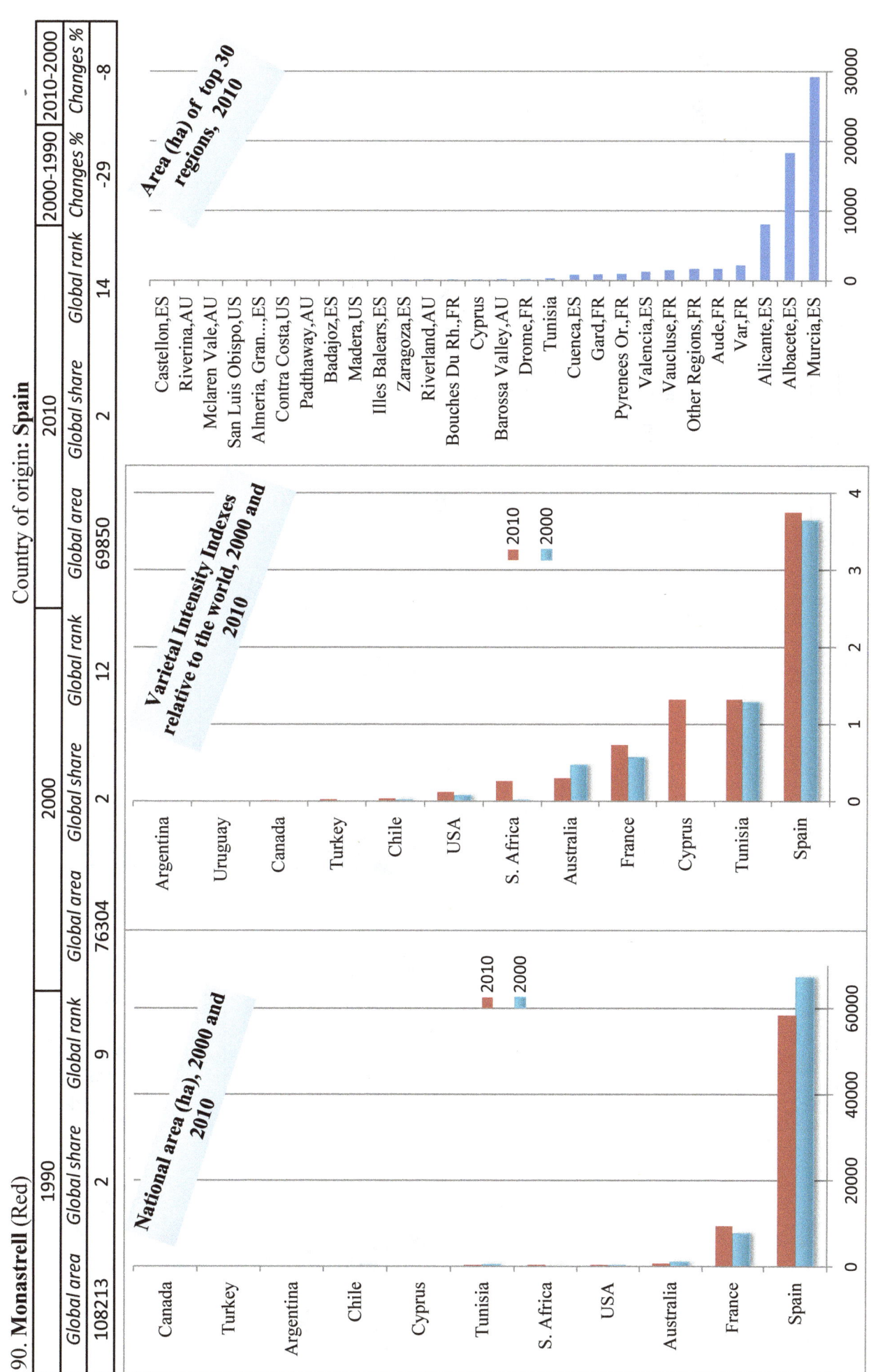

91. Montepulciano (Red)

Country of origin: Italy

	1990		2000			2010			2000-1990	2010-2000
	Global area	Global share	Global area	Global share	Global rank	Global area	Global share	Global rank	Changes %	Changes %
	32982	0.6	28679	0.6	37	34947	0.8	33	-13	22

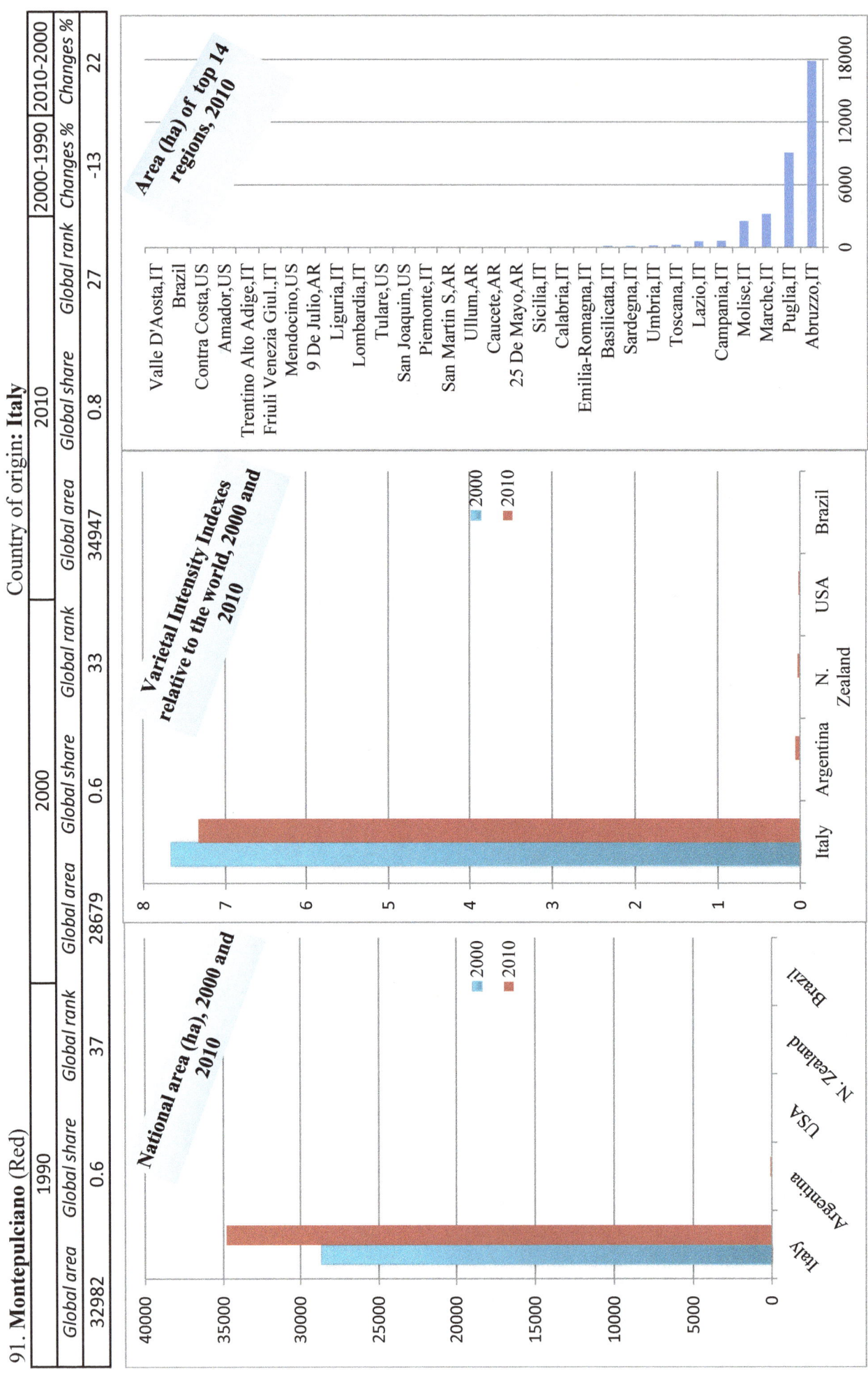

92. Müller Thurgau (White)

Country of origin: Germany

	1990			2000			2010		2000-1990	2010-2000
	Global area	Global share	Global rank	Global area	Global share	Global rank	Global area	Global share	Global rank	Changes %	Changes %
	36381	0.7	33	33572	0.7	28	22753	0.5	37	-8	-32

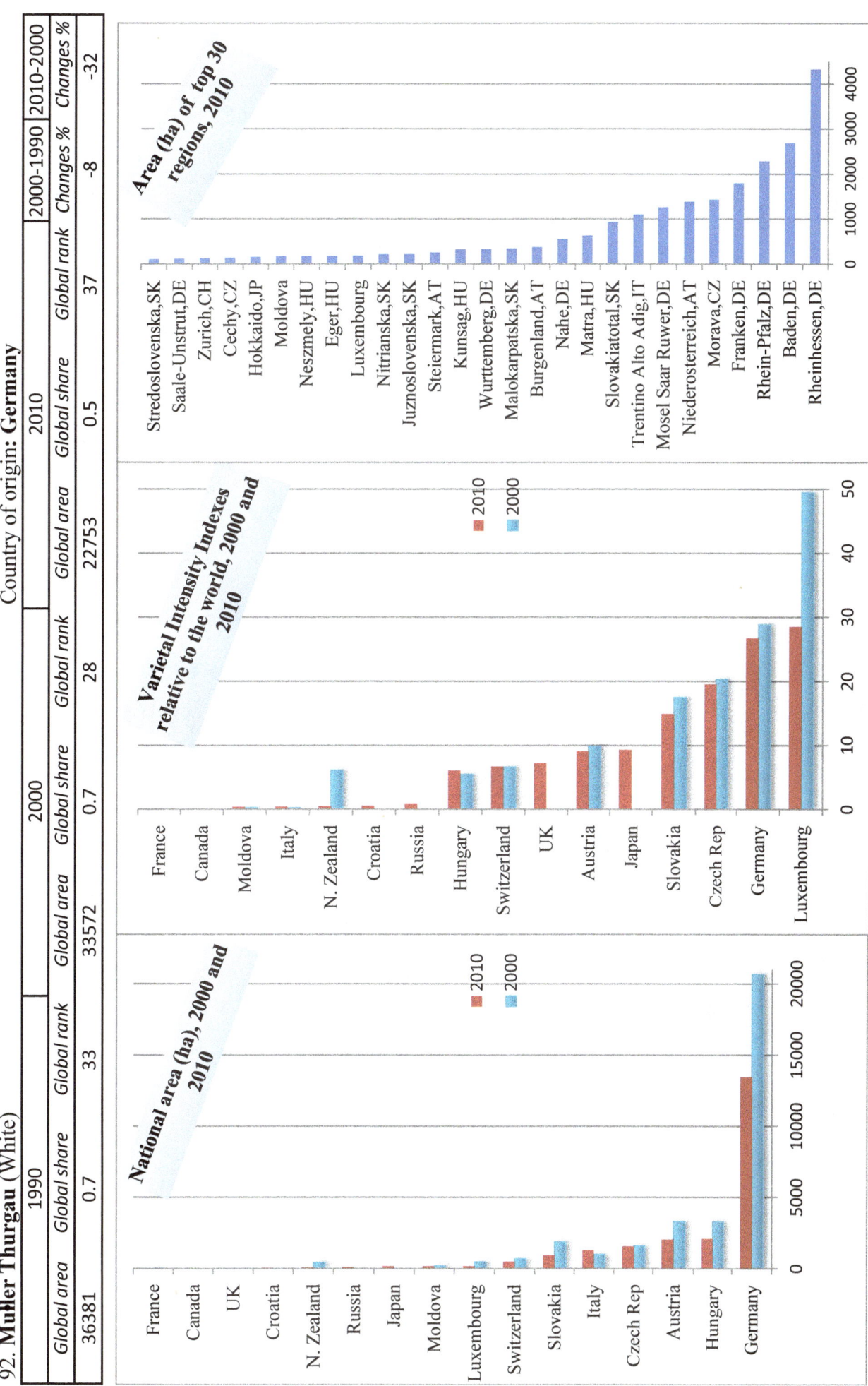

93. Muscat Blanc a Petits Grains (White)

Country of origin: Italy

	1990			2000			2010		2000-1990	2010-2000
Global area	Global share	Global rank	Global area	Global share	Global rank	Global area	Global share	Global rank	Changes %	Changes %
17806	0.3	50	28401	0.6	34	31112	0.7	33	60	10

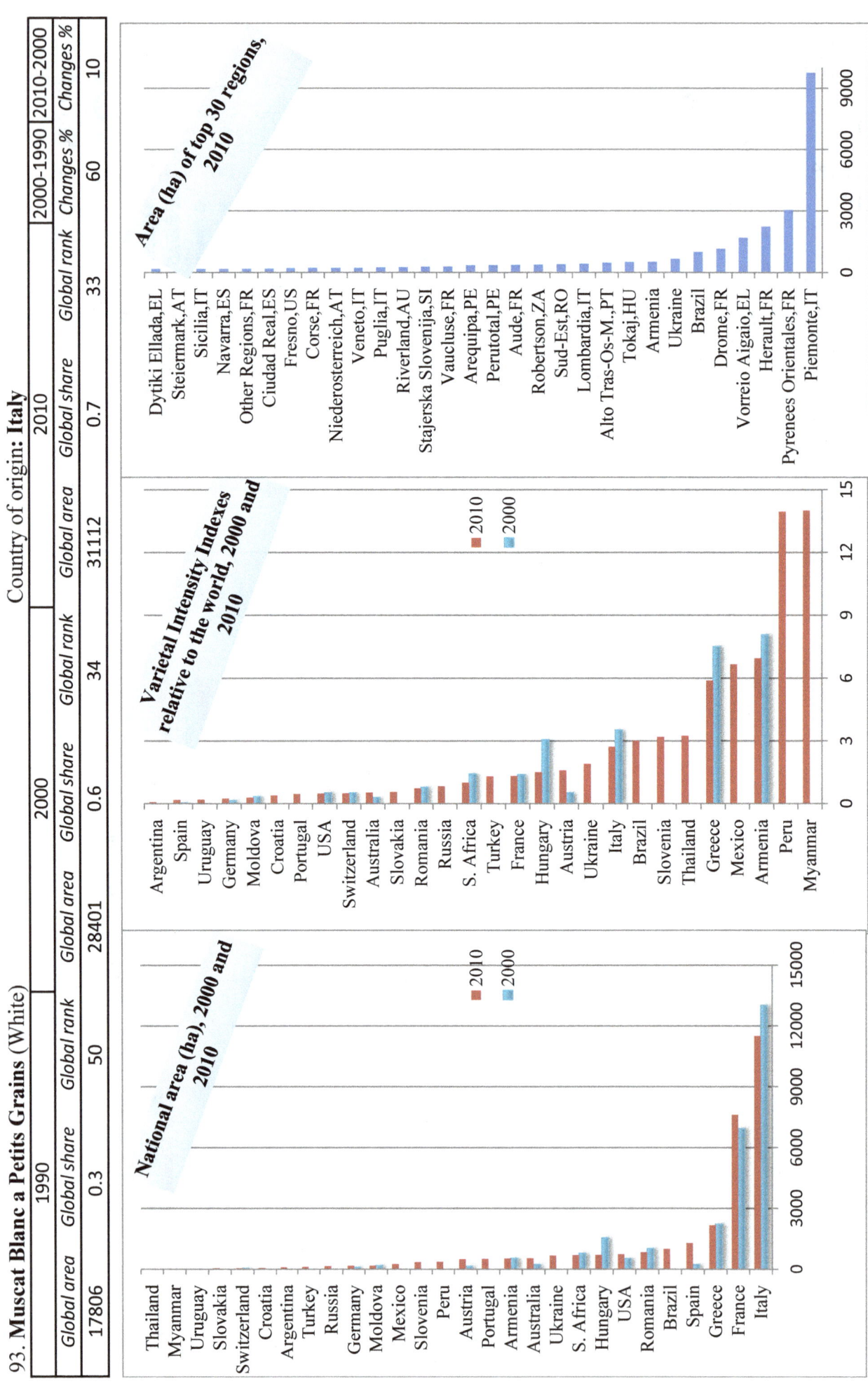

94. Muscat of Alexandria (White)

Country of origin: Greece

	1990		2000			2010			2000-1990	2010-2000
Global area	Global share	Global rank	Global area	Global share	Global rank	Global area	Global share	Global rank	Changes %	Changes %
64224	1.2	17	29411	0.6	32	26336	0.6	35	-54	-10

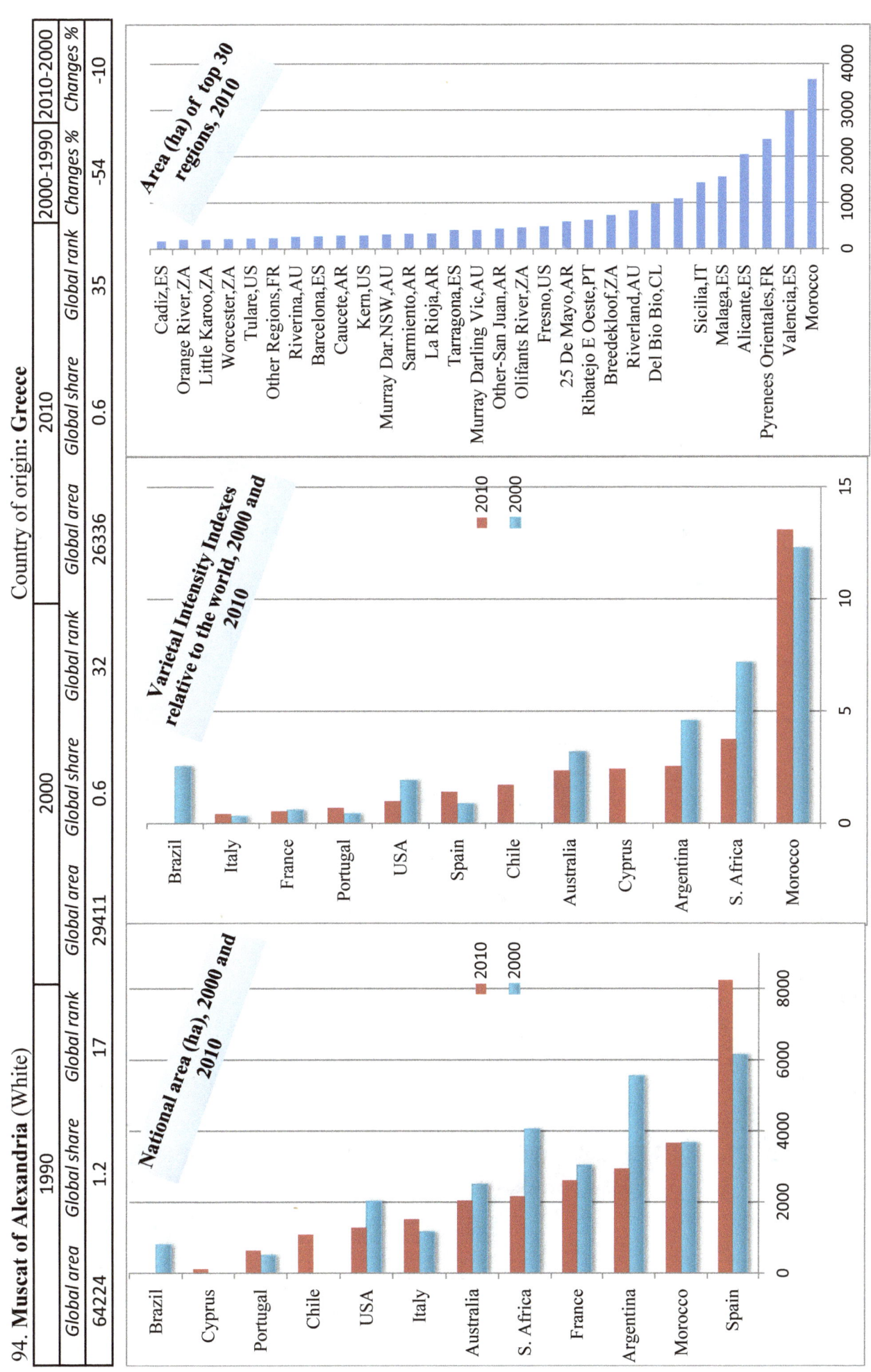

95. Nero d'Avola (Red)

Country of origin: Italy

	1990			2000			2010		2000-1990	2010-2000
	Global area	Global share	Global rank	Global area	Global share	Global rank	Global area	Global share	Global rank	Changes %	Changes %
	na			11318	0.2	66	16596	0.4	45		47

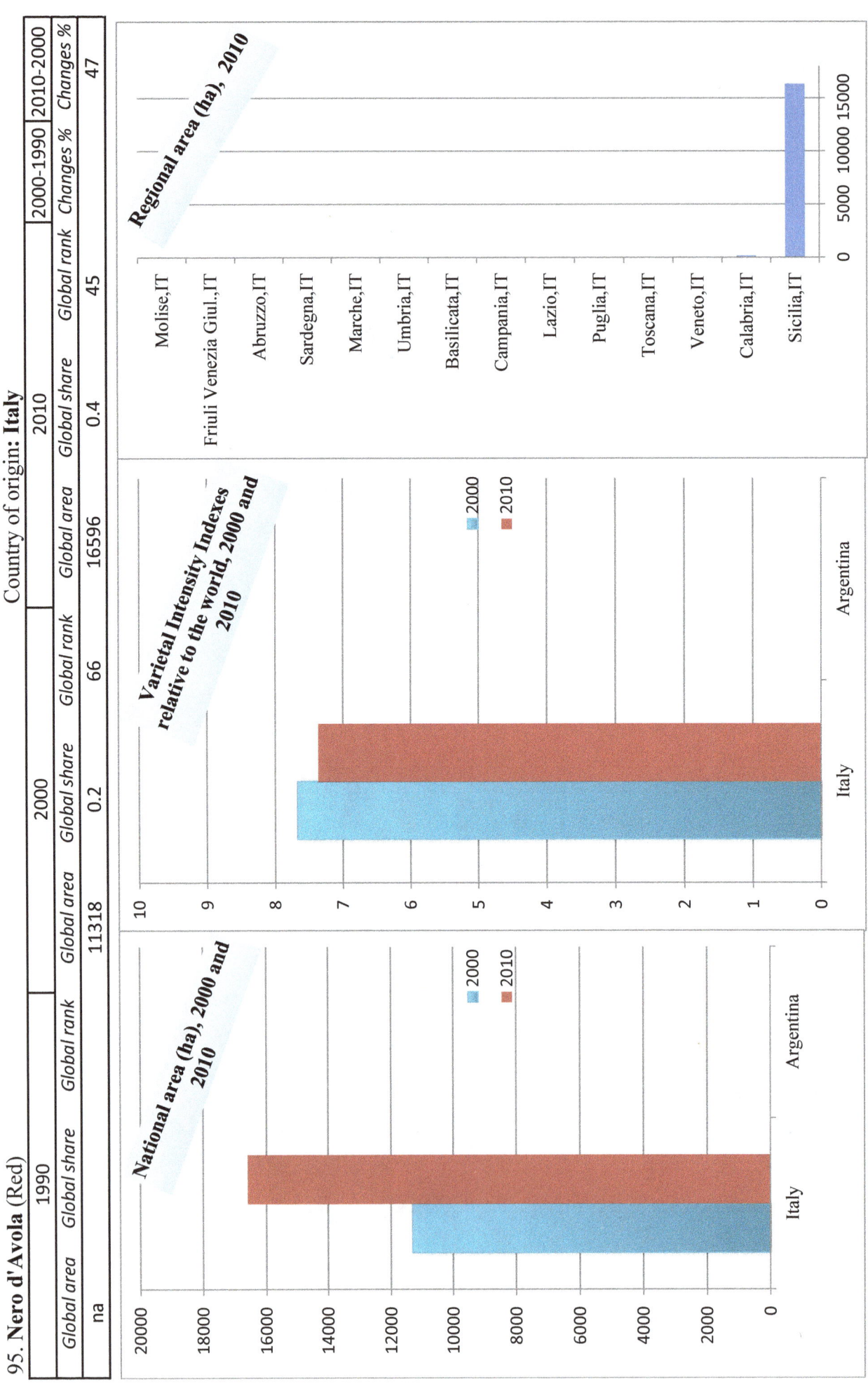

96. Palomino Fino (White)

Country of origin: **Spain**

	1990		2000			2010		2000-1990	2010-2000
Global area	Global share	Global area	Global share	Global rank	Global area	Global share	Global rank	Changes %	Changes %
50545	1.0	30297	0.6	22	22510	0.5	31	38	-40	-26

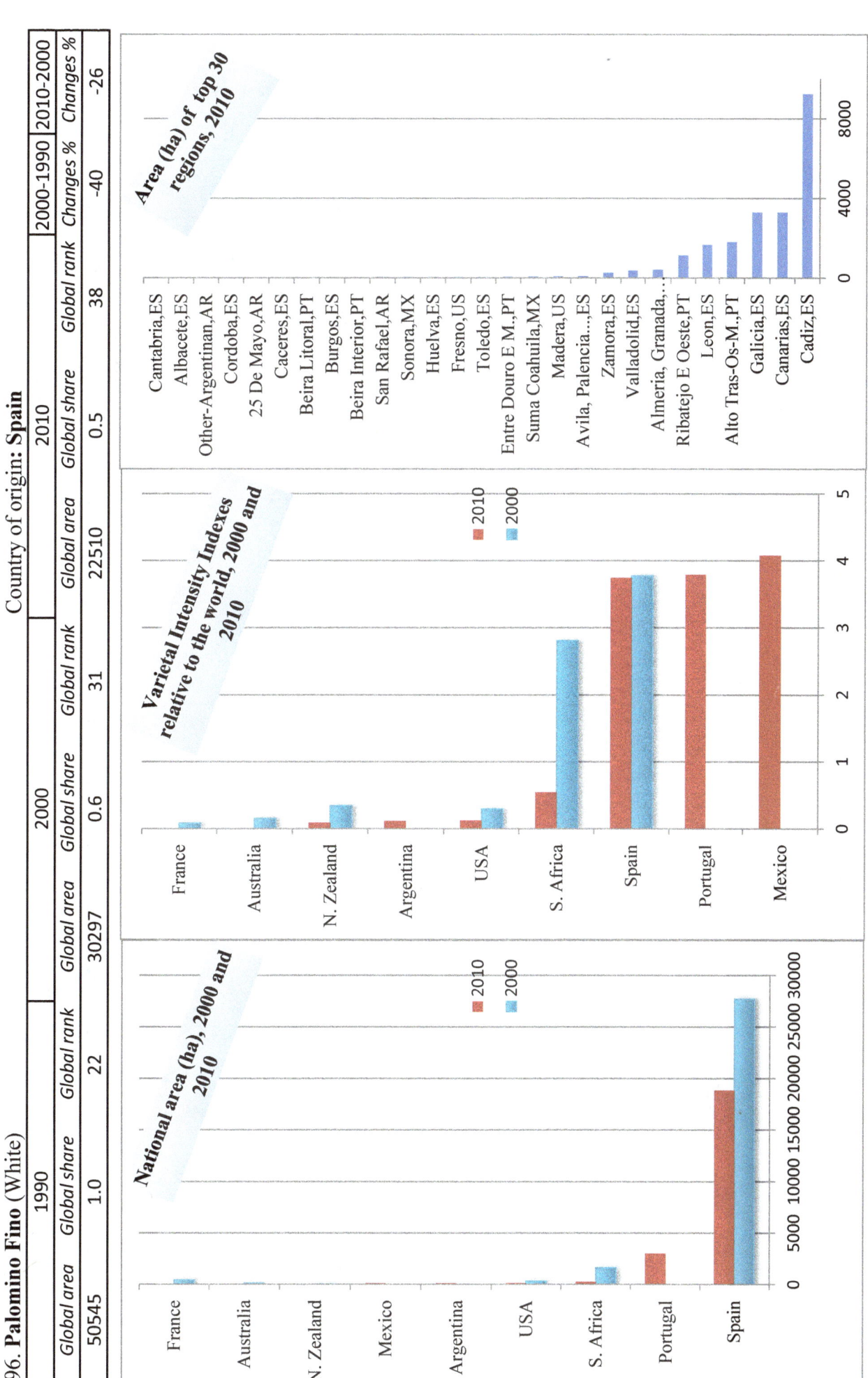

97. Pinot Gris (Grey)

Country of origin: France

	1990		2000			2010			2000-1990	2010-2000
	Global area	Global share	Global area	Global share	Global rank	Global area	Global share	Global rank	Changes %	Changes %
			18879	0.4	44	43563	0.9	19		131

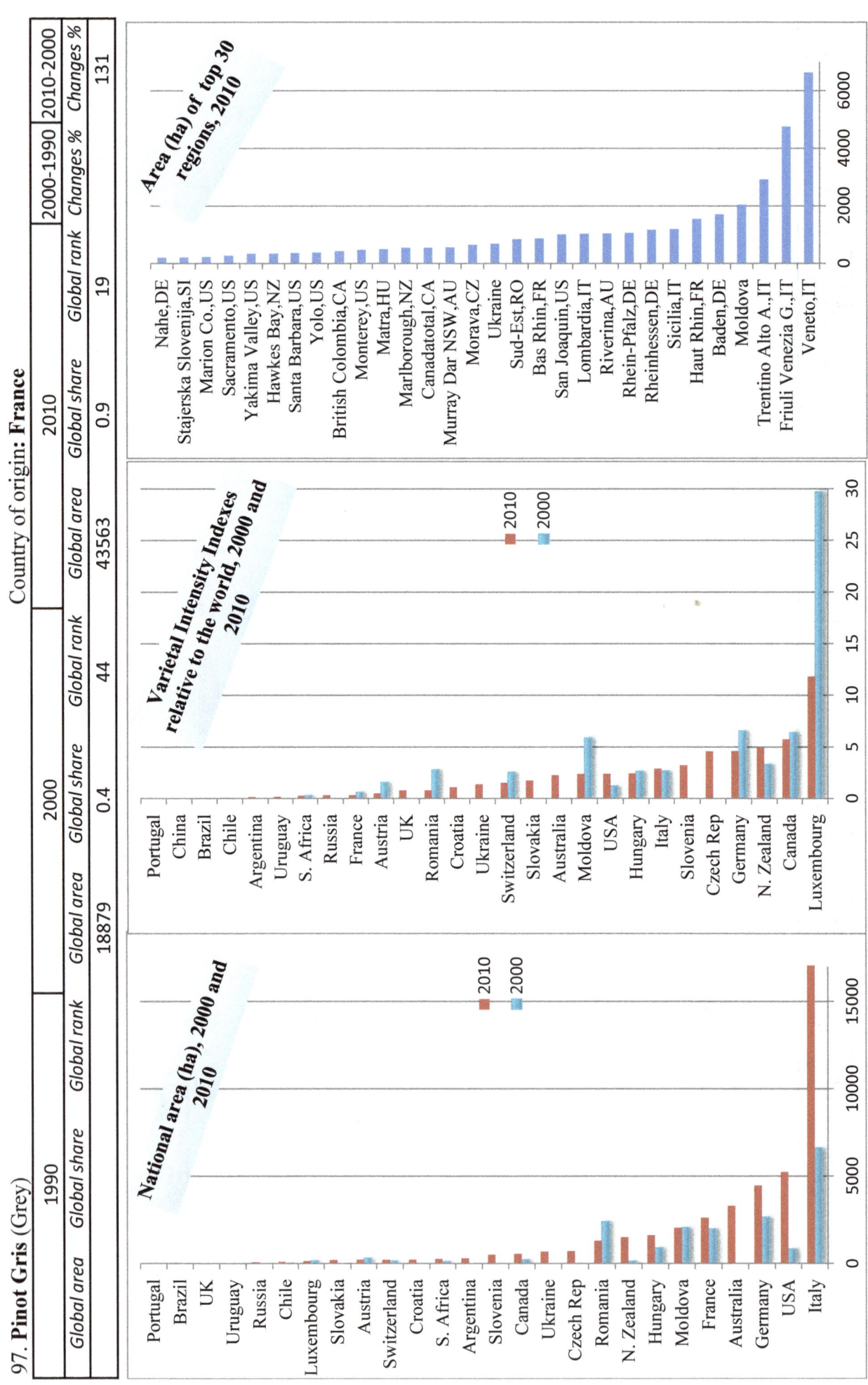

98. Pinot Noir (Red) — Country of origin: France

	1990		2000			2010		2000-1990	2010-2000
	Global area	Global share	Global rank	Global area	Global share	Global rank	Global area	Global share	Changes %	Changes %
	41539	1	30	60099	1	16	86662	2	10	45	44

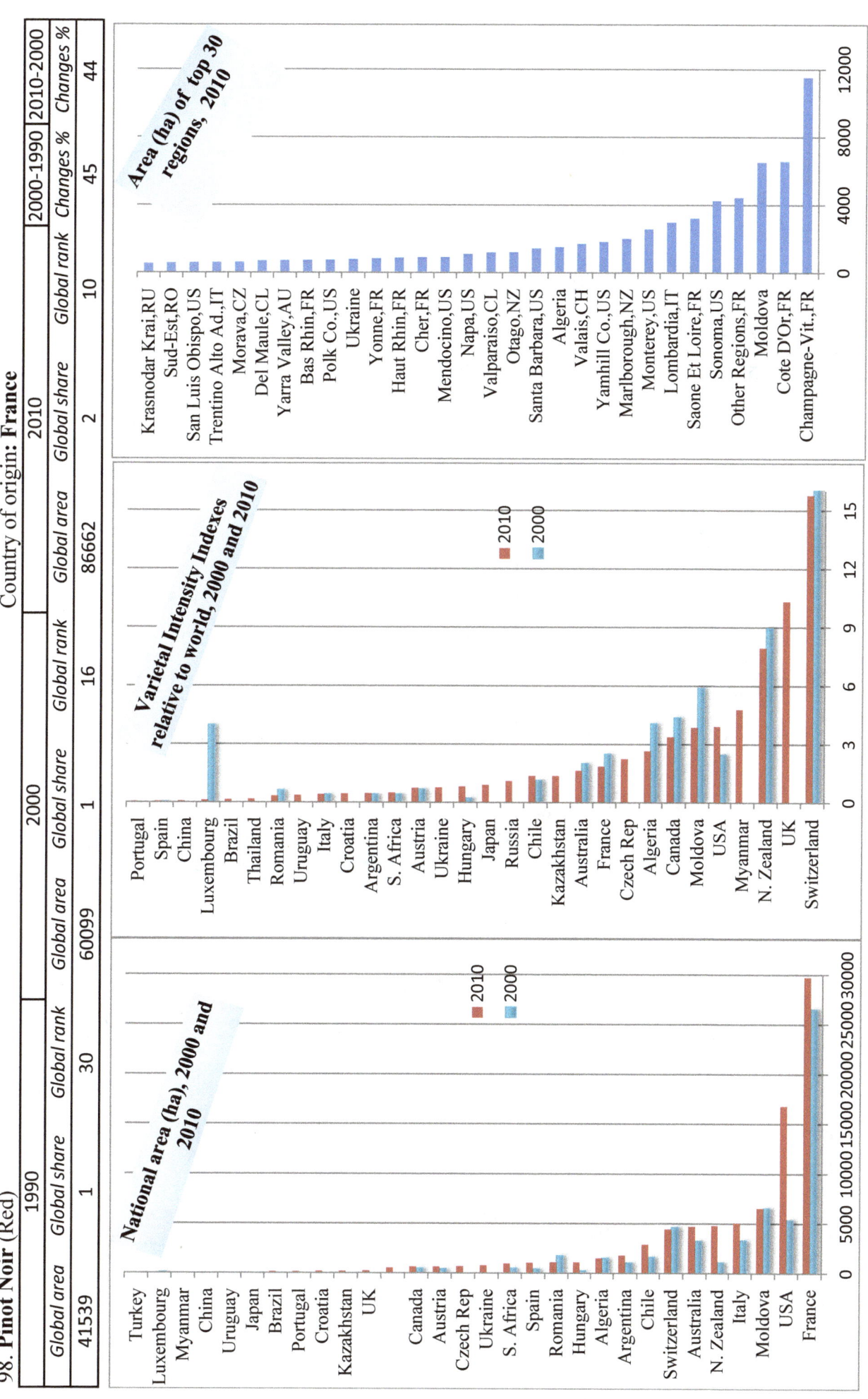

99. Prosecco (White)

Country of origin: Italy

	1990			2000			2010			2000-1990	2010-2000
	Global area	Global share	Global rank	Global area	Global share	Global rank	Global area	Global share	Global rank	Changes %	Changes %
	na	na	na	7498	0.2	84	18437	0.4	42		146

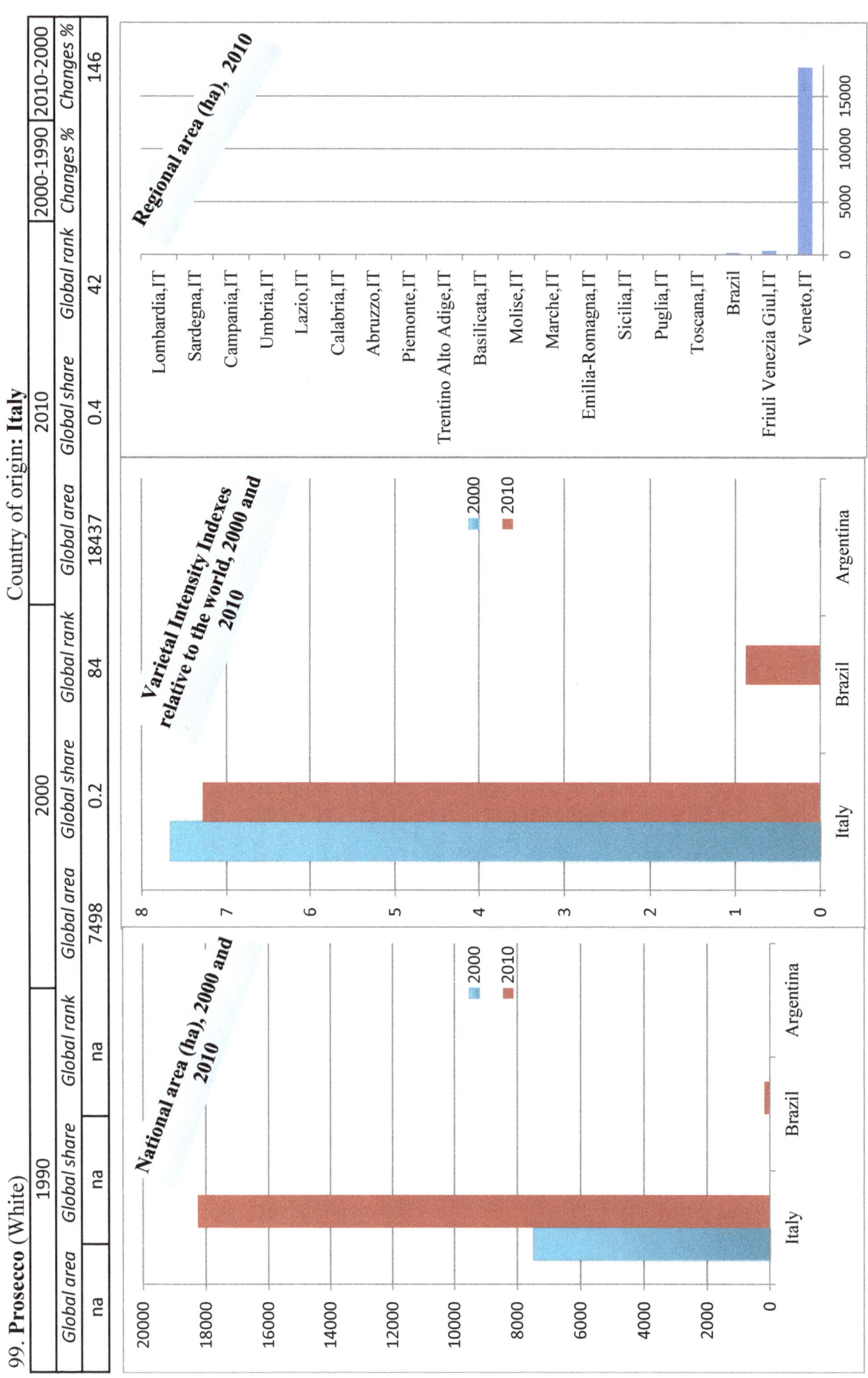

100. Riesling (white)

Country of origin: Germany

	1990		2000			2010		2000-1990	2010-2000
Global area	Global share	Global rank	Global area	Global share	Global rank	Global area	Global share	Changes %	Changes %
52164	1.0	21	43166	0.9	23	50060	1.1	18	-17	16

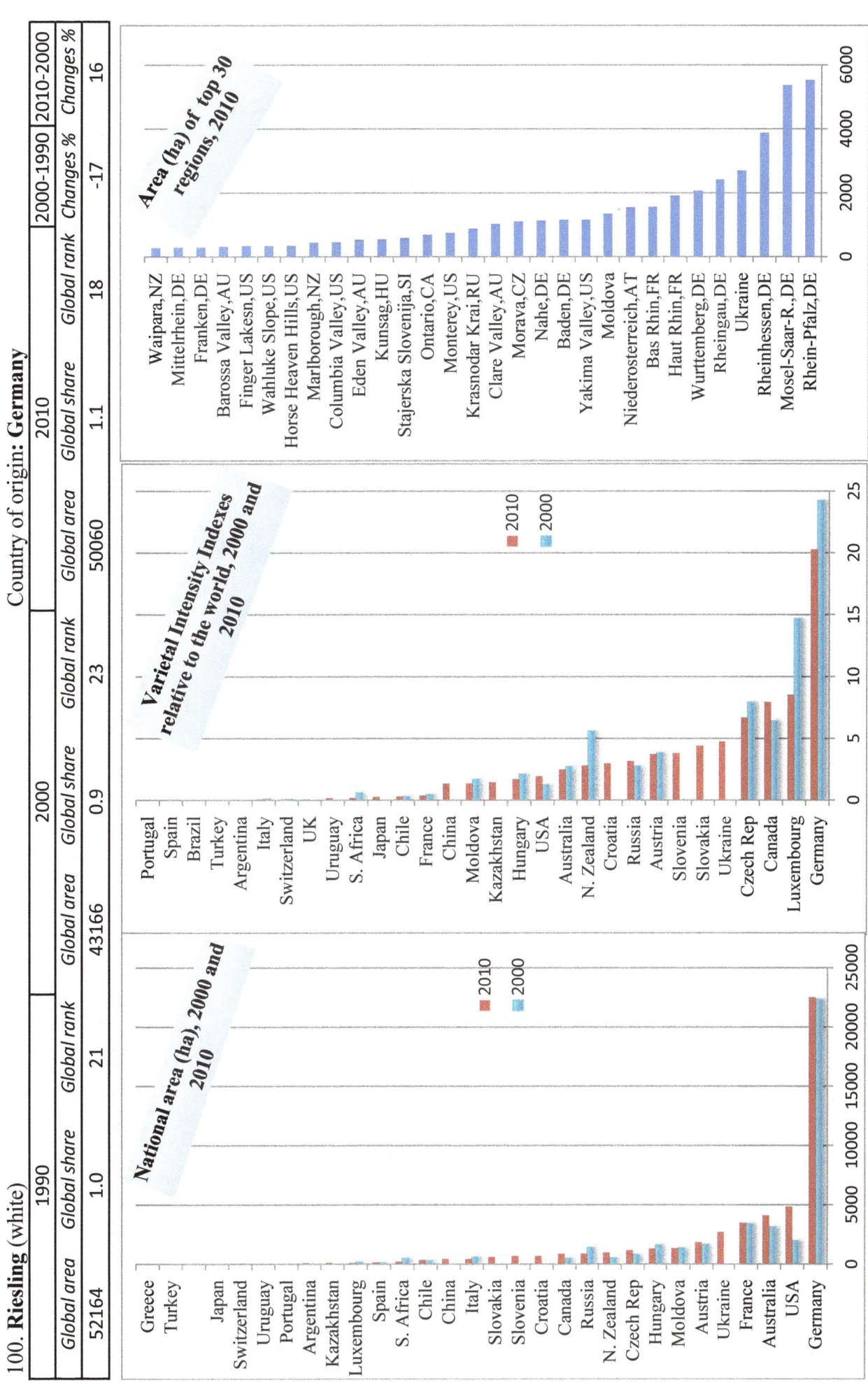

101. Rkatsiteli (White)

Country of origin: Georgia

	1990			2000			2010		2000-1990	2010-2000
Global area	Global share	Global rank	Global area	Global share	Global rank	Global area	Global share	Global rank	Changes %	Changes %
280569	5.3	3	67354	1.4	14	58641	1.3	16	-76	-13

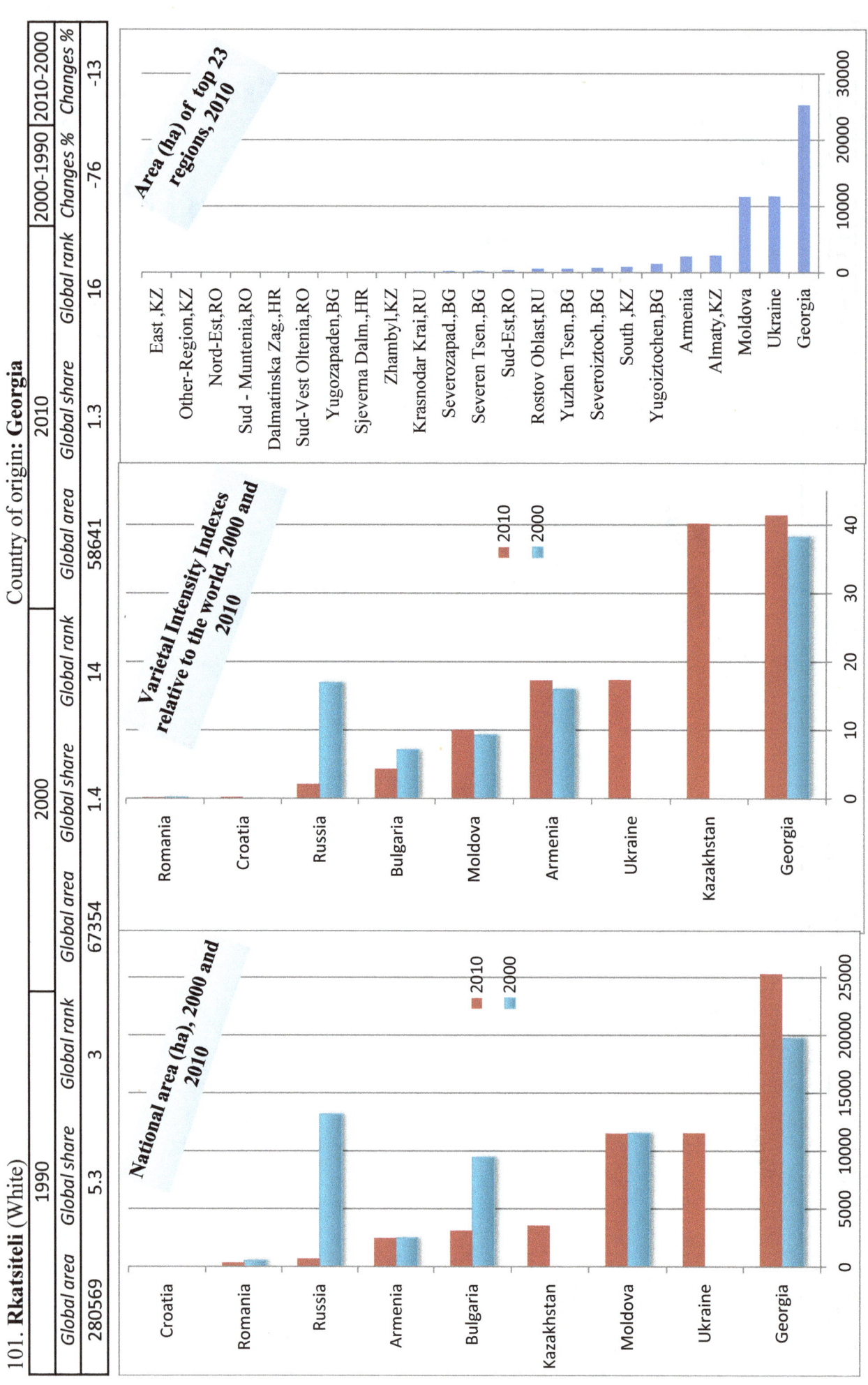

102. Sangiovese (Red)

Country of origin: **Italy**

	1990			2000			2010			2000-1990	2010-2000
Global area	Global share	Global rank	Global area	Global share	Global rank	Global area	Global share	Global rank	Changes %	Changes %
98946	2	11	68877	1	13	77709	2	13	-30	13

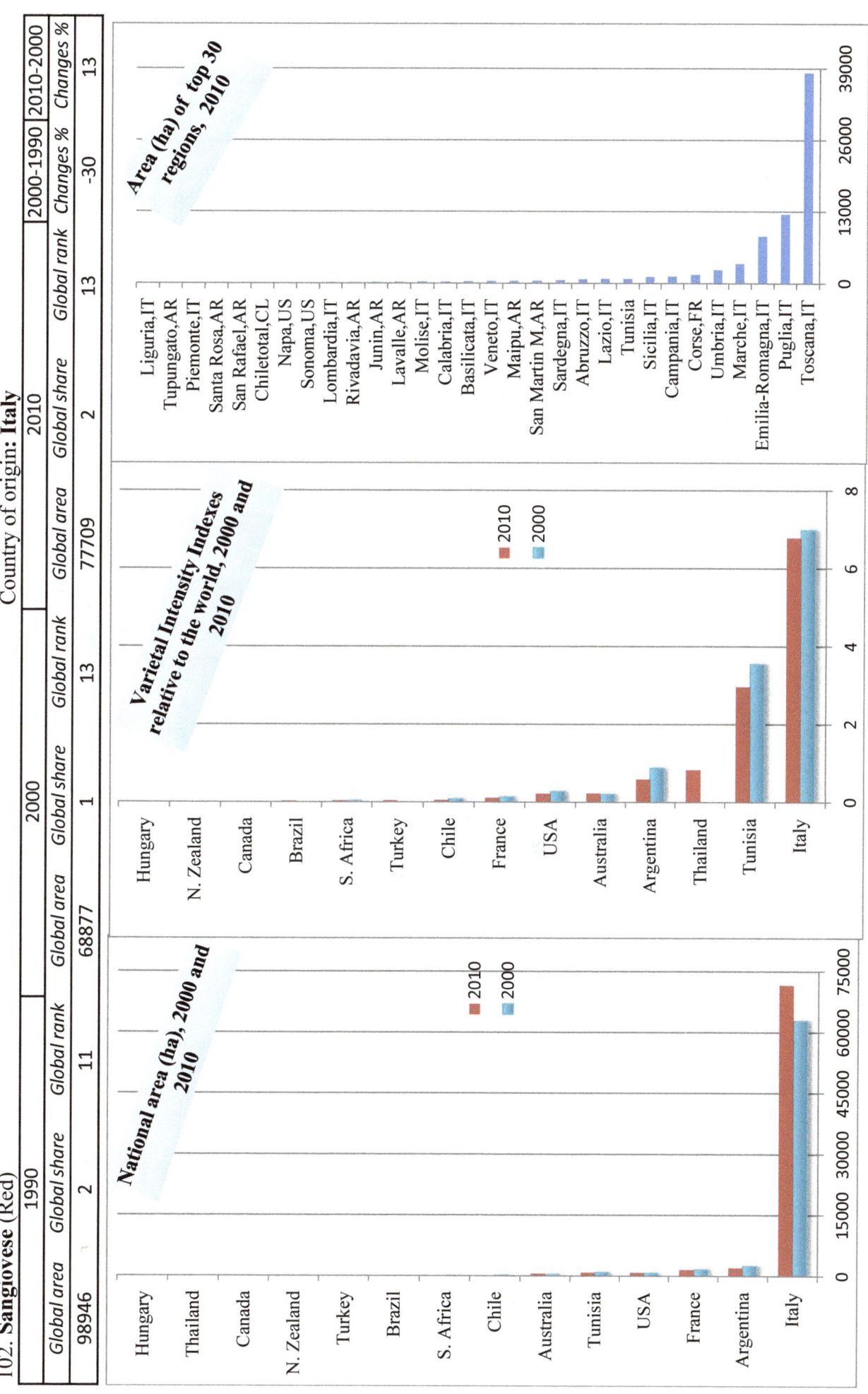

103. **Sauvignon Blanc** (White)

Country of origin: France

	1990			2000			2010		2000-1990	2010-2000
Global area	Global share	Global rank	Global area	Global share	Global rank	Global area	Global share	Global rank	Changes %	Changes %
44677	1	25	64889	1	15	110138	2	8	45	70

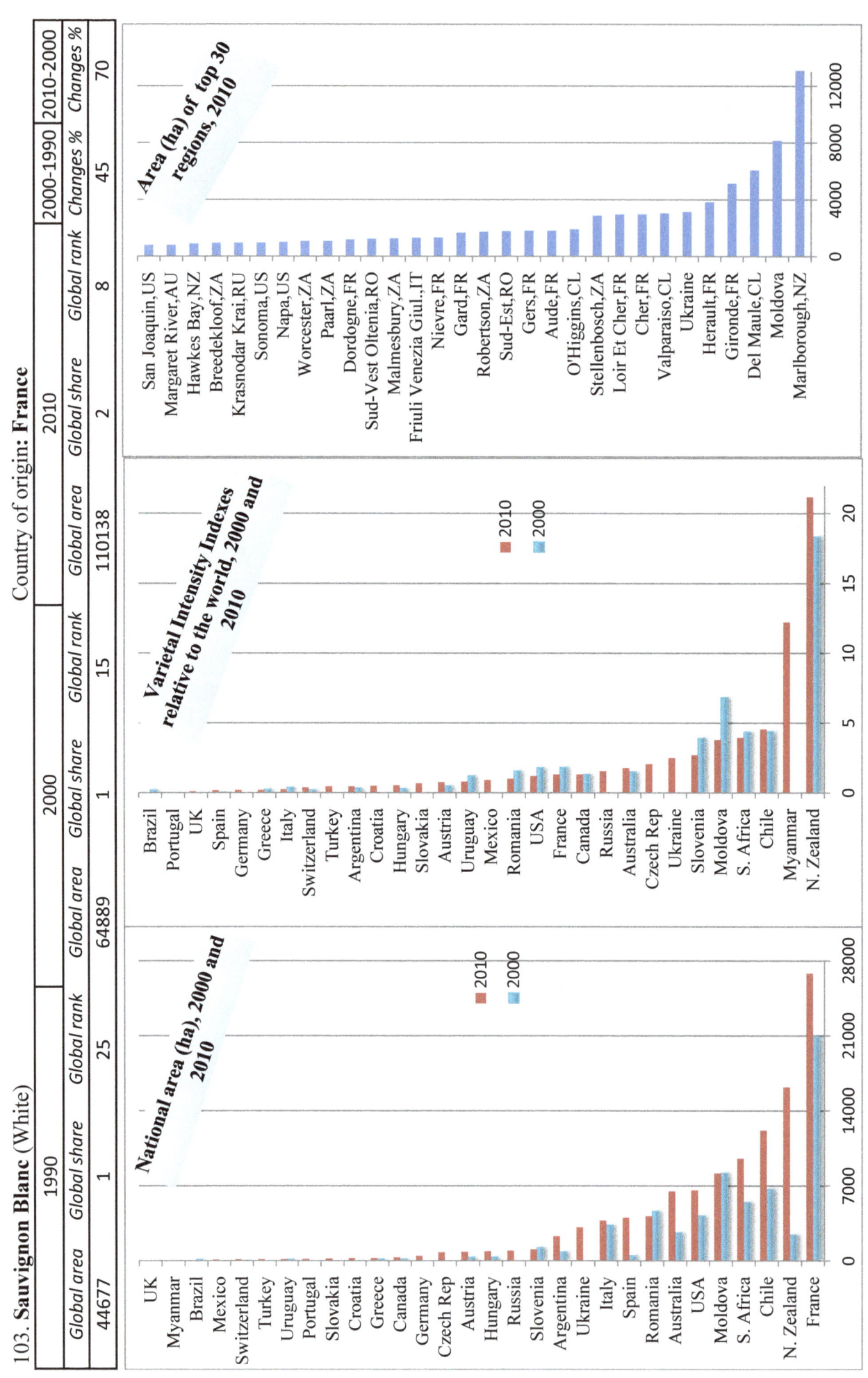

104. Semillon (White)

Country of origin: France

	1990			2000			2010		2000-1990	2010-2000
	Global area	Global share	Global rank	Global area	Global share	Global rank	Global area	Global share	Global rank	Changes %	Changes %
	31687	0.6		26230	0.5	38	22156	0.5	37	-17	-16

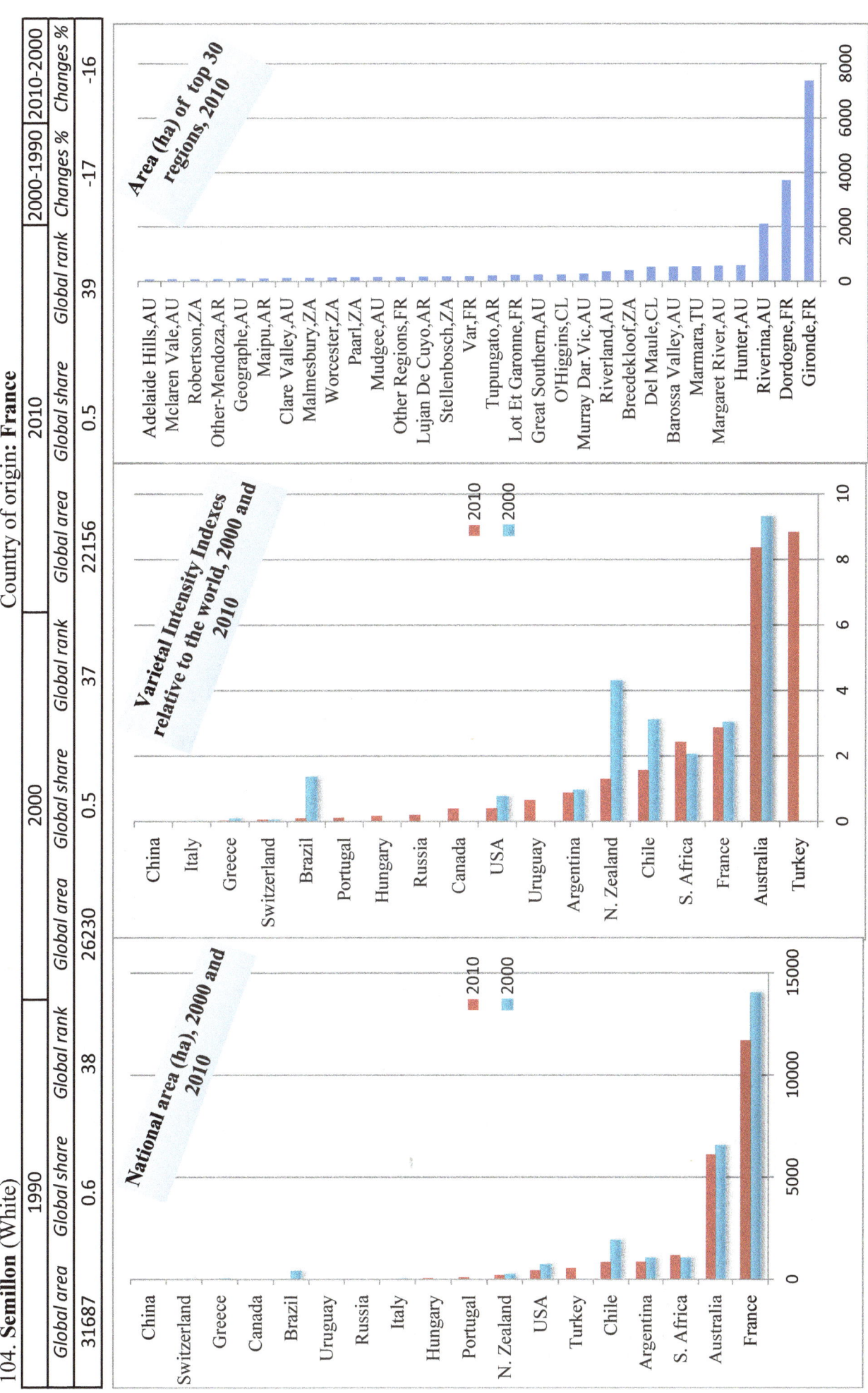

105. Syrah (Red)

Country of origin: France

	1990			2000			2010		2000-1990	2010-2000
	Global area	Global share	Global rank	Global area	Global share	Global rank	Global area	Global share	Global rank	Changes %	Changes %
	35086			101516		35	185568		8	4	6	189	83

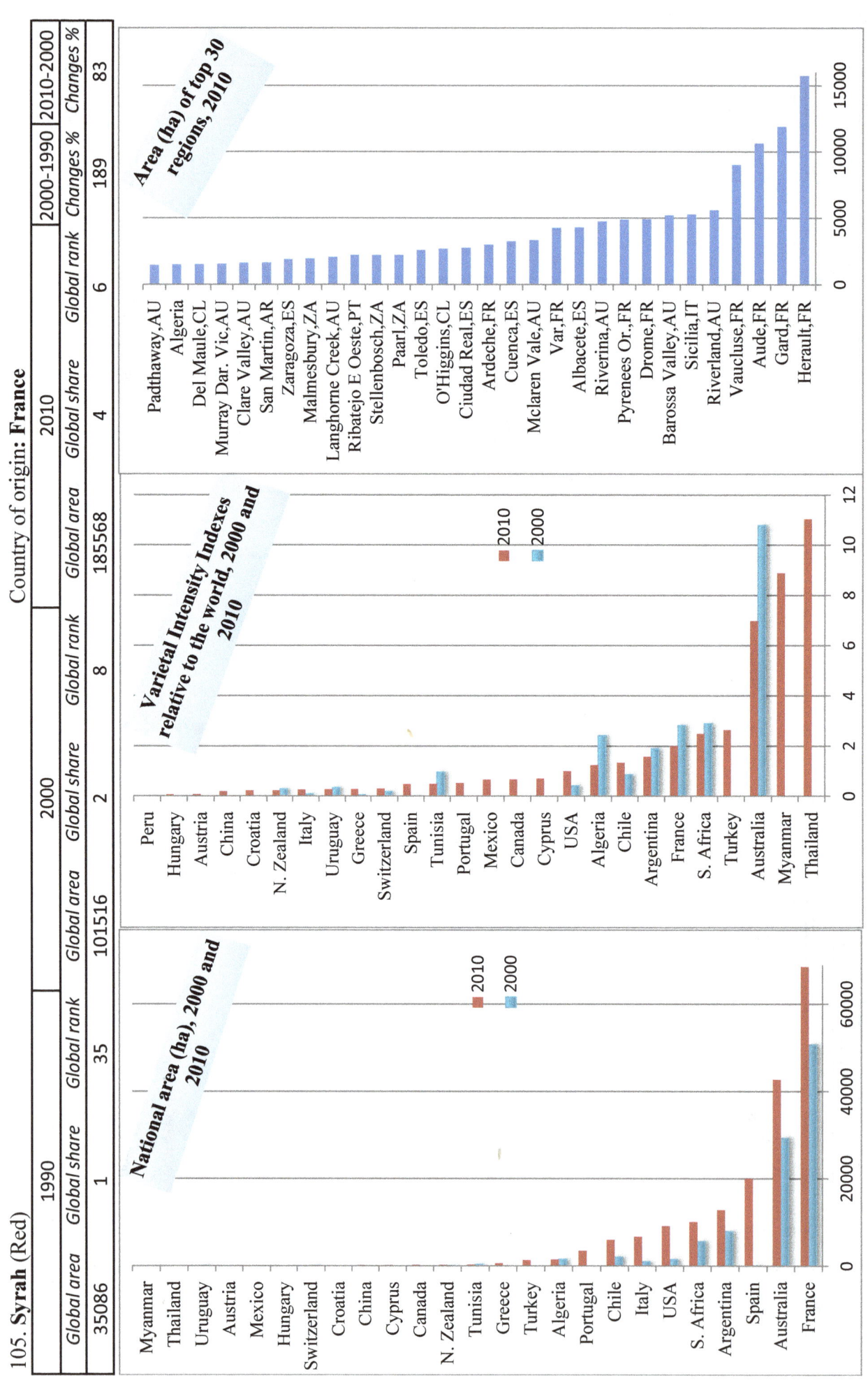

106. Tempranillo (Red)

Country of origin: **Spain**

	1990		2000			2010			2000-1990	2010-2000
Global area	Global share	Global rank	Global area	Global share	Global rank	Global area	Global share	Global rank	Changes %	Changes %
47429	1		92985	2	24	232561	5	4	96	150

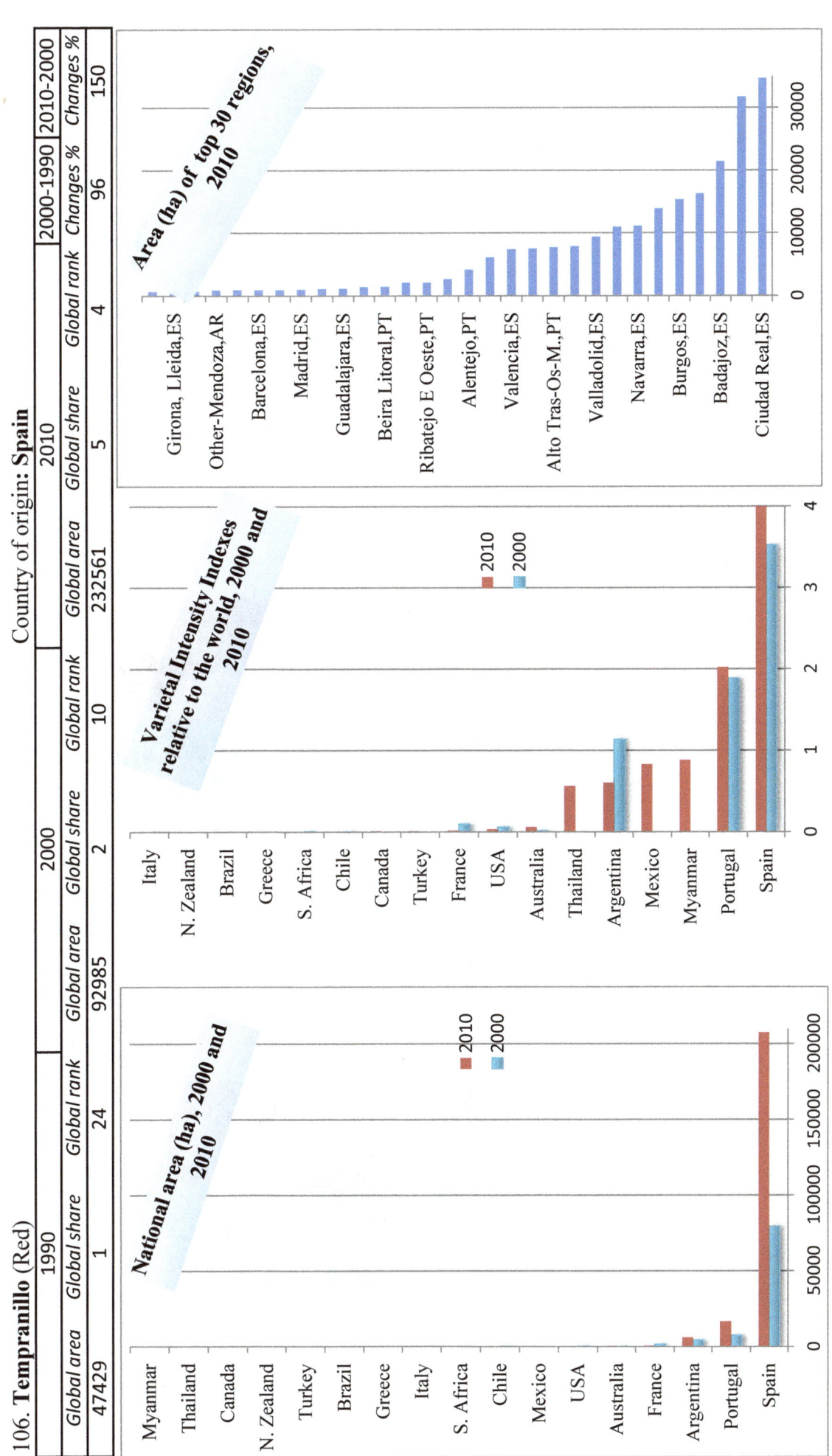

107. Trebbiano Romagnolo (White)
Country of origin: Italy
Global data

	1990			2000			2010		2000-1990	2010-2000
Global area	Global share	Global rank	Global area	Global share	Global rank	Global area	Global share	Global rank	Changes %	Changes %
na	na	na	19492	0.4	43	15893	0.3	49		-18

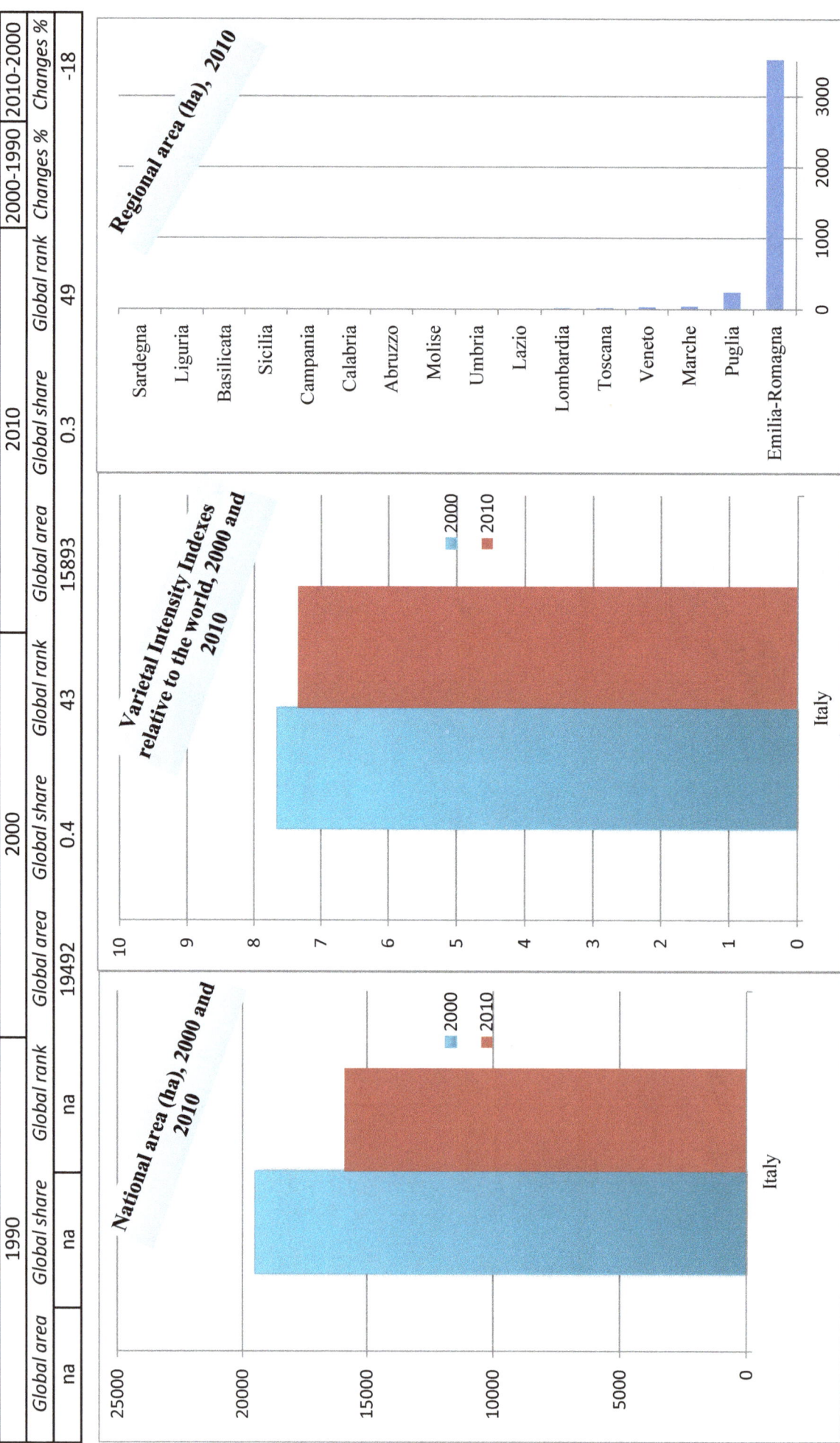

108. Trebbiano Toscano (White) — Country of origin: Italy

	1990		2000			2010		2000-1990	2010-2000
Global area	Global share	Global rank	Global area	Global share	Global rank	Global area	Global share	Changes %	Changes %
207442	4	5	136572	3	6	109772	2	9	-34	-20

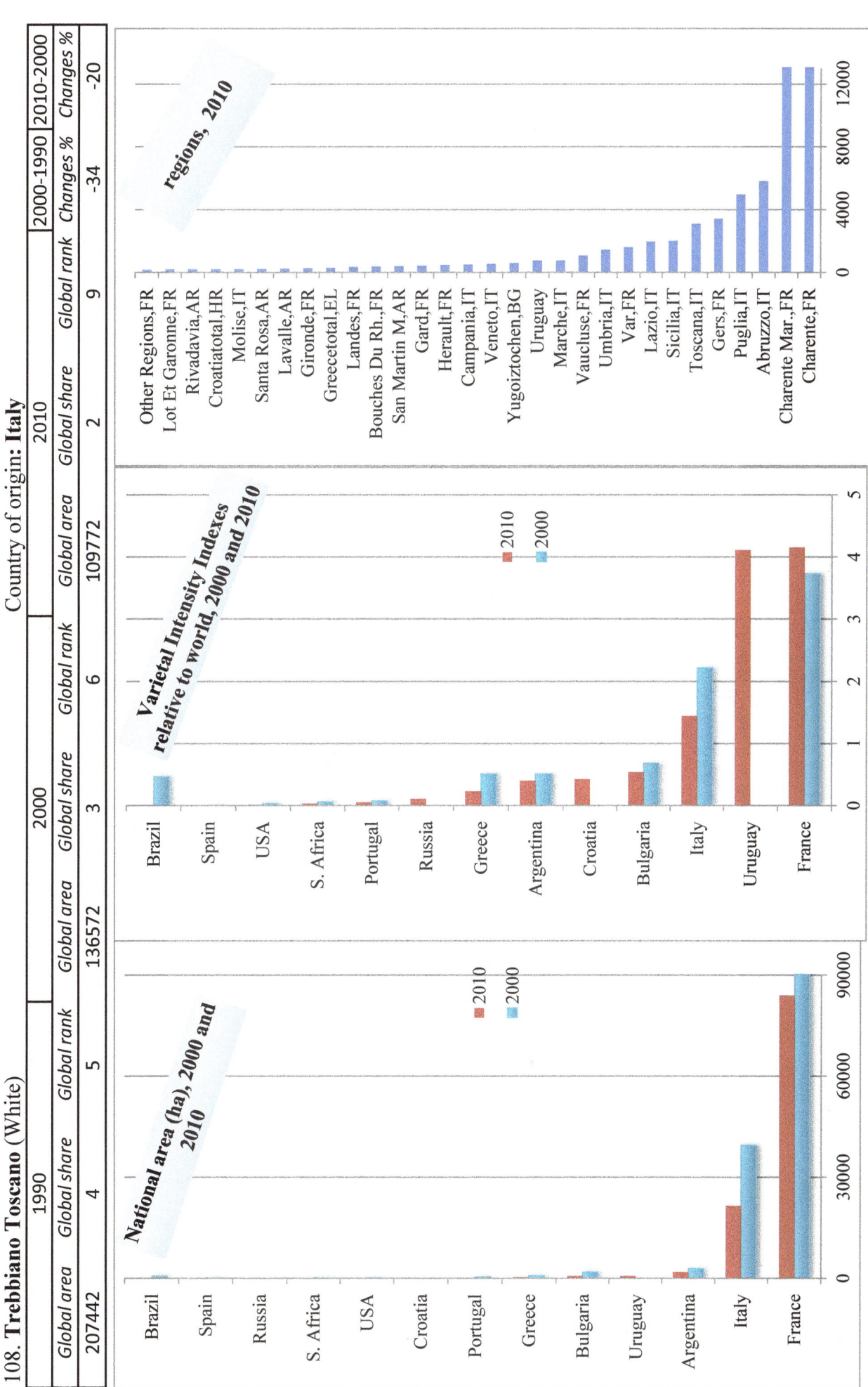

109. Tribidrag (Red)

Country of origin: Croatia

	1990		2000			2010			2000-1990	2010-2000
Global area	Global share	Global rank	Global area	Global share	Global rank	Global area	Global share	Global rank	Changes %	Changes %
41683	0.8	29	26915	0.6	36	32745	0.7	29	-35	22

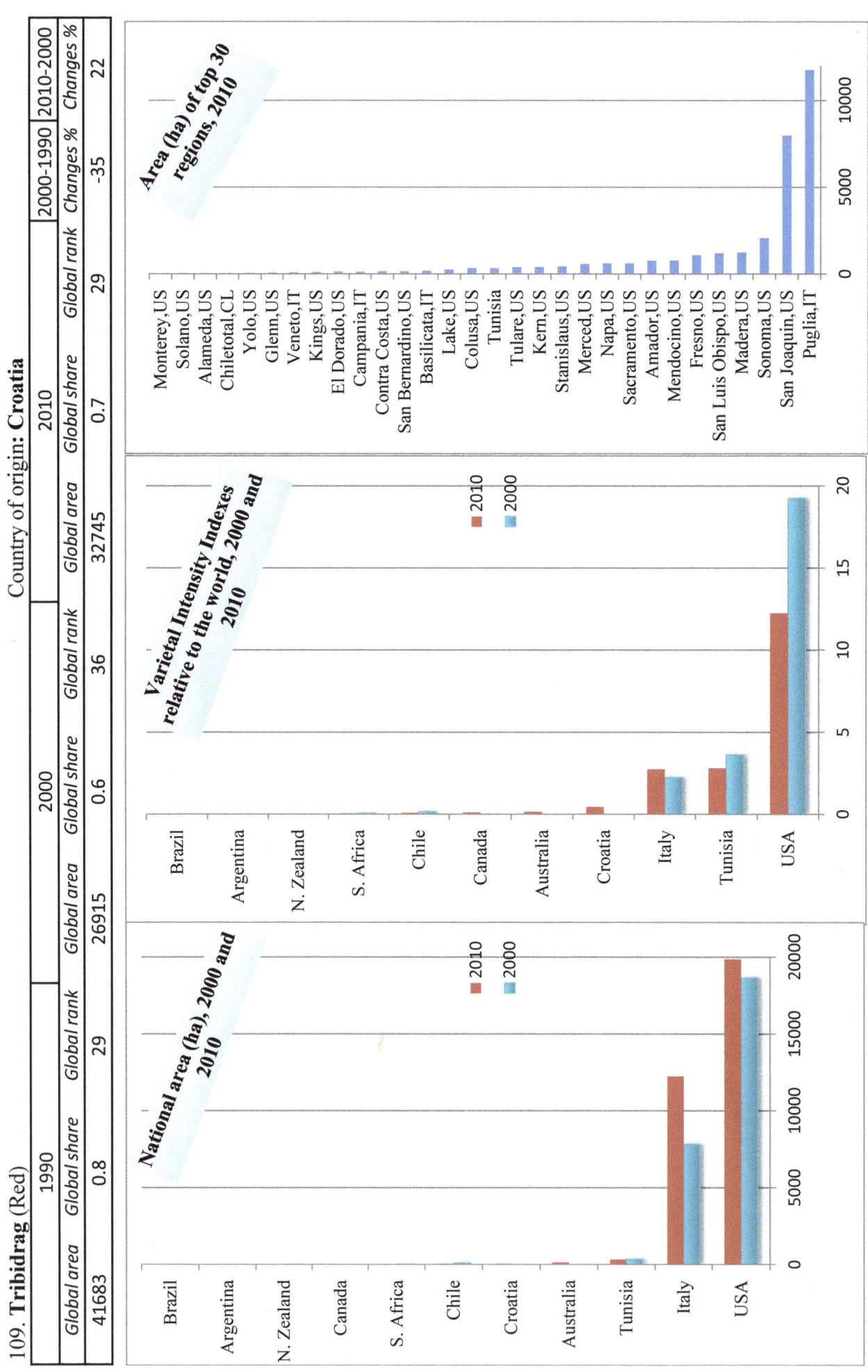

110. Verdejo (White)

Country of origin: **Spain**

	1990			2000			2010		2000-1990
Global area	Global share	Global rank	Global area	Global share	Global rank	Global area	Global share	Global rank	Changes %
na			4453	0.1	117	16578	0.4	46	272

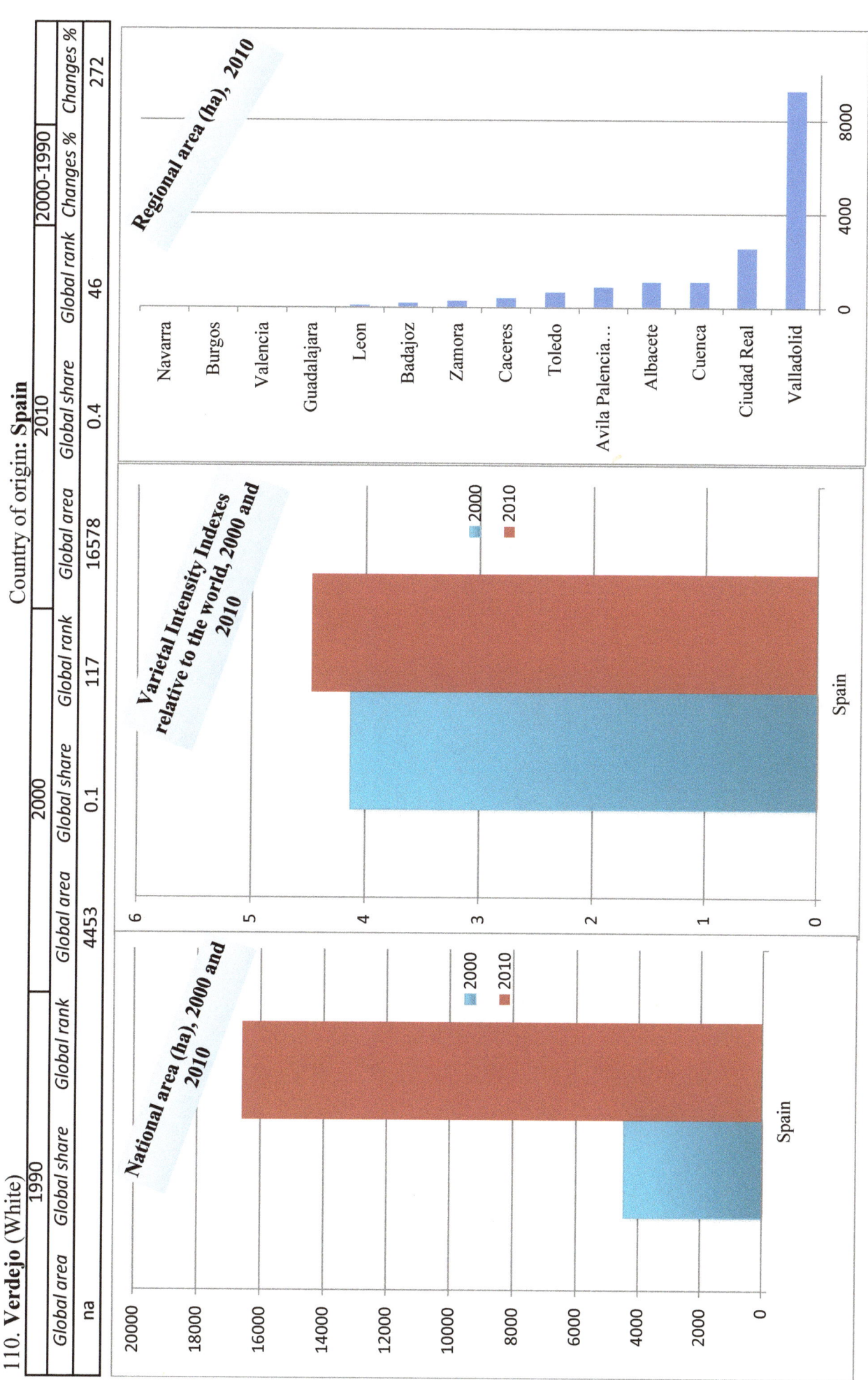

Table Section IX: Summary charts for each of the 44 countries

111. Algeria

Area		Changes in area (%)	Share (%) area of global total		No. of regions		No. of prime varieties	
2000	2010		2000	2010	2000	2010	2000	2010
30200	30200	0	0.61	0.65	1	1	8	8

Year	Share of top variety	Share of top 3 varieties	Share of top 10 varieties
2000	25	70	
2010	25	70	

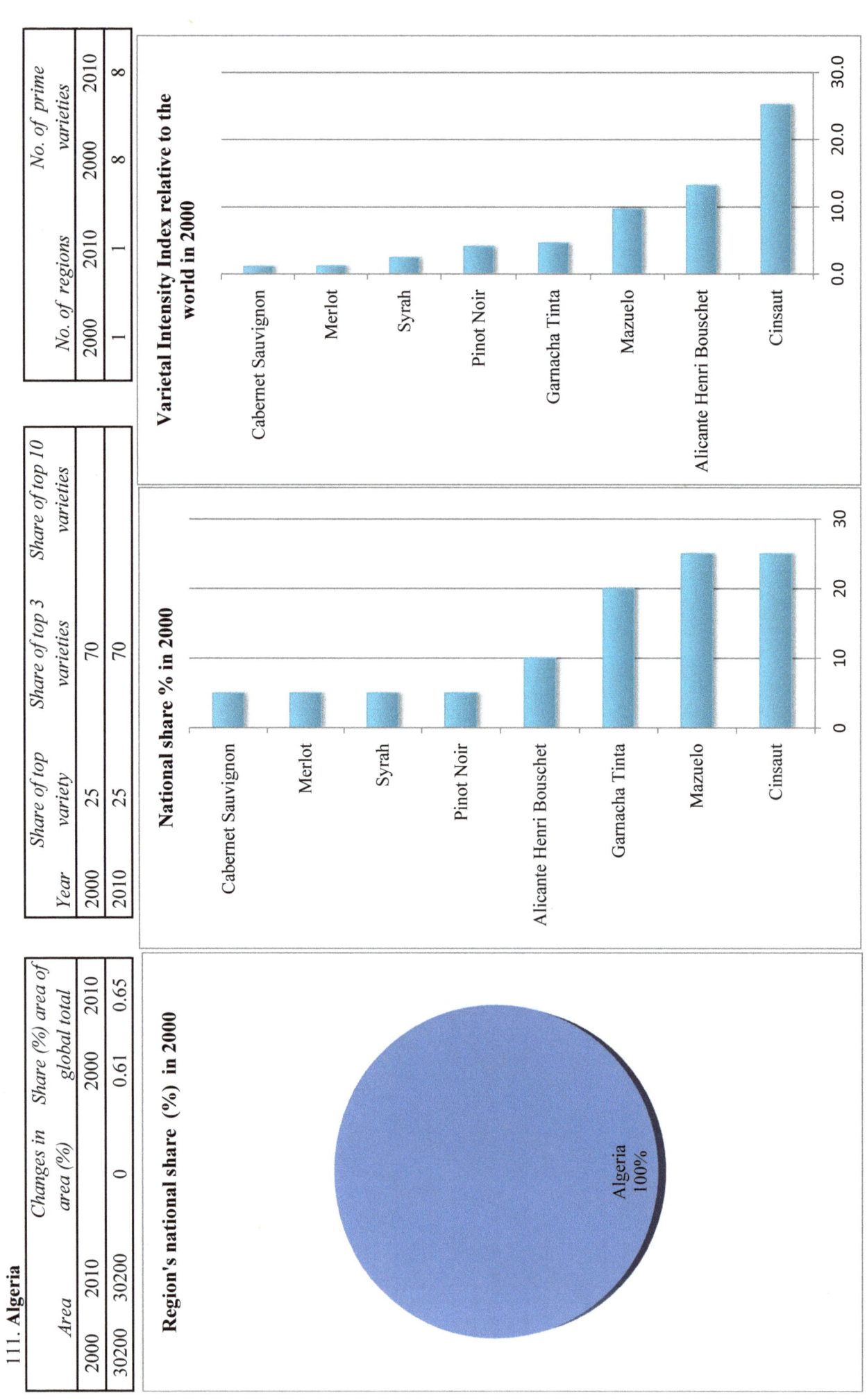

112. Argentina

Area		Changes in area (%)	Share (%) area of global total	
Year	2010		2000	2010
2000		0	4.08	4.33
2010	201060			

Year	Share of top variety	Share of top 3 varieties	Share of top 10 varieties	No. of regions		No. of prime varieties	
				2000	2010	2000	2010
2000	16	36	73	3	28	31	111
2010	15	39	79				

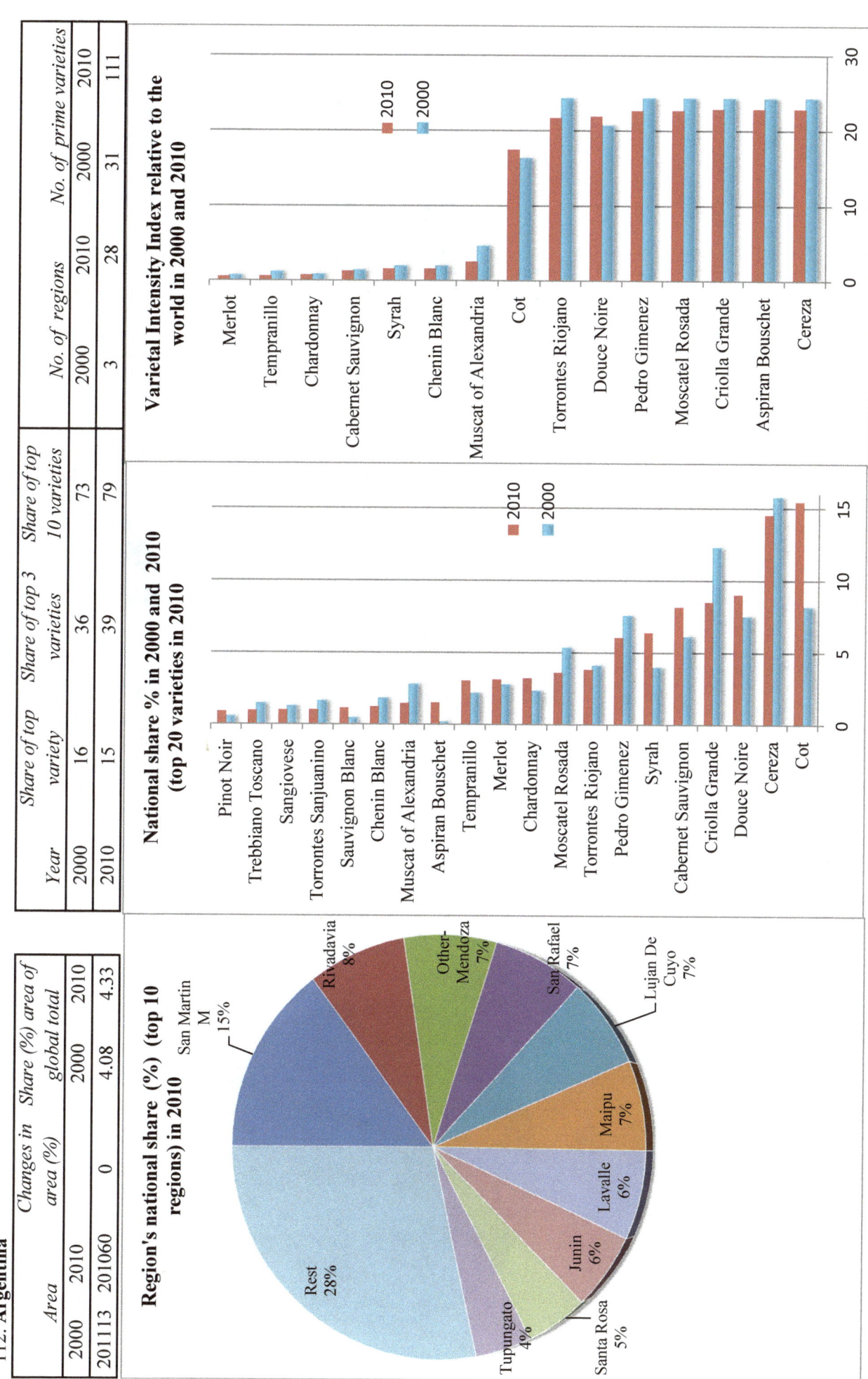

113. Armenia

Area		Changes in area (%)	Share (%) area of global total	
2000	2010		2000	2010
11206	11206	0	0.23	0.24

Year	Share of top variety	Share of top 3 varieties	Share of top 10 varieties	No. of regions		No. of prime varieties	
				2000	2010	2000	2010
2000	22	40		1	1	6	6
2010	22	40					

Varietal Intensity Index relative to the world in 2000

National share % in 2010

Region's national share (%) in 2000

114. Australia

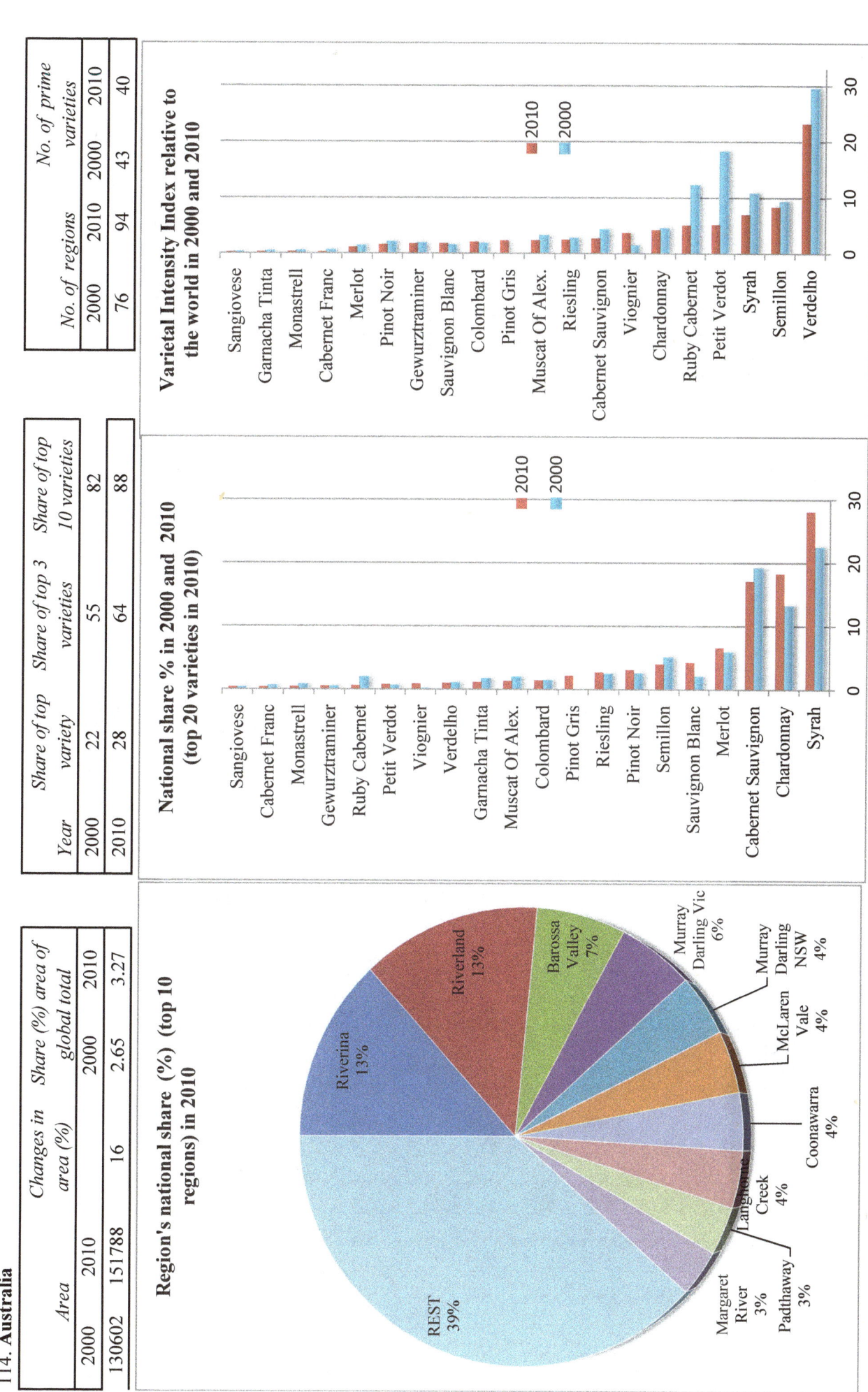

115. Austria

Area		Changes in area (%)	Share (%) area of global total	
2000	2010		2000	2010
48496	45533	-6	0.98	0.98

	No. of regions		No. of prime varieties	
	2000	2010	2000	2010
	4	4	33	35

Year	Share of top variety	Share of top 3 varieties	Share of top 10 varieties
2000	36	54	85
2010	30	51	80

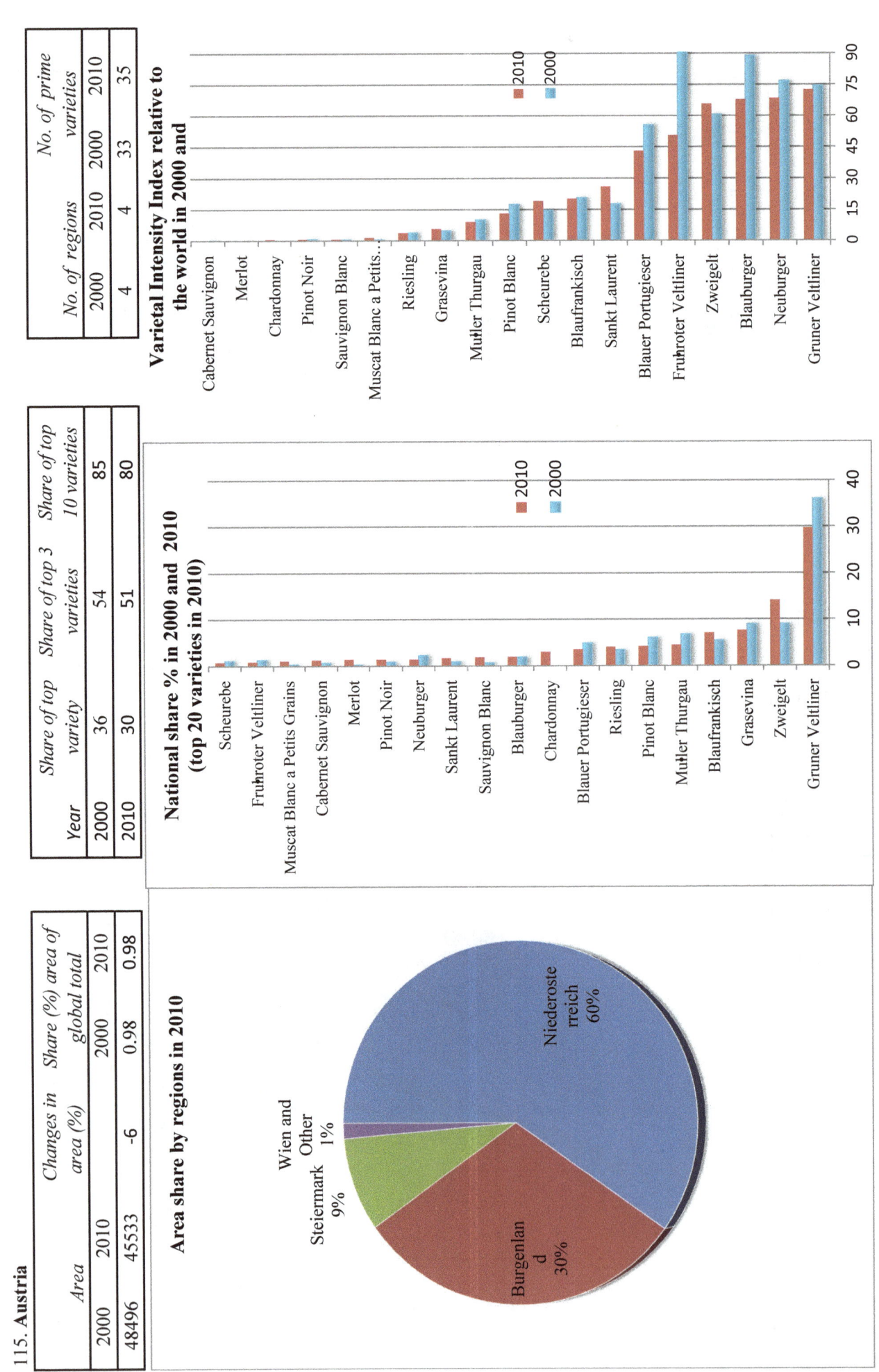

116. Brazil

Area		Changes in area (%)	Share (%) area of global total	
2000	2010		2000	2010
52840	49412	-6	1.07	1.06

Year	Share of top variety	Share of top 3 varieties	Share of top 10 varieties
2000	27	59	76
2010	37	61	86

No. of regions		No. of prime varieties	
2000	2010	2000	2010
1	1	19	101

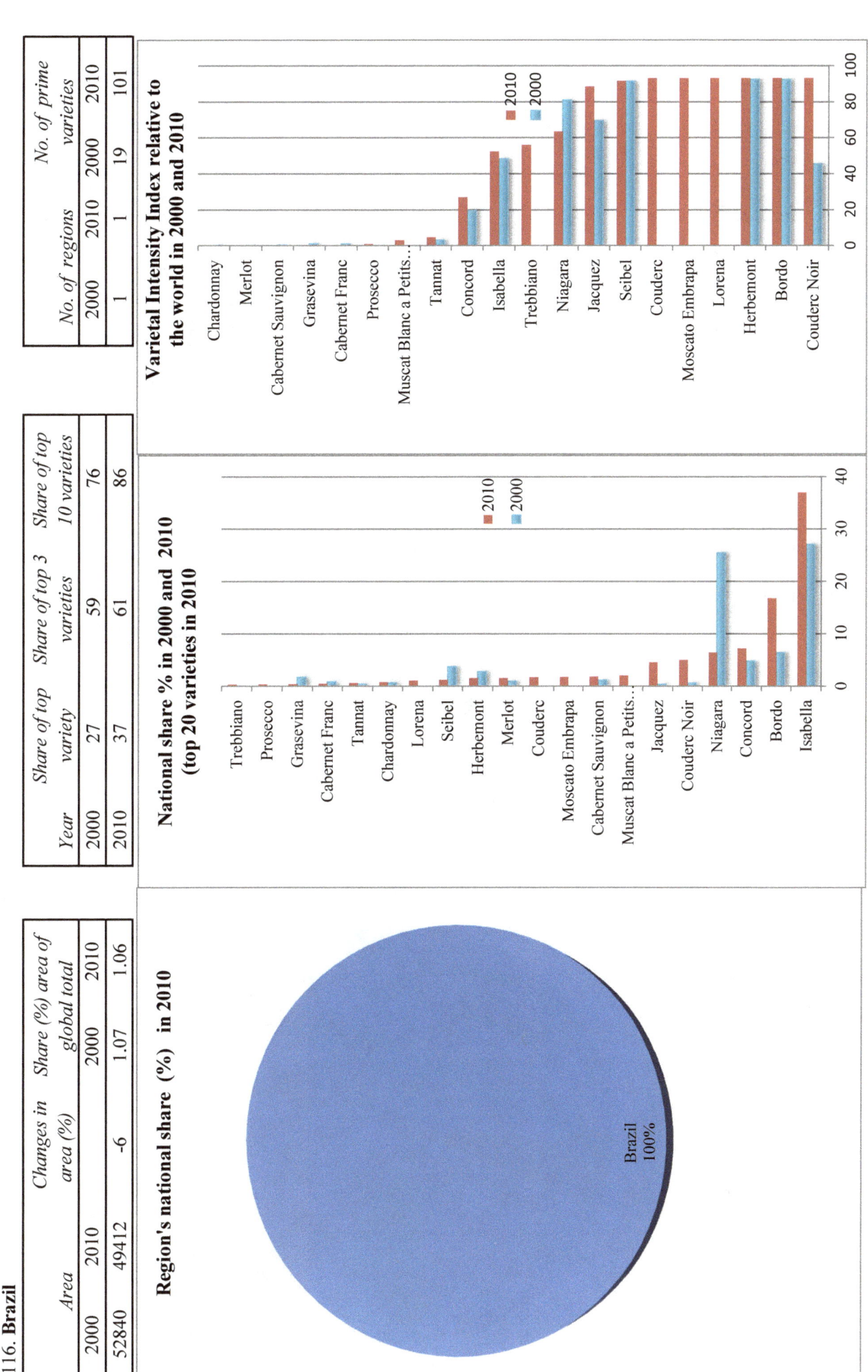

117. Bulgaria

Area		Changes in area (%)	Share (%) area of global total	
2000	2010		2000	2010
95997	56133	-42	1.95	1.21

Year	Share of top variety	Share of top 3 varieties	Share of top 10 varieties
2000	24	46	82
2010	19	46	78

No. of regions		No. of prime varieties	
2000	2010	2000	2010
1	6	21	16

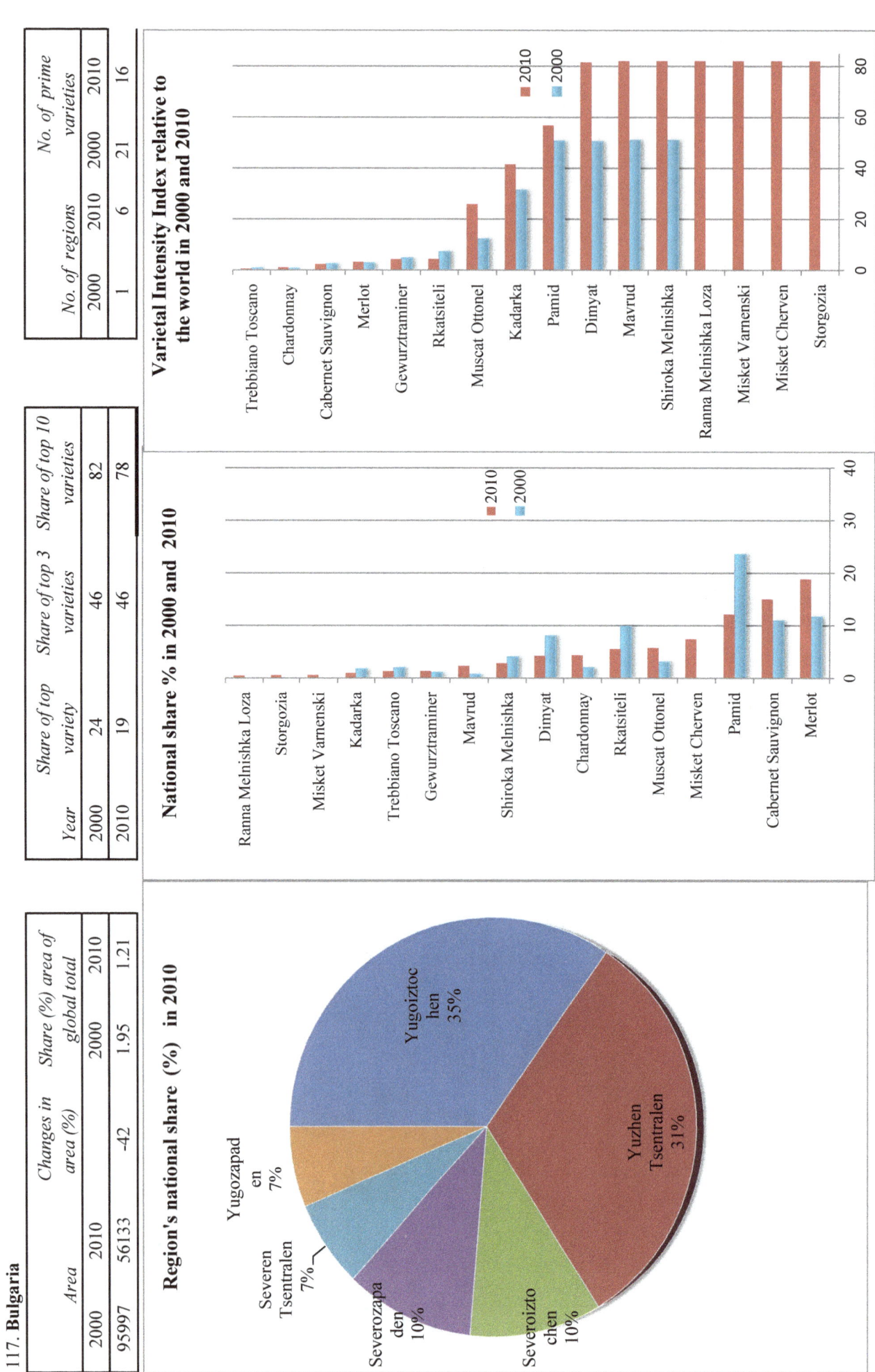

118. Canada

Area		Changes in area (%)	Share (%) area of global total	
2000	2010		2000	2010
8498	10096	19	0.17	0.22

Year	Share of top variety	Share of top 3 varieties	Share of top 10 varieties
2000	12	31	70
2010	13	34	74

No. of regions		No. of prime varieties	
2000	2010	2000	2010
1	2	20	76

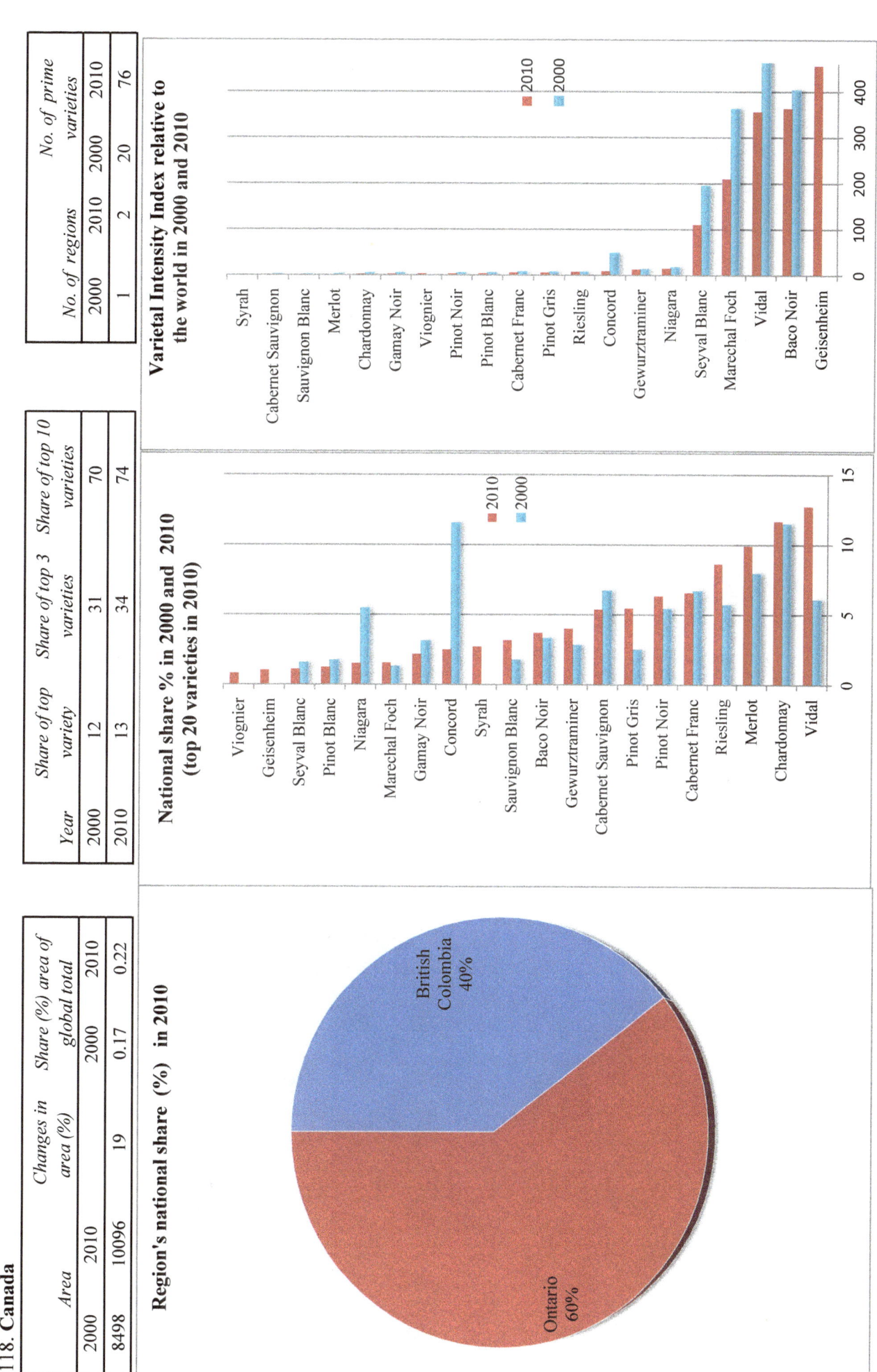

119. Chile

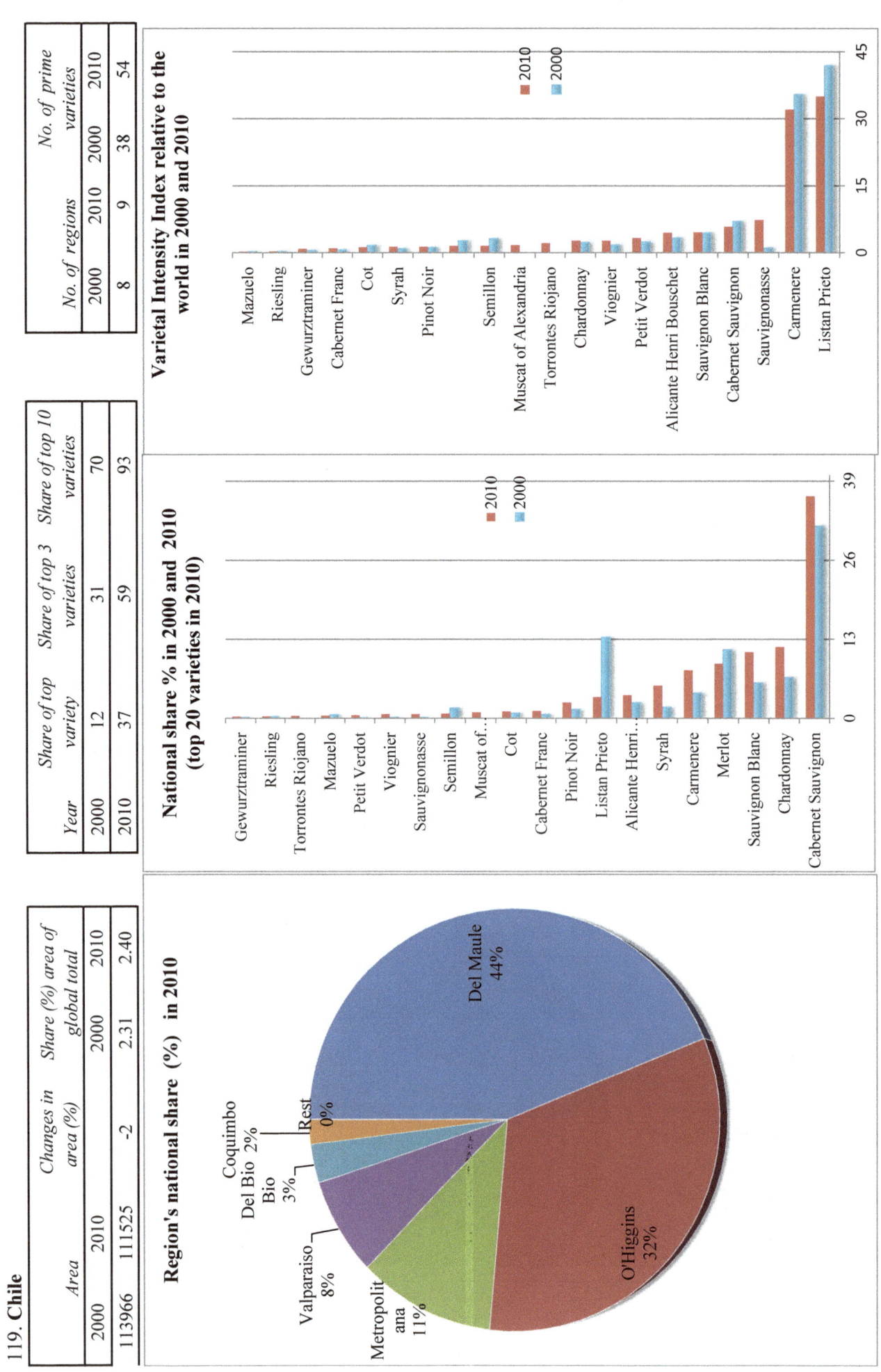

120. China

Area		Changes in area (%)	Share (%) area of global total	
2000	2010		2000	2010
na	29545	na	na	0.64

Year	Share of top variety	Share of top 3 varieties	Share of top 10 varieties
2000			
2010	77	93	100

No. of regions		No. of prime varieties	
2000	2010	2000	2010
	10		17

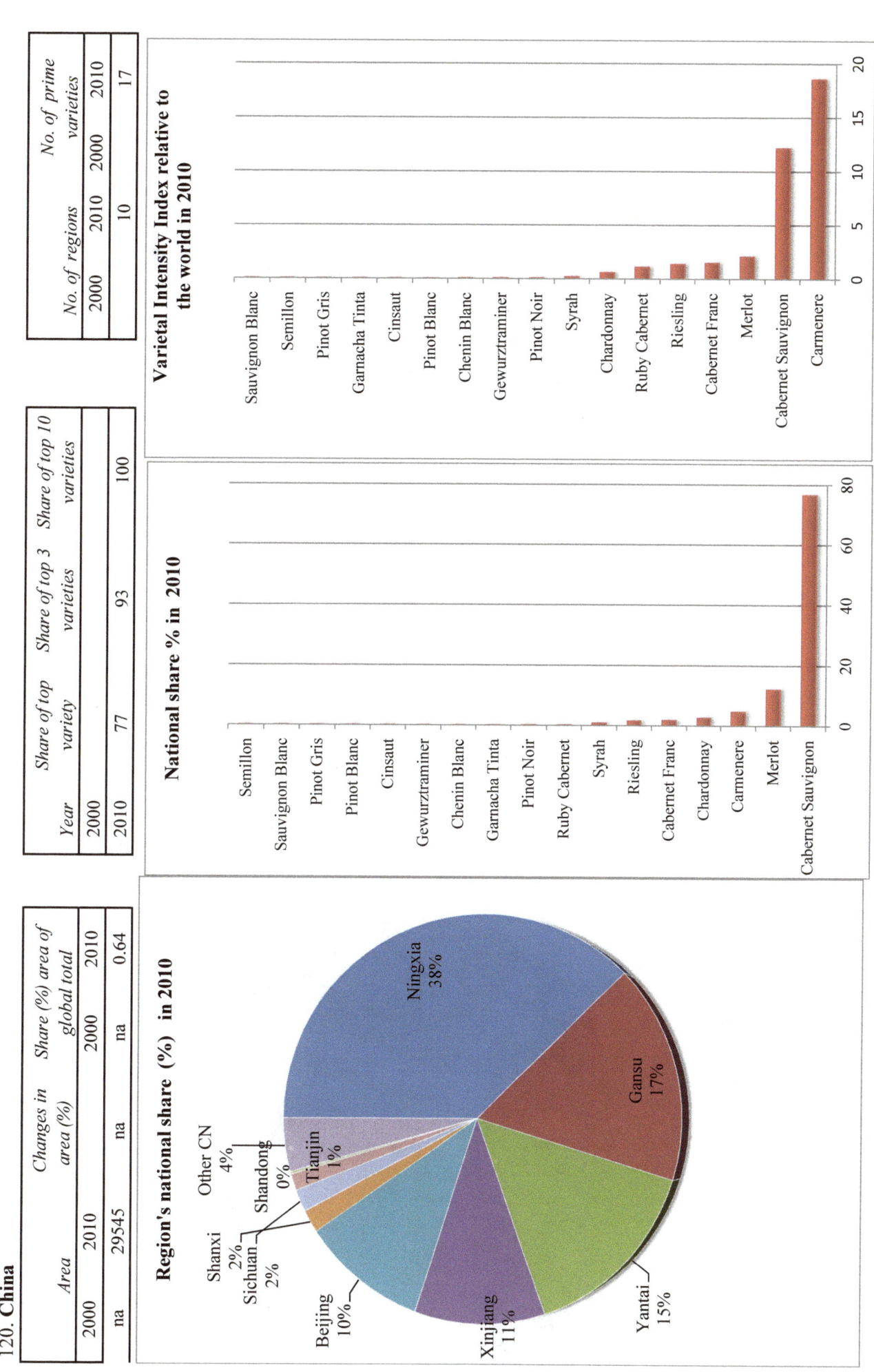

121. Croatia

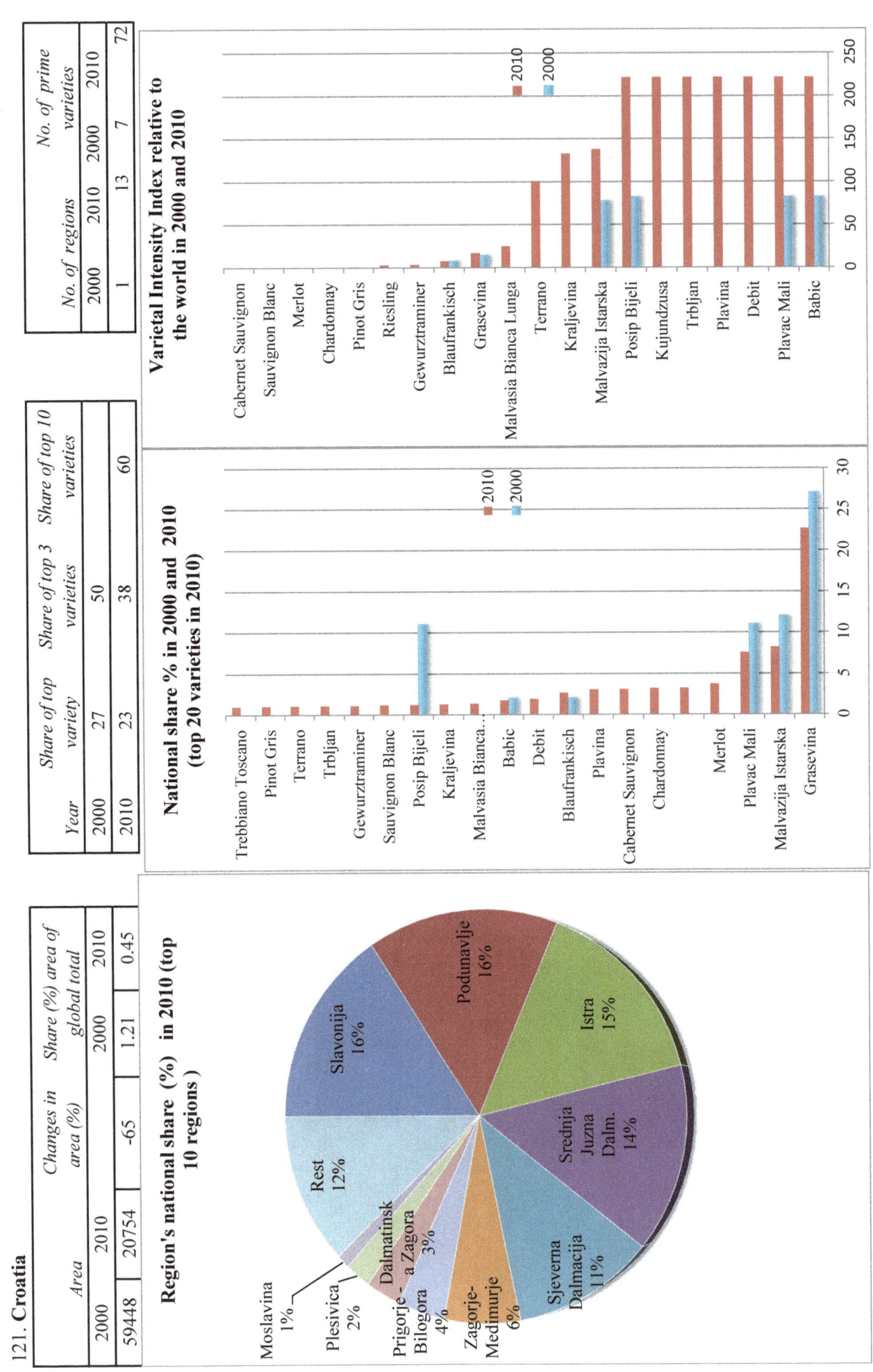

122. Cyprus

Area		Changes in area (%)	Share (%) area of global total		No. of regions		No. of prime varieties	
2000	2010		2000	2010	2000	2010	2000	2010
18282	8608	-53	0.37	0.19	1	1	2	15

Year	Share of top variety	Share of top 3 varieties	Share of top 10 varieties
2000	60		
2010	42	71	91

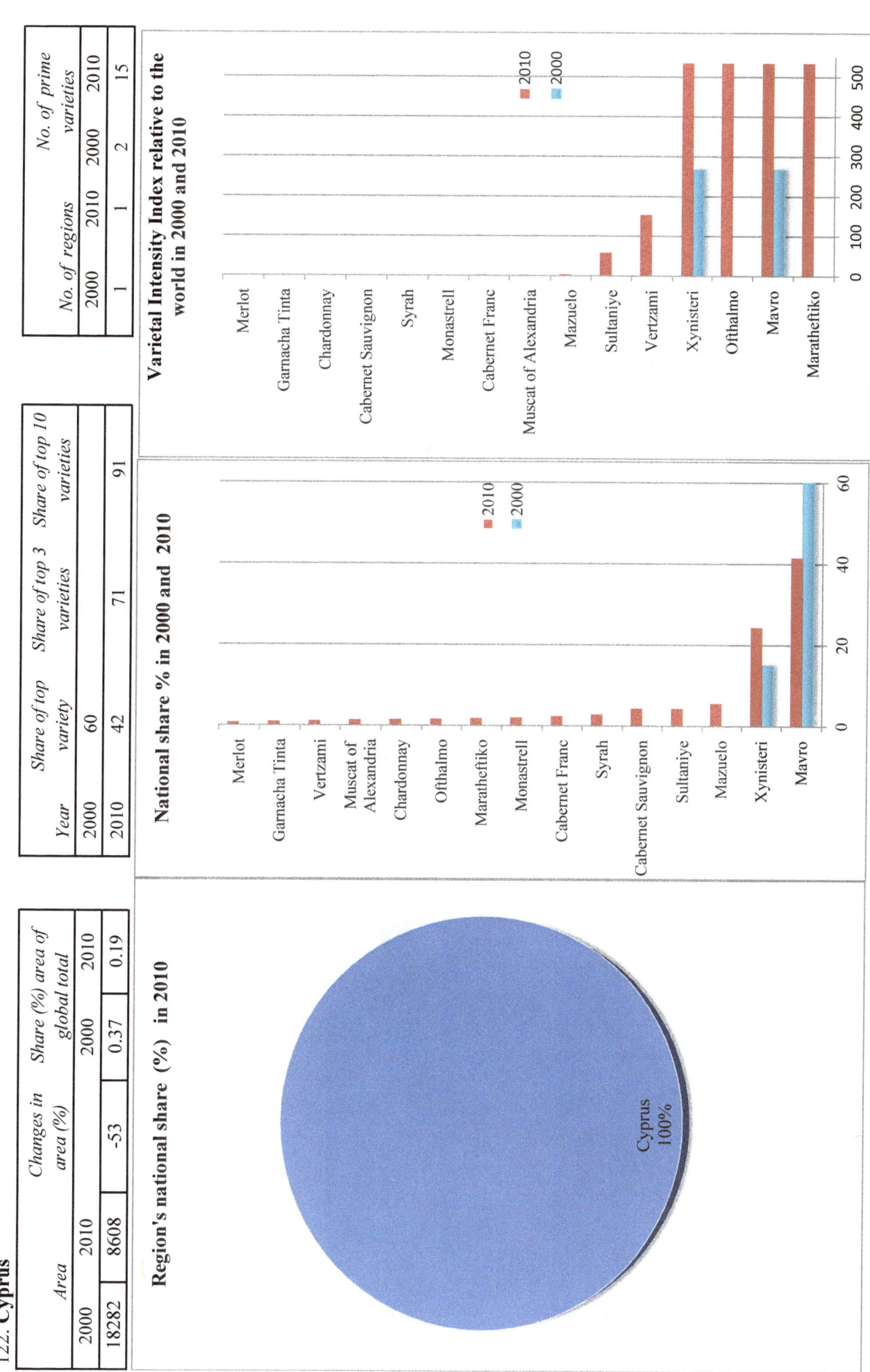

123. Czech Rep.

	Area		Changes in area (%)	Share (%) area of global total		No. of regions		No. of prime varieties	
	2000	2010		2000	2010	2000	2010	2000	2010
	11331	16242	43	0.23	0.35	1	2	10	32

Year	Share of top variety	Share of top 3 varieties	Share of top 10 varieties
2000	15	40	77
2010	10	27	68

Region's national share (%) in 2010

Morava 95%
Cechy 5%

National share % in 2000 and 2010 (top 20 varieties in 2010)

Varietal Intensity Index relative to the world in 2000 and 2010

124. France

Area		Changes in area (%)	Share (%) area of global total	
2000	2010		2000	2010
864846	846880	-2	17.54	18.23

Year	Share of top variety	Share of top 3 varieties	Share of top 10 varieties
2000	12	34	72
2010	14	35	72

	No. of regions		No. of prime varieties	
	2000	2010	2000	2010
	29	45	285	96

Region's national share (%) in 2010 (top 10 regins in 2010)

- Gironde 15%
- Herault 11%
- Aude 9%
- Gard 7%
- Vaucluse 6%
- Charente 5%
- Charente Maritime 5%
- Pyrenees Orientales 4%
- Var 4%
- Champagne-Viticole 4%
- Rest 30%

National share % in 2000 and 2010 (top 20 varieties in 2010)

Varietal Intensity Index relative to the world in 2000 and 2010

125. Georgia

Area		Changes in area (%)	Share (%) area of global total		No. of regions		No. of prime varieties	
2000	2010		2000	2010	2000	2010	2000	2010
37419	48001	28	0.76	1.03	1	1	21	21

Year	Share of top variety	Share of top 3 varieties	Share of top 10 varieties
2000	53	79	92
2010	53	79	92

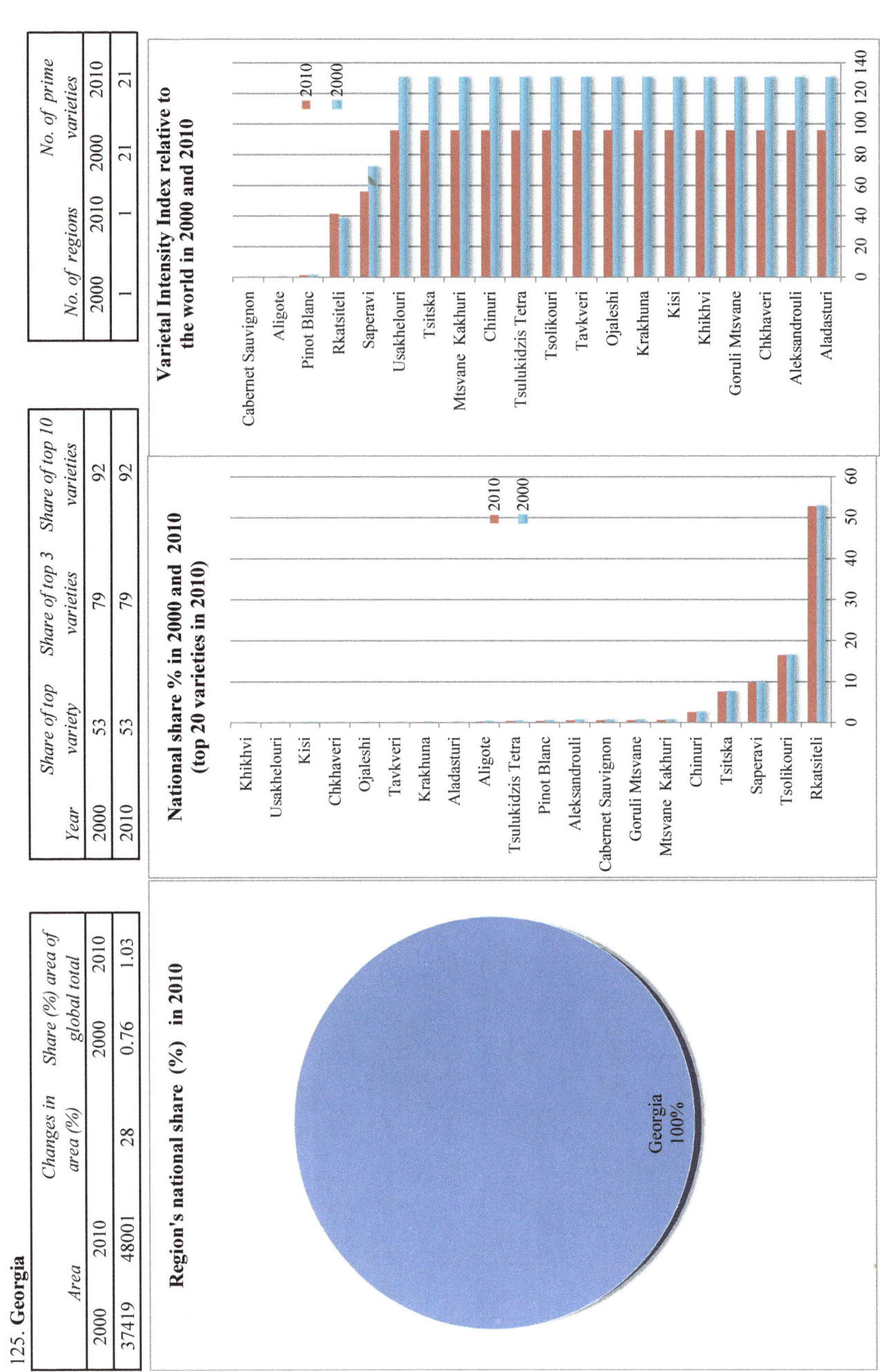

126. Germany

Area		Changes in area (%)	Share (%) area of global total	
2000	2010		2000	2010
104207	102060	-2	2.11	2.20

Year	Share of top variety	Share of top 3 varieties	Share of top 10 varieties
2000	21	48	65
2010	22	43	60

No. of regions		No. of prime varieties	
2000	2010	2000	2010
13	13	57	48

Region's national share (%) in 2010 (top 10 regions in 2010)

- Rheinhessen 26%
- Rhein-Pfalz 23%
- Baden 15%
- Wurttemberg 11%
- Mosel-Saar-Ruwer 9%
- Franken 6%
- Nahe 4%
- Rheingau 3%
- Saale-Unstrut 1%
- Rest 1%

National share % in 2000 and 2010 (top 20 varieties in 2010)

Varietal Intensity Index relative to the world in 2000 and 2010

641

127. Greece

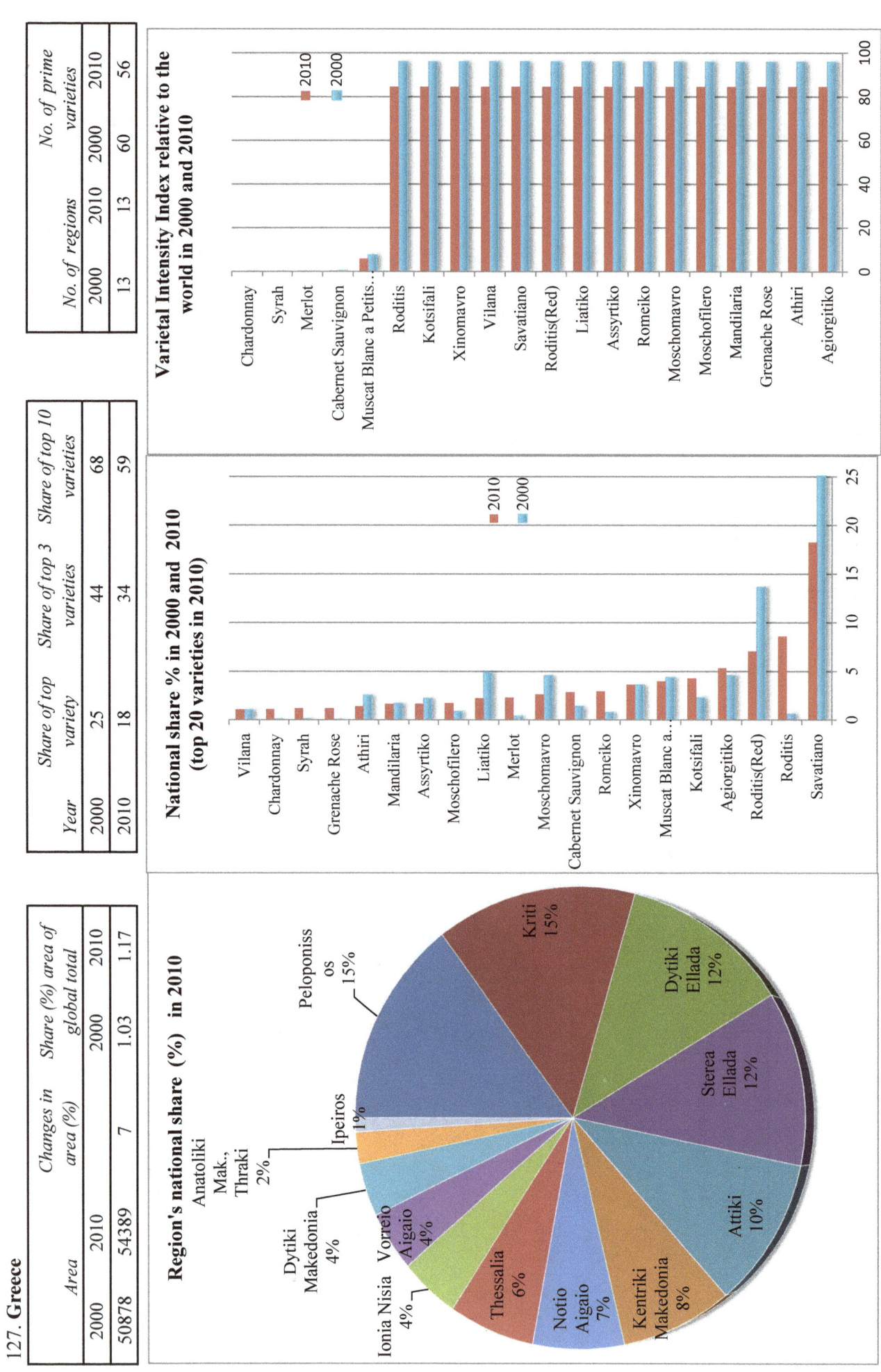

128. Hungary

	Area		Changes in area (%)	Share (%) area of global total	
	2000	2010		2000	2010
	86886	69715	-20	1.76	1.50

Year	Share of top variety	Share of top 3 varieties	Share of top 10 varieties
2000	8	20	42
2010	11	24	50

No. of regions		No. of prime varieties	
2000	2010	2000	2010
1	22	32	137

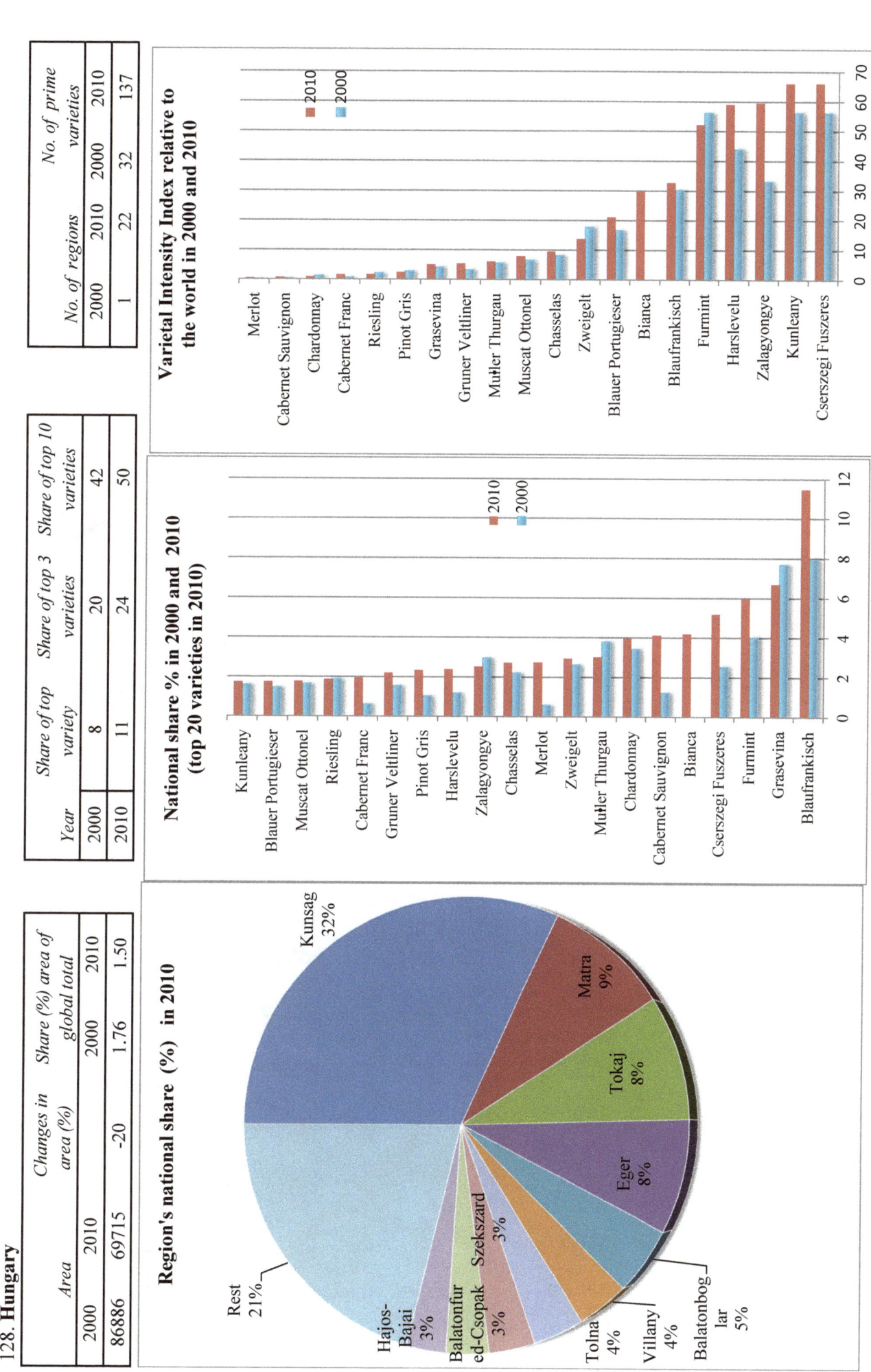

129. Italy

Area		Changes in area (%)	Share (%) area of global total	
2000	2010		2000	2010
636662	625700	-2	12.91	13.47

Year	Share of top variety	Share of top 3 varieties	Share of top 10 varieties
2000	10	24	47
2010	11	23	45

	No. of regions		No. of prime varieties	
	2000	2010	2000	2010
	103	20	323	396

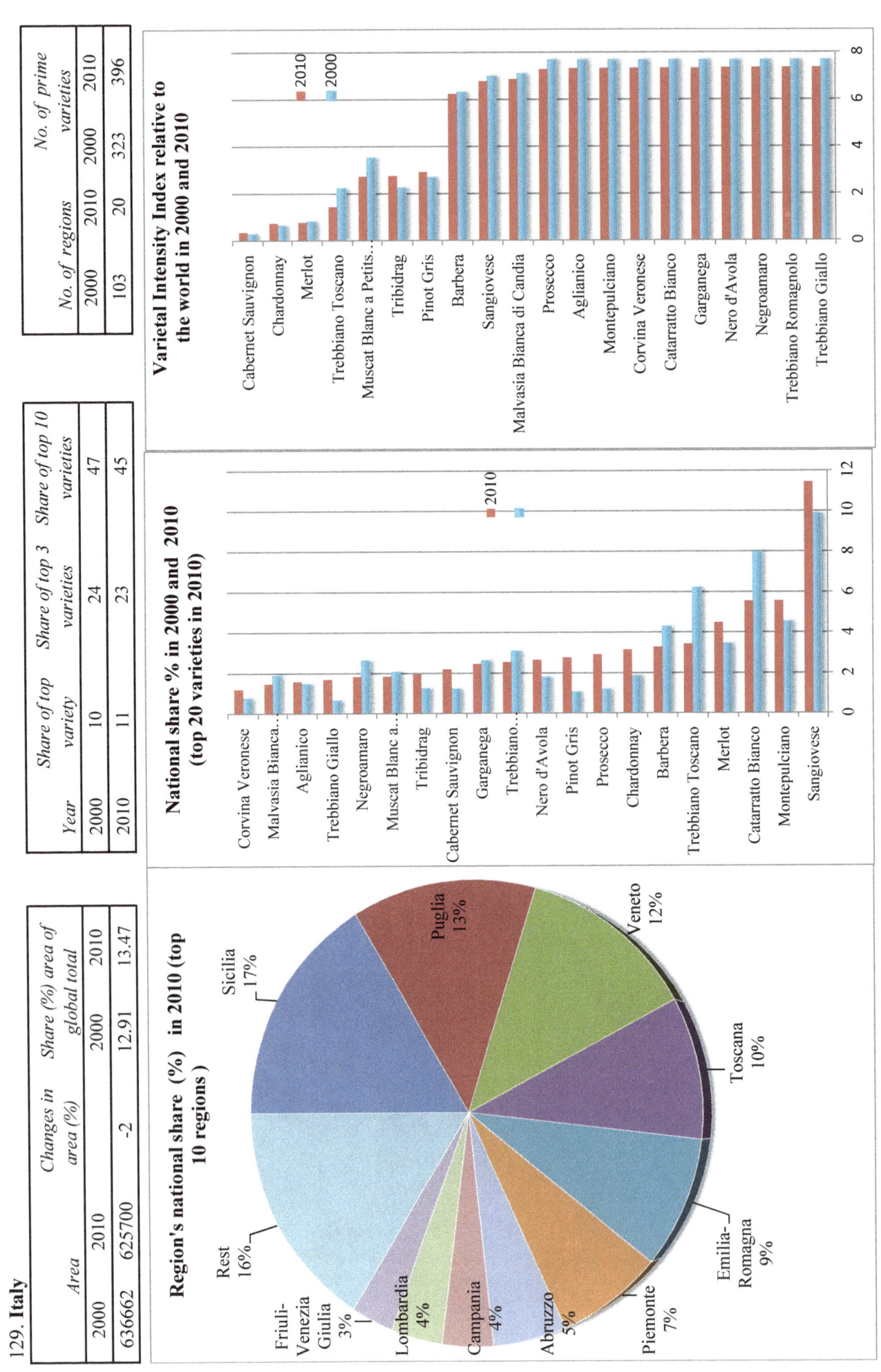

130. Japan

Area		Changes in area (%)	Share (%) area of global total		No. of regions		No. of prime varieties	
2000	2010		2000	2010	2000	2010	2000	2010
	3715			0.08		5		15

Year	Share of top variety	Share of top 3 varieties	Share of top 10 varieties
2000			
2010	22	51	95

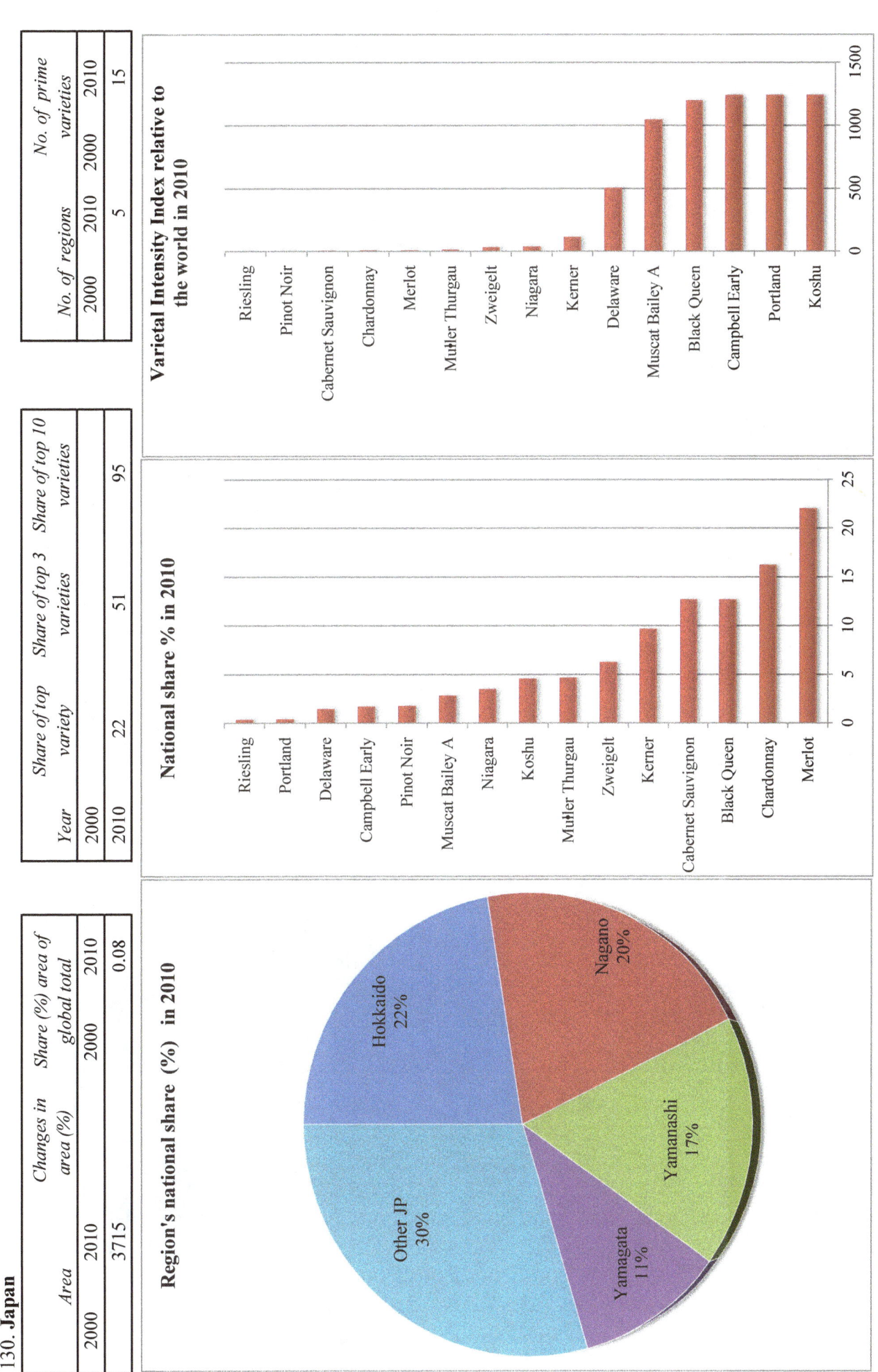

131. Kazakhstan

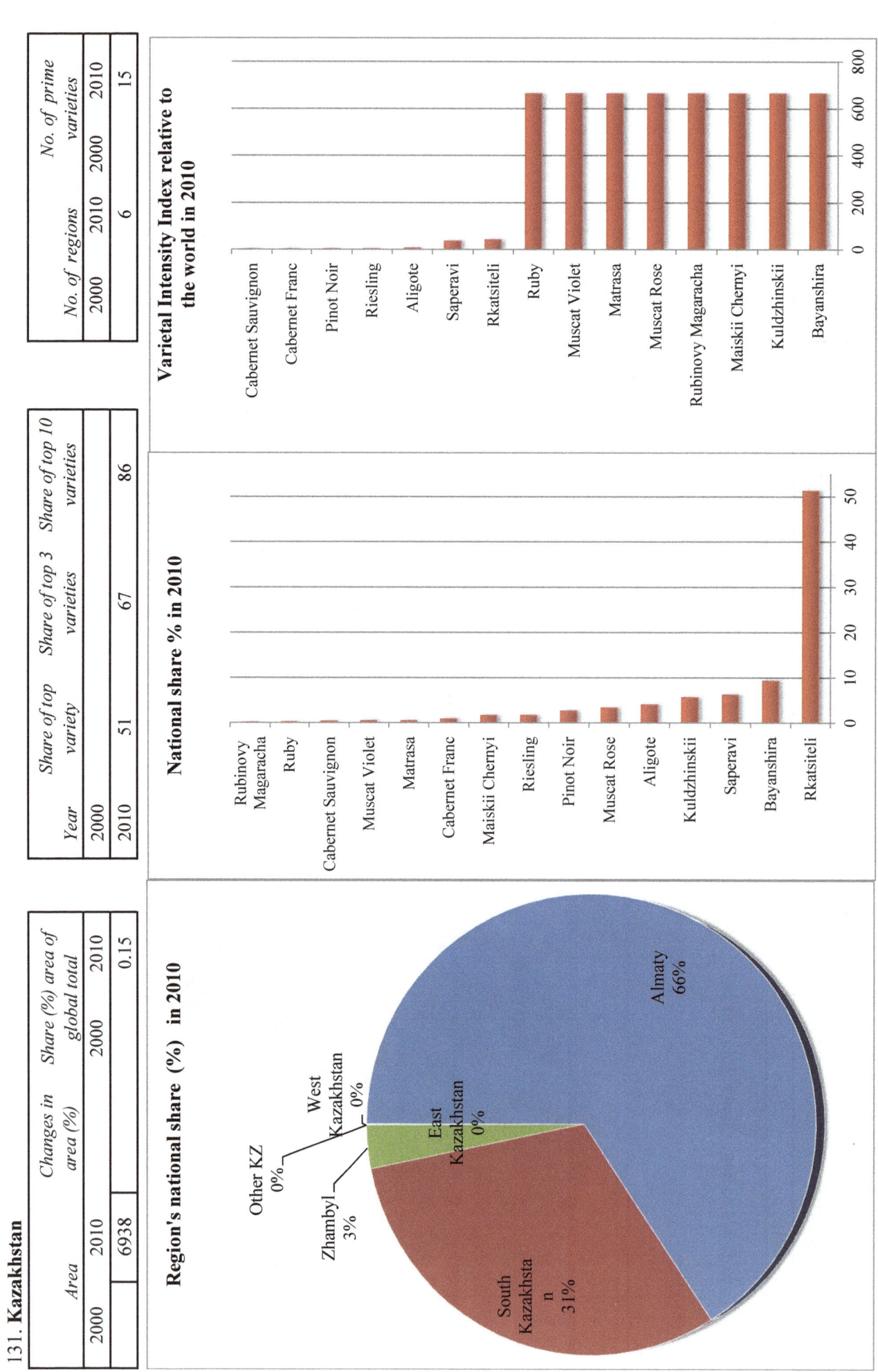

132. Luxembourg

Area		Changes in area (%)	Share (%) area of global total	
2000	2010		2000	2010
1348	1304	-3	0.03	0.03

Year	Share of top variety	Share of top 3 varieties	Share of top 10 varieties
2000	34	60	100
2010	28	57	100

No. of regions		No. of prime varieties	
2000	2010	2000	2010
1	1	11	10

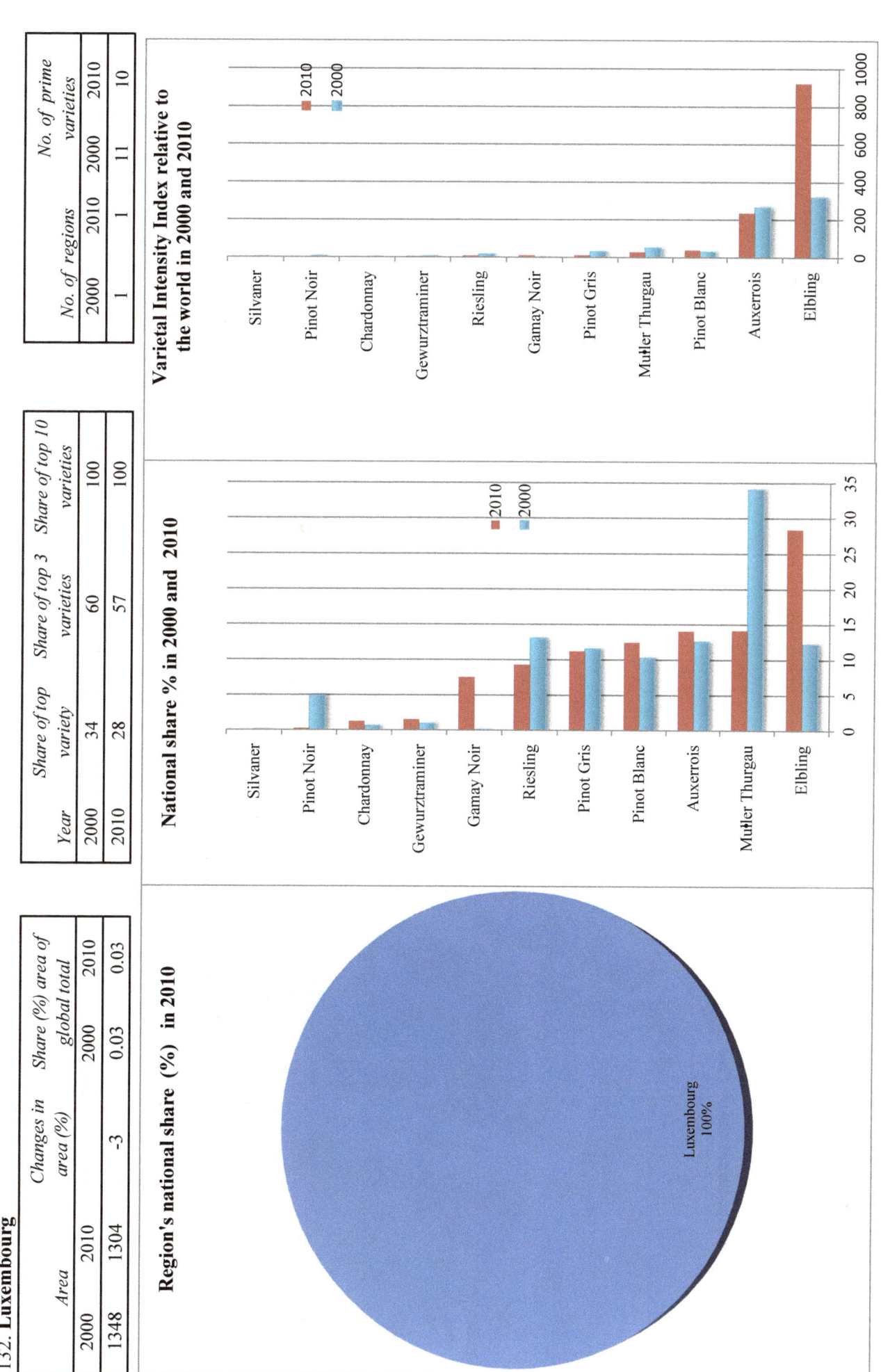

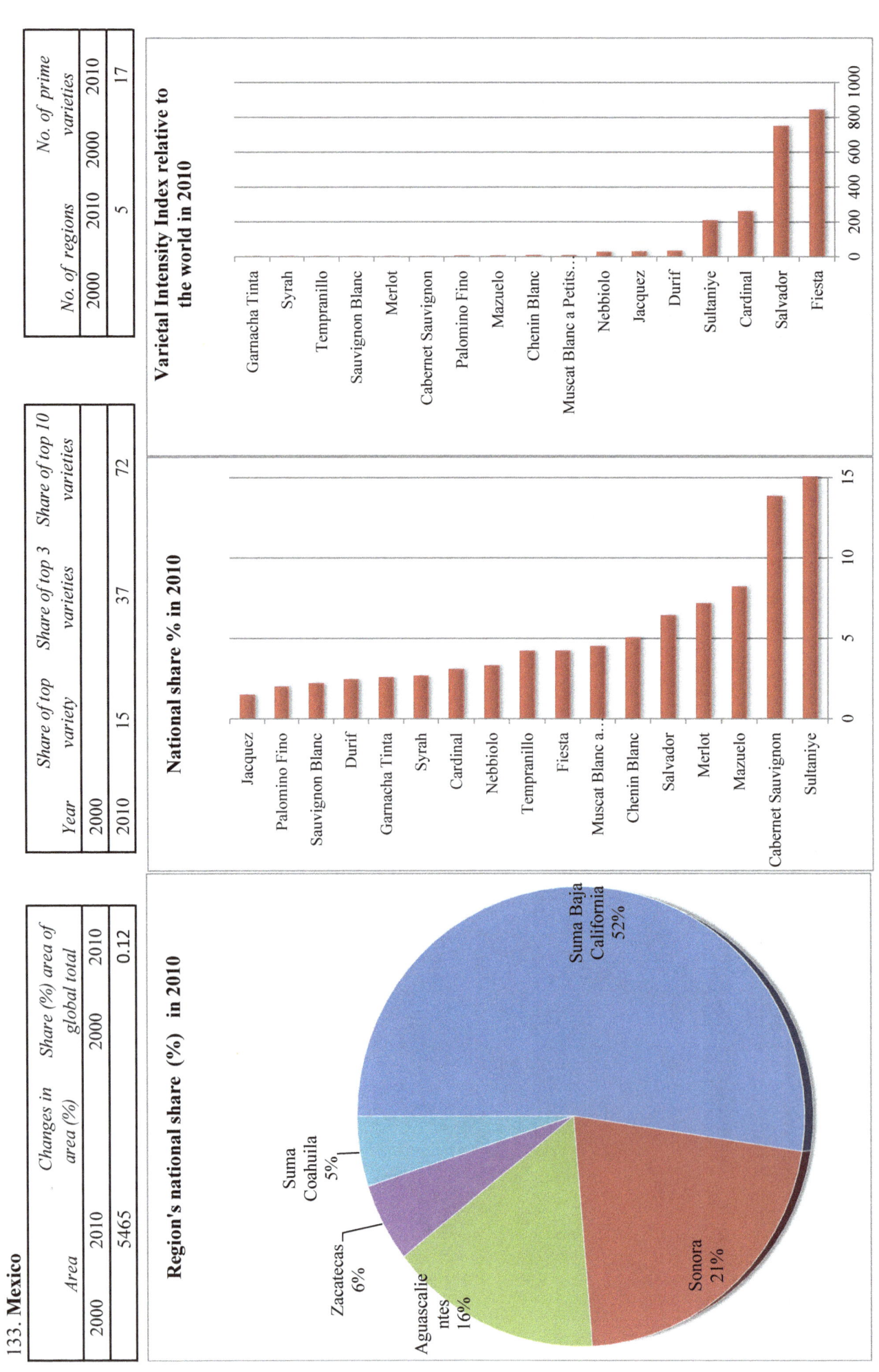

134. Moldova

Area		Changes in area (%)	Share (%) area of global total		No. of regions		No. of prime varieties	
2000	2010		2000	2010	2000	2010	2000	2010
89844	89844	0	1.82	1.93	1	1	39	39

Year	Share of top variety	Share of top 3 varieties	Share of top 10 varieties
2000	18	43	90
2010	18	43	90

Region's national share (%) in 2010

Moldova 100%

National share % in 2010 (top 20 varieties in 2010)

Silvaner, Muscat Blanc a..., Muller Thurgau, Pinot Blanc, Sukholimanskiy..., Saperavi, Bastardo..., Riesling, Muscat Ottonel, Pinot Gris, Gewurztraminer, Feteasca Alba, Chardonnay, Pinot Noir, Cabernet Sauvignon, Merlot, Sauvignon Blanc, Isabella, Rkatsiteli, Aligote

Varietal Intensity Index relative to the world 2010

Muscat Blanc a Petits..., Muller Thurgau, Pinot Blanc, Chardonnay, Cabernet Sauvignon, Riesling, Merlot, Silvaner, Pinot Gris, Sauvignon Blanc, Pinot Noir, Saperavi, Muscat Ottonel, Gewurztraminer, Rkatsiteli, Feteasca Alba, Sukholimanskiy Bely, Isabella, Aligote, Bastardo Magarachsky

135. Morocco

Area		Changes in area (%)	Share (%) area of global total		No. of regions		No. of prime varieties	
2000	2010		2000	2010	2000	2010	2000	2010
49600	49000	-1	1.01	1.05	1	1	8	8

Year	Share of top variety	Share of top 3 varieties	Share of top 10 varieties
2000	33	49	
2010	34	49	

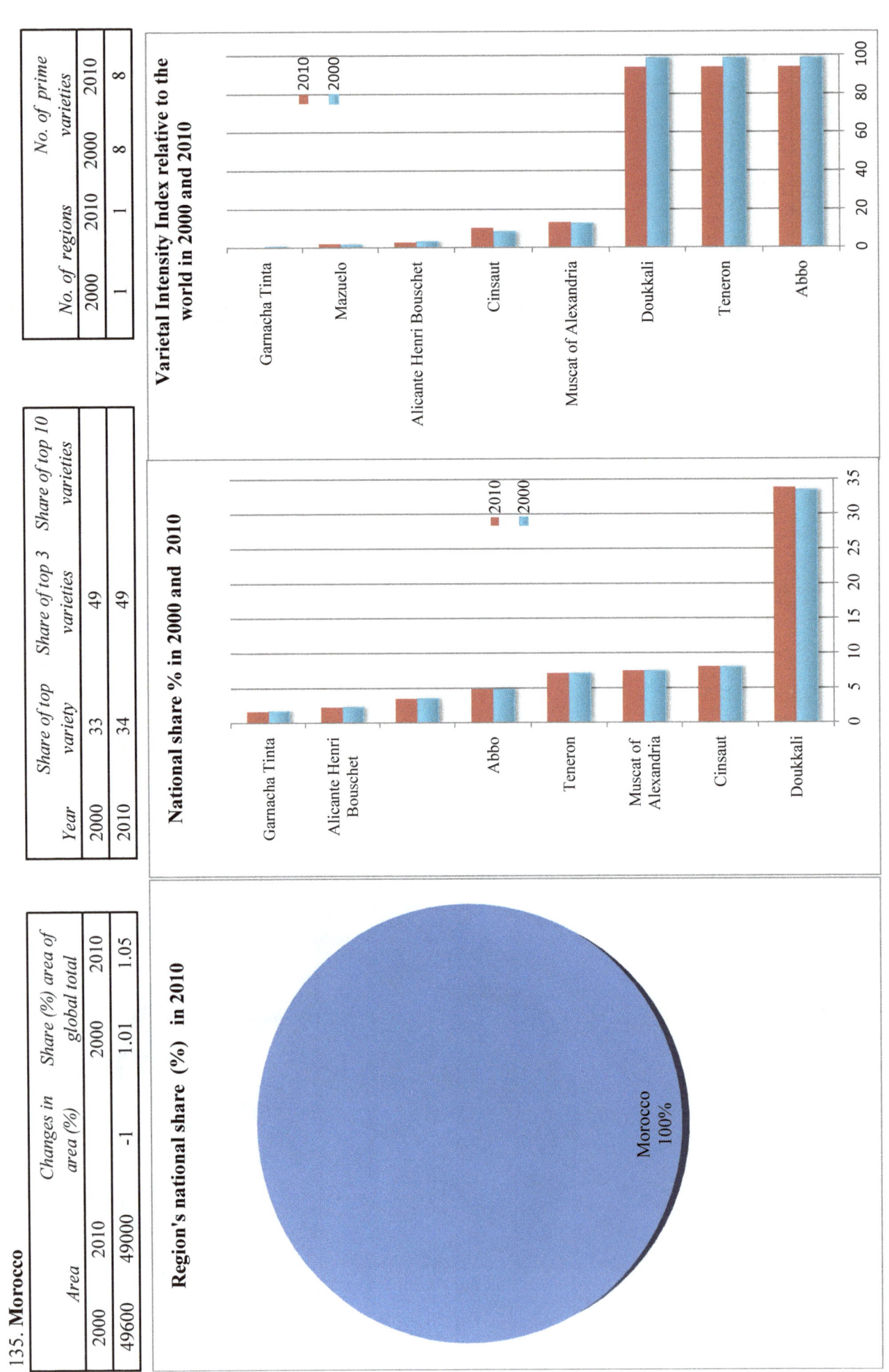

136. Myanmar

Area		Changes in area (%)	Share (%) area of global total	
2000	2010		2000	2010
	75			0.00

Year	Share of top variety	Share of top 3 varieties	Share of top 10 varieties
2000			
2010	36	75	100

No. of regions		No. of prime varieties	
2000	2010	2000	2010
	1		11

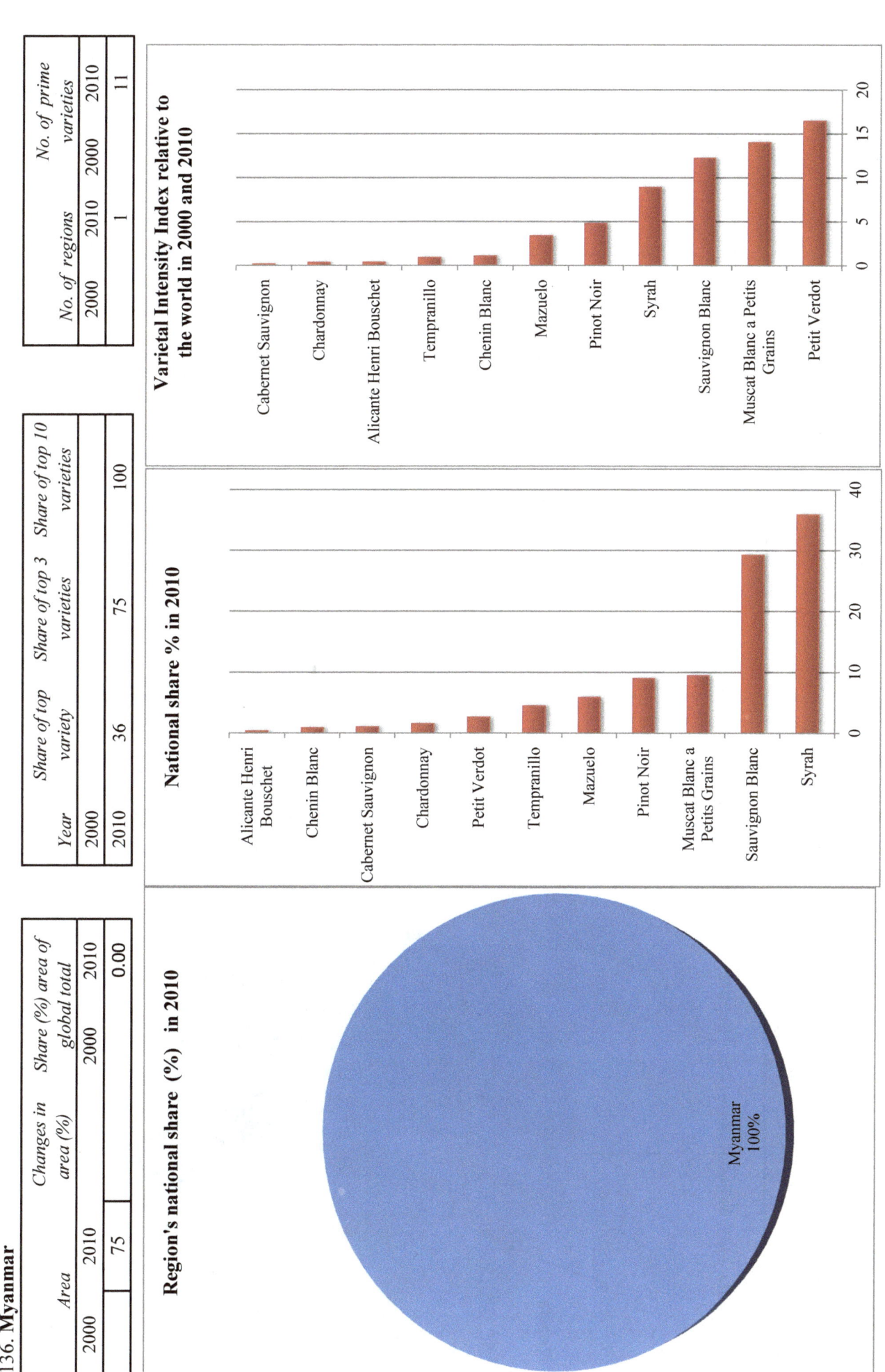

137. New Zealand

Area		Changes in area (%)	Share (%) area of global total	
2000	2010		2000	2010
9942	31964	221	0.20	0.69

Year	Share of top variety	Share of top 3 varieties	Share of top 10 varieties
2000	28	63	91
2010	51	78	94

No. of regions		No. of prime varieties	
2000	2010	2000	2010
10	11	22	45

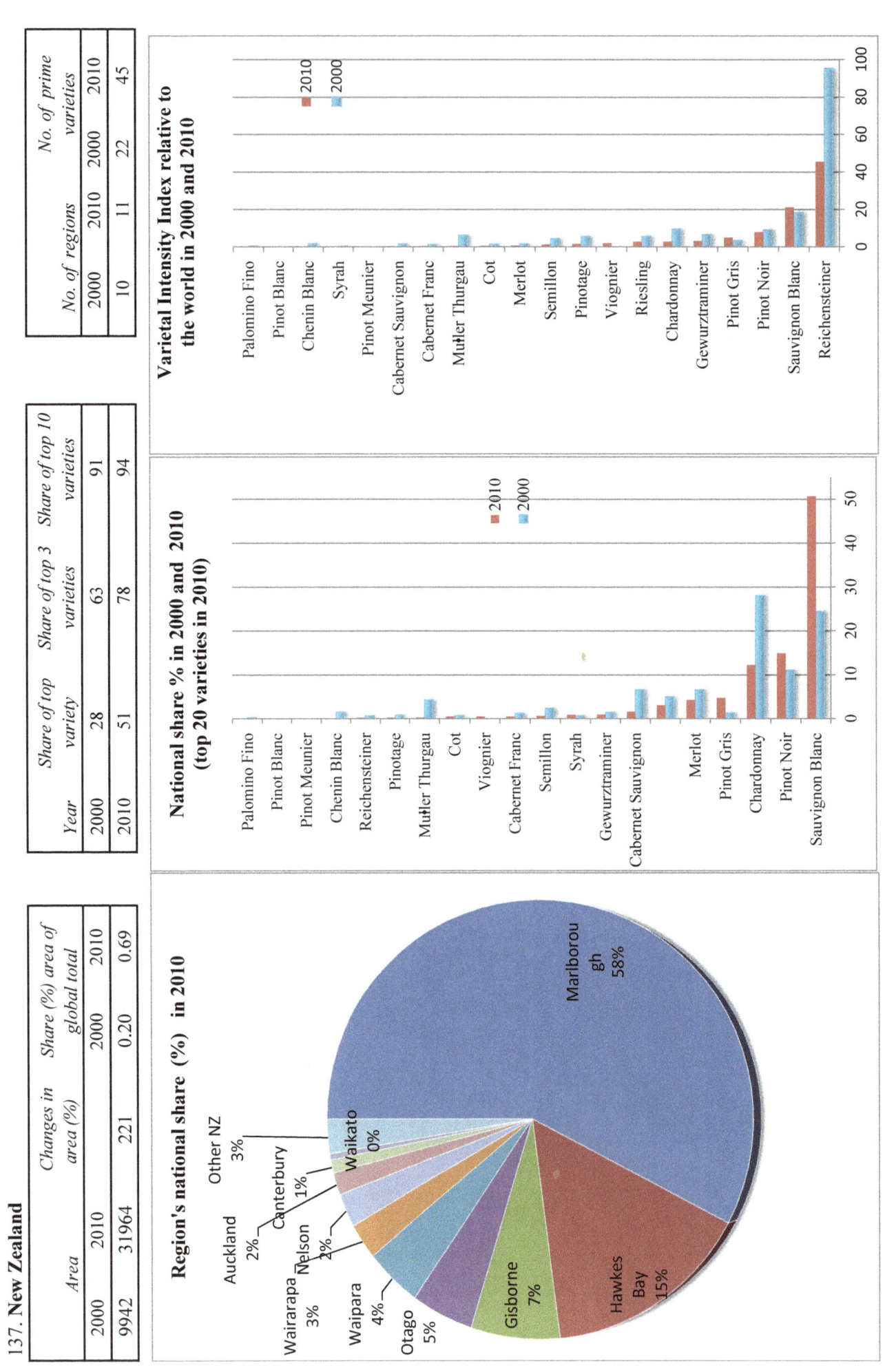

138. Peru

Area		Changes in area (%)	Share (%) area of global total	
2000	2010		2000	2010
	3831			0.08

Year	Share of top variety	Share of top 3 varieties	Share of top 10 varieties
2000			
2010	33	68	98

No. of regions		No. of prime varieties	
2000	2010	2000	2010
	4		30

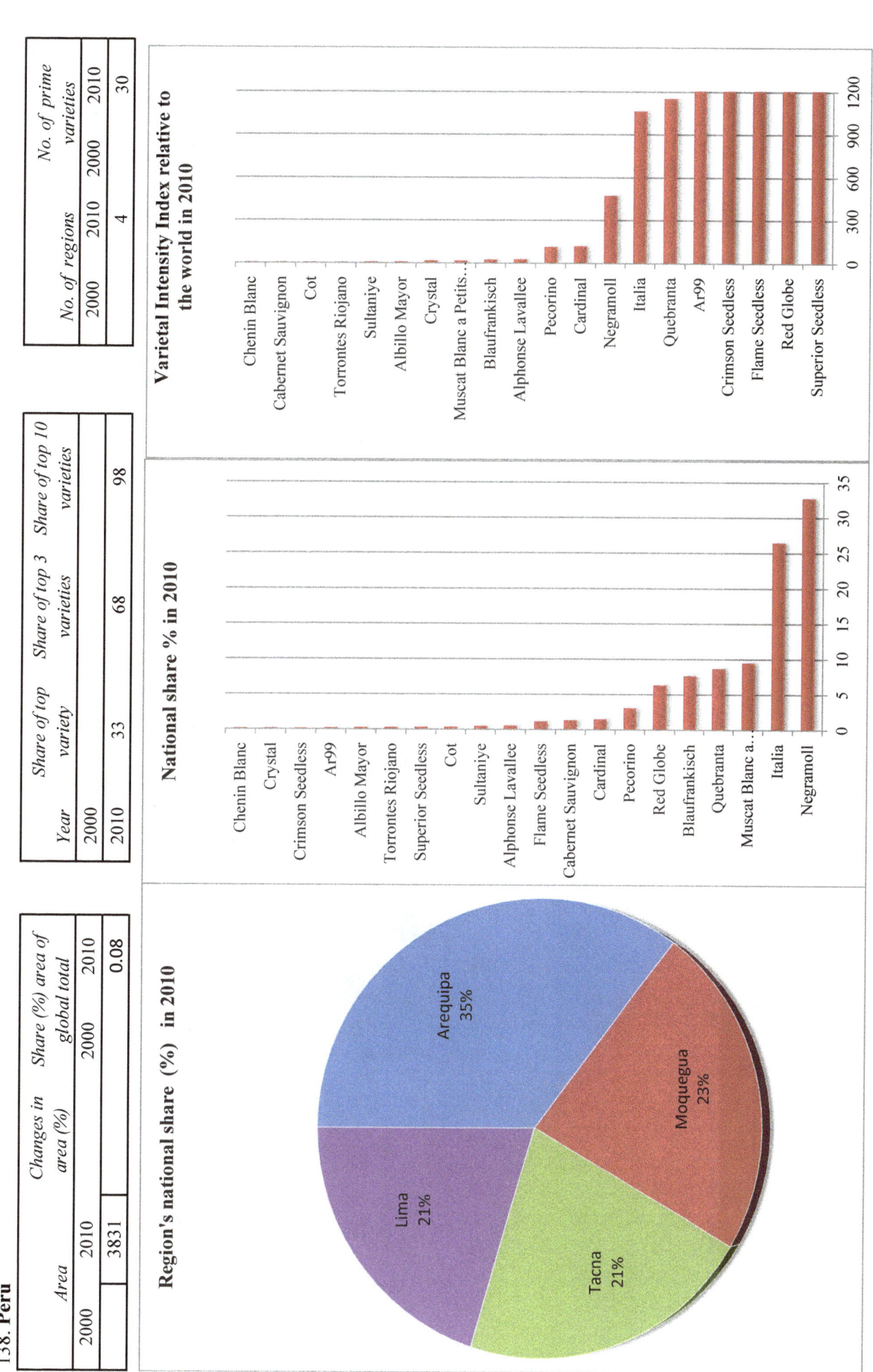

139. Portugal

Area		Changes in area (%)	Share (%) area of global total	
2000	2010		2000	2010
205003	163522	-20	4.16	3.52

Year	Share of top variety	Share of top 3 varieties	Share of top 10 varieties
2000	7	18	37
2010	10	24	55

No. of regions		No. of prime varieties	
2000	2010	2000	2010
9	9	80	266

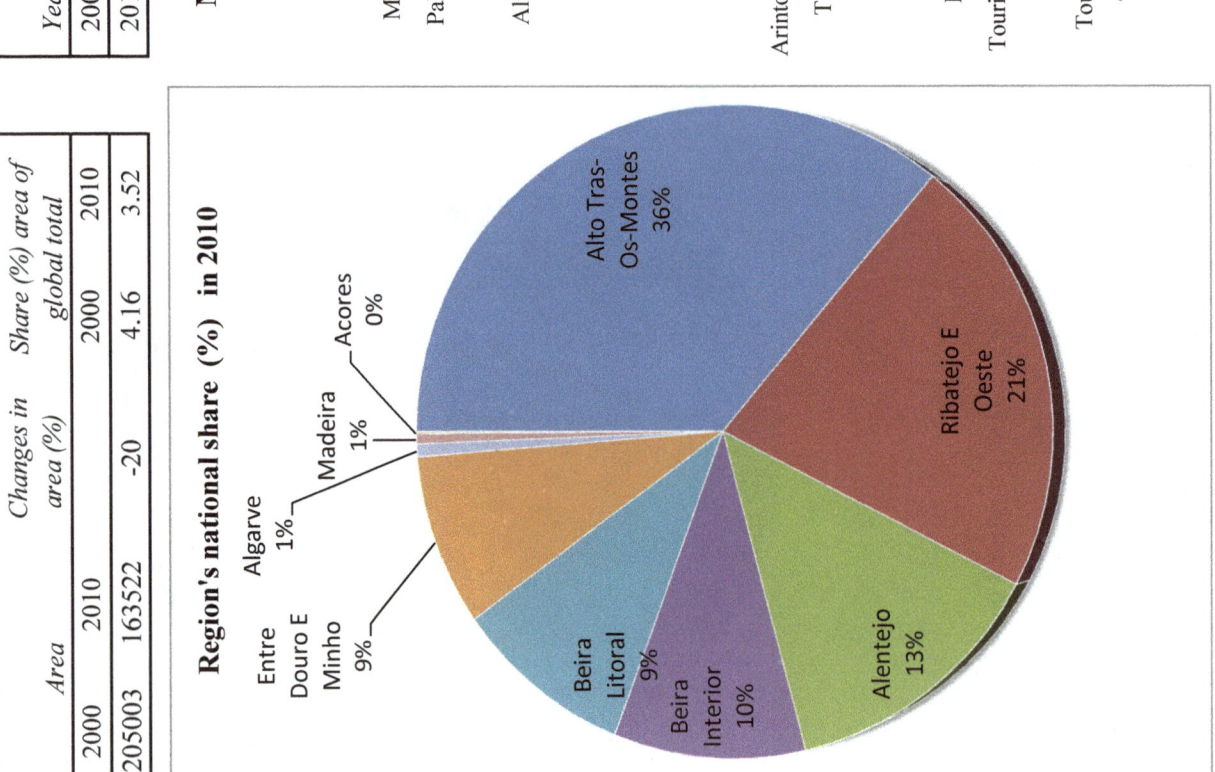

Region's national share (%) in 2010

National share % in 2000 and 2010 (top 20 varieties in 2010)

Varietal Intensity Index relative to the world in 2000 and 2010

140. Romania

Area		Changes in area (%)	Share (%) area of global total	
2000	2010		2000	2010
222173	170292	-23	4.51	3.67

Year	Share of top variety	Share of top 3 varieties	Share of top 10 varieties
2000	8	19	34
2010	8	22	41

No. of regions		No. of prime varieties	
2000	2010	2000	2010
1	8	18	25

Varietal Intensity Index relative to the world in 2000 and 2010

National share % in 2000 and 2010 (top 20 varieties in 2010)

Region's national share (%) in 2010

- Sud-Est 40%
- Sud-Vest Oltenia 19%
- Nord-Est 16%
- Sud-Muntenia 16%
- Nord-Vest 4%
- Centru 3%
- Vest 2%
- Bucuresti-Ilfov 0%

141. Russia

Area		Changes in area (%)	Share (%) area of global total	
2000	2010		2000	2010
56332	25628	-55	1.14	0.55

Year	Share of top variety	Share of top 3 varieties	Share of top 10 varieties
2000	23	33	54
2010	14	36	67

No. of regions		No. of prime varieties	
2000	2010	2000	2010
1	2	11	55

Region's national share (%) in 2010

Krasnodar Krai 83%
Rostov Oblast 17%

National share % in 2000 and 2010 (top 20 varieties in 2010)

Varieties: Podarok Magaracha, Viorica, Citronny Magarach, Saperavi Severny, Tsimlyansky..., Dunavski Lazur, Pinot Noir, Krasnostop..., Pinot Blanc, Rkatsiteli, Saperavi, Levokumsky, Riesling, Sauvignon Blanc, Aligote, Merlot, Chardonnay, Pervenets..., Bianca, Cabernet Sauvignon

Varieties (prime): Merlot, Pinot Noir, Sauvignon Blanc, Chardonnay, Rkatsiteli, Cabernet Sauvignon, Riesling, Aligote, Pinot Blanc, Saperavi, Bianca, Podarok Magaracha, Pervenets Magaracha, Viorica, Saperavi Severny, Dunavski Lazur, Levokumsky, Citronny Magarach, Tsimlyansky Cherny, Krasnostop Zolotovsky

142. Serbia

Area		Changes in area (%)	Share (%) area of global total	
2000	2010		2000	2010
68999	68999	0	1.40	1.49

Year	Share of top variety	Share of top 3 varieties	Share of top 10 varieties
2000	48	75	
2010	48	75	

No. of regions		No. of prime varieties	
2000	2010	2000	2010
1	1	4	4

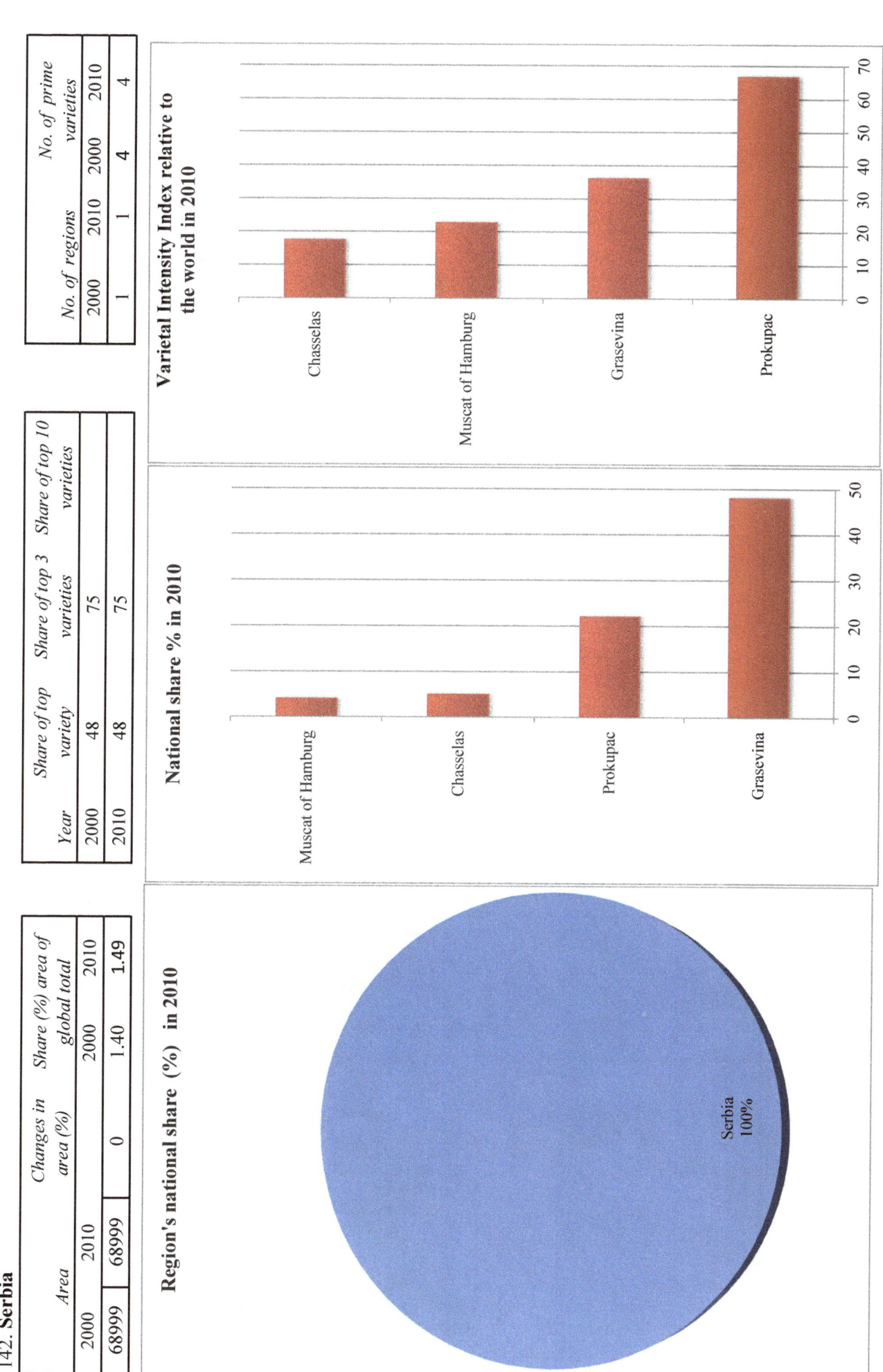

143. Slovakia

Area		Changes in area (%)	Share (%) area of global total	
2000	2010		2000	2010
15580	12637	-19	0.32	0.27

Year	Share of top variety	Share of top 3 varieties	Share of top 10 varieties
2000	25	56	82
2010	17	41	73

No. of regions		No. of prime varieties	
2000	2010	2000	2010
1	6	11	35

Region's national share (%) in 2010

- Juznoslovenska 33%
- Malokarpatska 29%
- Nitrianska 21%
- Stredoslovenska 9%
- Tokajska 4%
- Vychodoslovenska 4%

National share % in 2000 and 2010 (top 20 varieties in 2010)

Varietal Intensity Index relative to the world in 2000 and 2010

144. Slovenia

Area		Changes in area (%)	Share (%) area of global total	
2000	2010		2000	2010
23472	16354	-30	0.48	0.35

Year	Share of top variety	Share of top 3 varieties	Share of top 10 varieties
2000	15	27	
2010	14	30	65

No. of regions		No. of prime varieties	
2000	2010	2000	2010
1	10	6	21

Region's national share (%) in 2010

- Stajerska Slovenija 39%
- Vipavska Dolina 15%
- Goriska Brda 12%
- Slovenska Istra 10%
- Dolenjska 9%
- Bizeljsko Sremic 6%
- Prekmurje Kras 4%
- Prekmurje 3%
- Bela Krajina 2%
- Other SI 0%

National share % in 2000 and 2010 (top 20 varieties in 2010)

Varieties (ascending): Plavay, Barbera, Kraljevina, Sauvignonasse, Savagnin Blanc, Muscat Blanc a..., Cabernet Sauvignon, Pinot Gris, Pinot Blanc, Furmint, Riesling, Blaufrankisch, Malvazija Istarska, Ribolla Gialla, Zametovka, Merlot, Sauvignon Blanc, Chardonnay, Refosco, Grasevina

Varietal Intensity Index relative to the world in 2000 and 2010

Varieties (ascending): Cabernet Sauvignon, Merlot, Barbera, Chardonnay, Sauvignon Blanc, Muscat Blanc a Petits..., Pinot Gris, Riesling, Pinot Blanc, Grasevina, Blaufrankisch, Sauvignonasse, Savagnin Blanc, Furmint, Malvazija Istarska, Kraljevina, Ribolla Gialla, Refosco, Zametovka, Plavay

145. South Africa

Area		Changes in area (%)	Share (%) area of global total		No. of regions		No. of prime varieties	
2000	2010		2000	2010	2000	2010	2000	2010
93656	101016	8	1.90	2.17	9	9	68	68

Year	Share of top variety	Share of top 3 varieties	Share of top 10 varieties
2000	24	46	84
2010	18	42	87

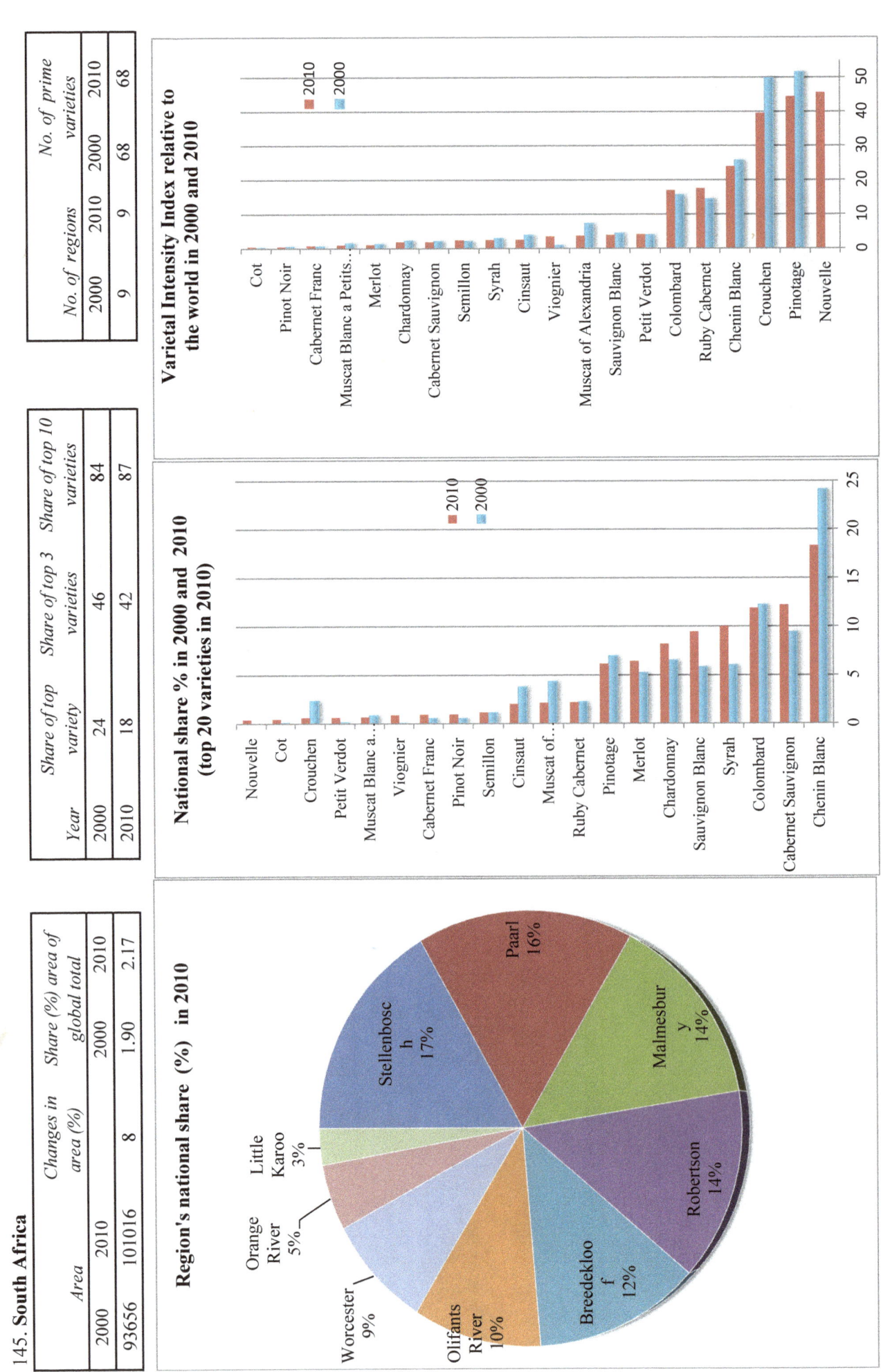

146. Spain

Area		Changes in area (%)	Share (%) area of global total	
2000	2010		2000	2010
1181805	1028258	-13	23.97	22.13

Year	Share of top variety	Share of top 3 varieties	Share of top 10 varieties
2000	33	49	75
2010	25	53	79

No. of regions		No. of prime varieties	
2000	2010	2000	2010
36	36	159	150

Region's national share (%) in 2010

- Ciudad Real 17%
- Rest 24%
- Toledo 12%
- Albacete 9%
- Cuenca 9%
- Badajoz 8%
- Valencia 6%
- Rioja 4%
- Murcia 4%
- Zaragoza 4%
- Tarragona 3%

National share % in 2000 and 2010 (top 20 varieties in 2010)

Varietal Intensity Index relative to the world in 2000 and 2010

147. Switzerland

Area		Changes in area (%)	Share (%) area of global total		No. of regions		No. of prime varieties	
2000	2010		2000	2010	2000	2010	2000	2010
15042	14820	-1	0.31	0.32	18	18	51	58

Year	Share of top variety	Share of top 3 varieties	Share of top 10 varieties
2000	36	79	95
2010	30	67	87

Region's national share (%) in 2010

National share % in 2000 and 2010 (top 20 varieties in 2010)

148. Thailand

Area		Changes in area (%)	Share (%) area of global total	
2000	2010		2000	2010
	149			0.00

Year	Share of top variety	Share of top 3 varieties	Share of top 10 varieties
2000			
2010	44	67	98

No. of regions		No. of prime varieties	
2000	2010	2000	2010
	1		13

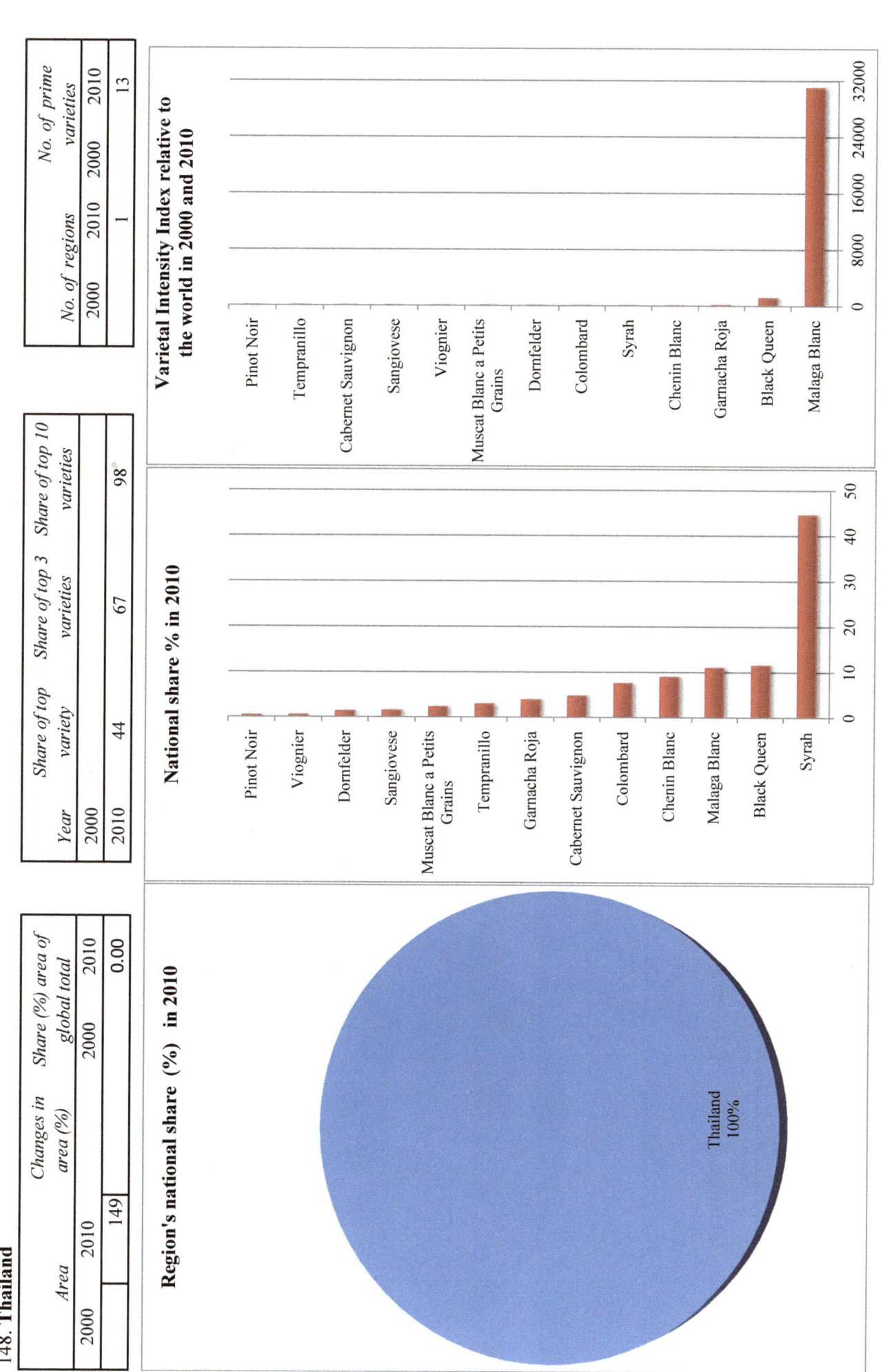

149. Tunisia

Area		Changes in area (%)	Share (%) area of global total	
2000	2010		2000	2010
16836	16836	0	0.34	0.36

Year	Share of top variety	Share of top 3 varieties	Share of top 10 varieties
2000	45	62	
2010	45	62	

No. of regions		No. of prime varieties	
2000	2010	2000	2010
1	1	9	9

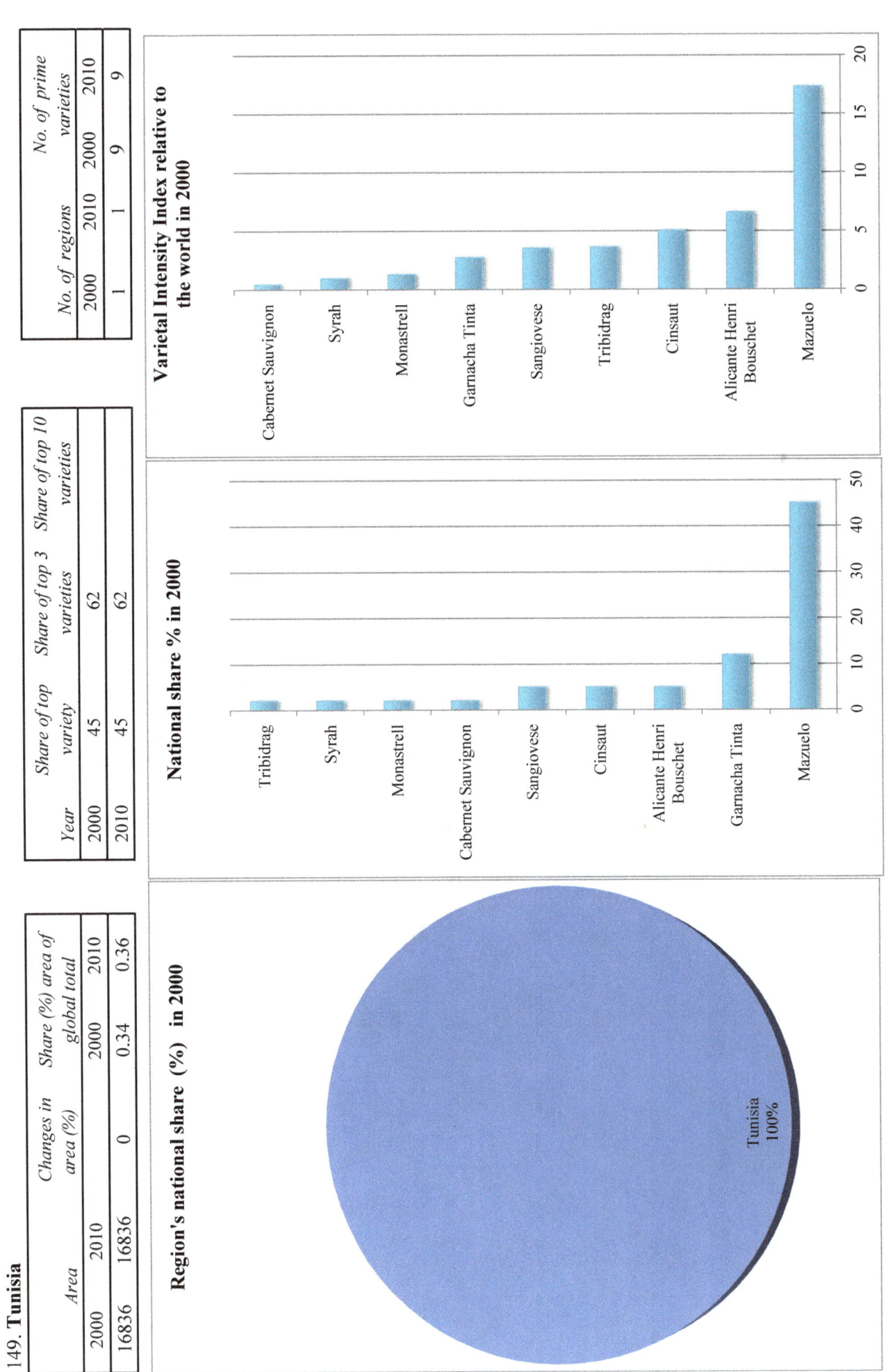

150. Turkey

Area		Changes in area (%)	Share (%) area of global total	
2000	2010		2000	2010
	12856			0.28

Year	Share of top variety	Share of top 3 varieties	Share of top 10 varieties
2000			
2010	14	36	78

	No. of regions		No. of prime varieties	
	2000	2010	2000	2010
		7		35

Region's national share (%) in 2010

- Ege 53%
- Orta Dogu 15%
- Marmara 14%
- Orta Guney 12%
- Guney Dogu 3%
- Orta Kuzey 3%
- Akdeniz 0%

National share % in 2010 (top 20 varieties)

(ascending) Mazuelo, Muscat Blanc a Petits..., Chardonnay, Sauvignon Blanc, Papazkarasi, Gamay Noir, Merlot, Cabernet Sauvignon, Alicante Henri Bouschet, Cinsaut, Semillon, Calkarasi, Emir, Narince, Kalecik Karasi, Dimrit, Bogazkere, Syrah, Okuzgozu, Sultaniye

Varietal Intensity Index relative to the world in 2010

Chardonnay, Mazuelo, Sauvignon Blanc, Merlot, Cabernet Sauvignon, Muscat Blanc a Petits..., Gamay Noir, Syrah, Alicante Henri Bouschet, Cinsaut, Semillon, Sultaniye, Papazkarasi, Calkarasi, Kalecik Karasi, Okuzgozu, Emir, Narince, Dimrit, Bogazkere

151. Ukraine

Area		Changes in area (%)	Share (%) area of global total	
2000	2010		2000	2010
	52293			1.13

Year	Share of top variety	Share of top 3 varieties	Share of top 10 varieties
2000			
2010	22	50	84

No. of regions		No. of prime varieties	
2000	2010	2000	2010
	1		22

Region's national share (%) in 2010

Ukraine 100%

National share % in 2010 (top 20 varieties in 2010)

Telti Kyryk, Pinot Blanc, Pervenets Magaracha, Muscat Blanc a Petits..., Pinot Gris, Pinot Noir, Kokur Bely, Gewurztraminer, Bastardo Magarachsky, Sukholimanskiy Bely, Saperavi, Isabella, Odessky Cherny, Riesling, Merlot, Chardonnay, Sauvignon Blanc, Cabernet Sauvignon, Aligote, Rkatsiteli

Varietal Intensity Index relative to the world in 2010

Pinot Noir, Merlot, Chardonnay, Pinot Gris, Cabernet Sauvignon, Muscat Blanc a Petits..., Pinot Blanc, Sauvignon Blanc, Riesling, Gewurztraminer, Isabella, Saperavi, Rkatsiteli, Pervenets Magaracha, Aligote, Bastardo Magarachsky, Sukholimanskiy Bely, Odessky Cherny, Telti Kyryk, Kokur Bely

152. United Kingdom

	Area		Changes in area (%)	Share (%) area of global total	
	2000	2010		2000	2010
	873	1198	37	0.02	0.03

Year	Share of top variety	Share of top 3 varieties	Share of top 10 varieties
2000	13	36	
2010	20	49	80

No. of regions		No. of prime varieties	
2000	2010	2000	2010
18	18	51	58

Region's national share (%) in 2010

United Kingdom 100%

National share % in 2000 and 2010 (top 20 varieties in 2010)

Varietal Intensity Index relative to the world in 2000 and 2010

153. United States

Area		Changes in area (%)	Share (%) area of global total	
2000	2010		2000	2010
175693	227948	30	3.56	4.91

Year	Share of top variety	Share of top 3 varieties	Share of top 10 varieties
2000	20	41	79
2010	18	43	77

No. of regions		No. of prime varieties	
2000	2010	2000	2010
61	89	84	130

Region's national share (%) in 2010 (top 10 regions)

Rest 35%, San Joaquin 12%, Sonoma 10%, Napa 8%, Fresno 7%, Monterey 7%, Madera 6%, San Luis Obispo 5%, Kern 4%, Chautauqua-Erie 3%, Sacramento 3%

National share % in 2000 and 2010 (top 20 varieties in 2010)

Varietal Intensity Index relative to the world in 2000 and 2010

154. Uruguay

Area		Changes in area (%)	Share (%) area of global total	
2000	2010		2000	2010
8880	7657	-14	0.18	0.16

Year	Share of top variety	Share of top 3 varieties	Share of top 10 varieties
2000	33	72	
2010	24	55	86

No. of regions		No. of prime varieties	
2000	2010	2000	2010
1	1	8	41

Region's national share (%) in 2010

Uruguay 100%

National share % in 2000 and 2010 (top 20 varieties in 2010)

Concord, Semillon, Gewurztraminer, Nebbiolo, Arinarnoa, Petit Verdot, Cot, Viognier, Pinot Noir, Syrah, Marselan, Sauvignon Blanc, Chardonnay, Isabella, Cabernet Franc, Cabernet Sauvignon, Trebbiano Toscano, Merlot, Muscat of Hamburg, Tannat

Varietal Intensity Index relative to the world in 2000 and 2010

Syrah, Pinot Noir, Chardonnay, Cot, Semillon, Sauvignon Blanc, Gewurztraminer, Concord, Cabernet Sauvignon, Merlot, Viognier, Nebbiolo, Petit Verdot, Cabernet Franc, Trebbiano Toscano, Isabella, Marselan, Muscat of Hamburg, Tannat, Arinarnoa

About the Wine Economics Research Centre

The Wine Economics Research Centre was established in 2010 by the School of Economics and the Wine2030 Research Network of the University of Adelaide, South Australia, having been previously a research program in the University's Centre for International Economic Studies. Its purpose is to promote and foster its growing research strength in the area of wine economics, and to complement the university's long-established strength in viticulture and oenology research.

The University of Adelaide is the Southern Hemisphere's premier wine research and teaching university and is part of the adjacent Wine Innovation Cluster which includes the University's School of Agriculture, Food and Wine and the Australian Wine Research Institute (established in 1955).

Adelaide is the capital of the state of South Australia, where nearly half of Australia's winegrapes and from where more than half of Australia's wine exports are shipped. Adelaide has four major wine regions and more than 200 cellar doors within an hour's drive (Adelaide Hills, Barossa Valley, McLaren Vale and Southern Fleurieu/Langhorne Creek), in addition to South Australia's three other key wine regions (Clare Valley, Coonawarra/Limestone Coast and Riverland). Adelaide University is also home to the National Wine Centre of Australia.

The Wine Economics Research Centre is unique in Australia and one of few similar centres around the world. It has close links with the Center for Wine Economics at the Robert Mondavi Institute for Wine and Food Science at the University of California, Davis, and with the American Association of Wine Economists' *Journal of Wine Economics*.

The key objectives of the Wine Economics Research Centre are to:

- publish wine economics research outputs and disseminate them to industry and government as well as academia
- contribute to economics journals, wine industry journals and related publications
- promote collaboration and sharing of information, data and analyses between industry and government agencies as well as research institutions
- sponsor wine economics seminars, workshops and conferences and contribute to other grape and wine meetings

The founding Executive Director of the Wine Economics Research Centre is Professor Kym Anderson. Contact details are as follows:

> Wine Economics Research Centre
> School of Economics
> University of Adelaide
> Adelaide SA 5005
> Australia
> Email: kym.anderson@adelaide.edu.au
> Website: www.adelaide.edu.au/wine-econ